EU SHIPPING LAW

VOLUME II

EU SHIPPING LAW

THIRD EDITION

VOLUME II

VINCENT POWER

B.C.L. (NUI), LL.M., Ph.D. (Cambridge), Solicitor
Partner, A&L Goodbody Solicitors
and
Adjunct Professor of Law, University College Cork
European Union Centre for Excellence Visiting Professor of European Union Law,
Dalhousie University, Canada

informa law
from Routledge

Third edition published 2019
by Informa Law from Routledge
2 Park Square, Milton Park, Abingdon, Oxon OX14 4RN

and by Informa Law from Routledge
711 Third Avenue, New York, NY 10017

Informa Law from Routledge is an imprint of the Taylor & Francis Group, an informa business

© 2019 Vincent Power

The right of Vincent Power to be identified as author of this work has been asserted by him in accordance with sections 77 and 78 of the Copyright, Designs and Patents Act 1988.

First edition published by Lloyd's of London 1992
Second edition published by LLP Reference Publishing 1998

British Library Cataloguing-in-Publication Data
A catalogue record for this book is available from the British Library

Library of Congress Cataloging-in-Publication Data
A catalog record has been requested for this book

ISBN: 978-1-843-11633-2 (hbk)
ISBN: 978-1-315-62614-7 (ebk)
ISBN: 978-0-367-02564-9 (volume II)

Typeset in Times New Roman
by Wearset Ltd, Boldon, Tyne and Wear

Printed and bound by CPI Group (UK) Ltd, Croydon, CR0 4YY

CHAPTER 19

European Union law relating to the maritime
environment: introduction; European Union
measures relating to the maritime environment
generally; and penalties for infringements

A. INTRODUCTION

19.001 This chapter sets the scene for a discussion over various other chapters on European Union ("EU") maritime[1] environmental law.

19.002 The protection of the marine environment is a very important element of EU shipping law.[2] The citizens of the EU would not now[3] forgive the EU if it does not do enough to protect the environment. Scenes of oil spills, dead birds and marine wildlife as well as incidents such as the *Amoco Cadiz*, the *Erika* and the *Prestige* have all stimulated calls from the EU's citizens and businesses to demand action by the EU in the area of environmental protection.

19.003 Yet, one might well ask whether it is *appropriate* for the EU to be involved in this area given the fact that the global specialised maritime organisation – the International Maritime Organization ("IMO") – is already involved in the area with technical expertise and near global membership. Equally, there are several international treaties outside the scope of the IMO already in place. Despite the presence of at least one specialised international organisation and several non-IMO treaties, the EU has become involved in issues relating to the maritime environment and will remain involved. It is not feasible now to undo the work of the EU in this area and it would be counterproductive because the EU is able to achieve deeper and higher standards in the EU – and sometimes quicker – than a near-global organisation or the international community generally can do so because of the EU's smaller, narrower and closer membership base. Indeed, the EU is,

---

1 This chapter deals with "maritime" (i.e. shipping) environmental law rather than marine environmental law.

2 See the legislative instruments, case law and literature cited throughout this chapter and the accompanying chapters in this book on the environment. See also, De La Rue et al., *Shipping and the Environment* (2009) generally, see also de Sadeleer, *EU Environmental Law and the Internal Market* (2014); Hedemann-Robinson, *Enforcement of European Union Environmental Law: Legal Issues and Challenges* (2015); Kramer, *Casebook on EU Environmental Law* (2002); Kramer, *EU Environmental Law* (2016); Langlet and Mahmoudi, *EU Environmental Law and Policy* (2016); and Lee, *EU Environmental Law, Governance and Decision Making* (2014). See also Born, Cliquet and Schoukens (eds), *The Habitats Directive in its EU Environmental Law Context: European Nature's Best Hope?* (2014).

3 It has not always been so. EU environmental law is of relatively recent origin and was not addressed in the Foundation Treaties even though they related to sectors such as coal and steel as well as various other economic sectors. Nowadays, given the fact that the environment is an issue of real concern to many people, it is very likely that most citizens would not now tolerate any situation where the EU did not protect the environment where it was possible for it to do so.

in many ways, better able to achieve compliance than the wider international organisations because Member States can be taken to the Court of Justice of the European Union ("CJEU") for failure to comply with EU law.

19.004 The EU is not involved in marine environmental matters to "make up the numbers" in terms of the agencies active in this area around the world. The first recital to Directive 2000/59 on port facilities[4] provides that the EU policy on the environment aims at a *high level of protection.* The first recital also states that this policy is based on the *precautionary principle* and the principles that the *polluter should pay* and that *preventive action* should be taken. The principles utilised in the maritime environment are thus comparable to the principles deployed in EU environmental law generally. Ultimately, provided they can reach agreement, the EU Member States can achieve more and enforce environmental law better in this area than States individually.

19.005 The EU is involved in this area not only for the sake of the citizens and the environment but also because it is important from the perspective of maritime transport generally because vessels and operations which are more environmentally robust are more likely to be safer and more efficient. The first recital to Directive 2000/59 on port facilities[5] provides that one important field of EU action in maritime transport generally concerns the reduction of the pollution of the seas and this

> "can be achieved through compliance with international conventions, codes and resolutions while maintaining the freedom of navigation as provided for by the United Nations Convention on the Law of the Sea and the freedom of providing services as provided for in [EU] law".

So, contemporary EU maritime environmental law can be seen as an amalgam of EU, international and national laws, but with the additional element of EU ambition, convergence and compliance.

19.006 The EU could have chosen to rely solely on enforcing its own rules on vessels flying the flag of a Member State but that would have left the EU very exposed. Relatively few vessels are flying the flag of a Member State and many of those which are likely to cause the greatest environmental damage (e.g. many tankers) do not do so. This would have been problematical because vessels of all nations sail by Member States and many of those even use the EU's 1,000 plus seaports (those seaports had approximately 834,481 calls by ships in 2012) so EU maritime environmental law tends to be flag-neutral and will apply to vessels in EU waters and EU ports irrespective of the flag of the vessel – as a general rule, EU shipping legislation applies in EU ports regardless of the flag of the vessel calling.[6]

19.007 The EU's approach to maritime environmental law is typified by the opening recitals to Directive 2000/59 of the European Parliament and of the Council of 27 November 2000 on port reception facilities for ship-generated waste and cargo residues[7] which provide:

> "(1) Community policy on the environment aims at a high level of protection. It is based on the precautionary principle and the principles that the polluter should pay and that preventive action should be taken.

---

4 OJ L332/81.
5 OJ L332/81.
6 In regard to the MSC Orchestra, see Case C-537/11 Manzi and Compagnia Naviera Orchestra v Capitaneria di Porto di Genova ECLI:EU:C:2014:19.
7 OJ L332/81, 28 December 2000.

(2) One important field of Community action in maritime transport concerns the reduction of the pollution of the seas. This can be achieved through compliance with international conventions, codes and resolutions while maintaining the freedom of navigation as provided for by the United Nations Convention on the Law of the Sea and the freedom of providing services as provided for in Community law."

B. CONTEXT AND FACTUAL BACKGROUND

The maritime environment is a challenge for the EU and not just the Member States individually

19.008 The EU Transport Council stated in its 7 May 2014 Athens Declaration "that European shipping faces significant challenges in relation to strengthened environmental requirements".[8] It would be theoretically possible for Member States to tackle maritime environmental issues on an individual or unilateral basis but that would lead to inconsistent results and dissatisfaction that the protection of the environment could be random – for example, it would be unfortunate if a vessel registered in one Member State which was lax in its adoption and enforcement of standards were to run aground in the waters of another Member State leading to an oil spillage which was very damaging to the latter Member State. It could also be difficult for some Member States to enforce the strongest rules if they acted unilaterally so it is better to act together. Today, unilateral and individual action is no longer really feasible (except in some circumstances where it may result in higher standards being applied) as opposed to the more successful collective action.

Level of environmental cleanliness of the shipping sector

19.009 Shipping is generally regarded as the cleanest mode of transport from the environmental perspective. For example, a product tanker would emit lower carbon dioxide ("CO_2") than an aircraft, a truck or a train. In overall terms, however, the shipping sector accounts for a higher proportion of CO_2 emissions than most other modes of transport: while estimates vary, a common belief is that international shipping represents 3% of the share of global CO_2 emissions with domestic shipping and fishing accounting for 0.6% but road transport accounted for 21.3%; however, because there is relatively less activity, international air transport represented only 1.9% and rail transport represented 0.5%.

19.010 It is important to ensure that the highest environmental standards are met for several reasons. First, the consequences of an individual environmental incident involving shipping can be quite dramatic as demonstrated by incidents involving *The Torrey Canyon*, *Braer*, *Erika* and so on. Second, shipping is so pervasive in the EU with almost 90% of the EU external freight trade being carried on ships and short sea shipping representing 40% of intra-EU exchanges in terms of ton-kilometres so it is imperative to have adequate protection and supervision of the rules.[9] Third, the impact of an environmental disaster can be pervasive across several Member States and several industries and ecosystems.

---

8 See www.gr2014.eu.
9 See chap. 2.

Costs

19.011 Compliance with higher environmental standards can be expensive. It is reckoned that building new LNG-powered ships can be 15–20% more expensive than traditional fuelled vessels. Equally, the costs of retrofitting ships with more environmentally friendly equipment can also be expensive. Most measures to ensure compliance with environmental protection involve spending rather than saving money.

The EU in the wider international arena

19.012 While the EU has more than two dozen Member States, the IMO has many more – the IMO has 171 Member States and three associated Member States.[10] Around 25% of world tonnage is registered under the EU flag and 40% of the world fleet is controlled by EU shipping companies. The IMO develops environmental policies through the Marine Environment Protection Committee ("MEPC"). Despite the IMO being broader than the EU in terms of the location of members and more representative in terms of tonnage associated with that membership (over six times as many members), the EU is able to achieve more sophisticated and stronger measures than the IMO. The EU is able to, and does, play an important role in addition to, but not in substitution for, the IMO.

C. THE EU INSTITUTIONAL DIMENSION

19.013 There is no single EU institution with responsibility for maritime environmental matters. Instead, it is a combination of institutions and bodies while the former may adopt legislation which binds Member States but the latter often perform important specialised functions. The European Commission deals with environmental issues in different ways. It is responsible for proposing laws and developing policy as well as bringing cases before the CJEU. The Council and the Parliament encourage and adopt legislation. The European Commission adopts secondary legislation. The CJEU decides cases on the issue including enforcement cases instituted by the Commission as well as hearing preliminary references from the Member States and certain tribunals. Bodies such as the European Maritime Safety Agency ("EMSA") have a key role to play in developing rules and proposals as well as enforcing the regime.[11]

D. OVERVIEW OF THE EU RESPONSES TO MARINE ENVIRONMENTAL ISSUES

Introduction

19.014 The EU has a battery of possible responses to environmental issues. It is not confined to a single type of instrument; in other words, it is able to deploy provisions in treaties as well provisions in regulations, directives and decisions. Nor is it confined to either binding or non-binding instruments because it can use "soft law" instruments such as encouragement, negotiation as well as naming and shaming. It can adapt a mixture of

---

10 The associated States are Faroes, Hong Kong and Macao.
11 See www.emsa.europa.eu.

instruments and all for different aims. The EU does not have the power to impose criminal liability (e.g. imprisonment and/or fines) but it has been able to get Member States to adopt rules which involve criminal liability at the Member State level.[12]

Aims

19.015 The aims of EU environmental law and policy in this area are manifold. Measures are aimed at achieving such objectives as: preventing environmental damage; ensuring that those who pollute are identified, punished and compensate the victims; responding to incidents; ensuring a consistent minimum level of environmental protection; aligning the position of EU Member States in dealing with institutional law issues; providing a minimum standard of protection across the EU; but permitting Member States to adopt more stringent regimes at a national level than at the EU level.

Form of measures

19.016 As mentioned above, there is no single type of measure which the EU has to adopt in this area – instead there is a plethora of measures available to the EU.

Treaties

19.017 There are now provisions in the Treaties dealing with the issue of the environment. The original Foundation Treaties did not contain provisions relating to the environment which is something which is surprising given the fact that the early days of what is now the EU involved coal and steel (by virtue of the European Coal and Steel Community ("ECSC")) and both of those sectors raise environmental issues but there was less interest in, and concern with, the environment in the 1950s than there is today.

Regulations

19.018 Regulations can be used in environmental matters where a general measure is possible. Such a measure allows general rules to be adopted without the need to have those rules implemented in the national laws of Member States.

Directives

19.019 Directives are used where there is a desire to adopt EU rules but it is not possible or desirable to adopt uniform rules across the EU (by way of regulations). Directives allow a certain degree of flexibility because Member States have some room for manoeuvre in terms of implementing directives (e.g. to take account of national circumstances) provided the Member States do not undermine the aim of the directive.

---

12 See below.

Decisions

19.020 Decisions are specific legally binding instruments. They are addressed at specific persons to deal with specific issues.

Recommendations and opinions

19.021 Recommendations and opinions are adopted to deal with some issues where legally binding measures are not possible or desirable or yet politically feasible. Such instruments have been useful in developing policy in the environmental arena and can be used as a soft law tool to nudge or encourage developments.

Strategy statements

19.022 Strategy statements or memoranda are also useful in developing policies including on environmental matters. For example, the EU's Maritime Transport Strategy 2009–2018 refers to the need to provide cost-efficient maritime transport adapted to the needs of sustainable economic growth of the EU. The aim would be zero-waste, zero-emission maritime transport.

White papers

19.023 White papers are another form of policy statements, for example, the 2011 White Paper is entitled *Roadmap to a Single European Transport Area*. The Commission advocated the need for a global level-playing field. The EU should, the White Paper suggested, strive in co-operation with the IMO for the universal application and enforcement of high standards of safety, security, environmental protection and working conditions and for eliminating piracy.

E. RELATIONSHIP BETWEEN EU AND INTERNATIONAL LEGISLATION

19.024 Environmental laws exist at the international, EU and national levels. There could also be regional laws as well involving several Member States in areas such as the North Sea, the Baltic or the Mediterranean. EU law can be more onerous and stringent than international law generally but that is because it can be easier to reach agreement between neighbouring States who are more experienced at reaching agreement on difficult issues and have more in common than a global collection of States. However, national laws must be compatible with EU law where there are national and EU laws on the same issue.

F. RANGE OF MARITIME ENVIRONMENTAL ISSUES

19.025 The EU has to deal with a range of maritime environmental law issues including ship source pollution, air pollution, greenhouse gases ("GHGs") and climate change, ballast water and invasive species, ship recycling, port reception facilities and antifouling. The range of issues is growing over time as new sources of environmental damage are being identified all the time.

G. GENERAL MEASURES

19.026 The EU has adopted a number of general measures on the maritime environment. It is useful to consider some of these general measures at this point. In particular, the EU has adopted measures on, for example, bunkers, land-based pollution, port reception facilities, low sulphur fuels, regional measures, CO_2 emissions, flag State requirements, port charges as well as penalties for environmental law breaches.

H. BUNKERS

Introduction

19.027 One of the most obvious sources of potential maritime pollution damage would be bunkers or fuel oil carried on board ships. The EU has taken action on this front as well.

Council Decision 2002/762 of 19 September 2002 authorising the Member States, in the interest of the Community, to sign, ratify or accede to the International Convention on Civil Liability for Bunker Oil Pollution Damage, 2001

19.028 On 19 September 2002, Council Decision 2002/762 was adopted to authorise the Member States, in the interest of the Community, to sign, ratify or accede to the International Convention on Civil Liability for Bunker Oil Pollution Damage, 2001 (the so-called "Bunkers Convention").[13]

19.029 The legal basis for Decision 2002/762 was the Treaty establishing the European Community ("TEC") generally, and in particular Article 61(c),[14] Article 67(1)[15] and Article 300(2)[16] of the TEC.

19.030 The background was the "Bunkers Convention" which was adopted on 23 March 2001 with the aim of ensuring adequate, prompt and effective compensation of persons who suffer damage caused by spills of oil, when carried as fuel in ships' bunkers.[17] The Bunkers Convention was seen (correctly) by the EU's Council as filling a significant gap in the international regulation of marine pollution liability.[18]

19.031 The second recital to Decision 2002/762 recalled that Articles 9 and 10 of the Bunkers Convention affect EU secondary legislation on jurisdiction and the recognition and enforcement of judgments, as laid down in Council Regulation 44/2001 of 22 December 2000 on jurisdiction and the recognition and enforcement of judgments in civil and commercial matters (i.e. the Brussels Regulation). The EU therefore had sole competence in relation to Articles 9 and 10 of the Bunkers Convention inasmuch as those Articles affect the rules laid down in the Brussels Regulation. The Member States retain their competence for matters covered by that convention which do not affect EU law – but this element needed EU action. However, under the Bunkers Convention, only sovereign

---

13 OJ L256/7, 25 September 2002.
14 The TFEU equivalents of Art. 61 include Arts 67, 68, 69, 70 and 71 TFEU.
15 There is no equivalent in the TFEU for Art. 67(1) TEC.
16 See Art. 218 TFEU.
17 Dec. 2002/762, Recital 1.
18 Dec. 2002/762, Recital 1.

States may be party to it; there are no plans, in the short term, to reopen negotiations for the purpose of taking into account EU competence for the matter. It was not therefore possible for the EU to sign, ratify or accede to the Bunkers Convention, nor was there any prospect that it will be able do so in the near future.[19] The Bunkers Convention was particularly important, given the interests of the EU and its Member States, because it makes for improved victim protection under international rules on marine pollution liability, in keeping with the 1982 United Nations Convention on the Law of the Sea ("UNCLOS").[20] The sixth recital to Decision 2002/76 provides that the substantive rules of the system established by the Bunkers Convention fall under the national competence of Member States and only the provisions of jurisdiction and the recognition and enforcement of the judgments are matters covered by exclusive EU competence. Given the subject matters and the aim of the Bunkers Convention, acceptance of the provisions of that convention which come under EU competence cannot be dissociated from the provisions which come under the competence of the Member States. Therefore, the seventh recital to Decision 2002/76 provides that the Council should therefore authorise the Member States to sign, ratify or accede to the Bunkers Convention in the interest of the EU, under the conditions set out in this decision 2002/76. The eighth recital to Decision 2002/76 therefore provided that Member States would have to make efforts to sign the Bunkers Convention before 30 September 2002 and finalise, within a reasonable time, their procedures for ratification of, or accession to, that convention in the interest of the EU. Member States should exchange information on the state of their ratification or accession procedures in order to prepare the deposit of their instruments of ratification of, or accession to, the convention.

19.032 In accordance with Articles 1 and 2 of the Protocol on the position of Denmark annexed to the Treaty on European Union and to the TEC, Denmark did not take part in the adoption of Decision 2002/76, and is not bound by it or subject to its application. (Denmark has largely remained outside the judgments convention/regulation regime.)

19.033 Article 1(1) of Decision 2002/762 provides that without prejudice to existing EU competence in the matter, the Council authorises the Member States to sign, ratify or accede to the Bunkers Convention in the interest of the EU, subject to the conditions set out in Decision 2002/76. Article 1(3) provides that the term "Member State", when used in the decision means all Member States with the exception of Denmark.

19.034 Article 2 provides that when signing, ratifying or acceding to the Bunkers Convention, Member States must make the following declaration:

"Judgments on matters covered by the Convention shall, when given by a court of all the Member States to which Decision 2002/76 is applicable except the Member Sate making the declaration and Denmark, be recognised and enforced in Member State making the declaration according to the relevant internal Community rules on the subject."

19.035 Article 3(1) provides that Member States have to make efforts to sign the Bunkers Convention before 30 September 2002. Member States have to take the necessary steps to deposit the instruments of ratification of, or accession to, the Bunkers Convention within a reasonable time with the Secretary-General of the IMO and, if possible, before 30 June 2006.[21] Member States have to inform the Council and the Commission,

---

19 Dec. 2002/76, Recital 4.
20 Dec. 2002/76, Recital 5.
21 Dec. 2002/76, Art. 3(2).

before 30 June 2004, of the prospective date of finalisation of their ratification or acces-sion procedures.[22] Member States must seek to exchange information on the state of their ratification or accession proceedings.[23]

19.036 When signing, ratifying or acceding to the Bunkers Convention, Member States shall inform the Secretary-General of the IMO in writing that such signing, ratifi-cation or accession has taken place in accordance with Decision 2002/76.[24]

19.037 Member States, at the earliest opportunity, use their best endeavours to ensure that the Bunkers Convention is amended to allow the EU to become a contracting party to it.[25]

19.038 Council Decision 2004/246 of 2 March 2004 authorising the Member States to sign, ratify or accede to, in the interest of the European Community ("EC"), the Protocol of 2003 to the International Convention on the Establishment of an International Fund for Compensation for Oil Pollution Damage, 1992, and authorising Austria and Luxembourg, in the interest of the EU, to accede to the underlying instruments.

I. OIL POLLUTION

Introduction

19.039 The most obvious and distressing symbol of maritime pollution is oil pollution. It is obviously and closely related to pollution from bunkers but can arise in its own regard as well as in, for example, where an oil tanker spills its load.

Council Decision 2004/246 of 2 March 2004 authorising the Member States to Sign, Ratify or Accede to, in the Interest of the European Community, the Protocol of 2003 to the International Convention on the Establishment of an International Fund for Compensation for Oil Pollution Damage, 1992, and Authorising Austria and Luxembourg, in the Interest of the European Community, to Accede to the Underlying Instruments

19.040 The first measure to be considered is Council Decision 2004/246 of 2 March 2004 authorising the Member States to Sign, Ratify or Accede to, in the Interests of the European Community, the Protocol of 2003 to the International Convention on the Estab-lishment of an International Fund for Compensation for Oil Pollution Damage, 1992, and Authorising Austria and Luxembourg, in the Interest of the European Community, to Accede to the Underlying Instruments.[26] It was amended by Council Decision 2004/664 of 24 September 2004 adapting Decision 2004/246 by reason of the accession of the Czech Republic, Estonia, Cyprus, Latvia, Lithuania, Hungary, Malta, Poland, Slovenia and Slovakia.[27]

---

22 Dec. 2002/76, Art. 3(3).
23 Dec. 2002/76, Art. 3(4).
24 Dec. 2002/76, Art. 4.
25 Dec. 2002/76, Art. 5.
26 OJ L78/22, 16 March 2004.
27 OJ L303/28, 30 September 2004.

19.041 The legal basis was the TEC generally and, in particular, Article 61(c), in conjunction with Article 300(2), first subparagraph, and Article 300(3), second subparagraph, of the TEC.[28]

19.042 The background to Decision 2004/2016 is clear-cut. The 1992 Protocol to the International Convention on the Establishment of an International Fund for Compensation for Oil Pollution Damage (known as the "Supplementary Fund Protocol") is aimed at ensuring adequate, prompt and effective compensation of persons who suffer damage caused by oil spills caused by tankers. It raised significantly the limits of compensation available in the pre-existing international system. The Supplementary Fund Protocol addressed a shortcoming in the international regulation of oil pollution liability. The second recital to the decision recalls that Articles 7 and 8 of the Supplementary Fund Protocol affects EU legislation on jurisdiction (namely, Regulation 44/2001 of 22 December 2000 on jurisdiction and the recognition and enforcement of judgments in civil and commercial matters). Under EU law, the EU has exclusive competence in relation to Articles 7 and 8 of the protocol in so far as those Articles affect the rules in Regulation 44/2001 with the Member States retaining competence in all other respects. However, there is a difficulty in that despite the Member States conferring on the EU the exclusive competence to deal with certain matters which are now addressed by the Supplementary Fund Protocol, only Member States may be parties to the protocol so the EU may not be. So, therefore, as an exceptional compromise, the Council authorises the Member States (by virtue of this decision) to sign and conclude the protocol in the interest of the EU under the conditions laid down in the decision. While all other States were subject to the regime, Denmark was not bound by the regime because of its unusual relationship with Regulation 44/2001. Austria and Luxembourg were also authorised to accede. So, the purpose of the decision is to provide that Member States, with the exception of Austria and Luxembourg had to sign or ratify the protocol, as far as possible before the end of June 2004. The choice of signing and subsequently ratifying the protocol, or signing it without reservation as to ratification, acceptance or approval, was left to the Member States.

19.043 Article 1(1) therefore provides that the Member States are authorised to sign, ratify or accede to, in the interest of the EU, the Protocol of 2003 to the International Convention on the Establishment of an International Fund for Compensation for Oil Pollution Damage, 1992 (the Supplementary Fund Protocol) subject to the conditions set out in the articles of Decision 2004/246. Article 1(2) provides the Czech Republic, Estonia, Luxembourg, Hungary, Austria and Slovakia are authorised to accede to the underlying instruments.

19.044 Article 1(3) of Decision 2004/246 provides that the text of the Supplementary Fund Protocol is attached in Annex I to Decision 2005/246. The text of the underlying instruments is attached in Annexes II and III to the decision. In Decision 2004/246, the term "underlying instruments" means the Protocol of 1992 to amend the International Convention on Civil Liability for Oil Pollution Damage, 1969 and the Protocol of 1992 to amend the International Convention on the Establishment of an International Fund for Compensation for Oil Pollution Damage, 1971. In Decision 2004/246, "Member State" means all the Member States with the exception of Denmark.[29]

---

28 For the TFEU equivalent of Art. 61 TEC, see Arts 67-71 TFEU and Art. 300 TEC, see Art. 218 TFEU.
29 Dec. 2004/246, Art. 1(5).

19.045 Article 2(1) provides that Member States must take the necessary steps to express their consent to be bound by the Supplementary Fund Protocol, pursuant to Article 19(2), within a reasonable time limit and, if possible, before 30 June 2004, with the exception of the Czech Republic, Estonia, Luxembourg, Hungary, Austria and Slovakia, which express their consent to be bound by the protocol subject to the conditions set out in paragraph 3 of Article 2. Article 2(2) provides that Member States must exchange information with the Commission within the Council, by 30 April 2004, on the date on which they expect their internal procedures to be completed. Article 2(3) provides that the Czech Republic, Estonia, Luxembourg, Hungary, Austria and Slovakia must take the necessary steps to express their consent to be bound by the underlying instruments and the Supplementary Fund Protocol, as far as possible by 31 December 2005.

19.046 Article 3 provides that when signing, ratifying or acceding to the instruments referred to in Article 1, Member States must inform the Secretary-General of the IMO in writing that such signature, ratification or accession has taken place in accordance with Decision 2004/246. This is quite a common provision.

19.047 Article 4 provides that Member States must, at the earliest opportunity, use their best endeavours to ensure that the Supplementary Fund Protocol, and the underlying instruments, are amended in order to allow the EU to become a Contracting Party to them.

19.048 Annex I contains the Protocol of 2003 to the International Convention on the Establishment of an International Fund for Compensation for Oil Pollution Damage, 1992.

J. LAND-BASED POLLUTION

Introduction

19.049 Land-based pollution is also an issue for the maritime environment.

Council Resolution of 3 March 1975 on the Convention for the Prevention of Marine Pollution from Land-Based Sources

19.050 The Council adopted a resolution on 3 March 1975 on the convention for the Prevention of Marine Pollution from Land-Based Sources is a non-binding measure.[30] This was a soft (i.e. non-legally binding) measure. The Council believed that it is in the interests of the Member States and the EU to take effective measures as quickly as possible to protect the sea from pollution, including pollution from land-based sources. The Council also adopted Decision 75/437 of 3 March 1975 concluding the Convention for the Prevention of Marine Pollution from Land-Based Sources.

19.051 The Council therefore invited the Member States affected by the Convention for the Prevention of Marine Pollution from Land-Based Sources to sign the convention as soon as possible, and in any case before 31 May 1975. The Council considered it advisable to ensure coherent implementation of the undertakings entered into under the convention, of those which may result from the European Convention for the Protection

---

30 OJ C168/1, 25 July 1975.

of International Watercourses against Pollution, being drawn up by the Council of Europe, and, more generally, of the other commitments arising from the carrying out of the programme of action of the Communities on the environment.[31]

19.052 Finally, the Council agreed that they would endeavour to examine the proposal for a decision on the reduction of pollution caused by certain dangerous substances discharged into the aquatic environment of the Community with a view to taking a decision by 30 June 1975.

Council Decision 75/437 of 3 March 1975 concluding the Convention for the Prevention of Marine Pollution from Land-Based Sources

19.053 The Council adopted Decision 75/437 on 3 March 1975 concluding the Convention for the Prevention of Marine Pollution from Land-Based Sources.[32]

19.054 The legal basis of Decision 75/437 was the Treaty establishing the European Economic Community ("EEC") generally, and in particular Article 235 of the Treaty. This would now be the Treaty on the Functioning of the European Union ("TFEU") and Article 352 of the TFEU respectively.

19.055 The recitals to Decision 75/437 recalled that the declaration of the Council of the European Communities and of the representatives of the governments of the Member States meeting in the Council of 22 November 1973 on the programme of action of the European Communities on the environment, emphasises that it is important for the Community to take measures to combat marine pollution in general, and provides amongst other things for Community action with a view to combating marine pollution from land-based sources. The recitals also recalled that the Convention for the Prevention of Marine Pollution from Land-Based Sources of 21 February 1974 also provides for the preparation and implementation of programmes intended either to eliminate or to reduce this type of pollution in the North-East Atlantic. The recitals also recalled that it appeared necessary for the Community to conclude this convention in order to attain, in the course of the operation of the common market, one of the objectives of the Community in the fields of the protection of the environment and the quality of life, and whereas no provision is made in the Treaty for the necessary powers. It also recalled that the representative of the EU within the Commission established under the convention should be designated.

19.056 Article 1 provides that the Convention for the Prevention of Marine Pollution from Land-Based Sources is concluded on behalf of the Community.

19.057 Article 2 provides that the President of the Council was authorised to designate the persons empowered to sign the convention and to confer on them the powers they require to bind the Community. Article 3 provides that the then community is represented by the Commission in the Commission established under Article 15 of the convention. The Commission must in that body put forward the position of the Community in accordance with such directives as the Council may give it.

---

31 OJ C112/1, 20 December 1973.
32 OJ L194/5, 25 July 1975.

K. PORT RECEPTION FACILITIES

Introduction

19.058 Damage to the marine environment is often typified by dumping or pollution at sea but it is also important to ensure that there is protection of the port environment as well. Dumping at ports of materials collected over days, weeks or months at sea can be very problematical. It is important therefore to have adequate and appropriate facilities at ports.

Directive 2000/59 on port facilities

19.059 On 27 November 2000, the Parliament and Council adopted Directive 2000/59 on port reception facilities for ship-generated waste and cargo residues.[33] It has been amended by: (a) Parliament and Council Directive 2002/84 of 5 November 2002;[34] (b) Commission Directive 2007/71;[35] (c) Parliament and Council Regulation 1137/2008;[36] and Commission Directive 2015/2087.[37] The directive was a concrete measure to address a serious environmental issue.

19.060 The background is clear from some of the recitals:

"(3) The Community is seriously concerned about the pollution of the seas and coastlines of the Member States caused by discharges of waste and cargo residues from ships, and in particular about the implementation of the International Convention for the Prevention of Pollution from Ships, 1973, as modified by the Protocol of 1978 relating thereto (Marpol 73/78) which regulates what wastes can be discharged from ships into the marine environment and requires States Parties to ensure the provision of adequate reception facilities in ports. All Member States have ratified Marpol 73/78.

(4) The protection of the marine environment can be enhanced by reducing discharges into the sea of ship-generated waste and cargo residues. This can be achieved by improving the availability and use of reception facilities and by improving the enforcement regime. In its Resolution of 8 June 1993 on a common policy on safe seas,[38] the Council included among its priority actions the development of availability and use of reception facilities within the Community.

(5) Council Directive 95/21/EC of 19 June 1995 concerning the enforcement, in respect of shipping using Community ports and sailing in the waters under the jurisdiction of the Member States, of international standards for ship safety, pollution prevention and shipboard living and working conditions (port State control)[39] provides that ships posing an unreasonable threat of harm to the marine environment may not proceed to sea.

(6) Pollution of the seas by its very nature has transboundary implications. In view of the subsidiarity principle, action at Community level is the most effective way of ensuring common environmental standards for ships and ports throughout the Community.

(7) In view of the proportionality principle, a Directive is the appropriate legal instrument, as it provides a framework for the Member States' uniform and compulsory application of environmental standards, while leaving each Member State the right to decide which implementation tools best fit its internal system.

---

33 OJ L332/81, 28 December 2000,
34 OJ L324/53, 29 November 2002.
35 OJ L329/33, 14 December 2007.
36 OJ L311/1, 21 November 2008.
37 OJ L302/99, 19 November 2015.
38 Ed., OJ C271/1, 7 October 1993.
39 Ed., OJ L157/1, 7 July 1995.

(8) Consistency with existing regional agreements, such as the 1974/1992 Convention on the Protection of the Marine Environment in the Baltic Sea Area, should be ensured.

(9) In the interest of improving pollution prevention and avoiding distortion of competition, the environmental requirements should apply to all ships, irrespective of the flag they fly, and adequate reception facilities should be made available in all ports of the Community.

(10) Adequate port reception facilities should meet the needs of users, from the largest merchant ship to the smallest recreational craft, and of the environment, without causing undue delay to the ships using them. The obligation to ensure the availability of adequate port reception facilities leaves the Member States with a high degree of freedom to arrange the reception of waste in the most suitable manner and permits them, inter alia, to provide fixed reception installations or to appoint service providers bringing to the ports mobile units for the reception of waste when needed. This obligation also implies the obligation to provide all services and/or other accompanying arrangements necessary for the proper and adequate use of these facilities.

(11) Adequacy of facilities can be improved by up-to-date waste reception and handling plans established in consultation with the relevant parties.

(12) The effectiveness of port reception facilities can be improved by requiring ships to notify their need to use reception facilities. Such notification would also provide information for effectively planned waste management. Waste from fishing vessels and from recreational craft authorised to carry no more than 12 passengers may be handled by the port reception facilities without prior notification.

(13) Discharges of ship-generated waste at sea can be reduced by requiring all ships to deliver their waste to port reception facilities before leaving the port. In order to reconcile the interest of the smooth operation of maritime transport with the protection of the environment, exceptions to this requirement should be possible taking into account the sufficiency of the dedicated storage capacity on board, the possibility to deliver at another port without risk of discharge at sea and specific delivery requirements adopted in accordance with international law.

(14) In view of the 'polluter pays' principle, the costs of port reception facilities, including the treatment and disposal of ship-generated waste, should be covered by ships. In the interest of protecting the environment, the fee system should encourage the delivery of ship-generated waste to ports instead of discharge into the sea. This can be facilitated by providing that all ships contribute to the costs for the reception and handling of ship-generated waste so as to reduce the economic incentives to discharge into the sea. In view of the subsidiarity principle, Member States should, in accordance with their national laws and current practices, retain the powers to establish whether and in what proportion the fees related to quantities actually delivered by the ships will be included in the cost recovery systems for using port reception facilities. Charges for using these facilities should be fair, non-discriminatory and transparent.

(15) Ships producing reduced quantities of ship-generated waste should be treated more favourably in the cost recovery systems. Common criteria would facilitate the identification of such ships.

(16) In order to avoid undue burden for the parties concerned, ships engaged in scheduled traffic with frequent and regular port calls may be exempted from certain obligations deriving from this Directive where there is sufficient evidence that there are arrangements to ensure the delivery of the waste and the payment of fees.

(17) Cargo residues should be delivered to port reception facilities in accordance with Marpol 73/78. Marpol 73/78 requires cargo residues to be delivered to port reception facilities to the extent necessary to comply with the tank cleaning requirements. Any fee for such delivery should be paid by the user of the reception facility, the user being normally specified in the contractual arrangements between the parties involved or in other local arrangements.

(18) It is necessary to undertake targeted inspections in order to verify compliance with this Directive. The number of such inspections, as well as the penalties imposed, should be sufficient to deter non-compliance with this Directive. For reasons of efficiency and

cost-effectiveness, such inspections may be undertaken within the framework of Directive 95/21, ... when applicable.

(19) Member States should ensure a proper administrative framework for the adequate functioning of the port reception facilities. Under Marpol 73/78, allegations of inadequate port reception facilities should be transmitted to the International Maritime Organisation (IMO). The same information could be simultaneously transmitted to the Commission for information purposes.

(20) An information system for the identification of polluting or potentially polluting ships would facilitate the enforcement of this Directive and would be helpful in evaluating the implementation thereof. The SIRENAC information system established under the Paris Memorandum of Understanding on Port State Control provides a large amount of the additional information needed for that purpose.

(21) It is necessary that a Committee consisting of representatives of the Member States assist the Commission in the effective application of this Directive. Since the measures necessary for implementing this Directive are measures of a general scope within the meaning of Article 2 of Council Decision 1999/468/EC of 28 June 1999 laying down the procedures for the exercise of implementing powers conferred on the Commission,[40] such measures should be adopted in accordance with the regulatory procedure provided for in Article 5 of that Decision.

(22) Certain provisions of this Directive may, without broadening its scope, be amended in accordance with that procedure in order to take into account Community or IMO measures which enter into force in the future so as to ensure their harmonised implementation".

Legal basis and history of Directive 2000/59

19.061 The legal basis for Directive 2000/59 is now the TFEU generally (it was the TEC when the directive was adopted) including, in particular Article 100(2) of the TFEU (then 80(2) of the TEC). The legislative history of Directive 2000/59 includes the proposal from the Commission,[41] the opinion of the Economic and Social Committee ("EESC")[42] and an opinion of the Committee of the Regions.[43]

Purpose of Directive 2000/59

19.062 Article 1 of the directive provides that the purpose of the directive is

"to reduce the discharges of ship-generated waste and cargo residues into the sea, especially illegal discharges, from ships using ports in the Community, by improving the availability and use of port reception facilities for ship-generated waste and cargo residues, thereby enhancing the protection of the marine environment".

Concepts in Directive 2000/59

19.063 Article 2 sets out some of the key concepts in Directive 2000/59:

"(a) 'ship' shall mean a seagoing vessel of any type whatsoever operating in the marine environment and shall include hydrofoil boats, air-cushion vehicles, submersibles and floating craft;

---

40 Ed., OJ L184/23, 17 July 1999.
41 OJ C271, 31 August 1998, p. 79 and OJ C148, 28 May 1999, p. 7.
42 OJ C138, 18 May 1999, p. 12.
43 OJ C198, 14 July 1999, p. 27.

(b) 'Marpol 73/78' shall mean the International Convention for the Prevention of Pollution from Ships, 1973, as modified by the Protocol of 1978 relating thereto, in its up-to-date version;

(c) 'ship-generated waste' shall mean all waste, including sewage, and residues other than cargo residues, which are generated during the service of a ship and fall under the scope of Annexes I, IV and V to Marpol 73/78 and cargo-associated waste as defined in the Guidelines for the implementation of Annex V to Marpol 73/78;

(d) 'cargo residues' shall mean the remnants of any cargo material on board in cargo holds or tanks which remain after unloading procedures and cleaning operations are completed and shall include loading/unloading excesses and spillage;

(e) 'port reception facilities' shall mean any facility, which is fixed, floating or mobile and capable of receiving ship-generated waste or cargo residues;

(f) 'fishing vessel' shall mean any ship equipped or used commercially for catching fish or other living resources of the sea;

(g) 'recreational craft' shall mean a ship of any type, regardless of the means of propulsion, intended for sports or leisure purposes;

(h) 'port' shall mean a place or a geographical area made up of such improvement works and equipment as to permit, principally, the reception of ships, including fishing vessels and recreational craft.

Without prejudice to the definitions in points (c) and (d), 'ship-generated waste' and 'cargo residues' shall be considered to be waste within the meaning of Article 1(a) of Council Directive 75/442/EEC of 15 July 1975 on waste."[44]

Scope of Directive 2000/59

19.064 Article 3 sets out the scope of Directive 2000/59. The directive applies to: (a) all ships, including fishing vessels and recreational craft, irrespective of their flag, calling at, or operating within, a port of a Member State, with the exception of any warship, naval auxiliary or other ship owned or operated by a State and used, for the time being, only on government non-commercial service; and (b) all ports of the Member States normally visited by ships falling under the scope of point (a). Member States must take measures to ensure that ships which are excluded from the scope of the directive under point (a) of the preceding paragraph deliver their ship-generated waste and cargo residues in a manner consistent, in so far as is reasonable and practicable, with the directive.

Port reception facilities

19.065 Article 4(1) of Directive 2000/59 provides that Member States must ensure the availability of port reception facilities adequate to meet the needs of the ships normally using the port without causing undue delay to ships.

19.066 Article 4(2) of Directive 2000/59 provides that in order to achieve adequacy, the reception facilities shall be capable of receiving the types and quantities of ship-generated waste and cargo residues from ships normally using that port, taking into account the operational needs of the users of the port, the size and the geographical location of the port, the type of ships calling at that port and the exemptions provided for under Article 9.

---

44 Ed., OJ L194/39, 25 July 1975.

19.067 Article 4(3) provides that Member States must establish procedures, in accordance with those agreed by the IMO, for reporting to the port State alleged inadequacies of port reception facilities.

Waste reception and handling plans

19.068 Waste reception and handling plans are addressed by Article 5. Article 5(1) provides that an appropriate waste reception and handling plan must be developed and implemented for each port following consultations with the relevant parties, in particular with port users or their representatives, having regard to the requirements of Articles 4, 6, 7, 10 and 12. Detailed requirements for the development of such plans are set out in Annex I. Article 5(2) provides that the waste reception and handling plans referred to in Article 5(1) may, where required for reasons of efficiency, be developed in a regional context with the appropriate involvement of each port, provided that the need for, and availability of, reception facilities are specified for each individual port. Member States must evaluate and approve the waste reception and handling plan, monitor its implementation and ensure its re-approval at least every three years and after significant changes in the operation of the port.[45]

19.069 Annex I sets out the requirements for waste reception and handling plans in ports. The Annex states:

"Plans shall cover all types of ship-generated waste and cargo residues originating from ships normally visiting the port and shall be developed according to the size of the port and the types of ships calling at that port.

The following elements shall be addressed in the plans:

- an assessment of the need for port reception facilities, in light of the need of the ships normally visiting the port;
- a description of the type and capacity of port reception facilities;
- a detailed description of the procedures for the reception and collection of ship-generated waste and cargo residues;
- description of the charging system;
- procedures for reporting alleged inadequacies of port reception facilities;
- procedures for ongoing consultations with port users, waste contractors, terminal operators and other interested parties; and
- type and quantities of ship-generated waste and cargo residues received and handled.

In addition, the plans should include:

- a summary of relevant legislation and formalities for delivery;
- identification of a person or persons to be responsible for the implementation of the plan;
- a description of the pre-treatment equipment and processes in the port, if any;
- a description of methods of recording actual use of the port reception facilities;
- a description of methods of recording amounts of ship-generated waste and cargo residues received; and
- a description of how the ship-generated waste and cargo residues are disposed of.

The procedures for reception, collection, storage, treatment and disposal should conform in all respects to an environmental management scheme suitable for the progressive reduction of the environmental impact of these activities. Such conformity is presumed if the procedures are in

---

45 Art. 5(3).

compliance with the Council Regulation (EEC) No 1836/93 of 29 June 1993 allowing voluntary participation by companies in the industrial sector in a Community eco-management and audit scheme.[46]

Information to be made available to all port users:

– brief reference to fundamental importance of proper delivery of ship-generated waste and cargo residues;
– location of port reception facilities applicable to each berth with diagram/map;
– list of ship-generated waste and cargo residues normally dealt with;
– list of contact points, the operators and the services offered;
– description of procedures for delivery;
– description of charging system; and
– procedures for reporting alleged inadequacies of port reception facilities."

Notification

19.070 Article 6(1) provides that the master of a ship, other than a fishing vessel or recreational craft authorised to carry no more than 12 passengers, bound for a port located in the EU shall complete truly and accurately the form in Annex II[47] and notify that information to the authority or body designated for this purpose by the Member State in which that port is located: (a) at least 24 hours prior to arrival, if the port of call is known; or (b) as soon as the port of call is known, if this information is available less than 24 hours prior to arrival; or (c) at the latest upon departure from the previous port, if the duration of the voyage is less than 24 hours. Member States may decide that the information will be notified to the operator of the port reception facility, who will forward it to the relevant authority.[48] Article 6(2) provides that the information referred to in paragraph 1 shall be kept on board at least until the next port of call and shall upon request be made available to the Member States' authorities.

Delivery of ship-generated waste

19.071 Article 7 deals with delivery of ship-generated waste. Article 7(1) provides that the master of a ship calling at an EU port must, before leaving the port, deliver all ship-generated waste to a port reception facility. It is not an absolute rule. Article 7(2) provides that notwithstanding Article 7(1), but subject to more stringent delivery requirements for ships adopted in accordance with international law,[49] a ship may proceed to the next port of call without delivering the ship-generated waste, if it follows from the information given in accordance with Article 6 and Annex II, that there is sufficient dedicated storage capacity for all ship-generated waste that has been accumulated and will be accumulated during the intended voyage of the ship until the port of delivery. If there are good reasons to believe that adequate facilities are not available at the intended port of delivery, or if

---

46 OJ L168, 10.7.1993, p. 1.
47 Annex II (as amended) deals with the information to be notified before entry into a port. This information includes: (1) name, call sign and, where appropriate, the IMO identification number of the ship; (2) the flag State; (3) the estimated time of arrival; (4) the estimated time of departure; (5) the previous port at which the vessel called; (7) the next port of call; (8) the last port and date when ship-generated waste was delivered; and (9) the type of waste to be discharged.
48 Art. 6(1).
49 Art. 7(3).

this port is unknown, and that there is therefore a risk that the waste will be discharged at sea, the Member State shall take all necessary measures to prevent marine pollution, if necessary by requiring the ship to deliver its waste before departure from the port.[50]

Fees for ship-generated waste

19.072 If ports were to impose excessive fees the ships could be deterred from using the facilities. Equally, an obligation to give facilities for free would be unfair on port authorities. Article 8 of the directive deals with fees for ship-generated waste. Member States shall ensure that the costs of port reception facilities for ship-generated waste, including the treatment and disposal of the waste, shall be covered through the collection of a fee from ships.[51] The cost recovery systems for using port reception facilities must provide no incentive for ships to discharge their waste into the sea and, to this end, the following principles shall apply to ships other than fishing vessels and recreational craft authorised to carry no more than 12 passengers:

(a) all ships calling at a port of a Member State shall contribute significantly to the costs referred to in paragraph 1, irrespective of actual use of the facilities. Arrangements to this effect may include incorporation of the fee in the port dues or a separate standard waste fee. The fees may be differentiated with respect to, inter alia, the category, type and size of the ship;

(b) the part of the costs which is not covered by the fee referred to in subparagraph (a), if any, shall be covered on the basis of the types and quantities of ship-generated waste actually delivered by the ship;

(c) fees may be reduced if the ship's environmental management, design, equipment and operation are such that the master of the ship can demonstrate that it produces reduced quantities of ship-generated waste.[52]

19.073 Article 8(3) provides that in order to ensure that the fees are fair, transparent, non-discriminatory and reflect the costs of the facilities and services made available and, where appropriate, used, the amount of the fees and the basis on which they have been calculated should be made clear for the port users. Article 8(4) goes on to provide that the Commission must, within three years of the date referred to in Article 16(1), submit a report to the European Parliament and to the Council, evaluating the impact of the variety of cost recovery systems adopted in accordance with paragraph 2 on the marine environment and waste flow patterns. That report must be drawn up in liaison with the competent authorities of the Member States and representatives of ports.

19.074 The Commission shall, if necessary in the light of this evaluation, submit a proposal to amend the directive by the introduction of a system involving the payment of an appropriate percentage, of no less than one-third, of the costs referred to in paragraph 1 by all ships calling at a port of a Member State irrespective of actual use of the facilities, or an alternative system with equivalent effects.

---

50 Art. 7(1).
51 Art. 8(1).
52 Art. 8(2).

Exemptions

19.075 Article 9 provides a number of exemptions to Directive 2000/59. Article 9(1) which provides that when ships are engaged in scheduled traffic with frequent and regular port calls and there is sufficient evidence of an arrangement to ensure the delivery of ship-generated waste and payment of fees in a port along the ship's route, Member States of the ports involved may exempt these ships from the obligations in Article 6, Article 7(1) and Article 8. Article 9(2) provides that Member States must inform the Commission of exemptions granted in accordance with Article 9(1) on a regular basis, at least once a year.

Delivery of cargo residues

19.076 Article 10 provides that the master of a ship calling at an EU port must ensure that cargo residues are delivered to a port reception facility in accordance with the provisions of MARPOL 73/78 and any fee for delivery of cargo residues shall be paid by the user of the reception facility.

Enforcement

19.077 The enforcement of Article 2000/59 is largely dealt with by Article 11. The Article provides, in paragraph 1, that Member States must ensure that any ship may be subject to an inspection in order to verify that it complies with Articles 7 and 10 and that a sufficient number of such inspections is carried out. Article 11(2) provides that for inspections concerning ships other than fishing vessels and recreational craft authorised to carry no more than 12 passengers:

"(a) in selecting ships for inspection, Member States shall pay particular attention to:

  – ships which have not complied with the notification requirements in Article 6;
  – ships for which the examination of the information provided by the master in accordance with Article 6 has revealed other grounds to believe that the ship does not comply with this Directive;

(b) such inspection may be undertaken within the framework of Directive 95/21, … when applicable; whatever the framework of the inspections, the 25% inspection requirement set out in that Directive shall apply;

(c) if the relevant authority is not satisfied with the results of this inspection, it shall ensure that the ship does not leave the port until it has delivered its ship-generated waste and cargo residues to a port reception facility in accordance with Articles 7 and 10;

(d) when there is clear evidence that a ship has proceeded to sea without having complied with Articles 7 or 10, the competent authority of the next port of call shall be informed thereof and such a ship shall, without prejudice to the application of the penalties referred to in Article 13, not be permitted to leave that port until a more detailed assessment of factors relating to the ship's compliance with this Directive, such as the accuracy of any information provided in accordance with Article 6, has taken place."

19.078 Article 11(3) goes on to provide that Member States must establish control procedures, to the extent required, for fishing vessels and recreational craft authorised to carry no more than 12 passengers to ensure compliance with the applicable requirements of the directive.

19.079 Article 12 ensures that Directive 2000/59 would not be alone. It provides for accompanying measures. Under Article 12(1), Member States must: (a) take all necessary measures to ensure that masters, providers of port reception facilities and other persons concerned are adequately informed of the requirements addressed to them under this directive and that they comply with them; (b) designate appropriate authorities or bodies for performing functions under the directive; (c) make provision for co-operation between their relevant authorities and commercial organisations to ensure the effective implementation of the directive; (d) ensure that the information notified by masters in accordance with Article 6 be appropriately examined; (e) ensure that the formalities relating to the use of port reception facilities are simple and expeditious in order to create an incentive for the master to use port reception facilities and to avoid undue delays to ships; (f) ensure that the Commission is provided with a copy of the allegations of inadequate port reception facilities referred to in Article 4(3); (g) ensure that the treatment, recovery or disposal of ship-generated waste and cargo residues shall be carried out in accordance with Directive 75/442 and other relevant EU waste legislation, in particular Council Directive 75/439 of 16 June 1975 on the disposal of waste oils[53] and Council Directive 91/689 of 12 December 1991 on hazardous waste;[54] and (h) ensure in accordance with their national legislation that any party involved in the delivery or reception of ship-generated waste or cargo residues can claim compensation for damage caused by undue delay.

19.080 Article 12(2) provides that delivery of ship-generated waste and cargo residues shall be considered as release for free circulation within the meaning of Article 79 of Council Regulation 2913/92 of 12 October 1992 establishing the Community Customs Code.[55] The customs authorities shall not require the lodging of a summary declaration in accordance with Article 45 of the Community Customs Code.

19.081 Article 12(3) states that Member States and the Commission must co-operate in establishing an appropriate information and monitoring system, covering at least the whole of the Community, to (a) improve the identification of ships which have not delivered their ship-generated waste and cargo residues in accordance with the directive; and (b) ascertain whether the goals set in Article 1 of the directive have been met. Moreover, Member States and the Commission must co-operate in establishing common criteria for identifying ships referred to in Article 8(2)(c).

Penalties

19.082 Article 13 provides for a penalties regime for breaches. Under the article, Member States must lay down a system of penalties for the breach of national provisions adopted pursuant to the directive and must take all the measures necessary to ensure that those penalties are applied. The penalties provided must be effective, proportionate and dissuasive.

---

53 OJ L194, 25 July 1975, p. 23.

54 OJ L377, 31 December 1991, p. 20. Directive as last amended by Directive 94/31 (OJ L168, 2 July 1994, p. 28).

55 OJ L302, 19 October 1992, p. 1. Regulation as last amended by Regulation (EC) No 955/1999 (OJ L119, 7 May 1999, p. 1).

Committee procedure

19.083 Article 14(1) provides that the Commission shall be assisted by the Committee on Safe Seas and the Prevention of Pollution from Ships ("COSS") set up by Article 3 of Regulation (EC) No 2099/2002 of the European Parliament and of the Council.[56],[57]

Amendment procedure

19.084 Article 15 deals with the amendment procedure. The annexes to the directive, the definition in Article 2(b) and references to Community and IMO instruments may be adapted by the Commission in order to bring them into line with Community or IMO measures which have entered into force, in so far as such amendments do not broaden the scope of the directive. The annexes to the directive may be amended by the Commission when necessary in order to improve the regime established by the directive, in so far as such amendments do not broaden the scope of the directive. Those measures, designed to amend non-essential elements of the directive, shall be adopted in accordance with the regulatory procedure with scrutiny referred to in Article 14(2).The amendments to the international instruments referred to in Article 2 may be excluded from the scope of the directive pursuant to Article 5 of Regulation 2099/2002.

Entry into force and implementation

19.085 Article 18 provides that the directive entered into force on the day of its publication in the *Official Journal*. Article 16 deals with implementation. Article 16(1) provides that Member States had to bring into force the laws, regulations and administrative provisions necessary to comply with the directive before 28 December 2002 and forthwith inform the Commission of their implementation of the directive. However, as far as sewage (as referred to in Article 2(c)) was concerned, the implementation of the directive was suspended until 12 months after the entry into force of Annex IV to MARPOL 73/78, while respecting the distinction made in the convention between new and existing ships. Article 16(2) provides that when Member States adopted these measures, they had to contain a reference to the directive or be accompanied by such a reference on the occasion of their official publication. The methods of making such a reference could be laid down by Member States.

EU evaluation of Directive 2000/59

19.086 Article 17 sensibly provides for evaluation of the operation of the directive. Article 17(1) provides that Member States shall submit to the Commission a status report concerning the implementation of the directive every three years. In turn, Article 17(2) provides that the Commission must submit an evaluation report on the operation of the system as provided for in the directive to the European Parliament and the Council, on the

---

56 OJ L324, 29 November 2002, p. 1.

57 Art. 14(2) provides that where reference is made to that paragraph, Art. 5a(1) to (4) and Art. 7 of Dec. 1999/468 shall apply, having regard to the provisions of Art. 8 thereof.

basis of the reports of the Member States as provided for in Article 17(1) together with proposals as necessary, concerning the implementation of the directive.

L. DISCHARGE OF HYDROCARBONS AT SEA COMMISSION DECISION 80/686 SETTING UP AN ADVISORY COMMITTEE ON THE CONTROL AND REDUCTION OF POLLUTION CAUSED BY OIL AND OTHER HARMFUL SUBSTANCES DISCHARGED AT SEA

19.087 On 25 June 1980 the Commission adopted Decision 80/686 of setting up an Advisory Committee on the control and reduction of pollution caused by oil and other harmful substances discharged at sea.[58] It was amended by Commission Decision OJ L188/11, 22 July 1980. The decision entered into force on 25 June 1980.[59] It was amended by Commission Decision of 25 March 1985[60] and Commission Decision of 13 February 1987.[61]

19.088 At its meetings in Copenhagen on 7 and 8 April 1978, in Bremen on 6 and 7 July 1978 and in Luxembourg on 27 and 28 April 1980, the European Council took the view that preventing and combating marine pollution, in particular by hydrocarbons, should be one of the EU's major "objectives of action";

"Whereas the European Communities' 1973 environment action programme (1), supplemented by that of 1977 (2), stressed that it was of paramount importance to western Europe that effective action be taken against the dangers inherent in the carriage of hydrocarbons, including the threat of serious coastal pollution as a result of accidents on the high seas, and specified that the protection of sea water in order to ensure the maintenance of ecological balances was a priority task;

Whereas on 26 June 1978 the Council adopted a resolution setting up an action programme of the European Communities on the control and reduction of pollution caused by hydrocarbons discharged at sea (3);

Whereas the Commission needs to seek advice from highly qualified experts in the Member States concerning pollution caused by hydrocarbons discharged at sea;

Whereas the Community also needs to have a forum where experts can meet for the purpose of collecting existing information and experience gained in Member States, thus facilitating the coordination of measures taken or planned at national, international or Community level…"

19.089 Article 1 provides that the Commission sets up an Advisory Committee on the control and reduction of pollution caused by oil and other harmful substances discharged at sea, hereinafter referred to as "the Committee".

19.090 Article 2 provides that the terms of reference of the Committee shall be: (1) to advise the Commission, at the request of the latter or on its own initiative, on all problems concerning the implementation of Community measures for the control and reduction of pollution caused by oil and other harmful substances discharged at sea: and (2) to allow the collection of existing information and experience gained in the Member States, on ways of controlling and reducing pollution caused by oil and other harmful substances discharged at sea, thus facilitating the co-ordination of measures taken or planned at national, international or EU level.

---

58 OJ L188/11, 22 July 1980.
59 Dec. 80/686, Art. 12.
60 OJ L89/64, 29 March 1985.
61 OJ L57/57, 27 February 1987.

19.091 Article 3(1) states that the Committee must consist of government experts with specialist knowledge of the areas referred to in Article 2 (two representatives per Member State).

19.092 Article 3(2) provides that committee members shall be chosen by the Commission on the basis of nominations by the Member States.

19.093 Article 3(3) provides that representatives of the departments of the Commission concerned shall take part in the meetings of the Committee.

19.094 An alternate must be appointed by each Committee member. Without prejudice to Article 9, an alternate shall attend Committee meetings and take part in the work of the Committee only if the full member in question is prevented from attending.[62]

19.095 The Commission must publish the membership list in the *Official Journal of the European Communities* as a matter of information.[63]

19.096 The Committee must be chaired by a Commission representative.[64]

19.097 Article 7 provides that where necessary, the Commission may invite one or more members who are particularly well qualified in the area in question to attend a meeting on an individual basis.

19.098 The departments of the Commission shall provide the secretariat of the Committee and of the bureau.[65]

19.099 Article 9 provides that the chairman may invite any person with expert knowledge of a subject on the agenda to take part in the work of the Committee. Experts must only take part in the discussions on the matter concerning which they have been invited to attend.

19.100 Without prejudice to Article 214 of the Treaty, Committee members shall be required not to disclose any information which has been acquired by them in the course of the work of the Committee or of the bureau where the Commission informs them that the opinion requested or the question raised concerns a confidential matter.[66]

M. LOW SULPHUR FUELS

Introduction

19.101 A key feature of the maritime environmental regime relates to low sulphur fuels. The Commission started early with a recommendation.

Commission Recommendation of 21 December 2009 on the safe implementation of the use of low sulphur fuel by ships at berth in Community ports

19.102 On 21 December 2009, the Commission adopted a recommendation on the safe implementation of the use of low sulphur fuel by ships at berth in Community ports.[67] The recommendation referred to the TFEU generally and, in particular, Article 292 of the TFEU.

---

62 Art. 4.
63 Art. 5.
64 Art. 6.
65 Art. 8.
66 Art. 11.
67 OJ L348/73, 29 December 2009.

19.103 The first recital to the recommendation recalled that Article 4b of Council Directive 1999/32 of 26 April 1999 relating to a reduction in the sulphur content of certain liquid fuels[68] (as amended) provided for the maximum sulphur content of marine fuels used by ships at berth in Community ports, including, as of 1 January 2010, the obligations for Member States to ensure that vessels do not use marine fuels with a sulphur content exceeding 0.1% by mass and that marine gas oils are not placed on the market in their territory if the sulphur content of those marine gas oils exceeds 0.1% by mass.

19.104 The second recital provided that Article 6 of the directive also provides that Member States shall check by sampling that the sulphur content of marine fuels complies with the relevant provision of Article 4b and that sampling commence from the date of entry into force of the requirement.

19.105 The third recital provided that as indicated in the Commission communication on notifications of postponements of attainment deadlines and exemptions from the obligation to apply certain limit values pursuant to Article 22 of Directive 2008/50 on ambient air quality and cleaner air for Europe,[69] concentrations in more than 40% of the zones and agglomerations in the Community currently exceed the daily PM10 limit value. Implementation of a low sulphur limit on fuel by ships while they are at berth in Community ports is essential to improve ambient air quality, as highlighted in the communication from the Commission to the European Parliament and to the Council on an EU strategy to reduce atmospheric emissions from seagoing ships[70] and the Thematic Strategy on Air Pollution adopted in 2005.[71]

19.106 The fourth recital provides that the requirements were adopted in October 2008 by the IMO in the context of the revision of the International Convention for the Prevention of Pollution from Ships (MARPOL Convention), to be implemented from 1 January 2015 for ships sailing within emission control areas as defined by Article 2(3e) of Directive 1999/32.

19.107 The fifth recital provided that the Commission, considering the safety risks at stake, deems it necessary to issue appropriate guidance to Member States in order to ensure a high level of safety and effective prevention of pollution from ships in the enforcement of the provisions of that directive throughout the EU.

19.108 The sixth recital is that from 1 January 2010, ships using heavy fuel oil while at sea are to switch to lighter marine fuels such as marine diesel or gas oil when at berth in EU ports as heavy fuel oil with a sufficiently low sulphur content is not generally available.

19.109 The seventh recital recalls sensibly that there may be operational problems and safety risks associated with the use of marine diesel and gas oil in ships that have not been designed to use such fuels or have not undergone the necessary technical adaptation. The Commission has considered the risks associated with the change of fuels and concluded that the main safety risk relates to use in ships' boilers which have not yet been assessed and certified for use with the required type of fuel. While boilers can use heavy fuel oil or distillate fuels, a risk arises because marine diesel and gas oils are less viscous

---

68 OJ L121/13, 11 May 1999.
69 COM (2008) 403.
70 COM (2002) 595.
71 COM (2005) 446.

and more volatile and heating of the fuel system, which is required for heavy fuel oil, is not necessary for distillate fuels. The number of affected ships and the probability of such occurrences are difficult to assess precisely.

19.110 The eighth to the tenth recitals then recall:

"(8) Directive 1999/32/EC allowed sufficient time for the shipping industry to bring about the technical adaptation to a maximum limit of 0,1% sulphur by mass for marine fuels used by ships at berth in Community ports. Technical solutions to limit the risks are available. However, to date, there are still ships that have not gone through the necessary modifications and very few ships have undergone the necessary verification and certification process.

(9) Technical solutions are available to mitigate potential consequences of switching fuel at berth. Limited demand from the shipping industry has delayed the development of the necessary technical solutions, resulting in subsequent delays in the verification and certification process.

(10) The information available to the Commission underlines that, for these ships that have not undergone the technical modifications, completion of the whole process should not take more than eight months.

(11) There is a need for boiler and engine manufacturers to develop specific recommendations and procedures for the retrofitting of these solutions, while shipowners should develop and implement specific operational procedures and provide appropriate training to crews."

19.111 The short recommendation itself read:

"1. As part of the Member States enforcement actions against ships which fail to comply with the requirement to use fuels with a maximum permitted sulphur content of 0,1% while at berth, Member States should request those ships to provide detailed evidence of the steps they are taking to achieve compliance. This should include a contract with a manufacturer and an approved retrofit plan which should be approved by the ship's classification society or, for ships flying the flag of a Member State, by the organisation having recognition in accordance with Regulation (EC) No 391/2009 of the European Parliament and of the Council.[72] The retrofit plan should clearly state the date of completion of the adaptation and certification process.

2. Member States may consider the existence of an approved retrofit plan when assessing the degree of penalties to be applied to non-complying ships.

3. Member States should take appropriate measures to raise awareness among owners, operators and seafarers of the safety risk related to fuel changeover in the absence of any necessary technical adaptation to a ship's fuel system and the necessity for training to be provided."

N. REGIONAL MEASURES

Introduction

19.112 In practical terms, the EU is not a singular maritime environmental region and it is therefore inevitable that regional arrangements would be adopted. Regional arrangements have been adopted for the likes of the Mediterranean and the Baltic and others could follow suit.

---

72 OJ L131/11, 28.5.2009.

MEDITERRANEAN

19.113 The Barcelona Convention for the Protection of the Mediterranean of 1976, amended in 1995, and the protocols drawn up in line with the convention aim to protect and improve the marine and coastal environment in the Mediterranean, while promoting regional and national plans contributing to sustainable development.

Mediterranean: Council Decision 77/585 of 25 July 1977 concluding the Convention for the protection of the Mediterranean Sea against pollution and the Protocol for the prevention of the pollution of the Mediterranean Sea by dumping from ships and aircraft

19.114 On 25 July 1977, the Council adopted Decision 77/585 of 25 July 1977 concluding the Convention for the Protection of the Mediterranean Sea against Pollution and the Protocol for the Prevention of the Pollution of the Mediterranean Sea by Dumping from Ships and Aircraft.[73] The recitals to the decision read:

"Whereas Article 24 of the Convention for the protection of the Mediterranean Sea against pollution provides that the Convention and the Protocols relating thereto shall be open for signature by the European Economic Community;

Having regard to the declaration of the Council of the European Communities and of the representatives of the Governments of the Member States meeting in the Council of 22 November 1973 on the programme of action of the European Communities on the environment;

Whereas that programme lays stress inter alia on the fact that marine pollution affects the whole Community, both because of the essential role played by the sea in the preservation and development of species and on account of the importance of sea transport for the harmonious economic development of the Community;

Whereas, furthermore, the action programme referred to above and Council Directive 76/464 ... of 4 May 1976 on pollution caused by certain dangerous substances discharged into the aquatic environment of the Community ... provide that certain measures are to be implemented by the Community in order to reduce the various types of marine pollution;

Whereas the Convention on the protection of the Mediterranean Sea against pollution provides in particular that suitable measures should be adopted to prevent and reduce pollution caused by dumping from ships and aircraft, pollution resulting from the exploration and exploitation of the continental shelf, the seabed and its subsoil and pollution from land-based sources;

Whereas Article 23 of the Convention provides that no party may become a Contracting Party thereto unless it becomes at the same time a Contracting Party to at least one of the Protocols and that no party may become a Contracting Party to a Protocol unless it is, or becomes at the same time, a Contracting Party to the Convention...

Whereas it appears necessary for the Community to conclude this Convention and the Protocol on the prevention of the pollution of the Mediterranean Sea by dumping from ships and aircraft in order to attain, in the course of the operation of the common market, one of the objectives of the Community in the field of the protection of the environment and of the quality of life; whereas, moreover no provision is made in the Treaty for the powers necessary to this end;

Whereas the Convention and the said Protocol were signed on behalf of the Community on 13 September 1976..."

19.115 Article 1 provides that the Convention for the Protection of the Mediterranean Sea against Pollution and the Protocol for the Prevention of Pollution of the

---

73 OJ L240/1, 19 September 1977.

Mediterranean Sea by Dumping from Ships and Aircraft are hereby concluded on behalf of the EEC. The texts of the convention and the protocol are annexed to the decision.

Mediterranean: Council Decision 83/101 of 28 February 1983 concluding the Protocol for the protection of the Mediterranean Sea against pollution from land-based sources

19.116 On 28 February 1983, the Council adopted Decision 83/101 on concluding the Protocol for the protection of the Mediterranean Sea against pollution from land-based sources.[74]

19.117 There has been a proposal from the Commission.[75] There also had been an opinion of the European Parliament.[76] The Council recalled the earlier declaration of the Council of the European Communities and of the representatives of the governments of the Member States meeting in the Council of 22 November 1973 on the programme of action of the European Communities on the environment.[77] The Council recalled that that programme had laid stress on, among other things, the fact that marine pollution affects the whole of the EU, both because of the essential role played by the sea in the preservation and development of species and on account of the importance of sea transport for the harmonious economic development of the EU. The decision also recalled that the Convention on the Protection of the Mediterranean Sea against Pollution provides, in particular, that suitable measures should be adopted to prevent and reduce pollution caused by dumping from ships and aircraft, pollution resulting from the exploration and exploitation of the continental shelf, the seabed and its subsoil and pollution from land-based sources. In adopting Decision 77/585, the Council approved the Convention for the Protection of the Mediterranean Sea against Pollution, and the Protocol for the Prevention of the Pollution of the Mediterranean Sea by Dumping from Ships and Aircraft.[78] The then Community had taken part in the negotiations concerning the conclusion of the convention protocol for the protection of the Mediterranean Sea against pollution from land-based sources and, on 17 May 1980, the then Community had signed the protocol. So the decision went further and said that

> "in order to attain, in the course of the operation of the common market, one of the objectives of the Community in the field of the protection of the environment and of the quality of life, it appears necessary to approve the said Protocol [and] since the specific powers of action required to adopt this Decision have not been provided for in the Treaty, it is necessary to invoke Article 235 thereof".

In other words, there was no specific treaty basis for the EU to take action but it nonetheless wanted to take action so it relied on the "catch-all" provision in Article 235 of the then EEC Treaty (which is now, in effect, Article 21 of the Treaty on the European Union). Article 235 of the then EEC Treaty was an interesting and useful measure which provided that if

---

74 OJ L67/1, 12 March 1983, http://eur-lex.europa.eu/legal-content/EN/TXT/HTML/?uri=CELEX:31994D0 157&from=EN.
75 OJ C4/3, 8 January 1982.
76 OJ C334/136, 20 December 1982.
77 OJ C112, 20 December 1973, p. 1.
78 OJ L240/1, 19 September 1977.

"action by the Community should prove necessary to attain, in the course of the operation of the common market, one of the objectives of the Community and this Treaty has not provided the necessary powers, the Council shall, acting unanimously on a proposal from the Commission and after consulting the European Parliament, take the appropriate measures".[79]

19.118 Article 1 provides that the Protocol for the protection of the Mediterranean Sea against pollution from land-based sources is hereby approved on behalf of the European Economic Community.

19.119 Article 2, under the President of the Council must deposit the Acts as provided for in Article 16(4) of the Protocol referred to in Article 1 hereof.

Mediterranean: Council Decision 2013/5 of 17 December 2012 on the accession of the European Union to the Protocol for the Protection of the Mediterranean Sea against pollution resulting from exploration and exploitation of the continental shelf and the seabed and its subsoil

19.120 On 17 December 2012, the Council adopted Decision 2013/5 on the accession of the European Union to the Protocol for the Protection of the Mediterranean Sea against pollution resulting from exploration and exploitation of the continental shelf and the seabed and its subsoil.[80] The decision entered into force on the date of its adoption.[81]

19.121 The legal basis of Decision 2014/5 is the TFEU generally and, in particular, Article 192(1), in conjunction with Article 218(6)(a) of the TFEU.

19.122 The first recital of Decision 2013/5 refers to the Convention for the Protection of the Mediterranean Sea against Pollution, which was subsequently renamed as the Convention for the Protection of the Marine Environment and the Coastal Region of the Mediterranean (the "Barcelona Convention"), was concluded on behalf of the EC by means of Council Decision 77/585[82] and amendments to the Barcelona Convention were accepted by means of Council Decision 1999/802.[83]

19.123 The second recital of Decision 2013/5 provides that in accordance with Article 7 of the Barcelona Convention, the Contracting Parties are to take all appropriate measures to prevent, abate, combat and to the fullest possible extent eliminate pollution of the Mediterranean Sea area resulting from exploration and exploitation of the continental shelf and the seabed and its subsoil. One of the protocols to the Barcelona Convention deals, according to the third recital of Decision 2013/5, with the protection of the Mediterranean Sea against pollution resulting from exploration and exploitation of the continental shelf and the seabed and its subsoil (the "Offshore Protocol") which entered into force on 24 March 2011. Albania, Cyprus, Libya, Morocco, Syria and Tunisia had ratified it. In addition to Cyprus, some other Member States that are Contracting Parties to the Barcelona Convention had announced just before they adopted Decision 2013/5 their intention to also ratify the protocol.

19.124 The Council estimated, according to the fourth recital, that there are more than 200 active offshore platforms in the Mediterranean and more installations are under

---

79 It is now mirrored in Art. 21 of the TEU.
80 OJ L4/13, 9 January 2013.
81 Dec. 2013/5, Art. 3.
82 OJ L240/1, 19 September 1997.
83 OJ L322/32, 14 December 1999.

consideration. Hydrocarbon exploration and exploitation activities are expected to increase after the discovery of large fossil fuels reserves in the Mediterranean. Due to the semi-enclosed nature and special hydrodynamics of the Mediterranean Sea, an accident of the kind that occurred in the Gulf of Mexico in 2010 could have immediate adverse transboundary consequences on the Mediterranean economy and fragile marine and coastal ecosystems. It is likely that in the medium term other mineral resources contained in the deep sea, seabed and subsoil will be the subject of exploration and exploitation activities.

19.125 It is clear from recital 5 that the Council believed that failure to address effectively the risks emanating from such activities could gravely compromise the efforts of all the Member States having the obligation to take the necessary measures to achieve and maintain good environmental status in their marine waters in the Mediterranean, as required by Directive 2008/56 of the European Parliament and of the Council of 17 June 2008 establishing a framework for community action in the field of marine environmental policy (the so-called "Marine Strategy Framework Directive").[84] In addition, taking the necessary action would contribute to meeting the commitments and respecting the obligations into which Greece, Spain, France, Italy, Cyprus, Malta, Slovenia and the Union itself have entered as Contracting Parties of the Barcelona Convention. The decision recalled (in the sixth recital) that the Offshore Protocol covers a broad range of provisions which will need to be implemented by different levels of administration. While it is appropriate for the Union to act in support of safety of offshore exploration and exploitation activities, bearing in mind, among other things, the high probability of cross-border effects of environmental problems related to such activities, the Member States and their relevant competent authorities should be responsible for certain detailed measures laid down in the Offshore Protocol. Ultimately, the aim of the decision was to enable the EU to accede to the Offshore Protocol.

19.126 The operative provisions were succinct. The accession of the European Union to the Protocol for the Protection of the Mediterranean Sea against pollution resulting from exploration and exploitation of the continental shelf and the seabed and its subsoil is hereby approved on behalf of the Union.[85] The President of the Council was authorised by the decision to designate the person(s) empowered to proceed, on behalf of the Union, to the deposit of the instrument of approval with the government of Spain which assumes the functions of Depositary, as provided for in Article 32(2) of the Offshore Protocol, in order to express the consent of the Union to be bound by the Offshore Protocol.[86]

Mediterranean: Council Decision 2010/631 of 13 September 2010 concerning the conclusion, on behalf of the European Union, of the Protocol on Integrated Coastal Zone Management in the Mediterranean to the Convention for the Protection of the Marine Environment and the Coastal Region of the Mediterranean

19.127 On 13 September 2010, the Council adopted Decision 2010/631 concerning the conclusion, on behalf of the European Union, of the Protocol on Integrated Coastal Zone

---

84 OJ L164, 25 June 2008, p. 19.

85 Art. 1.

86 The date of entry into force of the Offshore Protocol for the Union will be published in the Official Journal of the European Union by the General Secretariat of the Council.

Management in the Mediterranean to the Convention for the Protection of the Marine Environment and the Coastal Region of the Mediterranean.[87]

19.128 The recitals to Decision 2010/631 give the background to the decision:

"(1) The Convention for the Protection of the Mediterranean Sea against Pollution, which was subsequently renamed as the Convention for the Protection of the Marine Environment and the Coastal Region of the Mediterranean (hereinafter referred to as 'the Barcelona Convention') was concluded on behalf of the European Community by the Council in Decisions 77/585/EEC[88] and 1999/802/EC.[89]

(2) In accordance with Article 4.3(e) of the Barcelona Convention, the Contracting Parties shall commit themselves to promote the integrated management of the coastal zones, taking into account the protection of areas of ecological and landscape interest and the rational use of natural resources.

(3) The Recommendation of the European Parliament and of the Council of 30 May 2002, concerning the implementation of Integrated Coastal Zone Management in Europe,[90] and in particular Chapter V thereof, encourages the implementation by the Member States of integrated coastal zone management in the context of existing conventions with neighbouring countries, including non-Member States, in the same regional sea.

(4) The European Union promotes integrated management on a larger scale by means of horizontal instruments, including in the field of environmental protection, and by developing a sound scientific base for it, through its research programmes. These activities therefore contribute to integrated coastal zone management.

(5) Integrated Coastal Zone Management is one component of the EU Integrated Maritime Policy as endorsed by the European Council held in Lisbon on 13 and 14 December 2007 and as also detailed in the Commission Communication 'Towards an Integrated Maritime Policy for better governance in the Mediterranean' and later welcomed by the General Affairs Council in its conclusions on Integrated Maritime Policy of 16 November 2009.

(6) By Decision 2009/89/EC of 4 December 2008,[91] the Council signed the Protocol on Integrated Coastal Zone Management in the Mediterranean to the Barcelona Convention (hereinafter referred to as 'the ICZM Protocol') on behalf of the Community, subject to the subsequent conclusion of the ICZM Protocol at a later date.

(7) Following the entry into force of the Treaty of Lisbon on 1 December 2009, the European Union notified the Government of Spain as regards the European Union having replaced and succeeded the European Community.

(8) The Mediterranean coastal zones continue to experience severe environmental pressure and degradation of coastal resources. The ICZM Protocol provides a framework to stimulate a more concerted and integrated approach, involving public and private stakeholders including civil society and economic operators. Such an inclusive approach, based on best available scientific observation and knowledge, is required to address these problems more effectively and achieve a more sustainable development of the Mediterranean coastal zones.

(9) The ICZM Protocol covers a broad range of provisions which will need to be implemented by different levels of administration, having regard to the principles of subsidiarity and proportionality. While it is appropriate for the Union to act in support of integrated coastal zone management, bearing in mind, inter alia, the cross-border nature of most environmental problems, the Member States and their relevant competent authorities will be responsible for the design and implementation on the coastal territory of certain detailed measures laid down in the ICZM Protocol, such as the establishment of zones where construction is not allowed.

---

87 OJ L279/1, 23 October 2010.
88 Ed., OJ L240/1, 19 September 1997.
89 Ed., OJ L322/32, 14 December 1999.
90 Ed., OJ L148/24, 6 June 2002.
91 Ed., OJ L34/17, 4 April 2009.

(10) The ICZM Protocol should be approved."

19.129 Article 1 provides that the Protocol on Integrated Coastal Zone Management in the Mediterranean to the Convention for the Protection of the Marine Environment and the Coastal Region of the Mediterranean (i.e. "the ICZM Protocol") is hereby approved on behalf of the European Union.[92]

19.130 Article 2 provides that the President of the Council must designate the person(s) empowered to proceed, on behalf of the Union, to the deposit of the instrument of approval, with the Spanish Government which assumes the function of Depositary, provided for in Article 37 of the ICZM Protocol, in order to express the consent of the Union to be bound by the ICZM Protocol.

19.131 Article 3 provides that the decision entered into force on the day of its adoption (i.e., 13 September 2010). The date of entry into force of the ICZM Protocol was to be published in the Official Journal of the European Union.

Mediterranean: Council Decision 2004/575 on the conclusion, on behalf of the European Community, of the Protocol to the Barcelona Convention for the Protection of the Mediterranean Sea against Pollution, concerning cooperation in preventing pollution from ships and, in cases of emergency, combating pollution of the Mediterranean Sea

19.132 On 29 April 2004, the Council adopted Decision 2004/575 on the conclusion, on behalf of the European Community, of the Protocol to the Barcelona Convention for the Protection of the Mediterranean Sea against Pollution, concerning co-operation in preventing pollution from ships and, in cases of emergency, combating pollution of the Mediterranean Sea.[93]

19.133 The legal basis was the TEC generally, and, in particular, Article 175(1), in conjunction with the first sentence of Article 300(2) and the first subparagraph of Article 300(3) thereof.

19.134 The background to the decision is clear from the recitals:

"(1) European Community policy on the environment contributes to the pursuit of objectives which include preserving, protecting and improving the quality of the environment and promoting measures at international level to deal with regional or worldwide environmental problems.

(2) The European Community is a Contracting Party to the Convention for the Protection of the Mediterranean Sea against Pollution (Barcelona Convention), approved by Decision 77/585/EEC,[94] and its 1995 revision, approved by Decision 1999/802/EC.[95] The Community is also a Contracting Party to four protocols of the Barcelona Convention, including the Protocol concerning cooperation in combating pollution of the Mediterranean Sea by oil and other harmful substances in cases of emergency approved by Decision 81/420/EEC.[96]

---

92 The ICZM Protocol was published in OJ L34, 4 February 2009, p. 19, together with the decision on signature.

93 OJ L261, 6 August 2004, p. 40, http://eur-lex.europa.eu/legal-content/EN/TXT/HTML/?uri=OJ:JOL_2004_261_R_NS007&from=EN.

94 OJ L240/1, 19.9.1977.

95 OJ L322/32, 14.12.1999.

96 Ed., OJ L162/4, 19 June 1981.

(3) The Commission took part, on behalf of the Community, in the negotiations on the Protocol concerning cooperation in preventing pollution from ships and, in cases of emergency, combating pollution of the Mediterranean Sea (the Protocol), on the basis of the negotiating directives received from the Council on 25 January 2000.

(4) On 25 January 2002 in Malta, the Community signed the Protocol.

(5) The Protocol updates the legal instruments of the Barcelona Convention, to include cooperation on the prevention of pollution from ships, to make more effective cooperation in response to pollution incidents and to promote the implementation of the applicable international regulations.

(6) The Protocol, not affecting the right of Parties to adopt relevant stricter measures in conformity with international law, contains the measures needed to avoid there being any incoherence with Community legislation already in force in the areas covered by the Protocol.

(7) The Community should therefore approve the Protocol."

19.135 Article 1 provides that the Protocol to the Barcelona Convention for the Protection of the Mediterranean Sea against Pollution concerning co-operation in preventing pollution from ships and, in cases of emergency, combating pollution of the Mediterranean Sea, hereinafter referred to as the protocol, is approved on behalf of the EU.

19.136 Article 2 provides that the President of the Council is authorised to designate the person(s) empowered, on behalf of the EC, to deposit with the Spanish government the instrument of approval of the protocol, in accordance with the provisions of Article 23 of the protocol.

Mediterranean: Protocol Concerning Cooperation in Preventing Pollution from Ships and, in Cases of Emergency, Combating Pollution of the Mediterranean Sea

19.137 On 25 January 2002, the Protocol Concerning Cooperation in Preventing Pollution from Ships and, in Cases of Emergency, Combating Pollution of the Mediterranean Sea was adopted.[97] It was agreed at Valletta in Malta in the Arabic, English, French and Spanish languages with the four texts being equally authentic.

19.138 The background is clear from the recitals:

"Being Parties to the Convention for the Protection of the Mediterranean Sea against Pollution, adopted at Barcelona on 16 February 1976 and amended on 10 June 1995,

Desirous of implementing Articles 6 and 9 of the said Convention,

Recognising that grave pollution of the sea by oil and hazardous and noxious substances or a threat thereof in the Mediterranean Sea Area involves a danger for the coastal States and the marine environment,

Considering that the cooperation of all the coastal States of the Mediterranean Sea is called for to prevent pollution from ships and to respond to pollution incidents, irrespective of their origin,

Acknowledging the role of the International Maritime Organization and the importance of cooperating within the framework of this Organisation, in particular in promoting the adoption and the development of international rules and standards to prevent, reduce and control pollution of the marine environment from ships,

Emphasising the efforts made by the Mediterranean coastal States for the implementation of these international rules and standards,

Acknowledging also the contribution of the European Community to the implementation of international standards as regards maritime safety and the prevention of pollution from ships,

---

97 OJ L261/41, 6 August 2004.

Recognising also the importance of cooperation in the Mediterranean Sea Area in promoting the effective implementation of international regulations to prevent, reduce and control pollution of the marine environment from ships,

Recognising further the importance of prompt and effective action at the national, subregional and regional levels in taking emergency measures to deal with pollution of the marine environment or a threat thereof,

Applying the precautionary principle, the polluter pays principle and the method of environmental impact assessment, and utilising the best available techniques and the best environmental practices, as provided for in Article 4 of the Convention,

Bearing in mind the relevant provisions of the United Nations Convention on the Law of the Sea, done at Montego Bay on 10 December 1982, which is in force and to which many Mediterranean coastal States and the European Community are Parties,

Taking into account the international conventions dealing in particular with maritime safety, the prevention of pollution from ships, preparedness for and response to pollution incidents, and liability and compensation for pollution damage,

Wishing to further develop mutual assistance and cooperation in preventing and combating pollution..."

19.139 Article 1 sets out various definitions for the purpose of the protocol. First, the term "convention", means the Convention for the Protection of the Mediterranean Sea against Pollution, adopted at Barcelona on 16 February 1976 and amended on 10 June 1995. The term "pollution incident", means an occurrence or series of occurrences having the same origin, which results or may result in a discharge of oil and/or hazardous and noxious substances and which poses or may pose a threat to the marine environment, or to the coastline or related interests of one or more States, and which requires emergency action or other immediate response. The term "hazardous and noxious substances" means any substance other than oil which, if introduced into the marine environment, is likely to create hazards to human health, to harm living resources and marine life, to damage amenities or to interfere with other legitimate uses of the sea. The term "related interests", means the interests of a coastal State directly affected or threatened and concerning, among others: (i) maritime activities in coastal areas, in ports or estuaries, including fishing activities; (ii) the historical and tourist appeal of the area in question, including water sports and recreation; (iii) the health of the coastal population; (iv) the cultural, aesthetic, scientific and educational value of the area; and (v) the conservation of biological diversity and the sustainable use of marine and coastal biological resources. The expression "international regulations", means regulations aimed at preventing, reducing and controlling pollution of the marine environment from ships as adopted, at the global level and in conformity with international law, under the aegis of UN specialised agencies, and in particular of the IMO. The phrase "Regional Centre", means the Regional Marine Pollution Emergency Response Centre for the Mediterranean Sea ("REMPEC"), established by Resolution 7 adopted by the Conference of Plenipotentiaries of the Coastal States of the Mediterranean Region on the Protection of the Mediterranean Sea at Barcelona on 9 February 1976, which is administered by the IMO and the United Nations Environment Programme, and the objectives and functions of which are defined by the Contracting Parties to the convention.

19.140 Article 2 delineates the "Protocol area" and provides that the area to which the protocol applies shall be the Mediterranean Sea Area as defined in Article 1 of the convention.

19.141 Article 3 is termed "general provisions". Article 3(1) provides that the Parties must co-operate: (a) to implement international regulations to prevent, reduce and control pollution of the marine environment from ships; and (b) to take all necessary measures in cases of pollution incidents. Article 3(2) provides that in co-operating, the Parties should take into account as appropriate the participation of local authorities, non-governmental organisations and socioeconomic actors. Article 3(3) provides that each Party must apply the protocol without prejudice to the sovereignty or the jurisdiction of other Parties or other States. Any measures taken by a Party to apply the protocol shall be in accordance with international law.

19.142 Contingency plans and other means of preventing and combating pollution incidents are addressed by Article 4. Article 4(1) provides that the Parties shall endeavour to maintain and promote, either individually or through bilateral or multilateral co-operation, contingency plans and other means of preventing and combating pollution incidents. These means shall include, in particular, equipment, ships, aircraft and personnel prepared for operations in cases of emergency, the enactment, as appropriate, of relevant legislation, the development or strengthening of the capability to respond to a pollution incident and the designation of a national authority or authorities responsible for the implementation of the protocol. Article 4(2) goes on to provide that the parties shall also take measures in conformity with international law to prevent the pollution of the Mediterranean Sea Area from ships in order to ensure the effective implementation in that Area of the relevant international conventions in their capacity as flag State, port State and coastal State, and their applicable legislation. They shall develop their national capacity as regards the implementation of those international conventions and may co-operate for their effective implementation through bilateral or multilateral agreements. Under Article 4(3), the Parties shall inform the Regional Centre every two years of the measures taken for the implementation of Article 4. The Regional Centre shall present a report to the Parties on the basis of the information received.

19.143 Article 5 ("Monitoring") provides that the parties must develop and apply, either individually or through bilateral or multilateral co-operation, monitoring activities covering the Mediterranean Sea Area in order to prevent, detect and combat pollution, and to ensure compliance with the applicable international regulations.

19.144 Article 6 ("Cooperation in recovery operations") provides that in case of release or loss overboard of hazardous and noxious substances in packaged form, including those in freight containers, portable tanks, road and rail vehicles and shipborne barges, the Parties shall co-operate as far as practicable in the salvage of these packages and the recovery of such substances so as to prevent or reduce the danger to the marine and coastal environment.

19.145 Article 7 deals with the dissemination and exchange of information. Under Article 7(1), each party undertakes to disseminate to the other parties information concerning: (a) the competent national organisation or authorities responsible for combating pollution of the sea by oil and hazardous and noxious substances; (b) the competent national authorities responsible for receiving reports of pollution of the sea by oil and hazardous and noxious substances and for dealing with matters concerning measures of assistance between parties; (c) the national authorities entitled to act on behalf of the State in regard to measures of mutual assistance and co-operation between parties; (d) the national organisation or authorities responsible for the implementation of paragraph 2 of

Article 4, in particular those responsible for the implementation of the international conventions concerned and other relevant applicable regulations, those responsible for port reception facilities and those responsible for the monitoring of discharges which are illegal under MARPOL 73/78; (e) its regulations and other matters which have a direct bearing on preparedness for and response to pollution of the sea by oil and hazardous and noxious substances; and (f) new ways in which pollution of the sea by oil and hazardous and noxious substances may be avoided, new measures for combating pollution, new developments in the technology of conducting monitoring and the development of research programmes. Article 7(2) provides that the parties which have agreed to exchange information directly shall communicate such information to the Regional Centre and the latter shall communicate this information to the other Parties and, on a basis of reciprocity, to coastal States of the Mediterranean Sea Area which are not Parties to this protocol. Pursuant to Article 7(3), parties concluding bilateral or multilateral agreements within the framework of this protocol shall inform the Regional Centre of such agreements, which shall communicate them to the other parties.

19.146 Article 8 deals with the communication of information and reports concerning pollution incidents. Article 8 provides that the Parties undertake to co-ordinate the utilisation of the means of communication at their disposal in order to ensure, with the necessary speed and reliability, the reception, transmission and dissemination of all reports and urgent information concerning pollution incidents. The Regional Centre shall have the necessary means of communication to enable it to participate in this co-ordinated effort and, in particular, to fulfil the functions assigned to it by Article 12(2).

19.147 The reporting procedure is addressed by Article 9. The first paragraph provides that each Party must issue instructions to masters or other persons having charge of ships flying its flag and to the pilots of aircraft registered in its territory to report by the most rapid and adequate channels in the circumstances, following reporting procedures to the extent required by, and in accordance with, the applicable provisions of the relevant international agreements, to the nearest coastal State and to this party: (a) all incidents which result or may result in a discharge of oil or hazardous and noxious substances; (b) the presence, characteristics and extent of spillages of oil or hazardous and noxious substances, including hazardous and noxious substances in packaged form, observed at sea which pose or are likely to pose a threat to the marine environment or to the coast or related interests of one or more of the parties. Article 9(2) provides that without prejudice to the provisions of Article 20 of the protocol, each Party shall take appropriate measures with a view to ensuring that the master of every ship sailing in its territorial waters complies with the obligations under (a) and (b) of paragraph 1 and may request assistance from the Regional Centre in this respect. It shall inform the IMO of the measures taken. Under Article 9(3), each party shall also issue instructions to persons having charge of sea ports or handling facilities under its jurisdiction to report to it, in accordance with applicable laws, all incidents which result or may result in a discharge of oil or hazardous and noxious substances. Article 9(4) provides that in accordance with the relevant provisions of the Protocol for the Protection of the Mediterranean Sea against Pollution Resulting from Exploration and Exploitation of the Continental Shelf and the Seabed and its Subsoil, each Party shall issue instructions to persons having charge of offshore units under its jurisdiction to report to it by the most rapid and adequate channels in the circumstances, following reporting procedures it has prescribed, all incidents which result or may result in a discharge of oil or hazardous and noxious substances. Article 9(5) provides that in Article 9, paragraphs 1, 3 and 4 of Article 9, the term "incident" means an incident meeting the conditions described therein, whether or not it is a pollution incident. Under Article 9(6), the information collected in accordance with paragraphs 1, 3 and 4 shall be communicated to the Regional Centre in the case of a pollution incident. Article 9(7) provides that the information collected in accordance with paragraphs 1, 3 and 4 shall be immediately communicated to the other Parties likely to be affected by a pollution incident: (a) by the Party which has received the information, preferably directly or through the Regional Centre; or (b) by the Regional Centre. In case of direct communication between Parties, these shall inform the Regional Centre of the measures taken, and the Centre shall communicate them to the other Parties. Article 9(8) states that the parties shall use a mutually agreed standard form proposed by the Regional Centre for the reporting of pollution incidents as required under paragraphs 6 and 7 of Article 9. Under Article 9(9), in consequence of the application of the provisions of Article 9(7), the parties are not bound by the obligation laid down in Article 9(2) of the convention.

19.148 Article 10 deals with operational measures. Under Article 10(1), any party faced with a pollution incident shall: (a) make the necessary assessments of the nature, extent and possible consequences of the pollution incident or, as the case may be, the type and approximate quantity of oil or hazardous and noxious substances and the direction and speed of drift of the spillage; (b) take every practicable measure to prevent, reduce and, to the fullest possible extent, eliminate the effects of the pollution incident; (c) immediately inform all parties likely to be affected by the pollution incident of these assessments and of any action which it has taken or intends to take, and simultaneously provide the same information to the Regional Centre, which shall communicate it to all other parties; and (d) continue to observe the situation for as long as possible and report thereon in accordance with Article 9. Under Article 10(2), where action is taken to combat pollution originating from a ship, all possible measures shall be taken to safeguard: (a) human lives; and (b) the ship itself; in doing so, damage to the environment in general shall be prevented or minimised. Any party which takes such action shall inform the IMO either directly or through the Regional Centre. Emergency measures on board ships, on offshore installations and in ports are addressed by Article 11. Article 11(2) provides that each party shall take the necessary steps to ensure that ships flying its flag have on board a pollution emergency plan as required by, and in accordance with, the relevant international regulations. Article 11(2) provided that each Party shall require masters of ships flying its flag, in case of a pollution incident, to follow the procedures described in the shipboard emergency plan and in particular to provide the proper authorities, at their request, with such detailed information about the ship and its cargo as is relevant to actions taken in pursuance of Article 9, and to co-operate with these authorities. Article 11(3) provides that without prejudice to the provisions of Article 20 of the protocol, each Party shall take appropriate measures with a view to ensuring that the master of every ship sailing in its territorial waters complies with the obligation under paragraph 2 and may request assistance from the Regional Centre in this respect. It shall inform the IMO of the measures taken. Under Article 11(4) each Party shall require that authorities or operators in charge of sea ports and handling facilities under its jurisdiction as it deems appropriate have pollution emergency plans or similar arrangements that are co-ordinated with the national system established in accordance with Article 4 and approved in accordance with procedures established by the competent national authority. Finally, Article 11(5) provides that each Party shall require operators in charge of offshore installations under its jurisdiction to have a contingency plan to combat any pollution incident, which is co-ordinated with the national system established in accordance with Article 4 and in accordance with the procedures established by the competent national authority.

19.149 Assistance is dealt with by Article 12. Article 12(1) states that any Party requiring assistance to deal with a pollution incident may call for assistance from other Parties, either directly or through the Regional Centre, starting with the Parties which appear likely to be affected by the pollution. This assistance may comprise, in particular, expert advice and the supply to or placing at the disposal of the Party concerned of the required specialised personnel, products, equipment and nautical facilities. Parties so requested shall use their best endeavours to render this assistance. Article 12(2) provides that where the Parties engaged in an operation to combat pollution cannot agree on the organisation of the operation, the Regional Centre may, with the approval of all the Parties involved, co-ordinate the activity of the facilities put into operation by these Parties. Article 12(3) provides that in accordance with applicable international agreements, each Party must take the necessary legal and administrative measures to facilitate: (a) the arrival and utilisation in and departure from its territory of ships, aircraft and other modes of transport engaged in responding to a pollution incident or transporting personnel, cargoes, materials and equipment required to deal with such an incident; and (b) the expeditious movement into, through and out of its territory of the personnel, cargoes, materials and equipment referred to in subparagraph (a).

19.150 Reimbursement of costs of assistance is addressed by Article 13. Article 13(1) states that unless an agreement concerning the financial arrangements governing actions of Parties to deal with pollution incidents has been concluded on a bilateral or multilateral basis prior to the pollution incident, Parties shall bear the costs of their respective action in dealing with pollution in accordance with paragraph 2. Article 13(2) provides that (a) if the action was taken by one Party at the express request of another Party, the requesting party shall reimburse to the assisting Party the costs of its action. If the request is cancelled, the requesting party shall bear the costs already incurred or committed by the assisting Party; (b) if the action was taken by a party on its own initiative, that Party shall bear the cost of its action; and (c) the principles laid down in subparagraphs (a) and (b) above shall apply unless the Parties concerned otherwise agree in any individual case. Article 13(3) provides that unless otherwise agreed, the costs of the action taken by a Party at the request of another Party shall be fairly calculated according to the law and current practice of the assisting Party concerning the reimbursement of such costs. Article 13(4) provides that the Party requesting assistance and the assisting Party shall, where appropriate, co-operate in concluding any action in response to a compensation claim. To that end, they shall give due consideration to existing legal regimes. Where the action thus concluded does not permit full compensation for expenses incurred in the assistance operation, the Party requesting assistance may ask the assisting Party to waive reimbursement of the expenses exceeding the sums compensated or to reduce the costs which have been calculated in accordance with paragraph 3. It may also request a postponement of the reimbursement of such costs. In considering such a request, assisting Parties shall give due consideration to the needs of developing countries. Under Article 13(5), the provisions of this article shall not be interpreted as in any way prejudicing the rights of Parties to recover from third parties the costs of actions taken to deal with pollution incidents under other applicable provisions and rules of national and international law applicable to one or to the other Party involved in the assistance.

19.151 Port reception facilities are addressed by Article 14. Article 14(1) provides that the parties must individually, bilaterally or multilaterally take all necessary steps to ensure that reception facilities meeting the needs of ships are available in their ports and terminals. They shall ensure that these facilities are used efficiently without causing undue delay to ships. The parties are invited to explore ways and means to charge reasonable costs for the use of these facilities. Article 14 continues to provide: (a) the Parties shall also ensure the provision of adequate reception facilities for pleasure craft;[98] (b) the Parties must take all the necessary steps to ensure that reception facilities operate efficiently to limit any impact of their discharges to the marine environment; and (c) the Parties must take the necessary steps to provide ships using their ports with updated information relevant to the obligations arising from MARPOL 73/78 and from their legislation applicable in this field.[99]

19.152 Article 15 ("environmental risks of maritime traffic") provides that in conformity with generally accepted international rules and standards and the global mandate of the IMO, the Parties must individually, bilaterally or multilaterally take the necessary steps to assess the environmental risks of the recognised routes used in maritime traffic and shall take the appropriate measures aimed at reducing the risks of accidents or the environmental consequences thereof.

19.153 Article 16 deals with the difficult and controversial topic of the reception of ships in distress in ports and places of refuge. There is often a tension between the humanitarian desire to help ships in distress with the reality that ships in distress can cause considerable environmental damage to the coastal State providing refuge. Article 16 provides that the parties shall define national, subregional or regional strategies concerning reception in places of refuge, including ports, of ships in distress presenting a threat to the marine environment and they shall co-operate to this end and inform the Regional Centre of the measures they have adopted. Article 16 therefore does not prescribe or legislate too much for it (perhaps it could not do so) other than to plan and co-operate for the situation.

19.154 Subregional Agreements are addressed by Article 17 which provides that the parties may negotiate, develop and maintain appropriate bilateral or multilateral subregional agreements in order to facilitate the implementation of the protocol, or part of it. Upon request of the interested parties, the Regional Centre must assist them, within the framework of its functions, in the process of developing and implementing these subregional agreements.

19.155 The balance of the protocol deals with organisational matters. Article 18 deals with "Meetings". Article 18(1) provides that ordinary meetings of the Parties to the protocol must be held in conjunction with ordinary meetings of the Contracting Parties to the convention, held pursuant to Article 18 of the convention. The Parties to the protocol may also hold extraordinary meetings as provided in Article 18 of the convention. Article 18(2) provides that it shall be the function of the meetings of the Parties to this protocol,

---

98 Art. 14(2).
99 Art. 14(4).

in particular: (a) to examine and discuss reports from the Regional Centre on the implementation of this protocol, and particularly of its Articles 4, 7 and 16; (b) to formulate and adopt strategies, action plans and programmes for the implementation of this protocol; (c) to keep under review and consider the efficacy of these strategies, action plans and programmes, and the need to adopt any new strategies, action plans and programmes and to develop measures to that effect; and (d) to discharge such other functions as may be appropriate for the implementation of this protocol. The relationship with the convention is the subject matter of Article 19. Article 19(1) states that the provisions of the convention relating to any protocol shall apply with respect to the present protocol while Article 19(2) provides that the rules of procedure and the financial rules adopted pursuant to Article 24 of the convention shall apply with respect to this protocol, unless the Parties agree otherwise. Article 20 provides that in implementing the provisions of the protocol, the right of Parties to adopt relevant stricter domestic measures or other measures in conformity with international law, in the matters covered by the protocol, must not be affected. Article 21 provides that the Parties must, where appropriate, invite States that are not Parties to the protocol and international organisations to co-operate in the implementation of the protocol. There are other provisions on signature, ratification, acceptance, approval and accession

NORTH SEA AND OTHER AREAS: THE BONN AGREEMENT

19.156 Nine Member States and the EU have concluded the agreement for co-operation in dealing with pollution of the North Sea by oil and other harmful substances (the "Bonn Agreement"). The original agreement was concluded in 1983 and was amended in 2001.[100] The Bonn Agreement is, according to its accompanying website,[101] the

> "mechanism by which the North Sea States, and the European Union (the Contracting Parties), work together to help each other in combating pollution in the North Sea Area from maritime disasters and chronic pollution from ships and offshore installations; and to carry out surveillance as an aid to detecting and combating pollution at sea".

The contracting parties are the EU as well as Belgium, Denmark, France, Germany, Ireland, the Netherlands, Norway, Sweden and the UK.[102]

19.157 The Bonn Agreement covers not only the North Sea but now covers the Irish Sea and parts of the Atlantic west of Ireland, France and the UK.[103]

19.158 The contracting parties to the Bonn Agreement recognise that pollution of the sea by oil and other harmful substances in the North Sea area may threaten the marine environment and the interests of coastal States, note that such pollution has many sources and that casualties and other incidents at sea are of great concern, are convinced that an ability to combat such pollution as well as active co-operation and mutual assistance among States are necessary for the protection of their coasts and related interests,

---

100 See www.bonnagreement.org/policies for a copy of the text of the agreement.
101 www.bonnagreement.org.
102 For further information, see www.bonnagreement.org and the various publications cited and contained on that website.
103 See the map on www.bonnagreement.org as well as Art. 2 of the Bonn Agreement.

welcome the progress that has already been achieved within the framework of the agreement for co-operation in dealing with pollution of the North Sea by oil, signed at Bonn on 9 June 1969 and wish to develop further mutual assistance and co-operation in combating pollution.

19.159 Article 1 provides that the agreement applies whenever the presence or the prospective presence of oil or other harmful substances polluting or threatening to pollute the sea within the North Sea area, as defined in Article 2 of the agreement, presents a grave and imminent danger to the coast or related interests of one or more Contracting Parties. Article 1(2) provides that the agreement shall apply to surveillance conducted in the North Sea area as an aid to detecting and combating such pollution as to preventing violations of anti-pollution regulations.

19.160 Article 2 provides that for the purpose of the agreement, the Greater North Sea and its wider approaches means the area of sea comprising: (a) the North Sea proper southwards of latitude 63.38.10.68N; (b) the Skagerrak, the southern limit of which is determined east of the Skaw by the latitude 57.44.43.00N; (c) the English Channel and its approaches bounded on the south and west by the line defined in Part I of the annex to the agreement; and (d) the other waters comprising the Irish Sea, the Celtic Sea, the Malin Sea, the Great Minch, the Little Minch, part of the Norwegian Sea as well as parts of the north-east Atlantic, bounded on the west and north by the line defined in Part II of the annex to the agreement. The Bonn Agreement therefore is much wider than just the North Sea but has expanded over time.

19.161 Article 3(1) provides that the Contracting Parties consider that protection against pollution of the kind referred to in Article 1 of the agreement is a matter which calls for "active cooperation between them". Article 3(2) states that the Contracting Parties must jointly develop and establish guidelines for the practical, operational and technical aspects of joint action and co-ordinated surveillance as referred to in Article 6A. This element of surveillance is an additional element to the agreement.

19.162 Article 4 provides that the Contracting Parties (including the EU) undertake to inform the other Contracting Parties about: (a) their national organisation for dealing with pollution of the kind referred to in Article 1 of the agreement and for enforcing anti-pollution regulations; (b) the competent authority responsible for receiving and dispatching reports of such pollution and for dealing with questions concerning measures of mutual assistance between Contracting Parties and co-ordinated surveillance between the Contracting Parties; (c) their national means for avoiding or dealing with such pollution, which might be made available for international assistance; (d) new ways in which such pollution may be avoided and about new effective measures to deal with it; (e) major pollution incidents of this kind dealt with; (f) new developments in the technology of conducting surveillance; (g) their experience in the use of surveillance means and techniques in the detection of pollution and the prevention of violations of anti-pollution regulations, including use in co-operation with other Contracting Parties; (h) information of mutual interest derived from their surveillance activities; and (i) their national programmes for surveillance, including co-operative arrangements with other Contracting Parties. While some of these provisions are vague, they are well-intentioned and the regime works in practice.

19.163 Article 5(1) provides that whenever a Contracting Party is aware of a casualty or the presence of oil or other harmful substances in the North Sea area likely to constitute a serious threat to the coast or related interests of any other Contracting Party, it must inform that Party without delay through its competent authority. This is an important and useful reporting requirement. Article 5(2) provides that the Contracting Parties undertake to request the masters of all ships flying their flags and pilots of aircraft registered in their countries to report without delay through the channels which may be most practicable and adequate in the circumstances: (a) all casualties causing or likely to cause pollution of the sea; (b) the presence, nature and extent of oil or other harmful substances likely to constitute a serious threat to the coast or relating interests of one or more Contracting Parties. Article 5(3) concludes by providing that the Contracting Parties shall establish a standard form for the reporting of pollution as required under Article 5(1).

19.164 Article 6(1) provides that for the sole purpose of the agreement, the North Sea area is divided into the zones described in the annex to the agreement. The Contracting Party within whose zone a situation of the kind described in Article 1 of this agreement occurs, shall make the necessary assessments of the nature and extent of any casualty or, as the case may be, of the type and approximate quantity of oil or other harmful substances and the direction and speed of movement thereof.[104] Under Article 6(3), the Contracting Party concerned shall immediately inform all the other Contracting Parties through their competent authorities of its assessments and of any action which it has taken to deal with the oil or other harmful substances and shall keep these substances under observation as long as they are present in its zone. Article 6(4) provides that the obligations of the Contracting Parties under the provisions of Article 6 with respect to the zones of joint responsibility shall be the subject of special technical arrangements to be concluded between the Parties concerned. These arrangements shall be communicated to the other Contracting Parties.

19.165 A new provision, Article 6A, was added. It deals with surveillance. It provides that surveillance

> "shall be carried out, as appropriate, by the Contracting Parties in their zone of responsibility or zones of joint responsibility referred to in Article 6 of [the] Agreement. The Contracting Parties may bilaterally or multilaterally conclude agreements on or make arrangements for co-operation in the organisation of surveillance in the whole or part of the zones of the Parties concerned."

Article 9(3) (which was added to the agreement) provides that unless "otherwise specified in bilateral or multilateral agreements or arrangements, each Contracting Party shall bear the costs of its surveillance activities carried out in accordance with Article 6A".

19.166 Article 7 provides that a Contracting Party requiring assistance to deal with pollution or the prospective presence of pollution at sea or on its coast may call on the help of the other Contracting Parties. Contracting Parties requesting assistance shall specify the kind of assistance they require. The Contracting Parties called upon for help in accordance with this article shall use their best endeavours to bring such assistance as is within their power taking into account, particularly in the case of pollution by harmful substances other than oil, the technological means available to them.

19.167 Article 8 provides that the provisions of the agreement must not be interpreted as in any way prejudicing the rights and obligations of the Contracting Parties under international law, especially in the field of the prevention and combating of marine pollution.

---

104 Bonn Agreement, Art. 6(2).

Article 8(2) goes on to provide that in no case shall the division into zones referred to in Article 6 of the agreement be invoked as a precedent or argument in any matter concerning sovereignty or jurisdiction. Article 8(3) provides that the division into zones (referred to in Article 6 of the agreement) "shall in no way restrict the rights of Contracting Parties to carry out in accordance with international law surveillance activities beyond the limits of their zones".

19.168 The important issue of costs is addressed in Article 9 of the agreement. Article 9(1) provides that in the absence of an agreement concerning the financial arrangements governing actions of Contracting Parties to deal with pollution which might be concluded on a bilateral or multilateral basis or on the occasion of a joint combating operation, Contracting Parties must bear the costs of their respective actions in dealing with pollution in accordance with (a) or (b): (a) if the action was taken by one Contracting Party at the express request of another Contracting Party, the Contracting Party requesting such assistance shall reimburse to the assisting Contracting Party the costs of its action; and (b) if the action was taken by a Contracting Party on its own initiative, this Contracting Party must bear the costs of its action. Article 9(2) then provides that the Contracting Party requesting assistance may cancel its request at any time, but in that case it shall bear the costs already incurred or committed by the assisting Contracting Party. Article 9(3) (which was added to the agreement) provides that unless "otherwise specified in bilateral or multilateral agreements or arrangements, each Contracting Party shall bear the costs of its surveillance activities carried out in accordance with Article 6A". Under Article 10, unless otherwise agreed, the costs of action taken by a Contracting Party at the request of another Contracting Party must be calculated according to the law and current practice in the assisting country concerning the reimbursement of such costs by a person or entity liable.[105] Article 11 provides that Article 9 must not be interpreted as in any way prejudicing the rights of Contracting Parties to recover from third parties the costs of action to deal with pollution or the threat of pollution under other applicable provisions and rules of national and international law.

19.169 The practical matter of meetings is addressed by Article 12 of the agreement. Meetings of the Contracting Parties shall be held at regular intervals and at any time when, due to special circumstances, it is so decided in accordance with the Rules of Procedure.[106] The Contracting Parties at their first meeting to draw up Rules of Procedure and Financial Rules which had to be adopted by unanimous vote.[107]

19.170 Article 13, which has been updated, provides that within the areas of its competence, the EU is entitled to a number of votes equal to the number of its Member States which are Contracting Parties to the present agreement. The EEC shall not exercise its right to vote in cases where its Member States exercise theirs and conversely. If the UK leaves the EU then this could be significant in adjusting the voting balance. Article 14 provides that it shall be the duty of meetings of the Contracting Parties: (a) to exercise overall supervision over the implementation of this agreement; (b) to review the effectiveness of the measures taken under this agreement; and (c) to carry out such other functions as may be necessary under the terms of this agreement.

---

105 Art. 10.
106 Agreement, Art. 12(1).
107 Agreement, Art. 12(2).

19.171 Article 15 is largely administrative in nature. Article 15(1) provides that the Contracting Parties must make provision for the performance of secretariat duties in relation to the agreement, taking into account existing arrangements in the framework of other international agreements on the prevention of marine pollution in force for the same region as the agreement. Under Article 15(2), each Contracting Party shall contribute 2.5% towards the annual expenditure of the agreement. The balance of the agreement's expenditure shall be divided among Contracting Parties other than the EEC in proportion to their gross national product in accordance with the scale of assessment adopted regularly by the United Nations General Assembly. In no case shall the contribution of a Contracting Party to this balance exceed 20% of the balance.

19.172 Article 16(1) provides that without prejudice to Article 17 of the agreement, a proposal by a Contracting Party for the amendment of this agreement or its annex shall be considered at a meeting of the Contracting Parties. Following adoption of the proposal by unanimous vote the amendment shall be communicated by the Depositary Government to the Contracting Parties.

Article 16(2) provides that such an amendment shall enter into force on the first day of the second month following the date on which the Depositary Government has received notifications of approval from all Contracting Parties.

19.173 Article 17 provides that two or more Contracting Parties may modify the common boundaries of their zones described in the annex to this agreement and such a modification shall enter into force for all Contracting Parties on the first day of the sixth month following the date of its communication by the Depositary Government unless, within a period of three months following that communication, a Contracting Party has expressed an objection or has requested consultation on the matter.

19.174 Article 18(1) states that the agreement shall be open for signature by the governments of the States invited to participate in the Conference on the agreement for co-operation in dealing with pollution of the North Sea by oil and other harmful substances, held at Bonn on 13 September 1983, and by the then EEC (now the EU). Under Article 18(2), these States and the EU may become Parties to the agreement either by signature without reservation as to ratification, acceptance or approval or by signature subject to ratification, acceptance or approval followed by ratification, acceptance or approval. Instruments of ratification, acceptance or approval shall be deposited with the government of the Federal Republic of Germany.

19.175 Article 19(1) provides that this agreement shall enter into force on the first day of the second month following the date on which the governments of all the States mentioned in Article 18 of this agreement and the EEC have signed the agreement without reservation as to ratification, acceptance or approval. Article 19(2) provides that upon the entry into force of this agreement, the agreement for co-operation in dealing with pollution of the North Sea by oil, done at Bonn on 9 June 1969, shall cease to be in force.

19.176 Under Article 20(1), the Contracting Parties may unanimously invite any other coastal State of the north-east Atlantic area to accede to the agreement. In such a case Article 2 of the agreement and its annex shall be amended as necessary. The amendments shall be adopted by unanimous vote at a meeting of the Contracting Parties and shall take effect upon the entry into force of this agreement for the acceding State.[108]

---

108 Art. 20(2).

19.177 Article 21(1) provides that for each State acceding to the agreement, the agreement must enter into force on the first day of the second month following the date of deposit by such State of its instrument of accession. Under Article 21(2), instruments of accession must be deposited with the German government.

19.178 Article 22 states that after the agreement has been in force for five years, it may be denounced by any Contracting Party. Denunciation shall be effected by a notification in writing addressed to the Depositary Government which shall notify all the other Contracting Parties of any denunciation received and of the date of its receipt. A denunciation shall take effect one year after its receipt by the Depositary Government.

19.179 Article 23 provides that the Depositary Government shall inform the Contracting Parties and those referred to in Article 18 of the agreement of: (a) any signature of the agreement; (b) the deposit of any instrument of ratification, acceptance, approval or accession and of the receipt of any notice of denunciation; (c) the date of entry into force of the agreement; and (d) the receipt of any notification of approval relating to amendments to this agreement or its annex and of the date of entry into force of such amendments.

19.180 Article 24 provides that the original of the agreement, of which the English, French and German texts are equally authentic, shall be deposited with the government of the Federal Republic of Germany, which shall send certified copies thereof to the Contracting Parties and which shall transmit a certified copy to the Secretary-General of the United Nations for registration and publication in accordance with Article 102 of the Charter of the United Nations.

19.181 The annex to the agreement contains a description of the zones referred to in Article 6 of the agreement. It is a detailed description of the geographical application of the agreement.

NORTH-EAST ATLANTIC

Atlantic: the OSPAR Convention

19.182 The Convention for the Protection of the Marine Environment of the North-East Atlantic (the "OSPAR Convention") was open for signature at the Ministerial Meeting of the Oslo and Paris Commissions in Paris on 22 September 1992.[109] It was adopted together with a Final declaration and an Action Plan.

19.183 The convention has been signed and ratified by Belgium, Denmark, the EU, Finland, France, Germany, Iceland, Ireland, Luxembourg, the Netherlands, Norway, Portugal, Spain, Sweden, Switzerland and the UK.

19.184 The Contracting Parties are Belgium, Denmark, Finland, France, Germany, Iceland, Ireland, Luxembourg, the Netherlands, Norway, Portugal, Spain, Sweden, Switzerland and United Kingdom, together with the EU.

19.185 The OSPAR Convention entered into force on 25 March 1998. It replaced the Oslo and Paris Conventions but decisions, recommendations and all other agreements adopted under those conventions will continue to be applicable, unaltered in their legal

---

109 www.ospar.org/content/content.asp?menu=00340108070000_000000_000000. See also: www.ospar.org/convention/text for the text of the convention.

nature, unless they are terminated by new measures adopted under the 1992 OSPAR Convention. The working languages of the convention are English and French.

19.186 The OSPAR Convention has a series of annexes which deal with the following specific areas: Annex I: Prevention and elimination of pollution from land-based sources; Annex II: Prevention and elimination of pollution by dumping or incineration; Annex III: Prevention and elimination of pollution from offshore sources; and Annex IV: Assessment of the quality of the marine environment.

19.187 It is not proposed to consider the OSPAR Convention in depth in this book but it is proposed to mention the decision taken by the EU in regard to the OSPAR Convention.

Atlantic: Council Decision 98/249 of 7 October 1997 on the conclusion of the Convention for the protection of the marine environment of the north-east Atlantic[110]

19.188 On 7 October 1997, the Council adopted Decision 98/249 on the conclusion of the Convention for the protection of the marine environment of the north-east Atlantic.[111]

19.189 The decision recalled that the Commission, on behalf of the then EC, participated in the negotiations on the drafting of the Convention for the protection of the marine environment of the north-east Atlantic. The convention was signed on behalf of the EC on 22 September 1992. The convention aims to prevent and eliminate pollution and to protect the maritime area against the adverse effects of human activities. The decision recalled that the EC had adopted measures in the area covered by the convention and should therefore undertake international commitments in that area; whereas the Community's action is a necessary complement to that of the Member States directly concerned and its participation in the convention would appear to comply with the principle of subsidiarity.

19.190 Article 1 provides the Convention for the protection of the marine environment of the north-east Atlantic, as signed in Paris on 22 September 1992, is approved on behalf of the EU. Article 2 provides that the President of the Council is authorised to designate the person or persons empowered to deposit the instrument of approval with the government of the French Republic in accordance with the provisions of Article 26 of the convention. Article 3 finally provides that the EU shall be represented by the Commission as regards matters within the sphere of EU competence, in the commission established under Article 10 of the convention.

Atlantic: Lisbon Agreement: Council Decision 2010/655 of 19 October 2010 concerning the conclusion, on behalf of the European Union, of the Additional Protocol to the Cooperation Agreement for the Protection of the Coasts and Waters of the North-East Atlantic against Pollution

19.191 On 19 October 2010, the Council adopted Decision 2010/655 concerning the conclusion, on behalf of the EU, of the Additional Protocol to the Cooperation Agreement

---

110 OJ L104/1, 3 April 1998, http://eur-lex.europa.eu/legal-content/EN/TXT/HTML/?uri=CELEX:31998D0 249&from=EN.

111 OJ L104/1, 3 April 1998. It was signed by Jean-Claude Juncker in his capacity as a Luxembourgeois Minister – he was still involved in EU affairs 20 years later as President of the European Commission.

for the Protection of the Coasts and Waters of the North-East Atlantic against Pollution.[112] The decision entered into force on the date of its adoption.[113] The legal basis of Decision 2010/655 was the TFEU generally and, in particular, Articles 196(2) and 218(6)(a) of the TFEU.

19.192 The first recital states that the EU is a party to the Cooperation Agreement for the Protection of the Coasts and Waters of the North-East Atlantic against Pollution approved by Council Decision 93/550 (hereinafter referred to as the Lisbon Agreement).[114] A political dispute over the borders in Western Sahara prevented Spain and Morocco from ratifying the Lisbon Agreement. This dispute has now been resolved by the Additional Protocol to the Lisbon Agreement modifying Article 3(c) thereof. Following the adoption of the Council Decision on the signing, on behalf of the then EC, of the Additional Protocol to the Cooperation Agreement for the Protection of the Coasts and Waters of the North-East Atlantic against Pollution on 12 December 2008, the Additional Protocol was signed, on behalf of the EC, on 25 March 2009. The Additional Protocol to the Lisbon Agreement was open to ratification, acceptance or approval by the Parties. It was therefore appropriate for the EU to conclude the Additional Protocol to the Lisbon Agreement. The decision therefore was based on the notion that the EU and Member States Parties to the Lisbon Agreement should endeavour to deposit simultaneously, to the extent possible, their instruments of ratification, acceptance or approval of the Additional Protocol.

19.193 Article 1 of Decision 2010/655 provides that the Additional Protocol to the Cooperation Agreement for the Protection of the Coasts and Waters of the North-East Atlantic against Pollution is hereby approved on behalf of the EU.

19.194 Article 2(1) provides that the President of the Council must designate the person(s) empowered to proceed, on behalf of the EU, to the deposit of the instrument of approval with the government of Portugal, which assumes the function of Depositary, in accordance with Article 3(1) of the Additional Protocol, in order to express the consent of the Union to be bound by that protocol. Article 2(2) provides that the EU and Member States Parties to the Lisbon Agreement must endeavour to deposit simultaneously, to the extent possible, their instruments of ratification, acceptance or approval of the Additional Protocol.

Baltic Sea: Convention on the Protection of the Marine Environment in the Baltic Sea Area of 1992 (further to the earlier version of 1974) – the Helsinki Convention

19.195 The Convention on the Protection of the Marine Environment in the Baltic Sea Area of 1992 (further to the earlier version of 1974) is the so-called Helsinki Convention. It was signed by all the States bordering the Baltic Sea and the now EU. This convention is occasionally referred to as "HELCOM".

19.196 On 21 February 1994 the Council adopted Decision 94/156 on the accession of the Community to the Convention on the Protection of the Marine Environment of the Baltic Sea Area (1974 Helsinki Convention).[115] Also on the same day, the Council

---

112 OJ L285/1, 30 October 2010.
113 Dec. 2010/655, Art. 3.
114 OJ L267, 28 October 1993, p. 20.
115 OJ L73/1, 16 March 1994.

adopted Decision 94/157 on the conclusion, on behalf of the Community, of the Convention on the Protection of the Marine Environment of the Baltic Sea Area (Helsinki Convention as revised in 1992).[116] These two decisions enabled the Community to accede to the Convention on the Protection of the Marine Environment of the Baltic Sea Area (Helsinki Convention). The convention, which was signed in March 1974 by all the States bordering the Baltic Sea (Denmark, Germany, Sweden, Estonia, Finland, Latvia, Lithuania, Poland and Russia), aims to reduce pollution of the Baltic Sea area caused by discharges through rivers, estuaries, outfalls and pipelines, dumping and shipping operations as well as through airborne pollutants. The convention entered into force in 1980.

Baltic Sea: Council Decision 94/156 of 21 February 1994 on the accession of the Community to the Convention on the Protection of the Marine Environment of the Baltic Sea Area 1974 (Helsinki Convention)

19.197 On 21 February 1994, the Council adopted Decision 94/156 on the accession of the Community to the Convention on the Protection of the Marine Environment of the Baltic Sea Area 1974 (the Helsinki Convention).[117]

19.198 The legal basis was the TEC generally (now, the TFEU) and in particular Article 130s in conjunction with Article 228(3), first subparagraph, of the TEC. The legislative history included the proposal from the Commission[118] opinion of the European Parliament, and opinion of the EESC.[119] The background to the decision was set out in the recitals:

"Whereas, according to Article 130r of the TEC, Community policy on the environment is to contribute to the following objectives: preserving, protecting and improving the quality of the environment, protecting human health and the prudent and rational utilization of natural resources; whereas, furthermore, the Community and the Member States are cooperating, within the framework of their respective jurisdictions, with third countries and the relevant international organizations;

Whereas the Community has adopted measures in the area covered by the Convention on the Protection of the Marine Environment of the Baltic Sea Area 1974 (Helsinki Convention) and should act at international level in that area;

Whereas the Commission has been participating as an observer in the meetings of the Baltic Marine Environment Protection Commission since 19 February 1991;

Whereas the Commission has also been participating in the meetings of the ad hoc group set up to revise the Convention on the Protection of the Marine Environment of the Baltic Sea Area;

Whereas the Convention on the Protection of the Marine Environment of the Baltic Sea Area has been the subject of amendments intended to permit the accession of the Community."

19.199 Article 1 of Decision 94/156 provides that the EC shall accede to the Convention on the Protection of the Marine Environment of the Baltic Sea Area 1974 (i.e. the Helsinki Convention).

19.200 Article 2 of Decision 94/156 provides that the President of the Council shall be authorised to designate the person or persons empowered to deposit the instrument of accession in accordance with Article 26 of the convention.

---

116 OJ L73/19, 16 March 1994.
117 OJ L73/1, 16 March 1994.
118 OJ C222/13, 18 August 1933.
119 OJ C34/5, 2 February 1994.

Baltic Sea: Council Decision 94/157 of 21 February 1994 on the conclusion, on behalf of the Community, of the Convention on the Protection of the Marine Environment of the Baltic Sea Area (Helsinki Convention as revised in 1992)

19.201 On 21 February 1994, the Council adopted Decision 94/157 on the conclusion, on behalf of the Community, of the Convention on the Protection of the Marine Environment of the Baltic Sea Area (Helsinki Convention as revised in 1992).[120]

19.202 The background to Decision 94/157 is as described in the following recitals:

"Whereas the Commission, on behalf of the Community, took part in the negotiations of the drafting of the Helsinki Convention as revised in 1992;

Whereas that Convention was signed on behalf of the Community on 24 September 1992;

Whereas that Convention establishes a framework for regional cooperation to ensure the ecological rehabilitation of the Baltic Sea with a view to the self-regeneration of its marine environment and the preservation of its ecological balance;

Whereas the Community has adopted measures in the area covered by the Convention and should act at international level in that areas;

Whereas Community policy on the environment contributes to the pursuit of the objectives of preserving, protecting and improving the quality of the environment, protecting human health and the prudent and rational utilization of natural resources;

Whereas Community policy on the environment aims at a high level of protection; whereas it is based on the precautionary principle and on the principles that preventive action should be taken, that environmental damage should as a priority be rectified at source and that the polluter should pay;

Whereas, within the framework of their respective responsibilities, the Community and the Member States cooperate with third countries and with competent international organizations;

Whereas the conclusion of the Convention by the Community will help attain the objectives set out in Article 130r of the Treaty ..."

19.203 Article 1 provides that the Convention on the Protection of the Marine Environment of the Baltic Sea Area (Helsinki Convention as revised in 1992), signed in Helsinki (Finland) on 24 September 1992 was hereby approved on behalf of the EU.

19.204 Article 2 provides that the President of the Council must deposit the instrument of approval with the Finnish government in accordance with Article 38 of the convention.

O. CARBON DIOXIDE EMISSIONS

Introduction

19.205 GHG emissions are harmful to the environment. Shipping contributes some of these emissions – it is estimated that shipping represents about 3% of the world's GHG emissions and 4% of the EU's GHG emissions. In defence of shipping, it is clear that shipping emits far less per tonne/kilometre than any other mode of transport. Some in the shipping sector would advocate that the EU should switch to shipping away from other modes so as to reduce emissions.

---

120 OJ L73/19, 16 March 1994.

REGULATION 2015/757 ON THE MONITORING, REPORTING AND VERIFICATION OF CARBON DIOXIDE EMISSIONS FROM MARITIME TRANSPORT, AND AMENDING DIRECTIVE 2009/16/EC

Introduction

19.206 On 29 April 2015, the Parliament and Council adopted Regulation 2015/757 on the monitoring, reporting and verification of carbon dioxide emissions from maritime transport, and amending Directive 2009/16.[121] It has been amended by Commission Delegated Regulation 2016/2071 of 22 September 2016 which addresses and amends some of the details in the annexes.[122]

Chapter I of Regulation 2015/757: "general provisions"

19.207 Article 1 ("subject matter") provides that the regulation

"lays down rules for the accurate monitoring, reporting and verification of carbon dioxide (CO2) emissions and of other relevant information from ships arriving at, within or departing from ports under the jurisdiction of a Member State, in order to promote the reduction of CO2 emissions from maritime transport in a cost effective manner".

19.208 Article 2 sets out the scope of Regulation 2015/757. Under Article 2(1), the regulation applies to ships above 5,000 gt (g)[123] in respect of CO_2 emissions released during their voyages from their last port of call to a port of call under the jurisdiction of a Member State and from a port of call under the jurisdiction of a Member State to their next port of call, as well as within ports of call under the jurisdiction of a Member State. Article 2(2) provides that the regulation does not apply to warships, naval auxiliaries, fish-catching or fish-processing ships, wooden ships of a primitive build, ships not propelled by mechanical means, or government ships used for non-commercial purposes. So, it applies to the vast majority of ordinary vessels in the shipping sector.

19.209 Various definitions are set out in Article 3. For the purposes of the regulation, the following definitions apply. The term "CO_2 emissions" means the release of CO_2 into the atmosphere by ships. The phrase "port of call" means the port where a ship stops to load or unload cargo or to embark or disembark passengers; consequently, stops for the sole purposes of refuelling, obtaining supplies, relieving the crew, going into dry-dock or making repairs to the ship and/or its equipment, stops in port because the ship is in need of assistance or in distress, ship-to-ship transfers carried out outside ports, and stops for the sole purpose of taking shelter from adverse weather or rendered necessary by search and rescue activities are excluded.

19.210 The term "voyage" means any movement of a ship that originates from or terminates in a port of call and that serves the purpose of transporting passengers or cargo for commercial purposes.

---

121 OJ L123/55, 19 May 2015.
122 OJ L320/1, 26 November 2016.
123 This is a much larger size vessel than the type of vessel covered by other types of EU regime (e.g. 500 grt is the normal threshold).

19.211 The phrase "company" means the shipowner or any other organisation or person, such as the manager or the bareboat charterer, which has assumed the responsibility for the operation of the ship from the shipowner.

19.212 The expression "gross tonnage" ("gt") means the gross tonnage calculated in accordance with the tonnage measurement regulations contained in Annex I to the International Convention on Tonnage Measurement of Ships, adopted by the IMO in London on 23 June 1969, or any successor convention.

19.213 The word "verifier" means a legal entity carrying out verification activities which is accredited by a national accreditation body pursuant to Regulation (EC) No 765/2008 and this regulation.

19.214 The word "verification" means the activities carried out by a verifier to assess the conformity of the documents transmitted by the company with the requirements of Regulation 2015/757.

19.215 The expression "document of compliance" means a document specific to a ship, issued to a company by a verifier, which confirms that that ship has complied with the requirements of the regulation for a specific reporting period.

19.216 The phrase "other relevant information" means information related to CO_2 emissions from the consumption of fuels, to transport work and to the energy efficiency of ships, which enables the analysis of emission trends and the assessment of ships' performances.

19.217 The phrase "emission factor" means the average emission rate of a GHG relative to the activity data of a source stream, assuming complete oxidation for combustion and complete conversion for all other chemical reactions.

19.218 The word "uncertainty" means a parameter, associated with the result of the determination of a quantity, that characterises the dispersion of the values that could reasonably be attributed to the particular quantity, including the effects of systematic as well as of random factors, expressed as a percentage, and describes a confidence interval around the mean value comprising 95% of inferred values taking into account any asymmetry of the distribution of values.

19.219 The word "conservative" means that a set of assumptions is defined in order to ensure that no under-estimation of annual emissions or over-estimation of distances or amounts of cargo carried occurs.

19.220 The expression "reporting period" means one calendar year during which CO_2 emissions have to be monitored and reported. For voyages starting and ending in two different calendar years, the monitoring and reporting data shall be accounted under the first calendar year concerned.

19.221 The expression "ship at berth" means a ship which is securely moored or anchored in a port falling under the jurisdiction of a Member State while it is loading, unloading or hotelling, including the time spent when not engaged in cargo operations.

19.222 The phrase "ice class" means the notation assigned to the ship by the competent national authorities of the flag State or an organisation recognised by that State, showing that the ship has been designed for navigation in sea-ice conditions.

Chapter II of Regulation 2015/757: "monitoring and reporting"

19.223 Article 4 ("Common principles for monitoring and reporting") provides:

"1. In accordance with Articles 8 to 12, companies shall, for each of their ships, monitor and report on the relevant parameters during a reporting period. They shall carry out that monitoring and reporting within all ports under the jurisdiction of a Member State and for any voyages to or from a port under the jurisdiction of a Member State.

2. Monitoring and reporting shall be complete and cover CO_2 emissions from the combustion of fuels, while the ships are at sea as well as at berth. Companies shall apply appropriate measures to prevent any data gaps within the reporting period.

3. Monitoring and reporting shall be consistent and comparable over time. To that end, companies shall use the same monitoring methodologies and data sets subject to modifications assessed by the verifier.

4. Companies shall obtain, record, compile, analyse and document monitoring data, including assumptions, references, emission factors and activity data, in a transparent manner that enables the reproduction of the determination of CO_2 emissions by the verifier.

5. Companies shall ensure that the determination of CO_2 emissions is neither systematically nor knowingly inaccurate. They shall identify and reduce any source of inaccuracies.

6. Companies shall enable reasonable assurance of the integrity of the CO_2 emission data to be monitored and reported.

7. Companies shall endeavour to take account of the recommendations included in the verification reports issued pursuant to Article 13(3) or (4) in their subsequent monitoring and reporting."

19.224 Article 5 ("Methods for monitoring CO_2 emissions and other relevant information") provides:

"1. For the purposes of Article 4(1), (2) and (3), companies shall, for each of their ships, determine the CO_2 emissions in accordance with any of the methods set out in Annex I, and monitor other relevant information in accordance with the rules set out in Annex II or adopted pursuant to it.

2. The Commission shall be empowered to adopt delegated acts in accordance with Article 23 to amend the methods set out in Annex I and the rules set out in Annex II, in order to take into account relevant international rules as well as international and European standards. The Commission shall be also empowered to adopt delegated acts in accordance with Article 23 to amend Annexes I and II in order to refine the elements of the monitoring methods set out therein, in the light of technological and scientific developments."

19.225 The content and submission of the monitoring plan is addressed by Article 6:

"1. By 31 August 2017, companies shall submit to the verifiers a monitoring plan for each of their ships indicating the method chosen to monitor and report CO_2 emissions and other relevant information.

2. Notwithstanding paragraph 1, for ships falling under the scope of this Regulation for the first time after 31 August 2017, the company shall submit a monitoring plan to the verifier without undue delay and no later than two months after each ship's first call in a port under the jurisdiction of a Member State.

3. The monitoring plan shall consist of a complete and transparent documentation of the monitoring method for the ship concerned and shall contain at least the following elements:

(a) the identification and type of the ship, including its name, its IMO identification number, its port of registry or home port, and the name of the shipowner;

(b) the name of the company and the address, telephone and e-mail details of a contact person;

(c) a description of the following CO2 emission sources on board the ship: main engines, auxiliary engines, gas turbines, boilers and inert gas generators, and the fuel types used;

(d) a description of the procedures, systems and responsibilities used to update the list of CO2 emission sources over the reporting period;

(e) a description of the procedures used to monitor the completeness of the list of voyages;

(f) a description of the procedures for monitoring the fuel consumption of the ship, including:

    (i) the method chosen from among those set out in Annex I for calculating the fuel consumption of each CO2 emission source, including, where applicable, a description of the measuring equipment used,

    (ii) the procedures for the measurement of fuel uplifts and fuel in tanks, a description of the measuring equipment used and the procedures for recording, retrieving, transmitting and storing information regarding measurements, as applicable,

    (iii) the method chosen for the determination of density, where applicable,

    (iv) a procedure to ensure that the total uncertainty of fuel measurements is consistent with the requirements of this Regulation, where possible referring to national laws, clauses in customer contracts or fuel supplier accuracy standards;

(g) single emission factors used for each fuel type, or in the case of alternative fuels, the methodologies for determining the emission factors, including the methodology for sampling, methods of analysis and a description of the laboratories used, with the ISO 17025 accreditation of those laboratories, if any;

(h) a description of the procedures used for determining activity data per voyage, including:

    (i) the procedures, responsibilities and data sources for determining and recording the distance,

    (ii) the procedures, responsibilities, formulae and data sources for determining and recording the cargo carried and the number of passengers, as applicable,

    (iii) the procedures, responsibilities, formulae and data sources for determining and recording the time spent at sea between the port of departure and the port of arrival;

    (i) a description of the method to be used to determine surrogate data for closing data gaps;

(j) a revision record sheet to record all the details of the revision history.

4. The monitoring plan may also contain information on the ice class of the ship and/or the procedures, responsibilities, formulae and data sources for determining and recording the distance travelled and the time spent at sea when navigating through ice.

5. Companies shall use standardised monitoring plans based on templates. Those templates, including the technical rules for their uniform application, shall be determined by the Commission by means of implementing acts. Those implementing acts shall be adopted in accordance with the examination procedure referred to in Article 24(2)."

Article 7 allows for the monitoring plan to be modified. Under Article 7(1), companies are obliged to check regularly, and at least annually, whether a ship's monitoring plan reflects the nature and functioning of the ship and whether the monitoring methodology can be improved. Moreover, under Article 7(2), companies must modify the monitoring plan in any of the following situations: (a) where a change of company occurs; (b) where new CO_2 emissions occur due to new emission sources or due to the use of new fuels not yet contained in the monitoring plan;[124] (c) where a change in availability of data, due to the use of new types of measuring equipment, new sampling methods or analysis methods, or for other reasons, may affect the accuracy of the determination of CO_2 emissions;[125] (d) where data resulting from the monitoring method applied has been found to be incorrect;[126] or (e) where any part of the monitoring plan is identified as not being in conformity with the requirements of this regulation and the company is required to revise it pursuant to Article 13(1). Companies must, by virtue of Article 7(3), notify to the verifiers without undue delay any proposals for modification of the monitoring plan. Under Article 7(4), modifications of the monitoring plan under points (b), (c) and (d) of Article 7(2) must be subject to assessment by the verifier in accordance with Article 13(1). Following the assessment, the verifier shall notify the company whether those modifications are in conformity.

19.226 From 1 January 2018, companies have had to, by virtue of Article 8 and based on the monitoring plan assessed in accordance with Article 13(1), monitor CO_2 emissions for each ship on a per-voyage and an annual basis by applying the appropriate method for determining CO_2 emissions among those set out in Part B of Annex I and by calculating CO_2 emissions in accordance with Part A of Annex I.

19.227 Monitoring on a *per-voyage basis* is specified in Article 9. Under Article 9(1), based on the monitoring plan assessed in accordance with Article 13(1), for each ship arriving in or departing from, and for each voyage to or from, a port under a Member State's jurisdiction, companies shall monitor in accordance with Part A of Annex I and Part A of Annex II the following parameters: (a) port of departure and port of arrival including the date and hour of departure and arrival; (b) amount and emission factor for each type of fuel consumed in total; (c) CO_2 emitted; (d) distance travelled; (e) time spent at sea; (f) cargo carried; and (g) transport work. Companies may also monitor information relating to the ship's ice class and to navigation through ice, where applicable. Under Article 9(2) and by way of derogation from Article 9(1) and without prejudice to Article 10, a company shall be exempt from the obligation to monitor the information referred to in paragraph 1 of this article on a per-voyage basis in respect of a specified ship, if: (a) all of the ship's voyages during the reporting period either start from or end at a port under the jurisdiction of a Member State; and (b) the ship, according to its schedule, performs more than 300 voyages during the reporting period.

19.228 Monitoring on an *annual basis* is provided for in Article 10. Based on the monitoring plan assessed in accordance with Article 13(1), for each ship and for each calendar year, companies shall monitor in accordance with Part A of Annex I and with Part B of Annex II the following parameters: (a) amount and emission factor for each type of fuel consumed in total; (b) total aggregated CO_2 emitted within the scope of the regulation; (c) aggregated CO_2 emissions from all voyages between ports under a Member State's jurisdiction; (d) aggregated CO_2 emissions from all voyages which departed from ports under a Member State's jurisdiction; (e) aggregated CO_2 emissions from all voyages to ports under a Member State's jurisdiction; (f) CO_2 emissions which occurred within ports

---

124 Under Art. 7(4), modifications of the monitoring plan under this point of Art. 7(2) must be subject to assessment by the verifier in accordance with Art. 13(1). Following the assessment, the verifier must notify the company whether those modifications are in conformity.

125 Ibid.

126 Ibid.

under a Member State's jurisdiction at berth; (g) total distance travelled; (h) total time spent at sea; (i) total transport work; and (j) average energy efficiency. Companies may monitor information relating to the ship's ice class and to navigation through ice, where applicable. Companies may also monitor fuel consumed and CO_2 emitted, differentiating on the basis of other criteria defined in the monitoring plan.

19.229 The entire system is dependent on reporting. Article 11 therefore specifies the content of the emissions report. Article 12 deals with the format of the report.

19.230 Article 11 specifies in regard to the content of the report:

"1. From 2019, by 30 April of each year, companies shall submit to the Commission and to the authorities of the flag States concerned, an emissions report concerning the CO2 emissions and other relevant information for the entire reporting period for each ship under their responsibility, which has been verified as satisfactory by a verifier in accordance with Article 13.

2. Where there is a change of company, the new company shall ensure that each ship under its responsibility complies with the requirements of this Regulation in relation to the entire reporting period during which it takes responsibility for the ship concerned.

3. Companies shall include in the emissions report the following information:

    (a) data identifying the ship and the company, including:

        (i)   name of the ship,
        (ii) IMO identification number,
        (iii) port of registry or home port,
        (iv) ice class of the ship, if included in the monitoring plan,
        (v) technical efficiency of the ship (the Energy Efficiency Design Index (EEDI) or the Estimated Index Value (EIV) in accordance with IMO Resolution MEPC.215 (63), where applicable),
        (vi) name of the shipowner,
        (vii) address of the shipowner and its principal place of business,
        (viii) name of the company (if not the shipowner),
        (ix) address of the company (if not the shipowner) and its principal place of business,
        (x) address, telephone and e-mail details of a contact person;

    (b) the identity of the verifier that assessed the emissions report;
    (c) information on the monitoring method used and the related level of uncertainty;
    (d) the results from annual monitoring of the parameters in accordance with Article 10."

19.231 Article 12 deals with the format of the emissions report. Article 12(1) provides that the emissions report shall be submitted using automated systems and data exchange formats, including electronic templates. Under Article 12(2), the Commission shall determine, by means of implementing acts, technical rules establishing the data exchange formats, including the electronic templates. Those implementing acts shall be adopted in accordance with the examination procedure referred to in Article 24(2).

Chapter III of Regulation 2015/757: "verification and accreditation"

19.232 Article 13 deals with the scope of verification activities and verification report:

"1. The verifier shall assess the conformity of the monitoring plan with the requirements laid down in Articles 6 and 7. Where the verifier's assessment identifies non-conformities with those requirements, the company concerned shall revise its monitoring plan accordingly and submit the revised plan for a final assessment by the verifier before the reporting period starts. The company shall agree with the verifier on the timeframe necessary to introduce those revisions. That timeframe shall in any event not extend beyond the beginning of the reporting period.

2. The verifier shall assess the conformity of the emissions report with the requirements laid down in Articles 8 to 12 and Annexes I and II.

   In particular the verifier shall assess whether the CO2 emissions and other relevant information included in the emissions report have been determined in accordance with Articles 8, 9 and 10 and the monitoring plan.

3. Where the verification assessment concludes, with reasonable assurance from the verifier, that the emissions report is free from material misstatements, the verifier shall issue a verification report stating that the emissions report has been verified as satisfactory. The verification report shall specify all issues relevant to the work carried out by the verifier.

4. Where the verification assessment concludes that the emissions report includes misstatements or non-conformities with the requirements of this Regulation, the verifier shall inform the company thereof in a timely manner. The company shall then correct the misstatements or non-conformities so as to enable the verification process to be completed in time and shall submit to the verifier the revised emissions report and any other information that was necessary to correct the non-conformities identified. In its verification report, the verifier shall state whether the misstatements or non-conformities identified during the verification assessment have been corrected by the company. Where the communicated misstatements or non-conformities have not been corrected and, individually or combined, lead to material misstatements, the verifier shall issue a verification report stating that the emissions report does not comply with this Regulation."

19.233 The general obligations and principles for the verifiers are set down in Article 14:

"1. The verifier shall be independent from the company or from the operator of a ship and shall carry out the activities required under this Regulation in the public interest. For that purpose, neither the verifier nor any part of the same legal entity shall be a company or ship operator, the owner of a company, or be owned by them, nor shall the verifier have relations with the company that could affect its independence and impartiality.

2. When considering the verification of the emissions report and of the monitoring procedures applied by the company, the verifier shall assess the reliability, credibility and accuracy of the monitoring systems and of the reported data and information relating to CO2 emissions, in particular:

   (a) the attribution of fuel consumption to voyages;
   (b) the reported fuel consumption data and related measurements and calculations;
   (c) the choice and the employment of emission factors;
   (d) the calculations leading to the determination of the overall CO2 emissions;
   (e) the calculations leading to the determination of the energy efficiency.

3. The verifier shall only consider emissions reports submitted in accordance with Article 12 if reliable and credible data and information enable the CO2 emissions to be determined with a reasonable degree of certainty and provided that the following are ensured:

   (a) the reported data are coherent in relation to estimated data that are based on ship tracking data and characteristics such as the installed engine power;
   (b) the reported data are free of inconsistencies, in particular when comparing the total volume of fuel purchased annually by each ship and the aggregate fuel consumption during voyages;
   (c) the collection of the data has been carried out in accordance with the applicable rules; and
   (d) the relevant records of the ship are complete and consistent."

19.234 Article 15 addresses the verification procedures:

"1. The verifier shall identify potential risks related to the monitoring and reporting process by comparing reported CO_2 emissions with estimated data based on ship tracking data and characteristics such as the installed engine power. Where significant deviations are found, the verifier shall carry out further analyses.

2. The verifier shall identify potential risks related to the different calculation steps by reviewing all data sources and methodologies used.

3. The verifier shall take into consideration any effective risk control methods applied by the company to reduce levels of uncertainty associated with the accuracy specific to the monitoring methods used.

4. The company shall provide the verifier with any additional information that enables it to carry out the verification procedures. The verifier may conduct spot-checks during the verification process to determine the reliability of reported data and information.

5. The Commission shall be empowered to adopt delegated acts in accordance with Article 23, in order to further specify the rules for the verification activities referred to in this Regulation. When adopting these acts, the Commission shall take into account the elements set out in Part A of Annex III. The rules specified in those delegated acts shall be based on the principles for verification provided for in Article 14 and on relevant internationally accepted standards."

19.235 The accreditation of verifiers is addressed by Article 16:

"1. Verifiers that assess the monitoring plans and the emissions reports, and issue verification reports and documents of compliance referred to in this Regulation shall be accredited for activities under the scope of this Regulation by a national accreditation body pursuant to Regulation (EC) No 765/2008.

2. Where no specific provisions concerning the accreditation of verifiers are laid down in this Regulation, the relevant provisions of Regulation (EC) No 765/2008 shall apply.

3. The Commission shall be empowered to adopt delegated acts in accordance with Article 23, in order to further specify the methods of accreditation of verifiers. When adopting these acts, the Commission shall take into account the elements set out in Part B of Annex III. The methods specified in those delegated acts shall be based on the principles for verification provided for in Article 14 and on relevant internationally accepted standards."

Chapter IV of Regulation 2015/757: "compliance and publication of information"

19.236 Article 17 deals with the so-called "document of compliance" (it is not the documentation of compliance but the actual compliance document itself):

"1. Where the emissions report fulfils the requirements set out in Articles 11 to 15 and those in Annexes I and II, the verifier shall issue, on the basis of the verification report, a document of compliance for the ship concerned.

2. The document of compliance shall include the following information:

    (a) identity of the ship (name, IMO identification number and port of registry or home port);

    (b) name, address and principal place of business of the shipowner;

    (c) identity of the verifier;

    (d) date of issue of the document of compliance, its period of validity and the reporting period it refers to.

3. Documents of compliance shall be valid for the period of 18 months after the end of the reporting period.

4. The verifier shall inform the Commission and the authority of the flag State, without delay, of the issuance of any document of compliance. The verifier shall transmit the information referred to in paragraph 2 using automated systems and data exchange formats, including electronic templates.

5. The Commission shall determine, by means of implementing acts, technical rules for the data exchange formats, including the electronic templates. Those implementing acts shall be adopted in accordance with the examination procedure referred to in Article 24(2)."

19.237 There is an obligation to carry a valid document of compliance on board, by virtue of Article 18. It provides that by 30 June of the year following the end of a reporting period, ships arriving at, within or departing from a port under the jurisdiction of a Member State, and which have carried out voyages during that reporting period, shall carry on board a valid document of compliance.

19.238 Article 19 sets out the compliance regime for monitoring and reporting requirements and inspections:

"1. Based on the information published in accordance with Article 21(1), each Member State shall take all the measures necessary to ensure compliance with the monitoring and reporting requirements set out in Articles 8 to 12 by ships flying its flag. Member States shall regard the fact that a document of compliance has been issued for the ship concerned, in accordance with Article 17(4), as evidence of such compliance.

2. Each Member State shall ensure that any inspection of a ship in a port under its jurisdiction carried out in accordance with Directive 2009/16/EC includes checking that a valid document of compliance is carried on board.

3. For each ship in respect of which the information referred to in points (i) and (j) of Article 21(2), is not available at the time when it enters a port under the jurisdiction of a Member State, the Member State concerned may check that a valid document of compliance is carried on board."

19.239 Article 20 provides for penalties, information exchange and expulsion order. Importantly, given the current state of the development of EU law, it is the Member States (rather than the EU) which has the power to impose these penalties. So, Article 20(1) provides that Member States shall set up a system of penalties for failure to comply with the monitoring and reporting obligations set out in Articles 8 to 12 and shall take all the measures necessary to ensure that those penalties are imposed. The penalties provided for shall be effective, proportionate and dissuasive. Member States shall notify those provisions to the Commission by 1 July 2017, and shall notify to the Commission without delay any subsequent amendments. Under Article 20(2), Member States shall establish an effective exchange of information and effective co-operation between their national authorities responsible for ensuring compliance with monitoring and reporting obligations or, where applicable, their authorities entrusted with penalty procedures. National penalty procedures against a specified ship by any Member State shall be notified to the Commission, the EMSA, to the other Member States and to the flag State concerned. Article 20(3) provides that in the case of ships that have failed to comply with the monitoring and reporting requirements for two or more consecutive reporting periods and where other enforcement measures have failed to ensure compliance, the competent authority of the Member State of the port of entry may issue an expulsion order which shall be notified to the Commission, EMSA, the other Member States and the flag State concerned. As a result of the issuing of such an expulsion order, every Member State shall refuse entry of the ship concerned into any of its ports until the company fulfils its monitoring and reporting obligations in accordance with Articles 11 and 18. The fulfilment of those obligations shall be confirmed by the notification of a valid document of compliance to the competent national authority which issued the expulsion order. Article 20(3) shall, sensibly, be without prejudice to international maritime rules applicable in the case of ships in distress. Under Article 20(4), the shipowner or operator of a ship or its represent-ative in the Member States shall have the right to an effective remedy before a court or tribunal against an expulsion order and shall be properly informed thereof by the com-petent authority of the Member State of the port of entry. Member States shall establish and maintain appropriate procedures for this purpose. Finally, Article 20(5) provides that any Member State without maritime ports in its territory and which has closed its national ship register or has no ships flying its flag that fall within the scope of this regulation, and as long as no such ships are flying its flag, may derogate from the provisions of this article. Any Member State that intends to avail itself of that derogation shall notify the Commission at the latest on 1 July 2015. Any subsequent change shall also be communic-ated to the Commission.

19.240 Certain information is to be published and the Commission is to prepare a report. Article 21 addresses the issue. Under Article 21(1), by 30 June each year, the Commission shall make publicly available the information on CO_2 emissions reported in accordance with Article 11 as well as the information set out in Article 21(2). Article 21(2) goes on to provide that the Commission shall include the following in the informa-tion to be made publicly available: (a) the identity of the ship (name, IMO identification number and port of registry or home port); (b) the technical efficiency of the ship; (c) the annual CO_2 emissions; (d) the annual total fuel consumption for voyages; (e) the annual average fuel consumption and CO_2 emissions per distance travelled of voyages; (f) the annual average fuel consumption and CO_2 emissions per distance travelled and cargo carried on voyages; (g) the annual total time spent at sea in voyages; (h) the method applied for monitoring; (i) the date of issue and the expiry date of the document of com-pliance; (j) the identity of the verifier that assessed the emissions report; and (k) any other information monitored and reported on a voluntary basis in accordance with Article 10. Under Article 21(3), where, due to specific circumstances, disclosure of a category of aggregated data under Article 20(2), which does not relate to CO_2 emissions, would exceptionally undermine the protection of commercial interests deserving protection as a legitimate economic interest overriding the public interest in disclosure pursuant to Regu-lation 1367/2006 of the European Parliament and of the Council, a different level of aggregation of that specific data shall be applied, at the request of the company, so as to protect such interests.[127] Where application of a different level of aggregation is not pos-sible, the Commission shall not make those data publicly available. There is an obliga-tion, by virtue of Article 21(4) on the Commission to publish an annual report on CO_2 emissions and other relevant information from maritime transport, including aggregated and explained results, with the aim of informing the public and allowing for an assess-ment of the CO_2 emissions and the energy efficiency of maritime transport per size, type of ships, activity or any other category deemed relevant. Moreover, by virtue of Article

---

127 I.e. Reg. 1367/2006 of the European Parliament and of the Council of 6 September 2006 on the applica-tion of the provisions of the Aarhus Convention on Access to Information, Public Participation in Decision-making and Access to Justice in Environmental Matters to Community institutions and bodies (OJ L264/13, 25 September 2006).

21(5), the Commission shall assess every two years the maritime transport sector's overall impact on the global climate including through non-CO_2-related emissions or effects. Under Article 21(6), within the framework of its mandate, EMSA shall assist the Commission in its work to comply with this article and Articles 12 and 17 of this regulation, in accordance with Regulation 1406/2002 of the European Parliament and of the Council.[128]

Chapter V of Regulation 2015/757: "international cooperation"

19.241 Article 22 recognises that international co-operation is needed. It provides in Article 22(1) that the Commission shall inform the IMO and other relevant international bodies on a regular basis of the implementation of this regulation, without prejudice to the distribution of competences or to decision-making procedures as provided for in the Treaties. Article 22(2) provides that the Commission and, where relevant, the Member States shall maintain technical exchange with third countries, in particular the further development of monitoring methods, the organisation of reporting and the verification of emissions reports. Finally, under Article 22(3), if an international agreement on a global monitoring, reporting and verification system for GHG emissions or on global measures to reduce GHG emissions from maritime transport is reached, the Commission shall review the regulation and shall, if appropriate, propose amendments to this regulation in order to ensure alignment with that international agreement.

Chapter VI: "delegated and implementing powers and final provisions"

19.242 Article 23 deals with the exercise of delegation which is necessary in this context:

"1. The power to adopt delegated acts is conferred on the Commission subject to the conditions laid down in this Article. It is of particular importance that the Commission follow its usual practice and carry out consultations with experts, including Member States' experts, before adopting those delegated acts.
2. The power to adopt delegated acts referred to in Articles 5(2), 15(5) and 16(3) shall be conferred on the Commission for a period of five years from 1 July 2015. The Commission shall draw up a report in respect of the delegation of power not later than nine months before the end of the five-year period. The delegation of power shall be tacitly extended for periods of an identical duration, unless the European Parliament or the Council opposes such extension not later than three months before the end of each period.
3. The delegation of power referred to in Articles 5(2), 15(5) and 16(3) may be revoked at any time by the European Parliament or by the Council. A decision to revoke shall put an end to the delegation of the power specified in that decision. It shall take effect the day following the publication of the decision in the Official Journal of the European Union or at a later date specified therein. It shall not affect the validity of any delegated acts already in force.
4. As soon as it adopts a delegated act, the Commission shall notify it simultaneously to the European Parliament and to the Council.
5. A delegated act adopted pursuant to Articles 5(2), 15(5) and 16(3) shall enter into force only if no objection has been expressed either by the European Parliament or the Council within a period of two months of notification of that act to the European Parliament and the Council

---

128 I.e. Reg. 1406/2002 of the European Parliament and of the Council of 27 June 2002 establishing a European Maritime Safety Agency (OJ L208/1, 5 August 2002).

or if, before the expiry of that period, the European Parliament and the Council have both informed the Commission that they will not object. That period shall be extended by two months at the initiative of the European Parliament or of the Council."

19.243 Article 24 lays down the relevant committee procedure. It specifies that the Commission shall be assisted by the Committee established by Article 26 of Regulation 525/2013 of the European Parliament and of the Council.[129] That Committee shall be a committee within the meaning of Regulation 182/2011. Where the Committee delivers no opinion, the Commission shall not adopt the draft implementing act and the third subparagraph of Article 5(4) of Regulation 182/2011 shall apply.

19.244 Article 26 provided that the regulation entered into force on 1 July 2015.

19.245 There are various annexes and they should be consulted in specific cases but the level of detail in those annexes goes beyond what is practicable to present in this work. Annex I deals with the methods for monitoring CO_2 emissions. Annex II deals with the monitoring of other relevant information. Annex III sets out the elements to be taken into account for the delegated acts provided for in Articles 15 and 16.

COMMISSION IMPLEMENTING REGULATION (EU) 2016/1927 OF 4 NOVEMBER 2016 ON TEMPLATES FOR MONITORING PLANS, EMISSIONS REPORTS AND DOCUMENTS OF COMPLIANCE PURSUANT TO REGULATION (EU) 2015/757 OF THE EUROPEAN PARLIAMENT AND OF THE COUNCIL ON MONITORING, REPORTING AND VERIFICATION OF CARBON DIOXIDE EMISSIONS FROM MARITIME TRANSPORT

19.246 On 4 November 2016, the Commission adopted a detailed implementing regulation on templates for monitoring plans, emissions reports and documents of compliance under Regulation 2015/757.[130] Regard should be had to the 21-page Regulation for the detail on those plans, reports and documents.

COMMISSION IMPLEMENTING REGULATION 2016/1928 OF 4 NOVEMBER 2016 ON DETERMINATION OF CARGO CARRIED FOR CATEGORIES OF SHIPS OTHER THAN PASSENGER, RO-RO AND CONTAINER SHIPS PURSUANT TO REGULATION (EU) 2015/757 OF THE EUROPEAN PARLIAMENT AND OF THE COUNCIL ON THE MONITORING, REPORTING AND VERIFICATION OF CARBON DIOXIDE EMISSIONS FROM MARITIME TRANSPORT

19.247 On 4 November 2016, the Commission adopted Regulation 2016/1928 on determination of cargo carried for categories of ships other than passenger, ro-ro and container ships pursuant to Regulation (EU) 2015/757 of the European Parliament and of the Council on the monitoring, reporting and verification of carbon dioxide emissions from maritime transport.[131] It provides some detail on the operation of Regulation 2015/757.

---

129 I.e. Reg. 525/2013 of the European Parliament and of the Council of 21 May 2013 on a mechanism for monitoring and reporting greenhouse gas emissions and for reporting other information at national and Union level relevant to climate change and repealing Decision 280/2004 (OJ L165/13, 18 June 2013).

130 OJ L299/1, 5 November 2016.

131 OJ L299/22, 5 November 2016.

Article 4 provided that the regulation entered into force on the twentieth day following that of its publication in the *Official Journal*.

19.248 The background is clear from the recitals:

"(1) The rules on the monitoring of cargo carried and other relevant information are laid down in Annex II to Regulation ... 2015/757. In particular, the determination of cargo carried for categories of ships other than passenger ships, ro-ro ships and container ships is to be done in accordance with the parameters set out in point (g) of paragraph 1 of Part A to that Annex.

(2) In the case of oil tankers, chemical tankers, gas carriers, bulk carriers, refrigerated cargo ships and combination carriers, it is appropriate to ensure that the determination of the average operational energy efficiency indicator is in line with the IMO Guidelines for voluntary use of the Ship Energy Efficiency Operational Indicator (EEOI) ... since those Guidelines reflect industry practices.

(3) In the case of LNG carriers and container/ro-ro cargo ships, the parameter to be used for calculating cargo carried should reflect industry practices and ensure that the information provided is accurate and comparable over time.

(4) In the case of general cargo ships, the determination of cargo carried should follow a specifically developed approach that takes into account variations in cargo density significant for this ship category. It is appropriate to allow these data to be supplemented on a voluntary basis with additional data in line with the IMO Guidelines for voluntary use of the Ship Energy Efficiency Operational Indicator (EEOI).

(5) In the case of vehicle carriers, the determination of cargo carried should follow a flexible approach based on two different options. In order to better reflect the special relevance of volume, it is appropriate to allow for data on a different additional parameter to be provided on a voluntary basis.

(6) Ro-pax ships should be considered as a specific case in which particular conditions should apply. In view of the mixed service offered by ro-pax ships and to better reflect industry practices, two parameters should be applied to express cargo carried.

(7) For other ship types not falling under any of the above categories nor under those in points (d), (e) and (f) of paragraph 1 of Part A of Annex II to Regulation ... 2015/757, a flexible approach should be permitted so as to fully reflect the diversity of ships carrying very different types of cargo. In order to ensure consistency and comparability of data over time in accordance with Article 4(3) of Regulation ... 2015/757, the company's choice concerning the most appropriate cargo carried parameter is to be documented in the ship's monitoring plan and applied accordingly.

(8) The Commission has consulted parties concerned on the best industry practices on matters addressed by this Regulation. The consultation was carried out through the 'Shipping MRV monitoring subgroup' set up under the umbrella of the European Sustainable Shipping Forum.

(9) The measures provided for in this Regulation are in accordance with the opinion of the Climate Change Committee established by Article 26 of Regulation ... 525/2013 of the European Parliament and of the Council."

19.249 Article 1 ("subject matter") provides that the regulation lays down rules specifying the parameters applicable to the determination of cargo carried for categories of ships other than passenger ships, ro-ro ships and container ships for the purposes of monitoring of other relevant information on a per-voyage basis pursuant to Article 9(1) of Regulation 2015/757.

19.250 Article 2 ("definitions") provides that for the purpose of the regulation, the following definitions shall apply:

"(1) 'Oil tanker' means a ship constructed or adapted primarily to carry crude oil or petroleum products in bulk in its cargo spaces, other than combination carriers, noxious liquid substances (NLS) tankers or gas tankers;

(2) 'Chemical tanker' means a ship constructed or adapted for the carriage in bulk of any liquid product listed in Chapter 17 of the International Code for the Construction and Equipment of Ships carrying Dangerous Chemicals in Bulk ... or a ship constructed or adapted to carry a cargo of NLS in bulk;

(3) 'LNG carrier' means a tanker for the bulk carriage of liquefied natural gas (LNG) (primarily methane) in independent insulated tanks;

(4) 'Gas carrier' means a tanker for the bulk carriage of liquefied gases other than LNG;

(5) 'Bulk carrier' means a ship which is intended primarily to carry dry cargo in bulk, including types such as ore carriers as defined in Regulation 1 of Chapter XII of the 1998 International Convention for the Safety of Life at Sea (the SOLAS Convention), but excluding combination carriers;

(6) 'General cargo ship' means a ship with a multi-deck or single-deck hull designed primarily for the carriage of general cargo excluding specialised dry cargo ships, which are not included in the calculation of reference lines for general cargo ships, namely livestock carrier, barge carrier, heavy load carrier, yacht carrier, nuclear fuel carrier;

(7) 'Refrigerated cargo ship' means a ship designed exclusively for the carriage of refrigerated cargoes in holds;

(8) 'Vehicle carrier' means a multi-deck roll-on-roll-off cargo ship designed for the carriage of empty cars and trucks;

(9) 'Combination carrier' means a ship designed to load 100% deadweight with both liquid and dry cargo in bulk;

(10) 'Ro-pax ship' means a ship, which carries more than 12 passengers and which has roll-on/roll-off cargo space on board;

(11) 'Container/ro-ro cargo ship' means a hybrid of a container ship and a ro-ro cargo ship in independent sections;

(12) 'Deadweight carried' means, in metric tonnes, the measured volume displacement of a ship at a load draught condition multiplied by the relative water density at departure reduced by the ship's lightweight and by the weight of the fuel on board determined at the departure of the laden voyage concerned;

(13) 'Measured volume displacement' means, in cubic meters, the volume of the moulded displacement of the ship, excluding appendages, in a ship with a metal shell, and means the volume of displacement to the outer surface of the hull in a ship with a shell of any other material;

(14) 'Lightweight' means, in metric tonnes, the actual weight of the ship with no fuel, passengers, cargo, water and other consumables on board."

19.251 Article 3 sets out the parameters to determine the "cargo carried" per ship category.

"'Cargo carried' for the purpose of monitoring of other relevant information on a per-voyage basis pursuant to Article 9(1) of Regulation (EU) 2015/757, shall be determined as follows:

(a) for oil tankers, as the mass of the cargo on board;

(b) for chemical tankers, as the mass of the cargo on board;

(c) for LNG carriers, as the volume of the cargo on discharge, or if the cargo is discharged at several occasions during a voyage, the sum of the cargo discharged during a voyage and the cargo discharged at all subsequent ports of call until new cargo is loaded;

(d) for gas carriers, as the mass of the cargo on board;

(e) for bulk carriers, as the mass of the cargo on board;

(f) for general cargo ships, as deadweight carried for laden voyages and as zero for ballast voyages;

(g) for refrigerated cargo ships, as the mass of the cargo on board;

(h) for vehicle carriers, as the mass of the cargo on board, determined as the actual mass or as the number of cargo units or occupied lane meters multiplied by default values for their weight;

(i) for combination carriers, as the mass of the cargo on board;

(j) for ro-pax ships, as the number of passengers and as the mass of the cargo on board, determined as the actual mass or the number of cargo units (trucks, cars, etc.) or occupied lane meters multiplied by default values for their weight;

(k) for container/ro-ro cargo ships, as the volume of the cargo on board, determined as the sum of the number of cargo units (cars, trailers, trucks and other standard units) multiplied by a default area and by the height of the deck (the distance between the floor and the structural beam), of the number of occupied lane-metres multiplied by the height of the deck (for other ro-ro cargo) and of the number of TEUs multiplied by 38,3 m³;

(l) for other ship types not falling under any of the categories mentioned in points (a) to (k) nor under those in points (d), (e) and (f) of paragraph 1 of Part A of Annex II to Regulation (EU) 2015/757, as mass of cargo on board or as deadweight carried for laden voyages and zero for ballast voyages.

For the purposes of point (f) of the first paragraph, the mass of the cargo on board can be used on a voluntary basis as an additional parameter.

For the purposes of point (h) of the first paragraph, deadweight carried for laden voyages and zero for ballast voyages can be used on a voluntary basis as an additional parameter."

P. FLAG STATE REQUIREMENTS: DIRECTIVE 2009/21 OF THE EUROPEAN PARLIAMENT AND OF THE COUNCIL OF 23 APRIL 2009 ON COMPLIANCE WITH FLAG STATE REQUIREMENTS

19.252 On 23 April 2009, the Parliament and the Council adopted Directive 2009/21 on compliance with flag State requirements.[132]

19.253 The background is set out in the recitals which state:

"(1) The safety of Community shipping and of citizens using it and the protection of the environment should be ensured at all times.

(2) In respect of international shipping a comprehensive framework enhancing maritime safety and the protection of the environment with regard to pollution from ships has been set up through the adoption of a number of conventions for which the International Maritime Organisation (hereinafter the IMO) is the depository.

(3) Under the provisions of the United Nations Convention on the Law of the Sea, 1982 (UNCLOS) and of the conventions for which IMO is the depository (hereinafter the IMO Conventions), the States which are party to those instruments are responsible for promulgating laws and regulations and for taking all other steps which may be necessary to give those instruments full and complete effect so as to ensure that, from the point of view of safety of life at sea and protection of the marine environment, a ship is fit for the service for which it is intended and is manned with competent maritime personnel.

(4) Due account has to be taken of the Maritime Labour Convention, adopted by the International Labour Organisation (ILO) in 2006, which also addresses flag State-related obligations.

(5) On 9 October 2008, the Member States adopted a statement in which they unanimously recognised the importance of the application of the international conventions related to flag States obligations in order to improve maritime safety and to contribute to preventing pollution by ships.

---

132 OJ L131/132, 28 May 2009.

(6) Implementation of the procedures recommended by the IMO in MSC/Circ.1140/MEPC/ Circ.424 of 20 December 2004 on the transfer of ships between States should strengthen the provisions of the IMO Conventions and Community maritime safety legislation relating to a change of flag and should increase transparency in the relationship between flag States, in the interests of maritime safety.

(7) The availability of information on ships flying the flag of a Member State, as well as on ships which have left a register of a Member State, should improve the transparency of the performance of a high-quality fleet and contribute to better monitoring of flag State obligations and to ensuring a level playing field between administrations.

(8) In order to help Member States in further improving their performance as flag States, they should have their administration audited on a regular basis.

(9) A quality certification of administrative procedures in accordance with the standards of the International Organisation for Standardisation (ISO) or equivalent standards should further ensure a level playing field between administrations.

(10) The measures necessary for the implementation of this Directive should be adopted in accordance with Council Decision 1999/468/EC of 28 June 1999 laying down the procedures for the exercise of implementing powers conferred on the Commission.

(11) Since the objectives of this Directive, namely the introduction and implementation of appropriate measures in the field of maritime transport policy, cannot be sufficiently achieved by the Member States and can therefore, by reason of its scale and effects, be better achieved at Community level, the Community may adopt measures, in accordance with the principle of subsidiarity as set out in Article 5 of the Treaty. In accordance with the principle of proportionality, as set out in that Article, this Directive does not go beyond what is necessary in order to achieve those objectives."

19.254 Article 1(1) states that the purpose of the directive is: (a) to ensure that Member States effectively and consistently discharge their obligations as flag States; and (b) to enhance safety and prevent pollution from ships flying the flag of a Member State.

19.255 Article 2 states that the directive shall apply to the administration of the State whose flag the ship is flying.

19.256 There are a number of definitions in Article 3 which are set out for the purposes of the directive:

"(a) 'ship' means a ship or craft flying the flag of a Member State falling within the scope of the relevant IMO Conventions, and for which a certificate is required;

(b) 'administration' means the competent authorities of the Member State whose flag the ship is flying;

(c) 'recognised organisation' means an organisation recognised in accordance with Regulation (EC) No 391/2009 of the European Parliament and of the Council of 23 April 2009 on common rules and standards for ship inspection and survey organisations (recast)...;

(d) 'certificates' means statutory certificates issued in respect of the relevant IMO Conventions;

(e) 'IMO audit' means an audit conducted in accordance with the provisions of Resolution A.974(24) adopted by the IMO Assembly on 1 December 2005."

19.257 The conditions for allowing a ship to operate upon granting the right to fly the flag of a Member State are specified in Article 4:

"1. Prior to allowing a ship to operate, which has been granted the right to fly its flag, the Member State concerned shall take the measures it deems appropriate to ensure that the ship in question complies with the applicable international rules and regulations. In particular, it shall verify the safety records of the ship by all reasonable means. It shall, if necessary, consult with the losing flag State in order to establish whether any outstanding deficiencies or safety issues identified by the latter remain unresolved.

2. Whenever another flag State requests information concerning a ship which was previously flying the flag of a Member State, that Member State shall promptly provide details of outstanding deficiencies and any other relevant safety-related information to the requesting flag State."

19.258 The detention of a ship flying the flag of a Member State is addressed by Article 5 which provides that when the administration is informed that a ship flying the flag of the Member State concerned has been detained by a port State, it shall, according to the procedures it has established to this effect, oversee the ship being brought into compliance with the relevant IMO conventions.

19.259 Article 6 deals with the so-called "accompanying measures". It provides that Member States shall ensure that at least the following information concerning ships flying their flag is kept and remains readily accessible for the purposes of this directive: (a) particulars of the ship (name, IMO number, etc.); (b) dates of surveys, including additional and supplementary surveys, if any, and audits; (c) identification of the recognised organisations involved in the certification and classification of the ship; (d) identification of the competent authority which has inspected the ship under port State control provisions and the dates of the inspections; (e) outcome of the port State control inspections (deficiencies: yes or no; detentions: yes or no); (f) information on marine casualties; and (g) identification of ships which have ceased to fly the flag of the Member State concerned during the previous 12 months.

19.260 Article 8 ("quality management system and internal evaluation") provides:

"1. By 17 June 2012 each Member State shall develop, implement and maintain a quality management system for the operational parts of the flag State-related activities of its administration. Such quality management system shall be certified in accordance with the applicable international quality standards.
2. Member States which appear on the black list or which appear, for two consecutive years, on the grey list as published in the most recent annual report of the Paris Memorandum of Understanding on Port State Control (hereinafter the Paris MOU) shall provide the Commission with a report on their flag State performance no later than four months after the publication of the Paris MOU report.

The report shall identify and analyse the main reasons for the lack of compliance that led to the detentions and the deficiencies resulting in black or grey status."

19.261 Every five years, and for the first time by 17 June 2012, the Commission is obliged under Article 9 to present a report to the European Parliament and to the Council on the application of the directive and the report shall contain an assessment of the performance of the Member States as flag States. Article 10 provides for the assistance to be given to the Commission of the COSS. In terms of transposition in Member State law, Article 11(1) provides that Member States had to bring into force the laws, regulations and administrative provisions necessary to comply with the directive by 17 June 2011 at the latest. Article 12 provides that the directive entered into force on the twentieth day following its publication in the *Official Journal*.

Q. PORT CHARGES AND ENVIRONMENT-FRIENDLY MARITIME TRANSPORT ACTIVITIES AND SUSTAINABLE TRANSPORTATION

19.262 On 27 June 2017, the European Commission published a "Study on differenti-ated port infrastructure charges to promote environmentally friendly maritime transport activities and sustainable transportation".[133]

R. PENALTIES FOR ENVIRONMENTAL LAW BREACHES

Introduction

19.263 This part of the chapter considers, a high level, Council Framework Decision 2005/667,[134] Directive 2005/35 on ship-source pollution and on the introduction of penal-ties, including criminal penalties, for pollution offences[135] and the *Intertanko* litigation before the CJEU.

COUNCIL FRAMEWORK DECISION 2005/667

Introduction

19.264 On 12 July 2005, the Council adopted Council Framework Decision 2005/667/ JHA to strengthen the criminal-law framework for the enforcement of the law against ship-source pollution.[136] In terms of entry into force, Article 12 provided that the frame-work decision entered into force on the day following that of its publication in the *Official Journal* (i.e. it entered into force on 1 October 2005).

Background

19.265 The Treaty of Amsterdam enabled the EU to become more involved in matters which would be described as in the criminal regime. The recitals to the decision give some background to the decision:

"(1) The Action Plan of the Council and the Commission on how best to implement the provi-sions of the Treaty of Amsterdam on an area of freedom, security and justice ... and the conclusions of the Tampere European Council of 15 and 16 October 1999,[137] and in par-ticular point 48 thereof, call for proposals for legislation to combat environmental crime, in particular common penalties and comparable procedural guarantees.

(2) The fight against intentional or seriously negligent ship-source pollution constitutes one of the Union's priorities. Points 32 to 34 of the conclusions of the Copenhagen European Council of 12 and 13 December 2002 and the statement of the JHA Council of 19 Decem-ber 2002 following the shipwreck of the tanker Prestige, in particular, express the Union's determination to adopt all the measures needed to avoid recurrence of such damage.

---

133 https://ec.europa.eu/transport/sites/transport/files/2017-06-differentiated-port-infrastructure-charges-exec-summary.pdf and https://ec.europa.eu/transport/sites/transport/files/2017-06-differentiated-port-infrastructure-charges-exec-summary.pdf.

134 OJ L255, 30 September 2005, p. 11.

135 OJ L255/11, 30 September 2005.

136 OJ L255/164, 30 September 2005.

137 Ed., this was just before the Erika incident in December 1999.

(3) To this end, as the Commission stated in its Communication to the European Parliament and the Council on improving safety at sea in response to the Prestige accident,[138] the legislation of the Member States should be approximated.

(4) The purpose of Directive 2005/35 ... of the European Parliament and of the Council of 7 September 2005 on ship-source pollution and on the introduction of penalties for infringements ... and this framework Decision, which supplements Directive 2005/35 ... with detailed rules in criminal matters, is to carry out this approximation.

(5) This framework Decision, based on Article 34 of the Treaty on the European Union, is the correct instrument for imposing on the Member States the obligation to provide for criminal penalties.

(6) Due to the specific nature of the conduct, common penalties with regard to legal persons should be introduced.

(7) The 1982 United Nations Convention on the Law of the Sea, signed by all the Member States and with the European Community as a party, is particularly important in the context of cooperation.

(8) The best possible cooperation should be organised between Member States to guarantee the swift transmission of information from one Member State to another. Contact points should be designated and identified.

(9) Since the objectives of this framework Decision cannot be achieved adequately by the Member States and can therefore, by reason of the cross-border character of the damage which may be caused by the behaviour concerned, be better achieved at Union level, the Union may adopt measures, in accordance with the principle of subsidiarity as set out in Article 5 of the Treaty establishing the European Community. In accordance with the principle of proportionality, as set out in that Article, this framework Decision does not go beyond what is necessary in order to achieve those objectives.

(10) This framework Decision respects the fundamental rights and observes the principles recognised by Article 6 of the Treaty of the European Union and reflected in the Charter of Fundamental Rights of the European Union.

(11) This framework Decision does not contain an explicit obligation for Member States bordering straits used for international navigation subject to the regime for transit passage, as laid down in Part III, section 2 of the 1982 United Nations Convention on the Law of the Sea, to establish jurisdiction with regard to offences committed in such straits. The jurisdiction with regard to offences should be established in accordance with international law and in particular Article 34 of the 1982 United Nations Convention on the Law of the Sea.

(12) The practical application of the measures taken by the Member States in implementing this framework Decision, should be monitored by the Commission which should in five years from the date of implementation of this framework Decision, present a report to the Council. This report may include appropriate proposals."

Definitions and territorial scope

19.266 Article 1 states that, for the purposes of the framework decision, the definitions provided for in Article 2 of Directive 2005/35 shall apply (which are discussed below). Article 10 provides that the framework decision shall have the same territorial scope as Directive 2005/35.

Implementation

19.267 In terms of implementation, Article 11 is clear-cut:

"1. Member States shall adopt the measures necessary to comply with the provisions of this framework Decision by 12 January 2007.

---

138 Ed., the Prestige sunk in November 2002.

2. By 12 January 2007, Member States shall transmit to the General Secretariat of the Council and to the Commission the texts of the provisions transposing into their national law the obligations imposed on them by this framework Decision. On the basis of that information and a written report by the Commission, the Council shall, by 12 January 2009 at the latest, assess the extent to which Member States have complied with this framework Decision.

3. By 12 January 2012, the Commission shall, on the basis of information supplied by the Member States on the practical application of the provisions implementing this framework Decision, submit a report to the Council and make any proposals it deems appropriate which may include proposals to the effect that Member States shall, concerning offences committed in their territorial sea or in their exclusive economic zone or equivalent zone, consider a ship flying the flag of another Member State not to be a foreign ship within the meaning of Article 230 of the 1982 United Nations Convention on the Law of the Sea."

Criminal offences

19.268 The most significant aspect of the framework decision is Article 2 (entitled "criminal offences"). It does not provide that there would be criminal offences in EU law (that would not have been possible) but instead, Article 2(1) provides that subject to Article 4(2) of the framework decision, each Member State must take the measures necessary to ensure that an infringement within the meaning of Articles 4 and 5 of Directive 2005/35 shall be regarded as a criminal offence. This is an important and significant step: it is essentially the EU getting certain conduct criminalised by the "back door" by getting Member States to do so.

19.269 Article 2 is not an absolute criminalisation of conduct because Article 2(2) provides that Article 2(1)

> "shall not apply to crew members in respect of infringements that occur in straits used for international navigation, exclusive economic zones and on the high seas where the conditions set out in Annex I, Regulation 11(b) or in Annex II, Regulation 6(b), of the Marpol 73/78 Convention are satisfied".

This is a less significant exemption than might first appear because any significant coastal incident in the EU would probably be covered by the regime.

Aiding, abetting and inciting

19.270 Article 3 is designed to ensure that anyone who is aiding, abetting or inciting a breach (e.g. shore-based management or personnel) would also be punished. Article 3 states simply that each Member State shall, in accordance with national law, take the measures necessary to ensure that aiding, abetting or inciting an offence referred to in Article 2 is punishable.

Penalties

19.271 There is little point in having criminalisation unless there is also penalisation. This is where Article 4 of the framework decision becomes very interesting. There was a risk that different Member States would provide different levels of penalty. So, Article 4 addresses the issue straight on by specifying *minimum* penalties. Article 4 provides:

"1. Each Member State shall take the measures necessary to ensure that the offences referred to in Articles 2 and 3 are punishable by effective, proportionate and dissuasive criminal penalties which shall include, at least for serious cases, criminal penalties of a maximum of at least between one and three years of imprisonment.[139]

2. In minor[140] cases, where the act committed does not cause a deterioration of the quality of the water, a Member State may provide for penalties of a different type from those laid down in paragraph 1.

3. The criminal penalties provided for in paragraph 1 may be accompanied by other penalties or measures, in particular fines, or the disqualification for a natural person from engaging in an activity requiring official authorisation or approval,[141] or founding, managing or directing a company or a foundation, where the facts having led to his/her conviction show an obvious risk that the same kind of criminal activity may be pursued again.

4. Each Member State shall take the measures necessary to ensure that the intentionally committed offence referred to in Article 2 is punishable by a maximum of at least between five and ten years of imprisonment where the offence caused significant and widespread[142] damage to water quality, to animal or vegetable species or to parts of them and the death or serious injury of persons.

5. Each Member State shall take the measures necessary to ensure that the intentionally committed offence referred to in Article 2 is punishable by a maximum[143] of at least between two and five years of imprisonment where:

    (a) the offence caused significant and widespread damage to water quality, to animal or vegetable species or to parts of them; or

    (b) the offence was committed within the framework of a criminal organisation within the meaning of Council Joint Action 98/733/JHA of 21 December 1998 on making it a criminal offence to participate in a criminal organisation in the Member States of the European Union …, irrespective of the level of the penalty referred to in that Joint Action.

6. Each Member State shall take the measures necessary to ensure that the offence referred to in Article 2, when committed with serious negligence, is punishable by a maximum of at least between two and five years of imprisonment where the offence caused significant and widespread damage to water quality, to animal or vegetable species or to parts of them and the death or serious injury of persons.

7. Each Member State shall take the measures necessary to ensure that the offence referred to in Article 2, when committed with serious negligence, is punishable by a maximum of at least between one and three years of imprisonment where the offence caused significant and widespread damage to water quality, to animal or vegetable species or to parts of them.

8. Regarding custodial penalties, this Article shall apply without prejudice to international law and in particular Article 230 of the 1982 United Nations Convention on the Law of the Sea."

Liability of legal persons

19.272 The laws in different Member States differ on whether or not legal persons (e.g. companies) may be liable. The framework decision seeks to put the matter beyond doubt in Article 5:

---

139 Ed., this is quite prescriptive.

140 Ed., this is a somewhat vague term but is linked to the deterioration of the "quality" of the water.

141 Ed., e.g. a ship's master losing his or her licence/certificate/ticket.

142 Ed., the phrase "significant and widespread" is quite a vague one.

143 Ed., the use of the word "maximum" (and not "minimum" or "mandatory") is important because some Member States are more likely than others to imprison/incarcerate persons even though the law allows for the possibility.

"1. Each Member State shall take the measures necessary to ensure that legal persons can be held liable for the offences referred to in Articles 2 and 3, committed for their benefit by any persons acting either individually or as part of an organ of the legal person, who have a leading position within the legal person, based on:

(a) a power of representation of the legal person, or
(b) an authority to take decisions on behalf of the legal person, or
(c) an authority to exercise control within the legal person.

2. Apart from the cases provided for in paragraph 1, Member States shall take the measures necessary to ensure that a legal person can be held liable where lack of supervision or control by a person referred to in paragraph 1 has made possible the commission of the offence referred to in Article 2 for the benefit of the legal person by a person under its authority.

3. The liability of a legal person under paragraphs 1 and 2 shall not exclude criminal proceedings against natural persons who are involved as perpetrators, instigators or accessories in the offences referred to in Articles 2 and 3."

Penalties against legal persons

19.273 The framework decision is very interesting in that it lays down the maximum penalties for breaches committed by legal persons. The amounts are very substantial. Article 6 states:

"1. Each Member State shall take the measures necessary to ensure that a legal person held liable pursuant to Article 5(1) is punishable by effective, proportionate and dissuasive penalties. The penalties:

(a) Shall include criminal or non-criminal[144] fines, which, at least for cases where the legal person is held liable for offences referred to in Article 2, are:

(i) of a maximum of at least between EUR 150 000 and EUR 300 000;
(ii) of a maximum of at least between EUR 750 000 and EUR 1 500 000 in the most serious cases, including at least the intentionally committed offences covered by Article 4(4) and (5).

(b) may, for all cases, include penalties other than fines, such as:

(i) exclusion from entitlement to public benefits or aid;
(ii) temporary or permanent disqualification from engaging in commercial activities;
(iii) placing under judicial supervision;
(iv) a judicial winding-up order;
(v) the obligation to adopt specific measures in order to eliminate the consequences of the offence which led to the liability of the legal person.

2. For the purpose of the implementation of paragraph 1(a), and without prejudice to the first sentence of paragraph 1, Member States in which the euro has not been adopted shall apply the exchange rate between the euro and their currency as published in the Official Journal of the European Union on 12 July 2005.

3. A Member State may implement paragraph 1(a) by applying a system, whereby the fine is proportionate to the turnover of the legal person, to the financial advantage achieved or envisaged by the commission of the offence, or to any other value indicating the financial situation of the legal person, provided that such system allows for maximum fines, which are at least equivalent to the minimum for the maximum fines established in paragraph 1(a).

---

144 Ed., these are so-called "civil fines" which would involve a "fine" but at the civil standard of proof.

4. A Member State that implements the framework Decision in accordance with paragraph 3 shall notify the General Secretariat of the Council and the Commission that it intends to do so.

5. Each Member State shall take the measures necessary to ensure that a legal person held liable pursuant to Article 5(2) is punishable by effective, proportionate and dissuasive penalties or measures."

Jurisdiction

19.274 A central issue is when and how Member States would claim jurisdiction. The situation is complicated by such factors as the flag of the vessel, the place (or places) of the incident, the nationality of person being charged and the nationality of the legal person being charged. Article 7 therefore addresses the issue:

"1. Each Member State shall take the measures necessary to establish its jurisdiction, so far as permitted by international law,[145] with regard to the offences referred to in Articles 2 and 3 where the offence has been committed:

(a) fully or in part in its territory;

(b) in its exclusive economic zone or in an equivalent zone established in accordance with international law;

(c) on board of a ship flying its flag;

(d) by one of its nationals if the offence is punishable under criminal law where it was committed or if the place where it was committed does not fall under any territorial jurisdiction;

(e) for the benefit of a legal person with a registered office in its territory;

(f) outside of its territory but has caused or is likely to cause pollution in its territory or its economic zone, and the ship is voluntarily within a port or at an offshore terminal of the Member State;

(g) on the high seas, and the ship is voluntarily within a port or at an offshore terminal of the Member State.

2. AnyMember State may decide that it will not apply, or that it will apply only in specific cases or circumstances, the jurisdiction rules set out in:

(a) paragraph 1(d);

(b) paragraph 1(e).

3. Member States shall inform the General Secretariat of the Council accordingly where they decide to apply paragraph 2, where appropriate with an indication of the specific cases or circumstances in which the decision applies.

4. When an offence is subject to the jurisdiction of more than one Member State, the relevant Member States shall strive to coordinate their actions appropriately, in particular concerning the conditions for prosecution and the detailed arrangements for mutual assistance.

5. The following connecting factors shall be taken into account:

(a) the Member State in whose territory, exclusive economic zone or equivalent zone the offence was committed;

(b) the Member State in whose territory, exclusive economic zone or equivalent zone the effects of the offence are felt;

(c) the Member State in whose territory, exclusive economic zone or equivalent zone a ship from which the offence was committed is in transit;

(d) the Member State of which the perpetrator of the offence is a national or a resident;

---

145 Ed., it is therefore not an unfettered exertion of jurisdiction.

(e) the Member State in whose territory the legal person on whose behalf the offence was committed has its registered office;

(f) the Member State of the flag of the ship from which the offence was committed.

6. For the application of this Article, the territory includes the area referred to in Article 3(1)(a) and (b) of Directive 2005/35/EC."

Notification of information

19.275 Article 8 of the framework decision provides:

"1. Where a Member State is informed of the commission of an offence to which Article 2 applies or of the risk of the commission of such an offence which causes or is likely to cause imminent pollution, it shall immediately inform such other Member States as are likely to be exposed to this damage, and the Commission.[146]

2. Where a Member State is informed of the commission of an offence to which Article 2 applies or of the risk of the commission of such an offence which is likely to fall within the jurisdiction of a Member State, it shall immediately inform that other Member State.

3. Member States shall without delay notify the flag State or any other State concerned of measures taken pursuant to this framework Decision, and in particular Article 7."

Article 9 deals with the designation of contact points. Article 9(1) provides that each Member State shall designate existing contact points, or, if necessary, create new contact points, in particular for the exchange of information as referred to in Article 8. Article 9(2) goes on to provide that each Member State shall inform the Commission which of its departments acts or act as contact points in accordance with Article 9(1) and the Commission shall notify the other Member States of these contact points.

Conclusion

19.276 There is no doubt that the framework decision is a radical and significant move. It is not unwelcome in terms of ensuring (or attempting to ensure) stronger enforcement and hence greater compliance.

DIRECTIVE 2005/35 ON SHIP-SOURCE POLLUTION AND ON THE INTRODUCTION OF PENALTIES, INCLUDING CRIMINAL PENALTIES, FOR POLLUTION OFFENCES

Introduction

19.277 On 7 September 2005, the Parliament and Council adopted Directive 2005/35 on ship-source pollution and on the introduction of penalties, including criminal penalties, for pollution offences.[147] It was later amended by Directive 2009/123 of the European Parliament and of the Council.[148] There are very detailed annexes which are not discussed in this book (as it would be disproportionate to do so) but regard should be had to those annexes in any specific case.

---

146 Ed., this puts the Commission at the centre of the process.

147 OJ L255/11, 30 September 2005.

148 OJ L280/52, 27 October 2009.

Background to the directive

19.278 The recitals are very incisive in setting out the background:

"(1) The Community's maritime safety policy is aimed at a high level of safety and environmental protection and is based on the understanding that all parties involved in the transport of goods by sea have a responsibility for ensuring that ships used in Community waters comply with applicable rules and standards.[149]

(2) The material standards in all Member States for discharges of polluting substances from ships are based upon the Marpol 73/78 Convention; however these rules are being ignored on a daily basis by a very large number of ships sailing in Community waters, without corrective action being taken.[150]

(3) The implementation of Marpol 73/78 shows discrepancies among Member States[151] and there is thus a need to harmonise its implementation at Community level; in particular the practices of Member States relating to the imposition of penalties for discharges of polluting substances from ships differ significantly.

(4) Measures of a dissuasive nature form an integral part of the Community's maritime safety policy, as they ensure a link between the responsibility of each of the parties involved in the transport of polluting goods by sea and their exposure to penalties; in order to achieve effective protection of the environment there is therefore a need for effective, dissuasive and proportionate penalties.[152]

(5) To that end it is essential to approximate, by way of the proper legal instruments, existing legal provisions, in particular on the precise definition of the infringement in question, the cases of exemption and minimum rules for penalties, and on liability and jurisdiction.

(6) This Directive is supplemented by detailed rules on criminal offences and penalties as well as other provisions set out in Council Framework Decision 2005/667/JHA of 12 July 2005 to strengthen the criminal law framework for the enforcement of the law against ship-source pollution...

(7) Neither the international regime for the civil liability and compensation of oil pollution nor that relating to pollution by other hazardous or noxious substances provides sufficient dissuasive effects to discourage the parties involved in the transport of hazardous cargoes by sea from engaging in substandard practices; the required dissuasive effects can only be achieved through the introduction of penalties applying to any person who causes or contributes to marine pollution; penalties should be applicable not only to the shipowner or the master of the ship, but also the owner of the cargo, the classification society or any other person involved.

(8) Ship-source discharges of polluting substances should be regarded as infringements if committed with intent, recklessly or by serious negligence. These infringements are regarded as criminal offences by, and in the circumstances provided for in, Framework Decision 2005/667/JHA supplementing this Directive.

(9) Penalties for discharges of polluting substances from ships are not related to the civil liability of the parties concerned and are thus not subject to any rules relating to the limitation or channelling of civil liabilities, nor do they limit the efficient compensation of victims of pollution incidents.

(10) There is a need for further effective cooperation among Member States to ensure that discharges of polluting substances from ships are detected in time and that the offenders are identified. For this reason, the European Maritime Safety Agency set up by Regulation (EC) No 1406/2002 of the European Parliament and of the Council of 27 June 2002 ... has

---

149 Ed., the objective of providing for penalties is to ensure that there is greater compliance with, and enforcement of, the rules by ensuring tougher even criminal penalties which the EU itself could not impose but which can be imposed by Member State law at the instigation of the EU.

150 Ed., this is a very strong statement (e.g. on a "daily basis" is not proven) but provides the justification for the EU to intervene.

151 Ed., this is part of the justification for EU intervention.

152 Ed., this demonstrates the need for dissuasive/penalties to buttress the regime.

a key role to play in working with the Member States in developing technical solutions and providing technical assistance relating to the implementation of this Directive and in assisting the Commission in the performance of any task assigned to it for the effective implementation of this Directive.

(11) In order better to prevent and combat marine pollution, synergies should be created between enforcement authorities such as national coastguard services. In this context, the Commission should undertake a feasibility study on a European coastguard dedicated to pollution prevention and response, making clear the costs and benefits. This study should, if appropriate, be followed by a proposal on a European coastguard.

(12) Where there is clear, objective evidence of a discharge causing major damage or a threat of major damage, Member States should submit the matter to their competent authorities with a view to instituting proceedings in accordance with Article 220 of the 1982 United Nations Convention on the Law of the Sea.

(13) The enforcement of Directive 2000/59/EC of the European Parliament and of the Council of 27 November 2000 on port reception facilities for ship-generated waste and cargo residues ... is, together with this Directive, a key instrument in the set of measures to prevent ship-source pollution.

(14) The measures necessary for the implementation of this Directive should be adopted in accordance with Council Decision 1999/468/EC of 28 June 1999 laying down the procedures for the exercise of implementing powers conferred on the Commission ...

(15) Since the objectives of this Directive, namely the incorporation of the international ship-source pollution standards into Community law and the establishment of penalties – criminal or administrative – for violation of them in order to ensure a high level of safety and environmental protection in maritime transport, cannot be sufficiently achieved by the Member States and can therefore be better achieved at Community level, the Community may adopt measures, in accordance with the principle of subsidiarity as set out in Article 5 of the Treaty. In accordance with the principle of proportionality, as set out in that Article, this Directive does not go beyond what is necessary in order to achieve those objectives.

(16) This Directive fully respects the Charter of fundamental rights of the European Union; any person suspected of having committed an infringement must be guaranteed a fair and impartial hearing and the penalties must be proportional."

Purpose of the directive

19.279 Article 1 addresses the purpose of the directive. Article 1(1) provides that the purpose of the directive is to incorporate international standards for ship-source pollution into EU law and to ensure that persons responsible for discharges of polluting substances are subject to adequate penalties, including criminal penalties, in order to improve maritime safety and to enhance protection of the marine environment from pollution by ships. Under Article 1(2), the directive does not prevent Member States from taking more stringent measures against ship-source pollution in conformity with international law. There are two comments which should be made about Article 1. First, the directive is aimed at ensuring greater enforcement but recognises that Member States are the ones (not the EU) empowered to introduce criminal measures. Second, there is nothing stopping Member States adopting more stringent measures if they wish to do so.

Definitions

19.280 Article 2 sets out a series of definitions for the purpose of the directive:

"1. 'Marpol 73/78' shall mean the International Convention for the Prevention of Pollution from Ships, 1973 and its 1978 Protocol, in its up-to-date version;

2. 'polluting substances' shall mean substances covered by Annexes I (oil) and II (noxious liquid substances in bulk) to Marpol 73/78;
3. 'discharge' shall mean any release howsoever caused from a ship, as referred to in Article 2 of Marpol 73/78;
4. 'ship' shall mean a seagoing vessel, irrespective of its flag, of any type whatsoever operating in the marine environment and shall include hydrofoil boats, air-cushion vehicles, submersibles and floating craft;
5. 'Legal person' shall mean any legal entity in possession of such status under applicable national law, other than States themselves or public bodies in the exercise of State authority or public international organisations."

They are straightforward and uncontroversial at this stage.

Scope of the directive

19.281 Article 3 is very important. It deals with the scope of the Directive:

"1. This Directive shall apply, in accordance with international law, to discharges of polluting substances in:

(a) the internal waters, including ports, of a Member State, in so far as the Marpol regime is applicable;
(b) the territorial sea of a Member State;
(c) straits used for international navigation subject to the regime of transit passage, as laid down in Part III, section 2, of the 1982 United Nations Convention on the Law of the Sea, to the extent that a Member State exercises jurisdiction over such straits;
(d) the exclusive economic zone or equivalent zone of a Member State, established in accordance with international law; and
(e) the high seas.

2. This Directive shall apply to discharges of polluting substances from any ship, irrespective of its flag, with the exception of any warship, naval auxiliary or other ship owned or operated by a State and used, for the time being, only on government non-commercial service."[153]

19.282 Article 4 addresses the issue of infringements. Article 4(1) provides that Member States must ensure that ship-source discharges of polluting substances, including minor cases of such discharges, into any of the areas referred to in Article 3(1) are regarded as infringements if committed with intent, recklessly or with serious negligence which means that there is reduced room for Member States to condone such acts. Article 4(2) provides that each Member State must take the necessary measures to ensure that any natural or legal person having committed an infringement within the meaning of paragraph 1 can be held liable therefor. Article 4 is somewhat indicative that the EU does not entirely trust some of its Member States to enforce the regime without being forced to do so.

Exceptions

19.283 Article 5 provides:

---

153 This exception for naval and public service vessels is not unusual.

"1. A discharge of polluting substances into any of the areas referred to in Article 3(1) shall not be regarded as an infringement, if it satisfies the conditions set out in Annex I, Regulations 15, 34, 4,1 or 4,3 or in Annex II, Regulations 13, 3.1.1 or 3.1.3 of Marpol 73/78.

2. A discharge of polluting substances into the areas referred to in Article 3(1)(c), (d) and (e) shall not be regarded as an infringement for the owner, the master or the crew, if it satisfies the conditions set out in Annex I, Regulation 4,2 or in Annex II, Regulation 3.1.2 of Marpol 73/78."

Criminal offences as well as inciting, aiding and abetting

19.284 Article 5a is pivotal to understanding the directive. Article 5a provides:

"1. Member States shall ensure that infringements within the meaning of Articles 4 and 5 are regarded as criminal offences.

2. Paragraph 1 shall not apply to minor cases, where the act committed does not cause deterioration in the quality of water.

3. Repeated minor cases that do not individually but in conjunction result in deterioration in the quality of water shall be regarded as a criminal offence, if committed with intent, recklessly or with serious negligence."

19.285 Article 5b deals with inciting, aiding and abetting. It provides simply that Member States must ensure that any act of inciting, or aiding and abetting an offence committed with intent and referred to in Article 5a(1) and (3), is punishable as a criminal offence.

Enforcement measures with respect to ships within a port of a Member State

19.286 Article 6 deals with enforcement measures with respect to ships within a port of a Member State. Article 6(1) provides that if irregularities or information give rise to a suspicion that a ship which is voluntarily within a port or at an off-shore terminal of a Member State has been engaged in or is engaging in a discharge of polluting substances into any of the areas referred to in Article 3(1), then that Member State must ensure that an appropriate inspection, taking into account the relevant guidelines adopted by the IMO, is undertaken in accordance with its national law. Article 6(2) provides that, in so far as the inspection referred to in Article 6(1) reveals facts that could indicate an infringement within the meaning of Article 4, the competent authorities of that Member State and of the flag State must be informed.

Enforcement measures by coastal States with respect to ships in transit

19.287 Article 7(1) provides that if the suspected discharge of polluting substances takes place in the areas referred to in Article 3(1)(b), (c), (d) or (e) and the ship which is suspected of the discharge does not call at a port of the Member State holding the information relating to the suspected discharge, the following shall apply: (a) if the next port of call of the ship is in another Member State, the Member States concerned shall co-operate closely in the inspection referred to in Article 6(1) and in deciding on the appropriate measures in respect of any such discharge; and (b) if the next port of call of the ship is a port of a State outside the Community, the Member State shall take the necessary measures to ensure that the next port of call of the ship is informed about the suspected discharge and shall request the State of the next port of call to take the appropriate measures in respect of any such discharge. Pursuant to Article 7(2), where there is clear, objective evidence that a ship navigating in the areas referred to in Article 3(1)(b) or (d) has, in the area referred to in Article 3(1)(d), committed an infringement resulting in a discharge causing major damage or a threat of major damage to the coastline or related interests of the Member State concerned, or to any resources of the areas referred to in Article 3(1)(b) or (d), that State shall, subject to Part XII, Section 7 of the 1982 UNCLOS and provided that the evidence so warrants, submit the matter to its competent authorities with a view to instituting proceedings, including detention of the ship, in accordance with its national law. Article 7(3) provides that in any event, the authorities of the flag State must be informed.

Penalties

Introduction

19.288 Under Article 8, each Member State must take the necessary measures to ensure that infringements within the meaning of Articles 4 and 5 are punishable by effective, proportionate and dissuasive penalties.

Penalties against natural persons

19.289 Under Article 8a, each Member State must take the necessary measures to ensure that the offences referred to in Article 5a(1), and (3) and Article 5b are punishable by effective, proportionate and dissuasive criminal penalties.

Liability of legal persons

19.290 Under Article 8b(1), each Member State must take the necessary measures to ensure that legal persons can be held liable for the criminal offences referred to in Article 5a(1) and (3) and Article 5b, committed for their benefit by any natural person acting either individually or as part of an organ of the legal person, and who has a leading position within the structure of the legal person, based on: (a) a power of representation of the legal person; (b) authority to take decisions on behalf of the legal person; or (c) authority to exercise control within the legal person. Under Article 8(3), the liability of a legal person under paragraphs 1 and 2 shall not exclude criminal proceedings against natural persons involved as perpetrators, inciters or accessories in the criminal offences referred to in Article 5a(1) and (3) and Article 5b.

19.291 Under Article 8b(2), each Member State must also ensure that a legal person can be held liable where lack of supervision or control by a natural person referred to in paragraph 1 has made the commission of a criminal offence referred to in Article 5a(1) and (3) and Article 5b possible for the benefit of that legal person by a natural person under its authority. Under Article 8(3), the liability of a legal person under paragraphs 1 and 2 shall not exclude criminal proceedings against natural persons involved as perpetrators, inciters or accessories in the criminal offences referred to in Article 5a(1) and (3) and Article 5b.

Penalties against legal persons

19.292 Under Article 8c, each Member State shall take the necessary measures to ensure that a legal person held liable pursuant to Article 8b is punishable by effective, proportionate and dissuasive penalties.

Compliance with international law

19.293 Member States must apply the provisions of the directive without any discrimination in form or in fact against foreign ships and in accordance with applicable international law, including Section 7 of Part XII of the 1982 UNCLOS, and they must promptly notify the flag State of the vessel and any other State concerned of measures taken in accordance with the directive.[154]

Accompanying measures

19.294 Article 10(1) provides that for the purposes of Directive 2005/35, Member States and the Commission must co-operate, where appropriate, in close collaboration with the EMSA and taking account of the action programme to respond to accidental or deliberate marine pollution set up by Decision 2850/2000 and, if appropriate, of the implementation of Directive 2000/59 in order to: (a) develop the necessary information systems required for the effective implementation of this directive; (b) establish common practices and guidelines on the basis of those existing at international level, in particular for:

- the monitoring and early identification of ships discharging polluting substances in violation of this directive, including, where appropriate, on-board monitoring equipment,
- reliable methods of tracing polluting substances in the sea to a particular ship, and
- the effective enforcement of this directive.

19.295 Under Article 10(2), in accordance with its tasks as defined in Regulation 1406/2002, the EMSA must: (a) work with the Member States in developing technical solutions and providing technical assistance in relation to the implementation of this directive, in actions such as tracing discharges by satellite monitoring and surveillance; and (b) assist the Commission in the implementation of this directive, including, if appropriate, by means of visits to the Member States, in accordance with Article 3 of Regulation (EC) No 1406/2002.

Feasibility study

19.296 Article 11 provides that the Commission shall, before the end of 2006, submit to the European Parliament and the Council a feasibility study on a European coastguard dedicated to pollution prevention and response, making clear the costs and benefits.[155]

---

154 Art. 9.
155 Dir. 2005/35.

Reporting

19.297 Article 12 provides every three years Member States must transmit a report to the Commission on the application of this directive by the competent authorities. On the basis of these reports, the Commission shall submit a Community report to the European Parliament and the Council. In this report, the Commission shall assess, *inter alia*, the desirability of revising or extending the scope of this directive. It shall also describe the evolution of relevant case law in the Member States and shall consider the possibility of creating a public database containing such relevant case law.

Committee procedure

19.298 The Commission shall be assisted by the COSS.

Provision of information

19.299 The Commission must regularly inform the Committee set up by Article 4 of Decision 2850/2000 of any proposed measures or other relevant activities concerning the response to marine pollution.[156]

Amendment procedure

19.300 Article 15 provides that in accordance with Article 5 of Regulation 2099/2002 and following the procedure referred to in Article 13 of this directive; the COSS may exclude amendments to MARPOL 73/78 from the scope of this directive.

Implementation

19.301 Member States had to bring into force the laws, regulations and administrative provisions necessary to comply with this directive by 1 April 2007 and forthwith inform the Commission thereof.[157]

Entry into force

19.302 This directive shall enter into force on the day following its publication in the *Official Journal of the European Union*.[158]

Directive 2005/35 and the Charter of Fundamental Rights of the European Union

19.303 The sixteenth recital of Directive 2005/35 provides that the directive "fully respects the Charter of Fundamental Rights of the European Union; any person suspected of having committed an infringement must be guaranteed a fair and impartial hearing and the penalties must be proportional". Merely stating that the directive complies with the

---

156 Dir. 2005/35, Art. 14.
157 Art. 16.
158 Dir. 2005/35, Art. 17.

Charter does not make it so and this should not prevent the invocation of the Charter in appropriate cases.

THE *INTERTANKO* LITIGATION

Introduction

19.304 On 3 June 2008, the Grand Chamber of the Court decided *The Queen, on the application of International Association of Independent Tanker Owners (Intertanko), International Association of Dry Cargo Shipowners (Intercargo), Greek Shipping Co-operation Committee, Lloyd's Register, International Salvage Union v Secretary of State for Transport.*[159]

19.305 The case involved a reference for a preliminary ruling from the High Court of Justice of England and Wales (the Queen's Bench Division (Administrative Court)). The reference concerned the validity of Articles 4 and 5 of Directive 2005/35 and its relationship with the United Nations Convention on the Law of the Sea ("UNCLOS III") and the MARPOL 73/78 Convention. The reference was made in the course of proceedings brought by Intertanko, Intercargo, the Greek Shipping Co-operation Committee, Lloyd's Register and the International Salvage Union against the UK's Secretary of State for Transport concerning implementation of Directive 2005/35. The claimants were a group of organisations in the shipping industry. They were well-representative of the industry. They applied to the High Court of Justice of England and Wales, Queen's Bench Division (Administrative Court), for judicial review in relation to the implementation of Directive 2005/35 – it was essentially a challenge through the English courts to the EU regime.

19.306 The CJEU stated that the legal context to the case included both (a) international law and (b) EU law. The international law dimension could be subdivided into (a) the UNCLOS III and (ii) the International Convention for the Prevention of Pollution from Ships, signed in London on 2 November 1973, as supplemented by the protocol of 17 February 1978 ("MARPOL 73/78").

International law

19.307 The CJEU recalled that UNCLOS III had been approved on behalf of the then EC by Council Decision 98/392 of 23 March 1998.[160]

19.308 The CJEU then recalled several provisions of UNCLOS. It is useful to cite them. Article 2 of UNCLOS which refers to the legal status of the territorial sea:

> "1. The sovereignty of a coastal State extends, beyond its land territory and internal waters and, in the case of an archipelagic State, its archipelagic waters, to an adjacent belt of sea, described as the territorial sea
>
> ...
>
> 3. The sovereignty over the territorial sea is exercised subject to this Convention and to other rules of international law."

---

159 Case C-308/06. Judges Skouris (President), Jann, Timmermans, Rosas, Lenaerts, Bay Larsen, Schiemann, Makarczyk, Kūris, Malenovský (Rapporteur), Ó Caoimh, Lindh and Bonichot. The Advocate-General was AG Kokott.
160 OJ 1998 L179/1.

Article 17 of UNCLOS provides: "Subject to this Convention, ships of all States, whether coastal or land-locked, enjoy the right of innocent passage through the territorial sea."

Article 34 of UNCLOS specifies as follows the legal status of waters forming straits used for international navigation:

"1. The regime of passage through straits used for international navigation established in this Part shall not in other respects affect the legal status of the waters forming such straits or the exercise by the States bordering the straits of their sovereignty or jurisdiction over such waters and their airspace, bed and subsoil.

2. The sovereignty or jurisdiction of the States bordering the straits is exercised subject to this Part and to other rules of international law."

Article 42 of UNCLOS provides:

"1. Subject to the provisions of this section, States bordering straits may adopt laws and regulations relating to transit passage through straits, in respect of all or any of the following:

...

(b) the prevention, reduction and control of pollution, by giving effect to applicable international regulations regarding the discharge of oil, oily wastes and other noxious substances in the strait; ..."

The CJEU then recalled Part V of UNCLOS which lays down a specific legal regime governing the relatively new concept of the exclusive economic zone (or "EEZ"). In Part V, Article 56(1) provides:

"1. In the exclusive economic zone, the coastal State has:

(a) sovereign rights for the purpose of exploring and exploiting, conserving and managing the natural resources, whether living or non-living, of the waters superjacent to the sea-bed and of the sea-bed and its subsoil, and with regard to other activities for the economic exploitation and exploration of the zone, such as the production of energy from the water, currents and winds; ..."

While Article 58(1) provides:

"In the exclusive economic zone, all States, whether coastal or land-locked, enjoy, subject to the relevant provisions of this Convention, the freedoms referred to in Article 87 of navigation and overflight and of the laying of submarine cables and pipelines, and other internationally lawful uses of the sea related to these freedoms, such as those associated with the operation of ships, aircraft and submarine cables and pipelines, and compatible with the other provisions of this Convention."

And Article 79(1) of UNCLOS states: "All States are entitled to lay submarine cables and pipelines on the continental shelf, in accordance with the provisions of this Article."

Article 89 of UNCLOS goes on to provide: "No State may validly purport to subject any part of the high seas to its sovereignty."

Article 90 of UNCLOS provides: "Every State, whether coastal or land-locked, has the right to sail ships flying its flag on the high seas."

Article 116 of UNCLOS provides: "'All States have the right for their nationals to engage in fishing on the high seas."

The CJEU then recalled Part XII of UNCLOS which is devoted to protection and preservation of the marine environment. In Part XII, Article 211 provides:

"1. States, acting through the competent international organisation or general diplomatic conference, shall establish international rules and standards to prevent, reduce and control pollution of the marine environment from vessels and promote the adoption, in the same manner, wherever appropriate, of routeing systems designed to minimise the threat of accidents which might cause pollution of the marine environment, including the coastline, and pollution damage to the related interests of coastal States. Such rules and standards shall, in the same manner, be re-examined from time to time as necessary.

2. States shall adopt laws and regulations for the prevention, reduction and control of pollution of the marine environment from vessels flying their flag or of their registry. Such laws and regulations shall at least have the same effect as that of generally accepted international rules and standards established through the competent international organisation or general diplomatic conference

...

4. Coastal States may, in the exercise of their sovereignty within their territorial sea, adopt laws and regulations for the prevention, reduction and control of marine pollution from foreign vessels, including vessels exercising the right of innocent passage. Such laws and regulations shall, in accordance with Part II, section 3, not hamper innocent passage of foreign vessels.

5. Coastal States, for the purpose of enforcement as provided for in section 6, may in respect of their exclusive economic zones adopt laws and regulations for the prevention, reduction and control of pollution from vessels conforming to and giving effect to generally accepted international rules and standards established through the competent international organisation or general diplomatic conference."

19.309 The second element of the international legal context is the MARPOL 73/78, signed in London on 2 November 1973, as supplemented by the protocol of 17 February 1978, which establishes rules to combat pollution of the marine environment. The regulations for the prevention of pollution by oil are set out in Annex I to MARPOL 73/78. Regulation 9 of Annex I states that, subject to the provisions of Regulations 9(2), 10 and 11, any discharge into the sea of oil or oily mixtures from ships to which that Annex applies is to be prohibited except when certain exhaustively listed conditions are satisfied. Regulation 10 of Annex I lays down methods for the prevention of oil pollution from ships while operating in special areas. Regulation 11 of that Annex, headed "Exceptions", states:

"Regulations 9 and 10 of this Annex shall not apply to:

(a) the discharge into the sea of oil or oily mixture necessary for the purpose of securing the safety of a ship or saving life at sea; or

(b) the discharge into the sea of oil or oily mixture resulting from damage to a ship or its equipment:

    (i) provided that all reasonable precautions have been taken after the occurrence of the damage or discovery of the discharge for the purpose of preventing or minimising the discharge; and

    (ii) except if the owner or the master acted either with intent to cause damage, or recklessly and with knowledge that damage would probably result; or

(c) the discharge into the sea of substances containing oil, approved by the Administration [of the flag State], when being used for the purpose of combating specific pollution incidents in order to minimise the damage from pollution. Any such discharge shall be subject to the approval of any Government in whose jurisdiction it is contemplated the discharge will occur."

19.310 The regulations for the control of pollution by noxious liquid substances are set out in Annex II to MARPOL 73/78. Regulation 5 of Annex II prohibits discharge into the sea of the substances covered by that Annex, except when certain exhaustively listed conditions are satisfied. Regulation 6(a) to (c) of that Annex sets out, in analogous terms, the exceptions provided for in Regulation 11(a) to (c) of Annex I.

EU law

19.311 In terms of EU law, the CJEU cited Article 3(1) of Directive 2005/35 which provides:

"This Directive shall apply, in accordance with international law, to discharges of polluting substances in:

(a) the internal waters, including ports, of a Member State, in so far as the Marpol regime is applicable;

(b) the territorial sea of a Member State;

(c) straits used for international navigation subject to the regime of transit passage, as laid down in Part III, section 2, of [UNCLOS], to the extent that a Member State exercises jurisdiction over such straits;

(d) the exclusive economic zone or equivalent zone of a Member State, established in accordance with international law; and

(e) the high seas."

19.312 The CJEU then cited Article 4 of Directive 2005/35 which provides:

"Member States shall ensure that ship-source discharges of polluting substances into any of the areas referred to in Article 3(1) are regarded as infringements if committed with intent, recklessly or by serious negligence. These infringements are regarded as criminal offences by, and in the circumstances provided for in, Framework Decision 2005/667/JHA supplementing this Directive."

19.313 The CJEU went on to Article 5 of Directive 2005/35 which states:

"1. A discharge of polluting substances into any of the areas referred to in Article 3(1) shall not be regarded as an infringement if it satisfies the conditions set out in Annex I, Regulations 9, 10, 11(a) or 11(c) or in Annex II, Regulations 5, 6(a) or 6(c) of Marpol 73/78.

2. A discharge of polluting substances into the areas referred to in Article 3(1)(c), (d) and (e) shall not be regarded as an infringement for the owner, the master or the crew when acting under the master's responsibility if it satisfies the conditions set out in Annex I, Regulation 11(b) or in Annex II, Regulation 6(b) of Marpol 73/78."

19.314 Article 8 of Directive 2005/35 was also cited by the CJEU and it provides:

"1. Member States shall take the necessary measures to ensure that infringements within the meaning of Article 4 are subject to effective, proportionate and dissuasive penalties, which may include criminal or administrative penalties.

2. Each Member State shall take the measures necessary to ensure that the penalties referred to in paragraph 1 apply to any person who is found responsible for an infringement within the meaning of Article 4."

Questions referred to the CJEU for a preliminary ruling

19.315 The questions referred to the CJEU were:

"(1) In relation to straits used for international navigation, the exclusive economic zone or equivalent zone of a Member State and the high seas, is Article 5(2) of Directive 2005/35/EC invalid in so far as it limits the exceptions in Annex I Regulation 11(b) of [MARPOL] 73/78 and in Annex II Regulation (6)(b) of [MARPOL] 73/78 to the owners, masters and crew?

(2) In relation to the territorial sea of a Member State:
(a) Is Article 4 of the Directive invalid in so far as it requires Member States to treat serious negligence as a test of liability for discharge of polluting substances; and/or
(b) Is Article 5(1) of the Directive invalid in so far as it excludes the application of the exceptions in Annex I Regulation 11(b) of [MARPOL] 73/78 and in Annex II Regulation (6)(b) of [MARPOL] 73/78?

(3) Does Article 4 of the Directive, requiring Member States to adopt national legislation which includes serious negligence as a standard of liability and which penalises discharges in territorial sea, breach the right of innocent passage recognised in [UNCLOS], and if so, is Article 4 invalid to that extent?

(4) Does the use of the phrase 'serious negligence' in Article 4 of the Directive infringe the principle of legal certainty, and if so, is Article 4 invalid to that extent?"

Admissibility of the preliminary reference

19.316 Like many preliminary references, the first question was whether the preliminary reference was admissible at all. France questioned whether the reference was admissible. It argued that the UK court failed to set out the circumstances in which the case had been brought before it. In particular, France argued that the claimants had sought to bring an action contesting the transposition of Directive 2005/35 by the UK. The CJEU rejected France's claim because it was not obvious that the ruling sought by the national court on the validity of Directive 2005/35 bore no relation to the actual facts of the main action or its purpose or concerns a hypothetical problem.[161]

Consideration of the questions referred for a preliminary ruling

Questions 1 to 3

19.317 The CJEU summarised the first three questions posed by the English court and said that by

---

161 The CJEU stated: "31 ... when a question on the validity of a measure adopted by the institutions of the [EU] is raised before a national court, it is for that court to decide whether a decision on the matter is necessary to enable it to give judgment and, consequently, whether it should request the Court to rule on that question. Accordingly, where the national court's questions relate to the validity of a provision of [EU] law, the [CJEU] is obliged in principle to give a ruling. 32 It is possible for the [CJEU] to refuse to give a preliminary ruling on a question submitted by a national court only where, inter alia, it is quite obvious that the ruling sought by that court on the interpretation or validity of [EU] law bears no relation to the actual facts of the main action or its purpose or where the problem is hypothetical (British American Tobacco (Investments) and Imperial Tobacco, paragraph 35 and the case-law cited). 33 In the present case, it is clear from the order for reference that the claimants in the main proceedings have made an application to the High Court for judicial review of implementation of Directive 2005/35 in the United Kingdom and that they may make such an application even though, when the application was made, the period prescribed for implementation of the directive had not yet expired and no national implementing measures had been adopted. 34 Nor is it disputed before the Court of Justice that the questions submitted are relevant to the outcome of the main proceedings, as the adoption of national measures designed to transpose a directive into domestic law in the United Kingdom may be subject to the condition that the directive be valid (see British American Tobacco (Investments) and Imperial Tobacco, paragraph 37). 35 It is therefore not obvious that the ruling sought by the national court on the validity of Directive 2005/35 bears no relation to the actual facts of the main action or its purpose or concerns a hypothetical problem."

"its first three questions, the national court essentially requests the Court of Justice to assess the validity of Articles 4 and 5 of Directive 2005/35 in the light of Regulations 9 and 11(b) of Annex I, and Regulations 5 and 6(b) of Annex II, to Marpol 73/78 and in the light of the provisions of UNCLOS which define the conditions under which coastal States may exercise certain of their rights in the various marine zones".

19.318 The claimants as well as the Cypriot, Greek and Maltese governments argued that Articles 4 and 5 were incompatible with MARPOL 73/78 or UNCLOS. The CJEU summarised the arguments thus:

"37. The claimants in the main proceedings and the Greek, Cypriot and Maltese Governments[162] submit that Articles 4 and 5 of Directive 2005/35 do not comply with Marpol 73/78 or UNCLOS in several respects. In particular, by laying down that liability is to be incurred for serious negligence, those articles establish a stricter liability regime for accidental discharges than that laid down in Article 4 of Marpol 73/78, read in conjunction with Regulations 9 and 11(b) of Annex I, and Regulations 5 and 6(b) of Annex II, to that Convention.

38. The claimants in the main proceedings and the abovementioned governments proceed on the basis that the legality of Directive 2005/35 may be assessed in the light of UNCLOS, since the Community is a party thereto and it thus forms an integral part of the Community legal order.

39. In their submission, the directive's legality may also be assessed in the light of Marpol 73/78. They state that UNCLOS defines and governs the extent of the jurisdiction of the Contracting Parties in their actions on the high seas, in their exclusive economic zones and in international straits. Thus, the Community lacks the power to adopt legislation applying to discharges from ships not flying the flag of one of the Member States, save to the extent that UNCLOS accords the Community the right to adopt such legislation. Under UNCLOS, the Contracting Parties have the power only to adopt legislation implementing the international rules and standards in such marine areas, that is to say, in the present case, the provisions of Marpol 73/78. This power is specified with regard to the high seas in Article 211(1) and (2) of UNCLOS, with regard to international straits in Articles 42(1)(b) and 45 of that Convention and with regard to the exclusive economic zone in Article 211(5). The same holds for territorial waters, by virtue of Article 2(3) of UNCLOS.

40. The claimants in the main proceedings add that the legality of Directive 2005/35 must be assessed in the light of Marpol 73/78 for the further reason that the Community legislature seeks to implement the latter in Community law by means of that directive.

41. Furthermore, the field of maritime transport is a field where the Community has assumed the function of regulating the implementation of the international obligations of the Member States. The position is analogous to that under the General Agreement on Tariffs and Trade of 30 October 1947 ('GATT 1947') before the advent of the Agreement establishing the World Trade Organisation, where the Community, without becoming a party to GATT 1947, succeeded to the obligations of Member States through its actions under the common commercial policy. The field covered by GATT 1947 was thereby brought within the jurisdiction of the Community, its provisions having the effect of binding the Community."

19.319 The CJEU emphatically rejected the arguments. The CJEU recalled that the EU institutions are bound to comply with agreements concluded by the EU which means that those agreements have primacy over secondary EU law but ultimately it believed that there was no breach. Given the significance of the finding, it is useful to cite it in full:

"42. It is clear from Article 300(7) EC[163] that the Community institutions are bound by agreements concluded by the Community and, consequently, that those agreements have primacy

---

162 Ed., Member States are automatically able to intervene in all CJEU cases and argue their viewpoints.
163 Ed., see Art. 218 TFEU.

over secondary Community legislation (see, to this effect, Case C-61/94 *Commission v Germany* [1996] ECR I-3989, paragraph 52, and Case C-311/04 *Algemene Scheeps Agentuur Dordrecht* [2006] ECR I-609, paragraph 25).

43. It follows that the validity of a measure of secondary Community legislation may be affected by the fact that it is incompatible with such rules of international law. Where that invalidity is pleaded before a national court, the Court of Justice thus reviews, pursuant to Article 234 EC,[164] the validity of the Community measure concerned in the light of all the rules of international law, subject to two conditions.

44. First, the Community must be bound by those rules (see Joined Cases 21/72 to 24/72 *International Fruit Company and Others* [1972] ECR 1219, paragraph 7).

45. Second, the Court can examine the validity of Community legislation in the light of an international treaty only where the nature and the broad logic of the latter do not preclude this and, in addition, the treaty's provisions appear, as regards their content, to be unconditional and sufficiently precise (see to this effect, in particular, Case C-344/04 *IATA and ELFAA* [2006] ECR I-403, paragraph 39).

46. It must therefore be examined whether Marpol 73/78 and UNCLOS meet those conditions.

47. First, with regard to Marpol 73/78, it is to be observed at the outset that the Community is not a party to this Convention.

48. Furthermore, as the Court has already held, it does not appear that the Community has assumed, under the EC Treaty, the powers previously exercised by the Member States in the field to which Marpol 73/78 applies, nor that, consequently, its provisions have the effect of binding the Community (Case C-379/92 *Peralta* [1994] ECR I-3453, paragraph 16). In this regard, Marpol 73/78 can therefore be distinguished from GATT 1947 within the framework of which the Community progressively assumed powers previously exercised by the Member States, with the consequence that it became bound by the obligations flowing from that agreement (see to this effect, in particular, *International Fruit Company and Others*, paragraphs 10 to 18). Accordingly, this case-law relating to GATT 1947 cannot be applied to MARPOL 73/78.

49. It is true that all the Member States of the Community are parties to Marpol 73/78. Nevertheless, in the absence of a full transfer of the powers previously exercised by the Member States to the Community, the latter cannot, simply because all those States are parties to Marpol 73/78, be bound by the rules set out therein, which it has not itself approved.

50. Since the Community is not bound by Marpol 73/78, the mere fact that Directive 2005/35 has the objective of incorporating certain rules set out in that Convention into Community law is likewise not sufficient for it to be incumbent upon the Court to review the directive's legality in the light of the Convention.

51. Admittedly, as is clear from settled case-law, the powers of the Community must be exercised in observance of international law, including provisions of international agreements in so far as they codify customary rules of general international law (see, to this effect, Case C-286/90 *Poulsen and Diva Navigation* [1992] ECR I-6019, paragraphs 9 and 10; Case C-405/92 *Mondiet* [1993] ECR I-6133, paragraphs 13 to 15; and Case C-162/96 *Racke* [1998] ECR I-3655, paragraph 45). None the less, it does not appear that Regulations 9 and 11(b) of Annex I to Marpol 73/78 and Regulations 5 and 6(b) of Annex II to that Convention are the expression of customary rules of general international law.

52. In those circumstances, it is clear that the validity of Directive 2005/35 cannot be assessed in the light of Marpol 73/78, even though it binds the Member States. The latter fact is, however, liable to have consequences for the interpretation of, first, UNCLOS and, second, the provisions of secondary law which fall within the field of application of Marpol 73/78. In view of the customary principle of good faith, which forms part of general international law, and of Article 10 EC, it is incumbent upon the Court to interpret those provisions taking account of Marpol 73/78.

---

164 Ed., see Art. 267 TFEU.

53. Second, UNCLOS was signed by the Community and approved by Decision 98/392, thereby binding the Community, and the provisions of that Convention accordingly form an integral part of the Community legal order (see Case C-459/03 *Commission v Ireland* [2006] ECR I-4635, paragraph 82).

54. It must therefore be determined whether the nature and the broad logic of UNCLOS, as disclosed in particular by its aim, preamble and terms, preclude examination of the validity of Community measures in the light of its provisions.

55. UNCLOS's main objective is to codify, clarify and develop the rules of general international law relating to the peaceful cooperation of the international community when exploring, using and exploiting marine areas.

56. According to the preamble to UNCLOS, the Contracting Parties agreed to that end to establish through UNCLOS a legal order for the seas and oceans which would facilitate international navigation, which would take into account the interests and needs of mankind as a whole and, in particular, the special interests and needs of developing countries, and which would strengthen peace, security, cooperation and friendly relations among all nations.

57. From this viewpoint, UNCLOS lays down legal regimes governing the territorial sea (Articles 2 to 33), waters forming straits used for international navigation (Articles 34 to 45), archipelagic waters (Articles 46 to 54), the exclusive economic zone (Articles 55 to 75), the continental shelf (Articles 76 to 85) and the high seas (Articles 86 to 120).

58. For all those marine areas, UNCLOS seeks to strike a fair balance between the interests of States as coastal States and the interests of States as flag States, which may conflict. In this connection, as is apparent from numerous provisions of the Convention, such as Articles 2, 33, 34(2), 56 and 89, the Contracting Parties provide for the establishment of the substantive and territorial limits to their respective sovereign rights.

59. On the other hand, individuals are in principle not granted independent rights and freedoms by virtue of UNCLOS. In particular, they can enjoy the freedom of navigation only if they establish a close connection between their ship and a State which grants its nationality to the ship and becomes the ship's flag State. This connection must be formed under that State's domestic law. Article 91 of UNCLOS states in this regard that every State is to fix the conditions for the grant of its nationality to ships, for the registration of ships in its territory and for the right to fly its flag, and that there must exist a genuine link between the State and the ship. Under Article 92(1) of UNCLOS, ships are to sail under the flag of one State only and may not change their flag during a voyage or while in a port of call, save in the case of a real transfer of ownership or change of registry.

60. If a ship is not attached to a State, neither the ship nor the persons on board enjoy the freedom of navigation. In this connection, UNCLOS provides inter alia, in Article 110(1), that a warship which encounters a foreign ship on the high seas is justified in boarding it if there is reasonable ground for suspecting that the ship is without nationality.

61. It is true that the wording of certain provisions of UNCLOS, such as Articles 17, 110(3) and 111(8), appears to attach rights to ships. It does not, however, follow that those rights are thereby conferred on the individuals linked to those ships, such as their owners, because a ship's international legal status is dependent on the flag State and not on the fact that it belongs to certain natural or legal persons.

62. Likewise, it is the flag State which, under the Convention, must take such measures as are necessary to ensure safety at sea and, therefore, to protect the interests of other States. The flag State may thus also be held liable, vis-à-vis other States, for harm caused by a ship flying its flag to marine areas placed under those States' sovereignty, where that harm results from a failure of the flag State to fulfil its obligations.

63. Doubt is not cast on the foregoing analysis by the fact that Part XI of UNCLOS involves natural and legal persons in the exploration, use and exploitation of the sea-bed and ocean floor, and subsoil thereof, beyond the limits of national jurisdiction, since the present case does not in any way concern the provisions of Part XI.

64. In those circumstances, it must be found that UNCLOS does not establish rules intended to apply directly and immediately to individuals and to confer upon them rights or freedoms capable of being relied upon against States, irrespective of the attitude of the ship's flag State.

65. It follows that the nature and the broad logic of UNCLOS prevent the Court from being able to assess the validity of a Community measure in the light of that Convention.

66. Consequently, the answer to the first three questions must be that the validity of Directive 2005/35 cannot be assessed:

    – either in the light of Marpol 73/78,
    – or in the light of UNCLOS."

19.320 In the fourth question, the UK court asked whether Article 4 of Directive 2005/35 was invalid on the ground that, by using the term "serious negligence", it infringed the general principle of legal certainty.

19.321 The claimants argued:

"68. The claimants in the main proceedings and the Greek Government consider that Article 4 of Directive 2005/35 breaches the general principle of legal certainty which requires that rules should be clear and precise so that individuals may ascertain unequivocally what their rights and obligations are. They submit that, under this provision, liability of persons causing discharges of polluting substances is subject to the test of serious negligence, which is not defined at all by Directive 2005/35 and which consequently lacks clarity. Thus, the persons concerned are unable to ascertain the degree of severity of the rules to which they are subject."

19.322 The CJEU rejected these arguments too:

"69. The general principle of legal certainty, which is a fundamental principle of Community law, requires, in particular, that rules should be clear and precise, so that individuals may ascertain unequivocally what their rights and obligations are and may take steps accordingly (see Case C-110/03 *Belgium v Commission* [2005] ECR I-2801, paragraph 30, and *IATA and ELFAA*, paragraph 68).

70. Furthermore, in obliging the Member States to regard certain conduct as infringements and to punish it, Article 4 of Directive 2005/35, read in conjunction with Article 8 thereof, must also observe the principle of the legality of criminal offences and penalties (*nullum crimen, nulla poena sine lege*), which is one of the general legal principles underlying the constitutional traditions common to the Member States (Case C-303/05 *Advocaten voor de Wereld* [2007] ECR I-3633, paragraph 49) and is a specific expression of the general principle of legal certainty.

71. The principle of the legality of criminal offences and penalties implies that Community rules must define clearly offences and the penalties which they attract. This requirement is satisfied where the individual can know from the wording of the relevant provision and, if need be, with the assistance of the courts' interpretation of it, what acts and omissions will make him criminally liable (see, in particular, *Advocaten voor de Wereld*, paragraph 50, and the judgment of the European Court of Human Rights in *Coëme and Others v. Belgium*, nos. 32492/96, 32547/96, 32548/96, 33209/96 and 33210/96, Reports of Judgments and Decisions 2000-VII, § 145).

72. It is true that Article 4 of Directive 2005/35, read in conjunction with Article 8 thereof, obliges the Member States to punish ship-source discharges of polluting substances if committed 'with intent, recklessly or by serious negligence', without defining those concepts.

73. It is, however, to be pointed out, first of all, that those various concepts, in particular that of 'serious negligence' referred to by the national court's questions, correspond to tests for the incurring of liability which are to apply to an indeterminate number of situations that it is impossible to envisage in advance and not to specific conduct capable of being set out in detail in a legislative measure, of Community or of national law.

74. Next, those concepts are fully integrated into, and used in, the Member States' respective legal systems.

75. In particular, all those systems have recourse to the concept of negligence which refers to an unintentional act or omission by which the person responsible breaches his duty of care.

76. Also, as provided by many national legal systems, the concept of 'serious' negligence can only refer to a patent breach of such a duty of care.

77. Accordingly, 'serious negligence' within the meaning of Article 4 of Directive 2005/35 must be understood as entailing an unintentional act or omission by which the person responsible commits a patent breach of the duty of care which he should have and could have complied with in view of his attributes, knowledge, abilities and individual situation.

78. Finally, in accordance with Article 249 EC, Directive 2005/35 must be transposed by each of the Member States into national law. Thus, the actual definition of the infringements referred to in Article 4 of that directive and the applicable penalties are those which result from the rules laid down by the Member States.

79. In view of the foregoing, Article 4 of Directive 2005/35, read in conjunction with Article 8 thereof, does not infringe the general principle of legal certainty in so far as it requires the Member States to punish ship-source discharges of polluting substances committed by 'serious negligence', without defining that concept.

80. It follows that examination of the fourth question has revealed nothing capable of affecting the validity of Article 4 of Directive 2005/35 in the light of the general principle of legal certainty."

19.323 In summary, the CJEU ruled:

"1. The validity of Directive 2005/35/EC of the European Parliament and of the Council of 7 September 2005 on ship-source pollution and on the introduction of penalties for infringements cannot be assessed:

   – either in the light of the International Convention for the Prevention of Pollution from Ships, signed in London on 2 November 1973, as supplemented by the Protocol of 17 February 1978,
   – or in the light of the United Nations Convention on the Law of the Sea, signed in Montego Bay on 10 December 1982.

2. Examination of the fourth question has revealed nothing capable of affecting the validity of Article 4 of Directive 2005/35 in the light of the general principle of legal certainty."

19.324 Mention of the *Intertanko* case would be incomplete without mention of the ruling of the Grand Chamber of the CJEU on 23 October 2007.[165] The Commission sought, and succeeding in obtaining, the annulment of Council framework Decision 2005/667.

19.325 The CJEU outlined the dispute as follows:

"2. On 12 July 2005, acting on the initiative of the Commission, the Council … adopted Framework Decision 2005/667.

3. Based on Title VI of the EU Treaty, in particular on Articles 31(1)(e) EU and 34(2)(b) EU, the Framework Decision constitutes, as is clear from the first five recitals in its preamble, the instrument by which the European Union intends to approximate criminal-law legislation of the Member States by requiring them to provide for criminal penalties in order to combat ship-source pollution caused with intent or by serious negligence.

4. The Framework Decision supplements Directive 2005/35/EC of the European Parliament and of the Council of 7 September 2005 on ship-source pollution and on the introduction of penalties for infringements (OJ 2005 L255, p. 11), with a view to strengthening maritime safety by approximating the legislation of the Member States.

---

165 Case C-440/05. Composed of Judges Skouris (President), Jann, Timmermans, Rosas, Lenaerts, Tizzano, Schintgen (Rapporteur), Cunha Rodrigues, Ilešič, Malenovský, von Danwitz, Arabadjiev and Toader with AG Mazák being the Advocate-General.

5. Framework Decision 2005/667 provides that the Member States are to adopt a certain number of criminal-law-related measures with a view to attaining the objective pursued by Directive 2005/35, namely to ensure a high level of safety and environmental protection in relation to maritime transport.

...

24. At the time of adoption both of Directive 2005/35 and the Framework Decision, the Commission made statements in order to dissociate itself from the 'double-text' approach taken by the Council. The statement relating to the Framework Decision reads as follows:

> 'Given the importance of combating ship-source pollution, the Commission is in favour of the discharge of polluting substances by ships being made a criminal offence and of penalties being adopted at national level in the event of the infringement of Community regulations concerning ship-source pollution.
>
> The Commission is, however, of the opinion that the Framework Decision is not the appropriate legal instrument with which to impose on Member States an obligation to criminalise the illicit discharge of polluting substances at sea and to establish corresponding criminal penalties at national level.
>
> The Commission – as it is arguing in the Court of Justice in its appeal C-176/03 [Case C-176/03 *Commission v Council* [2005] ECR I-7879] against the Framework Decision on the protection of the environment through criminal law – considers that, within the competences which it possesses for the purpose of achieving the objectives set out in Article 2 of the Treaty establishing the European Community, the Community is empowered to require Member States to provide for penalties – including, if appropriate, criminal penalties – at national level, where this proves necessary in order to achieve a Community objective.
>
> This is the case with regard to questions of ship-source pollution, for which Article 80(2) of the Treaty establishing the European Community constitutes the legal basis.
>
> Pending the ruling on C-176/03, if the Council adopts the Framework Decision in spite of this Community competence, the Commission reserves all the rights conferred upon it by the Treaty.'

25. Considering that the Framework Decision had not been adopted on the correct legal basis and that Article 47 EU had thereby been infringed, the Commission brought the present action."

19.326 The CJEU then decided to annul the measure:

"52. Under Article 47 EU, none of the provisions of the EC Treaty is to be affected by a provision of the EU Treaty. The same rule is laid down in the first paragraph of Article 29 EU, which introduces Title VI of the EU Treaty, entitled 'Provisions on police and judicial cooperation in criminal matters'.

53. It is the task of the Court to ensure that acts which, according to the Council, fall within the scope of Title VI do not encroach upon the powers conferred by the EC Treaty on the Community (see Case C-170/96 *Commission v Council* [1998] ECR I-2763, paragraph 16, and Case C-176/03 *Commission v Council*, paragraph 39).

54. It is therefore necessary to determine whether or not the provisions of Framework Decision 2005/667 affect the Community's competence under Article 80(2) EC, in that they could have been adopted on the basis of that provision, as submitted by the Commission.

55. It should be borne in mind, firstly, that the common transport policy is one of the foundations of the Community, since Article 70 EC, read together with Article 80(1) EC, provides that the objectives of the Treaty are, in matters of transport by rail, road or inland waterway, to be pursued by the Member States within the framework of that policy (see Case 97/78 *Schumalla* [1998] ECR 2311, paragraph 4).

56. Next, it should be noted that, under Article 80(2) EC, the Council may decide whether, to what extent and by what procedure appropriate provisions may be laid down for sea transport (see, inter alia, Case C-18/93 *Corsica Ferries* [1994] ECR I-1783, paragraph 25), and the procedural provisions of Article 71 EC are to apply.

57. As evidenced by the Court's case-law, far from excluding the application of the EC Treaty to sea transport, Article 80(2) EC merely provides that the specific rules of the Treaty relating to the common transport policy, which are set out in Title V thereof, will not automatically apply to that sphere of activity (see, inter alia, Case C-178/05 *Commission v Greece* [2007] ECR I-0000, paragraph 52).

58. Since Article 80(2) EC does not lay down any explicit limitations as to the nature of the specific common rules which the Council may adopt on that basis in accordance with the procedural provisions laid down in Article 71 EC, the Community legislature has broad legislative powers under Article 80(2) EC and is competent – by virtue of that provision and in keeping with the other provisions of the EC Treaty relating to the common transport policy, in particular Article 71(1) EC – to lay down, inter alia, 'measures to improve transport safety' and 'any other appropriate provisions' in the field of maritime transport (see, to that effect, in respect of road transport, Joined Cases C-184/02 and C-223/02 *Spain and Finland v Parliament and Council* [2004] ECR I-7789, paragraph 28).

59. That finding, to the effect that, within the scope of the competence conferred on it by Article 80(2) EC, the Community legislature may adopt measures aimed at improving maritime transport safety, is not called into question by the fact that, in the present case, the Council has not considered it appropriate to adopt the provisions of Framework Decision 2005/667 on the basis of Article 80(2) EC. In fact, the existence of the legislative competence conferred by Article 80(2) EC is not dependent on a decision by the legislature actually to exercise that competence.

60. Moreover, since requirements relating to environmental protection, which is one of the essential objectives of the Community (see, inter alia, Case C-176/03 *Commission v Council*, paragraph 41), must, according to Article 6 EC, 'be integrated into the definition and implementation of ... Community policies and activities', such protection must be regarded as an objective which also forms part of the common transport policy. The Community legislature may therefore, on the basis of Article 80(2) EC and in the exercise of the powers conferred on it by that provision, decide to promote environmental protection (see, by analogy, Case C-336/00 *Huber* [2002] ECR I-7699, paragraph 36).

61. Lastly, it must be borne in mind that, according to the Court's settled case-law, the choice of legal basis for a Community measure must rest on objective factors which are amenable to judicial review, including in particular the aim and the content of the measure (see Case C-300/89 *Commission v Council (Titanium dioxide)* [1991] ECR I-2867, paragraph 10; *Huber*, paragraph 30; and Case C-176/03 *Commission v Council*, paragraph 45).

62. More specifically, in respect of Framework Decision 2005/667, the preamble thereto states that its purpose is to enhance maritime safety and improve protection of the marine environment against ship-source pollution. As evidenced by the second and third recitals in the preamble, that decision is intended to approximate certain legislation of the Member States in order to avoid a recurrence of damage like that brought about by the sinking of the oil tanker, the *Prestige*.

63. As is clear from the fourth recital in the preamble to Framework Decision 2005/667 and the sixth recital in the preamble to Directive 2005/35, the Framework Decision is intended to supplement the directive with detailed rules on criminal matters. As evidenced by the first and fifteenth recitals in the preamble to Directive 2005/35 and also in Article 1 thereof, it also aims to ensure a high level of safety and environmental protection in maritime transport. Its purpose, according to the fifteenth recital in the preamble and Article 1, is to incorporate international ship-source pollution standards into Community law and to establish penalties – criminal and administrative – for infringement of those rules, in order to ensure that they are effective.

64. As to the content of Framework Decision 2005/667, by virtue of Articles 2, 3 and 5 thereof, it introduces the obligation for Member States to provide for criminal penalties for persons, natural or legal, who have committed, aided, abetted or incited one of the offences referred to in Articles 4 and 5 of Directive 2005/35.

65. Moreover, the Framework Decision, according to which the criminal penalties must be effective, proportionate and dissuasive, lays down, in Articles 4 and 6, the type and level of

criminal penalty to be applied according to the damage caused by the offences to water quality, to animal or vegetable species or to persons.

66. Although it is true that, as a general rule, neither criminal law nor the rules of criminal procedure fall within the Community's competence (see, to that effect, Case 203/80 *Casati* [1981] ECR 2595, paragraph 27; Case C-226/97 *Lemmens* [1998] ECR I-3711, paragraph 19; and Case C-176/03 *Commission v Council*, paragraph 47), the fact remains that when the application of effective, proportionate and dissuasive criminal penalties by the competent national authorities is an essential measure for combating serious environmental offences, the Community legislature may require the Member States to introduce such penalties in order to ensure that the rules which it lays down in that field are fully effective (see, to that effect, Case C-176/03 *Commission v Council*, paragraph 48).

67. In the present case, the Court finds, firstly, that the provisions laid down in Framework Decision 2005/667 – like those of Framework Decision 2003/80, at issue in the proceedings which gave rise to the judgment in Case C-176/03 *Commission v Council* – relate to conduct which is likely to cause particularly serious environmental damage as a result, in this case, of the infringement of the Community rules on maritime safety.

68. Secondly, it is clear from the third, fourth, fifth, seventh and eighth recitals in the preamble to Directive 2005/35, read in conjunction with the first five recitals in the preamble to Framework Decision 2005/667, that the Council took the view that criminal penalties were necessary to ensure compliance with the Community rules laid down in the field of maritime safety.

69. Accordingly, since Articles 2, 3 and 5 of Framework Decision 2005/667 are designed to ensure the efficacy of the rules adopted in the field of maritime safety, non-compliance with which may have serious environmental consequences, by requiring Member States to apply criminal penalties to certain forms of conduct, those articles must be regarded as being essentially aimed at improving maritime safety, as well as environmental protection, and could have been validly adopted on the basis of Article 80(2) EC.

70. By contrast, and contrary to the submission of the Commission, the determination of the type and level of the criminal penalties to be applied does not fall within the Community's sphere of competence.

71. It follows that the Community legislature may not adopt provisions such as Articles 4 and 6 of Framework Decision 2005/667, since those articles relate to the type and level of the applicable criminal penalties. Consequently, those provisions were not adopted in infringement of Article 47 EU.

72. It should also be pointed out that the references made in Articles 4 and 6 of the Framework Decision to Articles 2, 3 and 5 thereof highlight the fact that, in the present case, those provisions are inextricably linked to the provisions concerning the criminal offences to which they relate.

73. As regards Articles 7 to 12 of Framework Decision 2005/667 – which respectively concern jurisdiction, notification of information between Member States, designation of contact points, territorial scope of application of the Framework Decision, the implementation obligation on Member States and the date of entry into force of the Framework Decision – it is sufficient to note, in the present case, that those articles are also inextricably linked to the provisions of the Framework Decision that are referred to in paragraphs 69 and 71 of this judgment, which means that it is not necessary to rule on the question whether they fall within the sphere of competence of the Community legislature.

74. In the light of the foregoing, it must be concluded that Framework Decision 2005/667, in encroaching on the competence which Article 80(2) EC attributes to the Community, infringes Article 47 EU and, being indivisible, must be annulled in its entirety."

CHAPTER 20

European Union law relating to the maritime environment: organotin

A. INTRODUCTION

20.001 The European Union ("EU") has stated that it is seriously concerned by the harmful environmental effects of organotin compounds used as anti-fouling systems on ships, and in particular of tributyltin ("TBT") coatings.[1]

20.002 Internationally, the International Convention on the Control of Harmful Anti-Fouling Systems on Ships (the "AFS-Convention") was adopted on 5 October 2001 at a Diplomatic Conference ("AFS-Conference") held under the aegis of the International Maritime Organization ("IMO"). The EU Member States attended the AFS-Conference.

20.003 The Commission has seen the AFS-Convention as a framework convention allowing the prohibition of harmful anti-fouling systems used on ships in accordance with well-defined procedures and having due regard to the precautionary principle expressed in the Rio Declaration on Environment and Development.[2]

20.004 The Commission believes that as the AFS-Convention in 2003 only prohibited the application of organotin compounds on ships, the Commission proposed further EU legislation (hence Regulation 782/2003 considered below).[3] It also noted that so-called "fixed application dates" have been included in the AFS-Convention (i.e. 1 January 2003 for the prohibition of the application of organotin compounds on ships and 1 January 2008 for the elimination of the presence of organotin compounds on ships) and the AFS-Convention will only enter into force 12 months after its ratification by at least 25 States representing at least 25% of the world's tonnage.[4]

B. REGULATION 782/2003 ON THE PROHIBITION OF ORGANOTIN COMPOUNDS ON SHIPS

Introduction

20.005 On 14 April 2003, the Parliament and the Council adopted Regulation (EC) No 782/2003 on the prohibition of organotin compounds on ships.[5]

---

1 Reg. 782/2003, OJ L115/1, 9 May 2003, Recital 1. For an electronic version, see http://eur-lex.europa.eu/legal-content/EN/TXT/?uri=CELEX%3A32003R0782.
2 Reg. 782/2003, Recital 3.
3 See para. 20.005.
4 Reg. 782/2003, Recitals 5 and 6.
5 OJ L115/1, 9 May 2003,

Legal basis

20.006 The legal basis for Regulation 782/2003 was the Treaty establishing the European Community ("TEC") generally and, in particular, Article 80(2). Under Article 11, the regulation entered into force on the day following that of its publication in the *Official Journal* and it was published on 9 May 2003.

Legislative history

20.007 The legislative history was a proposal from the Commission,[6] an opinion of the European Economic and Social Committee and a consultation with the Committee of the Regions.

20.008 The regulation provides in the seventh recital that Member States should ratify the AFS-Convention at the earliest opportunity. Moreover, the eighth recital states that Member States should be put in the best possible position for a speedy ratification of the AFS-Convention and any obstacle which might impede such ratification should be removed.

20.009 The background to the regulation is clear from the following recitals:

"(9) The AFS-Conference, aware that the time remaining until 1 January 2003 might not be sufficient to enable the entry into force of the AFS-Convention by that date, and desiring that organotin compounds should effectively cease to be applied in shipping as from 1 January 2003, requested in AFS-Conference Resolution No 1 that IMO Member States do their utmost to prepare for implementing the AFS-Convention as a matter of urgency, and urged the relevant industries to refrain from the marketing, sale and application of organotin compounds by that date.

(10) As an immediate follow-up to the AFS-Conference the Commission adopted Commission Directive 2002/62/EC of 9 July 2002 adapting to technical progress for the ninth time Annex I to Council Directive 76/769/EEC on the approximation of the laws, regulations and administrative provisions of the Member States relating to restrictions on the marketing and use of certain dangerous substances and preparations (organostannic compounds)[7] in order to prohibit, with effect from 1 January 2003, the marketing and use of organostannic compounds in anti-fouling systems for all ships, irrespective of their length.

(11) In the light of AFS-Conference Resolution No 1, additional steps are necessary for the implementation of measures concerning organotin compounds in order to ensure a general ban on TBT coating used on ships throughout the Community and its surrounding seas on the dates provided for by the AFS-Convention.

(12) A Regulation is the appropriate legal instrument as it imposes on shipowners and Member States, directly and within a short time frame, precise requirements to be implemented at the same time and in the same manner throughout the Community. This Regulation, which should seek solely to prohibit organotin compounds, should not duplicate the AFS-Convention.

(13) This Regulation should not affect the restrictions on the marketing and use of certain dangerous substances and preparations (organostannic compounds) laid down in Directive 76/769/EEC.[8]

(14) Uncertainty regarding the total prohibition of active TBT coatings should not be accepted at Community level; the world-wide shipping industry, which has to programme the

---

6 OJ C262/492 E, 29 October 2002.

7 Ed., OJ L183/58, 12 July 2002.

8 Ed., OJ L262/201, 27 September 1976. Directive as last amended by Commission Dir. 2003/3 (OJ L4/12, 9 January 2003).

maintenance of its ships, should be made aware clearly and in due time that, as from 1 January 2008, ships bearing an active TBT coating on their hulls will no longer be allowed in Community ports.

(15) Third countries, particularly if they cannot benefit from the added value of a supranational regulation, might experience legal technical difficulties in imposing, through their national legislation, the prohibition on applying TBT coatings to their ships from the day on which the prohibition enters into force under this Regulation. The application of the prohibition in this Regulation on applying TBT coatings should therefore be suspended as regards ships sailing under the flag of a third State for an interim period beginning on 1 July 2003 and ending on the date of entry into force of the AFS-Convention.

(16) Flag States which have banned the use of TBT coatings on their ships have an economic interest in ensuring that the AFS-Convention enters into force as soon as possible, in order to ensure a world-wide level playing field. This Regulation, which prohibits, as soon as possible, all ships flying the flag of a Member State from applying TBT coatings should constitute an incentive for flag States to ratify the AFS-Convention.

(17) The definitions used and requirements imposed in this Regulation should as far as possible be based upon those used in the AFS-convention.

(18) In order to ensure its application to offshore platforms, this Regulation should also apply to ships operating under the authority of a Member State. It should not apply to any warships or other government ships since the treatment of those ships is adequately covered under the AFS-Convention.

(19) Imposing, as from 1 July 2003, the prohibition of active TBT coatings on all ships which are entitled to fly the flag of a Member State and whose anti-fouling system has been applied, changed or replaced after that date, should be an incentive for the shipping industry to implement the recommendation of AFS-Conference Resolution No 1.

(20) It is appropriate to establish the same survey and certification regime as that provided for by the AFS-Convention. Under this Regulation all ships of 400 gross tonnage and above, irrespective of the nature of their voyage, should be surveyed, whilst ships of 24 metres or more in length but less than 400 gross tonnage should only have to carry a declaration of compliance with this Regulation or with the AFS-Convention. The Community should have the right to introduce a harmonised survey regime for these ships, if this proves necessary at a later stage.

(21) For ships less than 24 metres in length, it is not necessary to provide for a specific survey or declaration since these ships, mainly recreational craft and fishing vessels, will be adequately covered under the provisions of Directive 76/769/EEC.

(22) Certificates and documents issued in conformity with this Regulation, as well as AFS-Certificates and AFS-Declarations issued by Parties to the AFS-Convention, should be recognised.

(23) If the AFS-Convention has not entered into force by 1 January 2007, the Commission should be permitted to adopt appropriate measures allowing ships flying the flag of a third State to demonstrate their compliance with this Regulation, as well as measures to control the implementation of these provisions.

(24) The most appropriate regime for controlling the implementation of the prohibition of TBT coatings on ships and the requirements of the AFS-Convention is that laid down in Council Directive 95/21/EC of 19 June 1995 concerning the enforcement, in respect of shipping using Community ports and sailing in the waters under the jurisdiction of the Member States, of international standards for ship safety, pollution prevention and shipboard living and working conditions (port State control)[9] and amendments should be made to that Directive at the appropriate time. Having regard to the specific scope of that Directive, equivalent provisions should be applied to ships flying the flag of a Member State during the interim period.

---

9 Ed., OJ L157/1, 7 July 1995. Directive as last amended by Directive 2002/84 of the European Parliament and of the Council (OJ L324/53, 29 November 2002).

(25) The measures necessary for the implementation of this Regulation should be adopted in accordance with Council Decision 1999/468/EC of 28 June 1999 laying down procedures for the exercise of implementing powers conferred on the Commission.[10]

(26) In order to assess the achievement of the objective of this Regulation, the Commission should report to the European Parliament and the Council and propose, if necessary, any appropriate adjustments to the Regulation.

(27) The entry into force of this Regulation should be such as to allow the effective prohibition of organotin compounds on ships as soon as possible."

Objective of Regulation 782/2003

20.010 The purpose of Regulation 782/2003, according to Article 1, is to reduce or eliminate adverse effects on the marine environment and human health caused by organotin compounds, which act as active biocides in anti-fouling systems used on ships flying the flag of, or operating under the authority of, a Member State, and on ships, regardless of the flag they fly, sailing to or from ports of the Member States.

Concepts in Regulation 782/2003

20.011 Article 2 sets out a number of definitions for the purpose of the regulation. First, the term "anti-fouling system" means a coating, paint, surface treatment, surface or device that is used on a ship to control or prevent attachment of unwanted organisms. The phrase "gross tonnage" means the gross tonnage calculated in accordance with the tonnage measurement regulations contained in Annex 1 to the International Convention on Tonnage Measurement of Ships, 1969, or any successor convention. The term "length" means the length as defined in the International Convention on Load Lines, 1966, as modified by the Protocol of 1988 relating thereto, or any successor convention. The word "ship" means a vessel of any type whatsoever operating in the marine environment and includes hydrofoil boats, air-cushion vehicles, submersibles, floating craft, fixed or floating platforms, floating storage units ("FSUs") and floating production storage and off-loading units ("FPSOs"). The phrase "AFS-Convention" means the International Convention on the control of harmful anti-fouling systems on ships, adopted on 5 October 2001, irrespective of its entry into force. The phrase "recognised organisation" means a body recognised in accordance with the provisions of Council Directive 94/57 of 22 November 1994 on common rules and standards for ship inspection and survey organisations and for the relevant activities of maritime administrations.[11] The term "AFS-Certificate" means the certificate issued to ships in conformity with the provisions of Annex 4 to the AFS-Convention or, during the interim period, a certificate issued in accordance with the format laid down in Annex II to this regulation, when it is issued by the administration of any Member State or by a recognised organisation acting on its behalf. The term "AFS-Declaration" means a declaration drawn up under the provisions of Annex 4 to the AFS-Convention or, during the interim period, a declaration signed by the owner or the owner's authorised agent and drawn up in accordance with the format

---

10 OJ L184/23, 17.7.1999.

11 OJ L319/20, 12 December 1994. Directive as last amended by Directive 2002/84 of the European Parliament and of the Council.

laid down in Annex III to this regulation. The words "AFS-Statement of Compliance" means a document recording compliance with Annex 1 to the AFS-Convention, issued by a recognised organisation on behalf of the administration of a Member State. The concept of "interim period" means the period beginning on 1 July 2003 and ending on the date of entry into force of the AFS-Convention.

Scope of Regulation 782/2003

20.012 Article 3 provides the regulation shall apply to: (a) ships flying the flag of a Member State; (b) ships not flying the flag of a Member State but operating under the authority of a Member State, and (c) ships that enter a port or offshore terminal of a Member State but do not fall within points (a) or (b). Article 3(2) provides that the regulation shall not apply to any warship, naval auxiliary or other ship owned or operated by a State and used, for the time being, only on government non-commercial service.

Prohibition of the application of organotin compounds which act as biocides

20.013 Article 4 provides that as from 1 July 2003, organotin compounds which act as biocides in anti-fouling systems shall not be applied or re-applied on ships. However, during the interim period this provision shall only apply to ships referred to in points (a) or (b) of Article 3(1).

Prohibition of the bearing of organotin compounds which act as biocides

20.014 Article 5 provides:

"1. Ships entitled to fly the flag of a Member State as from 1 July 2003, and whose anti-fouling system has been applied, changed or replaced after that date, shall not bear organotin compounds which act as biocides in anti-fouling systems on their hulls or external parts and surfaces, unless they bear a coating that forms a barrier to such compounds to prevent them leaching from the underlying non-compliant anti-fouling system.
2. As from 1 January 2008 the ships referred to in Article 3(1) shall either not bear organotin compounds which act as biocides in anti-fouling systems on their hulls or external parts and surfaces, or bear a coating that forms a barrier to such compounds leaching from the underlying non-compliant anti-fouling system.
3. Paragraphs 1 and 2 shall not apply to fixed and floating platforms, FSUs and FPSOs constructed prior to 1 July 2003 that have not been in dry-dock on or after that date."

Survey and certification

20.015 Article 6 deals with survey and certification. Article 6(1) provides that the following rules shall apply as regards the survey and certification of ships flying the flag of a Member State: (a) ships of 400 gt and above, excluding fixed or floating platforms, FSUs and FPSOs, shall be surveyed and certified as from 1 July 2003 in accordance with the requirements laid down in Annex 1, before the ship is put into service for the first time, or when the anti-fouling systems are changed or replaced; (b) ships of 24 metres or more in length, but less than 400 gt, excluding fixed or floating platforms, FSUs and FPSOs, shall carry an AFS-Declaration to demonstrate compliance with Articles 4 and 5 and if necessary, the Commission, in accordance with the procedure referred to in Article 9(2), may establish a harmonised survey and certification regime for these ships; and (c) Member States may establish appropriate measures for ships not covered by points (a) and (b) in order to ensure compliance with this regulation. Article 6(2) provides that the following rules shall apply as regards the recognition of certificates, declarations and statements of compliance: (a) as from 1 July 2003, Member States shall recognise any AFS-Certificate; (b) until a year after the date referred to in point (a), Member States shall recognise any AFS-Statement of Compliance; and (c) as from 1 July 2003, Member States shall recognise any AFS-Declaration. These declarations shall be accompanied by appropriate documentation (such as a paint receipt or a contractor invoice) or contain an appropriate endorsement. Article 6(3) provides that if the AFS-Convention has not entered into force by 1 January 2007, the Commission, in accordance with the procedure referred to in Article 9(2), shall adopt appropriate measures in order to allow ships flying the flag of a third State to demonstrate their compliance with Article 5.

Port State control

20.016 Article 7 provides that during the interim period Member States shall apply control provisions equivalent to those laid down in Directive 95/21 to ships of 400 gt and above flying the flag of a Member State. With regard to the inspections and detection of breaches, Member States shall be guided by the provisions of Article 11 of the AFS-Convention. If the AFS-Convention has not entered into force by 1 January 2007, the Commission, in accordance with the procedure referred to in Article 9(2), shall establish appropriate procedures for these controls.

Adaptations

20.017 Article 8 states that in order to take account of developments at international level and in particular in the IMO, or to improve the effectiveness of this regulation in the light of experience, the references to the AFS-Convention, to the AFS-Certificate, to the AFS-Declaration and to the AFS-Statement of Compliance and/or the annexes to this regulation, including relevant IMO guidelines in relation to Article 11 of the AFS-Convention, may be amended in accordance with the procedure referred to in Article 9(2).

Committee

20.018 Article 9(1) provides that the Commission shall be assisted by the Committee on Safe Seas and the Prevention of Pollution from Ships ("COSS") established by Article 3 of Regulation (EC) No 2099/2002 of the European Parliament and of the Council of 5 November 2002 concerning the COSS and amending the regulations on maritime safety and the prevention of pollution from ships.[12] Article 9(2) provides that where reference is made to this paragraph, Articles 5 and 7 of Decision 1999/468 shall apply, having regard to the provisions of Article 8 thereof. The period laid down in Article 5(6) of Decision

---

12 OJ L324/1, 29 November 2002.

1999/468 shall be set at three months. Article 9(3) provides that the COSS shall adopt its rules of procedure.

Annexes

20.019 Of the annexes, Annex 1 is the more important. It deals with surveys and certification requirements for anti-fouling systems on ships flying the flag of a Member State.

Evaluation

20.020 Pursuant to Article 10, by 10 May 2004, the Commission had to report to the Parliament and the Council on the state of ratification of the AFS-Convention and provide information on the extent to which organotin compounds, which act as biocides in anti-fouling systems on ships, are still used on ships not flying the flag of a Member State operating to or from EU ports. In the light of this report the Commission may propose, if necessary, amendments to ensure accelerated reduction of the contribution by ships not flying the flag of a Member State to the presence of harmful anti-fouling compounds in the waters under the jurisdiction of Member States.

C. REGULATION 536/2008 GIVING EFFECT TO ARTICLE 6(3) AND ARTICLE 7 OF REGULATION 782/2003 ON THE PROHIBITION OF ORGANOTIN COMPOUNDS ON SHIPS AND AMENDING THAT REGULATION

Introduction

20.021 On 13 June 2008, the Commission adopted Regulation 536/2008 giving effect to Article 6(3) and Article 7 of Regulation 782/2003 of the European Parliament and of the Council on the prohibition of organotin compounds on ships and amending that regulation.[13]

20.022 The legal basis of the regulation is the TEC. The legal background was, in particular, Article 6(3), Article 7, second paragraph, and Article 8 of Regulation 782/2003. Under Article 6, the regulation entered into force on the twentieth day following that of its publication in the *Official Journal* and it was published on 14 June 2008.

20.023 It is useful to consider some of the recitals:

"(1) Regulation (EC) No 782/2003 requires the Commission to adopt a number of measures in order to give effect to that Regulation if the International Convention on the control of harmful anti-fouling systems on ships (hereinafter referred to as the AFS-Convention), adopted on 5 October 2001, has not entered into force by 1 January 2007.

(2) The AFS-Convention has not yet entered into force.

(3) It is therefore necessary to adopt measures in order to allow ships flying the flag of a third State to demonstrate their compliance with Article 5 of Regulation (EC) No 782/2003, and to provide for port State control.

(4) Article 8 of Regulation (EC) No 782/2003 provides that the Regulation may be amended in order to take account of developments at international level and in particular in the International Maritime Organisation (hereinafter referred to as the IMO), or to improve the effectiveness of the Regulation in the light of experience.

---

13 OJ L156/10, 14 June 2008.

(5) The IMO Marine Environment Protection Committee (hereinafter referred to as the MEPC), in accordance with Article 1(4)(a) of Annex 4 to the AFS-Convention, adopted Guidelines for Survey and Certification of Anti-Fouling Systems on Ships by means of Resolution MEPC.102(48) on 11 October 2002.

(6) The MEPC, in accordance with Article 11(2) of the AFS-Convention, adopted Guidelines for Inspection of Anti-Fouling Systems on Ships by means of Resolution MEPC.105(49) on 18 July 2003.

(7) The MEPC, in accordance with Article 11(1) of the AFS-Convention, adopted on Guidelines for Brief Sampling of Anti-Fouling Systems on Ships by means of Resolution MEPC.104(49) on 18 July 2003.

(8) Until the entry into force of the AFS-Convention, it is appropriate to apply its provisions to ships flying the flag of a State which is a Party to the said convention. Similarly, ships flying the flag of a State which is not a Party to the AFS-Convention should not receive a more favourable treatment within the Community.

(9) The measures provided for in this Regulation are in accordance with the opinion of the Committee on Safe Seas and the Prevention of Pollution from Ships, established by Regulation (EC) No 2099/2002 of the European Parliament and of the Council."[14]

Purpose of the regulation

20.024 Article 1 provides that the purpose of the regulation is to: (a) establish measures in order to allow ships flying the flag of a third State that enter a port or offshore terminal of a Member State to demonstrate their compliance with Article 5 of Regulation 782/2003; (b) establish procedures for control by the port State within the Community; and (c) amend the references to the AFS-Statement of Compliance in Regulation 782/2003 and Annex 1 to that regulation.

20.025 Article 2(1) provides that ships referred to in Article 3(1)(c) of Regulation 782/2003 shall demonstrate their compliance with Article 5 of that regulation in accordance with paragraphs 2, 3 and 4 of Article 2 of Regulation 536/2008. Article 2(2) provides that during the interim period ships flying the flag of a State which is a Party to the AFS-Convention shall demonstrate their compliance with Article 5 of Regulation 782/2003 by means of a Statement of Compliance in accordance with paragraph 5.4.1 of the guidelines for surveys and certification of anti-fouling systems on ships annexed to Resolution MEPC.102(48) of the Marine Environment Protection Committee of the IMO (""MEPC"). Article 2(3) provides that as from the entry into force of the AFS-Convention ships flying the flag of a State which is a Party to the AFS-Convention shall demonstrate their compliance with Article 5 of Regulation 782/2003 by means of an International Anti-Fouling System Certificate in accordance with Annex 4 to the AFS-Convention. Article 2(4) states that ships flying the flag of a State which is not a Party to the AFS-Convention, shall demonstrate their compliance with Article 5 of Regulation 782/2003 by means of a Statement of Compliance delivered by the Administration of the flag State by applying the provisions of Article 10 of the AFS-Convention, in conjunction with Annex 4 thereto and the guidelines for surveys and certification of anti-fouling systems on ships annexed to the resolution. For the purpose of this paragraph the references made in the said article, annex and guidelines to the International Anti-Fouling System Certificate shall be construed as references to the Statement of Compliance.

---

14 OJ L324, 29 November 2002, p. 1. Regulation as last amended by Commission Regulation (EC) No 93/2007 (OJ L22, 31 January 2007, p. 12).

20.026 Article 3(1) provides that during the interim period, Member States shall apply control provisions equivalent to those laid down in Council Directive 95/21[15] to ships falling within the scope of Regulation 782/2003 in accordance with paragraphs 2 and 3 of Article 3. Article 3(2) provides that with regard to the inspections and detection of breaches, and without prejudice to Article 2 of this regulation, Member States shall apply the provisions of Article 11 of the AFS-Convention and be guided by the guidelines for inspection of anti-fouling systems on ships annexed to Resolution MEPC.105(49) of the MEPC. Article 3(3) provides that Article 3(1) shall apply to ships referred to in Article 3(1)(c) of Regulation (EC) No 782/2003 from 1 January 2008.

20.027 Article 4 provides that in fulfilling their obligations pursuant to Articles 6 and 7 of Regulation 782/2003, Member States shall be guided by the guidelines for brief sampling of anti-fouling systems on ships annexed to Resolution MEPC.104(49) of the MEPC.

20.028 Article 5 amended Regulation 782/2003 in various ways which have been incorporated into the text above.[16]

D. CONCLUSIONS

20.029 The measures adopted by the EU have been important steps to address the very harmful effects of organotin compounds.[17]

---

15 OJ L157/1, 7 July 1995.

16 Art. 5 amended Art. 2, point 9, Art .6(2), point (b) and Annex I, para. 1.4 of Reg. 782/2002.

17 See http://eur-lex.europa.eu/legal-content/EN/TXT/?uri=URISERV%3Al24256 and http://www.ecomare. nl/en/encyclopedia/natural-environment/matter-and-materials/pesticides/organotin-compounds/.

CHAPTER 21

European Union law relating to the maritime environment: the hazardous and noxious substances by sea convention

A. INTRODUCTION

21.001 This chapter considers the European Union ("EU") law relating to the International Convention on Liability and Compensation for Damage in Connection with the Carriage of Hazardous and Noxious Substances by Sea, 1996 (the "HNS Convention"). The HNS Convention has generated considerable commentary[1] and, indeed, some controversy but the focus of this chapter is focused on the EU aspects of the convention.

21.002 The principal EU measure is Council Decision 2002/971 authorising the Member States, in the interest of the Community, to ratify or accede to the HNS Convention.[2]

21.003 The background, in part, to the decision is clear from the fact that the EU is not a member of the International Maritime Organization ("IMO"). The HNS Convention is a mixed agreement.

B. COUNCIL DECISION 2002/971 OF 18 NOVEMBER 2002 AUTHORISING THE MEMBER STATES, IN THE INTEREST OF THE COMMUNITY, TO RATIFY OR ACCEDE TO THE INTERNATIONAL CONVENTION ON LIABILITY AND COMPENSATION FOR DAMAGE IN CONNECTION WITH THE CARRIAGE OF HAZARDOUS AND NOXIOUS SUBSTANCES BY SEA, 1996 (THE "HNS CONVENTION")

21.004 On 18 November 2002, the Council adopted Decision 2002/971 authorising the Member States, in the interest of, what is now, the EU, to ratify or accede to the HNS Convention.[3] The fifth recital of the decision provides that the

"HNS Convention is particularly important, given the interests of the Community and its Member States, because it makes for improved victim protection under international rules on marine pollution liability, in keeping with the 1982 United Nations Convention on the Law of the Sea."

---

1 See Argyropoulou, The HNS Fund and its Implications: A Critical Approach of the Second Tier of the HNS Convention from the Time Prior to its Creation up to the Changes Incurred by the 2010 HNS Protocol (2011) and Argyropoulou, The HNS Convention and 2010 Protocol: Industry Implications (2012). See also Baughen, Shipping Law (6th ed., 2015), pp. 334–338 and Tsimplis in Baatz (ed.), Maritime Law (3rd ed., 2014), pp. 402–415.

2 OJ L337/55, 13 December 2002.

3 OJ L337/55, 13 December 2002.

21.005 The legal basis for Decision 2002/971 was the then Treaty establishing the European Community, and in particular Articles 61(c), 67(1) and 300(2).

21.006 The legislative history involved a proposal from the Commission[4] and an opinion of the European Parliament.[5]

21.007 The international legal background was the HNS Convention. This convention was aimed at ensuring adequate, prompt and effective compensation of persons who suffer damage caused by spills of hazardous and noxious substances, when carried by sea. The HNS Convention fills a significant gap in the international regulation of marine pollution liability.

21.008 Article 1(1) provides that without prejudice to the then existing European Community ("EC") competence in the matter, the Council authorised the Member States[6] to ratify or accede to the HNS Convention in the interest of the EU, subject to the conditions set out in the decision. In the decision, the term "Member State" means all Member States with the exception of Denmark.[7] The second recital to the decision provides that

"Articles 38, 39 and 40 of the HNS Convention affect Community secondary legislation on jurisdiction and the recognition and enforcement of judgments, as laid down in Council Regulation (EC) No 44/2001 of 22 December 2000 on jurisdiction and the recognition and enforcement of judgments in civil and commercial matters."[8]

The third recital therefore goes on to state that the

"Community therefore has sole competence in relation to Articles 38, 39 and 40 of the HNS Convention inasmuch as that Convention affects the rules laid down in Regulation (EC) No 44/2001. The Member States retain their competence for matters covered by that Convention which do not affect Community law."

21.009 The fourth recital to the decision provided that

"[p]ursuant to the HNS Convention, only sovereign States may be party to it; there are no plans, in the short term, to reopen negotiations for the purpose of taking into account Community competence for the matter. It is not therefore possible for the Community to ratify or accede to the HNS Convention at present, nor is there any prospect that it will be able to do so in the near future."

Article 2 provides that when ratifying or acceding to the HNS Convention, Member States must make the following declaration: "Judgments on matters covered by the Convention shall, when given by a court of ([a Member State][9]), be recognised and enforced

---

4 OJ C51 E, 26 February 2002, p. 370.

5 Opinion delivered on 11 June 2002.

6 The tenth recital records that in "accordance with Articles 1 and 2 of the Protocol on the position of Denmark annexed to the Treaty on European Union and to the Treaty establishing the European Community, Denmark is not taking part in the adoption of this Decision, and is not bound by it or subject to its application".

7 The ninth recital to the decision provides: "[the] United Kingdom and Ireland are taking part in the adoption and application of this Decision".

8 OJ L12, 16 January 2001, p. 1.

9 All the Member States to which this decision is applicable except the Member State making the declaration and Denmark.

in (^{10}) according to the relevant internal Community rules on the subject."^{11} The sixth to eighth recitals provides:

"(6) The substantive rules of the system established by the HNS Convention fall under the national competence of Member States and only the provisions of jurisdiction and the recognition and enforcement of the judgments are matters covered by exclusive Community competence. Given the subject matters and the aim of the HNS Convention, acceptance of the provisions of that Convention which come under Community competence cannot be dissociated from the provisions which come under the competence of the Member States.

(7) The Council should therefore authorise the Member States to ratify or accede to the HNS Convention in the interest of the Community, under the conditions set out in this Decision.

(8) Member States should finalise, within a reasonable time, their procedures for ratification of, or accession to, the HNS Convention in the interest of the Community. Member States should exchange information on the state of their ratification or accession procedures in order to prepare the deposit of their instruments of ratification of, or accession to, the Convention."

21.010 Article 3(1) provides that Member States must take the necessary steps to deposit the instruments of ratification of, or accession to, the HNS Convention within a reasonable time with the Secretary-General of the IMO and, if possible, before 30 June 2006. Article 3(2) provides that Member States must inform the Council and the Commission, before 30 June 2004, of the prospective date of finalisation of their ratification or accession procedures. Member States must seek to exchange information on the state of their ratification or accession procedures.

21.011 Article 4 provides that when ratifying or acceding to the HNS Convention, Member States shall inform the Secretary-General of the IMO in writing that such ratification or accession has taken place in accordance with this decision.

21.012 Article 5 provides that Member States must, at the earliest opportunity, use their best endeavours to ensure that the HNS Convention is amended to allow the Community to become a contracting party to it.

---

10 I.e. the Member State making the declaration.
11 At present, these rules are laid down in Reg. (EC) No 44/2001.

CHAPTER 22

European Union law relating to shipbuilding

A. INTRODUCTION

Purpose of this chapter

22.001 The purpose of this chapter is to examine the European Union ("EU") law relating to shipbuilding.[1] In some ways, it is a narrow topic with only four legislative instruments but, in other ways, it is an extremely important topic because of the strategic significance of shipbuilding and the associated technologies for the EU.

22.002 The four legislative instruments are: (a) Regulation 2016/1035 of the European Parliament and of the Council of 8 June 2016 on protection against injurious pricing of vessels;[2] (b) Commission Decision 98/157of 5 November 1997 concerning aid Spain proposed to grant to Astilleros Zamacona SA in respect of five tugboats;[3] (c) Commission Decision 92/569 of 31 July 1992 concerning proposed aid by Germany to the Chinese shipping company Cosco for the construction of container vessels;[4] and (d) Council Resolution of 19 September 1978 on the reorganisation of the shipbuilding industry.[5] Ultimately, only three of those four are legally binding (the last is a non-legally binding resolution) and of the three legally binding measures, only one is of general application as two are specific and targeted.

22.003 The apparent paucity of legislation is somewhat deceptive because there has been a string of measures spanning many years in the area of shipbuilding. These measures (mainly directives) were designed to stem the demise of the shipbuilding sector in the EU. It has been quite a struggle for the European shipyards to compete with yards elsewhere in the world (particularly in Asia). Many of the Asian yards benefited from lower costs and subsidies (e.g. cheaper steel than would be available in Europe). Ultimately, in so far as European yards survived (and some even prospered), it was because of focusing on technologically advanced products or specialist type vessels (e.g. ferries and cruise liners).

Overview of shipbuilding in the EU

22.004 The European Commission wrote in 2018:

"The shipbuilding industry deals with the production of larger (mainly seagoing) vessels intended for the merchant fleet (cargo or passenger transport), the off-shore energy industry or

---

1 The term "shipbuilding" is used in this chapter to include ship conversion and ship repair (unless the context requires otherwise).
2 OJ L176/1, 30 June 2016.
3 OJ L50/38, 20 February 1998.
4 OJ L367/29, 16 December 1992.
5 OJ C229/1, 27 September 1978.

military purposes. It also includes products and services supplied for the building, conversion, and maintenance of these ships. The European Commission promotes the industry's development and addresses competitiveness issues it faces.

Importance of the Shipbuilding Sector
The European shipbuilding industry is a dynamic and competitive sector. It is important from both an economic and social perspective. It is also linked to other sectors including transport, security, energy, research, and the environment.

- There are about 150 large shipyards in Europe. Around 40 of them are active in the global market for large seagoing commercial vessels;
- Some 120,000 people are employed by shipyards (civil and naval, new building, and repair yards) in the EU;
- With a market share of around 6% in terms of tonnage and 35% for marine equipment, Europe is a major player in the global shipbuilding industry (total turnover of EUR 60 billion in 2012);

Shipbuilding is an important and strategic industry in a number of EU countries. Shipyards contribute significantly to regional industrial infrastructure and national security interests (military shipbuilding).

The European shipbuilding industry is the global leader in the construction of complex vessels, such as cruise ships, ferries, mega-yachts, and dredgers. It also has a strong position in the building of submarines and other naval vessels.

The European marine equipment industry is a world leader for a wide range of products ranging from propulsion systems, large diesel engines, environmental, and safety systems, to cargo handling and electronics.

Challenges faced by the Shipbuilding Industry
The sector faces fierce international competition from countries like China and South Korea. The industry has also suffered from the absence of effective global trade rules and state supported over investment. This is because shipyards offer a wide range of technologies, employ a significant number of workers, and generate foreign currency income, due to the fact the global shipbuilding market is dollar-based.

What the Commission is doing
The Commission is addressing issues affecting the shipbuilding industry through a variety of policy measures, in particular LeaderSHIP 2015[6] and LeaderSHIP 2020 ...[7]

The shipbuilding industry impacts upon various other policy areas, in particular research and innovation, intellectual property, maritime clusters, safety, and the environment. The Commission also takes further policy action in these areas, including conducting studies on key issues."[8]

22.005 In total, there are about 150 large shipyards out of a total of around 300 shipyards in the EU but only 40 or so of those are active in the global market for large seagoing vessels. The numbers of people employed by these yards have fallen over time but the level of technology deployed by these yards has risen over time. Shipyards are centred mainly in countries such as Finland, France, Germany, Greece, Italy and Poland but are also important in many other Member States. The industry is extremely important for various policy objectives including those connected with regional, research and development, employment, social, innovation and commercial policies.

22.006 The EU's interest (and that of the European Commission in particular) is long established. In some ways, it has been a sad story. From the 1950s to the 1970s,

---

6 Ed., http://eur-lex.europa.eu/legal-content/EN/TXT/?uri=CELEX:52003DC0717&locale=en.
7 Ed., http://ec.europa.eu/DocsRoom/documents/10504/attachments/1/translations.
8 https://ec.europa.eu/growth/sectors/maritime/shipbuilding_en.

shipbuilding in Europe was a strong industry employing hundreds of thousands and was a world leader (if not, *the* world leader). Since then, the story has been largely one of decline. Many shipyards became uneconomic and were no longer viable because of the costs, challenges and competition which they faced. The EU has certainly done something to assist them but many of the closed yards would argue that it was not enough while the EU would argue that there was a limit to what it could achieve and that it had done a great deal through various initiatives including the LeaderShip 2015[9] and Leader-Ship 2020.[10]

Economic value of shipbuilding in the EU

22.007 The Commission has estimated that the value of exports from the EU shipbuilding sector in 2009 was in the order of €11.9 billion while EU shipbuilding imports in 2009 were worth €14.7 billion. While obviously, imports were higher in value, the absence of an EU shipbuilding capacity would have meant that the trade imbalance would have been even greater. Writing in 2013, the Commission believed that the "ships and maritime equipment industry employs more than 500,000 people and has an average annual turnover of around [€72 billion]".[11] The Commission saw this industry as comprising:

"Shipbuilding and Ship Repair
The European shipbuilding industry and ship repair industry is made up of around 300 yards of which more than 80% can be considered to be 'small to medium' (building ships of 60–150mt). The remaining yards can be defined as 'large'. Around 90% of the orderbook is for export markets.

Marine Equipment Manufacturing
The European marine equipment manufacturing and industry (propulsion, cargo handling, communication, automation, integrated systems, etc.) is made up of around 7,500 companies, the vast majority of which can be considered to be 'small to medium'. Around 70% of production is for export markets."[12]

Strategic significance for the EU of shipbuilding

22.008 A vital and competitive shipbuilding industry is important strategically for the EU. Shipbuilding is an important export industry because ships built in the EU are purchased by carriers around the world. The Preamble to the Seventh Shipbuilding Directive[13] encapsulates this notion very well:

---

9 See Communication from the Commission to the Council, the European Parliament, the European Economic and Social Committee and the Committee of the Regions – LeaderSHIP 2015 – Defining the Future of the European Shipbuilding and Repair Industry – Competitiveness through Excellence (COM/2003/0717 final).
10 https://ec.europa.eu/docsroom/documents/10504/attachments/1/translations/en/renditions/pdf.
11 LeaderShip 2020: https://ec.europa.eu/docsroom/documents/10504/attachments/1/translations/en/rendi tions/pdf.
12 Ibid.
13 Dir. 90/684, OJ 1990 L380/27. The Preamble to the Third Shipbuilding Directive (Dir. 75/432) had read: "Whereas a sound and competitive shipbuilding industry is necessary to the [EU]; whereas it contributes to its economic and social development, by providing a substantial market for a range of sectors, including those using advanced technology, and as an employer in a number of [EU] regions; whereas this is also the case with ship conversion and ship repair…"

"a competitive shipbuilding industry is of vital interest to the [EU] and contributes to its economic and social development by providing a substantial market for a range of industries, including those using advanced technology; whereas it contributes also to the maintenance of employment in a number of regions, including some which are already suffering a high rate of unemployment; whereas this is also true of ship conversion and ship repair."

Challenges for the EU shipbuilding sector

22.009 The EU shipbuilding sector has faced severe challenges in recent decades. The plight of shipbuilding in the EU[14] is, in large measure, dependent on the plight of EU shipping: because shipbuilding in the EU is, in turn, somewhat dependent on the fortunes of EU shipping. Given the troubles facing both the shipping and shipbuilding sectors in the EU (but particularly, shipbuilding), there is a need for an effective EU policy so as to ensure the survival of the sectors. The plight of some shipyards has led various governments to provide aids, subsidies and tax breaks so as to stimulate activity at such yards and so there is a need to co-ordinate at an EU level the response to such individual measures.

22.010 Writing in 2013, the Commission said:

"Reduction of New Orders and Overcapacity
The global maritime technology industry is facing serious challenges. New orders for ships have virtually collapsed from a pre-crisis speculative boom of 85 mln cgt to 16 mln cgt in 2009 and have remained low. The expected average order volume is 30–40 mln cgt annually.
At the same time the expanded global shipyard capacity reached new output records year on year peaking in 2012 at around 60 mln cgt. The capacity expansion in shipbuilding has mainly taken place in China, Korea and other emerging markets, however Europe has refrained from taking this approach. The long production cycle in shipbuilding means that the impact of low orders on the supply chain and on employment is only now being felt. This is particularly concerning for Europe."[15]

This observation, made in the aftermath of the economic downturn which started in earnest in 2008, is so symptomatic of the rollercoaster nature of the shipbuilding industry.

22.011 Shipbuilding in the EU has had its difficulties but these difficulties are not new. It has faced strong competition internationally (particularly, from the Far East). It has suffered because of government subsidies provided to some shipyards both inside and outside the EU. Many foreign yards have lower costs (particularly wages but also energy) than EU yards making them very competitive on price. Shipbuilding enjoyed a boom during the 1960s and early 1970s. Such a boom was caused by the success experienced and the growth expected in the world's economies during that time. During 1974–1976, production was about 33 million grt (gross registered tonnage). However, a depression in the shipbuilding sector (particularly in the EU sector) began in the mid-1970s. Between 1976 and 1979, vessel completions around the world fell by 37%. However, in the EU,

---

14 Bredima-Savopoulou and Tzoannos, The Common Shipping Policy of the EEC (1990), p. 54 et seq. and Bredima and Tzoannos, "In Search of a Common Shipping Policy for the EEC" (1981) 20 JCMS 95, at 111–112. See also "Plans to Help Former Shipyard Areas", Lloyd's List, 17 July 1987, p. 1; "European Call for Sanctions in Shipbuilding", Lloyd's List, 23 October 1987, p. 1; "Japan set to abolish shipyard subsidies", Lloyd's List, 10 December 1991, p. 1. See also the European Commission's Press Release, "Commission to Investigate Aid to Greek Shipbuilding" (IP(89)235). See "Euro Shipbuilding Bowed but Not Out" (2010) Fairplay 19.

15 https://ec.europa.eu/docsroom/documents/10504/attachments/1/translations/en/renditions/pdf.

this decline was 42%.[16] By the late 1980s, the crisis was serious and appeared irreversible.[17] So why did this depression occur? Such was the increase in orders for new tonnage that the crisis of the mid-1970s and 1980s might well have occurred due to over-capacity anyway, even without the oil crises of 1973 and 1978 and the economic crises of that era. This decline in the fortunes of shipbuilding was very notable in the EU. In 1976, the volume of output totalled 5,927 million cgrt (compensated gross registered tonnes)[18] but, by 1987, this had fallen to 1,719 million cgrt.[19] This was more than a three-fold drop and when translated into the EU's position in the world of shipbuilding, it meant a decline from 26.8% of world production to 18.6% by 1989.[20] In employment terms, 273,000 people were employed in EU shipyards in 1980, but this had fallen to 139,000 working in the 71 leading yards by 1987.[21] There were large-scale redundancies. In the EU, employment declined by some 36% between 1975 and 1979.[22] The decline did not end there but has been a theme running through the shipbuilding industry through the decades.

22.012 In part, the EU yards were not to blame for this decline. As already mentioned, there had been an over-capacity and over-ordering in the preceding years: between 1973 and 1987, the worldwide fleet volume increased by 30%, but transport volume decreased by 10%.[23] On the other hand, much of the decline in the fortunes of EU yards was due to the competitive pressure from South-East Asian and Japanese yards who benefited from (at the very least) better economies of scale and stronger links with other industries. South Korean yards benefited from government subsidies and low labour costs – for example, hourly labour costs in 1987 amounted to €17 per hour in South Korea, but some €62 in the Netherlands, €69 in Germany and €34 in the UK. The Commission in its communication to the Council of Ministers, entitled "Reorganisation of the Community Shipbuilding Industry",[24] stated that the "difficulties in new shipbuilding result from a world-wide structural imbalance between production capacity and demand; they are relatively worse for the [EU] industry on account of the competitive weakness of [EU] shipyards in comparison with non-European competitors". More thoroughly, the decline may be attributed to seven principal reasons. First, and foremost, while production facilities in some Member States had been modernised, EU shipbuilding generally was structurally inefficient. Second, there were more yards in the EU than the demand justified. Third, the competitors in Japan were integrated into large multi-sectoral industrial groups which could shelter the yards during bad times. Fourth, wages and social security costs were very high in the EU. Fifth, the decline in the EU fleet meant that more owners placed their orders close to home (i.e. outside the EU) (often because of the availability of grants), and there was a consequential decline in the orders placed at EU shipyards. Sixth, currency

---

16 See Bredima and Tzoannos, op. cit. at fn. 14, p. 111.

17 Newspaper coverage of this issue includes "Yard Crisis to Cost 45,000 EEC Jobs", Lloyd's List, 24 August 1987, p. 1.

18 See Panorama of EC Industry 1989, p. 15-1.

19 See Panorama of EC Industry 1989, p. 15-1.

20 In terms of the vessels actually built in the EU, it is worth noting that they are mainly in the categories of passenger vessels (in particular, ferries) and other non-cargo carrying vessels such as fishing vessels. See Panorama of EC Industry 1989, p. 15-2.

21 See Panorama of EC Industry 1989, p. 15-1.

22 Commission of the European Communities, Report on the State of the Shipbuilding Industry in the Community, COM(80)443 final.

23 See Panorama of EC Industry 1989, p. 15-1.

24 9 December 1977, Bull EC, Supp. 7/77, para. 1, footnote omitted.

movements played their part to make the EU yards less attractive. Seventh, smaller scale production in the EU was not as efficient as the South-East Asian competitors. On 12 May 1976, the EU Member States, as well as Norway, Sweden, Finland, Spain, Portugal[25] and Japan, signed, under the auspices of the Organisation for Economic Co-operation and Development ("OECD"), the so-called "General Guidelines for Government Policies in the Shipbuilding Industry".[26] This agreement was designed to restore, in the medium term, the balance between supply and demand.

22.013 The EU sought to intervene and solve the problems facing shipbuilding more generally; Bredima-Savopoulou and Tzoannos commented in 1981:

> "The Commission's intervention with respect to the problems of shipbuilding has three dimensions: (a) it attempts to harmonise government subsidies to the shipbuilding sector within the [EU], (b) it has proposed a number of measures at [EU] level which would encourage the shipbuilding industry to undertake the necessary structural changes in order to become competitive in the world market, whilst at the same time boosting demand in order to alleviate the social consequences of the crisis and (c) it has taken action at international level to induce other countries, especially Japan, to try and reduce shipbuilding overcapacity."

22.014 Individual EU Member States responded in a number of ways to the crisis in shipbuilding. First, some enlarged their navies and directed State shipping companies to place orders at home as opposed to foreign shipyards. Individual shipyards responded by banning overtime, introducing short-time working, reducing working hours and curbing new recruitment. In Italy, the State-owned shipping group, Finmare, had to place its orders for new ships with the state-owned shipbuilding group, Fincantieri. In Portugal, new ships to be built by Portuguese companies had to be built in Portuguese yards. As a general rule, shipyards in Member States rely quite heavily on orders from shipping companies in their own Member State.[27] Second, some Member States gave aid either to their shipyards (to subsidise prices), or shipping companies (to subsidise costs) or both. The aid given was huge but perhaps not very effective – it often kept yards open which ought to have been closed. Third, individual yards made staff redundant and restricted recruitment. Such nationalistic approaches could only go so far in attempting to solve an international crisis. There was need for action by the world shipbuilding community generally. There was a need to avoid individualist protectionist measures and therefore an EU-wide response was needed. This programme has been adopted (but amended from time to time) and the EU shipbuilding sector has fought back by concentrating, in many ways, on technologically intensive ships and high value ships (e.g. cruise ships and container vessels). Many believe that the future of EU shipyards lies in technologically advanced and high value vessels

22.015 Clearly State aid is very common in the shipbuilding sector but it does not necessarily help to resolve the difficulties of EU shipyards – the Commission has stated that it is "to be feared that uncoordinated measures by individual countries would be ineffective and, because of their protectionist effect, lead only to disruption of competition and a partitioning of the market".[28] It is submitted that the Commission's view is correct in so far as it relates to State aid which distorts competition. Nonetheless, it would be

---

25 Sweden, Finland, Spain and Portugal were not then EU Member States.
26 See below.
27 Bredima-Savopoulou and Tzoannos, op. cit. at fn. 14, p. 58.
28 COM(76)224 final, p. 9. The Commission could have added "and prolongation of the problems".

impossible to outlaw aid completely[29] – as the Preamble to the Seventh Shipbuilding Directive[30] states: "a complete abolition of aid to the sector is still not possible in view of the present market situation and in view of the need to encourage restructuring in many yards." So long as other States elsewhere in the world (i.e. non-EU Member States) are providing State aid, there will be a demand by EU shipyards and the shipping sector for aid. Indeed, it may never be quite possible to outlaw State aid entirely in this sector because it may be desirable in certain circumstances (e.g. the development of experimental or new ships which would be safer and less damaging to the environment). Nonetheless the Council continued in the same Preamble to the Seventh Shipbuilding Directive:

> "a tight and selective aid policy should be continued in order to support the present trend in production towards more technologically-advanced ships and in order to ensure fair and uniform conditions for intra-Community competition ... [and] such a policy constitutes the most appropriate approach in terms of ensuring the maintenance of a sufficient level of activity in European shipyards and, thereby, the survival of an efficient and competitive European shipbuilding industry".[31]

22.016 The Commission in its *First Report on Competition Policy*[32] stated:

> "168. Shipbuilding is one of the few industries to benefit from production aid throughout the world.
> This has led to a genuine 'aid rush' during the period 1969–1970 for which there are several reasons.
> As against other industries, shipbuilding cannot be protected by conventional commercial policy measures (customs duties and quantitative restrictions) without prejudicing shipbuilders who carry out their business on markets where competition is extremely active. The export of ships, therefore, also involves the export of certain manufactured products which are incorporated in the ships and which could, as such, not easily be exported without encountering certain obstacles, especially customs duties. Fostering an increase in tonnage by lowering prices of ships and maintaining freight prices at a low level could also be to the advantage of economies which are largely dependent upon seagoing trade.
> Thus, thanks to aid, some non-[EU] member countries have been able to build up an important, and in one particular case, a dominating position on the world market. This situation could not be ignored by the traditional shipbuilding countries of Western Europe, because of the regional and social considerations arising from the location of a number of shipyards. Their reactions were also motivated by shipping and industrial policy considerations, since shipbuilding, being essentially an assembly industry, considerably influences the economy as a whole.
> It would have been better to normalise the competition conditions on a world-wide basis rather than to adopt national protection measures which are bound to foster outbidding in the matter of aid. This was done within the OECD, which groups the world's main shipbuilding countries, but the effective results of this work have only started to show themselves in 1971. In the meantime, measures had to be taken in Europe, and in the [EU] in particular, both at national and at [EU] levels. Since 1972, to aid traditionally granted in France and Italy was added aid granted in Germany, followed by aid granted in the Netherlands and in Belgium from 1967 onwards.[33]
> For its part, the Commission submitted to the Council [of Ministers], in 1965, a draft directive concerning the granting of aid to shipbuilding with a view to correcting distortions of

---

29 The Council of Ministers stated in the Preamble to the Third Shipbuilding Directive (Dir. 75/432): "aid to shipbuilding should not ... adversely affect trading conditions to an extent contrary to the common interest".
30 Council Directive 90/684 of 21 December 1990 on aid to shipbuilding, OJ 1990 L380/27, recital 9.
31 Council Directive 90/684 of 21 December 1990 on aid to shipbuilding, OJ 1990 L380/27, recital 9.
32 1972.
33 This demonstrates the so-called "aid race" which can start once one state provides aid.

competition on the international shipbuilding market. The directive was only adopted by the Council in July 1969."[34]

22.017 A State's policy on shipbuilding can often (but not always) be directly linked to the State's policy on shipping generally[35] – thus, for example, a State wishing to foster and maintain its shipping fleet could well decide to also support its shipbuilding industry and, conversely, a State wishing to bolster its shipbuilding industry could well decide to oblige or incentivise its shipping companies to build a portion of their ships in home yards and even provide aid to facilitate this protectionism. However, irrespective of the correlation between shipping and shipbuilding, it is clear that shipbuilding is an important industry in its own right because, for example, it can represent a source of export revenue and facilitate the development of technology in other areas of the economy (e.g. engineering).

22.018 The shipbuilding sector has certain characteristics worldwide. It is a very cyclical sector. Its fortunes depend on demand for ships which is in turn dependent on various factors such as economic conditions generally (e.g. the levels of trade influence the level of demand for shipping services), market sentiment, changes in trade patterns, changes in technology and currency fluctuations. The industry is capital intensive. It is not a market where one can move easily in and out of (i.e. there are significant barriers to entry, expansion and exit) so there is relative inflexibility in terms of capacity. It is also an industry where a relatively small number of yards are capable of competing for some of the higher specification work – indeed the EU is probably the most competitive zone in the world for higher specification shipbuilding (e.g. liners and specialist ships). The sector is also characterised by the fact that its output is often highly specific and not always easy to sell elsewhere. Today, the situation is not much more optimistic; for example, writing in 2017, the Shipyards' & Maritime Equipment Association was quite pessimistic and observed that 2016 was the worst year in 20 years in terms of global order intake and while demand for passenger ships (mainly cruise liners) had doubled year on year, the demand for tankers, containerships and bulkers had plunged. It also recalled that China was the biggest contractor with 215 vessels accounting for 3.3 million cgt with Europe second with 2.7 million cgt followed by Korea (2 million cgt) and Japan (1.5 million cgt). Interestingly, European contracts accounted for 52% of the total value of new orders – worth €18 billion – with growth shown in passenger ships in particular.

22.019 It is useful to take a historical perspective to put the challenges into context. The reasons for the downturn change over time but some constant themes remained. The Seventh Commission report to the Council on the situation in world shipbuilding[36] stated:

"The countries or regions with the largest market shares in this sector are Japan, South Korea, China and the European Union. The sector is currently reeling from a deep crisis caused by three factors: past over-ordering, the global economic slowdown – and particularly the US slowdown – and the repercussions of September 11. Order intake worldwide fell by 12.3% from 2001 to 2002, following a decrease of 20.7% between 2000 and 2001. European shipyards have, however, been the worst affected by this slump, with orders generally down 50% on 2001 and by over 70% compared to 2000. The hardest hit vessels are container ships and cruise ships. Only

---

34 This was the first Shipbuilding Directive, OJ 1969 L206/25.

35 It could also be linked to a policy such as one on technology, regional development, employment or industry.

36 COM (2003) 232 final – not published in the Official Journal.

oil product tankers and bulk carriers have seen increased ordering, due to the replacement of old tonnage following new European Union maritime safety regulations and strong domestic demand in the Far East. The main shipbuilding regions have, however, been affected in different ways: Japanese yards have the advantage of strong domestic demand, especially for bulk carriers; South Korea and China are battling for tanker contracts; and the European Union is only really active in the ferries and small tankers segment, where replacement needs are building up, although it is possible that Korean shipbuilders might try to further penetrate this market segment. Prices: the statistics show that some categories of vessel are particularly affected by a major drop in market prices. Large container ships have seen their sales prices fall as a result of excessive price-cutting by Korean yards. The trend has been such that production costs have not always been covered. This is all the more surprising as the current weakness of the US dollar against the euro, won and yen should have led to an across-the-board increase in US dollar prices. Studies have also been carried out to investigate the relationship between the normal price, which is the full cost of production plus a profit margin of 5%, and the actual contract price charged by certain Korean shipyards. Given that production costs have risen in recent years, the gap between contract prices and normal prices has widened further. The studies are based on an analysis of several Korean yards and have revealed that the difference between the normal price and the contract price ranges from between –1% and –39%. All these results indicate a clear trend: Korean shipyards are trying to grab every order that appears in the market no matter the cost, despite assertions made to the contrary by the management of the different Korean groups. This strategy could be damaging if Korean yards fail to take certain factors into consideration, such as inflation and debt servicing, and major financial difficulties could ensue in the short term."

Earlier, the Sixth Commission report to the Council on the situation in world shipbuilding[37] stated:

"the crisis in world shipbuilding is deepening with very slow order intake in the major shipbuilding regions in the first six months of 2002. The main reasons are past over-supply, slowing economies around the world and the effects of 11 September. Only Japanese yards still manage to fill building slots. However, this is helped a lot by domestic demand, in particular for bulk carriers, as has been long-standing practice in this region. World-wide ordering of new ships in the first half of 2002 was down by almost two thirds compared to average quarterly figures in 2000, which was admittedly the best year ever for shipbuilding. In the EU the situation is even worse, with ordering down by almost 80% compared to 2000. Prices for new ships have declined further and are now at the lowest level for more than a decade. Yards in South Korea have further lowered offer prices despite increases in all major cost factors, and a number of Korean yards may find it difficult to meet their financial obligations if order intake is not increased soon."

The Fifth Commission report to the Council on the situation in world shipbuilding[38] was also bleak:

"the world shipbuilding market continues to face serious difficulties due to a substantial imbalance of supply and demand. Past expansion of shipyards, mainly in Korea, but now increasingly also in China, has led to price depression. Thanks to a historically high level of ordering in 2000, prices recovered to some extent, but the significant drop in orders in 2001 has led to a new reduction in prices. The year 2001 has been very problematic for the maritime industries worldwide: the recession in the United States and the terrorist attacks of 11 September have reduced the demand for sea trade and cruises respectively. The decline in ordering affected the container ship and cruise ship sectors most, leading to a drop in overall market shares for Korea and the EU, which are particularly strong in these segments. The detailed cost investigations undertaken by the Commission show that certain Korean yards continue to price ships below cost while others

---

37 COM (2002) 622 final – not published in the Official Journal.
38 COM (2002) 205 final – not published in the Official Journal.

are trying to improve their bottom line. Despite various rounds of talks with Korea, the Commission did not manage to convince the Korean authorities and yards to fully implement market principles and allow a shake-out of non-viable companies. An improvement in the market situation is therefore unlikely and the Commission has consequently proposed counter-measures to the Council, including preparing the ground for requesting a dispute settlement at the World Trade Organisation and the introduction of a temporary defensive mechanism for shipbuilding."

And similar observations were made in the Fourth Commission report to the Council on the situation in world shipbuilding,[39] Third Commission report on the situation in world shipbuilding,[40] Second Commission report on the situation in world shipbuilding[41] and First Commission report on the situation in world shipbuilding.[42]

EU's legislative competence in regard to shipbuilding

22.020 The EU's legislative competence in regard to shipbuilding is derived from the Treaty on the Functioning of the European Union ("TFEU") and various provisions in the Treaty and elsewhere. In particular, it has competence by virtue of the Treaty provisions on State aid (i.e. Article 107 of the TFEU), the Common Commercial Policy (i.e. Article 207 of the TFEU) and the EU's Industrial Policy (i.e. Article 173 of the TFEU).

22.021 This web of rules is somewhat entangled. For example, various forms of aid (chiefly from the European Regional Development Fund ("ERDF") and the European Social Fund) have been granted for the development of the regions and the retraining of workers affected by the crisis in the shipbuilding industry.

EU's aims in regard to shipbuilding

22.022 The EU's aims in regard to shipbuilding have been described by the European Parliament in the following terms:

"The EU is seeking to rationalize the shipbuilding industry by means of a controlled cut-back in capacity (a quantitative adjustment). While the workers made redundant should be retrained, the EU should obviously maintain some reserve capacity for strategic,[43] social, economic and industrial reasons. Assistance for existing shipyards should concentrate on modernizing and diversifying production machinery and on improving productivity and competitiveness (a qualitative adjustment)."[44]

22.023 The European Commission made the following interesting observations on the issue in 2006:

"Shipyards provide a good case study of how a traditional European maritime sector is facing up to increasing pressures of global competition, most notably from Asia. In the last decade, European shipbuilding has lost 36% of its jobs but gained 43% in productivity. This has resulted in a sector that is specialised in the production of sophisticated vessels. Ships produced in Europe are outstanding in terms of complexity, safety and environmental impact, often well beyond regulatory requirements. The EU shipbuilding industry (including yards and equipment

---

39 COM (2001) 219 final – not published in the Official Journal.
40 COM (2000) 730 final – not published in the Official Journal.
41 COM (2000) 263 final – not published in the Official Journal.
42 COM (1999) 474 final – not published in the Official Journal.
43 Ed., presumably this also includes a military dimension.
44 European Parliament Fact Sheet 4.7.3.

manufacturers) continues to be the technological world leader, with all major innovations coming from Europe. As a result, EU industry has a much higher turnover than the equivalent sectors in the Far East, despite the smaller volume of tonnage produced.

European shipbuilders and their suppliers, lead in market segments such as cruise and passenger ships, small merchant ships, naval vessels and specialised tonnage. Europe has a strong position in leisure boats and equipment, a highly competitive sector because of its modern and advanced production engineering. Innovation in these sectors is driven by societal demands for cleaner coasts as well as by evolving regulations.

Sound policy and programmes can boost competitiveness, as shown by LeaderSHIP 2015,[45] addressing the future competitiveness of the shipbuilding and ship-repair sector.

This is a co-operative effort based on cutting edge knowledge, entrepreneurship, innovation and stakeholder participation. The Commission believes that this example can be replicated more broadly. In a number of maritime sectors, such as shipping, shipbuilding and offshore energy, the introduction of new technology to ensure environmental sustainability of their activities creates business and export opportunities, notably as other countries move in the direction of sustainable development."[46]

Historical evolution of EU shipbuilding measures

22.024 Before considering the current position, it is useful to review the historical evolution – more detail is available in previous editions of this work. The EU has sought to reduce or limit State aid in progressive steps over time and by virtue of a series of directives. For example, in 1969, the EU adopted a directive to limit aid granted by the Member States to shipyards to a certain percentage of the value of new tonnage. This was the directive of 28 July 1969. The First Shipbuilding Directive, Directive 69/262EC,[47] provided that aid should be no more than 10% of the price contractually fixed before the beginning of the works, for the purchase of new vessels or for "works of transformation". Ten per cent was chosen because this was estimated to be the level of harm suffered by EU shipyards as a result of the distortion of competition in the world market.[48] The Second Shipbuilding Directive, Directive 72/273,[49] reduced the maximum permissible aid. The ceiling was lowered to 5% of the contract price in 1972 and 4% in 1973. The Third Shipbuilding Directive, Directive 75/432,[50] was adopted on 10 July 1975. It was due to apply until 31 December 1977.[51] Some of these measures contemplate, what seem now, quaint vessel sizes (e.g. 150grt). The Fourth Shipbuilding Directive, Directive 78/338,[52] was adopted on 4 April 1978. The legal bases for the directive were the then Articles 92(3)(d) and 113 of the then EEC Treaty. The plight of the EU's shipbuilding industry is obvious from one of the recitals of that directive which (like other directives) read:

> "the position of shipbuilding has considerably worsened during the last few years; whereas [EU] shipyards face a general fall in demand and acute price competition on a contracted world market; whereas the result of this has been a serious reduction in orders, aggravating the structural problems of the industry and indeed threatening its existence".

---

45 http://ec.europa.eu/enterprise/maritime/maritime_industrial/leadership_2015.htm.
46 Commission, Towards a Future Maritime Policy for the Union: A European Vision for the Oceans and Seas (2006), p. 10 (some footnotes omitted).
47 OJ 1969 L206/25.
48 First Report on Competition Policy, 1972, para. 168.
49 OJ 1972 L169/28.
50 OJ 1975 L192/27.
51 Dir. 75/432, Art. 9.
52 OJ 1978 L98/19.

In 1978, the Council of Ministers adopted a resolution stressing the need to maintain within the EU a competitive and healthy shipbuilding industry.[53] The resolution also stressed the need to make qualitative and quantitative adjustments to the shipbuilding sector. Directive 81/363 later summarised the resolution as stressing "the need to maintain within the EU a healthy and competitive shipbuilding industry whose scale of activity should be consistent with the size of the EU's seaborne trade and respect its economic, social and strategic importance".[54] The 1978 Council Resolution[55] led to the Commission proposing a scheme to promote the scrapping and building of new ships of new vessels in EU yards. This proposal was embodied in a communication from the Commission to the Council on a Scheme to Promote the Scrapping and Building of Ocean-Going Ships.[56] All to little avail. On 28 April 1981 the Fifth Shipbuilding Directive, Directive 81/363,[57] was adopted. On 26 January 1987, the Council of Ministers adopted the Sixth Shipbuilding Directive, Directive 86/167. In December 1990, the Council adopted the Seventh Directive (Directive 90/684) on state aid to the shipbuilding sector for a three-year period. On 16 December 1994, the Seventh Directive on aid to shipbuilding was extended. The European Parliament wanted the directive to remain in force until the situation became clearer internationally. The Seventh Shipbuilding Directive, Directive 90/684,[58] was adopted by the Council on 21 December 1990. It was rendered necessary by the fact that the Sixth Shipbuilding Directive, Directive 87/167 of 26 January 1987, was due to expire on 31 December 1990.[59] One of its purposes is to

"ensure fair competition at an international level among shipyards through a balanced and equitable elimination of all existing impediments to normal competition conditions and must provide a suitable instrument for counteracting all illegal practices and forms of assistance inconsistent with the agreement".[60]

The litany of measures was matched by the decline in the fortunes of the sector. The measures did not cause the decline but they could only arrest the decline to some extent. What was needed – but was elusive – was a global settlement of the issue.

B. THE OECD DIMENSION

22.025 It is impossible to understand contemporary EU shipbuilding law without understanding the role of the OECD.

22.026 An important characteristic of the shipbuilding sector, as is clear from the foregoing discussion, is the very high level of government subsidies to the sector worldwide.[61] It has not been possible for States to agree globally on how to control or end such

---

53 OJ 1978 C229/1.
54 Dir. 81/363, recital 3.
55 See above.
56 Bulletin of the European Communities, Supp. 7/79.
57 OJ 1981 L137/39.
58 OJ 1990 L380/27.
59 See Dir. 90/684, Recital 1.
60 Dir. 90/684, Recital 6.
61 Such subsidies exist because, for example, the costs are very high, the market is cyclical and so shipbuilding companies often turn to the deep pockets of States to support them, States sometimes see a military or defensive reason to maintain shipbuilding capacity in their countries and also some States see shipbuilding as a flagship industry which assists in terms of the development of technology in their States.

subsidies. For many years, the main shipbuilding nations have been trying to reach an agreement in the framework of the OECD on conditions for fair competition in the shipbuilding sector. However, these negotiations have often proved difficult.

22.027 On 17 July 1994, the EU, Japan, South Korea, Norway and the USA reached agreement on the ending of aid to the shipbuilding industry. This agreement was concluded within the confines of the OECD. The agreement was aimed at eliminating all existing measures or practices which constitute obstacles to normal competitive conditions, namely direct and indirect support, anti-competitive regulations and unfair practices. This so-called "OECD Agreement" was due to enter into force on 1 January 1996, but did not do so, because the USA had not ratified it[62] so it is still not in force. The OECD has helpfully summarised the background in the following terms:

"I. Background

1. In December 1994, the Commission of the European Communities, and the Governments of Finland, Japan, the Republic of Korea, Norway, Sweden and the United States signed the Final Act of the 'Agreement Respecting Normal Competitive Conditions in the Commercial Shipbuilding and Repair Industry'. The Agreement was scheduled to enter into force on 15 July 1996 after all Parties to it had concluded their national ratification procedures. However, the United States has still not ratified the Agreement, and as a consequence, the Agreement is not yet in force. The goal of the Agreement is to establish, in a legally binding manner, normal, i.e subsidy and dumping-free, competitive conditions in the shipbuilding industries of OECD countries. In this way, it will provide a 'level playing field' for nearly 80 per cent of the world shipbuilding industry.

2. The negotiations on the Agreement were launched by the US Government in the autumn of 1989, in the framework of the OECD Council Working Party on Shipbuilding. The intention of the US Government was to create a new discipline for all government support to shipbuilding. For its part, the European Commission proposed that 'unfair pricing' or dumping practices – later called 'injurious pricing' in the Agreement – also be covered. Government support and private dumping practices are thus the two targets of the Agreement. To ensure effectiveness, the Agreement was intended from the beginning of the negotiations to be legally binding, with provisions for dispute settlement, 'remedies' to be applied in case of violation, and 'sanctions' to enforce implementation of the remedies.

3. The Agreement can be seen as a response to some important features of shipbuilding, namely a strong tendency for governments to assist their industries, and a pronounced cyclicality of shipbuilding activity which induces companies in bad times to engage in the shipbuilding equivalent of price dumping, resulting in distortion of competition among countries and shipbuilding companies alike. These problems have existed for a long time and severe crises, such as in the 1970s and 1980s, have made them particularly apparent, prompting OECD governments to develop policy responses for one of the causes of distortion of competition, namely subsidies: an General Guidelines for Government Policies in the Shipbuilding Industry (first negotiated in 1969), a General Guidelines for Government Policies in the Shipbuilding Industry (1972), and General Guidelines for Government Policies in the Shipbuilding Industry (1976) were concluded over the years. But their effectiveness was limited because of their non-binding nature.

4. Much hope was placed in the Agreement Respecting Normal Competitive Conditions in the Commercial Shipbuilding and Repair Industry because of its legally binding character, because it deals with all kinds of State support – direct and indirect – and, moreover, because it also covers dumping practices of shipyards – which had been considered by some countries to be a problem that warranted the provision of offsetting subsidies. With an initial

---

62 See Bryceland, "State Aids and the Shipbuilding Industry" (1997) 3(4) International Transport Law Review 115.

coverage of about 80 per cent of the world shipbuilding market, the Agreement was expected to have a gravitational effect on other shipbuilding countries to accede to it once in force, thereby extending the area of fair competition beyond its initial boundaries (major other countries are Brazil, China, Russia and Ukraine)."[63]

22.028 The OECD then went on to describe the main elements of the agreement:

"Government Support

5. The Agreement sets a stringent discipline for government support to the shipbuilding industry, whether it is provided directly to the shipbuilder or indirectly through shipowners or other parties. The Agreement details, comprehensively, the kinds of support that would be prohibited in the future. This includes financial support as well as administrative regulations in favour of the domestic shipbuilding industry. In practice, direct subsidies, loans and guarantees are the most important types of support. However, the Agreement also prohibits other types, such as forgiveness of debts, provision of equity capital not consistent with usual investment practices, assistance to suppliers of goods and services, and others...

6. In order to prevent 'last minute' support from being given, there was an understanding among the Participants to the Agreement that they would not, from the signing of the Final Act (i.e. December 1994), increase the subsidy level of existing support measures or introduce new measures, pending entry into force of the Agreement. In the same spirit, all support, or undertaking to provide support, with regard to vessels that were to be delivered after 1998, was forbidden.

7. Although the catalogue of prohibited government support is comprehensive and detailed, not all government support to the shipbuilding industry would be banned under the Agreement. There were five exceptions, four of which were to be permanent. First, officially supported export credits would continue to be permitted on condition that they respect the provisions of the Understanding on Export Credits for Ships which severely limits any concessional element. This Understanding, which has existed since 1969, was revised in the context of the negotiations on the Agreement and was to become effective in its revised form upon the entry into force of the Agreement (but of course, this has not yet happened). Its main new provisions were the commercial interest reference rates (replacing the hitherto fixed interest rate of 8 per cent), the repayment period of 12 years (extended from previously 8½ years) to take account of the reality in ship financing, and the prohibition of aid credits for vessels that are commercially viable. This was in line with the 1992 revision of the OECD Arrangement on Guidelines for Officially Supported Export Credits.

8. Second, 'home credits', that is, government assisted loans and guarantees to domestic buyers of ships, intended for the modernisation of the domestic fleet would be allowed, subject to a stringent discipline. Such credits could be given only if they met specific conditions which are principally that they are no more 'concessional' than permitted for export credits – the logic being to treat domestic and foreign buyers of ships in an equal manner.

9. The third and fourth exceptions were support for research and development and for shipbuilding workers losing their employment. R&D and new technologies are increasingly playing a pivotal role in the shipbuilding industry, both in the development of high performance ships and in ship construction itself. Government support for R&D activities would therefore be permitted generously, but in descending order of intensity the closer the activity is to the market. In addition, R&D undertaken by small and medium sized ship yards as well as R&D related to safety and the environment could benefit from higher than 'normal' rates. The social dimension of the Agreement was reflected by provisions that permit support to be provided to workers who lose their employment or retirement benefits. Finally, the shipyard restructuring that was underway in some countries (Korea, Belgium, Portugal and Spain) was permitted to continue as planned at the time when the Agreement was concluded, but no new restructuring programmes could be permitted.

---

63 www.oecd.org/industry/industryandglobalisation/shipbuildingagreement-overview.htm.

10. A special feature of the Agreement was the treatment of the 'Jones Act' of the United States.[64] As an exception from the prohibition of official regulations and practices which favour the domestic shipbuilding industry, the United States retained the domestic build provision of some of its laws. However, this exception was to be subject to transparency and possible sanctions for abuse.

11. To ensure effectiveness of the Agreement, a binding dispute settlement and enforcement mechanism was devised to deal with violations of the discipline on Government support. In such a case, and if violation was confirmed by the binding judgement of an independent international panel, the illegal support measure would have to be eliminated and the illegal benefit paid back, with interest, by the shipbuilder who received it ('remedy'). Should the government not terminate the support, or the shipbuilder did not pay back the illegal benefit, 'sanctions' could be authorised. They could take two forms: the suspension by the party (or parties) adversely affected by the illegal benefit, of GATT concessions related to products associated with shipbuilding, and/or the denial to the illegally subsidised shipbuilder of the right to complain about dumping (injurious pricing) by other shipbuilders.

Injurious Pricing

12. The Injurious Pricing Code of the Agreement would make anti-dumping applicable to shipbuilding for the first time. The Code condemns injurious pricing (export sales of ships below normal value) if it causes or threatens injury to an established shipbuilding industry or retards the establishment of a domestic industry of another Party. It is based on the Anti Dumping Code of GATT 1994 and adjusts it to the particularities of shipbuilding. These are mainly the fact that ships are not normally imported for sale – and thus escape the GATT anti-dumping mechanism which is enforced through anti-dumping duties on imported goods – and the non-series production of ships.

13. If the shipbuilding industry in one Party to the Agreement claims to have been injured by the sale to a buyer within that country of a ship from another Party, at a price below that which it should normally command, the investigating authorities of the first may determine whether injurious pricing has indeed occurred. They would apply a multi-step approach: first, they would determine whether their industry had had a sufficient prospect of making the sale and whether it had met other criteria to be eligible to complain ('initiation'); second, they would determine the existence of injurious pricing (determination of injurious pricing') and the impact of the sale below normal value on the domestic industry (determination of injury).

14. As a rule, the provisions of the Injurious Pricing Code of the Agreement regarding the determination of injurious pricing and of injury would follow closely the Anti Dumping Code of GATT 1994. For example, in determining injurious pricing, the investigating authorities would compare the export price of the vessel in question with (1) the domestic price of the like vessel, or (2) the export price of a like vessel to a third country, or (3) the cost of production plus normal profit in the exporting country. In the examination of the impact on the domestic industry, i.e. the determination of injury, the investigating authorities would evaluate all relevant economic factors having a bearing on the state of the industry; this would include actual and potential decline in sales, profits, output, market share, productivity, return on investments, or utilisation of capacity; factors affecting domestic prices; the magnitude of the margin of injurious pricing; actual and potential negative effects on cash flow, inventories, employment, wages, growth, ability to raise capital or investments.

15. If the investigating authorities have to confirm injurious pricing and impose a levy upon the vessel in question, this 'injurious pricing charge' would have to be paid by the exporting shipbuilder – in contrast to the provisions in the GATT Anti Dumping Code, where the charge would be paid by the importer in the form of extra import duties. The shipbuilder would have to pay the charge within 180 days or later if payment within that period would render it insolvent. But the shipbuilder would have the option to void the sale in question or to comply with an alternative remedy.

---

64 Ed., this was a protectionist measure in US maritime law.

16. As in the case of illegally received Government support, 'sanctions' are foreseen if the ship-builder does not pay the injurious pricing charge (or void the sale, or comply with an altern-ative remedy). These are severe: the country that has investigated the injurious pricing case may, on its own initiative, deny onloading and offloading privileges for a maximum period of four years after delivery to certain vessels built by that shipbuilder (i.e. vessels contracted for during a period of four years after public notice). Because of the requirement of prior public notice this would discipline the shipbuilder via the threat of losing orders, but it would not injure innocent shipbuyers. A panel could extend or limit this countermeasure."[65]

22.029 The OECD then considered the outlook or future:

"17. When (and if) the Agreement enters into force, its functioning would be subject to close supervision through a 'Parties Group'. There would be regular consultations and permanent transparency on matters such as ship prices, provision of permitted assistance, and others. The procedures foreseen for dealing with violations, whether in the area of government support or of injurious pricing, are such that a balance between all parties would be assured and that there would always be the possibility of recourse to the Panel or the Parties Group in case of differences of views. Three years after the Agreement enters into force, a major review is foreseen to examine the experience to that date.

18. There is the expectation that if the Agreement were to come into force, it would have a sus-tained positive impact on the world shipbuilding market by repressing government support which has been a serious problem for years, and by punishing dumping practices that were judged to be damaging other shipbuilders. Non-availability of government support and the prosecution of injurious pricing would bring to light the economic advantages of the various countries and the true competitivity of individual shipbuilders.

19. Shipowners, for their part, would be confronted with a situation where ships are no longer available at subsidised or dumped prices. They may consequently change their expectation as to the profits they can make with a vessel, especially from speculative buying and selling of ships. Changed ordering behaviour for ships may, in turn, therefore contribute to stabil-ising the shipbuilding market and thus contribute to establishing normal competitive con-ditions in the shipbuilding industry."[66]

Pending the implementation of this OECD Agreement, the Council adopted Regulation 1540/98 of 29 June 1998.[67]

OECD Agreement

22.030 The actual 53-page agreement itself is too long to analyse here (and it is an OECD rather than an EU document) but Article 1 of the "Agreement Respecting Normal Competitive Conditions in the Commercial Shipbuilding and Repair Industry" sets out the essence of the agreement very neatly:

"Article 1
Restoration and Maintenance of Normal Competitive Conditions

1. The Parties shall, in accordance with the specific provisions set out in Annex II, eliminate all existing measures or practices which are inconsistent with normal competitive conditions in the commercial shipbuilding and repair industry pursuant to Annex I (hereafter referred to as 'measures of support').

2. The Parties shall not introduce any new measures of support.

---

65 www.oecd.org/industry/industryandglobalisation/shipbuildingagreement-overview.htm.
66 www.oecd.org/industry/industryandglobalisation/shipbuildingagreement-overview.htm.
67 OJ 1998 L202/1.

3. The Parties recognise that the sale of commercial ships at less than their normal value is to be condemned if it causes or threatens material injury to an established shipbuilding and repair industry in the territory of another Party, or materially retards the establishment of a domestic shipbuilding and repair industry. In order to remedy or prevent such injurious pricing, Annex III is applicable."

EU reaction

22.031 At the EU level, Regulation 3094/95[68] was adopted as a result of the 1994 OECD Agreement concluded in 1994 within the framework of the OECD. This regulation has now been replaced by Regulation 2016/1035[69] which is examined below.

C. COUNCIL RESOLUTION OF 19 SEPTEMBER 1978 ON THE REORGANISATION OF THE SHIPBUILDING INDUSTRY

22.032 On 19 September 1978, the Council adopted a resolution on the reorganisation of the shipbuilding industry:

"COUNCIL RESOLUTION of 19 September 1978 on the reorganization of the shipbuilding industry

THE COUNCIL OF THE EUROPEAN COMMUNITIES, – convinced of the need to maintain within the Community a healthy and competitive shipbuilding industry whose scale of activity should be consistent with the size of the Community's maritime trade and respect its economic, social and strategic importance;

- whereas the level of demand for new vessels from Community shipyards in the early 1980s is likely to be considerably lower than the level reached in 1974 and 1975;
- whereas, while the efforts necessary to adjust the quality and quantity of production capacity are first and foremost the responsibility of the industry itself, it is for public authorities in the Community to provide guidance and stimulus;

1. is of the opinion that the necessary structural adjustments should be made which will lead to the maintenance within the Community of a healthy, competitive industry on a scale of activity consistent with the size of the Community's maritime trade and respecting other essential interests of the Community and its Member States, in particular from a social and strategic point of view; such adjustments must take into account medium- and long-term market prospects;
2. urges the industry to continue and suitably intensify its efforts to adapt and restructure production capacity and to diversify its activities;
3. urges the industry to increase its competitiveness by improving management, research and production facilities;
4.1. requests the public authorities responsible at local, national and Community level to support and even, if necessary, to guide the industry's efforts referred to above;
4.2. requests these public authorities to lay particular stress on the creation of new jobs in conjunction with those progressively lost in the shipbuilding industry and urges them to limit the social consequences for those workers affected by a reduction in the industry's activity;
4.3. requests the authorities of the Member States and the Community to take account of all these objectives in their industrial, regional, social and general economic policies and to

---

68 OJ L332/1, 30 December 1995.
69 Art. 17 of Reg. 2016/1035 repealed Reg. 385/96.

make available adequate funds for this purpose in so far as budgetary requirements or other financial constraints permit;

5. considers that the Community must continue its efforts to obtain, through international cooperation, adequate solutions which will ensure that the inevitable reduction in world shipbuilding capacity may be achieved in the least damaging and most equitable way possible;

6.1. notes that the Commission will have medium- and long-term market surveys carried out by suitable organizations and will report to the Council on the outcome of these surveys, at the same time giving its opinion on the necessary structural adaptation of production;

6.2. notes that the Commission will submit proposals for the accompanying social measures at the earliest opportunity;

6.3. notes that certain measures in the field of shipping policy could be of some importance for the shipbuilding industry; therefore requests the Commission to communicate its opinion as to whether and to what extent certain measures might be likely to improve demand for new ships from Community shipyards so that this aspect may be taken into consideration during the preparation of the shipping policies of the Community and of the Member States;

7. notes that the Commission will prepare half-yearly reports on the state of the shipbuilding industry and on the progress made with its reorganization and will submit appropriate proposals as soon as possible."

22.033 This was a simple non-legally binding resolution but this was in tune with the approach at the time when EU shipping law was "finding its feet" by way of resolutions and similar measures which were non-invasive to the Member States. It laid the groundwork for future action by the EU in this area.[70]

22.034 This resolution built on work which had been done in the two previous years.

22.035 On 23 December 1976, the European Parliament's Committee on Economic and Monetary Affairs published its "Interim Report on the Community Shipping Industry".[71] The report recalled in paragraph 37 that the

"shipbuilding industry is extremely important to the [EU], directly employing more than 400,000 people, and also providing work for a further one million or so in various supply industries, whose deliveries of goods or services represent about 60% of shipyard turnover".

The report recorded some examples which would prove instructive:

"A recent report[72] states that 'yards in virtually every major shipbuilding country are now quoting for new orders on terms which contravene the intent, if not the letter, of the Organisation for Economic Cooperation and Development's Understanding on Export Credits'. A case is cited of a West German shipyard indicating to Egyptian officials seeking to order ships that the 30% down payment (which the understanding requires to be paid in the pre-delivery period) could be provided in the form of capital aid made available by the German government for development projects.

The Budgets Committee of the Bundestag voted at the beginning of April,[73] 'to lift a restriction which had barred German shipowners placing orders with German yards from claiming both interest rate subsidies under the country's shipyard aid scheme and direct subvention under the shipping line aid fund. It also decided to reduce the subventions that German shipping lines could claim when placing orders abroad'.

---

70 Some of the EU's actions and activity in this area has been to protect, re-train, re-educate and compensate redundant workers from shipyards across the EU which closed.

71 Doc. 479/76, Rapporteur: Mr J. L. Prescott.

72 The Times, London, 26 January 1976.

73 The Times, London, 12 April 1976.

The British Government has decided to extend to home shipowners the insurance inflation scheme which has been available to foreign customers on capital goods. This measure[74] had been delayed by difficulties over gaining approval from the [EU] authorities in Brussels. In response to pressure from the European Commission, this cost escalation scheme will cover goods imported from other Member States for incorporation into ships being built in the United Kingdom. The Commission's requirement of degressivity having also been complied with, the Commission has proposed that the Council should amend its directive 75/432/EEC on aid to shipbuilding to permit this British scheme.[75]

As a final example of increasing aids to shipbuilding, one notes that the West German Transport Ministry announced in April 1976 that the shipbuilding aid programme for the current year would be stepped up (from the [Deutsche Mark ('DM')] 110m originally planned) to DM 170m."

22.036 On 9 December 1977, the Commission sent a communication to the Council of Ministers on the Reorganisation of the Community Shipbuilding Industry.[76] Such an initiative was necessary because the EU's shipbuilding industry was in serious difficulties: there were serious fears for the jobs of many of the 165,000 people then employed in EU shipyards.[77] This communication dealt with three main issues: the problems of EU shipbuilding; the objectives of EU intervention; and EU action. First, it stated that the problems of EU shipbuilding may be expressed in these terms: in 1960, the first nine Member States of the EU represented 50.9% of the world's shipbuilding output; by 1970, this had fallen to 27.8% and, by 1975, it had fallen to 22.3%.[78] The communication recognised that the EU had a shipbuilding crisis[79] and that this crisis was particularly bad for the EU in the light of the competitive weakness of EU shipyards in comparison with non-EU competitors,[80] particularly, the South-East Asian yards. In the communication, the Commission stated that its interest in the problem of shipbuilding has "two aspects", namely:

"– competition: so far [EU] action on the industry has been almost entirely limited to successive directives coordinating aids to shipbuilding. Their main objective was to harmonise public intervention in the sector and reduce the level of those aids most damaging to intra-[EU] competition;
– financial: since its inception, the European Regional Development Fund ('ERDF') has paid out an estimated [€]78.65 million … in regions where there is a high concentration of shipbuilding. The sum covers 225 projects involving a total investment of [€]1,470 million … and the creation or preservation of 34,112 jobs in France, Germany, Italy and in the United Kingdom where, in addition, 111 industrial-infrastructure projects have been aided in the said regions."

And:

"[i]ntervention by the Social Fund to benefit workers in the industry has been modest and the Council did not take up the Commission's proposal for applying Art. 4 of the decision on the use of the Social Fund,[81] submitted in January 1974".[82]

---

74 The Times, London, 9 April 1976.
75 COM(76)321 final, 30 July 1976.
76 Bull. EC, Supp. 7/77.
77 See communication, para. 12.
78 The European Parliament's Committee on Economic and Monetary Affairs published its Interim Report on the Community Shipping Industry, para. 38.
79 Ibid., para. 1.
80 Ibid., para. 1.
81 OJ 1971 L28.
82 OJ 1974 C13.

The communication then identified that the first objective of EU policy on shipbuilding must be to make EU yards competitive in the world market.[83] Thus it wrote in 1977, the EU's

> "attention should be directed chiefly to the new building of seagoing non-naval ships,[84] since this is the segment of the industry in which the structural problem of over-capacity and competitiveness is acute. The other sub-sectors, while less affected by the structural problem, are more sensitive to the short-term economic situation."

Thus, the communication continued, there was a need to reorganise the yards in the EU so that they are competitive in the world market. In the debate on the balance between the interests of the shipping industry and the shipbuilding industry, the Commission declared "[a]s the cost of transport is a very important factor in the [EU's] economy, the Commission does not consider that the interests of the shipping industry should in any way be subordinated to those of shipbuilders".[85] The Commission was of the opinion that there was a need for a quantitative and qualitative adjustment of structures to foreseeable demand. It said that "[q]uantitatively, it will be necessary, in the industry's own interests as well as in the interests of the workers whose jobs in the shipyards will otherwise disappear entirely, to adjust production capacities to market prospects in an orderly fashion" and "[q]ualitatively, moves to adapt production capacities quantitatively must be accompanied by efforts to improve production facilities so that they may survive without aid and become competitive in the world market".[86] It is interesting to note the views of the Commission in relation to employment:

> "13. Once the objective of reorganisation has been defined for the industry, the consequences for employment must be drawn; these will be of two kinds:
>
> – retraining of workers within yards where the latter undertake internal conversion as part of the qualitative adaptation of production facilities;
> – redeployment outside the industry: here the [EU] should bring into play all its resources for creating jobs outside shipbuilding, both within the yards themselves and, more particularly, for those made redundant, every effort being made to site the activities in the same district or region as the affected yards, so that these new activities may benefit from the skills of the workers concerned; this process of creating new jobs must be accompanied by suitable social measures.
>
> In view of an expected level of demand of about 2.4 million cgrt in the early 1980s, the Commission estimates that an effective restructuring operation in this sector could affect approximately 75,000 jobs, 15,000 of which it is estimated will be vacated by natural wastage. If the operation is extended to directly related industries, these would be affected in the same proportion which would make approximately 30,000 persons redundant.
>
> 14. As such results can only be achieved gradually, it will be necessary to continue to resort to holding actions which are essential for the direct or indirect support of employment.
>
> The Commission considers that, if the objective is to be achieved, [EU] action would be acceptable to the general public and to the workers only if it takes full account of the different situations in the industry in each Member State, and the position the industry

---

83 Ibid., para. 10.

84 At this stage it does not seem appropriate to include warships because the building of these highly sophisticated vessels is not affected by the crisis.

85 Communication, para. 10.

86 Communication, para. 11.

occupies in the economy of the Member State or region. Whether this operation will be used to demonstrate the [EU's] solidarity will depend on the political will of the Council."[87]

The communication then mentioned that there was the transfer of a significant proportion of the world fleet to flags of convenience and this "has brought into the shipping market vessels which present both operating hazards (substandard ships) and a threat to the marine environment".[88] The Commission then recorded that international bodies were then "trying to devise means of combating this form of unfair competition. The [EU] should step up the action it is already taking in this direction by taking steps towards the adoption of practical measures in the near future."[89] It went on to suggest that "[c]ertain environmental measures could lead to a partial reduction of the excess capacity in tanker fleets and also appreciably stimulate the conversion of existing tankers"[90] and more

> "stringent safety regulations would remove unfair advantages enjoyed by ships of non-member countries, particularly those registered under flags of convenience, and thus act to the advantage of the shipbuilding industry, either directly (conversions and repairs), or indirectly (ships would be scrapped more quickly, and this would speed up the improvement of the transport market). Such regulations could also limit the trend for our shipowners to register their vessels under flags of convenience."[91]

The Commission then identified certain key courses of action which were indispensable for the successful reorganisation of the EU shipbuilding industry. These indispensable courses of action were:

> "– since (private or public) initiatives in the Member States do not cancel one another out the Commission continues with, and steps up, its measures to make these initiatives less opaque and to co-ordinate them;
> – the intervention concentrates less and less on maintaining hopeless situations and turns increasingly to re-establishing maximum efficiency in the undertakings and, above all, to creating new jobs in other activities;
> – contacts with all the parties concerned are maintained and strengthened; the Commission is already in regular contact with employer, managerial and trade union bodies and these contacts should be intensified; also, to obtain a clearer appreciation of the possibilities of meeting the type likely to face [EU] shipyards, these contacts should be extended to the industrial and trade union organisations concerned with Community shipping;
> – there is greater, permanent concentration between the Community's public authorities under Community auspices and with due regard for the spheres of competence deriving from the … Treaty;
> – [EU] action continues, with appropriate procedures, throughout the crisis situation in the industry."[92]

In terms of reorganising the shipbuilding sector, the Commission believed that reorganisation was contingent upon the determination of a quantitative "indicator" of the level of demand to which the shipbuilding industry's production should be geared – with such an indicator being geared to demand.[93] The topic of shipbuilding aids is a controversial one and the comments of the Commission in the communication deserve repetition in full:

---

87 Communication, p. 10 (footnote omitted).
88 Ibid., para. 15. In some ways, the availability of State aid can reduce the risk of substandard ships being continued in service because owners are able to replace the vessels more easily.
89 Ibid., para. 16.
90 Ibid., para. 16 (footnote omitted).
91 Ibid., para. 16.
92 Ibid., para. 19.
93 Ibid., para. 20.

"In order to avoid the situation whereby national aids granted to undertakings – in the vain hope of a recovery in the near future – divert the recipients' attention from the need to modernise their production facilities – a necessary condition of stability in [EU] shipbuilding – the Commission, in its proposal for a fourth directive, sought to co-ordinate these aids with a view to reorganising the sector in a manner consistent with the quantitative indicator.

With previous directives the [EU] tried to remove those barriers to competition in shipbuilding which were not in the common interest. The directives therefore covered a very wide range of aids affecting the shipbuilding market.

Against the current background of [the] imminent crisis in the industry the Commission has now made proposals specifically geared to enabling the Member States to deal with the situation.[94]

Such measures are, however, acceptable only within limits and only in so far as they do not worsen conditions of competition to an extent prejudicial to the common interest.

Measures of this type must also be in line with the reorganisation objectives, the aim of which is to make the industry competitive and capable of functioning without aid.

The Commission's proposal for a fourth directive, sent to the Council on 4 November 1977, takes abundant account of the industry's structural problems and should therefore not be regarded simply as a legal framework for limiting the granting of aids but as an essential element of an industrial approach.

The proposal also covers Member States' aids to shipowners and provides that such aids may not discriminate against shipyards of other Member States."[95]

22.037 The Commission concluded by calling on the Council of Ministers to set up, in order to permit a better understanding of the shipbuilding sector and its problems at an EU level, a standing body in the form of a committee of senior officials briefed to contribute to the progressive adjustment of production capacities to demand, as far as possible on the basis of national programmes, but taking account of changes in forecast worldwide supply and demand.[96] This Committee would be known as the Shipbuilding Committee and would advise the Council and the Commission as well as contribute towards the co-ordination of national and EU policies.[97] The purpose of the Committee would be, according to the Proposal, to monitor trends in the level of demand and contribute towards organising the adjustment of production capacities to that level and improving production structures.[98]

D. REGULATION 2016/1035 ON PROTECTION AGAINST INJURIOUS PRICING OF VESSELS

Introduction

22.038 The principal measure in EU shipbuilding law is Regulation 2016/1035 – on 8 June 2016, the Parliament and the Council adopted Regulation 2016/1035 on protection against injurious pricing of vessels.[99] It is a codification measure. It was sensible to adopt

---

94 Bull. EC, 10–1977, point 2.1.19.

95 Communication, para. 21.

96 Communication, para. 31. See Proposal for a Council decision setting up a Shipbuilding Committee, annexed to the communication.

97 See Art. 1 of the Proposal for a Council Decision setting up a Shipbuilding Committee, appended to the Reorganisation of the Community Shipbuilding Industry, ibid., at p. 21.

98 See Art. 2 of the Proposal for a Council Decision setting up a Shipbuilding Committee, appended to the Reorganisation of the Community Shipbuilding Industry, ibid., at p. 21.

99 OJ L176/1, 30 June 2016.

it because the previous measure, Council Regulation 385/96 of 29 January 1996 on protection against injurious pricing of vessels,[100] had been amended several times so, as first recital of Regulation 2106/1035 makes plain, in "the interests of clarity and rationality, that Regulation should be codified".

22.039 The legal basis of Regulation 2016/1035 is the TFEU generally and, in particular, Article 207(2) of the regulation. It was adopted in accordance with the ordinary legislative procedure.

22.040 Under Article 18, Regulation 2016/1035 entered into force on the twentieth day following that of its publication in the *Official Journal of the European Union* and it would apply from the date of entry into force of the Shipbuilding Agreement.[101] Article 18 also states, and this is largely historical now, the regulation shall not apply to vessels contracted for before the date of entry into force of the Shipbuilding Agreement, except for vessels contracted for after 21 December 1994 and for delivery more than five years from the date of the contract. Such vessels shall be subject to the regulation, unless the shipbuilder demonstrates that the extended delivery date was for normal commercial reasons and not to avoid the application of this regulation.

22.041 Regulation 2016/1035 is part of the wider dumping regime. This is typified by, for example, Article 15 which provides that the Commission shall include information on the implementation of this regulation in its annual report on the application and implementation of trade defence measures presented to the European Parliament and to the Council pursuant to Article 23 of Regulation 2016/1036.

22.042 Regulation 2016/1035 recalls the multilateral negotiations conducted under the auspices of the OECD which led to the conclusion, on 21 December 1994, of an Agreement Respecting Normal Competitive Conditions in the Commercial Shipbuilding and Repair Industry (the so-called "Shipbuilding Agreement") (which was set out above).

22.043 Under Article 16(1), Regulation 2016/1035 shall not preclude the application of: (a) any special rules laid down in agreements concluded between the Union and third countries; or (b) special measures, provided that such action does not run counter to obligations pursuant to the Shipbuilding Agreement.

22.044 The EU acknowledges in the third to the fifth recitals to Regulation 2016/1035 that the Shipbuilding Agreement recognises the problems of the sector:

"(3) It has been recognised in the framework of the Shipbuilding Agreement that the special characteristics of ship-purchase transactions have made it impractical to apply countervailing and anti-dumping duties, as provided for under Article VI of the General Agreement on Tariffs and Trade, the Agreement on Subsidies and Countervailing Measures, and the Agreement on Implementation of Article VI of the General Agreement on Tariffs and Trade 1994 ('the 1994 Anti-Dumping Agreement') annexed to the Agreement establishing the World Trade Organisation. The need to provide for an effective means of protection against sales of ships below their normal value which cause injury has led to the conclusion of a Shipbuilding Injurious Pricing Code which, together with its Basic Principles, constitutes Annex III to the Shipbuilding Agreement ('the IPI Code').

(4) The text of the IPI Code is mainly based on the 1994 Anti-Dumping Agreement, but deviates from that Agreement when warranted by the specific nature of ship-purchase transactions. Therefore, the language of the IPI Code should be reflected in Union legislation, to

---

100 OJ L56/21, 6 March 1996.
101 The date of entry into force of the Shipbuilding Agreement will be published in the Official Journal of the European Union, L series.

the extent possible on the basis of the text of Regulation (EU) 2016/1036 of the European Parliament and of the Council.[102]

(5) The Shipbuilding Agreement and the legislative provisions deriving therefrom are of significant importance for Union law."

Principles and definitions

22.045 Article 1 ("principles and definitions") sets out the basic rules in the regulation.

22.046 Article 1(1) sets down the simple rule that an "injurious pricing charge may be imposed on the builder of any injuriously priced vessel whose sale to a buyer other than a buyer of the country in which the vessel originates causes injury". This is a proposition which is loaded with meaning and needs to be analysed carefully.

22.047 Article 1(2) goes on to provide that a vessel is to "be considered as being injuriously priced if the export price of the vessel sold is less than a comparable price for a like vessel, in the ordinary course of trade, when sold to a buyer of the exporting country". This is a simple proposition to articulate but much more difficult to define with precision because ships are not like motor cars – there are rarely several vessels which are identical (unlike cars where there are thousands of the same make and model produced) so making a comparison between the particular vessel and a paradigm vessel is more complicated.

22.048 Article 1(3) defines some key elements in Article 1(2) and 1(3) for the purposes of the regulation generally.

22.049 Article 1(3)(a) defines "vessel" as meaning[103] "any self-propelled sea-going vessel of 100 gross tonnes and above, used for transportation of goods or persons or for performance of a specialised service (for example, ice breakers and dredgers) and any tug of 365 kW and above". This would cover almost all conventional vessels.

22.050 One of the practical difficulties is to find a comparator vessel. Article 1(3)(b) defines such a vessel – known in the regulation as a "like vessel" – as meaning "any vessel of the same type, purpose and approximate size as the vessel under consideration and possessing characteristics closely resembling those of the vessel under consideration". This could be a matter of some controversy because many vessels are one of a kind but the comparison exercise must be undertaken nonetheless.

22.051 The fact that there could be a vessel of the same general category is recognised by Article 1(3)(c) which provides that the phrase "same general category of vessel" means "any vessel of the same type and purpose, but of a significantly different size".

22.052 The word "sale" is defined by Article 1(3)(d) as covering "the creation or transfer of an ownership interest in the vessel, except for an ownership interest created or acquired solely for the purpose of providing security for a normal commercial loan".

22.053 The phrase "ownership interest" is defined by Article 1(3)(e) as including (so it is not an exhaustive definition)

"any contractual or proprietary interest which allows the beneficiary or beneficiaries of such interest to take advantage of the operation of the vessel in a manner substantially comparable to the way in which an owner may benefit from the operation of the vessel. In determining whether

---

102 Ed., Reg. 2016/1036 of the European Parliament and of the Council of 8 June 2016 on protection against dumped imports from countries not members of the EU.

103 It is an exhaustive definition but the list of specialised service vessels is not exhaustive.

such substantial comparability exists, the following factors shall be considered, inter alia: (i) the terms and circumstances of the transaction; (ii) commercial practice within the industry; (iii) whether the vessel subject to the transaction is integrated into the operations of the beneficiary or beneficiaries; and (iv) whether in practice there is a likelihood that the beneficiary or beneficiaries of such interests will take advantage of, and the risk for, the operation of the vessel for a significant part of the life-time of the vessel."

22.054 The word "buyer" is defined by Article 1(3)(f) as meaning

"any person who, or any company which, acquires an ownership interest, including by way of lease or long-term bareboat charter, in conjunction with the original transfer from the shipbuilder, either directly or indirectly, including a person who, or company which, owns or controls a buyer, or gives instructions to the buyer. A person or company owns a buyer when it has more than a 50% interest in the buyer. A person or company controls a buyer when the person or company is legally or operationally in a position to exercise restraint or direction over the buyer, which is presumed at a 25% interest. If ownership of a buyer is shown, separate control of it is presumed not to exist unless established otherwise. There may be more than one buyer of any one vessel."

22.055 The word "company" is given its ordinary meaning by Article 1(3)(g) as meaning "any company or firm constituted under civil or commercial law, including cooperative societies, and other legal persons governed by public or private law, including those which are non-profitmaking". It could be seen as being a business or undertaking.

22.056 The phrase "'Contracting Party" means any third country that is party to the Shipbuilding Agreement.

What is "injurious pricing"? How is it determined?

22.057 It is all very well condemning injurious pricing but how does one determine what is injurious pricing? Article 2 of the regulation ("determination of injurious pricing") seeks to provide a methodology to do so.

22.058 Pursuant to Article 2(1), the "normal value" (a term which is undefined in the regulation but the concept is referred to in both the Shipbuilding Agreement and the regulation) shall normally be based on the price paid or payable, in the ordinary course of trade, for a like vessel by an independent buyer in the exporting country. Prices between parties which appear to be associated or to have a compensatory arrangement with each other may not be considered to be in the ordinary course of trade and may not be used to establish the normal value unless it is determined that they are unaffected by the relationship.[104] In this context, it is useful to be aware of Article 2(13) which provides that the injurious pricing margin shall be the amount by which the normal value exceeds the export price and where injurious pricing margins vary, a weighted average injurious pricing margin may be established.

22.059 The more difficult question of what to do when there is no obvious comparator is addressed by Article 2(3):

"when there are no sales of like vessels in the ordinary course of trade, or where, because of the particular market situation, such sales do not permit a proper comparison, the normal value of

---

104 Reg. 2016/1035, Art. 2(2).

the like vessel shall be calculated on the basis of the export price of a like vessel, in the ordinary course of trade, to an appropriate third country, provided that this price is representative. If such sales to any appropriate third country do not exist or do not permit a proper comparison, the normal value of the like vessels shall be calculated on the basis of the cost of production in the country of origin plus a reasonable amount for selling, general and administrative costs and for profits."

This is still somewhat vague.

22.060 Article 2(4) provides that sales of like vessels in the domestic market of the exporting country, or export sales to a third country, at prices below unit production costs (fixed and variable) plus selling, general and administrative costs, may be treated as not being in the ordinary course of trade by reason of price, and may be disregarded in determining the normal value, only if it is determined that such sales are at prices which do not provide for the recovery of all costs within a reasonable period, which should normally be five years.

22.061 Costs are normally calculated on the basis of records kept by the shipbuilder under investigation, provided that such records are in accordance with the generally accepted accounting principles of the country concerned and that it is shown that the records reasonably reflect the costs associated with the production and sale of the vessel under consideration.[105] Consideration shall be given to evidence submitted on the proper allocation of costs, provided that it is shown that such allocations have been historically utilised. In the absence of a more appropriate method, preference shall be given to the allocation of costs on the basis of turnover. Unless already reflected in the cost allocations under this subparagraph, costs shall be adjusted appropriately for those non-recurring items of cost which benefit future and/or current production, or for circumstances in which costs are affected by start-up operations.[106]

22.062 Pursuant to Article 2(6), the amounts for selling, for general and administrative costs and for profits shall be based on actual data pertaining to production and sales, in the ordinary course of trade, of like vessels by the shipbuilder under investigation. When such amounts cannot be determined on that basis, the amounts may be determined on the basis of: (a) the weighted average of the actual amounts determined for other shipbuilders of the country of origin in respect of production and sales of like vessels in that country's domestic market; (b) the actual amounts applicable to production and sales, in the ordinary course of trade, of the same general category of vessels for the shipbuilder in question in the domestic market of the country of origin; and (c) any other reasonable method, provided that the amount for profit so established shall not exceed the profit normally realised by other shipbuilders on sales of vessels of the same general category in the domestic market of the country of origin. Article 2(6) goes on to emphasise that the profit added in constructing value shall, in all instances, be based upon the average profit realised over a reasonable period of time of normally six months both before and after the sale under investigation and shall reflect a reasonable profit at the time of such sale. In making such calculation, any distortion which is demonstrated to result in a profit which is not a reasonable one at the time of the sale shall be eliminated.

---

105 Reg. 2016/1035, Art. 2(5).
106 Ibid.

22.063 As the construction of a vessel can take a number of years from design to delivery, it is not surprising that Article 2(7) provides that

"given the long lead time between contract and delivery of vessels, a normal value shall not include actual costs which the shipbuilder demonstrates are due to *force majeure* and are significantly above the cost increase which the shipbuilder could reasonably have anticipated and taken into account when the material terms of sales were fixed."

This means that aberrations in cost due to *force majeure* can be controlled in the calculation.

22.064 While there are not many non-market economies left in the world, Article 2(8) has sought to control for this issue as well. It provides that in

"the case of sales from non-market-economy countries and, in particular, those to which Regulation … 2015/755 of the European Parliament and of the Council[107] applies, the normal value shall be determined on the basis of the price or constructed value in a market-economy third country, or the price from such a third country to other countries, including the Union, or, where those are not possible, on any other reasonable basis, including the price actually paid or payable in the Union for the like vessel, duly adjusted if necessary to include a reasonable profit margin."

Article 2(8) goes on to provide that an "appropriate market-economy third country shall be selected in a not unreasonable manner, due account being taken of any reliable information made available at the time of selection. Account shall also be taken of time limits" and that the "parties to the investigation shall be informed, shortly after its initiation, of the market-economy third country envisaged and shall be given 10 days to comment". In this context, the export price shall be the price actually paid or payable for the vessel under consideration.[108]

22.065 There will always be exceptions so Article 2(10) provides that in cases where there is no export price or where it appears that the export price is unreliable because of an association or a compensatory arrangement between the shipbuilder and the buyer or a third party, the export price may be constructed on the basis of the price at which the vessel is first resold to an independent buyer, or, if the vessel is not resold to an independent buyer or is not resold in the condition in which it was originally sold, on any reasonable basis. In those cases, adjustment for all costs, including duties and taxes, incurred between the original sale and resale, and for profits accruing, shall be made so as to establish a reliable export price. The items for which adjustment shall be made shall include[109] those normally borne by a buyer but paid by any party, either inside or outside the Union, which appears to be associated or to have a compensatory arrangement with the shipbuilder or buyer, including usual transport, insurance, handling, loading and ancillary costs, customs duties, and other taxes payable in the importing country by reason of the purchase of the vessel, and a reasonable margin for selling, general and administrative costs, and profit.[110]

22.066 Article 2(11) provides that a fair comparison must be made between the export price and the normal value. This comparison shall be made at the same level of trade and

---

107 Ed., Reg. 2015/755 of the European Parliament and of the Council of 29 April 2015 on common rules for imports from certain third countries (OJ L123/15, 19 May 2015).
108 Reg. 2016/1035, Art. 2(9).
109 Note that it is not an exhaustive list.
110 Reg. 2016/1035, Art. 2(10).

in respect of sales made at, as closely as possible, the same time, which will normally mean sales that take place within three months before or after the sale under investigation, or in the absence of such sales, any appropriate period. Due allowance shall be made in each case, on its merits, for differences which affect price comparability, including differences in conditions and terms of sale, contractual penalties, taxation, level of trade, quantities, physical characteristics and any other differences which are also demonstrated to affect price comparability. Where, in cases referred to in paragraph 10, price comparability has been affected, the normal value shall be established at a level of trade equivalent to the level of trade of the constructed export price, or due allowance made, as warranted, under this paragraph. Any duplication when making adjustments shall be avoided, in particular in relation to discounts and contractual penalties. When the price comparison requires a conversion of currencies, such conversion shall be made using the rate of exchange on the date of sale, except that when a sale of foreign currency on forward markets is directly linked to the export sale involved the rate of exchange in the forward sale shall be used. For the purpose of this provision, the date of sale shall be the date on which the material terms of sale are established, normally the date of contract. However, if the material terms of sale are significantly changed on another date, the rate of exchange on the date of the change should be applied. In such a case, appropriate adjustments shall be made to take into account any unreasonable effect on the injurious pricing margin due solely to exchange rate fluctuations between the original date of sale and the date of the change.

22.067 Article 2(12) provides that subject to the relevant provisions governing fair comparison, the existence of injurious pricing margins shall normally be established on the basis of a comparison of a weighted average normal value with a weighted average of prices of all sales, or by a comparison of individual normal values and individual export prices on a transaction-to-transaction basis. However, a normal value established on a weighted average basis may be compared to prices of all individual sales, if there is a significant difference in the pattern of export prices among different purchasers, regions or time periods, and should the methods specified in the first sentence of this paragraph not reflect the full degree of injurious pricing being practised.

The determination of "injury"

22.068 Article 3 ("determination of injury") sets out how "injury" is determined:

"1. Pursuant to this Regulation, the term 'injury' shall, unless otherwise specified, be taken to mean material injury to the Union industry, threat of material injury to the Union industry or material retardation of the establishment of such an industry and shall be interpreted in accordance with the provisions of this Article.

2. A determination of injury shall be based on positive evidence and shall involve an objective examination of:

   (a) the effect of the sale at less than normal value on prices in the Union market for like vessels; and
   (b) the consequent impact of that sale on the Union industry.

3. With regard to the effect of the sale at less than normal value on prices, consideration shall be given to whether there has been significant price undercutting by the sale at less than normal value as compared with the price of like vessels of the Union industry, or whether

1173

the effect of such sale is otherwise to depress prices to a significant degree or prevent price increases, which would otherwise have occurred, to a significant degree. No one or more of those factors can necessarily give decisive guidance.

4. Where sales of vessels from more than one country are simultaneously subject to injurious pricing investigations, the effects of such sales shall be cumulatively assessed only if it is determined that:

   (a) the margin of injurious pricing established in relation to the purchases from each country is more than *de minimis* as defined in Article 7(3); and
   (b) a cumulative assessment of the effects of the sales is appropriate in the light of the conditions of competition between vessels sold by non-Union shipbuilders to the buyer and the conditions of competition between such vessels and the like Union vessels.

5. The examination of the impact of the sale at less than normal value on the Union industry concerned shall include an evaluation of all relevant economic factors and indices having a bearing on the state of the industry, including the fact that an industry is still in the process of recovering from the effects of past dumping, injurious pricing or subsidisation; the magnitude of the actual margin of injurious pricing; actual and potential decline in sales, profits, output, market share, productivity, return on investments and utilisation of capacity; factors affecting Union prices; actual and potential negative effects on cash flow, inventories, employment, wages, growth, ability to raise capital or investments. This list is not exhaustive, nor can any one or more of these factors necessarily give decisive guidance.

6. It must be demonstrated, from all the relevant evidence presented in relation to paragraph 2, that the sale at less than normal value is causing, or has caused, injury within the meaning of this Regulation. Specifically, that shall entail demonstrating that the price levels identified pursuant to paragraph 3 are responsible for an impact on the Union industry as provided for in paragraph 5, and that that impact exists to a degree which enables it to be classified as material.

7. Known factors, other than the sale at less than normal value, which at the same time are injuring the Union industry shall also be examined to ensure that the injury caused by those other factors is not attributed to the sale at less than normal value under paragraph 6. Factors which may be considered in that respect shall include: the volume and prices of sales by shipbuilders of countries other than the exporting country not realised at less than normal value; contraction in demand or changes in the patterns of consumption; restrictive trade practices of, and competition between, third country and Union producers; developments in technology; and the export performance and productivity of the Union industry.

8. The effect of the sale at less than normal value shall be assessed in relation to the production of the Union industry of like vessels when available data permit the separate identification of that production on the basis of criteria such as the production process, producers' sales and profits. If such separate identification of that production is not possible, the effects of the sale at less than normal value shall be assessed by examination of the production of the narrowest group or range of vessels, which includes the like vessel, for which the necessary information can be provided.

9. A determination of a threat of material injury shall be based on facts and not merely on allegation, conjecture or remote possibility. The change in circumstances which would create a situation in which the sale at less than normal value would cause injury must have been clearly foreseen and must be imminent.

   In making a determination regarding the existence of a threat of material injury, consideration should be given to factors such as: (a) whether there is sufficient freely disposable capacity on the part of the shipbuilder or an imminent and substantial increase in such capacity indicating the likelihood of substantially increased sales at less than normal value, account being taken of the availability of other export markets to absorb any additional exports; (b) whether vessels are being exported at prices that would, to a significant degree, depress prices or prevent price increases which otherwise would have occurred, and would probably increase demand for further purchases from other countries.

No one of the factors listed above by itself can necessarily give decisive guidance, but the totality of the factors considered shall be such as to lead to the conclusion that further sales at less than normal value are imminent and that, unless protective action is taken, material injury will occur."

Definition of Union industry

22.069 The interesting and practical question of what constitutes "Union industry" is addressed by Article 4.[111] Article 4(1) provides that for the purposes of the regulation, the term "Union industry" shall be interpreted as referring to the Union producers as a whole capable of producing a like vessel with their present facilities or whose facilities can be adapted in a timely manner to produce a like vessel, or to those of them whose collective capability to produce a like vessel constitutes a major proportion, as defined in Article 5(6), of the total Union capability to produce a like vessel. However, when producers are related to the shipbuilder, exporters or buyers, or are themselves buyers of the allegedly injuriously priced vessel, the term "Union industry" may be interpreted as referring to the rest of the producers. In this context, producers shall (by virtue of Article 4(1)) be considered to be related to the shipbuilder, exporters or buyers only if: (a) one of them directly or indirectly controls the other; (b) both of them are directly or indirectly controlled by a third person; or (c) together they directly or indirectly control a third person, provided that there are grounds for believing or suspecting that the effect of the relationship is such as to cause the producer concerned to behave differently from non-related producers. For this purpose, one shall be deemed to control another when the former is legally or operationally in a position to exercise restraint or direction over the latter.

Initiation of proceedings

22.070 If there is an allegation of injurious pricing then proceedings are usually initiated. This is the subject matter of Article 5. The proceedings must generally be formal: Article 5(1) provides that except as provided for in Article 5(8), an investigation to determine the existence, degree and effect of any alleged injurious pricing shall be initiated upon a written complaint by any natural or legal person, or any association not having legal personality, acting on behalf of the Union industry. The complaint may be submitted to the Commission or, somewhat curiously but sensibly, to a Member State, which shall forward it to the Commission. The Commission shall send all Member States a copy of any complaint it receives. The complaint shall be deemed to have been lodged on the first working day following its delivery to the Commission by registered mail or the issuing of an acknowledgement of receipt by the Commission. Where, in the absence of any complaint, a Member State is in possession of sufficient evidence of injurious pricing and of resultant injury to the Union industry, it shall immediately communicate such evidence to the Commission.

22.071 Under Article 5(2), a complaint under Article 5(1) shall be filed no later than: (a) six months from the time that the complainant knew, or should have known, of the sale of the vessel, when: (i) the complainant was invited to tender a bid on the contract at

---

111 Reg. 2016/1035, Art. 4(3) provides that the provisions of Art. 3(8) shall be applicable to Art. 4.

issue through a broad multiple bid or any other bidding process; (ii) the complainant actually did tender a bid; and (iii) the bid of the complainant substantially met bid specifications; or (b) nine months from the time that the complainant knew, or should have known, of the sale of the vessel in the absence of an invitation to tender, provided that a notice of intent to apply, including information reasonably available to the complainant to identify the transaction concerned, had been submitted no later than six months from that time to the Commission or a Member State. In no event shall a complaint be filed later than six months from the date of delivery of the vessel. The complainant may be considered to have known of the sale of a vessel from the time of publication of the fact of the conclusion of the contract, along with very general information concerning the vessel, in the international trade press. For the purpose of Article 5, a broad multiple bid shall be interpreted to mean a bid in which the proposed buyer extends an invitation to bid to at least all the shipbuilders known to the buyer to be capable of building the vessel in question.

22.072 A complaint under Article 5(1) shall include evidence: (a) of injurious pricing;[112] (b) of injury; (c) of a causal link between the injuriously priced sale and the alleged injury; and (d) (i) that, if the vessel was sold through a broad multiple bid, the complainant was invited to tender a bid on the contract at issue, it actually did so, and the bid of the complainant substantially met bid specifications (namely, delivery date and technical requirements); or (ii) that, if the vessel was sold through any other bidding process and the complainant was invited to tender a bid on the contract at issue, it actually did so, and the bid of the complainant substantially met bid specifications; or (iii) that, in the absence of an invitation to tender a bid other than under a broad multiple bid, the complainant was capable of building the vessel concerned and, if the complainant knew, or should have known, of the proposed purchase, it made demonstrable efforts to conclude a sale with the buyer consistent with the bid specifications in question. The complainant may be considered to have known of the proposed purchase if it is demonstrated that the majority of the relevant industry has made efforts with that buyer to conclude a sale of the vessel in question, or if it is demonstrated that general information on the proposed purchase was available from brokers, financiers, classification societies, charterers, trade associations or other entities normally involved in shipbuilding transactions with whom the complainant had regular contacts or dealings. Under Article 6(10), the complaint may be withdrawn prior to initiation, in which case it shall be considered not to have been lodged.

22.073 The complaint must, by virtue of Article 5(4), contain such information as is reasonably available to the complainant on the following: (a) the identity of the complainant and a description of the volume and value of the Union production of the like vessel by the complainant. Where a written complaint is made on behalf of the Union industry, the complaint shall identify the industry on behalf of which the complaint is made by a list of all known Union producers capable of building the like vessel and, to the extent possible, a description of the volume and value of Union production of the like vessel accounted for by such producers; (b) a complete description of the allegedly injuriously priced vessel, the names of the country or countries of origin or export in question, the identity of each known exporter or foreign producer and the identity of the buyer of the vessel in question; (c) the prices at which such vessels are sold in the domestic markets of

---

112 See Reg. 2016/1035, Art. 2.

the country or countries of origin or export (or, where appropriate, the prices at which such vessels are sold from the country or countries of origin or export to a third country or countries or the constructed value of the vessel) and the export prices or, where appropriate, the prices at which such vessels are first resold to an independent buyer; and (d) the effect of the injuriously priced sale on prices of the like vessel on the Union market and the consequent impact of the sale on the Union industry, as demonstrated by relevant factors and indices having a bearing on the state of the Union industry, such as those listed in Article 3(3) and (5).

22.074 There is an initial filtration step. The Commission must, as far as possible, examine the accuracy and adequacy of the evidence provided in the complaint, to determine whether there is sufficient evidence to justify the initiation of an investigation.[113] An investigation shall not be initiated pursuant to Article 5(1) unless it has been determined, on the basis of an examination as to the degree of support for, or opposition to, the complaint expressed by Union producers capable of building the like vessel, that the complaint has been made by, or on behalf of, the Union industry.[114] The complaint shall be considered to have been made by, or on behalf of, the Union industry if it is supported by those Union producers whose collective capacity to produce the like vessel constitutes more than 50% of the total capacity of that portion of the Union industry expressing either support for, or opposition to, the complaint.[115] However, no investigation shall be initiated where Union producers expressly supporting the complaint account for less than 25% of total capacity of the Union producers capable of producing the like vessel.[116]

22.075 Interestingly, and to protect the EU's position, the authorities must avoid, unless a decision has been taken to initiate an investigation, any publicising of the complaint seeking the initiation of an investigation[117] but, before proceeding to initiate an investigation, the government of the exporting country concerned shall be notified.[118]

22.076 Usefully, the Commission may initiate an investigation of its own accord. This is useful because sometimes parties could be concerned about making a complaint (or being seen to make a complaint) so if the Commission can do so of its own initiative then that would be useful.[119] If, in special circumstances, the Commission decides to initiate an investigation without having received a written complaint by, or on behalf of, the Union industry for the initiation of such investigation, this shall be done on the basis of sufficient evidence of injurious pricing, injury, a causal link and that a member of the allegedly injured Union industry met the criteria referred to in Article 6(3)(d), to justify such initiation. Where appropriate, an investigation may also be initiated upon a written complaint by the authorities of a Contracting Party. Such a complaint must be supported by sufficient evidence to show that a vessel is being, or has been, injuriously priced and that the alleged sale to a Union buyer at less than normal value is causing, or has caused, injury to the domestic industry of the Contracting Party concerned.

---

113 Reg. 2016/1035, Art. 5(5).
114 Reg. 2016/1035, Art. 5(6).
115 Ibid.
116 Ibid.
117 Ibid.
118 Ibid.
119 Reg. 2016/1035, Art. 5(8).

22.077 The Commission must consider the evidence of injurious pricing and injury simultaneously. Article 6(9) provides that the evidence of both injurious pricing and injury shall be considered simultaneously in the decision on whether or not to initiate an investigation. A complaint shall be rejected where there is insufficient evidence of either injurious pricing or of injury to justify proceeding with the case.

22.078 If it is apparent that there is sufficient evidence to justify initiating proceedings, the Commission shall do so within 45 days of the date on which the complaint was lodged, or, in the case of initiation pursuant to paragraph 8, no later than six months from the time the sale of the vessel was known or should have been known, and shall publish a notice in the *Official Journal of the European Union*.[120] Where insufficient evidence has been presented, the complainant shall be so informed within 45 days of the date on which the complaint is lodged with the Commission.[121] The Commission shall provide information to the Member States once it has determined that there is a need to initiate such proceedings.[122]

22.079 Where the Commission initiates the proceedings then the notice of initiation of the proceedings shall announce the initiation of an investigation, indicate the name and country of the shipbuilder and the buyer or buyers and a description of the vessel concerned, give a summary of the information received, and provide that all relevant information is to be communicated to the Commission.[123] It shall state the periods within which interested parties may make themselves known, present their views in writing and submit information if such views and information are to be taken into account during the investigation. It shall also state the period within which interested parties may apply to be heard by the Commission in accordance with Article 6(5).[124]

22.080 The Commission is obliged to advise the exporter, the buyer or buyers of the vessel and representative associations of producers, exporters or buyers of such vessels known to it to be concerned, as well as representatives of the country the vessel of which is subject to such investigation and the complainants, of the initiation of the proceedings and, with due regard to the protection of confidential information, provide the full text of the written complaint received pursuant to Article 6(1) to the exporter, and to the authorities of the exporting country, and make it available upon request to other interested parties involved.[125]

The investigation

22.081 Turning from the initiation of the investigation to the actual investigation itself requires an analysis of Article 6 of the regulation.

22.082 Following the decision to initiate the proceedings, the Commission, acting in co-operation with the Member States[126] and, where appropriate, with the authorities of third countries, must commence an investigation at Union level.[127] Such an investigation

---

120 Reg. 2016/1035, Art. 5(11).
121 Ibid.
122 Ibid.
123 Reg. 2016/1035, Art. 5(12).
124 Ibid.
125 Reg. 2016/1035, Art. 5(13).
126 Presumably, this involves making all Member States aware of the issue but only some will want to participate.
127 Reg. 2016/1035, Art. 6(1).

must cover both injurious pricing and injury, and they shall be investigated simultaneously[128] (which is a recurrent theme in the regulation).

22.083 The parties receiving questionnaires used in an injurious pricing investigation must be given at least 30 days to reply[129] which seems relatively short given the complexity of the calculations involved. The time limit for exporters shall be counted from the date of receipt of the questionnaire, which for this purpose shall be deemed to have been received one week from the day on which it was sent to the exporter or transmitted to the appropriate diplomatic representative of the exporting country.[130] An extension to the 30-day period may be granted, due account being taken of the time limits of the investigation, provided that the party shows due cause for such an extension in terms of its particular circumstances.[131] The Commission may request the authorities of third countries, where appropriate, as well as the Member States, to supply information, and Member States shall take whatever steps are necessary in order to give effect to such requests.[132] They shall send to the Commission the information requested together with the results of all inspections, checks or investigations carried out.[133] Where that information is of general interest or where its transmission has been requested by a Member State, the Commission shall forward it to the Member States, provided that it is not confidential, in which case a non-confidential summary shall be forwarded.[134]

22.084 The Commission may request the authorities of third countries, where appropriate, as well as the Member States, to carry out all necessary checks and inspections, particularly among Union producers, and to carry out investigations in third countries, provided that the firms concerned give their consent and that the government of the country in question has been officially notified and raises no objection.[135] Of course, third countries are not obliged (as a matter of EU law) to co-operate with the Commission but Member States must take whatever steps are necessary in order to give effect to such requests from the Commission.[136] Officials of the Commission shall be authorised, if the Commission or a Member State so requests, to assist the officials of Member States in carrying out their duties. Likewise, officials of the Commission may assist the officials of the authorities of third countries in carrying out their duties, upon agreement between the Commission and such authorities.[137] The interested parties which have made themselves known in accordance with Article 5(12) shall be heard if they have, within the period prescribed in the notice published in the *Official Journal of the European Union*, made a written request for a hearing showing that they are an interested party likely to be affected by the result of the proceedings and that there are particular reasons why they should be heard.[138] Opportunities shall, on request, be provided for the shipbuilder, the buyer or buyers, representatives of the government of the exporting country, the complainants and

---

128 Ibid.
129 Reg. 2016/1035, Art. 6(2).
130 Ibid.
131 Ibid.
132 Reg. 2016/1035, Art. 6(3).
133 Ibid.
134 Ibid.
135 Reg. 2016/1035, Art. 6(4).
136 Ibid.
137 Ibid.
138 Reg. 2016/1035, Art. 6(5).

other interested parties, which have made themselves known in accordance with Article 5(12), to meet those parties with adverse interests, so that opposing views may be presented and rebuttal arguments offered.[139] Provision of such opportunities shall take account of the need to preserve confidentiality and of the convenience to the parties.[140] There shall be no obligation on any party to attend a meeting, and failure to do so shall not be prejudicial to that party's case.[141] Oral information provided under this paragraph shall be taken into account in so far as it is subsequently confirmed in writing.[142]

22.085 The complainants, the shipbuilder, the buyer or buyers and other interested parties, which have made themselves known in accordance with Article 5(12), as well as the representatives of the exporting country, may, upon written request, inspect all information, made available by any party to an investigation, as distinct from internal documents prepared by the authorities of the Union or its Member States, which is relevant to the presentation of their cases and not confidential within the meaning of Article 13, and is used in the investigation.[143] Such parties may respond to such information and their comments shall be taken into consideration, wherever they are sufficiently substantiated in the response.[144]

22.086 Apart from the circumstances provided for in Article 12, the information which is supplied by interested parties and upon which findings are based shall be examined for accuracy as far as possible.[145] For proceedings involving price to price comparison, where a like vessel has been delivered, the investigation shall be concluded no later than one year from the date of initiation.[146] For proceedings in which the like vessel is under construction, the investigation shall be concluded no later than one year from the date of delivery of that like vessel.[147] Investigations involving constructed value shall be concluded within one year of their initiation or within one year of delivery of the vessel, whichever is the later.[148] Those time limits shall be suspended to the extent that Article 16(2) is applied.[149]

22.087 It is worth noting Article 16(2) which provides that an investigation pursuant to the regulation shall not be carried out and measures shall not be imposed or maintained where such measures would be contrary to the EU's obligations emanating from the Shipbuilding Agreement or any other relevant international agreement. Moreover, the regulation shall not prevent the Union from fulfilling its obligations under the provisions of the Shipbuilding Agreement concerning dispute settlement.

---

139 Reg. 2016/1035, Art. 6(6).
140 Ibid.
141 Ibid.
142 Ibid.
143 Reg. 2016/1035, Art. 6(7).
144 Ibid.
145 Reg. 2016/1035, Art. 6(8).
146 Reg. 2016/1035, Art. 6(9).
147 Ibid.
148 Ibid.
149 Ibid.

Termination without measures, imposition and collection of injurious pricing charges

22.088 Proceedings can be terminated without measures, imposition and collection of injurious pricing charges. This is addressed by Article 7 of Regulation 2016/1035. Where the complaint is withdrawn, the proceedings "may" be terminated according to Article 7(1) but there is no obligation to do so. Where measures are unnecessary, the investigation or proceedings must be terminated.[150] The Commission must terminate the investigation in accordance with the examination procedure referred to in Article 10(2).[151] There is a *de minimis* type regime by virtue of Article 7(3) which provides that there shall be immediate termination of the proceedings where it is determined that the margin of injurious pricing is less than 2%, expressed as a percentage of the export price.[152]

Injurious pricing and injury

22.089 By contrast, where the facts as finally established show that there is injurious pricing and injury caused thereby, an injurious pricing charge shall be imposed on the shipbuilder by the Commission acting in accordance with the examination procedure referred to in Article 10(2) of Regulation 2016/1035.[153] The amount of the injurious pricing charge shall be equal to the margin of injurious pricing established[154] which means that there is no penalty but rather just an equalisation of the situation. The Commission must, after having informed the Member States, take the necessary measures for the implementation of its decision, in particular the collection of the injurious pricing charge.[155] Article 10(5) provides that the

> "shipbuilder shall pay the injurious pricing charge within 180 days of notification to it of the imposition of the charge, which for this purpose shall be deemed to have been received 1 week from the day on which it was sent to the shipbuilder".

The Commission may give the shipbuilder a reasonably extended period of time to pay where the shipbuilder demonstrates that payment within 180 days would render it insolvent or would be incompatible with a judicially supervised reorganisation, in which case interest shall accrue on any unpaid portion of the charge, at a rate equal to the secondary market yield on medium-term euro bonds in the Luxembourg stock exchange plus 50 basis points. If the payment was not made then presumably the Commission would (as it would be entitled to do legally) go into the Member State courts to seek recovery. However, Article 9 provides a very effective method of enforcement by, essentially, "blackballing" vessels which are built with the benefit of unlawful assistance (see below).

---

150 Reg. 2016/1035, Art. 7(2).
151 Ibid.
152 Reg. 2016/1035, Art. 7(3).
153 Reg. 2016/1035, Art. 7(4).
154 Ibid.
155 Ibid.

Alternative remedies

22.090 Article 8 provides for the possibility of alternative remedies. The investigation may be terminated without the imposition of an injurious pricing charge if the shipbuilder definitively and unconditionally voids the sale of the injuriously priced vessel or complies with an alternative, equivalent remedy accepted by the Commission. In this context, a sale shall be considered to have been voided only where all contractual relationships between the parties concerned by the sale in question have been terminated, all consideration paid in connection with the sale is reimbursed and all rights in the vessel concerned or parts thereof are returned to the shipbuilder.

Countermeasures – denial of loading and unloading rights

22.091 Article 9 provides – and it is worth citing the measure in full given its novelty:

"1. If the shipbuilder concerned does not pay the injurious pricing charge imposed under Article 7, countermeasures under the form of denial of loading and unloading rights shall be imposed by the Commission on the vessels built by the shipbuilder in question.

   The Commission shall provide information to the Member States once the grounds for countermeasures referred to in the first subparagraph arise.

2. The decision imposing the countermeasures shall enter into force 30 days after its publication in the *Official Journal of the European Union* and shall be repealed on full payment of the injurious pricing charge by the shipbuilder. The countermeasure shall cover all vessels contracted for during a period of 4 years from the date of entry into force of the decision. Each vessel shall be subject to the countermeasure for a period of 4 years after its delivery. Such periods may be reduced only following and in accordance with the outcome of an international dispute settlement procedure concerning the countermeasures imposed.

   The vessels subject to the denial of loading and unloading rights shall be specified by decision to be adopted by the Commission and published in the Official Journal of the European Union.

3. The Member States' customs authorities shall not grant permission to load or unload to vessels subject to the denial of loading and unloading rights."

22.092 This is a very clever and effective mechanism for ensuring payment. The shipyard will not want to have disputes with the vessel owner and the latter will not want disputes with the cargo owners or any charterer of the vessel.

Organisational issues

22.093 Article 10 provides for a committee procedure. Under Article 10(1), the Commission shall be assisted by the Committee established by Regulation 2016/1036[156] and that Committee shall be a committee within the meaning of Regulation 182/2011.[157] Where reference is made to Article 10(2) in the regulation, Article 5 of Regulation 182/2011 shall apply.

---

156 I.e. Reg. 2016/1036 of the European Parliament and of the Council of 8 June 2016 on protection against dumped imports from countries not members of the European Union (OJ L176/21, 30 June 2016). This has been amended by Reg. 2017/2321 of the European Parliament and of the Council of 12 December 2017 amending Reg. (EU) 2016/1036 on protection against dumped imports from countries not members of the European Union and Reg. (EU) 2016/1037 on protection against subsidised imports from countries not members of the European Union (OJ L338/1, 19 December 2017).

157 Reg. 2016/1035, Art. 10(1).

22.094 Article 11 deals with so-called verification visits. Article 11(1) provides that the Commission shall, where it considers it appropriate, carry out visits to examine the records of exporters, shipbuilders, traders, agents, producers, trade associations and organisations, to verify information provided on injurious pricing and injury. In the absence of a proper and timely reply, the Commission may choose not to carry out a verification visit. The Commission may carry out investigations in third countries as required, provided that it obtains the agreement of the firms concerned, that it notifies the representatives of the government of the country in question and that the latter does not object to the investigation.[158] As soon as the agreement of the firms concerned has been obtained, the Commission shall notify the authorities of the exporting country of the names and addresses of the firms to be visited and the dates agreed.[159] The firms concerned shall be advised of the nature of the information to be verified during verification visits and of any further information which needs to be provided during such visits, though this does not preclude requests, made during the verification, for further details to be provided in the light of information obtained.[160] In investigations carried out under Article 11(1), (2) and (3), the Commission shall be assisted by officials of those Member States which so request.

22.095 Article 12 deals with non-co-operation.[161]

---

158 Reg. 2016/1035, Art. 11(2).
159 Ibid.
160 Reg. 2016/1035, Art. 11(3).
161 Article 12:
"1. In cases in which any interested party refuses access to, or otherwise does not provide, necessary information within the time limits provided for in this Regulation, or significantly impedes the investigation, provisional or final findings, affirmative or negative, may be made on the basis of the facts available.
Where it is found that any interested party has supplied false or misleading information, that information shall be disregarded and use may be made of facts available.
Interested parties shall be made aware of the consequences of non-cooperation.
2. Failure to give a computerised response shall not be deemed to constitute non-cooperation, provided that the interested party shows that presenting the response as requested would result in an unreasonable extra burden or unreasonable additional cost.
3. Where the information submitted by an interested party is not ideal in all respects, it shall nevertheless not be disregarded, provided that any deficiencies are not such as to cause undue difficulty in arriving at a reasonably accurate finding and that the information is appropriately submitted in good time and is verifiable, and that the party has acted to the best of its ability.
4. If evidence or information is not accepted, the supplying party shall be informed forthwith of the reasons therefor and shall be granted an opportunity to provide further explanations within the time limit specified. If the explanations are considered unsatisfactory, the reasons for rejection of such evidence or information shall be disclosed and given in published findings.
5. If determinations, including those regarding normal value, are based on the provisions of paragraph 1, including the information supplied in the complaint, it shall, where practicable and with due regard to the time limits of the investigation, be checked by reference to information from other independent sources which may be available, such as published price lists, official statistics of sales and customs returns, or information obtained from other interested parties during the investigation.
6. If an interested party does not cooperate, or cooperates only partially, so that relevant information is thereby withheld, the result of the investigation may be less favourable to the party than if it had cooperated."

22.096 Confidentiality is protected by Article 13 of the regulation.[162]

22.097 Article 14 of the regulation deals with the issue of disclosure. Under Article 14(1), the complainants, the shipbuilder, the exporter, the buyer or the buyers of the vessel and their representative associations, and representatives of the exporting country, may request disclosure of the details underlying the essential facts and considerations on the basis of which it is intended to recommend the imposition of an injurious pricing charge, or the termination of an investigation or proceedings without the imposition of a charge. Article 14(2) goes on to provide that requests for final disclosure, as defined in Article 14(2), shall be addressed to the Commission in writing and be received within time limits set by the Commission. Final disclosure shall be given in writing.[163] It shall be made, due regard being had to the need to protect confidential information, as soon as possible and, normally, not less than one month before a definitive decision.[164] Where the Commission is not in a position to disclose certain facts or considerations at that time, they shall be disclosed as soon as possible thereafter.[165] Disclosure shall not prejudice any subsequent decision which may be taken by the Commission, but where such a decision is based on any different facts and considerations they shall be disclosed as soon as possible.[166] Representations made after disclosure is given shall be taken into consideration only if received within a period to be set by the Commission in each case, which shall be at least ten days, due consideration being given to the urgency of the matter.[167]

---

162 Article 13 provides:
   "1. Any information which is by nature confidential (for example, because its disclosure would be of significant competitive advantage to a competitor or would have a significantly adverse effect upon a person supplying the information or upon a person from whom the person supplying the information has acquired the information) or which is provided on a confidential basis by parties to an investigation shall, if good cause is shown, be treated as such by the authorities.
   2. Interested parties providing confidential information shall be required to provide non-confidential summaries thereof. Those summaries shall be in sufficient detail to permit a reasonable understanding of the substance of the information submitted in confidence. In exceptional circumstances, such parties may indicate that such information is not capable of being summarised. In such exceptional circumstances, a statement of the reasons why summarisation is not possible shall be provided.
   3. If it is considered that a request for confidentiality is not warranted and if the supplier of the information is either unwilling to make the information available or to authorise its disclosure in generalised or summary form, such information may be disregarded unless it can be satisfactorily demonstrated from appropriate sources that the information is correct. Requests for confidentiality shall not be arbitrarily rejected.
   4. This Article shall not preclude the disclosure of general information by the Union authorities, and, in particular, of the reasons on which decisions taken pursuant to this Regulation are based, or disclosure of the evidence relied on by the Union authorities insofar as is necessary to explain those reasons in court proceedings. Such disclosure shall take into account the legitimate interest of the parties concerned that their business secrets not be divulged.
   5. The Commission and the Member States, including the officials of either, shall not reveal any information received pursuant to this Regulation for which confidential treatment has been requested by its supplier, without specific permission from that supplier. Exchanges of information between the Commission and Member States, or any internal documents prepared by the authorities of the Union or the Member States, shall not be divulged except as specifically provided for in this Regulation.
   6. Information received pursuant to this Regulation shall be used only for the purpose for which it was requested."
163 Reg. 2016/1035, Art. 14(3).
164 Ibid.
165 Ibid.
166 Ibid.
167 Reg. 2016/1035, Art. 14(4).

E. COMMISSION DECISION 98/157 OF 5 NOVEMBER 1997 CONCERNING AID SPAIN PROPOSES TO GRANT TO ASTILLEROS ZAMACONA SA IN RESPECT OF FIVE TUGBOATS

22.098 On 5 November 1997, the Commission adopted Decision 98/157 concerning aid Spain proposed to grant to Astilleros Zamacona SA in respect of five tugboats.[168] The facts were quite specific and so there is no need to dwell on them now.

22.099 The case was an investigation under the EU State Aid rules (principally, Article 108(2)) and the then Council Directive 90/684 of 21 December 1990 on aid to shipbuilding,[169] as amended by Directive 94/73,[170] and in particular Article 4(3) thereof.

22.100 The facts were straightforward enough. In 1996, the Commission decided to open a procedure pursuant to, what is now, Article 108(2) of the TFEU to investigate a request by the Spanish authorities to extend the three-year delivery limit pursuant to Article 4(3) of Directive 90/684 in respect of five tugboats contracted in December 1991 by Astilleros Zamacona SA ("Zamacona"), a small shipyard in Bilbao. If this request were accepted the yard would be allowed to receive 9% aid per contract for the vessels in question (that is to say, up to the aid ceiling applicable in 1991). Under Article 4(3) of the shipbuilding aid directive, there were ceilings for aid levels except where there were delays. Spain denied that there was any breach. The Commission also received comments from the governments of two Member States (Denmark and the United Kingdom), both of which shared the Commission's doubts that the proposed extension of the delivery date was compatible with Directive 90/684, the United Kingdom in particular pointing out that it has a number of yards located in sensitive regional areas that are engaged in the construction of tugs and are in direct competition with Spanish yards such as Zamacona. Spain rejected the comments of the interveners. In their comments the Spanish authorities reiterated their view that, on the basis of the information previously supplied, the circumstances affecting Zamacona should be regarded as constituting "unexpected disruptions of a substantial and defensible nature in the working programme of the yard". Spain pointed to changes to port legislation, the construction of a new fitting-out wharf and the takeover of the Ardeag yard. Ultimately, the Commission concluded that there were serious doubts whether the five contracts were final contracts. It also concluded that the delay in the delivery of the five tugs covered by these contracts was not due to any unexpected disruption in Zamacona's working programme of a substantial and defensible nature. Accordingly, the conditions of the second subparagraph of Article 4(3) of Directive 90/684 had not been fulfilled and the level of aid granted for these five tugs was not to exceed the level of the aid ceiling prevailing three years prior to actual delivery of the vessels, namely 4.5%. The Commission stated that "to decide otherwise would create a dangerous precedent with serious implications for the inspection of State aid in the shipbuilding sector". As the Spanish authorities gave assurances that no aid above 4.5% had yet been granted for the contracts in question there was no need to order reimbursement. The Commission thus adopted a decision which was quite succinct:

---

168 OJ L50/38, 20 February 1998.
169 OJ L380/27, 31 December 1990.
170 OJ L351/10, 31 December 1994.

"Article 1
The proposal of Spain to grant aid in the form of a direct grant to Astilleros Zamacona SA of up to 9% of the contract value before aid for five tugboat contracts (Nos 300, 301, 318, 319 and 320) signed in December 1991 is incompatible with the common market, since the aid does not comply with Article 4(3) of Directive 90/684...

Article 2
Spain shall reduce the level of aid proposed for the five contracts in question so as to ensure that the level of aid in respect of each vessel does not exceed 4,5% of the contract value before aid, in accordance with the common maximum ceiling for 1992 and 1993 as fixed by the Commission in accordance with the provisions of Article 4(2), (3) and (4) of Directive 90/684...

Article 3
Spain shall inform the Commission, within two months of notification of this Decision, of the measures taken to comply therewith."

F. COMMISSION DECISION 92/569 OF 31 JULY 1992 CONCERNING PROPOSED AID BY GERMANY TO THE CHINESE SHIPPING COMPANY COSCO FOR THE CONSTRUCTION OF CONTAINER VESSELS

22.101 On 31 July 1992, the Commission adopted Decision 92/569 concerning proposed aid by Germany to the Chinese shipping company Cosco for the construction of container vessels.[171]

22.102 The case is quite specific and as it was over two decades ago and under a different regime, it is not proposed to dwell too long on it.

22.103 In 1991, an EU shipyard complained to the Commission of a distortion of competition that would result from the German government's intention to grant development aid to a Chinese shipping company for the construction of four container vessels. The Commission invited the German authorities to notify the project pursuant to Article 4(7) and 11(2)(c) of Directive 90/684. The German authorities stated that a negative decision had been taken on a request from a shipbuilding consortium (Bremer Vulkan, HDW and ex-GDR yards) for financial support on certain development aid conditions for the shipbuilding contract of Cosco (China Ocean Shipping Company). Following another complaint from the same yard during the same year, the Commission again invited the German authorities to notify the development aid plans relating to the Cosco contract. The German authorities stated that the question of whether and to what extent development aid could be granted for the Cosco contract was awaiting a project assessment by the Kreditanstalt fuer Wiederaufbau. However, the German authorities later notified to the OECD under the development aid provisions of the OECD Understanding on export credit for ships the terms and conditions of a subsidised loan related to a project to build three 3,765 teu (twenty foot equivalent unit) container vessels for Cosco. The Danish government complained to the Commission about the Cosco aid project. The Commission gave the German authorities a final ten working days to notify the Cosco aid project. Various Member States and other parties[172] concerned submitted comments. The

---

171 OJ L367, 16 December 1992, p. 29.
172 I.e. the UK, Denmark, the European Community Shipowners' Associations, the Association of Danish Shipbuilders and the Danish Shipowners' Association.

Commission analysis is interesting and shows the lengths to which it goes in terms of examining the facts:

"According to Article 4 (7) of Directive 90/684/EEC, aid for shipbuilding granted as development aid is not subject to the normal ceiling for operating aid and may be deemed compatible with the common market if it complies with the OECD Understanding on Export Credits for Ships. By letter of 3 January 1989, the Commission informed the Member States of its interpretation of Article 4 (7) of Directive 90/684/EEC. It repeated that any individual aid proposal was subject to prior notification to the Commission which would verify, on the basis of the notification, whether the proposed aid constituted development aid and whether it fell within the scope of the OECD Understanding. It also investigates whether the proposed aid complies with the criteria laid down in OECD Document C/WP6 (84)3 of 18 January 1984 concerning the interpretation of Article 6 of the Understanding on Export Credits for Ships according to which the following basic criteria must be adhered to by Member States granting development aid:

1. the aid may not be granted for the construction of ships which will be operated under a flag of convenience;
2. in the event that the aid cannot be classified as official development aid in the framework of the OECD Understanding the donor must confirm that the aid is part of an intergovernmental agreement;
3. the donor must provide proof that the owner is resident in the recipient country and that the recipient company is not a non-operational subsidiary of a foreign company;
4. the recipient must give undertakings not to sell the ship without prior Government approval;
5. the grant element must be at least 25% of the contract value in accordance with the OECD method of calculation (see OECD Document C/WP6 (85)62 of 21 October 1985);
6. the country involved must be on the Commission's list of countries eligible for development aid under Article 4 (7) of Directive 90/684/EEC.

It is clear from the above that the Commission is required to establish whether the aid granted in respect of each individual contract and liable to individual notification according to Article 11 (2) of the Directive constitutes development aid and whether the other criteria and conditions are met. In relation to the Cosco contracts, the Commission would make the following remarks:

1. The German authorities explain the higher contract price for the three ships by reference to the different specifications (higher speed, etc.) and the extra financial costs due to the soft loan conditions. Even after these explanations the price remains at the upper end of the prevailing market prices for this type of ship. However, the Commission is not in a position, on the basis of the information available to it, to demonstrate that the pricing package acts as an aid to the shipbuilding yards.
2. The German authorities point to China's increased transport needs and the resulting possibility of earning or saving more hard currencies through imports and exports. It also mentions China's objective of maintaining maximum independence from foreign countries for overseas transport and the relatively underdeveloped rail and inland waterways system. However, in assessing this aid the Commission must establish both that it is necessary and that it represents genuine development aid rather than an operating subsidy to German shipyards. The necessity of the aid is an essential condition for such assessment as has been stated by the Court of Justice in Case 730/79 *Philip Morris*...[173] Officially, Cosco currently has a fleet of 630 owned/long-term chartered vessels. Experts estimate that through its subsidiaries and other interests Cosco has control over an even higher number of ships. The vast majority of these vessels are operating in the time charter and spot charter markets all over the world. Around 80 of the above vessels are container ships, the fastest growing part of Cosco's fleet in recent years, making it the fifth largest container operator in the world.

---

173 Ed., Case 730/79 [1980] ECR 2671, ECLI:EU:C:1980:209.

The average age of the Cosco fleet is now 14 years and this accounts for its aim of engaging in long-term fleet renewal programmes. According to information available to the Commission the new container tonnage will be deployed on the Pacific and on the company's services to the Mediterranean and North West Europe. At the moment Cosco operates six 1 100/1 300 teu vessels on its Mediterranean service and a similar number on its North West Europe service. One of the company's major aims seems to be to set up an integrated network in Europe. Cosco has for the past two to three years been self-financing and any fleet renewal programmes must be self-generated.

This all leads to the conclusion that Cosco is not a company which needs development aid in order to contribute to China's development. The company is financially capable of buying new ships on the normal market and since it operates on international shipping routes with time charter and spot contracts, its operations are not directly linked to China's import or export trade. In view of this situation the granting of unjustified aid to Cosco carries the risk of creating a serious distortion of competition to an extent contrary to the common interest. Cosco is, because of its size and independence from the freight conferences, an important player in the world shipping market and is regarded by competitors as potentially a high destabilizing force in the Pacific/Far East and Far East/Europe trades.

3. This conclusion is reinforced by the fact that Cosco is willing and able to buy the smaller 2 700 teu container vessel without development aid at normal market prices. The German Government's information shows that the smaller vessel, to be delivered to a foreign subsidiary of Cosco, Rubymonte Maritime Inc. (Panama) and to be built by HDW, will not be supported with development aid. This makes it possible for the Commission to approve the contract for this ship and close the procedure in this respect.

On these grounds the Commission considers that the aid for the construction of three container vessels for Cosco cannot be considered as genuine development aid within the meaning of Article 4 (7) of Directive 90/684 ... and that the aid distorts or threatens to distort competition in the common market and affects trade between Member States both in the shipbuilding and in the shipping sectors to an extent contrary to the common interest within the meaning of Article [107(1)]."

22.104 Ultimately, the Commission decided:

"Article 1
The Commission has established that no development aid is involved in the Cosco contract for the construction of a 2 700 teu container ship by Howaldtswerke-Deutsche Werft AG, Kiel, and that the export credit terms applied are compatible with the common market.

Article 2
The proposed aid for the contract to build three further container vessels for the State-owned Chinese shipping company Cosco, at the Bremer Vulkan yard, Bremen, and the Mathias Thesen yard, Wismar, cannot be regarded as genuine development aid within the meaning of Article 4 (7) of Council Directive 90/684/EEC on aid to shipbuilding and is therefore incompatible with the common market.

Article 3
The German Government shall inform the Commission within two months of the date of notification of this Decision of the measures taken to comply herewith."

22.105 Germany appealed the Commission's decision to the CJEU.[174] Germany sought APPLICATION for the annulment of the decision or, in the alternative, the annulment of Articles 2 and 3 of that decision. Germany's appeal failed.

---

174 Case C-400/92 Germany v Commission [1994] ECR I-04701, ECLI:EU:C:1994:360.

G. CJEU AND COMMISSION CASE LAW ON SHIPBUILDING

Introduction

22.106 It is instructive to review some of the principal cases on shipbuilding before the Commission and the CJEU. Most of the cases are now of historical interest only as they related to now defunct shipbuilding directives but some are still interesting and, in the interests of space, a selection is outlined here.

French guarantee scheme for financing shipbuilding

22.107 On 16 May 2006, the Commission approved a French guarantee scheme for financing shipbuilding.[175] It was a State guarantee scheme introduced by France. Guarantees would be granted to financial institutions providing loans and loan guarantees to French shipyards to finance the construction of large ships. Guarantee premiums would be charged and vary according to the risk on a case by case basis. The premium level would cover the risks of payments and the administrative costs of the scheme, so that the scheme would be self-financing. The Commission considered that this measure therefore did not constitute State aid and did not threaten to distort competition in the internal market. Competition Commissioner Neelie Kroes said:

> "financial institutions remain reluctant to finance the construction of large ships, even for highly specialised, modern yards. I am therefore pleased to approve a scheme which is free of State aid and which can help French shipyards to raise finance."

The Commission believed that the scheme helped to solve the problems of the shipbuilding industry in accessing finance for the construction of ships, as identified in the Leader-SHIP 2015 report.[176] Loans, down payment guarantees ("cautions de restitution d'acompte") and performance bonds ("cautions de performance") granted to finance the construction of ships with a contract value larger than €40 million would be eligible for State guarantees under the scheme. The State guarantees would amount to a maximum of 80% of the guaranteed instrument. Yards in difficulties would be automatically excluded from this guarantee scheme. Premiums charged by the State would vary according to the risk of the guaranteed project and would exceed the premium received by the financial institution on the non-guaranteed part of the loan/bond/guarantee. Yearly guarantee premiums would amount to at least 0.8%. The premium level would be revised (and adjusted, if necessary) on a yearly basis in order to verify that it covers the risks of payments and the administrative costs generated by the scheme. The Commission had approved a similar scheme in Germany in December 2003[177] and in the Netherlands in July 2005.[178]

2006: Volkswerft Stralsund shipyard in Germany

22.108 On 6 December 2006, the Commission approved investment aid for the Volkswerft Stralsund shipyard in Germany.[179] The Commission had opened an in-depth

---

175 IP/06/633.
176 IP/03/1464.
177 IP/03/1740.
178 IP/05/982.
179 Commission Press Release IP/06/1696.

investigation in February 2006. The aid, amounting to €4.2 million, was for the Volkswerft Stralsund shipyard in Mecklenburg-Vorpommern (an assisted area) to enable it to build larger ships. The aid intensity of the aid was 22.5% as the total investment was €18.7 million. The aid was authorised under Article 107(3)(a) of the TFEU. The Commission had been concerned that it might have created new capacity. However, the Commission found that the aid was aimed at improving productivity and was unlikely to lead to a disproportionate capacity increase as the output of the yard would remain unchanged.

2006: Rolandwerft shipyard in Berne in Lower Saxony

22.109 On 20 December 2006, the Commission approved the granting by Germany of regional investment aid to the Rolandwerft shipyard in Berne in Lower Saxony (an assisted area where economic development is below the German average).[180] The Commission had conducted an in-depth investigation which had opened in February 2006. The total aid was €2.03 million which comprised €1.56 million towards a total investment of €13 million to modernise the yard (this corresponded to an aid intensity of 12%) and a further €0.47 million towards a total investment of €3.97 million to improve the yard's ship lift and to enable it to lift bigger and heavier ships at the lowest possible cost (this corresponded to an aid intensity of 11.84%). The aid could be authorised under Article 107(3)(c) of the TFEU because it was to promote the development on an area of under-development. The Commission had concerns about the proposed aid. The shipbuilding framework on state aid to shipbuilding[181] only allowed for investment for the upgrading and modernisation of existing infrastructure and not for new infrastructure (so as to avoid increasing capacity through State aid). The Commission had been concerned that the aid would not be limited to the modernisation of the existing yard and could lead to an increase in capacity at the yard which would thereby potentially distort competition. However, the Commission concluded, after its investigation, that the aid was aimed at improving productivity and was unlikely to lead to a disproportionate capacity increase (the output of the yard would remain unchanged).

2007: Italian oil and chemical tankers

22.110 On 7 February 2007, the Commission decided that an Italian scheme granting aid to shipping companies breaking up their single hull oil and chemical tankers which were over 15 years old (as at 31 December 2004) was not contrary to the EU State aid rules.[182] They were small ships used on the Italian cabotage trade.[183] The Commission approved the scheme under Article 107(3)(c) of the TFEU and the Community Guidelines on State Aid to Maritime Transport.[184] The Commission believed that the scheme would improve the safety of EU waters because it would remove those single hulled vessels even before the deadline provided for in Regulation 417/2002 on the accelerated

---

180 Commission Press Release IP/06/1850.
181 OJ 2003 C317/11.
182 Commission Press Release IP/07/148.
183 As the cabotage trade had been liberalised, the ships no longer had to be Italian-flagged so there was no inevitable discrimination.
184 OJ 2004 C13/3.

phasing-in of double hull or equivalent design requirements for single hull oil tankers.[185] The ships would be scrapped rather than transferred to non-EU Member State registers. The scheme was worth €12 million.

2007: German Peene-Werft shipyard

22.111 On 27 June 2007, the Commission approved, under the State aid rules, the grant of regional investment aid by Germany to the Peene-Werft shipyard in Mecklenburg-Vorpommern region which was an assisted area where the standard of living was abnormally low and there was serious underemployment.[186] Given the circumstances, the aid to promote the regional development of the area may generally be authorised under Article 107(3)(a) of the TFEU. However, the shipbuilding sector was covered by special and restrictive rules under the Commission Framework on State Aid to Shipbuilding.[187] The Commission only allowed investment for the upgrading and modernisation of existing installations and not for new ones (so as to avoid increasing capacity through State support). Germany had notified in January 2007 its plans to grant regional investment aid to the Peene-Werft shipyard. The aid package was worth €2.025 million which corresponded to an aid intensity of 22.5% (which was the maximum aid intensity under the Framework). The Commission approved the aid under the Framework because it would allow improvements to the productivity of the yard by increasing the degree of automation, reducing open-air work, improving the lay-out of the production process on the premises, building larger ships while maintaining the assembling duration in the dry dock and re-integrating works previously outsourced to sub-contractors. The Commission did not consider that the investments would lead to a disproportionate increase of capacity.

2001: Spanish shipyards

22.112 On 12 July 2001, the Commission opened an investigation into a transaction whereby Astilleras Espanoles ("AESA") sold two shipyards and a motor factor to Sociedad Estatal de Participaciones Industriales ("SEPI") for €60 million. The Commission had doubts as to whether SEPI's behaviour could be regarded as comparable to that of a private investor,[188] whether the possibly inflated purchase price constituted a capital injection to AESA and thereby aid to it and whether such aid would be compatible with the common market.[189]

22.113 On 28 November 2001, the Commission extended its State aid investigation into further restructuring of public shipyards in Spain. It thereby extended its already ongoing formal investigation on the restructuring of Spanish shipbuilding by including all transactions that led to the creation of the shipbuilding group IZAR. The Commission had doubts whether the price paid by Bazan/IZAR for a number of shipyards bought from

---

185 OJ 2002 L64/1.
186 IP/07/896.
187 OJ 2003 C317/11.
188 The private investor or market economy investor is a test to determine whether there is State aid.
189 IP/01/1672.

AESA and for SEPI was a genuine market transaction and therefore aid to the IZAR group.

2006: German Volkswert Stralsund shipyard

22.114 On 6 December 2006, the Commission announced that it had decided to approve under the EU State aid rules the grant of investment aid by Germany to the Volkswert Stralsund shipyard.[190] The investigation under what is now Article 108 of the TFEU had been announced in February 2006. The aid amounted to €4.2 million towards a total investment of €18.7 million to enable the yard to build larger vessels; the aid intensity was therefore 22.5%. The Commission authorised the aid under Article 107(3) (a) of the TFEU because the yard was located in an assisted area where the standard of living was below average and there was serious unemployment. The aid was covered by the EU's shipbuilding framework[191] which meant that investment was for the upgrading and modernisation of existing installations and not for new ones (in order to avoid increasing capacity through State support). The Commission believed that the aid was aimed at improving productivity and was unlikely to lead to a disproportionate capacity increase (i.e. the output of the yard as a whole would remain unchanged).

2015: Portuguese shipyard

22.115 On 7 May 2015, the Commission announced:

"State aid: Commission finds Portuguese shipyard operator ENVC received €290 million of incompatible aid; orders recovery from ENVC but not from new operator WestSea
… After an in-depth investigation, the … Commission has concluded that around €290 million of public support granted by Portugal to Estaleiros Navais de Viana do Castelo, S.A. (ENVC), the former operator of shipyards located in Viana do Castelo in Portugal, was not compatible with EU state aid rules. The Commission also found that the aid needs to be paid back by the ENVC and not the new shipyard operator WestSea, which has purchased part of ENVC's assets. There is no economic continuity between ENVC and WestSea because the assets were purchased at market conditions.
    ENVC made heavy losses since 2000. Since then, Portugal has directly and indirectly granted continuous subsidies to ENVC via numerous measures, including a capital increase in 2006, several loans granted between 2006 and 2011 to cover operating costs, comfort letters and guarantees to underwrite financing agreements between ENVC and commercial banks. The total value of the support measures amounts to approx. €290m.
    On the basis of its in-depth investigation opened in 2013, the Commission found that no private investor would have accepted to subsidise a loss-making company over 13 years. The measures were therefore not granted on market terms and constitute state aid within the meaning of the EU rules. They gave ENVC a significant economic advantage over its competitors, who had to operate without such subsidies. The Commission further concluded that the measures are not compatible with common rules, in particular the applicable 2004 Guidelines on rescue and restructuring aid, on the basis of which aid to companies in difficulty may be allowed subject to certain conditions:

– ENVC, at the time, had no realistic restructuring program to ensure the company's long-term viability without further state support.

---

190 Commission Press Release, IP/06/1696.
191 OJ 2003 C317/11.

– ENVC received repeated aid, at least over the last ten years, in breach of the 'one time last time' principle, which allows the grant of rescue or restructuring aid only once in a ten-year period. This is to avoid that market players rely on public money instead of running an effective business and competing on the merits.

Thus, the measures have distorted competition in the Single Market, in breach of EU state aid rules, and ENVC is liable to pay back the value of the advantage it has received.

The Commission decision has taken into account that ENVC is currently in the process of being wound up and that part of its assets (including a sub-concession of the land on which ENVC operated) has been acquired by the private operator WestSea, owned by Martifer and Navalria. Since WestSea only acquired part of the assets and has acquired them at market conditions following an open and competitive tender, the Commission has concluded that WestSea is not the economic successor of ENVC. The obligation to repay the incompatible aid therefore remains with ENVC and is not passed on to WestSea.

Background
ENVC was founded in 1944 and nationalised by Portugal in 1975. It used to operate the largest Portuguese shipyard. It is fully owned by the State through EMPORDEF, a 100% State-owned holding. ENVC has been heavily loss-making since at least 2000, and has had negative equity since at least 2009. In December 2013, the Portuguese state decided to liquidate ENVC and to start selling its assets. The shipyard was acquired by WestSea after an open and competitive tender.

Public interventions in companies that carry out economic activities can be considered free of state aid within the meaning of EU rules when they are made on terms that a private operator would have accepted under market conditions (the market economy investor principle – MEIP). If the MEIP is not respected, the public intervention constitutes state aid in the meaning of the EU rules (Article 107 of the Treaty on the Functioning of the European Union – TFEU), because it procures an economic advantage to the beneficiary that its competitors do not have. The Commission then proceeds to assess whether such aid can be found compatible with the common EU rules that allow certain categories of aid, such as the EU guidelines on rescue and restructuring aid.

Rescue and restructuring aid is very distortive, because it artificially keeps alive companies that would have exited the market without the aid. In order to avoid that inefficient companies rely on public subsidies rather than competing on the merits, such aid may be granted only under very strict conditions. Moreover, a company may receive rescue and restructuring aid only once in ten years.

To determine whether aid has been passed on to new owners in an asset sale, the Commission assesses whether there is economic continuity between the new and previous owner. The Commission uses a set of indicators, such as the scope of the assets sold (assets and liabilities, maintenance of workforce, bundle of assets), the sale price, the identity of the buyer(s), the moment of the sale and the economic logic of the operation. In this case it appears that no such economic continuity exists. Furthermore, as the assets were sold on the basis of an open, transparent and non-discriminatory tender process, the new owner has received the assets at their market value and hence free of aid."[192]

2018: Croatian shipyard Uljanik

22.116 It would be wrong to assume that the Commission only blocks aid. For example, on 22 January 2018, the Commission cleared rescue aid for Croatian shipbuilder Uljanik. The Commission approved a Croatian plan to grant the Uljanik shipyard a State guarantee for a €96 million loan. The measure would allow the company to meet urgent

---

192 IP/15/4940, see case number SA.35546 in the State Aid Register on the DG Competition website.

liquidity needs while preparing a restructuring plan, whilst competition distortions were limited. Competition Commissioner Vestager said:

> "the Croatian State guarantee will help the Uljanik shipyard to continue operating and maintain 1 800 jobs, while they work out a sound restructuring strategy to ensure its future. We approved it today. The restructuring plan must return the company to long-term viability without continued public support, to preserve jobs in Istria on a sustainable basis."[193]

---

193 IP/18/391, see case number SA.49619 in the State Aid Register on the DG Competition website.

CHAPTER 23

European Union law relating to ship repair

23.001 This is a very short chapter which is designed to encompass in a single chapter pointers to other chapters as they relate to the topic of ship repair.

23.002 There has not been very much European Union ("EU") law developed relating specifically to the topic of ship repair but there are various aspects of EU shipping law which impinge on the topic so it useful to bring the various strands together and act as a cross-reference to other topics.

23.003 If the ship repair is funded, directly or indirectly, by a Member State then issues of State aid law may arise. It would therefore be useful to have regard to chapter 15.

23.004 There can be environmental law aspects to ship repair and therefore regard should be had to chapters 19–21 as well as other aspects of the issue which are also considered in other chapters.

23.005 In so far as the ship repair amounts to shipbuilding then the previous chapter, chapter 22, would be relevant.

23.006 If there is any ship dismantling or ship recycling then regard should be had to the next chapter, namely, chapter 24.

23.007 Safety is always an issue in regard to ship repair and it is covered in various chapters in this book.

23.008 Before concluding, it is useful to consider the comments of the European Economic and Social Committee ("EESC") in its own-initiative 2013 opinion entitled: "*The European ship repair and conversion sector: a resilient industry, competitive in the world and committed to EU policies for sustainable growth*":[1]

1.1 The ship maintenance, repair and conversion sector (SMRC) is strategically important to Europe and its sustainable development, since it plays a key role in areas such as environmental protection, transport, security and energy efficiency.

1.2 The EESC believes that, on account of its advanced technical know-how, the current network of SMRC shipyards in the EU is well prepared and capable of meeting the growing demand for sustainable development, technology, innovation, workers' skills and shipyard equipment.

1.3 According to the Committee, opportunities for the sector are emerging despite the difficult economic climate. These relate to the enlargement of the world fleet and the increasing proportion of older ships, and in particular to the growing demand for conversion and modernisation due to environmental, energy and climate requirements. In the immediate term, this involves the growing demand for energy-efficient vessels, the operation and development of offshore wind energy facilities and extraction of natural resources from the sea.

---

1 10/12/2013, CCMI/111-EESC-2013-2301, Rapporteur: Krzaklewski (Workers – GR II/Poland) and Co-rapporteur: Calvet-Chambon (Employers – GR I/Spain): http://webapi.eesc.europa.eu/documentsanonymous/ces2301-2013_00_00_tra_ac_en.doc.

1.4 In the medium to long term, the opening up of Arctic sea routes and deep-sea mining provide further opportunities for the sector.

1.5 The Committee points out that despite these promising opportunities, the on-going crisis means that shipowners and SMRC shipyards are still facing financing bottlenecks, for example, access to credit and thus difficult business conditions for companies. A further challenge is maintaining a critical mass for the sector.

1.6 In order to address this, the SMRC sub-sector should work closely with the maritime value chain with the aim of raising its profile and obtaining support from the EU, the Member States and regions, given the existence of ever greater competition from third countries.

    1.6.1 The Committee believes that the following will be beneficial and useful for this sector:

- A broader and more active role for the EIB [European Investment Bank] in the sector within the framework of EIB objectives to support European industrial policy: this also concerns SMEs [small and medium-sized enterprises] from the SMRC sector, where the EIB and the EIF [European Investment Fund] have significant indirect scope for action;
- The organisation of workshops with the participation of the EIB, the European Commission and industry stakeholders (these workshops are proposed in the LeaderSHIP 2020 initiative), and measures to explore EIB financing opportunities;
- The possible use of the Europe 2020 Project Bond Initiative in areas relating to transport and energy; the allocation of regional funding (including funding relating to 'smart specialisation') to the maritime sector; decision by the Commission – which must be taken by the end of 2013 – on extending the framework on authorised State aid for the shipbuilding sector until the proposal and entry into force of new rules on both the general RDI [Research, Development and Innovation] framework and regional aid, which taken together should play the role of the current framework in future; steps should be taken to ensure that the expiry of the framework and its replacement with new rules does not produce new financial bottlenecks and every effort should be made to compensate the SMRC sector for the economic damage this may cause;
- The prioritisation of EU RDI funding under Horizon 2020 (which is to be a continuation of the Waterborne technology platform) for focused maritime projects with demonstration elements and innovation potential (including PPP [Public Private Partnership] for research purposes).

1.7 The EESC points out that although workers in the EU's SMRC sector have adequate skills, they should be continually assessed and updated. These measures should be supported as a matter of priority, for example within the framework of the LeaderSHIP 2020 initiative. There is a real risk of a loss of critical mass in this sector, given the ageing skilled workforce.

1.8 According to the EESC, generating interest in the sector among new and younger workers should be a main concern and this should be linked to measures aimed at improving the sector's image. This should be associated with financial support for schools and universities with specialisations covering SMRC.

1.9 The Committee believes that the Commission, together with the social partners and other stakeholders (using the concept of the sector council on skills, for example), should draw up a plan for the continual adaptation of skills to the new tasks of the SMRC sector, covering among other things off-shore facilities (platforms, wind farms, etc.), harbours, new technical floating units, facilities and ships for LNG bunkering, etc. This requires monitoring of skills, the permanent advancement of training and promotion of mobility within Europe.

1.10 A comprehensive set of principles and rules (environmental protection, security, ports, rules on transport, assembly, recycling) has a crucial impact on the way in which the sector functions and on demand for its services. In light of this, the EESC believes that the SMRC and newbuilding industry should carry out frequent and systematic consultations together with EMSA [European Maritime Safety Agency], with a view to ensuring that ships are safer and more environmentally-friendly and that they are monitored effectively.

1.11 According to the EESC, the collection of new rules and requirements relating to advanced technologies should not be regarded as harmful or problematic for the sector, but rather as an opportunity. In this regard, SMRC and newbuilding yards and the steel manufacturing sector should work together more closely to achieve better results. The Committee calls for DG MOVE [Directorate General for Mobility and Transport] to take into account the SMRC sector in its strategic policy developments (including on the matter of short-sea shipping).

The EESC believes that, in accordance with medium-term (3 year) forecasts pointing to strong demand for ship recycling carried out in Europe, the SMRC sector has the facilities to carry out such projects. It also has the human capital to meet requirements for recycling of ships that is not harmful to humans or the environment. At the same time, account is being taken in the sector of the fact that this is a new and different form of activity, with sensitive aspects and requiring a careful approach. The Committee believes that ship recycling will be an increasingly strategic activity for European industry.

1.12 According to the Committee, the key short-term objectives, which require public support with a view to financing conversions in the EU's SMRC sector, are the installation of cleaners and systems for the treatment of ballast water (this may affect up to 65 000 ships around the world according to the Lloyd's Register), and conversions associated with energy efficiency (including installation of LNG-powered [liquefied natural gas] engines, installation of facilities for LNG bunkering at sea and heat recovery systems as well as modernisation units for slow steaming, etc.).

1.13 The Committee firmly believes that the SMRC industry is of huge importance to the respective European naval fleets and that this subject should be included in other EESC opinions on the armaments sector.

1.14 The EESC believes that putting IMO [International Maritime Organization] rules in practice, particularly the Ballast Water Management Convention, is of key importance for the sector. This convention should therefore be implemented in a proper and efficient way with clear expectations.

23.009 Ultimately, the issues are very much connected with the shipbuilding sector so this chapter should be read in conjunction with chapter 22 along with the other chapters in the book.

CHAPTER 24

European Union law relating to ship dismantling and recycling

A. INTRODUCTION

24.001 While there is usually publicity surrounding the launching or maiden voyage of vessels, there is usually little coverage about the dismantling of vessels. In reality, the dismantling of vessels can have dramatic consequences: for example, employees working on the dismantling exercise can be injured, infected or killed due to the poor working conditions in so-called "breaker's yards" which could be nothing more than beaches. It is therefore not surprising that the world community and the European Union ("EU") have become concerned about ship dismantling. Given the significant environmental dimension then it is also not surprising that the notion that ships (or parts of ships) could be recycled has also come into focus. This chapter considers the interrelated issues of ship dismantling and ship recycling.

B. SHIP DISMANTLING

24.002 Ship dismantling could occur anywhere in the world but would often occur in South Asia. Sometimes, the process is undertaken in proper breaker's yards or shipyards but it could well be that it would occur simply on a beach. Vessels are deliberately run aground on the beach (typically on tidal mudflats) and then workers (including child labourers) climb on board to dismantle the vessels. There is little proper equipment or protective clothing to undertake the work and, moreover, little safety equipment available to the workers. There are frequent injuries and even fatalities. The world has reacted with some concern but the practice still continues.

C. SHIP RECYCLING

Introduction

24.003 Ships almost invariably have to be dismantled because not every ship can remain intact. So, the logical next step is to consider whether all or parts of ships can be recycled. Some parts are clearly capable of recycling while other parts are not suitable for recycling.

International level

24.004 At an international level, the 2009 Hong Kong International Convention for the Safe and Environmentally Sound Recycling of Ships (the "Hong Kong Convention") is aimed at encouraging safe and sustainable recycling of ships.[1] The Hong Kong Convention was adopted on 15 May 2009. It is designed to enter into force 24 months after ratification by 15 States which represent 40% of world merchant shipping by gross tonnage, and has a combined maximum annual ship recycling volume not less than 3% cent of their combined tonnage.

24.005 Recital 4 to Regulation 1257/2013 of the European Parliament and of the Council of 20 November 2013 on ship recycling and amending Regulation 1013/2006 and Directive 2009/16 gives some background to the Hong Kong Convention:

"The Hong Kong Convention was adopted on 15 May 2009 under the auspices of the International Maritime Organization. The Hong Kong Convention will enter into force only 24 months after the date of ratification by at least 15 states representing a combined merchant fleet of at least 40 per cent of the gross tonnage of the world's merchant shipping and whose combined maximum annual ship recycling volume during the preceding 10 years constitutes not less than three per cent of the gross tonnage of the combined merchant shipping of the same states. That Convention covers the design, the construction, the operation and the preparation of ships with a view to facilitating safe and environmentally sound recycling without compromising ship safety and operational efficiency. It also covers the operation of ship recycling facilities in a safe and environmentally sound manner, and the establishment of an appropriate enforcement mechanism for ship recycling."

24.006 The sixth recital to the same regulation provides:

"The Hong Kong Convention provides explicitly for its Parties to take more stringent measures consistent with international law, with respect to the safe and environmentally sound recycling of ships, in order to prevent, reduce or minimise any adverse effects on human health and the environment. Taking that into account, this Regulation should provide protection from the possible adverse effects of hazardous materials on board all ships calling at a port or anchorage of a Member State while ensuring compliance with the provisions applicable to those materials under international law. In order to ensure the monitoring of compliance with the requirements relating to hazardous materials under this Regulation, Member States should apply national provisions to implement Directive 2009/16 … of the European Parliament and of the Council.[2] Currently, port State control inspectors are tasked with the inspection of certification and with active testing for hazardous materials, including asbestos, under the International Convention for the Safety of Life at Sea ('SOLAS'). The Paris Memorandum of Understanding on Port State Control provides a harmonised approach for those activities."

EU level

24.007 At the EU level, the EU has also been keen to promote recycling where possible. This enthusiasm found expression in the adoption by the European Parliament and the Council of the Ship Recycling Regulation on 20 November 2013. The regulation aims at reducing the dangerous and negative impacts of the recycling of ships. It relates to

---

1 See   www.imo.org/en/About/Conventions/ListOfConventions/Pages/The-Hong-Kong-International-Convention-for-the-Safe-and-Environmentally-Sound-Recycling-of-Ships.aspx.

2 Ed., Dir. 2009/16 of the European Parliament and of the Council of 23 April 2009 on port State control (OJ L131/57, 28 May 2009).

vessels flying the flag of EU Member States. The regulation embodies the requirements of the 2009 Hong Kong Convention. The regulation also includes additional safety and environmental requirements (as authorised by Article 1(2) of the Hong Kong Convention). The EU has decided that to ensure legal clarity and avoid administrative burden, ships covered by the EU regime will be excluded from the scope of the Waste Shipment Regulation 1013/2006.[3] In this context, "ship recycling" means the activity of complete or partial dismantling of a ship at a ship recycling facility in order to recover components and materials for reprocessing, for preparation for re-use or for re-use, whilst ensuring the management of hazardous and other materials, and includes associated operations such as storage and treatment of components and materials on site, but not their further processing or disposal in separate facilities.

24.008 In June 2016, the European Commission published a special thematic issue of Science for Environment Policy focusing on the impacts of ship recycling.

24.009 In November 2016, the European Maritime Safety Agency ("EMSA"),[4] published a Best Practice Guidance on the Inventory of Hazardous Materials for practitioners on the field, shipowners and national authorities.

24.010 The Parliament and the Council recalled in the opening recitals to Regulation 1257/2013 various background issues:

> "(1) Ships which constitute waste and which are subject to a transboundary movement for recycling are regulated by the Basel Convention of 22 March 1989 on the Control of the Transboundary Movements of Hazardous Wastes and their Disposal ('the Basel Convention') and Regulation ... 1013/2006 of the European Parliament and of the Council.[5] Regulation ... 1013/2006 implements the Basel Convention as well as an amendment[6] to that Convention adopted in 1995, which has not yet entered into force at international level, and which establishes a ban on exports of hazardous waste to countries that are not members of the Organisation for Economic Cooperation and Development (OECD). Such ships are generally classified as hazardous waste and prohibited from being exported from the Union for recycling in facilities in countries that are not members of the OECD.
>
> (2) The mechanisms for monitoring the application of, and enforcing the current Union and international law are not adapted to the specificities of ships and international shipping. Efforts involving inter-agency cooperation between the International Labour Organisation (ILO), the International Maritime Organisation (IMO) and the Secretariat of the Basel Convention have been successful in reaching agreement on the introduction of mandatory requirements, at global level, aimed at ensuring an efficient and effective solution to unsafe and unsound ship recycling practices in the form of the Hong Kong International Convention for the Safe and Environmentally Sound Recycling of Ships ('the Hong Kong Convention').
>
> (3) Current ship recycling capacity in OECD countries which is legally accessible to ships flying the flag of a Member State is insufficient. Current safe and environmentally sound ship recycling capacity in countries which are not members of the OECD is sufficient to treat all ships flying the flag of a Member State and is expected to expand further by 2015 as the results of actions taken by recycling countries to meet the requirements of the Hong Kong Convention."

---

3 OJ L190/1, 12 July 2006.

4 See chap. 27.

5 Ed., Reg. 1013/2006 of the European Parliament and of the Council of 14 June 2006 on shipments of waste (OJ L190/1, 12 July 2006).

6 Amendment to the Basel Convention ("Ban amendment") adopted by Decision III/1 of the Parties to the Basel Convention.

D. REGULATION (EU) NO 1257/2013 OF THE EUROPEAN PARLIAMENT AND OF THE COUNCIL OF 20 NOVEMBER 2013 ON SHIP RECYCLING AND AMENDING REGULATION (EC) NO 1013/2006 AND DIRECTIVE 2009/16

Introduction

24.011 On 20 November 2013, the Parliament and Council adopted Regulation 1257/2013 of the European Parliament and of the Council of 20 November 2013 on Ship Recycling and Amending Regulation 1013/2006 and Directive 2009/16.[7] The legal basis was the Treaty on the Functioning of the European Union ("TFEU") generally and, in particular, Article 192(1) of the TFEU. The European Economic and Social Committee gave its views on the Commission proposal[8] which was adopted in accordance with the ordinary legislative procedure.[9] Pursuant to Article 31, the regulation entered into force on the twentieth day following that of its publication in the *Official Journal of the European Union* and it was published on 10 December 2013. However, the date from when the regulation would apply was more complex; Article 32 deals with the application of the regulation:

"1. This Regulation shall apply from the earlier of the following two dates, but not earlier than 31 December 2015:

(a) 6 months after the date that the combined maximum annual ship recycling output of the ship recycling facilities included in the European List constitutes not less than 2,5 million light displacement tonnes (LDT). The annual ship recycling output of a ship recycling facility is calculated as the sum of the weight of ships expressed in LDT that have been recycled in a given year in that facility. The maximum annual ship recycling output is determined by selecting the highest value occurring in the preceding 10-year period for each ship recycling facility, or, in the case of a newly authorised ship recycling facility, the highest annual value achieved at that facility; or

(b) on 31 December 2018.

2. However in relation to the following provisions the following dates of application shall apply:

(a) Article 2, the second subparagraph of Article 5(2), Articles 13, 14, 15, 16, 25 and 26 from 31 December 2014;

(b) the first and third subparagraphs of Article 5(2) and Article 12(1) and (8) from 31 December 2020.

3. The Commission shall publish in the Official Journal of the European Union a notice concerning the date of application of this Regulation when the conditions referred to in point (a) of paragraph 1 have been fulfilled.

4. If a Member State has closed its national ship register or, during a three year period, has had no ships registered under its flag, and as long as no ship is registered under its flag, that Member State may derogate from the provisions of this Regulation, except for Articles 4, 5, 11, 12, 13, 14, 16(6), 18, 19, 20, 21 and 22. Where a Member State intends to avail itself of this derogation, it shall notify the Commission at the latest on the date of application of this Regulation. Any subsequent change shall also be communicated to the Commission."

---

7 OJ L330/1, 10 December 2013.

8 OJ C299/158, 4 October 2012.

9 Position of the European Parliament of 22 October 2013 (not yet published in the Official Journal) and Decision of the Council of 15 November 2013.

24.012 The fifth recital to the regulation provides that the regulation is aimed at facilitating early ratification of the Hong Kong Convention both within the EU and in third countries by applying proportionate controls to ships and ship recycling facilities on the basis of that convention.

24.013 In that context, the purpose of the regulation is stated to be to reduce disparities[10] between operators in the EU, in Organisation for Economic Co-operation and Development ("OECD") countries and in relevant third countries in terms of health and safety at the workplace and environmental standards and to direct ships flying the flag of a Member State to ship recycling facilities that practise safe and environmentally sound methods of dismantling ships instead of directing them to substandard sites as is currently the practice. In this regard, the seventh recital provides:

> "The competitiveness of safe and environmentally sound recycling and treatment of ships in ship recycling facilities located in a Member State would thereby also be increased. The establishment of a European List of ship recycling facilities ('the European List') fulfilling the requirements set out in this Regulation would contribute to those objectives as well as to better enforcement by facilitating the control of ships going for recycling by the Member State whose flag the ship is flying. Those requirements for ship recycling facilities should be based on the requirements of the Hong Kong Convention. In this regard, ship recycling facilities approved in accordance with this Regulation should meet the necessary requirements to ensure protection of the environment, the health and safety of workers and the environmentally sound management of the waste recovered from recycled ships. For ship recycling facilities located in a third country, the requirements should achieve a high level of protection of human health and the environment that is broadly equivalent to that in the Union. Ship recycling facilities which do not meet those minimum requirements should therefore not be included in the European List."

24.014 The regulation is ambitious. In that regard, the ninth recital provides that Member States are encouraged to adopt appropriate measures to ensure that ships excluded from the scope of the regulation act in a manner that is consistent with the regulation, in so far as is reasonable and practicable.

Multiple regulation of the issue internationally

24.015 The EU has decided, sensibly, to avoid duplication or multiplication of regulation. In that regard, Recital 10 states that in order to avoid such a problem,

> "it is necessary to exclude ships flying the flag of a Member State falling under the scope of this Regulation from the scope of application of Regulation ... 1013/2006 and of Directive 2008/98 ... of the European Parliament and of the Council[11] respectively. Regulation ... 013/2006 applies to shipments of waste from the Union, subject to exclusions for certain categories of waste where an alternative regime applies. This Regulation subjects ships within its scope to controls throughout their life-cycle and aims to secure recycling of those ships in an environmentally sound manner. It is therefore appropriate to specify that a ship subject to the alternative control regime throughout its life-cycle under this Regulation should not be subject to Regulation ... 1013/2006. Ships neither covered by the scope of the Hong Kong Convention nor by this Regulation, and

---

10 The eighth recital provides that the principle of equality in EU law should be applied and its application monitored, in particular when establishing and updating the European List in respect of ship recycling facilities located in a Member State and ship recycling facilities located in a third country fulfilling the requirements set out in the regulation.

11 Ed., Dir. 2008/98 of the European Parliament and of the Council of 19 November 2008 on waste and repealing certain Directives (OJ L312/3, 22 November 2008).

any waste on board of a ship other than operationally generated waste, should continue to be subject to Regulation ... 1013/2006 and to Directives 2008/98 ... and 2008/99 ... of the European Parliament and of the Council,[12] respectively."

24.016 This issue of putting the EU measure into the broader international framework has meant that the EU has

"acknowledged that ships continue to be subject to other international conventions to ensure their safe operation at sea during the operational part of their life-cycle and, although they can exercise certain navigational rights and freedoms, ships are required to provide prior notice of entry into ports. Member States should be able to choose to apply further controls in accordance with other international treaties. Additional transit controls are therefore not considered necessary under this Regulation."

24.017 The thirteenth recital also seeks to avoid an ambiguity within EU law: for the purposes of the regulation, the term "recycling" should not have the same meaning as defined in Directive 2008/98 with the result that the Recycling Regulation has its own meaning.

Interpretation

24.018 When the Court of Justice of the European Union ("CJEU") or the Commission interprets the regulation, it obviously has to have regard to EU law. The twelfth recital adds a little complication when it states that when interpreting the requirements of this regulation, consideration should be given to the guidelines developed by the International Maritime Organization ("IMO guidelines") to support the Hong Kong Convention. It is probably fair to say that the EU institutions will have to take the IMO guidelines into "consideration" but would only be bound by EU law.

Hazardous materials

24.019 A critical part of the issue relates to hazardous materials. Recitals 14 and 15 are interesting in this regard:

"(14) Regulation ... 1272/2008 of the European Parliament and of the Council[13] implements at Union level the Globally Harmonised System for the classification and labelling of chemicals. That Regulation, together with Council Directive 67/548 ...[14] and Directive 1999/45/ EC of the European Parliament and of the Council, ...[15] provides useful guidance in determining what constitutes a hazardous material.

(15) Keeping an inventory of hazardous materials on board a ship throughout its life-cycle is a key requirement laid down in the Hong Kong Convention and in this Regulation. In

---

12 Ed., Dir. 2008/99 of the European Parliament and of the Council of 19 November 2008 on the protection of the environment through criminal law (OJ L328/28, 6 December 2008).

13 Ed., Reg. 1272/2008 of the European Parliament and of the Council of 16 December 2008 on classification, labelling and packaging of substances and mixtures, amending and repealing Dirs 67/548 and 1999/45 and amending Reg. 1907/2006 (OJ L353/1, 31 December 2008).

14 Ed., Council Dir. 67/548 of 27 June 1967 on the approximation of laws, regulations and administrative provisions relating to the classification, packaging and labelling of dangerous substances (OJ 196/1, 16 August 1967).

15 Ed., Dir. 1999/45 of the European Parliament and of the Council of 31 May 1999 concerning the approximation of the laws, regulations and administrative provisions of the Member States relating to the classification, packaging and labelling of dangerous preparations (OJ L200/1, 30 July 1999).

accordance with Regulation 8(2) of the Hong Kong Convention, a ship destined to be recycled should minimise the amounts of operationally generated waste in the period prior to entering the ship recycling facility. If the operationally generated waste is intended for delivery with the ship to a ship recycling facility, the approximate quantities and locations of that waste should be listed in Part II of the inventory."

Compliance

24.020 It is interesting to note that there is a real desire to ensure compliance:

"(16) Member States should take measures to prevent circumvention of ship recycling rules and to enhance transparency of ship recycling. As provided for in the Hong Kong Convention, Member States should report information concerning ships to which an inventory certificate has been issued, ships for which a statement of completion has been received and information regarding illegal ship recycling and follow-up actions that they have undertaken.

(17) Member States should lay down rules on penalties applicable to infringements of this Regulation and ensure that those penalties are applied so as to prevent circumvention of ship recycling rules. The penalties, which may be of a civil or administrative nature, should be effective, proportionate and dissuasive.

(18) In accordance with the case-law of the Court of Justice, the courts of the Member States are required to interpret, to the fullest extent possible, the procedural rules relating to the conditions to be met in order to bring administrative or judicial proceedings in accordance with the objectives of Article 9(3) of the Aarhus Convention.

(19) In the interest of protecting human health and the environment and having regard to the 'polluter pays' principle, the Commission should assess the feasibility of establishing a financial mechanism applicable to all ships calling at a port or anchorage of a Member State, irrespective of the flag they are flying, to generate resources that would facilitate the environmentally sound recycling and treatment of ships without creating an incentive to out-flag.

(20) In order to take into account developments regarding the Hong Kong Convention, the power to adopt acts in accordance with Article 290 of the Treaty on the Functioning of the European Union should be delegated to the Commission in respect of the updating of Annexes I and II to this Regulation. It is of particular importance that the Commission carry out appropriate consultations during its preparatory work, including at expert level. The Commission, when preparing and drawing up delegated acts, should ensure a simultaneous, timely and appropriate transmission of relevant documents to the European Parliament and to the Council.

(21) In order to ensure uniform conditions for the implementation of this Regulation, implementing powers should be conferred on the Commission. Those powers should be exercised in accordance with Regulation ... 182/2011 of the European Parliament and of the Council.[16]

(22) Since the objective of this Regulation, namely to prevent, reduce or eliminate adverse effects on human health and the environment caused by the recycling, operation and maintenance of ships flying the flag of a Member State, cannot be sufficiently achieved by the Member States due to the international character of shipping and ship recycling, but can rather by reason of its scale and effects, be better achieved at Union level, the Union may adopt measures, in accordance with the principle of subsidiarity as set out in Article 5 of the Treaty on European Union. In accordance with the principle of proportionality, as set out in that Article, this Regulation does not go beyond what is necessary in order to achieve that objective."

---

16 Ed., Reg. 182/2011 of the European Parliament and of the Council of 16 February 2011 laying down the rules and general principles concerning mechanisms for control by the Member States of the Commission's exercise of implementing powers (OJ L55/13, 28 February 2011).

Subject-matter and scope of the regulation and definitions in the regulation

24.021 Title I of the regulation deals with the subject-matter and scope of the regulation and the definitions in it.

24.022 Article 1 ("subject matter and purpose") provides that the purpose of the regulation is to prevent, reduce, minimise and, to the extent practicable, eliminate accidents, injuries and other adverse effects on human health and the environment caused by ship recycling. The purpose of the regulation is to enhance safety, the protection of human health and of the Union marine environment throughout a ship's life-cycle, in particular to ensure that hazardous waste from such ship recycling is subject to environmentally sound management. The regulation also lays down rules to ensure the proper management of hazardous materials on ships. The regulation also aims to facilitate the ratification of the Hong Kong Convention.

24.023 Article 2 ("scope") provides in Article 2(1) that the regulation, with the exception of Article 12, applies compulsorily to ships flying the flag of a Member State. Article 12 applies to ships flying the flag of a third country calling at a port or anchorage of a Member State. Article 2(2) provides some exceptions to the application of the regulation on the basis that the regulation does not apply to: (a) any warships, naval auxiliary or other ships owned or operated by a State and used, for the time being, only on government non-commercial service; (b) ships of less than 500 gt (gross tonnage); (c) ships operating throughout their life only in waters subject to the sovereignty or jurisdiction of the Member State whose flag the ship is flying.

Definitions

24.024 Article 3 contains various definitions for the purposes of the regulation. It is quite comprehensive but it is useful. Article 3(1) provides that for the purposes of the regulation, the following definitions apply.

24.025 The word "ship" means a vessel of any type whatsoever operating or having operated in the marine environment, and includes submersibles, floating craft, floating platforms, self-elevating platforms, Floating Storage Units ("FSUs"), and Floating Production Storage and Offloading Units ("FPSOs"), as well as a vessel stripped of equipment or being towed.

24.026 The phrase "new ship" means a ship for which either: (a) the building contract is placed on or after the date of application of this regulation; (b) in the absence of a building contract, the keel is laid or the ship is at a similar stage of construction six months after the date of application of the regulation or thereafter; or (c) the delivery takes place 30 months after the date of application of this regulation or thereafter.

24.027 The word "tanker" means an oil tanker as defined in Annex I to the Convention for the Prevention of Pollution from Ships ("MARPOL Convention") or a Noxious Liquid Substances ("NLS") tanker as defined in Annex II to that convention. The phrase "hazardous material" means any material or substance which is liable to create hazards to human health and/or the environment.

24.028 The expression "operationally generated waste" means waste water and residues generated by the normal operation of ships subject to the requirements of the MARPOL Convention.

24.029 The phrase "ship recycling" means the activity of complete or partial dismantling of a ship at a ship recycling facility in order to recover components and materials for reprocessing, for preparation for re-use or for re-use, whilst ensuring the management of hazardous and other materials, and includes associated operations such as storage and treatment of components and materials on site, but not their further processing or disposal in separate facilities.

24.030 The expression "ship recycling facility" means a defined area that is a yard or facility located in a Member State or in a third country and used for the recycling of ships.

24.031 The phrase "ship recycling company" means, the owner of the ship recycling facility or any other organisation or person who has assumed the responsibility for the operation of the ship recycling activity from the owner of the ship recycling facility.

24.032 The word "administration" means a governmental authority designated by a Member State as being responsible for duties related to ships flying its flag or to ships operating under its authority.

24.033 The expression "recognised organisation" means an organisation recognised in accordance with Regulation 391/2009 of the European Parliament and of the Council on common rules and standards for ship inspection and survey organisations.[17]

24.034 The phrase "competent authority" means a governmental authority or authorities designated by a Member State or a third country as responsible for ship recycling facilities, within a specified geographical area or an area of expertise, relating to all operations within the jurisdiction of that state.

24.035 The well-known phrase "gross tonnage" means the gross tonnage calculated in accordance with the tonnage measurement regulations contained in Annex I to the International Convention on Tonnage Measurement of Ships, 1969, or any successor convention.

24.036 The phrase "competent person" means a person with suitable qualifications, training and sufficient knowledge, experience and skill, for the performance of the specific work. Article 3(3) provides that for these purposes, a competent person may be a trained worker or a managerial employee capable of recognising and evaluating occupational hazards, risks and employee exposure to potentially hazardous materials or unsafe conditions in a ship recycling facility, and who is capable of specifying the necessary protection and precautions to be taken to eliminate or reduce those hazards, risks or that exposure. Indeed, the regulation also states that without prejudice to Directive 2005/36 of the European Parliament and of the Council,[18] the competent authority may define appropriate criteria for the designation of such persons and may determine the duties to be assigned to them.

24.037 The label "ship owner" means, for the purposes of the regulation,

> "the natural or legal person registered as the owner of the ship, including the natural or legal person owning the ship for a limited period pending its sale or handover to a ship recycling facility, or, in the absence of registration, the natural or legal person owning the ship or any other organisation or person, such as the manager or the bareboat charterer, who has assumed the responsibility for operation of the ship from the owner of the ship, and the legal person operating a state-owned ship".

---

17 OJ L131/11, 28 May 2009.

18 Dir. 2005/36 of the European Parliament and of the Council of 7 September 2005 on the recognition of professional qualifications (OJ L255/22, 30 September 2005).

24.038 The expression "new installation" means the installation of systems, equipment, insulation or other material on a ship after the date of application of the regulation.

24.039 The new bespoke phrase of "ship recycling plan" means a plan developed by the operator of the ship recycling facility for each specific ship to be recycled under its responsibility taking into account the relevant IMO guidelines and resolutions.

24.040 The phrase "ship recycling facility plan" means a plan prepared by the operator of the ship recycling facility and adopted by the board or the appropriate governing body of the ship recycling company that describes the operational processes and procedures involved in ship recycling at the ship recycling facility and that covers in particular workers' safety and training, protection of human health and the environment, roles and responsibilities of personnel, emergency preparedness and response, and systems for monitoring, reporting and record-keeping, taking into account the relevant IMO guidelines and resolutions.

24.041 The expression "safe-for-entry" means a space that meets all of the following criteria: (a) the oxygen content of the atmosphere and the concentration of flammable vapours are within safe limits; (b) any toxic materials in the atmosphere are within permissible concentrations; (c) any residues or materials associated with the work authorised by the competent person will not produce uncontrolled release of toxic materials or an unsafe concentration of flammable vapours under existing atmospheric conditions while maintained as directed.

24.042 The expression "safe-for-hot work" means a space in which all of the following criteria are met: (a) safe, non-explosive conditions, including gas-free status, exist for the use of electric arc or gas welding equipment, cutting or burning equipment or other forms of naked flame, as well as heating, grinding or spark-generating operations; (b) the safe-for-entry criteria set out in point 18 of Article 3[19] are met; (c) existing atmospheric conditions do not change as a result of the hot work; (d) all adjacent spaces have been cleaned, rendered inert or treated sufficiently to prevent the start or spread of fire.

24.043 The phrase "statement of completion" means a confirmatory statement issued by the operator of the ship recycling facility that the ship recycling has been completed in accordance with the regulation.

24.044 The phrase "inventory certificate" means a ship-specific certificate that is issued to ships flying the flag of a Member State in accordance with Article 9 and that is supplemented by an inventory of hazardous materials in accordance with Article 5.

24.045 The expression "ready for recycling certificate" means a ship-specific certificate that is issued to ships flying the flag of a Member State in accordance with Article 9(9) and that is supplemented by an inventory of hazardous materials in accordance with Article 5(7) and the approved ship recycling plan in accordance with Article 7.

24.046 The statement "statement of compliance" means a ship-specific certificate that is issued to ships flying the flag of a third country and that is supplemented by an inventory of hazardous materials in accordance with Article 12.

24.047 The expression "light displacement tonnes (LDT)" means the weight of a ship in tonnes without cargo, fuel, lubricating oil in storage tanks, ballast water, fresh water, feedwater, consumable stores, passengers and crew and their effects and it is the sum of the weight of the hull, structure, machinery, equipment and fittings of the ship.

---

19 See first description under para. 24.041.

Article 3(2) sets out definitions, for the purposes of Article 7(2)(d) and Articles 13, 15 and 16, of "waste", "hazardous waste", "treatment", "waste management", "site inspection", "site inspection" and "site inspection"; as these definitions are devised for the purposes of particular provisions, the definitions will be examined below in the context of those provisions.

24.048 The terms "waste", "hazardous waste", "treatment" and "waste management" have the same meaning as in Article 3 of Directive 2008/98. Article 3 of Directive 2008/98[20] defines "waste" as meaning any substance or object which the holder discards or intends or is required to discard. The latter article defines "hazardous waste" as waste which displays one or more of the hazardous properties listed in Annex III which lists the various characteristics. The term "treatment" means recovery or disposal operations, including preparation prior to recovery or disposal. "Waste management" is defined as meaning the collection, transport, recovery and disposal of waste, including the supervision of such operations and the after-care of disposal sites, and including actions taken as a dealer or broker.

24.049 The phrase "site inspection" means an inspection of the ship recycling facility assessing whether the conditions on site are consistent with those described in any relevant documentation provided.

24.050 The word "worker" means any person who performs work, either regularly or temporarily, in the context of an employment relationship, including the personnel working for contractors and subcontractors. It is a somewhat circular definition. It seems to exclude agency or temporary workers but includes those working for contractors and subcontractors.

24.051 The expression "environmentally sound management" is defined as meaning taking all practicable steps to ensure that waste and hazardous materials are managed in a manner which protects human health and the environment against the adverse effects which may result from such materials and waste.

Ships

Introduction

24.052 Title II of the regulation is entitled "ships".

Control of hazardous materials

24.053 Article 4 deals with the control of hazardous materials. The article provides that the installation or use of hazardous materials referred to in Annex I on ships is prohibited or restricted as specified in Annex I, without prejudice to other requirements of relevant EU law which may require further measures.

Inventory of hazardous materials

24.054 Article 5(1) provides that each new ship shall have on board an inventory of hazardous materials, which shall identify at least the hazardous materials referred to in

---

20 OJ L312/3, 22 November 2008, http://data.europa.eu/eli/dir/2008/98/2015-07-31.

Annex II and contained in the structure or equipment of the ship, their location and approximate quantities. Under Article 5(2), subject to point (b) of Article 32(2), existing ships shall comply, as far as practicable, with Article 5(1). In the case of ships going for recycling, they shall comply, as far as practicable, with paragraph 1 of this article from the date of the publication of the European List of ship recycling facilities ("the European List") as set out in Article 16(2). Subject to point (b) of Article 32(2), when the inventory of hazardous materials is developed it shall identify, at least, the hazardous materials listed in Annex I. Article 5(3) provides that the inventory of hazardous materials must: (a) be specific to each ship; (b) provide evidence that the ship complies with the prohibition or restrictions on installing or using hazardous materials in accordance with Article 4; (c) be compiled taking into account the relevant IMO guidelines; and (d) be verified either by the administration or a recognised organisation authorised by it. Under Article 5(4), in addition to Article 5(3), for existing ships a plan shall be prepared describing the visual or sampling check by which the inventory of hazardous materials is developed and taking into account the relevant IMO guidelines. Article 5(5) states that the inventory of hazardous materials shall consist of three parts: (a) a list of hazardous materials referred to in Annexes I and II, in accordance with the provisions of paragraphs 1 and 2 of this article, and contained in the structure or equipment of the ship, with an indication of their location and approximate quantities (Part I); (b) a list of the operationally generated waste present on board the ship (Part II); and (c) a list of the stores present on board the ship (Part III). Under Article 5(6), Part I of the inventory of hazardous materials shall be properly maintained and updated throughout the operational life of the ship, reflecting new installations containing any hazardous materials referred to in Annex II and relevant changes in the structure and equipment of the ship. Article 5(7) provides that prior to recycling, and taking into account the relevant IMO guidelines, the inventory of hazardous materials shall, in addition to the properly maintained and updated Part I, incorporate Part II for operationally generated waste and Part III for stores, and be verified by the administration or a recognised organisation authorised by it. Under Article 5(8), the Commission shall be empowered to adopt delegated acts in accordance with Article 24 concerning the updating of the list of items for the inventory of hazardous materials in Annexes I and II to ensure that the lists include at least the substances listed in Appendices I and II of the Hong Kong Convention. The Commission must adopt a separate delegated act in respect of each substance to be added or deleted from Annexes I or II.

General requirements for shipowners

24.055 Article 6 deals with general requirements for shipowners. Under Article 6(1), when preparing to send a ship for recycling, shipowners shall:

"(a) provide the operator of the ship recycling facility with all ship-relevant information, necessary for the development of the ship recycling plan set out in Article 7;

(b) notify in writing the relevant administration, within a timeframe to be determined by that administration, of the intention to recycle the ship in a specified ship recycling facility or facilities. The notification shall include at least:

(i) the inventory of hazardous materials; and
(ii) all ship-relevant information provided under point (a)."

24.056 By virtue of Article 6(2), shipowners shall ensure that ships destined to be recycled: (a) are only recycled at ship recycling facilities that are included in the European List; (b) conduct operations in the period prior to entering the ship recycling facility in such a way as to minimise the amount of cargo residues, remaining fuel oil and ship generated waste remaining on board; (c) hold a ready for recycling certificate issued by the administration or a recognised organisation authorised by it prior to any recycling of the ship and after the receipt of the ship recycling plan approved in accordance with Article 7(3). Under Article 6(3), shipowners must ensure that tankers arrive at the ship recycling facility with cargo tanks and pump rooms in a condition ready for certification as safe-for-hot work. Article 6(4) states that shipowners shall provide the operator of the ship recycling facility with a copy of the ready for recycling certificate issued in accordance with Article 9. By virtue of Article 6(5), shipowners shall be responsible for the ship and shall make arrangements to maintain that ship in compliance with the requirements of the administration of the Member State whose flag the ship is flying up until such time as the operator of the ship recycling facility accepts responsibility for that ship. The operator of the ship recycling facility may decline to accept the ship for recycling if the condition of the ship does not correspond substantially with the particulars of the inventory certificate, including where Part I of the inventory of hazardous materials has not been properly maintained and updated, reflecting changes in the ship's structure and equipment. In such circumstances, the shipowner shall retain responsibility for that ship and shall inform the administration thereof without delay.

Ship recycling plan

24.057 Article 7(1) provides that a ship-specific ship recycling plan must be developed prior to any recycling of a ship. The ship recycling plan must address any ship-specific considerations that are not covered in the ship recycling facility plan or that require special procedures.

24.058 By virtue of Article 7(2), the ship recycling plan must: (a) be developed by the operator of the ship recycling facility in accordance with the relevant provisions of the Hong Kong Convention and taking into account the relevant IMO guidelines and the ship-relevant information provided by the shipowner in accordance with Article 6(1)(a) so that its contents are consistent with the information contained in the inventory of hazardous materials; (b) clarify whether and to what extent any preparatory work, such as pre-treatment, identification of potential hazards and removal of stores, is to take place at a location other than the ship recycling facility identified in the ship recycling plan. The ship recycling plan should include the location where the ship will be placed during recycling operations and a concise plan for the arrival and safe placement of the specific ship to be recycled; (c) include information concerning the establishment, maintenance and monitoring of the safe-for-entry and safe-for-hot work conditions for the specific ship, taking into account features such as its structure, configuration and previous cargo, and other necessary information on how the ship recycling plan is to be implemented; (d) include information on the type and amount of hazardous materials and of waste to be generated by the recycling of the specific ship, including the materials and the waste identified in the inventory of hazardous materials, and on how they will be managed and stored in the ship recycling facility as well as in subsequent facilities; and (e) be prepared separately, in principle, for each ship recycling facility involved where more than one ship recycling facility is to be used, and identify the order of use and the authorised activities that will occur at those facilities.

24.059 Article 7(3) provides that the ship recycling plan must be tacitly or explicitly approved by the competent authority in accordance with the requirements of the state where the ship recycling facility is located, where applicable. Explicit approval shall be given when the competent authority sends a written notification of its decision on the ship recycling plan to the operator of the ship recycling facility, the shipowner and the administration. Tacit approval shall be deemed given, if no written objection to the ship recycling plan is communicated by the competent authority to the operator of the ship recycling facility, the shipowner and the administration within a review period laid down in accordance with the requirements of the state where the ship recycling facility is located, where applicable, and notified in accordance with Article 15(2)(b).

24.060 Under Article 7(4), Member States may require their administration to send to the competent authority of the state where the ship recycling facility is located the information provided by the shipowner pursuant to Article 6(1)(b) and the following details: (i) the date on which the ship was registered within the State whose flag it flies; (ii) the ship's identification number (IMO number); (iii) the hull number on new-building delivery; (iv) the name and type of the ship; (v) the port at which the ship is registered; (vi) the name and address of the shipowner as well as the IMO registered owner identification number; (vii) the name and address of the company; (viii) the name of any classification societies with which the ship is classed; and (ix) the ship's main particulars (LOA, breadth (moulded), depth (moulded), LDT, gross and net tonnage, and engine type and rating).

Surveys

24.061 Article 8 deals with "surveys". Article 8(1) provides that surveys of ships shall be carried out by officers of the administration, or of a recognised organisation authorised by it, taking into account the relevant IMO guidelines. Article 8(2) states that where the administration uses recognised organisations to conduct surveys, as described in paragraph 1, it shall, as a minimum, empower such recognised organisations to: require a ship that they survey to comply with this regulation; and carry out surveys if requested by the appropriate authorities of a Member State. By reason of Article 8(3), ships must be subject to the following surveys: (a) an initial survey; (b) a renewal survey; (c) an additional survey; and (d) a final survey. Under Article 8(4), the initial survey of a new ship shall be conducted before the ship is put in service, or before the inventory certificate is issued. For existing ships, an initial survey shall be conducted by 31 December 2020. The survey shall verify that Part I of the inventory of hazardous materials complies with the requirements of this regulation. Under Article 8(5), the renewal survey must be conducted at intervals specified by the administration, which shall not exceed five years. The renewal survey shall verify that Part I of the inventory of hazardous materials complies with the requirements of this regulation. Under Article 8(6), the additional survey, either general or partial depending on the circumstances, shall be conducted if requested by the shipowner after a change, replacement or significant repair of the structure, equipment, systems, fittings, arrangements and material, which has an impact on the inventory of hazardous materials. The survey shall be such as to ensure that any change, replacement or significant repair has been made in a manner that ensures that the ship continues to comply with the requirements of this regulation, and that Part I of the inventory of hazardous materials is amended as necessary. According to Article 8(7), the final survey shall be conducted prior to the ship being taken out of service and before the recycling of the ship has started. That survey must verify that: (a) the inventory of hazardous materials complies with the requirements of Article 5; (b) the ship recycling plan properly reflects the information contained in the inventory of hazardous materials and complies with the requirements of Article 7; and (c) the ship recycling facility where the ship is to be recycled is included in the European List. Article 8(8) provides that for existing ships intended for ship recycling, the initial survey and the final survey may be conducted at the same time.

Issuance and endorsement of certificates

24.062 Article 9 deals with the issuance and endorsement of certificates. After successful completion of an initial or renewal survey, the administration or a recognised organisation authorised by it shall issue an inventory certificate. That certificate shall be supplemented by Part I of the inventory of hazardous materials, referred to in Article 5(5) (a).[21] Where the initial survey and the final survey are conducted at the same time as provided for in Article 8(8), only the ready for recycling certificate referred to in Article 9(9) shall be issued.[22] The Commission must adopt implementing acts to establish the format of the inventory certificate to ensure it is consistent with Appendix 3 to the Hong Kong Convention. Those implementing acts shall be adopted in accordance with the examination procedure referred to in Article 25 of the regulation.[23] An inventory certificate must be endorsed at the request of the shipowner either by the administration or by a recognised organisation authorised by it after successful completion of an additional survey conducted in accordance with Article 8(6).[24] Article 9(3) and (4) should be read together:

"3. Subject to paragraph 4, the administration or recognised organisation authorised by it shall issue or endorse, as appropriate, an inventory certificate, where the renewal survey is successfully completed: (a) in the three month period before the expiry date of the existing inventory certificate, and the new certificate shall be valid from the date of completion of the renewal survey to a date not exceeding five years from the date of expiry of the existing one; (b) after the expiry date of the existing inventory certificate, and the new certificate shall be valid from the date of completion of the renewal survey to a date not exceeding five years from the date of expiry of the existing one; (c) more than three months before the expiry date of the existing inventory certificate, and the new certificate shall be valid from the date of completion of the renewal survey to a date not exceeding five years from the date of completion of the renewal survey.

4. Where a renewal survey has been successfully completed and a new inventory certificate cannot be issued or placed on board before the expiry date of the existing certificate, the administration or recognised organisation authorised by it shall endorse the existing certificate and such a certificate shall be accepted as valid for a further period which shall not exceed five months from the date of expiry."

---

21 Reg. 1257/2013, Art. 9(1).
22 Ibid.
23 Ibid.
24 Reg. 1257/2013, Art. 9(2).

24.063 In the case of an inventory certificate issued for a period of less than five years, the administration or the recognised organisation authorised by it may extend the validity of the existing certificate for a further period which shall not exceed five years.[25] In special circumstances as determined by the administration, a new inventory certificate need not be dated from the date of expiry of the existing certificate as required by points (a) and (b) of paragraph 3 and paragraphs 7 and 8.[26] In those circumstances, the new certificate shall be valid for a period not exceeding five years from the date of completion of the renewal survey.[27]

24.064 Article 9(7) is a practical measure to enable vessels to sail to a port or anchorage for inspection. Where a ship is not at the port or anchorage where it is to be surveyed when the inventory certificate expires, the administration may, if it is proper to do so, extend the period of validity of the inventory certificate for a period not exceeding three months to enable the ship to complete its voyage to the port in which it is to be surveyed. Any such extension granted shall be conditional on the survey being completed at that port before the ship leaves. A ship to which an extension is granted shall not, on its arrival in the port in which it is to be surveyed, be entitled, by virtue of such extension, to leave the port without having a new certificate. When the renewal survey is completed, the new inventory certificate shall be valid for a period not exceeding five years from the date of expiry of the existing certificate before the extension was granted. Article 9(8) provides a limitation on this Article 9(7) facility in that an inventory certificate for a ship engaged on short voyages and which has not been extended under the conditions referred to in Article 9(7) may be extended by the administration for a period of grace of up to one month from its expiry. When the renewal survey is completed, the new inventory certificate shall be valid for a period not exceeding five years from the date of expiry of the existing certificate before the extension was granted.

24.065 Under Article 9(9), after successful completion of a final survey in accordance with Article 8(7), the administration or a recognised organisation authorised by it shall issue a ready for recycling certificate. That certificate shall be supplemented by the inventory of hazardous materials and the ship recycling plan. The Commission shall adopt implementing acts to establish the format of the ready for recycling certificate to ensure it is consistent with Appendix 4 to the Hong Kong Convention. Those implementing acts shall be adopted in accordance with the examination procedure referred to in Article 25 of the regulation. A ready for recycling certificate issued after a final survey in accordance with the first subparagraph of this paragraph shall be accepted by the other Member States and regarded for the purposes of the regulation as having the same validity as a ready for recycling certificate issued by them.

Duration and validity of certificates

24.066 Article 10 of the regulation deals with duration and validity of certificates. It is quite simple in its approach:

---

25 Reg. 1257/2013, Art. 9(5).
26 Reg. 1257/2013, Art. 9(6).
27 Ibid.

"1. Subject to Article 9, an inventory certificate shall be issued for a period specified by the administration, which shall not exceed five years.

2. An inventory certificate issued or endorsed under Article 9 shall cease to be valid in any of the following cases:

    (a) if the condition of the ship does not correspond substantially with the particulars of that inventory certificate, including where Part I of the inventory of hazardous materials has not been properly maintained and updated, reflecting changes in ship structure and equipment, taking into account the relevant IMO guidelines;

    (b) where the renewal survey is not completed within the intervals specified in Article 8(5).

3. A ready for recycling certificate shall be issued by the administration or by a recognised organisation authorised by it for a period not exceeding three months.

4. A ready for recycling certificate issued under Article 9(9) shall cease to be valid where the condition of the ship does not correspond substantially with the particulars of the inventory certificate.

5. By way of derogation from paragraph 3, the ready for recycling certificate may be extended by the administration or by a recognised organisation authorised by it for a single point to point voyage to the ship recycling facility."

Port State control

24.067 Port State control ("PSC")[28] is dealt with by Article 11 of the regulation:

"1. Member States shall apply control provisions for ships in accordance with their national law having regard to Directive 2009/16/EC. Subject to paragraph 2, any such inspection shall be limited to checking that either an inventory certificate or a ready for recycling certificate is kept on board, which, if valid, shall be considered sufficient for the inspection to be approved.

2. A detailed inspection may be carried out by the relevant authority involved in port State control activities, taking into account the relevant IMO guidelines, where a ship does not carry a valid certificate or there are clear grounds for believing either that: (a) the condition of the ship or its equipment does not correspond substantially with the particulars of that certificate, Part I of the inventory of hazardous materials, or both; or (b) there is no procedure implemented on board the ship for the maintenance of Part I of the inventory of hazardous materials.

3. A ship may be warned, detained, dismissed or excluded from the ports or offshore terminals under the jurisdiction of a Member State in the event that it fails to submit to the relevant authorities of that Member State a copy of the inventory certificate or the ready for recycling certificate, as appropriate and on request of those authorities, without prejudice to Article 9. A Member State taking such action shall immediately inform the administration concerned. Failure to update the inventory of hazardous materials shall not constitute a detainable deficiency, but any inconsistencies in the inventory of hazardous materials shall be reported to the administration concerned and shall be rectified at the time of the next survey.

4. Access to a specific port or anchorage may be permitted by the relevant authority of a Member State in the event of force majeure or overriding safety considerations, or to reduce or minimise the risk of pollution or to have deficiencies rectified, provided that adequate measures to the satisfaction of the relevant authority of that Member State have been implemented by the owner, the operator or the master of the ship to ensure safe entry."

---

28 On PSC generally, see chap. 29.

Requirements for ships flying the flag of a third country

24.068 Article 12 deals with the requirements for ships flying the flag of a third country. Under Article 12(1):

"Subject to point (b) of Article 32(2),[29] when calling at a port or anchorage of a Member State, a ship flying the flag of a third country shall have on board an inventory of hazardous materials that complies with Article 5(2).

Notwithstanding the first subparagraph, access to a specific port or anchorage may be permitted by the relevant authority of a Member State in the event of force majeure or overriding safety considerations, or to reduce or minimise the risk of pollution or to have deficiencies rectified, provided that adequate measures to the satisfaction of the relevant authority of that Member State have been implemented by the owner, the operator or the master of the ship to ensure safe entry."

24.069 Article 12(2) provides that the installation of hazardous materials referred to in Annex I on ships flying the flag of a third country, while in a port or anchorage of a Member State, shall be prohibited or restricted as specified in Annex I. The paragraph also provides that the use of hazardous materials referred to in Annex I on ships flying the flag of a third country, while in a port or anchorage of a Member State, shall be prohibited or restricted as specified in Annex I, without prejudice to the exemptions and transitional arrangements applicable to those materials under international law. Article 12(2) should be read in conjunction with Article 12(3) which provides that the inventory of hazardous materials shall be specific to each ship, be compiled taking into account the relevant IMO guidelines and serve to clarify that the ship complies with Article 12(2). When the inventory of hazardous materials is developed it shall identify, at least, the hazardous materials listed in Annex I. A plan shall be established by the ship flying the flag of a third country describing the visual/sampling check by which the inventory of hazardous materials is developed taking into account the relevant IMO guidelines.

---

29 Ed., it is worth recalling Art. 32(2) in the context of the whole of Art. 32:
"Application
1. This Regulation shall apply from the earlier of the following two dates, but not earlier than 31 December 2015:
    (a) 6 months after the date that the combined maximum annual ship recycling output of the ship recycling facilities included in the European List constitutes not less than 2,5 million light displacement tonnes (LDT). The annual ship recycling output of a ship recycling facility is calculated as the sum of the weight of ships expressed in LDT that have been recycled in a given year in that facility. The maximum annual ship recycling output is determined by selecting the highest value occurring in the preceding 10-year period for each ship recycling facility, or, in the case of a newly authorised ship recycling facility, the highest annual value achieved at that facility; or
    (b) on 31 December 2018.
2. However in relation to the following provisions the following dates of application shall apply:
    (a) Article 2, the second subparagraph of Article 5(2), Articles 13, 14, 15, 16, 25 and 26 from 31 December 2014;
    (b) the first and third subparagraphs of Article 5(2) and Article 12(1) and (8) from 31 December 2020.
3. The Commission shall publish in the Official Journal of the European Union a notice concerning the date of application of this Regulation when the conditions referred to in point (a) of paragraph 1 have been fulfilled.
4. If a Member State has closed its national ship register or, during a three year period, has had no ships registered under its flag, and as long as no ship is registered under its flag, that Member State may derogate from the provisions of this Regulation, except for Articles 4, 5, 11, 12, 13, 14, 16(6), 18, 19, 20, 21 and 22. Where a Member State intends to avail itself of this derogation, it shall notify the Commission at the latest on the date of application of this Regulation. Any subsequent change shall also be communicated to the Commission."

24.070 Under Article 12(4), the inventory of hazardous materials shall be properly maintained and updated throughout the operational life of the ship, reflecting new installations containing any hazardous materials referred to in Annex II and relevant changes in the structure and equipment of the ship, taking into account the exemptions and transitional arrangements applicable to those materials under international law.

24.071 A ship flying the flag of a third country may, pursuant to Article 12(5), be warned, detained, dismissed or excluded from the ports or offshore terminals under the jurisdiction of a Member State in the event that it fails to submit to the relevant authorities of that Member State a copy of the statement of compliance in accordance with Article 12(6) and 12(7), together with the inventory of hazardous materials, as appropriate and on request from those authorities.[30] A Member State taking such action shall immediately inform the relevant authorities of the third country whose flag the ship concerned is flying. Failure to update the inventory of hazardous materials shall not constitute a detainable deficiency, but any inconsistencies in the inventory of hazardous materials shall be reported to the relevant authorities of the third country whose flag that ship is flying.

24.072 The statement of compliance shall be issued, by virtue of Article 12(6), after verification of the inventory of hazardous materials by the relevant authorities of the third country whose flag the ship is flying or an organisation authorised by them, in accordance with the national requirements. The statement of compliance may be modelled on the basis of Appendix 3 to the Hong Kong Convention.[31]

24.073 In the context of ships flying the flag of third states, a special rule applies by virtue of Article 12(8). This would apply, for example, to the UK post-Brexit in the absence of a special agreement to the contrary. Article 12(8) provides that subject to point (b) of Article 32(2), ships flying the flag of a third country applying to be registered under the flag of a Member State shall ensure that an inventory of hazardous materials, as provided for in Article 5(2), is kept on board or is established within six months of the registration under the flag of that Member State or during any of the next surveys under Article 8(3), whichever comes first.

Ship recycling facilities

Introduction

24.074 Title III of the regulation deals with ship recycling facilities.

24.075 Article 13 sets down the requirements necessary for ship recycling facilities to be included in the European List.

24.076 Under Article 13(1), in order to be included in the European List, a ship recycling facility must comply with the following requirements, in accordance with the relevant Hong Kong Convention provisions and taking into account the relevant guidelines of the IMO, the International Labour Organization, the Basel Convention and of the Stockholm Convention on Persistent Organic Pollutants and of other international guidelines:

---

30 Reg. 1257/2013, Art. 12(5).
31 Pursuant to Art. 12(7), the statement of compliance and the inventory of hazardous materials must be drawn up in an official language of the issuing relevant authorities of the third country whose flag the ship is flying and where the language used is not English, French or Spanish, the text shall include a translation into one of those languages.

(a) it is authorised by its competent authorities to conduct ship recycling operations; (b) it is designed, constructed and operated in a safe and environmentally sound manner; (c) it operates from built structures; (d) it establishes management and monitoring systems, procedures and techniques which have the purpose of preventing, reducing, minimising and to the extent practicable eliminating: (i) health risks to the workers concerned and to the population in the vicinity of the ship recycling facility, and (ii) adverse effects on the environment caused by ship recycling; (e) it prepares a ship recycling facility plan; (f) it prevents adverse effects on human health and the environment, including the demonstration of the control of any leakage, in particular in intertidal zones; (g) it ensures safe and environmentally sound management and storage of hazardous materials and waste, including: (i) the containment of all hazardous materials present on board during the entire ship recycling process so as to prevent any release of those materials into the environment; and in addition, the handling of hazardous materials, and of waste generated during the ship recycling process, only on impermeable floors with effective drainage systems; (ii) that all waste generated from the ship recycling activity and their quantities are documented and are only transferred to waste management facilities, including waste recycling facilities, authorised to deal with their treatment without endangering human health and in an environmentally sound manner; (h) it establishes and maintains an emergency preparedness and response plan; ensures rapid access for emergency response equipment, such as fire-fighting equipment and vehicles, ambulances and cranes, to the ship and all areas of the ship recycling facility; (i) it provides for worker safety and training, including ensuring the use of personal protective equipment for operations requiring such use; (j) it establishes records on incidents, accidents, occupational diseases and chronic effects and, if requested by its competent authorities, reports any incidents, accidents, occupational diseases or chronic effects causing, or with the potential for causing, risks to workers' safety, human health and the environment; (k) it agrees to comply with the requirements of paragraph 2.

24.077 Article 13(2) provides that the operator of a ship recycling facility must: (a) send the ship recycling plan, once approved in accordance with Article 7(3), to the shipowner and the administration or a recognised organisation authorised by it; (b) report to the administration that the ship recycling facility is ready in every respect to start the recycling of the ship; and (c) when the total or partial recycling of a ship is completed in accordance with this regulation, within 14 days of the date of the total or partial recycling in accordance with the ship recycling plan, send a statement of completion to the administration which issued the ready for recycling certificate for the ship. The statement of completion shall include a report on incidents and accidents damaging human health and/or the environment, if any.

24.078 Under Article 13(3), the Commission shall adopt implementing acts to establish the format of: (a) the report required by point (b) of paragraph 2 of this article to ensure it is consistent with Appendix 6 to the Hong Kong Convention; and (b) the statement required by point (c) of paragraph 2 of this article to ensure it is consistent with Appendix 7 to the Hong Kong Convention. Those implementing acts shall be adopted in accordance with the examination procedure referred to in Article 25 of the regulation.

Authorisation of ship recycling facilities located in a Member State

24.079 Article 14(1) provides that without prejudice to other relevant provisions of EU law,

"competent authorities [must] authorise ship recycling facilities located on their territory that comply with the requirements set out in Article 13 to conduct ship recycling. That authorisation may be granted to the respective ship recycling facilities for a maximum period of five years and renewed accordingly."

The paragraph continues that provided that the requirements of the regulation are complied with, any permit produced pursuant to other relevant national or EU law provisions may be combined with the authorisation under this article to form a single permit, where such a format obviates the unnecessary duplication of information and the duplication of work by the operator of the ship recycling facility or the ship recycling company or the competent authority. In those cases the authorisation may be extended in accordance with the permit regime referred to in the first subparagraph, but not exceeding a maximum period of five years. Article 14(2) provides that Member States must establish and update a list of the ship recycling facilities that they have authorised in accordance with Article 14(1). Pursuant to Article 14(3), the list referred to in Article 14(2) shall be communicated to the Commission without delay and not later than 31 March 2015. Under Article 14(4), where a ship recycling facility ceases to comply with the requirements set out in Article 13, the Member State where that ship recycling facility is located shall suspend or withdraw the authorisation given to it or require corrective actions by the ship recycling company concerned and shall inform the Commission thereof without delay. Finally, Article 14(5) provides that where a ship recycling facility has been authorised in accordance with paragraph 1, the Member State concerned shall inform the Commission thereof without delay.

Ship recycling facilities located in a third country

24.080 The so-called European List is central to the EU's recycling regime.[32] Article 15(1) provides that a ship recycling company owning a ship recycling facility located in a third country and intending to recycle ships flying the flag of a Member State shall submit an application to the Commission for inclusion of that ship recycling facility in the European List. Article 15(2) provides that the application referred to in Article 15(1) shall be accompanied by evidence that the ship recycling facility concerned complies with the requirements set out in Article 13 in order to conduct ship recycling and to be included in

---

32 The Commission has stated on its website (http://ec.europa.eu/environment/waste/ships/): "The European List of ship recycling facilities. From a date set in the Regulation to fall between mid-2017 and 31 December 2018, large commercial seagoing vessels flying the flag of an EU Member State may be recycled only in safe and sound ship recycling facilities included in the European List of ship recycling facilities. The List was first established on 19 December 2016. It will be updated in the future through Implementing Acts to add more compliant facilities or to remove facilities which have ceased to comply. To be included in the European List, any ship recycling facility irrespective of its location has to comply with a number of safety and environmental requirements. In April 2016, the Commission issued technical guidelines on these requirements. The Commission assesses applications received from the ship recycling facilities located in third countries. The template for applications of ship recycling facilities located outside the EU can be found here. For facilities located in the EU, it is the national authorities of the Member States which indicate to the Commission which facilities located on their territory are compliant."

the European List in accordance with Article 16. In particular, the ship recycling company shall: (a) identify the permit, licence or authorisation granted by its competent authorities to conduct the ship recycling and, where relevant, the permit, licence or authorisation granted by the competent authorities to all its contractors and sub-contractors directly involved in the process of ship recycling and specify all information referred to in Article 16(2); (b) indicate whether the ship recycling plan will be approved by the competent authority through a tacit or explicit procedure, specifying the review period relating to tacit approval, in accordance with national requirements, where applicable; (c) confirm that it will only accept a ship flying the flag of a Member State for recycling in accordance with the regulation; (d) provide evidence that the ship recycling facility is capable of establishing, maintaining and monitoring of the safe-for-hot work and safe-for-entry criteria throughout the ship recycling process; (e) attach a map of the boundary of the ship recycling facility and the location of ship recycling operations within it; (f) for each hazardous material referred to in Annex I and additional hazardous material which might be part of the structure of a ship, specify: (i) whether the ship recycling facility is authorised to carry out the removal of the hazardous material. Where it is so authorised, the relevant personnel authorised to carry out the removal shall be identified and evidence of their competence shall be provided; (ii) which waste management process will be applied within or outside the ship recycling facility such as incineration, landfilling or another waste treatment method, the name and address of the waste treatment facility if different from that of the ship recycling facility, and provide evidence that the applied process will be carried out without endangering human health and in an environmentally sound manner; (g) confirm that the company adopted a ship recycling facility plan, taking into account the relevant IMO guidelines; and (h) provide the information necessary to identify the ship recycling facility. The Commission is empowered, by virtue of Article 15(3), to adopt implementing acts to specify the format of the information required to identify the ship recycling facility. Those implementing acts shall be adopted in accordance with the examination procedure referred to in Article 25. In that context, in order to be included in the European List, compliance by ship recycling facilities located in third countries with the requirements set out in Article 13 shall be certified following a site inspection by an independent verifier with appropriate qualifications.[33] The certification shall be submitted to the Commission by the ship recycling company when applying for inclusion in the European List and, every five years thereafter, upon renewal of the inclusion in the European List.[34] The initial inclusion on the list and the renewal thereof shall be supplemented by a mid-term review to confirm compliance with the requirements set out in Article 13.[35] By applying for inclusion in the European List, ship recycling companies accept the possibility of the ship recycling facility concerned being subject to site inspections by the Commission or agents acting on its behalf prior to or after their inclusion in the European List in order to verify compliance with the requirements set out in Article 13.[36] The independent verifier, the Commission or agents acting on its behalf shall co-operate with the competent authorities of the third country where the ship recycling

---

33 Reg. 1257/2013, Art. 15(4).
34 Ibid.
35 Ibid.
36 Ibid.

facility is located in order to carry out those site inspections.[37] The Commission may issue technical guidance notes in order to facilitate such certification.[38] Indeed, Article 15(5) provides that for the purposes of Article 13, with regard to the waste recovery or disposal operation concerned, environmentally sound management may only be assumed to be in place provided the ship recycling company can demonstrate that the waste management facility which receives the waste will be operated in accordance with human health and environmental protection standards that are broadly equivalent to relevant international and EU standards. In this context, the ship recycling company must provide updated evidence without delay in the event of any changes to the information provided to the Commission and shall, in any event, three months prior to expiry of each five-year period of inclusion on the European List, declare that: (a) the evidence that it has provided is complete and up to date; and (b) the ship recycling facility continues and will continue to comply with the requirements of Article 13.

Establishment and updating of the European List

24.081 The establishment and updating of the European List is addressed by Article 16. Under Article 16(1), the Commission must adopt implementing acts to establish a European List of ship recycling facilities which: (a) are located in the Union and have been notified by the Member States in accordance with Article 14(3); and (b) are located in a third country and whose inclusion is based on an assessment of the information and supporting evidence provided or gathered in accordance with Article 15. Those implementing acts shall be adopted in accordance with the examination procedure referred to in Article 25. Under Article 16(2), the European List shall be published in the *Official Journal of the European Union* and on the website of the Commission not later than 31 December 2016.[39] It must be divided into two sub-lists indicating the ship recycling facilities located in a Member State and the ship recycling facilities located in a third country. The European List must include all of the following information about the ship recycling facility: (a) the method of recycling; (b) the type and size of ships that can be recycled; (c) any limitation and conditions under which the ship recycling facility operates, including as regards hazardous waste management; (d) details on the explicit or tacit procedure, as referred to in Article 7(3), for the approval of the ship recycling plan by the competent authority; and (e) the maximum annual ship recycling output. The European List must, by virtue of Article 16(3), indicate the date of expiry of the inclusion of the ship recycling facility. An inclusion shall be valid for a maximum period of five years and shall be renewable. The Commission must, by reason of Article 16(4), adopt implementing acts to regularly update the European List, in order to: (a) include a ship recycling facility in the European List where: (i) it has been authorised in accordance with Article 14; or (ii) its inclusion in the European List is decided in accordance with paragraph 1(b) of Article 16; (b) remove a ship recycling facility from the European List where: (i) the ship recycling facility ceases to comply with the requirements set out in Article 13; or (ii) the updated evidence is not provided at least three months prior to expiry of the five-year period as set

---

37 Ibid.
38 Ibid.
39 For the list, see http://ec.europa.eu/environment/waste/ships/list.htm.

out in paragraph 3 of Article 16. Those implementing acts shall be adopted, in accordance with the examination procedure referred to in Article 25. Finally, Article 16(5) provides that in establishing and updating the European List, the Commission must act in accordance with the principles enshrined in the Treaties and with the international obligations of the Union and Article 16(6) provides that Member States must communicate to the Commission all information that may be relevant in the context of updating the European List and the Commission shall forward all relevant information to the other Member States.

General administrative provisions

24.082 Title IV of the regulation deals with some general administrative provisions.

24.083 Article 17 ("Language") provides, in paragraph 1, that the

"ship recycling plan referred to in Article 7 shall be developed in a language accepted by the state authorising the ship recycling facility. Where the language used is not English, French or Spanish, the ship recycling plan shall be translated into one of those languages, except where the administration is satisfied that that is unnecessary."

Article 17(2) provides that the

"inventory certificate and the ready for recycling certificate issued pursuant to Article 9 shall be drawn up in an official language of the issuing administration. Where the language used is not English, French or Spanish, the text shall include a translation into one of those languages."

24.084 The designation of competent authorities and administrations is addressed by Article 18. Article 18(1) provides that Member States must designate the competent authorities and administrations responsible for the application of the regulation and shall notify the Commission of those designations. Member States must immediately notify the Commission of any changes in such information.[40] Article 18(2) provides that the Commission must publish on its website lists of the designated competent authorities and administrations and shall update those lists as appropriate.

24.085 The designation of contact persons is addressed by Article 19. Under Article 19(1), Member States and the Commission must each designate one or more contact persons responsible for informing or advising natural or legal persons making enquiries. The contact person of the Commission must forward to the contact persons of the Member States any questions received which concern the latter, and vice versa. Member States must, by virtue of Article 19(2), notify the Commission of the designation of contact persons. Member States shall immediately notify the Commission of any changes to that information. Article 19(3) states that the Commission shall publish on its website lists of the designated contact persons and shall update those lists as appropriate.

24.086 Article 20 deals with the so-called "meeting of contact persons". It provides that the Commission must

"if requested by Member States or where it considers it appropriate, periodically organise a meeting of the contact persons to discuss the questions raised by the implementation of this Regulation. Relevant stakeholders shall be invited to such meetings, or parts of meetings, where all Member States and the Commission are in agreement that it is appropriate to do so."

---

40 Reg. 1257/2013, Art. 18(1).

Reporting and enforcement

24.087 Title V deals with reporting and enforcement.

24.088 Article 21 relates to reports by the Member States. The article provides:

"1. Each Member State shall send to the Commission a report containing the following:

    (a) a list of the ships flying its flag to which a ready for recycling certificate has been issued, and the name of the ship recycling company and the location of the ship recycling facility as shown in the ready for recycling certificate;

    (b) a list of the ships flying its flag for which a statement of completion has been received;

    (c) information regarding illegal ship recycling, penalties and follow-up actions undertaken by the Member State.

2. Every three years, Member States shall electronically transmit the report to the Commission no later than nine months after the end of the three-year period covered by it.

    The first electronic report shall cover the period from the date of application of this Regulation to the end of the first regular three-year reporting period, specified in Article 5 of Council Directive 91/692/EEC,[41] falling after the starting date of the first reporting period.

    The Commission shall publish a report on the application of this Regulation no later than nine months after receiving the reports from the Member States.

3. The Commission shall enter this information in an electronic database that is permanently accessible to the public."

Enforcement in Member States

24.089 Enforcement in Member States is addressed by Article 22. Under Article 22(1), Member States must lay down provisions on penalties applicable to infringements of the regulation and shall take all the measures necessary to ensure that they are applied. The penalties provided for shall be effective, proportionate and dissuasive. Member States shall co-operate, bilaterally or multilaterally, with one another in order to facilitate the prevention and detection of potential circumvention and breach of this regulation.[42] Member States must designate those members of their permanent staff responsible for the co-operation referred to in Article 22(2).[43] That information must be sent to the Commission, which shall distribute to those members a compiled list.[44] Member States must communicate to the Commission the provisions of their national law relating to the enforcement of this regulation and the applicable penalties.[45]

Request for action

24.090 Article 23 deals with requests for action. Article 23(1) provides:

"1. Natural or legal persons affected or likely to be affected by a breach of Article 13 in conjunction with Article 15 and Article 16(1)(b) of this Regulation, or having a sufficient interest in environmental decision-making relating to the breach of Article 13 in conjunction

---

41 Ed., Council Dir. 91/692 of 23 December 1991 standardising and rationalising reports on the implementation of certain Directives relating to the environment (OJ L377/48, 31 December 1991).
42 Reg. 1257/2013, Art. 22(2).
43 Reg. 1257/2013, Art. 22(3).
44 Ibid.
45 Reg. 1257/2013, Art. 22(4).

with Article 15 and Article 16(1)(b) of this Regulation shall be entitled to request the Commission to take action under this Regulation with respect to such a breach or an imminent threat of such a breach.

The interest of any non-governmental organisation promoting environmental protection and meeting the requirements laid down in Article 11 of Regulation (EC) No 1367/2006 of the European Parliament and of the Council[46] shall be deemed sufficient for the purposes of the first subparagraph."

24.091 The request for action shall be accompanied by the relevant information and data supporting that request.[47] Where the request for action and the accompanying information and data show in a plausible manner that a breach of Article 13 in conjunction with Article 15 and Article 16(1)(b) has occurred, or that there is an imminent threat of such a breach, the Commission shall consider any such requests for action and information and data. In such circumstances, the Commission shall give the ship recycling company concerned an opportunity to make its views known with respect to the request for action and the accompanying information and data.[48] The Commission must, without delay and in accordance with the relevant provisions of EU law, inform the persons who submitted a request pursuant to Article 23(1), of its decision to accede to or refuse the request for action and shall provide the reasons for it.[49]

Final provisions in the regulation

Introduction

24.092 Title VI is entitled "final provisions". Article 24 ("Exercise of the Delegation") provides in paragraph 1 that the power to adopt delegated acts is conferred on the Commission subject to the conditions laid down in Article 24. Under Article 24(2), the power to adopt delegated acts referred to in Article 5(8) shall be conferred on the Commission for a period of five years from 30 December 2013. The Commission shall draw up a report in respect of the delegation of power no later than nine months before the end of the five-year period. The delegation of power shall be tacitly extended for periods of an identical duration, unless the European Parliament or the Council opposes such extension no later than three months before the end of each period. Article 24(3) provides that the delegation of power referred to in Article 5(8) may be revoked at any time by the European Parliament or by the Council. A decision to revoke shall put an end to the delegation of the power specified in that decision. It shall take effect the day following the publication of the decision in the *Official Journal of the European Union* or at a late date specified therein. It shall not affect the validity of any delegated acts already in force. Under Article 24(4), as soon as it adopts a delegated act, the Commission shall notify it simultaneously to the European Parliament and to the Council. Finally, Article 24(5) states that a delegated act adopted pursuant to Article 5(8) shall enter into force only if no objection

---

46 Ed., Reg. 1367/2006 of the European Parliament and of the Council of 6 September 2006 on the application of the provisions of the Aarhus Convention on Access to Information, Public Participation in Decision-making and Access to Justice in Environmental Matters to Community institutions and bodies (OJ L264/13, 25 September 2006).

47 Reg. 1257/2013, Art. 23(2).

48 Reg. 1257/2013, Art. 23(3).

49 Reg. 1257/2013, Art. 23(4).

has been expressed either by the European Parliament or the Council within a period of two months of notification of that act to the European Parliament and the Council or if, before the expiry of that period, the European Parliament and the Council have both informed the Commission that they will not object. That period shall be extended by two months at the initiative of the European Parliament or of the Council.

Committee procedure

24.093 Article 25 of the regulation establishes the committee procedure. Article 25(1) provides that the Commission shall be assisted by a committee and that committee shall be a committee within the meaning of Regulation 182/2011. Article 25(2) provides that when reference is made to Article 25(2), Article 5 of Regulation 182/2011 shall apply and where the committee delivers no opinion, the Commission shall not adopt the draft implementing act and the third subparagraph of Article 5(4) of Regulation 182/2011 shall apply.

Transitional provision

24.094 Article 26 contains a transition provision. As of the date of publication of the European List, Member States may, prior to the date of application of the regulation, authorise the recycling of ships in ship recycling facilities included in the European List. In such circumstances, Regulation 1013/2006 shall not apply.

Amendments

24.095 Articles 27 and 28 provide for amendments to two other EU measures. Article 27 amended Regulation 1013/2006 by adding an additional point in Article 1(3) of Regulation 1013/2006: "(i) ships flying the flag of a Member State falling under the scope of Regulation (EU) No 1257/2013 of the European Parliament and of the Council".[50] Article 28 amends Directive 2009/16[51] by adding a point (numbered 49) to Annex IV: "[a] certificate on the inventory of hazardous materials or a statement of compliance as applicable pursuant to Regulation (EU) No 1257/2013 of the European Parliament and of the Council".[52]

Financial incentive

24.096 Article 29 provides that the Commission had to, by 31 December 2016, submit to the European Parliament and to the Council a report on the feasibility of a financial instrument that would facilitate safe and sound ship recycling and shall, if appropriate, accompany it by a legislative proposal.

---

50 Reg. (EU) No 1257/2013 of the European Parliament and of the Council of 20 November 2013 on ship recycling and amending Reg. (EC) No 1013/2006 and Dir. 2009/16 (OJ L330, 10 December 2013, p. 1).

51 OJ L131, 28 May 2009, p. 57.

52 Reg. (EU) No 1257/2013 of the European Parliament and of the Council of 20 November 2013 on ship recycling and amending Reg. (EC) No 1013/2006 and Dir. 2009/16 (OJ L330, 10 December 2013, p. 1).

Review

24.097 Article 30 of the regulation deals with the review of the regulation:

"1. The Commission shall assess which infringements of this Regulation should be brought under the scope of Directive 2008/99/EC to achieve equivalence of the provisions related to infringements between this Regulation and Regulation (EC) No 1013/2006. The Commission shall report on its findings by 31 December 2014 to the European Parliament and to the Council and, if appropriate, accompany it by a legislative proposal.

2. The Commission shall review this Regulation not later than 18 months prior to the date of entry into force of the Hong Kong Convention and at the same time, submit, if appropriate, any appropriate legislative proposals to that effect. This review shall consider the inclusion of ship recycling facilities authorised under the Hong Kong Convention in the European List in order to avoid duplication of work and administrative burden.

3. The Commission shall keep this Regulation under review and, if appropriate, make timely proposals to address developments relating to international Conventions, including the Basel Convention, should it prove necessary.

4. Notwithstanding paragraph 2, the Commission shall, by five years after the date of application of this Regulation, submit a report to the European Parliament and to the Council on the application of this Regulation, accompanied, if appropriate, by legislative proposals to ensure that its objectives are being met and its impact is ensured and justified."

Annexes

24.098 Annex I deals with the control of hazardous materials and include substances such as asbestos.[53] Annex II enumerates the items for the Inventory of Hazardous Materials. They are: (1) any hazardous materials listed in Annex I; (2) cadmium and cadmium compounds; (3) hexavalent chromium and hexavalent chromium compounds; (4) lead and lead compounds; (5) mercury and mercury compounds; (6) polybrominated biphenyl ("PBBs"); (7) polybrominated diphenyl ethers ("PBDEs"); (8) polychlorinated naphthalenes (more than three chlorine atoms); (9) radioactive substances; (10) certain shortchain chlorinated paraffins (alkanes, C10-C13, chloro); and (11) brominated flame retardant ("HBCDD").

E. COMMISSION IMPLEMENTING DECISION (EU) 2016/2325 OF 19 DECEMBER 2016 ON THE FORMAT OF THE CERTIFICATE ON THE INVENTORY OF HAZARDOUS MATERIALS ISSUED IN ACCORDANCE WITH REGULATION (EU) NO 1257/2013 OF THE EUROPEAN PARLIAMENT AND OF THE COUNCIL ON SHIP RECYCLING

24.099 On 19 December 2016, the Commission Implementing Decision 2016/2325 on the format of the certificate on the inventory of hazardous materials was issued in accordance with Regulation 1257/2013 of the European Parliament and of the Council on ship recycling.[54] The decision is based, as a matter of law, on the TFEU generally. The background is Regulation 1257/2013 of the European Parliament and of the Council of 20 November 2013 on ship recycling and amending Regulation 1013/2006 and Directive

---

53 For details, see Annex I of Reg. 1257/2013.
54 OJ L345/131, 20 December 2016.

2009/16,[55] and in particular Article 9(1) thereof. The decision is a very short measure.[56] Article 1 provides that inventory certificates issued and endorsed in accordance with Article 9 of Regulation 1257/2013 shall comply with the format set out in the annex to the decision. Article 2 provides that the decision entered into force on the twentieth day following that of its publication in the *Official Journal of the European Union*.

---

55 OJ L330/1, 10 December 2013.

56 The background is clear from the recitals: "(1) Reg ... 1257/2013 lays down requirements for ship owners, administrations and recognised organisations regarding the development, surveying and certification of inventories of hazardous materials found in ships. (2) In accordance with the requirements of Article 5 of Reg ... 1257/2013, ships are to have on board an inventory of hazardous materials. (3) Pursuant to Article 32 of Regulation ... 1257/2013, the obligation to have on board an inventory of hazardous materials is to apply to existing ships from 31 December 2020, to new ships not later than 31 December 2018 and to ships going for recycling from the date of publication of the European List published in accordance with Reg ... 1257/2013. (4) Pursuant to Article 8 of Regulation ... 1257/2013, ships are to be subject to surveys by officers of administrations or of recognised organisations authorised by administrations. The surveys aim to confirm that the inventory of hazardous materials complies with the applicable requirements of the Regulation. (5) Pursuant to Article 9(1) of Reg ... 1257/2013, after successful completion of an initial or renewal survey, the administration or a recognised organisation authorised by it is to issue an inventory certificate. The format of the inventory certificate must be consistent with Appendix 3 to the International Convention for the Safe and Environmentally Sound Recycling of Ships adopted in Hong Kong on 15 May 2009 ('Hong Kong Convention'). (6) The measures provided for in this Decision are in accordance with the opinion of the Ship Recycling Regulation Committee established under Article 25 of Reg. 1257/2013."

CHAPTER 25

European Union external relations law and shipping

A. INTRODUCTION

25.001 This chapter examines selected aspects of the external dimension of European Union ("EU") shipping law.[1] The topic of the EU's external dimensions or foreign relations is an enormous topic so this chapter is necessarily selective in nature.

25.002 Traditionally, the topic of "external relations" was seen as somewhat esoteric but the topic could become even more significant if the UK leaves the EU (i.e. if "Brexit" occurs). It is not clear, at the time of writing, what will be the nature and terms of the relationship between the EU and the UK so the UK could be either a total stranger (in the

---

1 On EU external relations law generally, see Eeckhout, EU External Relations Law (2nd ed., 2012); Kuijper, Wouters, Hoffmeister, De Baere and Ramopoulos, The Law of EU External Relations: Cases, Materials, and Commentary on the EU as an International Legal Actor (2015); Van Vooren, EU External Relations Law and the European Neighbourhood Policy (2013); and Van Vooren and Wessel, EU External Relations Law: Text, Cases and Materials (2014). See also Ziegler, "The Relationship between EU Law and International Law", University of Leicester School of Law Research Paper No. 15-04, http://papers.ssrn.com/sol3/papers.cfm?abstract_id=2554069##. See De Baere, "EU External Action" in Barnard and Peers (eds), European Union Law (2014), chap. 24. This chapter does not consider the 1998 Agreement in the form of an Exchange of Letters between the European Community and the Republic of Lithuania on maritime transport (OJ L51/240, 20 February 1998) which was short but now of largely historical relevance only; for completeness, it read:

"AGREEMENT in the form of an Exchange of Letters between the European Community and the Republic of Lithuania on maritime transport

A. Letter from the Community

Sir,

We would be grateful if you would confirm that your Government agrees with the following:

When the Free Trade Agreement between the European Communities and Lithuania was signed, the Parties undertook to address in the appropriate manner, issues relating to the operation of shipping, particularly where the development of trade might be hindered. Mutually satisfactory solutions on shipping will be sought while the principle of free and fair competition on a commercial basis is observed.

It has likewise been agreed that such issues should also be discussed by the Association Council.

Please accept, Sir, the assurance of our highest consideration.

On behalf of the Council of the European Union

B. Letter from the Republic of Lithuania

Sir,

I have the honour to acknowledge receipt of your letter and to confirm that my Government agrees with the following:

'When the Free Trade Agreement between the European Communities and Lithuania was signed, the Parties undertook to address in the appropriate manner, issues relating to the operation of shipping, particularly where the development of trade might be hindered. Mutually satisfactory solutions on shipping will be sought while the principle of free and fair competition on a commercial basis is observed.

It has likewise been agreed that such issues should also be discussed by the Association Council.'

Please accept, Sir, the assurance of our highest consideration.

For the Government of the Republic of Lithuania."

case of a "hard Brexit") in which case the general EU external dimension would apply but if there is a special arrangement between the EU and the UK then the terms of that relationship could be more significant.

25.003 The external dimension to EU shipping law is complicated by such factors as that the EU participates as a contracting party to the United Nations Convention on the Law of the Sea ("UNCLOS III") but, conversely, the EU is not a member in its own right of the United Nations' International Maritime Organization ("IMO"). While the EU Member States are members of the IMO and vote in their own right, their views are co-ordinated by the EU (acting primarily through the Commission) so there is almost invariably a common view expressed at the IMO even though the EU is not a member. The situation becomes more complicated when the EU seeks to adopt a measure which is lawful according to the IMO rules but unlawful under EU law (e.g. because it would involve EU Member States engaging in discrimination in favour of, or against, EU Member States)

B. EU LAW GENERALLY ON EXTERNAL RELATIONS

Introduction

25.004 The EU is not a State but it is actively involved in international affairs. Indeed, in many respects, the EU is seen by many as having international legal personality.[2] Indeed, in some respects and in so far as Member States allow it, the EU even represents the interests not only of the EU itself but also its Member States in certain international matters (e.g. in certain international organisations).

The Treaty on European Union

25.005 As will be recalled from chapter 3, there are two main treaties in EU law: the Treaty on European Union ("TEU") and the Treaty on the Functioning of the European Union ("TFEU"). Both treaties are relevant to the topic of external relations and the external dimension to EU law.

25.006 Title V of the TEU has some provisions which are relevant to the external relations of the EU from the perspective of EU shipping law. Title V is entitled "General Provisions on the Union's External Action and Specific Provisions on the Common Foreign and Security Policy".

25.007 Chapter 1 of Title V is entitled "General Provisions on the Union's External Action".

25.008 Article 21(1) of the TEU (which is in Chapter 1 of Title V) provides that the EU's

---

2 Art. 47 of the TEU provides that "[t]he Union shall have legal personality". Declaration No. 24 Concerning the Legal Personality of the European Union (attached to the TFEU) provides: "The Conference confirms that the fact that the European Union has a legal personality will not in any way authorise the Union to legislate or to act beyond the competences conferred upon it by the Member States in the Treaties." It is possible that a third State might not recognise the EU as having legal personality but it has legal personality as far as the EU and its Member States are concerned.

"action on the international scene shall be guided by the principles which have inspired its own creation, development and enlargement, and which it seeks to advance in the wider world: democracy, the rule of law, the universality and indivisibility of human rights and fundamental freedoms, respect for human dignity, the principles of equality and solidarity, and respect for the principles of the United Nations Charter and international law."

The same provision goes on to say that the EU

"shall seek to develop relations and build partnerships with third countries, and international, regional or global organisations which share the principles referred to in the first subparagraph. It shall promote multilateral solutions to common problems, in particular in the framework of the United Nations."

Article 21(2) provides that the EU

"shall define and pursue common policies and actions, and shall work for a high degree of cooperation in all fields of international relations, in order to: (a) safeguard its values, fundamental interests, security, independence and integrity; (b) consolidate and support democracy, the rule of law, human rights and the principles of international law; (c) preserve peace, prevent conflicts and strengthen international security, in accordance with the purposes and principles of the United Nations Charter, with the principles of the Helsinki Final Act and with the aims of the Charter of Paris, including those relating to external borders; (d) foster the sustainable economic, social and environmental development of developing countries, with the primary aim of eradicating poverty; (e) encourage the integration of all countries into the world economy, including through the progressive abolition of restrictions on international trade; (f) help develop international measures to preserve and improve the quality of the environment and the sustainable management of global natural resources, in order to ensure sustainable development; (g) assist populations, countries and regions confronting natural or man-made disasters; and (h) promote an international system based on stronger multilateral cooperation and good global governance."

Article 21(3) provides that EU

"shall respect the principles and pursue the objectives set out in paragraphs 1 and 2 in the development and implementation of the different areas of the Union's external action covered by this Title and by Part Five of the Treaty on the Functioning of the European Union, and of the external aspects of its other policies. The Union shall ensure consistency between the different areas of its external action and between these and its other policies. The Council and the Commission, assisted by the High Representative of the Union for Foreign Affairs and Security Policy, shall ensure that consistency and shall cooperate to that effect."

25.009 In this context, Article 22(1) of the TEU provides that, on the basis of the principles and objectives set out in Article 21, the European Council must identify the strategic interests and objectives of the EU. Decisions of the European Council on the strategic interests and objectives of the Union shall relate to the common foreign and security policy (the "CFSP") and to other areas of the external action of the Union. Such decisions may concern the relations of the Union with a specific country or region or may be thematic in approach. They shall define their duration, and the means to be made available by the EU and the Member States. The European Council must act unanimously on a recommendation from the Council, adopted by the latter under the arrangements laid down for each area. Decisions of the European Council shall be implemented in accordance with the procedures provided for in the Treaties. The High Representative of the Union for Foreign Affairs and Security Policy, for the area of CFSP, and the Commission, for other areas of external action, may submit joint proposals to the Council.

25.010 Chapter 2 of Title V deals with specific provisions on the CFSP. Section 1 is entitled "Common Provisions".

25.011 Article 23 provides that the EU's action on the international scene, pursuant to the Chapter, shall be guided by the principles, shall pursue the objectives of, and be conducted in accordance with, the general provisions laid down in Chapter 1.

25.012 Article 24(1) provides that the EU's competence in matters of CFSP shall cover all areas of foreign policy and all questions relating to the Union's security, including the progressive framing of a common defence policy that might lead to a common defence. The CFSP is subject to specific rules and procedures. It shall be defined and implemented by the European Council and the Council acting unanimously, except where the Treaties provide otherwise. The adoption of legislative acts shall be excluded. The CFSP shall be put into effect by the High Representative of the Union for Foreign Affairs and Security Policy and by Member States, in accordance with the Treaties. The specific role of the European Parliament and of the Commission in this area is defined by the Treaties. The Court of Justice of the European Union ("CJEU") shall not have jurisdiction with respect to these provisions, with the exception of its jurisdiction to monitor compliance with Article 40 of the TEU and to review the legality of certain decisions as provided for by the second paragraph of Article 275 of the TFEU. Article 24(2) provides that within the framework of the principles and objectives of its external action, the EU must conduct, define and implement a CFSP, based on the development of mutual political solidarity among Member States, the identification of questions of general interest and the achievement of an ever-increasing degree of convergence of Member States' actions. Under Article 24(3), the Member States must support the EU's external and security policy actively and unreservedly in a spirit of loyalty and mutual solidarity and shall comply with the Union's action in this area. The Member States must work together to enhance and develop their mutual political solidarity. They shall refrain from any action which is contrary to the interests of the Union or likely to impair its effectiveness as a cohesive force in international relations. The Council and the High Representative must ensure compliance with these principles.

25.013 Under Article 25, the EU must conduct the CFSP by: (a) defining the general guidelines; (b) adopting decisions defining: (i) actions to be undertaken by the Union; (ii) positions to be taken by the Union; (iii) arrangements for the implementation of the decisions referred to in points (i) and (ii); and by (c) strengthening systematic co-operation between Member States in the conduct of policy.

25.014 Under Article 26(1), the European Council must identify the EU's strategic interests, determine the objectives of and define general guidelines for the CFSP, including for matters with defence implications. It must adopt the necessary decisions. If international developments so require, the President of the European Council shall convene an extraordinary meeting of the European Council in order to define the strategic lines of the EU's policy in the face of such developments. Under Article 26(2), the Council must frame the CFSP and take the decisions necessary for defining and implementing it on the basis of the general guidelines and strategic lines defined by the European Council. The Council and the High Representative of the Union for Foreign Affairs and Security Policy must ensure the unity, consistency and effectiveness of action by the Union. Under Article 26(3), the CFSP shall be put into effect by the High Representative and by the Member States, using national and EU resources.

25.015 Article 27(1) provides that the EU's "High Representative of the Union for Foreign Affairs and Security Policy", who shall chair the Foreign Affairs Council, shall contribute through his or her proposals to the development of the CFSP and shall ensure implementation of the decisions adopted by the European Council and the Council. The High Representative shall represent the EU for matters relating to the CFSP. He shall conduct political dialogue with third parties on the EU's behalf and shall express the Union's position in international organisations and at international conferences.[3] Article 27(3) provides that in fulfilling his mandate, the High Representative shall be assisted by a European External Action Service – this is the so-called "EEAS".[4] This service shall work in co-operation with the diplomatic services of the Member States and shall comprise officials from relevant departments of the General Secretariat of the Council and of the Commission as well as staff seconded from national diplomatic services of the Member States. The organisation and functioning of the EEAS shall be established by a decision of the Council. The Council shall act on a proposal from the High Representative after consulting the European Parliament and after obtaining the consent of the Commission.

25.016 Article 28(1) provides that where the international situation requires operational action by the EU, the Council shall adopt the necessary decisions. The Council shall lay down their objectives, scope, the means to be made available to the EU, if necessary their duration, and the conditions for their implementation. If there is a change in circumstances having a substantial effect on a question subject to such a decision, the Council shall review the principles and objectives of that decision and take the necessary decisions. Article 28(2) provides that the decisions referred to in Article 28(1) commit the Member States in the positions they adopt and in the conduct of their activity. Whenever there is any plan to adopt a national position or take national action pursuant to a decision as referred to in Article 28(1), information must be provided by the Member State concerned in time to allow, if necessary, for prior consultations within the Council.[5] The obligation to provide prior information must not apply to measures which are merely a national transposition of Council decisions.[6] There is some limited discretion: Article 28(4) provides that in cases of imperative need arising from changes in the situation and failing a review of the Council decision as referred to in Article 28(1), Member States may take the necessary measures as a matter of urgency having regard to the general objectives of that decision. The Member State concerned must inform the Council immediately of any such measures. Should there be any major difficulties in implementing a decision as referred to in this article, a Member State shall refer them to the Council which shall discuss them and seek appropriate solutions.[7] Such solutions must not run counter to the objectives of the decision referred to in Article 28(1) or impair its effectiveness.[8]

25.017 Article 29 goes on to provide that the Council must adopt decisions which shall define the approach of the EU to a particular matter of a geographical or thematic nature

---

3 TEU, Art. 27(2).
4 On the EEAS, see https://eeas.europa.eu/headquarters/headquarters-homepage_en.
5 TEU, Art. 28(3).
6 Ibid.
7 TEU, Art. 28(5).
8 Ibid.

and Member States must ensure that their national policies conform to the Union positions.

25.018 Article 30(1) provides that any Member State, the High Representative of the Union for Foreign Affairs and Security Policy, or the High Representative with the Commission's support, may refer any question relating to the CFSP to the Council and may submit to it, respectively, initiatives or proposals. By way of exception, Article 30(2) provides that in cases requiring a rapid decision, the High Representative, of his or her own motion, or at the request of a Member State, shall convene an extraordinary Council meeting within 48 hours or, in an emergency, within a shorter period.

25.019 Article 31 provides in paragraph 1 that decisions under Chapter 2 must be taken by the European Council and the Council acting unanimously, except where the Chapter provides otherwise while the adoption of legislative acts shall be excluded. When abstaining in a vote, any member of the Council may qualify its abstention by making a formal declaration. In that case, it is not obliged to apply the decision, but must accept that the decision commits the EU. In a spirit of mutual solidarity, the Member State concerned must refrain from any action likely to conflict with or impede Union action based on that decision and the other Member States shall respect its position. If the members of the Council qualifying their abstention in this way represent at least one-third of the Member States comprising at least one-third of the population of the Union, the decision must not be adopted. Paragraph 2[9] of Article 31 provides a derogation from the provisions of paragraph 1 when it states that the Council shall act by qualified majority: when adopting a decision defining a Union action or position on the basis of a decision of the European Council relating to the Union's strategic interests and objectives, as referred to in Article 22(1); when adopting a decision defining a Union action or position, on a proposal which the High Representative of the Union for Foreign Affairs and Security Policy has presented following a specific request from the European Council, made on its own initiative or that of the High Representative; when adopting any decision implementing a decision defining a Union action or position; and when appointing a special representative in accordance with Article 33. If a member of the Council declares that, for vital and stated reasons of national policy, it intends to oppose the adoption of a decision to be taken by qualified majority, a vote shall not be taken. The High Representative will, in close consultation with the Member State involved, search for a solution acceptable to it. If he or she does not succeed, the Council may, acting by a qualified majority, request that the matter be referred to the European Council for a decision by unanimity. Under the third paragraph of Article 31, the European Council may unanimously adopt a decision stipulating that the Council shall act by a qualified majority in cases other than those referred to in paragraph 2.[10] For procedural questions, Article 31(5) provides that the Council shall act by a majority of its members.

25.020 Article 32 provides that Member States must consult one another within the European Council and the Council on any matter of foreign and security policy of general interest in order to determine a common approach. Before undertaking any action on the international scene or entering into any commitment which could affect the Union's interests, each Member State shall consult the others within the European Council or the

---

9 This paragraph does not apply to decisions having military or defence implications.
10 This paragraph does not apply to decisions having military or defence implications.

Council. Member States shall ensure, through the convergence of their actions, that the Union is able to assert its interests and values on the international scene. Member States shall show mutual solidarity. When the European Council or the Council has defined a common approach of the Union within the meaning of the first paragraph, the High Representative of the Union for Foreign Affairs and Security Policy and the Ministers for Foreign Affairs of the Member States shall co-ordinate their activities within the Council. The diplomatic missions of the Member States and the Union delegations in third countries and at international organisations[11] must co-operate and shall contribute to formulating and implementing the common approach.

25.021 Article 33 provides that the Council may, on a proposal from the High Representative of the Union for Foreign Affairs and Security Policy, appoint a special representative with a mandate in relation to particular policy issues. The special representative must carry out his or her mandate under the authority of the High Representative.

25.022 Article 34(1) provides that Member States must co-ordinate their action in international organisations and at international conferences. They shall uphold the EU's positions in such forums. The High Representative of the Union for Foreign Affairs and Security Policy shall organise this co-ordination. In international organisations and at international conferences where not all the Member States participate, those which do take part shall uphold the Union's positions. In accordance with Article 24(3), Member States represented in international organisations or international conferences where not all the Member States participate shall keep the other Member States and the High Representative informed of any matter of common interest.[12] Member States which are also members of the United Nations Security Council will concert and keep the other Member States and the High Representative fully informed. Member States which are members of the Security Council will, in the execution of their functions, defend the positions and the interests of the Union, without prejudice to their responsibilities under the provisions of the United Nations Charter. When the Union has defined a position on a subject which is on the United Nations Security Council agenda, those Member States which sit on the Security Council shall request that the High Representative be invited to present the Union's position.

25.023 Under Article 35, the diplomatic and consular missions of the Member States and the Union delegations in third countries and international conferences, and their representations to international organisations, must co-operate in ensuring that decisions defining Union positions and actions adopted pursuant to this Chapter are complied with and implemented. They shall step up co-operation by exchanging information and carrying out joint assessments. They shall contribute to the implementation of the right of citizens of the Union to protection in the territory of third countries as referred to in Article 20(2)(c) of the TFEU and of the measures adopted pursuant to Article 23 of that Treaty.

25.024 Article 36 provides that the High Representative of the Union for Foreign Affairs and Security Policy must regularly consult the European Parliament on the main aspects and the basic choices of the CFSP and the common security and defence policy

---

11 E.g. the IMO.
12 TEU, Art. 34(2).

and inform it of how those policies evolve.[13] He or she must ensure that the views of the European Parliament are duly taken into consideration. Special representatives may be involved in briefing the European Parliament.[14] The European Parliament may address questions or make recommendations to the Council or the High Representative.[15] Twice a year it must hold a debate on progress in implementing the CFSP, including the common security and defence policy.[16]

25.025 The Union may conclude agreements with one or more States or international organisations in areas covered by Chapter 2.[17]

25.026 Article 38 provides:

"Without prejudice to Article 240 of the Treaty on the Functioning of the European Union, a Political and Security Committee shall monitor the international situation in the areas covered by the common foreign and security policy and contribute to the definition of policies by delivering opinions to the Council at the request of the Council or of the High Representative of the Union for Foreign Affairs and Security Policy or on its own initiative. It shall also monitor the implementation of agreed policies, without prejudice to the powers of the High Representative.

Within the scope of this Chapter, the Political and Security Committee shall exercise, under the responsibility of the Council and of the High Representative, the political control and strategic direction of the crisis management operations referred to in Article 43.

The Council may authorise the Committee, for the purpose and for the duration of a crisis management operation, as determined by the Council, to take the relevant decisions concerning the political control and strategic direction of the operation."

25.027 Article 39 provides in accordance with Article 16 of the TFEU and by way of derogation from paragraph 2 of Article 16, the Council must adopt a decision laying down the rules relating to the protection of individuals with regard to the processing of personal data by the Member States when carrying out activities which fall within the scope of this Chapter, and the rules relating to the free movement of such data. Compliance with these rules shall be subject to the control of independent authorities.

25.028 Article 40 provides that the implementation of the CFSP must not affect the application of the procedures and the extent of the powers of the institutions laid down by the Treaties for the exercise of the Union competences referred to in Articles 3 to 6 of the TFEU. Similarly, the implementation of the policies listed in those articles shall not affect the application of the procedures and the extent of the powers of the institutions laid down by the Treaties for the exercise of the Union competences under the Chapter.

25.029 Article 41(1) provides that administrative expenditure to which the implementation of the Chapter gives rise for the institutions shall be charged to the EU's budget. Article 41(2) provides that operating expenditure to which the implementation of the Chapter gives rise shall also be charged to the Union budget, except for such expenditure arising from operations having military or defence implications and cases where the Council acting unanimously decides otherwise. In cases where expenditure is not charged to the Union budget, it shall be charged to the Member States in accordance with the gross national product scale, unless the Council acting unanimously decides otherwise. As for expenditure arising from operations having military or defence implications,

---

13 TEU, Art. 36.
14 Ibid.
15 Ibid
16 Ibid.
17 TEU, Art. 37.

Member States whose representatives in the Council have made a formal declaration under Article 31(1), second subparagraph, shall not be obliged to contribute to the financing thereof. Article 41(3) provides that the Council must adopt a decision establishing the specific procedures for guaranteeing rapid access to appropriations in the Union budget for urgent financing of initiatives in the framework of the CFSP, and in particular for preparatory activities for the tasks referred to in Article 42(1) and Article 43. It shall act after consulting the European Parliament. Preparatory activities for the tasks referred to in Article 42(1) and Article 43 which are not charged to the Union budget shall be financed by a start-up fund made up of Member States' contributions. The Council shall adopt by a qualified majority, on a proposal from the High Representative of the Union for Foreign Affairs and Security Policy, decisions establishing: (a) the procedures for setting up and financing the start-up fund, in particular the amounts allocated to the fund; (b) the procedures for administering the start-up fund; and (c) the financial control procedures. When the task planned in accordance with Article 42(1) and Article 43 cannot be charged to the Union budget, the Council shall authorise the High Representative to use the fund. The High Representative shall report to the Council on the implementation of this remit.

25.030 Section 2 is entitled "Provisions on the Common Security and Defence Policy".

25.031 Article 42(1) of the TEU provides that the common security and defence policy shall be an integral part of the CFSP. It shall provide the EU with an operational capacity drawing on civilian and military assets. The EU may use them on missions outside the EU for peace-keeping, conflict prevention and strengthening international security in accordance with the principles of the United Nations Charter. The performance of these tasks shall be undertaken using capabilities provided by the Member States. Article 42(2) provides that the common security and defence policy shall include the progressive framing of a common Union defence policy. This will lead to a common defence, when the European Council, acting unanimously, so decides. It shall in that case recommend to the Member States the adoption of such a decision in accordance with their respective constitutional requirements. The policy of the EU in accordance with the Section shall not prejudice the specific character of the security and defence policy of certain Member States and shall respect the obligations of certain Member States, which see their common defence realised in the North Atlantic Treaty Organisation ("NATO"), under the North Atlantic Treaty and be compatible with the common security and defence policy established within that framework. Article 42(3) provides that Member States must make civilian and military capabilities available to the Union for the implementation of the common security and defence policy, to contribute to the objectives defined by the Council. Those Member States which together establish multinational forces may also make them available to the common security and defence policy. Member States must undertake progressively to improve their military capabilities. The Agency in the field of defence capabilities development, research, acquisition and armaments (the European Defence Agency ("EDA")) shall identify operational requirements, shall promote measures to satisfy those requirements, shall contribute to identifying and, where appropriate, implementing any measure needed to strengthen the industrial and technological base of the defence sector, shall participate in defining a European capabilities and armaments policy and shall assist the Council in evaluating the improvement of military capabilities. Article 42(4) provides that decisions relating to the common security and defence policy, including those initiating a mission as referred to in Article 42, must be adopted by the Council acting unanimously on a proposal from the High Representative of the Union for Foreign Affairs and Security Policy or an initiative from a Member State. The High Representative may propose the use of both national resources and Union instruments, together with the Commission where appropriate. The Council may entrust the execution of a task, within the Union framework, to a group of Member States in order to protect the Union's values and serve its interests.[18] The execution of such a task shall be governed by Article 44.[19] Those Member States whose military capabilities fulfil higher criteria and which have made more binding commitments to one another in this area with a view to the most demanding missions shall establish permanent structured co-operation within the Union framework. Such co-operation shall be governed by Article 46.[20] It does not affect the provisions of Article 43.[21] If a Member State is the victim of armed aggression on its territory, the other Member States shall have towards it an obligation of aid and assistance by all the means in their power, in accordance with Article 51 of the United Nations Charter.[22] This shall not prejudice the specific character of the security and defence policy of certain Member States.[23] Commitments and co-operation in this area shall be consistent with commitments under the NATO, which, for those States which are members of it, remains the foundation of their collective defence and the forum for its implementation.[24]

25.032 Article 43(1) provides that the tasks referred to in Article 42(1), in the course of which the EU may use civilian and military means, shall include joint disarmament operations, humanitarian and rescue tasks, military advice and assistance tasks, conflict prevention and peace-keeping tasks, tasks of combat forces in crisis management, including peace-making and post-conflict stabilisation. All these tasks may contribute to the fight against terrorism, including by supporting third countries in combating terrorism in their territories. Under Article 43(2), the Council must adopt decisions relating to the tasks referred to in paragraph 1, defining their objectives and scope and the general conditions for their implementation. The High Representative of the Union for Foreign Affairs and Security Policy, acting under the authority of the Council and in close and constant contact with the Political and Security Committee, shall ensure co-ordination of the civilian and military aspects of such tasks.

25.033 Article 44(1) provides that within the framework of the decisions adopted in accordance with Article 43, the Council may entrust the implementation of a task to a group of Member States which are willing and have the necessary capability for such a task. Those Member States, in association with the High Representative of the Union for Foreign Affairs and Security Policy, shall agree among themselves on the management of the task. Article 44(2) provides that Member States participating in the task shall keep the Council regularly informed of its progress on their own initiative or at the request of another Member State. Those States shall inform the Council immediately should the

---

18 TEU, Art. 42(5).
19 TEU, Art. 42(5).
20 TEU, Art. 42(6).
21 Ibid.
22 TEU, Art. 42(7).
23 Ibid.
24 Ibid.

completion of the task entail major consequences or require amendment of the objective, scope and conditions determined for the task in the decisions referred to in paragraph 1. In such cases, the Council shall adopt the necessary decisions.

25.034 Article 45(1) provides that the EDA referred to in Article 42(3), subject to the authority of the Council, shall have as its task to: (a) contribute to identifying the Member States' military capability objectives and evaluating observance of the capability commitments given by the Member States; (b) promote harmonisation of operational needs and adoption of effective, compatible procurement methods; (c) propose multilateral projects to fulfil the objectives in terms of military capabilities, ensure co-ordination of the programmes implemented by the Member States and management of specific co-operation programmes; (d) support defence technology research, and co-ordinate and plan joint research activities and the study of technical solutions meeting future operational needs; (e) contribute to identifying and, if necessary, implementing any useful measure for strengthening the industrial and technological base of the defence sector and for improving the effectiveness of military expenditure. Article 45(2) provides that the EDA shall be open to all Member States wishing to be part of it. The Council, acting by a qualified majority, shall adopt a decision defining the Agency's statute, seat and operational rules. That decision should take account of the level of effective participation in the Agency's activities. Specific groups shall be set up within the Agency bringing together Member States engaged in joint projects. The Agency shall carry out its tasks in liaison with the Commission where necessary.

25.035 Article 46(1) provides that those Member States which wish to participate in the permanent structured co-operation referred to in Article 42(6), which fulfil the criteria and have made the commitments on military capabilities set out in the protocol on permanent structured co-operation, shall notify their intention to the Council and to the High Representative of the Union for Foreign Affairs and Security Policy. Article 46(2) provides that within three months following the notification referred to in Article 46(1), the Council must adopt a decision establishing permanent structured co-operation and determining the list of participating Member States. The Council shall act by a qualified majority after consulting the High Representative. Article 46(3) provides that any Member State which, at a later stage, wishes to participate in the permanent structured co-operation shall notify its intention to the Council and to the High Representative. The Council shall adopt a decision confirming the participation of the Member State concerned which fulfils the criteria and makes the commitments referred to in Articles 1 and 2 of the protocol on permanent structured co-operation. The Council shall act by a qualified majority after consulting the High Representative. Only members of the Council representing the participating Member States shall take part in the vote. A qualified majority shall be defined in accordance with Article 238(3)(a) of the TFEU. If a participating Member State no longer fulfils the criteria or is no longer able to meet the commitments referred to in Articles 1 and 2 of the protocol on permanent structured co-operation, the Council may adopt a decision suspending the participation of the Member State concerned.[25] The Council shall act by a qualified majority.[26] Only members of the Council representing the participating Member States, with the exception of the Member State in

---

25 TEU, Art. 46(4).
26 Ibid.

question, shall take part in the vote.[27] A qualified majority shall be defined in accordance with Article 238(3)(a) of the TFEU.[28] Any participating Member State which wishes to withdraw from permanent structured co-operation shall notify its intention to the Council, which shall take note that the Member State in question has ceased to participate.[29] The decisions and recommendations of the Council within the framework of permanent structured co-operation, other than those provided for in paragraphs 2 to 5, shall be adopted by unanimity.[30] For the purposes of this paragraph, unanimity shall be constituted by the votes of the representatives of the participating Member States only.[31]

Treaty on the Functioning of the European Union

25.036 As well as Part V of the TEU, Part V of the TFEU also deals with the EU's regime relating to external dimension.

25.037 Title I of Part V of the TFEU deals with "General Provisions on the Union's External Action". Article 205 provides that the EU's action on the international scene, pursuant to Part V of the TFEU, must be guided by the principles, pursue the objectives and be conducted in accordance with the general provisions laid down in Chapter 1 of Title V of the TEU.

25.038 Title II of Part V of the TFEU deals with "Common Commercial Policy". Article 206 provides that by establishing a customs union in accordance with Articles 28 to 32 of the TFEU, the EU must contribute, in the common interest, to the harmonious development of world trade, the progressive abolition of restrictions on international trade and on foreign direct investment, and the lowering of customs and other barriers. Article 207(1) provides that the

"common commercial policy shall be based on uniform principles, particularly with regard to changes in tariff rates, the conclusion of tariff and trade agreements relating to trade in goods and services, and the commercial aspects of intellectual property, foreign direct investment, the achievement of uniformity in measures of liberalisation, export policy and measures to protect trade such as those to be taken in the event of dumping or subsidies. The common commercial policy shall be conducted in the context of the principles and objectives of the Union's external action."

Article 207(2) provides that the "European Parliament and the Council, acting by means of regulations in accordance with the ordinary legislative procedure, shall adopt the measures defining the framework for implementing the common commercial policy". Where agreements with one or more third countries or international organisations need to be negotiated and concluded, Article 218 shall apply, subject to the special provisions of Article 207.[32] The Commission must make recommendations to the Council, which shall authorise it to open the necessary negotiations. The Council and the Commission shall be responsible for ensuring that the agreements negotiated are compatible with internal

---

27 Ibid.
28 Ibid.
29 TEU, Art. 46(5).
30 Ibid.
31 Ibid.
32 TFEU, Art. 207(3).

Union policies and rules.[33] The Commission must conduct these negotiations in consultation with a special committee appointed by the Council to assist the Commission in this task and within the framework of such directives as the Council may issue to it.[34] The Commission must report regularly to the special committee and to the European Parliament on the progress of negotiations.[35] Article 206(4) provides that for the negotiation and conclusion of the agreements referred to in Article 206(3), the Council must act by a qualified majority. For the negotiation and conclusion of agreements in the fields of trade in services and the commercial aspects of intellectual property, as well as foreign direct investment, the Council must act unanimously where such agreements include provisions for which unanimity is required for the adoption of internal rules. Also under Article 206(4), the Council must also act unanimously for the negotiation and conclusion of agreements: (a) in the field of trade in cultural and audiovisual services, where these agreements risk prejudicing the Union's cultural and linguistic diversity; (b) in the field of trade in social, education and health services, where these agreements risk seriously disturbing the national organisation of such services and prejudicing the responsibility of Member States to deliver them. Importantly for the purposes of EU shipping law, Article 206(5) provides that the negotiation and conclusion of international agreements in the field of transport shall be subject to Title VI of Part Three and to Article 218 of the TFEU. Article 206(6) provides that the exercise of the competences conferred by Article 206 in the field of the common commercial policy must not affect the delimitation of competences between the EU and the Member States, and shall not lead to harmonisation of legislative or regulatory provisions of the Member States in so far as the Treaties exclude such harmonisation.

25.039 Title III is entitled "Cooperation with Third Countries and Humanitarian Aid". Chapter 1 is entitled "Development Cooperation".

25.040 Article 208(1) provides that EU policy in the field of development co-operation must be conducted within the framework of the principles and objectives of the EU's external action.[36] Indeed, the EU's development co-operation policy and that of the Member States complement and reinforce each other.[37] EU development co-operation policy must have as its primary objective the reduction and, in the long term, the eradication of poverty.[38] The EU must take account of the objectives of development co-operation in the policies that it implements which are likely to affect developing countries.[39] Article 208(2) provides that the EU and the Member States must comply with the commitments and take account of the objectives they have approved in the context of the United Nations and other competent international organisations.

25.041 Article 209(1) provides that the Parliament and the Council, acting in accordance with the ordinary legislative procedure, must adopt the measures necessary for the implementation of development co-operation policy, which may relate to multiannual co-operation programmes with developing countries or programmes with a thematic

---

33 Ibid.
34 Ibid.
35 Ibid.
36 TFEU, Art. 208(1).
37 Ibid.
38 Ibid.
39 Ibid.

approach. The EU may conclude with third countries and competent international organisations any agreement helping to achieve the objectives referred to in Article 21 of the TEU and in Article 208 of the TFEU. Article 209(3) provides that the European Investment Bank shall contribute, under the terms laid down in its Statute, to the implementation of the measures referred to in paragraph 1.

25.042 Under Article 210(1), in order to promote the complementarity and efficiency of their action, the EU and the Member States must co-ordinate their policies on development co-operation and shall consult each other on their aid programmes, including in international organisations and during international conferences. They may undertake joint action. Member States shall contribute if necessary to the implementation of EU aid programmes. Under Article 210(2), the Commission may take any useful initiative to promote the co-ordination referred to in Article 210(1). Within their respective spheres of competence, the EU and the Member States must co-operate with third countries and with the competent international organisations.[40] This is important in the context of, for example, the relationship between the EU and the Member States with the IMO.

25.043 Chapter 2 is entitled "Economic, Financial and Technical Cooperation with Third Countries".

25.044 Article 212(1) of the TFEU provides that without prejudice to the other provisions of the Treaties, and in particular Articles 208 to 211, the Union shall carry out economic, financial and technical co-operation measures, including assistance, in particular financial assistance, with third countries other than developing countries. Such measures shall be consistent with the development policy of the Union and shall be carried out within the framework of the principles and objectives of its external action. The Union's operations and those of the Member States shall complement and reinforce each other. Article 212(2) provides that the European Parliament and the Council, acting in accordance with the ordinary legislative procedure, shall adopt the measures necessary for the implementation of Article 212(1). Article 212(3) provides within their respective spheres of competence, the Union and the Member States shall co-operate with third countries and the competent international organisations. The arrangements for Union co-operation may be the subject of agreements between the Union and the third parties concerned. The first subparagraph is without prejudice to the Member States' competence to negotiate in international bodies and to conclude international agreements.

25.045 Article 213 provides simply that when the situation in a third country requires urgent financial assistance from the Union, the Council must adopt the necessary decisions on a proposal from the Commission.

25.046 Chapter 3 is entitled "Humanitarian Aid". It would have only some relevance for EU shipping law but there could be some relevance by virtue of the fact that ships are often used for the carriage of humanitarian aid.

25.047 Article 214(1) provides that the EU's operations in the field of humanitarian aid must be conducted within the framework of the principles and objectives of the external action of the Union. Such operations must be intended to provide ad hoc assistance and relief and protection for people in third countries who are victims of natural or man-made disasters, in order to meet the humanitarian needs resulting from these different situations. The EU's measures and those of the Member States must complement and

---

40 TFEU, Art. 211.

reinforce each other. Humanitarian aid operations must be conducted in compliance with the principles of international law and with the principles of impartiality, neutrality and non-discrimination.[41] The Parliament and the Council, acting in accordance with the ordinary legislative procedure, must establish the measures defining the framework within which the EU's humanitarian aid operations shall be implemented.[42] The EU may conclude with third countries and competent international organisations any agreement helping to achieve the objectives referred to in paragraph 1 and in Article 21 of the TEU[43] but this is without prejudice to Member States' competence to negotiate in international bodies and to conclude agreements.[44] In order to establish a framework for joint contributions from young Europeans to the humanitarian aid operations of the EU, a European Voluntary Humanitarian Aid Corps shall be set up.[45] The Parliament and the Council, acting by means of regulations in accordance with the ordinary legislative procedure, shall determine the rules and procedures for the operation of the Corps.[46] The Commission may take any useful initiative to promote co-ordination between actions of the Union and those of the Member States, in order to enhance the efficiency and complementarity of Union and national humanitarian aid measures.[47] The EU must ensure that its humanitarian aid operations are co-ordinated and consistent with those of international organisations and bodies, in particular those forming part of the United Nations system.[48]

25.048 Title IV of the TFEU is entitled "Restrictive Measures".

25.049 Article 215(1) provides where a decision, adopted in accordance with Chapter 2 of Title V of the TEU, provides for the interruption or reduction, in part or completely, of economic and financial relations with one or more third countries, the Council, acting by a qualified majority on a joint proposal from the High Representative of the Union for Foreign Affairs and Security Policy and the Commission, shall adopt the necessary measures. It shall inform the European Parliament thereof. Where a decision adopted in accordance with Chapter 2 of Title V of the TEU so provides, the Council may adopt restrictive measures under the procedure referred to in paragraph 1 against natural or legal persons and groups or non-State entities.[49] The acts referred to in Article 215 shall include necessary provisions on legal safeguards.[50]

25.050 Title V of the TFEU deals with "international agreements". Article 216(1) provides that the EU

> "may conclude an agreement with one or more third countries or international organisations where the Treaties so provide or where the conclusion of an agreement is necessary in order to achieve, within the framework of the Union's policies, one of the objectives referred to in the Treaties, or is provided for in a legally binding Union act or is likely to affect common rules or alter their scope."

---

41 TFEU, Art. 214(2).
42 TFEU, Art. 214(3).
43 TFEU, Art. 214(4).
44 Ibid.
45 TFEU, Art. 214(5).
46 Ibid.
47 TFEU, Art. 214(6).
48 TFEU, Art. 214(7).
49 TFEU, Art. 215(1).
50 TFEU, Art. 215(3).

Agreements concluded by the Union are binding upon the institutions of the Union and on its Member States.[51] Article 217 provides that the EU may conclude with one or more third countries or international organisations agreements establishing an association involving reciprocal rights and obligations, common action and special procedure. Article 218(1) provides that without prejudice to the specific provisions laid down in Article 207, agreements between the EU and third countries or international organisations shall be negotiated and concluded in accordance with the following procedure. The Council must authorise the opening of negotiations, adopt negotiating directives, authorise the signing of agreements and conclude them.[52] The Commission, or the High Representative of the Union for Foreign Affairs and Security Policy where the agreement envisaged relates exclusively or principally to the CFSP, shall submit recommendations to the Council, which shall adopt a decision authorising the opening of negotiations and, depending on the subject of the agreement envisaged, nominating the Union negotiator or the head of the EU's negotiating team.[53] The Council may address directives to the negotiator and designate a special committee in consultation with which the negotiations must be conducted.[54] The Council, on a proposal by the negotiator, shall adopt a decision authorising the signing of the agreement and, if necessary, its provisional application before entry into force.[55] Article 218(6)[56] provides that the Council, on a proposal by the negotiator, must adopt a decision concluding the agreement. Except where agreements relate exclusively to the CFSP, the Council must adopt the decision concluding the agreement: (a) after obtaining the consent of the European Parliament in the following cases: (i) association agreements; (ii) agreement on Union accession to the European Convention for the Protection of Human Rights and Fundamental Freedoms; (iii) agreements establishing a specific institutional framework by organising co-operation procedures; (iv) agreements with important budgetary implications for the Union; (v) agreements covering fields to which either the ordinary legislative procedure applies, or the special legislative procedure where consent by the European Parliament is required. The Parliament and the Council may, in an urgent situation, agree upon a time-limit for consent; and (b) after consulting the European Parliament in other cases. The European Parliament shall deliver its opinion within a time-limit which the Council may set depending on the urgency of the matter. In the absence of an opinion within that time-limit, the Council may act. The Council shall act by a qualified majority throughout the procedure.[57] However, it shall act unanimously when the agreement covers a field for which unanimity is required for the adoption of a Union act as well as for association agreements and the agreements

---

51 TFEU, Art. 216(2).
52 TFEU, Art. 218(2).
53 TFEU, Art. 218(3).
54 TFEU, Art. 218(4).
55 TFEU, Art. 218(5). Art. 218(7) provides that when concluding an agreement, the Council may, by way of derogation from paragraphs 5, 6 and 9, authorise the negotiator to approve on the Union's behalf modifications to the agreement where it provides for them to be adopted by a simplified procedure or by a body set up by the agreement. The Council may attach specific conditions to such authorisation.
56 Art. 218(7) provides that when concluding an agreement, the Council may, by way of derogation from paragraphs 5, 6 and 9, authorise the negotiator to approve on the Union's behalf modifications to the agreement where it provides for them to be adopted by a simplified procedure or by a body set up by the agreement. The Council may attach specific conditions to such authorisation.
57 TFEU, Art. 218(8).

referred to in Article 212 with the States which are candidates for accession.[58] The Council shall also act unanimously for the agreement on accession of the Union to the European Convention for the Protection of Human Rights and Fundamental Freedoms; the decision concluding this agreement shall enter into force after it has been approved by the Member States in accordance with their respective constitutional requirements.[59] The Council, on a proposal from the Commission or the High Representative of the Union for Foreign Affairs and Security Policy, shall adopt a decision suspending application of an agreement and establishing the positions to be adopted on the Union's behalf in a body set up by an agreement, when that body is called upon to adopt acts having legal effects, with the exception of acts supplementing or amending the institutional framework of the agreement.[60] The European Parliament must be immediately and fully informed at all stages of the procedure.[61] A Member State, the European Parliament, the Council or the Commission may obtain the opinion of the Court of Justice as to whether an agreement envisaged is compatible with the Treaties.[62] Where the opinion of the Court is adverse, the agreement envisaged may not enter into force unless it is amended or the Treaties are revised.[63]

25.051 Article 219(1) provides by way of derogation from Article 218, the Council, either on a recommendation from the European Central Bank ("ECB") or on a recommendation from the Commission and after consulting the ECB, in an endeavour to reach a consensus consistent with the objective of price stability, may conclude formal agreements on an exchange-rate system for the euro in relation to the currencies of third States. The Council shall act unanimously after consulting the European Parliament and in accordance with the procedure provided for in Article 219(3). The Council may, either on a recommendation from the ECB or on a recommendation from the Commission, and after consulting the ECB, in an endeavour to reach a consensus consistent with the objective of price stability, adopt, adjust or abandon the central rates of the euro within the exchange-rate system. The President of the Council must inform the European Parliament of the adoption, adjustment or abandonment of the euro central rates. Article 219(2) provides that in the absence of an exchange-rate system in relation to one or more currencies of third States as referred to in Article 219(1), the Council, either on a recommendation from the Commission and after consulting the ECB or on a recommendation from the ECB, may formulate general orientations for exchange-rate policy in relation to these currencies. These general orientations shall be without prejudice to the primary objective of the European System of Central Banks ("ESCB") to maintain price stability. Under Article 219(3), by way of derogation from Article 218, where agreements concerning monetary or foreign exchange regime matters need to be negotiated by the EU with one or more third States or international organisations, the Council, on a recommendation from the Commission and after consulting the ECB, shall decide the arrangements for the negotiation and for the conclusion of such agreements. These arrangements shall ensure that the Union expresses a single position. The Commission shall be fully associated with

---

58 Ibid.
59 Ibid.
60 TFEU, Art. 218(9).
61 TFEU, Art. 218(10).
62 TFEU, Art. 218(11).
63 Ibid.

the negotiations. Article 219(4) provides that without prejudice to EU competence and EU agreements as regards economic and monetary union, Member States may negotiate in international bodies and conclude international agreements.

25.052 Title VI is entitled the "Union's Relations with International Organisations and Third Countries and Union Delegations". Article 220(1) provides that the EU must establish all appropriate forms of co-operation with the organs of the United Nations and its specialised agencies, the Council of Europe, the Organization for Security and Co-operation in Europe and the Organisation for Economic Co-operation and Development. The Union must also maintain such relations as are appropriate with other international organisations. The High Representative of the Union for Foreign Affairs and Security Policy and the Commission shall implement this article.[64]

25.053 Article 221(1) of the TFEU states that EU delegations in third countries and at international organisations shall represent the EU. While Article 221(2) provides that EU delegations must be placed under the authority of the High Representative of the Union for Foreign Affairs and Security Policy. They shall act in close co-operation with Member States' diplomatic and consular missions.

25.054 Title VII is the somewhat controversial "Solidarity Clause".

25.055 Article 222(1) of the TFEU provides that the EU and its Member States must act jointly in a spirit of solidarity if a Member State is the object of a terrorist attack or the victim of a natural or man-made disaster. The EU must mobilise all the instruments at its disposal, including the military resources made available by the Member States, to: (a) prevent the terrorist threat in the territory of the Member States, protect democratic institutions and the civilian population from any terrorist attack, assist a Member State in its territory, at the request of its political authorities, in the event of a terrorist attack; (b) assist a Member State in its territory, at the request of its political authorities, in the event of a natural or man-made disaster. Should a Member State be the object of a terrorist attack or the victim of a natural or man-made disaster, the other Member States shall assist it at the request of its political authorities.[65] To that end, the Member States shall co-ordinate between themselves in the Council.[66] The arrangements for the implementation by the Union of the solidarity clause shall be defined by a decision adopted by the Council acting on a joint proposal by the Commission and the High Representative of the Union for Foreign Affairs and Security Policy.[67] The Council shall act in accordance with Article 31(1) of the TEU where this decision has defence implications. The European Parliament must be informed. For the purposes of Article 222(3) and without prejudice to Article 240, the Council shall be assisted by the Political and Security Committee with the support of the structures developed in the context of the common security and defence policy and by the Committee referred to in Article 71; the two committees shall, if necessary, submit joint opinions. The European Council must regularly assess the threats facing the Union in order to enable the Union and its Member States to take effective action.[68]

25.056 It is useful to consider a number of specific measures as they relate to external affairs and EU shipping law.

---

64 TFEU, Art. 220(2).
65 TFEU, Art. 222(2).
66 Ibid.
67 TFEU, Art. 222(3).
68 TFEU, Art. 222(4).

C. COUNCIL DECISION 83/573 OF 26 OCTOBER 1983 CONCERNING COUNTER-MEASURES IN THE FIELD OF INTERNATIONAL MERCHANT SHIPPING

25.057 On 26 October 1983, the Council adopted Decision 83/573 concerning counter-measures in the field of international merchant shipping.[69] The legal basis of the measure was the Treaty on the European Economic Community ("TEEC") generally and, in particular, Article 84(2) of it (i.e. essentially, this would now be Article 100(2) of the TFEU). The recitals to the decision provide:

"Whereas the results of the maritime information system set up under the provisions of Decisions 78/774/EEC,[70] 79/4/EEC,[71] 80/1181/EEC,[72] 81/189/EEC[73] and 82/870/EEC,[74] together with the experience of certain Member States, show that it would be advisable to define an appropriate Community procedure concerning counter-measures in the field of international merchant shipping in relation to third countries to be taken by the Member States concerned..."

25.058 Article 1 provides that a Member State which has adopted or intends to adopt counter-measures in the field of international merchant shipping in relation to third countries must consult the other Member States and the Commission in accordance with the consultation procedure established by Decision 77/587.[75]

25.059 Article 2(1) provides that the Member States must endeavour, within the framework of the consultation referred to in Article 1, to concert any counter-measures they may take. Article 2(2) provides that the Council may, acting unanimously, decide on the joint application by Member States of appropriate counter-measures forming part of their national legislation.

25.060 Article 3 provides:

"When engaging in the consultation referred to in Article 1, Member States should, if appropriate, specify as far as possible the following:

(a) the developments which have caused countermeasures to be taken;
(b) the shipping area to which the counter-measure is to apply;
(c) the nature of the shipping service affected (for example liner traffic);
(d) the nature of the counter-measures taken or to be taken;
(e) the duration of the counter-measure;
(f) the proportionality of the counter-measure to the damage suffered."

25.061 Article 4 recognises that Member States still have latitude and therefore provides that Member States shall remain free to apply national counter-measures unilaterally.

D. COUNCIL DECISION OF 17 SEPTEMBER 1987 RELATING TO MARITIME TRANSPORT BETWEEN ITALY AND ALGERIA

25.062 On 17 September 1987, the Council adopted Decision 87/475 relating to maritime transport between Italy and Algeria.[76] Article 1 provided that Italy may ratify its

---

69 OJ L332/37, 28 November 1983.
70 OJ No L258, 21.9.1978, p. 35.
71 OJ No L5, 9.1.1979, p. 31.
72 OJ No L350, 23.12.1980, p. 44.
73 OJ No L88, 2.4.1981, p. 32.
74 OJ No L368, 28.12.1982, p. 42.
75 OJ No L239, 17 September 1977, p. 23.
76 OJ L272/37, 25 September 1987.

Agreement on Maritime Transport and Navigation with the People's Democratic Republic of Algeria, signed on 28 February 1987, on the understanding that Italy: (a) will take the necessary steps to accede as soon as possible, in accordance with Regulation (EEC) No 954/79, to the United Nations Convention on a Code of Conduct for Liner Conferences; (b) will reiterate to Algeria that the provisions of the agreement will be implemented in accordance with Community law; and (c) will report to the Member States and the Commission, within not later than one year of notification of this decision, on the implementation of the agreement.

E. COOPERATION AGREEMENT BETWEEN THE EUROPEAN COMMUNITY AND THE KINGDOM OF CAMBODIA – JOINT DECLARATIONS – EXCHANGE OF LETTERS ON MARITIME TRANSPORT

25.063 On 29 April 1997, the EU and Cambodia agreed on a Cooperation Agreement on maritime transport.[77] Article 21 deals with the entry into force and renewal of the agreement. Article 21(1) provides that the agreement "shall enter into force on the first day of the month following the date on which the Parties notify each other of the completion of the procedures necessary for this purpose" while Article 21(2) provides that the "Agreement is concluded for a period of five years. It shall be renewed automatically from year to year unless one of the Parties denounces it six months before its expiry date."[78]

---

77 OJ L269, 19 October 1999, p. 18. Art. 20 (entitled "Annexes") provides that Annexes I and II to the Agreement forms an integral part thereof.

78 Annex I is entitled the "Joint Declaration on Article 19 – Non-execution of the Agreement". It provides: "(a) The Parties agree, for the purposes of the interpretation and practical application of this Agreement, that the term 'cases of special urgency' in Article 19 of the Agreement means a case of the material breach of the Agreement by one of the Parties. A material breach of the Agreement consists in: repudiation of the Agreement not sanctioned by the general rules of international law, violation of essential elements of the Agreement set out in Article 1 ... (b) The Parties agree that the 'appropriate measures' referred to in Article 19 are measures taken in accordance with international law. If a Party takes a measure in a case of special urgency as provided for under Article 19, the other Party may avail itself of the procedure relating to settlement of disputes." There was an exchange of letters on maritime transport. It provides:
"A. Letter from the Community ...
Sir,
With regard to the barriers to trade which may arise for the European Community and its Member States or the Kingdom of Cambodia as a result of the operation of shipping, it has been agreed that mutually satisfactory solutions should be sought with due regard for the principle of free and fair competition on a commercial and non-discriminatory basis.
I should be obliged if you would confirm that your Government is in agreement with the foregoing.
Please accept, Sir, the assurance of my highest consideration.
On behalf of the Council of the European Union"
The letter from Cambodia read:
"Sir,
I have the honour to acknowledge receipt of your letter of today's date, which reads as follows:
'With regard to the barriers to trade which may arise for the European Community and its Member States or the Kingdom of Cambodia as a result of the operation of shipping, it has been agreed that mutually satisfactory solutions should be sought with due regard for the principle of free and fair competition on a commercial and non-discriminatory basis.
I should be obliged if you would confirm that your Government is in agreement with the foregoing.'
I am able to confirm that my Government is in agreement with the contents of your letter.
Please accept, Sir, the assurance of my highest consideration.
For the Kingdom of Cambodia."

25.064 By way of background, the Parties wanted to create favourable conditions for the development of trade and investment between the EU and Cambodia. They recognised the need to adhere to the principles of international trade, the purpose of which is to promote trade liberalisation in a stable, transparent and non-discriminatory manner. They considered the need to support the then current process of economic reform in order to guarantee transition to a market economy, with due regard for the importance of the social development which should go hand in hand with economic development and the common commitment to respecting social rights. They equally considered the need to support the Cambodian government's efforts to improve the living conditions of the poorest and most disadvantaged sections of the population, with a special emphasis on the status of women. Finally, they considered the importance accorded by the Parties to the protection of the environment at all levels and to the sustainable management of natural resources, taking account of the links between the environment and development.

25.065 Article 1 set out the basis of the agreement which was expressed to be the respect for the democratic principles and fundamental human rights established by the Universal Declaration on Human Rights which "inspires the internal and international policies of the Community and of Cambodia and constitutes an essential element of the Agreement".

25.066 Article 2 enumerates the "objectives" of the agreement. The main objective of the agreement is to provide a framework for enhancing cooperation between the Parties, within their respective areas of jurisdiction. This objective had the following aims: (a) to accord each other most-favoured-nation treatment on trade in goods in all areas specifically covered by the agreement, save as regards advantages accorded by either Party within the context of customs unions or free trade areas, trade arrangements with neighbouring countries or specific obligations under international commodity agreements; (b) to promote and intensify trade between the Parties, and to encourage the steady expansion of sustainable economic co-operation, in accordance with the principles of equality and mutual advantage; (c) to strengthen co-operation in fields closely related to economic progress and benefiting both Parties; (d) to contribute to Cambodia's efforts to improve the quality of life and standards of living of the poorest sections of its population, together with measures for the country's reconstruction; (e) to encourage job creation in both the Community and Cambodia, with priority being accorded to programmes and operations which could have a favourable effect in this respect. The Parties shall also exchange views and information on their respective initiatives in this field, step up and diversify their economic links and establish conditions conducive to job creation; and (f) to take the requisite measures to protect the environment and manage natural resources sustainably.

25.067 Article 3 (entitled "Development Cooperation") provides that the EU recognises Cambodia's need for development assistance and is prepared to step up its co-operation in order to contribute to that country's own efforts to achieve sustainable economic development and the social progress of its people through concrete projects and programmes in accordance with the priorities set out in Council Regulation 443/92 of 25 February 1992 on financial and technical assistance to, and economic co-operation with, the developing countries in Asia and Latin America. The article also provides that in accordance with Regulation 443/92, assistance will be targeted mainly on the rehabilitation and reconstruction of the country and on the poorest sections of the population. In co-operation, priority will be given to schemes aimed at alleviating poverty, and in particular those likely to create jobs, foster development at grassroots level and promote the role of women in development. The Parties will also encourage the adoption of appropriate measures to prevent and combat AIDS and take steps to increase grassroots development and education on AIDS and the operational capacity of the health services. The agreement also provides that co-operation between the Parties will also address the problem of drugs to encourage and enhance training, education, health care and the rehabilitation of addicts. In Article 3 of the agreement, the parties acknowledge the importance of human resources development, social development, the improvement of living and working conditions, the development of skills and the protection of the most vulnerable sections of the population. Human resources and social development must be an integral part of economic and development co-operation. Appropriate consideration shall therefore be given to training objectives addressing institutional needs and specific vocational training activities aimed at enhancing the skills of the local workforce. In view of its major contribution to mine-clearance programmes in Cambodia, the Community will, in its future commitments, continue to concentrate on mutually agreed priorities to ensure that assistance is effective and lasting. EU co-operation in all its areas will be concentrated on mutually agreed priorities to ensure that assistance is effective and lasting. Development co-operation activities shall be compatible with the development strategies pursued under the auspices of the institutions of the Bretton Woods Agreement.

25.068 Trade co-operation is dealt with by Article 4 of the agreement. First, Article 4(1) provides that the Parties confirm their determination: (a) to take all appropriate measures to create favourable conditions for trade between them; (b) to do their utmost to improve the structure of their trade in order to diversify it further; and (c) to work towards the elimination of barriers to trade, and towards measures to improve transparency, in particular through the removal at an appropriate time of non-tariff barriers, in accordance with work undertaken in this connection by other international bodies while ensuring that personal data are suitably protected. Second, Article 4(2)[79] provides that in their trade relations, the Parties must accord each other most-favoured-nation treatment in all matters regarding: (a) customs duties and charges of all kinds, including the procedures for their collection; (b) the regulations, procedures and formalities governing customs clearance, transit, warehousing and transhipment; (c) taxes and other internal charges levied directly or indirectly on imports or exports; and (d) administrative formalities for the issue of import or export licences. Article 4(3) provides that within the areas of their respective areas of jurisdiction, the Parties must undertake: (a) to seek ways of establishing co-operation in the field of maritime transport leading to market access on a commercial and non-discriminatory basis, taking into account the work done in this connection by other international bodies;[80] (b) to improve customs co-operation between their respective authorities, especially with regard to vocational training, the simplification and harmonisation of customs procedures and administrative assistance in the matter of

---

79 Art. 4(4) provides that Art. 4(2) and Art. 4(3)(a) shall not apply to: (a) advantages accorded by either Party to States which are fellow members of a customs union or free trade area; (b) advantages accorded by either Party to neighbouring countries with a view to facilitating border trade; and (c) measures which either Party may take in order to meet its obligations under international commodity agreements.

80 Art. 4(4) provides that Art. 4(2) and Art. 4(3)(a) shall not apply to: (a) advantages accorded by either Party to States which are fellow members of a customs union or free trade area; (b) advantages accorded by either Party to neighbouring countries with a view to facilitating border trade; and (c) measures which either Party may take in order to meet its obligations under international commodity agreements.

customs fraud; and (c) to exchange information on mutually advantageous opportunities, in particular in the field of tourism and co-operation on statistical matters. Cambodia must improve conditions for the adequate and effective protection and enforcement of intellectual, industrial and commercial property rights in conformity with the highest international standards and, to this end, Cambodia shall accede to the relevant international conventions on intellectual, industrial and commercial property to which it is not yet a party. In order to enable Cambodia to fulfil the abovementioned obligations, technical assistance could be envisaged.[81] Within their respective areas of jurisdiction and in so far as their rules and regulations permit, the Parties shall agree to consult each other on all questions, problems or disputes which may arise in connection with trade.[82]

25.069 Article 5 dealt with environmental co-operation. The parties recognise that the way to improve environmental protection is to introduce appropriate environmental legislation, implement it effectively and integrate it into other policy areas. The main objective of environmental co-operation is to enhance the prospects of sustainable economic growth and social development by placing a high priority on respect for the natural environment including: (a) the drafting of an effective environment protection policy involving appropriate legislative measures and the resources needed to implement it. Proper implementation of these measures will be essential in helping to put an end to illegal logging activities. Such a policy will also encompass training, capacity building and the transfer of appropriate environmental technology; (b) co-operation in the development of sustainable and non-polluting energy sources, as well as solutions to urban and industrial pollution problems; (c) refraining from activities harmful to the environment, especially in regions with fragile ecosystems, while developing tourism as a sustainable source of revenue; (d) environmental impact assessment, which is a vital element in the preparation and implementation of any reconstruction or development project; (e) close co-operation to achieve the objectives of environmental agreements to which both Parties are signatories; and (f) particular priority and initiatives for the conservation of existing primary forests and for the sustainable development of new forest resources.

25.070 Economic co-operation is addressed by Article 6. Within the limits of their respective areas of jurisdiction and the financial resources available, the Parties undertake to foster economic co-operation to their mutual advantage. This co-operation is aimed at: (a) developing the economic environment in Cambodia by facilitating access to EU know-how and technology; (b) facilitating contacts between economic operators and taking other measures to promote trade; (c) encouraging, in accordance with their legislation, rules and policies, public- and private-sector investment programmes in order to strengthen economic co-operation, including co-operation between enterprises, technology transfers, licences and subcontracting; (d) facilitating the exchange of information and the adoption of initiatives, fostering co-operation on enterprise policy, particularly with regard to improving the business environment and encouraging closer contacts; and (e) reinforcing mutual understanding of the Parties' respective economic environments as a basis for effective co-operation. In these fields, the principal objectives must be: to assist Cambodia in its efforts to restructure its economy by creating the conditions for a suitable economic environment and business climate; to encourage synergies between the

---

81 Art. 4(5).
82 Art. 4(6).

Parties' respective economic sectors, and in particular their private sectors; and within the Parties' respective areas of jurisdiction, and in accordance with their legislation, rules and policies, to establish a climate conducive to private investment by improving conditions for the transfer of capital and, where appropriate, by supporting the conclusion of agreements between the Member States and Cambodia on the promotion and protection of investment. The Parties will together determine, to their mutual advantage, the areas and priorities for economic co-operation programmes and activities.

25.071 Article 15 deals with future developments. Article 15(1) provides that the Parties may, by mutual consent and within their respective areas of jurisdiction, extend the agreement to expand co-operation and add to it by means of agreements on specific sectors or activities. Within the framework of the agreement, Article 15(2) provides that either Party may put forward suggestions for expanding the scope of the co-operation, taking into account the experience gained in its application.

25.072 Article 16 deals with other agreements. It provides that without prejudice to the relevant provisions of the Treaties establishing the European Communities, neither the agreement nor any action taken thereunder shall in any way affect the powers of the Member States of the EU to undertake bilateral activities with Cambodia in the framework of economic co-operation or to conclude, where appropriate, new economic co-operation agreements with Cambodia.

25.073 Facilities are dealt with by Article 17. The article provides that to facilitate co-operation under this agreement, the Cambodian authorities will grant to Community officials and experts the guarantees and facilities necessary for the performance of their duties. The detailed provisions will be set out in a separate exchange of letters.

25.074 Under Article 18, the territorial application of the agreement is stated to be "on the one hand, to the territories in which the Treaty establishing the European Community is applied and under the conditions laid down in that Treaty and, on the other hand, to the territory of Cambodia".

25.075 Article 19 provides for the non-execution of the agreement. It states that if either Party considers that the other Party has failed to fulfil an obligation under the agreement, it may take appropriate measures. Before so doing, except in cases of special urgency, it must supply the Joint Committee with all relevant information required for a thorough examination of the situation with a view to seeking a solution acceptable to the Parties. In the selection of measures, priority must be given to those which least disturb the functioning of the agreement. These measures must be notified immediately to the Joint Committee and must be the subject of consultations within the Joint Committee if the other Party so requests.

F. CHINA: COUNCIL DECISION 2009/825 OF 26 OCTOBER 2009 CONCERNING THE CONCLUSION OF THE PROTOCOL AMENDING THE AGREEMENT ON MARITIME TRANSPORT BETWEEN THE EUROPEAN COMMUNITY AND ITS MEMBER STATES, OF THE ONE PART, AND THE GOVERNMENT OF THE PEOPLE'S REPUBLIC OF CHINA, OF THE OTHER PART

25.076 The Agreement on maritime transport between the European Community ("EC") and its Member States, of the one part, and the government of the People's

Republic of China, of the other part was signed in Brussels on 6 December 2002. It was subsequently concluded on 31 January 2008 pursuant to Council Decision 2008/143 and entered into force on 1 March 2008.

25.077 On 26 October 2009, the Council adopted Decision 2009/825 concerning the conclusion of the protocol amending the agreement on maritime transport between the EC and its Member States, of the one part, and the government of the People's Republic of China, of the other part.[83]

25.078 The legal basis was the TEC generally and Article 80(2) of the TEC (i.e. Article 100(2) of the TFEU) in conjunction with the first sentence of the first subparagraph of Article 300(2) and the first subparagraph of Article 300(3) thereof (i.e. Article 218 of the TFEU).

25.079 A protocol amending the agreement on maritime transport between the EC and its Member States, of the one part, and the government of the China, of the other part, to take account of the accession of the Czech Republic, Estonia, Cyprus, Latvia, Lithuania, Hungary, Malta, Poland, Slovenia and the Slovak Republic to the EU was signed in Beijing on 5 September 2005 and concluded pursuant to Council Decision 2008/144. In accordance with Article 6(2) of the 2005 Act of Accession, Bulgaria and Romania are to accede to the agreement by way of a protocol between the Council and China. The protocol amending the agreement on maritime transport between the EC and its Member States, of the one part, and the Chinese government, of the other part, to take account of the accession of Bulgaria and Romania to the EU was signed in Brussels on 31 March 2009.

25.080 Article 1 provides that the

"Protocol amending the Agreement on maritime transport between the European Community and its Member States, of the one part, and the Government of the People's Republic of China, of the other part, to take account of the accession of the Republic of Bulgaria and Romania to the European Union is hereby approved on behalf of the Community."

25.081 Article 2 provides that the President of the Council shall, on behalf of the EU and its Member States, give the notification provided for in Article 3 of the protocol.

G. BRAZIL: FRAMEWORK AGREEMENT FOR CO-OPERATION BETWEEN THE EUROPEAN ECONOMIC COMMUNITY AND THE FEDERATIVE REPUBLIC OF BRAZIL – EXCHANGE OF LETTERS ON MARITIME TRANSPORT

25.082 The Framework Agreement for co-operation between the European Economic Community ("EEC") and Brazil was embodied in an exchange of letters on maritime transport.[84] This 1982 agreement has been replaced by the 1992 Framework Agreement for Cooperation between the European Economic Community and the Federative Republic of Brazil – Exchange of Letters between the European Economic Community and the Federative Republic of Brazil on maritime transport.[85]

---

83 OJ L294/10, 11 November 2009. See http://eur-lex.europa.eu/legal-content/EN/TXT/HTML/?uri=CELE X:32009D0825&from=EN.
84 OJ L281/2, 4 October 1982.
85 OJ L262/54, 1 November 1995.

25.083 Under the 1982 Agreement, the then EEC and Brazil wanted to establish a direct link with each other which would support, complement and extend the relations existing between Brazil and the then EEC Member States. Both sides resolved

"to consolidate, deepen and diversify their commercial and economic relations to the full extent of their growing capacity, so as to meet each other's requirements on the basis of mutual benefit and exploration of the complementarity of their economies in a dynamic context",

were mindful "that the more dynamic trade relationship which both the [then EEC] and … Brazil desire calls for cooperation in the field of commercial and economic endeavour", were conscious "that such cooperation is between equal partners but will take into account their respective levels of economic development and … Brazil's membership of the Group of 77",[86] were persuaded "that such cooperation should be realized in evolutionary and pragmatic fashion as their policies develop" and recognised "the value of a Framework Agreement for the furtherance of the partner's economic growth and development objectives".

25.084 Article 1 was entitled "most-favoured-nation treatment". It provided that the Contracting Parties shall, in their commercial relations, accord each other most-favoured-nation treatment in accordance with the provisions of the General Agreement on Tariffs and Trade ("GATT").

25.085 Article 2 was entitled "commercial cooperation". It provided in Article 2(1) that the "Contracting Parties undertake to promote the development and diversification of their commercial exchanges to the highest possible level consistent with their respective economic situations." Article 2(2) provided that to "this end the Parties agree to study ways and means of overcoming trade barriers, in particular non-tariff and quasi-tariff barriers, taking into account the work carried out by international organizations in this field". Article 28(3) provides that the Contracting Parties shall, each in accordance with its legislation, conduct a policy aimed at: (a) granting each other the widest facilities for commercial transactions in which either Party has an interest; (b) co-operating bilaterally and at the multilateral level in the solution of commercial problems of common interest, including those relating to commodities, semi-manufactured and manufactured products; (c) taking fully into account their respective needs and interests regarding both access to and the further processing of resources and access to each Contracting Party's market for the other Party's semi-manufactured and manufactured products; (d) bringing together economic operators in the two regions with the aim of diversifying and expanding existing trade flows; and (e) studying and recommending trade promotion measures likely to encourage the expansion of imports and exports.

25.086 Article 3 was entitled "economic cooperation". It provided:

"1. The Contracting Parties, in the light of their mutual interests and taking into account their long-term economic aspirations, shall foster economic cooperation in all fields deemed suitable by the Parties. Among the objectives of such cooperation shall be:

– to encourage the development and prosperity of their respective industries,
– to open up new sources of supply and new markets,
– to encourage scientific and technological progress,
– generally to contribute to the development of their respective economies and standards of living.

---

86 The Group of 77 was a collection of relatively poorer States typically in the Third World.

2. As means to such ends, the Contracting Parties shall endeavour inter alia to facilitate and promote by appropriate means: (a) broad and harmonious cooperation between their respective industries, in particular in the form of joint ventures; (b) greater participation by their respective economic operators in the industrial development of the Contracting Parties on mutually advantageous terms; (c) scientific and technological cooperation; (d) cooperation in the field of energy; (e) cooperation in the agricultural sector; (f) favourable conditions for the expansion of investment on a basis of advantage for both Parties; and (g) cooperation in respect of third countries.

3. The Contracting Parties shall as appropriate encourage the regular exchange of information relating to commercial and economic cooperation.

4. Without prejudice to the relevant provisions of the Treaties establishing the European Communities, this Agreement and any action taken thereunder shall in no way affect the powers of the Member States of the Communities to undertake bilateral activities with the Federative Republic of Brazil in the field of economic cooperation and to conclude, where appropriate, new economic cooperation agreements with the Federative Republic of Brazil."

25.087 Article 4 dealt with the "Joint Cooperation Committee". Under Article 4(1), a Joint Cooperation Committee had to be established, consisting of representatives of the EU and of Brazil. It must meet once a year. Extraordinary meetings may be called by mutual agreement. Article 4(2) provides that the Committee must promote and keep under review the various commercial and economic co-operation activities envisaged between the Community and Brazil; it also provides that consultations must be held in the Committee at an appropriate level to facilitate the implementation of the agreement and to further the attainment of its general aims.

25.088 Article 5 ("Other agreements") provided that the agreement would replace the trade agreement between the EEC and Brazil which has been in application since 1 January 1974. Subject to the provisions concerning economic co-operation in Article 3(4), the provisions of the agreement shall replace the provisions of agreements concluded between Member States of the EC and Brazil where such provisions are either incompatible with or identical to the provisions of the agreement.

25.089 Article 8 dealt with territorial application. It provided that the agreement must apply, on the one hand, to the territories in which the Treaty establishing the then EEC is applied and under the conditions laid down in that Treaty and, on the other hand, to the territory of Brazil.

25.090 Article 9(1) ("Duration") provided that the agreement "shall enter into force on the first day of the month following the date on which the Contracting Parties have notified each other of the completion of the procedures necessary for this purpose". Article 9(2) provides that the agreement is concluded for a period of five years and shall be renewed on a yearly basis unless one of the Contracting Parties denounces it six months before the date of expiry.

25.091 There was an exchange of letters on sea transport:

"Your Excellency,
I have the honour to confirm the following:
In view of the concern expressed by the European Economic Community and the Member States on the occasion of the negotiation of the Agreement between the Community and Brazil, signed this day, as regards obstacles to trade resulting from sea transport conditions, it has been agreed that mutually satisfactory solutions will be sought as regards sea transport between Brazil and the Community and the Member States.

To this end, it has also been agreed that, at the first meeting of the Joint Committee, the problems mentioned in the first paragraph, which could affect the development of reciprocal trade, will be examined with a view to ensuring the harmonious conduct of such trade.

Please accept, Your Excellency, the assurance of my highest consideration.

For the Council of the European Communities and the Member States of the Community

Sir,

I have the honour to confirm the following:

In view of the concern expressed by the European Economic Community and the Member States on the occasion of the negotiation of the Agreement between the Community and Brazil, signed this day, as regards obstacles to trade resulting from sea transport conditions, it has been agreed that mutually satisfactory solutions will be sought as regards sea transport between Brazil and the Community and the Member States.

To this end, it has also been agreed that, at the first meeting of the Joint Committee, the problems mentioned in the first paragraph, which could affect the development of reciprocal trade, will be examined with a view to ensuring the harmonious conduct of such trade.

Please accept, Sir, the assurance of my highest consideration.

For the Government of Brazil"

H. BRAZIL: FRAMEWORK AGREEMENT FOR COOPERATION BETWEEN THE EUROPEAN ECONOMIC COMMUNITY AND THE FEDERATIVE REPUBLIC OF BRAZIL – EXCHANGE OF LETTERS BETWEEN THE EUROPEAN ECONOMIC COMMUNITY AND THE FEDERATIVE REPUBLIC OF BRAZIL ON MARITIME TRANSPORT

25.092 The Framework Agreement for Cooperation between the European Economic Community and the Federative Republic of Brazil – Exchange of Letters between the European Economic Community and the Federative Republic of Brazil on maritime transport was signed on 29 June 1992 and entered into force on 1 November 1995.[87]

25.093 The agreement begins in Article 1 by recalling the democratic basis for cooperation:

"[c]ooperation ties between the Community and Brazil and this Agreement in its entirety are based on respect for the democratic principles and human rights which inspire the domestic and international policies of both the Community and Brazil and which constitute an essential component of this Agreement."

25.094 Article 2 ("strengthening of cooperation") provides:

"1. The Contracting Parties hereby undertake to impart renewed vigour to relations between them. To achieve this essential objective, they resolve to promote in particular the development of cooperation relating to trade, investment, finance and technology, taking account of Brazil's special situation as a developing country. 2. The Contracting Parties acknowledge the value, in the light of the aims of this Agreement, of consulting each other on international issues of mutual interest."

25.095 Article 3 ("economic cooperation") provides:

"1. The Contracting Parties, taking into account their mutual interest and long- and medium-term economic objectives, undertake to establish economic cooperation of the widest possible scope. The aims of such cooperation shall be in particular: (a) generally to step up and

---

87 OJ L262/54, 1 November 1995.

diversify economic links between them; (b) to contribute to the sustainable development of their economies and standards of living; (c) to promote the expansion of trade in order to achieve diversification and open up new markets; (d) to encourage the flow of investment, the transfer of technology and strengthen the protection of investment; (e) to promote cooperation between economic operators, particularly small and medium-sized enterprises; (f) to establish conditions conducive to job-creation; (g) to protect and improve the environment; (h) to encourage rural development measures; (i) to strengthen the scientific foundation and capacity for innovation of the Contracting Parties; and (j) to support efforts and initiatives for regional integration.

2. Without excluding any area from the outset, the Contracting Parties shall, in their mutual interest and with regard to their respective competence and capacities, determine by common agreement the spheres to be covered by economic cooperation. Cooperation shall centre particularly on the following: (a) industry; (b) the use of natural resources against a background of sustainable development; (c) intellectual property, including industrial property, standards and quality criteria; (d) health and plant-health regulations; (e) services in general, and tourism and transport in particular; (f) data processing, electronics, telecommunications, the use of space technology; and (g) information on monetary matters.

3. In the interests of attaining the objectives of economic cooperation, the Contracting Parties shall, each in accordance with its laws, endeavour to promote activities including the following: (a) a continuous exchange of points of view and information in connection with cooperation, primarily by gaining access to existing databases or by setting up new ones; (b) encouragement of joint ventures, and in more general terms the development of partnerships which are suited to the needs of firms; (c) organizing visits, meetings and activities for promoting cooperation between individuals and delegations representing firms or economic organizations, and creating the appropriate machinery and institutions; (d) organizing seminars and meetings between businessmen, arranging and holding specialized fairs, exhibitions and symposia, and promoting contacts between economic operators at these events; (e) studies or evaluation reports concerning project feasibility or advance selection of new forms of cooperation; and (f) research projects and exchanges of scientists."

25.096 Article 4 ("Most-favoured-nation status") provides that the contracting parties must grant each other most-favoured-nation treatment in trade, in accordance with the GATT. Article 5 ("Development of Trade Cooperation") provides:

"1. The Contracting Parties undertake to develop and diversify trade to the highest possible degree, taking into account the economic situation of each of the Parties and facilitating trade transactions between them as far as possible.

2. To that end, the Contracting Parties shall endeavour to find methods of reducing and eliminating the obstacles hindering the development of trade, notably non-tariff and para-tariff barriers, taking account of work already accomplished in this field by international organizations.

3. The Contracting Parties agree to promote the interchange of information and to hold consultations on the issues of tariffs, health and technical requirements, trade laws and practices, and on any anti-dumping or countervailing duties which might apply.

4. Without prejudice to their rights and obligations under the GATT, the Contracting Parties undertake to consult each other on any disputes which may arise in connection with trade.

    If one of the Parties requests such consultation, it shall take place at the earliest opportunity. The Contracting Party making the request shall provide the other Party with all the information necessary for a detailed examination of the situation.

    Attempts shall be made through such consultations to resolve trade disputes as rapidly as possible.

5. In trade between the Contracting Parties, should allegations arise of dumping or subsidy leading to investigation by the competent authorities, each Contracting Party undertakes to examine requests made by the other Party in connection with the case in question.

The competent authorities of the Contracting Parties shall inform the interested parties at their request of the essential facts and considerations which will serve as the basis for a decision. Such information shall be provided before the definitive conclusions of the investigation are reached, and in sufficient time for the interested parties to defend their interests.

Before definitive anti-dumping and countervailing duties are imposed, the Contracting Parties shall do their utmost to bring about a constructive solution to the problem.

6. Paragraphs 3, 4 and 5 shall cease to apply when the new anti-dumping code and other GATT instruments currently being negotiated within the Uruguay Round enter into force in Brazil and the Community."

25.097 Article 6 ("means of achieving cooperation in trade") provides that in the interests of bringing about more active co-operation in trade, the Contracting Parties undertake to take steps, in conformity with their respective laws and considering the differences in their levels of development, including the following: (a) promoting meetings, interchange and contacts between entrepreneurs of each of the Parties, with the aim of identifying goods suitable for sale on the market of the other Party; (b) facilitating administrative co-operation between their customs services, in particular as regards vocational training, the simplification of procedures and preventing and detecting violations of customs regulations; (c) encouraging and providing support for trade promotion activities such as seminars, symposia, fairs and trade and industrial exhibitions, trade visits, reciprocal visits, business weeks and other activities, with the aim of supporting and accompanying efforts to expand trade, (d) providing support for their own organisations and firms, to enable them to engage in activities which are of benefit to both sides; (e) taking into consideration each other's interests with regard to market access for commodities, semi-finished and manufactured goods and with the aims agreed within the competent international organisations; and (f) examining methods of facilitating trade and eliminating barriers to trade, taking into consideration the work of international organisations.

25.098 Article 7 ("temporary admission of goods") provides that the Contracting Parties undertake to consider tax and duty exemption for temporary import into their territory of goods, in accordance with their respective laws and taking account, wherever possible, of existing international agreements in this field.

25.099 Article 8 ("Industrial cooperation") provides that the Contracting Parties shall promote the expansion and diversification of Brazil's production base in the industrial and service sectors, directing their co-operation activities at small and medium-sized enterprises in particular and encouraging steps to facilitate access on the part of these enterprises to sources of capital, to markets and to appropriate technology, and also fostering joint venture activities directed especially towards trade between the Parties and aimed at third country markets.

25.100 Article 9 ("Investment") provides that the Contracting Parties agree, so far as their competence, rules and regulations and policies permit: (a) to encourage an increase in mutually beneficial investment and (b) to examine the possibility of setting up operations and mechanisms to improve the climate for such investment in keeping with the guidelines of paragraph 38 of the Rome Declaration on relations between the then EEC and its Member States and the countries of the Rio Group.[88]

25.101 Article 15 deals with co-operation in the field of transport. It provides:

---

88 The Rio Group is a group of some of the countries in Central and South America as well as the Caribbean which was established in Rio de Janeiro in 1986 and allows for co-operation between the States involved.

"Recognizing the importance of transport to economic development and the intensification of trade, the Contracting Parties shall adopt the necessary measures to further cooperation in this field.

Cooperation in the area of air, road and rail transport and in that of infrastructure shall centre on the following:

- the interchange of information on subjects of common interest, including policies,
- training programmes aimed at economic operators and those in charge of public-sector departments,
- technical assistance particularly in connection with programmes for the modernization of infrastructure, replacement of rolling stock, vehicles and craft, and the introduction of technology relating to combined and multi-mode transport."

25.102 The annex contains the exchange of letters between the EEC and Brazil:

"ANNEX
EXCHANGE OF LETTERS between the European Economic Community and the Federative Republic of Brazil on maritime transport

A. Letter from the Community
Sir,
We should be obliged if you would confirm that your Government is in agreement with the following:

When the Framework Agreement for cooperation between the European Economic Community and the Federative Republic of Brazil was signed, the Parties undertook to address in the appropriate manner issues relating to the operation of shipping, particularly where the development of trade might be hindered. Mutually satisfactory solutions on shipping will be sought, while the principle of free and fair competition on a commercial basis is observed.

It has likewise been agreed that such issues should also be discussed by the Joint Committee.

Please accept, Sir, the assurance of my highest consideration.

On behalf of the Council of the European Communities

B. Letter from the Federative Republic of Brazil
Sir,
I have the honour to acknowledge receipt of your letter of today's date and confirm the agreement of my Government with the following:

'When the Framework Agreement for cooperation between the European Economic Community and the Federative Republic of Brazil was signed, the Parties undertook to address in the appropriate manner issues relating to the operation of shipping, particularly where the development of trade might be hindered. Mutually satisfactory solutions on shipping will be sought, while the principle of free and fair competition on a commercial basis is observed.

It has likewise been agreed that such issues should also be discussed by the Joint Committee.

Please accept, Sir, the assurance of my highest consideration.

For the Government of Brazil"

I. EU–AFRICAN RELATIONS IN SHIPPING LAW

25.103 In 2017, the European Parliament initiated an ambitious EU–Africa strategy. Shipping was part of that strategy. In particular, the strategy contemplates positive market liberalisation initiatives and investment in maritime infrastructure to improve trade and make market access easier for the maritime industry. The Parliament is contemplating a new collaboration leading to an Economic Partnership Agreement which would contribute to sustained growth on the African continent. One important aspect would be maritime infrastructure to enable the shipping industry to operate more easily in the African countries. It should ultimately lead to, if pursued and implemented, an increase in international trade. The European Parliament's rapporteur of the EU–Africa Strategy, Maurice Ponga MEP said:

> "This strategy will strengthen our neighbouring continent, which both the African and European citizens will benefit from. Open markets are a prerequisite to achieve the full potential of international trade and a stable framework for private investment, such as those in infrastructure. Therefore, maritime transport plays an important role in the eradication of extreme poverty and the pursuit of a substantial development."

J. CANADA–EU: COMPREHENSIVE ECONOMIC AND TRADE AGREEMENT

25.104 On 30 October 2016, Canada and the EU signed the Comprehensive Economic and Trade Agreement ("CETA").[89] It entered into force on 21 September 2017 provisionally. Around 47% of trade between Canada and the EU is carried by sea. CETA is designed to eliminate 98% of tariffs between the EU and Canada. Canada's Global Affairs Canada believes that CETA will lead to an increase of around 20% in terms of trade between Canada and the EU.

25.105 CETA has had some impact on demand for transatlantic maritime transportation between the EU and Canada. Some EU carriers have located ships in Canada for cabotage service.

25.106 Chapter 14 of CETA deals with various issues including the maritime sector. It seeks to liberalise the market because the Canadian regime has protected Canadian shipowners against competitors registered under foreign flags owing to cabotage restrictions by virtue of the Coasting Trade Act – traditionally only Canadian-flagged vessels or duty-paid vessels could carry goods or passengers between two Canadian ports. Non-Canadian shipowners had to apply for a coasting trade licence. It was difficult to obtain a licence because non-Canadian vessels were not allowed to ply their trade unless there was no Canadian vessel available and, even then, such a vessel was granted permission for only a limited timeframe. Under CETA, EU vessels are able to engage in cabotage trade in three circumstances:

(a) EU shipping lines may provide feeder services on both continuous and single trip bases between the ports of Montréal and Halifax so long as the service is part of carriage involving the importation of inbound goods into Canada or of outbound goods from the country. This would require an EU ship to ply exclusively between Montreal and Halifax or transport containers between those two Canadian ports while engaged in an international voyage;

(b) the repositioning of empty containers within Canada, but this service is not offered to third parties but is only on a non-revenue basis in terms of moving one's own containers;

(c) dredging services. Canadian companies may hire EU vessels to dredge in Canadian waters but Canadian federal government agencies must follow CETA's procurement rules if the contract is valued at more than C$8.81 million.

---

89 See http://ec.europa.eu/trade/policy/in-focus/ceta/ceta-explained/index_en.htm for a very useful summary. See also http://ec.europa.eu/trade/policy/in-focus/ceta/.

25.107 Foreign work permits could still be an issue. Most foreign nationals entering Canada on a vessel as crew members engaging in the coasting trade need a work permit from Immigration, Refugees and Citizenship Canada. Before hiring a foreign worker in Canada, employers also generally obliged to obtain a Labour Market Impact Assessment to demonstrate that there is a need for a foreign worker to fill the job.

CHAPTER 26

Maritime safety: introduction and European Union measures relating to maritime safety generally

A. INTRODUCTION

26.001 Safety has become a central and critical component of European Union ("EU") shipping law.[1] It is, in some ways, not too surprising as there have been various significant and tragic maritime safety incidents in EU waters including the *Herald of Free Enterprise*, the *Scandinavian Star*, the *Erika*, the *Prestige*, the *Betelgeuse* and, in earlier times, the likes of the *Torrey Canyon*. Not only have these terrible events occurred but there was also a need for the EU to be seen to respond to these incidents in the interests of the EU, its citizens and the various interests involved (e.g. coastal and economic (e.g. aquaculture and tourism)). If the EU did nothing or very little, EU citizens could be quite unforgiving of the EU. If the EU said that it should do nothing because of the presence of the likes of the International Maritime Organization ("IMO"), it is quite likely that the EU's citizenry and other interests would have been scathing about the EU because of its unwillingness to act and to introduce higher standards than might have been achievable in a near-global organisation such as the IMO which has to proceed at a slower pace than could be possible in a smaller and more agile organisation such as the EU.

26.002 There is a clear link between maritime safety and the maritime environment. A defect in safety can lead to a disaster in the environment. This chapter and the subsequent chapters on safety should be read in conjunction with the chapters on the environment.

26.003 In 2018, the European Commission described maritime safety in the following terms:

"Safety and Environment
In recent years, the European Union and its Member States have been at the forefront of improving maritime safety legislation and promoting high-quality standards. The aim is to eliminate substandard shipping, increase the protection of passengers and crews, reduce the risk of environmental pollution, and ensure that operators who follow good practices are not put at a commercial disadvantage compared to those prepared to take short cuts with vessel safety.

Whilst many flag States and owners are meeting their international obligations, their efforts are constantly undermined by those who do not play the game according to the rules. When operators break the rules on safety and environmental protection, they put crews and the environment at risk, and in addition benefit from unfair competition.

---

1 E.g. on 8 May 2014, the Council adopted Decision 2014/280 on the position to be adopted on behalf of the European Union at the International Maritime Organization during the 93rd session of the Maritime Safety Committee on the adoption of amendments to SOLAS Regulations II-1/29, II-2/3, 2/9.7, 2/13.4, 2/18, III/20, the Life Saving Appliances Code and the 2011 Enhanced Survey Programme Code (OJ L145/40, 16.5.2014) and the very first recital states: "[a]ction by the European Union in the sector of maritime transport should aim to improve maritime safety".

Shipping is of strategic importance to the EU's economy: every year, two billion tonnes of cargo are loaded and unloaded at EU ports, while one billion tonnes of oil transits through EU ports and EU waters. This is why the EU is constantly developing and intensifying its maritime safety policy to eradicate substandard shipping, essentially through a convergent application of internationally agreed rules.

EU action in the field of maritime safety and protection of the environment generates significant added value to the international legal framework, such as SOLAS [International Convention for the Safety of Life at Sea] and MARPOL [International Convention for the Prevention of Pollution by Ships], which is overseen by the International Maritime Organization (IMO). Furthermore, the transposition of IMO rules into the EU legal system ensures their 'harmonized application' across the entire EU. In addition, EU plays an important role in improving international standards by initiating and contributing directly to their development and adoption at international level.

The 'Erika' and the 'Prestige' accidents encouraged the EU to drastically reform its existing regime and to adopt new rules and standards for preventing accidents at sea, particularly those involving oil tankers. The EU considerably reinforced its legislative arsenal to combat flags of convenience and give Europe better protection against the risks of accidental oil spills. With the Third Maritime Safety Package adopted in 2009, the EU expanded its legislative arsenal covering all chains of responsibility in the maritime sector. The focus now is on proper implementation and enforcement as well as continuous evaluation to ensure that this legislation is fit for purpose. The European Commission can rely on the technical and scientific assistance of the European Maritime Safety Agency (EMSA)."[2]

26.004 It would be wrong to say that the EU cares more about one type of ship over another – a maritime casualty or tragedy of one type is as bad as another. However, there are probably two types of ship which have attracted most attention: passenger ships and oil tankers. The former because it directly impinges on citizens and can often involve the loss of life on a large scale. The latter because it causes enormous pollution and environmental damage.

26.005 In regard to passenger ships, the Commission commented in 2018:

"Safety of passenger ships
Passenger ships play an important role in the mobility of EU citizens – more than 400 million people pass every year through EU ports, with 120 million passengers being transported between ports of the same Member State.

EU legislation on passenger ship safety has been put in place over time following accidents such as the sinking of the Herald of Free Enterprise in 1987 and the Estonia in 1994, which resulted in the loss of 193 and 852 lives respectively. It complements international and national standards, provides for safer ships and more efficient handling of ship accidents.

Review of EU rules on passenger ship safety
On 30 November 2017, a number of legislative texts that simplify and improve the common rules on safety of ships carrying passengers in EU waters were published in the Official Journal of the European Union. They had been adopted by the European Parliament on 4 October 2017 and the Council on 23 October 2017.

The new rules enter into force 20 days after publication. Member States then have 2 years to transpose the updated rules into national legislation and shall apply them from 21 December 2019.

The package is a result of proposals made by the European Commission in June 2016, as a follow-up to the recommendations of the fitness check driven by the Commission's Regulatory Fitness and Performance (REFIT) Programme.

---

2 https://ec.europa.eu/transport/modes/maritime/safety_en.

The update is a response to lessons learnt, including from accidents, and technological progress. Its aim is to enhance safety and ensure that the competition takes place on equal footing. It does so by making the rules clearer, simpler and up-to-date with legal and technological developments.

The new rules will also provide for easier compliance by operators and better monitoring and enforcement for national competent authorities as well as the European Commission, assisted by the European Maritime Safety Agency (EMSA). The key changes to the safety standards and requirements for passenger ships sailing in EU waters include:

- Amendments to Directive 2009/45/EC on technical requirements for passenger ships on domestic voyages clarify that ships built in aluminium have to be certified according to this Directive and meet its fire safety requirements (in 10 years for new and 12 years for existing aluminium ships after the amendments enter into force). Passenger ships below 24 metres are excluded from the scope of the Directive.
- Amendments to Directive 98/41/EC on registration of persons on board introduce the requirement to register passenger data in a digital manner, using harmonised administrative procedures (the so-called single window established under Directive 2010/65/EU) to facilitate search and rescue operations in case of emergency. For a period of 6 years after entry into force, Member States may continue to apply the old rules, i.e. keeping data concerning persons on board by means of the company's registrar. The time allowed for reporting data on persons on board is shortened from 30 to 15 minutes after the ship's departure.
- A new Directive replacing and repealing Directive 1999/35/EC on surveys for passenger ferries and high-speed craft in regular service eliminates overlaps between various inspection regimes. This preserves the safety level while reducing the administrative burden on shipowners and rationalise the inspection efforts of Member States' authorities.

See also: 'Maritime Transport: Final adoption of the Passenger Ship Safety package' (23/10/2017)

Next steps

In the coming months, the Commission, assisted by the European Maritime Safety Agency, will follow-up on the remaining recommendations of the fitness check. In particular, it will:

1. Finalise the development of a new framework of goal-based standards for small passenger ships (i.e. smaller than 24m) built from innovative materials such as fibre-reinforced plastic, in view of creating a European market.

   To support next steps and facilitate the exchange of views with national administrations, industry stakeholders and passenger associations, the Commission has enlarged its expert group on passenger ship safety to observers from stakeholder organisations.

   See also: 'Consultation on common EU rules for small passenger ships' (25/07/2017–30/11/2017) and the roadmap.

2. Continue to support a preparatory study to assess whether the specific EU damage stability requirements for ro-ro passenger ships should be aligned with those applicable at the global level (adopted on 16 June 2017 within the International Maritime Organisation, IMO).

   See also: 'Maritime Transport: Commission welcomes international agreement to increase the safety of passenger ships' (16/06/2017)

EU passenger ship safety legislation

The most extensive EU legislative instrument is Directive 2009/45/EC, which covers passenger ships made of steel or equivalent material and high speed craft on domestic voyages. Where applicable and feasible, it is based on internationally agreed standards, namely the International Convention for the Safety of Life At Sea (SOLAS), establishing detailed technical requirements on vessel construction, stability, fire protection and life-saving equipment. It also includes specific access and public information requirements for persons with reduced mobility or disabilities.

In addition, Directive 2003/25/EC provides for additional measures for ro-ro passenger vessels throughout the Union, engaged on both international and domestic voyages, to ensure their stability following damage. Moreover, specific EU rules governing the mandatory inspections for ro-ro passenger ships and high-speed craft in regular service are in place (Directive (EU) 2017/2110 that has replaced and repealed Directive 1999/35/EC). Shipping companies also need to comply with the requirements of Directive 98/41/EC on registration of persons on board, in order to make search and rescue operations more effective and to facilitate proper management of the consequences of any accident (medical care, insurance, etc.).

Passenger carriers' liability
Passengers involved in maritime accidents must have an adequate level of compensation for any loss or damage they suffer. To ensure this, ship owners must have appropriate insurance arrangements in place.

The Regulation on the liability of carriers of passengers by sea in the event of accidents (Regulation (EC) 392/2009) lays down harmonised rules on liability and insurance for shipping companies and aims at an adequate level of compensation should an accident occur. This applies irrespective of the area of operation of the vessel, thus to all carriers engaging in international carriage, including between EU Member States, and certain types of domestic carriage (over 5 miles from the coastline). Passengers may claim compensation for death or personal injury, loss or damage to luggage or valuables, vehicle and mobility or other special equipment, provided that one of the following requirements are fulfilled:

- the ship flies the flag of a Member State or is registered in a Member State, or
- the carriage agreement was concluded in a Member State, or
- the point of departure and/or destination specified in the carriage agreement are located in a Member State

Enforcement of the rights and obligations under the Regulation relies mainly on flag State and port State control, and the relevant systems available in the EU.

The Commission has recently completed an ex-post evaluation of the application of the Regulation and concluded that on the whole it has performed as expected and not proposed any changes to the Regulation. The Commission Staff Working Document, the support study and connected documents relating to the passenger liability regulation were published in October 2017."[3]

26.006 The EU has taken action on safety (and environment protection) in various specific areas. Subsequent chapters consider specific measures while this chapter considers a number of general and earlier measures. The areas in which the EU has acted include classification societies, vessel traffic monitoring/maritime surveillance, port State control, maritime casualty investigation, insurance for maritime claims, ship-source pollution, compelling Member States to impose penalties for infringements of environmental law, rules on marine equipment and a wide range of measures on maritime safety generally. The maritime safety measures have covered areas (and there is an overlap) such as passenger safety, port State control, vessel traffic monitoring and reporting formalities, flag state and recognised organisations, seafarers, pollution prevention, casualty investigation, insurance and liability, technical safety requirements, the EMSA and the Committee on Safe Seas and the Prevention of Pollution from Ships ("COSS").

26.007 As mentioned above, this chapter considers some of the general measures while later chapters consider the more specific measures.

---

3 https://ec.europa.eu/transport/modes/maritime/safety-and-environment/safety-passenger-ships_en.

B. 1978: COUNCIL RECOMMENDATION 78/584 ON THE RATIFICATION OF CONVENTIONS ON SAFETY IN SHIPPING

26.008 On 26 June 1978, the Council adopted Recommendation 78/584 on the ratification of conventions on safety in shipping.[4] It followed on from a number of maritime incidents but also an awakening in the then European Communities that it could and should tackle maritime issues.[5] The preamble was lucid and clear as to what was involved:

"Whereas the European Council of 7 and 8 April 1978 declared that the prevention of and the fight against marine pollution, particularly from hydrocarbons, must be a major objective for Community action;

Whereas it asked the Council, acting on a proposal from the Commission, and the Member States to take appropriate measures without delay within the Community and to adopt common attitudes in the appropriate international bodies on the swift implementation of existing international rules in this field, in particular those regarding minimum standards for the operation of ships;

Whereas there is a fundamental interest in seeing effective action undertaken to reduce the risks inherent in the transport of hydrocarbons, in particular the danger of severe coastal pollution as the result of accidents on the high seas, and whereas this fundamental interest is underlined by the European Communities' environment action programmes;

Whereas safety in shipping must be improved and the living and working conditions of crews and their level of competence better safeguarded;

Whereas Community action in this field in the framework of specialized international bodies, particularly the IMCO [Intergovernmental Maritime Consultative Organization] and the ILO [International Labour Organization] and their respective Conventions, may be jeopardized if too long a period were to elapse between the conclusion of those Conventions and their entry into force;

Whereas the 1974 International Convention for the safety of life at sea (SOLAS) and the 1978 Protocol relating thereto and ILO Convention No 147 concerning minimum standards in merchant ships of 1976, which have not yet entered into force, can make a substantial contribution towards improving both technical and welfare standards affecting, respectively, the safety of ships and their equipment and the living and working conditions of their crews;

Whereas the 1973 Convention for the prevention of pollution by ships (MARPOL), as amended by the 1978 Protocol, can make a substantial contribution towards protecting the marine environment against pollution by ships, particularly oil tankers;

Whereas the signing and ratification by or the accession of all the Member States could accelerate the entry into force and increase the effectiveness of these Conventions..."

26.009 The recommendation which followed the preamble was equally clear but it was a sign that the EU had started on its journey to cajole and compel Member States into action in regard to safety and the environment. The EU was taking the upper hand and, some would say, the strong hand vis-à-vis the Member States:

"HEREBY RECOMMENDS:

- that, where they have not already done so, the Member States, where appropriate, sign the following international conventions and ratify or accede to them:
- the 1974 International Convention for the safety of life at sea (SOLAS),
- the 1978 Protocol relating to the 1974 International Convention for the safety of life at sea,

---

4 OJ L194/17, 19 July 1978.
5 See chap. 5.

- the 1973 International Convention for the prevention of pollution by ships (MARPOL), as amended by the 1978 Protocol,
- Convention No 147 concerning minimum standards in merchant ships, adopted by the International Labour Conference in 1976;
- that signing, ratification or accession by the Member States, as the case may be, take place by the following dates:
- the 1974 SOLAS Convention: ratification or accession as soon as possible and, in any event, by 1 January 1979,
- the Protocol thereto (1978): – signing as soon as possible and by 1 March 1979 at the latest,
- ratification as soon as possible and, in any event, by 30 June 1979,
- the Protocol (1978) amending and supplementing the MARPOL Convention (1973) and Annex I thereto:
- signing by 1 June 1979,
- ratification by 1 June 1980,
- ILO Convention No 147:
- ratification or accession by 1 April 1979;
- that the Member States inform in writing the Secretary-General of the Inter-Governmental Maritime Consultative Organization or the International Labour Organization, as appropriate, that their signing, ratification or accession has had regard to this recommendation."

This was clearly a case of the EU cajoling and encouraging Member States to adopt these measures.

C. 1993: COUNCIL RESOLUTION OF 8 JUNE 1993 ON A COMMON POLICY ON SAFE SEAS

26.010 On 8 June 1993, the Council adopted a non-binding resolution on a common policy on safe seas. Again, one sees that the EU was beginning to become more involved and testing its way somewhat by means of a resolution.[6]

"THE COUNCIL OF THE EUROPEAN COMMUNITIES,

Reaffirming the conclusions of the extraordinary Council of 25 January 1993, stating the Council's intention to improve maritime safety and to contribute to the prevention of maritime pollution in the seas surrounding the Community through the development and implementation of international standards concerning ships, personnel and navigation procedures and through the development of navigation infrastructures and emergency facilities;

Stressing the role of the International Maritime Organization (IMO) and, where appropriate, of the International Labour Organization (ILO) for maritime safety and pollution prevention, in particular through the establishment of standards for vessels, personnel and maritime infrastructures;

Stressing the role of European cooperation within the Paris Memorandum of Understanding on port State control (MOU) for the application of IMO standards;

Calling again upon the Community and its Member States to support and promote further and more coordinated and firm action in the ongoing work at IMO and MOU;

Recognizing the need for intensified action as appropriate at Community or national level to ensure an adequate response to the requirements of maritime safety and the prevention of marine pollution;

Welcoming the Commission communication on 'A common policy on safe seas', including its coherent action programme on priority measures to be taken by the Community and its Member States to enhance maritime safety and pollution prevention,

---

6 OJ C271/1.

I

1. NOTES with satisfaction that the objectives and main initiatives outlined in the said communication correspond, to a large extent, to the conclusions of the aforementioned extraordinary Council;
2. FULLY SUPPORTS the objectives of the communication;
3. EMPHASIZES that Community measures in the field of maritime safety and of the prevention of maritime pollution, in particular for the convergent application of IMO standards, should apply in principle to ships of all flags in Community waters, by which is meant waters of the Member States of the Community, in order to protect the Community coastlines, human life, fauna and flora and other marine resources, and not to jeopardize the competitiveness of the Community fleet, while taking due account of the international nature of shipping;
4. STRESSES in this context that further Community action should be framed on the basis of the following main objectives:

   – to strengthen inspection, in particular to reinforce measures concerning standards of operation and measures against substandard crews, and to take measures designed to remove all substandard ships from Community waters,
   – to improve the safety of maritime navigation,
   – to identify, on the basis of existing legislation and international guidelines, environmentally sensitive areas within the Community and propose to IMO specific measures for them.

II

1. AGREES that the abovementioned main objectives should be implemented while respecting the following priorities for a Community action programme that takes proper account of international conventions and work at IMO, MOU and ILO:

   (a) effective and uniform implementation of international rules:

   – to develop common criteria for more thorough port State control and to harmonize rules on port State inspection and detention, including the possibility of refusing access to Community ports to ships found to be below internationally agreed standards and which refuse to be upgraded as required and including the possibility of publishing the results of the inspections,
   – to identify IMO resolutions considered to be necessary for improving maritime safety of vessels of any flags entering Community waters and to ensure their mandatory application,
   – to elaborate common standards for classification societies,
   – to harmonize the implementation of IMO standards and the approval procedures for marine equipment,
   – to encourage work directed towards the introduction of a Community register (Euros) as a register of high-safety standard ships;

   (b) enhanced training and education:

   – to develop common standards for minimum training levels of key personnel, including the question of a common language on board Community vessels, as well as of port inspectors and vessel traffic services (VTS) operators;

   (c) improvement of maritime infrastructures and of traffic procedures

   (i) to identify the need for maritime infrastructures for the protection of environmentally sensitive areas of the Community and to propose to IMO specific measures for them;

1266

(ii) to develop further VTS infrastructures, to harmonize VTS procedures and to impose mandatory ship reporting in certain areas through IMO, where appropriate;

(iii) to adopt, in accordance with Article 13 of the Council Directive concerning minimum requirements for vessels bound for or leaving Community ports and carrying dangerous or polluting goods, a fuller reporting system;

(iv) to develop the availability and use of reception facilities within the Community;

(v) to devise a European radionavigation plan and, if appropriate, to examine the possibility of introducing a mechanism whereby the costs of providing radionavigational aids are recoverable from users taking account of the international law of the sea;

(vi) to strengthen coordinated Community emergency planning through enhanced responsibility by way of towing and salvage facilities;

(d) civil liability:

– to ratify as soon as possible:

– the 1969 International Convention on civil liability for oil pollution damage (CLC) and the 1971 International Convention on the establishment of an international fund for compensation for oil pollution damage (FUND) where they have not yet been ratified,

– the protocols to the 1969 Liability Convention and to the 1971 Fund Convention, as agreed upon in 1984 and revised in 1992, concerning increased compensation amounts;

– to continue to study the questions of liability for environmental damage including the possibility of a liability and FUND convention covering hazardous and noxious substances;

(e) safety of passenger vessels: to harmonize criteria for the determination of the number and qualification of lifeboatmen on board passenger ships engaged in short international voyages;

(f) risk assessment: to consider whether and, if so, how the principles of potential risk assessment developed for other major risks can be applied to the sea transport of freight;

2. APPROVES in principle the establishment of a Committee on Safe Seas, in accordance with Council Decision 87/373/EEC of 13 July 1987 laying down the procedures for the exercise of implementing powers conferred on the Commission,[7] with the purpose of:

(a) centralizing the duties of Committees, created by the implementation of the aforementioned Decision in existing or future Community legislation, concerning maritime safety matters;

(b) assisting and advising the Commission in all maritime safety matters and matters of prevention or limitation of environmental pollution due to maritime activities;

3. AGREES to a more effective common monitoring of the work of IMO and MOU and the preparation of, or contribution to, a closer coordination of Member States towards a common position in these organizations, achieved through the usual Council procedures.

III
Therefore:

1. WELCOMES the fact that the Commission has presented proposals concerning:

---

7 Ed., OJ L197/33, 18 July 1987.

- common rules and standards for ship inspection and survey organizations (classification societies),[8]
- the minimum level of training for maritime occupations;

2. URGES the Commission to submit as soon as possible to the Council suggestions for specific action and formal proposals concerning:

- the implementation of Article 13 of the Council Directive concerning minimum requirements for vessels bound for or leaving Community ports and carrying dangerous or polluting goods,
- criteria for the inspection of ships, including the harmonization of detention rules, and including the possibility of publication of the results of the inspections and refusal of access,
- enforcement, within the Community, of relevant IMO resolutions, in particular:
- IMO resolution A 722(17) on application of tonnage measurement of ballast spaces in segregated ballast tanks (SBT),
- IMO resolution on the IMO identification number for ships;
- a revised proposal on the introduction of a Community register (Euros) also with a view to safety at sea under European flags,
- common safety rules for marine equipment used on board of commercial and passenger vessels,
- safety rules for passenger vessels in domestic voyages,
- a Committee on Safe Seas,
- measures for traffic surveillance and aid, including VTS;

3. COMMITS ITSELF to make every effort to come to conclusions on these suggestions and decide upon proposals before the end of 1993;
4. INVITES the Commission to submit an interim report by the end of 1993;
DECIDES to embark upon, before the end of 1994 and on the basis of a report by the Commission, a revision and update of the objectives and priority action programme of this resolution."

D. REGULATION (EC) NO 2099/2002 OF THE EUROPEAN PARLIAMENT AND OF THE COUNCIL OF 5 NOVEMBER 2002 ESTABLISHING A COMMITTEE ON SAFE SEAS AND THE PREVENTION OF POLLUTION FROM SHIPS (COSS) AND AMENDING THE REGULATIONS ON MARITIME SAFETY AND THE PREVENTION OF POLLUTION FROM SHIPS

26.011 On 5 November 2002, the Parliament and Council adopted Regulation 2099/2002 establishing a Committee on Safe Seas and the Prevention of Pollution from Ships (COSS) and amending the regulations on maritime safety and the prevention of pollution from ships.[9] It has been amended several times since: Commission Regulation 415/2004 of 5 March 2004;[10] Commission Regulation 93/2007 of 30 January 2007;[11] Regulation 596/2009 of the European Parliament and of the Council of 18 June 2009;[12] Regulation 530/2012 of the European Parliament and of the Council of 13 June 2012;[13]

---

8 Ed., OJ 162/13, 18. 6. 1993.
9 OJ L324/1 29 November 2002.
10 OJ L68/10, 6 March 2004.
11 OJ L22/12, 31 January 2007.
12 OJ L188/14, 18 July 2009.
13 OJ L172/3, 30 June 2012.

and Commission Regulation 2016/103 of 27 January 2016.[14] The background to the regulation is clear from the recitals.[15] Under Article 12, the regulation entered into force on

---

14 OJ L21/67, 28 January 2016.
15 The recitals provide:

"(1) The measures implementing the existing Regulations and Directives in the field of maritime safety were adopted by a regulatory procedure involving the Committee set up by Council Directive 93/75/EEC of 13 September 1993 concerning minimum requirements for vessels bound for or leaving Community ports and carrying dangerous or polluting goods [Ed., OJ L247/19, 5 October 1993] and, in certain cases, an ad hoc committee. These committees were governed by the rules set out in Council Decision 87/373/EEC of 13 July 1987 laying down the procedures for the exercise of implementing powers conferred on the Commission...

(2) By its Resolution of 8 June 1993 on a common policy on safe seas ..., the Council approved in principle the establishment of a Committee on Safe Seas and the Prevention of Pollution from Ships (COSS) and called on the Commission to present a proposal to set up such a committee.

(3) The role of COSS is to centralise the tasks of the committees set up under the Community legislation on maritime safety, the prevention of pollution from ships and the protection of shipboard living and working conditions and to assist and advise the Commission on all matters of maritime safety and prevention or reduction of pollution of the environment by shipping activities.

In keeping with the Resolution of 8 June 1993, a Committee on Safe Seas and the Prevention of Pollution from Ships should be set up and assigned the tasks previously devolved to the committees established under the aforesaid legislation. All new Community legislation adopted in the field of maritime safety should stipulate recourse to the Committee thereby set up.

(5) Decision 87/373/EEC has been replaced by Council Decision 1999/468/EC of 28 June 1999 laying down the procedures for the exercise of implementing powers conferred on the Commission [Ed., OJ L184/23, 17 July 1999], the provisions of which should therefore be applied to COSS. The purpose of the latter decision is to define the Committee procedures applicable and ensure more comprehensive information to the European Parliament and the public on the work of the committees.

(6) The measures required to implement the aforesaid legislation should be adopted in accordance with Decision 1999/468/EC.

(7) The aforesaid legislation should also be amended to substitute COSS for the Committee set up by Directive 93/75/EEC or, where appropriate, for the ad hoc committee established under any particular act. This Regulation should in particular amend the relevant provisions of Council Regulations (EEC) No 613/91 of 4 March 1991 on the transfer of ships from one register to another within the Community ..., (EC) No 2978/94 of 21 November 1994 on the implementation of IMO Resolution A.747(18) on the application of tonnage measurement of ballast spaces in segregated ballast oil tankers ..., (EC) No 3051/95 of 8 December 1995 on the safety management of roll-on/roll-off passenger ferries (ro-ro ferries) [Ed., OJ L320/14, 30 December 1995. Regulation as amended by Commission Regulation 179/98 (OJ L19/35, 24 January 1998)] and Regulation (EC) No 417/2002 of the European Parliament and of the Council of 18 February 2002 on the accelerated phasing-in of double hull or equivalent design requirements for single hull oil tankers and repealing Council Regulation (EC) No 2978/94 [Ed., see OJ L64/1, 7 March 2002], in order to insert a reference to COSS and to stipulate the regulatory procedure laid down in Article 5 of Decision 1999/468/EC.

(8) Moreover, the aforesaid legislation is based on the application of rules resulting from international instruments in force at the date of adoption of the Community act in question, or at the date specified by the latter. As a consequence, Member States cannot apply the subsequent amendments to these international instruments until the Community Directives or Regulations have been amended. This has major disadvantages owing to the difficulty of ensuring that the date of entry into force of the amendment at international level coincides with that of the Regulation integrating this amendment into Community law, not least the delayed application within the Community of the most recent and most stringent international safety standards.

(9) However, it is necessary to draw a distinction between the provisions of a Community act making reference, for the purposes of their application, to an international instrument and Community provisions reproducing an international instrument in full or in part. In the latter case, the most recent amendments to the international instruments cannot in any case be rendered applicable until the Community provisions concerned have been amended.

(10) Member States should therefore be permitted to apply the most recent provisions of international instruments, with the exception of those explicitly incorporated in a Community act. This can be done by stating that the international convention applicable for the purposes of the Directive or Regulation concerned is that 'in its up-to-date version', without mentioning the date.

(11) For reasons of transparency, the relevant amendments to international instruments that are integrated in Community maritime legislation should be made public in the Community through their publication in the Official Journal of the European Communities.

the twentieth day following that of its publication in the *Official Journal*. The regulation is binding in its entirety and directly applicable in all Member States.

26.012 Article 1 sets out the purpose of the regulation. It is to improve the implementation of the EU legislation referred to in Article 2(2) of the regulation on maritime safety, the prevention of pollution from ships and shipboard living and working conditions: (a) by centralising the tasks of the committees set up under Community maritime legislation and replaced by this regulation by establishing a single Committee on Safe Seas and the Prevention of Pollution from Ships, to be known as COSS; and (b) by accelerating the update of, and facilitating subsequent amendments to, Community maritime legislation in the light of developments in the international instruments referred to in Article 2(1) of the regulation.

26.013 Article 2(2) enumerates most of the key instruments on EU maritime safety. Article 2(2) defines, for the purposes of the regulation, "Community maritime legislation" as meaning the following acts:

(a) Council Regulation 2978/94 of 21 November 1994 on the implementation of IMO Resolution A.747(18) on the application of tonnage measurement of ballast spaces in segregated ballast oil tankers;[16]

(b) Council Directive 96/98 of 20 December 1996 on marine equipment;[17]

(c) Council Directive 97/70 of 11 December 1997 setting up a harmonised safety regime for fishing vessels of 24 metres in length and over;[18]

(d) Council Directive 98/41 of 18 June 1998 on the registration of persons sailing on board passenger ships operating to or from ports of the Member States of the Community;[19]

(e) Council Directive 1999/32 of 26 April 1999 relating to a reduction in the sulphur content of certain liquid fuels and amending Directive 93/12[20] for the purpose of implementation of its Article 4(d)(2);

(f) Council Directive 1999/35 of 29 April 1999 on a system of mandatory surveys for the safe operation of regular ro-ro ferry and high-speed passenger craft services;[21]

(g) Directive 2000/59 of the European Parliament and of the Council of 27 November 2000 on port reception facilities for ship-generated waste and cargo residues;[22]

(h) Directive 2001/96 of the European Parliament and of the Council of 4 December

---

(12) A specific conformity checking procedure should, however, be set up to enable the Commission, after consulting COSS, to take whatever measures may be necessary to exclude the risk of amendments to the international instruments being incompatible with the aforesaid legislation or Community policy on maritime safety, the prevention of pollution from ships and the protection of shipboard living and working conditions in force or with the objectives pursued by that legislation. Such a procedure should also prevent international amendments from lowering the standard of maritime safety achieved in the Community.

(13) The conformity checking procedure will only be fully effective if the planned measures are adopted as speedily as possible, but at all events before the expiry of the deadline for the entry into force of the international amendment. Consequently, the time available to the Council to act on the proposed measures in accordance with Article 5(6) of Decision 1999/468/EC should be one month."

16 OJ L319/1, 12 December 1994.
17 OJ L46/25, 17 February 1997.
18 OJ L34/1, 9 February 1998.
19 OJ L188/355, 2 July 1998.
20 OJ L121/13, 11 May 1999.
21 OJ L138/1, 1 June 1999.
22 OJ L332/81, 28 December 2000.

2001 establishing harmonised requirements and procedures for the safe loading and unloading of bulk carriers;[23]

(i) Directive 2002/59 of the European Parliament and of the Council of 27 June 2002 establishing a Community vessel traffic monitoring and information system and repealing Council Directive 93/75;

(j) Regulation 782/2003 of the European Parliament and of the Council of 14 April 2003 on the prohibition of organotin compounds on ships;[24]

(k) Directive 2003/25 of the European Parliament and of the Council of 14 April 2003 on specific stability requirements for ro-ro passenger ships;[25]

(l) Regulation 789/2004 of the European Parliament and of the Council of 21 April 2004 on the transfer of cargo and passenger ships between registers within the Community and repealing Council Regulation 613/91;[26]

(m) Directive 2005/35 of the European Parliament and of the Council of 7 September 2005 on ship-source pollution and on the introduction of penalties, including criminal penalties, for pollution offences;[27]

(n) Regulation 336/2006 of the European Parliament and of the Council of 15 February 2006 on the implementation of the International Safety Management Code within the Community and repealing Council Regulation 3051/95;[28]

(o) Directive 2008/106 of the European Parliament and of the Council of 19 November 2008 on the minimum level of training of seafarers;[29]

(p) Directive 2009/15 of the European Parliament and of the Council of 23 April 2009 on common rules and standards for ship inspection and survey organisations and for the relevant activities of maritime administrations;[30]

(q) Directive 2009/16 of the European Parliament and of the Council of 23 April 2009 on port State control;[31]

(r) Directive 2009/18 of the European Parliament and of the Council of 23 April 2009 establishing the fundamental principles governing the investigation of accidents in the maritime transport sector and amending Council Directive 1999/35 and Directive 2002/59 of the European Parliament and of the Council;[32]

(s) Directive 2009/21 of the European Parliament and of the Council of 23 April 2009 on compliance with flag State requirements;[33]

(t) Regulation 391/2009 of the European Parliament and of the Council of 23 April 2009 on common rules and standards for ship inspection and survey organisations;[34]

---

23 OJ L13/9, 16 January 2002.
24 OJ L115/1, 9 May 2003.
25 OJ L123/22, 17 May 2003.
26 OJ L138/19, 30 April 2004.
27 OJ L255/11, 30 September 2005.
28 OJ L64/1, 4 March 2006.
29 OJ L323/33, 3 December 2008.
30 OJ L131/47, 28 May 2009.
31 OJ L131/57, 28 May 2009.
32 OJ L131/114, 28 May 2009.
33 OJ L131/132, 28 May 2009.
34 OJ L131/11, 28 May 2009.

(u) Regulation 392/2009 of the European Parliament and of the Council of 23 April 2009 on the liability of carriers of passengers by sea in the event of accidents;[35]

(v) Directive 2009/45 of the European Parliament and of the Council of 6 May 2009 on safety rules and standards for passenger ships;[36]

(w) Regulation 530/2012 of the European Parliament and of the Council of 13 June 2012 on the accelerated phasing-in of double-hull or equivalent design requirements for single-hull oil tankers;[37]

(x) Commission Regulation 788/2014 of 18 July 2014 laying down detailed rules for the imposition of fines and periodic penalty payments and the withdrawal of recognition of ship inspection and survey organisations pursuant to Articles 6 and 7 of Regulation 391/2009 of the European Parliament and of the Council;[38]

(y) Directive 2014/90 of the European Parliament and of the Council of 23 July 2014 on marine equipment and repealing Council Directive 96/98.[39]

26.014 Article 2 sets out a number of other definitions for the purposes of the regulation. In particular, the term "international instruments" shall mean the conventions, protocols, resolutions, codes, compendia of rules, circulars, standards and provisions adopted by an international conference, the IMO, the ILO or the parties to a memorandum of understanding referred to in the provisions of the Community maritime legislation in force.

26.015 Article 3 ("Establishment of a Committee") establishes the COSS. Article 3(1) provides that the Commission shall be assisted by a Committee on Safe Seas and the Prevention of Pollution from Ships ("COSS"). Article 3(2) provides that where reference is made to Article 3(2) then Articles 5 and 7 of Decision 1999/468 shall apply, having regard to the provisions of Article 8 thereof. The period laid down in Article 5(6) of Decision 1999/468 shall be set at one month. Article 3(3) provides where reference is made to this paragraph, Article 5a(1) to (4) and Article 7 of Decision 1999/468 shall apply, having regard to the provisions of Article 8 thereof.

26.016 Article 4 ("integration of amendments to international instruments in Community law") provides that for the purposes of EU maritime legislation, the applicable international instruments shall be those which have entered into force, including the most recent amendments thereto, with the exception of the amendments excluded from the scope of the EU maritime legislation resulting from the conformity checking procedure established by Article 5.

26.017 The conformity checking procedure is addressed by Article 5:

"1. For the purposes of this Regulation and with a view to reducing the risks of conflict between the Community maritime legislation and international instruments, Member States and the Commission shall cooperate, through coordination meetings and/or any other appropriate means, in order to define, as appropriate, a common position or approach in the competent international fora.

2. A conformity checking procedure is hereby established in order to exclude from the scope of the Community maritime legislation any amendment to an international instrument only if,

---

35 OJ L131/24, 28 May 2009.
36 OJ L163/1, 25 June 2009.
37 OJ L172/3, 30 June 2012.
38 OJ L214/12, 19 July 2014.
39 OJ L257/146, 28 August 2014.

on the basis of an evaluation by the Commission, there is a manifest risk that the international amendment, within the scope of the Regulations or the Directives referred to in Article 2(2), will lower the standard of maritime safety, of prevention of pollution from ships or of protection of shipboard living and working conditions established by Community maritime legislation, or be incompatible with the latter.

The conformity checking procedure may be used solely to make amendments to the Community maritime legislation in the fields expressly covered by the regulatory procedure and strictly within the framework of exercise of implementing powers conferred on the Commission.

3. In the circumstances referred to in paragraph 2, the conformity checking procedure shall be initiated by the Commission, which, where appropriate, may act at the request of a Member State.

The Commission shall submit to the COSS, without delay, after the adoption of an amendment to an international instrument a proposal for measures with the aim of excluding the amendment in question from the Community text concerned.

The conformity checking procedure, including, if applicable, the procedures set up in Article 5(6) of Decision 1999/468/EC, shall be completed at least one month before the expiration of the period established internationally for the tacit acceptance of the amendment concerned or the envisaged date for the entry into force of said amendment.

4. In the event of a risk as referred to in the first subparagraph of paragraph 2, Member States shall refrain, during the period of the conformity checking procedure, from any initiative intended to integrate the amendment in national legislation or to apply the amendment to the international instrument concerned."

26.018 Article 6 ("information") provides that all relevant amendments to international instruments that are integrated in Community maritime legislation, in accordance with Articles 4 and 5, shall be published, for information purposes, in the *Official Journal of the European Communities*.

26.019 The powers of COSS are set out in Article 7:

"COSS shall exercise the powers conferred on it by virtue of the Community legislation in force. Article 2(2) may be amended in accordance with the regulatory procedure with scrutiny referred to in Article 3(3) in order to include a reference to the Community acts conferring implementing power on COSS that have entered into force following the adoption of this Regulation. Those measures, designed to amend non-essential elements of this Regulation, shall be adopted in accordance with the procedure referred to in Article 3(3)."

26.020 The regulation also amends Regulations 613/91, 2978/94 and 3051/95.

E. COUNCIL DECISION (EU) 2016/2077 OF 17 OCTOBER 2016 ON THE POSITION TO BE ADOPTED ON BEHALF OF THE EUROPEAN UNION AT THE INTERNATIONAL MARITIME ORGANIZATION (IMO) DURING THE 70TH SESSION OF THE MARINE ENVIRONMENT PROTECTION COMMITTEE AND THE 97TH SESSION OF THE MARITIME SAFETY COMMITTEE, ON THE ADOPTION OF AMENDMENTS TO MARPOL ANNEX VI, SOLAS REGULATIONS II-1, SOLAS REGULATIONS III/1.4, III/30 AND III/37, SOLAS REGULATIONS II-2/1 AND II-2/10, SOLAS REGULATION II-1/3–12, THE STCW CONVENTION AND CODE, THE FIRE SAFETY SYSTEMS CODE AND THE 2011 ENHANCED SURVEY PROGRAMME CODE

26.021 On 17 October 2016, the Council adopted Decision 2016/2077 on the position to be adopted on behalf of the European Union at the International Maritime Organization

(IMO) during the 70th session of the Marine Environment Protection Committee and the 97th session of the Maritime Safety Committee, on the adoption of amendments to MARPOL Annex VI, SOLAS Regulations II-1, SOLAS Regulations III/1.4, III/30 and III/37, SOLAS Regulations II-2/1 and II-2/10, SOLAS Regulation II-1/3–12, the STCW Convention and Code, the Fire Safety Systems Code and the 2011 Enhanced Survey Programme Code.[40]

26.022 The background is that the EU

"is neither a member of the IMO nor a contracting party to the relevant conventions and codes. It is therefore necessary for the Council to authorise the Member States to express the position of the Union and express their consent to be bound by those amendments, to the extent that they fall under the exclusive competence of the Union."[41]

The legal basis is the TFEU generally and, in particular, Article 100(2), in conjunction with Article 218(9) of the TFEU. The background is clear from the recitals.[42]

---

40 OJ L320/36, 26 November 2016.

41 Dec. 2016/2077, Recital 14.

42 "(2) The Marine Environment Protection Committee ('MEPC') of the International Maritime Organization ('IMO'), meeting at its 69th session, agreed on the establishment of a mandatory data collection system for fuel consumption and the necessary amendments to Chapter 4 of Annex VI to the International Convention for the Prevention of Pollution from Ships ('MARPOL Annex VI'). Those amendments are expected to be adopted during the 70th session of the MEPC to be held in October 2016.

(3) The Maritime Safety Committee (MSC) of the IMO, meeting at its 95th and 96th sessions, approved amendments to Regulation II-1, Regulations III/1.4, III/30 and III/37, Regulations II-2/1 and II-2/10 and Regulation II-1/3-12 of the International Convention for the Safety of Life at Sea (SOLAS), to the International Convention and Code on Standards of Training, Certification and Watchkeeping for Seafarers ('STCW Convention and Code'), to the International Code for Fire Safety Systems ('FSS Code') and to the 2011 Enhanced Survey Programme Code (the '2011 ESP Code'). Those amendments are expected to be adopted during the 97th session of the MSC to be held in November 2016.

(4) The amendments to Chapter 4 of MARPOL Annex VI will establish a mandatory global data collection system for the data to be collected and reported annually by certain ships, the verification processes related to reported data, the establishment of statements of compliance, situations concerning ownership transfer, submission of the data to the IMO, anonymisation of and access to the data, as well as procedures for confirming compliance of ships flying the flag of non-parties to MARPOL Annex VI. Regulation ... 2015/757 of the European Parliament and of the Council [Ed., Reg. 2015/757 of the European Parliament and of the Council of 29 April 2015 on the monitoring, reporting and verification of carbon dioxide emissions from maritime transport, and amending Dir. 2009/16 (OJ L123/55, 19 May 2015)] sets out an EU system to monitor, report and verify (MRV) CO2 emissions and energy efficiency from shipping. It applies to all ships over 5 000 gross tons arriving at, within or departing from ports under the jurisdiction of a Member State from 1 January 2018 onwards, irrespective of where the ships are registered.

(5) Article 22 of Regulation (EU) 2015/757 includes a review clause in the event of an international agreement in this field. The adoption of the amendments to Chapter 4 of MARPOL Annex VI will start such a review process, which may lead to a proposal to amend Regulation (EU) 2015/757 in order to ensure alignment, to the extent appropriate, with the global data collection system agreed in the IMO.

(6) The amendments to SOLAS Regulations II-1/1, II-1/2, II-1/3, II-1/4, II-1/5, II-1/6, II-1/7, II-1/8-1, II-1/9, II-1/10, II-1/12, II-1/13, II-1/15–17, II-1/19, II-1/21–22 and II-1/35 will introduce editorial and consequential changes, as well as changes that concern subdivision and damage stability requirements to improve passenger ship survivability in case of damage. Directive 2009/45/EC of the European Parliament and of the Council [Ed., Dir. 2009/45of the European Parliament and of the Council of 6 May 2009 on safety rules and standards for passenger ships (OJ L163/1, 25 June 2009)] applies to passenger ships and high-speed passenger craft which are engaged in domestic voyages. Article 6(2)(a)(i) of that Directive provides that new passenger ships of Class A are to comply entirely with the requirements of the 1974 SOLAS Convention, as amended.

(7) The amendments to SOLAS Regulation II-1/1.2, the new SOLAS Regulation II-1/19-1, and the amendments to SOLAS Regulations III/1.4, III/30 and III/37 concerning damage control drills form part of a comprehensive approach to enhance the survivability after flooding with the intention of improving safety on new and existing passenger ships. Directive 2008/106/EC of the European Parliament and of the Council, [Ed., Dir. 2008/106 of the European Parliament and of the Council of 19 November 2008 on the minimum level of

26.023 Article 1 provides that the position to be adopted on behalf of the Union at the seventieth session of the IMO Marine Environment Protection Committee shall be to agree to the adoption of the amendments to Chapter 4 of MARPOL Annex VI, as laid down in Annex 7 to IMO document MEPC 69/21/Add.1.

26.024 Article 2 gives some detail on the position to be adopted:

---

training of seafarers (OJ L323/33, 3 December 2008)] and in particular Regulation V/2 of Chapter V of Annex I, includes mandatory minimum requirements for the training and qualifications of masters, officers, ratings and other personnel on passenger ships. The STCW Convention, which has been incorporated into Union law by means of Directive 2008/106/EC, includes training requirements on ship stability in the relevant tables of competences of the STCW Code.

(8) The amendments to SOLAS Regulations II-2/1 and II-2/10 will provide that foam-type extinguishers of at least 135 l capacity are no longer to be required in boiler rooms in the case of domestic boilers of less than 175 kW, or boilers protected by fixed water-based local application fire-extinguishing systems. Article 6(2)(a)(i) of Directive 2009/45/EC provides that new passenger ships of Class A are to comply entirely with the requirements of the 1974 SOLAS Convention, as amended. In addition, SOLAS Regulations II-2/1 and II-2/10 are applicable to new Class B, C and D and existing Class B passenger ships in accordance with Annex I, Chapter II-2 Part A, point 6.7 ('Fire-extinguishing arrangements in machinery spaces') of Directive 2009/45/EC, in which it is established that machinery spaces and boiler rooms should be equipped with portable systems.

(9) The amendments to SOLAS Regulation II-1/3-12 will address a gap in the current Regulation concerning the application of the Code on Noise Levels on Board Ships for ships for which the building contract is placed before 1 July 2014 and the keels of which are laid or which are at a similar stage of construction on or after 1 January 2015 and the delivery of which is not before 1 July 2018. Article 3 of Directive 2003/10/EC of the European Parliament and of the Council [Ed., Dir. 2003/10 of the European Parliament and of the Council of 6 February 2003 on the minimum health and safety requirements regarding the exposure of workers to the risks arising from physical agents (noise) (OJ L42/38, 15 February 2003)] lays down minimum requirements for the protection of workers and sets exposure limit values and exposure action values. Furthermore, as relevant secondary legislation, Article 6(2)(a)(i) of Directive 2009/45/EC makes the application of the 1974 SOLAS Convention, as amended, applicable to new Class A ships, and Annex I PART C, Regulation 15 of that Directive lays down measures for noise reduction in machinery spaces for new Class B, C and D ships.

(10) The amendments to the STCW Convention and Code relating to passenger-ship specific training and to Parts A and B of the STCW Code will address new challenges posed by the increased size of modern cruise ships and the large number of passengers on board and comprise four distinct levels of training and familiarization: passenger ship emergency familiarization, passenger ship crowd management training, passenger ship crisis management and human behaviour training, and ro-ro passenger ship training. Directive 2008/106/EC, in particular Regulation V/2 of Chapter V of Annex I, includes mandatory minimum requirements for the training and qualifications of masters, officers, ratings and other personnel on passenger ships.

(11) The amendments to Chapter 13 of the FSS Code will clarify that the calculations of the dimension of means of escape, which are made on the basis of the total number of persons expected to escape by the stairway and through doorways, corridors and landings, are to be made separately for two different cases of occupancy of the specified spaces. Article 6(2)(a)(i) of Directive 2009/45/EC establishes that new passenger ships of Class A are to comply entirely with the requirements of the 1974 SOLAS Convention, as amended. Furthermore, Chapter II-2, Part A, of Annex I of Directive 2009/45/EC applies the FSS Code adopted by Resolution MSC.98(73), to Class B, C and D ships constructed on or after 1 January 2003.

(12) To the extent that the amendments to SOLAS Regulations II-1/1, II-1/2, II-1/3, II-1/4, II-1/5, II-1/6, II-1/7, II-1/8-1, II-1/9, II-1/10, II-1/12, II-1/13, II-1/15–17, II-1/19, II-1/21–22 and II-1/35, SOLAS Regulations II-2/1 and II-2/10 and Chapter 13 of the FSS Code may affect the provisions of Directive 2009/45/EC regarding passenger ships and high-speed passenger craft which are engaged on domestic voyages, those amendments fall under the exclusive competence of the Union.

(13) The amendments to the 2011 ESP Code will provide alignment with the updated Unified Requirements Z10 series of the International Association of Classification Societies Uniform Requirements (IACS UR Z10 series), which concern survey and certification requirements. Articles 5 and 6 of Regulation (EU) No 530/2012 of the European Parliament and of the Council [Ed., Reg. 530/2012 of the European Parliament and of the Council of 13 June 2012 on the accelerated phasing-in of double-hull or equivalent design requirements for single-hull oil tankers (OJ L172/3, 30 June 2012)] make mandatory the application of the IMO's Condition Assessment Scheme (CAS) to single hull oil tankers above 15 years of age. The Enhanced Programme of Inspections during surveys of Bulk Carriers and Oil tankers or Enhanced Survey Programme (ESP) specifies how to undertake this intensified assessment. As CAS uses ESP as the tool to achieve its aim, any changes to the ESP inspections will automatically be applicable through Regulation (EU) No 530/2012."

"1. The position to be adopted on behalf of the Union at the 97th session of the IMO Maritime Safety Committee shall be to agree to the adoption of the following amendments to:

(a) SOLAS Regulations II-1/1, II-1/2, II-1/3, II-1/4, II-1/5, II-1/6, II-1/7, II-1/8–1, II-1/9, II-1/10, II-1/12, II-1/13, II-1/15–17, II-1/19, II-1/21–22 and II-1/35 as laid down in Annex 1 to IMO Circular Letter No 3644 of 20 May 2016;

(b) SOLAS Regulation II-1/1.2, a new regulation II-1/19–1, and amendments to SOLAS Regulations III/1.4, III/30 and III/37 as laid down in Annex 1 to IMO Circular Letter No 3644 of 20 May 2016;

(c) SOLAS Regulations II-2/1 and II-2/10 as laid down in Annex 1 to IMO Circular Letter No 3644 of 20 May 2016;

(d) SOLAS Regulation II-1/3–12 as laid down in Annex 1 to IMO Circular Letter No 3644 of 20 May 2016;

(e) The STCW Convention and Code relating to passenger-ship specific training and to parts A and B of the STCW Code as laid down in Annexes 8, 9 and 10 to IMO Document MSC 96/25/Add.1;

(f) Chapter 13 of the FSS Code as laid down in Annex 2 to IMO Circular Letter No 3644 of 20 May 2016;

(g) The 2011 ESP Code as laid down in Annex 4 to IMO Circular Letter No 3644 of 20 May 2016.

2. If the amendments to SOLAS Regulation II-1/6 referred to in point (a) of paragraph 1 are reviewed at the 97th session of the IMO Maritime Safety Committee, the position to be adopted on behalf of the Union shall be to agree to changes to those amendments that improve the current safety levels."

26.025 Article 3 provides quite simply that the position to be adopted on behalf of the EU as set out in Articles 1 and 2 shall be expressed by the Member States, which are members of the IMO, acting jointly in the interest of the Union and that minor changes to the positions referred to in Articles 1 and 2 may be agreed upon without further decision of the Council.

26.026 Article 4 provides that Member States are hereby authorised to give their consent to be bound, in the interest of the EU, by the amendments referred to in Articles 1 and 2, to the extent that they fall under the exclusive competence of the EU.

F. COUNCIL RECOMMENDATION OF 25 JULY 1983 ON THE RATIFICATION OF OR ACCESSION TO THE 1979 INTERNATIONAL CONVENTION ON MARITIME SEARCH AND RESCUE (SAR)

26.027 On 25 July 1983, the Council adopted Recommendation 83/419 on the ratification of or accession to the 1979 International Convention on Maritime Search and Rescue ("SAR").[43] It is a straightforward non-legally binding measure:

"Having regard to the Treaty establishing the European Economic Community,

Whereas on 27 April 1979 an International Convention on Maritime Search and Rescue was approved in Hamburg under the auspices of the Intergovernmental Maritime Consultative Organization (IMCO);

Whereas, in view of the great importance of the said Convention with regard to the search for and rescue of persons in distress at sea, the Convention should enter into force as soon as possible;

---

43 OJ L237/34, 26 August 1983.

Whereas ratification or accession by all the Member States will not only help to bring the Convention into force in accordance with the principles of international law but will also ensure a unified search and rescue service in the coastal waters of the Community and thereby increase the effectiveness of the Convention,

HEREBY RECOMMENDS:
that inasmuch as they have not already done so, the Member States ratify or accede to the 1979 International Convention on Maritime Search and Rescue as soon as they can."

G. COMMISSION REGULATION (EU) NO 802/2010 OF 13 SEPTEMBER 2010 IMPLEMENTING ARTICLE 10(3) AND ARTICLE 27 OF DIRECTIVE 2009/16 OF THE EUROPEAN PARLIAMENT AND OF THE COUNCIL AS REGARDS COMPANY PERFORMANCE

26.028 On 13 September 2010, the Commission Regulation 802/2010 implementing Article 10(3) and Article 27 of Directive 2009/16 of the European Parliament and of the Council as regards company performance.[44] The regulation was amended by Commission Implementing Regulation (EU) No 1205/2012 of 14 December 2012.[45]

26.029 The background included Directive 2009/16 of the European Parliament and of the Council of 23 April 2009 on port State control,[46] and in particular Article 10(3) and Article 27 thereof. The background is clear from the recitals to the directive which provide:

"(1)   Company performance is one of the generic parameters determining the risk profile of a ship.

(2)   With a view to determining the performance of companies within the meaning of Directive 2009/16, … it is necessary that, when inspecting a ship, inspectors record the IMO number assigned to a company.

(3)   In order to assess company performance, the deficiency and detention rates of all ships in a company's fleet, which have been subject to an inspection within the Union and within the region covered by the Paris Memorandum of Understanding on port State control (Paris MoU), should be taken into account.

(4)   It is necessary to build upon the expertise acquired through the application of the Paris MoU with regard to the methodology used for assessing company performance.

(5)   The Commission should rely on the European Maritime Safety Agency established by Regulation (EC) No 1406/2002 of the European Parliament and of the Council[47] for the publication on a public website of the list of companies with a low or very low performance.

(6)   The measures provided for in this Regulation are in accordance with the opinion of the Committee on Safe Seas and the Prevention of Pollution from Ships."

26.030 Article 1 provides for the identification of companies:

"Member States shall ensure that the company as defined in Article 2(18) of Directive 2009/16/EC is identified through the IMO number where the ship has to comply with the International Safety Management Code (ISM Code) as referred to in Chapter IX of the International Convention for the Safety of Life at Sea (SOLAS Convention)."

---

44   OJ L241/4, 14 September 2010.
45   OJ L347/10, 15 December 2012.
46   OJ L131/57, 28 May 2009.
47   Ed., OJ L208/1, 5 August 2002.

26.031 Article 2 sets out the criteria for assessing the company performance:

"1. With a view to assessing the company performance referred to in point (e) of Part I.1 of Annex I to Directive 2009/16/EC, the criteria set out in the Annex to this Regulation shall be used.

2. The level of company performance shall be updated daily and calculated on the basis of the 36 months preceding the assessment. For that purpose the calculation shall be made on the basis of data collected from 17 June 2009. Where less than 36 months have elapsed since 17 June 2009, the calculation shall be made on the basis of the available data.

3. The companies shall be ranked as having a very low, low, medium or high performance as listed in point 3 of the Annex."

26.032 Article 3 is entitled "publication of lists of companies with a low and very low performance". It provides in Article 3(1) that the Commission

"shall be assisted by the European Maritime Safety Agency (EMSA) with a view to the regular publication on a public website of information on companies with a low and very low performance in accordance with Article 27 of Directive 2009/16/EC."

Under Article 3(2), EMSA must publish, from 1 January 2014, and update on a daily basis on its public website the following information: (a) the list of companies whose performance has been very low for a continuous period of 36 months; (b) the list of companies whose performance has been low or very low for a continuous period of 36 months; and (c) the list of companies whose performance has been low for a continuous period of 36 months.

26.033 The regulation entered into force, under Article 4, on the twentieth day following its publication in the *Official Journal of the European Union*. It applied from 1 January 2011.

26.034 The annex (entitled "Company Performance Criteria") (referred to in Article 10(3) of Directive 2009/16) provides:

"1. Detention index of a company
The detention index is the ratio of the number of detentions of all ships in a company's fleet to the number of inspections of all the ships in the company's fleet within the previous 36 months, compared with the average detention ratio for all ships inspected in the region covered by the Paris MoU over the previous 36 months.

The detention index shall be considered average if it is within a margin of 2 percentage points above or below the average detention ratio for all ships inspected in the region covered by the Paris MoU during the previous 36 months.

The detention index shall be considered above average if it is more than 2 percentage points above the average detention ratio for all ships inspected in the region covered by the Paris MoU during the previous 36 months.

The detention index shall be considered below average if it is more than 2 percentage points below the average detention ratio for all ships inspected in the region covered by the Paris MoU during the previous 36 months.

The detention index of a company shall be considered above average irrespective of all other inspection results if a refusal of access order in accordance with Directive 2009/16/EC is issued within the previous 36 months to any ship in the fleet of that company.

2. Deficiency index of a company
The deficiency index is the ratio of the total points of all deficiencies of all ships in a company's fleet to the number of inspections of all ships in the company's fleet during the previous 36 months, compared with the average deficiency ratio for all ships inspected in the region covered by the Paris MoU over the previous 36 months.

For the purposes of the first subparagraph ISM Code related deficiencies shall be weighted at 5 points while any other deficiencies shall be weighted at 1 point. The average deficiency ratio within the region covered by the Paris MoU shall be weighted taking into account the average occurrence of ISM Code related deficiencies and any other deficiencies per inspection.

The deficiency index shall be considered average if it is within a margin of 2 percentage points above or below the weighted average of deficiencies in the region covered by the Paris MoU during the previous 36 months.

The deficiency index shall be considered above average if it is more than 2 percentage points above the weighted average of deficiencies in the region covered by the Paris MoU during the previous 36 months.

The deficiency index shall be considered below average if it is more than 2 percentage points below the weighted average of deficiencies in the region covered by the Paris MoU during the previous 36 months.

3.   Company performance matrix
     Company performance shall be ranked as follows:

'Detention index	Deficiency index	Company performance
above average	above average	very low
above average	average	low
above average	below average	
average	above average	
below average	above average	
average	average	medium
average	below average	
below average	average	
below average	below average	High'

… However, if a company has no previous records of inspections carried on its fleet or is not required to have an IMO number, it shall be considered as having medium performance."

H. COMMISSION REGULATION (EU) NO 801/2010 OF 13 SEPTEMBER 2010 IMPLEMENTING ARTICLE 10(3) OF DIRECTIVE 2009/16 OF THE EUROPEAN PARLIAMENT AND OF THE COUNCIL AS REGARDS THE FLAG STATE CRITERIA

26.035 On 13 September 2010, the Commission adopted Regulation 801/2010 of 13 September 2010 implementing Article 10(3) of Directive 2009/16 of the European Parliament and of the Council as regards the flag State criteria.[48] The legal background was the TFEU generally and, in particular, Directive 2009/16 of the European Parliament and of the Council of 23 April 2009 on port State control,[49] and in particular Article 10(3) of the directive. The background is clear from the four recital which provide: (1) flag State performance is one of the generic parameters determining the risk profile of ships; (2) in order to assess the risk profile of a ship, the detention rate within the Union and within the region covered by the Paris Memorandum of Understanding on port State control (the "Paris MoU") should be taken into account; (3) it is necessary to build upon the expertise acquired through the application of the Paris MoU with regard to the methodology to be

---

48 OJ L24/1, 14 September 2010.
49 OJ L131, 28 May 2009, p. 57.

used for assessing flag State performance; and (4) the measures provided for in this regulation are in accordance with the opinion of the COSS.

26.036 The regulation itself is quite short. Article 1 deals with the categorisation of flag States based on the detention rates:

"1. With a view to establishing flag State performance within the meaning of Directive 2009/16/EC, flag States shall be classified into black, grey or white lists, adopted in accordance with the Paris MoU on the basis of the total inspections and detentions over a three year period. Additionally, flag States listed in the black list shall be divided into very high, high, medium to high or medium risk depending on their detention rate. The classification shall be updated yearly.

2. Classification of a flag State into the black, grey or white list requires a minimum of thirty port state control inspections.

3. The methodology and formulas to be used to categorize the flag States shall comply with the flag State criteria as set out in the Annex."

26.037 Article 2 deals with "flag State performance based on the IMO audit":

"The compliance referred to in point (c) (iii) of Part I.1 of Annex I to Directive 2009/16/EC required for ships to be considered as posing a lower risk, shall be regarded as demonstrated when the Commission receives a written confirmation from the flag State that a final audit report has been completed and where relevant, a corrective action plan submitted. Audits carried out before 17 June 2009 shall be taken into account equally."

26.038 Article 3 deals with entry into force and application. The regulation entered into force on the twentieth day following its publication in the *Official Journal of the European Union*. It applied from 1 January 2011.

26.039 The annex deals with flag State criteria (as referred to in Article 10(3)(a) of Directive 2009/16).[50]

I. COUNCIL DECISION 2014/826 OF 10 NOVEMBER 2014 ON THE POSITION TO BE ADOPTED ON BEHALF OF THE EUROPEAN UNION WITHIN THE INTERNATIONAL MARITIME ORGANIZATION DURING THE 94TH SESSION OF THE MARITIME SAFETY COMMITTEE ON THE ADOPTION OF AMENDMENTS TO THE 2011 ENHANCED SURVEY PROGRAMME CODE

26.040 On 10 November 2014, the Council Decision 2014/826 on the position to be adopted on behalf of the European Union within the International Maritime Organization during the 94th session of the Maritime Safety Committee on the adoption of amendments to the 2011 Enhanced Survey Programme Code.[51] The legal basis was the TFEU generally and, in particular, Articles 100(2) and 218(9) of the TFEU. The background to the measure is that the EU

"is neither a member of the IMO nor a contracting party to the conventions and codes concerned. It is therefore necessary for the Council to authorise the Member States to express the position of the Union and express their consent to be bound by the amendments to the 2011 ESP Code."[52]

---

50 As the annex is quite detailed, see the annex for the detail.
51 OJ L335/17, 22 November 2014.
52 Dec. 2014/826, recital 5. The background generally is apparent from the recitals which state, in part:
"(1) Action by the European Union in the sector of maritime transport should aim to improve maritime safety.

26.041 Article 1 provides:

"1. The position of the Union at the 94th session of the IMO Maritime Safety Committee shall be to agree to the adoption of the amendments to the 2011 ESP Code, as laid down in Annex 22, Annex B, part B, of the IMO document MSC 93/22/Add.3, for the purposes referred to in Articles 5 and 6 of Regulation (EU) No 530/2012.

2. The position of the Union as set out in paragraph 1 shall be expressed by the Member States, which are members of IMO, acting jointly in the interest of the Union.

3. Formal and minor changes to this position may be agreed without requiring that position to be amended."

26.042 Article 2 states that Member States are hereby authorised to give their consent to be bound, in the interest of the EU, by the amendments referred to in Article 1(1).

J. COUNCIL DECISION 2014/280 OF 8 MAY 2014 ON THE POSITION TO BE ADOPTED ON BEHALF OF THE EUROPEAN UNION AT THE INTERNATIONAL MARITIME ORGANIZATION DURING THE 93RD SESSION OF THE MARITIME SAFETY COMMITTEE ON THE ADOPTION OF AMENDMENTS TO SOLAS REGULATIONS II-1/29, II-2/3, 2/9.7, 2/13.4, 2/18, III/20, THE LIFE SAVING APPLIANCES CODE AND THE 2011 ENHANCED SURVEY PROGRAMME CODE

26.043 On 8 May 2014, the Council adopted Decision 2014/280 on the position to be adopted on behalf of the European Union at the International Maritime Organization during the 93rd session of the Maritime Safety Committee on the adoption of amendments to SOLAS Regulations II-1/29, II-2/3, 2/9.7, 2/13.4, 2/18, III/20, the Life Saving Appliances Code and the 2011 Enhanced Survey Programme Code.[53] The legal basis was the TFEU generally and, in particular, Articles 100(2) and 218(9) of the TFEU.

26.044 The background to this decision, which is addressed to Member States,[54] is that the EU

"is neither a member of the IMO nor a contracting party to the conventions and codes concerned [so it] is therefore necessary for the Council to authorise the Member States to express the position of the Union and express their consent to be bound by these amendments, to the extent that they fall under the exclusive competence of the Union."[55]

---

(2) The IMO Maritime Safety Committee (MSC) meeting at its 93rd session approved amendments to the 2011 Enhanced Survey Programme (ESP) Code. Those amendments are expected to be adopted at the 94th session of the MSC, to be held in November 2014.

(3) The amendments to the 2011 ESP Code bring it in line with the practices of classification societies and also allow, under certain conditions, hydrostatic testing of cargo tanks by the ship's crew, under the direction of the master, in lieu of carrying out such testing in the presence of a surveyor.

(4) Articles 5 and 6 of Regulation (EU) No 530/2012 of the European Parliament and of the Council [Reg. (EU) No 530/2012 of the European Parliament and of the Council of 13 June 2012 on the accelerated phasing-in of double-hull or equivalent design requirements for single-hull oil tankers (OJ L172/3, 30 June 2012)] provide for the mandatory application of the IMO's Condition Assessment Scheme (CAS). The CAS is complemented by the 2011 ESP Code, adopted by the IMO Assembly by Resolution A.1049(27). Annex B, part B, of the 2011 ESP Code concerns inspections during surveys of oil tankers other than double-hull oil tankers and specifies how to undertake the intensified assessment. As a consequence, any changes to the 2011 ESP Code, as far as single-hull oil tankers above 15 years of age are concerned, will automatically be applicable through Regulation (EU) No 530/2012."

53 OJ L145/40, 16 May 2014.
54 Dec. 2014/280, Art.3.
55 Dec. 2014/280, Recital 11.

26.045 The essence[56] of the decision is clear from Articles 1 and 2. Article 1 states:

---

56 The background to the decision is clear from the recitals which state in part:

"(1) … The main reference framework for the safety standards should be the 1974 International Convention for the Safety of Life at Sea (the 1974 SOLAS Convention), as amended, which encompasses internationally agreed standards for passenger ships and high-speed passenger craft engaged on international voyages.

(2) The IMO Maritime Safety Committee (MSC) meeting at its 92nd session approved, among others, amendments to SOLAS Regulations II-1/29, II-2/3, 2/9.7, 2/13.4, 2/18, III/20, the Life Saving Appliances Code and the 2011 Enhanced Survey Programme Code. Those amendments are expected to be adopted in the 93rd session of the MSC, to be held in May 2014.

(3) The amendments to the SOLAS regulations II-2/3 and II-2/9.7 concerning fire resistance of ventilation ducts for new ships will introduce new requirements for ventilation systems in ships, including for passenger ships carrying more than 36 passengers. The provisions of Regulation 12, Part A and of Regulation 9, Part B of Chapter II-2 of Annex 1 to Directive 2009/45/EC of the European Parliament and of the Council [Dir. 2009/45 of the European Parliament and of the Council of 6 May 2009 on safety rules and standards for passenger ships (OJ L163/1, 25 June 2009)] on ventilation duct penetration provisions and on ventilation systems for ships carrying more than 36 passengers cover these issues and are derived from these SOLAS provisions which are now expected to be amended.

(4) The amendments to SOLAS Regulation II-2/13.4 will introduce additional means of escape from machinery spaces for new passenger and cargo ships. The provisions of Regulation 6, Part B, Chapter II-2 of Annex 1 to Directive 2009/45/EC (Means of escape) covers these issues and are derived from the SOLAS provisions which are now expected to be amended.

(5) The amendments to SOLAS Regulation II-2/18 concerning helicopter landing areas on ro-ro passenger ships for new ships will include a requirement for fire-fighting foam application systems to be in accordance with IMO Circular MSC.1/Circ.1431 of 31 May 2012 on Guidelines for the approval of helicopter facility foam fire-fighting appliances. Regulation 18, Part B, Chapter II-2 of Annex 1 to Directive 2009/45/EC provides that ships equipped with helidecks shall comply with the requirements of the SOLAS regulation as revised per 1 January 2003 which are now expected to be amended.

(6) The amendments to SOLAS Chapter III, Regulation 20 and associated requirements for periodic servicing and maintenance of lifeboats and rescue boats for all ships aim to make these detailed requirements mandatory. Chapter III of Annex 1 to Directive 2009/45/EC provides that maintenance and inspections of life-saving appliances shall be carried out in accordance with the same requirements of SOLAS Regulation III/20, which are now expected to be amended.

(7) The amendments to the Life-Saving Appliances (LSA) Code concerning lifejackets Reference Test Devices (RTDs) will introduce new requirements for RTDs. Regulation 2.2, Chapter III of Directive 2009/45/EC indicates that all such personal life-saving appliances comply with the LSA Code. In addition, Article 5(1) of Council Directive 96/98/EC [Council Dir. 96/98 of 20 December 1996 on marine equipment (OJ L46/25, 17 February 1997)] stipulates that equipment listed in its Annex A.1 placed on board a Community ship meet the applicable requirements of the international instruments referred to in that Annex. In the table in Annex A.1, entry A.1.1.4, the applicable standard for life jackets is IMO Resolution MSC 48(66) – the LSA Code, which is now expected to be amended.

(8) The amendments to SOLAS regulation II-1/29 concerning requirements for steering gear trials will introduce further requirements to demonstrate compliance during sea trials. Regulations 6 and 7, Part C, Chapter II-1 of Annex 1 to Directive 2009/45/EC are derived from and replicate the same provisions of SOLAS in Chapter II-1, Part C Regulation 29 on requirements for the main and auxiliary steering gear which are now expected to be amended.

(9) The above amendments to SOLAS Regulations II-1/29, II-2/3, 2/9.7, 2/13.4, 2/18, III/20 and the Life Saving Appliances Code, will apply to passenger ships and high-speed passenger craft which are engaged on domestic voyages, pursuant to Articles 1 and 3 of Directive 2009/45/EC. Therefore, to the extent that they affect passenger ships and high-speed passenger craft which are engaged on domestic voyages, these amendments fall under the exclusive competence of the Union.

(10) The amendments to the 2011 Enhanced Survey Programme (ESP) Code bring it into line with the practices of classification societies. Articles 5 and 6 of Regulation (EU) No 530/2012 of the European Parliament and of the Council [Reg. (EU) No 530/2012 of the European Parliament and of the Council of 13 June 2012 on the accelerated phasing-in of double-hull or equivalent design requirements for single-hull oil tankers (OJ L172/3, 30 June 2012)] make mandatory the application of the IMO's Condition Assessment Scheme (CAS) to single hull oil tankers above 15 years of age. The Enhanced Programme of Inspections during surveys of Bulk Carriers and Oil tankers or Enhanced Survey Programme (ESP) specifies how to undertake this intensified assessment. As CAS uses ESP as the tool to achieve its aim, any changes to the ESP inspections will automatically be applicable through Regulation (EU) No 530/2012."

"1. The position of the Union at the 93rd session of the IMO Maritime Safety Committee shall be to agree to the adoption of the amendments to SOLAS Regulations II-2/3, 2/9.7, 2/13.4 and 2/18 as laid down in Annex 13 to the IMO document MSC 92/26.Add.1, and to the adoption of the amendments to SOLAS Regulations II-1/29 and III/20, the Life Saving Appliances Code and the 2011 Enhanced Survey Programme Code as laid down in Annexes 31, 32, 33, 34, 35 and 36 respectively to the IMO document MSC 92/26/Add.2.

2. The position of the Union as set out in paragraph 1 shall be expressed by the Member States, which are members of IMO, acting jointly in the interest of the Union.

3. Formal and minor changes to this position may be agreed without requiring that position to be amended."

26.046 Article 2 states that "Member States are hereby authorised to give their consent to be bound, in the interest of the Union, by the amendments referred to in Article 1(1) to the extent that they fall under the exclusive competence of the Union".

K. CONCLUSIONS

26.047 The purpose of this chapter was to introduce the topic. Other more specific issues in EU maritime safety law are examined in other chapters throughout this book.

CHAPTER 27

Maritime safety: the European Maritime Safety Agency

A. INTRODUCTION

27.001 The European Maritime Safety Agency ("EMSA") now plays a central role in the European Union's ("EU") maritime safety agenda. As a specialised and dedicated agency, it can take the EU's work in regard to maritime safety to a new higher level than the Commission which is more concerned with policy issues and has a wider agenda.[1] This chapter focuses on the EMSA while subsequent chapters consider particular aspects of EU maritime safety law and particular aspects of the work of EMSA.

27.002 Article 1(1) of Regulation 1406/2002 established EMSA "for the purpose of ensuring a high, uniform and effective level of maritime safety, maritime security, prevention of, and response to, pollution caused by ships as well as response to marine pollution caused by oil and gas installations".[2]

B. BACKGROUND TO THE ESTABLISHMENT OF EMSA

27.003 The stimuli for the establishment of EMSA included two incidents, namely, the *Erika* in 1999 and the *Prestige* in 2002 which resulted in serious oil spills in EU waters. These two incidents followed many others over time.

27.004 The first recital to the regulation[3] which established the EMSA recalled that a large number of legislative measures have been adopted in the EU in order to enhance safety and prevent pollution in maritime transport but in order to be effective such legislation must be applied in a proper and uniform manner throughout the EU. The recital also stated that such a move "will ensure a level playing field, reduce the distortion of competition resulting from the economic advantages enjoyed by non-complying ships and will reward the serious maritime players".

27.005 The establishment of EMSA was the creation of a "specialised expert body"[4] to execute certain tasks which had previously been executed at EU or Member State level. EMSA was needed because

---

1 This is not a negative reflection on the excellent staff in the Commission dealing with the issue but a reflection of the fact that a dedicated team can take the issue further and deeper.

2 OJ L208/1, 5 August 2002. A consolidated version is available at: https://eur-lex.europa.eu/legal-content/EN/TXT/HTML/?uri=CELEX:02002R1406-20161006&qid=1525711266034&from=EN.

3 Reg. 1406/2002, OJ L208/1, 5 August 2002.

4 Ibid., recital 2. EMSA is a "body" but not an "institution" so it is not a law-making entity.

"there is a need for technical and scientific support and a high level of stable expertise to properly apply the [EU] legislation in the fields of maritime safety and ship pollution prevention, to monitor its implementation and to evaluate the effectiveness of the measures in place."[5]

C. LEGAL REGIME RELATING TO EMSA

27.006 EMSA was established by Regulation 1406/2002 of the European Parliament and of the Council of 27 June 2002 establishing a European Maritime Safety Agency.[6] This regulation was amended by Regulation 1644/2003 of the European Parliament and of the Council of 22 July 2003,[7] Regulation 724/2004 of the European Parliament and of the Council of 31 March 2004,[8] Regulation 2038/2006 of the European Parliament and of the Council of 18 December 2006,[9] Regulation 100/2013 of the European Parliament and of the Council of 15 January 2013[10] and Regulation 2016/1625 of the European Parliament and of the Council of 14 September 2016.[11] The legal regime is likely to be amended on an ongoing basis.

D. LOCATION OF EMSA

27.007 EMSA is based in Lisbon in Portugal. Its address is European Maritime Safety Agency, PraÁa" Europa 4, Cais do Sodré, 1249-206 LISBOA, Portugal. Its website is www.emsa.europa.eu/.

E. LEGAL STATUS AND STANDING OF EMSA

27.008 EMSA is a body rather than an institution[12] which means that it does not have law-making power. EMSA has legal personality pursuant to Article 5(1) of Regulation 1406/2002.[13] Article 5(2) of the same regulation provides that in

"each of the Member States, the Agency shall enjoy the most extensive legal capacity accorded to legal persons under their laws. It may in particular, acquire or dispose of movable and immovable property and may be a party to legal proceedings."

EMSA is represented by its Executive Director.[14]

27.009 In respect of EMSA's contractual liability, the eighth recital to Regulation 1406/2002[15] provides that for

---

5 Reg. 1406/2002, OJ L208/1, 5 August 2002, recital 2.

6 OJ L208/1, 5 August 2002. The legal basis for Reg. 1406/2002 was the TEC and in particular Art. 80(2) thereof (which is now Art. 100(2) of the TFEU). Art. 24 of Reg. 1406/2002 provides that the regulation entered into force on the twentieth day following its publication in the Official Journal (it was published on 5 August 2002).

7 OJ L245/10, 29 September 2003.

8 OJ L129/1, 29 April 2004.

9 OJ L394/1, 30 December 2006.

10 OJ L39/30, 9 February 2013.

11 OJ L251/77, 16 September 2016.

12 Reg. 1406/2002, Art. 5(1).

13 OJ L208/1, 5 August 2002.

14 Reg. 1406/2002, OJ L208/1, 5 August 2002, Art. 5(4).

15 OJ L208/1, 5 August 2002.

"the contractual liability of the Agency, which is governed by the law applicable to the contracts concluded by the Agency, the Court of Justice should have jurisdiction to give judgment pursuant to any arbitration clause contained in the contract. The Court of Justice should also have jurisdiction in disputes relating to compensation for any damage arising from the non-contractual liability of the Agency."

27.010 Article 5(3) of Regulation 1406/2002 provides that at the request of the Commission, the Administrative Board may decide, with the agreement of and in co-operation with the Member States concerned and with due regard to budgetary implications, including any contribution the Member States concerned may provide, to establish the regional centres necessary in order to carry out, in the most efficient and effective way, some of EMSA's tasks. When taking such a decision, the Administrative Board must define the precise scope of activities of the regional centre while avoiding unnecessary financial costs and enhancing co-operation with existing regional and national networks.

F. STRUCTURE AND GOVERNANCE OF EMSA

Introduction

27.011 The ninth and tenth recitals to Regulation 1406/2002 set the scene for the structure and governance of EMSA:

"(9) In order to effectively ensure the accomplishment of the functions of the Agency, the Member States and the Commission should be represented on an Administrative Board entrusted with the necessary powers to establish the budget, verify its execution, adopt the appropriate financial rules, establish transparent working procedures for decision making by the Agency, approve its work programme, examine requests for technical assistance from Member States, define a policy for visits to the Member States and appoint the Executive Director. In the light of the highly technical and scientific mission and tasks of the Agency, it is appropriate for the Administrative Board to consist of one representative of each Member State and four representatives of the Commission, being members with a high level of expertise. In order further to ensure the highest level of expertise and experience in the Administrative Board and with a view to involving the sectors most closely concerned in the tasks of the Agency, the Commission should nominate independent professionals from these sectors as board members without the right to vote, on the basis of their personal merit and experience in the field of maritime safety and prevention of pollution by ships and not as representatives of particular professional organisations.
(10) The good functioning of the Agency requires that its Executive Director be appointed on the grounds of merit and documented administrative and managerial skills, as well as competence and experience relevant for maritime safety and prevention of pollution by ships and that he/she performs his/her duties with complete independence and flexibility as to the organisation of the internal functioning of the Agency. To this end, the Executive Director should prepare and take all necessary steps to ensure the proper accomplishment of the working programme of the Agency, should prepare each year a draft general report to be submitted to the Administrative Board, should draw up estimates of the revenues and expenditure of the Agency and should implement the budget."

Administrative Board

27.012 Article 10 (as amended) of Regulation 1406/2002 deals with the creation and powers of EMSA's Administrative Board:

"1. An Administrative Board is hereby set up.

2. The Administrative Board shall:

    (a) appoint the Executive Director pursuant to Article 16;[16]

    (b) adopt the annual report on the Agency's activities and forward it each year by 15 June to the European Parliament, the Council, the Commission, the Court of Auditors and the Member States.

    The Agency shall forward annually to the budgetary authority all information regarding the outcome of the evaluation procedures;

    (c) examine and approve, in the framework of the preparation of the work programme, requests for assistance to the Commission, as referred to in Article 2(2)(d), requests from Member States for technical assistance, as referred to in Article 2(3), and requests for technical assistance, as referred to in Article 2(5) as well as requests for assistance as referred to in Article 2a;

        (ca) examine and adopt a multiannual strategy for the Agency for a period of five years taking the written opinion of the Commission into account;

        (cb) examine and adopt the multiannual staff policy plan of the Agency;

        (cc) consider draft administrative arrangements, as referred to in Article 15(2)(ba);

    (d) adopt, by 30 November each year, and taking the opinion of the Commission into account, the work programme of the Agency for the coming year and forward it to the Member States, the European Parliament, the Council and the Commission; this work programme shall be adopted without prejudice to the annual Community budgetary procedure. In the event that the Commission expresses, within 15 days from the date of adoption of the work programme, its disagreement with the said programme, the Administrative Board shall re-examine the programme and adopt it, possibly amended, within a period of two months, in second reading either with a two-thirds majority, including the Commission representatives, or by unanimity of the representatives of the Member States;

    (e) adopt the final budget of the Agency before the beginning of the financial year, adjusting it, where necessary, according to the Community contribution and any other revenue of the Agency;

---

16 Ed., Art. 16 ("Appointment and dismissal of the Executive Director and the Heads of Department") provides: "1. The Executive Director shall be appointed and dismissed by the Administrative Board. The appointment shall be made for a period of five years on grounds of merit and documented administrative and managerial competence, as well as documented experience in the fields referred to in Article 1 after hearing the opinion of the observer as referred to in Article 10. The Executive Director shall be appointed from a list of at least three candidates proposed by the Commission after an open competition, following publication of the post in the Official Journal of the European Union, and elsewhere, of a call for expression of interest. The candidate selected by the Administrative Board may be invited to make a statement before the competent committee of the European Parliament and answer questions put by its members. The Administrative Board shall deliberate on dismissal at the request of the Commission or of one third of its members. The Administrative Board shall take its decisions on appointment or dismissal by a four-fifths majority of all members with the right to vote. 2. The Administrative Board, acting on a proposal from the Commission, taking into account the evaluation report may extend once the term of office of the Executive Director for not more than four years. The Administrative Board shall take its decision by a four-fifths majority of all members with the right to vote. The Administrative Board shall inform the European Parliament about its intention to extend the Executive Director's term of office. Within a month before the extension of his/her term of office, the Executive Director may be invited to make a statement before the competent committee of the European Parliament and answer questions put by its members. If the term of office is not extended, the Executive Director shall remain in office until the appointment of his/her successor. 3. The Executive Director may be assisted by one or more Heads of Department. If the Executive Director is absent or indisposed, one of the Heads of Department shall take his/her place. 4. The Heads of Department shall be appointed on grounds of merit and documented administrative and managerial skills, as well as professional competence and experience in the fields referred to in Article 1. The Heads of Department shall be appointed or dismissed by the Executive Director after having received a positive opinion of the Administrative Board."

(f) establish procedures for decision-making by the Executive Director;

(g) establish the methodology for the visits to be carried out pursuant to Article 3. In the event that the Commission expresses, within 15 days from the date of adoption of the methodology, its disagreement, the Administrative Board shall re-examine and adopt it, possibly amended, in second reading either with a two-thirds majority, including the Commission representatives, or by unanimity of the representatives of the Member States;

(h) perform its duties in relation to the Agency's budget pursuant to Articles 18, 19 and 21 and monitor and ensure adequate follow-up to the findings and recommendations stemming from various audit reports and evaluations, whether internal or external;

(i) exercise disciplinary authority over the Executive Director and the Heads of Department referred to in Article 16;

(j) establish its rules of procedure;

(k) adopt, following the procedures set out in (d), a detailed plan for the Agency's pollution preparedness and response activities, aiming at the optimum use of the financial means available to the Agency;

(l) review the financial execution of the detailed plan referred to in point (k) of this paragraph and the budgetary commitments provided for in Regulation (EC) No 2038/2006 of the European Parliament and of the Council of 18 December 2006 on multiannual funding for the action of the European Maritime Safety Agency in the field of response to pollution caused by ships;[17]

(m) appoint an observer from amongst its members to follow the selection procedure by the Commission for the appointment of the Executive Director."

27.013 The composition of the Administrative Board is addressed in Article 11. Article 11(1) provides:

"The Administrative Board shall be composed of one representative of each Member State and four representatives of the Commission, as well as of four professionals from the sectors most concerned, nominated by the Commission, without the right to vote.

Administrative Board members shall be appointed on the basis of their degree of relevant experience and expertise in the fields referred to in Article 1. The Member States and the Commission shall each strive for a balanced representation between men and women on the Administrative Board."

27.014 Each Member State and the Commission shall appoint their members of the Administrative Board as well as an alternate who will represent the member in his/her absence.[18] The duration of the term of office shall be four years. The term of office may be renewed.[19] Article 11(4) of Regulation 1406/2002 provides that when appropriate, the participation of representatives of third countries and the conditions thereof shall be established in the arrangements referred to in Article 17(2) of the regulation.[20]

27.015 The meetings of the Administrative Board shall be convened by its Chairperson.[21] The Executive Director of the Agency shall take part in the deliberations.[22] The

---

17 Ed., OJ L394/1, 30 December 2006.

18 Reg. 1406/2002, Art. 11(2).

19 Reg. 1406/2002, Art. 11(3).

20 Art. 17 ("Participation of third countries") provides: "1. The Agency shall be open to the participation of third countries, which have entered into agreements with the European Community, whereby they have adopted and are applying the Community law in the field of maritime safety, maritime security, prevention of pollution and response to pollution caused by ships. 2. Under the relevant provisions of these agreements, arrangements will be developed which shall, inter alia, specify the nature and the extent of the detailed rules for the participation by these countries in the work of the Agency, including provisions on financial contributions and staff."

21 Reg. 1406/2002, Art. 13(1).

22 Ibid.

Administrative Board shall hold an ordinary meeting twice a year.[23] In addition, it shall meet on the initiative of the Chairperson or at the request of the Commission or of one-third of the Member States.[24] When there is a matter of confidentiality or conflict of interest, the Administrative Board may decide to examine specific items of its agenda without the presence of the members concerned. Detailed rules for the application of this provision shall be laid down in the rules of procedure.[25] The Administrative Board may invite any person whose opinion can be of interest to attend its meetings as an observer.[26] The members of the Administrative Board may, subject to the provisions of its rules of procedure, be assisted by advisers or experts.[27] The secretariat for the Administrative Board shall be provided by the Agency.[28]

Chairmanship of the Administrative Board

27.016 Article 12(1) of Regulation 1406/2002 provides that the Administrative Board shall elect a Chairperson and a Deputy-Chairperson from among its members. The Deputy Chairperson shall automatically take the place of the Chairperson if he/she is prevented from attending to his/her duties. While Article 12(2) provides that the terms of office of the Chairperson and Deputy Chairperson shall be three years and shall expire when they cease to be members of the Administrative Board and the terms of office shall be renewable once.

Voting in the Administrative Board

27.017 Article 14 of Regulation 1406/2002 sets out the rules on voting in the Administrative Board. The Administrative Board shall take its decisions by a two-thirds majority of all members with the right to vote.[29] Each member shall have one vote. The Executive Director of the Agency shall not vote.[30] In the absence of a member, his/her alternate shall be entitled to exercise his/her right to vote.[31] The rules of procedure shall establish the more detailed voting arrangements, in particular, the conditions for a member to act on behalf of another member.[32]

Executive Director

27.018 EMSA is represented by its Executive Director.[33] The Administrative Board appoints the Executive Director pursuant to Article 16 of Regulation 1406/2002. The Executive Director shall take part in the deliberations of the Administrative Board[34] but

---

23 Reg. 1406/2002, Art. 13(3).
24 Ibid.
25 Reg. 1406/2002, Art. 13(4).
26 Reg. 1406/2002, Art. 13(5).
27 Reg. 1406/2002, Art. 13(6).
28 Reg. 1406/2002, Art. 13(7).
29 Reg. 1406/2002, Art. 14(1).
30 Reg. 1406/2002, Art. 14(2).
31 Ibid.
32 Reg. 1406/2002, Art. 14(3).
33 Reg. 1406/2002, Art. 5(4).
34 Reg. 1406/2002, Art. 13(2).

does not vote in its deliberations.[35] Article 15 of Regulation 1406/2002 describes the duties and powers of the Executive Director. It provides that EMSA is managed by its Executive Director, who is completely independent in the performance of his/her duties, without prejudice to the respective competencies of the Commission and the Administrative Board.[36] Under Article 15(2), the Executive Director has the following duties and powers:

"(a) he/she shall prepare the multiannual strategy of the Agency and submit it to the Administrative Board after consultation of the Commission at least eight weeks before the relevant Administrative Board meeting, taking into account views and suggestions made by members of the Administrative Board;

   (aa) he/she shall prepare the multiannual staff policy plan of the Agency and submit it to the Administrative Board after consultation of the Commission at least four weeks before the relevant Administrative Board meeting;

   (ab) he/she shall prepare the annual work programme, with an indication of the expected human and financial resources allocated to each activity, and the detailed plan for the Agency's pollution preparedness and response activities, and submit them to the Administrative Board after consultation of the Commission at least eight weeks before the relevant Board meeting, taking into account views and suggestions made by members of the Administrative Board. He/she shall take the necessary steps for their implementation. He/she shall respond to any requests for assistance from a Member State in accordance with Article 10(2)(c);

(b) he/she shall decide to carry out the visits and inspections provided for in Article 3, after consultation of the Commission and following the methodology for visits established by the Administrative Board in accordance with Article 10(2)(g);

   (ba) he/she may enter into administrative arrangements with other bodies working in the Agency's fields of activities provided that the draft arrangement has been submitted for consultation to the Administrative Board and provided that the Administrative Board does not object within four weeks;

(c) he/she shall take all necessary steps, including the adoption of internal administrative instructions and the publication of notices, to ensure the functioning of the Agency in accordance with the provisions of this Regulation;

(d) he/she shall organise an effective monitoring system in order to be able to compare the Agency's achievements with its objectives and tasks as laid down in this Regulation. To this end, he/she shall establish, in agreement with the Commission and the Administrative Board, tailored performance indicators allowing for an effective assessment of the results achieved. He/she shall ensure that the Agency's organisational structure will be regularly adapted to the evolving needs within the available financial and human resources. On this basis the Executive Director shall prepare a draft general report each year and submit it for consideration by the Administrative Board. The report shall include a dedicated section concerning the financial execution of the detailed plan for the Agency's pollution preparedness and response activities and give an update of the status of all actions funded under that plan. He/she shall establish regular evaluation procedures that meet recognised professional standards;

(e) he/she shall exercise, in respect of the staff, the powers laid down in Article 6(2);

---

35 Reg. 1406/2002, Art. 14(2).
36 Reg. 1406/2002, Art. 15(1).

(f) he/she shall draw up estimates of the Agency's revenue and expenditure, in accordance with Article 18,[37] and shall implement the budget in accordance with Article 19.[38]"

27.019 Interestingly, under Article 15(3), the Executive Director must, as appropriate, report to the European Parliament and the Council on the carrying out of his/her tasks. In

---

37 Ed., Art. 18 ("Budget") provides: "1. The Agency's revenues shall consist of: (a) a contribution from the Community; (b) possible contributions from any third country which participates in the work of the Agency in accordance with Article 17; (c) fees and charges for publications, training and/or any other services provided by the Agency. 2. The Agency's expenditure shall cover staff and administrative, infrastructure and operational expenses. 3. The Executive Director shall draw up a draft statement of estimates of the Agency's revenue and expenditure for the following year, on the basis of activity-based budgeting, and shall forward it to the Administrative Board, together with a draft establishment plan. 4. Revenue and expenditure shall be in balance. 5. Each year the Administrative Board, on the basis of a draft statement of estimates of revenue and expenditure, shall produce a statement of estimates of revenue and expenditure for the Agency for the following financial year. 6. This statement of estimates, which shall include a draft establishment plan together with the provisional work programme, shall by 31 March at the latest be forwarded by the Administrative Board to the Commission and to the States with which the Community has concluded agreements in accordance with Article 17. 7. The statement of estimates shall be forwarded by the Commission to the European Parliament and the Council (the 'budgetary authority') together with the draft general budget of the European Union. 8. On the basis of the statement of estimates, the Commission shall enter in the draft general budget of the European Union the estimates it deems necessary for the establishment plan and the amount of the subsidy to be charged to the general budget, which it shall place before the budgetary authority in accordance with Article 314 TFEU, together with a description of and justification for any difference between the Agency's statement of estimates and the subsidy to be charged to the general budget. 9. The budgetary authority shall authorise the appropriations for the subsidy to the Agency. The budgetary authority shall adopt the establishment plan for the Agency. 10. The budget shall be adopted by the Administrative Board. It shall become final following final adoption of the general budget of the European Union. Where appropriate, it shall be adjusted accordingly, together with the annual work programme. 11. The Administrative Board shall, as soon as possible, notify the budgetary authority of its intention to implement any project which may have significant financial implications for the funding of the budget, in particular any projects relating to property such as the rental or purchase of buildings. It shall inform the Commission thereof. Where a branch of the budgetary authority has notified its intention to deliver an opinion, it shall forward its opinion to the Administrative Board within a period of six weeks after the date of notification of the project."

38 Ed., Art. 19 (" Implementation and control of the budget") provides: "1. The Executive Director shall implement the Agency's budget. 2. By 1 March at the latest following each financial year, the Agency's accounting officer shall communicate the provisional accounts to the Commission's accounting officer together with a report on the budgetary and financial management for that financial year. The Commission's accounting officer shall consolidate the provisional accounts of the institutions and decentralised bodies in accordance with Article 128 of the general Financial Regulation. 3. By 31 March at the latest following each financial year, the Commission's accounting officer shall forward the Agency's provisional accounts to the Court of Auditors, together with a report on the budgetary and financial management for that financial year. The report on the budgetary and financial management for the financial year shall also be forwarded to the European Parliament and the Council. 4. On receipt of the Court of Auditors' observations on the Agency's provisional accounts, under Article 129 of the general Financial Regulation, the Executive Director shall draw up the Agency's final accounts under his own responsibility and submit them to the Administrative Board for an opinion. 5. The Administrative Board shall deliver an opinion on the Agency's final accounts. 6. The Executive Director shall, by 1 July at the latest following each financial year, forward the final accounts to the European Parliament, the Council, the Commission and the Court of Auditors, together with the Administrative Board's opinion. 7. The final accounts shall be published. 8. The Executive Director shall send the Court of Auditors a reply to its observations by 30 September at the latest. He shall also send this reply to the Administrative Board. 9. The Executive Director shall submit to the European Parliament, at the latter's request, all information necessary for the smooth application of the discharge procedure for the financial year in question, as laid down in Article 146(3) of the general Financial Regulation. 10. The European Parliament, on a recommendation from the Council acting by a qualified majority, shall, before 30 April of year $N+2$, give a discharge to the Executive Director in respect of the implementation of the budget for year N." There are other provisions on combating fraud (Art. 20) and financial provisions (Art. 21). There have also been other specific measures on financing of EMSA but they fall outside the scope of this work (e.g. Reg. 1891/2006 of the European Parliament and of the Council of 18 December 2006 on multiannual funding for the action of the European Maritime Safety Agency in the field of response to pollution caused by ships and amending Regulation 1406/2002 (OJ L394/1, 30 December 2006)).

particular, he/she must present the state of play with regard to the preparation of the multiannual strategy and the annual work programme. It is interesting that the Executive Director reports to the Parliament rather than the Council and Commission – which gives the Parliament a stronger role in these matters.

G. STAFF, PRIVILEGES, LIABILITY AND LANGUAGES OF EMSA

Staff

27.020 Today, EMSA has a total staff complement of over 200 which is a substantial increase from the 30 in 2003.[39] Article 6 of Regulation 1406/2002 provides:

"1. The Staff Regulations of officials of the European Communities, the Conditions of employment of other servants of the European Communities and the rules adopted jointly by the institutions of the European Communities for the purposes of the application of those Staff Regulations and conditions of Employment shall apply to the staff of the Agency. The Administrative Board, in agreement with the Commission, shall adopt the necessary detailed rules of application.
2. Without prejudice to Article 16, the powers conferred on the appointing authority by the Staff Regulations and the Conditions of employment of other servants shall be exercised by the Agency in respect of its own staff.
3. The Agency's staff shall consist of officials assigned or seconded by the Commission or Member States on a temporary basis and of other servants recruited by the Agency as necessary to carry out its tasks."

Privileges

27.021 Article 7 of Regulation 1406/2002 provides that the Protocol on the Privileges and Immunities of the European Communities applies to the Agency and to its staff.

Liability

27.022 Liability can be an important issue for EMSA given its activities (e.g. in regard to environmental and safety issues, there are often issues arising). Article 8 of Regulation 1406/2002 provides:

"1. The contractual liability of the Agency shall be governed by the law applicable to the contract in question.
2. The Court of Justice shall have jurisdiction to give judgment pursuant to any arbitration clause contained in a contract concluded by the Agency.
3. In the case of non-contractual liability, the Agency shall, in accordance with the general principles common to the laws of the Member States, make good any damage caused by its departments or by its servants in the performance of their duties.
4. The Court of Justice shall have jurisdiction in disputes relating to the compensation for damage referred to in paragraph 3.
5. The personal liability of its servants towards the Agency shall be governed by the provisions laid down in the Staff Regulations or Conditions of employment applicable to them."

---

39 See www.emsa.europa.eu/emsa-documents/latest/download/3671/2494/23.html.

Languages

27.023 Article 9(1) of Regulation 1406/2002 provides that the provisions laid down in Regulation No 1 of 15 April 1958 determining the languages to be used in the European Economic Community[40] shall apply to EMSA. Article 9(2) goes on to provide that the translation services required for the functioning of the EMSA shall be provided by the Translation Centre of the bodies of the EU.

H. BUDGET OF EMSA

27.024 The eleventh recital to Regulation 1406/2002 provides that in order "to guarantee the full autonomy and independence of the Agency, it is considered necessary to grant it an autonomous budget whose revenue comes essentially from a contribution from the [EU]". The twelfth recital goes on to say that over

"the past years, as more decentralised agencies have been created, the budgetary authority has looked to improve transparency and control over the management of the [EU] funding allocated to them, in particular concerning the budgetisation of the fees, financial control, power of discharge, pension scheme contributions and the internal budgetary procedure (code of conduct). In a similar way, Regulation 1073/1999 of the European Parliament and of the Council of 25 May 1999 concerning investigations conducted by the European Anti-Fraud Office (OLAF)[41] should apply without restriction to the Agency, which should accede to the Interinstitutional Agreement of 25 May 1999 between the European Parliament, the Council of the European Union and the Commission of the European Communities concerning internal investigations by the European Anti-Fraud Office (OLAF).[42]"

EMSA's 2016 Budget was in the region of €55 million which demonstrates that it is a substantial player in maritime safety issues.

I. FUNCTIONS OF EMSA: INTRODUCTION

27.025 EMSA's aim is to seek to ensure a high, uniform and effective level of maritime safety and maritime security in the EU. In that context, it also works to prevent pollution and respond to pollution caused by ships or by oil and gas installations.[43] There has long been a strong connection in EU shipping history between pollution and safety but there does not have to be and EMSA's role is evolving over time including into areas relating to migration.[44]

27.026 EMSA is largely a technical, rather than policy, body. The third recital to Regulation 1409/2002 states that in

"general terms, the Agency should represent the technical body providing the [EU] with the necessary means to act effectively to enhance overall maritime safety and ship pollution prevention rules. The Agency should assist the Commission in the continuous process of updating and developing [EU] legislation in the field of maritime safety and prevention of pollution by ships and should provide the necessary support to ensure the convergent and effective implementation

---

40 OJ 17, 6 October 1958, p. 385/58. Regulation as last amended by the 1994 Act of Accession.
41 Ed, OJ L136/1, 31 May 1999.
42 Ed., OJ L136/15, 31 May 1999.
43 Reg. 1406/2002, Art. 1(1).
44 See COM(2015) 667 final.

of such legislation throughout the Community by assisting the Commission in performing the tasks assigned to the latter by existing and future [EU] legislation on maritime safety and ship pollution prevention."[45]

In this regard, EMSA provides technical assistance and support to the Commission and Member States in regard to the development, application and evaluation of EU law on maritime safety, security and pollution. This technical approach is reflected in Article 1(2) of Regulation 1406/2002 which provides that in order to achieve the aim set out in Article 1(1) that EMSA was established "for the purpose of ensuring a high, uniform and effective level of maritime safety, maritime security, prevention of, and response to, pollution caused by ships as well as response to marine pollution caused by oil and gas installations", EMSA:

"shall cooperate with the Member States and the Commission and provide them with technical, operational and scientific assistance in the fields mentioned in paragraph 1 of this Article within the limits of the core tasks set out in Article 2 and, as and when applicable, the ancillary tasks set out in Article 2a, in particular in order to help the Member States and the Commission to apply the relevant legal acts of the Union properly. As regards the field of response to pollution, the Agency shall provide operational assistance only upon the request of the affected State(s)."

27.027 Article 1(3) of Regulation 1406/2002 states that by EMSA

"providing the assistance referred to in [Article 1(2)], the Agency shall, where appropriate, contribute to the overall efficiency of maritime traffic and maritime transport as set out in this Regulation, so as to facilitate the establishment of a European Maritime Transport Space without Barriers."

27.028 The fourth recital to Regulation 1406/2002 provides that for

"the proper achievement of the purposes for which the Agency is established, it is appropriate that the Agency carries out a number of other important tasks aimed at enhancing maritime safety and ship pollution prevention in the waters of the Member States."

The regulation gives some examples:

"the Agency should work with Member States to organise appropriate training activities on port State control and flag State related issues and to provide technical assistance related to the implementation of [EU] legislation ...
    [it] should facilitate cooperation between the Member States and the Commission as provided for in Directive 2002/59/EC of the European Parliament and of the Council of 27 June 2002 establishing a Community vessel traffic monitoring and information system and repealing Council Directive 93/75/EEC,[46] namely by developing and operating any information system necessary for the objectives of that Directive, and in the activities concerning the investigations related to serious maritime accidents ...
    [it] should provide the Commission and the Member States with objective, reliable and comparable information and data on maritime safety and on ship pollution prevention to enable them to take any necessary initiatives to enhance the measures in place and to evaluate their effectiveness ...
    [it] should place the [EU] maritime safety know-how at the disposal of the States applying for accession [and]

---

45 Reg. 1406/2002, recital 3.
46 Ed., OJ L208/10, 5 August 2002.

[it] should be open to the participation of these States and to other third countries which have concluded agreements with the [EU] whereby they adopt and implement [EU] legislation in the field of maritime safety and prevention of pollution by ships."

27.029 EMSA should also, according to the fifth recital,

"favour the establishment of better cooperation between the Member States and should develop and disseminate best practices in the [EU]. This in turn should contribute to enhancing the overall maritime safety system in the [EU] as well as reducing the risk of maritime accidents, marine pollution and the loss of human lives at sea."

27.030 It would be wrong if EMSA operated in isolation of the Member States. So, the sixth recital to Regulation 1406/2002 provides that it in

"order properly to carry out the tasks entrusted to the Agency, it is appropriate that its officials carry out visits to the Member States in order to monitor the overall functioning of the [EU] maritime safety and ship pollution prevention system. The visits should be carried out in accordance with a policy to be established by the Agency's Administrative Board and should be facilitated by the authorities of the Member States."

J. FUNCTIONS OF EMSA: CORE TASKS OF EMSA

27.031 EMSA has certain "core tasks" under Article 2 of Regulation 1406/2002. It is useful to consider the functions individually.[47]

27.032 The first group of functions relate to EMSA's work to assist the Commission. Article 2(2) sets out those functions.

27.033 Article 2(2)(a) provides that EMSA must assist the Commission "in the preparatory work for updating and developing relevant legal acts of the Union, in particular in line with the development of international legislation". This is an important task because EMSA is able to provide technical input into the Commission's work.

27.034 Article 2(2)(b) states that EMSA must assist the Commission

"in the effective implementation of relevant binding legal acts of the Union, in particular by carrying-out visits and inspections as referred to in Article 3 of this Regulation and by providing technical assistance to the Commission in the performance of the inspection tasks assigned to it pursuant to Article 9(4) of Regulation ... 725/2004 of the European Parliament and of the Council of 31 March 2004 on enhancing ship and port facility security.[48] In this regard, it may address suggestions to the Commission for any possible improvements of those binding legal acts."

27.035 In regard to research projects, Article 2(2)(c) provides that "in the analysis of ongoing and completed research projects relevant to the objectives of the Agency; this may include the identification of possible follow-up measures resulting from specific research projects".

27.036 The Commission may give other functions to EMSA because Article 2(2)(d) provides that EMSA must assist the Commission "in the performance of any other task assigned to the Commission in legislative acts of the Union regarding the objectives of the Agency".

---

47 Art. 2(1) of Reg. 1406/2002 provides that "[i]n order to ensure that the objectives set out in Article 1 are met in the appropriate manner, the Agency shall perform the core tasks listed in this Article [2]".

48 Ed., OJ L129/6, 29 April 2004.

27.037 The second group of functions involve those where EMSA must work with the Member States to achieve certain functions. Article 2(3) sets out those functions.

27.038 Article 2(3)(a) provides that EMSA must work with the Member States to "organise, where appropriate, relevant training activities in fields which are the responsibility of the Member States".

27.039 Article 2(3)(b) provides that EMSA must work with the Member States to "develop technical solutions, including the provision of relevant operational services, and provide technical assistance, to the building up of the necessary national capacity for the implementation of relevant legal acts of the Union".

27.040 EMSA must work with the Member States, by virtue of Article 2(3)(c) of Regulation 1406/2002, to

> "provide, at the request of a Member State, appropriate information resulting from the inspections referred to in Article 3 in order to support the monitoring of the recognised organisations that carry out certification tasks on behalf of the Member States in accordance with Article 9 of Directive 2009/15/EC of the European Parliament and of the Council of 23 April 2009 on common rules and standards for ship inspection and survey organisations and for the relevant activities of maritime administrations[49] without prejudice to the rights and obligations of the flag State."

Article 3 (entitled "Visits to Member States and Inspections") provides:

> "1. In order to perform the tasks entrusted to it and to assist the Commission in fulfilling its duties under the TFEU, and in particular the assessment of the effective implementation of relevant Union law, the Agency shall carry out visits to Member States in accordance with the methodology established by the Administrative Board.
> 2. The Agency shall inform the Member State concerned in good time of the planned visit, the names of the authorised officials, and the date on which the visit starts and its expected duration. The Agency officials delegated to carry out such visits shall do so on presentation of a decision in writing from the Executive Director of the Agency specifying the purpose and the aims of their mission.
> 3. The Agency shall carry out inspections on behalf of the Commission as required by binding legal acts of the Union regarding organisations recognised by the Union in accordance with Regulation ... 391/2009 of the European Parliament and of the Council of 23 April 2009 on common rules and standards for ship inspection and survey organisations),[50] and regarding the training and certification of seafarers in third countries in accordance with Directive 2008/106...
> 4. At the end of each visit or inspection, the Agency shall draw up a report and send it to the Commission and to the Member State concerned.
> 5. Where appropriate, and in any case when a cycle of visits or inspections is concluded, the Agency shall analyse reports from that cycle with a view to identifying horizontal findings and general conclusions on the effectiveness and cost-efficiency of the measures in place. The Agency shall present this analysis to the Commission for further discussion with Member States in order to draw any relevant lessons and facilitate the dissemination of good working practices."

27.041 Article 2(3)(d) provides that EMSA must work with the Member States to

> "support with additional means in a cost efficient way pollution response actions in case of pollution caused by ships as well as marine pollution caused by oil and gas installations, when a request has been presented by the affected Member State under the authority of which the

---

49 OJ L131/47, 28.5.2009.
50 Ed., OJ L131/11, 28 May 2009.

cleaning operations are conducted, without prejudice to the responsibility of coastal States to have appropriate pollution response mechanisms in place while respecting existing cooperation between Member States in this field. As appropriate, requests for mobilisation of anti-pollution actions shall be relayed through the EU Civil Protection Mechanism established by Council Decision 2007/779/EC, Euratom."[51]

27.042 The third group of functions relate to the facilitation of co-operation between the Member States and the Commission. This is the longest list of functions.

27.043 EMSA must facilitate co-operation between the Member States and the Commission in the field of traffic monitoring covered by Directive 2002/59,[52] indeed EMSA must

"in particular promote cooperation between riparian States in the shipping areas concerned, as well as develop and operate the European Union Long-Range Identification and Tracking of Ships European Data Centre and the Union Maritime Information and Exchange System (Safe-SeaNet) as referred to in Articles 6b and 22a of that Directive as well as the International Long-Range Identification and Tracking information data exchange system in accordance with the commitment made in the International Maritime Organisation ('IMO')."[53]

27.044 EMSA must facilitate co-operation between the Member States and the Commission

"by providing, upon request and without prejudice to national and Union law, relevant vessel positioning and Earth observation data to the competent national authorities and relevant Union bodies within their mandate in order to facilitate measures against threats of piracy and of intentional unlawful acts as provided for in applicable Union law or under internationally agreed legal instruments in the area of maritime transport, subject to applicable data protection rules and in accordance with administrative procedures to be established by the Administrative Board or the High Level Steering Group established in accordance with Directive 2002/59/EC, as appropriate. The provision of long-range identification and tracking of ships data shall be subject to the consent of the flag State concerned."[54]

27.045 Article 2(4)(c) of Regulation 1406/2002 provides that

"in the field of the investigation of marine casualties and incidents in accordance with Directive 2009/18/EC of the European Parliament and of the Council of 23 April 2009 establishing the fundamental principles governing the investigation of accidents in the maritime transport sector)[55]; the Agency shall, if requested by the relevant Member States and assuming that no conflict of interest arises, provide operational support to these Member States concerning investigations related to serious or very serious casualties and it shall carry out analysis of safety investigation reports with a view to identify added value at Union level in terms of any relevant lessons to be drawn. On the basis of data provided by the Member States, in accordance with Article 17 of that Directive, the Agency shall compile a yearly overview of marine casualties and incidents."

This is an extremely important and valuable activity of EMSA in the context of cross-border incidents or, more commonly, where there is a cross-border element to the issues involved.

---

51 OJ L314/9, 1 December 2007.
52 See www.emsa.europa.eu/emsa-documents/legislative-texts/weblink/32/1300/1.html.
53 Reg. 1406/2002, Art. 2(4)(a).
54 Reg. 1406/2002, Art. 2(4)(b).
55 OJ L131/114, 28.5.2009.

27.046 EMSA must, according to Article 2(4)(d) of Regulation 1406/2002, facilitate co-operation between the Member States and the Commission

"in providing objective, reliable and comparable statistics, information and data, to enable the Commission and the Member States to take the necessary steps to improve their actions and to evaluate the effectiveness and cost-efficiency of existing measures. Such tasks shall include the collection, recording and evaluation of technical data, the systematic exploitation of existing databases, including their cross-fertilisation, and, where appropriate, the development of additional databases. On the basis of the data collected, the Agency shall assist the Commission in the publication of information relating to ships pursuant to Directive 2009/16/EC of the European Parliament and of the Council of 23 April 2009 on port State control."[56]

27.047 EMSA must, by virtue of Article 2(4)(e) of Regulation 1406/22 facilitate co-operation between the Member States and the Commission "in gathering and analysing data on seafarers provided and used in accordance with Directive 2008/106 of the European Parliament and of the Council of 19 November 2008 on the minimum level of training of seafarers".[57]

27.048 Article 2(4)(f) provides that EMSA must facilitate co-operation between the Member States and the Commission "in improving the identification and pursuit of ships making unlawful discharges in accordance with Directive 2005/35/EC of the European Parliament and of the Council of 7 September 2005 on ship-source pollution and on the introduction of penalties for infringements".[58]

27.049 It is clear, by virtue of Article 2(4)(g) of Regulation 1406/2002 that EMSA must facilitate co-operation between the Member States and the Commission "regarding marine oil pollution caused by oil and gas installations, by using the European Satellite Oil Monitoring Service (CleanSeaNet) to monitor the extent and environmental impact of such pollution".

27.050 EMSA must, by virtue of Article 2(4)(h) of Regulation 1406/22 facilitate co-operation between the Member States and the Commission

"in providing technical assistance necessary for the Member States and the Commission to contribute to the relevant work of the technical bodies of the IMO, the International Labour Organisation as far as shipping is concerned, and the Paris Memorandum of Understanding on Port State Control ('Paris MoU') and relevant regional organisations to which the Union has acceded, with regard to matters of Union competence."

27.051 EMSA must, by virtue of Article 2(4)(i) of Regulation 1406/22 facilitate co-operation between the Member States and the Commission

"with regard to the implementation of Directive 2010/65/EU of the European Parliament and of the Council of 20 October 2010 on reporting formalities for ships arriving in and/or departing from ports of the Member States,[59] in particular by facilitating the electronic transmission of data through SafeSeaNet and by supporting the development of the single window."

---

56 OJ L131/57, 28 May 2009.
57 OJ L323/33, 3 December 2008.
58 OJ L255/11, 30 September 2005.
59 OJ L283/1, 29.10.2010.

K. FUNCTIONS OF EMSA: ANCILLARY TASKS OF EMSA

Introduction

27.052 EMSA has certain "core tasks" under Article 2 of Regulation 1406/2002 but it also has so-called "ancillary tasks". If there is any conflict between the "core" tasks in Article 2 and the "ancillary" tasks in Article 2a then the former shall prevail over the ancillary tasks. It is useful to consider the ancillary tasks individually.

27.053 Article 2a(1) provides that without prejudice to the core tasks referred to in Article 2, EMSA must assist the Commission and the Member States, as appropriate, in the development and implementation of the Union activities set out in Article 2a, paragraphs 2 and 3 related to EMSA's objectives, in so far as EMSA has established and recognised expertise and tools. The ancillary tasks set out in Article 3 are aimed to (a) create substantiated added value; (b) avoid duplication of efforts; (c) be in the interest of the Union maritime transport policy; (d) not be detrimental to the Agency's core tasks; and (e) not infringe upon Member States' rights and obligations, in particular as flag States, port States and coastal States.

EMSA's assistance of the Commission

27.054 Article 2a(2) sets out six ancillary tasks by which the Commission would assist the Commission.

27.055 Article 2a(2)(a) of Regulation 1406/2002 provides that EMSA shall assist the Commission

"in the context of the implementation of Directive 2008/56/EC of the European Parliament and of the Council (Marine Strategy Framework Directive),[60] by contributing to the objective of achieving good environmental status of marine waters with its shipping-related elements and in exploiting the results of existing tools such as SafeSeaNet and CleanSeaNet."

27.056 Under Article 2a(2)(b) of Regulation 1406/2002 provides that EMSA shall assist the Commission "providing technical assistance in relation to greenhouse gas emissions from ships, in particular in following up ongoing international developments".

27.057 Article 2a(2)(c) of Regulation 1406/2002 provides that EMSA shall assist the Commission "as concerns the Global Monitoring for Environment and Security programme ('GMES'), in promoting the use of GMES data and services for maritime purposes, within the GMES governance framework".

27.058 EMSA must assist the Commission under Article 2a(2)(d) in the development of a Common Information Sharing Environment for the EU maritime domain.

27.059 EMSA must assist the Commission under Article 2a(2)(e) with respect to mobile offshore oil and gas installations, in examining IMO requirements and in gathering basic information on potential threats to maritime transport and the marine environment.

27.060 EMSA must assist the Commission under Article 2a(2)(f) by providing relevant information with regard to classification societies for inland waterway vessels in accordance with Directive 2006/87 of the European Parliament and of the Council of

---

60 OJ L164/19, 25.6.2008.

12 December 2006 laying down technical requirements for inland waterway vessels.[61] This information shall also be part of the reports referred to in Article 3(4) and (5) of this regulation.

EMSA's assistance of the Commission and the Member States

27.061 Article 2a(3) sets out six ancillary tasks by which the Commission would assist the Commission and the Member States.

27.062 Article 2a(3)(a) provides that EMSA shall assist the Commission and the Member States in the examination of the feasibility and the implementation of policies and projects supporting the establishment of the European Maritime Transport Space without Barriers, such as the Blue Belt concept and e-Maritime, as well as Motorways of the Sea. This shall be done in particular by exploring additional functionalities to Safe-SeaNet, without prejudice to the role of the High Level Steering Group established in accordance with Directive 2002/59.[62]

27.063 Article 2a(3)(b) provides that EMSA shall assist the Commission and the Member States by exploring with competent authorities for the River Information Services System the possibility of sharing information between this system and maritime transport information systems on the basis of the report provided for in Article 15 of Directive 2010/65.[63]

27.064 Article 2a(3)(c) provides that EMSA shall assist the Commission and the Member States by facilitating voluntary exchange of best practices in maritime training and education in the Union and by providing information on Union exchange programmes relevant to maritime training while fully respecting Article 166 of the TFEU. Article 166 of the TFEU deals with the EU's vocational training programme.

European co-operation on coast guard functions

27.065 Given the migrant crisis which beset Europe in recent years, it is not surprising that the role of EMSA was going to expand. Article 2b ("European cooperation on coast guard functions") provides the detail on these additional functions:

"Article 2b
European cooperation on coast guard functions

1. The Agency shall, in cooperation with the European Border and Coast Guard Agency, established by Regulation ... 2016/1624 of the European Parliament and of the Council,[64] and the European Fisheries Control Agency, established by Council Regulation ... 768/2005,[65] each

---

61 OJ L389/1, 30 December 2006.
62 OJ L208/10, 5 August 2002.
63 OJ L283/1, 29 October 2010.
64 Ed., Reg. 2016/1624 of the European Parliament and of the Council of 14 September 2016 on the European Border and Coast Guard and amending Reg. 2016/399 of the European Parliament and of the Council and repealing Reg. 863/2007 of the European Parliament and of the Council, Council Reg. 2007/2004 and Council Dec. 2005/267 (OJ L251/1, 16 September 2016).
65 Ed., Council Reg. 768/2005 of 26 April 2005 establishing a Community Fisheries Control Agency and amending Reg. 2847/93 establishing a control system applicable to the common fisheries policy (OJ L128/1, 21 May 2005).

within their mandate, support national authorities carrying out coast guard functions at national and Union level and, where appropriate, at international level by:

    (a) sharing, fusing and analysing information available in ship reporting systems and other information systems hosted by or accessible to those agencies, in accordance with their respective legal bases and without prejudice to the ownership of data by Member States;

    (b) providing surveillance and communication services based on state-of-the-art technology, including space-based and ground infrastructure and sensors mounted on any kind of platform;

    (c) building capacity by drawing up guidelines and recommendations and by establishing best practices as well as by providing training and exchange of staff;

    (d) enhancing the exchange of information and cooperation on coast guard functions including by analysing operational challenges and emerging risks in the maritime domain;

    (e) sharing capacity by planning and implementing multipurpose operations and by sharing assets and other capabilities, to the extent that these activities are coordinated by those agencies and are agreed to by the competent authorities of the Member States concerned.

2.   Without prejudice to the powers of the Administrative Board of the Agency set out in Article 10(2), the precise forms of cooperation on coast guard functions between the Agency, the European Border and Coast Guard Agency and the European Fisheries Control Agency shall be determined in a working arrangement, in accordance with their respective mandates and the financial rules applicable to those agencies. Such an arrangement shall be approved by the Administrative Board of the Agency, the Administrative Board of the European Fisheries Control Agency and the management board of the European Border and Coast Guard Agency.

3.   The Commission shall, in close cooperation with the Member States, the Agency, the European Border and Coast Guard Agency and the European Fisheries Control Agency, make available a practical handbook on European cooperation on coast guard functions. That handbook shall contain guidelines, recommendations and best practices for the exchange of information. The Commission shall adopt the handbook in the form of a recommendation.

4.   The tasks set out in this Article shall not be detrimental to the Agency's tasks referred to in Article 2 and shall not infringe upon Member States' rights and obligations, in particular as flag States, port States or coastal States."

27.066 These additional Article 2b tasks are difficult but important aspects of the contemporary role of the EMSA.

L. RELATIONS WITH MEMBER STATES

27.067 EMSA does not control or supervise the Member States. Instead, it assists the Member States.

27.068 Articles 2 and 2a of Regulation 1406/2002 sets out the tasks and ancillary tasks of the EMSA. These have been discussed above.

27.069 Article 3 deals with visits to Member States and inspections. It should be borne in mind that these visits are, at a technical level, intrusions on the Member States but are, in appropriate cases, necessary for the fulfilment of EMSA's work so the fact that there is regime established around them is not surprising.

27.070 Article 3 provides:

"1. In order to perform the tasks entrusted to it and to assist the Commission in fulfilling its duties under the TFEU, and in particular the assessment of the effective implementation of relevant Union law, the Agency shall carry out visits to Member States in accordance with the methodology established by the Administrative Board.

2. The Agency shall inform the Member State concerned in good time of the planned visit, the names of the authorised officials, and the date on which the visit starts and its expected duration. The Agency officials delegated to carry out such visits shall do so on presentation of a decision in writing from the Executive Director of the Agency specifying the purpose and the aims of their mission.

3. The Agency shall carry out inspections on behalf of the Commission as required by binding legal acts of the Union regarding organisations recognised by the Union in accordance with Regulation (EC) No 391/2009 of the European Parliament and of the Council of 23 April 2009 on common rules and standards for ship inspection and survey organisations,[66] and regarding the training and certification of seafarers in third countries in accordance with Directive 2008/106…

4. At the end of each visit or inspection, the Agency shall draw up a report and send it to the Commission and to the Member State concerned.

5. Where appropriate, and in any case when a cycle of visits or inspections is concluded, the Agency shall analyse reports from that cycle with a view to identifying horizontal findings and general conclusions on the effectiveness and cost-efficiency of the measures in place. The Agency shall present this analysis to the Commission for further discussion with Member States in order to draw any relevant lessons and facilitate the dissemination of good working practices."

M. RELATIONS WITH NON-MEMBER STATES

27.071 In a "core task",[67] Article 2(5) of Regulation 1406/2002 provides that EMSA

"may, upon the request of the Commission, provide technical assistance, including the organisation of relevant training activities, as regards relevant legal acts of the Union, to States applying for accession to the Union, and, where applicable, to European Neighbourhood partner countries and to countries taking part in the Paris MoU.[68] The Agency may also provide assistance in case of pollution caused by ships as well as marine pollution caused by oil and gas installations affecting those third countries sharing a regional sea basin with the Union, in line with the EU Civil Protection Mechanism established by Decision 2007/779/EC, Euratom, and by analogy with the conditions applicable to Member States as referred to in paragraph (3)(d) of this Article. These tasks shall be coordinated with the existing regional cooperation arrangements related to marine pollution."

N. RELATIONS WITH THE PUBLIC, TRANSPARENCY AND PROTECTION OF INFORMATION

27.072 The seventh recital to Regulation 1406/2002 provides that EMSA

"should apply the relevant [EU] legislation concerning public access to documents and the protection of individuals with regard to the processing of personal data. It should give the public and any interested party objective, reliable and easily understandable information with regard to its work."

It is imperative that there is adequate and appropriate transparency given EMSA's important work.

---

66 OJ L131, 28.5.2009, p. 11.
67 See the language of Art. 2a(1) of Reg. 1406/2002 which contrasts EMSA's "core" and "ancillary" tasks.
68 Ed., this is the Paris Memorandum of Understanding relating to port State control (see chap. 29).

27.073 Article 4 of Regulation 1406/2002 provides:

"1. Regulation ... 1049/2001 of the European Parliament and of the Council of 30 May 2001 regarding public access to European Parliament, Council and Commission documents[69] shall apply to documents held by the Agency.

2. The Agency may communicate on its own initiative in the fields within its mission. It shall ensure in particular that the public and any interested party are rapidly given objective, reliable and easily understandable information with regard to its work.

3. The Administrative Board shall adopt the practical arrangements for the application of paragraphs 1 and 2, including, where appropriate, arrangements regarding consultation with Member States before the publication of information.

4. The information collected and processed in accordance with this Regulation by the Commission and the Agency shall be subject to Regulation (EC) No 45/2001 of the European Parliament and of the Council of 18 December 2000 on the protection of individuals with regard to the processing of personal data by the Community institutions and bodies and on the free movement of such data[70] and the Agency shall take the necessary measures to ensure the safe handling and processing of confidential information.

5. Decisions taken by the Agency pursuant to Article 8 of Regulation (EC) No 1049/2001 may form the subject of a complaint to the Ombudsman or of an action before the Court of Justice of the European Communities, under Articles 195 and 230 of the EC Treaty respectively."

O. THE EU'S RE-EVALUATION OF EMSA

27.074 The eleventh recital to Regulation 1406/2002 provides that within

"five years from the date of the Agency having taken up its responsibilities, the Administrative Board should commission an independent external evaluation in order to assess the impact of this Regulation, the Agency and its working practices on establishing a high level of maritime safety and prevention of pollution by ships."

Article 22 of Regulation 1406/22 (entitled "Evaluation") provides:

"1. At regular intervals and at least every five years, the Administrative Board shall commission an independent external evaluation on the implementation of this Regulation. The Commission shall make available to the Agency any information the latter considers relevant to that evaluation.

2. The evaluation shall assess the impact of this Regulation as well as the utility, relevance, achieved added value and effectiveness of the Agency and its working practices. The evaluation shall take into account the views of stakeholders, at both European and national level. It shall, in particular, address the possible need to modify the Agency's tasks. The Administrative Board shall issue specific terms of reference in agreement with the Commission, following consultations with the parties involved.

3. The Administrative Board shall receive the evaluation and issue recommendations regarding changes to this Regulation, the Agency and its working practices to the Commission. Both the evaluation findings and recommendations shall be forwarded by the Commission to the European Parliament and to the Council and shall be made public. An action plan with a timetable shall be included, if appropriate."

27.075 Article 22 of Regulation 1406/2002 (entitled "Progress report") gives specificity to this by saying that by

---

69 OJ L145, 31.5.2001/43.
70 OJ L8, 12.1.2001/1.

"2 March 2018, and taking into account the evaluation report referred to in Article 22, the Commission shall submit a report to the European Parliament and the Council setting out how the Agency has undertaken the additional responsibilities assigned by this Regulation with a view to identifying further efficiency gains and, if necessary, the case for modifying its objectives and tasks."

P. CONCLUSIONS

27.076 As is clear not only from this chapter, other chapters in this book and the detail on EMSA's website,[71] EMSA has already made a significant and substantial contribution to the evolution of maritime safety in the EU. The European Commission had worked diligently in the area but a specialised technical agency dedicated to maritime safety could complement the Commission's work in this area that is often policy-driven. Aspects of the detailed work of EMSA are examined in other chapters on maritime safety throughout this book. EMSA's work has included holding workshops and training sessions for personnel throughout the EU. Its publications have disseminated a great deal of knowledge and information on maritime safety issues[72] including manuals.[73] It is irrefutable that EMSA has made a very tangible and substantial contribution to EU shipping.

---

71 See www.emsa.europa.eu.
72 www.emsa.europa.eu/emsa-documents.html.
73 http://emsa.europa.eu/publications/guidelines-manuals-and-inventories.html.

CHAPTER 28

Maritime safety: port State control

A. INTRODUCTION

28.001 Port State control ("PSC") is an important part of the maritime safety toolkit. It *complements* Flag State Control ("FSC"). Unlike FSC which relies on the supervision of standards (i.e. control) by the country of the ship's registration (i.e. the flag State), PSC involves supervision by the State in which the port is located irrespective of the ship's flag. PSC means that shipowners may not circumvent regulations by flagging out to flag States who are not committed to adopting or enforcing rules, but such shipowners will, instead, face scrutiny in every port into which the vessels sails (i.e. port State control). PSC is an increasingly world-wide phenomenon and not just a European Union ("EU") one. This chapter considers some of the global aspects but concentrates on the EU aspects of PSC.[1]

28.002 The European Maritime Safety Agency ("EMSA") has described the background and rules relating to PSC very well:

"The coastline of the European Union is many thousands of kilometres in length and contains well over 1000 individual ports. These handle around 90% of EU external trade and around 40% of trade between EU countries. This involves handling 3.5 billion tonnes of goods and 350 million passengers being transported on thousands of ship journeys each year.

Consequently, it is vital that EU maritime transport operates in a safe, secure and environmentally friendly way. In support of these goals, and in addition to the systems and procedures in place in each country, the EU has put in place specific maritime legislation. The port State control Directive 2009/16 … as amended[2] and its 3 implementing regulations[3] form a significant

---

1 On the EU law aspects of PSC see http://eur-lex.europa.eu/legal-content/EN/TXT/?uri=uriserv%3Atr0022. On the EMSA and PSC, see www.emsa.europa.eu/implementation-tasks/port-state-control.html. See also various presentations on the EMSA website (www.emsa.europa.eu) including, for example, a Frequently Asked Questions section: www.emsa.europa.eu/implementation-tasks/port-state-control/item/505-how-is-the-mss-rota-organised.html. On port State control generally, see Ozcayir, Port State Control (2004). See also International Maritime Organization, Procedures for Port State Control (2012). See also Pimm, "Commentary on Directive 2009/16/EC of the European Parliament and of the Council of 23 April 2009 on Port State Control" in Jessen and Werner (eds), EU Transport Law: Brussels Commentary on EU Maritime Transport Law (2016), pp. 856–901.

2 Directive 2009/16/EC entered into force on 17 June 2009 and started being applied from 1 January 2011. This Directive replaced Directive 95/21/EC. The Directive has been amended by the Directive 2013/38/EU which has entered into force on 20 August 2013, allowing PSCOs to enforce MLC convention. The amended provisions will be applied following transposition into national legislation of the Member States, but no later than 21 November 2014.

3 Commission Regulation (EU) No 428/2010 implementing Article 14 of Directive 2009/16/EC of the European Parliament and of the Council as regards expanded inspection of ships, Commission Regulation (EU) No 801/2010 of 13 September 2010 implementing Article 10(3) of Directive 2009/16/EC of the European Parliament and of the Council as regards the flag State criteria, Commission Regulation (EU) No 802/2010 of 13 September 2010 implementing Article 10(3) and Article 27 of Directive 2009/16/EC of the European Parliament and of the Council as regards company performance amended by Regulation (EU) 1205/2012 of 14 December 2012.

part thereof. This legislation aims to ensure that there is effective control of compliance with international standards by ships in EU ports and, thereby, ensure that ships sailing in EU waters have been appropriately constructed and are adequately maintained. In addition, Directive 1999/35 ... provides for a system of mandatory surveys for the ro-ro ferries and high speed passenger crafts to be carried out by the host States.

Against this background, EMSA has been given the technical responsibility for monitoring of port State control at EU level. This involves assessing the functioning of the port State inspection systems set up by individual EU members, undertaking a comprehensive analysis of global statistics relating to vessels calling at EU ports, as well as analysis of data on individual ship inspections. Risk assessment studies combined with statistical research provide results which are used to develop objectives and procedures for the continuous improvement of EU port State control performance.

In addition, the Agency carries out a number of supporting tasks in this area in order to ensure the overall effectiveness of the EU port State control system. These tasks include:

- Providing technical assistance to the Commission and Member States in relation to the implementation of the Directive 2009/16/EC as amended;
- Providing, upon the request of the Commission, technical assistance, including the organization of relevant training activities, to States applying for accession to the Union, to European Neighbourhood partner countries and to countries taking part in the Paris MoU;[4]
- Assisting the Commission in the publication of information relating to ship pursuant to the Directive 2009/16/EC;
- Providing statistics, information and data to the Commission and Member States;
- Providing technical assistance necessary for the Member States and the Commission to contribute to the relevant work of the technical bodies of the IMO, the ILO and Paris MoU;
- Developing and implementing, in cooperation with Member States and the Commission, the information system (THETIS)[5] which supports the inspection regime for port State control;

---

4 Ed., the MoU is the Memorandum of Understanding.
5 Ed., EMSA describes THETIS in the following terms:

"THETIS is the information system that supports the new Port State Control inspection regime (NIR). This information system is crucial for the implementation of the new regime, which is laid down in the new Directive 2009/16/EC on Port State Control and its four implementing regulations, Directive 99/35/EC on ro-ro ferries and high-speed passenger crafts, Directive 2009/17/EC on vessel traffic monitoring, Directive 2009/15/EC on Recognised Organisations and the related Regulation (EC) No 319/2009 and, from July 2013, Directive 2009/20/EC on insurance for maritime claims and Regulation (EC) No 392/2009 on liability for the carriage of passengers.

The system serves both the EU Community and the wider region of the Paris Memorandum of Understanding on PSC (Paris MOU) which includes Canada, Iceland, Norway and the Russian Federation.

The working name for the system is THETIS – who, fittingly, was a goddess of the sea in mythology.

To facilitate planning of inspections, the new system is linked to the Community's SafeSeaNet system. SafeSeaNet provides information on ships in, or expected at, all ports of the Member States. THETIS indicates which ships have priority for inspection and allows the results of inspections to be recorded. Via THETIS these reports are made available to all port State control authorities in the Community and the Paris MOU ...

THETIS also interfaces with a number of other maritime safety-related databases including those of the EU-recognised classification societies, Community and national information systems and other port State control regimes so as to exchange data and provide a full picture for the inspector. Inspection results are also available through a public website.

In 2013 a new component for the statistical analysis of data stored in the THETIS database, known as Jasper, was created and made available to the Member States.

The Agency had provided project management, financing and the development of the system. The development began in November 2008, in close cooperation with Member States and the European Commission and the system, together with the SafeSeaNet-THETIS interface, was ready for use end November 2010. The system was fully operational, ready for the implementation of the new inspection regime on 1 January 2011. Comprehensive training for Paris MOU users had been delivered in advance.

Today, 18 000 inspections per year are recorded in the system by 600 authorised users from 27 connected countries. Each day more than 3 000 arrivals at any port in the region are recorded in the system, collected through SafeSeaNet."

- Developing and implementing a 'Harmonized Community Scheme' for the training and assessment of competences of port state control inspectors by Member States;
- Organising and delivering training through seminars for Port State Control Officers;
- Developing, managing and operating a distance learning program for Port State Control Officers;
- Developing, managing and operating a database (RuleCheck) of relevant documents published by IMO, ILO and port state control related document and procedures, to support PSCOs activity."

B. BACKGROUND TO PSC

28.003 The background to PSC falls outside the scope of EU shipping law[6] but a brief sketch would be helpful. At the 1976 International Labour Organisation's ("ILO") conference's maritime session, the Convention concerning Minimum Standards in Merchant Ships (the so-called "ILO Convention 147") ("ILO 147") was adopted. It was aimed at ensuring minimum standards in merchant shipping. The measure was aimed at ensuring inspection of vessels entering the ports of ILO Member States. Eight States, and later nine States, decided among themselves that the ILO 147 needed a follow up. Those eight States were Belgium, Denmark, France, Germany, the Netherlands, Norway, Sweden and the United Kingdom. (Greece joined them on 1 November 1980.) The action by eight States led to the adoption of the so-called Hague Memorandum on 2 March 1978. Ultimately, the EU decided to adopt the same approach.[7]

C. DIRECTIVE 2009/16 ON PSC

Introduction

28.004 The EU PSC regime is embodied primarily in Directive 2009/16 of the European Parliament and of the Council of 23 April 2009 on port State control (as amended).[8] The directive has been amended several times.[9] It entered into force on 17 June 2009. It applied from 1 January 2011. It was not the first directive on PSC – see, for example, Council Directive 95/21 of 19 June 1995 on port State control of shipping[10] – because PSC is best seen as an evolutionary regime. Directive 2009/16 is, in many ways, a recast/consolidation measure but also one which takes the law further on various issues. The directive has itself been amended since. It was part of the EU's Third Maritime Safety Package following incidents such as the *Erika* (1999) and *Prestige* (2001).

Purpose of Directive 2009/16

28.005 Article 1 provides that the purpose of Directive 2009/16 is to help to reduce drastically substandard shipping in the waters under the jurisdiction of Member States by:

---

6 See Ozcayir, op. cit. at fn. 1, chaps 1–5.

7 Ibid., chap. 7.

8 OJ L131/57, 28 May 2009.

9 Dir. 2013/38 (OJ L218/1, 14 August 2013), Reg. 1257/2014 (OJ L330/1, 10 December 2013) and Reg. 2015/757 (OJ L123/55, 19 May 2015). See also a corrigendum at OJ L32/23, 1 February 2013. An unofficial consolidated version is available at https://eur-lex.europa.eu/legal-content/EN/TXT/HTML/?uri=CELEX:02009L0016-20151231&qid=1525516413657&from=EN.

10 OJ L157/1, 7 July 1995.

(a) increasing compliance with international and relevant EU legislation on maritime safety, maritime security, protection of the marine environment and on-board living and working conditions of ships of *all* flags and not just Member State flags; (b) establishing common criteria for control of ships by the port State and harmonising procedures on inspection and detention, building upon the expertise and experience under the Paris Memorandum of Understanding on port State control ("Paris MoU"); and (c) implementing within the EU a PSC system based on the inspections performed within the EU and the Paris MoU region, aiming at the inspection of all ships with a frequency depending on their risk profile, with ships posing a higher risk being subject to a more detailed inspection carried out at more frequent intervals.

Entry into force

28.006 Article 38 of Directive 2009/16 provided that the directive would enter into force on the twentieth day following its publication in the *Official Journal of the European Union*. It was published on 28 May 2009. It entered into force on 17 June 2009. It applied from 1 January 2011.

Legal basis and history of Directive 2009/16

28.007 The legal basis for Directive 2009/16 was the Treaty establishing the European Community ("TEC") generally and, in particular, Article 80(2) of it (this would now be the Treaty on the Functioning of the European Union ("TFEU") generally and Article 100(2) of the TFEU respectively).

Scope of Directive 2009/16

28.008 Article 3 sets out the scope of Directive 2009/16. As a general rule,[11] the directive applies to any ship and its crew calling at a port or anchorage of a Member State to engage in a ship/port interface.[12] If a Member State performs an inspection of a ship in waters within its jurisdiction, other than at a port, it must be considered as an inspection for the purposes of the directive.[13] Nothing in Article 3 may affect the rights of intervention available to a Member State under the relevant conventions.[14] Member States which do not have seaports and which can verify that of the total number of individual vessels calling annually over a period of the three previous years at their river ports, less than 5% are ships covered by the directive, may derogate from the provisions of the directive.[15] Member States which do not have seaports must communicate to the Commission at the latest on the date of transposition of the directive the total number of vessels and the

---

11 The exception, set out in Art. 3(1), provides that France may decide that the ports and anchorages covered by Art. 3(1) do not include ports and anchorages situated in the overseas departments referred to in Art. 299(2) of the TEC (now Art. 349 of the TFEU).

12 Dir. 2009/16, Art. 3(1).

13 Ibid.

14 Ibid.

15 Ibid.

number of ships calling at their ports during the three-year period referred to above and must inform the Commission of any subsequent change to the abovementioned figures.[16]

28.009 If the gross tonnage of a ship is less than 500 grt (gross registered tonnage), then Member States must apply those requirements of a relevant convention which are applicable and must, to the extent that a convention does not apply, take such action as may be necessary to ensure that the ships concerned are not clearly hazardous to safety, health or the environment. In applying Article 3(2), Member States must be guided by Annex 1 to the Paris MoU.[17]

28.010 When inspecting a ship flying the flag of a State which is not a party to a convention, Member States must ensure that the treatment of that ship and its crew is not more favourable than that of a ship flying the flag of a State party to that convention.[18] Such a ship shall be subject to a more detailed inspection in accordance with procedures established by the Paris MoU.[19]

28.011 Fishing vessels, warships, naval auxiliaries, wooden ships of a primitive build, government ships used for non-commercial purposes and pleasure yachts not engaged in trade are excluded from the scope of the directive.[20]

28.012 Measures adopted to give effect to Directive 2009/16 must not lead to a reduction in the general level of protection of seafarers under EU social law in the areas to which the directive applies, as compared to the situation which already prevails in each Member State.[21] In implementing those measures, if the competent authority of the port State becomes aware of a clear violation of EU law on board ships flying the flag of a Member State, it must, in accordance with national law and practice, forthwith inform any other relevant competent authority in order for further action to be taken as appropriate.[22]

Background to Directive 2009/16

28.013 Directive 2009/16 was the result of a Commission proposal followed by an opinion of the European Economic and Social Committee[23] and an opinion of the Committee of the Regions.[24] The adoption of the measure required the use of the Conciliation Committee.

28.014 The sixth recital to Directive 2009/16 emphasises the role of flag state control:

"Responsibility for monitoring the compliance of ships with the international standards for safety, pollution prevention and on-board living and working conditions lies primarily with the flag State. Relying, as appropriate, on recognised organisations, the flag State fully guarantees the completeness and efficiency of the inspections and surveys undertaken to issue the relevant certificates. Responsibility for maintenance of the condition of the ship and its equipment after survey to comply with the requirements of Conventions applicable to the ship lies with the ship

---

16 Ibid.
17 Dir. 2009/16, Art. 3(2).
18 Dir. 2009/16, Art. 3(3).
19 Ibid.
20 Dir. 2009/16, Art. 3(4).
21 Ibid.
22 Dir. 2009/16, Art. 3(5). An example might be a breach of employment or environmental law.
23 OJ C318/195, 23 December 2006.
24 OJ C229/38, 22 September 2006.

company. However, there has been a serious failure on the part of a number of flag States to implement and enforce international standards. Henceforth, as a second line of defence against substandard shipping, the monitoring of compliance with the international standards for safety, pollution prevention and on-board living and working conditions should also be ensured by the port State, while recognising that port State control inspection is not a survey and the relevant inspection forms are not seaworthiness certificates."

28.015 EMSA has an important role in regard to PSC. The tenth recital to Directive 2009/16 provides:

"The European Maritime Safety Agency (EMSA) established by Regulation (EC) No 1406/2002 of the European Parliament and of the Council,[25] should provide the necessary support to ensure the convergent and effective implementation of the port State control system. EMSA should in particular contribute to the development and implementation of the inspection database set up in accordance with this Directive and of a harmonised Community scheme for the training and assessment of competences of port State control inspectors by Member States."

28.016 The eleventh recital to Directive 2009/16 provides:

"An efficient port State control system should seek to ensure that all ships calling at ports and anchorages within the Community are regularly inspected. Inspection should concentrate on substandard ships, while quality ships, meaning those which have satisfactory inspection records or which fly the flag of a State complying with the Voluntary International Maritime Organisation (IMO) Member State Audit Scheme, should be rewarded by undergoing less frequent inspections. In particular to this effect, Member States should give overall priority to ships due for inspections with a high risk profile."

28.017 The twelfth recital of Directive 2009/16 provides:

"Such new inspection arrangements should be incorporated into the Community port State control system as soon as its various aspects have been defined and on the basis of an inspection-sharing scheme whereby each Member State contributes fairly to the achievement of the Community objective of a comprehensive inspection scheme and the volume of inspections is shared in an equitable manner among the Member States. This inspection-sharing scheme should be revised taking into account the experience gained with the new port State control system with a view to improving its effectiveness. Moreover, Member States should recruit and retain the requisite number of staff, including qualified inspectors, taking into account the volume and characteristics of shipping traffic at each port."

28.018 The thirteenth recital provides:

"The inspection system set up by this Directive takes into account the work carried under the Paris MOU. Since any developments arising from the Paris MOU should be agreed at Community level before being made applicable within the EU, close coordination should be established and maintained between the Community and the Paris MOU in order to facilitate as much convergence as possible."

28.019 The fourteenth recital provides:

"The Commission should manage and update the inspection database, in close collaboration with the Paris MOU. The inspection database should incorporate inspection data of Member States and all signatories to the Paris MOU. Until the Community maritime information system, Safe-SeaNet, is fully operational and allows for an automatic record of the data concerning ships' calls in the inspection database, Member States should provide the Commission with the information needed to ensure a proper monitoring of the application of this Directive, in

---

25 Ed., OJ L208/1, 5 August 2002.

particular concerning the movements of ships. On the basis of the inspection data provided by Member States, the Commission should retrieve from the inspection database data on the risk profile of ships, on ships due for inspections and on the movement of ships and should calculate the inspection commitments for each Member State. The inspection database should also be capable of interfacing with other Community maritime safety databases."

28.020 Member States should endeavour to review the method of drawing the white, grey and black list of flag States in the framework of the Paris MoU, in order to ensure its fairness, in particular with respect to the way it treats flag States with small fleets.[26]

28.021 The sixteenth recital provides that the rules and procedures for PSC inspections, including criteria for the detention of ships, should be harmonised to ensure consistent effectiveness in all ports, which would also drastically reduce the selective use of certain ports of destination to avoid the net of proper control.

28.022 The seventeenth recital provides that periodic and additional inspections should include an examination of pre-identified areas for each ship, which will vary according to the type of ship, the type of inspection and the findings of previous PSC inspections. The inspection database should indicate the elements to identify the risk areas to be checked at each inspection.

28.023 The eighteenth recital provides that certain categories of ships present a major accident or pollution hazard when they reach a certain age and should therefore be subject to an expanded inspection and the details of such expanded inspection should be laid down.

28.024 Under the inspection system set up by Directive 2009/16, the intervals between periodic inspections on ships depend on their risk profile that is determined by certain generic and historical parameters. For high risk ships this interval should not exceed six months.[27]

28.025 In order to provide the competent PSC authorities with information on ships in ports or anchorages, port authorities or bodies or the authorities or bodies designated for that purpose should forward notifications on arrivals of ships, on receipt to the extent possible.[28]

28.026 The twenty-first recital provides:

"Some ships pose a manifest risk to maritime safety and the marine environment because of their poor condition, flag performance and history. It is therefore legitimate for the Community to dissuade those ships from entering the ports and anchorages of Member States. The refusal of access should be proportionate and could result in a permanent refusal of access, if the operator of the ship persistently fails to take corrective action in spite of several refusals of access and detentions in ports and anchorages within the Community. Any third refusal of access can only be lifted if a number of conditions designed to ensure that the ship concerned can be operated safely in Community waters, in particular relating to the flag State of the ship and the managing company, are fulfilled. Otherwise, the ship should be permanently refused access to ports and anchorages of the Member States. In any case, any subsequent detention of the ship concerned should lead to a permanent refusal of access to ports and anchorages of the Member States. In the interests of transparency, the list of ships refused access to ports and anchorages within the Community should be made public."

---

26 Dir. 2009/16, Recital 15.
27 Dir. 2009/16, Recital 19.
28 Dir. 2009/16, Recital 20.

28.027 The twenty-second recital provides that with a view to reducing the burden placed on certain administrations and companies by repetitive inspections, surveys under Council Directive 1999/35 of 29 April 1999 on a system of mandatory surveys for the safe operation of regular ro-ro ferry and high-speed passenger craft services,[29] carried out on ro-ro ferries or high-speed passenger craft by a host State which is not the flag State of the vessel, and which include at least all the items of an expanded inspection, should be taken into account when calculating the risk profile of a ship, the intervals between inspections and the fulfilment of the inspection commitment of each Member State. In addition, the Commission should examine whether it is appropriate that Directive 1999/35 be amended in the future with a view of enhancing the level of safety required for the operation of ro-ro ferries and high-speed passenger craft to and from ports of Member States.

28.028 Pilots and port authorities or bodies should be enabled to provide useful information on apparent anomalies found on board ships.[30]

28.029 Complaints from persons with a legitimate interest regarding on-board living and working conditions should be investigated and any person lodging a complaint should be informed of the follow-up action taken with regard to that complaint.[31]

Concepts in Directive 2009/16

28.030 Article 2 contains definitions for the purposes of Directive 2009/16.

28.031 The term "conventions" means the following conventions, with the protocols and amendments thereto, and related codes of mandatory status, in their up-to-date version: (a) the International Convention on Load Lines, 1966 ("LL 66"); (b) the International Convention for the Safety of Life at Sea, 1974 ("SOLAS 74"); (c) the International Convention for the Prevention of Pollution from Ships, 1973, and the 1978 Protocol relating thereto ("MARPOL 73/78"); (d) the International Convention on Standards of Training, Certification and Watchkeeping for Seafarers, 1978 ("STCW 78/95"); (e) the Convention on the International Regulations for Preventing Collisions at Sea, 1972 ("Colreg 72"); (f) the International Convention on Tonnage Measurement of Ships, 1969 ("ITC 69"); (h) the International Convention on Civil Liability for Oil Pollution Damage, 1992 ("CLC 92"); (i) the Maritime Labour Convention, 2006; (j) the International Convention on the Control of Harmful Anti-fouling Systems on Ships, 2001 ("AFS 2001"); and (k) the International Convention on Civil Liability for Bunker Oil Pollution Damage, 2001 (Bunkers Convention, 2001).

28.032 The term "Paris MOU" means the Memorandum of Understanding on Port State Control, signed in Paris on 26 January 1982, in its up-to-date version.

28.033 The term "framework and procedures for the Voluntary IMO Member State Audit Scheme" means IMO Assembly Resolution A.974(24). The term "Paris MOU region" means the geographical area in which the signatories to the Paris MoU conduct inspections in the context of the Paris MoU. The term "Ship" means any seagoing vessel to which one or more of the conventions apply, flying a flag other than that of the port State.

---

29 OJ L138/1, 1 June 1999.
30 Dir. 2009/16, recital 26.
31 Dir. 2009/16, recital 27.

28.034 The term "ship/port interface" means the interactions that occur when a ship is directly and immediately affected by actions involving the movement of persons or goods or the provision of port services to or from the ship.

28.035 The term "ship at anchorage" means a ship in a port or another area within the jurisdiction of a port, but not at berth, carrying out a ship/port interface.

28.036 The term "inspector" means a public-sector employee or other person, duly authorised by the competent authority of a Member State to carry out PSC inspections, and responsible to that competent authority.

28.037 The term "competent authority" means a maritime authority responsible for PSC in accordance with this directive.

28.038 The term "night time" means any period of not less than seven hours, as defined by national law, and which must include, in any case, the period between midnight and 05.00.

28.039 The term "initial inspection" means a visit on board a ship by an inspector, in order to check compliance with the relevant conventions and regulations and including at least the checks required by Article 13(1).

28.040 The term "more detailed inspection" means an inspection where the ship, its equipment and crew as a whole or, as appropriate, parts thereof are subjected, in the circumstances specified in Article 13(3), to an in-depth examination covering the ship's construction, equipment, manning, living and working conditions and compliance with on-board operational procedures.

28.041 The term "expanded inspection" means an inspection, which covers at least the items listed in Annex VII. An expanded inspection may include a more detailed inspection whenever there are clear grounds in accordance with Article 13(3).

28.042 The term "complaint" means any information or report submitted by any person or organisation with a legitimate interest in the safety of the ship, including an interest in safety or health hazards to its crew, on-board living and working conditions and the prevention of pollution.

28.043 The term "detention" means the formal prohibition for a ship to proceed to sea due to established deficiencies which, individually or together, make the ship unseaworthy.

28.044 The term "refusal of access order" means a decision issued to the master of a ship, to the company responsible for the ship and to the flag State notifying them that the ship will be refused access to all ports and anchorages of the Community.

28.045 The term "stoppage of an operation" means a formal prohibition for a ship to continue an operation due to established deficiencies which, individually or together, would render the continued operation hazardous.

28.046 The term "company" means the owner of the ship or any other organisation or person such as the manager, or the bareboat charterer, who has assumed the responsibility for operation of the ship from the owner of the ship and who, on assuming such responsibility, has agreed to take over all the duties and responsibilities imposed by the International Safety Management ("ISM") Code.

28.047 The term "recognised organisation" means a classification company or other private body, carrying out statutory tasks on behalf of a flag State administration.

28.048 The term "statutory certificate" means a certificate issued by or on behalf of a flag State in accordance with conventions.

28.049 The term "classification certificate" means a document confirming compliance with SOLAS 74, Chapter II-1, Part A-1, Regulation 3-1.

28.050 The term "inspection database" means the information system contributing to the implementation of the PSC system within the Community and concerning the data related to inspections carried out in the Community and the Paris MoU region.

28.051 The term "maritime labour certificate" means the certificate referred to in Regulation 5.1.3 of the Maritime Labour Convention 2006.

28.052 The term "declaration of maritime labour compliance" means the declaration referred to in Regulation 5.1.3 of the Maritime Labour Convention 2006.

Inspection powers

28.053 Article 4(1) provides that Member States must take all necessary measures, in order to be legally entitled to carry out the inspections referred to in the directive on board foreign ships, in accordance with international law. Member States must maintain appropriate competent authorities, to which the requisite number of staff, in particular qualified inspectors, for the inspection of ships is assigned, for example, through recruitment, and must take appropriate measures to ensure that inspectors perform their duties as laid down in the directive and in particular that they are available for carrying out the inspections required in accordance with the directive.[32]

Inspection system and annual inspection commitment

28.054 The inspection system and annual inspection commitment are addressed by Article 5 of Directive 2009/16. Member States must carry out inspections in accordance with the selection scheme described in Article 12 and the provisions in Annex I.[33] To comply with its annual inspection commitment, each Member State must: (a) inspect all Priority I ships, referred to in Article 12(a), calling at its ports and anchorages; and (b) carry out annually a total number of inspections of Priority I and Priority II ships, referred to in Article 12(a) and (b), corresponding at least to its share of the total number of inspections to be carried out annually within the Community and the Paris MoU region.[34] The inspection share of each Member State shall be based on the number of individual ships calling at ports of the Member State concerned in relation to the sum of the number of individual ships calling at ports of each State within the Community and the Paris MoU region.[35]

Modalities of compliance with the inspection commitment

28.055 Article 6 deals with the modalities of compliance with the inspection commitment. A Member State which fails to carry out the inspections required in Article 5(2)(a),

---

32 Dir. 2009/16, Art. 4(2).
33 Dir. 2009/16, Art. 5(1).
34 Art. 5(3) of Dir. 2009/16 provides that with a view to calculating the share of the total number of inspections to be carried out annually within the EU and the Paris MoU region referred to in point (b) of paragraph 2, ships at anchorage shall not be counted unless otherwise specified by the Member State concerned.
35 Dir. 2009/16, Art. 5(2).

complies with its commitment in accordance with that provision if such missed inspections do not exceed: (a) 5% of the total number of Priority I ships with a high risk profile calling at its ports and anchorages; and (b) 10% of the total number of Priority I ships other than those with a high risk profile calling at its ports and anchorages. Notwithstanding the percentages in (a) and (b), Member States must prioritise inspection of ships, which, according to the information provided by the inspection database, call at ports within the EU infrequently. Notwithstanding the percentages in (a) and (b), for Priority I ships calling at anchorages, Member States must prioritise inspection of ships with a high risk profile, which, according to the information provided by the inspection database, call at ports within the EU infrequently.

Modalities allowing a balanced inspection share within the EU

28.056 A Member State in which the total number of calls of Priority I ships exceeds its inspection share referred to in Article 5(2)(b), must be regarded as complying with such commitment, if a number of inspections on Priority I ships carried out by that Member State corresponds at least to such inspection share and if that Member State does not miss more than 30% of the total number of Priority I ships calling at its ports and anchorages.[36] A Member State, in which the total number of calls of Priority I and Priority II ships is less than the inspection share referred to in Article 5(2)(b), must be regarded as complying with such commitment, if that Member State carries out the inspections of Priority I ships required under Article 5(2)(a) and inspections on at least 85% of the total number of Priority II ships calling at its ports and anchorages.[37]

28.057 The Commission shall, in its review referred to in Article 35, examine in particular the impact of this article on the inspection commitment, taking into account the expertise and the experience gained in the Community and under the Paris MoU.[38] The review shall take into account the objective of inspecting all ships calling at ports and anchorages within the Community. If appropriate, the Commission shall propose complementary measures with a view to improving the effectiveness of the inspection system applied in the Community, and, if necessary, a new review of the impact of this article at a later stage.[39]

28.058 Article 8 deals with the postponement of inspections and exceptional circumstances. Article 8(l) provides that a Member State may decide to postpone the inspection of a Priority I ship in the following circumstances: (a) if the inspection may be carried out at the next call of the ship in the same Member State, provided that the ship does not call at any other port in the Community or the Paris MoU region in between and the postponement is not more than 15 days; or (b) if the inspection may be carried out in another port of call within the Community or the Paris MoU region within 15 days, provided the State in which such port of call is located has agreed in advance to perform the inspection. If an inspection is postponed in accordance with point (a) or (b) and recorded in the inspection database, a missed inspection shall not be counted as a missed inspection against the Member States which postponed the inspection. Nevertheless, where an inspection of a

---

36 Dir. 2009/16, Art. 7(1).
37 Dir. 2009/16, Art. 7(2).
38 Dir. 2009/16, Art. 7(3).
39 Ibid.

Priority I ship is not performed, the relevant ship shall not be exempted from being inspected at the next port of call within the Community in accordance with this directive.

28.059 Article 8(2) provides where an inspection is not performed on Priority I ships for operational reasons, it shall not be counted as a missed inspection, provided that the reason for missing the inspection is recorded in the inspection database and the following exceptional circumstances occur: (a) in the judgment of the competent authority the conduct of the inspection would create a risk to the safety of inspectors, the ship, its crew or to the port, or to the marine environment; or (b) the ship call takes place only during night time. In this case Member States shall take the measures necessary to ensure that ships which call regularly during night time are inspected as appropriate.

28.060 Article 8(3) provides that if an inspection is not performed on a ship at anchorage, it shall not be counted as a missed inspection if: (a) the ship is inspected in another port or anchorage within the EU or the Paris MoU region in accordance with Annex I within 15 days; or (b) the ship call takes place only during night time or its duration is too short for the inspection to be carried out satisfactorily, and the reason for missing the inspection is recorded in the inspection database; or (c) in the judgment of the competent authority the conduct of the inspection would create a risk to the safety of inspectors, the ship, its crew or to the port, or to the marine environment, and the reason for missing the inspection is recorded in the inspection database.

Notification of arrival of ships

28.061 Article 9(l) provides that the operator, agent or master of a ship which, in accordance with Article 14, is eligible for an expanded inspection and bound for a port or anchorage of a Member State, must notify its arrival in accordance with the provisions laid down in Annex III. On receipt of the notification referred to in paragraph 1 of this article and in Article 4 of Directive 2002/59 of the European Parliament and of the Council of 27 June 2002 establishing a Community vessel traffic monitoring and information system,[40] the port authority or body or the authority or body designated for that purpose shall forward such information to the competent authority.[41] Electronic means must be used whenever possible for any communication provided for in this article.[42] The procedures and formats developed by Member States for the purposes of Annex III to this directive must comply with the relevant provisions laid down in Directive 2002/59 regarding ships' notifications.[43]

Ship risk profile

28.062 Article 10 provides that all ships calling at a port or anchorage of a Member State must, in the inspection database, be attributed a ship risk profile which determines their respective priority for inspection, the intervals between the inspections and the scope of inspections.[44] The risk profile of a ship must be determined by a combination of generic

---

40 OJ L208/10, 5 August 2002.
41 Dir. 2009/16, Art. 9(2)
42 Dir. 2009/16, Art. 9(3)
43 Dir. 2009/16, Art. 9(4)
44 Dir. 2009/16, Art. 10(l).

and historical risk parameters as follows: (a) generic parameters based on the type, age, flag, recognised organisations involved and company performance in accordance with Annex I, Part I.1 and Annex II; and (b) historical parameters based on the number of deficiencies and detentions during a given period in accordance with Annex I, Part I.2 and Annex II.

28.063 Article 10(3) provides that implementing powers must be conferred on the Commission to implement a methodology for the consideration of generic risk parameters relating in particular to the flag State criteria and company performance criteria. Those implementing acts shall be adopted in accordance with the examination procedure referred to in Article 31(3).

Frequency of inspections

28.064 Article 11 provides that ships calling at ports or anchorages within the EU must be subject to periodic inspections or to additional inspections as follows:

"(a) Ships shall be subject to periodic inspections at predetermined intervals depending on their risk profile in accordance with Annex I, Part I. The interval between periodic inspections of ships shall increase as the risk decreases. For high risk ships, this interval shall not exceed six months.

(b) Ships shall be subject to additional inspections regardless of the period since their last periodic inspection as follows:

– the competent authority shall ensure that ships to which overriding factors listed in Annex I, Part II 2A, apply are inspected,
– ships to which unexpected factors listed in Annex I, Part II 2B, apply may be inspected. The decision to undertake such an additional inspection is left to the professional judgement of the competent authority."

Selection of ships for inspection

28.065 The competent authority shall ensure that ships are selected for inspection on the basis of their risk profile as described in Annex I, Part I, and when overriding or unexpected factors arise in accordance with Annex I, Part II 2A and 2B.[45] With a view to the inspection of ships, the competent authority:

"(a) shall select ships which are due for a mandatory inspection, referred to as 'Priority I' ships, in accordance with the selection scheme described in Annex I, Part II 3A; (b) may select ships which are eligible for inspection, referred to as 'Priority II' ships, in accordance with Annex I, Part II 3B."[46]

Initial and more detailed inspections

28.066 Article 13 provides Member States must ensure that ships which are selected for inspection in accordance with Article 12 are subject to an initial inspection or a more detailed inspection as follows:

---

45 Dir. 2009/16. Art. 12.
46 Dir. 2009/16. Art. 12.

"1. On each initial inspection of a ship, the competent authority shall ensure that the inspector, as a minimum:

    (a) checks the certificates and documents listed in Annex IV required to be kept on board in accordance with Community maritime legislation and Conventions relating to safety and security;

    (b) verifies, where appropriate, whether outstanding deficiencies found during the previous inspection carried out by a Member State or by a State signatory to the Paris MOU have been rectified;

    (c) satisfies himself of the overall condition of the ship, including the hygiene of the ship, including engine room and accommodation.

2. When, after an inspection referred to in point 1, deficiencies to be rectified at the next port of call have been recorded in the inspection database, the competent authority of such next port may decide not to carry out the verifications referred to in point 1(a) and (c).

3. A more detailed inspection shall be carried out, including further checking of compliance with on-board operational requirements, whenever there are clear grounds for believing, after the inspection referred to in point 1, that the condition of a ship or of its equipment or crew does not substantially meet the relevant requirements of a Convention.

'Clear grounds' shall exist when the inspector finds evidence which in his professional judgement warrants a more detailed inspection of the ship, its equipment or its crew.

Examples of 'clear grounds' are set out in Annex V."

Expanded inspections

28.067 Article 14 provides:

"1. The following categories of ships are eligible to an expanded inspection in accordance with Annex I, Part II 3A and 3B:

    – ships with a high risk profile,

    – passenger ships, oil tankers, gas or chemical tankers or bulk carriers, older than 12 years of age,

    – ships with a high risk profile or passenger ships, oil tankers, gas or chemical tankers or bulk carriers, older than 12 years of age, in cases of overriding or unexpected factors,

    – ships subject to a re-inspection following a refusal of access order issued in accordance with Article 16.

2. The operator or master of the ship shall ensure that sufficient time is available in the operating schedule to allow the expanded inspection to be carried out.

Without prejudice to control measures required for security purposes, the ship shall remain in the port until the inspection is completed.

3. On receipt of a pre-notification provided by a ship eligible for a periodic expanded inspection, the competent authority shall inform the ship if no expanded inspection will be carried out.

4. The scope of an expanded inspection, including the risk areas to be covered, is set out in Annex VII. The Commission may adopt detailed measures to ensure uniform conditions for the application of Annex VII. Those implementing acts shall be adopted in accordance with the examination procedure referred to in Article 31(3)."

Safety and security guidelines and procedures

28.068 Article 15 deals with Safety and Security guidelines and procedures. Member States must ensure that their inspectors follow the procedures and guidelines specified in Annex VI to Directive 2009/16, Article 15(1). As far as security checks are concerned, Member States must apply the relevant procedures set out in Annex VI to Directive 2009/16 to all ships referred to in Article 3(1), 3(2) and 3(3) of Regulation 725/2004 of the European Parliament and of the Council,[47] calling at their ports and anchorages, unless they fly the flag of the port State of inspection.[48] The provisions of Article 14 of Directive 2009/16 concerning expanded inspections shall apply to ro-ro ferries and high-speed passenger craft, referred to in Article 2(a) and (b) of Directive 1999/35.[49]

28.069 When a ship has been surveyed in accordance with Articles 6 and 8 of Directive 1999/35 by a host State which is not the flag State of the ship, such specific survey shall be recorded as a more detailed or an expanded inspection, as relevant, in the inspection database and taken into account for the purposes of Articles 10, 11 and 12 of Directive 2009/16 and for calculating the fulfilment of the inspection commitment of each Member State in as much as all the items referred to in Annex VII to this directive are covered.

28.070 Without prejudice to a prevention of operation of a ro-ro ferry or a high-speed passenger craft decided in accordance with Article 10 of Directive 1999/35, the provisions of Directive 2009/16 concerning rectification of deficiencies, detention, refusal of access, follow-up to inspections, detentions and refusal of access, as appropriate, shall apply. The Commission may adopt detailed measures to ensure uniform application of the procedures referred to in paragraph 1 and of the security checks referred to in paragraph 2 of this article. Those implementing acts shall be adopted in accordance with the examination procedure referred to in Article 31(3).

Access refusal measures concerning certain ships

28.071 Article 16(1) deals with access refusal measures concerning certain ships. A Member State must ensure that any ship which:

"– flies the flag of a State whose detention rate falls into the black list, adopted in accordance with the Paris MOU on the basis of information recorded in the inspection database and as published annually by the Commission, and has been detained or has been issued with a prevention of operation order under Directive 1999/35/EC more than twice in the course of the preceding 36 months in a port or anchorage of a Member State or of a State signatory of the Paris MOU, or

– flies the flag of a State whose detention rate falls into the grey list, adopted in accordance with the Paris MOU on basis of information recorded in the inspection database and as published annually by the Commission, and has been detained or has been issued with a prevention of operation order under Directive 1999/35/EC more than twice in the course of the preceding 24 months in a port or anchorage of a Member State or of a State signatory of the Paris MOU, is refused access to its ports and anchorages, except in the situations described in Article 21(6).

---

47 OJ L129/6, 29 April 2009.
48 Dir. 2009/16, Art. 15(2).
49 Dir. 2009/16, Art. 15(3).

Refusal of access shall become applicable as soon as the ship leaves the port or anchorage where it has been the subject of a third detention and where a refusal of access order has been issued."

28.072 The refusal of access order must be lifted only after a period of three months has passed from the date of issue of the order and when the conditions in paragraphs 3 to 9 of Annex VIII are met.[50] If the ship is subject to a second refusal of access, the period shall be 12 months.[51]

28.073 Article 16(3) provides:

"Any subsequent detention in a port or anchorage within the Community shall result in the ship being refused access to any port and anchorage within the Community. This third refusal of access order may be lifted after a period of 24 months has passed from the issue of the order and only if:

– the ship flies the flag of a State whose detention rate falls neither into the black list nor the grey list referred to in paragraph 1,
– the statutory and classification certificates of the ship are issued by an organisation or organisations recognised under Regulation (EC) No 391/2009 of the European Parliament and of the Council of 23 April 2009 on common rules and standards for ship inspection and survey organisations (recast) …,
– the ship is managed by a company with a high performance according to Annex I, Part I.1, and
– the conditions in paragraphs 3 to 9 of Annex VIII are met.

Any ship not meeting the criteria specified in this paragraph, after a period of 24 months has passed from the issue of the order, shall be permanently refused access to any port and anchorage within the Community."

28.074 Any subsequent detention in a port or anchorage within the EU after the third refusal of access shall result in the ship being permanently refused access to any port and anchorage within the EU.[52] For the purpose of Article 16, Member States must comply with the procedures laid down in Annex VIII.[53]

Report of inspection to the master

28.075 On completion of an inspection, a more detailed inspection or an expanded inspection, the inspector shall draw up a report in accordance with Annex IX.[54] The ship's master shall be provided with a copy of the inspection report. Where, following a more detailed inspection, the living and working conditions on the ship are found not to conform to the requirements of the Maritime Labour Convention 2006, the inspector shall forthwith bring the deficiencies to the attention of the master of the ship, with required deadlines for their rectification. In the event that the inspector considers such deficiencies to be significant, or if they relate to a possible complaint under point 19 of Part A of Annex V, the inspector shall also bring the deficiencies to the attention of the appropriate seafarers' and shipowners' organisations in the Member State in which the inspection is

---

50 Dir. 2009/16, Art. 16(2).
51 Ibid.
52 Dir. 2009/16, Art. 16(4).
53 Dir. 2009/16, Art. 16(5).
54 Dir. 2009/16, Art. 17.

carried out, and may: (a) notify a representative of the flag State; and (b) provide the competent authorities of the next port of call with the relevant information.

28.076 In respect of matters concerning the Maritime Labour Convention 2006, the Member State in which the inspection is carried out shall have the right to transmit a copy of the inspector's report, to be accompanied by any reply received from the competent authorities of the flag State within the prescribed deadline, to the Director-General of the International Labour Office with a view to such action as may be considered appropriate and expedient in order to ensure that a record is kept of such information and that it is brought to the attention of parties who might be interested in availing themselves of relevant recourse procedures.

Complaints

28.077 All complaints must be subject to a rapid initial assessment by the competent authority.[55] This assessment shall make it possible to determine whether a complaint is justified.[56] Should that be the case, the competent authority shall take the necessary action on the complaint, in particular, ensuring that anyone directly concerned by that complaint can make their views known.[57] Where the competent authority deems the complaint to be manifestly unfounded, it shall inform the complainant of its decision and of the reasons therefor.[58] The identity of the complainant shall not be revealed to the master or the shipowner of the ship concerned.[59] The inspector shall take appropriate steps to safeguard the confidentiality of complaints made by seafarers, including ensuring confidentiality during any interviews of seafarers.[60] Member States must inform the flag State administration, with a copy to the ILO if appropriate, of complaints not manifestly unfounded and of follow-up actions taken.[61]

Onshore Maritime Labour Convention 2006 complaint-handling procedures

28.078 A complaint by a seafarer alleging a breach of the requirements of the Maritime Labour Convention 2006 (including seafarers' rights) may be reported to an inspector in the port at which the seafarer's ship has called. In such cases, the inspector shall undertake an initial investigation.[62] Where appropriate, given the nature of the complaint, the initial investigation shall include consideration of whether the on-board complaint procedures provided for under Regulation 5.1.5 of the Maritime Labour Convention 2006 have been pursued.[63] The inspector may also conduct a more detailed inspection in accordance with Article 13 of this directive.[64] The inspector must, where appropriate, seek to promote a resolution of the complaint at the ship-board level.[65] In the event that

---

55 Dir. 2009/16, Art. 18.
56 Ibid.
57 Ibid.
58 Ibid.
59 Ibid.
60 Ibid.
61 Ibid.
62 Dir. 2009/16, Art. 18a(1).
63 Dir. 2009/16, Art. 18a(2).
64 Ibid.
65 Dir. 2009/16, Art. 18a(3).

the investigation or the inspection reveals a non-conformity that falls within the scope of Article 19, that article shall apply. Where Article 18(4) does not apply and a complaint by a seafarer related to matters covered by the Maritime Labour Convention 2006 has not been resolved at the ship-board level, the inspector shall forthwith notify the flag State, seeking, within a prescribed deadline, advice and a corrective plan of action to be submitted by the flag State. A report of any inspection carried out shall be transmitted by electronic means to the inspection database referred to in Article 24.[66]

28.079 Where the complaint has not been resolved following action taken in accordance with paragraph 5, the port State shall transmit a copy of the inspector's report to the Director-General of the International Labour Office.[67] The report must be accompanied by any reply received within the prescribed deadline from the competent authority of the flag State.[68] The appropriate seafarers' and shipowners' organisations in the port State shall be similarly informed.[69] In addition, statistics and information regarding complaints that have been resolved shall be regularly submitted by the port State to the ILO's Director-General.[70] Such submissions are provided in order that, on the basis of such action as may be considered appropriate and expedient, a record is kept of such information and brought to the attention of parties, including seafarers' and shipowners' organisations, which might be interested in availing themselves of relevant recourse procedures.[71]

28.080 To ensure uniform conditions for the implementation of Article 18a, implementing powers shall be conferred on the Commission regarding the setting-up of a harmonised electronic format and procedure for the reporting of follow-up actions taken by Member States. Those implementing acts shall be adopted in accordance with the examination procedure referred to in Article 31(3).[72]

28.081 Article 18a is without prejudice to Article 18.[73] The fourth paragraph of Article 18 shall also apply to complaints relating to matters covered by the Maritime Labour Convention 2006.[74]

Rectification and detention

28.082 The competent authority shall be satisfied that any deficiencies confirmed or revealed by the inspection are, or will be, rectified in accordance with the conventions.[75]

28.083 In the case of deficiencies which are clearly hazardous to safety, health or the environment, the competent authority of the port State where the ship is being inspected shall ensure that the ship is detained or that the operation in the course of which the deficiencies are revealed is stopped. The detention order or stoppage of an operation shall not be lifted until the hazard is removed or until such authority establishes that the ship can,

---

66 Dir. 2009/16, Art. 18a(5).
67 Dir. 2009/16, Art. 18a(6).
68 Ibid.
69 Ibid.
70 Ibid.
71 Ibid.
72 Dir. 2009/16, Art. 18a(7).
73 Dir. 2009/16, Art. 18a(8).
74 Ibid.
75 Dir. 2009/16, Art. 19(1).

subject to any necessary conditions, proceed to sea or the operation be resumed without risk to the safety and health of passengers or crew, or risk to other ships, or without there being an unreasonable threat of harm to the marine environment.[76]

28.084 In the case of living and working conditions on board which are clearly hazardous to the safety, health or security of seafarers or deficiencies which constitute a serious or repeated breach of the Maritime Labour Convention 2006 requirements (including seafarers' rights), the competent authority of the port State where the ship is being inspected shall ensure that the ship is detained or that the operation in the course of which the deficiencies are revealed is stopped.[77] The detention order or stoppage of an operation shall not be lifted until those deficiencies have been rectified or if the competent authority has accepted a plan of action to rectify those deficiencies and it is satisfied that the plan will be implemented in an expeditious manner. Prior to accepting a plan of action, the inspector may consult the flag State.[78]

28.085 When exercising his professional judgment as to whether or not a ship is to be detained, the inspector shall apply the criteria set out in Annex X.[79]

28.086 If the inspection reveals that the ship is not equipped with a functioning voyage data recorder, when use of such recorder is compulsory in accordance with Directive 2002/59, the competent authority shall ensure that the ship is detained.[80] If such deficiency cannot be readily rectified in the port of detention, the competent authority may either allow the ship to proceed to the appropriate repair yard nearest to the port of detention where it may be readily rectified or require the deficiency to be rectified within a maximum period of 30 days, as provided for in the guidelines developed by the Paris MoU. For these purposes, the procedures laid down in Article 21 shall apply.[81]

28.087 In exceptional circumstances, where the overall condition of a ship is obviously substandard, the competent authority may suspend the inspection of that ship until the responsible parties take the steps necessary to ensure that it complies with the relevant requirements of the conventions.[82]

28.088 In the event of detention, the competent authority shall immediately inform, in writing and including the report of inspection, the flag State administration or, when this is not possible, the Consul or, in his absence, the nearest diplomatic representative of that State, of all the circumstances in which intervention was deemed necessary.[83] In addition, nominated surveyors or recognised organisations responsible for the issue of classification certificates or statutory certificates in accordance with conventions shall also be notified where relevant. Moreover, if a ship is prevented from sailing due to serious or repeated breach of the requirements of the Maritime Labour Convention 2006 (including seafarers' rights) or due to the living and working conditions on board being clearly hazardous to the safety, health or security of seafarers, the competent authority shall forthwith notify the flag State accordingly and invite a representative of the flag State to be

---

76 Dir. 2009/16, Art. 19(2).
77 Dir. 2009/16, Art. 19(2a).
78 Ibid.
79 Dir. 2009/16, Art. 19(3).
80 Dir. 2009/16, Art. 19(4).
81 Ibid.
82 Dir. 2009/16, Art. 19(5).
83 Dir. 2009/16, Art. 19(6).

present, if possible, requesting the flag State to reply within a prescribed deadline.[84] The competent authority must also inform forthwith the appropriate seafarers' and ship-owners' organisations in the port State in which the inspection was carried out.

28.089 This Directive 2009/16 is without prejudice to the additional requirements of the conventions concerning notification and reporting procedures related to PSC.[85]

28.090 When PSC is exercised under Directive 2009/16, all possible efforts shall be made to avoid a ship being unduly detained or delayed.[86] If a ship is unduly detained or delayed, the owner or operator shall be entitled to compensation for any loss or damage suffered.[87] In any instance of alleged undue detention or delay the burden of proof shall lie with the owner or operator of the ship.[88]

28.091 In order to alleviate port congestion, a competent authority may allow a detained ship to be moved to another part of the port if it is safe to do so.[89] However, the risk of port congestion shall not be a consideration when deciding on a detention or on a release from detention.[90] Port authorities or bodies must co-operate with the competent authority with a view to facilitating the accommodation of detained ships.[91]

28.092 The port authorities or bodies must be informed at the earliest convenience when a detention order is issued.[92]

Right of appeal

28.093 The owner or operator of a ship or his representative in the Member State shall have a right of appeal against detention or refusal of access by the competent authority.[93] An appeal shall not cause the detention or refusal of access to be suspended.[94] Member States must establish and maintain appropriate procedures for this purpose in accordance with their national legislation.[95] The competent authority must properly inform the master of a ship referred to in Article 20(1) of the right of appeal and the practical arrangements relating thereto.[96] When, as a result of an appeal or of a request made by the owner or the operator of a ship or his representative, a detention order or a refusal of access order is revoked or amended: (a) Member States shall ensure that the inspection database is amended accordingly without delay; and (b) the Member State where the detention order or refusal of access order is issued shall, within 24 hours of such a decision, ensure that the information published in accordance with Article 26 is rectified.[97]

---

84 Ibid.
85 Dir. 2009/16, Art. 19(7).
86 Dir. 2009/16, Art. 19(8).
87 Ibid.
88 Ibid.
89 Dir. 2009/16, Art. 19(9).
90 Ibid.
91 Ibid.
92 Dir. 2009/16, Art. 19(10).
93 Dir. 2009/16, Art. 20(1).
94 Ibid.
95 Dir. 2009/16, Art. 20(2).
96 Dir. 2009/16, Art. 20(3).
97 Dir. 2009/16, Art. 20(4).

Follow-up to inspections and detentions

28.094 Article 21 deals with follow-up to inspections and detentions which deal with the situation where the issue cannot be dealt with on the spot.

28.095 Article 21(1) provides that where deficiencies referred to in Article 19(2) cannot be rectified in the port of inspection, the competent authority of that Member State may allow the ship concerned to proceed without undue delay to the appropriate repair yard nearest to the port of detention, as chosen by the master and the authorities concerned, where follow-up action can be taken, provided that the conditions determined by the competent authority of the flag State and agreed by that Member State are complied with. Such conditions shall ensure that the ship can proceed without risk to the safety and health of passengers or crew, or risk to other ships, or without there being an unreasonable threat of harm to the marine environment. It is clear from Article 21(2) that where the decision to send a ship to a repair yard is due to a lack of compliance with IMO Resolution A.744(18), either with respect to a ship's documentation or with respect to a ship's structural failures and deficiencies, the competent authority may require that the necessary thickness measurements be carried out in the port of detention before the ship is allowed to sail. In the circumstances referred to in Article 29(1) then pursuant to Article 29(3), the competent authority of the Member State in the port of inspection shall notify the competent authority of the State where the repair yard is situated, the parties mentioned in Article 19(6) and any other authority as appropriate of all the conditions for the voyage. The competent authority of a Member State receiving such notification must inform the notifying authority of the action taken. Article 29(4) states that Member States must take measures to ensure that access to any port or anchorage within the EU is refused to ships referred to in Article 21(1) which proceed to sea: (a) without complying with the conditions determined by the competent authority of any Member State in the port of inspection; or (b) which refuse to comply with the applicable requirements of the conventions by not calling into the indicated repair yard. Such refusal shall be maintained until the owner or operator provides evidence to the satisfaction of the competent authority of the Member State where the ship was found defective, demonstrating that the ship fully complies with all applicable requirements of the conventions. In the circumstances referred to in Article 21(4)(a), the competent authority of the Member State where the ship was found defective shall immediately alert the competent authorities of all the other Member States. In the circumstances referred to in Article 21(4)(b), the competent authority of the Member State in which the repair yard lies must immediately alert the competent authorities of all the other Member States. Before denying entry, the Member State may request consultations with the flag administration of the ship concerned. By way of derogation from Article 21(4), access to a specific port or anchorage may be permitted by the relevant authority of that port State in the event of force majeure or overriding safety considerations, or to reduce or minimise the risk of pollution or to have deficiencies rectified, provided that adequate measures to the satisfaction of the competent authority of such Member State have been implemented by the owner, the operator or the master of the ship to ensure safe entry.

Professional profile of inspectors

28.096 Article 22 provides that inspections must be carried out only by inspectors who fulfil the qualification criteria specified in Annex XI and who are authorised to carry out PSC by the competent authority. Such a restriction or limitation is reasonable and fair given the intrusive nature of, and extensive power involved in, inspections.

28.097 When the required professional expertise cannot be provided by the competent authority of the port State, the inspector of that competent authority may be assisted by any person with the required expertise. It will be noted that the latter person is *assisting* the inspector but not conducting the inspection.

28.098 The competent authority, the inspectors carrying out PSC and the persons assisting them shall have no commercial interest either in the port of inspection or in the ships inspected, nor shall the inspectors be employed by, or undertake work on behalf of, non-governmental organisations which issue statutory and classification certificates or which carry out the surveys necessary for the issue of those certificates to ships. Such independence is critical to the integrity of the system and any lack of independence (in a non-trivial manner) should be seen as fatal to the independence of the inspection.

28.099 Each inspector shall carry a personal document in the form of an identity card issued by his competent authority in accordance with Commission Directive 96/40 of 25 June 1996 establishing a common model for an identity card for inspectors carrying out PSC.[98]

28.100 Member States shall ensure that the competence of inspectors and their compliance with the minimum criteria referred to in Annex XI are verified, before authorising them to carry out inspections and periodically thereafter in the light of the training scheme referred to in paragraph 7.

28.101 Member States shall ensure that inspectors receive appropriate training in relation to changes to the PSC system applied in the EU as laid down in this directive and amendments to the conventions.

28.102 In co-operation with Member States, the Commission shall develop and promote a harmonised EU scheme for the training and assessment of competences of PSC inspectors by Member States.

Reports from pilots and port authorities

28.103 Article 23 deals with pilots and port authorities being suitable monitors for the system. Member States shall take appropriate measures to ensure that their pilots engaged on the berthing or unberthing of ships or engaged on ships bound for a port or in transit within a Member State immediately inform the competent authority of the port State or the coastal State, as appropriate, whenever they learn in the course of their normal duties that there are apparent anomalies which may prejudice the safe navigation of the ship, or which may pose a threat of harm to the marine environment. If port authorities or bodies, in the course of their normal duties, learn that a ship within their port has apparent anomalies which may prejudice the safety of the ship or poses an unreasonable threat of harm to the marine environment, such authority or body shall immediately inform the competent authority of the port State concerned. Member States shall require pilots and

---

98 OJ L196/8, 7 August 1996.

port authorities or bodies to report at least the following information, in electronic format whenever possible: (a) ship information (name, IMO identification number, call sign and flag); (b) sailing information (last port of call, port of destination); and (c) description of apparent anomalies found on board. Member States must ensure that proper follow-up action is taken on apparent anomalies notified by pilots and port authorities or bodies and shall record the details of action taken. Implementing powers must be conferred on the Commission to adopt measures for the implementation of this article, including harmonised procedures for the reporting of apparent anomalies by pilots and port authorities or bodies and of follow-up actions taken by Member States. Those implementing acts shall be adopted in accordance with the examination procedure referred to in Article 31(3).

Inspection database

28.104 There is a need to ensure that information on inspections is collated in, and available from, a database. Article 24 addresses that issue. The Commission shall develop, maintain and update the inspection database, building upon the expertise and experience under the Paris MoU. The inspection database must contain all the information required for the implementation of the inspection system set up under this directive and shall include the functionalities set out in Annex XII. Equally, Member States must take the appropriate measures to ensure that the information on the actual time of arrival and the actual time of departure of any ship calling at their ports and anchorages, together with an identifier of the port concerned, is transferred within a reasonable time to the inspection database through the Community maritime information exchange system "SafeSeaNet" referred to in Article 3(s) of Directive 2002/59. Once they have transferred such information to the inspection database through SafeSeaNet, Member States are exempted from the provision of data in accordance with paragraphs 1.2 and 2(a) and (b) of Annex XIV to the directive. Member States must ensure that the information related to inspections performed in accordance with the directive is transferred to the inspection database as soon as the inspection report is completed or the detention lifted. Within 72 hours, Member States must ensure that the information transferred to the inspection database is validated for publication purposes. On the basis of the inspection data provided by Member States, the Commission shall be able to retrieve from the inspection database any relevant data concerning the implementation of this directive, in particular on the risk profile of the ship, on ships due for inspections, on ships' movement data and on the inspection commitments of each Member State. Member States must have access to all the information recorded in the inspection database which is relevant for implementing the inspection procedures of the directive. Interestingly, and going beyond the EU, Member States and third signatories to the Paris MoU shall be granted access to any data they have recorded in the inspection database and to data on ships flying their flag.

Exchange of information and co-operation

28.105 Each Member State must, by virtue of Article 25, ensure that its port authorities or bodies and other relevant authorities or bodies provide the competent PSC authority with the following types of information in their possession: (a) information notified in accordance with Article 9 and Annex III; (b) information concerning ships which have failed to notify any information according to the requirements of this directive, and to Directive 2000/59 of the European Parliament and of the Council of 27 November 2000 on port reception facilities for ship-generated waste and cargo residues[99] and Directive 2002/59, as well as, if appropriate, with Regulation (EC) No 725/2004; (c) information concerning ships which have proceeded to sea without having complied with Articles 7 or 10 of Directive 2000/59; (d) information concerning ships which have been denied entry or expelled from port on security grounds; and (e) information on apparent anomalies in accordance with Article 23.

Publication of information

28.106 The Commission must, pursuant to Article 26, make available and maintain on a public website the information on inspections, detentions and refusals of access in accordance with Annex XIII, building upon the expertise and experience under the Paris MoU.

Publication of a list of companies with a low and very low performance

28.107 The Commission must, by virtue of Article 27, establish and publish regularly on a public website information relating to companies whose performance, in view of determining the ship risk profile referred to in Annex I Part I, has been considered as low and very low for a period of three months or more. Implementing powers must be conferred on the Commission to establish the detailed arrangements for publication of the information referred to in the first paragraph, the criteria for aggregating the relevant data and the frequency of updates. Those implementing acts shall be adopted in accordance with the examination procedure referred to in Article 31(3).

Reimbursement of costs

28.108 Article 28 provides that should the inspections referred to in Articles 13 and 14 confirm or reveal deficiencies in relation to the requirements of a convention warranting the detention of a ship, all costs relating to the inspections in any normal accounting period shall be covered by the shipowner or the operator or by his representative in the port State. This is reasonable. All costs relating to inspections carried out by the competent authority of a Member State under the provisions of Articles 16 and 21(4) shall be charged to the owner or operator of the ship. This is also reasonable and acts as a deterrent. In the case of detention of a ship, all costs relating to the detention in port shall be borne by the owner or operator of the ship. The detention shall not be lifted until full payment is made or a sufficient guarantee is given for reimbursement of the costs.

Data to monitor implementation

28.109 Member States must, under Article 29, provide the Commission with the information listed in Annex XIV at the intervals stated in that Annex.[100]

---

99 OJ L332/81, 28 December 2000.
100 Dir. 2009/16, Art. 29.

Monitoring of compliance and performance of Member States

28.110 In order to ensure the effective implementation of the directive and to monitor the overall functioning of the Community's PSC regime in accordance with Article 2(b)(i) of Regulation 1406/2002, the Commission shall collect the necessary information and carry out visits to Member States.

Delegated acts

28.111 The Commission is, under Article 30a, empowered to adopt delegated acts in accordance with Article 30b, concerning amendments to Annex VI, in order to add to the list set out in that annex further instructions relating to PSC adopted by the Paris MoU Organisation. Article 30b provides that the power to adopt delegated acts is conferred on the Commission subject to the conditions laid down in Article 30.

28.112 The power to adopt delegated acts referred to in Article 30a shall be conferred on the Commission for a period of five years from 20 August 2013. The Commission shall draw up a report in respect of the delegation of power not later than nine months before the end of the five-year period. The delegation of power shall be tacitly extended for periods of an identical duration, unless the European Parliament or the Council opposes such extension not later than three months before the end of each period.

28.113 The delegation of power referred to in Article 30a may be revoked at any time by the European Parliament or by the Council. A decision to revoke shall put an end to the delegation of the power specified in that decision. It shall take effect the day following the publication of the decision in the *Official Journal of the European Union* or at a later date specified therein. It shall not affect the validity of any delegated acts already in force.

28.114 As soon as it adopts a delegated act, the Commission shall notify it simultaneously to the European Parliament and to the Council.

28.115 A delegated act adopted pursuant to Article 30a shall enter into force only if no objection has been expressed either by the European Parliament or the Council within a period of two months of notification of that act to the European Parliament and the Council or if, before the expiry of that period, the European Parliament and the Council have both informed the Commission that they will not object. That period shall be extended by two months at the initiative of the European Parliament or of the Council.

Committee

28.116 By virtue of Article 31, the Commission shall be assisted by the Committee on Safe Seas and the Prevention of Pollution from Ships ("COSS") established by Article 3 of Regulation 2099/2002 of the European Parliament and the Council. That Committee shall be a committee within the meaning of Regulation 182/2011. Where reference is made to this paragraph, Article 5 of Regulation 182/2011 shall apply. Where the committee delivers no opinion on a draft implementing act to be adopted pursuant to Articles 10(3), 23(5) and the second paragraph of Article 27 respectively, the Commission shall not adopt the draft implementing act and the third subparagraph of Article 5(4) of Regulation 182/2011 shall apply.

Implementing rules

28.117 Article 33 provides that when establishing the implementing rules referred to in Articles 10(3), 14(4), 15(4), 18a(7), 23(5) and 27 in accordance with the procedures referred to in Article 31(3), the Commission must take specific care that those rules take into account the expertise and experience gained with the inspection system in the EU and build upon the expertise of the Paris MoU.

Penalties

28.118 The system would be deficient and ineffective if there were no penalties. Article 34 therefore provides that Member States must lay down a system of penalties for the breach of national provisions adopted pursuant to the directive and shall take all the measures necessary to ensure that those penalties are applied. The penalties provided for shall be effective, proportionate and dissuasive. The reason why the directive mandates the Member States to provide for penalties but does not contain those penalties itself lies in the limited competence of the EU to impose such penalties itself.

Review

28.119 Article 35 provided that the Commission must review the implementation of the directive no later than 30 June 2012. The review was to examine, *inter alia*, the fulfilment of the overall EU inspection commitment laid down in Article 5, the number of PSC inspectors in each Member State, the number of inspections carried out, and the compliance with the annual inspection commitment by each Member State and the implementation of Articles 6, 7 and 8. The Commission would communicate the findings of the review to the European Parliament and the Council and would determine on the basis of the review whether it was necessary to propose an amending directive or further legislation in this area.

Implementation and notification

28.120 Member States must, by virtue of Article 36, adopt and publish, by 31 December 2010, the laws, regulations and administrative provisions necessary to comply with the directive. They have had to apply those provisions since 1 January 2011. When Member States adopt those measures, they must contain a reference to the directive or be accompanied by such a reference on the occasion of their official publication. They shall also include a statement that references in existing laws, regulations and administrative provisions to the directive repealed by the directive shall be construed as references to the directive. Member States shall determine how such reference is to be made and how that statement is to be formulated. Member States must communicate to the Commission the text of the main provisions of national law adopted in the field covered by the directive. Additionally, the Commission must inform the European Parliament and the Council on a regular basis of progress in the implementation of the directive within the Member States, in particular with a view to a uniform application of the inspection system in the EU.

Elements of the Community Port State Inspection System

28.121 Annex I is entitled "Elements of the Community Port State Inspection System". It is relevant to Article 5 of the directive. Annex II deals with "Design of Ship Risk Profile". It is relevant to Article 10(2) of the directive. Annex III is entitled "Notification". It is referred to in Article 9(1) of the directive. Annex IV is entitled "List of Certificates and Documents". Annex IV contains a list of certificates and documents. It is referred to in Article 13(1). Annex V contains examples of "clear grounds". This is referred to in Article 13(3). Annex VI is entitled "procedures for the control of ships". This is referred to in Article 15(1). Annex VII is entitled "expanded inspection of ships". This is referred to in Article 14. Annex VIII is entitled "provisions concerning refusal of access to ports and anchorages within the Community". This is referred to in Article 16. Annex IX is entitled "Inspection Report". It is referred to in Article 17 of the directive. Annex X is entitled "Criteria for Detention of a Ship". It is referred to in Article 19(3) of the directive. Annex XI is entitled "Minimum Criteria for Inspectors". It is referred to in Articles 22(1) and (5). Annex XII is entitled "Functionalities of the Inspection Database". It is referred to in Article 24(1). Annex XIII is entitled "Publication of Information related to Inspections, Detentions and Refusals of Access in Ports and Anchorages of Member States". It is referred to in Article 26. Annex XIV is entitled "Data Provided in the Context of Monitoring Implementation". It is referred to in Article 29. Annex XV deals with the repealed directive with its successive amendments (referred to in Article 37) and the list of time limits for transposition into national law (referred to in Article 37). Annex XXI is a correlation table.

D. DIRECTIVE 2009/15 OF 23 APRIL 2009 OF THE EUROPEAN PARLIAMENT AND OF THE COUNCIL ON THE COMMON RULES AND STANDARDS FOR SHIP INSPECTION AND SURVEY ORGANISATIONS AND FOR THE RELEVANT ACTIVITIES OF MARITIME ADMINISTRATIONS

Introduction

28.122 On 23 April 2009, Directive 2009/15 was adopted by the Parliament and Council setting out common rules and standards for ship inspection and survey organisations and for the relevant activities of maritime administrations.[101] Directive 2009/15 has been amended by Commission Implementing Directive 2014/11 of 17 December 2014.[102] The measure was based on the TEC generally (which would now be the TFEU) and, in particular, Article 80(2) of that treaty (which would now be Article 100(2) of the TFEU). Article 15 provides that the directive entered into force on the twentieth day following its publication in the *Official Journal of the European Union*. While Article 13 provides for the entry into force of the directive:

> "1. Member States shall bring into force the laws, regulations and administrative provisions necessary to comply with this Directive by 17 June 2011. They shall forthwith inform the Commission thereof.

---

101 OJ L131/47, 28 May 2009.
102 OJ L366/83, 20 December 2014.

When they are adopted by Member States, these measures shall contain a reference to this Directive or shall be accompanied by such reference on the occasion of their official publication. They shall also include a statement that references in existing laws, regulations and administrative provisions to the directives repealed by this Directive shall be construed as references to this Directive. The methods of making such references shall be laid down by Member States.

2.   Member States shall communicate to the Commission the text of the main provisions of national law which they adopt in the field covered by this Directive."

28.123 The background to the directive is clear from the recitals:

"(1)   Council Directive 94/57 ... of 22 November 1994 on common rules and standards for ship inspection and survey organisations and for the relevant activities of maritime administrations[103] has been substantially amended several times. Since further amendments are to be made, it should be recast in the interests of clarity.

(2)   In view of the nature of the provisions of Directive 94/57 ... it seems appropriate that its provisions be recast in two different Community legal instruments, namely a Directive and a Regulation.

(3)   In its Resolution of 8 June 1993 on a common policy on safe seas, the Council set the objective of removing all substandard vessels from Community waters and gave priority to Community action designed to secure the effective and uniform implementation of international rules by drawing up common standards for classification societies.

(4)   Safety and pollution prevention at sea may be effectively enhanced by strictly applying international conventions, codes and resolutions while furthering the objective of freedom to provide services.

(5)   The control of compliance of ships with the uniform international standards for safety and prevention of pollution of the seas is the responsibility of flag and port States.

(6)   Member States are responsible for the issuing of international certificates for safety and the prevention of pollution provided for under conventions such as the International Convention for the Safety of Life at Sea of 1 November 1974 (SOLAS 74), the International Convention on Load Lines of 5 April 1966 and the International Convention for the Prevention of Pollution from Ships of 2 November 1973 (Marpol), and for the implementation of those conventions.

(7)   In compliance with such conventions all Member States may authorise to a varying extent recognised organisations for the certification of such compliance and may delegate the issue of the relevant certificates for safety and the prevention of pollution.

(8)   Worldwide a large number of the existing organisations recognised by International Maritime Organisation (IMO) Contracting Parties do not ensure either adequate implementation of the rules or sufficient reliability when acting on behalf of national administrations as they do not have reliable and adequate structures and experience to enable them to carry out their duties in a highly professional manner.

(9)   In accordance with SOLAS 74 Chapter II-1, Part A-1, Regulation 3-1, Member States are responsible for ensuring that ships flying their flag are designed, constructed and maintained in compliance with the structural, mechanical and electrical requirements of organisations, recognised by administrations. These organisations therefore produce and implement rules for the design, construction, maintenance and inspection of ships and they are responsible for inspecting ships on behalf of the flag States and certifying that those ships meet the requirements of the international conventions for the issue of the relevant certificates. To enable them to carry out that duty in a satisfactory manner they need to have strict independence, highly specialised technical competence and rigorous quality management.

(10)   Ship inspection and survey organisations play an important role in Community legislation concerning maritime safety.

---

103   OJ L319, 12.12.1994, p. 20.

(11) Ship inspection and survey organisations should be able to offer their services throughout the Community and compete with each other while providing equal levels of safety and of environmental protection. The necessary professional standards for their activities should therefore be uniformly established and applied across the Community.

(12) The issue of the cargo ship safety radio certificate may be entrusted to private bodies having sufficient expertise and qualified personnel.

(13) A Member State may restrict the number of recognised organisations it authorises in accordance with its needs, based on objective and transparent grounds, subject to control exercised by the Commission in accordance with a committee procedure.

(14) This Directive should ensure freedom to provide services in the Community; accordingly the Community should agree with those third countries where some of the recognised organisations are located, to ensure equal treatment for the recognised organisations located in the Community.

(15) A tight involvement of the national administrations in ship surveys and in the issue of the related certificates is necessary to ensure full compliance with the international safety rules even if the Member States rely upon recognised organisations, which are not part of their administration for carrying out statutory duties. It is appropriate, therefore, to establish a close working relationship between the administrations and the recognised organisations authorised by them, which may require that the recognised organisations have a local representation on the territory of the Member State on behalf of which they perform their duties.

(16) When a recognised organisation, its inspectors, or its technical staff issue the relevant certificates on behalf of the administration, Member States should consider enabling them, as regards these delegated activities, to be subject to proportionate legal safeguards and judicial protection, including the exercise of appropriate rights of defence, apart from immunity, which is a prerogative that can only be invoked by Member States as an inseparable right of sovereignty and therefore that cannot be delegated.

(17) Divergence in terms of financial liability regimes among the recognised organisations working on behalf of the Member States would impede the proper implementation of this Directive. In order to contribute to solving this problem it is appropriate to bring about a degree of harmonisation at Community level of the liability arising out of any marine casualty caused by a recognised organisation, as decided by a court of law, including settlement of a dispute through arbitration procedures.

(18) The measures necessary for the implementation of this Directive should be adopted in accordance with Council Decision 1999/468 ... of 28 June 1999 laying down the procedures for the exercise of implementing powers conferred on the Commission...

(19) In particular the Commission should be empowered to amend this Directive in order to incorporate subsequent amendments to the international conventions, protocols, codes and resolutions related thereto. Since those measures are of general scope and are designed to amend non-essential elements of this Directive, inter alia by supplementing it with new non-essential elements, they must be adopted in accordance with the regulatory procedure with scrutiny provided for in Article 5a of Decision 1999/468...

(20) Member States should nevertheless be left with the possibility of suspending or withdrawing their authorisation of a recognised organisation while informing the Commission and the other Member States of their decisions and giving substantiated reasons therefor.

(21) Member States should periodically assess the performance of the recognised organisations working on their behalf and provide the Commission and all the other Member States with precise information related to such performance.

(22) As port authorities, Member States are required to enhance safety and prevention of pollution in Community waters through priority inspection of ships carrying certificates of organisations which do not fulfil the common criteria, thereby ensuring that ships flying the flag of a third State do not receive more favourable treatment.

(23) At present there are no uniform international standards to which all ships must conform either at the building stage or during their entire lifetime, as regards hull, machinery and electrical and control installations. Such standards may be fixed according to the rules of

recognised organisations or to equivalent standards to be decided by the national adminis-trations in accordance with the procedure laid down in Directive 98/34 ... of the European Parliament and of the Council of 22 June 1998 laying down a procedure for the provision of information in the field of technical standards and regulations and of rules on Informa-tion Society services.[104]

(24) Since the objective of this Directive, namely to establish measures to be followed by the Member States in their relationship with organisations entrusted with the inspection, survey and certification of ships, operating in the Community, cannot be sufficiently achieved by the Member States and can therefore, by reason of the scale of the action, be better achieved at Community level, the Community may adopt measures, in accordance with the principle of subsidiarity as set out in Article 5 of the Treaty. In accordance with the prin-ciple of proportionality, as set out in that Article, this Directive does not go beyond what is necessary in order to achieve that objective.

(25) The obligation to transpose this Directive into national law should be confined to those pro-visions which represent a substantive change as compared with the Directive 94/57. ... The obligation to transpose the provisions which are unchanged arises under that Directive.

(26) This Directive should be without prejudice to the obligations of the Member States relating to the time limits for transposition into national law of the Directives set out in Annex I, Part B.

(27) In accordance with point 34 of the Interinstitutional Agreement on better law-making,[105] Member States are encouraged to draw up, for themselves and in the interest of the Com-munity, their own tables, illustrating, as far as possible, the correlation between this Direc-tive and the transposition measures, and to make them public.

(28) Measures to be followed by ship inspection and survey organisations are laid down in Regulation ... 391/2009 of the European Parliament and the Council of 23 April 2009 on common rules and standards for ship inspection and survey organisations (recast)..."

Purpose of the directive

28.124 The directive establishes measures to be followed by the Member States in their relationship with organisations entrusted with the inspection, survey and certifica-tion of ships for compliance with the international conventions on safety at sea and pre-vention of marine pollution, while furthering the objective of freedom to provide services.[106] This includes the development and implementation of safety requirements for hull, machinery and electrical and control installations of ships falling under the scope of the international conventions.

Definitions used in the directive

28.125 Article 2 sets out various definitions for the purpose of the directive. The term "ship" means a ship falling within the scope of the international conventions. The phrase "ship flying the flag of a Member State" means a ship registered in and flying the flag of a Member State in accordance with its legislation. Ships not corresponding to this defini-tion are assimilated to ships flying the flag of a third country. The expression "inspections and surveys" means inspections and surveys that are mandatory under the international conventions. The phrase "international conventions" means the SOLAS 74 with the

---

104 OJ L204/37, 21.7.1998.
105 OJ C321/1, 31.12.2003.
106 Art. 1.

exception of chapter XI-2 of the annex thereto, the LL 66 and the MARPOL of 2 November 1973, together with the protocols and amendments thereto, and the related codes of mandatory status in all Member States, with the exception of paragraphs 16.1, 18.1 and 19 of part 2 of the IMO Instruments Implementation Code, and of sections 1.1, 1.3, 3.9.3.1, 3.9.3.2 and 3.9.3.3 of part 2 of the IMO Code for Recognized Organizations, in their up-to-date version. The word "organisation" means a legal entity, its subsidiaries and any other entities under its control, which jointly or separately carry out tasks falling under the scope of the directive. The term "control" means, for the purpose of the word "organisation", rights, contracts or any other means, in law or in fact, which, either separately or in combination confer the possibility of exercising decisive influence on a legal entity or enable that entity to carry out tasks falling under the scope of the directive. The expression "recognised organisation" means an organisation recognised in accordance with Regulation 391/2009. The word "authorisation" means an act whereby a Member State grants an authorisation or delegates powers to a recognised organisation. The expression "statutory certificate" means a certificate issued by or on behalf of a flag State in accordance with the international conventions. The term "rules and procedures" means a recognised organisation's requirements for the design, construction, equipment, maintenance and survey of ships. The phrase "class certificate" means a document issued by a recognised organisation certifying the fitness of a ship for a particular use or service in accordance with the rules and procedures laid down and made public by that recognised organisation. The expression "cargo ship safety radio certificate" means the certificate introduced by the 1988 Protocol amending SOLAS, adopted by the International Maritime Organization ("IMO").

Article 3: Appropriate enforcement

28.126 Article 3 provides:

"1. In assuming their responsibilities and obligations under the international conventions, Member States shall ensure that their competent administrations can ensure appropriate enforcement of the provisions thereof, in particular with regard to the inspection and survey of ships and the issue of statutory certificates and exemption certificates as provided for by the international conventions. Member States shall act in accordance with the relevant provisions of the Annex and the Appendix to IMO Resolution A.847(20) on guidelines to assist flag States in the implementation of IMO instruments.
2. Where for the purpose of paragraph 1 a Member State decides with respect to ships flying its flag:

(i) to authorise organisations to undertake fully or in part inspections and surveys related to statutory certificates including those for the assessment of compliance with the rules referred to in Article 11(2) and, where appropriate, to issue or renew the related certificates; or
(ii) to rely upon organisations to undertake fully or in part the inspections and surveys referred to in point (i);

it shall entrust these duties only to recognised organisations.
    The competent administration shall in all cases approve the first issue of the exemption certificates.
    However, for the cargo ship safety radio certificate these duties may be entrusted to a private body recognised by a competent administration and having sufficient expertise and

qualified personnel to carry out specified safety assessment work on radio-communication on its behalf.

3.   This Article does not concern the certification of specific items of marine equipment."

Article 4: Member States may generally not refuse to authorise any of the recognised organisations to undertake certain functions

28.127   Article 4 provides that in applying Article 3(2), Member States shall in principle not refuse to authorise any of the recognised organisations to undertake such functions, subject to the provisions of paragraph 2 of Article 4 and Articles 5 and 9. However, they may restrict the number of organisations they authorise in accordance with their needs provided there are transparent and objective grounds for so doing. At the request of a Member State, the Commission shall, in accordance with the regulatory procedure referred to in Article 6(2), adopt appropriate measures to ensure the correct application of the first subparagraph of this paragraph as regards refusal of authorisation and of Article 8 as regards those cases where authorisation is suspended or withdrawn. In order for a Member State to accept that a recognised organisation located in a third State is to carry out fully or in part the duties mentioned in Article 3 it may request the third State in question to grant reciprocal treatment to those recognised organisations which are located in the EU. In addition, the EU may request the third State where a recognised organisation is located to grant reciprocal treatment to those recognised organisations which are located in the EU.

Article 5: Working relationship

28.128   Article 5 is worth studying:

"1.   Member States which take a decision as described in Article 3(2) shall set out a 'working relationship' between their competent administration and the organisations acting on their behalf.

2.   The working relationship shall be regulated by a formalised written and non-discriminatory agreement or equivalent legal arrangements setting out the specific duties and functions assumed by the organisations and including at least:

(a)   the provisions set out in Appendix II of IMO Resolution A.739(18) on guidelines for the authorisation of organisations acting on behalf of the administration, while drawing inspiration from the Annex, Appendices and Attachment to IMO MSC/Circular 710 and MEPC/Circular 307 on a model agreement for the authorisation of recognised organisations acting on behalf of the administration;

(b)   the following provisions concerning financial liability:

(i)   if liability arising out of any marine casualty is finally and definitely imposed on the administration by a court of law or as part of the settlement of a dispute through arbitration procedures, together with a requirement to compensate the injured parties for loss of or damage to property or personal injury or death, which is proved in that court of law to have been caused by a wilful act or omission or gross negligence of the recognised organisation, its bodies, employees, agents or others who act on behalf of the recognised organisation, the administration shall be entitled to financial compensation from the recognised organisation to the extent that that loss, damage, injury or death was, as decided by that court, caused by the recognised organisation;

(ii) if liability arising out of any marine casualty is finally and definitely imposed on the administration by a court of law or as part of the settlement of a dispute through arbitration procedures, together with a requirement to compensate the injured parties for personal injury or death, which is proved in that court of law to have been caused by any negligent or reckless act or omission of the recognised organisation, its employees, agents or others who act on behalf of the recognised organisation, the administration shall be entitled to financial compensation from the recognised organisation to the extent that that personal injury or death was, as decided by that court, caused by the recognised organisation; the Member States may limit the maximum amount payable by the recognised organisation, which must, however, be at least equal to EUR 4 million;

(iii) if liability arising out of any marine casualty is finally and definitely imposed on the administration by a court of law or as part of the settlement of a dispute through arbitration procedures, together with a requirement to compensate the injured parties for loss of or damage to property, which is proved in that court of law to have been caused by any negligent or reckless act or omission of the recognised organisation, its employees, agents or others who act on behalf of the recognised organisation, the administration shall be entitled to financial compensation from the recognised organisation, to the extent that that loss or damage was, as decided by that court, caused by the recognised organisation; the Member States may limit the maximum amount payable by the recognised organisation, which must, however, be at least equal to EUR 2 million;

(c) provisions for a periodical audit by the administration or by an impartial external body appointed by the administration into the duties the organisations are undertaking on its behalf, as referred to in Article 9(1);

(d) the possibility for random and detailed inspections of ships;

(e) provisions for compulsory reporting of essential information about their classed fleet, and changes, suspensions and withdrawals of class.

3. The agreement or equivalent legal arrangement may require the recognised organisation to have a local representation on the territory of the Member State on behalf of which it performs the duties referred to in Article 3. A local representation with legal personality under the law of the Member State and subject to the jurisdiction of its national courts may satisfy such a requirement.

4. Each Member State shall provide the Commission with precise information on the working relationship established in accordance with this Article. The Commission shall subsequently inform the other Member States thereof."

Role of the Committee on Safe Seas and the Prevention of Pollution from Ships

28.129 The Commission is, by virtue of Article 6, assisted by the COSS established by Regulation 2099/2002 of the European Parliament and of the Council.

28.130 Article 7 enables the directive to be amended (in limited circumstances):

"1. This Directive may, without broadening its scope, be amended in order to:

(a) incorporate, for the purposes of this Directive, subsequent amendments to the international conventions, protocols, codes and resolutions related thereto referred to in Articles 2(d), 3(1) and 5(2), which have entered into force;

(b) alter the amounts specified in points (ii) and (iii) of Article 5(2)(b).

These measures designed to amend non-essential elements of this Directive shall be adopted in accordance with the regulatory procedure with scrutiny referred to in Article 6(3).

2. Following the adoption of new instruments or protocols to the international conventions referred to in Article 2(d), the Council, acting on a proposal from the Commission, shall decide, taking into account the Member States' parliamentary procedures as well as the relevant procedures within the IMO, on the detailed arrangements for ratifying those new instruments or protocols, while ensuring that they are applied uniformly and simultaneously in the Member States.

The amendments to the international instruments referred to in Article 2(d) and Article 5 may be excluded from the scope of this Directive, pursuant to Article 5 of Regulation (EC) No 2099/2002."

Suspension or revocation of an authorisation

28.131 Article 8 provides that notwithstanding the minimum criteria specified in Annex I of Regulation 391/2009, where a Member State considers that a recognised organisation can no longer be authorised to carry out on its behalf the tasks specified in Article 3, it may suspend or withdraw such authorisation. In such case, the Member State must inform the Commission and the other Member States of its decision without delay and shall give substantiated reasons therefor.

Competence of organisations

28.132 Each Member State must, by virtue of Article 9, satisfy itself that the recognised organisations acting on its behalf for the purpose of Article 3(2) effectively carry out the functions referred to in that article to the satisfaction of its competent administration. In order to carry out the task referred to in Article 9(1), each Member State must, at least on a biennial basis, monitor every recognised organisation acting on its behalf and shall provide the other Member States and the Commission with a report on the results of such monitoring activities at the latest by 31 March of the year following the year in which the monitoring was carried out.[107]

Reporting to the Commission

28.133 In exercising their inspection rights and obligations as port States, Member States must (by virtue of Article 10) report to the Commission and to other Member States, and inform the flag State concerned, if they find that valid statutory certificates have been issued by recognised organisations acting on behalf of a flag State to a ship which does not fulfil the relevant requirements of the international conventions, or in the event of any failure of a ship carrying a valid class certificate and relating to items

---

107 An action was brought on 26 June 2017 by the Commission against Portugal (Case C-383/17). Portugal asked the Court to: "declare that by failing to provide the Commission with any report of the results of the monitoring of every recognised organisation acting on its behalf, the Portuguese Republic fails to fulfil its obligations under Article 9(2) of Directive 2009/15". The Commission argued that Art. 9(2) of the Directive clearly lays down that each Member State must, at least on a biennial basis, monitor every recognised organisation acting on its behalf and provide the other Member States and the Commission with a report on the results of such monitoring activities at the latest by 31 March of the year following the year in which the monitoring was carried out. The Commission also argued that since the time limit for transposing the Directive into national law expired on 17 June 2011 in accordance with Art. 13(1) of that Directive, Portugal ought to have provided the first report by 31 March 2013 at the latest, as it could have opted to carry out the first monitoring during 2011 or 2012. As of the date of the application (i.e. June 2017), Portugal had still not provided a report.

covered by that certificate. Only cases of ships representing a serious threat to safety and the environment or showing evidence of particularly negligent behaviour of the recognised organisations shall be reported for the purposes of this article. The recognised organisation concerned shall be advised of the case at the time of the initial inspection so that it can take appropriate follow-up action immediately.

Obligations on Member States

28.134 Member States are placed under various obligations by virtue of Article 11 to ensure that the regime works. First, by virtue of Article 11(1), each Member State must ensure that ships flying its flag are designed, constructed, equipped and maintained in accordance with the rules and procedures relating to hull, machinery and electrical and control installation requirements of a recognised organisation. This obligation is amplified by Article 11(2) which provides that a Member State may decide to use rules which it considers *equivalent* (but not identical) to the rules and procedures of a recognised organisation only on the proviso that it immediately notifies them to the Commission in conformity with the procedure under Directive 98/34 and to the other Member States and they are not objected to by another Member State or the Commission and are held, through the regulatory procedure referred to in Article 6(2) of this directive, not to be equivalent. By virtue of Article 11(3), Member States must co-operate with the recognised organisations which they authorise in the development of the rules and procedures of those organisations and, moreover, they must confer with the recognised organisations with a view to achieving consistent interpretation of the international conventions.

Vigilance

28.135 The Commission must, by virtue of Article 12, on a biennial basis, inform the European Parliament and the Council of progress in the implementation of the directive in the Member States.

E. COUNCIL DECISION 2015/873 OF 18 MAY 2015 ON THE POSITION TO BE ADOPTED, ON BEHALF OF THE EUROPEAN UNION, AT THE 48TH SESSION OF THE PORT STATE CONTROL COMMITTEE OF THE PARIS MEMORANDUM OF UNDERSTANDING ON PORT STATE CONTROL

28.136 On 18 May 2015, the Council adopted Decision 2015/873 on the position to be adopted, on behalf of the European Union, at the 48th session of the Port State Control Committee of the Paris Memorandum of Understanding on Port State Control. The legal basis was the TFEU generally and, in particular, Article 100(2) and Article 218(9) of the TFEU.

28.137 Before considering the essence of the decision, it is useful to review the recitals which give some of the background not only to the measure but also maritime safety and PSC generally.

28.138 The preamble to the decision explains its background very well:

"(1) Maritime safety, pollution prevention and on-board living and working conditions may be effectively enhanced through a drastic reduction of substandard ships in Union waters, by strictly applying relevant Conventions, international codes and resolutions.

(2) While the primary responsibility for monitoring the compliance of ships with the international standards for safety, pollution prevention and on-board living and working conditions lies with the flag State, responsibility for maintenance of the condition of the ship and its equipment after survey to comply with the requirements of Conventions applicable to the ship lies with the ship company. There has, however, been a serious failure on the part of a number of flag States to implement and enforce those international standards.

(3) Therefore, as a second line of defence against substandard shipping, the monitoring of compliance with the international standards for safety, pollution prevention and on-board living and working conditions should also be ensured by port States, while recognising that port State control inspection is not a survey and the relevant inspection forms are not seaworthiness certificates. A harmonised approach to the effective enforcement of those international standards by coastal Member States of the Union in respect of ships sailing in the waters under their jurisdiction and using their ports should avoid distortions of competition.

(4) Directive 2009/16/EC of the European Parliament and of the Council sets out the Union regime on port State control, reformulating and reinforcing the previous Union legislation in this field in force since 1995. The Union regime is based on the pre-existing structure of the Paris Memorandum of Understanding on Port State Control (the 'Paris MOU'), signed in Paris on 26 January 1982.

(5) As regards Union Member States, Directive 2009/16/EC effectively brings certain procedures, tools and work of the Paris MOU within the scope of Union law. By virtue of Directive 2009/16, … certain decisions taken by the appropriate competent body of the Paris MOU become binding on Member States of the Union.

(6) The Port State Control Committee (PSCC) of the Paris MOU will hold its 48th session from 18 to 22 May 2015. During that session, the PSCC is expected to decide on certain issues which have direct legal effect on Directive 2009/16…

(7) The PSCC is expected to consider and, subsequently, adopt the updated 2014 inspection statistics, including the new white, grey and black flag performance lists and the recognised organisations performance list which will be used for targeting purposes as from 1 July 2015. As the Paris MOU inspection statistics are essential for the implementation of the inspection regime established by Directive 2009/16, … the Member States, on behalf of the Union, should support their adoption.

(8) The PSCC is also expected to consider and, subsequently, adopt the regional commitment and the fair share calculation in accordance with Annex 11 to the Paris MOU. Given the importance of the inspection commitment being shared in an equitable manner among Member States and that each Member State contributes fairly to the achievement of the Union objective as set out in Article 5 of Directive 2009/16, … the Member States, on behalf of the Union, should support those actions of the PSCC.

(9) The PSCC is also expected to confirm the average detention and deficiency ratios. Bearing in mind Commission Regulation … 802/2010 and Commission Implementing Regulation … 205/2012, the Member States, on behalf of the Union, should support their adoption.

(10) Furthermore, the PSCC is expected to discuss the follow-up detention (FUD) forms and the procedures in the event of failure to recycle a vessel as agreed and to consider an amendment of the procedures and guidelines of the Paris MOU. Bearing in mind the importance of an effective, proportionate and dissuasive detention, access refusal and follow-up to inspection system under Articles 16, 19 and 21 of Directive 2009/16/EC, the Member States, on behalf of the Union, should oppose the proposal in point 2.6 of the amended guideline set out in Annex II to document PSCC48/4.3.8, which concerns a definitive and permanent ban on vessels, as opposed to a temporary ban, as that proposal is not in line with Directive 2009/16/EC.

(11) Pursuant to Article 218(9) of the Treaty on the Functioning of the European Union, the position to be adopted on behalf of the Union in a body set up by an agreement, when that

body is called upon to adopt acts having legal effects, is to be adopted by Council decision, on a proposal from the Commission.

(12) The Union is not a contracting party to the Paris MOU. It is therefore necessary for the Council to authorise the Member States to express the position to be adopted on behalf of the Union and express their consent to be bound by the decisions taken by the PSCC."

28.139 Article 1 provides that the positions to be adopted on behalf of the EU at the forty-eighth session of the Port State Control Committee ("PSCC") of the Paris MoU when that body is called upon to adopt decisions having legal effects are set out in the annex. The annex provides:

"The positions to be adopted, on behalf of the Union, at the 48th session of the Port State Control Committee of the Paris Memorandum of Understanding on Port State Control shall be to:

    (a) endorse the actions proposed in document PSCC48/3.3 A, paragraph 9.1;
    (b) endorse the actions proposed in document PSCC48/4.2.2B, paragraph 5.1;
    (c) endorse the actions proposed in document PSCC48/4.2.2C, paragraph 6.1; and
    (d) oppose the proposed amendment in point 2.6 of the amended guideline in document PSCC48/4.3.8."

28.140 Article 2 provides that the positions to be adopted on behalf of the EU as referred to in Article 1 shall be expressed by the Member States, which are bound by the Paris MoU, acting jointly in the interest of the EU.

28.141 Article 3 provides that formal and minor changes to the positions referred to in Article 1 may be agreed without requiring those positions to be amended.

28.142 Article 4 completes the decision by providing that Member States are hereby authorised to give their consent to be bound, in the interest of the EU, by the decisions referred to in Article 1.

F. COUNCIL DECISION 2016/381 OF 14 MARCH 2016 ON THE POSITION TO BE ADOPTED, ON BEHALF OF THE EUROPEAN UNION, WITHIN THE PORT STATE CONTROL COMMITTEE OF THE PARIS MEMORANDUM OF UNDERSTANDING ON PORT STATE CONTROL

28.143 On 14 March 2016, the Council adopted Decision 2016/381 on the position to be adopted, on behalf of the European Union, within the Port State Control Committee of the Paris Memorandum of Understanding on Port State Control.[108] The legal basis was the TFEU generally and, in particular, Article 100 and Article 218(9) of it.

28.144 Before examining the operative provisions, it is useful to consider the recitals which set out the background:

"(1) Maritime safety, maritime security, pollution prevention and on-board living and working conditions may be effectively enhanced by means of a drastic reduction of substandard ships in the waters under the jurisdiction of Member States, by strictly applying relevant Conventions, international codes and resolutions.

(2) While the primary responsibility for monitoring the compliance of ships with the international standards for safety, security, pollution prevention and on-board living and working conditions lies with the flag State, responsibility for maintenance of the condition

---

108 OJ L72/53, 17 March 2016. See http://eur-lex.europa.eu/legal-content/EN/TXT/?toc=OJ%3AL%3A2016%3A072%3ATOC&uri=uriserv%3AOJ.L_.2016.072.01.0053.01.ENG.

of the ship and its equipment after survey to comply with the requirements of the Conventions applicable to the ship lies with the ship company. There has, however, been a serious failure on the part of a number of flag States to implement and enforce those international standards.

(3)   Therefore, as a second line of defence against substandard shipping, the monitoring of compliance with the international standards for safety, security, pollution prevention and on-board living and working conditions should also be ensured by port States, while recognising that port State control inspection is not a survey and the relevant inspection forms are not seaworthiness certificates. A harmonised approach to the effective enforcement of those international standards by coastal Member States of the Union in respect of ships sailing in the waters under their jurisdiction and using their ports should avoid distortions of competition.

(4)   Directive 2009/16/EC of the European Parliament and of the Council[109] sets out the Union regime on port State control, reformulating and reinforcing the previous Union legislation in this field in force since 1995. The Union regime is based on the pre-existing structure of the Paris Memorandum of Understanding on Port State Control (the 'Paris MOU'), signed in Paris on 26 January 1982.

(5)   As regards the Union Member States, Directive 2009/16/EC effectively brings certain procedures, tools and activities of the Paris MOU within the scope of Union law. By virtue of that Directive, certain decisions taken by the appropriate competent body of the Paris MOU become binding on the Union Member States.

(6)   The Port State Control Committee ('PSCC') of the Paris MOU meets annually and during its deliberations decides on certain issues which have legal effects.

(7)   Pursuant to Article 218(9) of the … TFEU, … the position to be adopted on behalf of the Union in a body set up by an agreement, when that body is called upon to adopt acts having legal effects, is to be adopted by Council decision, on a proposal from the Commission.

(8)   As the internal rules of the Paris MOU make it difficult to establish a position to be adopted on behalf of the Union in accordance with Article 218(9) TFEU in a timely manner for each individual meeting of the PSCC, it is efficient in this case to establish such a position on a multiannual basis, consisting of guiding principles and orientations, together with a framework for its year-to-year specification. At the same time, most of the topics discussed at the individual meetings of the PSCC concern port State control matters and are generally covered by a single Union legal act, namely Directive 2009/16 … .In the particular circumstances that apply to the Paris MOU, it is therefore possible to establish a general position to be adopted on behalf of the Union for several of those meetings.

(9)   The Union is not a contracting party to the Paris MOU. It is therefore necessary for the Council to authorise the Member States to act in accordance with the position to be adopted on behalf of the Union and express their consent to be bound by the decisions taken by the PSCC.

(10)   The current method for drawing up the white, grey and black list of flag States has proven to have disproportionate and unintended consequences for flag States with small fleets. At the same time, progress on the development of an alternative calculation method has been slow. It is therefore important to rapidly develop an alternative method in order to ensure fairness.

(11)   Technical discussions and cooperation with third country members of the Paris MOU within the PSCC are of great importance in ensuring the effectiveness and the good functioning of the Paris MOU.

(12)   This decision should cover the period from 2016 to 2019.'

28.145 Article 1 provides that the position to be adopted on behalf of the EU within the annual PSCC meeting of the Paris MoU when that body is called upon to adopt deci-

---

109 Directive 2009/16/EC of the European Parliament and of the Council of 23 April 2009 on port State control (OJ L131, 28.5.2009, p. 57).

sions having legal effects is set out in Annex I which is entitled "The Position to be adopted on Behalf of the Union within the Port State Control Committee of the Paris Memorandum of Understanding on Port State Control". Annex I provides:

"Guiding Principles
In the framework of the PSCC of the Paris MOU, the Member States which are bound by the Paris MOU, acting jointly in the interest of the Union, shall:

(a) act in accordance with the objectives pursued by Directive 2009/16/EC, notably to improve maritime safety, maritime security, pollution prevention and on-board living and working conditions by means of a drastic reduction of substandard ships by strictly applying relevant Conventions, international codes and resolutions;

(b) promote the implementation of a harmonised approach by Members of the Paris MOU to the effective enforcement of the international standards in respect of ships sailing in the waters under their jurisdiction and using their ports;

(c) work together within the Paris MOU to achieve a comprehensive inspection scheme and the sharing of the inspection burden in an equitable manner, in particular by adopting the annual inspection commitment drawn up in accordance with the agreed methodology set out in Annex 11 to the Paris MOU;

(d) work within the Paris MOU to maintain appropriate competent authorities, to which the requisite number of staff, in particular qualified inspectors, for the inspection of ships is assigned, for example, through recruitment;

(e) ensure that measures adopted within the Paris MOU are consistent with international law, and in particular with the relevant Conventions, international codes and resolutions relating to maritime safety, maritime security, pollution prevention and on-board living and working conditions;

(f) promote the development of common approaches with other bodies carrying out port State control;

(g) ensure consistency with other Union policies notably in the areas of external relations, security, environment and others.

Orientations
The Member States which are bound by the Paris MOU, acting jointly in the interest of the Union, shall endeavour to support the following actions by the Paris MOU:

A. in order to ensure the smooth year-to-year functioning of the Union's port State control regime in accordance with Directive 2009/16/EC, the adoption of:

1. the following elements of the ship risk profile used to target vessels for inspection:

   (a) the white, grey and black flag list in accordance with the formula developed by the Paris MOU and set out in the Annex to Commission Regulation (EU) No 801/2010;

   (b) the performance list for recognised organisations in accordance with the methodology adopted by the PSCC at its 37th session in May 2004 (Agenda Item point 4.5.2);

   (c) the average deficiency and detention ratio for the company performance formula on the basis of the Annex to Commission Regulation (EU) No 802/2010.

2. changes or updates to the procedures and guidelines of the Paris MOU having legal effects that are consistent with the objectives pursued by Directive 2009/16/EC, notably to improve maritime safety, maritime security, pollution prevention and on-board living and working conditions.

B. the development as soon as possible of an alternative method of drawing up the white, grey and black list of flag States in order to ensure its fairness, regardless of the size of the fleet."

28.146 Article 2 states that the year-to-year specification of the position to be adopted on behalf of the Union within the annual PSCC meeting of the Paris MoU shall be conducted in accordance with Annex II. Annex II is entitled: "Year-to-Year Specification of the Position to be Adopted on Behalf of the Union within the Port State Control Committee of the Paris Memorandum of Understanding on Port State Control". Annex II provides:

"Before each annual PSCC meeting of the Paris MOU, the necessary steps shall be taken so that the position to be expressed on the Union's behalf takes account of all relevant information transmitted to the European Commission as well as any document to be discussed which falls within Union competence in accordance with the guiding principles and orientations set out in Annex I.
   To this effect and based on that information, a preparatory document setting out the particulars of the envisaged Union position shall be transmitted by the Commission services, in sufficient time before the PSCC meeting, to the Council or to its preparatory bodies for consideration and approval."

28.147 Article 3 provides that the Member States which are bound by the Paris MoU shall act in accordance with the position to be adopted on behalf of the Union as referred to in Article 1, acting jointly in the interest of the Union.

28.148 Article 4 stated that the decision entered into force on 1 April 2016. It will expire on 31 December 2019.

G. COMMISSION REGULATION 428/2010 OF 20 MAY 2010 IMPLEMENTING ARTICLE 14 OF DIRECTIVE 2009/16 OF THE PARLIAMENT AND COUNCIL AS REGARDS EXPANDED INSPECTIONS OF SHIPS

28.149 On 20 May 2010, the Commission adopted Regulation 428/2010 implementing Article 14 of Directive 2009/16 of the Parliament and of the Council as regards expanded inspections of ships.[110] The background to the regulation is Directive 2009/16 of the Parliament and the Council of 23 April 2009 on PSC,[111] and in particular Article 14(4) thereof. The background is that when carrying out an expanded inspection of a ship, the PSC officer should be guided by a list of specific items to be verified, subject to their practical feasibility or any constraints relating to the safety of persons, the ship or the port. With regard to the identification of the specific items to be verified in the course of an expanded inspection of any of the risk areas listed in Annex VII to Directive 2009/16, the Commission believed it was necessary to build upon the expertise of the Paris MoU. The Commission believed that the PSC Officers should use their professional judgment to determine the applicability of and the appropriate depth of examination of, each specific item.

28.150 Article 1 ("list of specific items to be verified in an expanded inspection") provides that an expanded inspection as referred to in Article 14 of Directive 2009/16 shall, where applicable, as a minimum comprise the verification of the specific items listed in the annex to the regulation. In the case where no specific areas are indicated for a particular type of ship, as defined in Directive 2009/16, the inspector shall use his professional judgment to decide which items must be inspected, and to what extent, in order to

---

110 OJ L125/2, 21 May 2010.
111 OJ L131/57, 28 May 2009.

check the overall condition in these areas. Article 2 provides that the regulation entered into force on the twentieth day following its publication in the *Official Journal*. It applied from 1 January 2011.

28.151 The annex contains "Specific Items to be Verified during an Expanded Inspection", as referred to in Article 14(4) of Directive 2009/16, and deals with the various criteria to be applied to the vessels under inspection. The criteria cover issues as diverse as structural issues, radio communications, lighting, steering gear, fire safety, alarms, living and working conditions, lifesaving appliances and pollution prevention. The annex also deals with various types of ships and the specific items to be verified depending on the type of vessel.

H. COMMISSION DIRECTIVE 96/40 OF 25 JUNE 1996 ESTABLISHING A COMMON MODEL FOR AN IDENTITY CARD FOR INSPECTORS CARRYING OUT PORT STATE CONTROL

28.152 On 25 June 1996, the Commission adopted Directive 96/40 of 25 June 1996 establishing a common model for an identity card for inspectors carrying out PSC.[112] The directive had

"regard to Council Directive 95/21/EC of 19 June 1995 concerning the enforcement, in respect of shipping using Community ports and sailing in the waters under the jurisdiction of the Member States, of international standards for ship safety, pollution prevention and shipboard living and working conditions (port State control),[113] and in particular Article 12(4) thereof."

The recitals to the directive provide in part:

"Whereas Directive 95/21/EC provides for the establishment of a common model for an identity card for port State control inspectors;

Whereas it is necessary that the identity card contains at least the following information: name of the issuing authority, full name of the holder of the identity card, a picture of the holder of the identity card, the signature of the holder of the identity card and a statement to the effect that the holder is authorized to carry out inspections in accordance with the national legislation adopted pursuant to the Directive;

Whereas to serve the purpose of identifying the inspector to the ship master and crew members it is necessary that the identity card contains a translation into the English language if that is not the main language used;

Whereas the exact format of the identity card should be left to the Member States;

Whereas the measures provided for in this Directive are in accordance with the opinion of the Committee set up pursuant to Article 12 of Council Directive 93/75/EEC, ..."[114]

28.153 Article 1 provides that the identity card referred to in Article 12 (4), of Directive 95/21 shall comply with the requirements set out in the annex. The annex provides:

"REQUIREMENTS FOR THE IDENTITY CARD FOR PORT STATE CONTROL INSPECTORS
(as referred to in Article 12 (4) of Directive 95/21/EC)
The identity card shall contain at least the following information:

(a) Name of the issuing authority
(b) Full name of the holder of the identity card

---

112 OJ L196/8, 7 August 1996.
113 OJ No L157, 7.7.1995, p. 1.
114 OJ No L247, 5 October 1993, p. 19.

(c) An up-to-date picture of the holder of the identity card
(d) The signature of the holder of the identity card
(e) A statement to the effect that the holder of the identity card is authorized to carry out inspections in accordance with the national legislation adopted pursuant to the Directive.

If the main language used on the identity card is not English, it must include a translation into that language.
The format of the identity card is left to the discretion of the competent authorities."

28.154 Article 2(1) provides that Member States must bring into force the laws, regulations and administrative provisions necessary to comply with the directive no later than 1 February 1997. They must immediately inform the Commission thereof. Article 2(1) also provides that when these provisions are adopted by Member States, they shall contain a reference to the directive or be accompanied by such a reference at the time of their official publication. The procedure for making such a reference shall be laid down by Member States. Article 2(2) provides that Member States must communicate to the Commission the provisions of national law which they adopt in the field governed by the directive.

28.155 Article 3 provides that the directive entered into force on the twentieth day following its publication in the *Official Journal of the European Communities*.

I. COMMISSION REGULATION 801/2010 OF 13 SEPTEMBER 2010 IMPLEMENTING ARTICLE 10(3) OF DIRECTIVE 2009/16 OF THE PARLIAMENT AND COUNCIL AS REGARDS THE FLAG STATE CRITERIA

28.156 On 13 September 2010, the Commission adopted Regulation 801/2010 implementing Article 10(3) of Directive 2009/16 of the European Parliament and of the Council as regards the flag State criteria.[115] It applied from 1 January 2011. The background to Regulation 801/2010 is Directive 2009/16 of the Parliament and the Council of 23 April 2009 on PSC, and in particular Article 10(3) thereof. The first recital recalls that flag State performance is one of the generic parameters determining the risk profile of ships. The second recital recalls that in order to assess the risk profile of a ship, the detention rate within the EU and within the region covered by the Paris MoU should be taken into account. It is necessary, according to the third recital, to build upon the expertise acquired through the application of the Paris MoU with regard to the methodology to be used for assessing flag State performance.

28.157 Article 1 of the regulation deals with the categorisation of flag States based on the detention rates. Article 1(1) provides that with a view to establishing flag State performance within the meaning of Directive 2009/16, flag States shall be classified into black, grey or white lists, adopted in accordance with the Paris MoU on the basis of the total inspections and detentions over a three-year period. Additionally, flag States listed in the black list shall be divided into very high, high, medium to high or medium risk depending on their detention rate. The classification shall be updated yearly. Article 1(2) provides that classification of a flag State into the black, grey or white list requires a minimum of 30 PSC inspections. Article 1(3) provides that the methodology and formu-

---

115 OJ L241/1, 14 September 2010.

las to be used to categorise the flag States shall comply with the flag State criteria as set out in the annex.

28.158 Flag State performance based on the IMO audit is addressed in Article 2 of the regulation. The compliance referred to in point (c) (iii) of Part I.1 of Annex I to Directive 2009/16 required for ships to be considered as posing a lower risk, shall be regarded as demonstrated when the Commission receives a written confirmation from the flag State that a final audit report has been completed and where relevant, a corrective action plan submitted. Audits carried out before 17 June 2009 must be taken into account equally. The annex sets out the flag State criteria (as referred to in Article 10(3)(a) of Directive 2009/16).

J. MEMBER STATE HAVING TOO FEW INSPECTIONS: *COMMISSION V FRANCE*

28.159 What if a Member State has too few inspections? On 22 June 2004, the Court of Justice of the European Union ("CJEU") delivered its judgment in *Commission v France*[116] and declared that, by failing to carry out inspections of at least 25% of the number of individual vessels which entered its ports in 1999 and 2000, France had failed to fulfil its obligations under Article 5(1) of Council Directive 95/21 of 19 June 1995 concerning the enforcement, in respect of shipping using Community ports and sailing in the waters under the jurisdiction of the Member States, of international standards for ship safety, pollution prevention and shipboard living and working conditions (PSC).[117] The French authorities had stated to the Commission that they were under constraints in their use of human resources and the organisation of their services. According to France, because of the demographic structure of the bodies carrying out vessel inspections, numerous members of staff had retired. Those retirements coincided with a suspension of certain types of recruitment linked to the creation of a body of inspectors of maritime affairs. Thus, the number of inspectors able to carry out the inspections required by Directive 95/21 fell from 70 to 54 between 1994 and 1999. The budgetary and recruitment efforts made since that time have made it possible to increase the inspection percentages by a substantial proportion. France also pointed to the quality of the inspections carried out, which is shown by a percentage of ship detentions higher than the European average (11% of ships detained in 1999 and 17% in 2000, compared to the European average of 9.15% in 1999 and 9.50% in 2000). The Commission did not accept those arguments and instituted proceedings and ultimately, the CJEU found that France was in breach. The reasoning of the Court was succinct given the relative simplicity of the case:

"Findings of the Court

14. In the present case, it is common ground that the French Republic has failed to fulfil its obligation under Article 5(1) of the directive, which requires each Member State to carry out inspections of at least 25% of the number of individual vessels entering its ports during a representative calendar year.

---

116 Case C-439/02 Commission v France EU:C:2004:380. The fifth chamber was composed of Judges Gulmann (President of the Chamber), von Bahr and R Silva de Lapuerta (Rapporteur). The Advocate-General was AG Jacobs but the court proceeded to judgment without the need for an opinion.
117 OJ 1995 L157/1.

15. Furthermore, the Court has repeatedly held that a Member State cannot plead provisions, practices or situations in its internal legal order to justify the absence of implementation of a directive within the period prescribed (see, inter alia, Case C-352/01 *Commission v Spain* [2002] ECR I-10263, paragraph 8).
16. The action brought by the Commission must therefore be considered well founded.
17. Consequently, it must be held that, by failing to carry out inspections of at least 25% of the number of individual vessels which entered its ports in 1999 and 2000, the French Republic has failed to fulfil its obligations under Article 5(1) of Directive 95/21."

In essence, the CJEU decided that by failing to carry out inspections of at least 25% of the number of individual vessels which entered its ports in 1999 and 2000, the French Republic has failed to fulfil its obligations under Article 5(1) of Council Directive 95/21 of 19 June 1995.

28.160 As an aside, it would be interesting to speculate if a Member State had what appeared to be too many inspections. Whether the Member State would be liable should be determined by reference to the purpose and the effect of such inspections. For example, if the real purpose was to distort and hinder inter-State trade then the Member State might well be liable.

CHAPTER 29

Maritime safety: ship inspection and survey organisations

A. INTRODUCTION

29.001 Ship inspection and survey organisations[1] are long-established, necessary and systemically important to shipping. In terms of longevity, their origins lie in, at least, the mid-eighteenth century so they have provided useful and important services to the shipping community, and beyond, for at least 250 years. They are systemically important because they allow insurers to insure ships and cargoes, provide a protective layer in the fight to ensure safety of shipping and give some reassurance to the shipping community participants. They therefore serve both public and private functions. The tenth recital to Directive 2009/15[2] provides that "ship inspection and survey organisations play an important role in [European Union ("EU")] legislation concerning maritime safety."

29.002 The EU believes that ship inspection and survey organisations should be able to offer their services throughout the EU and compete[3] with each other while providing equal levels of safety and environmental protection. The necessary professional standards for their activities should therefore be uniformly established and applied across the EU.[4] It is interesting to see how the EU seeks to achieve two aims simultaneously: a competitive regime but also a top quality one operating to the highest standards. One sees this twin track approach within the European Commission with DG Mobility and Transport paying attention to the safety dimension while the Directorate General for Competition is paying attention to the competition dimensions. The two aims are not incompatible and

---

1 On classification organisations, see Basedow and Wurmnest, Third Party Liability of Classification Societies (2005); Broad, Marine Classification Society Surveying (2009); and Lux (ed.), Classification Societies (1993). See also Begines, "The EU Law on Classification Societies" (2005) JMLC 487; Boisso, "Classification Societies and Safety at Sea" (1994) Marine Policy 363; de Bruyne and Vanleenhove, "An EU Perspective on the Liability of Classification Societies: Selected Current Issues and Private International Law Aspects" (2014) 20 JIML 103. On classification societies and EU competition law, see Dohms and Rieder, "Commitment Decision in the Ship Classification Case: Paving the Way for More Competition", European Commission Competition Policy Newsletter, No. 1, 2010, p. 41.

2 I.e. Dir. 2009/15 of the European Parliament and of the Council of 23 April 2009 on common rules and standards of ships inspections and survey organisation and for the relevant activities of maritime administration (OJ L131/47, 28 May 2009).

3 Despite their roles in safety, they are still expected to compete with each other for the purposes of EU competition law.

4 Reg. 391/2009 (OJ L131/1, 28 May 2009), third recital which is reflected in the fourth and twenty-third recitals and Art. 1. See Jessen, "Commentary on Regulation EC/391/2009 on Common Rules and Standards for Ship Inspection and Survey Organisations and Directive 2009/15/EC on Common Rules and Standards for Ship Inspection and Survey Organisations and for the Relevant Activities of Maritime Administrations" in Jessen and Werner (eds), EU Maritime Transport Law (2016), p. 713. Presumably, there could be higher standards in certain circumstances where they do not undermine the EU regime.

are both laudable; presumably, if there was a contest between safety and competition then the former would prevail

B. REGULATION 391/2009 ON COMMON RULES AND STANDARDS FOR SHIP INSPECTION AND SURVEY ORGANISATIONS

Introduction

29.003 On 23 April 2009, the Parliament and the Council adopted Regulation 391/2009 on common rules and standards for ship inspection and survey organisations.[5] Article 19 of Regulation 391/2009 provides that the regulation entered into force on the twentieth day following its publication in the *Official Journal*; as it was published on 29 May 2009, it therefore entered into force on 17 June 2009.

29.004 Regulation 391/2009 was amended by Commission Implementing Regulation 1355/2014 of 17 December 2014.[6] On 23 April 2009, the Parliament and the Council also adopted Directive 2009/15 on common rules and standards for ship inspection and survey organisations and for the relevant activities of maritime administrations.[7]

29.005 The legal basis for Regulation 391/2009 was the Treaty establishing the European Community ("TEC") (now, with amendments, the Treaty on the Functioning of the European Union ("TFEU")) and, in particular, Article 80(2) of the TEC (now Article 100(2) of the TFEU).

29.006 The legislative history of Regulation 391/2009 included a proposal by the Commission, an opinion of the European Economic and Social Committee[8] and an opinion of the Committee of the Regions.[9]

29.007 Part of the background to Regulation 391/2009 was Council Directive 94/57 of 22 November 1994 on common rules and standards for ship inspection and survey organisations and for the relevant activities of maritime administrations[10] – this latter measure had been amended substantially several times. As further amendments were to be made by 2009, the original Directive 94/57 was recast but largely in the interests of clarity.[11] However, in view of the nature of the provisions of Directive 94/57, the EU decided that it was appropriate that its provisions be recast in two different EU legal instruments, namely, a directive and a regulation.[12]

29.008 The EU was mindful of the need to harmonise the EU approach with that of the International Maritime Organization ("IMO") so the fourth recital to Regulation 391/2009 provides that the objective of recasting Directive 94/57

"should be pursued through measures that adequately tie in with the work of the International Maritime Organisation ('IMO') and, where appropriate, build on and complement it. Furthermore, the Member States and the Commission should promote the development by the IMO of an international code for recognised organisations."[13]

---

5 OJ L131/1, 28 May 2009.
6 OJ L365/82, 19 December 2014, it was also corrected by a corrigendum, OJ L74/1, 22 March 2010.
7 OJ L131/47, 28 May 2009.
8 OJ C318/195, 23 December 2006.
9 OJ C229/38, 22 September 2006.
10 OJ L319/20, 12 December 1994.
11 Reg. 391/2009, Recital 1.
12 Reg. 391/2009, Recital 2.
13 Reg. 391/2009, Recital 4.

29.009 The fifth recital to Regulation 391/2009 provides that minimum criteria for recognition of organisations should be laid down with a view to enhancing the safety of, and preventing pollution from, ships and the aim is that the minimum criteria laid down in Directive 94/57 should therefore be strengthened.

29.010 In order to grant initial recognition to the organisations wishing to be authorised to work on behalf of the Member States, the sixth recital provides that compliance with the minimum criteria laid down in Regulation 391/2009 could be assessed more effectively in a harmonised and centralised manner by the Commission together with the Member States requesting the recognition.

29.011 The seventh recital provides that recognition should be granted only on the basis of the quality and safety performance of the organisation. The recital also recalls that it should be ensured that the extent of that recognition be at all times in keeping with the actual capacity of the organisation concerned. The recital also recalled that recognition should furthermore take into account the differences in legal status and corporate structure of recognised organisations while continuing to ensure uniform applications of the minimum criteria laid down in the regulation and the effectiveness of EU controls. Regardless of the corporate structure, the organisation to be recognised should provide services worldwide and its legal entities should be subject to global joint and several liability.

29.012 Interestingly, the eighth recital provides that the measures necessary for the implementation of Regulation 391/2009 should be adopted in accordance with Council Decision 1999/468 of 28 June 1999 laying down the procedures for the exercise of implementing powers conferred on the Commission[14] which meant that the Commission was given greater powers. For example, under the ninth recital, the Commission should be empowered to amend Regulation 391/2009 in order to incorporate subsequent amendments to the international conventions, protocols, codes and resolutions related thereto, to update the minimum criteria in Annex I and to adopt the criteria to measure the effectiveness of the rules and procedures as well as the performance of the recognised organisations as regards the safety of, and the prevention of pollution from, their classed ships. Since those measures are of general scope and are designed to amend non-essential elements of the regulation, among other things, by supplementing it with new non-essential elements, they must be adopted in accordance with the regulatory procedure with scrutiny provided for in Article 5a of Decision 1999/468.

29.013 As the system is so dependent on organisations doing the correct thing, the tenth recital states that it is of the utmost importance that failure by a recognised organisation to fulfil its obligations can be addressed in a prompt, effective and proportionate manner. The primary objective should be to correct any deficiencies with a view to removing any potential threat to safety or the environment at an early stage. The Commission should therefore be given, the tenth recital goes on, the necessary powers to require that the recognised organisation undertake the necessary preventive and remedial action, and to impose fines and periodic penalty payments as coercive measures. When exercising these powers, the Commission should do so in a manner that complies with fundamental rights and should ensure that the organisation can make its views known throughout the procedure.

---

14 OJ L184/23, 17 July 1999.

29.014 An organisation may lose its recognition under EU law which would prevent it operating. In accordance with the EU-wide approach, the decision to withdraw the recognition of an organisation must be taken at EU level and therefore by the Commission on the basis of a committee procedure where the organisation fails to fulfil the obligations set out in Regulation 391/2009 if the various measures under the regulation prove ineffective or the organisation otherwise presents an unacceptable threat to safety or the environment.

29.015 The regulation makes clear in the twelfth recital that the continuous a posteriori[15] monitoring of the recognised organisation to assess their compliance with the regulation can be carried out more effectively in a harmonised and centralised manner. Therefore, the regulation is premised on the notion that it is appropriate that the Commission, together with the Member State requesting the recognition, be entrusted with this task on behalf of the EU

29.016 The frames of the regulation believed that as part of the monitoring of the operations of recognised organisations, it is crucial that Commission inspectors have access to ships and ship files regardless of the ship's flag in order to ascertain whether the recognised organisations are complying with the minimum criteria laid down in the regulation in respect of all ships in their respective classes.[16] Indeed, the ability of recognised organisations to identify rapidly and correct weaknesses in their rules, processes and internal controls is critical for the safety of the ships they inspect and certify.[17] That ability should be enhanced, the regulation contemplates, by means of a quality assessment and certification entity, which should be independent of commercial or political interests, can propose common action for the sustained improvement of all recognised organisations and ensure fruitful co-operation with the Commission.[18] Not surprisingly, the regulation states that the rules and procedures of recognised organisations are a key factor for increasing safety and preventing accidents and pollution.[19] The recognised organisations have initiated a process that should lead to harmonisation of their rules and procedures.[20] That process should be encouraged and supported by EU legislation, as it should have a positive impact on maritime safety as well as on the competitiveness of the European shipbuilding industry.[21]

29.017 The harmonisation of the rules of recognised organisations for the design, construction and periodic survey of merchant ships is, the regulation recognises, an ongoing process and it will remain ongoing.[22] Therefore, the obligation to have a set of own rules or the demonstrated ability to have own rules should be seen in the context of the process of harmonisation and should not constitute an obstacle to the activities of recognised organisations or potential candidates for recognition.[23]

29.018 The regulation goes on to provide that recognised organisations should be obliged to update their technical standards and enforce them consistently in order to

---

15 I.e. a reasoned monitoring based on observations or experiences.
16 Reg. 391/2009, Recital 13.
17 Reg. 391/2009, Recital 14.
18 Ibid.
19 Reg. 391/2009, Recital 15.
20 Ibid.
21 Ibid.
22 Reg. 391/2009, Recital 18.
23 Reg. 391/2009, Recital 18.

harmonise safety rules and ensure uniform implementation of international rules within the EU.[24] Where the technical standards of recognised organisations are identical or very similar, mutual recognition of certificates for materials, equipment and components should be considered in appropriate cases, taking the most demanding and rigorous standards as the reference.[25]

29.019 While each recognised organisation, in principle, should be held responsible solely and exclusively in relation to the parts it certifies, the liability of recognised organisations and manufacturers will follow the agreed conditions or, as the case may be, the applicable law in each individual case.[26]

29.020 Transparency is very important so the nineteenth recital provides that

"transparency and exchange of information between interested parties, as well as public right of access to information, are fundamental tools for preventing accidents at sea, recognised organisations should provide all relevant statutory information concerning the conditions of the ships in their class to the port State control authorities and make it available to the general public."[27]

29.021 The twentieth recital recognises a practical problem: in "order to prevent ships from changing class to avoid carrying out necessary repairs, recognised organisations should exchange all relevant information among themselves concerning the conditions of ships changing class and involve the flag State when necessary".

29.022 The twenty-first recital deals with intellectual property rights: the "protection of intellectual property rights of maritime stakeholders including shipyards, equipment suppliers and shipowners, should not prevent normal business transactions and contractually agreed services between these parties".

29.023 The twenty-second recital recalls that the European Maritime Safety Agency ("EMSA") provides the necessary support to ensure the application of Regulation 391/2009.

29.024 The penultimate recital, the twenty-third, provides

"since the objective of the Regulations, namely the establishment of measures to be followed by organisations entrusted with the inspection, survey and certification of ships, operating in the [EU], cannot be sufficiently achieved by the Member States and can therefore, by reason of the scale of the action, be better achieved at [EU] level, the [EU] may adopt measures, in accordance with the principles of subsidiary as set out in [Article 5 of the EC Treaty which has been repealed but it is now effectively Article 4(3) of the TFEU]. In accordance with the principle of proportionality, as set out in the Article, this Regulation does not go beyond what is necessary in order to achieve that objective."

29.025 The final recital, the twenty-fourth, states:

"measures to be followed by the Member States in their relationship with ship inspections and survey organisations are laid down by Directive 2009/15 … of the European Parliament and of the Council of 23 April 2009 on 'common rules and standards for ship inspection and survey organisations and for the relevant activities of maritime administrations'.[28]"

---

24 Reg. 391/2009, Recital 17.
25 Ibid.
26 Reg. 391/2009, Recital 18.
27 Reg. 391/2009, Recital 19.
28 Ed., OJ L 131/47.

Objectives of Regulation 391/2009

29.026 Article 1 provides that Regulation 391/2009 establishes those measures to be followed by organisations[29] entrusted with the inspection, survey and certification of ships for compliance with the international conventions on safety at sea and prevention of marine pollution, while furthering the EU's objective of freedom to provide services. This includes the development and implementation of safety requirements for hull, machinery and electrical and control installations of ships falling under the scope of the international conventions.

29.027 Article 1 reflects the twenty-third recital (along with the third and fourth recitals of the regulation). The twenty-third recital states that since

"the objective of this Regulation, namely the establishment of measures to be followed by organisations entrusted with the inspection, survey and certification of ships, operating in the [EU], cannot be sufficiently achieved by the Member States and can therefore, by reason of the scale of the action, be better achieved at [EU] level, the [EU] may adopt measures, in accordance with the principle of subsidiarity as set out in Article 5 of the [EC] Treaty.[30] In accordance with the principle of proportionality, as set out in that Article, this Regulation does not go beyond what is necessary in order to achieve that objective."

This provision reflects the concepts of the subsidiary and proportionality.

Definitions of key concepts in Regulation 391/2009

29.028 Article 2 sets out a number of definitions for the purpose of Regulation 391/2009.

29.029 The term "ship" means a ship falling within the scope of the "international conventions" – this is not overly specific but allows flexibility.

29.030 The phrase "international conventions" means the International Convention for the Safety of Life at Sea of 1 November 1974 ("SOLAS 74") with the exception of chapter XI-2 of the annex thereto, the International Convention on Load Lines of 5 April 1966 and the International Convention for the Prevention of Pollution from Ships of 2 November 1973 ("MARPOL"), together with the protocols and amendments thereto, and the related codes of mandatory status in all Member States, with the exception of paragraphs 16.1, 18.1 and 19 of part 2 of the IMO Instruments Implementation Code, and of sections 1.1, 1.3, 3.9.3.1, 3.9.3.2 and 3.9.3.3 of part 2 of the IMO Code for Recognized Organizations, in their up-to-date version.

29.031 The word "organisation" means, under Article 2(c) of Regulation 391/2009, a legal entity, its subsidiaries and any other entities under its control, which jointly or separately carry out tasks falling under the scope of this regulation.

29.032 The term "control" means, for the purpose of Article 2(c), rights, contracts or any other means, in law or in fact, which, either separately or in combination confer the possibility of exercising decisive influence on a legal entity or enable that entity to carry out tasks falling under the scope of this regulation.

---

29 The word "organisation" means, under Art. 2(c), a legal entity, its subsidiaries and any other entities under its control, which jointly or separately carry out tasks falling under the scope of the regulation.

30 Ed., now effectively Art. 4(3) of the Treaty on the European Union ("TEU").

29.033 The phrase "recognised organisation" means an organisation recognised in accordance with the regulation.

29.034 The word "authorisation" means an act whereby a Member State grants an authorisation or delegates powers to a recognised organisation.

29.035 The phrase "statutory certificate" means a certificate issued by or on behalf of a flag State in accordance with the international conventions.

29.036 The phrase "rules and procedures" means a recognised organisation's requirements for the design, construction, equipment, maintenance and survey of ships.

29.037 The term "class certificate" means a document issued by a recognised organisation certifying the fitness of a ship for a particular use or service in accordance with the rules and procedures laid down and made public by that recognised organisation.

29.038 The word "location" means the place of the registered office, central administration or principal place of business of an organisation.

Requests for initial authorisation/recognition

29.039 Article 3(1) of Regulation 301/2009 provides that Member States which wish to grant an authorisation to any organisation which is not yet recognised shall submit a request for recognition to the Commission together with complete information on, and evidence of, the organisation's compliance with the minimum criteria set out in Annex I and on the requirement and its undertaking that it shall comply with the provisions of Articles 8(4), 9, 10 and 11. Article 3(2) of Regulation 301/2009 provides that the Commission, together with the respective Member States submitting the request, shall carry out assessments of the organisations for which the request for recognition was received in order to verify that the organisations meet and undertake to comply with the requirements referred to in paragraph 1. Article 3(3) of Regulation 301/2009 provides that the Commission must, in accordance with the regulatory procedure referred to in Article 12(3), refuse to recognise organisations which fail to meet the requirements referred to in paragraph 1 or whose performance is considered an unacceptable threat to safety or the environment on the basis of the criteria laid down in accordance with Article 14.

Granting initial authorisation/recognition

29.040 Recognition must be granted by the Commission in accordance with the regulatory procedure referred to in Article 12(3).[31] Recognition must only be granted to organisations which meet the requirements referred to in Article 3.[32] Recognition must be granted to the relevant legal entity, which is the parent entity of all legal entities that constitute the recognised organisation.[33] The recognition must encompass all legal entities that contribute to ensuring that that organisation provides cover for their services worldwide. The Commission, acting in accordance with the regulatory procedure referred to in Article 12(3), may limit the recognition as regards certain types of ships, ships of a certain size, certain trades, or a combination thereof, in accordance with the proven capacity and

---

31 Reg. 391/2009, Art. 4(1).
32 Reg. 391/2009, Art. 4(2).
33 Reg. 391/2009, Art. 4(3).

expertise of the organisation concerned.[34] In such a case, the Commission shall state the reasons for the limitation and the conditions under which the limitation shall be removed or can be widened. The limitation may be reviewed at any time. The Commission must draw up and regularly update a list of the organisations recognised in accordance with this article. That list shall be published in the *Official Journal*.[35] Article 4 reflects the seventh recital which provides that recognition should be granted only on the basis of the quality and safety performance of the organisation – laudable and necessary criteria. Recognition should be always in keeping with the actual capacity of the organisation concerned. Recognition should furthermore take into account the differences in legal status and corporate structure of recognised organisations while continuing to ensure uniform application of the minimum criteria laid down in Regulation 391/2009 and the effectiveness of the EU controls. Regardless of the corporate structure, the organisation to be recognised should provide services worldwide and its legal entities should be subject to global joint and several liability.

Failure by a recognised organisation to comply with the minimum criteria in the regulation

29.041 Article 5 provides that where the Commission considers that a recognised organisation has failed to fulfil the minimum criteria set out in Annex I or its obligations under the regulation, or that the safety and pollution prevention performance of a recognised organisation has worsened significantly, without, however, it constituting an unacceptable threat to safety or the environment, it shall require the recognised organisation concerned to undertake the necessary preventive and remedial action within specified deadlines to ensure full compliance with those minimum criteria and obligations and, in particular, remove any potential threat to safety or the environment, or to otherwise address the causes of the worsening performance. The preventive and remedial action may include interim protective measures when the potential threat to safety or the environment is immediate. However, and without prejudice to their immediate implementation, the Commission must give to all Member States which have granted an authorisation to the recognised organisation concerned, advance notice of the measures that it intends to take.

Fines and periodic penalties on organisations in breach

29.042 Article 6 of Regulation 391/2009[36] provides:

"1. In addition to the measures taken under Article 5, the Commission may, in accordance with the advisory procedure referred to in Article 12(2), impose fines on a recognised organisation:

(a) – whose serious or repeated failure to fulfil the minimum criteria set out in Annex I or its obligations under Articles 8(4), 9, 10 and 11,

---

34 Reg. 391/2009, Art. 4(4).
35 Reg. 391/2009, Art. 4(5).
36 Note the Corrigendum to Reg. (EC) No 391/2009 of the European Parliament and of the Council of 23 April 2009 on common rules and standards for ship inspection and survey organisations OJ L74/1, 22 March 2010 which corrected the layout of Art. 6(1).

or

    – whose worsening performance reveals serious shortcomings in its structure, systems, procedures or internal controls;

or

    (b) which has deliberately provided incorrect, incomplete or misleading information to the Commission in the course of its assessment pursuant to Article 8(1) or otherwise obstructed that assessment.

2. Without prejudice to paragraph 1, where a recognised organisation fails to undertake the preventive and remedial action required by the Commission, or incurs unjustified delays, the Commission may impose periodic penalty payments on that organisation until the required action is fully carried out.
3. The fines and periodic penalty payments referred to in paragraphs 1 and 2 shall be dissuasive and proportionate to both the gravity of the case and the economic capacity of the recognised organisation concerned, taking into account, in particular, the extent to which safety or the protection of the environment has been compromised.

    They shall be imposed only after the recognised organisation and the Member States concerned have been given the opportunity to submit their observations.

    The aggregate amount of the fines and periodic penalty payments imposed shall not exceed 5% of the total average turnover of the recognised organisation in the preceding three business years for the activities falling under the scope of this Regulation.
4. The Court of Justice of the European Communities shall have unlimited jurisdiction to review decisions whereby the Commission has fixed a fine or periodic penalty payment. It may cancel, reduce or increase the fine or periodic penalty payment imposed."

Withdrawal of Regulation 391/2009

29.043 Under Article 7(1) of Regulation 391/2009, the Commission must withdraw the recognition of an organisation: (a) whose repeated and serious failure to fulfil the minimum criteria set out in Annex I or its obligations under this regulation is such that it constitutes an unacceptable threat to safety or the environment;[37] (b) whose repeated and serious failure in its safety and pollution prevention performance is such that it constitutes an unacceptable threat to safety or the environment;[38] (c) which prevents or repeatedly obstructs the assessment by the Commission; (d) which fails to pay the fines and/or periodic penalty payments referred to in Article 6(1) and (2); or (e) which seeks to obtain financial cover or reimbursement of any fines imposed on it pursuant to Article 6.

29.044 Article 7(3) provides that withdrawal of recognition shall be decided by the Commission, upon its own initiative or at the request of a Member State, in accordance

---

37 Art. 7(2) provides that for the purpose of point (a) of para. 1, the Commission shall decide on the basis of all the available information, including: (a) the results of its own assessment of the recognised organisation concerned pursuant to Art. 8(1); (b) reports submitted by Member States pursuant to Art. 10 of Dir. 2009/15; (c) analyses of casualties involving ships classed by the recognised organisations; (d) any recurrence of the shortcomings referred to in point (a) of Art. 6(1); (e) the extent to which the fleet in the recognised organisation's class is affected; and (f) the ineffectiveness of the measures referred to in Art. 6(2).

38 Art. 7(2) provides that for the purpose of point (b) of para. 1, the Commission shall decide on the basis of all the available information, including: (a) the results of its own assessment of the recognised organisation concerned pursuant to Art. 8(1); (b) reports submitted by Member States pursuant to Art. 10 of Dir. 2009/15; (c) analyses of casualties involving ships classed by the recognised organisations; (d) any recurrence of the shortcomings referred to in point (a) of Art. 6(1); (e) the extent to which the fleet in the recognised organisation's class is affected; and (f) the ineffectiveness of the measures referred to in Art. 6(2).

with the regulatory procedure referred to in Article 12(3) and after the recognised organisation concerned has been given the opportunity to submit its observations.

Assessment of organisations

29.045 Article 8(1) of Regulation 391/2009 provides that all the recognised organisations must be assessed by the Commission, together with the Member State which submitted the relevant request for recognition, on a regular basis and at least every two years to verify that they meet the obligations under Regulation 391/2009 and fulfil the minimum criteria set out in Annex I. The assessment shall be confined to those activities of the recognised organisations, which fall within the scope of Regulation 301/2009.

29.046 Article 8(2) provides that in selecting the recognised organisations for assessment, the Commission must pay particular attention to the safety and pollution prevention performance of the recognised organisation, to the casualty records and to the reports produced by Member States in accordance with Article 10 of Directive 2009/15.

29.047 Article 8(3) states that the assessment may include a visit to regional branches of the recognised organisation as well as random inspection of ships, both in service and under construction, for the purpose of auditing the recognised organisation's performance. In this case the Commission shall, where appropriate, inform the Member State in which the regional branch is located. The Commission shall provide the Member States with a report on the results of the assessment.

29.048 Under Article 8(4), each recognised organisation shall make available the results of its quality system management review to the Committee referred to in Article 12(1), on an annual basis.

Access to information from organisations

29.049 Article 9(1) provides that recognised organisations must ensure that the Commission has access to the information necessary for the purposes of the assessment referred to in Article 8(1). No contractual clauses may be invoked to restrict this access. Recognised organisations shall ensure in their contracts with shipowners or operators for the issue of statutory certificates or class certificates to a ship that such issue shall be made conditional on the parties not opposing the access of the Commission inspectors on board that ship for the purposes of Article 8(1).[39]

Consultation

29.050 Article 10(1) sets out the basis rules on consultation. Recognised organisations shall consult with each other periodically with a view to maintaining equivalence and aiming for harmonisation of their rules and procedures and the implementation thereof. They shall co-operate with each other with a view to achieving consistent interpretation of the international conventions, without prejudice to the powers of the flag States. Recognised organisations shall, in appropriate cases, agree on the technical and procedural conditions under which they will mutually recognise the class certificates for

---

39 Art. 9(2).

materials, equipment and components based on equivalent standards, taking the most demanding and rigorous standards as the reference. Where mutual recognition cannot be agreed upon for serious safety reasons, recognised organisations shall clearly state the reasons therefor. Where a recognised organisation ascertains by inspection or otherwise that material, a piece of equipment or a component is not in compliance with its certificate, that organisation may refuse to authorise the placing on board of that material, piece of equipment or component. The recognised organisation shall immediately inform the other recognised organisations, stating the reasons for its refusal. Recognised organisations shall recognise, for classification purposes, certificates of marine equipment bearing the wheel mark in accordance with Council Directive 96/98 of 20 December 1996 on marine equipment.[40] They must provide the Commission and the Member States with periodic reports on fundamental progress in standards and mutual recognition of certificates for materials, equipment and components.

29.051 Article 10(2) provides that the Commission had to submit a report to the European Parliament and the Council by 17 June 2014, based on an independent study, on the level reached in the process of harmonising the rules and procedures and on mutual recognition of certificates for materials, equipment and components.

29.052 Article 10(3) provides that the recognised organisations must co-operate with port State control ("PSC") administrations where a ship of their class is concerned, in particular in order to facilitate the rectification of reported deficiencies or other discrepancies.

29.053 Under Article 10(4), the recognised organisations must provide to all Member States' administrations which have granted any of the authorisations provided for in Article 3 of Directive 2009/15 and to the Commission all relevant information about their classed fleet, transfers, changes, suspensions and withdrawals of class, irrespective of the flag the ships fly. Information on transfers, changes, suspensions, and withdrawals of class, including information on all overdue surveys, overdue recommendations, conditions of class, operating conditions or operating restrictions issued against their classed ships, irrespective of the flag the ships fly, shall also be communicated electronically to the common inspection database used by the Member States for the implementation of Directive 2009/16 of the European Parliament and of the Council of 23 April 2009 on PSC[41] at the same time as it is recorded within the recognised organisation's own systems and in any case no later than 72 hours after the event that gave rise to the obligation to communicate the information. That information, with the exception of recommendations and conditions of class which are not overdue, shall be published on the website of these recognised organisations.

29.054 Article 10(5) provides that the recognised organisations shall not issue statutory certificates to a ship, irrespective of its flag, which has been declassed or is changing class for safety reasons, before giving the opportunity to the competent administration of the flag State to give its opinion within a reasonable time as to whether a full inspection is necessary.

29.055 Article 10(6) provides that in cases of transfer of class from one recognised organisation to another, the losing organisation shall, without undue delay, provide the

---

40 OJ L46/25, 17 February 1997.
41 OJ L131/S7, 28 May 2009.

gaining organisation with the complete history file of the ship and, in particular, inform it of: (a) any overdue surveys; (b) any overdue recommendations and conditions of class; (c) operating conditions issued against the ship; and (d) operating restrictions issued against the ship. New certificates for the ship may be issued by the gaining organisation only after all overdue surveys have been satisfactorily completed and all overdue recommendations or conditions of class previously issued in respect of the ship have been completed as specified by the losing organisation. Prior to the issue of the certificates, the gaining organisation must advise the losing organisation of the date of issue of the certificates and confirm the date, place and action taken to satisfy each overdue survey, overdue recommendation and overdue condition of class. Recognised organisations must establish and implement appropriate common requirements concerning cases of transfer of class where special precautions are necessary. Those cases shall, as a minimum, include the transfer of class of ships of 15 years of age or over and the transfer from a non-recognised organisation to a recognised organisation. Recognised organisations must co-operate with each other in properly implementing the provisions of this paragraph.

Establishment and maintenance of an independent quality assessment and certification entity

29.056 Article 11(1) of Regulation 391/2009 provides that recognised organisations had to establish by 17 June 2011 and then maintain an independent quality assessment and certification entity in accordance with the applicable international quality standards where the relevant professional associations working in the shipping industry may participate in an advisory capacity.

29.057 Under Article 11(2), the quality assessment and certification entity must carry out the following tasks: (a) frequent and regular assessment of the quality management systems of recognised organisations, in accordance with the ISO 9001 quality standard criteria; (b) certification of the quality management systems of recognised organisations, including organisations for which recognition has been requested in accordance with Article 3; (c) issue of interpretations of internationally recognised quality management standards, in particular to take account of the specific features of the nature and obligations of recognised organisations; and (d) adoption of individual and collective recommendations for the improvement of recognised organisations' processes and internal control mechanisms.

29.058 Article 11(3) provides that the quality assessment and certification entity shall have the necessary governance and competences to act independently of the recognised organisations and shall have the necessary means to carry out its duties effectively and to the highest professional standards, safeguarding the independence of the persons performing them. Article 11(3) also provides that the quality assessment and certification entity will lay down its working methods and rules of procedure.

29.059 Article 11(4) provides that the quality assessment and certification entity may request assistance from other external quality assessment bodies.

29.060 Pursuant to Article 11(5), the quality assessment and certification entity must provide the interested parties, including flag States and the Commission, with full information on its annual work plan as well as on its findings and recommendations, particularly with regard to situations where safety might have been compromised.

29.061 Article 11(6) ensures continual review of the quality assessment and certification entity by virtue of it being periodically assessed by the Commission.

29.062 The Commission must report to the Member States on the results and follow-up of its assessment.[42]

Committee on Safe Seas and the Prevention of Pollution from Ships (COSS) and interaction with selected other EU instruments

29.063 Article 12(1) provides that the Commission must be assisted by the Committee on Safe Seas and the Prevention of Pollution from Ships ("COSS") established by Regulation 2099/2002 of the European Parliament and of the Council.[43] The second paragraph provides that where reference is made to that paragraph, Articles 3 and 7 of Decision 1999/468 shall apply, having regard to the provisions of Article 8 thereof. Wherever there is a reference to Article 12(3), Articles 5 and 7 of Decision 1999/468 shall apply, having regard to the provisions of Article 8 thereof and the period laid down in Article 5(6) of Decision 1999/468 shall be set at three months.[44] Article 12(4) provides that where reference is made to that paragraph, Article 5a(1) to (4) and Article 7 of Decision 1999/468 shall apply, having regard to the provisions of Article 8 thereof.

Amendment of Regulation 391/2009

29.064 Article 13(1) provides that the regulation may, without broadening its scope, be amended in order to update the minimum criteria set out in Annex I taking into account, in particular, the relevant decisions of the IMO. These measures designed to amend non-essential elements of the regulation must be adopted in accordance with the regulatory procedure with scrutiny referred to in Article 12(4). Article 13(2) provides that amendments to the international conventions defined in Article 2(b) of this regulation may be excluded from the scope of this regulation, pursuant to Article 5 of Regulation 2099/2002.

Adoption and publication of criteria

29.065 Article 14(1) of Regulation 391/2009 provides that the Commission must adopt and publish:

> "(a) criteria to measure the effectiveness of the rules and procedures as well as the performance of the recognised organisations as regards the safety of, and the prevention of pollution from, their classed ships, having particular regard to the data produced by the Paris Memorandum of Understanding on Port State Control and/or by other similar schemes; and (b) criteria to determine when such performance is to be considered an unacceptable threat to safety or the environment, which may take into account specific circumstances affecting smaller-sized or highly specialised organisations."

These measures designed to amend non-essential elements of the regulation by supplementing it shall be adopted in accordance with the regulatory procedure with scrutiny referred to in Article 12(4).

---

42 Reg. 391/2009, Art. 11(7).
43 Ed., OJ L324/1, 29 November 2002.
44 Reg. 391/2009, Art. 12(3).

29.066 The measures designed to amend non-essential elements of Regulation 391/2009 by supplementing it relating to the implementation of Article 6 and, if appropriate, Article 7 shall be adopted in accordance with the regulatory procedure with scrutiny referred to in Article 12(4).[45]

29.067 Article 14(3) provides that without prejudice to the immediate application of the minimum criteria set out in Annex I, the Commission may, in accordance with the regulatory procedure referred to in Article 12(3), adopt rules on their interpretation and may consider the establishment of objectives for the general minimum criteria referred to in point 3, Part A of Annex I.

Continuation of recognition

29.068 Article 15(1) of Regulation 391/2009 provides that the organisations which, at the entry into force of the regulation, had been granted recognition in accordance with Directive 94/57 shall retain their recognition, subject to the provisions of Article 15(2) which goes on to provide that without prejudice to Articles 5 and 7, the Commission must re-examine all limited recognitions granted under Directive 94/57 in light of Article 4(3) of the regulation by 17 June 2010, with a view to deciding, in accordance with the regulatory procedure referred to in Article 12(3), whether the limitations are to be replaced by others or removed. The limitations must continue to apply until the Commission has taken a decision.

Verification of the holder of recognition

29.069 Article 16 provides that in the course of the assessment pursuant to Article 8(1), the Commission must verify that the holder of the recognition is the relevant legal entity within the organisation to which the provisions of this regulation shall apply. If that is not the case, the Commission shall take a decision amending that recognition. Where the Commission amends the recognition, the Member States shall adapt their agreements with the recognised organisation to take account of the amendment.

Commission must keep the Parliament and the Council informed on the application of Regulation 391/2009

29.070 The Commission must, on a biennial basis, inform the European Parliament and the Council on the application of the regulation.[46]

29.071 Article 18 of Regulation 391/2009 provides that references in EU and national law to Directive 94/57 (i.e. the predecessor measure to Regulation 391/2009) must be construed, as appropriate, as being made to Regulation 391/2009 and must be read in accordance with the correlation table in Annex II. Annex I of Regulation 391/2009 is entitled "minimum criteria for organisations to obtain or to continue to enjoy community recognition". It provides:

---

45 Reg. 391/2009, Art. 14(2).
46 Reg. 391/2009, Art. 17.

"A. GENERAL MINIMUM CRITERIA

1. A recognised organisation must have legal personality in the State of its location. Its accounts shall be certified by independent auditors.
2. The recognised organisation must be able to document extensive experience in assessing the design and construction of merchant ships.
3. The recognised organisation must be equipped at all times with significant managerial, technical, support and research staff commensurate with the size of the fleet in its class, its composition and the organisation's involvement in the construction and conversion of ships. The recognised organisation must be capable of assigning to every place of work, when and as needed, means and staff commensurate with the tasks to be carried out in accordance with general minimum criteria under points 6 and 7 and with the specific minimum criteria under part B.
4. The recognised organisation must have and apply a set of own comprehensive rules and procedures, or the demonstrated ability thereto, for the design, construction and periodic survey of merchant ships, having the quality of internationally recognised standards. They must be published and continually upgraded and improved through research and development programmes.
5. The recognised organisation must have its register of ships published on an annual basis or maintained in an electronic database accessible to the public.
6. The recognised organisation must not be controlled by shipowners or shipbuilders, or by others engaged commercially in the manufacture, equipping, repair or operation of ships. The recognised organisation is not substantially dependent on a single commercial enterprise for its revenue. The recognised organisation does not carry out class or statutory work if it is identical to or has business, personal or family links to the shipowner or operator. This incompatibility shall also apply to surveyors employed by the recognised organisation.
7. The recognised organisation must operate in accordance with the provisions set out in the Annex to IMO Resolution A.789(19) on specifications on the survey and certification functions of recognised organisations acting on behalf of the administration, in so far as they cover matters falling within the scope of this Regulation.

B. SPECIFIC MINIMUM CRITERIA

1. The recognised organisation must provide worldwide coverage by its exclusive surveyors or, in exceptional and duly justified cases, through exclusive surveyors of other recognised organisations.
2. The recognised organisation must be governed by a code of ethics.
3. The recognised organisation must be managed and administered in such a way as to ensure the confidentiality of information required by the administration.
4. The recognised organisation must provide relevant information to the administration, to the Commission and to interested parties.
5. The recognised organisation, its surveyors and its technical staff shall carry out their work without in any way harming the intellectual property rights of shipyards, equipment suppliers, and shipowners, including patents, licences, know-how, or any other kind of knowledge whose use is legally protected at international, Community or national level; under no circumstances, and without prejudice to the assessment powers of Member States and the Commission and in particular under Article 9, may either the recognised organisation or the surveyors and technical staff, whom it employs pass on or divulge commercially relevant data obtained in the course of their work of inspecting, checking, and monitoring ships under construction or repair.
6. The recognised organisation's management must define and document its policy and objectives for, and commitment to, quality and must ensure that this policy is understood, implemented and maintained at all levels in the recognised organisation. The recognised organisation's policy must refer to safety and pollution prevention performance targets and indicators.

7. The recognised organisation must ensure that:

   (a) its rules and procedures are established and maintained in a systematic manner;
   (b) its rules and procedures are complied with and an internal system to measure the quality of service in relation to these rules and procedures is put in place;
   (c) the requirements of the statutory work for which the recognised organisation is authorised are satisfied and an internal system to measure the quality of service in relation to compliance with the international conventions is put in place;
   (d) the responsibilities, powers and interrelation of personnel whose work affects the quality of the recognised organisation's services are defined and documented;
   (e) all work is carried out under controlled conditions;
   (f) a supervisory system is in place which monitors the actions and work carried out by surveyors and technical and administrative staff employed by the recognised organisation;
   (g) surveyors have an extensive knowledge of the particular type of ship on which they carry out their work as relevant to the particular survey to be carried out and of the relevant applicable requirements;
   (h) a system for qualification of surveyors and continuous updating of their knowledge is implemented;
   (i) records are maintained, demonstrating achievement of the required standards in the items covered by the services performed, as well as the effective operation of the quality system;
   (j) a comprehensive system of planned and documented internal audits of the quality related activities is maintained in all locations;
   (k) the statutory surveys and inspections required by the harmonised system of survey and certification for which the recognised organisation is authorised are carried out in accordance with the provision set out in the Annex and Appendix to IMO Resolution A.948(23) on survey guidelines under the harmonised system of survey and certification;
   (l) clear and direct lines of responsibility and control are established between the central and the regional offices of the recognised organisation and between the recognised organisations and their surveyors.

8. The recognised organisation must have developed, implemented and must maintain an effective internal quality system based on appropriate parts of internationally recognised quality standards and in compliance with EN ISO/IEC 17020:2004 (inspection bodies) and with EN ISO 9001:2000 (quality management systems, requirements), as interpreted and certified by the quality assessment and certification entity referred to in Article 11(1).

9. The rules and procedures of the recognised organisation must be implemented in such a way that the organisation remains in a position to derive from its own direct knowledge and judgment a reliable and objective declaration on the safety of the ships concerned by means of class certificates on the basis of which statutory certificates can be issued.

10. The recognised organisation must have the necessary means of assessing, through the use of qualified professional staff and pursuant to the provisions set out in the Annex to IMO Resolution A.913(22) on guidelines on implementation of the International Safety Management (ISM) Code by administrations, the application and maintenance of the safety management system, both shore-based and on board ships, intended to be covered in the certification.

11. The recognised organisation must allow participation in the development of its rules and procedures by representatives of the administration and other parties concerned."

C. DIRECTIVE 2009/15 ON COMMON RULES AND STANDARDS FOR SHIP INSPECTION AND SURVEY ORGANISATIONS AND FOR THE RELEVANT ACTIVITIES OF MARITIME ADMINISTRATIONS

Introduction

29.072 On 23 April 2009, the Parliament and the Council adopted Directive 2009/15 on common rules and standards for ship inspection and survey organisations and for the relevant activities of maritime administrations.[47] Article 15 of Directive 2009/5 provided that the directive would enter into force on the twentieth day following its publication in the *Official Journal of the European Union*. As it was published on 28 May 2000, it entered into force on 17 June 2009. Directive 2009/95 should be read in conjunction with Commission Implementing Directive 2009/111.[48]

29.073 The legal basis for Directive 2009/15 was the TEC, and in particular Article 80(2) of the TEC, which would now be the TFEU and, in particular, Article 100(2) of the TFEU.

29.074 The legislative history of Directive 2009/15 included the usual proposal from the Commission, an opinion of the European Economic and Social Committee[49] and an opinion of the Committee of the Regions.[50]

29.075 It was recognised by the first recital to Directive 2009/15 that the pre-existing measure, Council Directive 94/57 of 22 November 1994 on common rules and standards for ship inspection and survey organisations and for the relevant activities of maritime administrations[51] had been substantially amended several time and since further amendments were to be made, it should be recast in the interests of clarity.

The EU decided not to replace the earlier directive with another directive. The second recital provides that in view of the nature of the provisions of Directive 94/57 it seemed appropriate that its provisions be recast in two different EU legal instruments, namely a directive and a regulation.

29.076 It is useful to recall the safety background to the measure by looking at certain recitals. The background to the directive is clear, in part, from the following:

"(3) In its Resolution of 8 June 1993 on a common policy on safe seas, the Council set the objective of removing all substandard vessels from Community waters and gave priority to Community action designed to secure the effective and uniform implementation of international rules by drawing up common standards for classification societies.

(4) Safety and pollution prevention at sea may be effectively enhanced by strictly applying international conventions, codes and resolutions while furthering the objective of freedom to provide services.

(5) The control of compliance of ships with the uniform international standards for safety and prevention of pollution of the seas is the responsibility of flag and port States.

(6) Member States are responsible for the issuing of international certificates for safety and the prevention of pollution provided for under conventions such as the International Convention for the Safety of Life at Sea of 1 November 1974 (SOLAS 74), the International Convention on Load Lines of 5 April 1966 and the International Convention for the Prevention

---

47 OJ L131/17, 28.5.2009.
48 OJ L366/83, 20 December 2014.
49 OJ C318/195, 23 December 2006.
50 OJ C229/38, 22 September 2006.
51 OJ L319/20, 12 December 1994.

of Pollution from Ships of 2 November 1973 (Marpol), and for the implementation of those conventions.

(7) In compliance with such conventions all Member States may authorise to a varying extent recognised organisations for the certification of such compliance and may delegate the issue of the relevant certificates for safety and the prevention of pollution.

(8) Worldwide a large number of the existing organisations recognised by International Maritime Organisation (IMO) Contracting Parties do not ensure either adequate implementation of the rules or sufficient reliability when acting on behalf of national administrations as they do not have reliable and adequate structures and experience to enable them to carry out their duties in a highly professional manner.

(9) In accordance with SOLAS 74 Chapter II-1, Part A-1, Regulation 3-1, Member States are responsible for ensuring that ships flying their flag are designed, constructed and maintained in compliance with the structural, mechanical and electrical requirements of organisations, recognised by administrations. These organisations therefore produce and implement rules for the design, construction, maintenance and inspection of ships and they are responsible for inspecting ships on behalf of the flag States and certifying that those ships meet the requirements of the international conventions for the issue of the relevant certificates. To enable them to carry out that duty in a satisfactory manner they need to have strict independence, highly specialised technical competence and rigorous quality management.

(11) Ship inspection and survey organisations should be able to offer their services throughout the Community and compete with each other while providing equal levels of safety and of environmental protection. The necessary professional standards for their activities should therefore be uniformly established and applied across the [EU].

29.077 There are other issues addressed by the recitals of the directive. It is recognised that the issue of the cargo ship safety radio certificate may be entrusted to private bodies having sufficient expertise and qualified personnel.

29.078 The directive recognises that a Member State must be able to restrict the number of recognised organisations it authorises in accordance with its needs, based on objective and transparent grounds, subject to control exercised by the Commission in accordance with a committee procedure.[52]

29.079 The fourteenth recital to the directive puts the directive into the broader context of the freedom to provide services: the "Directive should ensure freedom to provide services in the [EU]; accordingly the [EU] should agree with those third countries where some of the recognised organisations are located, to ensure equal treatment for the recognised organisations located in the [EU]".

29.080 The directive contemplates that there is an interaction between the EU and the Member State authorities:

"A tight involvement of the national administrations in ship surveys and in the issue of the related certificates is necessary to ensure full compliance with the international safety rules even if the Member States rely upon recognised organisations, which are not part of their administration for carrying out statutory duties. It is appropriate, therefore, to establish a close working relationship between the administrations and the recognised organisations authorised by them, which may require that the recognised organisations have a local representation on the territory of the Member State on behalf of which they perform their duties."[53]

---

52 Dir. 2005/15, Recital 13.
53 Dir. 2009/15, Recital 15.

29.081 The directive also addresses various other aspects of the issue:

"(16) When a recognised organisation, its inspectors, or its technical staff issue the relevant certificates on behalf of the administration, Member States should consider enabling them, as
regards these delegated activities, to be subject to proportionate legal safeguards and judicial protection, including the exercise of appropriate rights of defence, apart from immunity, which is a prerogative that can only be invoked by Member States as an inseparable
right of sovereignty and therefore that cannot be delegated.

(17) Divergence in terms of financial liability regimes among the recognised organisations
working on behalf of the Member States would impede the proper implementation of this
Directive. In order to contribute to solving this problem it is appropriate to bring about a
degree of harmonisation at Community level of the liability arising out of any marine
casualty caused by a recognised organisation, as decided by a court of law, including settlement of a dispute through arbitration procedures.

(18) The measures necessary for the implementation of this Directive should be adopted in
accordance with Council Decision 1999/468/EC of 28 June 1999 laying down the procedures for the exercise of implementing powers conferred on the Commission.[54]

(19) In particular the Commission should be empowered to amend this Directive in order to
incorporate subsequent amendments to the international conventions, protocols, codes and
resolutions related thereto. Since those measures are of general scope and are designed to
amend non-essential elements of this Directive, inter alia by supplementing it with new
non-essential elements, they must be adopted in accordance with the regulatory procedure
with scrutiny provided for in Article 5a of Decision 1999/468/EC.

(20) Member States should nevertheless be left with the possibility of suspending or withdrawing their authorisation of a recognised organisation while informing the Commission and
the other Member States of their decisions and giving substantiated reasons therefor.

(21) Member States should periodically assess the performance of the recognised organisations
working on their behalf and provide the Commission and all the other Member States
with precise information related to such performance.

(22) As port authorities, Member States are required to enhance safety and prevention of pollution in Community waters through priority inspection of ships carrying certificates of
organisations which do not fulfil the common criteria, thereby ensuring that ships flying
the flag of a third State do not receive more favourable treatment.

(23) At present there are no uniform international standards to which all ships must conform
either at the building stage or during their entire lifetime, as regards hull, machinery and
electrical and control installations. Such standards may be fixed according to the rules of
recognised organisations or to equivalent standards to be decided by the national administrations in accordance with the procedure laid down in Directive 98/34/EC of the European Parliament and of the Council of 22 June 1998 laying down a procedure for the
provision of information in the field of technical standards and regulations and of rules on
Information Society services.[55]

(24) Since the objective of this Directive, namely to establish measures to be followed by the
Member States in their relationship with organisations entrusted with the inspection,
survey and certification of ships, operating in the Community, cannot be sufficiently
achieved by the Member States and can therefore, by reason of the scale of the action, be
better achieved at Community level, the Community may adopt measures, in accordance
with the principle of subsidiarity as set out in Article 5 of the Treaty.[56] In accordance with
the principle of proportionality, as set out in that Article, this Directive does not go
beyond what is necessary in order to achieve that objective.

(25) The obligation to transpose this Directive into national law should be confined to those
provisions which represent a substantive change as compared with the Directive 94/57 ...

---

54 Ed., OJ L184/23, 17 July 1999.
55 Ed., OJ L204/37, 21 July 1998.
56 Ed., this is now, effectively, TEU, Art. 4(3).

The obligation to transpose the provisions which are unchanged arises under that Directive.

(26) This Directive should be without prejudice to the obligations of the Member States relating to the time limits for transposition into national law of the Directives set out in Annex I, Part B.

(27) In accordance with point 34 of the Interinstitutional Agreement on better law-making,[57] Member States are encouraged to draw up, for themselves and in the interest of the Community, their own tables, illustrating, as far as possible, the correlation between this Directive and the transposition measures, and to make them public.

Measures to be followed by ship inspection and survey organisations are laid down in Regulation (EC) No 391/2009 of the European Parliament and the Council of 23 April 2009 on common rules and standards for ship inspection and survey organisations (recast).[58]"

Objective of Directive 2009/15

29.082 Article 1 of Directive 2009/15 provides that the directive

"establishes measures to be followed by the Member States in their relationship with organisations entrusted with the inspection, survey and certification of ships for compliance with the international conventions on safety at sea and prevention of marine pollution, while furthering the objective of freedom to provide services. This includes the development and implementation of safety requirements for hull, machinery and electrical and control installations of ships falling under the scope of the international conventions."

Concepts in Directive 2009/15

29.083 Article 2 of Directive 2009/15 provides that for the purpose of the directive the following definitions shall apply:

"(a) 'ship' means a ship falling within the scope of the international conventions;

(b) 'ship flying the flag of a Member State' means a ship registered in and flying the flag of a Member State in accordance with its legislation. Ships not corresponding to this definition are assimilated to ships flying the flag of a third country;

(c) 'inspections and surveys' means inspections and surveys that are mandatory under the international conventions;

(d) 'international conventions' means the International Convention for the Safety of Life at Sea of 1 November 1974 (SOLAS 74) with the exception of chapter XI-2 of the Annex thereto, the International Convention on Load Lines of 5 April 1966 and the International Convention for the Prevention of Pollution from Ships of 2 November 1973 (MARPOL), together with the protocols and amendments thereto, and the related codes of mandatory status in all Member States, with the exception of paragraphs 16.1, 18.1 and 19 of part 2 of the IMO Instruments Implementation Code, and of sections 1.1, 1.3, 3.9.3.1, 3.9.3.2 and 3.9.3.3 of part 2 of the IMO Code for Recognized Organizations, in their up-to-date version;

(e) 'organisation' means a legal entity, its subsidiaries and any other entities under its control, which jointly or separately carry out tasks falling under the scope of this Directive;

(f) 'control' means, for the purpose of point (e), rights, contracts or any other means, in law or in fact, which, either separately or in combination confer the possibility of exercising decisive influence on a legal entity or enable that entity to carry out tasks falling under the scope of this Directive;

---

57 Ed., OJ C321/1, 31 December 2003.
58 Ed., OJ L131/11.

(g) 'recognised organisation' means an organisation recognised in accordance with Regulation (EC) No 391/2009;

(h) 'authorisation' means an act whereby a Member State grants an authorisation or delegates powers to a recognised organisation;

(i) 'statutory certificate' means a certificate issued by or on behalf of a flag State in accordance with the international conventions;

(j) 'rules and procedures' means a recognised organisation's requirements for the design, construction, equipment, maintenance and survey of ships;

(k) 'class certificate' means a document issued by a recognised organisation certifying the fitness of a ship for a particular use or service in accordance with the rules and procedures laid down and made public by that recognised organisation;

(l) 'cargo ship safety radio certificate' means the certificate introduced by the 1988 Protocol amending SOLAS, adopted by the International Maritime Organisation (IMO)."

Enforcement of Directive 2009/15

29.084 Article 3(3) of Directive 2009/15 provides that Article 3 does not concern the certification of specific items of marine equipment.

29.085 Article 3(1) provides that in assuming their responsibilities and obligations under the international conventions, Member States must ensure that their competent administrations can ensure appropriate enforcement of the provisions thereof, in particular with regard to the inspection and survey of ships and the issue of statutory certificates and exemption certificates as provided for by the international conventions. Member States must act in accordance with the relevant provisions of the annex and the appendix to IMO Resolution A.847(20) on guidelines to assist flag States in the implementation of IMO instruments.

29.086 Article 3(2) goes on to provide that where:

"for the purpose of Article 3(1), a Member State shall entrust these duties only to recognise organisations where it decides with respect to ships flying its flag:

(i) to authorise organisations to undertake fully or in part inspections and surveys related to statutory certificates including those for the assessment of compliance with the rules referred to in Article 11(2) and, where appropriate, to issue or renew the related certificates; or

(ii) to rely upon organisations to undertake fully or in part the inspections and surveys referred to in point (i). The competent administration shall in all cases approve the first issue of the exemption certificates. However, for the cargo ship safety radio certificate these duties may be entrusted to a private body recognised by a competent administration and having sufficient expertise and qualified personnel to carry out specified safety assessment work on radio-communication on its behalf. Article 3(3) provides that Article 3 does not concern the certification of specific items of marine equipment."

Article 4: Recognition of organisations

29.087 Article 4(1) states that in applying Article 3(2), Member States must, in principle, not refuse to authorise any of the recognised organisations to undertake such functions, subject to the provisions of Article 4(2) and Articles 5 and 9. However, they may restrict the number of organisations they authorise in accordance with their needs provided there are transparent and objective grounds for so doing. At the request of a Member State, the Commission shall, in accordance with the regulatory procedure referred to in Article 6(2), adopt appropriate measures to ensure the correct application of the first subparagraph of this paragraph as regards refusal of authorisation and of Article 8 as regards those cases where authorisation is suspended or withdrawn. Article 4(2) provides that in order for a Member State to accept that a recognised organisation located in a third State is to carry out fully or in part the duties mentioned in Article 3 it may request the third State in question to grant reciprocal treatment to those recognised organisations which are located in the EU. In addition, the EU may request the third State where a recognised organisation is located to grant reciprocal treatment to those recognised organisations which are located in the EU.

Article 5: Working relationships

29.088 Article 5(1) provides that Member States which take a decision as described in Article 3(2) must set out a "working relationship" between their competent administration and the organisations acting on their behalf.

29.089 Article 5(2) provides:

"The working relationship shall be regulated by a formalised written and non-discriminatory agreement or equivalent legal arrangements setting out the specific duties and functions assumed by the organisations and including at least:

  (a) the provisions set out in Appendix II of IMO Resolution A.739(18) on guidelines for the authorisation of organisations acting on behalf of the administration, while drawing inspiration from the Annex, Appendices and Attachment to IMO MSC/Circular 710 and MEPC/Circular 307 on a model agreement for the authorisation of recognised organisations acting on behalf of the administration;

  (b) the following provisions concerning financial liability:

   (i) if liability arising out of any marine casualty is finally and definitely imposed on the administration by a court of law or as part of the settlement of a dispute through arbitration procedures, together with a requirement to compensate the injured parties for loss of or damage to property or personal injury or death, which is proved in that court of law to have been caused by a wilful act or omission or gross negligence of the recognised organisation, its bodies, employees, agents or others who act on behalf of the recognised organisation, the administration shall be entitled to financial compensation from the recognised organisation to the extent that that loss, damage, injury or death was, as decided by that court, caused by the recognised organisation;

   (ii) if liability arising out of any marine casualty is finally and definitely imposed on the administration by a court of law or as part of the settlement of a dispute through arbitration procedures, together with a requirement to compensate the injured parties for personal injury or death, which is proved in that court of law to have been caused by any negligent or reckless act or omission of the recognised organisation, its employees, agents or others who act on behalf of the recognised organisation, the administration shall be entitled to financial compensation from the recognised organisation to the extent that that personal injury or death was, as decided by that court, caused by the recognised organisation; the Member States may limit the maximum amount payable by the recognised organisation, which must, however, be at least equal to EUR 4 million;

   (iii) if liability arising out of any marine casualty is finally and definitely imposed on the administration by a court of law or as part of the settlement of a dispute through arbitration procedures, together with a requirement to compensate the injured parties for loss of or damage to property, which is proved in that court of law to have been caused by any negligent or reckless act or omission of the recognised organisation, its employees, agents or others who act on behalf of the recognised organisation, the administration shall be entitled to financial compensation from the recognised organisation, to the extent that that loss or damage was, as decided by that court, caused by the recognised organisation; the Member States may limit the maximum amount payable by the recognised organisation, which must, however, be at least equal to EUR 2 million;

(c) provisions for a periodical audit by the administration or by an impartial external body appointed by the administration into the duties the organisations are undertaking on its behalf, as referred to in Article 9(1);

(d) the possibility for random and detailed inspections of ships;

(e) provisions for compulsory reporting of essential information about their classed fleet, and changes, suspensions and withdrawals of class."

29.090 Article 5(3) provides that the agreement or equivalent legal arrangement may require the recognised organisation to have a local representation on the territory of the Member State on behalf of which it performs the duties referred to in Article 3. Article 5(3) also provides that a local representation with legal personality under the law of the Member State and subject to the jurisdiction of its national courts may satisfy such a requirement.

29.091 Each Member State must provide the Commission with precise information on the working relationship established in accordance with the article and the Commission must subsequently inform the other Member States thereof.

Article 6: assistance by COSS to the Commission

29.092 Article 6(1) provides that the Commission must be assisted by the COSS established by Regulation (EC) No 2099/2002 of the European Parliament and of the Council.[59] Where reference is made to Article 6(2) then Articles 5 and 7 of Decision 1999/468 shall apply, having regard to the provisions of Article 8 thereof. The period laid down in Article 5(6) of Decision 1999/468 shall be set at three months. Article 6(3) provides that where reference is made to the paragraph then Article 5a(1) to (4) and Article 7 of Decision 1999/468 shall apply, having regard to the provisions of Article 8 thereof.

Article 7: amendments to the regime

29.093 Article 7 provides:

"1. This Directive may, without broadening its scope, be amended in order to:

(a) incorporate, for the purposes of this Directive, subsequent amendments to the international conventions, protocols, codes and resolutions related thereto referred to in Articles 2(d), 3(1) and 5(2), which have entered into force;

(b) alter the amounts specified in points (ii) and (iii) of Article 5(2)(b).

These measures designed to amend non-essential elements of this Directive shall be adopted in accordance with the regulatory procedure with scrutiny referred to in Article 6(3).

---

59 OJ L324/1, 29 November 2002.

2. Following the adoption of new instruments or protocols to the international conventions referred to in Article 2(d), the Council, acting on a proposal from the Commission, shall decide, taking into account the Member States' parliamentary procedures as well as the relevant procedures within the IMO, on the detailed arrangements for ratifying those new instruments or protocols, while ensuring that they are applied uniformly and simultaneously in the Member States.

The amendments to the international instruments referred to in Article 2(d) and Article 5 may be excluded from the scope of this Directive, pursuant to Article 5 of Regulation (EC) No 2099/2002."

Article 8: amendments to the regime

29.094 Article 8 states that notwithstanding the minimum criteria specified in Annex I of Regulation 391/2009, where a Member State considers that a recognised organisation can no longer be authorised to carry out on its behalf the tasks specified in Article 3, it may suspend or withdraw such authorisation. In such a case, the Member State must inform the Commission and the other Member States of its decision without delay and give substantiated reasons therefor.

Article 9: supervision of recognised organisations

29.095 Article 9(1) provides that each Member State must satisfy itself that the recognised organisations acting on its behalf for the purpose of Article 3(2) effectively carry out the functions referred to in that article to the satisfaction of its competent administration. Article 9(2) goes on to provide that in order to carry out the task referred to in Article 9(1), each Member State must, at least on a biennial basis, monitor every recognised organisation acting on its behalf and shall provide the other Member States and the Commission with a report on the results of such monitoring activities at the latest by 31 March of the year following the year in which the monitoring was carried out.

Article 10: Member State reports to the Commission

29.096 Article 10 provides that in exercising their inspection rights and obligations as port States, Member States must report to the Commission and to other Member States, and inform the flag State concerned, if they find that valid statutory certificates have been issued by recognised organisations acting on behalf of a flag State to a ship which does not fulfil the relevant requirements of the international conventions, or in the event of any failure of a ship carrying a valid class certificate and relating to items covered by that certificate. Only cases of ships representing a serious threat to safety and the environment or showing evidence of particularly negligent behaviour of the recognised organisations shall be reported for the purposes of Article 10. The recognised organisation concerned shall be advised of the case at the time of the initial inspection so that it can take appropriate follow-up action immediately.

Article 11: Member State obligation relating to vessels flying its flag

29.097 Article 11(1) provides that each Member State must ensure that ships flying its flag are designed, constructed, equipped and maintained in accordance with the rules and procedures relating to hull, machinery and electrical and control installation requirements of a recognised organisation. Article 11(2) states that a Member State may decide to use rules it considers equivalent to the rules and procedures of a recognised organisation only on the proviso that it immediately notifies them to the Commission in conformity with the procedure under Directive 98/34 and to the other Member States and they are not objected to by another Member State or the Commission and are held, through the regulatory procedure referred to in Article 6(2) of Directive 2009/15, not to be equivalent. Article 11(3) provides that Member States must co-operate with the recognised organisations they authorise in the development of the rules and procedures of those organisations. They shall confer with the recognised organisations with a view to achieving consistent interpretation of the international conventions.

Article 12: Commission reports to the Parliament and Council

29.098 Article 12 provides that the Commission must, on a biennial basis, inform the European Parliament and the Council of progress in the implementation of Directive 2009/15 in the Member States.

Article 13: entry into force of the directive

29.099 Article 13(1) provides that Member States had to bring into force the laws, regulations and administrative provisions necessary to comply with Directive 2009/15 by 17 June 2011. They had to forthwith inform the Commission. When they are adopted by Member States, these measures must contain a reference to Directive 2009/15 shall be accompanied by such reference on the occasion of their official publication. They shall also include a statement that references in existing laws, regulations and administrative provisions to the directives repealed by this directive shall be construed as references to this directive. The methods of making such references shall be laid down by Member States. Article 12(2) provides that a Member States must communicate to the Commission the text of the main provisions of national law which they adopt in the field covered by the directive.

Article 14: repeal

29.100 Article 14 provides that Directive 94/57, as amended by the directives listed in Annex I, Part A, must be repealed with effect from 17 June 2009, without prejudice to the obligations of the Member States relating to the time limits for transposition into national law of the directives set out in Annex I, Part B.

D. COMMISSION DECISION 2005/311 OF 18 APRIL 2005 ON THE EXTENSION OF THE LIMITED RECOGNITION OF "RINAVE – REGISTRO INTERNACIONAL NAVAL"

29.101 On 18 April 2005, the Commission adopted Decision 2005/311 on the extension of the limited recognition of "RINAVE – Registro Internacional Naval, SA".[60] The

---

60 OJ L99/15, 19 April 2005.

background to the decision was Council Directive 94/57 of 22 November 1994 on common rules and standards for ship inspection and survey organisations and for the relevant activities of maritime administrations,[61] and in particular Article 4(3). The Commission had received letters in 2003 from Portugal, requesting the extension of the limited recognition of "RINAVE – Registro Internacional Naval, SA" (hereafter RINAVE) in accordance with Article 4(2) and (3) of Directive 93/57, for unlimited time.

29.102 It is useful to consider the background to the decision. The first recital of Decision 2005/311 provides that the limited recognition under Article 4(3) of Directive 94/57 is a recognition granted to organisations (classification societies) which fulfil all criteria other than those set out under paragraphs 2 and 3 of the section "General" of the annex, but which is limited in time and scope in order for the organisation concerned to further gain experience.

29.103 The Commission went on to recall other facts or factors. Commission Decision 2000/481[62] recognised RINAVE on the basis of Article 4(3) for Portugal, for a period of three years. The Commission verified that RINAVE met all the criteria in the annex of the abovementioned directive other than those set out under paragraphs 2 and 3 of the section "General" of the annex, including the new provisions referred to in Article 4(5). The assessment carried out by the Commission furthermore revealed the organisation's dependence on the technical rules of another recognised organisation. During the period 2000 to 2003, the safety and pollution prevention performance records of RINAVE as published by the Paris Memorandum of Understanding on port State control were consistently of the highest level.

29.104 The Commission recalled that therefore the measures provided for in the decision were in accordance with the opinion of the Committee set out in Article 7 of Directive 94/57.

29.105 Article 1 therefore provided that the limited recognition of RINAVE was extended pursuant to Article 4(3) of Directive 94/57 for a period of three years as from the date of adoption of the decision. By virtue of Article 2, the effects of the extended recognition were limited to Portugal.

E. COMMISSION REGULATION 788/2014 OF 18 JULY 2014 LAYING DOWN DETAILED RULES FOR THE IMPOSITION OF FINES AND PERIODIC PENALTY PAYMENTS AND THE WITHDRAWAL OF RECOGNITION TO ARTICLES 6 AND 7 OF REGULATION (EC) NO 391/2009 OF THE EUROPEAN PARLIAMENT AND OF THE COUNCIL

Introduction

29.106 It was anticipated by the Parliament and Council, when adopting Regulation 391/2009[63] that the Commission would adopt detailed rules for the imposition of fines and periodic penalties pursuant to Articles 6 and 7 of the regulation.

29.107 On 18 July 2014, the Commission adopted

---

61 OJ L319, 12 December 1994, p. 20. Directive as last amended by Directive 2002/84 of the European Parliament and of the Council (OJ L324, 29 November 2002, p. 53).
62 OJ L193/91, 29 July 2000.
63 OJ L131, 28 May 2009.

"Regulation 788/2014 laying down detailed rules for the imposition of fines and periodic penalty payments and the withdrawal of recognition of ship inspection and survey organisations pursuant to Articles 6 and 7 of Regulation (EC) No 391/2009 of the European Parliament and of the Council."[64]

29.108 Articles 6 and 7 of Regulation (EC) No 391/2009 empower the Commission to impose fines and periodic penalty payments on recognised organisations, as defined in Article 2 of that regulation, or to withdraw their recognition, in order to ensure the enforcement of the criteria and obligations established under that regulation with a clear view to removing any potential threat to safety or the environment. These are not criminal fines in the domestic law sense, but are fines.

29.109 The Commission believes that it is in the interest of transparency to lay down, in accordance with Article 14(2) of Regulation (EC) No 391/2009, detailed rules of procedure for decision-making, as well as the methodology for the calculation of fines and periodic penalty payments by the Commission so that it is known in advance by the organisations concerned, including specific criteria for the Commission to appraise the gravity of the case and the extent to which safety or the protection of the environment has been compromised.[65]

29.110 The Commission hopes that through the introduction of fines and periodic penalty payments the Commission should have a supplementary tool, allowing it to give a more nuanced, flexible and graduated response to a breach of the rules contained in Regulation 391/2009 by a recognised organisation, compared to the withdrawal of its recognition.[66] Whether this happens will only be capable of judging with the passage of time.

29.111 Periodic penalty payments should, according to the Commission, be effective in ensuring that any breach of the obligations and requirements laid down in Regulation 391/2009 is promptly and appropriately remedied.[67] Therefore, according to the Commission, Regulation 391/2009 empowers the Commission to apply periodic penalty payments where a recognised organisation has failed to undertake the preventive and remedial actions required by the Commission, after a reasonable period and until such time as the required actions have been taken by the recognised organisation concerned.[68] If necessary, in light of the circumstances of the case, the daily amount of the periodic penalty payments may gradually be increased to reflect the urgency of the requested actions.[69]

29.112 The calculation of fines and periodic penalty payments as a fraction of the turnover of the organisation, bearing in mind the maximum ceiling established in accordance with Regulation 391/2009, is, according to the Commission, "a simple method to make the fines and periodic penalty payments dissuasive while remaining proportionate to both the gravity of the case and the economic capacity of the organisation concerned, in light of the diverse sizes of recognised organisations".[70] It is a method of calculating fines elsewhere in EU law including competition law.

---

64 OJ L214/12, 19 July 2014. Corrigendum was published at: OJ L234/15, 7 August 2014.
65 Reg. 788/2014, recital 2.
66 Reg. 788/2014, recital 3.
67 Reg. 788/2014, recital 4.
68 Ibid.
69 Ibid.
70 Reg. 788/2014, recital 5.

29.113 The Commission recalls in recital 6 to Regulation 788/2014 that the application of the maximum aggregate amount ceiling to the fines and periodic penalty payments should be clearly set out taking into account the different circumstances where this would apply, in the interests of transparency and legal certainty.

29.114 The Commission also recalls that for the same reasons, the way in which the total average turnover in the preceding three business years for the activities falling under the scope of Regulation 391/2009 is calculated for each recognised organisation should also be laid down.[71]

29.115 The regulation provides that it is appropriate that a decision to withdraw the recognition of an organisation on the basis of the conditions laid down in Article 7(1) of Regulation 391/2009 should consider all factors linked to the overarching objective of monitoring the recognised organisations' operations and overall performance, including the effectiveness of any fines and periodic penalty payments already imposed for repeated and serious breaches of that regulation.[72]

29.116 The eighth recital provides that a specific procedure should be laid down in order to enable the Commission, be it at its own initiative or at the request of Member State(s), to withdraw the recognition of an organisation pursuant to Regulation 391/2009, further to the Commission's powers to assess recognised organisations and to impose fines and periodic penalty payments with the associated procedures set out in this regulation.[73]

29.117 The ninth recital provides that it is important that a decision to impose fines, periodic penalty payments or the withdrawal of recognition in accordance with Regulation 788/2014 is based exclusively on grounds on which the recognised organisation concerned has been able to comment.

29.118 The tenth recital provides that Regulation 788/2014 respects the fundamental rights and observes the principles recognised by the Charter of Fundamental Rights of the European Union, in particular the right of defence and the principles of confidentiality and *ne bis in idem*, in accordance with the general principles of law of the Court of Justice of the European Union ("CJEU") but whether this is so will be tested over time and it is simply not a matter of affirmation.

29.119 The regulation also provides that decisions imposing fines and periodic penalty payments in accordance with this regulation should be enforceable in accordance with Article 299 of the TFEU and can be subject to review by the CJEU.[74]

29.120 Time limits are also provided for in the regulation. The twelfth recital provides that for the purpose of ensuring fairness and legal certainty in the conduct of the procedure, it is necessary to lay down detailed rules for the calculation of time limits set by the Commission in the course of the procedure and of the limitation periods that apply to the Commission for the imposition and enforcement of fines and periodic penalty payments, taking into account also the date of entry into force of Regulation 391/2009.

29.121 The thirteenth recital recognises that the enforcement of Regulation 788/2014 requires effective co-operation between the Member States concerned, the Commission and the EMSA, so the regulation seeks to clarify the rights and obligations of each of

---

71 Reg. 788/2014, recital 6.
72 Reg. 788/2014, recital 5.
73 Reg. 788/2014, recital 8.
74 Reg. 788/2014, recital 11.

these parties in the procedures laid down in this regulation, in order to ensure the effective conduct of the inquiry, decision-making and follow-up process pursuant to Articles 6 and 7 of Regulation 391/2009.

General provisions

29.122 Chapter 1 is entitled "General Provision" and consists simply of two articles.

29.123 Article 1 ("Subject matter") provides that the regulation: (a) lays down rules for the implementation of Articles 6 and 7 of Regulation 391/2009 by the Commission; and (b) sets out the criteria for establishing the amount of fines and periodic penalty payments, the decision-making procedure to impose a fine and a periodic penalty payment or to withdraw the recognition of a recognised organisation on the Commission's own initiative or at the request of a Member State.

29.124 Article 2 ("Definitions") provides that for the purposes of the regulation, the definitions set out in Article 2 of Regulation 391/2009 shall apply. The term "Member State concerned" means any Member State that has entrusted a recognised organisation with the inspection, survey and certification of ships flying its flag for compliance with the international conventions, in accordance with Directive 2009/15 of the European Parliament and of the Council of 23 April 2009 on common rules and standards for ship inspection and survey organisations and for the relevant activities of maritime administrations,[75] including the Member State that has submitted the request for recognition of that organisation to the Commission, in accordance with Article 3 of Regulation 391/2009.

Fines and periodic penalty payments

29.125 Article 3 ("Identification of infringements") provides:

"1. The Commission shall identify an infringement under Article 6(1) of Regulation (EC) No 391/2009 where:

    (a) the serious or repeated failure by a recognised organisation to fulfil one of the minimum criteria set out in Annex I of Regulation (EC) No 391/2009 or its obligations under Articles 8(4), 9, 10 and 11 of Regulation (EC) No 391/2009 reveals serious shortcomings in a recognised organisation's structure, systems, procedures or internal controls;

    (b) a recognised organisation's worsening performance, taking into account Commission Decision … 2009/491,[76] reveals serious shortcomings in that organisation's structure, systems, procedures or internal controls;

    (c) a recognised organisation has deliberately provided incorrect, incomplete or misleading information to the Commission in the course of its assessment or otherwise obstructed that assessment.

2. In any infringement procedure under this Regulation, the burden of proving an infringement shall rest on the Commission."

---

75 OJ L131/97, 28 May 2009.
76 OJ L162/6, 25.6.2009.

29.126 Article 4 deals with the calculation of fines. Article 4(1) provides that a basic fine of 0.6% of the total average turnover of the recognised organisation, as determined in accordance with Article 9, shall be initially assigned to each infringement established on the basis of Article 6(1) of Regulation 391/2009. Article 4(2) provides that for the calculation of the individual fine for each infringement the basic fine referred to in paragraph 1 shall be increased or reduced, on the basis of the seriousness and of the effects of the infringement, in particular the extent to which safety or the protection of the environment have been compromised, in accordance with Articles 5 and 6 respectively. Under Article 4(3), the maximum amount of each individual fine shall not exceed 1.8% of the total average turnover of the recognised organisation. Where one action or omission of the recognised organisation forms the sole basis of two or more infringements under Article 6(1)(a) of Regulation 391/2009 identified in accordance with Article 3(1)(a) of Regulation 788/2014, the concurrent individual fine shall be the highest of the individual fines calculated for the underlying infringements.[77] These fines are much lower than the fines imposed for breaches of competition law.

The total fine imposed on a recognised organisation in one decision shall be the sum of all individual fines resulting from the application of paragraphs 1 to 4 of Article 4, without prejudice to the maximum ceiling established under Article 6(3) of Regulation 391/2009, as detailed in Article 8 of Regulation 788/2014.[78]

29.127 Article 5 deals with the assessment of the seriousness of an infringement:

"When assessing the seriousness of each infringement the Commission shall take into account all relevant aggravating and mitigating circumstances, in particular the following:

    (a) whether the organisation has acted with negligence or intent;
    (b) the number of actions or omissions of the recognised organisation which give rise to the infringement;
    (c) whether the infringement affects isolated offices, geographical areas or the entire organisation;
    (d) the recurrence of the actions or omissions of the recognised organisation giving rise to the infringement;
    (e) the duration of the infringement;
    (f) a misrepresentation of the actual condition of ships in the certificates and documents of compliance delivered by the recognised organisation, or the inclusion of incorrect or misleading information therein;
    (g) prior sanctions, including fines, imposed on the same recognised organisation;
    (h) whether the infringement results from an agreement between recognised organisations or a concerted practice, which have as their object or effect the breach of the criteria and obligations provided in Regulation … 391/2009;
    (i) the degree of diligence and cooperation of the recognised organisation in the discovery of the relevant actions or omissions, as well as in the determination of the infringements by the Commission."

29.128 The assessment of the effects of an infringement is addressed by Article 6:

"When assessing the effects of each infringement, in particular the extent to which safety and the protection of the environment have been compromised, the Commission shall take into account all relevant aggravating and mitigating circumstances, in particular the following:

---

77 Reg. 788/2014, Art. 4(4).
78 Ibid.

(a) the nature and extent of the deficiencies actually or potentially affecting the fleet certified by the organisation, which the said organisation, as a result of the infringement, has failed to detect or may not be able to detect, or has failed to or may not be able to request the timely correction of, taking into account in particular the criteria for the detention of a ship laid down in Annex X of Directive 2009/16/EC of the European Parliament and of the Council[79] on port State control;

(b) the proportion of the fleet certified by the organisation actually or potentially affected;

(c) any other circumstances posing specific identifiable risks, such as the type of the ships actually or potentially affected."

29.129 Article 7 provides for periodic penalty payments, which are a helpful proportionate step short of a fine. The article provides:

"1. Periodic penalty payments as referred to in Article 6(2) of Regulation 391/2009 may be imposed by the Commission on the organisation concerned, without prejudice to the fines imposed pursuant to Article 3, in order to ensure that preventive and remedial action is taken as required by the Commission in the course of its assessment of the recognised organisation.

2. In the decision imposing fines pursuant to Article 3 the Commission may also establish periodic penalty payments to be imposed on the recognised organisation if, and for as long as, it fails to undertake remedial action or incurs unjustified delays in bringing the infringement to an end.

3. The decision imposing the periodic penalty payments shall determine the time limit within which the recognised organisation has to comply with the required action.

4. Periodic penalty payments shall apply as from the day following the expiry of the time limit established in accordance with paragraph 3 until the day on which appropriate remedial action has been undertaken by the organisation, provided that the remedial action is considered satisfactory by the Commission.

5. The basic amount per day of the periodic penalty payments for each infringement shall be 0,0033% of the total average turnover of the recognised organisation calculated in accordance with Article 9. For the calculation of the individual amount of periodic penalty payments for each infringement, the basic amount shall be adjusted based on the seriousness of the infringement and taking into account the extent to which safety or the protection of the environment has been compromised, in the light of Articles 5 and 6 of this Regulation.

6. The Commission may decide, in light of the circumstances of the case, and in particular in view of the urgency of the remedial action to be undertaken by the organisation concerned, to increase the daily amount for periodic penalty payments up to the following limits:

(a) when the recognised organisation exceeds the time limit established pursuant to paragraph 3 by more than 120 days, from the 121st to the 300th day from the expiry of the time limit, 0,005% per day of the organisation's total average turnover, calculated in accordance with Article 9;

(b) when the recognised organisation exceeds the time limit established pursuant to paragraph 3 by more than 300 days, from the 301st day from the expiry of the time limit, 0,01% per day of the organisation's total average turnover, calculated in accordance with Article 9.

7. The total amount of periodic penalty payments imposed under this Article, individually or in addition to fines, shall not exceed the maximum ceiling established under Article 6(3) of Regulation 391/2009, as detailed in Article 8 of this Regulation."

29.130 Article 8 (entitled "Determination of maximum aggregate amount of fines and periodic penalty payments") provides a ceiling for fines and periodic penalty payments.

---

79 Ed., OJ L131/57, 23 May 2009.

"The maximum aggregate amount of fines and periodic penalty payments imposed to the recognised organisation, as established in Article 6(3) of Regulation 391/2009, shall be determined as follows:

(a) the aggregate amount of the fines imposed on a recognised organisation in accordance with Article 4 within one business year for that organisation, taking into account the date of the decision to impose the fines and, in case of more than one decision imposing fines to that organisation, the date of the first decision imposing a fine on that organisation, shall not exceed 5% of the total average turnover of that organisation calculated in accordance with Article 9;

(b) the aggregate amount of the fines imposed on a recognised organisation in accordance with Article 4 within one business year for that organisation, determined in accordance with paragraph 1, and the periodic penalty payments imposed in the same decisions in accordance with Article 7(2) and accrued for as long as appropriate remedial action is not undertaken by the organisation shall not exceed 5% of the total average turnover of that organisation calculated in accordance with Article 9. Without prejudice to Article 21, recovery by the Commission of the periodic penalty payments shall not exceed the 5% ceiling;

(c) the aggregate amount of the periodic penalty payments imposed on a recognised organisation in accordance with Article 7(1) and accrued for as long as appropriate preventive or remedial action is not undertaken by the organisation shall not exceed 5% of the total average turnover of that organisation calculated in accordance with Article 9. Without prejudice to Article 21, recovery by the Commission of the periodic penalty payments shall not exceed the 5% ceiling."

29.131 Whenever fines are calculated by reference to turnover, there is a need to define turnover. The method chosen by Regulation 788/2014 pays attention to turnover over the previous three years rather than, as in competition law, over the last year. Article 9 ("Calculation of Turnover") provides:

"1. For the purposes of this Regulation the total average turnover of the recognised organisation concerned shall be one third of the amount obtained by adding, over the three business years preceding the Commission's decision, the aggregate turnover of the parent entity holding the recognition and all legal entities which are encompassed in that recognition at the end of each year.

2. In the case of a group with certified consolidated accounts, the turnover referred to in paragraph 1 shall be, as regards the parent entity and all legal entities included in that group which are encompassed in the recognition at the end of each business year, the consolidated revenue of those entities.

3. In the application of paragraphs 1 and 2 only the activities falling under the scope of Regulation 391/2009 shall be taken into account."

29.132 Chapter III of the regulation deals with "Withdrawal of Recognition". Article 10 deals with withdrawal of recognition.

"1. Upon its own initiative or at the request of a Member State, the Commission may adopt a decision to withdraw the recognition of an organisation, in the cases referred to in Article 7(1) points (a) to (e) of Regulation 391/2009.

2. In order to determine whether a repeated and serious failure constitutes an unacceptable threat to safety or the environment in accordance with Article 7(1)(a) and (b) of Regulation 391/2009, the following elements shall be taken into account:

(a) the information and circumstances referred to in Article 7(2) of Regulation 391/2009, particularly in light of the circumstances referred to in Articles 5 and 6 of this Regulation;

(b) the criteria and, as the case may be, thresholds defined in Commission Decision 2009/491 …

3. When fines and periodic penalty payments imposed on a recognised organisation reach the maximum ceiling established in accordance with Article 6(3) of Regulation 391/2009 and appropriate corrective action has not been taken by the recognised organisation, the Commission may consider that these measures have not attained their objective of removing any potential threat to safety or the environment."

29.133 The procedure to withdraw recognition at the request of a Member State is addressed by Article 11:

"1. Where a Member State requests the Commission to withdraw the recognition of an organisation in accordance with Article 7(3) of Regulation … 391/2009, it shall address that request in writing to the Commission.
2. The requesting Member State shall explain the reasons for its request in full detail and by reference, as appropriate, to the criteria listed in Article 7(1) and the circumstances listed in Article 7(2) of Regulation … 391/2009, as well as the circumstances listed in paragraphs 2 and 3 of Article 10 of this Regulation.
3. The requesting Member State shall provide the Commission with all necessary documentary evidence supporting its request, duly classified and numbered.
4. The Commission shall acknowledge receipt of the Member State's request in writing.
5. Where the Commission considers that additional information, clarification or evidence is necessary in order to take a decision, it shall inform the requesting Member State and invite it to supplement its submission as appropriate within a designated time limit, which shall not be less than four weeks. The Member State's request shall not be considered complete until all necessary information has been provided.
6. Within one year of receipt of a complete request, the Commission shall, if it concludes that the Member State's request is justified, address a statement of objections to the organisation concerned in accordance with Article 12, with a view to withdrawing its recognition in accordance with this Regulation. In this case, the requesting Member State shall be granted the consideration and rights of a Member State concerned under Chapter IV of this Regulation.
    If, within the same time limit, the Commission concludes that the Member State's request is unjustified, it shall inform the requesting Member State, stating the reasons thereof and inviting that to submit its observations within a designated time limit, which shall not be less than three months. Within six months of receipt of these observations, the Commission shall either confirm that the request is unjustified or issue a statement of objections in accordance with the first subparagraph.
7. If the Commission concludes that the Member State's request is unjustified or that it remains incomplete after the expiry of the time limit referred to in paragraph 5, the Commission may choose to incorporate all or part of that request and its accompanying evidence into the assessment of the recognised organisation undertaken in accordance with Article 8 of Regulation (EC) No 391/2009.
8. The Commission shall report yearly to the COSS on the requests for withdrawal submitted by the Member States as well as the on-going withdrawal procedures initiated by the Commission."

29.134 Chapter IV ("Common Provisions") deals with statement of objections, requests for information, oral hearings and periodic penalty payments for non-co-operation. Article 12 deals with the statement of objections:

"1. Where the Commission considers that there are grounds to impose a fine and periodic penalty payments on a recognised organisation in accordance with Article 6 of Regulation … 391/2009, or to withdraw an organisation's recognition in accordance with Article 7 of that Regulation, it shall address a statement of objections to the organisation and notify the Member States concerned.

2. The statement of objections shall include:

> (a) a detailed account of the recognised organisation's actions and omissions, including the description of the relevant facts and the identification of the provisions of Regulation ... 391/2009, which the Commission considers to have been breached by the recognised organisation;
>
> (b) an identification of the evidence on which the relevant findings are based, including by reference to inspection reports, assessment reports, or any other relevant documents which have been previously communicated to the organisation concerned by the Commission or by the European Maritime Safety Agency acting on the Commission's behalf;
>
> (c) a notice that fines and periodic penalty payments or the withdrawal of recognition may be imposed by the Commission in accordance with Articles 6 or 7 of Regulation ... 391/2009.

3. When notifying the statement of objections, the Commission shall invite the recognised organisation and the Member States concerned to submit written observations within a designated time limit, which shall not, in any event, be less than six weeks of the date of receipt of the statement of objections. The Commission shall not be obliged to take into account submissions received after the expiry of that time limit, without prejudice to the provisions of Article 24 paragraph 4 of this Regulation.

4. The notification of a statement of objections shall not suspend the assessment of the organisation concerned. At any moment prior to the adoption of a decision to impose a fine and periodic penalty payments, or the withdrawal of recognition in accordance with this Regulation, the Commission may decide to carry out additional inspections of an organisation's offices and facilities, to visit ships certified by the organisation or to request the recognised organisation in writing to provide additional information relating to its compliance with the criteria and obligations under Regulation ... 391/2009.

5. At any moment prior to the adoption of a decision to impose a fine and periodic penalty payments, or the withdrawal of recognition in accordance with this Regulation, the Commission may amend its assessment of the recognised organisation concerned. If the new assessment is different to the assessment which gave rise to the statement of objections, because new facts have been discovered, or because new infringements or new circumstances concerning the seriousness of an infringement or its effects on safety and the environment have been identified, the Commission shall issue a new statement of objections."

29.135 Article 13 is entitled "Requests for information". It provides that in order to clarify the facts for the purposes of Article 12, the Commission may request in writing the recognised organisation to provide written or oral explanations, or particulars or documents, within a designated time limit, which shall not, in any event, be less than 4 weeks. In such a case the Commission shall inform the recognised organisation of the periodic penalty payments and fines that may be imposed for failing to comply with the request or when incurring unjustified delays in the provision of information or providing deliberately incorrect, incomplete or misleading information to the Commission.

29.136 Article 14 deals with the oral hearing. At the request of the recognised organisation to which a statement of objections has been addressed, the Commission shall offer that organisation the opportunity to present its arguments at an oral hearing.[80] The Commission shall invite the competent authorities of Member States concerned, and may, on its own initiative or at the request of Member States concerned, invite any other persons

---

80 Art. 14(1).

with a legitimate interest in the infringements to take part in the oral hearing.[81] The Commission may choose to be assisted by the EMSA.[82] Natural or private legal persons invited to attend shall either appear in person or be represented by legal or authorised representatives. Member States shall be represented by officials of that Member State.[83] The oral hearing shall not be public.[84] Each person invited to attend may be heard separately or in the presence of other persons invited to attend, having regard to the legitimate interest of the recognised organisation and other parties in the protection of their business secrets and other confidential information.[85] The statements made by each person heard must be recorded.[86] Upon request, the recording of the hearing must be made available to the persons who attended the hearing and to Member States concerned.[87] The hearings seem comparable to (but not identical to) the competition law hearings held by the European Commission in EU competition law matters.

29.137 Article 15 of the regulation provides for periodic penalty payments for non-co-operation:

"1. Where the Commission intends to adopt a decision imposing periodic penalty payments as referred to in Article 7(1) to a recognised organisation that has failed to undertake or incurs unjustified delays in undertaking preventive and remedial action requested by the Commission, it shall first notify the recognised organisation in writing.
2. The notification by the Commission in accordance with paragraph 1 shall make reference to the specific preventive and remedial action that has not been undertaken by the recognised organisation and the supporting evidence, as well as inform the recognised organisation of the periodic penalty payments that are being considered by the Commission thereon.
3. The Commission shall set a time limit in which the recognised organisation may submit written observations to the Commission. The Commission shall not be obliged to take into account written observations received after the expiry of the time limit."

29.138 Article 16 deals with access to the file. In essence, there is access to the file but it is not unbridled access and the internal documents of the European Commission or the EMSA shall ordinarily be protected:

"1. At the request of the recognised organisation to which a statement of objections has been addressed, the Commission shall grant access to the file containing documents and other evidence compiled by the Commission on the alleged infringement.
2. The Commission shall set the date and make the relevant practical arrangements for the recognised organisation's access to the file, which may be granted in electronic form only.
3. The Commission shall make available to the recognised organisation concerned, upon request, a list of all the documents contained in the file.
4. The recognised organisation concerned shall have the right to access the documents and information contained in the file. When granting such access, the Commission shall have due regard to business secrets, confidential information or the internal character of documents issued by the Commission or the European Maritime Safety Agency.
5. For the purposes of paragraph 4, internal documents of the Commission and the European Maritime Safety Agency may include:

---

81 Art. 14(2).
82 Ibid.
83 Art. 14(3).
84 Art. 14(4).
85 Ibid.
86 Art. 14(5).
87 Ibid.

(a) documents or parts of documents pertaining to the internal deliberations of the Commission and its services and of the European Maritime Safety Agency, including the opinions and recommendations of the European Maritime Safety Agency addressed to the Commission;

(b) documents or parts of documents forming part of the correspondence between the Commission and the European Maritime Safety Agency or between the Commission and Member States."

29.139 Article 17 deals with legal representation. It provides that the recognised organisation shall have the right to legal representation at all stages of the proceedings under the regulation. This is reasonable and the absence of legal representation rights would have been problematical.

29.140 Article 18 deals with confidentiality, professional secrecy and the right to remain silent:

"1. Proceedings under this Regulation shall be carried out subject to the principles of confidentiality and of professional secrecy.

2. The Commission, the European Maritime Safety Agency, and the authorities of the Member States concerned, as well as their officials, servants and other persons working under their supervision shall not disclose information acquired or exchanged by them pursuant to this Regulation and of the kind covered by the obligation of professional secrecy and confidentiality.

3. Any recognised organisation or other person who submits information or observations pursuant to this Regulation shall clearly identify any material considered to be confidential, giving the reasons for it, and provide a separate non-confidential version by the date set by the Commission.

4. The Commission may also require recognised organisations and other interested parties to identify any part of a report, of the statement of objections or of a decision by the Commission, which in their view contains business secrets.

5. In the absence of the identification referred to in paragraphs 3 and 4, the Commission may assume that the documents or observations concerned do not contain confidential information.

6. Without prejudice to Article 9 of Regulation … 391/2009, recognised organisations shall have the right to remain silent in situations where it would otherwise be compelled to provide answers which might involve an admission on their part of the existence of a breach."

While Article 18 may appear to be conferring new rights, it is really recognising rights which would almost certainly exist as a matter of law.

29.141 Article 19 deals with the decisions to impose fines, provide payments or to withdraw recognition:

"1. A decision to impose fines, periodic penalty payments, or the withdrawal of recognition in accordance with this Regulation shall be based exclusively on the grounds on which the recognised organisation concerned has been able to submit its observations.

2. The decision to impose a fine or a periodic penalty payment and the determination of the appropriate amount shall take into account the principles of effectiveness, proportionality and dissuasiveness.

3. When taking measures in accordance with this Regulation and deciding on the seriousness and effect of the relevant actions or omissions on safety and the environment the Commission shall take into account national measures already taken on the basis of the same facts against the recognised organisation concerned, in particular where that organisation has already been subject to judicial or enforcement proceedings.

4. Actions or omissions of a recognised organisation on the basis of which measures have been taken in accordance with this Regulation shall not be subject to further measures. However, these actions or omissions may be taken into account in subsequent decisions adopted in accordance with this Regulation in order to assess recurrence.

5. A decision to impose periodic penalty payments or a decision imposing fines and periodic penalty payments shall be adopted by the Commission in accordance with the procedure applicable pursuant to Article 12(2) of Regulation ... 391/2009.

6. A decision to withdraw the recognition of a recognised organisation shall be adopted by the Commission in accordance with the procedure applicable pursuant to Article 12(3) of Regulation ... 391/2009."

29.142 The somewhat technical (but important) process of judicial remedies, notification and publication are addressed by Article 20:

"1. The Commission shall inform the recognised organisation concerned of the judicial remedies available to it.

2. The Commission shall notify its decision to the European Maritime Safety Agency and to the Member States for information.

3. When justified, in particular on grounds of safety or protection of the environment, the Commission may make its decision public. When publishing details of its decision or informing the Member States, the Commission shall have regard to the legitimate interests of the recognised organisation concerned and other interested persons."

29.143 Article 21 deals with recovery of fines and penalty payments. It provides that the Commission must

"proceed with the recovery of the fines and the penalty payments by establishing a recovery order and issuing a debit note addressed to the recognised organisation concerned in accordance with Articles 78 to 80 and 83 of Regulation 966/2012 of the European Parliament and of the Council[88] and Articles 80 to 92 of Commission Delegated Regulation ... 1268/2012.[89]"

29.144 Article 22 ("limitation periods for the imposition of fines and periodic penalty payments") provides in paragraph 1 that the right of the Commission to impose fines and/or periodic penalty payments to a recognised organisation in accordance with this regulation shall expire after five years from the date when the action or omission of the recognised organisation giving rise to an infringement identified in accordance with Article 3 of the regulation was committed. However, in case of continuing or repeated actions or omissions giving rise to an infringement, time shall begin to run on the day on which the action or omission ceases. The right of the Commission to impose periodic penalty payments to a recognised organisation in accordance with Article 15 of the regulation must expire after three years from the date when the action or omission of the recognised organisation, for which the Commission requested appropriate preventive and remedial action, was committed. Paragraph 2 provides that any action taken by the Commission or the EMSA for the purpose of the assessment or the infringement procedure in relation to an action or omission of the recognised organisation shall interrupt the relevant limitation period established under Article 23 paragraph 1. The limitation period shall be interrupted with effect from the date on which the action of the Commission or the Agency is notified to the recognised organisation.[90] Each interruption must start time running afresh.[91] The

---

88 Ed., OJ L298/1, 26 October 2012.
89 Ed., OJ L362/1, 31 December 2012.
90 Reg. 788/2014, Art. 22(12).
91 Reg. 788/2014, Art. 22(3).

limitation period shall, however, not exceed a period equal to twice the initial limitation period, except where limitation is suspended pursuant to paragraph 4 of Article 23(1).[92] The limitation period for the imposition of periodic penalty payments shall be suspended for as long as the decision of the Commission is the subject of proceedings pending before the CJEU.[93]

29.145 Article 23 ("limitation periods for the collection of fines and periodic penalty payments") provides in paragraph 1 that the right to start a recovery procedure for fines and/or periodic penalty payments shall expire one year after the decision pursuant to Article 19 has become final. Article 23(2) provides that the limitation period referred to in paragraph 1 shall be interrupted by any action of the Commission or of a Member State acting at the request of the Commission, aimed at enforcing payment of the fines and/or periodic penalty payments. Article 23(3) provides that each interruption shall start time running afresh. Article 23(4) states that the limitation periods referred to in paragraphs 1 and 2 shall be suspended for as long as: (a) time to pay is allowed; and (b) enforcement of payment is suspended pursuant to a decision of the CJEU.

Time limits

29.146 Article 24 deals with the application of time limits:

"1. The time limits laid down in this Regulation shall run from the day following receipt of the Commission's communication or delivery thereof by hand.
2. In the case of a communication addressed to the Commission, the relevant time limits shall be deemed to have been met when that communication has been dispatched by registered post before the relevant time limit expires.
3. In setting the time limits, the Commission shall have regard both to due process rights and the specific circumstances of each decision-making procedure under this Regulation.
4. Where appropriate and upon reasoned request made before the expiry of the original time limit, time limits may be extended."

National competent authorities

29.147 Article 25 provides for co-operation with national competent authorities. This is important at a practical level in operating the regulation. Article 24 provides:

"Information provided by the national competent authorities in response to a request from the Commission must be used by the Commission only for the following purposes: (a) to carry out the tasks entrusted to it for the recognition and supervision of recognised organisations under Regulation 391/2009; and (b) as evidence for the purposes of decision-making under the Regulation, without prejudice to Articles 16 and 18 of the Regulation."

It is therefore a safeguard and protection in respect of the use (or misuse) of information.

29.148 Chapter V is entitled "Final Provisions". Article 26 provides that events which occurred before the date of entry into force of Regulation 391/2009 shall not give rise to any measures in accordance with the regulation. Article 27 deals with the entry into force of the regulation; it provides that the regulation entered into force on the twentieth day following that of its publication in the *Official Journal of the European Union*. (i.e. twenty days following 19 July 2014).

---

92 Ibid.
93 Reg. 788/2014, Art. 22(4).

F. COMMISSION IMPLEMENTING DECISION (EU) 2015/668 OF 24 APRIL 2015 ON AMENDING THE RECOGNITIONS OF CERTAIN ORGANISATIONS IN ACCORDANCE WITH ARTICLE 16 OF REGULATION (EC) NO 391/2009 OF THE EUROPEAN PARLIAMENT AND OF THE COUNCIL

29.149 On 24 April 2015, the Commission adopted Implementing Regulation 2015/668 of 24 April 2015 on amending the Recognitions of Certain Organisations in Accordance with Article 16 of Regulation 391/2009 of the European Parliament and of the Council.[94] It is a simple implementing measure.

29.150 The background is Regulation 391/2009 of the European Parliament and of the Council of 23 April 2009 on the common rules and standards for ship inspection and survey organisations[95] and in particular Article 4(1) and Article 16 of that measure. The background is amplified by the recitals which are self-explanatory:

"(1) Pursuant to Article 16 of Regulation … 391/2009, the Commission has to verify that the holder of the recognition granted in accordance with Article 4(3) and Article 2(c) of that Regulation is the relevant legal entity within the organisation to which the provisions of that Regulation apply. If that is not the case, the Commission has to take a decision amending that recognition.

(2) Commission Decision 2007/42 …[96] referred to the organisations recognised by the Member States in accordance with Council Directive 94/57 …[97] by providing that the Director-General for Energy and Transport shall publish in the Official Journal of the European Union an updated list of organisations recognised in compliance with Directive 94/57/EC by 1 July each year.

(3) The latest list of organisations recognised on the basis of Directive 94/57/EC was published in the Official Journal of the European Union[98] in 2007.

(4) The recognitions of Lloyd's Register of Shipping (LR), Korean Register of Shipping (KR), Nippon Kaiji Kyokai (NK) and Registro Italiano Navale (RINA) were granted in accordance with Directive 94/57 …

(5) In accordance with Article 15(1) of Regulation … 391/2009, the organisations which on 17 June 2009 had been granted recognition in accordance with Directive 94/57/EC retained their recognition.

(6) In the case of Korean Register of Shipping (KR), the relevant parent entity of all legal entities that constitute the recognised organisation was renamed as 'KR (Korean Register)'.

(7) In the case of Nippon Kaiji Kyokai (NK), the relevant parent entity of all legal entities that constitute the recognised organisation has changed its legal status under Japanese law from a 'Foundation' to a 'General Incorporated Foundation'. As such, the complete name of the entity to which the recognition should be granted is 'Nippon Kaiji Kyokai General Incorporated Foundation (ClassNK)'.

(8) In the case of Lloyd's Register of Shipping (LR), the originally recognised organisation was first renamed Lloyd's Register and subsequently renamed Lloyd's Register Group Limited as a result of the company converting from a society incorporated under the United Kingdom's Industrial & Provident Societies Act of 1965, as amended, into a company incorporated under the United Kingdom's Companies Act of 2006. As such, the new name

---

94 OJ L110/22, 29 April 2015.

95 OJ L131/11, 28 May 2009.

96 Ed., Comm. Dec. 2007/421 of 14 June 2007 repealing Dec. 96/587 on the publication of the list of recognised organisations which have been notified by Member States in accordance with Council Dir. 94/57 (OJ L157/18, 19 June 2007).

97 Ed., Council Dir. 94/57 of 22 November 1994 on common rules and standards for ship inspection and survey organisations and for the relevant activities of maritime administrations (OJ L319/20, 12 December 1994).

98 Ed., OJ C135/4, 19 June 2007.

of the entity to which the recognition should be granted is 'Lloyd's Register Group LTD (LR)'.

(9) In the case of Registro Italiano Navale (RINA), all activities falling under Regulation (EC) No 391/2009 have been transferred from Registro Italiano Navale to RINA S.p.A., a fully owned subsidiary of RINA, followed by the transfer of these activities to RINA Services S.p.A. which is a fully owned subsidiary of RINA S.p.A. Therefore, 'RINA Services S.p.A.' is the relevant parent entity of all legal entities that constitute the recognised organisation and to which recognition should be granted.

(10) The changes in the identity of the mentioned relevant parent entities do not impact the capability of the respective organisations to comply with the requirements laid down in Regulation ... 391/2009.

(11) The measures provided for in this Decision are in accordance with the opinion of the Committee, on Safe Seas and the Prevention of Pollution from Ships established by Regulation (EC) No 2099/2002 of the European Parliament and of the Council.[99]"

29.151 Article 1 provides that the holder of the recognition previously granted to Korean Register of Shipping ("KR") shall be, from the date of entry into force of the decision, "KR (Korean Register)", which is the parent entity of all legal entities that constitute the recognised organisation for the purpose of Regulation 391/2009.

29.152 Article 2 states that the holder of the recognition previously granted to Lloyd's Register of Shipping (LR) shall be, from the date of entry into force of the decision, "Lloyd's Register Group LTD (LR)", which is the parent entity of all legal entities that constitute the recognised organisation for the purpose of Regulation 391/2009.

29.153 Article 3 provides that the holder of the recognition previously granted to Nippon Kaiji Kyokai (NK) shall be, from the date of entry into force of the decision, "Nippon Kaiji Kyokai General Incorporated Foundation (ClassNK)", which is the parent entity of all legal entities that constitute the recognised organisation for the purpose of Regulation 391/2009.

29.154 Article 4 provides that the holder of the recognition previously granted to Registro Italiano Navale (RINA) shall be, from the date of entry into force of the decision, "RINA Services S.p.A.", which is the parent entity of all legal entities that constitute the recognised organisation for the purpose of Regulation 391/2009.

G. COMMISSION IMPLEMENTING DECISION 2013/765 OF 13 DECEMBER 2013 AMENDING THE RECOGNITION OF DET NORSKE VERITAS PURSUANT TO REGULATION (EC) NO 391/2009 OF THE EUROPEAN PARLIAMENT AND OF THE COUNCIL ON COMMON RULES AND STANDARDS FOR SHIP INSPECTION AND SURVEY ORGANISATIONS

29.155 On 13 December 2013, the Commission adopted Implementing Decision 2013/765 amending the recognition of Det Norske Veritas pursuant to Regulation 391/2009 of the European Parliament and of the Council on common rules and standards for ship inspection and survey organisations.[100] It referred to Regulation 391/2009 of the European Parliament and of the Council of 23 April 2009 on common rules and standards

---

99 Ed., Reg. 2099/2002 of the European Parliament and of the Council of 5 November 2002 establishing a Committee on Safe Seas and the Prevention of Pollution from Ships (COSS) and amending the regulations on maritime safety and prevention of pollution from ships (OJ L324/1, 29 November 2002).

100 OJ L338/107, 17 December 2013.

for ship inspection and survey organisations,[101] and in particular Article 4(1) and Article 16 thereof. Decision 2013/765 was a technical measure.[102] Article 1 is the operative provision. It states that the holder of the recognition granted to Det Norske Veritas shall be, from the date of entry into force of this decision, DNV GL AS, which is the parent entity of all legal entities that constitute the recognised organisation for the purpose of Regulation (EC) No 391/2009. Due to the transfer of ownership of GL SE to DNV GL AS, the recognition of Germanischer Lloyd, initially granted to GL SE, ceases to apply.

H. COMMISSION IMPLEMENTING DECISION 2014/281 OF 14 MAY 2014 GRANTING EU RECOGNITION TO THE CROATIAN REGISTER OF SHIPPING PURSUANT TO REGULATION (EC) NO 391/2009 OF THE EUROPEAN PARLIAMENT AND OF THE COUNCIL ON COMMON RULES AND STANDARDS FOR SHIP INSPECTION AND SURVEY ORGANISATIONS

29.156 On 14 May 2014, the Commission adopted Implementing Decision 2014/281 granting EU recognition to the Croatian Register of Shipping pursuant to Regulation 391/2009 of the European Parliament and of the Council on common rules and standards

---

101 OJ L131/11, 28 May 2009.

102 The background was clear from the recitals: "(1) Pursuant to Article 16(1) of Regulation … 391/2009, the Commission is to verify that the holder of the recognition granted in accordance with Article 2(c) and Article 4(3) of that Regulation is the relevant legal entity within the organisation to which the provisions of that Regulation apply. If that is not the case, the Commission is to take a decision amending that recognition. (2) The recognitions of the two organisations Det Norske Veritas and Germanischer Lloyd ('the Parties') were granted in 1995 under Council Directive 94/57. … (3) Pursuant to Article 15(1) of Regulation … 391/2009, the Parties retained their respective recognitions at the entry into force of that Regulation. (4) The initial recognition of Det Norske Veritas was granted to the legal entity DNV Classification AS, later on renamed DNV AS, which operated under the non-operational entity DNV Group AS, financially controlled by the non-profit foundation Stiftelsen Det Norske Veritas ('SDNV'), established in Norway. (5) The initial recognition of Germanischer Lloyd was granted to the legal entity Germanischer Lloyd AG, later on established as Germanischer Lloyd SE ('GL SE'), which operated under the non-operational entity GL Group, financially controlled by the holding Mayfair, established in Germany. (6) On 10 June 2013, the Commission received a notification of a proposed concentration pursuant to Article 4 of Council Regulation (EC) No 139/2004 (3) by which SDNV acquires, within the meaning of Article 3(1)(b) of that Regulation, sole control of GL SE and combines it with its subsidiary DNV Group AS, thereafter to be renamed DNV GL Group AS. (7) On 15 July 2013, the Commission adopted a decision pursuant to Article 6(1)(b) of the Merger Regulation to not oppose the concentration, referred to as 'Case COMP/M.6885 – SDNV/Germanischer Lloyd', and to declare it compatible with the internal market. (8) The non-operational entity DNV GL Group AS, established in Norway, became effective on 12 September 2013. The Parties informed the Commission that, until the start of joint operations, the legacy organisations DNV AS and GL SE continued to exist and to operate independently under the umbrella of DNV GL Group AS in accordance with their respective legacy rules, procedures and systems … (9) The ownership of GL SE was transferred to DNV AS, thereafter renamed DNV GL AS. From this moment, which marks the commencement of joint operations, DNV GL AS, with its subsidiaries, is responsible for all classification and certification activities falling within the scope of Regulation … 391/2009. DNV GL AS is therefore the relevant parent entity of all legal entities that constitute the recognised organisation, and to which the recognition should be granted. (10) Conversely, GL SE is no longer the relevant parent entity of the organisation, to which the provisions of Regulation (EC) No 391/2009 should apply. Therefore, its recognition pursuant to Article 4 of that Regulation should cease. (11) The information supplied to the Commission by the Parties indicates that, from the start of joint operations and until a common production system is in place, existing ships and ongoing projects should be handled separately, according to the legacy rules, procedures and systems of DNV AS and GL SE respectively. Functions and systems should be gradually integrated to ensure continuous compliance with the obligations and criteria of Regulation … 391/2009. (12) The measures provided for in this Decision are in accordance with the opinion of the Committee on Safe Seas and the Prevention of Pollution from Ships established by Regulation … 2099/2002 of the European Parliament and of the Council."

for ship inspection and survey organisations.[103] It referred to Regulation 391/2009 of the European Parliament and of the Council of 23 April 2009 on common rules and standards for ship inspection and survey organisations,[104] and in particular Article 4(1) thereof. It was a technical measure. It was prompted by letters of 23 July 2010 and of 25 February 2014 from the Croatian authorities requesting the Commission to grant EU recognition to the Croatian Register of Shipping (the "CRS").[105] The operative provision, Article 1, states that the "Croatian Register of Shipping" is recognised pursuant to Article 4(1) of Regulation 391/2009.

---

103 OJ L145/43, 16 May 2014.

104 OJ L131/11, 28 May 2009.

105 The background is clear from the recitals: "(1) Pursuant to Article 3(1) of Regulation ... 391/2009, Member States wishing to grant an authorisation to an organisation which is not yet recognised shall submit a request for recognition to the Commission. (2) On 23 July 2010, the Republic of Croatia provided information on and evidence of CRS complying with the requirements of Regulation ... 391/2009. Taking into account that the recognition process may extend over a longer period of time following the request and that as from accession and until the process is completed the Croatian government would not be entitled to delegate statutory tasks to CRS, the Commission started preparatory stages of the assessment of CRS before Croatia became a Member State of the Union. (3) On 25 February 2014, Croatia reiterated its request to the Commission to grant EU recognition to the CRS following Croatia's accession to the Union. (4) The Commission, with the assistance of the European Maritime Safety Agency, verified that the CRS meets all the minimum criteria set out in Annex I of Regulation ... 391/2009. (5) The assessment was based on the examination of the documentation submitted by the Croatian authorities, as well as on the results of two inspections of the CRS offices carried out by experts from the European Maritime Safety Agency in October 2011 and one inspection carried out in October 2013 to verify the implementation of remedial actions undertaken by the CRS in response to the shortcomings identified by the Commission in the course of the assessment. (6) Where shortcomings were identified, the CRS implemented appropriate and sufficient remedial actions in all cases. The CRS cooperated effectively during the assessment process and demonstrated its capacity to improve its organisation and procedures in a proactive fashion. (7) The implementation of a number of remedial actions is still in progress and will be monitored, in particular the opening of a branch office in Shanghai, China. This however does not call into question the overall quality of the organisation's systems and control mechanisms. (8) The Commission also verified that the CRS has undertaken to comply with the provisions of Articles 8(4), 9, 10 and 11 of Regulation ... 391/2009. (9) The CRS's safety and pollution performance, albeit slightly below the average performance of other EU recognised organisations, is satisfactory. In particular, it shows a positive trend under the Paris Memorandum of Understanding on Port State Control, with an average rate of detention of 0,51 % in the period 2010–2012, compared to 0,89 % in the period 2009–2011 and 1,44 % in the period 2008–2010. Also, the CRS did not record any 'recognised organisation related' detention in 2010, 2011 and 2012 under the United States Coast Guard Port State Control regime. (10) In order to ensure that the organisation maintains at all times its capacity to operate in accordance with the requirements of Regulation ... 391/2009, and given the relative small size of the fleet currently certified by the CRS, the Commission considers that any substantial growth of the organisation's activities should be accompanied by an appropriate increase in its technical and managerial capacities, including if necessary with regards to the expansion of the office network. (11) CRS's legal entity is established in Split, Croatia, as a public institution pursuant to the 'Law on the Croatian Register of Shipping' of 20 September 1996 (Official Gazette No 81/96) and in the 'Croatian Register of Shipping Charter' of 1 June 1997. It holds the name 'Croatian Register of Shipping' ('Hrvatski registar brodova'). (12) The measures provided for in this Decision are in accordance with the opinion of the Committee on Safe Seas and the Prevention of Pollution from Ships established by Regulation ... 2099/2002 of the European Parliament and of the Council [Ed., i.e. Reg. 2099/2002 of the European Parliament and of the Council of 5 November 2002 establishing a Committee on Safe Seas and the Prevention of Pollution from Ships (COSS) and amending the regulations on maritime safety and the prevention of pollution from ships (OJ L324/1, 29 November 2002)].

I. COMMISSION REGULATION (EU) NO 428/2010 OF 20 MAY 2010 IMPLEMENTING ARTICLE 14 OF DIRECTIVE 2009/16 OF THE EUROPEAN PARLIAMENT AND OF THE COUNCIL AS REGARDS EXPANDED INSPECTIONS OF SHIPS

29.157 On 20 May 2010, Commission Regulation 428/2010 implementing Article 14 of Directive 2009/16 of the European Parliament and of the Council as regards expanded inspections of ships was adopted.[106] The Commission referred to Directive 2009/16 of the European Parliament and of the Council of 23 April 2009 on PSC and in particular Article 14(4) thereof.[107] It was a technical measure.[108] The operative provision, Article 1, dealt with the list of specific items to be verified in an expanded inspection and then the annex set out those items.[109] The annex sets out the specific items to be verified during an extended inspection.

---

106 OJ L125/2, 21 May 2010.

107 OJ L131/57, 28 May 2009.

108 The background to the measure is clear from the recitals: "(1) When carrying out an expanded inspection of a ship, the port State control officer should be guided by a list of specific items to be verified, subject to their practical feasibility or any constraints relating to the safety of persons, the ship or the port. (2) With regard to the identification of the specific items to be verified in the course of an expanded inspection of any of the risk areas listed in Annex VII to Directive 2009/16/EC, it appears necessary to build upon the expertise of the Paris Memorandum of Understanding on Port State Control. (3) The Port State Control Officers should use their professional judgement to determine the applicability of and the appropriate depth of examination of, each specific item. (4) The measures provided for in this Regulation are in accordance with the opinion of the Committee on Safe Seas and the Prevention of Pollution from Ships (COSS)."

109 Art. 1 provides that an expanded inspection as referred to in Art. 14 of Dir. 2009/16 shall, where applicable, as a minimum comprise the verification of the specific items listed in the Annex to the regulation. In the case where no specific areas are indicated for a particular type of ship, as defined in Dir. 2009/16, the inspector shall use his professional judgment to decide which items must be inspected, and to what extent, in order to check the overall condition in these areas.

CHAPTER 30

Maritime safety: casualty and accident investigation

A. INTRODUCTION

30.001 The purpose of this chapter is to consider the investigation of maritime casualties.

B. INVESTIGATION OF MARITIME CASUALTIES GENERALLY

30.002 The investigation of maritime casualties is a very important aspect of any maritime regime. Such investigations enable the collation of information as to what happened so as to ensure, in so far as possible, that comparable events are not repeated. These investigations can lead to palpable results such as the saving of lives and property. So much of European Union ("EU") shipping law is about direct prevention of casualties (e.g. the safety and environmental measures) but there is one measure which addresses the investigation of casualties: this is Directive 2009/18. As the first recital to Directive 2009/18 recognises: a "high general level of safety should be maintained in maritime transport in Europe and every effort should be made to reduce the number of marine casualties and incidents" while the second recital to Directive 2009/18 draws the link to investigations: the "expeditious holding of technical investigations into marine casualties improves maritime safety, as it helps to prevent the recurrence of such casualties resulting in loss of life, loss of ships and pollution of the marine environment".

C. NATIONAL AND INTERNATIONAL LEGAL DIMENSION ON MARITIME ACCIDENT INVESTIGATION

30.003 Traditionally, maritime accident investigation has been outside the remit of the EU. Member States have conducted their investigations without an EU dimension. This right of coastal States to conduct their own investigations is implicit in Article 2 of the United Nations Convention on the Law of the Sea ("UNCLOS")[1] which provides:

> *"Legal status of the territorial sea, of the air space over the territorial sea and of its bed and subsoil*
>
> 1. The sovereignty of a coastal State extends, beyond its land territory and internal waters and, in the case of an archipelagic State, its archipelagic waters, to an adjacent belt of sea, described as the territorial sea.

---

1 10 December 1982, www.un.org/depts/los/convention_agreements/texts/unclos/unclos_e.pdf.

2. This sovereignty extends to the air space over the territorial sea as well as to its bed and subsoil.
3. The sovereignty over the territorial sea is exercised subject to this Convention and to other rules of international law."

30.004 The fourth recital to Directive 2009/18 provides that Article 2 of UNCLOS

"establishes the right of coastal States to investigate the cause of any marine casualty occurring within their territorial seas which might pose a risk to life or to the environment, involve the coastal State's search and rescue authorities, or otherwise affect the coastal State."

The fourth recital is correct in its assertion but it is more accurate to say that it is implicit, rather than explicit, in Article 2 of UNCLOS.

30.005 It is fair to say that the opportunity to conduct investigations is not confined to coastal States because flag States also have a role to play. Article 94 of UNCLOS (and particular attention should be paid to Article 94(7)) provides:

"Duties of the flag State

1. Every State shall effectively exercise its jurisdiction and control in administrative, technical and social matters over ships flying its flag.
2. In particular every State shall:

   (a) maintain a register of ships containing the names and particulars of ships flying its flag, except those which are excluded from generally accepted international regulations on account of their small size; and
   (b) assume jurisdiction under its internal law over each ship flying its flag and its master, officers and crew in respect of administrative, technical and social matters concerning the ship.

3. Every State shall take such measures for ships flying its flag as are necessary to ensure safety at sea with regard, inter alia, to:

   (a) the construction, equipment and seaworthiness of ships;
   (b) the manning of ships, labour conditions and the training of crews, taking into account the applicable international instruments;
   (c) the use of signals, the maintenance of communications and the prevention of collisions.

4. Such measures shall include those necessary to ensure:

   (a) that each ship, before registration and thereafter at appropriate intervals, is surveyed by a qualified surveyor of ships, and has on board such charts, nautical publications and navigational equipment and instruments as are appropriate for the safe navigation of the ship;
   (b) that each ship is in the charge of a master and officers who possess appropriate qualifications, in particular in seamanship, navigation, communications and marine engineering, and that the crew is appropriate in qualification and numbers for the type, size, machinery and equipment of the ship;
   (c) that the master, officers and, to the extent appropriate, the crew are fully conversant with and required to observe the applicable international regulations concerning the safety of life at sea, the prevention of collisions, the prevention, reduction and control of marine pollution, and the maintenance of communications by radio.

5. In taking the measures called for in paragraphs 3 and 4 each State is required to conform to generally accepted international regulations, procedures and practices and to take any steps which may be necessary to secure their observance.

6. A State which has clear grounds to believe that proper jurisdiction and control with respect to a ship have not been exercised may report the facts to the flag State. Upon receiving such a report, the flag State shall investigate the matter and, if appropriate, take any action necessary to remedy the situation.

7. Each State shall cause an inquiry to be held by or before a suitably qualified person or persons into every marine casualty or incident of navigation on the high seas involving a ship flying its flag and causing loss of life or serious injury to nationals of another State or serious damage to ships or installations of another State or to the marine environment. The flag State and the other State shall cooperate in the conduct of any inquiry held by that other State into any such marine casualty or incident of navigation."

30.006 The fifth recital to Directive 2009/18 provides that Article 94 of UNCLOS "establishes that flag States are to cause an inquiry to be held, by or before a suitably qualified person or persons, into certain casualties or incidents of navigation on the high seas".

30.007 While UNCLOS is the main international instrument on the law of the sea, the sixth, seventh and eighth recitals to Directive 2009/18 go on to recall:

"(6) Regulation I/21 of International Convention for the Safety of Life at Sea of 1 November 1974 (hereinafter referred to as SOLAS 74), the International Convention of Load Lines of 5 April 1966 and the International Convention for the Prevention of Pollution from Ships of 2 November 1973 lay down the responsibilities of flag States to conduct casualty investigations and to supply the International Maritime Organisation (IMO) with relevant findings.

(7) The Code for the Implementation of Mandatory IMO Instruments annexed to Resolution A.996(25) of the IMO Assembly of 29 November 2007 recalls the obligation of flag States to ensure that marine safety investigations are conducted by suitably qualified investigators, competent in matters relating to marine casualties and incidents. That Code further requires flag States to be prepared to provide qualified investigators for that purpose, irrespective of the location of the casualty or incident.

(8) Account should be taken of the Code for the Investigation of Marine Casualties and Incidents annexed to Resolution A.849(20) of the IMO Assembly of 27 November 1997 (hereinafter referred to as the IMO Code for the Investigation of Marine Casualties and Incidents),[2] which provides for implementation of a common approach to the safety investigation of marine casualties and incidents and for cooperation between States in identifying the contributing factors leading to marine casualties and incidents. Account should also be taken of Resolution A.861(20) of the IMO Assembly of 27 November 1997 and Resolution MSC.163(78) of the IMO Maritime Safety Committee of 17 May 2004, which provide a definition of voyage data recorders."

---

2 Ed., Art. 3(1) of the directive provides that the term "IMO Code for the Investigation of Marine Casualties and Incidents" shall mean the Code for the Investigation of Marine Casualties and Incidents annexed to Res. A.849(20) of the IMO Assembly of 27 November 1997, in its up-to-date version.

D. DIRECTIVE 2009/18 OF THE EUROPEAN PARLIAMENT AND OF THE COUNCIL OF 23 APRIL 2009 ESTABLISHING THE FUNDAMENTAL PRINCIPLES GOVERNING THE INVESTIGATION OF ACCIDENTS IN THE MARITIME TRANSPORT SECTOR AND AMENDING COUNCIL DIRECTIVE 1999/35 AND DIRECTIVE 2002/59 OF THE EUROPEAN PARLIAMENT AND OF THE COUNCIL

Introduction

30.008 Directive 2009/18 of the European Parliament and of the Council of 23 April 2009 established the fundamental principles governing the investigation of accidents in the maritime transport sector, amending Council Directive 1999/35 and Directive 2002/59 of the European Parliament and of the Council.[3]

30.009 The directive had a long gestation with discussions commencing on it in March 2006. There was then the start of discussions about the methodology and guidelines in May 2007, followed by a meeting of an ad hoc subgroup of the Consultative Technical Group for Cooperation in Marine Accident Investigation ("CTG CMAI") on methodology and, finally, the measure was adopted in June 2009. Nonetheless, it is a very welcome measure.

30.010 The directive is supplemented by the Commission Implementing Regulation, namely Regulation 651/2011.[4]

30.011 It is worth stating at the outset that while Directive 2009/18 uses the term "accident", the word "casualty" seems more appropriate as not all maritime casualties are "accidents".

30.012 Directive 2009/18 establishes the fundamental principles governing the investigation of accidents in the maritime transport sector and amends Council Directive 1999/35[5] and Directive 2002/59[6] of the European Parliament and of the Council. Directive 2009/18 is known as the Accident Investigation Directive. The term "accident" is a little unfortunate and the term "casualty" (which covers accidents and non-accidents) would be more accurate: nonetheless the directive is very welcome.

30.013 Directive 2009/18 was adopted as part of the Third Maritime Package. Its legal basis was the Treaty on the European Union ("TEC") (now the Treaty on the Functioning of the European Union ("TFEU")) generally and what is now Article 100(2) of the TFEU in particular. It was quite challenging to adopt a measure which was usable across the Member States given the difference in approaches between Member States. These differences were (and remain) across different areas including legal, cultural and social.

30.014 The legislative history of the measure included the fact that the European Parliament, in its resolution of 21 April 2004 on improving safety at sea,[7] had urged the Commission to present a proposal for a directive on investigating shipping accidents. The

---

3 OJ L131/114, 28 May 2009. See Floch, "SAFEMED II: EU Directive on Accident Investigation" available at www.euromedtransport.eu/En/image.php?id=2206.

4 OJ L177/18, 6 July 2011, http://eur-lex.europa.eu/LexUriServ/LexUriServ.do?uri=OJ:L:2011:177:0018:00 23:EN:PDF.

5 Dir. 1999/35 relates to a system of mandatory surveys for the safe operation of regular ro-ro ferry and high-speed passenger craft services (OJ L138/1, 1 June 1999). See Marinho de Bastas, "The Need for a European Union Approach to Accident Investigations" (2004) Journal of Hazardous Materials 111(1–3).

6 OJ L208/10, 5 August 2002.

7 OJ C104 E, 30 April 2004, p. 730.

directive was also preceded by opinions of the European Parliament,[8] the European Economic and Social Committee[9] as well as the Committee of the Regions.[10]

30.015 To understand and construe Directive 2009/18 fully, one has to have regard to a number of other measures. Article 3 sets out some definitions of various terms used in the directive.[11]

Directive 2009/18 and Member State law

30.016 Article 25 of Directive 2009/18 provided for the transposition of the directive into Member State law. Article 25(1) provided that Member States had to bring into force by 17 June 2011 the laws, regulations and administrative provisions necessary to comply with the directive. When Member States adopted those measures, they had to contain a reference to the directive or be accompanied by such a reference on the occasion of their official publication. Member States could determine how such reference is to be made. Member States also had, pursuant to Article 25(2) to communicate to the Commission the text of the main provisions of national law which they adopt in the field covered by this directive. The directive also deleted two provisions in earlier measures, namely, Article 12 of Directive 1999/35 and Article 11 of Directive 2002/59.

30.017 Article 22 (entitled "Penalties") provides that Member States must lay down the rules on penalties applicable to infringements of the national provisions adopted pursuant to this directive and shall take all measures necessary to ensure that they are implemented. The penalties provided for must be effective, proportionate and dissuasive.

30.018 Member States may adopt other measures over and above what is contained in Directive 2009/18. Article 21 ("Additional measures") provides that

> "[n]othing contained in this Directive shall prevent a Member State from taking additional measures on maritime safety which are not covered by it, provided that such measures neither infringe this Directive nor in any way adversely affect the attainment of its objective, nor jeopardise the achievement of its objective."

---

8 OJ C74 E, 30 March 2008, p. 546.

9 OJ C318/195, 23 December 2006.

10 OJ C229/38, 22 September 2006.

11 Art. 3(2) provides that for the purposes of the directive "the following terms shall be understood in accordance with the definitions contained in the IMO Code for the Investigation of Marine Casualties and Incidents: (a) 'marine casualty'; (b) 'very serious casualty'; (c) 'marine incident'; (d) 'marine casualty or incident safety investigation'; (e) 'lead investigating State'; (f) 'substantially interested State". Art. 3(3) provides that "the term 'serious casualty' shall be understood in accordance with the updated definition contained in Circular MSC-MEPC.3/Circ.3 of the IMO Maritime Safety Committee and Marine Environment Protection Committee of 18 December 2008". Art. 3(4) provides that the term "'IMO guidelines on the fair treatment of seafarers in the event of a maritime accident' shall mean the guidelines as annexed to Resolution LEG.3(91) of the IMO Legal Committee of 27 April 2006 and as approved by the Governing Body of the International Labour Organisation in its 296th session of 12 to 16 June 2006". Art. 3(5) provides that "the terms 'ro-ro ferry' and 'high-speed passenger craft' shall be understood in accordance with the definitions contained in Article 2 of Directive 1999/35". Art. 3(6) provides that the term "'voyage data recorder' (or 'VDR') shall be understood in accordance with the definition contained in Resolution A.861(20) of the IMO Assembly and Resolution MSC.163(78) of the IMO Maritime Safety Committee". Art. 3(7) provides that the term "'safety recommendation' shall mean any proposal made, including for the purposes of registration and control, by: (a) the investigative body of the State conducting, or leading, the safety investigation on the basis of information derived from that investigation; or, where appropriate, (b) the Commission, acting on the basis of an abstract data analysis and the results of safety investigations carried out."

If Member States choose to do then they should ensure that the measures do not undermine what is contained in the directive.

Purpose of Directive 2009/18

30.019 Article 1(1) of Directive 2009/18 provides:

"The purpose of this Directive is to improve maritime safety and the prevention of pollution by ships, and so reduce the risk of future marine casualties, by:

(a) facilitating the expeditious holding of safety investigations and proper analysis of marine casualties and incidents in order to determine their causes; and

(b) ensuring the timely and accurate reporting of safety investigations and proposals for remedial action."

30.020 Experience internationally demonstrates that effect marine casualty investigation requires all involved to be able to speak openly and honestly without fear of recrimination. In other words, the object of the exercise is to understand what happened so that it would not recur rather than to apportion blame and liability (other different fora can do that), so Article 1(2) of Directive 2009/18 provides:

"Investigations under this Directive shall not be concerned with determining liability or apportioning blame. However, Member States shall ensure that the investigative body or entity (hereinafter referred to as the investigative body) is not refraining from fully reporting the causes of a marine casualty or incident because fault or liability may be inferred from the findings."

30.021 Recital 26 of the directive reflects that approach: since "the aim of the technical safety investigation is the prevention of marine casualties and incidents, the conclusions and the safety recommendations should in no circumstances determine liability or apportion blame".

30.022 Experience internationally also shows that seafarers need to be protected. Article 18 (entitled "fair treatment of seafarers") provides that in accordance with their national law, Member States must take into account the relevant provisions of the IMO guidelines on the fair treatment of seafarers in the event of a maritime accident in the waters under their jurisdiction. This is also reflected in the ninth recital to the directive which provides:

"Seafarers are recognised as a special category of worker and, given the global nature of the shipping industry and the different jurisdictions with which they may be brought into contact, need special protection, especially in relation to contacts with public authorities. In the interests of increased maritime safety, seafarers should be able to rely on fair treatment in the event of a maritime accident. Their human rights and dignity should be preserved at all times and all safety investigations should be conducted in a fair and expeditious manner. To that end, Member States should, in accordance with their national legislation, further take into account the relevant provisions of the IMO guidelines on the fair treatment of seafarers in the event of a maritime accident."

Scope of Directive 2009/18

30.023 Article 2(1) of the directive provides that the directive shall apply to marine casualties and incidents that: (a) involve ships flying the flag of one of the Member States;

(b) occur within Member States' territorial sea and internal waters as defined in UNCLOS; or (c) involve other substantial interests of the Member States.

30.024 Article 2(2) of the directive provides that the directive shall not apply to marine casualties and incidents involving only: (a) ships of war and troop ships and other ships owned or operated by a Member State and used only on government non-commercial service; (b) ships not propelled by mechanical means, wooden ships of primitive build, pleasure yachts and pleasure craft not engaged in trade, unless they are or will be crewed and carrying more than 12 passengers for commercial purposes; (c) inland waterway vessels operating in inland waterways; (d) fishing vessels with a length of less than 15 metres; and (e) fixed offshore drilling units.

Status of safety investigations

30.025 Article 4 of Directive 2009/18 sets out the "status" of safety investigations which fall within its scope. Article 4(1) provides that Member States must define, in accordance with their legal systems, the legal status of the safety investigation in such a way that such investigations can be carried out as effectively and rapidly as possible. It goes on to say that Member States must ensure, in accordance with their legislation and, where appropriate, through collaboration with the authorities responsible for the judicial inquiry, that safety investigations are: (a) independent of criminal or other parallel investigations held to determine liability or apportion blame; and (b) not unduly precluded, suspended or delayed by reason of such investigations.

30.026 Article 4(2) provides that the rules to be established by the Member States must include, in accordance with the permanent co-operation framework referred to in Article 10, provisions for allowing: (a) co-operation and mutual assistance in safety investigations led by other Member States, or the delegation to another Member State of the task of leading such an investigation in accordance with Article 7; and (b) co-ordination of the activities of their respective investigative bodies to the extent necessary to attain the objective of the directive.

Obligation to investigate

30.027 Interestingly, Article 5 imposes an obligation on Member States to conduct investigations in certain circumstances. This is useful for anyone who believes that there ought to be an investigation but the particular Member State is not agreeing to an investigation because it may be possible to go into the Member State courts and force an investigation based on Article 5 of the directive in appropriate circumstances.

30.028 Article 5(1) provides that each Member State must ensure that a safety investigation is carried out by the investigative body referred to in Article 8 after very serious marine casualties: (a) involving a ship flying its flag, irrespective of the location of the casualty; (b)occurring within its territorial sea and internal waters as defined in UNCLOS, irrespective of the flag of the ship or ships involved in the casualty; or (c) involving a substantial interest of the Member State, irrespective of the location of the casualty and of the flag of the ship or ships involved. Moreover, Article 5(2) goes on to provide:

"In addition, in the case of serious casualties, the investigative body shall carry out a preliminary assessment in order to decide whether or not to undertake a safety investigation. Where the investigative body decides not to undertake a safety investigation, the reasons for that decision shall be recorded and notified in accordance with Article 17(3).

In the case of any other marine casualty or incident, the investigative body shall decide whether or not a safety investigation is to be undertaken.

In the decisions referred to in the first and second subparagraphs, the investigative body shall take into account the seriousness of the marine casualty or incident, the type of vessel and/or cargo involved, and the potential for the findings of the safety investigation to lead to the prevention of future casualties and incidents."

30.029 Article 5(3) provides that the scope and practical arrangements for the conduct of safety investigations must be determined by the investigative body of the lead investigating Member State in co-operation with the equivalent bodies of the other substantially interested States, in such manner as appears to it most conducive to achieving the objective of this directive, and with a view to preventing future casualties and incidents.

30.030 Article 5(4) provides that when carrying out safety investigations, the investigative body must follow the common methodology for investigating marine casualties and incidents developed pursuant to Article 2(e) of Regulation 1406/2002. Investigators may depart from that methodology in a specific case where this can be justified as "necessary",[12] in their professional judgment, and if needed to achieve the aims of the investigation. The Commission also had to adopt or modify the methodology for the purposes of the directive, taking into account any relevant lessons drawn from safety investigations. That measure, designed to amend non-essential elements of this directive, *inter alia*, by supplementing it, had to be adopted in accordance with the regulatory procedure with scrutiny referred to in Article 19(3).

30.031 In terms of timing, Article 5(5) provides that a safety investigation must be started as promptly as is practicable after the marine casualty or incident occurs and, in any event, no later than two months after its occurrence.

Obligation to notify

30.032 Article 6 provides that a Member State must require, in the framework of its legal system, that its investigative body be notified without delay, by the responsible authorities and/or by the parties involved, of the occurrence of all casualties and incidents falling within the scope of the directive.

Leading of, and participation in, safety investigations

30.033 Article 7 deals with aspects of the process of the investigation. It provides:

"1. In principle, each marine casualty or incident shall be subject to only one investigation carried out by a Member State or a lead investigating Member State with the participation of any other substantially interested Member State.

In cases of safety investigations involving two or more Member States, the Member States concerned shall therefore cooperate with a view to rapidly agreeing which of them is to be the lead investigating Member State. They shall make every effort to agree on the procedures to

---

12 "Necessary" is a high standard – it is not just desirable, it must be necessary.

investigate. In the framework of this agreement, other substantially interested States shall have equal rights and access to witnesses and evidence as the Member State conducting the safety investigation. They shall also have the right to see their point of view taken into consideration by the lead investigating Member State.

The conduct of parallel safety investigations into the same marine casualty or incident shall be strictly limited to exceptional cases. In such cases, Member States shall notify the Commission of the reasons for conducting such parallel investigations. Member States conducting parallel safety investigations shall cooperate with each other. In particular, the investigative bodies involved shall exchange any pertinent information gathered in the course of their respective investigations, in particular in order to reach, as far as possible, shared conclusions.

Member States shall abstain from any measure which could unduly preclude, suspend or delay the conduct of a safety investigation falling within the scope of this Directive.

2. Notwithstanding paragraph 1, each Member State shall remain responsible for the safety investigation and coordination with other substantially interested Member States until such time as it is mutually agreed which of them is to be the lead investigating State.

3. Without prejudice to its obligations under this Directive and international law, a Member State may, on a case-by-case basis, delegate by mutual agreement to another Member State the task of leading a safety investigation or specific tasks for the conduct of such an investigation.[13]

4. When a ro-ro ferry or high-speed passenger craft is involved in a marine casualty or incident, the safety investigation procedure shall be launched by the Member State in whose territorial sea or internal waters as defined in UNCLOS the accident or incident occurs or, if occurring in other waters, by the last Member State visited by that ferry or craft. That State shall remain responsible for the safety investigation and coordination with other substantially interested Member States until it is mutually agreed which of them is to be the lead investigating State."

Investigative bodies

30.034 Without the directive, Member States could decide on different types of investigative bodies. Article 8(1) provides that Member States must ensure that safety investigations are conducted under the responsibility of an impartial permanent investigative body, endowed with the necessary powers, and by suitably qualified investigators, competent in matters relating to marine casualties and incidents. It also provides that in order to carry out a safety investigation in an unbiased manner, the investigative body shall be independent in its organisation, legal structure and decision-making of any party whose interests could conflict with the task entrusted to it. Interestingly, the last subparagraph of Article 8(1) provides that landlocked Member States which have neither ships nor vessels flying their flag will identify an independent focal point to co-operate in the investigation pursuant to Article 5(1)(c).

30.035 Not only must the investigation body be independent etc. but the investigators must be competent: Article 8(2) provides that the "investigative body shall ensure that individual investigators have a working knowledge of, and practical experience in, those subject areas pertaining to their normal investigative duties. Additionally, the investigative body shall ensure ready access to appropriate expertise, as necessary."

---

13 Ed., Recital 18 provides that a "Member State may delegate to another Member State the task of leading a marine casualty or incident safety investigation (hereinafter referred to as safety investigation) or specific tasks of such investigation, if mutually agreed."

30.036 Article 8(3) provides that the activities entrusted to the investigative body may be extended to the gathering and analysis of data relating to maritime safety, in particular for prevention purposes, in so far as these activities do not affect its independence or entail responsibility in regulatory, administrative or standardisation matters.

30.037 Article 8(4) provides:

"Member States, acting in the framework of their respective legal systems, shall ensure that the investigators of its investigative body, or of any other investigative body to which it has delegated the task of safety investigation, where appropriate in collaboration with the authorities responsible for the judicial inquiry, be provided with any information pertinent to the conduct of the safety investigation and therefore be authorised to:

(a) have free access to any relevant area or casualty site as well as to any ship, wreck or structure including cargo, equipment or debris;

(b) ensure immediate listing of evidence and controlled search for and removal of wreckage, debris or other components or substances for examination or analysis;

(c) require examination or analysis of the items referred to in point (b), and have free access to the results of such examinations or analysis;

(d) have free access to, copy and have use of any relevant information and recorded data, including VDR data, pertaining to a ship, voyage, cargo, crew or any other person, object, condition or circumstance;

(e) have free access to the results of examinations of the bodies of victims or of tests made on samples taken from the bodies of victims;

(f) require and have free access to the results of examinations of, or tests made on samples taken from, people involved in the operation of a ship or any other relevant person;

(g) interview witnesses in the absence of any person whose interests could be considered as hampering the safety investigation;

(h) obtain survey records and relevant information held by the flag State, the owners, classification societies or any other relevant party, whenever those parties or their representatives are established in the Member State;

(i) call for the assistance of the relevant authorities in the respective States, including flag-State and port-State surveyors, coastguard officers, vessel traffic service operators, search and rescue teams, pilots or other port or maritime personnel."

30.038 Article 8(5) provides that the investigative body shall be enabled to respond immediately on being notified at any time of a casualty, and to obtain sufficient resources to carry out its functions independently. Its investigators shall be afforded status giving them the necessary guarantees of independence.

30.039 Article 8(6) goes on to provide that the investigating body may combine its tasks under this directive with the work of investigating occurrences other than marine casualties on condition that such investigations do not endanger its independence.

Confidentiality

30.040 Article 9 provides for confidentiality:

"Without prejudice to Directive 95/46/EC, Member States, acting in the framework of their legal systems, shall ensure that the following records are not made available for purposes other than the safety investigation, unless the competent authority in that Member State determines that there is an overriding public interest in the disclosure of:

(a) all witness evidence and other statements, accounts and notes taken or received by the investigative body in the course of the safety investigation;[14]

(b) records revealing the identity of persons who have given evidence in the context of the safety investigation;

(c) information relating to persons involved in a marine casualty or incident which is of a particularly sensitive and private nature, including information concerning their health and private nature, including information concerning their health."

Costs

30.041 Article 11 of the directive ("costs") provides in less than clear language that where safety investigations involve two or more Member States, the respective activities shall be free of charge[15] and where assistance is requested of a Member State that is not involved in the safety investigation, Member States shall agree on the reimbursement of costs incurred.[16] Recital 19 of the directive provides that Member States "should"[17] make

"every effort not to charge for costs for assistance requested in the framework of safety investigations involving two or more Member States. Where assistance is requested from a Member State that is not involved in the safety investigation, Member States should agree on the reimbursement of costs incurred."

Review process

30.042 Article 23 of the directive (entitled "implementation report") provides that the Commission "shall, every five years, submit a report to the European Parliament and the Council on the implementation of, and compliance with, this directive, and, if necessary, propose further measures in the light of the recommendations set out therein."

Permanent co-operation framework

30.043 A permanent co-operation framework was established by Article 10 of the directive:

"1. Member States shall, in close cooperation with the Commission, establish a permanent cooperation framework enabling their respective investigative bodies to cooperate among themselves to the extent necessary to attain the objective of this Directive.

2. The rules of procedure of the permanent cooperation framework and the organisation arrangements required therefor shall be decided in accordance with the regulatory procedure referred to in Article 19(2).

3. Within the permanent cooperation framework, the investigative bodies in the Member States shall agree, in particular, upon the best modalities of cooperation in order to:

(a) enable investigative bodies to share installations, facilities and equipment for the technical investigation of wreckage and ship's equipment and other objects relevant to the

---

14 Ed., recital (10) provides that "Member States, acting in the framework of their legal systems, should protect witness statements following an accident and prevent them from being used for purposes other than safety investigations, with the objective of avoiding any discriminatory or retaliatory measures being taken against witnesses because of their participation in the investigations".

15 Dir. 2009/18, Art. 11(1).

16 Dir. 2009/18, Art. 11(2).

17 Note that the recital says "should" rather than "shall".

safety investigation, including the extraction and evaluation of information from VDRs and other electronic devices;

(b) provide each other with the technical cooperation or expertise needed to undertake specific tasks;

(c) acquire and share information relevant for analysing casualty data and making appropriate safety recommendations at Community level;

(d) draw up common principles for the follow-up of safety recommendations and for the adaptation of investigative methods to the development of technical and scientific progress;

(e) manage appropriately the early alerts referred to in Article 16;

(f) establish confidentiality rules for the sharing, in the respect of national rules, of witness evidence and the processing of data and other records referred to in Article 9, including in relations with third countries;

(g) organise, where appropriate, relevant training activities for individual investigators;

(h) promote cooperation with the investigative bodies of third countries and with the international maritime accidents investigation organisations in the fields covered by this Directive;

(i) provide investigative bodies conducting safety investigations with any pertinent information."

30.044 This finds expression in Commission Implementing Regulation for so-called "PCF" (i.e. permanent co-operation framework), namely, Regulation 651/2011.[18]

Co-operation with substantially interested third countries

30.045 Article 12 of the directive deals with the need for co-operation with so-called "third countries". The article provides:

"1. Member States shall cooperate, to the maximum extent possible, with other substantially interested third countries in safety investigations.

2. Substantially interested third countries shall, by mutual agreement, be allowed to join a safety investigation led by a Member State under this Directive at any stage of the investigation.

3. The cooperation of a Member State in a safety investigation conducted by a substantially interested third country shall be without prejudice to the conduct and reporting requirements of safety investigations under this Directive. Where a substantially interested third country is leading a safety investigation involving one or more Member States, Member States may decide not to carry out a parallel safety investigation, provided that the safety investigation led by the third country is conducted in accordance with the IMO Code for the Investigation of Marine Casualties and Incidents.[19]"

Preservation of evidence

30.046 As in any investigation, the preservation of evidence is very important in marine accident investigations. It is often difficult to achieve because unlike, say, an investigation of an incident on land, the ship in question could simply sail away and indeed may have to do so to meet obligations to the cargo owners or passengers on board.

---

18 OJ L177/18, 6 July 2011, http://eur-lex.europa.eu/LexUriServ/LexUriServ.do?uri=OJ:L:2011:177:0018:0023:EN:PDF.

19 Ed., Art. 3(1) of the directive provides that the term "IMO Code for the Investigation of Marine Casualties and Incidents" shall mean the Code for the Investigation of Marine Casualties and Incidents annexed to Res. A.849(20) of the IMO Assembly of 27 November 1997, in its up-to-date version.

Article 13 therefore provides that Member States must adopt measures to ensure that the parties concerned by casualties and incidents under the scope of this directive make every effort to: (a) save all information from charts, log books, electronic and magnetic recording and video tapes, including information from VDRs and other electronic devices relating to the period preceding, during and after an accident; (b) prevent the overwriting or other alteration of such information; (c) prevent interference with any other equipment which might reasonably be considered pertinent to the safety investigation of the accident; and (d) collect and preserve all evidence expeditiously for the purposes of the safety investigations.

Accident reports

30.047 The key output of the investigation is the so-called "accident report" (again, "casualty report" would be the better term). Article 14 of the directive provides:

"1. Safety investigations carried out under this Directive shall result in a published report presented in a format defined by the competent investigative body and in accordance with the relevant sections of Annex I.

Investigative bodies may decide that a safety investigation which does not concern a very serious or, as the case may be, a serious marine casualty and the findings of which do not have the potential to lead to the prevention of future casualties and incidents shall result in a simplified report to be published.

2. Investigative bodies shall make every effort to make the report referred to in paragraph 1, including its conclusions and any possible recommendations, available to the public, and especially to the maritime sector, within 12 months of the date of the casualty. If it is not possible to produce the final report within that time, an interim report shall be published within 12 months of the date of the casualty.

3. The investigative body of the lead investigating Member State shall send a copy of the final, simplified or interim report to the Commission. It shall take into account the possible technical observations of the Commission on final reports not affecting the substance of the findings for improving the quality of the report in the way most conducive to achieving the objective of this Directive."

30.048 Annex I sets out the rubric and framework for the report:

"Safety investigation report content
Foreword
This identifies the sole objective of the safety investigation and indicates that a safety recommendation shall in no case create a presumption of liability or blame and that the report has not been written, in terms of content and style, with the intention of it being used in legal proceedings.

(The report should make no reference to witness evidence nor link anyone who is referred to in the report to a person who has given evidence during the course of the safety investigation.)

1. SUMMARY
This part outlines the basic facts of the marine casualty or incident: what happened, when, where and how it happened; it also states whether any deaths, injuries, damage to the ship, cargo, third parties or environment occurred as a result.

2. FACTUAL INFORMATION
This part includes a number of discrete sections, providing sufficient information that the investigating body interprets to be factual, substantiate the analysis and ease understanding. These sections include, in particular, the following information:

2.1. Ship particulars
Flag/register,
Identification,
Main characteristics,
Ownership and management,
Construction details,
Minimum safe manning,
Authorised cargo.

2.2. Voyage particulars
Ports of call,
Type of voyage,
Cargo information,
Manning.

2.3. Marine casualty or incident information
Type of marine casualty or incident,
Date and time,
Position and location of the marine casualty or incident,
External and internal environment,
Ship operation and voyage segment,
Place on board,
Human factors data,
Consequences (for people, ship, cargo, environment, other).

2.4. Shore authority involvement and emergency response
Who was involved,
Means used,
Speed of response,
Actions taken,
Results achieved.

3. NARRATIVE
This part reconstructs the marine casualty or incident through a sequence of events, in a chronological order leading up to, during and following the marine casualty or incident and the involvement of each actor (i.e. person, material, environment, equipment or external agent). The period covered by the narrative depends on the timing of those particular accidental events that directly contributed to the marine casualty or incident. This part also includes any relevant details of the safety investigation conducted, including the results of examinations or tests.

4. ANALYSIS
This part includes a number of discrete sections, providing an analysis of each accidental event, with comments relating to the results of any relevant examinations or tests conducted during the course of the safety investigation and to any safety action that might already have been taken to prevent marine casualties.
    These sections should cover issues such as:

– accidental event context and environment,
– human erroneous actions and omissions, events involving hazardous material, environmental effects, equipment failures, and external influences,
– contributing factors involving person-related functions, shipboard operations, shore management or regulatory influence.

The analysis and comment enable the report to reach logical conclusions, establishing all of the contributing factors, including those with risks for which existing defences aimed at preventing an accidental event, and/or those aimed at eliminating or reducing its consequences, are assessed to be either inadequate or missing.

5. CONCLUSIONS

This part consolidates the established contributing factors and missing or inadequate defences (material, functional, symbolic or procedural) for which safety actions should be developed to prevent marine casualties.

6. SAFETY RECOMMENDATIONS

When appropriate, this part of the report contains safety recommendations derived from the analysis and conclusions and related to particular subject areas, such as legislation, design, procedures, inspection, management, health and safety at work, training, repair work, maintenance, shore assistance and emergency response.

The safety recommendations are addressed to those that are best placed to implement them, such as ship owners, managers, recognised organisations, maritime authorities, vessel traffic services, emergency bodies, international maritime organisations and European institutions, with the aim of preventing marine casualties.

This part also includes any interim safety recommendations that may have been made or any safety actions taken during the course of the safety investigation.

7. APPENDICES

When appropriate, the following non-exhaustive list of information is attached to the report in paper and/or electronic form:

- photographs, moving images, audio recordings, charts, drawings,
- applicable standards,
- technical terms and abbreviations used,
- special safety studies,
- miscellaneous information."

Safety recommendations

30.049 Article 15 deals with the safety recommendations which could flow from an investigation:

"1. Member States shall ensure that safety recommendations made by the investigative bodies are duly taken into account by the addressees and, where appropriate, be given an adequate follow-up in accordance with Community and international law.
2. Where appropriate, an investigative body or the Commission shall make safety recommendations on the basis of an abstract data analysis and of the overall results of safety investigations carried out.
3. A safety recommendation shall in no circumstances determine liability or apportion blame for a casualty."

30.050 Interestingly, recital 25 goes a little wider by providing that the "safety recommendations resulting from a safety investigation should be duly taken into account by the Member States and the Community".

30.051 Occasionally, something will emerge during an investigation which is of such importance that the sector needs to be advised of the discovery (e.g. a particular practice or piece of equipment needs to be changed) and Article 16 provides for a so-called "early alert system" by providing that without prejudice

"to its right to give an early alert, the investigative body of a Member State shall, at any stage of a safety investigation, if it takes the view that urgent action is needed at Community level to prevent the risk of new casualties, inform the Commission without delay of the need to give an early alert" and if "necessary, the Commission shall issue a note of warning for the attention of the responsible authorities in all the other Member States, the shipping industry, and to any other relevant party".

European database for marine casualties

30.052 In a very welcome move, Article 17 of Directive 2009/18 provides for the establishment of a database known as the European Marine Casualty Information Platform ("EMCIP"):

> "1. Data on marine casualties and incidents shall be stored and analysed by means of a European electronic database to be set up by the Commission, which shall be known as the European Marine Casualty Information Platform (EMCIP).
> 2. Member States shall notify the Commission of the entitled authorities that will have access to the database.
> 3. The investigative bodies of the Member States shall notify the Commission on marine casualties and incidents in accordance with the format in Annex II. They shall also provide the Commission with data resulting from safety investigations in accordance with the EMCIP database scheme.
> 4. The Commission and the Member States shall develop the database scheme and a method for the notification of data within the appropriate timescale."

30.053 This is a very welcome initiative.[20]

Role of COSS in the area of marine accident investigation

30.054 Article 19(1) of the directive provides that the Commission shall be assisted by the COSS which was established by Regulation 2099/2002 of the European Parliament and the Council.[21]

Amendments to the regime

30.055 Recital 29 to the directive provides that, in particular, the Commission should be empowered to amend the directive in order to apply subsequent amendments to the international conventions, protocols, codes and resolutions related thereto and to adopt or modify the common methodology for investigating marine casualties and incidents. The recital continues that since those measures are of general scope and are designed to amend non-essential elements of this directive, *inter alia*, by supplementing it with new non-essential elements, they must be adopted in accordance with the regulatory procedure with scrutiny provided for in Article 5a of Decision 1999/468. Thus, Article 20 of the directive provides that the Commission may update definitions in the directive, and the references made to Community acts and to IMO instruments in order to bring them into line with Community or IMO measures which have entered into force, subject to observance of the limits of this directive. Those measures, designed to amend non-essential elements of this directive, *inter alia*, by supplementing it, shall be adopted in accordance with the regulatory procedure with scrutiny referred to in Article 19(3).

---

20 See www.emsa.europa.eu/marine-casualties-a-incidents.html.
21 OJ L324/1, 29 November 2002.

Acting in accordance with the same procedure, the Commission may also amend the annexes. Amendments to the IMO Code for the Investigation of Marine Casualties and Incidents[22] may be excluded from the scope of this directive pursuant to Article 5 of Regulation 2099/2002.

Observations

30.056 While Member States could continue to investigate casualties on an ad hoc or individual basis, there must be benefits attached to engaging in cross-border co-operation. The output of the EMSA in this area (e.g. the annual overview of marine casualties and incidents)[23] has contributed an enormous amount to knowledge on the area but, perhaps more importantly, to the prevention of casualties and other incidents which means that lives have probably been saved because of a measure such as this one.

Common methodology for investigating marine casualties and incidents

30.057 The directive contains a common methodology for investigating marine casualties and incidents:

"A. PURPOSE, SCOPE AND APPLICATION
The purpose of safety investigations into marine accidents is to reduce the risk of future casualties and incidents and reduce their serious consequences including loss of life, loss of ships and pollution of the marine environment.

The purpose of this document is to provide a common methodology for investigative bodies of the Member States to conduct marine safety investigations in accordance with Directive 2009/18/EC. It is based on the scope and definitions of Directive 2009/18/EC, taking into account the IMO instruments referred to in the Directive.

The methodology aims to establish common approach in principle applicable in all investigations carried out in accordance with the Directive and it outlines the characteristics of a good safety investigation. It is not a check list. The investigators shall exercise their professional judgment and training to take into account the circumstances of each case.

In this way, through application of this common methodology and an objective and systemic approach to the investigation, the investigative body should best be able to draw lessons from each accident and so enhance maritime safety.

Proper identification of the causes of a marine casualty or incident requires timely and methodical investigation, going beyond the immediate evidence and looking for underlying conditions which may cause other future occurrences. Investigation may therefore be seen as a means of identifying not only immediate causes, but also issues in the total environment from regulation and policy through to implementation.

B. CONTENT
1. Operational readiness

    1.1.   Each investigative body shall plan in advance in order to ensure that unnecessary delays, after the notification and during the initiation of any investigation, do not occur as a result of a lack of relevant/prerequisite information, preparedness or

---

22 Art. 3(1) of the directive provides that the term "IMO Code for the Investigation of Marine Casualties and Incidents" shall mean the Code for the Investigation of Marine Casualties and Incidents annexed to Res. A.849(20) of the IMO Assembly of 27 November 1997, in its up-to-date version.

23 E.g. for the 2014 output: see www.emsa.europa.eu/implementation-tasks/accident-investigation/items. html?cid=141&id=2303.

knowledge. Such preparedness plan shall ensure resources and procedures are, as far as possible, immediately available to meet the requirements, including sufficient suitably qualified investigators and any necessary co-ordination, nationally and internationally, to enable initial actions to be taken promptly, after notification of a casualty or incident is first received.

1.2. Arrangements shall be put in place to ensure prompt receipt of casualty and incident notifications by the accident investigation body on a twenty-four hour basis.

2. Initial assessment and response

2.1. On being notified, the investigative bodies shall assess the situation. The initial assessment is critical for investigative bodies to gather an overview as quickly as possible, minimise the potential loss of evidence, and determine the scope of information required to decide the appropriate action.

2.2. This assessment shall include, as far as possible, an understanding of

– the overall events,
– key timings,
– the personnel involved, and
– the category of the event.

In addition to the factors listed in Article 5(2) of Directive 2009/18/EC, the following may amongst others also be considered in deciding which non very serious casualties or incidents to investigate:

– the potential safety value that may be gained by conducting an investigation
– whether the casualty is part of an identifiable trend
– the potential consequences of the casualty
– the extent of resources available and projected to be available in the event of conflicting priorities and the extent of any investigation backlog
– any risks associated with not investigating
– serious injuries occurring on-board to crew and/or passengers
– the pollution of environmentally sensitive areas
– ships subject to significant structural damages
– casualties which disrupt, or have the potential to disrupt, major port operations

2.3. After a decision is taken to investigate a serious casualty or another marine casualty or incident, the investigation shall normally be conducted with the same immediacy as that for a very serious casualty.

Where an investigation is to be carried out, the investigative bodies shall take immediate action as far as practicable to ensure preservation of evidence, coordination with other substantially interested parties and the appointment of a lead investigating state.

3. Strategy and evidence collection

3.1. The investigative body of the lead investigating Member State, in close liaison with those of the other substantially interested States, shall expeditiously develop a strategy for the scope, direction and timing of the investigation.

3.2. The investigative body shall keep the plan under review during the course of the investigation; by the end of the evidence collection phase the investigative body shall, as far as practicable, have ensured the completeness of evidence from all areas that could have influenced the casualty or incident.

3.3. The scope of a safety investigation and the procedure to be followed shall be sufficient as to eliminate uncertainty and ambiguity to the maximum extent possible and so enable robust logical assessments to be made of what led to the marine casualty or incident.

3.4. Investigative bodies of substantially interested Member States shall provide support to the lead investigating Member State, in a timely fashion, to the extent practicable.

3.5. The lead investigative body shall nominate an investigator to carry out the investigation, deploy appropriate resources and start the collection of evidence as soon as possible, as the quality of evidence, particularly that relying on the accuracy of human recollection, can deteriorate rapidly with time; and also in recognition that any ship involved in a marine casualty or incident should not be delayed more than is absolutely necessary by the need to gather evidence.

3.6. During the initial stage of every investigation, investigators shall collect as much of the relevant evidence as possible which may help understanding the incident and determining its causes, keeping in mind the possible breadth of any investigation.

3.7. In addition to that gained during the initial notification stage, investigators shall obtain appropriate background and reference information. This can include evidence or data requested from any monitoring system, from the traffic control system, from the maritime administration, from the rescue services, from the shipping company and the casualty vessel.

3.8. Where appropriate, the investigative body shall query databases, including that of European Marine Casualty Information Platform, and other sources of information to help identify potential safety issues that may be relevant to the marine casualty or incident under investigation.

3.9. In principle, investigators shall, if feasible visit the casualty and/or occurrence site in order to obtain undisturbed evidence and to gain an initial appreciation of the incident. Where it has not been possible to preserve the site, arrangements shall, where possible, be made to obtain appropriate documentation of the scene for example by photographs, audio-visual recordings, sketches or any other means available with the object of gathering important evidence and possibly recreating the circumstances at a later stage.

3.10. Where a VDR is fitted, the investigators shall make every effort in order to obtain and preserve the information recorded on it. In particular they shall take early action to ensure that the VDR is 'saved' to prevent it being overwritten. They also shall make every effort to obtain any relevant information from electronic sources, both on the ship and ashore. They shall review, in the order they find appropriate, any available, relevant documents, procedures and records.

3.11. Interviews shall be conducted with all available witnesses considered by the lead investigative body to be relevant. Investigators shall identify which witnesses they wish to interview initially and develop an interview plan. This plan shall, among other things, take into account fatigue (of both the witness and the investigator), the fragility of human evidence and the intended movements of the prospective witnesses.

Potential witnesses may include, among others:

– persons directly involved in the marine casualty or incident and its consequences
– eyewitnesses to the marine casualty or incident
– emergency response personnel
– company personnel, port officials, designers, repair personnel technical experts

If it is not possible to speak directly with some witnesses, the lead investigative body shall take steps to gain the evidence by other means.

Evidence may be obtained from them through telephone interviews or by asking other trained safety investigators to conduct the interview on behalf of the lead investigative State. In the latter case, the person conducting the interview will need to be carefully briefed by the investigator carrying out the investigation. Many key witnesses may need to be re-interviewed perhaps more than once.

3.12. Information shall be verified whenever possible. Statements made by different witnesses may conflict and further supporting evidence may be needed. To ensure that all of the relevant facts are uncovered, the broad questions of 'who', 'what', 'when', 'how' and 'why' shall be asked.

3.13. Human factors form an integral part of most investigations, and safety investigators must be trained appropriately. The success of the investigation of human factors depends largely on the type and quality of the information collected. As no two occurrences are the same, the investigative body shall determine the type and quality of data to be collected and reviewed. As a rule, the investigator shall be over-inclusive in gathering information initially and set aside superfluous data as the investigation unfolds.

3.14. If need be, the investigative body will have to secure some physical evidence in particular in order to obtain a scientific examination, inspection or testing ashore. In these cases, the investigators shall keep in mind that the passage of time could pollute the available evidence and therefore proceed with their removal as soon as appropriate. Prior to removal, such evidence shall be if possible photographed in situ. Their removal and their preservation shall be made with all the appropriate precautions in order to avoid affecting their examination.

3.15. If they appear to be relevant to the occurrence as part of their investigation, the investigative bodies may have to conduct or to order specialist examination, in particular technical examination of the vessel and of the different systems and equipment on board, if necessary by appropriate experts.

3.16. While gathering evidence, the investigative bodies shall try to identify any evidence that may be missing.

4. Analysis

4.1. Having collected evidence and related additional data, the investigative body of the lead investigating Member State, in cooperation with other substantially interested States as appropriate, shall analyse it with a view to identifying causal and contributing factors.

In that respect, the investigators shall take into account the variable value of the evidences they have collected and shall consider how best to resolve any ambiguities or conflicts of evidence.

4.2. Proper identification of causal factors requires timely and methodical investigation, going beyond the immediate evidence and looking for underlying conditions, which may be remote from the site of the marine casualty or incident, and which may cause other future marine casualties and marine incidents. Marine safety investigations should therefore in principle serve as a means of identifying not only immediate causal factors but also conditions that may be present in the whole operational process. To achieve this, the analysis of the evidence collected shall be thorough and iterative.

4.3. If a gap of information cannot be resolved and is filled in by logical extrapolation and reasonable assumptions, such extrapolation and assumptions shall be made clear in the wording of the report. A useful tool in this process can be the identification of all options and their analytical reduction to reach the most likely hypotheses.

5. Safety recommendations

5.1. Any safety recommendations shall be based on the analysis. They shall be addressed to those organisations or individuals best placed to take remedial action.

5.2. They may be based on safety investigations, or on research and abstract data analysis. Their formulation may be achieved in cooperation and consultation with the relevant stakeholders since these are often well-placed to identify and implement appropriate safety actions. The final decision on the content and addressees of safety recommendations shall, however, rest with the lead investigative body.

5.3. Where a causal or contributing factor is considered so serious that it should be addressed urgently, appropriate follow-up action shall be taken such as, for instance, issuing an interim safety recommendation.

5.4. To facilitate as much as possible acceptance and implementation by the recipients, any recommendation shall be:

- Necessary
- Likely to be effective
- Practicable
- Relevant
- Targeted
- Stated in a clear, concise and direct manner
- Stated so that it can be the basis for corrective action plans, highlighting the safety gap that needs to be addressed.

6. Reports

6.1. The investigative body of the lead investigating Member State shall produce a draft report in liaison with other substantially interested States. It shall clearly present, in a consistent and concise style, the facts and analysis which are used to support the conclusions and recommendations.

6.2. Where practicable, the draft report, or appropriate parts thereof, shall be circulated in confidence for consultation to any person or organisation that could be affected by it. The investigative body shall publish the final report, amended as appropriate.

7. Follow-up

The investigative bodies shall endeavour to ascertain details of action taken in response to safety recommendations."

30.058 This is a very comprehensive and useful document which will guide casualty investigators and those involved in casualties more constructively than anything which had existed previously in EU law.

CHAPTER 31

Maritime safety: minimum training of seafarers

A. INTRODUCTION

31.001 This chapter considers Directive 2008/106 on the minimum level of training of seafarers.[1]

31.002 On 19 November 2008, the Parliament and the Council adopted Directive 2008/106 on the minimum level of training of seafarers.[2]

31.003 Directive 2008/106 was amended by Directive 2012/35 of 21 November 2012.[3] The legal basis of Directive 2008/106 was the Treaty establishing the European Union ("TEC") and, in particular, Article 80(2) of the TEC (this is now the Treaty on the functioning of the European Union ("TFEU") and Article 100(2) of the TFEU respectively). The legislative history included a proposal from the Commission, an opinion of the European Economic and Social Committee and a consultation with the Committee of the Regions. An earlier measure was Directive 2001/25 of the European Parliament and of the Council of 4 April 2001 on the minimum level of training of seafarers[4] had been significantly amended on several occasions. So the first recital to Directive 2008/106 provided that new amendments are being made to that directive so it was desirable, for reasons of clarity, that the provisions in question should be recast.

31.004 Directive 2008/106 provides, in the second recital, that actions to be taken at European Union ("EU") level in the field of maritime safety and pollution prevention at sea should be in line with internationally agreed rules and standards.

31.005 Directive 2008/106 recognises that in order to maintain and develop the level of knowledge and skills in the maritime sector in the EU, it is important to pay appropriate attention to maritime training and the status of seafarers in the EU.[5] While a consistent level of training for the award of vocational competency certificates to seafarers should be ensured in the interests of maritime safety.[6]

B. BACKGROUND TO DIRECTIVE 2008/106

31.006 The background to the directive is also clear from such recitals as:

"(6) The mutual recognition of diplomas and certificates provided for under Directive 2005/36/
EC does not always ensure a standardised level of training for all seafarers serving on board

---

1 OJ L323/33, 3 December 2008. For an unofficial consolidated version, see http://eur-lex.europa.eu/legal-content/EN/TXT/?qid=1470569247469&uri=CELEX:02008L0106-20130103.
2 OJ L323/33, 3 December 2008.
3 OJ L343/78, 14 December 2012.
4 OJ L255/17, 18 May 2001.
5 Dir. 2009/106, Recital 3.
6 Dir. 1008/106, Recital 4.

vessels flying the flag of a Member State. This is, however, vital from the viewpoint of maritime safety.

(7) It is therefore essential to define a minimum level of training for seafarers in the Community. That level should be based on the standards of training already agreed at international level, namely the International Maritime Organisation (IMO) Convention on Standards of Training, Certification and Watchkeeping for Seafarers, 1978 (STCW Convention),[7] as revised in 1995. All Member States are Parties to that Convention.

(8) Member States may establish standards higher than the minimum standards laid down in the STCW Convention and this Directive.

(9) The Regulations of the STCW Convention annexed to this Directive should be supplemented by the mandatory provisions contained in Part A of the Seafarers' Training, Certification and Watchkeeping Code (STCW Code). Part B of the STCW Code contains recommended guidance intended to assist Parties to the STCW Convention and those involved in implementing, applying or enforcing its measures to give the Convention full and complete effect in a uniform manner.

(10) For the enhancement of maritime safety and pollution prevention at sea, provisions on minimum rest periods for watchkeeping personnel should be established in this Directive in accordance with the STCW Convention. Those provisions should be applied without prejudice to the provisions of Council Directive 1999/63/EC of 21 June 1999 concerning the Agreement on the organisation of working time of seafarers concluded by the European Community Shipowners' Association (ECSA) and the Federation of Transport Workers' Unions in the European Union (FST).[8]

(11) Member States should take and enforce specific measures to prevent and penalise fraudulent practices associated with certificates of competency as well as pursue their efforts within the IMO to achieve strict and enforceable agreements on the worldwide combating of such practices.

(12) In order to enhance maritime safety and prevent loss of human life and maritime pollution, communication among crew members on board ships sailing in Community waters should be improved.

(13) Personnel on board passenger ships nominated to assist passengers in emergency situations should be able to communicate with the passengers.

(14) Crews serving on board tankers carrying noxious or polluting cargo should be capable of coping effectively with accident prevention and emergency situations. It is paramount that a proper communication link between the master, officers and ratings is established, covering the requirements provided for in this Directive.

(15) It is essential to ensure that seafarers holding certificates issued by third countries and serving on board Community ships have a level of competence equivalent to that required by the STCW Convention. This Directive should lay down procedures and common criteria for the recognition by the Member States of certificates issued by third countries, based on the training and certification requirements as agreed in the framework of the STCW Convention.

(16) In the interests of safety at sea, Member States should recognise qualifications proving the required level of training only where these are issued by or on behalf of Parties to the STCW Convention which have been identified by the IMO Maritime Safety Committee (MSC) as having been shown to have given, and still to be giving, full effect to the standards set out in that Convention. To bridge the time gap until the MSC has been able to carry out such identification, a procedure for the preliminary recognition of certificates is needed.

---

7 Ed., the term "STCW Convention" means the International Maritime Organization (IMO) Convention on Standards of Training, Certification and Watchkeeping for Seafarers, 1978, as it applies to the matters concerned taking into account the transitional provisions of Article VII and Regulation I/15 of the convention and including, where appropriate, the applicable provisions of the STCW Code, all being applied in their up-to-date versions.

8 Ed., OJ L167/33, 2 July 1999.

(17) Where appropriate, maritime institutes, training programmes and courses should be inspected. Criteria for such inspection should therefore be established.

(18) The Commission should be assisted by a committee in carrying out the tasks related to the recognition of certificates issued by training institutes or administrations of third countries.

(19) The European Maritime Safety Agency established by Regulation ... 1406/2002 of the European Parliament and of the Council[9] should assist the Commission in verifying that Member States comply with the requirements laid down in this Directive.

(20) Member States, as port authorities, are required to enhance safety and prevention of pollution in Community waters through priority inspection of vessels flying the flag of a third country which has not ratified the STCW Convention, thereby ensuring no more favourable treatment to vessels flying the flag of a third country.

(21) It is appropriate to include in this Directive provisions on port State control, pending the amendment of Council Directive 95/21/EC[10] on port State control of shipping in order to transfer to that Directive the provisions on port State control which are included in this Directive.

(22) It is necessary to provide for procedures for adapting this Directive to changes in international conventions and codes.

(23) The measures necessary for the implementation of this Directive should be adopted in accordance with Council Decision 1999/468/EC of 28 June 1999 laying down the procedures for the exercise of implementing powers conferred on the Commission.[11]

(24) In particular the Commission should be empowered to amend this Directive in order to apply, for the purposes of this Directive, subsequent amendments to certain international codes and any relevant amendment to Community legislation. Since those measures are of general scope and are designed to amend non-essential elements of this Directive, they must be adopted in accordance with the regulatory procedure with scrutiny provided for in Article 5a of Decision 1999/468/EC.

(25) The new elements introduced into this Directive only concern the committee procedures. They therefore do not need to be transposed by the Member States.

(26) This Directive should be without prejudice to the obligations of the Members States relating to the time limits for transposition into national law of the Directives set out in Annex III, Part B."

It is clear that there is a need to ensure a standardised level of training (as in the sixth recital) and a need for a minimum level of training for seafarers (as in the seventh recital). Member States may establish standards which are higher than the minimum standards laid down in the STCW Convention and the directive. The directive is therefore aimed at imposing the minimum training of seafarers.

C. DEFINITIONS IN DIRECTIVE 2008/106

31.007 Article 1 of Directive 2008/106 sets out a number of definitions for the purposes of the directive.

31.008 The term "master" is defined as meaning the person having command of a ship.

31.009 The word "officer" means a member of the crew, other than the master, designated as such by national law or regulations or, in the absence of such designation, by collective agreement or custom.

---

9 Ed., OJ L208/1, 5 August 2002.
10 Ed., OJ L157/1, 7 July 1995.
11 Ed., OJ L184/23, 17 July 1999.

31.010 The phrase "deck officer" means an officer qualified in accordance with the provisions of Chapter II of Annex I.

31.011 The term "chief mate" means the officer next in rank to the master upon whom the command of the ship will fall in the event of the incapacity of the master.

31.012 The phrase "engineer officer" means an officer qualified in accordance with the provisions of Chapter III of Annex I.

31.013 The title "chief engineer officer" means the senior engineer officer responsible for the mechanical propulsion and the operation and maintenance of the mechanical and electrical installations of the ship.

31.014 The rank of "second engineer officer" means the engineer officer next in rank to the chief engineer officer upon whom the responsibility for the mechanical propulsion and the operation and maintenance of the mechanical and electrical installations of the ship will fall in the event of the incapacity of the chief engineer officer.

31.015 The position of "assistant engineer officer" means a person under training to become an engineer officer and designated as such by national law or regulations.

31.016 The rank of "radio operator" means a person holding an appropriate certificate issued or recognised by the competent authorities under the provisions of the Radio Regulations.

31.017 The word "rating" means a member of the ship's crew other than the master or an officer.

31.018 The phrase "seagoing ship" means a ship other than those which navigate exclusively in inland waters or in waters within, or closely adjacent to, sheltered waters or areas where port regulations apply.

31.019 The term "ship flying the flag of a Member State" means a ship registered in and flying the flag of a Member State in accordance with its legislation; a ship not corresponding to this definition shall be regarded as a ship flying the flag of a third country.

31.020 The term "near-coastal voyages" means voyages in the vicinity of a Member State as defined by that Member State.

31.021 The phrase "propulsion power" means the total maximum continuous rated output power in kilowatts of all of a ship's main propulsion machinery which appears on the ship's certificate of registry or other official document.

31.022 The phrase "oil-tanker" means a ship constructed and used for the carriage of petroleum and petroleum products in bulk.

31.023 The term "chemical tanker" means a ship constructed or adapted and used for the carriage in bulk of any liquid product listed in Chapter 17 of the International Bulk Chemical Code, in its up-to-date version.

31.024 The phrase "liquefied-gas tanker" means a ship constructed or adapted and used for the carriage in bulk of any liquefied gas or other product listed in Chapter 19 of the International Gas Carrier Code, in its up-to-date version.

31.025 The term "Radio Regulations" means the radio regulations annexed to, or regarded as being annexed to, the International Telecommunication Convention, as amended.

31.026 The phrase "passenger ship" means a ship as defined in the International Convention for the Safety of Life at Sea, 1974 ("SOLAS 74"), as amended.

31.027 The phrase "fishing vessel" shall mean a vessel used for catching fish or other living resources of the sea.

31.028 The term "STCW Convention" means the IMO Convention on Standards of Training, Certification and Watchkeeping for Seafarers, 1978, as it applies to the matters concerned taking into account the transitional provisions of Article VII and Regulation I/15 of the convention and including, where appropriate, the applicable provisions of the STCW Code, all being applied in their up-to-date versions.

31.029 The phrase "radio duties" includes, as appropriate, watchkeeping and technical maintenance and repairs conducted in accordance with the Radio Regulations, SOLAS 74 and, at the discretion of each Member State, the relevant recommendations of the IMO, in their up-to-date versions.

31.030 The term "ro-ro passenger ship" means a passenger ship with ro-ro cargo spaces or special-category spaces as defined in the SOLAS 74, in its up-to-date version.

31.031 The Phrase "STCW Code" means the Seafarers' Training, Certification and Watchkeeping ("STCW") Code as adopted by the 1995 Conference resolution 2, in its up-to-date version.

31.032 The word "function" means a group of tasks, duties and responsibilities, as specified in the STCW Code, necessary for ship operation, safety of life at sea or protection of the marine environment.

31.033 The word "company" means the owner of the ship or any other organisation or person such as the manager or the bareboat charterer who has assumed the responsibility for operation of the ship from the shipowner and who, on assuming such responsibility, has agreed to take over all the duties and responsibilities imposed on the company by Directive 2008/106.

31.034 The phrase "seagoing service" means service on board a ship relevant to the issue or revalidation of a certificate of competency, certificate of proficiency or other qualification.

31.035 The term "approved" means approved by a Member State in accordance with the directive.

31.036 The phrase "third country" means any country which is not an EU Member State.

31.037 The term "month" means a calendar month or 30 days made up of periods of less than one month. The expression "GMDSS radio operator" means a person qualified in accordance with Chapter IV of Annex I.

31.038 The phrase "ISPS Code" means the International Ship and Port Facility Security Code adopted on 12 December 2002, by resolution 2 of the Conference of Contracting Governments to the SOLAS 74, in its up-to-date version.

31.039 The expression "ship security officer" means the person on board a ship, accountable to the master, designated by the company as responsible for the security of the ship including implementation and maintenance of the ship security plan and liaison with the company security officer and port facility security officers.

31.040 The term "security duties" is said to include all security tasks and duties on board ships as defined by Chapter XI/2 of the SOLAS 74, as amended, and by the ISPS Code.

31.041 The term "certificate of competency" means a certificate issued and endorsed for masters, officers and GMDSS radio operators in accordance with Chapters II, III, IV or VII of Annex I, and entitling the lawful holder thereof to serve in the capacity and perform the functions involved at the level of responsibility specified therein.

31.042 The term "certificate of proficiency" means a certificate, other than a certificate of competency, issued to a seafarer stating that the relevant requirements of training, competencies or seagoing service in Directive 2008/106 have been met.

31.043 The expression "documentary evidence" is defined as meaning documentation, other than a certificate of competency or certificate of proficiency, used to establish that the relevant requirements in Directive 2008/106 have been met.

31.044 The phrase "electro-technical officer" means an officer qualified in accordance with Chapter III of Annex I.

31.045 The term "able seafarer deck" means a rating qualified in accordance with Chapter II of Annex I.

31.046 The phrase "able seafarer engine" means a rating qualified in accordance with Chapter III of Annex I.

31.047 Finally, the term "electro-technical rating" means a rating qualified in accordance with Chapter III of Annex I.

D. SCOPE OF DIRECTIVE 2008/106

31.048 Article 2 sets out the scope of the directive. It applies to the seafarers mentioned in the directive serving on board seagoing ships flying the flag of a Member State with the exception of: (a) warships, naval auxiliaries or other ships owned or operated by a Member State and engaged only on government non-commercial service; (b) fishing vessels; (c) pleasure yachts not engaged in trade; and (d) wooden ships of primitive build.

E. TRAINING AND CERTIFICATION

31.049 Article 3 addresses the issue of training and certification. Article 3(1) provides that Member States must take the measures necessary to ensure that seafarers serving on ships as referred to in Article 2 are trained as a minimum in accordance with the requirements of the STCW Convention, as laid down in Annex I to this directive, and hold certificates as defined in points (36) and (37) of Article 1, and/or documentary evidence as defined in point (38) of Article 1. Article 3(2) goes on to provide that Member States must take the measures necessary to ensure that those crew members that must be certified in accordance with Regulation III/10.4 of the SOLAS 74 are trained and certificated in accordance with the directive.

F. CERTIFICATES OF COMPETENCY, CERTIFICATES OF PROFICIENCY AND ENDORSEMENTS

31.050 Article 5 deals with certificates of competency, certificates of proficiency and endorsements. Under Article 5(1), Member States must ensure that certificates of competency and certificates of proficiency are issued only to candidates who comply with the requirements of Article 5. Certificates for masters, officers and radio operators shall be endorsed by the Member State as prescribed in Article 5.[12] Certificates of competency and certificates of proficiency must be issued in accordance with Regulation I/2, paragraph 3

---

12 Dir. 2008/106, Art. 5(2).

of the annex to the STCW Convention.[13] Certificates of competency must be issued only by the Member States, following verification of the authenticity and validity of any necessary documentary evidence and in accordance with the provisions laid down in Article 5.[14] Under Article 5(4), it is clear that in respect of radio operators, Member States may: (a) include the additional knowledge required by the relevant regulations in the examination for the issue of a certificate complying with the Radio Regulations; or (b) issue a separate certificate indicating that the holder has the additional knowledge required by the relevant regulations. Under Article 5(5), at the discretion of a Member State, endorsements may be incorporated in the format of the certificates being issued as provided for in section A-I/2 of the STCW Code. If they are incorporated then the form used must be that set out in section A-I/2, paragraph 1.[15] If issued otherwise, the form of endorsements used must be that set out in paragraph 2 of that section.[16] Endorsements must be issued in accordance with Article VI, paragraph 2, of the STCW Convention.[17]

31.051 Endorsements attesting the issue of a certificate of competency and endorsements attesting a certificate of proficiency issued to masters and officers in accordance with the Regulations V/1-1 and V/1-2 of Annex I shall be issued only if all the requirements of the STCW Convention and this directive have been complied with.

31.052 Article 5(6) provides that a Member State which recognises a certificate of competency, or a certificate of proficiency, issued to masters and officers in accordance with Regulations V/1-1 and V/1-2 of the annex to the STCW Convention under the procedure laid down in Article 19(2) of the directive must endorse that certificate to attest its recognition only after ensuring the authenticity and validity of the certificate. The form of the endorsement used must be that set out in paragraph 3 of Section A-I/2 of the STCW Code.

31.053 Under Article 5(7), the endorsements referred to in paragraphs 5 and 6: (a) may be issued as separate documents; (b) must be issued by Member States only; (c) must each be assigned a unique number, except for endorsements attesting the issue of a certificate of competency, which may be assigned the same number as the certificate of competency concerned, provided that that number is unique; and (d) must each expire as soon as the endorsed certificate of competency or certificate of proficiency issued to masters and officers in accordance with Regulations V/1-1 and V/1-2 of the annex to the STCW Convention expires or is withdrawn, suspended or cancelled by the Member State or third country which issued it and, in any case, within five years of their date of issue.

31.054 The capacity in which the holder of a certificate is authorised to serve must be identified in the form of endorsement in terms identical to those used in the applicable safe-manning requirements of the Member State concerned.[18] A Member State may use a format different from the format laid down in section A-I/2 of the STCW Code, provided that, as a minimum, the required information is provided in Roman characters and Arabic figures, taking account of the variations permitted under section A-I/2.[19]

---

13 Dir. 2008/106, Art. 5(3).
14 Dir. 2008/106, Art. 5(3)(a).
15 Dir. 2008/106, Art. 5(5).
16 Ibid.
17 Ibid.
18 Dir. 2008/116, Art. 5(8).
19 Dir. 2008/116, Art. 5(9).

31.055 Article 5(10)(13) provides:

"10. Subject to Article 19(7) any certificate required by this Directive shall be kept available in its original form on board the ship on which the holder is serving.

11. Candidates for certification shall provide satisfactory proof:

   (a) of their identity;

   (b) that their age is not less than that prescribed in the Regulations listed in Annex I relevant to the certificate of competency or certificate of proficiency applied for;

   (c) that they meet the standards of medical fitness, specified in Section A-I/9 of the STCW Code;

   (d) that they have completed the seagoing service and any related compulsory training prescribed in the Regulations listed in Annex I for the certificate of competency or certificate of proficiency applied for; and

   (e) that they meet the standards of competence prescribed in the Regulations listed in Annex I for the capacities, functions and levels that are to be identified in the endorsement of the certificate of competency.

   This paragraph shall not apply to recognition of endorsements under Regulation I/10 of the STCW Convention.

12. Each Member State shall undertake:

   (a) to maintain a register or registers of all certificates of competency and certificates of proficiency and endorsements for masters and officers and, where applicable, ratings which are issued, have expired or have been revalidated, suspended, cancelled or reported as lost or destroyed, as well as of dispensations issued;

   (b) to make available information on the status of certificates of competency, endorsements and dispensations to other Member States or other Parties to the STCW Convention and companies which request verification of the authenticity and validity of certificates of competency and/or certificates issued to masters and officers in accordance with Regulations V/1-1 and V/1-2 of Annex I produced to them by seafarers seeking recognition, under Regulation I/10 of the STCW Convention, or employment on board ship.

13. As of 1 January 2017, the information required to be available in accordance with point (b) of paragraph 12 shall be made available by electronic means."

31.056 Article 5a provides that each Member State must make available to the Commission on a yearly basis the information indicated in Annex V to Directive 2008/106 on certificates of competency, endorsements attesting the recognition of certificates of competency as well as, on a voluntary basis, certificates of proficiency issued to ratings in accordance with Chapters II, III and VII of the annex to the STCW Convention, for the purposes of statistical analysis only and exclusively for use by Member States and the Commission in policy-making.

G. TRAINING REQUIREMENTS

31.057 Article 6 provides that the training required pursuant to Article 3 must be in a form appropriate to the theoretical knowledge and practical skills required by Annex I, in particular the use of life saving and fire-fighting equipment, and approved by the competent authority or body designated by each Member State.

H. PRINCIPLES GOVERNING NEAR-COASTAL VOYAGES

31.058 Article 7(1) provides that when defining near-coastal voyages Member States must not impose training, experience or certification requirements on seafarers serving on board ships entitled to fly the flag of another Member State or another Party to the STCW Convention and engaged in such voyages in a manner resulting in more stringent requirements for such seafarers than for seafarers serving on board ships entitled to fly their own flag. In no case must a Member State impose requirements in respect of seafarers serving on board ships flying the flag of another Member State or of another Party to the STCW Convention in excess of those of this directive in respect of ships not engaged in near-coastal voyages. Article 7(1)(a) provides a Member State, for ships afforded the benefits of the near-coastal voyage provisions of the STCW Convention, which includes voyages off the coast of other Member States or of Parties to the STCW Convention within the limits of their near-coastal definition, must enter into an undertaking with the Member States or Parties concerned specifying both the details of the trading areas involved and other relevant provisions.

31.059 Article 7(2) provides that with respect to ships entitled to fly the flag of a Member State regularly engaged in near-coastal voyages off the coast of another Member State or of another Party to the STCW Convention, the Member State the flag of which a ship is entitled to fly shall prescribe training, experience and certification requirements for seafarers serving on such ships at least equal to those of the Member State or the Party to the STCW Convention off the coast of which the ship is engaged, provided that they do not exceed the requirements of Directive 2008/106 in respect of ships not engaged in near-coastal voyages. Seafarers serving on a ship which extends its voyage beyond what is defined as a near-coastal voyage by a Member State and enters waters not covered by that definition must fulfil the appropriate requirements of the directive.

31.060 Article 7(3) provides that a Member State may afford a ship which is entitled to fly its flag the benefits of the near-coastal voyage provisions of the directive when it is regularly engaged off the coast of a non-Party to the STCW Convention on near-coastal voyages as defined by that Member State. Article 7(3a) provides that the certificates of competency of seafarers issued by a Member State or a Party to the STCW Convention for its defined near-coastal voyage limits may be accepted by other Member States for service in their defined near-coastal voyage limits, provided the Member States or Parties concerned enter into an undertaking specifying the details of the trading areas involved and other relevant conditions thereof. Article 7(3b) provides that Member States defining near-coastal voyages, in accordance with the requirements of this article, must: (a) meet the principles governing near-coastal voyages specified in Section A-I/3 of the STCW Code; and (b) incorporate the near-coastal voyage limits in the endorsements issued pursuant to Article 5.

31.061 Article 7(4) provides that upon deciding on the definition of near-coastal voyages and the conditions of education and training required thereof in accordance with the requirements of paragraphs 1, 2 and 3 of Article 7, Member States must communicate to the Commission the details of the provisions they have adopted.

I. PREVENTION OF FRAUD AND OTHER UNLAWFUL PRACTICES

31.062 Article 8 deals with the important topic of the prevention of fraud and other unlawful practices:

"1. Member States shall take and enforce appropriate measures to prevent fraud and other unlawful practices involving certificates and endorsements issued, and shall provide for penalties that are effective, proportionate and dissuasive.

2. Member States shall designate the national authorities competent to detect and combat fraud and other unlawful practices and exchange information with the competent authorities of other Member States and of third countries concerning the certification of seafarers.

   Member States shall forthwith inform the other Member States and the Commission of the details of such competent national authorities.

   Member States shall also forthwith inform any third countries with which they have entered into an undertaking in accordance with Regulation I/10, paragraph 1.2 of the STCW Convention of the details of such competent national authorities.

3. At the request of a host Member State, the competent authorities of another Member State shall provide written confirmation or denial of the authenticity of seafarers' certificates, corresponding endorsements or any other documentary evidence of training issued in that other Member State."

J. PENALTIES OR DISCIPLINARY MEASURES

31.063 Article 9 provides:

"1. Member States shall establish processes and procedures for the impartial investigation of any reported incompetence, act, omission or compromise to security that may pose a direct threat to safety of life or property at sea or to the marine environment, on the part of the holders of certificates of competency and certificates of proficiency or endorsements issued by that Member State in connection with their performance of duties relating to their certificates of competency and certificates of proficiency and for the withdrawal, suspension and cancellation of such certificates of competency and certificates of proficiency for such cause and for the prevention of fraud.

2. Member States shall take and enforce appropriate measures to prevent fraud and other unlawful practices involving certificates of competency and certificates of proficiency and endorsements issued.

3. Penalties or disciplinary measures shall be prescribed and enforced in cases in which:

   (a) a company or a master has engaged a person not holding a certificate as required by this Directive;
   (b) a master has allowed any function or service in any capacity which under this Directive must be performed by a person holding an appropriate certificate to be performed by a person not holding the required certificate, a valid dispensation or having the documentary proof required by Article 19(7); or
   (c) a person has obtained by fraud or forged documents an engagement to perform any function or serve in any capacity which under this Directive must be performed or fulfilled by a person holding a certificate or dispensation.

4. Member States within the jurisdiction of which any company which or any person who is believed on clear grounds to have been responsible for or to have knowledge of any apparent non-compliance with this Directive specified in paragraph 3, is located shall extend cooperation to any Member State or other Party to the STCW Convention which advises them of its intention to initiate proceedings under its jurisdiction."

K. QUALITY STANDARDS

31.064 Article 10 provides:

"1. Each Member State shall ensure that:

> (a) all training, assessment of competence, certification, including medical certification, endorsement and revalidation activities carried out by non-governmental agencies or entities under their authority are continuously monitored through a quality standards system to ensure the achievement of defined objectives, including those concerning the qualifications and experience of instructors and assessors, in accordance with Section A-I/8 of the STCW Code;
>
> (b) where governmental agencies or entities perform such activities, there is a quality standards system in accordance with Section A-I/8 of the STCW Code;
>
> (c) education and training objectives and related quality standards of competence to be achieved are clearly defined and that the levels of knowledge, understanding and skills appropriate to the examinations and assessments required under the STCW Convention are identified;
>
> (d) the fields of application of the quality standards cover the administration of the certification systems, all training courses and programmes, examinations and assessments carried out by or under the authority of each Member State and the qualifications and experience required of instructors and assessors, having regard to the policies, systems, controls and internal quality-assurance reviews established to ensure achievement of the defined objectives.

The objectives and related quality standards referred to in point (c) of the first subparagraph may be specified separately for different courses and training programmes and shall cover the administration of the certification system.

2. Member States shall also ensure that independent evaluations of the knowledge, understanding, skills and competence acquisition and assessment activities, and of the administration of the certification system, are conducted at intervals of not more than five years by qualified persons who are not themselves involved in the activities concerned in order to verify that:

> (a) all internal management control and monitoring measures and follow-up actions comply with planned arrangements and documental procedures and are effective in ensuring that the defined objectives are achieved;
>
> (b) the results of each independent evaluation are documented and brought to the attention of those responsible for the area evaluated;
>
> (c) timely action is taken to correct deficiencies;
>
> (d) all applicable provisions of the STCW Convention and Code, including amendments are covered by the quality standards system. Member States may also include within this system the other applicable provisions of this Directive.

3. A report relating to each evaluation carried out pursuant to paragraph 2 shall be communicated by the Member State concerned to the Commission, in accordance with the format specified in Section A-I/7 of the STCW Code, within six months of the date of the evaluation."

L. MEDICAL STANDARDS

31.065 Article 11 provides:

"1. Each Member State shall establish standards of medical fitness for seafarers and procedures for the issue of a medical certificate in accordance with this Article and Section A-I/9 of the STCW Code, taking into account, as appropriate, Section B-I/9 of the STCW Code.

2. Each Member State shall ensure that those responsible for assessing the medical fitness of seafarers are medical practitioners recognised by that Member State for the purpose of seafarer medical examinations, in accordance with the Section A-I/9 of the STCW Code.

3. Every seafarer holding a certificate of competency or a certificate of proficiency, issued under the provisions of the STCW Convention, who is serving at sea shall also hold a valid medical certificate issued in accordance with this Article and Section A-I/9 of the STCW Code.

4. Candidates for medical certification shall:

   (a) be not less than 16 years of age;
   (b) provide satisfactory proof of their identity; and
   (c) meet the applicable medical fitness standards established by the Member State concerned.

5. Medical certificates shall remain valid for a maximum period of two years unless the seafarer is under the age of 18, in which case the maximum period of validity shall be one year.

6. If the period of validity of a medical certificate expires in the course of a voyage, Regulation I/9 of the Annex to the STCW Convention shall apply.

7. In urgent cases, a Member State may permit a seafarer to work without a valid medical certificate. In such cases, Regulation I/9 of the Annex to the STCW Convention shall apply."

M. REVALIDATION OF CERTIFICATES OF COMPETENCY AND CERTIFICATES OF PROFICIENCY

31.066 Article 12 provides:

"1. Every master, officer and radio operator holding a certificate issued or recognised under any chapter of Annex I other than Chapter VI who is serving at sea or intends to return to sea after a period ashore shall, in order to continue to qualify for seagoing service, be required at intervals not exceeding five years:

   (a) to meet the standards of medical fitness prescribed by Article 11; and
   (b) to establish continued professional competence in accordance with section A-I/11 of the STCW Code.

2. Every master, officer and radio operator shall, for continuing seagoing service on board ships for which special training requirements have been internationally agreed upon, successfully complete approved relevant training.

2a. Every master and officer shall, for continuing seagoing service on board tankers, meet the requirements of paragraph 1 of this Article and be required, at intervals not exceeding five years, to establish continued professional competence for tankers in accordance with paragraph 3 of Section A-I/11 of the STCW Code.

3. Each Member State shall compare the standards of competence which are required of candidates for certificates of competency issued until 1 January 2017 with those specified for the relevant certificate of competency in Part A of the STCW Code, and shall determine the need to require the holders of such certificates of competency to undergo appropriate refresher and updating training or assessment.

4. Each Member State shall, in consultation with those concerned, formulate or promote the formulation of a structure of refresher and updating courses as provided for in section A-I/11 of the STCW Code.

5. For the purpose of updating the knowledge of masters, officers and radio operators, each Member State shall ensure that the texts of recent changes in national and international regulations concerning the safety of life at sea, security and the protection of the marine environment are made available to ships entitled to fly its flag, while respecting point (b) of Article 14(3) and Article 18."

N. USE OF SIMULATORS

31.067 Article 13 provides:

"1. The performance standards and other provisions set out in section A-I/12 of the STCW Code and such other requirements as are prescribed in Part A of the STCW Code for any certificate concerned shall be complied with in respect of:

    (a) all mandatory simulator-based training;
    (b) any assessment of competence required by Part A of the STCW Code which is carried out by means of a simulator;
    (c) any demonstration, by means of a simulator, of continued proficiency required by Part A of the STCW Code."

O. RESPONSIBILITIES OF COMPANIES

31.068 Article 14 deals with responsibilities of companies.

31.069 Under Article 14(1), in accordance with paragraphs 2 and 3 of Article 14, Member States must hold companies responsible for the assignment of seafarers for service in their ships in accordance with the directive, and must require every company to ensure that: (a) each seafarer assigned to any of its ships holds an appropriate certificate in accordance with the provisions of the directive and as established by the Member State; (b) its ships are manned in accordance with the applicable safe-manning requirements of the Member State; (c) documentation and data relevant to all seafarers employed on its ships are maintained and readily accessible, and include, without being limited to, documentation and data on their experience, training, medical fitness and competence in assigned duties; (d) on being assigned to any of its ships seafarers are familiarised with their specific duties and with all ship arrangements, installations, equipment, procedures and ship characteristics that are relevant to their routine or emergency duties; (e) the ship's complement can effectively co-ordinate their activities in an emergency situation and in performing functions vital to safety or to the prevention or mitigation of pollution; (f) seafarers assigned to any of its ships have received refresher and updating training as required by the STCW Convention; and (g) at all times on board its ships there shall be effective oral communication in accordance with paragraphs 3 and 4 of Chapter V of Regulation 14, of the SOLAS 74, as amended.

31.070 Article 14(2) provides that companies, masters and crew members must each have responsibility for ensuring that the obligations set out in Article 14 are given full and complete effect and that such other measures as may be necessary are taken to ensure that each crew member can make a knowledgeable and informed contribution to the safe operation of the ship.

31.071 Under Article 14(3), the company must provide written instructions to the master of each ship to which this directive applies, setting out the policies and the procedures to be followed to ensure that all seafarers who are newly employed on board the ship are given a reasonable opportunity to become familiar with the shipboard equipment, operating procedures and other arrangements needed for the proper performance of their duties, before being assigned to those duties. Such policies and procedures shall include:

"(a) the allocation of a reasonable period of time during which each newly employed seafarer will have an opportunity to become acquainted with:

  (i) the specific equipment the seafarer will be using or operating; and

  (ii) hip-specific watchkeeping, safety, environmental protection and emergency procedures and arrangements the seafarer needs to know to perform the assigned duties
properly;

(b) the designation of a knowledgeable crew member who will be responsible for ensuring that
each newly employed seafarer is given an opportunity to receive essential information in a
language the seafarer understands."

31.072 Article 14(4) provides that companies must ensure that masters, officers and
other personnel assigned specific duties and responsibilities on board their ro-ro passenger
ships shall have completed familiarisation training to attain the abilities that are appropriate to the capacity to be filled and duties and responsibilities to be taken up, taking into
account the guidance given in Section B-I/14 of the STCW Code.

P. FITNESS FOR DUTY

31.073 Article 15 provides:

"1. For the purpose of preventing fatigue, Member States shall:

 (a) establish and enforce rest periods for watchkeeping personnel and those whose duties
involve designated safety, security and prevention of pollution duties in accordance
with paragraphs 3 to 13;

 (b) require that watch systems are arranged in such a way that the efficiency of watchkeeping personnel is not impaired by fatigue, and that duties are organised in such a
way that the first watch at the start of a voyage and subsequent relieving watches are
sufficiently rested and otherwise fit for duty.

2. Member States shall, for the purpose of preventing drug and alcohol abuse, ensure that adequate measures are established in accordance with the provisions laid down in this Article.

3. Member States shall take account of the danger posed by fatigue of seafarers, especially
those whose duties involve the safe and secure operation of a ship.

4. All persons who are assigned duty as officer in charge of a watch or as a rating forming part
of a watch, and those whose duties involve designated safety, prevention of pollution and
security duties shall be provided with a rest period of not less than:

 (a) a minimum of 10 hours of rest in any 24-hour period; and

 (b) 77 hours in any seven-day period.

5. The hours of rest may be divided into no more than two periods, one of which shall be at
least six hours in length, and the intervals between consecutive periods of rest shall not
exceed 14 hours.

6. The requirements for rest periods laid down in paragraphs 4 and 5 need not be maintained in
the case of an emergency or in other overriding operational conditions. Musters, firefighting
and lifeboat drills, and drills prescribed by national laws and regulations and by international
instruments, shall be conducted in a manner that minimises the disturbance of rest periods
and does not induce fatigue.

7. Member States shall require that watch schedules be posted where they are easily accessible.
The schedules shall be established in a standardised format in the working language or languages of the ship and in English.

8. When a seafarer is on call, such as when a machinery space is unattended, the seafarer shall
have an adequate compensatory rest period if the normal period of rest is disturbed by call-
outs to work.

1426

9. Member States shall require that records of daily hours of rest of seafarers be maintained in a standardised format, in the working language or languages of the ship and in English, to allow monitoring and verification of compliance with this Article. Seafarers shall receive a copy of the records pertaining to them, which shall be endorsed by the master, or by a person authorised by the master, and by the seafarers.

10. Notwithstanding the rules laid down in paragraphs 3 to 9, the master of a ship shall be entitled to require a seafarer to perform any hours of work necessary for the immediate safety of the ship, persons on board or cargo, or for the purpose of giving assistance to other ships or persons in distress at sea. Accordingly, the master may suspend the schedule of hours of rest and require a seafarer to perform any hours of work necessary until the normal situation has been restored. As soon as practicable after the normal situation has been restored, the master shall ensure that any seafarers who have performed work in a scheduled rest period are provided with an adequate period of rest.

11. With due regard for the general principles of the protection of the health and safety of workers and in line with Directive 1999/63/EC Member States may, by means of national laws, regulations or a procedure for the competent authority, authorise or register collective agreements permitting exceptions to the required hours of rest set out in point (b) of paragraph 4 and in paragraph 5 of this Article provided that the rest period is no less than 70 hours in any seven-day period and respects the limits set out in paragraphs 12 and 13 of this Article. Such exceptions shall, as far as possible, follow the standards set out but may take account of more frequent or longer leave periods, or the granting of compensatory leave for watchkeeping seafarers or seafarers working on board ships on short voyages. Exceptions shall, as far as possible, take into account the guidance regarding prevention of fatigue laid down in Section B-VIII/1 of the STCW Code. Exceptions to the minimum hours of rest provided for in point (a) of paragraph 4 of this Article shall not be allowed.

12. Exceptions referred to in paragraph 11 to the weekly rest period provided for in point (b) of paragraph 4 shall not be allowed for more than two consecutive weeks. The intervals between two periods of exceptions on board shall not be less than twice the duration of the exception.

13. In the framework of possible exceptions to paragraph 5 referred to in paragraph 11, the minimum hours of rest in any 24-hour period provided for in point (a) of paragraph 4 may be divided into no more than three periods of rest, one of which shall be at least six hours in length and neither of the two other periods shall be less than one hour in length. The intervals between consecutive periods of rest shall not exceed 14 hours. Exceptions shall not extend beyond two 24-hour periods in any seven-day period.

14. Member States shall establish, for the purpose of preventing alcohol abuse, a limit of not greater than 0,05% blood alcohol level (BAC) or 0,25 mg/l alcohol in the breath or a quantity of alcohol leading to such alcohol concentration for masters, officers and other seafarers while performing designated safety, security and marine environmental duties."

Q. DISPENSATION

31.074 Article 16 deals with dispensation. Article 16(1) provides that in circumstances of exceptional necessity, competent authorities may, if in their opinion this does not cause danger to persons, property or the environment, issue a dispensation permitting a specified seafarer to serve in a specified ship for a specified period not exceeding six months in a capacity, other than that of the radio operator, except as provided by the relevant Radio Regulations, for which he or she does not hold the appropriate certificate, provided that the person to whom the dispensation is issued shall be adequately qualified to fill the vacant post in a safe manner to the satisfaction of the competent authorities. However, dispensations shall not be granted to a master or chief engineer officer, except in circumstances of *force majeure* and then only for the shortest possible period. Article 16(2) provides that any dispensation granted for a post shall be granted only to a person properly certificated to fill the post immediately below. Where certification of the post below is not required, a dispensation may be issued to a person whose qualification and experience are, in the opinion of the competent authorities, of a clear equivalence to the requirements for the post to be filled, provided that, if such a person holds no appropriate certificate, he or she shall be required to pass a test accepted by the competent authorities as demonstrating that such a dispensation may safely be issued. In addition, the competent authorities shall ensure that the post in question is filled by the holder of an appropriate certificate as soon as possible.

R. RESPONSIBILITIES OF MEMBER STATES WITH REGARD TO TRAINING AND ASSESSMENT

31.075 Article 17 deals with the responsibilities of Member States with regard to training and assessment. Under Article 17(1), Member States must designate the authorities or bodies which shall: (a) give the training referred to in Article 3; (b) organise and/or supervise the examinations where required; (c) issue the certificates referred to in Article 5; and (d) grant the dispensations provided for in Article 16.

31.076 Article 17(2) provides that Member States must ensure that:

"(a) all training and assessment of seafarers is:

(i)   structured in accordance with the written programmes, including such methods and media of delivery, procedures and course material as are necessary to achieve the prescribed standard of competence; and

(ii) conducted, monitored, evaluated and supported by persons qualified in accordance with points (d), (e) and (f);

(b) persons conducting in-service training or assessment on board ship do so only when such training or assessment will not adversely affect the normal operation of the ship and they can dedicate their time and attention to training or assessment;

(c) instructors, supervisors and assessors are appropriately qualified for the particular types and levels of training or assessment of competence of seafarers either on board or ashore;

(d) any person conducting in-service training of a seafarer, either on board or ashore, which is intended to be used in qualifying for certification under this Directive:

(i)   has an appreciation of the training programme and an understanding of the specific training objectives for the particular type of training being conducted;

(ii) is qualified in the task for which training is being conducted; and

(iii) if conducting training using a simulator:

– has received appropriate guidance in instructional techniques involving the use of simulators, and

– has gained practical operational experience on the particular type of simulator being used;

(e) any person responsible for the supervision of the in-service training of a seafarer intended to be used in qualifying for certification has a full understanding of the training programme and the specific objectives for each type of training being conducted;

(f) any person conducting in-service assessment of the competence of a seafarer, either on board or ashore, which is intended to be used in qualifying for certification under this Directive:

    (i)   has an appropriate level of knowledge and understanding of the competence to be assessed;

   (ii) is qualified in the task for which the assessment is being made;

  (iii) has received appropriate guidance in assessment methods and practice;

  (iv) has gained practical assessment experience; and

   (v) if conducting assessment involving the use of simulators, has gained practical assessment experience on the particular type of simulator under the supervision and to the satisfaction of an experienced assessor;

(g) when a Member State recognises a course of training, a training institution, or a qualification granted by a training institution, as part of its requirements for the issue of a certificate, the qualifications and experience of instructors and assessors are covered in the application of the quality standard provisions of Article 10; such qualification, experience and application of quality standards shall incorporate appropriate training in instructional techniques and training and assessment methods and practice and comply with all applicable requirements of points (d), (e) and (f)."

S. ON-BOARD COMMUNICATION

31.077 Article 18 provides:

"Member States shall ensure that:

(a) without prejudice to points (b) and (d), there are at all times, on board all ships flying the flag of a Member State, means in place for effective oral communication relating to safety between all members of the ship's crew, particularly with regard to the correct and timely reception and understanding of messages and instructions;

(b) on board all passenger ships flying the flag of a Member State and on board all passenger ships starting and/or finishing a voyage in a Member State port, in order to ensure effective crew performance in safety matters, a working language is established and recorded in the ship's log-book;

the company or the master, as appropriate, shall determine the appropriate working language; each seafarer shall be required to understand and, where appropriate, give orders and instructions and report back in that language;

if the working language is not an official language of the Member State, all plans and lists that must be posted shall include translations into the working language;

(c) on board passenger ships, personnel nominated on muster lists to assist passengers in emergency situations are readily identifiable and have communication skills that are sufficient for that purpose, taking into account an appropriate and adequate combination of any of the following factors:

    (i)   the language or languages appropriate to the principal nationalities of passengers carried on a particular route;

   (ii) the likelihood that an ability to use elementary English vocabulary for basic instructions can provide a means of communicating with a passenger in need of assistance whether or not the passenger and crew member share a common language;

  (iii) the possible need to communicate during an emergency by some other means (e.g. by demonstration, hand signals, or calling attention to the location of instructions, muster stations, life-saving devices or evacuation routes) when verbal communication is impractical;

  (iv) the extent to which complete safety instructions have been provided to passengers in their native language or languages;

(v) the languages in which emergency announcements may be broadcast during an emergency or drill to convey critical guidance to passengers and to facilitate crew members in assisting passengers;

(d) on board oil tankers, chemical tankers and liquefied gas tankers flying the flag of a Member State, the master, officers and rating are able to communicate with each other in (a) common working language(s);

(e) there are adequate means for communication between the ship and the shore-based authorities; these communications shall be conducted in accordance with Chapter V, Regulation 14, paragraph 4, of the SOLAS 74;

(f) when carrying out port State control under Directive 95/21/EC, Member States also check that ships flying the flag of a State other than a Member State comply with this Article."

T. RECOGNITION OF CERTIFICATES OF COMPETENCY AND/OR CERTIFICATES OF PROFICIENCY

31.078 Article 19 provides:

"1. Seafarers who do not possess the certificates of competency issued by Member States and/or the certificates of proficiency issued by Member States to masters and officers in accordance with Regulations V/1-1 and V/1-2 of the STCW Convention, may be allowed to serve on ships flying the flag of a Member State provided that a decision on the recognition of their certificates of competency and certificates of proficiency has been adopted through the procedures set out in paragraphs 2 to 6 of this Article.

2. A Member State which intends to recognise, by endorsement, the certificates of competency and/or the certificates of proficiency referred to in paragraph 1 issued by a third country to a master, officer or radio operator, for service on ships flying its flag, shall submit a request for recognition of that third country to the Commission, stating its reasons.

   The Commission, assisted by the European Maritime Safety Agency and with the possible involvement of any Member State concerned, shall collect the information referred to in Annex II and shall carry out an assessment of the training and certification systems in the third country for which the request for recognition was submitted, in order to verify whether the country concerned meets all the requirements of the STCW Convention and whether the appropriate measures have been taken to prevent fraud involving certificates.

3. The decision on the recognition of a third country shall be taken by the Commission. Those implementing acts shall be adopted in accordance with the examination procedure referred to in Article 28(2), within 18 months of the date of the request for the recognition. The Member State submitting the request may decide to recognise the third country unilaterally until a decision is taken under this paragraph.

4. A Member State may decide, with respect to ships flying its flag, to endorse certificates issued by the third countries recognised by the Commission, account being taken of the provisions contained in Annex II, points (4) and (5).

5. Recognitions of certificates issued by recognised third countries and published in the Official Journal of the European Union, C series, before 14 June 2005 shall remain valid.

   These recognitions may be used by all Member States unless the Commission has subsequently withdrawn them pursuant to Article 20.

6. The Commission shall draw up and update a list of the third countries that have been recognised. The list shall be published in the Official Journal of the European Union, C series.

7. Notwithstanding Article 5(6), a Member State may, if circumstances require, allow a seafarer to serve in a capacity other than radio officer or radio operator, except as provided by the Radio Regulations, for a period not exceeding three months on board a ship flying its flag, while holding an appropriate and valid certificate issued and endorsed as required by a third country, but not yet endorsed for recognition by the Member State concerned so as to render it appropriate for service on board a ship flying its flag.

Documentary proof shall be kept readily available that application for an endorsement has been submitted to the competent authorities."

U. NON-COMPLIANCE WITH THE REQUIREMENTS OF THE STCW CONVENTION

31.079 Article 20 of the directive provides:

"1. Notwithstanding the criteria specified in Annex II, when a Member State considers that a recognised third country no longer complies with the requirements of the STCW Convention, it shall notify the Commission immediately, giving substantiated reasons therefore.

The Commission shall without delay refer the matter to the Committee referred to in Article 28(1).

2. Notwithstanding the criteria set out in Annex II, when the Commission considers that a recognised third country no longer complies with the requirements of the STCW Convention, it shall notify the Member States immediately, giving substantiated reasons therefor.

The Commission shall without delay refer the matter to the Committee referred to in Article 28(1).

3. When a Member State intends to withdraw the endorsements of all certificates issued by a third country it shall without delay inform the Commission and the other Member States of its intention, giving substantiated reasons therefor.

4. The Commission, assisted by the European Maritime Safety Agency, shall reassess the recognition of the third country concerned in order to verify whether that country failed to comply with the requirements of the STCW Convention.

5. Where there are indications that a particular maritime training establishment no longer complies with the requirements of the STCW Convention, the Commission shall notify the country concerned that recognition of that country's certificates will be withdrawn in two months' time unless measures are taken to ensure compliance with all the requirements of the STCW Convention.

6. The decision on the withdrawal of the recognition shall be taken by the Commission. Those implementing acts shall be adopted in accordance with the examination procedure referred to in Article 28(2). The Member States concerned shall take appropriate measures to implement the decision.

7. Endorsements attesting recognition of certificates, issued in accordance with Article 5(6) before the date on which the decision to withdraw recognition of the third country is taken, shall remain valid. Seafarers holding such endorsements may not claim an endorsement recognising a higher qualification, however, unless that upgrading is based solely on additional seagoing service experience."

V. REASSESSMENT

31.080 Article 21 provides:

"1. The third countries that have been recognised under the procedure referred to in the first subparagraph of Article 19(3), including those referred to in Article 19(6), shall be reassessed by the Commission, with the assistance of the European Maritime Safety Agency, on a regular basis and at least every five years to verify that they fulfil the relevant criteria set out in Annex II and whether the appropriate measures have been taken to prevent fraud involving certificates.

2. The Commission shall define the priority criteria for assessment of third countries on the basis of performance data provided by the port State control pursuant to Article 23, as well as the information relating to the reports of the independent evaluations communicated by third countries pursuant to section A-I/7 of the STCW Code.

3. The Commission shall provide the Member States with a report on the results of the assessment."

W. PORT STATE CONTROL

31.081 Article 22 provides:

"1. Irrespective of the flag it flies, each ship, with the exception of those types of ships excluded by Article 2, shall, while in the ports of a Member State, be subject to port State control by officers duly authorised by that Member State to verify that all seafarers serving on board who are required to hold a certificate of competency and/or a certificate of proficiency and/ or documentary evidence under the STCW Convention, hold such a certificate of competency or valid dispensation and/or certificate of proficiency and/or documentary evidence.
2. When exercising port State control under this Directive, Member States shall ensure that all relevant provisions and procedures laid down in Directive 95/21/EC are applied."

X. PORT STATE CONTROL PROCEDURES

31.082 Article 23 states:

"1. Without prejudice to Directive 95/21/EC, port State control pursuant to Article 22 shall be limited to the following:

   (a) verification that e1very seafarer serving on board who is required to hold a certificate of competency and/or a certificate of proficiency in accordance with the STCW Convention holds such a certificate of competency or valid dispensation and/or certificate of proficiency, or provides documentary proof that an application for an endorsement attesting recognition of a certificate of competency has been submitted to the authorities of the flag State;
   (b) verification that the numbers and certificates of the seafarers serving on board are in accordance with the safe-manning requirements of the authorities of the flag State.

2. The ability of the ship's seafarers to maintain watchkeeping and security standards, as appropriate, as required by the STCW Convention shall be assessed in accordance with Part A of the STCW Code if there are clear grounds for believing that such standards are not being maintained because any of the following has occurred:

   (a) the ship has been involved in a collision, grounding or stranding;
   (b) there has been a discharge of substances from the ship when under way, at anchor or at berth which is illegal under an international convention;
   (c) the ship has been manoeuvred in an erratic or unsafe manner whereby routing measures adopted by the IMO, or safe navigation practices and procedures have not been followed;
   (d) the ship is otherwise being operated in such a manner as to pose a danger to persons, property or the environment, or to compromise security;
   (e) a certificate has been fraudulently obtained or the holder of a certificate is not the person to whom that certificate was originally issued;
   (f) the ship is flying the flag of a country which has not ratified the STCW Convention, or has a master, officer or rating holding a certificate issued by a third country which has not ratified the STCW Convention.

3. Notwithstanding verification of the certificate, assessment under paragraph 2 may require the seafarer to demonstrate the relevant competence at the place of duty. Such a demonstration may include verification that operational requirements in respect of watchkeeping standards have been met and that there is a proper response to emergency situations within the seafarer's level of competence."

Y. DETENTION

31.083 Article 24 provides:

"Without prejudice to Directive 95/21/EC, the following deficiencies, in so far as they have been determined by the officer carrying out the port State control that they pose a danger to persons, property or the environment, shall be the only grounds under this Directive on which a Member State may detain a ship:

(a) failure of seafarers to hold certificates, to have appropriate certificates, to have valid dispensations or provide documentary proof that an application for an endorsement attesting recognition has been submitted to the authorities of the flag State;

(b) failure to comply with the applicable safe-manning requirements of the flag State;

(c) failure of navigational or engineering-watch arrangements to conform to the requirements specified for the ship by the flag State;

(d) absence in a watch of a person qualified to operate equipment essential to safe navigation, safety radio communications or the prevention of marine pollution;

(e) failure to provide proof of professional proficiency for the duties assigned to seafarers for the safety of the ship and the prevention of pollution;

(f) inability to provide for the first watch at the commencement of a voyage and for subsequent relieving watches persons who are sufficiently rested and otherwise fit for duty."

Z. REGULAR MONITORING OF COMPLIANCE

31.084 Article 25 provides for regular monitoring of compliance. It provides that without prejudice to the powers of the Commission under Article 226 of the TEC (which is largely Article 258 of the TFEU now), the Commission, assisted by the European Maritime Safety Agency, must verify on a regular basis and at least every five years that Member States comply with the minimum requirements laid down by the directive.

AA. INFORMATION FOR STATISTICAL PURPOSES

31.085 Article 25a of the directive provides:

"1. The Member States shall communicate the information listed in Annex V to the Commission for the purposes of statistical analysis only. Such information may not be used for administrative, legal or verification purposes, and is exclusively for use by Member States and the Commission in policy-making.

2. That information shall be made available by Member States to the Commission on a yearly basis and in electronic format and shall include information registered until 31 December of the previous year. Member States shall retain all property rights to the information in its raw data format. Processed statistics drawn up on the basis of such information shall be made publicly available in accordance with the provisions on transparency and protection of information set out in Article 4 of Regulation (EC) No 1406/2002.

3. In order to ensure the protection of personal data, Member States shall anonymise all personal information as indicated in Annex V by using software provided or accepted by the Commission before transmitting it to the Commission. The Commission shall use this anonymised information only.

4. Member States and the Commission shall ensure that measures for collecting, submitting, storing, analysing and disseminating such information are designed in such a way that statistical analysis is made possible.

For the purposes of the first subparagraph, the Commission shall adopt detailed measures regarding the technical requirements necessary to ensure the appropriate management of the statistical data. Those implementing acts shall be adopted in accordance with the examination procedure referred to in Article 28(2)."

AB. REPORTS

31.086 Article 26 provides:

"1. Not later than 14 December 2008 the Commission shall submit an evaluation report to the European Parliament and the Council, based on a detailed analysis and evaluation of the provisions of the STCW Convention, the implementation thereof and new insights gained with regard to the correlation between safety and the level of training of ships' crews.
2. Not later than 20 October 2010 the Commission shall submit to the European Parliament and the Council an evaluation report drawn up on the basis of the information obtained pursuant to Article 25.

In the report the Commission shall analyse the Member States' compliance with this Directive and, where necessary, make proposals for additional measures."

AC. AMENDMENT TO THE DIRECTIVE

31.087 Article 27 provides that the Commission must be empowered to adopt delegated acts, in accordance with Article 27a, amending Annex V to the directive with respect to specific and relevant content and details of the information that needs to be reported by Member States provided that such acts are limited to taking into account the amendments to the STCW Convention and Code and respect the safeguards on data protection. Such delegated acts shall not change the provisions of anonymisation of data as required by Article 25a(3).

AD. EXERCISE OF THE DELEGATION OF POWERS

31.088 Article 27a provides:

"1. The power to adopt delegated acts is conferred on the Commission subject to the conditions laid down in this Article.
2. The delegation of power referred to in Article 27 shall be conferred on the Commission for a period of five years from 3 January 2013. The Commission shall draw up a report in respect of the delegation of power not later than 4 April 2017. The delegation of power shall be tacitly extended for periods of an identical duration, unless the European Parliament or the Council opposes such extension not later than three months before the end of each period.
3. The delegation of power referred to in Article 27 may be revoked at any time by the European Parliament or by the Council. A decision to revoke shall put an end to the delegation of the power specified in that decision. It shall take effect the day following the publication of the decision in the Official Journal of the European Union or at a later date specified therein. It shall not affect the validity of any delegated acts already in force.
4. As soon as it adopts a delegated act, the Commission shall notify it simultaneously to the European Parliament and to the Council.
5. A delegated act adopted pursuant to Article 27 shall enter into force only if no objection has been expressed either by the European Parliament or the Council within a period of two months of notification of that act to the European Parliament and the Council or if, before the expiry of that period, the European Parliament and the Council have both informed the Commission that they will not object. That period shall be extended by two months at the initiative of the European Parliament or the Council."

AE. COMMITTEE PROCEDURE

31.089 Article 28 states:

"1. The Commission shall be assisted by the Committee on Safe Seas and the Prevention of Pollution from Ships (COSS) established by Regulation (EC) No 2099/2002 of the European Parliament and of the Council .... That committee shall be a committee within the meaning of Regulation (EU) No 182/2011 of the European Parliament and of the Council of 16 February 2011 laying down the rules and general principles concerning mechanisms for control by Member States of the Commission's exercise of implementing powers ....

2. Where reference is made to this paragraph, Article 5 of Regulation (EU) No 182/2011 shall apply. Where the Committee delivers no opinion, the Commission shall not adopt the draft implementing act and the third subparagraph of Article 5(4) of Regulation (EU) No 182/2011 shall apply."

AF. PENALTIES

31.090 Article 29 provides that Member States must lay down systems of penalties for breaching the national provisions adopted pursuant to Articles 3, 5, 7, 9 to 15, 17, 18, 19, 22, 23, 24 and Annex I, and must take all the measures necessary to ensure that they are implemented. The penalties provided for must be, according to Article 28, effective, proportionate and dissuasive – which enables the EU to set the standard but the Member States, exercising sovereignty, to decide the exact penalties (such measures, like the measure to implement the directive search, have to be communicated to the Commission under Article 31 of the directive).

AG. TRANSITIONAL PROVISIONS

31.091 Article 30 provides that in respect of those seafarers who commenced approved seagoing service, an approved education and training programme or an approved training course before 1 July 2013, Member States were able to continue to issue, recognise and endorse, until 1 January 2017, certificates of competency in accordance with the requirements of this directive as they were before 3 January 2013. Moreover, until 1 January 2017, Member States were entitled to continue to renew and revalidate certificates of competency and endorsements in accordance with the requirements of this directive as they were before 3 January 2013.

AH. REPEAL

31.092 Article 32 provides that Directive 2001/25, as amended by the directives listed in Annex III, Part A, was repealed, without prejudice to the obligations of the Member States relating to the time limits for transposition into national law of the directives set out in Annex III, Part B. References to the repealed directive have to be construed as references to Directive 2008/106 and shall be read in accordance with the correlation table in Annex IV. There are a number of annexes. First, Annex I deals with the training requirements of the STCW Convention (referred to in Article 3). Chapter I sets out the "general provisions". Chapter II deals with the master and deck department. Chapter III deals with the engine department. Chapter IV deals with radio communication and radio operators. Chapter V deals with special training requirements for personnel on certain types of ships. Chapter VI relates to emergency, occupational, safety, security, medical care and survival functions. Chapter VII is entitled alternative certification. Second, Annex II deals with the criteria for the recognition of third countries that have issued a certificate or under the authority of which was issued a certificate (referred to in Article 19(2)). Third, Annex III deals with the repealed directive with a list of successive amendments. Fourth, Annex IV contains a correlation table. Finally, Annex V sets out the type of information to be communicated to the Commission for statistical purposes. In particular, it relates to the following information specified in Section A-I/2, paragraph 9 of the STCW Code for all certificates of competency or endorsements attesting their issue.

CHAPTER 32

Maritime safety: minimum safety and health requirements for improved medical treatment on board vessels

A. INTRODUCTION

32.001 This chapter considers the European Union ("EU") shipping law aspects of the minimum safety and health requirements for improved medical treatment on board vessels.

32.002 While any workplace poses some health and safety risks, ships pose particular difficulties because those on board are often far away from treatment, facilities and medicine. This fact has long been recognised by the EU.[1] At a theoretical level, it would be easy to prescribe that all vessels should have medically trained personnel along with treatment facilities, equipment and medicines but that would be unrealistic and impractical – it would damage the competitiveness of EU vessels even though it would be laudable at a human level. Hence, a balance has to be struck.

B. BACKGROUND TO DIRECTIVE 92/29

32.003 The principal measure dealing with the minimum safety and health requirements for improved medical treatment on board vessels is Council Directive 92/29 of 31 March 1992 on the minimum safety and health requirements for improved medical treatment on board vessels.[2] It has been amended by Regulation 1882/2003 of the European Parliament and of the Council of 29 September 2003,[3] Directive 2007/30 of the European Parliament and of the Council of 20 June 2007[4] and Regulation 1137/2008 of the European Parliament and of the Council of 22 October 2008.[5]

32.004 The Commission proposed the measure after consultation with the Advisory Committee on Safety, Hygiene and Health Protection at Work. The background to the measure is apparent from the recitals to the final directive which say:

---

1 The 22 December 1994 Council Resolution on the Safety of Roll-on/Roll-off Passenger Ferries invites in para. 3(c): "the Member States and the Commission to submit or support proposals that the [International Maritime Organization] should undertake ... (c) a review of the requirements for qualified medical personnel on board roll-on/roll-off passenger ferries undertaking long voyages".

2 OJ L113/19, 30 April 1992, http://eur-lex.europa.eu/legal-content/EN/TXT/HTML/?uri=CELEX:31992L0 029&from=EN. Consolidated version: http://eur-lex.europa.eu/legal-content/EN/TXT/?uri=CELEX:01992L002 9-20081211. For details of implementation in Member State law, see http://eur-lex.europa.eu/search.html?type= advanced&qid=1456076432250&DN=71992L0029*. For further information on the topic, see http://eur-lex. europa.eu/legal-content/EN/LSU/?uri=CELEX:31992L0029.

3 OJ L284/1, 31 October 2003, http://eur-lex.europa.eu/legal-content/EN/TXT/?uri=celex:32003R1882.

4 OJ L165/21, 27 June 2007, http://eur-lex.europa.eu/legal-content/EN/TXT/?uri=celex:32007L0030.

5 OJ L311/1, 21 November 2008, http://eur-lex.europa.eu/legal-content/EN/TXT/?uri=celex:32008R1137.

"Whereas the Commission communication on its programme concerning safety, hygiene and health at work[6] envisages measures to ensure medical treatment at sea;

Whereas the safety and health of workers on board a vessel, which constitutes a workplace involving a wide range of risks, bearing in mind, inter alia, its geographical isolation, where appropriate, require special attention ...;

Whereas vessels should have adequate medical supplies, kept in good order and checked at regular intervals, so that workers can obtain the necessary medical treatment at sea;

Whereas, in order to ensure appropriate medical treatment at sea, training and information of seafarers should be encouraged as regards the use of medical supplies;

Whereas the use of long-distance medical-consultation methods constitutes an efficient way of contributing to the protection of the safety and health of workers ..."

In its proposal the Commission made clear that a vessel is "a workplace which requires special attention on account of its mobility, its geographical isolation, and the potentially high risks to safety and health of the workers on board", thus, the Commission contended,

"there is a need for vessels to have on board adequate medical equipment and medicines, properly maintained and checked at regular intervals, to permit the effective treatment of the crew and, in certain cases, avoid disembarkations at sea or diversions of vessels, which are not only costly but can also delay treatment."

The improvement of medical treatment at sea would then make it "desirable to promote training in and information on the use of medical supplies and of the various remote medical consultation facilities".

Legal basis

32.005 The legal basis of the directive was the European Economic Community ("EEC") Treaty generally and Article 118A in particular. The directive recognises that a vessel constitutes "a workplace involving a wide range of risks, bearing in mind, inter alia, its geographical isolation, where appropriate, requires special attention".

C. BASIC CONCEPTS IN DIRECTIVE 92/29

Antidote

32.006 An antidote is defined, for the purposes of the directive, by Article 1 of the directive as being: "a substance used to prevent or treat a harmful effect or effects, direct or indirect, of one or more substances included in the list of dangerous substances in Annex III [of the directive]".

Medical supplies

32.007 Medical supplies are defined, for the purposes of the directive, by Article 1 of the directive as being: "medicines, medical equipment and antidotes, including any antidotes that may be required under the terms of Article 3(1) a non-exhaustive list of which is given in Annex II [of the directive]". Annex II is entitled "MEDICAL SUPPLIES

---

6 Ed., OJ C28/3, 3 February 1988.

(NON-EXHAUSTIVE LIST)". Annex II contains a long list of medicines, items of medical equipment and antidotes. It is non-exhaustive but quite extensive.

Owner

32.008 Article 1 of the directive provides that the term "owner" means, for the purposes of that directive,

> "the registered owner of a vessel unless that vessel has been chartered by demise or is managed, either wholly or in part, by a natural or legal person other than the registered owner under the terms of a management agreement; in that case the owner shall be construed as the demise charterer or natural or legal person managing the vessel as appropriate."

Vessel

32.009 A vessel is defined, for the purposes of the directive, by Article 1 of the directive as being:

> "any vessel flying the flag of a Member State, or registered under the plenary jurisdiction of a Member State, seagoing or estuary-fishing, publicly or privately owned, excluding:
>
> – inland navigation vessels,
> – warships,
> – pleasure boats used for non-commercial purposes and not manned by professional crews,
> – tugs operating in harbour areas.
>
> Vessels shall be classed in three categories in accordance with Annex I."

32.010 Annex I of Directive 92/29 classifies vessels into three categories: (a) seagoing or sea-fishing vessels, with no limitation on length of trips; (b) seagoing or sea-fishing vessels making trips of less than 150 nautical miles from the nearest port with adequate medical equipment;[7] and (c) harbour vessels, boats and craft staying very close to shore or with no cabin accommodation other than a wheelhouse.

Worker

32.011 A worker is defined, for the purposes of the directive, by Article 1 of the directive as being: "any person who is employed or retained in whatever capacity on board a vessel, including trainees and apprentices, but excluding pilots".

D. OBLIGATION TO HAVE MEDICAL SUPPLIES ON BOARD

32.012 Member States are obliged under Article 2 of the directive to take measures necessary to ensure that the vessels under their jurisdiction always have adequate medicines and medical equipment on board. The quantities to be carried would have to take

---

7 Category B shall be extended to seagoing or sea-fishing vessels which make trips of less than 175 nautical miles from the nearest port with adequate medical equipment and which remain continuously within range of helicopter rescue services.

account of the nature and destination of the trip and the number of crew members. The contents of the medical supplies are to be detailed on a checklist. Article 2 provides:

"Medicines and medical equipment – Sick-bay – Doctor
Each Member State shall take the measures necessary to ensure that:

1. (a) every vessel flying its flag or registered under its plenary jurisdiction always carries on board medical supplies which meet at least, in terms of quality, the specifications of Annex II[8] sections I[9] and II[10] for the category of vessel to which it belongs;
   (b) the quantities of medicinal products and medical equipment to be carried depend on the nature of the voyage – in particular ports of call, destination, duration – the type or types of work to be carried out during the voyage, the nature of the cargo and the number of workers;
   (c) the content of the medicines and medical equipment included in the medical supplies shall be detailed on a checklist corresponding at least to the general framework laid down in Annex IV,[11] sections A,[12] B[13] and C[14] II[15] 1 and II 2;

2. (a) for each of its life-rafts and life-boats, every vessel flying its flag or registered under its plenary jurisdiction carries a watertight medicine chest at least containing the medical supplies specified in Annex II, sections I and II, for category C vessels;
   (b) the content of these chests is also detailed on the checklist referred to in paragraph 1 (c);

3. Every vessel flying its flag or registered under its plenary jurisdiction, of more than 500 gross registered tonnes, with a crew of 15 or more workers and engaged on a voyage of more than three days, has a sick-bay in which medical treatment can be administered under satisfactory material and hygienic conditions;

4. Every vessel flying its flag or registered under its plenary jurisdiction, with a crew of 100 or more workers and engaged on an international voyage of more than three days, has a doctor responsible for the medical care of the workers on board."

E. OBLIGATION ON SHIPS TO CARRY ANTIDOTES

32.013 Article 3 of the directive deals with dangerous substances. Member States would have two separate obligations depending on the type of vessel involved. First, Member States are obliged to ensure that any vessel under their jurisdiction carrying any of the dangerous substances set out in Section III of Annex III[16] to the directive has medical supplies, including the appropriate antidotes set out in Annex II of the directive. Second, Member States would be obliged in the case of ferry-type vessels, whose conditions of operation do not always allow them to know well enough in advance the nature of the dangerous substances being transported, all the antidotes listed in Section III of Annex II are carried on board. However, on a regular route where the crossing is due to last less than two hours, the antidotes may be limited to those which have to be administered within a period not exceeding the duration of the crossing.

---

8 Ed., entitled "MEDICAL SUPPLIES (NON-EXHAUSTIVE LIST)".
9 Ed., i.e. medicines.
10 Ed., i.e. medical equipment.
11 Ed., entitled "GENERAL FRAMEWORK FOR THE INSPECTION OF VESSELS' MEDICAL SUPPLIES".
12 Ed., entitled "SECTION A. CATEGORY A VESSELS".
13 Ed., entitled "SECTION B. CATEGORY B VESSELS".
14 Ed., entitled "SECTION C. CATEGORY C VESSELS".
15 Ed., entitled "Medical Supplies".
16 Entitled "DANGEROUS SUBSTANCES".

F. ALLOCATION OF RESPONSIBILITIES

32.014 Article 4 of Directive 92/29 provides:

"Member States will be obliged to ensure that:
Each Member State shall take the measures necessary to ensure that:

1. (a) the provision and replenishment of the medical supplies of any vessel flying its flag or registered under its plenary jurisdiction are undertaken on the exclusive responsibility of the owner, without any expense to the workers;
   (b) the management of the medical supplies is placed under the responsibility of the captain of the vessel; he may, without prejudice to this responsibility, delegate the use and maintenance of the medical supplies to one or more workers specially designated by reason of their competence;

2. the medical supplies are maintained in good condition and replenished and/or replaced as soon as possible, and in every case as a priority part of normal revictualling procedures;

3. in an emergency established by the captain as far as possible after having obtained a medical opinion, the required medicines, medical equipment and antidotes which are not available on board are made available as soon as possible."

G. INFORMATION AND TRAINING

32.015 Article 5 of the directive provides:

"Each Member State shall take the measures necessary to ensure that:

1. medical supplies are accompanied by one or more guides to their use, including instructions for use of at least the antidotes required in Annex II section III;
2. all persons receiving professional maritime training and intending to work on board ship have been given basic training in the medical and emergency measures to be taken immediately in the event of an accident or serious medical emergency;
3. the captain and any worker or workers to whom he delegates the use of the medical supplies pursuant to Article 4 (1) (b) have received special training updated periodically, at least every five years, taking into account the specific risks and needs connected with the different categories of vessel and in accordance with the general guidelines set out in Annex V."

32.016 The Member States are obliged to take appropriate measures to ensure that the medical supplies are accompanied by a guide to their use, including instructions for the use of the antidotes.

32.017 The directive envisages general training for the crew, as well as special training for the captain and those members of the crew who have been specially delegated to use the ship's medical supplies. In terms of general training, the proposed directive provides that Member States would be obliged to take all appropriate measures to ensure that during their professional maritime training all persons intending to work on board are given instruction in the medical and emergency measures to be taken immediately in the event of an accident or serious emergency. In terms of special training, the directive provides that Member States would be obliged to take all appropriate measures to ensure that the captain and the worker or workers to whom he or she delegates the use of the ship's medical supplies have received special training, taking into account the specific risks and needs connected with the different categories of vessels and in accordance with the general guidelines set out in Annex V of the directive. Annex V is entitled "Medical Training of The Captain and Designated Workers" and provides:

"I.
1. Basic understanding of physiology, symptomatology and therapeutics.
2. Elements of preventive medicine, notably individual and collective hygiene, and elements of possible prophylactic measures.
3. Ability to perform basic types of treatment and supervise emergency disembarkation at sea. Person responsible for treatment aboard category A vessels should if possible receive their practical training in hospitals.
4. Detailed knowledge of how to use the various remote medical consultation facilities.

II.
This training should take account of the programmes of instruction detailed in relevant recent international documents."

H. MEDICAL CONSULTATIONS BY RADIO

32.018 Article 6 of the directive provides:

"1. To ensure better emergency treatment for workers, each Member State shall take the measures necessary to ensure that:

   (a) one or more centres are designated to provide workers with free medical advice by radio;
   (b) some of the doctors providing their services for the radio consultation centres have been trained in the special conditions prevailing on board ship.

2. In order to optimize the advice given, the radio consultation centres may keep personal medical records, with the agreement of the workers concerned.

Such records shall remain confidential."

I. INSPECTION

32.019 Article 7 of the directive provides:

"1. Each Member State shall take the measures necessary to ensure that a competent person or a competent authority carries out an annual inspection to check that on board all vessels flying its flag:

   – the medical supplies meet the minimum requirements of this Directive;
   – the checklist provided for in Article 2 (1) (c) confirms that the medical supplies comply with those minimum requirements;
   – the medical supplies are correctly stored;
   – any expiry dates have been respected.

2. Inspections of the medical supplies stored on life-rafts shall be carried out in the course of those life-rafts' annual maintenance.

Those inspections may exceptionally be postponed for up to five months."

J. COMMITTEE PROCEDURE

32.020 Article 8 of the directive provides:

"Committee procedure

1. The Commission shall be assisted by a committee to make purely technical adaptations of the Annexes to this Directive in the light of technical progress or changes in international regulations or specifications and new findings in the field.

   Those measures, designed to amend non-essential elements of this Directive, shall be adopted in accordance with the regulatory procedure with scrutiny referred to in paragraph 2. On imperative grounds of urgency, the Commission may have recourse to the urgency procedure referred to in paragraph 3.

2. Where reference is made to this paragraph, Article 5a(1) to (4) and Article 7 of Decision 1999/468/EC shall apply, having regard to the provisions of Article 8 thereof.

3. Where reference is made to this paragraph, Article 5a(1), (2), (4) and (6) and Article 7 of Decision 1999/468/EC shall apply, having regard to the provisions of Article 8 thereof."

K. ENTRY INTO FORCE

32.021 The directive provided in Article 9(1) that Member States were obliged to bring into force the laws, regulations and administrative provisions necessary for compliance with the directive by 31 December 1994. Article 9a provides for an implementation report every five years:

"the Member States shall submit to the Commission a report on the practical implementation of this Directive in the form of a specific chapter of the single report referred to in Article 17a(1), (2) and (3) of Directive 89/391/EEC, which serves as a basis for the Commission's evaluation, in accordance with Article 17a(4) of that Directive."

L. CONCLUSION

32.022 There is little doubt that the adoption of the directive is welcome because "there is a need to provide for additional measures for medical assistance at sea in order to take account of technological and medical progress and thus ensure better protection of the health and safety"[17] of seafarers. The precise success of the initiative may never emerge but there is little doubt that lives will have been saved and injuries treated better and earlier than would have been the case without such a measure.

---

17 Dir. 92/29, Recital 5.

CHAPTER 33

Maritime safety: international safety management code for the safe operation of ships and for pollution prevention

A. INTRODUCTION

33.001 This chapter considers the European Union ("EU") shipping law aspects of the International Management Code for the Safe Operation of Ships and for Pollution Prevention (the "ISM Code").

33.002 The ISM Code was adopted by the International Maritime Organization (the "IMO") in 1993. The Code was applied gradually to most ships sailing on international voyages with the adoption in May 1994 of Chapter IX (i.e. "Management for the Safe Operation of Ships") of the International Convention for the Safety of Life at Sea ("SOLAS"), 1974. The ISM Code was amended by the IMO by Resolution MSC.104(73) which was adopted on 5 December 2000. Guidelines on Implementation of the ISM Code by Administrations were adopted by IMO Resolution A.788(19) on 23 November 1995. These Guidelines were amended by Resolution A.913(22) which was adopted on 29 November 2001.

B. REGULATION 336/2006 ON THE IMPLEMENTATION OF THE INTERNATIONAL SAFETY MANAGEMENT CODE WITHIN THE COMMUNITY AND REPEALING COUNCIL REGULATION 3051/95

Introduction

33.003 On 15 February 2006, the Parliament and Council adopted Regulation 336/2006 on the implementation of the International Safety Management Code within the Community and repealing Council Regulation 3051/95.[1] The regulation has been amended by: (a) Commission Regulation 540/2008 of 16 June 2008 amending Annex II to Regulation 336/2006 of the European Parliament and of the Council on the implementation of the ISM Code within the Community, as regards format of forms;[2] and (b) European Parliament and Council Regulation 1137/2008 of 22 October 2008 of the European Parliament and of the Council of 22 October 2008 adopting a number of instruments subject to the procedure laid down in Article 251 of the Treaty to Council Decision 1999/468, with regard to the regulatory procedure with scrutiny – Adaptation of the regulatory procedure with scrutiny – Part One.[3]

---

1 OJ L64/1, 4 March 2006.
2 OJ L157/15, 17 June 2008.
3 OJ L311/1, 21 November 2008.

33.004 The legal basis of Regulation 336/2006 was the Treaty on the European Union ("TEC") generally and, in particular, Article 80(2) – this would now be the Treaty on the Functioning of the European Union ("TFEU") and, in particular, Article 100(2).

33.005 The legislative history of Regulation 336/2006 included a proposal from the Commission, an opinion of the European Economic and Social Committee and a consultation of the Committee of the Regions.

33.006 Under Article 14, Regulation 336/2006 entered into force on the twentieth day following its publication in the *Official Journal* – it was published on 4 March 2006. As concerns cargo and passenger ships, which are not already required to comply with the ISM Code, this regulation applied from 24 March 2008.

33.007 The ninth recital to the regulation provides that the adoption of a new regulation with direct applicability should ensure the enforcement of the ISM Code on the understanding that it is left to the Member States to decide whether to implement the Code for ships, regardless of their flag, operating exclusively in port areas. This is because regulations are directly applicable and, unlike directives, do not have to be implemented in national law.

Background

33.008 Council Regulation 3051/95 of 8 December 1995 on the safety management of roll-on/roll-off passenger ferries (ro-ro ferries)[4] made the ISM Code mandatory at EU level with effect from 1 July 1996 for all ro-ro passenger ferries operating on a regular service to, and from, ports of the Member States, on both domestic and international voyages and regardless of their flag. This was a first step towards ensuring uniform and coherent implementation of the ISM Code in all Member States.

33.009 On 1 July 1998, the ISM Code became mandatory under the provisions of Chapter IX of SOLAS for companies operating passenger ships, including high-speed passenger craft, oil tankers, chemical tankers, gas carriers, bulk carriers and cargo high-speed craft of 500 gt (gross tonnage) and upwards, on international voyages.

33.010 On 1 July 2002, the ISM Code became mandatory for companies operating other cargo ships and mobile offshore drilling units of 500 gt and upwards, on international voyages.

33.011 If a Member State considers it difficult in practice for companies to comply with specific provisions of Part A of the ISM Code for certain ships or categories of ships exclusively engaged on domestic voyages in that Member State, it may derogate wholly or partly from those provisions by imposing measures ensuring equivalent achievement of the objectives of the Code. It may, for such ships and companies, establish alternative certification and verification procedures.

33.012 The recitals recall:

"(13) It is also necessary to take into account Council Directive 94/57/EC of 22 November 1994 on common rules and standards for ship inspection and survey organisations and for the relevant activities of maritime administrations,[5] in order to define the recognised organisations for the purpose of this Regulation, and Council Directive 98/18/EC of 17 March

---

4 OJ L320/14, 30 December 1995.
5 Ed., OJ L319/20, 12 December 1994. The directive as last amended by Dir. 2002/84.

1998 on safety rules and standards for passenger ships,[6] for the purpose of establishing the scope of application of this Regulation as regards passenger ships engaged on domestic voyages.

(14) The measures necessary for amending Annex II should be adopted in accordance with Council Decision 1999/468/EC of 28 June 1999 laying down the procedures for the exercise of implementing powers conferred on the Commission.[7]

(15) Since the objectives of this Regulation, namely to enhance the safety management and safe operation of ships as well as the prevention of pollution from ships, cannot be sufficiently achieved by the Member States and can therefore be better achieved at Community level, the Community may adopt measures, in accordance with the principle of subsidiarity as set out in Article 5 of the Treaty. In accordance with the principle of proportionality, as set out in that Article, this Regulation does not go beyond what is necessary in order to achieve those objectives."

Objective of the regulation

33.013 Article 1 provides that the objective of the regulation is to enhance the safety management and safe operation of ships as well as the prevention of pollution from ships, referred to in Article 3(1), by ensuring that companies operating those ships comply with the ISM Code by means of: (a) the establishment, implementation and proper maintenance by companies of the shipboard and shore-based safety management systems; and (b) the control thereof by flag and port State administrations.

Concepts in the regulation

33.014 Article 2 sets out some definitions for the purpose of the regulation. The term the "ISM Code" means the International Management Code for the Safe Operation of Ships and for Pollution Prevention adopted by the International Maritime Organization by Assembly Resolution A.741(18) of 4 November 1993, as amended by Maritime Safety Committee Resolution MSC.104(73) of 5 December 2000 and set out in Annex I to this regulation, in its up-to-date version. The phrase "recognised organisation" means a body recognised in accordance with Directive 94/57.[8] The term "company" means the owner of the ship or any other organisation or person, such as the manager or the bareboat charterer, who has assumed responsibility for the operation of the ship from the shipowner and who, on assuming such responsibility, has agreed to take over all the duties and responsibilities imposed by the ISM Code. The phrase "passenger ship" means a ship, including a high-speed craft, carrying more than 12 passengers, or a passenger submersible craft. The word "passenger" means every person other than: (a) the master and the members of the crew or other persons employed or engaged in any capacity on board a ship on the business of that ship; and (b) a child under one year of age. The phrase "high-speed craft" means a high-speed craft as defined in Regulation X-1/2 of SOLAS, in its up-to-date version. For high-speed passenger craft, the limitations indicated in Article 2(f) of Directive 98/18 shall apply. The phrase "cargo ship" means a ship, including a high-speed craft, which is not a passenger ship. The term "international voyage" means a

---

6 Ed., OJ L144/1, 15 May 1998. The directive as last amended by Commission Dir. 2003/75 (OJ L190, 30 July 2003, p. 6).

7 Ed., OJ L184/23, 17 July 1999.

8 OJ L319/20, 12.12.1994, http://eur-lex.europa.eu/legal-content/EN/TXT/?uri=celex:31994L0057.

voyage by sea from a port of a Member State or any other State to a port outside that State, or vice versa. The phrase "domestic voyage" means a voyage in sea areas from a port of a Member State to the same or another port within that Member State. The term "regular shipping service" means a series of ship crossings operated so as to serve traffic between the same two or more points, either: (a) according to a published timetable; or (b) with crossings so regular or frequent that they constitute a recognisable systematic series. The phrase "ro-ro passenger ferry" means a seagoing passenger vessel as defined in Chapter II-1 of SOLAS, in its up-to-date version. The term "passenger submersible craft" means a passenger-carrying mobile vessel which primarily operates under water and relies on surface support, such as a surface ship or shore-based facilities, for monitoring and for one or more of the following: (a) recharging of power supply; (b) recharging high pressure air; and (c) recharging life-support. The term "mobile offshore drilling unit" means a vessel capable of engaging in drilling operations for the exploration for or exploitation of resources beneath the seabed such as liquid or gaseous hydrocarbons, sulphur or salt. Finally, the term "gross tonnage" means the gross tonnage of a ship determined in accordance with the International Convention on Tonnage Measurement of Ships, 1969 or, in the case of ships engaged exclusively on domestic voyages and not measured in accordance with the said convention, the gross tonnage of the ship determined in accordance with national tonnage measurement regulations.

Scope of regulation 336/2006

33.015 Article 3(1) provides that the regulation shall apply to the following types of ships and to companies operating them: (a) cargo ships and passenger ships, flying the flag of a Member State, engaged on international voyages; (b) cargo ships and passenger ships engaged exclusively on domestic voyages, regardless of their flag; (c) cargo ships and passenger ships operating to or from ports of the Member States, on a regular shipping service, regardless of their flag; and (d) mobile offshore drilling units operating under the authority of a Member State.

33.016 Article 3(2) provides that the regulation shall not apply to the following types of ships or to the companies operating them: (a) ships of war and troopships and other ships owned or operated by a Member State and used only on government non-commercial service; (b) ships not propelled by mechanical means, wooden ships of primitive build, pleasure yachts and pleasure craft, unless they are or will be crewed and carrying more than 12 passengers for commercial purposes; (c) fishing vessels; (d) cargo ships and mobile offshore drilling units of less than 500 gt; and (e) passenger ships, other than ro-ro passenger ferries, in sea areas of Class C and D as defined in Article 4 of Directive 98/18.

Compliance

33.017 Article 4 of Regulation 336/2006 provides that Member States shall ensure that all companies operating ships falling within the scope of this regulation comply with the provisions of the regulation.

Safety management requirements

33.018 Article 5 of Regulation 336/2006 provides that the ships referred to in Article 3(1) of Regulation 336/2006 and the companies operating them shall comply with the requirements of Part A of the ISM Code.

Certification and verification

33.019 Article 6 of Regulation 336/2006 provides that for the purposes of certification and verification, Member States shall comply with the provisions of Part B of the ISM Code.

Derogation

33.020 Article 7 of Regulation 336/2006 provides for some derogation. Article 7(1) provides a Member State may, if it considers it difficult in practice for companies to comply with paragraphs 6, 7, 9, 11 and 12 of Part A of the ISM Code for certain ships or categories of ships exclusively engaged on domestic voyages in that Member State, derogate wholly or partly from those provisions by imposing measures ensuring equivalent achievement of the objectives of the Code. Article 7(2) provides that a Member State may, for ships and companies for which a derogation has been adopted by virtue of paragraph 1, if it considers it difficult in practice to apply the requirements laid down in Article 6, establish alternative certification and verification procedures. Article 7(3) provides that in the circumstances set out in paragraph 1 and, if applicable, paragraph 2, the following procedure shall apply: (a) the Member State concerned shall notify the Commission of the derogation and of the measures which it intends to adopt; (b) if, within six months of the notification, it is decided, in accordance with the procedure referred to in Article 12(2), that the proposed derogation is not justified or that the proposed measures are not sufficient, the Member State shall be required to amend or refrain from adopting the proposed provisions; and (c) the Member State shall make any adopted measures public with a direct reference to paragraph 1 and, if applicable, paragraph 2. Article 7(4) provides that following a derogation under paragraph 1 and, if applicable, paragraph 2, the Member State concerned shall issue a certificate in accordance with the second subparagraph of Annex II, Part B, Section 5, indicating the applicable operational limitations.

Validity, acceptance and recognition of certificates

33.021 Article 8 of Regulation 336/2006 deals with the validity, acceptance and recognition of certificates:

"1. The Document of Compliance shall remain valid for up to five years from the date of its issue. The Safety Management Certificate shall remain valid for up to five years from the date of its issue.
2. In cases of renewal of the Document of Compliance and the Safety Management Certificate, the relevant provisions of Part B of the ISM Code shall apply.
3. Member States shall accept Documents of Compliance, Interim Documents of Compliance, Safety Management Certificates and Interim Safety Management Certificates issued by the

administration of any other Member State or on behalf of this administration by a recognised organisation.

4. Member States shall accept Documents of Compliance, Interim Documents of Compliance, Safety Management Certificates and Interim Safety Management Certificates issued by, or on behalf of, the administrations of third countries.

However, for ships engaged on a regular shipping service, compliance with the ISM Code by the Documents of Compliance, Interim Documents of Compliance, Safety Management Certificates and Interim Safety Management Certificates issued on behalf of administrations of third countries shall be verified, by any appropriate means, by or on behalf of the Member State(s) concerned, unless they were issued by the administration of a Member State or by a recognised organisation."

Penalties

33.022 Article 9 of Regulation 336/2006 provides that Member States must lay down the rules on penalties applicable to infringements of the regulation and must take all the measures necessary to ensure that they are implemented. The penalties provided must be effective, proportionate and dissuasive.

Reporting

33.023 Article 10(1) of Regulation 336/2006 provides Member States must report to the Commission every two years on the implementation of the regulation. Article 10(2) provides that the Commission must, in accordance with the procedure referred to in Article 12(2), establish a harmonised specimen form for such reports. Article 10(3) provides that the Commission must, with the assistance of the European Maritime Safety Agency and within six months of receiving the reports from Member States, prepare a consolidated report concerning the implementation of this regulation, with any proposed measures, if appropriate. This report must be addressed to the European Parliament and the Council.

Amendments

33.024 Article 11 of Regulation 336/2006 deals with amendments. Article 11(1) provides that amendments to the ISM Code may be excluded from the scope of Regulation 336/2006 pursuant to Article 5 of Regulation 2099/2002 of the Parliament and Council of 5 November 2002 establishing a Committee on Safe Seas and the Prevention of Pollution from Ships ("COSS").[9] Article 11(2) states that adaptations to Annex II, designed to amend non-essential elements of this regulation, must be adopted in accordance with the regulatory procedure with scrutiny referred to in Article 12(3).

---

9 Ed., OJ L324/1, 29 November 2002. Regulation as amended by Commission Reg. (EC) No 415/2004 (OJ L68, 6 March 2004, p. 10).

Committee procedure

33.025 Article 12 of Regulation 336/2006 sets out that the Commission shall be assisted by the COSS set up by Article 3 of Regulation 2099/2002 of the Parliament and Council.[10]

Repeal

33.026 Article 13(1) of Regulation 336/2006 provides that Regulation 3051/95[11] was repealed with effect from 24 March 2006.

Annexes

33.027 Annex I sets out the ISM Code and Annex II deals with provisions for the administration concerning the implementation of the ISM Code. There is a great deal of detail in the annexes on the safety management code.

---

10 Ed., OJ L324/1, 29 November 2002.

11 I.e. Council Regulation (EC) No 3051/95 of 8 December 1995 on the safety management of roll-on/roll-off passenger ferries (ro-ro ferries), OJ L320/14, 30 December 1995, http://eur-lex.europa.eu/legal-content/EN/TXT/?uri=celex:31995R3051.

CHAPTER 34

Maritime safety: ferries and ro-ro vessels

A. INTRODUCTION

34.001 This chapter examines selected aspects of European Union ("EU") shipping law as they relate to the safety of ferries and roll-on/roll-off ("ro-ro") vessels.[1]

34.002 Ferry traffic is of enormous significance in the EU. It is believed that more than 400 million people sail in, or out of, EU ports annually with around 280 million passengers being on international voyages and around 120 million passengers sailing on cabotage voyages between ports of the same Member State.[2]

34.003 As the EU needs support from its citizens, it is imperative that citizens see the EU doing enough to protect them and their families when they travel on ferries and other passenger vessels. Equally, citizens want to see ferries being safe for passengers, cars and freight as well as their crews. Therefore it is not surprising that the EU has adopted various measures to ensure such protection.

34.004 At the outset, these measures were non-legally binding resolutions but have since been in the nature of legally binding measures. Therefore, there has been an evolution of measures. Some of these measures have been adopted in the aftermath of various events (for example, incidents such as the *Herald of Free Enterprise*,[3] the *Scandinavian Star*,[4] the *Estonia*,[5] the *Costa Concordia*[6] (though this was a cruise liner) and the *Norman Atlantic*[7]) while others have been influenced by policy, experience, lessons learned from casualties and technology developments as well as reflection on how safety could be improved.

34.005 The EU measures are not a complete code of laws in their own right but form part of a body of national and international rules on ferry safety.

34.006 This chapter has to be read in conjunction with the other chapters in the book on safety because the general rules relating to maritime safety apply equally to ferries.

---

1 It is also worth considering other measures which are considered in other chapters including, for example, Dir. 98/41 on registration of persons on board (OJ L188/35, 2 July 1998).

2 European Commission at: https://ec.europa.eu/transport/modes/maritime/safety-and-environment/safety-passenger-ships_en.

3 The Herald of Free Enterprise sank in 1987 in the port of Zeebrugge in Belgium with the loss of 193 lives. The ferry left the Belgian port with its bow door open with the result that sea water flooded the car deck and the vessel capsized within minutes.

4 The Scandinavian Star caught fire in 1990 with the loss of 159 people.

5 The Estonia sank in 1994 with the loss of 852 lives. There had been 989 persons on board (803 passengers and 186 crew) and amounted to one of the worst disasters ever in peacetime.

6 This Italian cruise ship ran aground and capsized in shallow water in 2012 off the Isola del Giglio. A total of 32 people lost their lives out of the 3,216 passengers and 1,013 crewmembers aboard.

7 The Norman Atlantic caught fire in the Adriatic Sea in 2014 with the loss of 28 lives in connection with the loss and two other lives were lost during the salvage operation.

B. RESOLUTION OF THE COUNCIL AND OF THE REPRESENTATIVES OF THE GOVERNMENTS OF THE MEMBER STATES, MEETING WITHIN THE COUNCIL OF 19 JUNE 1990 ON IMPROVING PASSENGER FERRY SAFETY

34.007 The 19 June 1990 saw the adoption of a Resolution of the Council and of the representatives of the governments of the Member States, meeting within the Council of 19 June 1990 on improving passenger ferry safety.[8] The resolution recognised an awareness of: the large number of passengers who travel by passenger ferries in European waters; the essentially international nature of such operations; the necessity of crews being able to function in a satisfactory manner in the event of an emergency; the dangers which can arise from management and communication failures; the potentially large-scale intervention which could be required in the event of an accident involving a passenger ferry; the fact that the transport of passengers in European waters is carried out by vessels registered both inside and outside the EU, thus requiring any necessary improvement of passenger ferry safety, including the question of crewing, to take place in a broad international context; and a wish to improve the safety of passenger ferries.

34.008 The resolution calls on the Member States and the Commission, in their capacity as members or as observer of: (a) the International Maritime Organization of the United Nations; (b) the memorandum of understanding on port State control "to press for the urgent identification, elaboration, adoption and implementation of measures which will improve safety of passenger ferries on an international basis in the framework of the aforementioned fora".

C. COUNCIL RESOLUTION OF 22 DECEMBER 1994 ON THE SAFETY OF ROLL-ON/ROLL-OFF PASSENGER FERRIES

34.009 On 22 December 1994, the Council adopted a resolution on the safety of ro-ro passenger ferries (i.e. Resolution 94/C 379/05).[9] It recalled the Commission's communication on "A common policy on safe seas" and the related Council resolution of 8 June 1993.[10] It expressed deep concern about the incident involving the ro-ro passenger ferry *Estonia* which capsized on a voyage from Tallinn to Stockholm on 28 September 1994 with the tragic loss of more than 900 lives. The Council indicated that it was "aware of the fact that similar accidents with roll-on/roll-off passenger ferries have occurred in European waters in recent years" and it was convinced

> "that in the light of these casualties the operation of roll-on/roll-off passenger ferries in European waters and, in particular, the design and equipment, the quality of the crews and the responsibility of the owners and operators of this type of ship, must be reviewed and improved."

It referred to Council Directive 94/58 of 22 November 1994 on the minimum level of training of seafarers,[11] and in particular to Article 8(1) and (2) thereof, which, among

---

8 OJ C206/3, 18 August 1990, http://eur-lex.europa.eu/legal-content/EN/TXT/HTML/?uri=CELEX:41990X0818&from=EN.

9 OJ C379/8, 31 December 1994, http://eur-lex.europa.eu/legal-content/EN/TXT/HTML/?uri=CELEX:31994Y1231(06)&from=EN.

10 OJ No C271/1, 7 October 1993.

11 OJ No L319/28, 12 December 1994.

other things, establishes specific requirements for communication on board passenger ships. The body of the resolution stated:

"1. WELCOMES the International Maritime Organization (IMO) initiative of an ad hoc panel of maritime experts to recommend improvements in the safety of roll-on/roll-off passenger ferries;

2. CALLS upon the Member States and the Commission to fully support the IMO initiative and to cooperate in such a way that the panel of experts can present its conclusions and recommendations by May 1995; calls upon the Member States and the Commission to cooperate in ensuring that the panel addresses not only the technical elements but also the wider human element;

3. INVITES the Member States and the Commission to submit or support proposals that the IMO should undertake:

   (a) an urgent and thorough review of the intact and damage stability requirements applied to roll-on/roll-off passenger ferries with the aim of significantly enhancing the survivability of such vessels;
   (b) a review of the evacuation procedures applying to roll-on/roll-off passenger ferries including the procedures, equipment and crew training requirements for rapid evacuation, effective and understandable communication of safety information and for giving evacuation instructions to passengers on board;
   (c) a review of the requirements for qualified medical personnel on board roll-on/roll-off passenger ferries undertaking long voyages;
   (d) preparatory work for the amendment of the Solas Convention or the preparation of a free-standing Convention to provide for the investigation of marine casualties and cooperation between States in the investigation of such casualties;
   (e) an examination of the necessary technical specifications for the mandatory fitting out of roll-on/roll-off passenger ferries with voyage recorders as an aid to accident investigation following a marine casualty;
   (f) the necessary steps to allow application of the standards set out in the 'Agreement concerning the stability of existing ro-ro passenger ships operating services to or from ports within a designated sea area of north west Europe' as a 'regional' standard and to enable Member States to apply these standards to all roll-on/roll-off passenger ferries operating to and from all ports of this specific region;
   (g) improved focusing and acceleration of the work of the Subcommittee on Flag State Implementation (FSI) of the IMO;
   (h) consideration of the need to prepare operational guidelines for use in adverse weather conditions given the size/type of ro-ro ships concerned and their area of operation;

4. INVITES the Member States and the Commission to strive within the framework of the Paris Memorandum to apply as soon as possible but by 1 January 1995 at the latest the provisions related to expanded inspection embodied in the draft Directive on port-State control;

II
INVITES the Commission to submit proposals for Council decisions concerning:

1. the advance mandatory application of the International Safety Management Code (IMO Resolution A.741(18)) by 1 July 1996 to all regular roll-on/roll-off passenger ferry services operating to or from European ports, in compliance with international law;

2. a mandatory requirement that all regular roll-on/roll-off vessels carrying passengers to or from ports of the European Union on voyages lasting a number of hours yet to be determined, be equipped with a system indicating accurately the number and names, and on voyages of short duration the number only, of passengers and crews on board the vessel at any time except in case of specific derogation for voyages of very short duration. Such information should be communicated to the shore before the vessel leaves its berth for a place to which the relevant authorities have immediate access;

3. an expanded mandatory survey regime, including operational inspections etc., for all roll-on/roll-off passenger ferries operating to or from ports of the European Union prior to the start of a new service and subsequently at regular intervals;

4. a regime compatible with international law and the need to avoid arbitrary interference with the freedom to trade, for the control by Member States of the safety of all roll-on/roll-off passenger ferries serving European Union ports including the right of investigation of marine casualties as mentioned in the relevant IMO Resolutions;

III

1. TAKES NOTE of the Commission's intention to submit as soon as possible the proposals mentioned in its action programme and requested by the Council and which could favourably affect the safety of roll-on/roll-off passenger ferries, notably those relating to:
   – the application of appropriate working hours and working conditions ensuring safety on board such passenger ships,

   – common safety rules for marine equipment used on board commercial and passenger vessels, including rescue facilities, in particular on board vessels with high sides,
   – mandatory application of the relevant provisions of certain IMO Assembly Resolutions,
   – safety rules for passenger vessels engaged in domestic trade;

2. INVITES the Commission to investigate the effect of competition upon the safe operation of ferries and to report to the Council;

3. INVITES the Commission to report, one year after the implementation by the Member States of Council Directive 94/58/EC, on the effectiveness of the communication arrangements for passengers provided for in that Directive;

IV

1. URGES Member States to inform the Commission of any difficulty they encounter in the implementation of their Global Maritime Distress and Safety System (GMDSS) obligations;

2. URGES Member States to ensure that their requirements for the application of the guidelines for securing arrangements for the transport of road vehicles on board roll-on/roll-off ferries, and in particular those regarding lashings (IMO Resolution A.581(14)), are correctly fulfilled by roll-on/roll-off passenger ferry operators;

3. URGES all classification societies and in particular those who are European Members of the International Association of Classification Societies (IACS) to assess and tighten up their rules governing the structural elements of roll-on/roll-off ferries. Special consideration should be given to the construction and means of securing the doors of roll-on/roll-off passenger ferries which allow vehicle access to vehicle decks;

4. UNDERLINES the need to ensure that adequate search and rescue facilities are available;

V

DECIDES to keep the matter of ferry safety on its agenda."

D. COUNCIL DIRECTIVE 1999/35 ON A SYSTEM OF MANDATORY SURVEYS FOR THE SAFE OPERATION OF REGULAR RO-RO FERRY AND HIGH-SPEED PASSENGER CRAFT SERVICES

Introduction

34.010 On 29 April 1999, the Council adopted Directive[12] 1999/35 on a system of mandatory surveys for the safe operation of regular ro-ro ferry and high-speed passenger

---

12 As a directive, it requires implementation in Member State law.

craft services.[13] The legal basis for Directive 1999/35 was the TEC generally and, in particular, Article 84(2) of the TEC (now, Article 100(2) of the TFEU). The legislative history included a proposal from the Commission[14] and an opinion of the Economic and Social Committee. Directive 1999/35 entered into force on 2 June 1999 in accordance with Article 21.[15]

34.011 The Council recalled the background to the adoption of Directive 1999/35 and it is useful to review it in detail because it is quite brief.

"(1) Whereas within the framework of the common transport policy further measures must be taken to improve safety in the maritime transport of passengers;

(2) Whereas the Community is seriously concerned by shipping accidents involving ro-ro ferries which have resulted in a massive loss of life; whereas persons using ro-ro ferries and high-speed passenger craft throughout the EU have the right to expect and to be able to rely on an appropriate level of safety;

(3) Whereas the Council invited the Commission, in its resolution of 22 December 1994 on the safety of roll-on/roll-off passenger ferries,[16] to submit proposals for a mandatory survey and control regime for the safety of all ro-ro passenger ferries operating to or from ports of the Community, including the right of investigation of marine casualties;

(4) Whereas in view, in particular, of the internal market dimension of maritime passenger transport, action at Community level is the most effective way of establishing a common minimum level of safety for ships throughout the EU;

(5) Whereas action at EU level is the best way to ensure the harmonised enforcement of some principles agreed on within the International Maritime Organisation (IMO), thus avoiding distortions of competition between different EU ports and ro-ro ferries and high-speed passenger craft;

(6) Whereas, in view of the proportionality principle, a Council Directive is the appropriate legal instrument as it provides a framework for the Member States' uniform and compulsory application of the common safety standards, while leaving each Member State the right to decide which implementation tools best fit its internal system;

(7) Whereas the safety of ships is primarily the responsibility of flag States; whereas each Member State should ensure compliance with the safety requirements applicable to the ro-ro ferries and high speed passenger craft flying the flag of that Member State and to the companies that operate them;

(8) Whereas port State control does not provide for regular in-depth preventive surveys and verifications for ro-ro ferries and high speed passenger craft; whereas it therefore should be verified that companies and their ferries and craft comply with the safety standards agreed within the IMO and, where appropriate, at regional level, through a system of regular mandatory inspections by host States; whereas companies should be prevented from operating such ferries and craft if these inspections reveal dangerous non-conformity with these safety standards;

(9) Whereas this Directive addresses the Member States in their capacity as host States; whereas the responsibilities exercised in that capacity are based on specific port State responsibilities that are fully in line with the 1982 United Nations Convention on the Law of the Sea (UNCLOS);

---

13 OJ L138/1, 1 June 1999. It was amended by Dir. 2002/84 of the European Parliament and of the Council of 5 November 2002 (OJ L324/53, 29 November 2002); (b) Reg. (EC) No 219/2009 of the European Parliament (OJ L87 109, 31 March 2009) and of the Council of 11 March 2009; and (c) Dir. 2009/18 of the European Parliament (OJ L131 114, 28 May 2009) and of the Council text with EEA relevance of 23 April 2009. A consolidated version of Dir. 1999/35 is available at http://eur-lex.europa.eu/legal-content/EN/TXT/?qid=14690112142 99&uri=CELEX:01999L0035-20090617.

14 OJ C108/122, 7 April 1998.

15 OJ C407/106, 28 December 1998.

16 OJ C379/8, 31.12.1994.

(10) Whereas in the interest of improving safety and avoiding distortion of competition, the common safety standards should apply to all ro-ro ferries and high-speed passenger craft, regardless of the flag they fly, providing regular services to or from a port in the Member States both on international voyages and on domestic voyages in sea areas beyond 20 miles from a coast line where shipwrecked persons can land, while leaving the possibility to the Member States to extend the scope of application of the Directive to ro-ro ferries and high-speed passenger craft operating on domestic voyages in sea areas within 20 miles from a coast line;

(11) Whereas it is necessary that host States check whether the ro-ro ferries and high-speed passenger craft operating to and from EU ports conform to certain harmonised requirements for certification and survey by the flag State;

(12) Whereas those ro-ro ferries and high-speed passenger craft should also conform, at the building stage and during their entire lifetime, with the applicable classification standards as regards the construction and maintenance of their hull, main and auxiliary machinery, electrical installation and control installation and should be fitted with a voyage data recorder complying with the relevant international requirements;

(13) Whereas host States should check that the companies providing those services operate their ro-ro ferries and high-speed passenger craft so as to guarantee maximum safety; whereas interested Member States, other than the flag State, should be allowed to participate fully in any investigation of a marine casualty;

(14) Whereas it is fundamental to check that third flag State administrations concur with the companies' commitments to cooperate with any investigation of a marine casualty or incident and to comply with the rules of recognised organisations for classification and, where applicable, for certification; whereas such administrations should accept the use of harmonised survey and certification procedures;

(15) Whereas, in order to ensure continuous compliance of ro-ro ferries and high-speed passenger craft with the requirements of this Directive, host States should carry out surveys prior to the start of a service and thereafter at regular intervals and whenever a significant change occurs in the operating circumstances;

(16) Whereas in order to reduce the burden placed on companies, due account should be taken of previous verifications and surveys; ro-ro ferries and high-speed passenger craft should be exempted from surveys where it has been confirmed that they comply with this Directive for operation on similar routes and replacement ferries and craft should benefit from special arrangements; whereas ro-ro ferries and high-speed passenger craft which have been surveyed to the satisfaction of the host State should not be subjected to expanded inspections under Council Directive 95/21/EC of 19 June 1995 concerning the enforcement, in respect of shipping using Community ports and sailing in the waters under the jurisdiction of the Member States, of international standards for ship safety, pollution prevention and shipboard living and working conditions (port State control);[17]

(17) Whereas Member States should cooperate to exercise their responsibilities as host States;

(18) Whereas Member States might find it useful to be assisted in the performance of their tasks by recognised organisations which meet the requirements of Council Directive 94/57/EC of 22 November 1994 on common rules and standards for ship inspection and survey organisations and for the relevant activities of marine administrations;[18]

(19) Whereas due account should be taken, in planning the surveys, of the operational and maintenance schedules of the ro-ro ferries and high-speed passenger craft;

(20) Whereas Member States should ensure that their internal legal systems enable them and any other substantially interested Member States to participate or cooperate in, or conduct, accident investigations on the basis of the provisions of the IMO Code for the investigation of marine casualties; whereas the outcome of such investigations should be made publicly available;

---

17 OJ L157/1, 7.7.1995.
18 OJ L319/20, 12.12.1994.

(21) Whereas a set of accompanying measures in the areas of navigational guidance systems, contingency planning and local operational restrictions will further improve safety;

(22) Whereas, in order to enable the monitoring of the application of this Directive, a database should be established based on the information derived from the surveys;

(23) Whereas it is necessary for a committee consisting of representatives of the Member States to assist the Commission in the effective application of this Directive; whereas the Committee set up in Article 12 of Council Directive 93/75/EEC of 13 September 1993 concerning minimum requirements for vessels bound for or leaving EU ports and carrying dangerous or polluting goods,[19] can undertake that function;

(24) Whereas certain provisions of the Directive may be adapted by that Committee to bring them into line with Community or IMO measures and to improve its regime to take into account future amendments to the 1974 International Convention for the Safety of Life at Sea (SOLAS) which have entered into force and to ensure a harmonised implementation of amendments to some IMO resolutions without broadening its scope ..."

These recitals encapsulate very well the purpose of the measure but it is worth considering in more detail the purpose of the measure.

Purpose of Directive 1999/35

34.012 Article 1 provides that the purpose of Directive 1999/35

"is to lay down a system of mandatory surveys which will provide a greater assurance of safe operation of regular ro-ro ferries and high-speed passenger craft services to or from ports in the Member States of the [EU] and to provide for the right of Member States to conduct, participate in or cooperate with any investigation of maritime casualties or incidents on these services."

This system of mandatory surveys is designed to promote safety of ro-ro vessels.

Concepts in Directive 1999/35

34.013 Article 2 of Directive 1999/35 sets out a number of concepts and definitions for the purposes of the directive. First, the term "ro-ro ferry" means a seagoing passenger vessel with facilities to enable road or rail vehicles to roll on and roll off the vessel, and carrying more than 12 passengers. This is the conventional ferry but also includes fast craft. Second, the term "high Speed Passenger Craft" shall mean a high speed craft as defined in Regulation X/1 of the 1974 Solas Convention, in its up-to-date version, which carries more than 12 passengers. Third, a "passenger" is defined as every person other than: (i) the master and the members of the crew or other persons employed or engaged in any capacity on board a ship on the business of that ship, and (ii) a child under one year of age. Fourth, the phrase "1974 Solas Convention" means the International Convention for the Safety of Life at Sea, together with protocols and amendments thereto, in its up-to-date version. Fifth, "high Speed Craft Code" ("HSC Code") means the "International Code for Safety of High Speed Craft" contained in IMO Maritime Safety Committee Resolution MSC 36 (63) of 20 May 1994, in its up-to-date version. The term "regular service" means a series of ro-ro ferry or high-speed passenger craft crossings operated so as to serve traffic between the same two or more ports, or a series of voyages from and to the same port without intermediate calls, either: (i) according to a published timetable; or

---

19 OJ L247/19, 5.10.1993.

(ii) with crossings so regular or frequent that they constitute a recognisable systematic series. The term "sea area" means any sea area included in a list established in accordance with Article 4 of Council Directive 98/18 of 17 March 1998 on safety rules and standards for passenger ships.[20] The word "certificates" means: (i) for ro-ro ferries and high-speed passenger craft engaged on international voyages, the safety certificates issued under the 1974 SOLAS Convention as amended, together with the relevant records of equipment and where appropriate exemption certificates and permits to operate; (ii) for ro-ro ferries and high-speed passenger craft engaged on domestic voyages, the safety certificates issued in accordance with Directive 98/18 together with the relevant records of equipment and where appropriate exemption certificates and permits to operate. The term "exemption certificate" means any certificate issued under the provisions of Regulation I B/12(a) (vi) of the 1974 SOLAS Convention. The all-important "administration of the flag State" is defined as meaning the competent authorities of the State whose flag the ro-ro ferry or the high-speed passenger craft is entitled to fly. The term "host State" means a Member State to or from whose port(s) a ro-ro ferry or a high-speed passenger craft is engaged on a regular service. An "international voyage" is defined as meaning a voyage by sea from a port of a Member State to a port outside that Member State, or conversely. The phrase "domestic voyage" means a voyage in sea areas from a port of a Member State to the same or another port within that Member State. The term "recognised organisation" means an organisation recognised in accordance with Article 4 of Directive 94/57. The word "company" means a company operating one or more ro-ro ferries to which a document of compliance has been issued in compliance with Article 5(2) of Regulation 3051/95 of 8 December 1995 on the safety management of ro-ro passenger ferries or a company operating high speed passenger craft, to which a document of compliance has been issued in accordance with Regulation IX/4 of the 1974 Solas Convention, in its up-to-date version. The phrase "Code for the investigation of marine casualties" means the Code for the investigation of marine casualties and incidents adopted by the IMO by means of Assembly Resolution A.849(20) of 27 November 1997. The words "specific survey" means a survey by the host State as specified in Articles 6 and 8. The phrase "qualified inspector" means a public-sector employee or other person, duly authorised by the competent authority of a Member State to carry out surveys and inspections related to the certificates and fulfilling the criteria of qualification and independence specified in Annex V. Finally, the term "deficiency" means a condition found not to be in compliance with the requirements of the directive.

Scope of Directive 1999/35

34.014 Article 3(1) provides that Directive 1999/35 shall apply to all ro-ro ferries and high-speed passenger craft operating to or from a port of a Member State on a regular service, regardless of their flag, when engaged on international voyages or on domestic voyages in sea areas covered by Class A as referred to in Article 4 of Directive 98/18. Article 3(2) provides that Member States may apply the directive to ro-ro ferries and high-speed passenger craft engaged on domestic voyages in sea areas other than those referred to in paragraph 1. In those circumstances, the relevant rules shall be applied to all

---

20 OJ L144/1, 15 May 1998.

ro-ro ferries or high-speed passenger craft operating under the same conditions, without discrimination in respect of flag, nationality or place of establishment of the company.

Initial verifications required in relation to ro-ro ferries and high-speed passenger craft

34.015 Article 4(1) of Directive 1999/35 provides that prior to the start of operation by a ro-ro ferry or high-speed passenger craft on a regular service, or within 12 months of the date referred to in Article 19(1) for a ro-ro ferry or high-speed passenger craft already operating a regular service on that date, host States must check that ro-ro ferries and high-speed passenger craft: (a) carry valid certificates, issued by the administration of the flag State or by a recognised organisation acting on its behalf; (b) have been surveyed for the issue of certificates in accordance with the relevant procedures and guidelines annexed to IMO Assembly Resolution A.746(18) on survey guidelines under the harmonised system of survey and certification, as they stand at the time of adoption of this directive or with procedures designed to achieve the same goal; (c) comply with the standards specified for classification by the rules of a recognised organisation, or rules accepted as equivalent by the administration of the flag State for construction and maintenance of their hull, machinery and electrical and control installation; (d) are fitted with a voyage data recorder ("VDR") for the purpose of providing information for the benefit of a possible casualty investigation. The VDR shall meet the performance standards of IMO Assembly Resolution A.861(20) of 27 November 1997 and comply with the testing standards laid down in International Electrotechnical Commission ("IEC") standard No 61996. However, for VDRs to be placed on board ro-ro ferries and high-speed passenger craft built before the entry into force of this directive, exemptions for compliance with some of the requirements may be granted. These exemptions and the conditions under which they can be granted shall be adopted in accordance with the regulatory procedure referred to in Article 16(2); and, finally, (e) but this only applies to high speed passenger craft only where appropriate, comply with specific stability requirements adopted at regional level, and transposed into their national legislation in accordance with the notification procedure laid down in Directive 98/34 of the European Parliament and of the Council of 22 June 1998 laying down a procedure for the provision of information in the field of technical standards and regulations and of rules on information society services,[21] when operating in that region a service covered by that national legislation, provided those requirements do not exceed those specified in the annex on Resolution 14 (Stability Requirements Pertaining to the Agreement) of the 1995 SOLAS Conference and have been notified to the Secretary-General of the IMO, in accordance with the procedures specified in point 3 of that resolution.

Initial verifications required in relation to companies and flag states

34.016 Article 5 provides that prior to the start of operation by a ro-ro ferry or high-speed passenger craft on a regular service, or within 12 months of the date referred to in Article 19(1) for a ro-ro ferry or high-speed passenger craft already operating on a regular

---

21 OJ L204/37, 21 July 1998.

service on that date, host States shall: (a) check that companies which operate or intend to operate such a ferry or craft on regular service: (i) take the necessary measures to ensure that the specific requirements laid down in Annex I are applied and provide the evidence of compliance with this paragraph and with Article 4 to the host States involved in the regular service; and (ii) will agree in advance that host States and any substantially interested Member State may conduct, participate fully in or co-operate with any investigation of a marine casualty or incident in accordance with Article 12, and will give them access to the information retrieved from the VDR of their ferry or craft involved in such a casualty or incident; and (b) check for such a ferry or craft flying a flag other than that of a Member State, the concurrence of that flag State that it has accepted the company's commitment to meet the requirements of the directive.

Initial specific surveys

34.017 Article 6(1) provides that prior to the start of operation by a ro-ro ferry or high-speed passenger craft on a regular service, or within 12 months of the date referred to in Article 19(1) for a ro-ro ferry and high-speed passenger craft already operating a regular service on that date, host States shall carry out an initial specific survey, in accordance with Annexes I and III, to satisfy themselves that the ro-ro ferry or high-speed passenger craft fulfils the necessary requirements for safe operation of a regular service. Article 6(2) provides that where Article 6 is applied prior to the start of operation, host States shall set a date for the initial specific survey which is no more than one month after receipt of the evidence necessary to complete the verification under Articles 4 and 5.

Special provisions

34.018 Article 7(1) provides that when a ro-ro ferry or high-speed passenger craft is to be engaged on another regular service, a new host State shall take the utmost account of verifications and surveys previously carried out for that ferry or craft for operation on a previous regular service covered by the directive. Provided that the new host State is satisfied with these previous verifications and surveys and that they are relevant to the new operational conditions, Articles 4, 5 and 6 need not be applied prior to the ro-ro ferry or high-speed passenger craft starting operation on the new regular service. Article 7(2) provides that Articles 4, 5 and 6 need not apply when a ro-ro ferry or high-speed passenger craft which complies with the directive already operating a regular service covered by the directive transfers to another regular service where the route characteristics are agreed by the relevant host States to be similar, and the host States all agree that the ro-ro ferry or high-speed passenger craft fulfils all the requirements for safe operation on that service. At the request of a company, the host States concerned may confirm in advance their agreement as to where route characteristics are similar. Article 7(3) provides that in cases where, following unforeseen circumstances, a replacement ro-ro ferry or high-speed passenger craft must be introduced rapidly to ensure continuity of service, and paragraphs 1 and 2 of Article 7 are not applicable then the host State may allow the ferry or craft to start operating provided that: (a) a visual inspection and document check raise no concerns that the ro-ro ferry or high-speed passenger craft does not fulfil the necessary requirements for safe operation, and (b) the host State completes the verifications and surveys under Articles 4, 5 and 6 within one month.

Regular specific surveys and other surveys

34.019 Article 8(1) provides that host states must, once in every 12-month period, carry out: (a) a specific survey, in accordance with Annex III, and (b) a survey during a regular service, which shall aim to cover enough items listed in Annexes I, III and IV in order to satisfy the host State that the ferry or craft continues to fulfil all the necessary requirements for safe operation. An initial specific survey in accordance with Article 6 counts as a specific survey for the purposes of this article. Article 8(3) provides that should the surveys confirm or reveal deficiencies in relation to the requirements of this directive warranting a prevention of operation, all costs relating to the surveys in any normal accounting period shall be covered by the company.

34.020 Pursuant to Article 8(2), a host State must carry out a specific survey in accordance with Annex III each time the ro-ro ferry or high-speed passenger craft undergoes repairs, alterations and modifications of a major character, or when there is a change in management or flag, or a transfer of class. However, in case of change in management or flag, or transfer of class, the host State may, after taking account of verifications and surveys previously issued for the ferry or craft, and provided that the safe operation of the ferry or craft is not affected by this change or transfer, dispense the ferry or craft from the specific survey required by this paragraph. The term "major changes" is not defined but is likely to be a question of fact in each case.

Notification

34.021 Article 9 provides that host States must inform companies promptly, in writing, of the outcome of verifications and surveys under Articles 4, 5, 6 and 8.

Prevention of operation

34.022 Article 10 deals with when the Member State may prevent the operation of a ferry. Under Article 10(1), a host State must – until the host State has established that the danger has been removed and the requirements of the directive are met – prevent the operation of a ro-ro ferry or high-speed passenger craft on a regular service: (a) when it has been unable to confirm compliance with the requirements in Articles 4 and 5; (b) whenever deficiencies are found during the surveys referred to in Articles 6 and 8 which pose an immediate danger to life, the ferry or craft, its crew and passengers; (c) when there is an established failure to comply with the Community instruments listed in Annex II which poses an immediate danger of life, the ferry or craft, its crew and passengers;[22]

---

22 Annex II lists various EU instruments for the purposes of Article 10(1c). I.e. for complete information, see Annex II and the instruments as amended: Council Dir. 93/75 of 13 September 1993 concerning minimum requirements for vessels bound for or leaving Community ports and carrying dangerous or polluting goods (OJ L247/19, 5 October1993); Council Dir. 94/58 of 22 November 1994 on the minimum level of training of seafarers (OJ L319/28, 12 December 1994); Council Reg. 3051/95 of 8 December 1995 on the safety management of roll on/roll off passenger ferries (ro-ro ferries) (OJ L320/14, 30 December 1995).

(d) whenever it has not been consulted by the flag State on the matters referred to in Article 13(1) or (5). The host State must inform the company in writing of the decision to prevent that ro-ro ferry or high-speed passenger craft operating, giving full reasoning.

34.023 Article 10(2) provides that, as an exception to the general rule set out in Article 10(1), where the ro-ro ferry or high-speed passenger craft is already operating a regular service and deficiencies are established, host States must require the company to take the necessary measures for their prompt rectification or within a well-defined and reasonable period of time, provided they do not pose an immediate danger to the safety of the ferry or craft, its crew and passengers. After rectification of the deficiencies, the host States concerned must verify that the rectification has been carried out to their full satisfaction. If this is not the case, they must prevent the ferry or craft from operating.

34.024 Under Article 10(3), Member States must, in accordance with national legislation, establish and maintain appropriate procedures covering the right of appeal by a company against a decision to prevent operation. The paragraph provides that appeals should be dealt with expeditiously. An appeal must not cause the decision to be automatically suspended. The competent authority must duly inform the company of its right of appeal.

34.025 In cases where Articles 4, 5 and 6 are applied prior to the start of operation by a ro-ro ferry or high-speed passenger craft on a regular service, a decision to prevent a ship operating must be taken within one month of the initial specific survey and communicated to the company immediately.[23]

Procedures related to initial and regular specific surveys

34.026 Article 11(1) provides that ro-ro ferries and high-speed passenger craft that have been subject to the specific surveys to the satisfaction of the involved host State(s) must be exempted by these host State(s) from expanded inspections referred to in Article 7(4) of Directive 95/21 and from the expanded inspections based on the clear grounds that they belong to the category of passenger ships referred to in Article 7(1) and Annex V.A.3 of that directive.

34.027 Administrations of two or more host States involved in a specific survey of the same ship or craft must co-operate with each other.[24] The specific surveys shall be carried out by a team composed of qualified inspectors of the involved host State(s). Wherever there is a need for qualitative assessment of the fulfilment of class-related provisions, host States must ensure the necessary expertise is included in the team, where appropriate by including a surveyor of a recognised organisation.[25] The inspectors must report deficiencies to the administrations of the host States.[26] The host State shall communicate this information to the flag State, if that State is not a host State involved in the survey.

34.028 An involved host State may agree to carry out a survey at the request of another involved host State.[27] Host States, when requested by companies, must invite the administration of the flag State which is not a host State to be represented in any specific survey

---

23 Dir. 1999/35, Art. 10(4).
24 Dir. 1999/35, Art. 11(2).
25 Ibid.
26 Ibid.
27 Dir. 1999/35, Art. 11(3).

under the provisions of Directive 1999/35.[28] Host States, in planning a survey in accordance with Articles 6 and 8, must take due account of the operational and maintenance schedule of the ferry or craft[29] – this is a pragmatic exception but one which must not be abused.

34.029 The findings of the specific surveys must be recorded in a report of which the format shall be established in accordance with the regulatory procedure referred to in Article 16(2).[30] In case of persistent disagreement between host States on the fulfilment of the requirements of Articles 4 and 5(1), the administration of any host State involved in a specific survey must immediately notify to the Commission the reasons of the disagreement.[31] The Commission must immediately start proceedings in order to take a decision in accordance with the regulatory procedure referred to in Article 16(2).[32]

Accompanying measures

34.030 Article 13(1) of Directive 1999/35 provides that Member States issuing or recognising an exemption certificate shall work together with the involved host State or administration of the flag State to resolve any disagreement concerning the suitability of the exemptions prior to the initial specific survey.

34.031 Article 13(2) goes on to provide that Member States should operate shore-based navigational guidance systems and other information schemes in accordance with IMO Resolution A.795(19) to assist ro-ro ferries and high-speed passenger craft in the safe conduct of the regular service, or part of it, for the safety of which they bear responsibility. Each Member State must provide to the Commission copies of the survey reports referred to in Article 11(6), with the IMO identification number where applicable.[33] The Commission may, in accordance with the regulatory procedure referred to in Article 16(2), decide on appropriate means for allocating an identification number to other vessels.[34] If two or more host States are involved in the regular service, the data may be provided by one of these host States.[35] The Commission must set up and maintain a database containing the information provided.[36] Conditions of access to the database must be decided in accordance with the regulatory procedure referred to in Article 16(2).[37] Member States must ensure that companies operating ro-ro ferries or high-speed passenger craft on regular services to or from their ports are able to maintain and implement an integrated system of contingency planning for shipboard emergencies.[38] To this end they shall make use of the framework provided by IMO Assembly Resolution A.852(20) on guidelines for a structure of an integrated system of contingency.[39] If two or more Member States are involved as host States in the regular service they shall jointly

---

28 Dir. 1999/35, Art. 11(4).
29 Dir. 1999/35, Art. 11(5).
30 Dir. 1999/35, Art. 11(6).
31 Dir. 1999/35, Art. 11(7).
32 Dir. 1999/35, Art. 11(8).
33 Dir. 1999/35, Art. 13(3).
34 Ibid.
35 Ibid.
36 Ibid.
37 Ibid.
38 Ibid.
39 Ibid.

establish a plan for the different routes.[40] Member States must ensure that they have been fully involved in their capacity as host State by the administration of the flag State, before the issuance of the permit to operate high speed craft, in accordance with the provisions of paragraph 1.9.3 of the HSC Code.[41] They must ensure that operational restrictions required by local situations, necessary to protect life, natural resources and coastal activities are established or maintained and they must take measures to ensure the enforcement of these restrictions.

Co-operation between host States

34.032 Under Article 14 of Directive 1999/35, host States involved in the same regular service must liaise with each other when applying the directive. This is very important in the context of regular ferry services. It is, again, a practical and pragmatic measure.

Supporting measures

34.033 Article 15 of Directive 1999/35 provides that the Member States must inform third States which have either flag State responsibilities or responsibilities similar to those of a host State for ro-ro ferries and high-speed passenger craft falling under the scope of the directive and operating between a port of a Member State and a port of a third State of the requirements imposed by the directive on any company providing a regular service to or from a port of the EU.

Committee procedure

34.034 Article 16(1) provides that the Commission is to be assisted by the COSS established by Article 3 of Regulation 2099/2002 of the European Parliament and of the Council.[42] Article 16(2) provides that where reference is made to Article 16(2) of Directive 1999/35 then Articles 5 and 7 of Decision 1999/468 shall apply, having regard to the provisions of Article 8 thereof.[43] The period laid down in Article 5(6) of Decision 1999/46 must be set at two months.[44] Under Article 16(3), where reference is made to Article 16(3), Article 5a(1) to (4) and Article 7 of Decision 1999/468 must apply, having regard to the provisions of Article 8 thereof.[45]

Amendment procedure

34.035 Article 17 provides that the annexes[46] to Directive 1999/35, the definitions, the references to EU instruments and references to IMO instruments may be adapted to the

---

40 Ibid.
41 Ibid.
42 OJ L324/l, 29 November 2002.
43 Dir. 1999/35, Art. 16(2).
44 Ibid.
45 Dir. 1999/35, Art. 16(3).
46 Annex I dealt with specific requirements to be fulfilled by companies as referred to in Art. 5(1), and Arts 6 and 8. Annex II listed the EU instruments referred to in Art. 10(1c). Annex III deals with procedures for specific surveys. Annex IV deals with indicative guidelines for qualified inspectors when carrying out unscheduled surveys during a regular crossing (as referred to in Art. 8(1)). Annex V lists the criteria of qualification and independence for qualified inspectors.

extent necessary to bring them into line with EU or IMO measures which have entered into force, but without broadening the scope of the directive. The annexes may also be adapted when it is necessary to improve the arrangements established by the directive, but without broadening its scope. Those measures, designed to amend non-essential elements of the directive, shall be adopted in accordance with the regulatory procedure with scrutiny referred to in Article 16(3). The amendments to the international instruments referred to in Article 2 may be excluded from the scope of the directive pursuant to Article 5 of Regulation 2099/2002.

Penalties

34.036 Under Article 18, Member States must lay down the system of penalties for breaching the national provisions adopted pursuant to the directive and must take all the measures necessary to ensure that those penalties are applied. The penalties thus provided for must be effective, proportionate and dissuasive. The rationale behind Article 18 is to provide for effective sanctions but as the EU either lacks competence or is not the appropriate party to adopt such sanctions then EU law obliges Member States to adopt such measures.

Application

34.037 Article 19 of Directive 1999/35 deals with the application of the directive. Article 19(1) provides that Member States had to bring into force the laws, regulations and administrative provisions necessary to comply with the directive not later than 1 December 2000 and inform the Commission. Article 19(2) states that the provisions of Article 4(1)(d) shall be applied no later than 30 months after the publication date of IEC standard No 61996 or by 1 January 2001, whichever of these dates came later. Under Article 19(3), when Member States adopt these measures, they must contain a reference to this directive or shall be accompanied by such reference on the occasion of their official publication. The methods of making such reference shall be laid down by the Member States. Under Article 19(4), the Member States had to immediately notify to the Commission all provisions of domestic law which they adopt in the field governed by the directive. The Commission then had to inform the other Member States thereof.

Assessment of application of Directive 1999/35

34.038 Under Article 20 three years after 1 December 2000, the Commission had to assess, on the basis of information to be provided by the Member States in accordance with Article 13, the application of the directive.

Proposed amendments

34.039 On 6 June 2016, the Commission proposed a directive of the European Parliament and of the Council on a system of inspections for the safe operation of ro-ro ferry and high-speed passenger craft in regular service and amending Directive 2009/16 of the European Parliament and of the Council on port State control and repealing Council

Directive 1999/35.[47] This was part of the Commission's REFIT and Better Regulation agenda and as a response to the fitness check on EU passenger ship safety legislation.[48]

E. DIRECTIVE 2003/25 ON SPECIFIC STABILITY REQUIREMENTS FOR RO-RO PASSENGER SHIPS

Introduction

34.040 On 14 April 2003, the Parliament and Council adopted Directive 2003/25 on specific stability requirements for ro-ro passenger ships.[49] The directive entered into force on 19 May 2003.[50] It was amended by Commission Regulation 2005/12[51] and Regulation 1137/2008 of the European Parliament and Council of 22 October 2008.[52]

34.041 The legal basis for Directive 2003/25 was the TEC generally and, in particular Article 80(2) so the legal basis is now the TFEU and Article 100(2) of the TFEU. The legislative history included a proposal from the Commission,[53] an opinion of the European Economic and Social Committee ("EESC") and a consultation with the Committee of the Regions.

34.042 The background to Directive 2003/25 is clear from a number of the recitals including the following:

"(3) The survivability of ro-ro passenger ships following collision damage, as determined by their damage stability standard, is an essential factor for the safety of passengers and crew and is particularly relevant for search and rescue operations; the most dangerous problem for the stability of a ro-ro passenger ship with an enclosed ro-ro deck, following collision damage, is the one posed by the effect of a build up of significant amounts of water on that deck.

(4) Persons using ro-ro passenger ships and crew employed on board such vessels throughout the EU should have the right to demand the same high level of safety regardless of the area in which ships operate.

(5) In view of the internal market dimension of maritime transport of passengers, action at Community level is the most effective way of establishing a common minimum level of safety for ships throughout the EU.

(6) Action at EU level is the best way to ensure the harmonised enforcement of principles agreed on within the International Maritime Organisation (IMO), thus avoiding distortions of competition between the operators of ro-ro passenger ships operating in the EU.

(7) General stability requirements for ro-ro passenger ships in damaged condition were established at international level by the 1990 Safety of Life at Sea (SOLAS 90) Conference and were included in Regulation II-1/B/8 of the SOLAS Convention (SOLAS 90 standard). These requirements are applicable in the entire Community owing to the direct application to international voyages of the SOLAS Convention and the application to domestic voyages of Council Directive 98/18/EC of 17 March 1998 on safety rules and standards for passenger ships.[54]

---

47 COM (2016) 371 final, 6 June 2016.
48 See COM(2015) 508.
49 OJ L123/22, 17 May 2003.
50 Dir. 2003/25, Art. 14.
51 OJ L48/19, 19 February 2005.
52 OJ L311/1, 21 November 2008.
53 OJ C20 E, 28 January 2003, p. 21.
54 Ed., OJ L144/1, 15 May 1998.

(8) The SOLAS 90 damage stability standard implicitly includes the effect of water entering the ro-ro deck in a sea state of the order of 1,5 m significant wave height.

(9) IMO Resolution 14 of the 1995 SOLAS Conference, allowed IMO members to conclude regional agreements if they consider that prevailing sea conditions and other local conditions require specific stability requirements in a designated area.

(10) Eight northern European countries, including seven Member States, agreed in Stockholm on 28 February 1996 to introduce a higher stability standard for ro-ro passenger ships in damaged condition in order to take into account the effect of water accumulation on the ro-ro deck and to enable the ship to survive in more severe states than the SOLAS 90 standard, up to 4 m significant wave heights.

(11) Under this agreement, known as the Stockholm Agreement, the specific stability standard is directly related to the sea area in which the vessel operates and more particularly to the significant wave height recorded in the area of operation; the significant wave height of the area where the ship operates determines the height of water on the car deck that would arise following the occurrence of accidental damage.

(12) At the conclusion of the Conference at which the Stockholm Agreement was adopted, the Commission noted that the Agreement was not applicable in other parts of the Community and announced its intention to examine the prevailing local conditions under which ro-ro passenger ships sail in all European waters and to take appropriate initiatives.

(13) The Council entered a statement in the minutes of the 2074th Council meeting of 17 March 1998 stressing the need to ensure the same level of safety for all passenger ferries operating in similar conditions, whether on international or on domestic voyages.

(14) In its Resolution of 5 October 2000 on the sinking of the Greek ferry 'Samina' ..., the European Parliament expressly stated that it awaited the evaluation by the Commission of the effectiveness of the Stockholm Agreement and other measures for improving the stability and safety of passenger ships.

(15) Following an expert study by the Commission, the wave height conditions in south European waters were found to be similar to those in the north. While meteorological conditions may be generally more favourable in the south, the stability standard determined in the context of the Stockholm Agreement is based solely on the significant wave height parameter and the way this influences the accumulation of water on the ro-ro deck.

(16) The application of EU safety standards regarding the stability requirements for ro-ro passenger ships is essential for the safety of these vessels and has to be part of the common maritime safety framework.

(17) In the interests of improving safety and avoiding distortion of competition, the common safety standards regarding stability should apply to all ro-ro passenger ships, regardless of the flag that they fly, providing regular services to or from a port in the Member States on international voyages.

(18) The safety of ships is primarily the responsibility of flag States and therefore each Member State should ensure compliance with the safety requirements applicable to the ro-ro passenger ships flying the flag of that Member State.

(19) Member States should also be addressed in their capacity as host States. The responsibilities exercised in that capacity are based on specific port State responsibilities that are fully in line with the 1982 United Nations Convention on the Law of the Sea (UNCLOS).

(20) The specific stability requirements introduced by this Directive should be based on a method, as set out in the Annexes to the Stockholm Agreement, which calculates the height of water on the ro-ro deck following collision damage in relation to two basic parameters: the ship's residual freeboard and the significant wave height in the sea area where the ship operates.

(21) Member States should determine and publicise the significant wave heights in the sea areas crossed by ro-ro passenger ships on regular service to or from their ports. For international routes the significant wave heights should, wherever applicable and possible, be established in agreement between the States at both ends of the route. Significant wave heights for seasonal operation in the same sea areas may also be determined.

(22) Every ro-ro passenger ship engaged in voyages within the scope of this Directive should fulfil the stability requirements in relation to the significant wave heights determined for its area of operation. It should carry a certificate of compliance issued by the Administration of the flag State, which should be accepted by all other Member States.

(23) The SOLAS 90 Standard provides a level of safety equivalent to the specific stability requirements established by this Directive for ships operating in sea areas where the significant wave height is equal to or less than 1,5 m.

(24) In view of the structural modifications that the existing ro-ro passenger ships may need to undergo in order to comply with the specific stability requirements, those requirements should be introduced over a period of years in order to allow to the part of the industry affected sufficient time to comply: to that end, a phasing-in timetable for existing ships should be provided. This phasing-in timetable should not affect the enforcement of the specific stability requirements in the sea areas covered by the Annexes to the Stockholm Agreement.

(25) Article 4(1)(e) of Council Directive 1999/35/EC of 29 April 1999 on a system of mandatory surveys for the safe operation of regular ro-ro ferry and high-speed passenger craft services[55] provides that host States are to check that ro-ro passenger ferries and high-speed passenger craft comply with specific stability requirements adopted at regional level and transposed into their national legislation, when these ships operate a service covered by that national legislation in the region concerned.

(26) High-speed passenger craft as defined in Regulation 1 of Chapter X of the SOLAS Convention, as amended, should not be required to comply with the provisions of this Directive, provided that they comply entirely with the provisions of the IMO 'International code for safety of high-speed craft', as amended.

(27) The measures necessary for the implementation of this Directive should be adopted in accordance with Council Decision 1999/468/EC of 28 June 1999 laying down the procedures for the exercise of implementing powers conferred on the Commission.[56]

(28) Since the objective of the proposed action, namely to safeguard human life at sea by improving the survivability of ro-ro passenger ships in the event of damage, cannot be sufficiently achieved by the Member States and can therefore, by reason of the scale and effects of the action, be better achieved at EU level, the EU may adopt measures, in accordance with the principle of subsidiarity. ... In accordance with the principle of proportionality, ... this Directive does not go beyond what is necessary in order to achieve that objective."

Purpose of Directive 2003/25

34.043 Article 1 provides that the purpose of Directive 2003/25 is to lay down a uniform level of specific stability requirements for ro-ro passenger ships, which will improve the survivability of this type of vessel in case of collision damage and provide a high level of safety for the passengers and the crew.

Concepts in Directive 2003/25

34.044 Article 2 sets out the definitions for various concepts in the directive. The term "ro-ro passenger ship" is defined as meaning a ship carrying more than 12 passengers, having ro-ro cargo spaces or special category spaces, as defined in Regulation II-2/3 of the SOLAS Convention, as amended. The term "new ship" means a ship the keel of which is laid or which is at a similar stage of construction on or after 1 October 2004: a

---

55 Ed., OJ L138/1, 1 June 1999.
56 Ed., OJ L184/23, 17 July 1999.

similar stage of construction means the stage at which: (i) construction identifiable with a specific ship begins; and (ii) assembly of that ship has commenced comprising at least 50 tonnes or 1% of the estimated mass of structural material, whichever is less. By contrast, an "existing ship" means a ship which is not a new ship. The term "a passenger" means every person other than the master and the members of the crew or other persons employed or engaged in any capacity on board a ship on the business of that ship and other than a child under one year of age. The phrase "international Conventions" means the 1974 SOLAS Convention, and the 1966 International Convention on Load Lines, together with protocols and amendments thereto in force. The term "regular service" means a series of ro-ro passenger ship crossings serving traffic between the same two or more ports, which is operated either: (i) according to a published timetable; or (ii) with crossings so regular or frequent that they constitute a recognisable systematic series. The phrase "Stockholm Agreement" means the agreement concluded at Stockholm on 28 February 1996 in pursuance of SOLAS 95 Conference Resolution 14 "Regional agreements on specific stability requirements for ro-ro passenger ships", adopted on 29 November 1995. The term "administration of flag State" means the competent authorities of the State whose flag the ro-ro passenger ship is entitled to fly. The term "host State" means a Member State to or from whose ports a ro-ro passenger ship is engaged on a regular service. The term "international voyage" means a sea voyage from a port of a Member State to a port outside that Member State, or vice versa. The phrase "specific stability requirements" means the stability requirements set out in Annex I. The concept "significant wave height" means the average height of the highest third of wave heights observed over a given period. The term "residual freeboard" ("fr") means the minimum distance between the damaged ro-ro deck and the final waterline at the location of the damage, without taking into account the additional effect of the sea water accumulated on the damaged ro-ro deck.

Scope of Directive 2003/25

34.045 Article 3 describes the scope of the directive. Article 3(1) provides that the directive shall apply to all ro-ro passenger ships operating to or from a port of a Member State on a regular service, regardless of their flag, when engaged on international voyages. By virtue of Article 3(2), each Member State, in its capacity as host State, shall ensure that ro-ro passenger ships, flying the flag of a State which is not a Member State, comply fully with the requirements of the directive before they may be engaged on voyages from or to ports of that Member State in accordance with Article 4 of Directive 1999/35.

Significant wave heights ("hs")

34.046 Article 4 of Directive 2003/25 provides that the significant wave heights shall be used for determining the height of water on the car deck when applying the specific stability requirements contained in Annex I. The figures of significant wave heights shall be those which are not exceeded by a probability of more than 10% on a yearly basis.

Sea areas

34.047 Article 5(1) provides that host States had to establish, not later than 17 May 2004, a list of sea areas crossed by ro-ro passenger ships operating on regular service to or from their ports as well as the corresponding values of significant wave heights in these areas. Article 5(2) provides that the sea areas and the applicable values of the significant wave height in these areas shall be defined by agreement between the Member States or, wherever applicable and possible, between Member States and third countries at both ends of the route. Where the ship's route crosses more than one sea area, the ship shall satisfy the specific stability requirements for the highest value of significant wave height identified for these areas. Article 5(3) states that the list shall be notified to the Commission and published in a public database available in the internet site of the competent maritime authority. The location of such information as well as any updates to the list and the reasons for such updates shall also be notified to the Commission.

Specific stability requirements

34.048 Stability of ro-ro ferries is a significant issue and instability has given rise to various incidents. Article 6 thus provides:

"1. Without prejudice to the requirements of Regulation II-I/B/8 of the SOLAS Convention (SOLAS 90 standard) relating to watertight subdivision and stability in damaged condition, all ro-ro passenger ships referred to in Article 3(1) shall comply with the specific stability requirements set out in Annex I to this Directive.
2. For ro-ro passenger ships operating exclusively in sea areas where the significant wave height is equal to or lower than 1,5 metres, compliance with the requirements of the regulation referred to in paragraph 1 shall be considered equivalent to compliance with the specific stability requirements set out in Annex I.
3. In applying the requirements set out in Annex I, Member States shall use the guidelines set out in Annex II, in so far this is practicable and compatible with the design of the ship in question."

Introduction of the specific stability requirements

34.049 Article 7 continues the theme of stability. It provides:

"1. New ro-ro passenger ships shall comply with the specific stability requirements as set out in Annex I.
2. Existing ro-ro passenger ships, with the exception of those ships to which Article 6(2) applies, shall comply with the specific stability requirements as set out in Annex I not later than 1 October 2010.
   Existing ro-ro passenger ships which on 17 May 2003 are in compliance with the requirements of the regulation referred to in Article 6(1) shall comply with the specific stability requirements as set out in Annex I not later than 1 October 2015.
3. This Article shall be without prejudice to Article 4(1)(e) of Directive 1999/35."

Certificates

34.050 Article 8(1) provides that all new and existing ro-ro passenger ships flying the flag of a Member State must carry a certificate confirming compliance with the specific stability requirements established in Article 6 and Annex I. This certificate, which must be issued by the administration of the flag State and may be combined with other related certificates, will indicate the significant wave height up to which the ship can satisfy the specific stability requirements. The certificate must remain valid as long as the ship operates in an area with the same or a lower value of significant wave height. Article 8(2) then provides that each Member State acting in its capacity as host State shall recognise certificates issued by another Member State in pursuance of Directive 2003/25. Under Article 8(3), each Member State acting in its capacity as host State must accept certificates issued by a third country certifying that a ship complies with the specific stability requirements established.

Seasonal and short-time period operations

34.051 It is sometimes difficult to envisage that the full rigours of the regime should apply to short term or seasonal services but every life is precious so there is an element of balance involved. So Article 9 provides:

"1. If a shipping company operating a regular service on a year-round basis wishes to introduce additional ro-ro passenger ships to operate for a shorter period on that service, it shall notify the competent authority of the host State or States not later than one month before the said ships are operated on that service. However, in cases where, following unforeseen circumstances, a replacement ro-ro passenger ship must be introduced rapidly to ensure continuity of service, Directive 1999/35/EC shall apply.
2. If a shipping company wishes to operate seasonally a regular service for a shorter time period not exceeding six months a year, it shall notify the competent authority of the host State or States not later than three months before such operation takes place.
3. Where such operations take place under conditions of lower significant wave height than those established for the same sea area for all-year-round operation, the significant wave height value applicable for this shorter time period may be used by the competent authority for determining the height of water on the deck when applying the specific stability requirements contained in Annex I. The value of the significant wave height applicable for this shorter time period shall be agreed between the Member States or, wherever applicable and possible, between Member States and third countries at both ends of the route.
4. Following agreement of the competent authority of the host State or States for operations within the meaning of paragraphs 1 and 2, the ro-ro passenger ship which undertakes such operations shall be required to carry a certificate confirming compliance with the provisions of this Directive, as provided for in Article 8(1)."

Adaptations and committee procedure

34.052 Article 10 of Directive 2003/25 provides that Annex I sets out the "specific stability requirements for Ro-Ro passenger ships" as referred to in Article 6. Annex II contains the indicative guidelines to national administrations as referred to in Article 6(3). The directive may be amended by the Commission in order to take account of developments at international level, in particular in the IMO, and to improve the effectiveness of this directive in the light of experience and technical progress. Those measures, designed to amend non-essential elements of this directive, shall be adopted in accordance with the regulatory procedure with scrutiny referred to in Article 11(2). Article 11 deals with the Committee procedure.

Committee procedure

34.053 Article 11(1) provides that the Commission must be assisted by the COSS established by Article 3 of Regulation 2099/2002 of the European Parliament and of the Council.[57] Where reference is made to Article 11(2) then, Article 5a(1) to (4) and Article 7 of Decision 1999/468 shall apply, having regard to the provisions of Article 8 thereof.

Penalties

34.054 Member States must lay down the rules on penalties applicable to infringements of the national provisions adopted pursuant to the directive and must take all the measures necessary to ensure that they are implemented.[58] The penalties provided for shall be effective, proportionate and dissuasive.[59] This formulation is deliberate: it obliges Member States to adopt penalties but leaves to the Member State the choice of penalties so long as the penalties chosen conform with the criteria set out in the directive. This is an attempt to reconcile the ambition of the EU (particularly the Commission) with the reality that sovereignty remains with the Member State.

Implementation

34.055 Under Article 13, Member States had to bring into force the laws, regulations and administrative provisions necessary to comply with the directive before 17 November 2004. They had to forthwith inform the Commission of such measures. When Member States adopted these measures, they had to contain a reference to the directive or be accompanied by such a reference on the occasion of their official publication. The methods of making such reference were to be laid down by the Member States.

F. DIRECTIVE 2009/45 OF THE EUROPEAN PARLIAMENT AND OF THE COUNCIL OF 6 MAY 2009 ON SAFETY RULES AND STANDARDS FOR PASSENGER SHIPS

Introduction

34.056 Directive 2009/45 of the European Parliament and of the Council of 6 May 2009 on safety rules and standards for passenger ships[60] is a cornerstone of the EU legislation as safety rules and standards for passenger ships. It is not just confined to ro-ro vessels but covers passenger ships and high-speed craft. It introduced uniform safety standards for such vessels. It does not apply to vessels with fewer than 12 passengers. It entered into force on the twentieth day following its publication of the directive in the *Official Journal* – it was published on 25 June 2009.

---

57 OJ L324/1, 29 November 2002.
58 Dir. 2003/25, Art. 1.
59 Dir. 2003/25, Art. 1.
60 OJ L163/1, 25 June 2009.

34.057 Directive 2009/45 was amended by: (a) Commission Directive 2010/36 of 1 June 2010[61] and (b) Commission Directive 2016/844 of 27 May 2016.[62] A corrigendum has also been published.[63]

34.058 The legal basis for Directive 2009/45 was the TEC and, in particular, Article 80(2) of the TEC. This provision is now Article 100(2) of the TFEU.

34.059 The legislative history included the proposal from the Commission, an opinion of the EESC and a consultation with the Committee of the Regions. It repealed, by virtue of Article 17, Directive 98/18. It entered into force, by virtue of Article 18, on the twentieth day following its publication in the *Official Journal* it was published on 25 June 2009.

34.060 The background is clear from the recitals of the directive as adopted originally:

"(1) Council Directive 98/18 ... of 17 March 1998 on safety rules and standards for passenger ships[64] has been substantially amended several times. ... Since further amendments are to be made, it should be recast in the interests of clarity.

(2) Within the framework of the common transport policy measures must be adopted to enhance safety in maritime transport.

(3) The EU is seriously concerned about shipping casualties in which passenger ships were involved resulting in a massive loss of life. Persons using passenger ships and high-speed passenger craft throughout the EU have the right to expect and to rely on an appropriate level of safety on board.

(4) Work equipment and personal protective equipment of workers are not covered by this Directive, because the provisions of Council Directive 89/391 ... of 12 June 1989 on the introduction of measures to encourage improvements in the safety and health of workers at work[65] and the relevant provisions of its relevant individual directives are applicable to the use of such equipment on passenger ships engaged on domestic voyages.

(5) The provision of maritime passenger transport services between Member States has already been liberalised by Council Regulation ... 4055/86 of 22 December 1986 applying the principle of freedom to provide services to maritime transport between Member States and between Member States and third countries.[66] The application of the principle of freedom to provide services to maritime transport within Member States (maritime cabotage) has been provided for by Council Regulation ... 3577/92.[67]

(6) To attain a high level of safety, and to remove barriers to trade, it is necessary to establish harmonised safety standards at an appropriate level for passenger ships and craft operating domestic services. Standards for vessels operating international voyages are being developed within the International Maritime Organization (IMO). Procedures to request action at the IMO in order to bring the standards for international voyages into line with the standards of this Directive should be available.

(7) In view, in particular, of the internal market dimension of maritime passenger transport, action at Community level is the only possible way to establish a common level of safety for ships throughout the Community.

(8) In view of the principle of proportionality, a Directive is the appropriate legal instrument as it provides a framework for a uniform and compulsory application of the safety standards by Member States, while leaving to each Member State the right to decide the implementation tools that best fit its internal system.

---

61 OJ L162/1, 29 June 2010.
62 OJ L141/51, 28 May 2016.
63 OJ L193/117, 19 July 2016.
64 Ed., OJ L144/1, 15 May 1998.
65 Ed., OJ L183/1, 29 June 1989.
66 Ed., OJ L378/1, 31 December 1986. See chap. 7.
67 Ed., OJ L364/7, 12 December 1992. See chap. 7.

(9)   In the interests of improving safety and avoiding distortions of competition the common safety requirements should apply to passenger ships and high-speed passenger craft engaged on domestic voyages in the Community, irrespective of the flag they fly. It is, however, necessary to exclude some categories of ships for which the rules of this Directive are technically unsuitable or economically unviable.

(10)   Passenger ships should be divided into different classes depending upon the range and conditions of the sea areas in which they operate. High-speed passenger craft should be categorised in accordance with the provisions of the High-Speed Craft Code established by the IMO.

(11)   The main reference framework for the safety standards should be the 1974 International Convention for the Safety of Life at Sea (the 1974 SOLAS Convention), as amended, which encompasses internationally agreed standards for passenger ships and high-speed passenger craft engaged on international voyages, as well as appropriate Resolutions adopted by the IMO and other measures complementing and interpreting that Convention.

(12)   The various classes of both new and existing passenger ships require a different approach for establishing safety requirements guaranteeing an equivalent safety level in view of the specific needs and limitations of those various classes. It is appropriate to make distinctions in the safety requirements to be respected as between new and existing ships since imposing the rules for new ships on existing ships would involve such extensive structural changes as to make them economically unviable.

(13)   The financial and technical implications arising from the upgrading of existing ships to the standards provided for by this Directive justify certain transitional periods.

(14)   In view of the substantial differences in the design, construction and use of high-speed passenger craft compared to traditional passenger ships, such craft should be required to respect special rules.

(15)   Shipborne marine equipment, complying with the provisions of Council Directive 96/98 ... of 20 December 1996 on marine equipment,[68] when installed on board a passenger ship, should not be subject to additional tests since such equipment is already subject to the standards and procedures of that Directive.

(16)   Directive 2003/25 ... of the European Parliament and of the Council of 14 April 2003 on specific stability requirements for ro-ro passenger ships[69] introduced strengthened stability requirements for ro-ro passenger vessels operating on international services to and from Community ports, and this enhanced measure should also apply to certain categories of such vessels operating on domestic services under the same sea conditions. Failure to apply such stability requirements should be grounds for phasing out ro-ro passenger ships after a certain number of years of operation. In view of the structural modifications that the existing ro-ro passenger ships may need to undergo in order to comply with the specific stability requirements, those requirements should be introduced over a period of years in order to give the part of the industry affected sufficient time to comply: to that end, provision should be made for a phasing-in timetable for existing ships. This phasing-in timetable should not affect the enforcement of the specific stability requirements in the sea areas covered by the Annexes to the Stockholm Agreement of 28 February 1996.

(17)   It is important to apply appropriate measures to ensure access in safe conditions for persons with reduced mobility to passenger ships and high-speed passenger craft operating on domestic services in the Member States.

(18)   Subject to control under the Committee procedure, Member States may adopt additional safety requirements if justified by local circumstances, permit the use of equivalent standards, or adopt exemptions from the provisions of this Directive under certain operating conditions, or adopt safeguard measures in exceptional dangerous circumstances.

(19)   Regulation ... 2099/2002 of the European Parliament and of the Council of 5 November 2002 establishing a Committee on Safe Seas and the Prevention of Pollution from Ships

---

68 Ed., OJ L46/25, 17 February 1997.
69 Ed., OJ L123/22, 17 May 2003.

(COSS)[70] centralised the tasks of the committees established under the pertinent Community legislation on maritime safety, the prevention of pollution from ships and the protection of shipboard living and working conditions.

(20) The measures necessary for the implementation of this Directive should be adopted in accordance with Council Decision 1999/468/EC of 28 June 1999 laying down the procedures for the exercise of implementing powers conferred on the Commission.[71]

(21) In particular, the Commission should be empowered to adapt certain provisions of this Directive, including its Annexes, to take account of developments at international level and specifically amendments to International Conventions. Since those measures are of general scope and are designed to amend non-essential elements of this Directive, they must be adopted in accordance with the regulatory procedure with scrutiny provided for in Article 5a of Decision 1999/468/EC.

(22) In order to monitor the effective implementation and enforcement of this Directive, surveys should be carried out on new and existing passenger ships and craft. Compliance with this Directive should be certified by or on behalf of the Administration of the flag State.

(23) In order to ensure full application of this Directive, Member States should lay down a system of penalties for breach of the national provisions adopted pursuant to this Directive and should monitor compliance with the provisions of this Directive on the basis of provisions modelled on those laid down in Council Directive 95/21/EC of 19 June 1995 on port State control of shipping.[72]

(24) The new elements introduced into this Directive only concern the committee procedures. They therefore do not need to be transposed by the Member States.

(25) This Directive should be without prejudice to the obligations of the Member States relating to the time-limits for transposition into national law and application of the Directives set out in Annex IV, Part B."

Purposes of Directive 2009/45

34.061 The purpose of Directive 2009/45 is described in Article 1 which states that the purpose of the directive is to introduce a uniform level of safety of life and property on new and existing passenger ships and high-speed passenger craft, when both categories of ships and craft are engaged on domestic voyages, and to lay down procedures for negotiation at international level with a view to a harmonisation of the rules for passenger ships engaged on international voyages.[73]

Definitions for the purposes of Directive 2009/45

34.062 For the purposes of Directive 2009/45, Article 2 sets out a number of definitions:

"(a) 'International Conventions' means the 1974 International Convention for the Safety of Life at Sea (the 1974 SOLAS Convention), as amended, and the 1966 International Convention on Load Lines, together with the Protocols and amendments thereto;

(b) 'Intact Stability Code' means the 'Code on Intact Stability for all types of ships covered by IMO Instruments' contained in IMO Assembly Resolution A.749(18) of 4 November 1993, as amended;

---

70 Ed., OJ L324/1, 29 November 2002.
71 Ed., OJ L184/23, 17 July 1999.
72 Ed., OJ L157/1, 3 July 1995.
73 Dir. 2009/45, Art. 1.

(c) 'High Speed Craft Code' means the 'International Code for Safety of High Speed Craft' contained in IMO Resolution MSC 36 (63) of 20 May 1994, or the International Code for Safety of High-Speed Craft, 2000 (2000 HSC Code), contained in IMO Resolution MSC.97(73) of December 2000, in their up-to-date versions;

(d) 'GMDSS' means the Global Maritime Distress and Safety System as laid down in Chapter IV of the 1974 SOLAS Convention, as amended;

(e) 'a passenger ship' means a ship which carries more than 12 passengers;

(f) 'ro-ro passenger ship' means a ship carrying more than 12 passengers, having ro-ro cargo spaces or special category spaces, as defined in Regulation II-2/A/2 contained in Annex I;

(g) 'high-speed passenger craft' means a high-speed craft as defined in Regulation X/1 of the 1974 SOLAS Convention, as amended, which carries more than 12 passengers, with the exception of passenger ships engaged on domestic voyages in sea areas of Class B, C or D when: (i) their displacement corresponding to the design waterline is less than 500 m3; and (ii) their maximum speed, as defined in Regulation 1.4.30 of the 1994 High Speed Craft Code and Regulation 1.4.37 of the 2000 High Speed Craft Code, is less than 20 knots;

(h) 'new ship' means a ship the keel of which was laid or which was at a similar stage of construction on or after 1 July 1998; a 'similar stage of construction' means the stage at which:

(i) construction identifiable with a specific ship begins; and (ii) assembly of that ship has commenced comprising at least 50 tonnes or 1% of the estimated mass of all structural material, whichever is less;

(i) 'existing ship' means a ship which is not a new ship;

(j) 'age' means the age of the ship, expressed in terms of the number of years after the date of its delivery;

(k) 'passenger' means every person other than: (i) the master and the members of the crew or other persons employed or engaged in any capacity on board a ship on the business of that ship; and (ii) a child under one year of age;

(l) 'length of a ship', unless expressly provided otherwise, means 96% of the total length on a water line at 85% of the least moulded depth measured from the top of the keel, or the length from the fore side of the stem to the axis of the rudder stock on that waterline, if that be greater. In ships designed with a rake of keel the waterline on which this length is measured shall be parallel to the designed waterline;

(m) 'bow height' means the bow height defined in Regulation 39 of the 1966 International Convention on Load Lines as the vertical distance at the forward perpendicular between the waterline corresponding to the assigned summer freeboard and the designed trim and the top of the exposed deck at side;

(n) 'ship with a full deck' means a ship that is provided with a complete deck, exposed to weather and sea, which has permanent means of closing all openings in the weatherpart thereof and below which all openings in the sides of the ship are fitted with permanent means of at least weathertight closing;

the complete deck may be a watertight deck or equivalent structure consisting of a non-watertight deck completely covered by a weathertight structure of adequate strength to maintain the weathertight integrity and fitted with weathertight closing appliances;

(o) 'international voyage' means a voyage by sea from a port of a Member State to a port outside that Member State, or conversely;

(p) 'domestic voyage' means a voyage in sea areas from a port of a Member State to the same or another port within that Member State;

(q) 'sea area' means an area as established pursuant to Article 4(2);

however, for the application of the provisions on radiocommunication, the definitions of sea areas will be those defined in Regulation 2, Chapter IV of the 1974 SOLAS Convention, as amended;

(r) 'port area' means an area other than a sea area, as defined by the Member States, extending to the outermost permanent harbour works forming an integral part of the harbour system, or to the limits defined by natural geographical features protecting an estuary or similar sheltered area;

(s) 'place of refuge' means any naturally or artificially sheltered area which may be used as a shelter by a ship or craft under conditions likely to endanger its safety;

(t) 'Administration of the flag State' means the competent authorities of the State whose flag the ship or craft is entitled to fly;

(u) 'host State' means a Member State to or from whose port(s) a ship or craft, flying a flag other than the flag of that Member State, is carrying out domestic voyages;

(v) 'recognised organisation' means an organisation recognised in conformity with Article 4 of Council Directive 94/57/EC of 22 November 1994 on common rules and standards for ship inspection and survey organisations and for the relevant activities of maritime administrations;

(w) 'a mile' is 1 852 metres;

(x) 'significant wave height' means the average height of the highest third of wave heights observed over a given period;

(y) 'persons with reduced mobility' means anyone who has a particular difficulty when using public transport, including elderly persons, disabled persons, persons with sensory impairments and wheelchair users, pregnant women and persons accompanying small children."

Scope of Directive 2009/45

34.063 Article 3(1) of Directive 2009/45 provides that the directive applies to the following passenger ships and craft, regardless of their flag,[74] when engaged on domestic voyages: (a) new passenger ships; (b) existing passenger ships of 24 metres in length and above; and (c) high-speed passenger craft. Each Member State, in its capacity as host State, must ensure that passenger ships and high-speed passenger craft, flying the flag of a State which is not a Member State, fully comply with the requirements of the directive, before they may be engaged on domestic voyages in that Member State.

34.064 Article 3(2) limits the scope of the directive by stating that the directive does not apply to: (a) passenger ships which are: (i) ships of war and troopships; (ii) ships not propelled by mechanical means; (iii) vessels constructed in material other than steel or equivalent and not covered by the standards concerning High Speed Craft (Resolution MSC 36 (63) or MSC.97 (73)) or Dynamically Supported Craft (Resolution A.373 (X)); (iv) wooden ships of primitive build; (v) original, and individual replicas of, historical passenger ships designed before 1965, built predominantly with the original materials; (vi) pleasure yachts unless they are or will be crewed and carrying more than 12 passengers for commercial purposes; or (vii) ships exclusively engaged in port areas; and (b) high-speed passenger craft which are: (i) craft of war and troopcraft; (ii) pleasure craft, unless they are or will be crewed and carrying more than 12 passengers for commercial purposes; or (iii) craft exclusively engaged in port areas. So, in reality, the limitation is limited.

Classes of passenger ships

34.065 Article 4(1) provides that passenger ships are divided into the following classes according to the sea area in which they operate:

" 'Class A' means a passenger ship engaged on domestic voyages other than voyages covered by Classes B, C and D.

---

74 This is important because it avoids the possibility of circumventing the regime by simply flagging out.

'Class B' means a passenger ship engaged on domestic voyages in the course of which it is at no time more than 20 miles from the line of coast, where shipwrecked persons can land, corresponding to the medium tide height.

'Class C' means a passenger ship engaged on domestic voyages in sea areas where the probability of exceeding 2,5 metres significant wave height is smaller than 10% over a one-year period for all-year-round operation, or over a specific restricted period of the year for operation exclusively in such period (e.g. summer period operation), in the course of which it is at no time more than 15 miles from a place of refuge, nor more than 5 miles from the line of coast, where shipwrecked persons can land, corresponding to the medium tide height.

'Class D' means a passenger ship engaged on domestic voyages in sea areas where the probability of exceeding 1,5 metres significant wave height is smaller than 10% over a one-year period for all-year-round operation, or over a specific restricted period of the year for operation exclusively in such period (e.g. summer period operation), in the course of which it is at no time more than 6 miles from a place of refuge, nor more than 3 miles from the line of coast, where shipwrecked persons can land, corresponding to the medium tide height."

34.066 Article 4(2) provides that each Member State must: (a) establish, and update when necessary, a list of sea areas under its jurisdiction, delimiting the zones for all-year-round operation and, where appropriate, restricted periodical operation of the classes of ships, using the criteria for classes set out in Article 4(1); (b) publish the list in a public database available on the internet site of the competent maritime authority; and (c) notify to the Commission the location of such information, and when modifications are made to the list.

34.067 Under Article 4(3), for high speed passenger craft the categories defined in Chapter 1 (1.4.10) and (1.4.11) of the HSC Code 1994, or Chapter 1 (1.4.12) and (1.4.13) of the HSC Code 2000 shall apply.

Application of Directive 2009/45

34.068 Article 5(1) provides that both new and existing passenger ships and high-speed passenger craft, when engaged on domestic voyages, must comply with the relevant safety rules and standards laid down in the directive. Member States must not withhold from operation, for reasons arising from the directive, passenger ships or high-speed passenger craft, when engaged on domestic voyages, which comply with the requirements of this directive, including any additional requirements imposed by a Member State in accordance with Article 9(1). Each Member State, acting in its capacity as host State, must recognise the High Speed Craft Safety Certificate and Permit to Operate issued by another Member State for high-speed passenger craft, when engaged on domestic voyages, or the Passenger Ship Safety Certificate referred to in Article 13 issued by another Member State for passenger ships when engaged on domestic voyages. A host State may inspect a passenger ship or a high-speed passenger craft, when engaged on domestic voyages, and audit its documentation, in accordance with the provisions of Directive 95/21.[75] All shipborne marine equipment, as listed in Annex A.1 to Directive 96/98 and complying with the provisions of the latter, shall be considered to be in conformity with the provisions of the directive, whether or not Annex I to this directive requires equipment to be approved and subjected to tests to the satisfaction of the Administration of the flag State.[76]

---

75 Dir. 2009/45, Art. 5(3).
76 Dir. 2009/45, Art. 5(4).

Safety requirements

34.069 Article 6(1) states that with regard to new and existing passenger ships of Classes A, B, C and D:

"(a) the construction and maintenance of the hull, main and auxiliary machinery, electrical and automatic plants shall comply with the standards specified for classification by the rules of a recognised organisation, or equivalent rules used by an Administration in accordance with Article 14(2) of Directive 94/57/EC;

(b) the provisions of Chapters IV, including the 1988 GMDSS amendments, V and VI of the 1974 SOLAS Convention, as amended, shall apply;

(c) the provisions for shipborne navigational equipment of Regulations 17, 18, 19, 20 and 21, Chapter V of the 1974 SOLAS Convention, in its up-to-date version, shall apply. Shipborne navigational equipment, as listed in Annex A(1) to Directive 96/98/EC and complying with the provisions of the latter, is considered to be in conformity with the type approval requirements of Regulation 18.1, Chapter V of the 1974 SOLAS Convention."

34.070 Article 6(2) then provides with regard to new passenger ships:

"(a) general requirements:

    (i) new passenger ships of Class A shall comply entirely with the requirements of the 1974 SOLAS Convention, as amended, and with the specific relevant requirements specified in this Directive; for those regulations for which the 1974 SOLAS Convention, as amended, leaves the interpretation to the discretion of the Administration, the Administration of the flag State shall apply the interpretations as contained in Annex I to this Directive;

    (ii) new passenger ships of Classes B, C, and D shall comply with the specific relevant requirements specified in this Directive;

(b) load line requirements:

    (i) all new passenger ships of 24 metres in length and above shall comply with the 1966 International Convention on Load Lines;

    (ii) criteria with a level of safety equivalent to those of the 1966 International Convention on Load Lines shall be applied, in relation to length and Class, to new passenger ships of less than 24 metres in length;

    (iii) notwithstanding points (i) and (ii), new passenger ships of Class D are exempted from the minimum bow height requirement laid down in the 1966 International Convention on Load Lines;

    (iv) new passenger ships of Classes A, B, C, and D shall have a full deck."

34.071 Article 6(3) deals with existing passenger ships:

"(a) existing passenger ships of Class A shall comply with the regulations for existing passenger ships defined in the 1974 SOLAS Convention, as amended, and with the specific relevant requirements in this Directive; for those regulations for which the 1974 SOLAS Convention, as amended, leaves the interpretation to the discretion of the Administration, the Administration of the flag State shall apply the interpretations as contained in Annex I to this Directive;

(b) existing passenger ships of Class B shall comply with the specific relevant requirements in this Directive;

(c) existing passenger ships of Classes C and D shall comply with the specific relevant requirements in this Directive and in respect of matters not covered by such requirements with the rules of the Administration of the flag State; such rules shall provide an equivalent level of safety to that of Chapters II-1 and II-2 of Annex I, while taking into account the specific local operational conditions related to the sea areas in which ships of such classes may operate;

before existing passenger ships of Classes C and D can be engaged on regular domestic voyages in a host State, the Administration of the flag State shall obtain concurrence of the host State on such rules;

(d) where a Member State is of the view that rules required by the Administration of the host State pursuant to point (c) are unreasonable, it shall immediately notify the Commission thereof; the Commission shall initiate proceedings in order to take a decision in accordance with the procedure referred to in Article 11(2);

(e) repairs, alterations and modifications of a major character and outfitting related thereto shall be in compliance with the requirements for new ships as prescribed in point (a) of paragraph 2; alterations made to an existing ship which are intended solely to achieve a higher survivability standard shall not be regarded as modifications of a major character;

(f) the provisions of point (a), unless earlier dates are specified in the 1974 SOLAS Convention, as amended, and the provisions of points (b) and (c), unless earlier dates are specified in Annex I to this Directive, shall not be applied in relation to a ship the keel of which was laid or which was at a similar stage of construction:

>   (i)   before 1 January 1940: until 1 July 2006;
>   (ii) on or after 1 January 1940 but before 31 December 1962: until 1 July 2007;
>   (iii) on or after 1 January 1963 but before 31 December 1974: until 1 July 2008;
>   (iv) on or after 1 January 1975 but before 31 December 1984: until 1 July 2009;
>   (v)   on or after 1 January 1985 but before 1 July 1998: until 1 July 2010."

34.072 Article 6(4) deals with high-speed passenger craft:

"(a) high speed passenger craft constructed or subjected to repairs, alterations or modifications of a major character on or after 1 January 1996 shall comply with the requirements of Regulation X/2 and X/3 of the 1974 SOLAS Convention, unless

>   – their keel was laid or they were at a similar stage of construction not later than June 1998, and
>   – delivery and commissioning has taken place not later than December 1998, and
>   – they fully comply with the requirements of the Code of Safety for Dynamically Supported Craft (DSC Code) in IMO Resolution A.373(X) as amended by IMO Resolution MSC.37(63);

(b) high-speed passenger craft constructed before 1 January 1996 and complying with the requirements of the High-Speed Craft Code shall continue operation certified under that Code;

high-speed passenger craft constructed before 1 January 1996 and not complying with the requirements of the High-Speed Craft Code may not be engaged on domestic voyages unless they were already in operation on domestic voyages in a Member State on 4 June 1998, in which case they may be allowed to continue their domestic operation in that Member State; such craft shall comply with the requirements of the DSC Code;

(c) the construction and maintenance of high-speed passenger craft and their equipment shall comply with the rules for the classification of high-speed craft of a recognised organisation, or equivalent rules used by an Administration in accordance with Article 14(2) of Directive 94/57."

Stability requirements and phasing-out of ro-ro passenger ships

34.073 Article 7(1) provides that all ro-ro passenger ships of Classes A, B and C, the keel of which was laid or which were at a similar stage of construction on or after 1 October 2004 shall comply with Articles 6, 8 and 9 of Directive 2003/25. Article 7(2) states that all ro-ro passenger ships of Classes A and B the keel of which was laid or which were at a similar stage of construction before 1 October 2004 shall comply with Articles 6, 8 and 9 of Directive 2003/25 by 1 October 2010, unless they are phased out on that date or on a later date on which they reach the age of 30 years, but in any case not later than 1 October 2015.

Safety requirements for persons with reduced mobility

34.074 Article 8(1) provides that Member States must ensure that appropriate measures are taken, based, where practicable, on the guidelines in Annex III, to enable persons with reduced mobility to have safe access to all passenger ships of Classes A, B, C and D and to all high-speed passenger craft used for public transport the keel of which was laid or which were at a similar stage of construction on or after 1 October 2004.

34.075 Article 8(2) provides that Member States must co-operate with and consult organisations representing persons with reduce mobility on the implementation of the guidelines included in Annex III.

34.076 Article 8(3) provides that for the purpose of modification of passenger ships of Classes A, B, C and D and high-speed passenger craft used for public transport the keel of which was laid or which were at a similar stage of construction before 1 October 2004, Member States shall apply the guidelines in Annex III as far as reasonable and practicable in economic terms. Member States must draw up a national action plan on how the guidelines are to be applied to such ships and craft. They had to forward that plan to the Commission not later than 17 May 2005.

34.077 Article 8(4) provides that Member States had to, no later than 17 May 2006, report to the Commission on the implementation of this article as regards all passenger ships referred to in paragraph 1, passenger ships referred to in paragraph 3 certified to carry more than 400 passengers and all high-speed passenger craft.

Additional safety requirements, equivalents, exemptions and safeguard measures

34.078 Article 9(1) states that if a Member State or group of Member States considers that the applicable safety requirements should be improved in certain situations due to specific local circumstances and if the need therefor is demonstrated, they may, subject to the procedure laid down in paragraph 4, adopt measures to improve the safety requirements.

34.079 Under Article 9(2), a Member State may, subject to the procedure laid down in paragraph 4, adopt measures allowing equivalents for the regulations contained in Annex I, provided that such equivalents are at least as effective as such regulations.

34.080 Article 9(3) states that provided there is no reduction in the level of safety and subject to the procedure laid down in paragraph 4, a Member State may adopt measures to exempt ships from certain specific requirements of this directive for domestic voyages to be carried out in that State, including in its archipelagic sea areas sheltered from open sea effects, under certain operating conditions, such as smaller significant wave height, restricted year period, voyages only during daylight time or under suitable climatic or weather conditions, or restricted trip duration, or proximity of rescue services.

34.081 Article 9(4) provides that a Member State which avails itself of the provisions of paragraph 1, 2 or 3 must proceed in accordance with the Member State and must notify the Commission of the measures which it intends to adopt, including particulars to the extent necessary to confirm that the level of safety is adequately maintained. If, within a period of six months from the notification, it is decided, in accordance with the procedure referred to in Article 11(2), that the proposed measures are not justified, the said Member State shall be required to amend or not to adopt the proposed measures. The adopted measures must be specified in the relevant national legislation and communicated to the Commission, which shall inform the other Member States of all particulars thereof. Any such measures shall be applied to all passenger ships of the same Class or to craft when operating under the same specified conditions, without discrimination with regard to their flag or to the nationality or place of establishment of their operator. These measures referred to in paragraph 3 shall apply only for as long as the ship or craft operates under the specified conditions.

34.082 Article 6(5) provides that where a Member State considers that a passenger ship or craft operating on a domestic voyage within that State, notwithstanding the fact that it is complying with the provisions of the directive, creates a risk of serious danger to safety of life or property, or environment, the operation of that ship or craft may be suspended or additional safety measures may be imposed, until such time as the danger is removed. In these circumstances, the following procedure shall apply: (a) the Member State must inform the Commission and the other Member States of its decision without delay, giving substantiated reasons therefor; (b) the Commission must examine whether the suspension or the additional measures are justified for reasons of serious danger to safety and to the environment; (c) it shall be decided, in accordance with the procedure referred to in Article 11(2), whether or not the decision of the Member State to suspend the operation of such ship or craft or to impose the additional measures is justified for reasons of serious danger to safety of life or property, or to the environment, and, if the suspension or the measures are not justified, that the Member State concerned shall be required to withdraw the suspension or the measures.

Adaptations

34.083 Article 10(1) provides that the following may be adapted in order to take account of developments at international level, in particular within the IMO: (a) the definitions in points (a), (b), (c), (d) and (v) of Article 2; (b) the provisions relating to procedures and guidelines for surveys referred to in Article 12; (c) the provisions concerning the 1974 SOLAS Convention, as amended, and the HSC Code, including its subsequent amendments, laid down in Articles 4(3), 6(4), 12(3) and 13(3); (d) the specific references to the "International Conventions" and IMO resolutions referred to in points (g), (m) and (q) of Article 2, point (a) of Article 3(2), points (b) and (c) of Article 6(1), point (b) of Article 6(2) and Article 13(3).

34.084 Under Article 10(2) annexes may be amended in order to (a) apply, for the purpose of the directive, amendments made to the International Conventions; (b) improve the technical specifications thereof, in the light of experience.

34.085 The measures referred to in Article 10(1) and (2), designed to amend non-essential elements of the directive, must be adopted in accordance with the regulatory procedure with scrutiny referred to in Article 11(3).

34.086 Under Article 10(4) the amendments to the international instruments referred to in Article 2 of the directive may be excluded from the scope of the directive, pursuant to Article 5 of Regulation 2099/2002.

COSS Committee

34.087 Article 11 sets out the details on the COSS Committee. Article 11(1) provides that the Commission shall be assisted by the COSS established by Article 3 of Regulation 2099/2002. Article 11(2) provides that where reference is made to Article 11(2) then Articles 5 and 7 of Decision 1999/468 shall apply, having regard to the provisions of Article 8 thereof. The period laid down in Article 5(6) of Decision 1999/468 shall be set at two months. Article 11(3) provides that where reference is made to Article 11(3) then, Article 5a(1) to (4) and Article 7 of Decision 1999/468 shall apply, having regard to the provisions of Article 8 thereof.

Surveys

34.088 Each new passenger ship must, under Article 12, be subjected by the administration of the flag State to the surveys specified in points (a), (b) and (c): (a) a survey before the ship is put into service; (b) a periodical survey once every 12 months; and (c) additional surveys, as the occasion arises. Under Article 12(2), each existing passenger ship must be subjected by the Administration of the flag State to the surveys specified in points (a), (b) and (c): (a) an initial survey, before the ship is put into service on domestic voyages in a host State, for existing ships engaged on domestic voyages in the Member State the flag of which they are entitled to fly; (b) a periodical survey once every 12 months; and (c) additional surveys, as the occasion arises.

34.089 Each high-speed passenger craft having to comply, in accordance with the provisions of Article 6(4) of the directive, with the requirements of the HSC Code, must by virtue of Annex 12(3) be made subject by the Administration of the flag State to the surveys required in that Code. High-speed passenger craft having to comply, in accordance with Article 6(4) of this directive, with the requirements of the DSC Code must be made subject by the Administration of the flag State to the surveys required in the DSC Code.

34.090 Article 12(4) provides that the relevant procedures and guidelines for surveys for the Passenger Ship Safety Certificate specified in IMO Resolution A.997(25), as amended, "Survey guidelines under the harmonized system of survey and certification, 2007" or procedures designed to achieve the same goal, must be followed.

34.091 The surveys mentioned in Article 12(1), (2) and (3) must be carried out exclusively by the surveyors of the Administration of the flag State itself, or of a recognised organisation or of the Member State authorised by the flag State to carry out surveys, with the purpose of ensuring that all applicable requirements of the directive are complied with.[77]

---

77 Dir. 2009/45, Art. 12(5).

Certificates

34.092 Article 13(1) provides that all new and existing passenger ships must be provided with a Passenger Ship Safety Certificate in compliance with the directive.[78] The certificate must have a format as laid down in Annex II. This certificate must be issued by the Administration of the flag State after an initial survey, as described in point (a) of Article 12(1) and point (a) of Article 12(2), has been carried out. The Passenger Ship Safety Certificate must be issued for a period not exceeding 12 months.[79] The period of validity of the certificate may be extended by the Administration of the flag State for a period of grace of up to one month from the date of expiry stated on it.[80] When an extension has been granted, the new period of validity of the certificate shall start from the expiry date of the existing certificate before its extension.[81] Renewal of the Passenger Ship Safety Certificate must be issued after a periodical survey, as described in point (b) of Article 12(1) and point (b) of Article 12(2), has been carried out. Article 13(3) provides that for high-speed passenger craft complying with the requirements of the HSC Code, a High Speed Craft Safety Certificate and a Permit to Operate High Speed Craft must be issued by the Administration of the flag State, in accordance with the provisions of the HSC Code.

34.093 For high-speed passenger craft complying with the requirements of the DSC Code, a DSC Construction and Equipment Certificate and a DSC Permit to Operate must be issued by the Administration of the flag State, in accordance with the provisions of the DSC Code.

34.094 Before issuing the Permit to Operate for high-speed passenger craft engaged on domestic voyages in a host State, the Administration of the flag State shall concur with the host State on any operational conditions associated with operation of the craft in that State. Any such conditions shall be shown by the Administration of the flag State on the Permit to Operate. Exemptions granted to ships or craft under and in accordance with the provisions of Article 9(3) shall be noted on the ship's or the craft's certificate.

1974 SOLAS Convention regulations

34.095 Article 14(1) provides that with regard to passenger ships engaged on international voyages the EU must submit requests to the IMO: (a) to expedite the ongoing work within the IMO to revise the regulations of Chapters II-1, II-2 and III of the 1974 SOLAS Convention, as amended, containing issues left to the discretion of the Administration, to establish harmonised interpretations for those regulations and to adopt amendments to the latter accordingly; and (b) to adopt measures for mandatory application of the principles underlying the provisions of MSC Circular 606 on Port State Concurrence with SOLAS Exemptions. Article 14(2) provides that the requests referred to in paragraph 1 must be made by the Presidency of the Council and by the Commission, on the basis of the harmonised regulations laid down in Annex I. All Member States must do their utmost to ensure that the IMO undertakes the development of the said regulations and measures expeditiously.

---

78 This effectively unifies the approach of all Member States across the EU.
79 Dir. 2009/45, Art. 13(2).
80 Ibid.
81 Ibid.

Penalties

34.096 Under Article 15 Member States must lay down the rules on penalties applicable to infringements of the national provisions adopted pursuant to the directive and must take all the measures necessary to ensure that they are implemented. The penalties provided for must be effective, proportionate and dissuasive. This is the way in which the EU achieves the ambition of an effective regime but leaves it to the Member States to specify the exact penalty.

Notifications

34.097 Member States must immediately notify to the Commission the main provisions of national law which they adopt in the field covered by Directive 2009/45.[82] The Commission must inform the other Member States thereof.[83]

G. COMMISSION DECISION 2003/587 OF 5 AUGUST 2003 ON COMPLIANCE OF THE FIRE-EXTINGUISHING SYSTEM USED ON THE RO-RO FERRY "FINNSAILOR" (IMO NO 8401444) WITH COUNCIL DIRECTIVE 1999/35 OF 29 APRIL 1999

34.098 For completeness, it is proposed to examine a narrow and specific measure. In a decision addressed to Finland, the Commission adopted Decision 2003/587 on 5 August 2003 on compliance of the fire-extinguishing system used on the ro-ro ferry *Finnsailor* (IMO No 8401444) with Council Directive 1999/35 of 29 April 1999.[84] The decision became applicable 12 months after the date of its adoption.[85]

34.099 The background is clear from the recitals:

"(1) Council Directive 1999/35/EC provides for a system of mandatory surveys of ro-ro ferries on regular services to or from ports in the Member States to ensure that the ship carries valid certificates; and it also provides for cooperation between the administrations of two or more host States involved in a specific survey of the same ship or craft.

(2) In case of persistent disagreement between host States on the results of a specific survey, the administration of any host State involved in this survey shall immediately notify the Commission of the reasons of the disagreement, according to Article 11(7) of Directive 1999/35/EC.

(3) According to Article 11(8) of Council Directive 1999/35/EC, the Commission shall take a decision, based on the opinion of the Committee, set up by article 16 of the Directive, should there be persistent disagreement between these administrations.

(4) ... Sweden, in its capacity as host State, on 3 July 2002 notified the Commission of a persistent disagreement with the Republic of Finland, regarding the fire-extinguishing system used in the motor vehicle deck of the ro-ro ferry 'Finnsailor' (IMO[86] No 8401444)[87] sailing under Finnish flag, and that in the view of Sweden this ship fails to comply with the International Convention on the Safety of Life at Sea (SOLAS) requirements for areas of a ship to which passengers have access during the voyage, as well as during loading and unloading.

---

82 Dir. 2009/45, Art. 16.
83 Ibid.
84 OJ L198/17, 6 August 2003. Notified under document number C(2003) 2819.
85 Dec. 2003/587, Art. 2.
86 International Maritime Organisation.
87 In the event of a change of name of the ship, the IMO number shall apply as identification.

(5)   The special category space of a ship as defined in Regulation II-2/3.18 of SOLAS, is 'an enclosed space above or below the bulkhead deck intended for the carriage of motor vehicles with fuel in their tanks for their own propulsion, into and from which such vehicles can be driven and to which passengers have access'; the motor vehicle deck to which passengers have access during at least the loading and unloading, shall be considered a 'special category space' and a 'passenger space'.

(6)   According to SOLAS, special category spaces shall be fitted with a fixed fire-extinguishing system according to Regulation II-2/37.1.3, such as a fixed pressure water spraying system, or other system that is not less effective, according to IMO Resolution A.123(V), in controlling fires likely to occur in such spaces at any time.

(7)   A gas-based fixed fire-extinguishing system, such as a carbon-dioxide-based system, is not considered sufficiently effective in controlling fires that are likely to occur in special category spaces, in particular during loading or unloading, when the space is not closed, and hence not gas-tight; in addition a fire-extinguishing system giving off toxic gases in quantities as to endanger persons is not permitted, and therefore its gas connections shall be blanked in cargo spaces, when used as passenger spaces, for instance during loading and unloading.

(8)   For the relevant certificates to be valid, a water-based fixed fire-extinguishing system shall therefore be installed in special category spaces.

(9)   The measure provided for in this Decision is in accordance with the opinion of the Committee on Safe Seas, set up by Regulation (EC) No 2099/2002 of the European Parliament and of the Council." [88]

34.100 Article 1 provides that the motor vehicle decks of the ro-ro passenger ferry *Finnsailor* (IMO No 8401444) shall be considered special category spaces, and shall therefore have a water-based fixed fire-extinguishing system installed, in compliance with SOLAS Chapter II-2. Article 2 simply states the decision is addressed to Finland.

H. 2016 COMMISSION PROPOSALS TO AMEND THE COMMON RULES ON SAFETY OF SHIPS CARRYING PASSENGERS IN EU WATERS

34.101 On 6 June 2016, the Commission adopted a number of proposals to amend the common rules on safety of ships carrying passengers in EU waters.[89] The review is aimed at simplifying the regime and benefiting from the experience gained in recent years.

34.102 There is a proposal[90] to amend Directive 2009/45 on technical requirements for passenger ships on domestic voyages to: (a) clarify that ships built of aluminium have to be certified according to the directive and meet its fire safety requirements; and (b) exclude ships below 24 metres from the scope of the directive (for which its prescriptive standards

---

88 Ed., OJ L324/1, 29 November 2002.

89 The Commission has stated: "[t]he review delivers on the recommendations of the fitness check driven by the Commission's Regulatory Fitness and Performance [see REFIT: http://ec.europa.eu/smart-regulation/refit/index_en.htm] Programme. The fitness check showed that the EU passenger ship safety legislation has resulted in improved safety of life but there is scope to remove outdated, ambiguous or disproportionate requirements, and to further improve the effectiveness of search and rescue operations. Results of the fitness check and the corresponding follow-up actions were described in the Commission's report, including the proposals for a review of EU rules on passenger ship safety, further detailed in the roadmap. ... See also: 'European Commission adopts proposals to simplify and improve passenger ship safety rules' (6/06/2016) [https://ec.europa.eu/transport/modes/maritime/news/2016-06-06-passenger_ship_safety_rules_en]."

90 Proposal for a Directive of the European Parliament and of the Council amending Directive 2009/45 on safety rules and standards for passenger ships, COM/2016/0369 final – 2016/0170 (COD), http://eur-lex.europa.eu/legal-content/EN/TXT/?uri=CELEX:52016PC0369.

proved to be difficult to adapt in practice) because the Commission believes that national rules for such ships can generally take better account of local circumstances.

34.103 There is a proposal[91] to amend Directive 98/41 on registration of persons on board to introduce the requirement to register passenger data in a digital manner, using harmonised administrative procedures (the so-called National Single Window established under Directive 2010/65) to facilitate search and rescue operations in case of emergency. Under the current regime, data concerning persons on board are kept by the companies' registrar. The proposal also proposes more flexibility for operators on shorter voyages.

34.104 There is also a proposal[92] to replace and repeal Directive 1999/35 on surveys for passenger ferries and high-speed craft in regular service. The aim of the proposal is to eliminate overlaps between various inspection regimes. It would also preserve the safety level while reducing the administrative burden on shipowners and rationalise the inspection efforts of Member States' authorities.

34.105 The proposals were accompanied by so-called "Staff working documents" which contained an Implementation Plan[93] and measures aimed at the Simplification of EU Passenger Ship Safety Legislation.[94]

---

91 "Proposal for a Directive of the European Parliament and of the Council Directive 98/41/EC on the registration of persons sailing on board passenger ships operating to or from ports of the Member States of the Community and amending Directive 2010/65/EU of the European Parliament and of the Council on reporting formalities for ships arriving in and/or departing from ports of the Member States", COM/2016/0370 final – 2016/0171 (COD), http://eur-lex.europa.eu/legal-content/EN/TXT/?uri=CELEX:52016PC0370.

92 "Proposal for a Directive of the European Parliament and of the Council on a system of inspections for the safe operation of ro-ro ferry and high-speed passenger craft in regular service and amending Directive 2009/16/EC of the European Parliament and of the Council on port State control and repealing Council Directive 1999/35/EC", COM/2016/0371 final – 2016/0172 (COD), http://eur-lex.europa.eu/legal-content/EN/TXT/?uri=CELEX:52016PC0371.

93 Commission Staff Working Document, "Implementation Plan Accompanying the document Proposal for a Directive of the European Parliament and of the Council amending Directive 2009/45/EC on safety rules and standards for passenger ships Proposal for a Directive of the European Parliament and of the Council amending Council Directive 98/41/EC on the registration of persons sailing on board passenger ships operating to or from ports of the Member States of the Community and amending Directive 2010/65/EU of the European Parliament and of the Council on reporting formalities for ships arriving in and/or departing from ports of the Member States Proposal for a Directive of the European Parliament and of the Council on a system of inspections for the safe operation of ro-ro ferry and high-speed passenger craft in regular service and amending Directive 2009/16/EC of the European Parliament and of the Council on port State control and repealing Council Directive 1999/35/EC", SWD/2016/0189 final – 2016/0170 (COD), http://eur-lex.europa.eu/legal-content/EN/TXT/?uri=CELEX:52016SC0189.

94 Commission Staff Working Document, "Simplification of EU Passenger Ship Safety Legislation Accompanying the document Proposal for a Directive of the European Parliament and of the Council amending Directive 2009/45/EC on safety rules and standards for passenger ships Proposal for a Directive of the European Parliament and of the Council amending Council Directive 98/41/EC on the registration of persons sailing on board passenger ships operating to or from ports of the Member States of the Community and amending Directive 2010/65/EU of the European Parliament and of the Council on reporting formalities for ships arriving in and/or departing from ports of the Member States Proposal for a Directive of the European Parliament and of the Council on a system of inspections for the safe operation of ro-ro ferry and high-speed passenger craft in regular service and amending Directive 2009/16/EC of the European Parliament and of the Council on port State control and repealing Council Directive 1999/35/EC", SWD/2016/0190 final – 2016/0170 (COD), http://eur-lex.europa.eu/legal-content/EN/TXT/?uri=CELEX:52016SC0190.

I. COMMISSION IMPLEMENTING DECISION 2013/795 OF 19 DECEMBER 2013 ON A NOTIFICATION BY THE UNITED KINGDOM OF MEASURES IT INTENDS TO ADOPT IN ACCORDANCE WITH ARTICLE 9(2) AND (3) OF DIRECTIVE 2009/45 OF THE EUROPEAN PARLIAMENT AND OF THE COUNCIL ON SAFETY RULES AND STANDARDS FOR PASSENGER SHIPS

34.106 On 19 December 2013, the Commission adopted Decision 2013/95 on a notification by the United Kingdom of measures it intends to adopt in accordance with Article 9(2) and (3) of Directive 2009/45 of the European Parliament and of the Council on safety rules and standards for passenger ships.[95]

34.107 The background is Directive 2009/45 of the European Parliament and of the Council of 6 May 2009 on safety rules and standards for passenger ships,[96] and in particular Article 9(4) thereof. Directive 2009/45 lays down a uniform level of safety requirements for passenger ships of whatever flag engaged on domestic voyages. Article 9(2) of the abovementioned directive permits Member States to adopt measures allowing equivalents for the regulations contained in Annex I to the directive provided that such equivalents are at least as effective as such regulations and subject to the procedure in Article 9(4). Article 9(3) of the directive permits Member States to adopt measures to exempt ships from certain specific requirements provided there is no reduction in the level of safety and subject to the procedure in Article 9(4).

34.108 Article 9(4) provides that a Member State which avails itself of the provisions of Article 9(2) and (3) should notify the Commission of the measures it intends to adopt, including particulars to the extent necessary to confirm that the level of safety is adequately maintained. If within a period of six months from the notification it is decided in accordance with the procedure in Article 11(2) that the measures are not justified, the said Member State shall be required to amend or not to adopt the proposed measures.

34.109 The UK originally transmitted to the Commission a notification of a national measure on exemptions and equivalencies to the directive's requirements for domestic passenger ships under Article 9(2) and (3) of Directive 2009/45 on 17 February 2011. The Commission requested additional technical details and explanations on the UK proposal on 25 March 2011.

34.110 The UK resubmitted a notification on 19 March 2013 on a national measure granting 21 equivalents and exemptions under Article 9(2) and (3) of Directive 2009/45. This notification replaced the notification transmitted on 17 February 2011; it mainly addressed technical and operational alternatives to the directive's requirements covering the specific needs of small passenger ships operating on the coast of the UK. The Commission requested on 12 June 2013 further information and clarification on the request for exemptions and equivalencies. The Commission indicated that the six-month period provided in Article 9(4) of the directive, starting from the original reception of the notification, was stopped until the complete reception of the information necessary to finalise the analysis. The UK replied on 13 July 2013. A meeting was held between the representatives of the Commission, the European Maritime Safety Agency and the UK authorities on 23 September 2013 to further explore the details of this complex notification.

---

95 OJ L349/107, 21 December 2013.
96 OJ L163/1, 25 June 2005.

34.111 By 1 October 2013, the UK had decided to withdraw 11 of the original exemptions/equivalencies. The UK also updated the remaining exemptions/equivalencies and clarified the operational conditions where the requested exemptions would be applied.

34.112 The Commission considered that nine of the exemptions/equivalencies requested were justified and the procedure laid down under Article 11(2) of Directive 2009/45 was not applicable.

34.113 The remaining request concerned the requirement under Regulation III/2.1 of Annex I to Directive 2009/45 on the "Provision of spare liferafts". This measure included an exemption and an equivalent proposal. The United Kingdom requested to exempt from the requirement under Regulation III/2.1 vessels of Classes C and D, under 24 metres in length, engaged only on voyages in favourable weather, in daylight and in summer, and carrying not more than 130 persons. The United Kingdom proposed as equivalency to such a regulation that these passenger ships should carry life rafts for 100% of persons on board, and buoyant apparatus for 20%.

34.114 The Commission considered that this remaining request to exempt vessels of Classes C and D, under 24 metres in length, from the requirement under Regulation III/2.1 of Annex I to Directive 2009/45 on the "Provision of spare liferafts", could not be accepted. The United Kingdom had not demonstrated that there was no reduction in safety under the proposed operating conditions of vessels engaged only on voyages in favourable weather, in daylight and in summer. Furthermore, the United Kingdom had not demonstrated that the risk of a life raft being unavailable is low, and the proposed equivalent measure of on-board buoyant apparatus for 20% of the persons on board was unacceptable as it implied that the persons using it will be in the water. In some of the areas covered by the measure, the sea temperature in the defined summer period can be very low, reaching in some cases 5 °C.

34.115 The Commission therefore considered that the intended measures on Regulation III/2.1 of Annex I to Directive 2009/45 were not justified. The measure provided in the decision is in accordance with the opinion of the COSS.

34.116 Article 1 states that the UK is required not to adopt its intended exemption to the requirement "Provision of spare liferafts" of Regulation III/2.1 of Annex I to Directive 2009/45 for the passenger ships of Classes C and D, under 24 metres and the equivalency proposed for those vessels to carry life rafts for 100%, and buoyant apparatus for 20% of persons on board. Article 2 provides that the decision is addressed to the UK.

CHAPTER 35

Maritime safety: organisation of working time of seafarers

A. INTRODUCTION

35.001 This chapter considers Council Directive 1999/63 of 21 June 1999 concerning the Agreement on the Organisation of Working Time of Seafarers concluded by the European Community Shipowners' Association ("ECSA") and the Federation of Transport Workers' Unions in the European Union ("FST").[1] Council Directive 1999/63 was amended by Council Directive 2009/13 of 16 February 2009.[2] Greaves has commented that two directives had been adopted, Directive 1999/63[3] and Directive 1999/95,[4] in respect of seafarers' hours on board ship:

> "[t]hese measures are examples of the Commission's policy to put forward Community proposals which give effect to internationally agreed standards, yet also include additional requirements not found in the international agreement itself but which will be enforced on board ships flying the flag of a Member State."[5]

35.002 Council Directive 1999/63 was somewhat unusual in that it related to an agreement between two associations, namely, ECSA and the FST rather than the more usual type of measure which involves legislation adopted by the European Union ("EU") and its institutions. The legal basis was the Treaty establishing the European Community ("TEC") generally but, in particular, Article 139(2) of the TEC (which would now be Article 155 of the TFEU).

B. BACKGROUND TO THE DIRECTIVE

35.003 The stimulus for the measure for the directive is recited in the opening recitals:

> "(1) following the entry into force of the Treaty of Amsterdam, the provisions of the Agreement on social policy annexed to the Protocol 14 on social policy, annexed to the Treaty establishing the European Community, as amended by the Treaty of Maastricht, have been incorporated into Articles 136 to 139 of the Treaty establishing the European Community;

---

1 OJ L167/33, 2 July 1999. An unofficial consolidated version is available at: http://eur-lex.europa.eu/legal-content/EN/TXT/?qid=1470518275765&uri=CELEX:01999L0063-20090520. For background, see https://osha.europa.eu/en/legislation/directives/copy_of_council-directive-1999-63-ec-working-time-of-seafarers.
2 OJ L124/30, 20 May 2009.
3 OJ 1999 L167/33.
4 OJ 2000 L14/29.
5 "European Community Transport Law", (2002) 51(1) ICLQ 175 at 185.

(2)   management and labour ('the social partners'), may in accordance with Article 139(2) of the Treaty, request jointly that agreements at Community level be implemented by a Council decision on a proposal from the Commission;

(3)   the Council adopted Directive 93/104/EC of 23 November 1993 concerning certain aspects of the organisation of working time;[6] whereas sea transport was one of the sectors of activity excluded from the scope of that Directive;

(4)   account should be taken of the relevant Conventions of the International Labour Organisation with regard to the organisation of working time, including in particular those relating to the hours of work of seafarers;

(5)   the Commission, in accordance with Article 3(2) of the Agreement on social policy, has consulted management and labour on the possible direction of Community action with regard to the sectors and activities excluded from Directive 93/104/EC;

(6)   after that consultation the Commission considered that Community action was desirable in that area, and once again consulted management and labour at Community level on the substance of the envisaged proposal in accordance with Article 3(3) of the said Agreement;

(7)   the European Community Shipowners' Association (ECSA) and the Federation of Transport Workers' Unions in the European Union (FST) informed the Commission of their desire to enter into negotiations in accordance with Article 4 of the Agreement on social policy;

(8)   the said organisations concluded, on 30 September 1998, an Agreement on the working time of seafarers; this Agreement contains a joint request to the Commission to implement the Agreement by a Council decision on a proposal from the Commission, in accordance with Article 4(2) of the Agreement on social policy;

(9)   the Council, in its resolution of 6 December 1994 on certain aspects for a European Union social policy: a contribution to economic and social convergence in the Union[7] asked management and labour to make use of the opportunities for concluding agreements, since they are close to social reality and to social problems;

(10) the Agreement applies to seafarers on board every seagoing ship, whether publicly or privately owned, which is registered in the territory of any Member State and is ordinarily engaged in commercial maritime operations;

(11) the proper instrument for implementing the Agreement is a Directive within the meaning of Article 249 of the Treaty; it therefore binds the Member States as to the result to be achieved, whilst leaving national authorities the choice of form and methods;

(12) in accordance with the principles of subsidiarity and proportionality as set out in Article 5 of the Treaty, the objectives of this Directive cannot be sufficiently achieved by the Member States and can therefore be better achieved by the Community; this Directive does not go beyond what is necessary for the attainment of those objectives;

(13) with regard to terms used in the Agreement which are not specifically defined therein, this Directive leaves Member States free to define those terms in accordance with national law and practice, as is the case for other social policy Directives using similar terms, providing that those definitions respect the content of the Agreement;

(14) the Commission has drafted its proposal for a Directive, in accordance with its communication of 20 May 1998 on adapting and promoting the social dialogue at Community level, taking into account the representative status of the signatory parties and the legality of each clause of the Agreement;

(15) the Commission informed the European Parliament and the Economic and Social Committee, in accordance with its communication of 14 December 1993 concerning the application of the Agreement on social policy, by sending them the text of its proposal for a Directive containing the Agreement;

(16) the implementation of the Agreement contributes to achieving the objectives under Article 136 of the Treaty."

---

6 OJ L307/18, 13.12.1993.

7 OJ C368/6, 23.12.1994.

C. PURPOSE OF THE DIRECTIVE

35.004 Article 1 of Directive 1999/63 provides that the purpose of the directive is to put into effect the agreement on the organisation of working time of seafarers concluded on 30 September 1998 between the organisations representing management and labour in the maritime sector (i.e. the ECSA and FST) as set out in the annex to the directive.

D. MINIMUM REQUIREMENTS

35.005 Article 2 of Directive 1999/63 is entitled "minimum requirements". Article 2(1) provides that Member States may maintain or introduce more favourable provisions than those laid down in the directive. Article 2(2) goes on to provide that the implementation of the directive shall, under no circumstances, constitute sufficient grounds for justifying a reduction in the general level of protection of workers in the fields covered by the directive. This shall be without prejudice to the rights of Member States and/or management and labour to lay down, in the light of changing circumstances, different legislative, regulatory or contractual arrangements to those prevailing at the time of the adoption of this directive, provided always that the minimum requirements laid down in this directive are adhered to.

E. TRANSPOSITION

35.006 Article 3 deals with transposition. Under Article 3(1), Member States must bring into force the laws, regulations and administrative provisions necessary to comply with the directive by 30 June 2002, or had to ensure that, by that date at the latest, management and labour have introduced the necessary measures by agreement, the Member States being required to take any necessary measure to enable them at any time to be in a position to guarantee the results imposed by the directive. They shall forthwith inform the Commission thereof. Under Article 3(2), when Member States adopt the provisions referred to in Article 3(1), these shall contain a reference to the directive or shall be accompanied by such reference at the time of their official publication. The methods of making such reference shall be laid down by the Member States.

F. ANNEX TO DIRECTIVE 1999/63

35.007 The annex to Directive 1999/63 contains the European Agreement on the Organisation of Working Time of Seafarers.

35.008 Clause 1 provides

"1. The Agreement applies to seafarers on board every seagoing ship, whether publicly or privately owned, which is registered in the territory of any Member State and is ordinarily engaged in commercial maritime operations. For the purpose of this Agreement a ship that is on the register of two States is deemed to be registered in the territory of the State whose flag it flies.

2. In the event of doubt as to whether or not any ships are to be regarded as seagoing ships or engaged in commercial maritime operations for the purpose of the Agreement, the question shall be determined by the competent authority of the Member State. The organisations of shipowners and seafarers concerned should be consulted.

3. In the event of doubt as to whether any categories of persons are to be regarded as seafarers for the purpose of this Agreement, the question shall be determined by the competent authority in each Member State after consultation with the shipowners' and seafarers' organisations concerned with this question. In this context due account shall be taken of the Resolution of the 94th (Maritime) Session of the General Conference of the International Labour Organisation concerning information on occupational groups."

35.009 Clause 2 sets out a number of definitions for the purpose of the agreement. The term "hours of work" means time during which a seafarer is required to do work on account of the ship. The term "hours of rest" means time outside hours of work; this term does not include short breaks. The term "seafarer" means any person who is employed or engaged or works in any capacity on board a ship to which this agreement applies. The term "shipowner" means the owner of the ship or another organisation or person, such as the manager, agent or bareboat charterer, who has assumed the responsibility for the operation of the ship from the owner and who, on assuming such responsibility, has agreed to take over the duties and responsibilities imposed on shipowners in accordance with this agreement, regardless of whether any other organisation or persons fulfil certain of the duties or responsibilities on behalf of the shipowner.

35.010 Clause 3 provides that within the limits set out in Clause 5, there must be fixed either a maximum number of hours of work which shall not be exceeded in a given period of time, or a minimum number or hours of rest which shall be provided in a given period of time.

35.011 Under Clause 4, without prejudice to Clause 5, the normal working hours standard of seafarers is, in principle, based on an eight-hour day with one day of rest per week and rest on public holidays. Member States may have procedures to authorise or register a collective agreement which determines seafarers' normal working hours on a basis less favourable than this standard.

35.012 Clause 5 is worth reciting in detail:

"1. The limits on hours of work or rest shall be either:

  (a) maximum hours of work which shall not exceed
     (i) fourteen hours in any 24 hour period; and
     (ii) 72 hours in any seven-day period;

or

  (b) minimum hours of rest which shall not be less than:

     (i) ten hours in any 24 hour period; and
     (ii) 77 hours in any seven-day period.

2. Hours of rest may be divided into no more than two periods, one of which shall be at least six hours in length and the interval between consecutive periods of rest shall not exceed 14 hours.

3. Musters, fire-fighting and lifeboat drills, and prescribed by national laws and regulations and by international instruments shall be conducted in a manner that minimises the disturbance of rest periods and does not induce fatigue.

4. In respect of situations when a seafarer is on call, such as when a machinery space is unattended, the seafarer shall have an adequate compensatory rest period if the normal period of rest is disturbed by call-outs to work.

5. With regard to paragraphs 3 and 4, where no collective agreement or arbitration award exists or if the competent authority determines that the provisions in the agreement or award are

inadequate, it would be for the competent authority to determine such provisions to ensure that the seafarers concerned have sufficient rest.

6. With due regard for the general principles of the protection of the health and safety of workers, Member States may have national laws, regulations or a procedure for the competent authority to authorise or register collective agreements permitting exceptions to the limits set out in paragraphs 1 and 2. Such exceptions shall, as far as possible, follow the standards set out but may take account of more frequent or longer leave periods, or the granting of compensatory leave for watchkeeping seafarers or seafarers working on board ship on short voyages.

7. A table shall be posted, in an easily accessible place, with the shipboard working arrangements, which shall contain for every position at least:

  (a) the schedule of service at sea and service in port; and
  (b) the maximum hours of work or the minimum hours of rest required by the laws, regulations or collective agreements in force in the Member States.

8. The table referred to in paragraph 7 shall be established in a standardised format in the working language or languages of the ship and in English."

35.013 Clause 6 provides that night work of seafarers under the age of 18 must be prohibited. For the purposes of Clause 6, "night" shall be defined in accordance with national law and practice. It shall cover a period of at least nine hours starting no later than midnight and ending no earlier than 5 a.m. An exception to strict compliance with the night work restriction may be made by the competent authority when: (a) the effective training of the seafarers concerned, in accordance with established programmes and schedules, would be impaired; or (b) the specific nature of the duty or a recognised training programme requires that the seafarers covered by the exception perform duties at night and the authority determines, after consultation with the shipowners' and seafarers' organisations concerned, that the work will not be detrimental to their health or well-being. The employment, engagement or work of seafarers under the age of 18 shall be prohibited where the work is likely to jeopardise their health or safety. The types of such work shall be determined by national laws or regulations or by the competent authority, after consultation with the shipowners' and seafarers' organisations concerned, in accordance with relevant international standards.

35.014 Under Clause 7, the master of a ship shall have the right to require a seafarer to perform any hours of work necessary for the immediate safety of the ship, persons on board or cargo, or for the purpose of giving assistance to other ships or persons in distress at sea. In accordance with paragraph 1, the master may suspend the schedule of hours of work or hours of rest and require a seafarer to perform any hours of work necessary until the normal situation has been restored. As soon as practicable after the normal situation has been restored, the master shall ensure that any seafarer who have performed work in a scheduled rest period are provided with an adequate period of rest.

35.015 Clause 8 provides:

"1. Records of seafarers' daily hours of work or of their daily hours of rest shall be maintained to allow monitoring of compliance with the provisions set out in Clause 5. The seafarer shall receive a copy of the records pertaining to him or her which shall be endorsed by the master, or a person authorised by the master, and by the seafarer.

2. Procedures shall be determined for keeping such records on board, including the intervals at which the information shall be recorded. The format of the records of the seafarers' hours of work or of their hours of rest shall be established taking into account any available

international guidelines. The format shall be established in the language provided by Clause 5, paragraph 8.

3. A copy of the relevant provisions of the national legislation pertaining to this Agreement and the relevant collective agreements shall be kept on board and be easily accessible to the crew."

35.016 Clause 9 provides that the records referred to in Clause 8 must be examined and endorsed at appropriate intervals, to monitor compliance with the provisions governing hours of work or hours of rest that give effect to this agreement.

35.017 Under Clause 10, when determining, approving or revising manning levels, it is necessary to take into account the need to avoid or minimise, as fast as practicable, excessive hours of work, to ensure sufficient rest and to limit fatigue. If the records or other evidence indicate infringement of provisions governing hours of work or hours of rest, measures, including if necessary the revision of the manning of the ship, shall be taken so as to avoid future infringements. All ships to which this agreement applies shall be sufficiently, safely and efficiently manned, in accordance with the minimum safe manning document or an equivalent issued by the competent authority.

35.018 Clause 11 provides that no person under 16 years of age shall work on a ship.

35.019 Under Clause 12, the shipowner must provide the master with the necessary resources for the purpose of compliance with obligations under this agreement, including those relating to the appropriate manning of the ship. The master shall take all necessary steps to ensure that the requirements on seafarers' hours of work and rest arising from this agreement are complied with.

35.020 Clause 13 is quite detailed. It provides that seafarers shall not work on a ship unless they are certified as medically fit to perform their duties. Exceptions can only be permitted as prescribed in the agreement. The competent authority shall require that, prior to beginning work on a ship, seafarers hold a valid medical certificate attesting that they are medically fit to perform the duties they are to carry out at sea. In order to ensure that medical certificates genuinely reflect seafarers' state of health, in light of the duties they are to perform, the competent authority shall, after consultation with the shipowners' and seafarers' organisations concerned, and giving due consideration to applicable international guidelines, prescribe the nature of the medical examination and certificate. The agreement is without prejudice to the International Convention on Standards of Training, Certification and Watchkeeping for Seafarers, 1978, as amended ("STCW"). A medical certificate issued in accordance with the requirements of STCW shall be accepted by the competent authority, for the purpose of points 1 and 2 of this Clause. A medical certificate meeting the substance of those requirements, in the case of seafarers not covered by STCW, shall similarly be accepted. The medical certificate must be issued by a duly qualified medical practitioner or, in the case of a certificate solely concerning eyesight, by a person recognised by the competent authority as qualified to issue such a certificate. Practitioners must enjoy full professional independence in exercising their medical judgment in undertaking medical examination procedures. Seafarers that have been refused a certificate or have had a limitation imposed on their ability to work, in particular with respect to time, field of work or trading area, shall be given the opportunity to have a further examination by another independent medical practitioner or by an independent medical referee. Each medical certificate shall state in particular that: (a) the hearing and sight of the seafarer concerned, and the colour vision in the case of a seafarer to be employed in capacities where fitness for the work to be performed is liable to be affected by defective colour vision, are all satisfactory; and (b) the seafarer concerned is not suffering from any medical condition likely to be aggravated by service at sea or to render the seafarer unfit for such service or to endanger the health of other persons on board. Unless a shorter period is required by reason of the specific duties to be performed by the seafarer concerned or is required under STCW: (a) a medical certificate shall be valid for a maximum period of two years unless the seafarer is under the age of 18, in which case the maximum period of validity shall be one year; (b) a certification of colour vision shall be valid for a maximum period of six years. In urgent cases the competent authority may permit a seafarer to work without a valid medical certificate until the next port of call where the seafarer can obtain a medical certificate from a qualified medical practitioner, provided that: (a) the period of such permission does not exceed three months; and (b) the seafarer concerned is in possession of an expired medical certificate of recent date. If the period of validity of a certificate expires in the course of a voyage, the certificate shall continue in force until the next port of call where the seafarer can obtain a medical certificate from a qualified medical practitioner, provided that the period shall not exceed three months. The medical certificates for seafarers working on ships ordinarily engaged on international voyages must as a minimum be provided in English. The nature of the health assessment to be made and the particulars to be included in the medical certificate shall be established after consultation with the shipowners' and seafarers' organisations concerned. All seafarers shall have regular health assessments. Watchkeepers suffering from health problems certified by a medical practitioner as being due to the fact that they perform night work shall be transferred, wherever possible, to day work to which they are suited. The health assessment referred to in points 13 and 14 shall be free and comply with medical confidentiality. Such health assessments may be conducted within the national health system.

35.021 Clause 14 provides that shipowners shall provide information on watchkeepers and other night workers to the national competent authority if they so request.

35.022 Clause 15 states that seafarers must have safety and health protection appropriate to the nature of their work. Equivalent protection and prevention services or facilities with regard to the safety and health of seafarers working by day or by night shall be available.

35.023 Clause 16 provides that every seafarer is entitled to paid annual leave. The annual leave with pay entitlement shall be calculated on the basis of a minimum of 2.5 calendar days per month of employment and pro rata for incomplete months. The minimum period of paid annual leave may not be replaced by an allowance in lieu, except where the employment relationship is terminated.

CHAPTER 36

Maritime safety: Maritime Labour Convention 2006

A. INTRODUCTION

36.001 This short chapter considers the position in European Union ("EU") law of the 2006 Maritime Labour Convention of the International Labour Organization ("ILO"). The purpose of this chapter is to consider the EU law aspects rather than the detail of the Maritime Labour Convention itself. However, it is useful to review briefly the Maritime Labour Convention in Part B before considering the EU law aspects.

B. MARITIME LABOUR CONVENTION 2006

36.002 The Maritime Labour Convention was adopted on 7 February 2006 by the ILO's maritime session of the International Labour Conference in Geneva. This convention, which resulted from five years of negotiation, aimed at consolidating a number of previous international conventions; it was a measure designed to "create a single, coherent instrument embodying as far as possible all up-to-date standards of existing international maritime labour conventions and recommendations, as well as the fundamental principles to be found in other international conventions".[1] It entered into force on 20 August 2013. The EU has positively encouraged its Member States to ratify the Maritime Labour Convention.

C. COUNCIL DECISION 2007/431 AUTHORISING MEMBER STATES TO RATIFY, IN THE INTERESTS OF THE EUROPEAN COMMUNITY, THE MARITIME LABOUR CONVENTION, 2006, OF THE INTERNATIONAL LABOUR ORGANISATION

36.003 On 7 June 2007, the Council adopted Decision 2007/431 authorising Member States to ratify, in the interests of the European Community, the Maritime Labour Convention, 2006, of the International Labour Organisation.[2] The convention "lays the foundations for an international maritime labour code by setting minimum labour standards".[3]

36.004 The second recital to the decision recalls that the convention

---

1 Preamble to the Maritime Labour Convention.
2 OJ L161/63, 22 June 2007,
3 Dec. 2007/431, Recital 3.

"brings a major input in the shipping sector at international level in promoting decent living and working conditions for seafarers and fairer competition conditions for operators and shipowners and it is therefore desirable that its provisions should be applied as soon as possible."

36.005 The legal basis of the decision was the then Treaty establishing the European Community ("TEC"), and in particular Article 42 in conjunction with the first sentence of the first subparagraph of Article 300(2) and the first subparagraph of Article 300(3) of the TEC.

36.006 The Council adopted the decision because the EU sought to achieve the establishment of a level playing field in the maritime industry.[4]

36.007 Article 19, paragraph 8 of the ILO Constitution states that

"in no case, shall the adoption of any Convention or Recommendation by the Conference, or the ratification of any Convention by any Member, be deemed to affect any law, award, custom or agreement which ensures more favourable conditions to the workers concerned than those provided for in the Convention or Recommendation".

36.008 The sixth recital to Decision 2007/431 provides that some provisions of the Convention fall within the Community's exclusive competence as regards the co-ordination of social security schemes. However, the seventh recital to the decision provides that the "Community cannot ratify the Convention, as only states can be parties thereto" while the eighth recital provides that the

"Council should therefore authorise the Member States which are bound by the Community rules on the coordination of social security schemes based on Article 42 of the Treaty to ratify the Convention in the interests of the Community, under the conditions laid down in this Decision."

36.009 Article 1 of the decision provides that Member States are authorised, by the decision, to ratify, for the parts falling under Community competence, the Maritime Labour Convention 2006, of the ILO, adopted on 7 February 2006.

36.010 Article 2 provides that Member States

"should make efforts to take the necessary steps to deposit their instruments of ratification of the Convention with the Director-General of the International Labour Office as soon as possible, preferably before 31 December 2010. The Council will review the progress of the ratification before January 2010."

36.011 Article 3 provides that the decision is addressed to the Member States in accordance with the TEC (now the Treaty on the Functioning of the European Union "TFEU").

D. DIRECTIVE 2013/54 OF THE EUROPEAN PARLIAMENT AND OF THE COUNCIL OF 20 NOVEMBER 2013 CONCERNING CERTAIN FLAG STATE RESPONSIBILITIES FOR COMPLIANCE WITH AND ENFORCEMENT OF THE MARITIME LABOUR CONVENTION 2006

Introduction

36.012 On 20 November 2013, the European Parliament and Council adopted Directive 2013/54 concerning certain flag State responsibilities for compliance with and

---

4 Dec. 2007/431, Recital 4.

enforcement of the Maritime Labour Convention, 2006.[5] At the time of the adoption of the directive, the Commission made a short statement: "[t]he Commission considers that the title does not properly reflect the scope of the Directive".

36.013 The legal basis of Directive 2013/54 is the TFEU generally and in particular Article 100(2) of the TFEU.[6]

36.014 The background to Directive 2013/54 provides that EU "action in the field of maritime transport aims, *inter alia*, to improve the shipboard living and working conditions of seafarers, security and safety at sea and to prevent pollution caused by maritime accidents". The directive provides that the EU was "aware of the fact that most accidents at sea are directly caused by human factors, especially fatigue".[7] The directive also recalled that one of "the main objectives of the maritime safety policy of the Union is to eradicate substandard shipping".[8]

36.015 The directive recalled that on 23 February 2006, the ILO, "desiring to create a single, coherent and up-to-date instrument that also embodies the fundamental principles to be found in other international labour conventions, adopted the Maritime Labour Convention, 2006 (MLC 2006)".[9]

36.016 According to Article VIII of the Maritime Labour Convention 2006, the Maritime Labour Convention 2006 was to enter into force 12 months after the date on which there have been registered ratifications by at least 30 Members of the ILO with a total share in the world gross tonnage of ships of 33%. This condition was fulfilled on 20 August 2012, and the Maritime Labour Convention 2006 therefore entered into force on 20 August 2013. Council Decision 2007/431[10] authorised the Member States to ratify the Maritime Labour Convention 2006, and Member States are urged to do so as soon as possible. The Maritime Labour Convention 2006 sets out "minimum global standards to ensure the right of all seafarers to decent living and working conditions, irrespective of their nationality and irrespective of the flag of the ships on which they serve, and to establish a level playing field".[11]

36.017 The eighth recital to Directive 2013/54 provides that

"various parts of MLC 2006 have been introduced into different Union instruments both as regards flag State and port State obligations. The aim of this Directive is to introduce certain compliance and enforcement provisions, envisaged in Title 5 of MLC 2006, which relate to those parts of MLC 2006 in respect of which the required compliance and enforcement provisions have not yet been adopted. Those parts correspond to the elements set out in the Annex to Council Directive 2009/13/EC."[12]

---

5 OJ L329/1, 10 December 2013.

6 Art. 100 of the TFEU provides: "1. The provisions of this Title shall apply to transport by rail, road and inland waterway. 2. The European Parliament and the Council, acting in accordance with the ordinary legislative procedure, may lay down appropriate provisions for sea and air transport. They shall act after consulting the Economic and Social Committee and the Committee of the Regions."

7 Dir. 2013/54, Recital 2.

8 Dir. 2013/54, Recital 3.

9 Dir. 2013/54, Recital 4.

10 I.e. Council Dec. 2007/431 of 7 of June 2007 authorising Member States to ratify, in the interests of the European Community, the Maritime Labour Convention, 2006, of the International Labour Organisation (OJ L161/63, 22 June 2007).

11 Dir. 2013/54, Recital 7.

12 I.e. Council Dir. 2009/13 of 16 February 2009 implementing the agreement concluded by the European Community Shipowners' Associations (ECSA) and the European Transport Workers' Federation (ETF) on the Maritime Labour Convention, 2006 and amending Directive 1999/63 (OJ L124/30, 20 May 2009).

36.018 The ninth recital recalls that Directive 2009/13 implements the Agreement concluded by the European Community Shipowners' Associations ("ECSA") and the European Transport Workers' Federation ("ETF") on the Maritime Labour Convention 2006, annexed thereto.

36.019 The tenth recital provides that although Directive 2009/21 of the European Parliament and of the Council[13] governs flag State responsibilities, incorporating the voluntary IMO Member States audit scheme into Union law, and introducing the certification of quality of national maritime authorities, a separate directive covering the maritime labour standards would be more appropriate and would more clearly reflect the different purposes and procedures, without affecting Directive 2009/21.

36.020 The eleventh recital provides that Directive 2009/21 applies to IMO conventions. In any event, Member States could develop, implement and maintain a quality management system for the operational parts of the flag State-related activities of their maritime administration falling within the scope of the directive.

36.021 The twelfth recital provides that Member States should ensure the effective discharge of their obligations as flag States with respect to the implementation, by ships flying their flag, of the relevant parts of the Maritime Labour Convention 2006. In establishing an effective system for monitoring mechanisms, including inspections, a Member State could, where appropriate, grant authorisation to public institutions, or to other organisations within the meaning of Regulation 5.1.2 of the Maritime Labour Convention 2006, under the conditions set out therein.

36.022 The thirteenth recital provides that according to Article 2(3)(c) of Regulation 1406/2002 of the European Parliament and of the Council[14] the mandate of the European Maritime Safety Agency includes, as a core task, that the Agency should work with the Member States to provide, at the request of a Member State, appropriate information in order to support the monitoring of recognised organisations acting on behalf of that Member State, without prejudice to the rights and obligations of the flag State.

36.023 The fourteenth recital provides that since the objectives of the directive cannot be sufficiently achieved by the Member States but can rather, by reason of the scale and effects of the action, be better achieved at the level of the Union, the Union may adopt measures, in accordance with the principle of subsidiarity as set out in Article 5 of the Treaty on the European Union. In accordance with the principle of proportionality, as set out in that article, this directive does not go beyond what is necessary in order to achieve those objectives.

36.024 The fifteenth recital provides that under no circumstances should the application of this directive lead to a reduction in the level of protection currently enjoyed by seafarers under EU law.

Subject matter of Directive 2013/54

36.025 Article 1 provides that the directive lays down rules to ensure that Member States effectively discharge their obligations as flag States with respect to the

---

13 Dir. 2009/21 of the European Parliament and of the Council of 23 April 2009 on compliance with flag State requirements (OJ L131, 28 May 2009, p. 132).

14 Reg. 1406/2002 of the European Parliament and of the Council of 27 June 2002 establishing a European Maritime Safety Agency (OJ L208/1, 5 August 2002).

implementation of the relevant parts of the Maritime Labour Convention 2006. This directive is without prejudice to Directives 2009/13 and 2009/21 and to any higher standards for living and working conditions for seafarers set out therein.

Definitions in Directive 2013/54

36.026 Article 2 provides that for the purposes of Directive 2013/54, the following definition shall apply in addition to the relevant definitions set out in the annex to Directive 2009/13: "relevant parts of the Maritime Labour Convention 2006" means "the parts of MLC 2006 of which the content shall be considered as corresponding to the provisions in the Annex to Directive 2009/13/EC".

Monitoring of compliance with Directive 2013/54

36.027 Article 3 of Directive 2013/54 provides:

"1. Member States shall ensure that effective and appropriate enforcement and monitoring mechanisms, including inspections at the intervals provided for in MLC 2006, are established in order to ensure that the living and working conditions of seafarers on ships flying their flag meet, and continue to meet, the requirements of the relevant parts of MLC 2006.

2. With respect to ships of less than 200 gross tonnage not engaged in international voyages, Member States may, in consultation with the shipowners' and seafarers' organisations concerned, decide to adapt, pursuant to Article II, paragraph 6 of MLC 2006, monitoring mechanisms, including inspections, to take account of the specific conditions relating to such ships.

3. When fulfilling their obligations under this Article, Member States may, where appropriate, authorise public institutions or other organisations, including those of another Member State, if the latter agrees, which they recognise as having sufficient capacity, competence and independence, to carry out inspections. In all cases, a Member State shall remain fully responsible for the inspection of the living and working conditions of the seafarers concerned on ships that fly the flag of that Member State. This provision is without prejudice to Directive 2009/15/EC of the European Parliament and of the Council.[15]

4. Member States shall establish clear objectives and standards covering the administration of their inspection systems, as well as adequate overall procedures for their assessment of the extent to which those objectives and standards are being attained.

5. A Member State shall ensure that seafarers on board ships flying the flag of that Member State have access to a copy of the Agreement. The access may be provided electronically."

Personnel in charge of compliance monitoring

36.028 Article 4 deals with personnel in charge of compliance monitoring:

"1. Member States shall ensure that personnel, including staff from institutions or other organisations ('recognised organisations' within the meaning of MLC 2006), authorised to carry out inspections in accordance with Article 3(3) and in charge of verifying the proper implementation of the relevant parts of MLC 2006, have the training, competence, terms of reference, full legal authority, status and independence necessary or desirable to enable them to carry out that verification and to ensure compliance with the relevant parts of MLC 2006. In

---

15 Ed., Dir. 2009/15 of the European Parliament and of the Council of 23 April 2009 on common rules and standards for ship inspection and survey organisations and for the relevant activities of maritime administrations (OJ L131/47, 28 May 2009).

accordance with MLC 2006, inspectors shall be empowered to take steps, as appropriate, to prohibit a ship from leaving port until necessary actions are taken.

2. All authorisations granted with respect to inspections shall, as a minimum, empower the recognised organisation to require the rectification of deficiencies that it identifies in seafarers' living and working conditions, and to carry out inspections in that regard at the request of a port State.

3. Each Member State shall establish:

   (a) a system to ensure the adequacy of work performed by recognised organisations, which includes information on all applicable national laws and regulations and relevant international instruments; and

   (b) procedures for communication with and oversight of such organisations.

4. Each Member State shall provide the International Labour Office with a current list of any recognised organisations authorised to act on its behalf, and shall keep this list up to date. The list shall specify the functions that the recognised organisations have been authorised to carry out."

On-board complaint procedures, handling of complaints and corrective measures

36.029 Article 5 deals with on-board complaint procedures, handling of complaints and corrective measures. Article 5(1) provides that each Member State must ensure that, in its laws or regulations, appropriate on-board complaint procedures are in place. Article 5(2) provides that if

"a Member State receives a complaint which it does not consider manifestly unfounded or obtains evidence that a ship that flies its flag does not conform to the requirements of the relevant parts of MLC 2006 or that there are serious deficiencies in its implementing measures, that Member State shall take the steps necessary to investigate the matter and ensure that action is taken to remedy any deficiencies found."

Personnel dealing with or becoming aware of complaints must treat as confidential the source of any grievance or complaint alleging a danger or deficiency in relation to seafarers' living and working conditions or a violation of laws and regulations and shall give no intimation to the shipowner, the shipowner's representative or the operator of the ship that an inspection was made as a consequence of such a grievance or complaint.[16]

Reports

36.030 Article 6 deals with reports under the directive. The Commission must, in the context of its reports to be established in accordance with Article 9 of Directive 2009/21, include matters falling within the scope of Directive 2013/54.[17] Article 6(2) provides that no later than 31 December 2018, the Commission must submit a report to the European Parliament and to the Council on the implementation and application of Regulation 5.3 of the Maritime Labour Convention 2006 regarding labour-supplying responsibilities. Article 6(2) also provides that if appropriate, the report may include proposals for measures to enhance living and working conditions in the maritime sector.

---

16 Dir. 2013/54, Art. 5(3).
17 Dir. 2013/54, Art. 6(1).

Transposition of Directive 2013/54

36.031 The directive entered into force on the twentieth day following that of its publication in the *Official Journal of the European Union*.[18] Member States had to bring into force the laws, regulations and administrative provisions necessary to comply with the directive by 31 March 2015.[19] When Member States adopt those measures, they shall contain a reference to this directive or shall be accompanied by such a reference on the occasion of their official publication. The methods for making such references shall be laid down by Member States.[20] The States also had to communicate to the Commission the text of the main measures of national law which they adopt in the field covered by the directive.[21]

E. DECISION 2014/346 ON THE POSITION TO BE ADOPTED ON BEHALF OF THE EUROPEAN UNION AT THE 103RD SESSION OF THE INTERNATIONAL LABOUR CONFERENCE CONCERNING AMENDMENTS TO THE CODE OF THE MARITIME LABOUR CONVENTION

36.032 On 26 May 2014, the Council adopted Decision 2014/346, addressed to the Member States, on the position to be adopted on behalf of the European Union at the 103rd session of the International Labour Conference concerning amendments to the Code of the Maritime Labour Convention.[22] It will be recalled that the ILO's 2006 Maritime Labour Convention "establishes minimum working and living standards for all seafarers working on ships flying the flags of ratifying countries".[23]

36.033 The legal basis of Decision 2014/346 is the TFEU generally and, in particular, Article 218(9), in conjunction with Article 153(1)(b) and 153(2)(b), of the TFEU.

36.034 The second recital to Decision 2014/346 provides that amendments to the Code of the Convention (referred to in the decision as the "amendments"), have been adopted by the "Special Tripartite Committee" established under the convention (referred to in the decision as the "Committee"), at its meeting on 7–11 April 2014. The amendments were submitted for approval to the 103rd session of the International Labour Conference on 28 May to 12 June 2014. These amendments concern the liability of shipowners with respect to compensation for claims due to death, personal injury and abandonment of seafarers.

36.035 The third recital to Decision 2014/346 provides that the amendments concern the liability of shipowners with respect to compensation for claims due to death, personal injury and abandonment of seafarers.

36.036 The fourth recital to Decision 2014/346 provides:

"Parts of the rules under the Convention and the amendments are falling within the Union's competence and concern matters in respect of which the Union has adopted rules. The amendments will interplay with existing acquis, in particular in the areas of social policy and transport. In particular, most of the provisions of the Convention have been the subject of Council Directive

---

18 Dir. 2013/54, Art. 8.
19 Dir. 2013/54, Art. 7(1). They had to forthwith communicate to the Commission the text of those provisions.
20 Dir. 2013/54, Art. 7(1).
21 Dir. 2013/54, Art. 7(2).
22 OJ L172/28, 12 June 2014.
23 Dec. 2014/346, Recital 1.

2009/13/EC of 16 February 2009 implementing the Agreement concluded by the European Community Shipowners' Associations (ECSA) and the European Transport Workers' Federation (ETF) on the Maritime Labour Convention, 2006, and amending Directive 1999/63/EC.[24] The implementation of the Convention in the Union is further ensured by Directive 2009/16/EC of the European Parliament and of the Council of 23 April 2009 on 'Port State Control',[25] as amended by Directive 2013/38/EU of the European Parliament and of the Council[26] and the 'Flag State Directive' 2013/54/EU of the European Parliament and of the Council[27] enforcing the Annex to Directive 2009/13/EC."

36.037 The fifth recital provides:

"The amendments to the Code of the Convention approved by the International Labour Conference will enter into force for all Parties in accordance with and under the conditions provided for by Article XV of the Convention. It follows that the amendments to the Code of the Maritime Labour Convention will constitute an act of a body set up by an international agreement which will produce legal effects."

36.038 The sixth recital recalls:

"Given the above, in accordance with Article 218(9) TFEU, it is necessary that the Council adopts a decision to establish the position to be adopted on the Union's behalf, as regards matters falling within the Union's competence and in respect of which the Union has adopted rules, authorising at the same time Member States to act jointly in the interest of the Union, which is not a member of the ILO."

36.039 Article 1(1) provides that the position of the EU at

"the 103rd session of the International Labour Conference shall be to support, as regards matters falling within the Union's competence and in respect of which the Union has adopted rules, the approval of the amendments to the Code of the Convention, adopted by the Committee at its meeting on 7–11 April 2014."

The text of the amendments is attached to Decision 2014/346.

36.040 Article 1(2) goes on to provide that the EU's position as set out in Article 1(1) "shall be taken by the Member States, acting jointly in the interest of the Union when approving the amendments to the Code of the Convention at the 103rd session of the International Labour Conference".

36.041 The annex to the decision contains the detail to the decision but as the annex is extremely detailed, it falls outside the scope of this chapter.

---

24 OJ L124, 20.5.2009, p. 30.

25 OJ L131, 28.5.2009, p. 57.

26 Directive 2013/38/EU of the European Parliament and of the Council of 12 August 2013 amending Directive 2009/16/EC on port State control (OJ L218, 14.8.2013, p. 1).

27 Directive 2013/54/EU of the European Parliament and of the Council of 20 November 2013 concerning certain flag State responsibilities for compliance with and enforcement of the Maritime Labour Convention, 2006 (OJ L329, 10.12.2013, p. 1).

CHAPTER 37

Maritime safety: marine equipment

A. INTRODUCTION

37.001 This chapter considers the European Union ("EU") shipping law aspects of marine equipment. EU law aims to enhance the safety and quality of marine equipment on board ships so as to increase levels of maritime safety generally. The spin-offs from improved standards for marine equipment include not only improved safety and well-being but enhanced protection of the environment.

37.002 In their 7 May 2014 Athens Declaration entitled *Mid-Term Review of the EU's Maritime Transport Policy until 2018 and Outlook to 2020,*[1] the EU's Transport Ministers emphasised "that Europe strives to keep its leadership in maritime technology, equipment and innovative maritime services and at the same time taking under consideration respective competition by other regions of the world". In the same Declaration, the Ministers went on to state:

"VI. Europe should be the world leader in maritime research and innovation

21. EMPHASIZE the need to reinforce targeted R&D and innovation efforts, including demonstration projects, to maintain European global leadership in sustainable and competitive shipping and SUPPORT the European manufacturing and shipbuilding industry serving maritime transport to find innovative solutions towards safer, more efficient and cleaner ships, highlighting that Horizon 2020 is a key tool in this context."

B. DIRECTIVE 2014/90 OF THE EUROPEAN PARLIAMENT AND OF THE COUNCIL OF 23 JULY 2014 ON MARINE EQUIPMENT AND REPEALING COUNCIL DIRECTIVE 96/98

Introduction

37.003 The principal directive on marine safety equipment is Directive 2014/90 of the European Parliament and of the Council of 23 July 2014 on marine equipment and repealing Council Directive 96/98.[2] Under Article 41 of the directive, Directive 2014/90 entered into force on the twentieth day following that of its publication in the *Official Journal of the European Union*. It was published on 28 August 2014. The legal basis of Directive 2014/90 is the Treaty on the Functioning of the European Union ("TFEU") generally and Article 100(2) in particular.

---

1 http://ec.europa.eu/transport/modes/maritime/consultations/doc/2015-mts-review/council-conclusions-on-mid-term-review-of-eu-maritime-policy.pdf.
2 OJ L257/146, 28 August 2014.

Background

37.004 It was recognised in the first recital to Directive 2014/90 that the

"international maritime safety conventions require flag States to ensure that the equipment carried on board ships complies with certain safety requirements as regards design, construction and performance, and to issue the relevant certificates. To that end, detailed performance and testing standards for certain types of marine equipment have been developed by the International Maritime Organization (IMO) and by the international and European standardisation bodies."

This may seem like a statement of the obvious but it is an important statement nonetheless.

37.005 The second recital provides that

"international instruments leave a significant margin of discretion to the flag administrations. In the absence of harmonisation, this leads to varying levels of safety for products which the competent national authorities have certified as complying with those conventions and standards; as a result, the smooth functioning of the internal market is affected as it becomes difficult for the Member States to accept equipment certified in another Member State to be placed on board ships flying their flags without further verification."

The third recital recalls that harmonisation by the EU was aimed at resolving these problems. Council Directive 96/98 (which was repealed by Directive 2014/90) thus laid down common rules to eliminate differences in the implementation of international standards by means of a clearly identified set of requirements and uniform certification procedures. So, it is clear, from the second and third recitals, that the EU measure is designed to minimise the gap.

37.006 The fourth recital of Directive 2014/90 provides that there are various other instruments of EU law which lay down requirements and conditions, *inter alia*, in order to ensure the free movement of goods within the internal market or for environmental purposes, for certain products which are similar in nature to equipment used on board ships but which do not meet the international standards – which may substantially differ from the internal legislation of the EU and are in constant evolution. Those products cannot therefore be certified by the Member States in accordance with the relevant international maritime safety conventions. Equipment to be placed on board EU ships in accordance with international safety standards should therefore be regulated exclusively by the directive, which should in any event be considered the *lex specialis*; furthermore, a specific marking should be established to indicate that equipment bearing that mark complies with the requirements laid down in the relevant international conventions and instruments which have entered into force.

37.007 It is clear from the fifth recital that as well as setting out detailed performance and testing standards for marine equipment, the international instruments sometimes allow for measures that deviate from the prescriptive requirements but which, under certain conditions, are suitable to satisfy the intent of those requirements. The SOLAS[3] allows for alternative designs and arrangements which could be applied by individual Member States acting under their own responsibility.

37.008 It is useful to consider the other recitals:

---

3 I.e. the 1974 International Convention for the Safety of Life at Sea.

"(6) Experience in the implementation of Directive 96/98/EC has shown that it is necessary to take additional measures in order to enhance the implementation and enforcement mechanisms of that Directive and simplify the regulatory environment while guaranteeing that IMO requirements are applied and implemented in a harmonised way across the Union.

(7) Requirements should therefore be established for marine equipment to meet the safety standards laid down in the applicable international instruments, including the relevant testing standards, in order to ensure that equipment which complies with those requirements can circulate unimpeded within the internal market and be placed on board ships flying the flag of any Member State.

(8) In order to allow for fair competition in the development of marine equipment, every effort should be made to promote the use of open standards in order to make them available freely or at a nominal charge, and permissible to all to copy, distribute and use for no fee or at a nominal fee.

(9) Decision No 768/2008/EC of the European Parliament and of the Council ... lays down common principles and reference provisions intended to apply across sectoral legislation in order to provide a coherent basis for revision or recasts of that legislation. That Decision constitutes a general framework of a horizontal nature for future legislation harmonising the conditions for the marketing of products and a reference text for existing legislation. That general framework provides appropriate solutions to the problems identified in the implementation of Directive 96/98/EC. It is therefore necessary to incorporate the definitions and reference provisions of Decision No 768/2008/EC into this Directive by making the adaptations which are required by the specific features of the marine equipment sector.

(10) In order to provide market surveillance authorities with additional, specific means to facilitate their task, an electronic tag could supplement or replace the wheel mark in due time.

(11) The responsibilities of the economic operators should be laid down in a way which is proportionate and non-discriminatory for those economic operators who are established within the Union, taking into account the fact that a significant proportion of the marine equipment falling within the scope of this Directive may never be imported and distributed in the territory of the Member States.

(12) Given that marine equipment is placed on board ships at the time of their construction or repair all over the world, market surveillance becomes particularly difficult and cannot be effectively supported by border controls. Therefore, the respective obligations of Member States and of economic operators within the Union should be clearly specified. Member States should ensure that only compliant equipment is installed on board ships flying their flags and that this obligation is fulfilled through issuance, endorsement or renewal of the certificates of such ships by the flag State administration under the international conventions, as well as through national market surveillance arrangements in place in accordance with the Union market surveillance framework laid down in Chapter III of Regulation (EC) No 765/2008 of the European Parliament and of the Council .... Member States should be supported in fulfilling those obligations by the information systems made available by the Commission for the assessment, notification and monitoring of bodies authorised to carry out conformity assessment tasks, the sharing of information in relation to approved marine equipment, applications withdrawn or refused, and non-compliance of equipment.

(13) In the first instance, the affixing of the wheel mark to the marine equipment by the manufacturer or, where relevant, the importer should be the guarantee pursuant to their obligations under this Directive that the equipment is compliant and may be placed on the market with a view to being placed on board an EU ship. Thereafter, certain provisions are necessary for the safe continuation and applicability of the wheel mark after it has been affixed and for the effective discharge of the task of national market surveillance authorities. The manufacturer or, where relevant, the importer or the distributor, should be obliged to provide the competent authorities with full and truthful information in relation to the equipment it has wheel marked to ensure that marine equipment remains safe. The manufacturer should be obliged to cooperate with market surveillance authorities, including as regard standards against which it has manufactured and certified equipment, and should also exercise due diligence in relation to marine equipment it places on the market. In this regard, a

manufacturer located outside the Union should appoint an authorised representative in order to ensure cooperation with competent national authorities.

(14) Compliance with international testing standards could best be demonstrated by means of conformity assessment procedures such as those laid down in Decision No 768/2008/EC. However, only those conformity assessment procedures which meet the requirements of the international instruments should be made available to manufacturers.

(15) In order to ensure a fair and efficient procedure when examining suspected non-compliance, the Member States should be encouraged to take all measures conducive to an exhaustive and objective evaluation of the risks;. if the Commission is satisfied that this condition has been met, it should not be obliged to repeat that evaluation when reviewing the restrictive measures adopted by the Member States as regards non-compliant equipment.

(16) When performing its investigative duties with regard to notified bodies, the Commission should keep Member States informed and should cooperate with them as far as possible, taking due account of its independent role.

(17) When the surveillance authorities of a Member State consider that marine equipment covered by this Directive is liable to present a risk to maritime safety, to health or to the environment, they should carry out evaluations or tests in relation to the equipment concerned. In cases where a risk is detected, the Member State should call upon the economic operator concerned to take the appropriate corrective action, or even to withdraw or recall the equipment concerned.

(18) The use of marine equipment not bearing the wheel mark should be allowed in exceptional circumstances, especially when it is not possible for a ship to obtain equipment bearing the wheel mark in a port or installation outside the Union or when equipment bearing the wheel mark is not available in the market.

(19) It is necessary to ensure that the attainment of the objectives of this Directive is not impaired by the absence of international standards or serious weaknesses or anomalies in existing standards, including testing standards, for specific items of marine equipment falling within the scope of this Directive. It is also necessary to identify the specific items of marine equipment which could benefit from electronic tagging. Moreover, it is necessary to keep up to date a non-essential element of this Directive, namely the references to standards as referred to in Annex III, when new standards become available. The power to adopt acts in accordance with Article 290 of the Treaty on the Functioning of the European Union should therefore be delegated to the Commission in respect of the adoption, under certain conditions and on an interim basis, of harmonised technical specifications and testing standards and in order to amend those references. It is of particular importance that the Commission carry out appropriate consultations during its preparatory work, including at expert level. The Commission, when preparing and drawing up delegated acts, should ensure a simultaneous, timely and appropriate transmission of relevant documents to the European Parliament and to the Council.

(20) In order to meet the objectives of this Directive, the international instruments should be uniformly implemented in the internal market. It is therefore necessary, for each item of marine equipment for which the approval of the flag State is required by the international conventions, to identify in a clear and timely way the design, construction and performance requirements as well as the associated testing standards laid down in the international instruments for that equipment, and to adopt common criteria and procedures, including timeframes, for the implementation of those requirements and standards by notified bodies, Member State authorities and economic operators, including any operator responsible for placing equipment on board an EU ship. It is also necessary to ensure that the attainment of the objectives of this Directive is not impaired by shortcomings in the applicable technical specifications and testing standards or in cases where the IMO has failed to produce appropriate standards for marine equipment falling within the scope of this Directive.

(21) The international instruments, with the exception of testing standards, should automatically apply in their up-to-date version. In order to mitigate the risk that the introduction of new testing standards into Union legislation causes disproportionate difficulties for the Union fleet and for economic operators, from the standpoint of clarity and legal certainty, the

entry into force of such new testing standards should not be automatic but, rather, should be explicitly indicated by the Commission.

(22) In order to ensure uniform conditions for the implementation of this Directive, implementing powers should be conferred on the Commission. Those powers should be exercised in accordance with Regulation (EU) No 182/2011 of the European Parliament and of the Council ....

(23) In order to facilitate a harmonised, rapid and simple implementation of this Directive, implementing acts adopted pursuant to this Directive should take the form of Commission Regulations.

(24) In line with established practice, the committee referred to in this Directive can play a useful role in examining matters concerning the application of this Directive raised either by its chair or by a representative of a Member State in accordance with its rules of procedure.

(25) When matters relating to this Directive, other than its implementation or infringements, are being examined, for example, in a Commission expert group, the European Parliament should, in line with existing practice, receive full information and documentation and, where appropriate, an invitation to attend meetings.

(26) The Commission is assisted by the European Maritime Safety Agency, in accordance with Regulation (EC) No 1406/2002 of the European Parliament and of the Council ..., in the effective implementation of relevant binding legal acts of the Union and in the performance of the tasks therein entrusted to the Commission.

(27) The competent authorities and all economic operators should make all possible efforts to facilitate written communication in accordance with international practice, with a view to finding common means of communication.

(28) Since the objectives of this Directive, namely to enhance safety at sea and the prevention of marine pollution through the uniform application of the relevant international instruments relating to equipment to be placed on board ships, and to ensure the free movement of such equipment within the Union, cannot be sufficiently achieved by the Member States but can rather, by reason of the scale of the action, be better achieved at Union level, the Union may adopt measures, in accordance with the principle of subsidiarity as set out in Article 5 of the Treaty on European Union. In accordance with the principle of proportionality, as set out in that article, this Directive does not go beyond what is necessary in order to achieve those objectives.

(29) The measures to be adopted represent a major modification of the provisions of Directive 96/98/EC and therefore, in the interests of clarity, that Directive should be repealed and replaced by this Directive."

Chapter 1 of the directive is entitled "General Provisions": Chapter 2 deals with the "Wheel Mark" which is a stamp of compliance.

Objective of Directive 2014/90

37.009 Article 1 provides that the objective of Directive 2014/90 is to enhance safety at sea and to prevent marine pollution through the uniform application of the relevant international instruments relating to marine equipment to be placed on board EU ships, and to ensure the free movement of such equipment within the EU.

Definitions used in Directive 2014/90

37.010 Article 2 sets out 22 definitions for the purposes of the directive.

37.011 Article 2(1) provides that the phrase "marine equipment" means equipment falling within the scope of the directive in accordance with Article 3 of the directive.

37.012 Article 2(2) provides that the term "EU Ship" means "a ship flying the flag of a Member State and falling within the scope of the international conventions".

37.013 Article 2(3) provides that the phrase "International Conventions" means the following conventions, together with their protocols and codes of mandatory application, adopted under the auspices of the International Maritime Organization ("IMO"), which have entered into force and which lay down specific requirements for the approval by the flag State of equipment to be placed on board ships: (a) the 1972 Convention on the International Regulations for Preventing Collisions at Sea ("Colreg"); (b) the 1973 International Convention for the Prevention of Pollution from Ships ("MARPOL"); and (c) the 1974 SOLAS.

37.014 The terms "testing standards" means the testing standards for marine equipment set by: the IMO; the International Organization for Standardization ("ISO"); the International Electrotechnical Commission ("IEC"); the European Committee for Standardization ("CEN"); the European Committee for Electrotechnical Standardization ("CENELEC"); the International Telecommunications Union ("ITU"); the European Telecommunications Standards Institute ("ETSI"); the European Commission (in accordance with Article 8 and 27(6) of the directive); and the regulatory authorities recognised in the mutual recognition agreement to which the EU is a party.

37.015 The phrase "international instruments" is defined as meaning the international conventions, together with the resolutions and circulars of the IMO giving effect to those conventions in their up-to-date version, and the testing standards.[4]

37.016 The directive is curious in that it embodies a symbol which has an important role. The symbol is the "wheel mark" which is a symbol referred to in Article 9 and set out in Annex I of the directive or, as appropriate, the electronic tag referred to in Article 11.[5]

37.017 The term "notified body" is used in the directive and means an organisation designated by the competent national administration of a Member State in accordance with Article 17.[6]

37.018 The phrase "making available on the market" means any supply of marine equipment on the EU market in the course of a commercial activity whether in return for payment or free of charge.[7] In that context, the expression "placing on the market" means the first making available of marine equipment on the EU market.[8]

37.019 The word "manufacturer" is defined as meaning (i.e. it is a closed and not an embracive definition) "any natural or legal person who manufacturers marine equipment or has marine equipment designed or manufactured, and markets that equipment under its name or trademark".[9] So the definition is broad enough to cover those who contract manufacture rather than manufacture in their own right. Such a person would be an "economic operator" for the purposes of Article 2(14) of the directive.

37.020 The phrase "authorised representative" means "any natural or legal person established within the Union who has received a written mandate from a manufacturer to

---

4 Dir. 2014/90, Art. 2(5).
5 Dir. 2014/90, Art. 2(6).
6 Dir. 2014/90, Art. 2(7).
7 Dir. 2014/90, Art. 2(8).
8 Dir. 2014/90, Art. 2(9).
9 Dir. 2014/90, Art. 2(10).

act on its behalf in relation to specified tasks".[10] The requirement for a written mandate is absolute and an oral arrangement would appear to fall outside the regime. Such a person would be an "economic operator" for the purposes of Article 2(14) of the directive.

37.021 The word "importer" means any natural or legal person established within the EU who places marine equipment from a third country on the Union market.[11] Such a person would be an "economic operator" for the purposes of Article 2(14) of the directive.

37.022 The term "distributor" means "any natural or legal person in the supply chain, other than the manufacturer or the importer, who makes marine equipment available on the market".[12] This is a conventional definition but would probably include an "agent" as well as a "distributor". Such a person would be an "economic operator" for the purposes of Article 2(14) of the directive.

37.023 The phrase "economic operators" is defined in a closed sense as meaning the manufacturer, the authorised representative, the importer and the distributor[13] – with each of those terms being, in turn, defined, in the directive itself.

37.024 The word "accreditation" means, under Article 2(15) of the directive, "accreditation as defined in point 10 of Article 2 of Regulation 765/2008".[14] In turn, point 10 of Article 2 of Regulation 765/2008[15] provides that

> "[a]ccreditation, though so far not regulated at Community level, is carried out in all Member States. The lack of common rules for that activity has resulted in different approaches and differing systems throughout the Community, with the result that the degree of rigour applied in the performance of accreditation has varied between Member States. It is therefore necessary to develop a comprehensive framework for accreditation and to lay down at Community level the principles for its operation and organisation."

37.025 The phrase "national accreditation body" is defined by Article 2(16) as meaning a national accreditation body as defined in point 11 of Article 2 of Regulation 765/2008 which is, in turn, defined as the "establishment of a uniform national accreditation body should be without prejudice to the allocation of functions within Member States".

37.026 The phrase "conformity assessment" is defined as meaning the process carried out by the notified bodies, in accordance with Article 15 of the directive, demonstrating whether marine equipment complies with the requirements laid down in the directive.[16] This should be read in conjunction with the next definition considered, that of "conformity assessment body".

37.027 A definition of "conformity assessment body" is provided by Article 2(18) as meaning "a body that performs conformity assessment activities including calibration, testing, certification and inspection". Obviously, the concept of "conformity assessment" should be seen in the light of the definition just discussed of "conformity assessment".

---

10 Dir. 2014/90, Art. 2(11).
11 Dir. 2014/90, Art. 2(12).
12 Dir. 2014/90, Art. 2(13).
13 Dir. 2014/90, Art. 2(14).
14 OJ L218/30, 13 August 2008.
15 Ibid.
16 Dir. 2014/90, Art. 2(17).

37.028 Recalls are extremely important in the context of marine equipment with manufacturers (in the broadest sense of that term) being liable to recall equipment so as to ensure safety standards. The term "recall" is defined by Article 2(19) as meaning "any measure aimed at achieving the return of marine equipment that has already been placed on board EU ships or purchased with the intention of being placed on board EU ships".[17]

37.029 The word "withdrawal" means "any measure aimed at preventing marine equipment in the supply chain from being made available on the market"[18] so it is quite a wide definition.

37.030 The phrase "EU declaration of conformity" means a "statement issued by the manufacturer in accordance with Article 16".[19]

37.031 The word "product" means an "item of marine equipment".[20]

Scope of Directive 2014/90

37.032 Article 3(1) provides that the directive shall apply to equipment placed or to be placed on board an EU ship and for which the approval of the flag State administration is required by the international instruments, regardless of whether the ship is situated in the Union at the time when it is fitted with the equipment. Notwithstanding the fact that this equipment may also fall within the scope of instruments of Union law other than the directive, that equipment shall, for the purpose set out in Article 1 of the directive, be subject only to the directive.[21]

Requirements for marine equipment

37.033 Article 4(1) provides that marine equipment that is placed on board an EU ship on or after the date referred to in the second subparagraph of Article 39(1) must meet the design, construction and performance requirements of the international instruments as applicable at the time when that equipment is placed on board. Compliance of marine equipment with the requirements referred to in paragraph 1 must be demonstrated solely in accordance with the testing standards and by means of the conformity assessment procedures referred to in Article 15.[22] These requirements and standards must be implemented in a uniform manner, in accordance with Article 35(2). The international instruments must apply, without prejudice to the conformity checking procedure set out in Article 5 of Regulation 2099/2002 of the Parliament and of the Council.[23]

Application of the directive

37.034 Article 5 deals with the application of Directive 2014/90. Article 5(1) provides that when Member States issue, endorse or renew the certificates of the ships flying their

---

17 Dir. 2014/90, Art. 2(19).
18 Dir. 2014/90, Art. 2(20).
19 Dir. 2014/90, Art. 2(21).
20 Dir. 2014/90, Art. 2(22).
21 Dir. 2014/90, Art. 3(2).
22 Dir. 2014/90, Art. 4(2).
23 Dir. 2014/90, Art. 4(4).

flag as required by the international conventions, they must ensure that the marine equipment on board those ships complies with the requirements of Directive 2014/90. Under Article 5(2), Member States must take the necessary measures to ensure that marine equipment on board ships flying their flag complies with the requirements in the international instruments which are applicable to equipment already placed on board. Implementing powers must be conferred upon the Commission to ensure the uniform application of those measures, in accordance with Article 35(3).

Functioning of the internal market

37.035 Member States must not prohibit the placing on the market or the placing on board an EU ship of marine equipment which complies with the directive, nor refuse to issue the certificates relating thereto to the ships flying their flag, or to renew the said certificates.[24]

Transfer of a ship to the flag of a Member State

37.036 The EU has long been concerned with trying to facilitate the transfer of ships between and to EU flags. Article 7 of the directive deals with the flagging in of vessels. Article 7(1) provides that in the case of a non-EU ship which is to be transferred to the flag of a Member State, that ship shall, during transfer, be subject to inspection by the receiving Member State to verify that the actual condition of its marine equipment corresponds to its safety certificates and either complies with the directive and bears the wheel mark or its equivalent, to the satisfaction of that Member State's administration, to marine equipment certified in accordance with the directive as of 18 September 2016. Article 7(2) provides that in cases where the date of installation on board of marine equipment cannot be established, Member States may determine satisfactory requirements of equivalence, taking into account relevant international instruments. Unless the equipment either bears the wheel mark or the administration considers it to be equivalent, it shall be replaced.[25] Marine equipment which is considered equivalent pursuant to Article 7 shall be issued with a certificate by the Member State which shall at all times be carried with the equipment.[26] That certificate shall give the flag Member State's permission for the equipment to be retained on board the ship and impose any restrictions or lay down any provisions relating to the use of the equipment.[27]

Standards for marine equipment

37.037 Article 8 is a detailed provision dealing with the all-important standards for marine equipment. In some ways, this is the heart of the directive.

---

24 Dir. 2014/90, Art. 6.
25 Dir. 2014/90, Art. 7(3).
26 Dir. 2014/90, Art. 7(4).
27 Ibid.

37.038 Article 8(1) provides that without prejudice to Directive 98/34 of the European Parliament and the Council,[28] as amended by Regulation 1025/2012 of the European Parliament and of the Council,[29] the EU shall pursue the development by the IMO and by standardisation bodies of appropriate international standards, including detailed technical specifications and testing standards, for marine equipment whose use or installation on board ships is deemed necessary to enhance maritime safety and the prevention of marine pollution.[30] The Commission is obliged to monitor such developments on a regular basis.[31] In the absence of an international standard for a specific item of marine equipment, in exceptional circumstances where duly justified by an appropriate analysis and in order to remove a serious and unacceptable threat to maritime safety, to health or to the environment and taking into account any ongoing work at IMO level, the Commission is to be empowered to adopt, by means of delegated acts in accordance with Article 37,[32] harmonised technical specifications and testing standards for that specific item of marine equipment.[33] Article 8(2) states that it is of particular importance that the Commission carry out consultations with experts, including Member States' experts, during the preparation of such delegated acts. Those technical specifications and testing standards are stated to apply on an interim basis until such time as the IMO has adopted a standard for that specific item of marine equipment. Article 8(3) provides that in exceptional circumstances where duly justified by an appropriate analysis and if it is necessary to remove an identified unacceptable threat to maritime safety, to health or to the environment due to a serious weakness or anomaly in an existing standard for a specific item of marine equipment indicated by the Commission pursuant to Article 35(2) or (3) and taking into account any ongoing work at IMO level, the Commission shall be empowered to adopt, by means of delegated acts in accordance with Article 37, harmonised technical specifications and testing standards for that specific item of marine equipment, to the extent necessary to remedy the serious weakness or anomaly only. Article 8(3) goes on to provide that it is of particular importance that the Commission carry out consultations with experts, including Member States' experts, during the preparation of such delegated acts. Those technical specifications and testing standards shall apply on an interim basis until such time as the IMO has reviewed the standard applicable to that specific item of marine equipment. The technical specifications and standards adopted in accordance with Article 8(2) and (3) shall, by virtue of Article 8(4), be made accessible free of charge by the Commission.

---

28 Directive 98/34 of the European Parliament and the Council of 22 June 1998 laying down a procedure for the provision of information in the field of technical standards and regulations (OJ L204, 21 July 1998, p. 37).

29 Regulation (EU) No 1025/2012 of the European Parliament and of the Council of 25 October 2012 on European standardisation, amending Council Dirs 89/686 and 93/15 and Dirs 94/9, 94/25, 95/16, 97/23, 98/34, 2004/22, 2007/23, 2009/23 and 2009/105 of the European Parliament and of the Council and repealing Council Dec. 87/95 and Dec. 1673/2006 of the European Parliament and of the Council (OJ L316, 14 November 2012, p. 12).

30 Dir. 2014/90, Art. 8(1).

31 Ibid.

32 Art. 37 deals with the exercise of the delegation of the Commission's functions.

33 Dir. 2014/90, Art. 8(2).

The wheel mark

37.039 Chapter 2 of the directive deals with the "wheel mark". The "wheel mark" is a key feature of the EU marine equipment regime and Chapter 2 sets out the rules on the subject.

37.040 Article 9 ("The Wheel Mark") provides, in the somewhat curiously drafted paragraph 1, that "[m]arine equipment the compliance of which with the requirements laid down in this Directive has been demonstrated in accordance with the relevant conformity assessment procedures shall have the wheel mark affixed to it". The wheel mark shall not be affixed to any other product.[34] The form of the wheel mark to be used shall be as set out in Annex I.[35] The use of the wheel mark is subject to the general principles set out in paragraphs 1 and 3 to 6 of Article 30 of Regulation 765/2008, where any reference to the Conformité Européene ("CE") marking shall be construed as a reference to the wheel mark.[36]

37.041 Annex I describes the "Wheel Mark". It provides that the mark of conformity must take the following form: if the wheel mark is reduced or enlarged the proportions given in the graduated drawing must be respected; the various components of the wheel mark must have substantially the same vertical dimension, which may not be less than 5 mm; but that minimum dimension may be waived for small devices. Annex II is entitled "Conformity Assessment Procedures". Annex III is entitled "Requirements to be met by Conformity Assessment Bodies in order to become Notified Bodies". Annex IV is entitled "Notification Procedure". Annex V sets out the "Requirements to be Met by Notifying Authorities".

Rules and conditions for affixing the wheel mark

37.042 The wheel mark must be affixed visibly, legibly and indelibly to the product or to its data plate and, where relevant, embedded in its software.[37] Where that is not possible or not warranted on account of the nature of the product, it shall be affixed to the packaging and to the accompanying documents.[38] The wheel mark must be affixed at the end of the production phase.[39] The wheel mark must be followed by the identification number of the notified body, where that body is involved in the production control phase, and by the year in which the mark is affixed.[40] The identification number of the notified body shall be affixed by the body itself or, under its instructions, by the manufacturer or the manufacturer's authorised representative.[41]

---

34 Dir. 2014/90, Art. 9(3).
35 Ibid.
36 Ibid.
37 Dir. 2014/90, Art. 10(1).
38 Ibid.
39 Dir. 2014/90, Art. 10(2).
40 Dir. 2014/90, Art. 10(3).
41 Dir. 2014/90, Art. 10(4).

Electronic tag

37.043 In order to facilitate market surveillance and prevent the counterfeiting of specific items of marine equipment referred to in Article 11(3), manufacturers may use an appropriate and reliable form of electronic tag instead of, or in addition to, the wheel mark.[42] In such a case, Articles 9 and 10 shall apply, as appropriate, *mutatis mutandis*.[43] The Commission must carry out a cost–benefit analysis concerning the use of the electronic tag as a supplement to, or a replacement of, the wheel mark.[44] The Commission may adopt delegated acts, in accordance with Article 37,[45] in order to identify the specific items of marine equipment which can benefit from electronic tagging. It is of particular importance that the Commission carry out consultations with experts, including Member States' experts, during the preparation of such delegated acts.

37.044 Implementing powers shall be conferred upon the Commission in order to lay down, in the form of Commission regulations and in accordance with the examination procedure referred to in Article 38(2), appropriate technical criteria as regards the design, performance, affixing and use of electronic tags.[46]

37.045 For the equipment identified in accordance with Article 38(3), the wheel mark may, within three years after the date of adoption of the appropriate technical criteria referred to in Article 38(4), be supplemented by an appropriate and reliable form of electronic tag.[47]

37.046 Article 11(6) provides that for the equipment identified in accordance with Article 11(3), the wheel mark may be replaced, five years after the date of adoption of the appropriate technical criteria referred to in Article 11(4), by an appropriate and reliable form of electronic tag.

Obligations of economic operators

37.047 Chapter 3 is entitled "Obligations of Economic Operators". There are three articles: Article 12 ("Obligations of Manufacturers"); Article 13 ("Authorised Representatives"); and Article 14 ("Other economic operators").

Obligations of manufacturers

37.048 Article 12 is entitled "Obligations of Manufacturers". By affixing the wheel mark, manufacturers must take on responsibility for guaranteeing that the marine equipment to which the mark is affixed has been designed and manufactured in accordance with the technical specifications and standards implemented in accordance with Article 35(2), and shall assume the obligations laid down in paragraphs 2 to 9 of the article.[48] Manufacturers must draw up the required technical documentation and have the

---

42 Dir. 2014/90, Art. 11(1).
43 Ibid.
44 Dir. 2014/90, Art. 11(2).
45 Art. 37 deals with the delegation of the Commission's powers.
46 Dir. 2014/90, Art. 11(4).
47 Dir. 2014/90, Art. 11(5).
48 Dir. 2014/90, Art. 12(1). See Art. 13(2) which is discussed below.

applicable conformity assessment procedures carried out.[49] Article 12(3) provides that where the compliance of marine equipment with the applicable requirements has been demonstrated by the conformity assessment procedure, manufacturers must draw up an EU declaration of conformity in accordance with Article 16 and affix the wheel mark in accordance with Articles 9 and 10 of the directive. Equally, under Article 12(4), manufacturers must keep the technical documentation and the EU declaration of conformity referred to in Article 16 for at least ten years after the wheel mark has been affixed and in no case for a period shorter than the expected life of the marine equipment concerned. Under Article 12(5), manufacturers must ensure that procedures are in place for series production to remain in conformity while changes in marine equipment design or characteristics and changes in the requirements in the international instruments as referred to in Article 4, on the basis of which conformity of marine equipment is declared, must be taken into account. When necessary in accordance with Annex II, manufacturers shall have a new conformity assessment carried out.[50] Manufacturers must ensure that their products bear a type, batch or serial number or other element allowing their identification, or, where the size or nature of the product does not allow it, that the required information is provided on the packaging or in a document accompanying the product or both, as appropriate.[51]

37.049 Manufacturers must indicate their name, registered trade name or registered trade mark and the address at which they can be contacted on the product or, where that is not possible, on its packaging or in a document accompanying the product or both, as appropriate. The address must indicate a single point at which the manufacturer can be contacted.[52]

37.050 Manufacturers must ensure that the product is accompanied by instructions and all necessary information for safe installation on board and safe use of the product, including limitations of use, if any, that can be easily understood by the users, together with any other documentation required by the international instruments or testing standards.[53]

37.051 Manufacturers who consider or have reason to believe that a product to which they have affixed the wheel mark is not in conformity with the applicable design, construction and performance requirements and with the testing standards implemented in accordance with Article 35(2) and (3), shall immediately take the necessary corrective measures to bring that product into conformity, to withdraw it or to recall it, if appropriate. In addition, where the product presents a risk, manufacturers shall immediately inform the competent national authorities of the Member States, giving details, in particular, of the non-compliance and of any corrective measures taken. Article 12(10) provides that manufacturers must, further to a reasoned request from a competent authority, promptly provide it with all the information and documentation necessary to demonstrate the conformity of the product, in a language which can be easily understood by or is acceptable to that authority, grant that authority access to their premises for market surveillance purposes in accordance with Article 19 of Regulation 765/2008 and provide

---

49 Dir. 2014/90, Art. 12(2).
50 Dir. 2014/90, Art. 12(5).
51 Dir. 2014/90, Art. 12(6).
52 Dir. 2014/90, Art. 12(7).
53 Dir. 2014/90, Art. 12(8).

samples or access to samples in accordance with Article 25(4) of Directive 2014/90. They shall co-operate with that authority, at its request, on any action taken to eliminate the risks posed by products which they have placed on the market.

Obligations of authorised representatives

37.052 Article 13 deals with the authorised representatives. Under Article 13(1), a manufacturer who is not located in the territory of at least one Member State must, by a written mandate, appoint an authorised representative for the EU and must indicate in the mandate the name of the authorised representative and the address at which it can be contacted. Fulfilment of the obligations laid down in Article 12(1) and the drawing-up of technical documentation must not form part of the authorised representative's mandate.[54] Under Article 13(3), an authorised representative must perform the tasks specified in the mandate received from the manufacturer. Moreover, under the same provision, the mandate must allow the authorised representative to do at least the following: (a) keep the EU declaration of conformity and the technical documentation at the disposal of national surveillance authorities for at least ten years after the wheel mark has been affixed and in no case for a period shorter than the expected life of the marine equipment concerned; (b) further to a reasoned request from a competent authority, provide that authority with all the information and documentation necessary to demonstrate the conformity of a product; and (c) co-operate with the competent authorities, at their request, on any action taken to eliminate the risks posed by products covered by its mandate.

Other economic operators

37.053 Article 14(1) provides that importers must indicate their name, registered trade name or registered trade mark and the address at which they can be contacted on the product or, where that is not possible, on its packaging or in a document accompanying the product or both, as appropriate.

37.054 Importers and distributors must, further to a reasoned request from a competent authority, provide it with all the information and documentation necessary to demonstrate the conformity of a product in a language which can be easily understood by, or is acceptable to, that authority.[55] They shall co-operate with that authority, at its request, on any action taken to eliminate the risks posed by products which they have placed on the market.[56]

37.055 An importer or distributor must be considered a manufacturer for the purposes of Directive 2014/90 and shall be subject to the obligations of the manufacturer under Article 12, where it places marine equipment on the market or on board an EU ship under its name or trademark or modifies marine equipment already placed on the market in such a way that compliance with the applicable requirements may be affected.[57]

37.056 Moreover, for a period of at least ten years after the wheel mark has been affixed and in no case for a period shorter than the expected life of the marine equipment

---

54 Dir. 2014/90, Art. 13(2).
55 Dir. 2014/90, Art. 14(2).
56 Ibid.
57 Dir. 2014/90, Art. 14(3).

concerned, economic operators must, on request, identify the following to the market surveillance authorities: (a) any economic operator who has supplied them with a product; and (b) any economic operator to whom they have supplied a product.

Conformity assessment and notification of conformity assessment bodies

37.057 Chapter 4 deals with conformity assessment and notification of conformity assessment bodies.

37.058 Article 15 sets out the conformity assessment procedures. Put simply, the conformity assessment procedures are as set out in Annex II.[58] Member States must ensure that the manufacturer or the manufacturer's authorised representative has the conformity assessment carried out, through a notified body, for a specific item of marine equipment, by using one of the options provided by means of implementing acts adopted by the Commission in accordance with the examination procedure referred to in Article 38(2), from among one of the following procedures: (a) where the EC type examination (module B) is to be used, before being placed on the market, all equipment shall be subject to (i) production-quality assurance (module D); or (ii) product-quality assurance (module E); or (iii) product verification (module F); (b) where sets of marine equipment are produced individually or in small quantities and not in series or in mass, the conformity assessment procedure may be the EC unit verification (module G).[59] The Commission must, by means of the information system made available for that purpose, keep an up-to-date list of approved marine equipment and applications withdrawn or refused and shall make that list available to interested parties.[60]

EU declaration of conformity

37.059 Article 16 addresses the important issue of the "EU declaration of conformity". This is not a protectionist measure but rather it is designed to ensure safety and conformity with the relevant standards. Article 16(1) provides that the EU declaration of conformity must state that the fulfilment of the requirements laid down in accordance with Article 4 has been demonstrated. Under Article 16(2), the EU declaration of conformity shall follow the model structure set out in Annex III to Decision 768/2008.[61] It shall contain the elements specified in the relevant modules set out in Annex II to this directive and shall be kept up to date. By drawing up the EU declaration of conformity, the manufacturer must assume the responsibility and the obligations referred to in Article 12(1).[62] When marine equipment is placed on board an EU ship, a copy of the EU declaration of conformity covering the equipment concerned must be provided to the ship, and must be kept on board until the equipment is removed from the ship.[63] It must be translated by the manufacturer into the language or languages required by the flag Member State, including

---

58 Dir. 2014/90, Art. 15(1).
59 Dir. 2014/90, Art. 14(2).
60 Dir. 2014/90, Art. 14(3).
61 I.e. Decision 768/2008 of the European Parliament and of the Council of 9 July 2008 on a common framework for the marketing of products, and repealing Council Decision 93/465 (OJ L218/82, 13 August 2008).
62 Dir. 2014/90, Art. 16(3).
63 Dir. 2014/90, Art. 16(4).

at least a language commonly used in the maritime transport sector.[64] A copy of the EU declaration of conformity must be provided to the notified body or to the bodies which carried out the relevant conformity assessment procedures.[65]

Notification of conformity assessment bodies

37.060 Member States must, by means of the information system made available by the Commission for that purpose, notify the Commission and the other Member States of bodies authorised to carry out conformity assessment tasks under Directive 2014/90.[66] Notified bodies must comply with the requirements laid down in Annex III.[67]

Notifying authorities

37.061 Article 18 deals with notifying authorities. Article 18(1) provides that Member States must designate a notifying authority that shall be responsible for setting up and carrying out the necessary procedures for the assessment and notification of conformity assessment bodies and the monitoring of notified bodies, including compliance with Article 20. Under Article 18(2), notified bodies must be monitored at least every two years and, in what may seem like an intrusion in sovereignty, the Commission may choose to participate as an observer in the monitoring exercise. Member States may decide that the assessment and monitoring referred to in Article 18(1) are to be carried out by a national accreditation body.[68] Where the notifying authority delegates or otherwise entrusts the assessment, notification or monitoring referred to in paragraph 1 to a body which is not a governmental entity, that body shall be a legal entity and shall comply *mutatis mutandis* with the requirements laid down in Annex V[69] and it shall also have in place arrangements to cover liability arising out of its activities[70] – in this context, the notifying authority must take full responsibility for the tasks performed by this body. The notifying authority shall also comply with the requirements laid down in Annex V.[71]

Information obligation on notifying authorities

37.062 Member States must inform the Commission of their procedures for the assessment and notification of conformity assessment bodies and the monitoring of such bodies, and of any changes thereto.[72] Moreover, the Commission must, by means of the information system made available for that purpose, make that information publicly available.[73]

---

64 Ibid.
65 Dir. 2014/90, Art. 16(5).
66 Dir. 2014/90, Art. 17(2).
67 Ibid.
68 Dir. 2014/90, Art. 18(3).
69 Dir. 2014/90, Art. 18(4).
70 Ibid.
71 Dir. 2014/90, Art. 18(5).
72 Dir. 2014/90, Art. 19(1).
73 Dir. 2014/90, Art. 19(2).

Subsidiaries of, and subcontracting by, notified bodies

37.063 Where a notified body subcontracts specific tasks connected with conformity assessment or has recourse to a subsidiary, it shall ensure that the subcontractor or the subsidiary meets the requirements set out in Annex III and shall inform the notifying authority accordingly.[74] Notified bodies must take full responsibility for the tasks performed by subcontractors or subsidiaries wherever these are established.[75] Activities may be subcontracted or carried out by a subsidiary only with the agreement of the client.[76] Notified bodies must keep at the disposal of the notifying authority the relevant documents concerning the assessment of the qualifications of the subcontractor or the subsidiary and the work carried out by such subcontractor or subsidiary under this directive.[77]

Changes to notifications

37.064 Where a notifying authority has ascertained, or has been informed, that a notified body no longer meets the requirements laid down in Annex III, or that it is failing to fulfil its obligations under the directive, the notifying authority must restrict, suspend or withdraw notification as appropriate, depending on the seriousness of the failure to meet those requirements or fulfil those obligations. It shall, by means of the information system made available by the Commission for that purpose, immediately inform the Commission and the other Member States accordingly.[78] If there is a restriction, suspension or withdrawal of notification, or where the notified body has ceased its activity, the notifying Member State must take appropriate steps to ensure that the files of that body are either processed by another notified body or kept available for the responsible notifying and market surveillance authorities at their request.[79]

Challenges to the competence of notified bodies

37.065 The Commission must investigate all cases where it doubts, based on the information available to it or brought to its attention, the competence of a notified body or the continued fulfilment by a notified body of the requirements and responsibilities to which it is subject.[80] The notifying Member State must provide the Commission, on request, with all information relating to the basis for the notification or the maintenance of the competence of the body concerned.[81] Indeed, the Commission must ensure that all sensitive information obtained in the course of its investigations is treated confidentially.[82] Where the Commission ascertains that a notified body does not meet, or no longer meets, the requirements for its notification, it must without delay inform the notifying Member

---

74 Dir. 2014/90, Art. 20(1).
75 Dir. 2014/90, Art. 20(2).
76 Dir. 2014/90, Art. 20(3).
77 Dir. 2014/90, Art. 20(4).
78 Dir. 2014/90, Art. 21(1).
79 Dir. 2014/90, Art. 21(2).
80 Dir. 2014/90, Art. 22(1).
81 Dir. 2014/90, Art. 22(2).
82 Dir. 2014/90, Art. 22(3).

State accordingly and request it to take the necessary corrective measures without delay, including de-notification if necessary.[83]

Operational obligations of notified bodies

37.066 Notified bodies must carry out conformity assessments or have them carried out in accordance with the procedures provided for in Article 15.[84] Where a notified body finds that the obligations laid down in Article 12 have not been met by a manufacturer, it shall require that manufacturer to take appropriate corrective measures without delay and shall not issue a conformity certificate.[85] Where, in the course of monitoring conformity following the issue of a conformity certificate, a notified body finds that a product no longer complies, it must require the manufacturer to take appropriate corrective measures without delay and shall suspend or withdraw the certificate if necessary. Where corrective measures are not taken or do not have the required effect, the notified body shall restrict, suspend or withdraw the certificate, as appropriate.[86]

Obligation of notified bodies to provide information

37.067 Notified bodies must inform the notifying authority of the following: (a) any refusal, restriction, suspension or withdrawal of a conformity certificate; (b) any circumstances affecting the scope of, and the conditions for notification; (c) any request for information which they have received from market surveillance authorities regarding conformity assessment activities; (d) on request, conformity assessment activities performed within the scope of their notification and any other activity performed, including cross-border activities and subcontracting.[87] Notified bodies must provide the Commission and the Member States, on request, with relevant information concerning issues relating to negative and positive conformity assessment results.[88] Notified bodies must provide the other notified bodies carrying out conformity assessment activities covering the same products with information concerning negative and, on request, positive conformity assessment results.[89]

Union market surveillance, control of products, safeguard provisions

37.068 Chapter 5 is entitled "Union Market Surveillance, Control of Products, Safeguard Provisions". Article 25 deals with EU market surveillance framework.

EU market surveillance framework

37.069 In the context of marine equipment, the Member States must undertake market surveillance in accordance with the EU market surveillance framework laid down in

---

83 Dir. 2014/90, Art. 22(4).
84 Dir. 2014/90, Art. 23(1).
85 Dir. 2014/90, Art. 23(2).
86 Dir. 2014/90, Art. 23(3).
87 Dir. 2014/90, Art. 24(1).
88 Dir. 2014/90, Art. 24(2).
89 Ibid.

Chapter III of Regulation 765/2008, subject to paragraphs 2 and 3 of this article.[90] National market surveillance infrastructures and programmes must take into account the specific features of the marine equipment sector, including the various procedures carried out as part of the conformity assessment, and in particular the responsibilities placed on the flag State administration by the international conventions.[91] Market surveillance may include documentary checks as well as checks of marine equipment which bears the wheel mark, whether or not it has been placed on board ships.[92] Checks of marine equipment already placed on board shall be limited to such examination as can be carried out while the equipment concerned remains fully functional on board.[93] Where the market surveillance authorities of a Member State, as defined in Regulation 765/2008, intend to carry out sample checks, they may, when it is reasonable and practicable to do so, request the manufacturer to make the necessary samples available or to give on-the-spot access to the samples at the manufacturer's own cost.[94]

Procedure for dealing with marine equipment presenting a risk at national level

37.070 Where the market surveillance authorities of a Member State have sufficient reason to believe that marine equipment covered by Directive 2014/90 presents a risk to maritime safety, to health or to the environment, they shall carry out an evaluation in relation to the marine equipment concerned covering all the requirements laid down in Directive 2014/90.[95] The relevant economic operators must co-operate as necessary with the market surveillance authorities.[96] Where, in the course of that evaluation, the market surveillance authorities find that the marine equipment does not comply with the requirements laid down in the directive, they shall without delay require the relevant economic operator to take all appropriate corrective actions to bring the marine equipment into compliance with those requirements, to withdraw the marine equipment from the market, or to recall it within such reasonable period, commensurate with the nature of the risk, as they may prescribe.[97] The market surveillance authorities must inform the relevant notified body accordingly.[98]

37.071 Article 26(2) provides that where the market surveillance authorities consider that non-compliance is not restricted to their national territory or to ships flying their flag, they must inform the Commission and the other Member States, by means of the information system made available by the Commission for market surveillance purposes, of the results of the evaluation carried out under Article 26(1) and of the actions which they have required the economic operator to take. Article 21 of Regulation 765/2008 shall apply to the measures referred to in Article 26(2) of Directive 2014/90.

37.072 The economic operator must ensure that all appropriate corrective action is taken in respect of all the products concerned that it has made available on the market

---

90 Dir. 2014/90, Art. 25(1).
91 Dir. 2014/90, Art. 25(2).
92 Dir. 2014/90, Art. 25(3).
93 Ibid.
94 Ibid.
95 Dir. 2014/90, Art.26(1).
96 Ibid.
97 Ibid.
98 Ibid.

throughout the EU or, as the case may be, placed or delivered to be placed on board EU ships.[99] Where the relevant economic operator does not take adequate corrective action within the period prescribed by the market surveillance authorities in accordance with the second subparagraph of Article 26(1),[100] or otherwise fails to meet its obligations under the directive, the market surveillance authorities must take all appropriate provisional measures to prohibit or restrict the marine equipment being made available on their national market or placed on board ships flying their flag, to withdraw the product from that market or to recall it.[101] The market surveillance authorities must inform the Commission and the other Member States, without delay, of those measures.[102]

37.073 The information on the measures taken by the market surveillance authorities referred to in Article 26(4) must include all available details, in particular the data necessary for the identification of the non-compliant marine equipment, the origin of the product, the nature of the alleged non-compliance and the risk involved, the nature and duration of the national measures taken and the arguments put forward by the economic operator concerned. In particular, the market surveillance authorities must indicate whether the non-compliance is due to either: (a) failure of the marine equipment to comply with the applicable design, construction and performance requirements as laid down pursuant to Article 4; (b) non-compliance with the testing standards referred to in Article 4 during the conformity assessment procedure; and (c) shortcomings in those testing standards.

37.074 Article 26(6) provides that Member States other than the Member State initiating the procedure must, without delay, inform the Commission and the other Member States of any measures adopted and of any additional information at their disposal relating to the non-compliance of the marine equipment concerned, and, in the event of disagreement with the notified national measure, of their objections.

37.075 Where, within four months of receipt of the information concerning the measures taken by the market surveillance authorities, as referred to in paragraph 4, no objection has been raised by a Member State or by the Commission in respect of a provisional measure taken by a Member State, that measure shall be deemed justified.[103] Member States must ensure that appropriate restrictive measures in respect of the marine equipment concerned, such as withdrawal of the product from their market, are taken without delay.[104]

---

99 Dir. 2014/90, Art. 26(3).

100 I.e. the provision in Art. 26(1) which states: "[w]here, in the course of that evaluation, the market surveillance authorities find that the marine equipment does not comply with the requirements laid down in this Directive, they shall without delay require the relevant economic operator to take all appropriate corrective actions to bring the marine equipment into compliance with those requirements, to withdraw the marine equipment from the market, or to recall it within such reasonable period, commensurate with the nature of the risk, as they may prescribe".

101 Dir. 2014/90, Art. 26(4).

102 Ibid.

103 Dir. 2014/90, Art. 26(7).

104 Dir. 2014/90, Art. 26(8).

EU safeguard procedure

37.076 Article 27(1) provides that where, on completion of the procedure set out in Article 26(3) and (4), objections are raised against a measure taken by a Member State, or where the Commission considers that a national measure may be contrary to EU legislation, the Commission must without delay enter into consultation with the Member States and the relevant economic operator or operators and shall evaluate the relevant national measure.[105] On the basis of the results of that evaluation, the Commission shall decide whether or not the relevant national measure is justified.[106]

37.077 For the purposes of Article 27(1), where the Commission is satisfied that the procedure followed in the adoption of the national measure is appropriate for an exhaustive and objective evaluation of the risk and that the national measure complies with Article 21 of Regulation 765/2008, it may limit itself to examining the appropriateness and proportionality of the relevant national measure in relation to the said risk.

37.078 The Commission must address its decision to all Member States and must immediately communicate it to them and to the relevant economic operator or operators.[107]

37.079 If the relevant national measure is considered justified, all Member States must take the measures necessary to ensure that the non-compliant marine equipment is withdrawn from their market, and, where necessary, recalled.[108] They must inform the Commission accordingly. If the relevant national measure is considered unjustified, the Member State concerned must withdraw it.[109]

> "6. Where the non-compliance of the marine equipment is attributed to shortcomings in the testing standards referred to in Article 4, the Commission may, in order to fulfil the objective of the Directive, confirm, modify or revoke a national safeguard measure by means of implementing acts in accordance with the examination procedure referred to in Article 38(2)."

The Commission shall furthermore be empowered to adopt, by means of delegated acts in accordance with the procedure referred to in Article 37, interim harmonised requirements and testing standards for that specific item of marine equipment.[110] The criteria laid down in Article 8(3) must apply accordingly.[111] These requirements and testing standards must be made accessible free of charge by the Commission.[112]

37.080 Where the testing standard concerned is a European standard, the Commission must inform the relevant European standardisation body or bodies and must bring the matter before the committee set up by Article 5 of Directive 98/34.[113] That committee must consult the relevant European standardisation body or bodies and deliver its opinion without delay.

---

105 Dir. 2014/90, Art. 27(1).
106 Ibid.
107 Dir. 2014/90, Art. 27(3).
108 Dir. 2014/90, Art. 27(4).
109 Dir. 2014/90, Art. 27(5).
110 Dir. 2014/90, Art. 27(6).
111 Dir. 2014/90, Art. 27(7).
112 Dir. 2014/90, Art. 27(8).
113 Dir. 2014/90, Art. 27(7).

Compliant products which present a risk to maritime safety, to health or to the environment

37.081 Where, having performed an evaluation under Article 26(1), a Member State finds that marine equipment which is in compliance with this directive nevertheless presents a risk to maritime safety, to health or to the environment, it shall require the economic operator concerned to take all appropriate measures to ensure that the marine equipment concerned, when placed on the market, no longer presents that risk, to withdraw the marine equipment from the market or to recall it within such reasonable period, commensurate with the nature of the risk, as it may prescribe.[114]

37.082 The economic operator must ensure that corrective action is taken in respect of all the products concerned that it has made available on the market throughout the EU or placed on board EU ships.[115] The Member State must immediately inform the Commission and the other Member States.[116] The information provided must include all available details, in particular the data necessary for the identification of the marine equipment concerned, the origin and the supply chain of the marine equipment, the nature of the risk involved and the nature and duration of the national measures taken.

37.083 The Commission must without delay enter into consultation with the Member States and the relevant economic operator or operators and must evaluate the national measures taken.[117] On the basis of the results of that evaluation, the Commission shall decide whether or not the measure is justified and shall where necessary propose appropriate measures. Article 27(2) shall apply *mutatis mutandis* for this purpose.[118]

37.084 The Commission must address its decision to all Member States and must immediately communicate it to them and to the relevant economic operator or operators.

Formal non-compliance

37.085 Article 29(1) provides that without prejudice to Article 26, where a Member State makes one of the following findings, it must require the relevant economic operator to put an end to the non-compliance concerned: (a) the wheel mark has been affixed in violation of Articles 9 or 10; (b) the wheel mark has not been affixed; (c) the EU declaration of conformity has not been drawn up; (d) the EU declaration of conformity has not been drawn up correctly; (e) technical documentation is either not available or not complete; and (f) the EU declaration of conformity has not been sent to the ship. Article 29(2) goes on to provide that where the non-compliance referred to in Article 29(1) persists, the Member State concerned shall take all appropriate measures to restrict or to prohibit the marine equipment being made available on the market or to ensure that it is recalled or withdrawn from the market.

---

114 Dir. 2014/90, Art. 28(1).
115 Dir. 2014/90, Art. 28(2).
116 Dir. 2014/90, Art. 28(3).
117 Dir. 2014/90, Art. 28(4).
118 Ibid.

Exemptions based on technical innovation

37.086 Article 30(1) provides that in exceptional circumstances of technical innovation, the flag State administration may permit marine equipment which does not comply with the conformity assessment procedures to be placed on board an EU ship if it is established by trial or otherwise to the satisfaction of the flag State administration that such equipment meets the objectives of the directive. Article 30(2) provides that the trial procedures shall in no way discriminate between marine equipment produced in the flag Member State and marine equipment produced in other States. Under Article 30(3), marine equipment covered by Article 30 shall be given a certificate by the flag Member State which shall at all times be carried with the equipment and which gives the flag Member State's permission for the equipment to be placed on board the ship and imposes any restrictions or lays down any provisions relating to the use of the equipment.

37.087 Article 30(4) provides that where a Member State allows marine equipment covered by Article 30 to be placed on board an EU ship, that Member State must forthwith communicate the particulars thereof together with the reports of all relevant trials, assessments and conformity assessment procedures to the Commission and to the other Member States. Within 12 months of receipt of such a communication, the Commission, if it considers that the conditions laid down in Article 30(1) are not met, may require the Member State concerned to withdraw the permission granted within a specified deadline. For this purpose, the Commission must act by means of implementing acts. Those implementing acts shall be adopted in accordance with the examination procedure referred to in Article 38(2).[119] Where a ship with marine equipment on board which is covered by Article 30(1) is transferred to another Member State, the receiving flag Member State may take the necessary measures, which may include tests and practical demonstrations, to ensure that the equipment is at least as effective as equipment which does comply with the conformity assessment procedures.[120]

Exemptions for testing or evaluation

37.088 A flag State administration may permit marine equipment which does not comply with the conformity assessment procedures or which is not covered by Article 30 to be placed on board an EU ship for reasons of testing or evaluation, if the following cumulative conditions are complied with: (a) the marine equipment shall be given a certificate by the flag Member State which shall at all times be carried with the equipment, state that Member State's permission for the equipment to be placed on board the EU ship, impose all necessary restrictions and lay down any other appropriate provisions as regards the use of the equipment concerned; (b) the permission shall be limited to the period considered by the flag State as being necessary to complete the testing, which should be as short as possible; and (c) the marine equipment shall not be relied on in place of equipment which meets the requirements of this directive and shall not replace such equipment, which shall remain on board the EU ship in working order and ready for immediate use.[121]

---

119 Dir. 2014/90, Art. 30(5).
120 Dir. 2014/90, Art. 30(6).
121 Dir. 2014/90, Art. 31.

Exemptions in exceptional circumstances

37.089 Article 32 deals with exemptions in exceptional circumstances. As it is quite an involved provision, it is worth setting it out in full:

"1. In exceptional circumstances, which shall be duly justified to the flag State administration, when marine equipment needs to be replaced in a port outside the Union where it is not practicable in terms of reasonable time, delay and cost to place on board equipment which bears the wheel mark, other marine equipment may be placed on board subject to paragraphs 2 to 4.

2. The marine equipment placed on board shall be accompanied by documentation issued by a Member State of the IMO which is a party to the relevant conventions, certifying compliance with the relevant IMO requirements.

3. The flag State administration shall be informed at once of the nature and characteristics of such other marine equipment.

4. The flag State administration shall, at the earliest opportunity, ensure that the marine equipment referred to in paragraph 1, along with its testing documentation, complies with the relevant requirements of the international instruments and of this Directive.

5. Where it has been demonstrated that specific marine equipment bearing the wheel mark is not available on the market, the flag Member State may authorise other marine equipment to be placed on board, subject to paragraphs 6 to 8.

6. The authorised marine equipment shall comply, as much as possible, with the requirements and testing standards referred to in Article 4.

7. The marine equipment placed on board shall be accompanied by an interim certificate of approval issued by the flag Member State or by another Member State, stating the following: (a) the equipment bearing the wheel mark which the certified equipment is due to replace; (b) the exact circumstances under which the certificate of approval has been issued, and in particular the unavailability in the market of equipment bearing the wheel mark; (c) the exact design, construction and performance requirements against which the equipment has been approved by the certifying Member State; (d) the testing standards applied, if any, in the relevant approval procedures.

8. The Member State issuing an interim certificate of approval shall inform the Commission forthwith. If the Commission considers that the conditions of paragraphs 6 and 7 have not been met, it may require that Member State to revoke that certificate or take other appropriate measures by means of implementing acts. Those implementing acts shall be adopted in accordance with the examination procedure referred to in Article 38(2)."

Final provisions

37.090 Chapter 6 (entitled "Final Provisions") contains: Article 33 ("Exchange of Experience"); Article 34 ("Coordination of Notified Bodies"); Article 35 ("Implementing Measures").

Exchange of experience

37.091 The Commission must provide for the organisation of exchanges of experience between the Member States' national authorities responsible for notification policy, especially as regards market surveillance.[122]

---

122 Dir. 2014/90, Art. 33.

Co-ordination of notified bodies

37.092 The Commission must ensure that appropriate co-ordination and co-operation between notified bodies are put in place and properly operated in the form of a sectoral group of notified bodies.[123] Member States must ensure that the bodies notified by them participate in the work of the sectoral group, directly or by means of designated representatives.[124]

Implementing measures

37.093 Article 35(1) provides that the Member States must, by means of the information system made available by the Commission for that purpose, notify to the Commission the name and contact details of the authorities in charge of the implementation of the directive. The Commission must draw up, periodically update and make public a list of those authorities. Under Article 35(2), for each item of marine equipment for which the approval of the flag State administration is required by the international conventions, the Commission shall indicate by means of implementing acts the respective design, construction and performance requirements and the testing standards provided for in the international instruments. When adopting those acts, the Commission shall explicitly indicate the dates from which those requirements and testing standards are to apply, including the dates for placing on the market and placing on board, in accordance with the international instruments, and taking into consideration timeframes for ship-building. The Commission may also specify the common criteria and detailed procedures for their application. The Commission must, by means of implementing acts, indicate the respective design, construction and performance requirements newly provided for in the international instruments and which apply to equipment already placed on board, in order to ensure that equipment placed on board EU ships complies with the international instruments.[125] The Commission must establish and maintain a database containing at least the following information: (a) the list and essential details of the conformity certificates issued pursuant to the directive, as provided by the notified bodies; (b) the list and essential details of the declarations of conformity issued pursuant to the directive, as provided by the manufacturers; (c) an up-to-date list of the applicable international instruments, and of the requirements and testing standards applicable by virtue of Article 4(4); (d) the list and full text of the criteria and procedures referred to in paragraph 2; (e) the requirements and conditions for electronic tagging referred to in Article 11, when applicable; and (f) any other useful information with a view to facilitating correct implementation of the directive by the Member States, the notified bodies and the economic operators.

That database shall be made accessible to the Member States. It shall also be made available to the public for information purposes only. The implementing acts referred to in this article shall be adopted in the form of Commission regulations in accordance with the examination procedure referred to in Article 38(2).[126]

---

123 Dir. 2014/90, Art. 34(1).
124 Dir. 2014/90, Art. 34(2).
125 Dir. 2014/90, Art. 35(3).
126 Dir. 2014/90, Art. 35(5).

Amendments

37.094 The Commission is empowered to adopt delegated acts in accordance with Article 37 in order to update the references to standards, as referred to in Annex III, when new standards become available.[127]

Exercise of the delegation

37.095 The power to adopt delegated acts is conferred on the Commission subject to the conditions laid down in Article 37.[128] The power to adopt delegated acts referred to in Articles 8, 11, 27 and 36 shall be conferred on the Commission for a period of five years from 17 September 2014.[129] The Commission shall draw up a report in respect of the delegation of power not later than nine months before the end of the five-year period. The delegation of power shall be tacitly extended for periods of an identical duration, unless the European Parliament or the Council opposes such extension not later than three months before the end of each period.[130] The delegation of power referred to in Articles 8, 11, 27 and 36 may be revoked at any time by the European Parliament or by the Council.[131] A decision to revoke must put an end to the delegation of the power specified in that decision.[132] It shall take effect the day following the publication of the decision in the *Official Journal of the European Union* or at a later date specified therein. It shall not affect the validity of any delegated acts already in force.[133] As soon as it adopts a delegated act, the Commission shall notify it simultaneously to the European Parliament and to the Council.[134] A delegated act adopted pursuant to Articles 8, 11, 27 and 36 shall enter into force only if no objection has been expressed either by the European Parliament or the Council within a period of two months of notification of that act to the European Parliament and the Council or if, before the expiry of that period, the European Parliament and the Council have both informed the Commission that they will not object.[135] That period shall be extended by two months at the initiative of the European Parliament or of the Council.[136]

Committee on Safe Seas and the Prevention of Pollution from Ships ("COSS")

37.096 The Commission is to be assisted, in regard to the directive, by the COSS established by Regulation 2099/2002.[137] That Committee shall be a committee within the meaning of Regulation 182/2011.[138] Where reference is made to Article 38(1) then Article

---

127 Dir. 2014/90, Art. 36.
128 Dir. 2014/90, Art. 37(1).
129 Dir. 2014/90, Art. 37(2).
130 Dir. 2014/90, Art. 37(3).
131 Ibid.
132 Dir. 2014/90, Art. 37(3).
133 Dir. 2014/90, Art. 37(4).
134 Ibid.
135 Dir. 2014/90, Art. 37(5).
136 Ibid.
137 Dir. 2014/90, Art. 38(1).
138 Ibid.

5 of Regulation 182/2011 shall apply.[139] Where the Committee delivers no opinion, the Commission shall not adopt the draft implementing act and the third subparagraph of Article 5(4) of Regulation 182/2011 shall apply.

Transposition

37.097 Article 39(1) provides that Member States had to adopt and publish, by 18 September 2016 at the latest, the laws, regulations and administrative provisions necessary to comply with the directive. They had to forthwith communicate to the Commission the text of those provisions. They had to apply those provisions from 18 September 2016. When Member States adopt those provisions, they have to contain a reference to the directive or be accompanied by such a reference on the occasion of their official publication. Member States must determine how such reference is to be made. Article 39(2) provides that Member States shall communicate to the Commission the text of the main provisions of national law which they adopt in the field covered by the directive.

Repeal

37.098 Article 40 repealed Directive 96/98 with effect from 18 September 2016. The requirements and testing standards for marine equipment applicable on 18 September 2016 pursuant to the provisions of national law adopted by the Member States in order to comply with Directive 96/98 shall continue to apply until the entry into force of the implementing acts referred to in Article 35(2). References to the repealed directive shall be construed as references to Directive 2014/90.

C. COMMISSION IMPLEMENTING REGULATION 2017/306 OF 6 FEBRUARY 2017 INDICATING DESIGN, CONSTRUCTION AND PERFORMANCE REQUIREMENTS AND TESTING STANDARDS FOR MARINE EQUIPMENT

37.099 On 6 February 2017, the Commission adopted implementing Regulation 2017/306 indicating design, construction and performance requirements and testing standards for marine equipment.[140] Article 3 provides that the regulation entered into force on the twentieth day following that of its publication in the *Official Journal* and it was published on 24 February 2017. The legal basis was the TFEU. The legal background included Directive 2014/90 of the European Parliament and of the Council of 23 July 2014 on marine equipment and repealing Council Directive 96/98,[141] and in particular Article 35(2) of that directive.

37.100 The background to Directive 2017/306 is set out in the recitals:

"(1) In order to facilitate a harmonised, rapid and simple implementation of Directive 2014/90/ EU, implementing acts adopted pursuant to that Directive should take the form of Commission Regulations.

(2) Directive 2014/90/EU requires the Commission to indicate the design, construction and performance requirements and testing standards provided for in the international

---

139 Dir. 2014/90, Art. 38(2).
140 OJ L48/1, 24 February 2017.
141 OJ L257/146, 28 August 2014.

instruments, as well as the dates from which those requirements and testing standards are to apply.

(3) Equipment newly subject to harmonised Union requirements as part of Directive 2014/90/ EU and its implementing acts should be explicitly listed as a new item in column 1 of the Annex to this Regulation.

(4) It is reasonable and proportionate to allow a new item which is in conformity with the national requirements for type-approval in force in a Member State before the entry into force of this Regulation to be placed on the market and on board an EU ship for a transitional period.

(5) The measures provided for in this Regulation are in accordance with the opinion of the Committee on Safe Seas and the Prevention of Pollution from Ships (COSS)."

37.101 Article 1 states simply that the design, construction and performance requirements and the testing standards provided for in the international instruments shall apply to each item of marine equipment as set out in the annex to the regulation.

37.102 Article 2 provides that equipment listed as a new item in column 1 of the annex to the regulation, which complies with the national requirements for type-approval in force before 16 March 2017 in a Member State, may continue to be placed on the market and on board a Union ship until 16 March 2020. Further information on the regulation and its annex is set out in the regulation itself.

D. COMMISSION RECOMMENDATION 2010/167 OF 19 MARCH 2010 ON THE AUTHORISATION OF SYSTEMS FOR MOBILE COMMUNICATION SERVICES ON BOARD VESSELS (MCV SERVICES)

37.103 On 19 March 2010, the Commission adopted Recommendation 2010/167 on the Authorisation of Systems for Mobile Communication Services on Board Vessels (MCV Services).[142]

"Having regard to Directive 2002/21/EC of the European Parliament and of the Council of 7 March 2002 on a common regulatory framework for electronic communications networks and services (Framework Directive) …, and in particular Article 19(1) thereof, …

(1) The i2010 policy, as the strategic framework for a European Information Society, promotes an open and competitive digital economy in the European Union, emphasises ICT as a driver of inclusion and quality of life, and stresses the benefits of ready access to information and communication resources in all areas of daily life.

(2) Mobile communication services on board vessels (MCV services) are used on board freight and passenger vessels sailing within the territorial seas in the European Union and in international waters and are often pan-European or inter-State in nature. Systems providing MCV services ('MCV systems') aim to complement existing mobile connectivity when operating in those areas of the territorial seas of the EU Member States, as defined in the United Nations Convention on the Law of the Sea, that are not covered by land-based mobile networks.

(3) An MCV system ('dedicated MCV system') generally consists of one or more pico-cell base stations on board a vessel (vessel-BS), providing access to a GSM [Global System for Mobile Communications] core network via a backhaul link, for example via satellite. The vessel-BS of such a system serve roaming GSM mobile terminals carried by ship passengers or crew.

---

142 OJ L72/42, 20 March 2010.

(4) MCV services are currently operated commercially using only the GSM standard and only in bands 880–915 MHz and 1 710-1 785 MHz for uplink (terminal transmit and base station receive) and 925–960 MHz and 1 805-1 880 MHz for downlink (base station transmit and terminal receive). In future, however, they may be extended to other terrestrial public mobile communication systems, operating in accordance with other standards and in other frequency bands.

(5) The operation of dedicated MCV systems should be distinguished from the extended coverage provided by land-based mobile electronic communications networks in territorial seas to the extent that this is based on operators' rights to establish and operate land-based mobile networks.

(6) A coordinated approach to the regulation of MCV services would help to facilitate the provision of these services across the European Union, thereby contributing to achievement of the objectives of the EU single market. It would also help to ensure seamless mobile connectivity for consumers and business users and would enhance the potential of innovative maritime communication services.

(7) When authorising use of spectrum for the provision of MCV services, Member States must comply with Directive 2002/21/EC and with Directive 2002/20/EC of the European Parliament and of the Council of 7 March 2002 on the authorisation of electronic communications networks and services (Authorisation Directive).[143] In particular, under Article 9(1) and (2) of Directive 2002/21/EC, Member States should ensure the effective management of radio frequencies for electronic communication services in their territory and promote harmonisation of the use of radio frequencies across the European Union, consistent with the need to ensure effective and efficient use thereof.

(8) Under Directive 2002/21/EC, national regulatory authorities in the Member States should contribute to the development of the single market, inter alia, by removing remaining obstacles to the provision of electronic communications networks, associated facilities and services, and electronic communication services at European level and by encouraging the establishment and development of trans-European networks, the interoperability of pan-European services, and end-to-end connectivity. They should also promote competition in the provision of electronic communications networks, electronic communication services and associated facilities and services by, inter alia, encouraging efficient use and ensuring the effective management of radio frequencies and numbering resources.

(9) Pursuant to Directive 2002/20/EC, the least onerous authorisation system possible should be used to allow the provision of electronic communications networks and services in order to stimulate the development of new electronic communication services and pan-European communications networks and services and to allow service providers and consumers to benefit from the economies of scale of the single market.

(10) In accordance with Article 3(2) of Directive 2002/20/EC, the provision of electronic communications networks or the provision of electronic communication services may, without prejudice to the specific obligations referred to in Article 6(2) or rights of use referred to in Article 5, only be subject to a general authorisation.

(11) Following Article 5(1) of Directive 2002/20/EC, Member States should, where possible, in particular where the risk of harmful interference is negligible, not make the use of radio frequencies subject to individual rights of use but to general authorisations that include the conditions of their usage.

(12) Provided the technical conditions set out in Commission Decision 2010/166/EU[144] are fulfilled, the risk of harmful interference caused by MCV operation will be negligible, so, in principle, general authorisations should be granted by Member States for the use of the radio spectrum for the provision of MCV services.

(13) Some Member States currently make the use of spectrum for the provision of MCV services subject to individual rights. This authorisation approach should be reassessed,

---

143 Ed., OJ L108/21, 24 April 2002.
144 Ed., OJ L72/38, 20 March 2010.

including on the basis of any experience as regards the provision of MCV services in the territorial seas of Member States.

(14) According to Article 1 of Directive 2009/114/EC of the European Parliament and of the Council of 16 September 2009 amending Council Directive 87/372/EEC on the frequency bands to be reserved for the coordinated introduction of public pan-European cellular digital land-based mobile communications in the Community[145] Member States should examine whether the existing assignment of the 900 MHz band to the competing mobile operators in their territory is likely to distort competition in the mobile markets concerned and should address such distortions in accordance with Article 14 of Directive 2002/20/EC. Member States should, where appropriate, consider using this occasion to change any existing exclusive rights of use granted to operators of land-based mobile networks so that they do not exclude the provision of MCV services in the relevant frequencies.

(15) Member States should share information amongst each other and with the Commission in order to resolve any harmful interference issues caused by MCV services. In as much as involvement of the Communications Committee and the Radio Spectrum Committee could facilitate the resolution of such issues, these Committees should be informed by the Commission.

(16) Pursuant to Directive 2002/22/EC of the European Parliament and of the Council of 7 March 2002 on universal service and users' rights relating to electronic communications networks and services (Universal Service Directive)[146] Member States should ensure that transparent and up-to-date information on applicable prices and tariffs, and on standard terms and conditions, in respect of access to and use of publicly available telephone services is available to end-users and consumers. The Directive also calls upon Member States to ensure that, where subscribing to services providing connection and/or access to the public telephone network, consumers have a right to a contract with an undertaking or undertakings providing such services, specifying, among other things particulars of prices and tariffs and the means by which up-to-date information on all applicable tariffs and maintenance charges may be obtained.

(17) International agreements in the area of maritime safety and/or public security should not be prejudiced by the operation of MCV services.

(18) The regulatory and technical elements of the common approach to authorisation of the use of spectrum for the provision of MCV services in the European Union should be kept under scrutiny to ensure that they remain satisfactory for the overall purpose of avoiding harmful interference, failing which appropriate remedial measures will be considered.

(19) The measures provided for in this Recommendation are in accordance with the opinion of the Communications Committee,

37.104 The recommendation is very straightforward at one level:

"1. This Recommendation aims to coordinate national authorisation conditions and procedures relating to the use of the radio spectrum for mobile communication services on board vessels (MCV services) in the territorial seas of Member States in order to facilitate the deployment of such services across the European Union while avoiding harmful interference caused by MCV services to land-based mobile electronic communication services.

The national authorisation conditions and procedures referred to in this Recommendation will apply without prejudice to legal obligations concerning maritime safety and public security and regulations and/or administrative provisions concerning equipment for MCV services put in place by Member States, in compliance with European Union law, in particular Directive 1999/5/EC of the European Parliament and of the Council of 9 March 1999 on radio equipment and telecommunications terminal equipment and the mutual recognition

---

145 Ed., OJ L274/25, 20 October 2009.
146 Ed., OJ L108/51, 24 April 2002.

of their conformity[147] and any applicable EU and international instruments concerning maritime equipment.

2. 'Mobile communication services on board vessels (MCV services)' means electronic communication services, as defined in Article 2(c) of Directive 2002/21/EC, provided by an undertaking to enable persons on board a vessel to communicate via public communication networks using a GSM system without establishing direct connections with land-based mobile networks.

3. This Recommendation applies to authorisation of the use of radio spectrum in the frequency bands defined in Decision 2010/166/EU for the provision of MCV services in the territorial seas of Member States, as defined in the United Nations Convention on the Law of the Sea. The provision of MCV services in the high seas, satellite communications between vessels and space stations, and the provision of mobile satellite services (MSS) to end-users on board vessels are outside the scope of this Recommendation.

4. No later than 12 months after adoption of this Recommendation, Member States should take all steps necessary to be able to authorise, in the frequency bands or sub-bands made available in accordance with Decision 2010/166/EU, the use of spectrum for the provision of MCV services in their territorial seas on board vessels of their nationality and the use of spectrum for the provision of MCV services in their territorial seas, as applicable.

5. Member States should not authorise use of spectrum for the provision of MCV services, unless such use satisfies the technical conditions set out in Decision 2010/166/EU.

6. Member States may require that MCV systems only use the specific frequency bands or sub-bands made available, in accordance with Decision 2010/166/EU, for the operation of MCV systems in their territorial seas.

7. Member States should make use of spectrum for the provision of MCV services subject to general authorisation. Without prejudice to Article 5(1) of Directive 2002/20/EC, where the use of spectrum for the provision of MCV services is subject to individual rights, Member States should reassess the need for such individual rights with the objective of incorporating the conditions attached to such rights into a general authorisation as soon as possible and at the latest within three years after adoption of this Recommendation.

8. No later than 12 months after adoption of this Recommendation, Member States should not require any additional authorisation for the use of spectrum made available for the provision of MCV services in their territorial seas if the use of spectrum by the relevant MCV system is already authorised by another Member State, in accordance with its authorisation regime and in compliance with this Recommendation.

9. Member States should consider not requiring an additional authorisation for the use of spectrum in their territorial seas for the provision of MCV services on board vessels of third country nationality, provided that the use of spectrum for the provision of MCV services on such vessels is already authorised by the relevant countries under the same conditions as those set out in Decision 2010/166/EU.

10. Member States that, prior to the adoption of this Recommendation, have granted in the frequency bands or sub-bands made available for operation of MCV systems, exclusive individual rights of use for the provision of land-based mobile electronic communications networks and/or services extending to their territorial seas should, on the occasion of the first review, modification, extension or renewal of such exclusive rights of use, based on either EU or national law, where appropriate, change such rights of use in order to allow for the operation of MCV systems in their territorial seas. Pending such first review, modification, extension or renewal, the Member States concerned should promote the provision of MCV services in their territorial seas on the basis of spectrum trading, spectrum sharing or any other comparable arrangements with the land-based mobile operators enjoying the relevant exclusive rights.

---

147 Ed., OJ L91/10, 7 April 1999.

11. Member States should cooperate actively, constructively and in a spirit of solidarity, using existing procedures where appropriate, to manage any issues concerning harmful interference allegedly caused by the operation of MCV systems.
12. Member States should promptly bring issues concerning harmful interference allegedly caused by the operation of an MCV system falling under the jurisdiction of another Member State to the attention of the latter Member State and should inform the Commission. Where appropriate, the Commission should inform the Communications Committee and the Radio Spectrum Committee of the abovementioned issues in order to seek solutions to any difficulties.
13. Member States that have jurisdiction over the MCV systems suspected of interfering harmfully with services in the territory of another Member State should respond and promptly resolve any such interference.
14. Member States should take any appropriate measures in order to ensure that consumers and other end-users are adequately informed about the terms and conditions for the use of MCV services.
15. Member States should keep the use of spectrum for the provision of MCV services under scrutiny, in particular concerning actual or potential harmful interference, and should report their findings to the Commission in order to allow a timely review of this Recommendation if necessary."

CHAPTER 38

Piracy

A. INTRODUCTION

38.001 Until recently, one would have been forgiven for thinking that piracy was consigned to the history books. However, the reality in recent years is that piracy has become a very significant issue in various parts of the world, most notably, off Somalia.[1] The situation off Somalia has intensified since the mid-2000s. While piracy exists in various parts of the world, it is the situation off Somalia which has caught the attention of the European Union ("EU") more than any other area. This chapter considers the EU law aspects of piracy.[2]

38.002 The first recital to the Council's 2010 Recommendation on Measures for Self-Protection and the Prevention of Piracy and Armed Robbery against Ships[3] recalls that

> "the resurgence of acts of piracy off the coast of Somalia led the Maritime Safety Committee of the International Maritime Organisation ('IMO') to adopt a series of measures at its 86th session from 27 May to 5 June 2009. It issued a number of circulars either updating the general recommendations in force on the measures to combat piracy and armed robbery against ships or defining specific measures to tackle piracy in the Gulf of Aden and off the coast of Somalia."

38.003 The EU's response to the crisis has been interesting from the legal perspective. The response has not involved the adoption of legally binding rules but has instead consisted of non-legally binding measures such as guidelines and recommendations. This has been a more practical approach. There was relatively little point in adopting legally binding measures which would have had little or no impact in Somalia or other areas where piracy was occurring. By contrast, by the EU adopting practical guidance and measures, the EU was able to address the issue in a concrete and practical manner.

38.004 The IMO has been particularly interested in the issue. Recitals 2 to 8 of the EU's 2010 Recommendation on Measures for Self-Protection and the Prevention of Piracy and Armed Robbery against Ships[4] recalls:

---

1 See Koutrakos and Skordas (eds), The Law and Practice of Piracy at Sea: European and International Perspectives (2014) and, in particular, Gosalbo-Bono and Boelaert, "The European Union's Comprehensive Approach to Combating Piracy at Sea: Legal Aspects" and Thym, "Transfer Agreements for Pirates Concluded by the EU: A Case Study on the Human Rights Accountability of the Common Security and Defence Policy" at pp. 81 and 167 respectively. See also Treves, "Piracy, Law of the Sea, and Use of Force: Developments off the Coast of Somalia" (2009) 20 (2) Eur J Int Law 399. See also Guilfoyle, "Piracy off Somalia: A Sketch of the Legal Framework" at www.ejiltalk.org/piracy-off-somalia-a-sketch-of-the-legal-framework/ and a UK parliamentary report entitled "Combating Somali Piracy: The EU's Naval Operation Atalanta – European Union Committee" at www.publications.parliament.uk/pa/ld200910/ldselect/ldeucom/103/10304.htm.

2 See http://eunavfor.eu/mission/.

3 OJ L67/13, 17 March 2010, http://eur-lex.europa.eu/legal-content/EN/TXT/HTML/?uri=CELEX:32010H0 159&from=EN. For the press release, see http://europa.eu/rapid/press-release_IP-10-267_en.htm?locale=en.

4 OJ L67/13, 17 March 2010, http://eur-lex.europa.eu/legal-content/EN/TXT/HTML/?uri=CELEX:32010H0 159&from=EN. For the press release, see http://europa.eu/rapid/press-release_IP-10-267_en.htm?locale=en.

"(2) Circular MSC.1/Circ.1334 of 23 June 2009 offers 'Guidance to ship owners and ship operators, shipmasters and crews on preventing and suppressing acts of piracy and armed robbery against ships'. The circular lists a comprehensive series of measures that can be taken onboard ships under any circumstances to prevent attacks or, when they occur, to minimise the risks to the crew and ship.

(3) Circular MSC.1/Circ.1332 of 16 June 2009 lists the best management practices to avoid, deter or delay acts of piracy in the Gulf of Aden and off the coast of Somalia, devised by maritime industry organisations on a voluntary basis and supported and encouraged by the contracting parties on account of the urgent need to combat attacks off the coast of Somalia. The maritime industry organisations updated these measures in version 2, which was published as circular MSC.1/Circ. 1335 of 29 September 2009.

(4) Although the measures set out in these IMO circulars are not compulsory or binding, the clear need to improve maritime security means that ships flying the flag of a Member State should protect themselves as best they can using current know-how when they are exposed in navigation regions with a high risk of piracy and armed robbery.

(5) By their very nature, acts of piracy and armed robbery against ships are often violent and pose a serious threat in several regions of the world, beyond the current situation off the coast of Somalia and in the Gulf of Aden and Indian Ocean.

(6) Piracy figures for 2008 are the highest since the International Maritime Bureau began collecting data in 1991, with 293 attacks on ships, 49 captures, 889 seamen held hostage, 11 killed, and 21 missing and presumed dead. Since 2008, there has been a sharp increase in the number of ships attacked and hijacked off the coast of Somalia and in the Gulf of Aden and Indian Ocean. Numerous ships have been attacked and detained by pirates, who hold the crew hostage until a ransom is paid for their release. The periods of captivity last several weeks or even months and are as unacceptable as they are traumatic for the seamen detained.

(7) The number of attacks in the Indian Ocean and Gulf of Aden has increased since the beginning of 2009, despite a brief respite in the summer on account of the monsoon and the difficult sailing conditions for pirates. Pirates carried out at least 164 attacks in 2009, 48 of which led to a ship being captured.

(8) The best management practices urge maritime companies and ships to register on the website of the Maritime Security Centre – Horn of Africa (MSCHOA (www.mschoa.org) before passing through the Gulf of Aden. Ships that register receive all the information available on the current situation in this particular navigation region and are tracked by the EU NAVFOR-ATALANTA operation forces, reducing the risk of attack. Yet more than one third of ships in transit are still not registered with the MSCHOA and, as a result, cannot benefit from the measures in place to safeguard their transit through this region."

The EU has become involved in the issue for various reasons including the reality that its citizens and its property interests have been affected badly by piracy. The impact on seafarers alone would justify intervention. One should not underestimate the trauma and stress to seafarers.[5] Siim Kallas, the then Commission Vice-President responsible for transport said in 2010:

"piracy poses a terrible threat to the men and women on board vessels and is a real danger for the maritime sector and for world trade. Crews should be fully protected against acts of piracy and their employers must ensure that they are able to work with optimum safety when they are in areas with a high risk of piracy."[6]

---

5 For a first-hand account, see http://ec.europa.eu/transport/modes/maritime/events/doc/2010_03_03_ piracy/2010_03_03_nightmare_comes_true.pdf (presented at the Commission's seminar "Piracy and Armed Robbery at Sea: How Best to Protect Seafarers?", 3 March 2010.

6 See http://europa.eu/rapid/press-release_IP-10-267_en.htm?locale=en.

38.005 The Commission organised on 3 March 2010 a seminar for representatives from the shipping industry, including seafarers' representatives, politicians, international organisations and seafarers' associations.[7] The seminar made it possible to raise the extreme importance of careful preparation of crews, of greater exchange of information and of co-operation in the waters at risk as well as the need to provide social support for seafarers and their families during and after any period of captivity.[8]

38.006 The EU's 2010 Recommendation 2010/159 recalls that

"MSCHOA was set up by the European Union (EU) as part of a European Security and Defence Policy initiative to combat piracy in the Horn of Africa. This work commenced with the establishment of EU NAVCO in September 2008. This coordination cell working in Brussels established links with a broad cross-section of the maritime community and provided coordination with EU forces operating in the region. In November 2008, the Council of the European Union took a major step further by setting up a naval mission – EU NAVFOR ATALANTA – to improve maritime security off the Somali coast by preventing and deterring pirate attacks and by helping to safeguard merchant shipping in the region."

The EU's 2010 Recommendation 2010/159 recalls that

"[t]he UK Maritime Trade Operations (UKMTO Dubai) office in Dubai acts as a point of contact for industry liaison with the combined military forces (CMF). UKMTO Dubai also administers the voluntary reporting scheme, under which merchant ships are encouraged to send daily reports, providing their position and ETA at their next port, whilst transiting the region bound by Suez, 78° E and 10° S. UKMTO Dubai subsequently tracks ships, and the positional information is passed to CMF and EU headquarters. Emerging and relevant information affecting commercial traffic can then be passed directly to ships, rather than by company offices, improving responsiveness to any incident and saving time."

38.007 From a legal perspective, the EU's intervention in the area to date has been largely in terms of recommendations rather than legally binding instruments. Moreover, the EU sees this as very much for the Member States to deal with – as the eleventh recital to the Commission recommendation on measures for self-protection and the prevention of piracy and armed robbery against ships[9] states: "it is the responsibility of the Member States to implement the measures aimed at strengthening maritime security and to ensure that all necessary means are allocated and provided to that end".

EU NAVFOR is the co-ordinating authority which operates the Maritime Security Centre (Horn of Africa).[10] The ninth and tenth recitals to the 2010 Recommendation on Measures for Self-Protection and the Prevention of Piracy and Armed Robbery against Ships[11] recall:

"(9) On 15 June 2009, the Council of the European Union decided to extend the EU NAVFOR–ATALANTA military operation by one year from 13 December 2009 in order to help deter, prevent and suppress acts of piracy and armed robbery off the coast of Somalia. This military operation is the first naval operation conducted under the European Security and

---

7 http://ec.europa.eu/transport/maritime/events/2010_03_03_piracy_en.htm.

8 For a summary of the seminar, see http://ec.europa.eu/transport/modes/maritime/events/doc/2010_03_03_piracy/2010_03_03_piracy_summary.pdf.

9 OJ L67/13, 17 March 2010. For the press release, see http://europa.eu/rapid/press-release_IP-10-267_en.htm?locale=en.

10 See http://eunavfor.eu.

11 OJ L67/13, 17 March 2010, http://eur-lex.europa.eu/legal-content/EN/TXT/HTML/?uri=CELEX:32010H0159&from=EN. For the press release, see http://europa.eu/rapid/press-release_IP-10-267_en.htm?locale=en.

Defence Policy (ESDP), the Council having observed that piracy off the coast of Somalia continued to pose a significant threat to sea transport in the region.

(10) Since they are complementary to measures taken under the EU NAVFOR–ATALANTA operation, the effective and harmonised implementation of the preventive measures recommended by circulars MSC.1/Circ. 1334 and MSC.1/Circ. 1335 can but increase the effectiveness of the naval protection measures adopted by the Council to combat piracy off the coast of Somalia."

B. EUROPEAN COMMISSION RECOMMENDATION OF 11 MARCH 2010 ON MEASURES FOR SELF-PROTECTION AND THE PREVENTION OF PIRACY AND ARMED ROBBERY AGAINST SHIPS

Introduction

38.008 On 11 March 2010, the Commission adopted a recommendation on measures for self-protection and the prevention of piracy and armed robbery against ships.[12] It was Recommendation 2010/159. As a recommendation, it is not legally binding in its own right. The recommendation was addressed to the Member States to ensure the effective application of measures for self-protection and for preventing acts of piracy and armed attacks against ships. These measures are known as "Best Management Practices" ("BMP") and had have been adopted by the IMO.

Legal basis

38.009 The legal basis for the recommendation was the Treaty on the Functioning of the European Union ("TFEU") generally but Article 292 in particular. Article 292 of the TFEU is a simple procedural provision which states that

"the Council shall adopt recommendations. It shall act on a proposal from the Commission in all cases where the Treaties provide that it shall adopt acts on a proposal from the Commission. It shall act unanimously in those areas in which unanimity is required for the adoption of a Union act. The Commission, and the European Central Bank in the specific cases provided for in the Treaties, shall adopt recommendations."

Essence of the recommendation

38.010 Articles 1–3 contain the essence of the recommendation:

"1. The Member States are requested to ensure the effective and harmonised application of preventive measures to deal with the threats which ships may face during acts of piracy and armed robbery. These measures, which have been inventoried and consolidated, have received wide support from the IMO and maritime industry organisations.

2. General measures

    2.1. The Member States are requested to inform operators registered with them of circular MSC.1/Circ.1334 adopted at the 86th session of the IMO's Maritime Safety Committee, which sets out and updates preventive measures for self-protection that ships and shipping companies are called on to implement in order to combat piracy and

---

12 OJ L67/13, 17 March 2010. For the press release, see http://europa.eu/rapid/press-release_IP-10-267_en.htm?locale=en.

armed robbery wherever such risk occurs, in accordance with the International Ship and Port Facility Security Code (ISPS Code).

2.2. The Member States are requested to ensure above all that their ships are sufficiently and effectively manned in accordance with Rule 4.28 of Part B of the ISPS Code, which has become compulsory under Article 3(5) of Regulation (EC) No 725/2004 of the European Parliament and of the Council.[13]

3. Measures specific to the situation off the coast of Somalia

3.1. The Member States are requested to inform operators registered with them of circular MSC.1/Circ.1332 adopted at the 86th session of the IMO's Maritime Safety Committee, supplemented by circular MSC.1/Circ.1335, which endorse best management practices at global level to avoid, deter or delay piracy in the Gulf of Aden and off the coast of Somalia, which are published and updated by maritime industry organisations on a regular basis.

3.2. The Member States are requested to take all necessary steps to ensure the dissemination, pass on the regular updates and verify the implementation of the best management practices to deter piracy off the coast of Somalia, which are set out in the Annex to this Recommendation."

Best practices as set out in the recommendation

38.011 The annex to the recommendation deals with the Best Management Practices to Deter Piracy in the Gulf of Aden and Off the Coast of Somalia. Version 2 was adopted in August 2009. The best practices are widely published so as to ensure that ships and their crew are safe. Paradoxically, publishing the guidance means that the information is available to the pirates as well. The best management practices are supported by several international industry representatives[14] and this helps to maximise their acceptance because the organisations consulted on the best practices document represent the vast majority of shipowners and operators transiting the region. The title of the recommendation is "Suggested planning and operational practices for owners, operators, managers and masters of ships transiting the Gulf of Aden and off the coast of Somalia".

38.012 In terms of the purpose of the recommendation, paragraph 1 states that the purpose of the document is to provide BMP to assist companies and ships in avoiding piracy attacks, deterring attacks and delaying successful attacks in the Gulf of Aden ("GoA") and off the coast of Somalia. These organisations will encourage their members to utilise these BMP and will endeavour to promulgate these to other shipping interests as BMP for combating piracy in the region. This document complements guidance provided in the IMO MSC Circular MSC.1/Circ.1334.

---

13 OJ L129, 29.4.2004, p. 6.

14 The representatives supporting the August 2009 version were the International Association of Independent Tanker Owners (Intertanko); the International Chamber of Shipping (ICS); the Oil Companies International Marine Forum (OCIMF); the Baltic and International Maritime Council (BIMCO); the Society of International Gas Tanker and Terminal Operators (SIGTTO); the International Association of Dry Cargo Ship Owners (Intercargo); the International Group of Protection and Indemnity Clubs (IGP & I); the Cruise Lines International Association (CLIA); the International Union of Marine Insurers (IUMI); the Joint War Committee (JWC) and Joint Hull Committee (JHC); the International Maritime Bureau (IMB) and the International Transport Workers Federation (ITF). The best management practices are also supported by: the Maritime Security Centre Horn of Africa (MSCHOA); the UK Maritime Trade Organisation (UKMTO Dubai); and the Maritime Liaison Office (MARLO).

38.013 The recommendation recollects the typical attack profiles and lessons learnt. It recalls that during 2008 and the first half of 2009, an increase in the number of pirate attacks on merchant ships occurred throughout the GoA and off the coast of Somalia and within the wider north-west Indian Ocean. The recommendation recalled that the majority of attacks were initially clustered around the northern side of the GoA but attacks have occurred further off the east coast of Somalia. The recommendation recalled that analysis of successful attacks indicates that the following common vulnerabilities are exploited by the pirates: (a) low speed; (b) low freeboard; (c) inadequate planning and procedures; (d) visibly low state of alert and/or lack of evident self-protective measures; (e) where a slow response by the ship is evident. The Recommendation recalled that commonly two or more small high-speed (up to 25 knots) open boats/"skiffs" are used in attacks often approaching from the port quarter and/or stern. The use of a pirate "mother ship", which is a larger ship carrying personnel, equipment, supplies and smaller attack craft, has enabled attacks to be successfully undertaken at a greater range from the shore. The recommendation also recalled that vigilance should be highest at first light and last light, as the majority of the attacks have taken place during these periods. Higher speed vessels (15 knots and above) should not presume to be safe from attack but speed is an effective form of defence. The use of small arms fire, rocket-propelled grenades ("RPGs"), in an effort to intimidate masters of vessels to reduce speed has occurred within the area. Maintaining full sea speed in such circumstances has been shown to be effective. The recommendation noted that the majority of attempted hijacks have been repelled by ship's crew who have planned and trained in advance of the passage and employed passive countermeasures to good effect. It also noted that prevailing weather and sea state conditions also greatly influence attackers' ability to operate. Wind strengths in excess of 18 knots and wave heights above 2 metres are considered sufficient to provide protection for all but the most vulnerable vessels, particularly where masters are taking full account of best management practices.

38.014 The recommended BMPs are as follows:

"1. Introduction

(a) Whilst recognising the absolute discretion of the master at all times to adopt appropriate measures to avoid, deter or delay piracy attacks in this region, this document of best practices is provided for ship owners and ship operators, masters and their crews.

(b) Not all measures discussed in this document may be applicable for each ship. Therefore, as part of the risk analysis, an assessment is recommended to determine which of the BMP will be most suitable for the ship. The following have, however, generally proved effective:

2. Prior to transit – general planning

(a) General

(i) UKMTO Dubai is the first point of contact for ships in the region. The day-to-day interface between masters and the military is provided by UKMTO Dubai, who talk to the ships and liaise directly with MSCHOA and the naval commanders at sea. UKMTO Dubai require regular updates on the position and intended movements of ships. They use this information to help the naval units maintain an accurate picture of shipping. (See Glossary at Annex A for further details.)

(ii) The Maritime Security Centre – Horn of Africa (MSCHOA), is the planning and coordination authority for EU forces (EU NAVFOR) in the Gulf of Aden and the area off the coast of Somalia. (See Glossary at Annex A.)

(iii) The Marine Liaison Office (MARLO) operates as a conduit for information exchange between the Combined Maritime Forces (CMF) and the commercial shipping community within the region. (See Glossary at Annex A.)

(iv) Prior to transiting the high-risk area, the owner and master should carry out their own risk assessment to assess the likelihood and consequences of piracy attacks on the ship, based on the latest available information. The outcome of this risk assessment should identify measures for prevention, mitigation and recovery and will mean combining statutory requirements with supplementary measures to combat piracy.

(v) Company crisis management procedures should consider appropriate measures to meet the threat of piracy by adopting IMO and other industry recommended practices as appropriate to the particular circumstances and ship type.

(vi) Advanced notice of a vessel's intended passage is required by the naval authorities so that they can identify vulnerabilities and plan suitable protection. This is achieved by primarily:

1. initial report to UKMTO Dubai (e-mail or fax);
2. initial report to MARLO (e-mail or fax);
3. additionally, if planning to transit the Gulf of Aden, or navigate within the area bound by 12° N, 58° E and 10° S: register the vessel movement with MSCHOA (either, online or by e-mail or fax).

(vii) Whilst measures should be taken to prevent pirates boarding, the safety of crew and passengers is paramount.

(b) Company planning

It is strongly recommended that managers and/or the operations department register for access to the restricted sections of the MSCHOA website (www.mschoa.eu), review the information contained therein and share this as appropriate within their fleet.

(i) 4–5 days before the vessel enters the international recommended transit corridor (IRTC), or area bound by 12 degrees north or 58 degrees east or 10 degrees south, ensure that a 'Vessel movement registration' submission has been logged with MSCHOA (online, e-mail or fax). Note: This can be done by either the ship or the company.

(ii) Review the ship security assessment (SSA) and implementation of the ship security plan (SSP) as required by the International Ship and Port Facility Code (ISPS Code) to counter the piracy threat.

(iii) The company security officer (CSO) is encouraged to see that a contingency plan for the high-risk passage is in place, exercised, briefed and discussed with the master and the ship security officer (SSO).

(iv) Be aware of the particular high-risk sea areas that have been promulgated.

(v) Offer their ship's master guidance with regard to the preferred and available methods of transiting the region (group transit, escorted group transit, national convoy, etc.).

(vi) Conduct periodic crew training sessions.

(vii) The use of additional private security guards is at the discretion of the company but the use of armed guards is not recommended.

(viii) Consider additional resources to enhance watchkeeping numbers.

(ix) Consider the outfitting of ships with self-protection measures (SPM) prior to transiting high-risk areas.

(c) Ship's master planning

    (i)   Communication of 'Initial report' to UKMTO Dubai and MARLO (e-mail or fax) when entering the reporting area between Suez, and 78 degrees east 10 degrees south, see anti-piracy planning chart Q6099.

   (ii) 4–5 days before entering the IRTC, or the area within 12 degrees north, 58 degrees east or 10 degrees south, ensure that a 'Vessel movement registration' submission has been logged with MSCHOA (online, e-mail or fax). Note: This can be done by either the ship or the company. If it is completed by the company, masters should satisfy themselves with their companies that their details are correctly registered with MSCHOA.

  (iii) Prior to transit of the region it is recommended that the crew should be thoroughly briefed.

  (iv) The anti-piracy contingency plan has been shown to be most effective when implemented in advance. A drill is conducted prior to arrival in the area, the plan reviewed and all personnel briefed on their duties, including familiarity with the alarm signal signifying a piracy attack.

   (v) Masters are advised to also prepare an emergency communication plan, to include all essential emergency contact numbers and pre-prepared messages, which should be ready at hand or permanently displayed near the communications panel (e.g. telephone numbers of MSCHOA, IMB PRC, CSO etc. – see Contact List at Annex B).

  (vi) Define the ship's AIS [automatic identification systems] policy: SOLAS [International Convention for the Safety of Life at Sea] permits the master the discretion to switch off AIS if he believes that its use increases the ship's vulnerability. However, in order to provide naval forces with tracking information within the GoA it is recommended that AIS transmission is continued but restricted to ship's identity, position, course, speed, navigational status and safety-related information. Off the coast of Somalia the decision is again left to the master's discretion, but current naval advice is to turn it off completely. If in doubt this can be verified with MSCHOA.

3.   Prior to transit voyage planning

  (a) Vessels are encouraged to report their noon position, course, speed, estimated and actual arrival times to UKMTO Dubai and MARLO whilst operating in the region.

  (b) Vessels are also encouraged to increase the frequency of such reports when navigating in known high-risk/piracy areas and further report upon passing point A or B in the GoA, as shown on anti-piracy chart Q6099.

  (c) Inside the GoA

    (i)   EU NAVFOR strongly recommends that ships conduct their passage within the IRTC. Westbound ships should bias themselves to the northern portion of the corridor, and eastbound ships to the southern portion. Group transit (GT) guidance within the GoA for times and speeds are on the MSCHOA website, if a GT is contemplated.

   (ii) Ships should avoid entering Yemeni territorial waters (YTWs) while on transit. This is for reasons of customary international law, as it is not possible for international military forces (non-Yemeni) to protect ships that are attacked inside YTWs.

  (iii) Ships may be asked to make adjustments to passage plans to conform to MSCHOA routeing advice.

  (iv) During GTs ships should not expect to be permanently in the company of a warship. But all warships in the GoA, whether part of EU NAVFOR or coordinating with them, will be aware of the GoA GTs and will have access to the full details of vulnerable shipping.

(v) MSCHOA strongly recommends masters make every effort to plan transit periods of highest risk areas of the GoA for night passage (MSCHOA will advise ships). Very few successful attacks have occurred at night.

(d) Outside the GoA

(i) Ships navigating off the east coast of Somalia should consult with the MSCHOA website or UKMTO Dubai in order to obtain the most recent routeing advice.

(ii) Masters should still update UKMTO Dubai in the usual manner with their ship's course and details.

(e) A list of useful contact details are contained in Annex B.

4. Prior to transit – defensive measures

(a) Taking into account the manning levels, ensure that ship routines are adjusted sufficiently in advance so that well-rested and well-briefed crew are on watch and sufficient watchkeepers are available. The master and officers of the watch should be familiar with the impact of zigzag manoeuvres onboard their particular ship (in all sea conditions) and in particular the impact that these manoeuvres can have upon reducing the speed of the vessel.

(b) Consider minimising external communications (radios, handsets and AIS information) to essential safety- and security-related communication and SOLAS information only during transit of the GoA and passing the coast of Somalia.

(c) Increase readiness and redundancy by running additional auxiliary machinery, including generators and steering motors.

(d) Increase lookouts/bridge manning.

(e) Man the engine room.

(f) Secure and control access to the bridge, engine room, steering gear room, and all accommodation/internal spaces. All potential access points (doors, portholes, vents, etc.) should be risk-assessed and adequately secured, especially where the potential access point is considered large enough for an attacker to gain entry. Access to and from the accommodation and internal work spaces should be reduced to a single point of entry when transiting the high-risk areas. Any measures employed should not obstruct an emergency exit from within the internal space, whilst remaining secure from access by pirates outside.

(g) In case of emergency, warships can be contacted on VHF Ch. 16 (Backup Ch.08).

(h) Check all ladders and outboard equipment are stowed or up on deck.

(i) Check that self-protection measures put in place in advance remain securely fitted and function as intended. Be mindful that temporary devices may work loose and consequently may only provide a reduced level of protection.

(j) If the ship has a comparatively low freeboard, consider the possibility of extending the width of the gunwales to prevent grappling hooks from gaining hold. Check the MSCHOA website for examples of such measures.

(k) It is recommended that a piracy attack muster point or 'citadel' be designated and lock-down procedures rehearsed in order to delay access to control of the ship and buy time. Ideally this should be away from external bulkheads and portholes. Due to the ongoing debate on the use of citadels and their method of employment, masters are recommended to check regularly with MSCHOA.

(l) Consider the use of dummies at the rails to simulate additional lookouts. However, if ship design creates lookout black spots and the security assessment identifies this risk, then it may have to be covered by manpower.

(m) It is suggested fire pumps and/or hoses should be pressurised and ready for discharge overboard around the vessel, particularly at the most vulnerable points.

(n) Consideration should also be given to creating a water curtain around the vessel to further deter boarding.

(o) Consider the use of razor wire/physical barriers around stern/lowest points of access, commensurate with crew safety and escape.

(p) Consider the use of passive defence equipment.

(q) Consider providing night vision optics for use during the hours of darkness.

(r) Operate CCTV (if fitted).

5. In transit – operations

(a) Ship's crew should not be exposed to undue risk when employing self-protective measures (SPM).

(b) All ships inside the GoA are strongly urged to use the IRTC and follow MSCHOA GT advice and timings as promulgated on the MSCHOA website.

(c) Attention of mariners is also drawn to IMO circular SN.1 Circ. 281 dated 4 August 2009, 'Information on internationally recognised transit corridor (IRTC) for ships transiting the Gulf of Aden' where advice is provided that the IRTC is subject to change by military authorities according to prevailing circumstances. Mariners are therefore urged to obtain up-to-date information from the 'MSCHOA' website www. mschoa.org or NAV warnings promulgated for that area.

(d) If you intend to follow a group transit (GT) through the IRTC: transit at the group transit speed, but remain aware of the ship's limitations. (Current advice, for example, is that if your full sea speed is 16 knots, consider joining a 14-knot GT and keep those 2 knots in reserve.)

(e) If you do not intend to follow a GT through the IRTC: maintain full sea speed through the high-risk area. (Current advice is that if the full sea speed of the ship is more than 18 knots, then do not slow down for a GT. Instead, maintain full sea speed and aim to transit as much of the high-risk area in darkness as possible.)

(f) Ships should comply with the International Rules for Prevention of Collision at Sea at all times. Masters should endeavour not to impede the safe navigation of other vessels when joining and leaving the IRTC. Navigation lights should not be turned off at night. Follow the guidance given by flag State authority.

(g) Provide deck lighting only as required for safety. Lighting in the shadow zones around the ship's hull may extend the area of visibility for lookouts, but only where consistent with safe navigation. Where fitted, and deemed suitable, consider the immediate use of 'remotely operated' ship searchlights, if suspicious activity around the vessel is observed, the use of searchlights may startle and deter a potential attack. (Current naval advice is to transit with navigation lights only).

(h) Keep photographs of pirate 'mother ships' on the bridge. Report immediately if sighted. Report all sightings of suspect mother ships to UKMTO Dubai and the IMB PRC. (See Annex C for an example of a piracy report for passing on such information or reporting on any other attack or sighting.)

(i) The master should try to make as early an assessment of a threat as possible. As soon as the master feels that a threat is developing he should immediately call the UKMTO Dubai.

(j) Keep a good lookout by all available means for suspicious craft, especially from astern and each quarter.

(k) Protect the crew from exposure to undue risk. Only essential work on deck should occur in transit of the high-risk area. Masters should, in so far as possible, keep crew members clear from external deck spaces during hours of darkness, whilst being mindful of their obligation to maintain a full and proper lookout at all times.

(l) Use light, alarm bells and crew activity to alert suspected pirates that they have been detected.

(m) A variety of other additional commercially available non-lethal defensive measures are available that could be considered; however these should be assessed by companies on their merits and on the particular characteristics and vulnerability of the ship concerned.

6. If attacked by pirates

(a) Follow the ship's pre-prepared contingency plan.

(b) Activate the emergency communication plan, and report the attack immediately to the single primary point of contact in the event of an attack, which is UKMTO Dubai. (MSCHOA, as the continually manned maritime security watch centre for piracy attacks in the region, will continue to function as a back-up contact point in the event of an attack.)

(c) Activate the ship security alert system (SSAS), which will alert your company security officer and flag state. Post attack reports should be communicated as quickly as possible to all relevant piracy reporting centres as explained in section 9.

(d) If the master has exercised his right to turn off the automatic identification system (AIS) during transit of the piracy area, this should be turned on once the ship comes under pirate attack.

(e) Sound the emergency alarm and make a 'pirate attack' (PA) announcement in accordance with the ship's emergency plan.

(f) Make a 'mayday' call on VHF Ch. 16 (and backup Ch. 08, which is monitored by naval units). Send a distress message via the DSC (digital selective calling) system and Inmarsat-C, as applicable. Establish telephone communication with UKMTO Dubai.

(g) Prevent skiffs closing on the ship by altering course and increasing speed where possible.[15] Pirates have great difficulty boarding a ship that is:

(i) making way at over 15 knots;

(ii) manoeuvring – it is suggested that as early as possible masters undertake continuous small zigzag manoeuvres to further deter boarding whilst maintaining speed. Consider increasing the pirates' exposure to wind/waves and using bow wave and stern wash to restrict pirate craft coming alongside. Masters and the officer of the watch (OOW) should be aware of the handling and manoeuvring characteristics of the vessel. Particular attention should be given to the effects of varying helm orders and the impact these can have on the ship's speed.

(h) Activate fire pump defensive measures.

(i) Consider turning on forward facing deck lights to draw attention to your vessel and aid positive identification by arriving military forces as a vessel under attack.

(j) Muster all remaining crew in accordance with the ship's contingency plan.

7. If boarded by pirates

(a) Before pirates gain access to the bridge, inform UKMTO Dubai and, if time permits, the company.

(b) Offer no resistance; this could lead to unnecessary violence and harm to the crew.

(c) If the bridge/engine room is to be evacuated, then the main engine should be stopped; all way taken off the vessel if possible and the ship navigated clear of other ships.

(d) Remain calm and cooperate fully with the pirates.

(e) Ensure all crew, other than the bridge team, stay together in one location.

---

15 If you can buy time until the military forces arrive, this often leads the pirates to abort their attack. This is why early registration with MSCHOA, use of group transit timings and updating your position with UKMTO Dubai are all essential: it gives a better probability that naval support will be nearby if the pirates attack.

(f) If in a locked down 'citadel' ensure internal protection/cover is available in case the pirates attempt to force entry. Keep clear of entry point/doors and portholes/windows – do not resist entry. Use citadel emergency communication methods to communicate with authorities.

8. In the event of military action

   (a) Crew should be advised NOT to use cameras with flash at any time when any military action is under way.
   (b) In the event that military personnel take action onboard the ship, all personnel should keep low to the deck, cover their heads with both hands, with hands visible and empty.
   (c) Be prepared to answer questions on identity and status onboard.
   (d) Be aware that English is not the working language of all naval units in the region.
   (e) Military forces may initially secure all persons encountered. This is standard practice. Brief and prepare ship's personnel to expect this and to cooperate fully during the initial stages of military action onboard.

9. Post incident reporting (reference Annex C).

   (a) Following any piracy attack or suspicious activity, it is vital that a detailed report of the event is reported to MSCHOA, UKMTO DUBAI and the IMB.
   (b) This will ensure full analysis and trends in piracy activity are established as well as enabling assessment of piracy techniques or changes in tactics, in addition to ensuring appropriate warnings can be issued to other merchant shipping in the vicinity.
   (c) Masters are therefore requested to complete the standardised piracy report form contained in Annex C.

   Updating best management practices

   1. It is anticipated that these BMP will be periodically updated based upon operational experience and lessons learned. The parties to this document will endeavour to meet regularly to update these BMP and to circulate revisions to their respective members and other interested organisations.
   2. If in doubt, consult the MSCHOA website where additional relevant information will always be posted (noting that this may not be endorsed by all of the above-listed organisations)."

There is a follow-up report known as the "Piracy Attack Report".

"Additional guidance for vessels engaged in fishing, supplementary to the best management practices to deter piracy in the Gulf of Aden and off the coast of Somalia

I. Recommendations to vessels in fishing zones
1. Non-Somali fishing vessels should avoid operating or transiting within 200 nm of the coast of Somalia, irrespective of whether or not they had been issued with licences to do so.
2. Do not start fishing operations when the radar indicates the presence of unidentified boats.
3. If polyester skiffs of a type typically used by pirates are sighted, move away from them full speed, sailing into wind and sea to make their navigation more difficult.
4. Avoid stopping at night, be alert and maintain bridge, deck and engine room watch.
5. During fishing operations, when the vessel is more vulnerable, be alert and maintain radar watch in order to give maximum notice to the authorities if an attack is in course.
6. While navigating at night, use only the mandatory navigation and safety lights so as to prevent the glow of lighting attracting pirates who sometimes are in boats without radars and are just lurking around.

7. While the vessel is drifting while fishing at night, keep guard at the bridge on deck and in the engine room. Use only mandatory navigation and safety lights. The engine must be ready for an immediate start up.
8. Keep away from unidentified ships.
9. Use VHF as little as possible to avoid being heard by pirates and make location more difficult.
10. Activate AIS when maritime patrol aircraft are operating in the area to facilitate identification and tracking

II. Identification
1. Managers are strongly recommended to register their fishing vessels with MSCHOA for the whole period of activity off the coast of Somalia. This should include communicating a full list of the crewmen on board and their vessels' intentions, if possible.
2. Carry out training prior to passage or fishing operations in the area.
3. Whenever fishing vessels are equipped with VMS devices, their manager should provide MSCHOA with access to VMS data.
4. Fishing vessels should avoid sailing through areas where they have been informed that suspected pirate 'mother ships' had been identified and should use all means to detect, as soon as possible, any movement of large or small vessels that could be suspicious.
5. Fishing vessels should always identify themselves upon request from aircraft or ships from Operation ATALANTA or other international or national anti-piracy operation.
6. Military, merchant and fishing vessels should respond without delay to any identification request made by a fishing vessel being approached (in order to facilitate early action to make escape possible, especially if the vessel is fishing).

III. In case of attack
1. In case of an attack or sighting a suspicious craft, warn the authorities (UKMTO and MSCHOA) and the rest of the fleet.
2. Communicate the contact details of the second master of the vessel (who is on land) whose knowledge of the vessel could contribute to the success of a military intervention.

    Recommendations only for purse-seiners
3. Evacuate all personnel from the deck and the crow's nest.
4. If pirates have taken control of the vessel and the purse-seine is spread out, encourage the pirates to allow the nets to be recovered. If recovery of the purse-seine is allowed, follow the instructions for its stowage and explain the functioning of the gear in order to avoid misunderstanding."

Assessment of the recommendation

38.015 The measure was helpful in that it raised the profile of the issue of piracy and clearly stated that the EU was keen to address it. Moreover, in the measure, the Commission urged the Member States to ensure measures to prevent maritime piracy are applied so it was a very sensible move by the EU institutions to get the Member States to mobilise and take specific actions to deal with the issue. On the other hand, critics of the measure would say that it was merely a recommendation which did not do anything other than "curse the dark", it itemised the steps which one might take to defend a pirate attack so it was curious to put on public record the "play book" of a ship under attack.

C. 2011: STRATEGIC FRAMEWORK FOR THE HORN OF AFRICA

38.016 On 14 November 2011, the EU Council of Ministers adopted a "Strategic Framework for the Horn of Africa".[16] Its objective was to set out the EU's multi-sectoral engagement in the region. It defines five priorities for EU action: building robust and accountable political structures; contributing to conflict resolution and prevention; mitigating security threats emanating from the region; promoting economic growth; and supporting regional economic co-operation. It describes the way in which the EU pursues its strategic approach, working in partnership with the region itself, in particular the African Union, and key international partners. The executive summary of the document is instructive:

"The political evolution of the Horn of Africa[17] over the past 50 years has been unusually turbulent. The objective of the European Union is therefore to support the people of the region in achieving greater peace, stability, security, prosperity and accountable government."

38.017 The EU's engagement in the Horn will be supportive of a regional and country-level environment conducive to peace, security and justice, of good governance based on the democratic principles of inclusion, the rule of law and respect for human rights, and of socio-economic development based on the attainment of the Millennium Development Goals with due consideration to equity, climate change and sustainable livelihoods.

38.018 The EU's interests in the Horn of Africa are defined by the region's geo-strategic importance, the EU's historic engagement with the countries of the region, its desire to support the welfare of the people and help lift them from poverty into self-sustaining economic growth, and the need for the EU to protect its own citizens from the threats that emanate from some parts of the region and address common challenges. To achieve its objective of peace, stability, security, prosperity and accountable government, the EU will: (1) assist all countries in the region to build robust and accountable political structures, including civil and civic institutions, allowing the people of the Horn to express their legitimate political aspirations and ensure that their basic human rights and freedoms are respected; (2) work with the countries of the region and with international organisations (especially the United Nations and African Union) to resolve current conflicts, particularly in Somalia and Sudan, and avoid future potential conflicts between or within countries; (3) ensure that, until that is achieved, the insecurity in the region does not threaten the security of others beyond its borders, e.g. through piracy, terrorism or irregular migration; (4) support efforts to promote the economic growth of all countries and people in the region, to enable them to reduce poverty, increase prosperity and enjoy not suffer from the benefits globalisation can bring; and (5) support political and economic regional cooperation and bolster the role of the Regional Economic Communities ("RECs") to tap into positive trends and developments across national borders.

To enhance the coherence, quality, impact and visibility of the EU's multifaceted action in the region, an EU Special Representative ("EUSR"), in close consultation with

---

16 www.consilium.europa.eu/uedocs/cms_data/docs/pressdata/EN/foraff/126052.pdf.

17 Ed., for the purpose of the Commission's paper, the Horn of Africa is defined as the countries belonging to the Inter-Governmental Authority for Development (IGAD) – Djibouti, Eritrea, Ethiopia, Kenya, Somalia, Sudan, South Sudan and Uganda.

the EUSR for Sudan and South Sudan, will contribute to the EU's regional approach to the interrelated challenges facing the Horn.

38.019 The Framework proposes a number of ways the EU can pursue this strategic approach that will enable it to do so in partnership with the region itself and key partners. It identifies areas for action, but specific actions, in the form of sub-strategies and action plans, will be subject to subsequent decisions by the Commission, Council and Member States.

38.020 The High Representative and the European External Action Service ("EEAS"), the EUSR, EU Delegations in the region, the European Commission and Member States will work together to implement this Framework.

38.021 To co-ordinate these efforts, since 1 January 2012, the EU has a Special Representative to the Horn of Africa, Alexander Rondos. He was tasked to initially focus on Somalia and the regional dimensions of the conflict there, as well as on piracy, which has its root causes in the instability of Somalia. More recently, the EU co-organised with the Somali federal government the Conference on a "New Deal for Somalia" in Brussels on 16 September 2013, where a strategic framework and broader objectives were set out for the country.

D. JUDICIAL INTERVENTION

38.022 Judicial intervention has had to develop to fight piracy. Over 1,200 suspects have been prosecuted in 21 countries (both EU Member States and third States). The EU is assisting the United Nations Development Programme and the United Nations Office for Drugs and Crime ("UNODC") to establish sufficient conditions to allow fair and efficient piracy trials in Somalia but this will take time. The EU has signed transfer agreements with the Seychelles and Mauritius. Transfers to Kenya are possible on a case by case basis. A joint EU/UNODC programme of support for the justice system in Kenya was launched in May 2009 to provide Kenya with practical assistance to cope with the extra demands associated with the prosecution and detention of piracy suspects. Similar support programmes were designed for the Seychelles and Mauritius.

E. OPERATION ATALANTA

38.023 In 2008, the EU launched "European Naval Force Somalia – Operation Atlanta (EU NAVFOR–ATALANTA)"[18] under the European Common Security and Defence

---

18 The European Union's External Action Service states on its website (http://eunavfor.eu/mission/): "EU NAVFOR operates in an Area of Operations covering the Southern Red Sea, the Gulf of Aden and a large part of the Indian Ocean, including the Seychelles, Mauritius and Comoros. The Area of Operations also includes the Somali coastal territory, as well as its territorial and internal waters. This represents an area of about 4,700,000 square nautical miles (approximately 8,700,000 square kilometres). Within the Area of Operations, EU NAVFOR units conduct tasks in accordance with the Mandate. Close co-operation with WFP and AMISOM ensures that no vessel transporting humanitarian aid (or logistics for the African Union mission) will travel unprotected along the Somali coastline. EU NAVFOR warships also conduct patrols in the Internationally Recommended Transit Corridor (IRTC) in the Gulf of Aden and the Indian Ocean. Furthermore, warships and Maritime Patrol and Reconnaissance Aircraft (MPRA) conduct reconnaissance and surveillance operations. Warships and their boarding teams routinely conduct visual or physical checks of vessels transiting the High Risk Area. Meetings with local seafarers, or 'friendly approaches', are conducted to gather a better understanding of maritime practices by talking with the crews of fishing and trading vessels in the region and to make

Policy ("CSDP") and the relevant UN Security Council Resolutions. The objectives of Operation ATALANTA are: (a) the protection of vessels of the World Food Programme ("WFP") delivering food aid to displaced persons in Somalia and the protection of African Union Mission in Somalia ("AMISOM") shipping; (b) the deterrence, prevention and repression of acts of piracy and armed robbery off the Somali coast; (c) the protection of vulnerable shipping off the Somali coast on a case by case basis; and (d) the monitoring of fishing activities off the coast of Somalia. EU NAVFOR–ATALANTA consists of combat vessels, auxiliary ships as well as military patrol and reconnaissance aircraft deployed in the area of operation.

F. POLITICAL AND SECURITY COMMITTEE DECISION ATALANTA/4/2014 OF 24 JULY 2014 ON THE APPOINTMENT OF THE EU FORCE COMMANDER FOR THE EUROPEAN UNION MILITARY OPERATION TO CONTRIBUTE TO THE DETERRENCE, PREVENTION AND REPRESSION OF ACTS OF PIRACY AND ARMED ROBBERY OFF THE SOMALI COAST (ATALANTA) AND REPEALING DECISION ATALANTA/1/2014 (2014/500/ CFSP)

38.024 The EU's Political and Security Committee adopted a decision appointing EU Force Commander for the European Union military operation to contribute to the deterrence, prevention and repression of acts of piracy and armed robbery off the Somali coast (Atalanta) as from 6 August 2014.[19]

G. CONCLUSIONS

38.025 On 21 November 2014, the Council of the EU had extended the Mandate of Operation ATALANTA until December 2016. The Operation has now been extended by the European Council until December 2020.

38.026 Today, EU NAVFOR operates alongside other CSDP Missions in the region including: EUCAP Nestor (this is a civilian mission augmented with military expertise designed to support regional maritime capacity-building) and the EUTM – Somalia (this is the EU Training Mission – Somalia which is an EU military training mission which aims to strengthen the Somali national government and the institutions of

---

ships' masters aware of the Best Management Practices (BMP) for protection against Somali-based piracy, i.e. self-protection measures. A significant objective of EU NAVFOR is the deterrence and disruption of acts of piracy and armed robbery on the high seas. Warships apprehend suspected pirates following intelligence reports of pirate activity or sightings by merchant vessels and MPRAs. When EU NAVFOR assets locate suspicious vessels, and further investigation confirms the suspicion, the pirate groups will be disrupted. This means action will be taken in order to render a suspected group incapable of further pirate operations. Suspected pirates may be detained with the aim to transfer them to competent national authorities for prosecution. Their equipment is often confiscated for evidence purposes. A disruption of a pirate logistics dump was also carried out on the Somali coastline as part of a focused and deliberate operation in May 2012. In addition, EU NAVFOR warships regularly come to the aid of vessels in distress, either because of a pirate attack or because the vessel is otherwise in an emergency situation at sea. EU NAVFOR assets also support UN Food and Agriculture Organization (FAO)'s programmes to monitor fishing activity in the area."

19 Political and Security Committee Decision Atalanta/3/2014 on the appointment of the EU Force Commander for the European Union military operation to contribute to the deterrence, prevention and repression of acts of piracy and armed robbery off the Somali coast (Atalanta) and repealing Decision Atalanta/1/2014.

Somalia, by providing military training to members of the Somali National Armed Forces).

38.027 For various reasons (including the actions of the EU), the situation off Somalia has eased considerably. The situation was at its worst in January 2011 when 736 hostages taken captive and 32 ships were being held by pirates. The situation has improved and, in recent years (particularly in 2015–2018), the number of ships and hostages has dropped significantly.

CHAPTER 39

Navigation

A. INTRODUCTION

Introduction

39.001 This chapter deals with two separate but related topics: navigation and short sea shipping.

Navigation

39.002 At one level, it is extraordinary that the European Union ("EU") has become involved in navigational issues. One would expect that those issues would be left to organisations such as the International Maritime Organization ("IMO") which are specialist maritime organisations. Yet, it is really impossible for the EU not to deal with navigational issues given the cross-over between navigation and various issues which are readily dealt with by the EU such as safety, pilotage, the environment and marine equipment. However, it is notable that the measures which relate to navigation are largely (but not entirely) recommendations and therefore not legally binding in their own right. This chapter deals with various measures which have been adopted by the EU in regard to navigation, including, Decision 92/143 of 25 February 1992 on radionavigation systems for Europe,[1] Decision 2004/71 on essential requirements relating to marine radio communication equipment which is intended to be used on non-International Convention for the Safety of Life at Sea ("SOLAS") vessels and to participate in the Global Maritime Distress and Safety System ("GMDSS").[2]

Short sea shipping

39.003 Short sea shipping,[3] as its name suggests, is the concept of maritime transport over short distances – near shipping in other words.[4] It is also referred to as coastal shipping

---

1 OJ L59/17, 4 March 1992.

2 OJ L16/54, 23 January 2004.

3 See www.shortsea.info for information on short sea shipping. See also www.wctrs-society.com/wp/wp-content/uploads/abstracts/rio/selected/1432.pdf for a copy of a paper on the competitiveness of the short sea shipping sector. See also Suárez-Alemán, "Short Sea Shipping in Today's Europe: A Critical Review of Maritime Transport Policy", Marit Econ Logist (2015), doi:10.1057/mel.2015.10. See also European Conference of Ministers of Transport, Short Sea Shipping in Europe (2001).

4 The EU's statistics agency, Eurostat, has stated (http://ec.europa.eu/eurostat/statistics-explained/index.php/Glossary:Short_sea_shipping_(SSS)): "Short sea shipping, abbreviated as SSS, is the maritime transport of goods over relatively short distances, as opposed to the intercontinental cross-ocean deep sea shipping. In the context of European Union (EU) transport statistics it is defined as maritime transport of goods between ports in the EU-27 (sometimes also including candidate countries and EFTA [European Free Trade Association] countries) on one hand, and ports situated in geographical Europe, on the Mediterranean and Black Seas on the other

and can either be cabotage (between two parts in the same State) or at least involving no more than two neighbouring or contiguous States. It is attractive from an environmental perspective in that it diverts traffic from road or rail to sea but it can be slower and more awkward because it is less direct and usually longer. The EU has adopted various measures including a communication from the Commission to the Council, the European Parliament, the European Economic and Social Committee ("EESC") and the Committee of the Regions on Short Sea Shipping.[5] The desirability of encouraging and promoting short sea shipping has been emphasised a number of times – for example, it was reiterated in the 7 May 2014 Athens Declaration. Short sea shipping is growing in popularity. In the 1990s, short sea shipping was the only mode of transport that proved able to keep up with the fast growth of road transport. Between 1995 and 2002, the tonne-kilometre performance of both short sea shipping and road grew by 25%. In 2001, short sea shipping performed 40% of all tonne-kilometres in Europe while the share of road transport was 45%.

B. COUNCIL DECISION 92/143 ON RADIONAVIGATION SYSTEMS FOR EUROPE

Introduction

39.004 On 25 February 1992, the Council adopted Decision 92/143 of on radio-navigation systems for Europe.[6]

Legal background to the decision

39.005 The legal basis for the decision was Article 84(2) of the then European Economic Treaty ("EEC") Treaty which is equivalent now to Article 100(2) of the Treaty on the Functioning of the European Union ("TFEU"). The legislative history included a proposal from the Commission,[7] an opinion of the European Parliament[8] as well as an opinion of the EESC.[9]

Factual background to the decision

39.006 The background to Decision 92/143 is clear from the recitals to the decision which state in part:

---

hand, i.e. ports in: (a) EU-27 countries (actually only the 22 maritime Member States: Belgium, Bulgaria, Cyprus, Denmark, Estonia, Finland, France, Germany, Greece, Ireland, Italy, Latvia, Lithuania, Malta, the Netherlands, Poland, Portugal, Romania, Slovenia, Spain, Sweden and the United Kingdom); (b) EEA [European Economic Area] countries (Iceland and Norway); (c) candidate countries (Croatia (now a Member State), Montenegro and Turkey); (d) the Baltic Sea area (Russia); (e) the Mediterranean Sea area (Albania, Algeria, Bosnia-Herzegovina, Egypt, Israel, Lebanon, Libya, Morocco, Occupied Palestinian territory, Syria, and Tunisia); and (f) the Black Sea area (Georgia, Moldova, Russia and Ukraine). This definition is derived from Commission Communication COM (1999) 317 final of June 1999 on the development of SSS in Europe. ... As a result, short sea shipping also includes feeder services: a short-sea network between ports with the objective of consolidating or redistributing freight to or from a deep sea service in one of these ports, the so-called hub port."

5 Com (2004) 452.
6 OJ L59/17, 4 March 1992.
7 OJ C53/71, 28 February 1991 and OJ C317/16, 7 December 1991.
8 OJ C280/32, 28 October 1991.
9 OJ C159/22, 17 June 1991.

"Whereas the 1974 International Convention for the Safety of Life at Sea (Solas 1974) drafted under the auspices of the International Maritime Organization (IMO), requires contracting parties to arrange for the establishment and maintenance of such aids to navigation as the volume of traffic and the degree of risk warrant;

Whereas, in its Resolution A.666 (16), the IMO refers both to the need for a worldwide radionavigation system and to the possibility of regional applications of terrestrial systems such as Chayka, Decca Navigator, Loran-C, Omega and Differential Omega;

Whereas the International Association of Lighthouse Authorities confirms that, in order to meet the needs of maritime navigation, a terrestrial radionavigation system is necessary until general-purpose satellite systems are widely available, and also thereafter in parallel to such systems for the foreseeable future;

Whereas it is a concern of the Community to ensure the highest degree of safety of navigation and protection of the marine environment;

Whereas the United States Coastguard has decided to terminate its Loran-C commitments outside the United States of America as from 1994 and intends to offer the Loran-C facilities to the relevant host nations;

Whereas certain Member States intend to participate in one or more regional agreements on the establishment of Loran-C chains covering North-West Europe and the North Atlantic, the Mediterranean, the Iberian Peninsula and the Baltic, while a number of these areas are already covered by terrestrial systems, such as Decca and Omega;

Whereas Member States are not required to abandon existing radionavigation systems, such as Decca and Omega, provided they fulfil their Loran-C obligations in accordance with regional agreements;

Whereas the Loran-C system in particular satisfies international requirements and its more general application does not prejudice the development of satellite aids to navigation, especially as combined coverage by satellite and Loran-C will offer an excellent degree of system verification and continuity of radionavigation coverage for the benefit of maritime safety and environmental protection;

Whereas the establishment of regional Loran-C systems must ensure coherent and complete coverage of the European maritime area, avoiding as much as possible the imposition of additional costs upon the users of existing terrestrial radionavigation systems..."

Operative provisions in the decision

39.007 Article 1(1) of the decision provides that without prejudice to the then existing radionavigation systems, Member States which participate in or join regional agreements on Loran-C must do so in a way which fulfils international objectives. Article 1(2) goes on to provide that with regard to their participation in the regional agreements referred to in Article 1(1), Member States must seek to achieve the radionavigation configurations which cover the widest possible geographical area in Europe and in neighbouring waters.

39.008 Article 2 of the decision then goes on to provide that the Commission must:

"– ensure coordination between the Member States participating in the regional agreements referred to in paragraph 1 with a view to ensuring compatibility between the Loran-C chains introduced at regional level,

– encourage the development of receivers, which take account of the ongoing development of satellite systems and the enhancement of the present Loran-C system,

– pursue its work with a view to setting up a radionavigation plan which takes into account the development of satellite navigation systems, of existing terrestrial systems and of the radionavigation plans of the Member States, and

– propose the necessary measures to the Council should the need arise."

39.009 Article 3 of the decision provides that as

"members or observers within the International Association of Lighthouse Authorities, Member States and the Commission shall support efforts to set up a worldwide radionavigation system including European regional Loran-C chains with the purpose of enlarging worldwide Loran-C coverage in order to improve the safety of navigation and protection of the marine environment."

C. NAVIGATION: REPEALED: COMMISSION DECISION 2004/71 ON ESSENTIAL REQUIREMENTS RELATING TO MARINE RADIO COMMUNICATION EQUIPMENT WHICH IS INTENDED TO BE USED ON NON-SOLAS VESSELS AND TO PARTICIPATE IN THE GLOBAL MARITIME DISTRESS AND SAFETY SYSTEM (GMDSS)

Introduction

39.010 On 4 September 2003, the Commission adopted Decision 2004/71 on essential requirements relating to marine radio communication equipment which is intended to be used on non-SOLAS vessels and to participate in the Global Maritime Distress and Safety System (GMDSS).[10] Commission Decision 2004/71 was repealed by Decision 2013/638.[11] It is useful to recall its contents for completeness but it has been repealed.

Legal background

39.011 The legal basis for the decision was the then Economic Community ("EC") Treaty generally – this would now be the TFEU.

Factual background

39.012 The factual background to the decision is clear from the recitals:

"Having regard to Directive 1999/5/EC of the European Parliament and of the Council of 9 March 1999 on radio equipment and telecommunications terminal equipment and the mutual recognition of their conformity,[12] and in particular Article 3(3)(e),

(1) A number of Member States have implemented or intend to implement common safety principles and rules for radio equipment on non-SOLAS (Safety of Life At Sea) vessels.

(2) The harmonisation of radio services should contribute to a safer navigation of non-SOLAS vessels, particularly in case of distress and bad weather conditions.

(3) Maritime Safety Committee (MSC) Circular 803 on the participation of non-SOLAS ships in the Global Maritime Distress and Safety System (GMDSS) and Resolution MSC.77(69) of the International Maritime Organisation (IMO) invite Governments to apply the Guidelines for the participation of non-SOLAS ships in the GMDSS and urges Governments to require certain features to be implemented in relation to the GMDSS on radio equipment to be used on all vessels.

(4) The International Telecommunications Union (ITU) Radio Regulations specify certain frequencies that are designated for use by the GMDSS. All radio equipment operating on those frequencies which is intended for use in times of distress should be compatible with

---

10 OJ L16/54, 23 January 2004.

11 OJ L296/22, 7 November 2013, http://data.europa.eu/eli/dec/2013/638/oj.

12 Ed., OJ L91/10, 7 April 1999.

the designated use of those frequencies and it should provide a reasonable guarantee of assurance that it will function correctly in times of distress.

(5) The scope of Commission Decision 2000/638/EC of 22 September 2000 on the application of Article 3(3)(e) of Directive 1999/5/EC to marine communication equipment intended to be fitted to seagoing non-SOLAS vessels and which is intended to participate in the global maritime distress and safety system (GMDSS) and not covered by Council Directive 96/98/EC on marine equipment[13] is limited to equipment which is intended to be fitted to seagoing vessels. The scope of that Decision should be broadened to cover GMDSS equipment for use on all non-SOLAS vessels. It is considered that the high level of safety given by this Decision is relevant for all vessels and therefore the scope of the Decision should be amended so that the same requirements apply to cover the use of GMDSS equipment on vessels outside the scope of SOLAS and the Marine equipment Directive whether or not they are seagoing. Decision 2000/638/EC should therefore be replaced.

(6) The measures set out in this Decision are in accordance with the opinion of the Telecommunications Conformity Assessment and Market Surveillance Committee."

Scope of the decision

39.013 Article 1 sets out the scope of application of the decision. It applies to radio equipment intended for use on non-SOLAS vessels and intended to participate in the GMDSS as laid down in Chapter IV of the SOLAS Convention operating in (a) the maritime mobile service as defined in Article 1.28 of the International Telecommunications Union ("ITU") Radio Regulations, or (b) the maritime mobile satellite service as defined in Article 1.29 of the ITU Radio Regulations. Pursuant to Article 4, the decision has applied since 4 September 2004.

Effect of the decision

39.014 Article 2 then provides that radio equipment falling within the scope of the decision (as specified in Article 1), shall be designed so as to ensure correct functioning under exposure to a marine environment, meet all the operational requirements of the GMDSS under distress conditions and provide clear and robust communications with a high degree of fidelity of the analogue or digital communications link. Article 3 repealed Decision 2000/638. Ultimately, Decision 2004/71 was repealed by Decision 2013/638.[14]

D. NAVIGATION: COMMISSION DECISION 2013/638 OF 12 AUGUST 2013 ON ESSENTIAL REQUIREMENTS RELATING TO MARINE RADIO COMMUNICATION EQUIPMENT WHICH IS INTENDED TO BE USED ON NON-SOLAS VESSELS AND TO PARTICIPATE IN THE GLOBAL MARITIME DISTRESS AND SAFETY SYSTEM (GMDSS)

39.015 On 12 August 2013, the Commission adopted Decision 2013/638 of 12 August 2013 on essential requirements relating to marine radio communication equipment which is intended to be used on non-SOLAS vessels and to participate in the Global Maritime

---

13 Ed., OJ L269/52, 21 October 2000.
14 OJ L296/22, 7 November 2013, http://data.europa.eu/eli/dec/2013/638/oj.

Distress and Safety System (GMDSS).[15] Decision 2013/638 was addressed to the Member States.

39.016 The legal basis of Decision 2013/638 was the TFEU generally. The decision has regard to Directive 1999/5 of the European Parliament and of the Council of 9 March 1999 on radio equipment and telecommunications terminal equipment and the mutual recognition of their conformity,[16] and in particular Article 3(3)(e) of Directive 1999/5.

39.017 The first recital to Decision 2013/638 provided that a number of Member States have implemented or intend to implement common safety principles and rules for radio equipment on vessels to which the 1974 SOLAS does not apply (hereinafter "non-SOLAS vessels").

39.018 The second recital provides that the harmonisation of radio services should contribute to a safer navigation of non-SOLAS vessels, particularly in case of distress and bad weather conditions.

39.019 The third recital provides that Maritime Safety Committee ("MSC") Circular 803 on the participation of non-SOLAS ships in the GMDSS and Resolution MSC.131 (75) of the IMO invite States to apply the Guidelines for the participation of non-SOLAS ships in the GMDSS and urges States to require certain features to be implemented in relation to the GMDSS on radio equipment to be used on all vessels.

39.020 The fourth recital states that the ITU Radio Regulations specify certain frequencies that are designated for use by the GMDSS. All radio equipment operating on those frequencies which is intended for use in times of distress should be compatible with the designated use of those frequencies and it should provide a reasonable guarantee of assurance that it will function correctly in times of distress.

39.021 The fifth recital provides that it is necessary to clarify that Commission Decision 2004/71 of 4 September 2003 on essential requirements relating to marine radio communication equipment which is intended to be used on non-SOLAS vessels and to participate in the GMDSS[17] applies to GMDSS equipment for use on all non-SOLAS vessels, which is not covered by Council Directive 96/98 of 20 December 1996 on marine equipment.[18]

39.022 The sixth recital provides that implementation of requirements to be complied with by GMDSS equipment destined for non-SOLAS vessels should be consistent across all Member States and in line with relevant IMO guidelines.

39.023 Given the number of changes to be made to Decision 2004/71, the seventh recital provides that the decision should be replaced, in the interest of clarity.

39.024 The eighth recital provides that the measures set out in this decision are in accordance with the opinion of the Telecommunications Conformity Assessment and Market Surveillance Committee.

39.025 Article 1 provides that the decision shall apply to all radio equipment not within the scope of Directive 96/98 and which are intended for use on all vessels to which the 1974 SOLAS does not apply (non-SOLAS vessels) and which are intended to participate in the GMDSS, as laid down in Chapter IV of the SOLAS Convention operating in either of the following services: (a) the maritime mobile service as defined in Article 1.28

---

15 OJ L296/22, 7 November 2013, http://data.europa.eu/eli/dec/2013/638/oj.
16 OJ L91/10, 7 April 1999.
17 OJ L16/54, 23 January 2004.
18 OJ L46/25, 17 February 1997.

of the ITU Radio Regulations; and (b) the maritime mobile satellite service as defined in Article 1.29 of the ITU Radio Regulations.

39.026 Article 2 states that without prejudice to Directive 2009/45 of the European Parliament and of the Council[19] radio equipment shall be designed so as to ensure correct functioning under exposure to a marine environment, meet all the operational requirements of the GMDSS applicable to non-SOLAS vessels, in accordance with the relevant provisions of the IMO, and provide clear and robust communications with a high degree of fidelity of the analogue or digital communications link.

39.027 Article 3 repealed Decision 2004/71 of 4 September 2003 on essential requirements relating to marine radio communication equipment which is intended to be used on non-SOLAS vessels to participate in the GMDSS.[20]

E. COMMISSION RECOMMENDATION 2010/167 OF 19 MARCH 2010 ON THE AUTHORISATION OF SYSTEMS FOR MOBILE COMMUNICATION SERVICES ON BOARD VESSELS (MCV SERVICES)

39.028 On 19 March 2010, the Commission adopted Recommendation 2010/167 on the Authorisation of Systems for Mobile Communication Services on Board Vessels (MCV Services).[21] The recommendation had regard to Directive 2002/21 of the European Parliament and of the Council of 7 March 2002 on a common regulatory framework for electronic communications networks and services (Framework Directive),[22] and in particular Article 19(1) of it.

39.029 The recitals to the recommendation 2010/167 provides:

"Whereas:

(1) The i2010 policy, as the strategic framework for a European Information Society, promotes an open and competitive digital economy in the European Union, emphasises ICT as a driver of inclusion and quality of life, and stresses the benefits of ready access to information and communication resources in all areas of daily life.

(2) Mobile communication services on board vessels (MCV services) are used on board freight and passenger vessels sailing within the territorial seas in the European Union and in international waters and are often pan-European or inter-State in nature. Systems providing MCV services ('MCV systems') aim to complement existing mobile connectivity when operating in those areas of the territorial seas of the EU Member States, as defined in the United Nations Convention on the Law of the Sea, that are not covered by land-based mobile networks.

(3) An MCV system ('dedicated MCV system') generally consists of one or more pico-cell base stations on board a vessel (vessel-BS), providing access to a GSM [Global System for Mobile Communications] core network via a backhaul link, for example via satellite. The vessel-BS of such a system serve roaming GSM mobile terminals carried by ship passengers or crew.

(4) MCV services are currently operated commercially using only the GSM standard and only in bands 880–915 MHz and 1 710-1 785 MHz for uplink (terminal transmit and base station receive) and 925–960 MHz and 1 805-1 880 MHz for downlink (base station transmit and terminal receive). In future, however, they may be extended to other terrestrial public

---

19 OJ L163/1, 25 June 2009.
20 OJ L16/54, 23 January 2004.
21 OJ L72/42, 20 March 2010.
22 OJ L108/33, 24 April 2002.

mobile communication systems, operating in accordance with other standards and in other frequency bands.

(5) The operation of dedicated MCV systems should be distinguished from the extended coverage provided by land-based mobile electronic communications networks in territorial seas to the extent that this is based on operators' rights to establish and operate land-based mobile networks.

(6) A coordinated approach to the regulation of MCV services would help to facilitate the provision of these services across the European Union, thereby contributing to achievement of the objectives of the EU single market. It would also help to ensure seamless mobile connectivity for consumers and business users and would enhance the potential of innovative maritime communication services.

(7) When authorising use of spectrum for the provision of MCV services, Member States must comply with Directive 2002/21/EC and with Directive 2002/20/EC of the European Parliament and of the Council of 7 March 2002 on the authorisation of electronic communications networks and services (Authorisation Directive) …. In particular, under Article 9(1) and (2) of Directive 2002/21/EC, Member States should ensure the effective management of radio frequencies for electronic communication services in their territory and promote harmonisation of the use of radio frequencies across the European Union, consistent with the need to ensure effective and efficient use thereof.

(8) Under Directive 2002/21/EC, national regulatory authorities in the Member States should contribute to the development of the single market, inter alia, by removing remaining obstacles to the provision of electronic communications networks, associated facilities and services, and electronic communication services at European level and by encouraging the establishment and development of trans-European networks, the interoperability of pan-European services, and end-to-end connectivity. They should also promote competition in the provision of electronic communications networks, electronic communication services and associated facilities and services by, inter alia, encouraging efficient use and ensuring the effective management of radio frequencies and numbering resources.

(9) Pursuant to Directive 2002/20/EC, the least onerous authorisation system possible should be used to allow the provision of electronic communications networks and services in order to stimulate the development of new electronic communication services and pan-European communications networks and services and to allow service providers and consumers to benefit from the economies of scale of the single market.

(10) In accordance with Article 3(2) of Directive 2002/20/EC, the provision of electronic communications networks or the provision of electronic communication services may, without prejudice to the specific obligations referred to in Article 6(2) or rights of use referred to in Article 5, only be subject to a general authorisation.

(11) Following Article 5(1) of Directive 2002/20/EC, Member States should, where possible, in particular where the risk of harmful interference is negligible, not make the use of radio frequencies subject to individual rights of use but to general authorisations that include the conditions of their usage.

(12) Provided the technical conditions set out in Commission Decision 2010/166/EU … are fulfilled, the risk of harmful interference caused by MCV operation will be negligible, so, in principle, general authorisations should be granted by Member States for the use of the radio spectrum for the provision of MCV services.

(13) Some Member States currently make the use of spectrum for the provision of MCV services subject to individual rights. This authorisation approach should be reassessed, including on the basis of any experience as regards the provision of MCV services in the territorial seas of Member States.

(14) According to Article 1 of Directive 2009/114/EC of the European Parliament and of the Council of 16 September 2009 amending Council Directive 87/372/EEC on the frequency bands to be reserved for the coordinated introduction of public pan-European cellular

digital land-based mobile communications in the Community[23] Member States should examine whether the existing assignment of the 900 MHz band to the competing mobile operators in their territory is likely to distort competition in the mobile markets concerned and should address such distortions in accordance with Article 14 of Directive 2002/20/EC. Member States should, where appropriate, consider using this occasion to change any existing exclusive rights of use granted to operators of land-based mobile networks so that they do not exclude the provision of MCV services in the relevant frequencies.

(15) Member States should share information amongst each other and with the Commission in order to resolve any harmful interference issues caused by MCV services. In as much as involvement of the Communications Committee and the Radio Spectrum Committee could facilitate the resolution of such issues, these Committees should be informed by the Commission.

(16) Pursuant to Directive 2002/22/EC of the European Parliament and of the Council of 7 March 2002 on universal service and users' rights relating to electronic communications networks and services (Universal Service Directive) ... Member States should ensure that transparent and up-to-date information on applicable prices and tariffs, and on standard terms and conditions, in respect of access to and use of publicly available telephone services is available to end-users and consumers. The Directive also calls upon Member States to ensure that, where subscribing to services providing connection and/or access to the public telephone network, consumers have a right to a contract with an undertaking or undertakings providing such services, specifying, among other things particulars of prices and tariffs and the means by which up-to-date information on all applicable tariffs and maintenance charges may be obtained.

(17) International agreements in the area of maritime safety and/or public security should not be prejudiced by the operation of MCV services.

(18) The regulatory and technical elements of the common approach to authorisation of the use of spectrum for the provision of MCV services in the European Union should be kept under scrutiny to ensure that they remain satisfactory for the overall purpose of avoiding harmful interference, failing which appropriate remedial measures will be considered.

(19) The measures provided for in this Recommendation are in accordance with the opinion of the Communications Committee."

Purpose of the recommendation

39.030 Paragraph 1 of the recommendation provides that the recommendation aims:

"to coordinate national authorisation conditions and procedures relating to the use of the radio spectrum for mobile communication services on board vessels (MCV services) in the territorial seas of Member States in order to facilitate the deployment of such services across the European Union while avoiding harmful interference caused by MCV services to land-based mobile electronic communication services.

The national authorisation conditions and procedures referred to in this Recommendation will apply without prejudice to legal obligations concerning maritime safety and public security and regulations and/or administrative provisions concerning equipment for MCV services put in place by Member States, in compliance with European Union law, in particular Directive 1999/5/EC of the European Parliament and of the Council of 9 March 1999 on radio equipment and telecommunications terminal equipment and the mutual recognition of their conformity[24] and any applicable EU and international instruments concerning maritime equipment."

39.031 Paragraph 2 provides that "mobile communication services on board vessels (MCV services)" means electronic communication services, as defined in Article 2(c) of

---

23 OJ L274/25, 20.10.2009.
24 Ed., OJ L91/10, 7 April 1999.

Directive 2002/21, provided by an undertaking to enable persons on board a vessel to communicate via public communication networks using a GSM system without establishing direct connections with land-based mobile networks.

39.032 Paragraph 3 provides that the recommendation applies to authorisation of the use of radio spectrum in the frequency bands defined in Decision 2010/166 for the provision of MCV services in the territorial seas of Member States, as defined in the UNCLOS of 10 December 1982. The provision of MCV services in the high seas, satellite communications between vessels and space stations, and the provision of mobile satellite services to end-users on board vessels are outside the scope of the recommendation.

39.033 Paragraph 4 provides that no later than 12 months after adoption of this recommendation, Member States should take all steps necessary to be able to authorise, in the frequency bands or sub-bands made available in accordance with Decision 2010/166, the use of spectrum for the provision of MCV services in their territorial seas on board vessels of their nationality and the use of spectrum for the provision of MCV services in their territorial seas, as applicable.

39.034 Paragraph 5 provides that Member States should not authorise use of spectrum for the provision of MCV services, unless such use satisfies the technical conditions set out in Decision 2010/166.

39.035 The sixth paragraph provides that Member States may require that MCV systems only use the specific frequency bands or sub-bands made available, in accordance with Decision 2010/166, for the operation of MCV systems in their territorial seas.

39.036 The seventh paragraph provides that Member States should make use of spectrum for the provision of MCV services subject to general authorisation. Without prejudice to Article 5(1) of Directive 2002/20, where the use of spectrum for the provision of MCV services is subject to individual rights, Member States should reassess the need for such individual rights with the objective of incorporating the conditions attached to such rights into a general authorisation as soon as possible and at the latest within three years after adoption of this recommendation.

39.037 Under the eighth paragraph, no later than 12 months after adoption of the recommendation, Member States should not require any additional authorisation for the use of spectrum made available for the provision of MCV services in their territorial seas if the use of spectrum by the relevant MCV system is already authorised by another Member State, in accordance with its authorisation regime and in compliance with this recommendation.

39.038 The ninth paragraph provides that the Member States should consider not requiring an additional authorisation for the use of spectrum in their territorial seas for the provision of MCV services on board vessels of third country nationality, provided that the use of spectrum for the provision of MCV services on such vessels is already authorised by the relevant countries under the same conditions as those set out in Decision 2010/166.

39.039 The tenth paragraph provides that Member States, prior to the adoption of the recommendation, have granted in the frequency bands or sub-bands made available for operation of MCV systems, exclusive individual rights of use for the provision of land-based mobile electronic communications networks and/or services extending to their territorial seas should, on the occasion of the first review, modification, extension or renewal of such exclusive rights of use, based on either EU or national law, where appropriate, change such rights of use in order to allow for the operation of MCV systems in their territorial seas. Pending such first review, modification, extension or renewal, the Member States concerned should promote the provision of MCV services in their territorial seas on the basis of spectrum trading, spectrum sharing or any other comparable arrangements with the land-based mobile operators enjoying the relevant exclusive rights.

39.040 Member States should co-operate actively, constructively and in a spirit of solidarity, using existing procedures where appropriate, to manage any issues concerning harmful interference allegedly caused by the operation of MCV systems;[25] (b) Member States should promptly bring issues concerning harmful interference allegedly caused by the operation of an MCV system falling under the jurisdiction of another Member State to the attention of the latter Member State and should inform the Commission and, where appropriate, the Commission should inform the Communications Committee and the Radio Spectrum Committee of the abovementioned issues in order to seek solutions to any difficulties;[26] (c) Member States that have jurisdiction over the MCV systems suspected of interfering harmfully with services in the territory of another Member State should respond and promptly resolve any such interference;[27] (d) Member States should take any appropriate measures in order to ensure that consumers and other end-users are adequately informed about the terms and conditions for the use of MCV services;[28] and (e) Member States should keep the use of spectrum for the provision of MCV services under scrutiny, in particular concerning actual or potential harmful interference, and should report their findings to the Commission in order to allow a timely review of this recommendation if necessary.

F. THE *JAN DE NUL NV V HAUPTZOLLAMT OLDENBURG* CASE

39.041 On 1 March 2007, the Court of Justice of the European Union ("CJEU") gave a preliminary ruling in *Jan De Nul NV v Hauptzollamt Oldenburg*.[29] This case considered the concept of "navigation within Community waters". It raised the question of whether there was, in the context of excise duties, an exemption from excise duty on mineral oils paying attention to Directive 92/81. The case originated in a preliminary reference to the CJEU by the Finanzgericht Hamburg in Germany.

39.042 The request to the CJEU for a preliminary ruling concerned the interpretation of the first subparagraph of Article 8(1)(c) of Council Directive 92/81 of 19 October 1992 on the harmonisation of the structures of excise duties on mineral oils[30] as amended by Council Directive 94/74 of 22 December 1994[31] ("Directive 92/81"). The request had been submitted in the context of proceedings between Jan De Nul NV ("Jan De Nul") and the Hauptzollamt (Principal Customs Office) Oldenburg (the "Hauptzollamt") concerning the latter's refusal to exempt from excise duty on mineral oils (the "duty") certain quantities of mineral oils used for the operation of a hopper dredger.

---

25 Para. 11.
26 Para. 12.
27 Para. 13.
28 Para. 14.
29 Case C-391/05 [2007] ECR I-01793, ECLI:EU:C:2007:126. The court composed of Judges Lenaerts (President of the Chamber), Juhász, Silva de Lapuerta (Rapporteur), Arestis and Malenovský. The Advocate-General was AG Bot.
30 OJ 1992 L316/12.
31 OJ 1994 L365/46.

39.043 Article 8(1) and (2) of Directive 92/81 provided:

"1. In addition to the general provisions set out in Directive 92/12/EEC on exempt uses of excisable products, and without prejudice to other Community provisions, Member States shall exempt the following from the harmonised excise duty under conditions which they shall lay down for the purpose of ensuring the correct and straightforward application of such exemptions and of preventing any evasion, avoidance or abuse:

...

(c) mineral oils supplied for use as fuel for the purposes of navigation within Community waters (including fishing), other than in private pleasure craft.

For the purposes of this Directive, 'private pleasure craft' shall mean any craft used by its owner or the natural or legal person who enjoys its use either through hire or through any other means, for other than commercial purposes and in particular other than for the carriage of passengers or goods or for the supply of services for consideration or for the purposes of public authorities.

2. Without prejudice to other Community provisions, Member States may apply total or partial exemptions or reductions in the rate of duty to mineral oils used under fiscal control:

...

(b) for navigation on inland waterways other than for private pleasure craft;

...

(g) in respect of dredging operations in navigable waterways and in ports."

39.044 The CJEU then considered the German national legislation:

"4. In Germany, the national provisions relating to the exemption of mineral oils from excise duty are contained in the Law on excise duty on mineral oils (Mineralölsteuergesetz) of 21 December 1992 (BGBl 1992 I, p. 2150 and 2185, 'the MinöStG') and in the Regulation implementing the Law on excise duty on mineral oils (Mineralölsteuer-Durchführungsverordnung) of 15 September 1993 (BGBl 1993 I, p. 1602).

5. Paragraph 4(1)(4) of the MinöStG provides that, subject to Paragraph 12 thereof, mineral oils may be used on an exempt-from-duty basis as motor or heating fuel on vessels deployed exclusively for commercial navigation and associated ancillary activities such as pilotage, towing and other services, and for work purposes and on warships and public authority boats, sea rescue boats and dedicated fishing boats.

6. In accordance with the statutory power conferred on the legislative authority by Paragraph 31(2)(5) of the MinöStG, Paragraph 17(5)(2) of the Regulation implementing the Law on excise duty on mineral oils excluded certain types of floating constructions from the definition of 'vessels' within the meaning of Paragraph 4(1)(4) of the MinöStG. Thus, dredgers, cranes and grain elevators are not considered to be vessels within the meaning of that last provision, with the result that the fuels which are used on board as motor or heating fuel cannot benefit from an exemption from excise duty."

39.045 It is useful to consider the dispute in the proceedings. Jan De Nul was the claimant and carried on hydraulic engineering activities. Jan De Nul sought to benefit from an exemption from duty for certain quantities of mineral oils used for the operation of a hopper dredger[32] called *Christoforo Colombo*, a vessel with a capacity of 10 062 tonnes, in respect of dredging operations carried out in an area between Hamburg and Cuxhaven. Jan De Nul declared the quantities of mineral oils which had been consumed

---

32 A hopper dredger sucks up sand, gravel and other materials from the water bed and pours them into its hold using pumped water. Subsequently, those materials are transported to dumping sites where they are discharged.

during the operations of pumping and discharge of materials. Later, the Hauptzollamt informed that company that duty was also payable on the quantities of mineral oils used during the unladen journeys of the vessel and the manoeuvres which it carried out in the course of its operations. The supplementary excise duty return by Jan De Nul, resulted in outstanding duty in the amount of DEM183,127. In 2002, the Hauptzollamt dismissed the objection lodged by Jan De Nul with a view to obtaining remission of that amount. Jan De Nul brought an action before the Finanzgericht Hamburg (i.e. the Hamburg Finance Court) seeking exemption from excise duty for the quantities of mineral oils used, not for the activities of the dredger itself, but for its unladen journeys. Jan De Nul asserted before the referring court that the activity of the hopper dredger must be equated with that of a special vessel involved in commercial navigation, the fuel consumption of which benefits from the exemption provided for in Article 8(1)(c) of Directive 92/81, irrespective of the purpose of that dredger's journey. The Hauptzollamt maintained before the same court that the area in which the hopper dredger pursued its operations constitutes an inland waterway, with the result that the exemption which Member States may apply, as provided in Article 8(2)(b) of Directive 92/81, arises from the legislative power of the national authorities. By an amending notice, the Hauptzollamt amended the excise duty return in the light of a judgment delivered on 3 February 2004 by the Bundesfinanzhof (Federal Finance Court) and accepted that the consumption of mineral oils on the unladen journeys of a hopper dredger had to benefit from the exemption from excise duty provided for in Paragraph 4(1)(4) of the MinöStG. Consequently, the amount of duty owing was reduced by DEM164,372. The parties to the main proceedings were therefore in agreement that the action has become devoid of purpose in so far as it concerns the components of the excisable amount giving rise to that reduction in the amount of the excise duty and that the dispute is therefore limited to the question whether Jan De Nul is required to pay that excise duty on the quantities of mineral oils consumed in the course of manoeuvres involved in dredging operations. In those circumstances, the Finanzgericht Hamburg, taking the view that the outcome of the proceedings before it hinged on the interpretation of the term "navigation within Community waters", decided to stay the proceedings and to refer the following questions to the CJEU for a preliminary ruling:

"(a) What interpretation should be given to the term 'Community waters' in the first subparagraph of Article 8(1)(c) of Directive 92/81 in contrast to the term 'inland waterways' for the purposes of Article 8(2)(b) of Directive 92/81?

(b) Should the operation of a suction and holding vessel (so-called 'hopper dredger') in Community waters always be regarded as navigation within the meaning of the first subparagraph of Article 8(1)(c) of Directive 92/81 or is it necessary to draw a distinction between the various forms of activity during the course of its use?"

39.046 In its first question, the CJEU said that the referring court asked the CJEU how it should interpret the term "Community waters" within the meaning of the first subparagraph of Article 8(1)(c) of Directive 92/81 in contrast to the term "inland waterways" within the meaning of Article 8(2)(b) of Directive 92/81. The CJEU responded that in order to reply to the question raised, it is necessary to recall at the outset that Directive 92/81 was adopted on the basis of Article 99 of the EC Treaty (now Article 121 TFEU), which authorises the Council, acting unanimously on a proposal from the Commission, to adopt, *inter alia*, provisions for the harmonisation of legislation concerning excise duties to the extent to which such harmonisation is necessary to ensure the establishment and the functioning of the internal market. The CJEU continued that in the context of the harmonised system of the structures of excise duties implemented at Community level, Directive 92/81 provides in Article 8(1) for a number of obligatory exemptions, such as that relating to mineral oils supplied for use as fuel for the purposes of navigation within Community waters, including fishing, other than in private pleasure craft. The CJEU stated that concerning "the term 'Community waters'", which appears in Article 8(1)(c) and is not defined, it should be mentioned that the interpretation of a provision of Community law must particularly take into account the context in which it occurs and the objects of the rules of which it is part.[33] The CJEU stated:

"21. To that effect, it appears from the third and fifth recitals in the preamble to Directive 92/81 that the latter is intended to render more precise a number of common definitions for mineral oil products which are to be subject to the general excise system and to lay down certain exemptions relating to those products which are obligatory at Community level (see C-389/02 *Deutsche See-Bestattungs-Genossenschaft* [2004] ECR I-3537, paragraphs 17 and 18). It is also apparent both from those recitals and from the title of Directive 92/81 that those common definitions and the exemptions laid down are intended to promote the establishment and proper functioning of the internal market and to set up a harmonised system in respect of the structures of excise duties on mineral oils at Community level.

22. Consequently, the definitions relating to the products governed by Directive 92/81 and the exemptions applicable to them should be interpreted independently on the basis of the wording of the provisions in question and on the purpose of the directive (see *Deutsche See-Bestattungs-Genossenschaft*, paragraph 19).

23. An independent interpretation of those exemptions is all the more essential because Article 8(1) of Directive 92/81 imposes on the Member States the obligation not to levy the harmonised excise duty on mineral oils supplied for use as fuel for a number of activities set out in that provision (see Case C-346/97 *Braathens* [1999] ECR I-3419, paragraph 31, and *Deutsche See-Bestattungs-Genossenschaft*, paragraph 20). Any divergent interpretation at national level of those exemption obligations provided for in Directive 92/81 would not only undermine the objectives of the Community legislation and legal certainty, but could introduce unequal treatment between the economic operators concerned (see Deutsche See-Bestattungs-Genossenschaft, paragraph 21).

24. With regard to Article 8(1), it must be noted that the obligatory exemption for mineral oils used as fuel for the purposes of navigation within Community waters is designed to facilitate intracommunity trade, particularly the movement of goods and the freedom to provide services capable of taking place on the waters concerned.

25. By the exemption concerned, the Community legislature intended to promote the equality of certain tax conditions under which the transport undertakings or other services which ply the waters concerned operate.

26. It follows that the term 'Community waters' must be understood as including all the waters in which maritime navigation is normally practised for commercial ends. That navigation concerns all sea-going vessels, including those which have the greatest capacity.

27. Moreover, as the Commission points out, such an interpretation alone can ensure the equality of economic conditions between sea ports within the Community, irrespective of the geographical position of each port in relation to the nearest coast from which the above-mentioned activities are carried on.

28. Finally, it should be noted that Directive 92/81 also has as its objective to ensure the free movement of mineral oils in the internal market, and to avoid distortions of competition which could stem from variations in the structures of excise duties from one Member State

---

33 The CJEU cited C-17/03 VEMW and Others [2005] ECR I-4983, ECLI:EU:C:2005:362, para. 41 and the case law cited.

to another (see C-240/01 *Commission v Germany* [2004] ECR I-4733, paragraphs 39 and 44).[34]

29.   In those circumstances, the system laid down by Article 8(2) of Directive 92/81, which concerns the possibility for Member States of applying total or partial exemptions or reductions in the rate of duty to mineral oils used under fiscal control, and particularly the concept of navigation on inland waterways, appearing in Article 8(2)(b), cannot be a conclusive factor in interpreting the extent of the obligatory exemptions provided for in Article 8(1).

30.   It is common ground that vessels appropriate for navigation for commercial purposes on maritime waters can also pursue those purposes on certain internal waterways as far as certain sea ports, although they are not situated on the coast. To exclude from the scope of obligatory exemption the navigation thus practised from the moment when it is carried out on those waterways towards sea ports would harm intracommunity trade since such an exclusion, in placing economic operators concerned by such navigation at a disadvantage, would risk diverting some of that sea traffic away from those ports. It would thus place the operators at a disadvantage in relation to those who operate in coastal ports.

31.   Thus, the optional system provided for in Article 8(2)(b) of Directive 92/81 can only be residual in that it would be applicable to navigation on inland waterways only in so far as that is engaged in beyond the waters on which maritime navigation for commercial purposes can be carried on.

32.   The answer to the first question raised must therefore be that the term 'Community waters' within the meaning of the first subparagraph of Article 8(1)(c) of Directive 92/81 relates to all waters which can be used by all sea-going vessels, including those which have the greatest capacity, capable of travelling maritime waterways for commercial purposes."

39.047 The CJEU stated that by its second question, the referring court asked, in substance, whether or not certain operations performed by a hopper dredger may be regarded as coming within the scope of the term "navigation" as used in the first paragraph of Article 8(1)(c) of Directive 92/81. The CJEU opined:

"34.   As follows from paragraph 15 above, the dispute between the parties to the main proceedings is limited to the question whether the quantities of mineral oils consumed in the course of manoeuvres involved in dredging operations are capable of benefiting from the exemption provided for by the provision in question, as Jan De Nul has accepted the imposition of excise duty on the quantities of mineral oils used for the operations of pumping and discharge of materials.

35.   It is also apparent from the order for reference that the consumption of mineral oils during the unladen journeys of the hopper dredger were included in the benefit of the exemption from excise duty.

36.   As for the term 'navigation' within the meaning of the first subparagraph of Article 8(1)(c) of Directive 92/81, the Court, at paragraph 23 of its judgment in *Deutsche See-Bastattungs-Genosenschaft*, declared that all navigation activity for commercial purposes comes within the scope of the exemption from the harmonised excise duty provided for in that provision. At paragraph 25 of that judgment, the Court stated that that provision does not make any distinction as to the purpose of the navigation referred to, given that the distortions of competition which the provisions of that directive are intended to avoid can arise whatever the type of commercial navigation at issue.

37.   It thus follows from the judgment in Deutsche See-Bestattungs-Genossenschaft that the purpose for which the journey is effected is irrelevant since it concerns navigation involving a provision of services for consideration.

38.   As for the case in the main proceedings, it is common ground that the hopper dredger has a propulsion system which permits it to be autonomous in its movements. That vessel has

---

34 Ed., this is ECLI:EU:C:2004:251.

therefore the technical characteristics necessary for navigation allowing it to carry out such a provision of services.

39. Concerning the system provided for in Article 8(2)(g) of Directive 92/81, under which the Member States may apply total or partial exemptions or reductions in the rate of duty to mineral oils used for dredging operations in navigable waterways and in ports, suffice it to observe, as was pointed out at paragraph 29 above, that that exemption capacity granted to the Member States cannot influence the interpretation to be given to Article 8(1).

40. Consequently, the answer to the second question must be that manoeuvres carried out by a hopper dredger during its operations of pumping and discharge of materials, that is to say, journeys inherent in the carrying out of dredging activities, come within the scope of the term 'navigation' as used in the first subparagraph of Article 8(1)(c) of Directive 92/81."

39.048 Ultimately, the CJEU ruled:

"1. The term 'Community waters' within the meaning of the first subparagraph of Article 8(1) (c) of Council Directive 92/81 ... of 19 October 1992 on the harmonisation of the structures of excise duties on mineral oils, as amended by Council Directive 94/74 ... of 22 December 1994, relates to all waters which can be used by all sea-going vessels, including those which have the greatest capacity, capable of travelling maritime waterways for commercial purposes.

2. Manoeuvres carried out by a hopper dredger during its operations of pumping and discharge of materials, that is to say, journeys inherent in the carrying out of dredging activities, come within the scope of the term 'navigation' as used in the first subparagraph of Article 8(1)(c) of Directive 92/81, as amended by Directive 94/74."

G. COUNCIL DECISION 87/475 OF 17 SEPTEMBER 1987 RELATING TO MARITIME TRANSPORT BETWEEN ITALY AND ALGERIA

39.049 On 17 September 1987, the Council adopted Decision 87/475 relating to maritime transport between Italy and Algeria.[35] It was addressed to Italy.[36] The background is clear from some of the recitals:

"Having regard to Council Regulation ... 4055/86 of 22 December 1986 applying the principle of freedom to provide services to maritime transport between Member States and between Member States and third countries,[37] and in particular Article 6(2) thereof, ...

Having regard to the proposal from the Commission,

Whereas the question of Algerian practices of cargo reservation was raised by the Italian delegation in July 1985 in the context of the consultation procedure on shipping matters established by Council Decision 77/587 ...[38] and led to a Community demarche in October 1985;

Whereas the Italian Government submitted to the Commission on 17 March 1987 the text of an Agreement on Maritime Transport and Navigation between the Italian Republic and the People's Democratic Republic of Algeria which was signed on 28 February 1987 but has not been ratified;

Whereas this submission is exceptionally to be treated as information for the purposes of Article 6 (1) of Regulation (EEC) No 4055/86;

Whereas Article 6 (2) of Regulation (EEC) No 4055/86 provides that the Council shall decide on the necessary action where a Member State's nationals or shipping companies do not have an effective opportunity to ply for trade to and from a particular third country;

---

35 OJ L272/37, 25 September 1987.
36 Dec. 87/475, Art. 2.
37 Ed., OJ L378/1, 31 December 1986.
38 Ed., OJ L239/23, 17 September 1977.

Whereas Algeria recently ratified the United Nations Convention on a Code of Conduct for Liner Conference, which entered into force for that country on 12 June 1987;

Whereas the provisions of the aforementioned Agreement need to be applied in such a way as to avoid a conflict with the obligations of the Member States under Community law, in particular with respect to fair, free and non-discriminatory access to cargoes by Community nationals or shipping companies, including independent lines;

Whereas Italy may in these circumstances ratify the Agreement..."

39.050 Article 1 provides that Italy may ratify its Agreement on Maritime Transport and Navigation with Algeria, signed on 28 February 1987, on the understanding that Italy: (a) will take the necessary steps to accede as soon as possible, in accordance with Regulation 954/79,[39] to the United States Convention on a Code of Conduct for Liner Conferences; (b) will reiterate to Algeria that the provisions of the agreement will be implemented in accordance with EU law; and (c) will report to the Member States and the Commission, within not later than one year of notification of the decision, on the implementation of the agreement.

H. DIRECTIVE 2002/59 OF 27 JUNE 2002 OF THE EUROPEAN PARLIAMENT AND OF THE COUNCIL ESTABLISHING A COMMUNITY VESSEL TRAFFIC MONITORING AND INFORMATION SYSTEM AND REPEALING COUNCIL DIRECTIVE 93/75

Introduction

39.051 On 27 June 2002, the Parliament and Council adopted Directive 2002/59 establishing a Community vessel traffic monitoring and information system and repealing Council Directive 93/75.[40] It was amended by: Directive 2009/17 of the European Parliament and of the Council of 23 April 2009;[41] Directive 2009/18 of the European Parliament and of the Council of 23 April 2009;[42] Commission Directive 2011/15;[43] and Commission Directive 2014/100 of 28 October 2014.[44]

39.052 After three introductory articles (on purpose, scope and definitions), the rest of the directive is divided into four titles: Title I relates to ship reporting and monitoring; Title II is entitled "notification of dangerous or polluting goods on board ships (HAZMAT)"; Title III deals with monitoring of hazardous ships and intervention in the event of incidents and accidents at sea; and Title IV deals with accompanying measures.

Purpose of the directive

39.053 The purpose of Directive 2002/59 has remained unchanged despite several amendments to other aspects of the measure. Article 1 states that the purpose of the directive

---

39 OJ L121/1, 17 May 1979.
40 OJ L208/10, 5 August 2002.
41 OJ L131/101, 28 May 2009.
42 OJ L131/114, 28 May 2009.
43 OJ L49/33, 24 February 2011.
44 OJ L308/82, 29 October 2014.

"is to establish in the [EU] a vessel traffic monitoring and information system with a view to enhancing the safety and efficiency of maritime traffic, improving the response of authorities to incidents, accidents or potentially dangerous situations at sea, including search and rescue operations, and contributing to a better prevention and detection of pollution by ships. Member States shall monitor and take all necessary and appropriate measures to ensure that the masters, operators or agents of ships, as well as shippers or owners of dangerous or polluting goods carried on board such ships, comply with the requirements under this Directive."

Scope of the directive

39.054 Article 2 is drafted in such a way that the measure has quite a wide scope. As a general rule, the directive applies to ships of 300 gt (gross tonnage) and upwards, unless stated otherwise. There are some exceptions but they are limited. Unless otherwise provided, this directive shall not apply to: (a) warships, naval auxiliaries and other ships owned or operated by a Member State and used for non-commercial public service; (b) fishing vessels, traditional ships and recreational craft with a length of less than 45 metres; and (c) bunkers on ships below 1,000 gt and ships' stores and equipment for use on board all ships.

Definitions in the directive

39.055 The directive defines in Article 3 various terms for the purposes of the directive. The definitions are uncontroversial but helpful. The definitions are closed definitions (i.e. not "includes" but rather "means") so there is a degree of precision involved.

"(a) 'Relevant international instruments' means the following instruments, in their up-to-date version:

- MARPOL means the International Convention for the Prevention of Pollution from Ships, 1973 and the 1978 Protocol thereto;
- SOLAS means the International Convention for the Safety of Life at Sea, together with the protocols and amendments thereto;
- the International Convention on Tonnage Measurement of Ships, 1969;
- the International Convention relating to Intervention on the High Seas in Cases of Oil Pollution Casualties, 1969 and its 1973 Protocol relating to Intervention on the High Seas in Cases of Pollution by Substances other than Oil;
- SAR Convention means the International Convention on Maritime Search and Rescue, 1979;
- ISM Code means the International Safety Management Code;
- IMDG Code means the International Maritime Dangerous Goods Code;
- IBC Code means the IMO International Code for the construction and equipment of ships carrying dangerous chemicals in bulk;
- IGC Code means the IMO International Code for the construction and equipment of ships carrying liquefied gases in bulk;
- BC Code means the IMO Code of Safe Practice for Solid Bulk Cargoes;
- INF Code means the IMO Code for the Safe Carriage of Irradiated Nuclear Fuel, Plutonium and High-Level Radioactive Wastes in Flasks on board Ships;
- IMO Resolution A.851(20) means International Maritime Organisation Resolution 851(20) entitled 'General principles for ship reporting systems and ship reporting requirements, including guidelines for reporting incidents involving dangerous goods, harmful substances and/or marine pollutants';

- IMO Resolution A.917(22) means International Maritime Organisation Resolution 917(22) entitled Guidelines for the onboard use of AIS, as amended by IMO Resolution A.956(23);
- IMO Resolution A.949(23) means International Maritime Organisation Resolution 949(23) entitled Guidelines on places of refuge for ships in need of assistance;
- IMO Resolution A.950(23) means International Maritime Organisation Resolution 950(23) entitled Maritime assistance services (MAS);
- IMO guidelines on the fair treatment of seafarers in the event of a maritime accident means the guidelines as annexed to resolution LEG. 3(91) of the IMO Legal Committee of 27 April 2006 and as approved by the Governing Body of the ILO in its 296th session of 12 to 16 June 2006;

(b) 'operator' means the owner or manager of a ship;

(c) 'agent' means any person mandated or authorised to supply information on behalf of the operator of the ship;

(d) 'shipper' means any person by whom or in whose name or on whose behalf a contract of carriage of goods has been concluded with a carrier;

(e) 'company' means a company within the meaning of Regulation 1(2) of Chapter IX of the SOLAS Convention;

(f) 'ship' means any sea-going vessel or craft;

(g) 'dangerous goods' means:

- goods classified in the IMDG Code,
- dangerous liquid substances listed in Chapter 17 of the IBC Code,
- liquefied gases listed in Chapter 19 of the IGC Code,
- solids referred to in Appendix B of the BC Code.

Also included are goods for the carriage of which appropriate preconditions have been laid down in accordance with paragraph 1.1.3 of the IBC Code or paragraph 1.1.6 of the IGC Code;

(h) 'polluting goods' means:

- oils as defined in Annex I to the MARPOL Convention,
- noxious liquid substances as defined in Annex II to the MARPOL Convention,
- harmful substances as defined in Annex III to the MARPOL Convention;

(i) 'cargo transport unit' means a road freight vehicle, a railway freight wagon, a freight container, a road tank vehicle, a railway wagon, or portable tank;

(j) 'address' means the name and the communication links whereby contact may, where necessary, be made with the operator, agent, port authority, competent authority or any other authorised person or body in possession of detailed information regarding the ship's cargo;

(k) 'competent authorities' means the authorities and organisations designated by Member States to perform functions under this Directive;

(l) 'port authority' means the competent authority or body designated by Member States for each port to receive and pass on information reported pursuant to this Directive;

(m) 'place of refuge' means a port, the part of a port or another protective berth or anchorage or any other sheltered area identified by a Member State for accommodating ships in distress;

(n) 'coastal station' means any of the following, designated by Member States pursuant to this Directive: a vessel traffic service; a shore-based installation responsible for a mandatory reporting system approved by the IMO; or a body responsible for coordinating search and rescue operations or operations to tackle pollution at sea;

(o) 'vessel traffic service (VTS)' means a service designed to improve the safety and efficiency of vessel traffic and to protect the environment, which has the capability to interact with the traffic and to respond to traffic situations developing in the VTS area;

(p) 'ship's routing system' means any system of one or more routes or routing measures aimed at reducing the risk of casualties; it includes traffic separation schemes, two-way routes, recommended tracks, areas to be avoided, inshore traffic zones, roundabouts, precautionary areas and deep-water routes;

(q) 'traditional ships' means all kinds of historical ships and their replicas including those designed to encourage and promote traditional skills and seamanship, that together serve as living cultural monuments, operated according to traditional principles of seamanship and technique;

(r) 'casualty' means a casualty within the meaning of the IMO Code for the investigation of marine casualties and incidents;

(s) 'SafeSeaNet' means the Community maritime information exchange system developed by the Commission in cooperation with the Member States to ensure the implementation of Community legislation;

(t) 'scheduled service' means a series of ship crossings operated so as to serve traffic between the same two or more ports, either according to a published timetable or with crossings so regular or frequent that they constitute a recognisable systematic series;

(u) 'fishing vessel' means any vessel equipped for commercial exploitation of living aquatic resources;

(v) 'ship in need of assistance' means, without prejudice to the provisions of the SAR Convention concerning the rescue of persons, a ship in a situation that could give rise to its loss or an environmental or navigational hazard;

(w) 'LRIT' means a system for the long-range identification and tracking of ships in accordance with SOLAS regulation V/19–1."

Notification prior to entry into ports of the Member States

39.056 Article 4 contains a very useful and practical obligation to notify Member State ports of the arrival of a vessel. Article 4(1) states that the operator, agent or[45] master of a ship bound for a port of a Member State must notify the information in Annex I(1) of the directive to the port authority: (a) at least 24 hours in advance; or (b) at the latest, at the time the ship leaves the previous port, if the voyage time is less than 24 hours; or (c) if the port of call is not known or it is changed during the voyage, as soon as this information is available. Pursuant to Article 4(2), ships coming from a port outside the Community and bound for a port of a Member State carrying dangerous or polluting goods, shall comply with the notification obligations of Article 13.

Monitoring of ships entering the area of mandatory ship reporting systems

39.057 There are areas where there are mandatory ship reporting systems in operation as part of the IMO operation. Article 5 addresses this. Article 5(1) provides that the Member State concerned must monitor and take all necessary and appropriate measures to ensure that all ships entering the area of a mandatory ship reporting system, adopted by the IMO according to Regulation 11 Chapter V of the SOLAS Convention and operated by one or more States, of which at least one is a Member State, in accordance with the relevant guidelines and criteria developed by the IMO, comply with that system in reporting the information required without prejudice to additional information required by a Member State in accordance with IMO Resolution A.851(20). Equally, under Article 5(2), when submitting a new mandatory ship reporting system to the IMO for adoption or

---

45 Note any one suffices.

a proposal to amend an existing reporting system, a Member State shall include in its proposal at least the information referred to in Annex I(4).

Use of automatic identification systems

39.058 Any ship calling at a port of a Member State must, in accordance with the timetable set out in Annex II(I), be fitted with an automatic identification system ("AIS") which meets the performance standards drawn up by the IMO.[46] Ships fitted with an AIS, shall maintain it in operation at all times except where international agreements, rules or standards provide for the protection of navigational information.[47]

39.059 Article 6b provides for the use of systems for the long-range identification and tracking of ships ("LRIT"). Article 6b(1) provides that ships to which SOLAS Regulation V/19–1 and the performance standards and functional requirements adopted by the IMO apply shall carry LRIT equipment complying with that regulation, when calling at a port of a Member State. Member States and the Commission must co-operate to determine the requirements concerning the fitting of equipment for transmitting LRIT information on board ships sailing in waters within the coverage of AIS fixed-based stations of Member States, and shall submit to the IMO any appropriate measures. The Commission must co-operate with Member States to establish an LRIT European Data Centre in charge of processing LRIT information.

Use of ship's routing systems

39.060 Member States are obliged to monitor and take all necessary and appropriate measures to ensure that all ships entering the area of a mandatory ships' routing system adopted by the IMO according to Regulation 10 Chapter V of the SOLAS Convention and operated by one or more States, of which at least one is a Member State, use the system in accordance with the relevant guidelines and criteria developed by the IMO.[48] When implementing a ship's routing system, which has not been adopted by the IMO, under their responsibility, Member States must take into account, wherever possible, the guidelines and criteria developed by the IMO and promulgate all information necessary for the safe and effective use of the ship's routing system.[49]

Monitoring of the compliance of ships with vessel traffic services

39.061 Member States must monitor and take all necessary and appropriate measures to ensure that: (a) ships entering the area of applicability of a vessel traffic service ("VTS") operated by one or more States, of which at least one is a Member State, within their territorial sea and based on the guidelines developed by the IMO, participate in, and comply with, the rules of that VTS; (b) ships flying the flag of a Member State or ships bound for a port of a Member State and entering the area of applicability of such a VTS

---

46 Dir. 2002/59, Art. 6(1). Art. 6a deals with the use of AIS by fishing vessels but falls outside the scope of this book.
47 Dir. 2002/59, Art. 6(2).
48 Dir. 2002/59, Art. 7(1).
49 Dir. 2002/59, Art. 7(2).

outside the territorial sea of a Member State and based on the guidelines developed by the IMO, comply with the rules of that VTS; (c) ships flying the flag of a third State and not bound for a port in a Member State entering a VTS area outside the territorial sea of a Member State, follow the rules of that VTS wherever possible. Member States should report to the flag State concerned any apparent serious breach of those rules in such a VTS area.

Infrastructure for ship reporting systems, ships' routing systems and VTS

39.062 Pursuant to Article 9(1), Member States shall take all necessary and appropriate measures to provide themselves gradually, on a time-schedule compatible with the timetable set out in Annex II(I), with appropriate equipment and shore-based installations for receiving and utilising the AIS information taking into account a necessary range for transmission of the reports. Article 9(2) provides that the process of building up all necessary equipment and shore-based installations for implementing this directive shall be completed by the end of 2007. Member States shall ensure that the appropriate equipment for relaying the information to, and exchanging it between, the national systems of Member States shall be operational at the latest one year thereafter. Under Article 9(3), Member States must ensure that the coastal stations in charge of monitoring the compliance with VTS and ships' routing systems have sufficient and properly qualified staff available, as well as appropriate means of communication and ship monitoring and that they operate in accordance with the relevant IMO guidelines.

Voyage data recorder systems

39.063 Article 10(1) provides that Member States must monitor and take all necessary and appropriate measures to ensure that ships calling at a port of a Member State are fitted with a voyage data recorder ("VDR") system in accordance with the rules laid down in Annex II(II). Any exemptions granted to ro-ro ferries or high-speed passenger craft under Article 4(1)(d) of Council Directive 1999/35 of 29 April 1999 on a system of mandatory surveys for the safe operation of regular ro-ro ferry and high-speed passenger craft services[50] shall terminate on 5 August 2002. Under Article 9(2), data which have been collected from a VDR system shall be made available to the Member State concerned in the event of an investigation following a casualty occurring within the waters under the jurisdiction of a Member State. Member States shall ensure that such data are used in the investigation and are properly analysed. Member States shall ensure that the findings of the investigation are published as soon as possible after its conclusion.

Notification of dangerous or polluting goods on board ships (HAZMAT)

39.064 Title II contains various provisions which set out detailed rules for the notification of dangerous or polluting goods on board ships. Under Article 12, there are various

---

50 OJ L138/1, 1 June 1999.

information and notification requirements concerning the transport of dangerous goods.[51] Then there must be notification of dangerous or polluting goods carried on board.[52] There is also a computerised exchange of data between Member States and those States are obliged to co-operate in that regard.[53] There are some, but limited exemptions by virtue of Article 15 of the directive.[54]

---

51 Art. 12 states:

"1. No dangerous or polluting goods shall be offered for carriage or taken on board any ship, irrespective of its size, in the port of a Member State unless a declaration has been delivered to the master or operator before the goods are taken on board containing the following information:

    (a) the information listed in Annex I(2);

    (b) for the substances referred to in Annex I to the Marpol Convention, the safety data sheet detailing the physico-chemical characteristics of the products, including, where applicable, their viscosity expressed in cSt at 50 °C and their density at 15 °C and the other data contained in the safety data sheet in accordance with IMO Resolution MSC.286(86);

    (c) the emergency numbers of the shipper or any other person or body in possession of information on the physico-chemical characteristics of the products and on the action to be taken in an emergency.

2. Vessels coming from a port outside the Community and calling at a port of a Member State which have dangerous or polluting goods on board shall be in possession of a declaration, as provided for by the shipper, containing the information required under paragraph 1(a), (b) and (c).

3. It shall be the duty and responsibility of the shipper to deliver to the master or operator such a declaration, and to ensure that the shipment offered for carriage is indeed the one declared in accordance with paragraph 1."

52 Art. 13 states:

"1. The operator, agent or master of a ship, irrespective of its size, carrying dangerous or polluting goods and leaving a port of a Member State shall, at the latest at the moment of departure, notify the information indicated in Annex I(3) to the competent authority designated by that Member State.

2. The operator, agent or master of a ship, irrespective of its size, carrying dangerous or polluting goods coming from a port located outside the Community and bound for a port of a Member State or an anchorage located in a Member State's territorial waters shall, at the latest upon departure from the loading port or as soon as the port of destination or the location of the anchorage is known, if this information is unavailable at the moment of departure, notify the information indicated in Annex I(3) to the competent authority of the Member State in which the first port of destination or anchorage is located.

3. Member States may put in place a procedure authorising the operator, agent or master of a ship referred to in paragraphs 1 and 2 to notify the information listed in Annex I(3) to the port authority of the port of departure or destination in the Community, as appropriate.

The procedure put in place must ensure that the competent authority has access to the information indicated in Annex I(3) at all times should it be needed. To this end, the port authority concerned shall retain the information listed in Annex I(3) long enough for it to be usable in the event of an incident or accident at sea. The port authority shall take the necessary measures to provide this information electronically and without delay to the competent authority, 24 hours a day upon request.

4. The operator, agent or master of the ship must communicate the cargo information indicated in Annex I(3) to the port authority or the competent authority.

The information must be transferred electronically whenever practicable. The electronic message exchange must use the syntax and procedures set out in Annex III."

53 Art. 14 provides that "Member States shall cooperate to ensure the interconnection and interoperability of the national systems used to manage the information indicated in Annex I. Communication systems set up pursuant to the first subparagraph must display the following features: (a) data exchange must be electronic and enable messages notified in accordance with Article 13 to be received and processed; (b) the system must allow information to be transmitted 24 hours a day; (c) upon request, through SafeSeaNet, and if needed for the purpose of maritime safety or security or the protection of the maritime environment, Member States shall be able to send information on the ship and the dangerous or polluting goods on board to the national and local competent authorities of another Member State without delay."

54 Art. 15 provides:

"1. Member States may exempt scheduled services performed between ports located on their territory from the requirements of Articles 4 and 13 provided the following conditions are met:

Monitoring of hazardous ships and intervention in the event of incidents and accidents at sea

39.065 The monitoring of hazardous ships and intervention in the event of incidents and accidents at sea is addressed by Title III. Article 16 deals with the transmission of information concerning certain ships.[55] There is a very specific obligation under Article 17 to report incidents and accidents at sea. Article 17 provides:

   (a) the company operating those scheduled services keeps and updates a list of the ships concerned and sends that list to the competent authority concerned;

   (b) for each voyage performed, the information listed in Parts 1 or 3, as appropriate, of Annex I is kept available for the competent authority upon request. The company shall establish an internal system to ensure that, upon request 24 hours a day and without delay, such information can be sent to the competent authority electronically, in accordance with Article 4(1) or Article 13(4), as appropriate;

   (c) any deviations from the estimated time of arrival at the port of destination or pilot station of three hours or more are notified to the port of arrival or to the competent authority in accordance with Article 4 or Article 13, as appropriate;

   (d) exemptions are only granted to individual vessels as regards a specific service.

For the purposes of the first subparagraph, the service shall not be regarded as a scheduled service unless it is intended to be operated for a minimum of one month.

Exemptions from the requirements of Articles 4 and 13 shall be limited to voyages of a scheduled duration of up to 12 hours.

2. When an international scheduled service is operated between two or more States, of which at least one is a Member State, any of the Member States involved may request the other Member States to grant an exemption for that service. All Member States involved, including the coastal States concerned, shall collaborate in granting an exemption to the service concerned in accordance with the conditions set out in paragraph 1.

3. Member States shall periodically check that the conditions set out in paragraphs 1 and 2 are being met. Where at least one of these conditions is no longer being met, Member States shall immediately withdraw the benefit of the exemption from the company concerned.

4. Member States shall communicate to the Commission a list of companies and ships to which an exemption has been granted under this Article, as well as any updates to that list."

55 Art. 16 provides:

"1. Ships meeting the criteria set out below shall be considered to be ships posing a potential hazard to shipping or a threat to maritime safety, the safety of individuals or the environment:

   (a) ships which, in the course of their voyage:

     – have been involved in incidents or accidents at sea as referred to in Article 17; or

     – have failed to comply with the notification and reporting requirements imposed by this Directive; or

     – have failed to comply with the applicable rules in ships' routing systems and VTS placed under the responsibility of a Member State;

   (b) ships in respect of which there is proof or presumptive evidence of deliberate discharges of oil or other infringements of the MARPOL Convention in waters under the jurisdiction of a Member State;

   (c) ships which have been refused access to ports of the Member States or which have been the subject of a report or notification by a Member State in accordance with Annex I-1 to Council Directive 95/21/EC of 19 June 1995 on port State control of shipping …;

   (d) ships which have failed to notify, or do not have, insurance certificates or financial guarantees pursuant to any Community legislation and international rules;

   (e) ships which have been reported by pilots or port authorities as having apparent anomalies which may prejudice their safe navigation or create a risk for the environment.

2. Coastal stations holding relevant information on the ships referred to in paragraph 1 shall communicate it to the coastal stations concerned in the other Member States located along the planned route of the ship.

"1. Without prejudice to international law and with a view to preventing or mitigating any significant threat to maritime safety, the safety of individuals or the environment, Member States shall monitor and take all appropriate measures to ensure that the master of a ship sailing within their search and rescue region/exclusive economic zone or equivalent, immediately reports to the coastal station responsible for that geographical area:

    (a) any incident or accident affecting the safety of the ship, such as collision, running aground, damage, malfunction or breakdown, flooding or shifting of cargo, any defects in the hull or structural failure;

    (b) any incident or accident which compromises shipping safety, such as failures likely to affect the ship's manoeuvrability or seaworthiness, or any defects affecting the propulsion system or steering gear, the electrical generating system, navigation equipment or communications equipment;

    (c) any situation liable to lead to pollution of the waters or shore of a Member State, such as the discharge or threat of discharge of polluting products into the sea;

    (d) any slick of polluting materials and containers or packages seen drifting at sea.

2. The report message sent in application of paragraph 1 shall include at least the ship's identity, its position, the port of departure, the port of destination, the address from which information may be obtained on the dangerous and polluting goods carried on board, the number of persons aboard, details of the incident and any relevant information referred to in IMO Resolution A.851(20)."

39.066 There is also an interesting obligation to address incidents in the event of exceptionally bad weather. Article 18 provides:

"1. Where the competent authorities designated by Member States consider, in the event of exceptionally bad weather or sea conditions, that there is a serious threat of pollution of their shipping areas or coastal zones, or of the shipping areas or coastal zones of other States, or that the safety of human life is in danger:

    (a) they should, where possible, fully inform the master of a ship which is in the port area concerned, and intends to enter or leave that port, of the sea state and weather conditions and, when relevant and possible, of the danger they may present to his/her ship, the cargo, the crew and the passengers;

    (b) they may take, without prejudice to the duty of assistance to ships in distress and in accordance with Article 20, any other appropriate measures, which may include a recommendation or a prohibition either for a particular ship or for ships in general to enter or leave the port in the areas affected, until it has been established that there is no longer a risk to human life and/or to the environment;

    (c) they shall take appropriate measures to limit as much as possible or, if necessary, prohibit the bunkering of ships in their territorial waters.

2. The master shall inform the company of the appropriate measures or recommendations referred to under paragraph 1. These do not however prejudice the decision of the master on the basis of his/her professional judgement corresponding to the SOLAS Convention. Where the decision taken by the master of the ship is not in accordance with the measures referred to under paragraph 1, he/she shall inform the competent authorities of the reasons for his/her decision.

---

3   Member States shall ensure that the information communicated to them under paragraph 2 is transmitted to the relevant port authorities and/or any other authority designated by the Member State. Within the limits of their available staff capacity, Member States shall carry out any appropriate inspection or verification in their ports either on their own initiative or at the request of another Member State, without prejudice to any port State control obligation. They shall inform all Member States concerned of the results of the action they take."

3. The appropriate measures or recommendations, referred to under paragraph 1, shall be based upon a sea state and weather forecast provided by a qualified meteorological information service recognised by the Member State."

39.067 There is also a provision relating to ice incidents.[56]

39.068 There are other provisions in regard to measures relating to incidents or accidents at sea generally (i.e. Article 19) which provides:

"1. In the event of incidents or accidents at sea as referred to in Article 17, Member States shall take all appropriate measures consistent with international law, where necessary to ensure the safety of shipping and of persons and to protect the marine and coastal environment.

Annex IV sets out a non-exhaustive list of measures available to Member States pursuant to this Article.

2. The operator, the master of the ship and the owner of the dangerous or polluting goods carried on board must, in accordance with national and international law, cooperate fully with the competent national authorities, at the latter's request, with a view to minimising the consequences of an incident or accident at sea.

To this end they shall communicate to the competent national authorities, on request, the information referred to in Article 12.

3. The master of a ship to which the provisions of the ISM Code are applicable shall, in accordance with that Code, inform the company of any incident or accident, as referred to in Article 17(1), which occurs at sea. As soon as it has been informed of such a situation, the company must contact the competent coastal station and place itself at its disposal as necessary.

4. In accordance with their national law, Member States shall take into account the relevant provisions of the IMO guidelines on the fair treatment of seafarers in the event of a maritime accident in the waters under their jurisdiction."

39.069 The directive then addresses the issue of ships in distress. First, Article 20 identifies the competent authority for the accommodation of ships in need of assistance:

"1. Member States shall designate one or more competent authorities which have the required expertise and the power, at the time of the operation, to take independent decisions on their own initiative concerning the accommodation of ships in need of assistance.

2. The authority or authorities referred to in paragraph 1 may, as appropriate and in particular in the event of a threat to maritime safety and protection of the environment, take any of the measures included in the list set out in Annex IV, which is non-exhaustive.

3. The authority or authorities referred to in paragraph 1 shall meet regularly to exchange expertise and improve measures taken pursuant to this Article. They may meet at any time on account of specific circumstances."

---

56 Art. 18a provides:

"1. Where the competent authorities consider, in view of ice conditions, that there is a serious threat to the safety of human life at sea or to the protection of their shipping areas or coastal zones, or of the shipping areas or coastal zones of other States:

    (a) they shall supply the master of a ship which is in their area of competence, or intends to enter or leave one of their ports, with appropriate information on the ice conditions, the recommended routes and the icebreaking services in their area of competence;

    (b) they may, without prejudice to the duty of assistance to ships in need of assistance and other obligations flowing from relevant international rules, request that a ship which is in the area concerned and intends to enter or leave a port or terminal or to leave an anchorage area document that it satisfies the strength and power requirements commensurate with the ice situation in the area concerned.

2. The measures taken pursuant to paragraph 1 shall be based, as regards the data concerning the ice conditions, upon ice and weather forecasts provided by a qualified meteorological information service recognised by the Member State."

39.070 Second, Article 20a gives details of the plans for the accommodation of ships in need of assistance:

"1. Member States shall draw up plans for the accommodation of ships in order to respond to threats presented by ships in need of assistance in the waters under their jurisdiction, including, where applicable, threats to human life and the environment. The authority or authorities referred to in Article 20(1) shall participate in drawing up and carrying out those plans.
2. The plans referred to in paragraph 1 shall be prepared after consultation of the parties concerned, on the basis of IMO Resolutions A.949(23) and A.950(23), and shall contain at least the following:

> (a) the identity of the authority or authorities responsible for receiving and handling alerts;
> (b) the identity of the competent authority for assessing the situation and taking a decision on acceptance or refusal of a ship in need of assistance in the place of refuge selected;
> (c) information on the coastline of Member States and all elements facilitating a prior assessment and rapid decision regarding the place of refuge for a ship, including a description of environmental, economic and social factors and natural conditions;
> (d) the assessment procedures for acceptance or refusal of a ship in need of assistance in a place of refuge;
> (e) the resources and installations suitable for assistance, rescue and combating pollution;
> (f) procedures for international coordination and decision-making;
> (g) the financial guarantee and liability procedures in place for ships accommodated in a place of refuge.

3. Member States shall publish the name and contact address of the authority or authorities referred to in Article 20(1) and of the authorities appointed for receiving and handling alerts.

  Member States shall communicate on request the relevant information concerning plans to neighbouring Member States.

  In implementing the procedures provided for in the plans for accommodating ships in need of assistance, Member States shall ensure that relevant information is made available to the parties involved in the operations.

  If requested by Member States, those receiving information in accordance with the second and third subparagraphs shall be bound by an obligation of confidentiality.

4. Member States shall inform the Commission by 30 November 2010 of the measures taken in application of this Article."

39.071 It is often quite a difficult decision for coastal States as to whether to give assistance to a ship which needs accommodation. So Article 20b provides that the

"authority or authorities referred to in Article 20(1) shall decide on the acceptance of a ship in a place of refuge following a prior assessment of the situation carried out on the basis of the plans referred to in Article 20a. The authority or authorities shall ensure that ships are admitted to a place of refuge if they consider such an accommodation the best course of action for the purposes of the protection of human life or the environment."

39.072 Given that a ship needing accommodation could cause damage, Article 20c deals with "financial security and cooperation". It provides:

"1. The absence of an insurance certificate within the meaning of Article 6 of Directive 2009/20/EC of the European Parliament and of the Council of 23 April 2009 on the insurance of shipowners for maritime claims … shall not exonerate a Member State from the preliminary assessment and decision referred to in Article 20b, and shall not in itself be considered sufficient reason for a Member State to refuse to accommodate a ship in a place of refuge.

2. Without prejudice to paragraph 1, when accommodating a ship in a place of refuge, a Member State may request the ship's operator, agent or master to present a insurance certificate within the meaning of Article 6 of Directive 2009/20/EC. The act of requesting the certificate shall not lead to a delay in accommodating the ship."

39.073 The Commission can examine the issues involved by virtue of Article 20d:

"The Commission shall examine existing mechanisms within Member States for the compensation of potential economic loss suffered by a port or a body as a result of a decision taken pursuant to Article 20(1). It shall, on the basis of that examination, put forward and evaluate different policy options. By 31 December 2011, the Commission shall report to the European Parliament and to the Council on the results of the examination."

39.074 Article 21 deals with the information of the parties concerned:

"1. The competent coastal station of the Member State concerned shall, as necessary, broadcast within the relevant areas any incident or accident notified under Article 17(1) and information with regard to any ship that poses a threat to maritime safety, the safety of individuals or the environment.

2. Competent authorities holding information notified in accordance with Articles 13 and 17 shall make adequate arrangements to provide such information at any time upon request for safety reasons by the competent authority of another Member State.

3. Any Member State the competent authorities of which have been informed, pursuant to this Directive or in some other way, of facts which involve or increase the risk for another Member State of a hazard being posed to certain shipping areas and coastal zones, shall take the appropriate measures to inform any interested Member State thereof as soon as possible and consult it regarding the action being envisaged. Where appropriate, Member States shall cooperate with a view to pooling the arrangements for joint action.

Each Member State shall make the necessary arrangements to use fully the reports which ships are required to transmit to them pursuant to Article 17."

Accompanying measures

39.075 There are a number of accompanying measures dealing with the designation and publication of a list of competent bodies,[57] co-operation between Member States and

---

57 Art. 22 provides:

"1. Each Member State shall designate the competent authorities, port authorities and coastal stations to which the notifications required by this Directive must be made.

2. Each Member State shall ensure that the shipping industry is properly informed and regularly updated, notably via nautical publications, regarding the authorities and stations designated pursuant to paragraph 1, including where appropriate the geographical area for which they are competent, and the procedures laid down for notifying the information required by this Directive.

3. Member States shall send the Commission a list of the authorities and stations they designate pursuant to paragraph 1, as well as any updating thereof."

the Commission,[58] and the processing and management of maritime safety information.[59] It is proposed to highlight one particular provision – Article 22a deals with "SafeSeaNet":

> "1. Member States shall establish maritime information management systems, at national or local level, to process the information referred to in this Directive.
> 2. The systems set up pursuant to paragraph 1 shall allow the information gathered to be used operationally and shall satisfy, in particular, the conditions laid down in Article 14.
> 3. To guarantee an effective exchange of the information referred to in this Directive, Member States shall ensure that national or local systems set up to gather, process and preserve that information can be interconnected with SafeSeaNet. The Commission shall ensure that Safe-SeaNet is operational on a 24 hour-a-day basis. The description and principles of SafeSeaNet are laid down in Annex III.
> 4. Without prejudice to paragraph 3, where operating under intra-Community agreements or in the framework of cross-border interregional or transnational projects within the Community, Member States shall ensure that information systems or networks comply with the requirements of this Directive and are compatible with and connected to SafeSeaNet."

I. COMMISSION DECISION (EU) 2016/566 OF 11 APRIL 2016 ON ESTABLISHING THE HIGH-LEVEL STEERING GROUP FOR GOVERNANCE OF THE DIGITAL MARITIME SYSTEM AND SERVICES AND REPEALING DECISION 2009/584

39.076 On 11 April 2016, the Commission adopted Commission Decision (EU) 2016/566 of 11 April 2016 on Establishing the High-Level Steering Group for Governance of the Digital Maritime System and Services and Repealing Decision 2009/584.[60]

---

58 Art. 23 provides:

"Member States and the Commission shall cooperate in attaining the following objectives:

(a) making optimum use of the information notified pursuant to this Directive, notably by developing appropriate telematic links between coastal stations and port authorities with a view to exchanging data relating to ships' movements, their estimated times of arrival in ports and their cargo;

(b) developing and enhancing the effectiveness of telematic links between the coastal stations of the Member States with a view to obtaining a clearer picture of traffic, improving the monitoring of ships in transit, and harmonising and, as far as possible, streamlining the reports required from ships en route;

(c) extending the cover of the Community vessel traffic monitoring and information system, and/or updating it, with a view to enhanced identification and monitoring of ships, taking into account developments in information and communication technologies. To this end, Member States and the Commission shall work together to put in place, where necessary, mandatory reporting systems, mandatory maritime traffic services and appropriate ship's routing systems, with a view to submitting them to the IMO for approval. They shall also collaborate, within the regional or international bodies concerned, on developing long-range identification and tracking systems;

(d) drawing up, if appropriate, concerted plans to accommodate ships in distress;

(e) ensuring the interconnection and interoperability of the national systems used for managing the information referred to in Annex I, and developing and updating SafeSeaNet."

59 Art. 24 provides:

"1. Member States shall, in accordance with Community or national legislation, take the necessary measures to ensure the confidentiality of information sent to them pursuant to this Directive, and shall only use such information in compliance with this Directive.

2. The Commission shall investigate possible network and information security problems and propose appropriate amendments to Annex III for improving the security of the network."

60 OJ L96/46, 12 April 2016.

39.077 The subject matter of the decision is clear from Article 1: the "high-level steering group for governance of the digital maritime system and services is hereby set up (hereinafter referred to as 'the HLSG')."

39.078 Article 2 describes the HLSG's tasks. It provides that the HLSG's tasks, without prejudice to the ownership of data by Member States, shall be (and it is a non-exhaustive list): (a) as stipulated in point 2.2 of Annex III of Directive 2002/59; (b) to assist the Commission in the fulfilment of its tasks set out in Article 3(2) of Directive 2010/65, in particular assist in developing technical mechanisms for the harmonisation and co-ordination of reporting formalities within the Union enhancing integration, re-use and sharing of information reported into the system, enabling reporting once and thereby supporting the facilitation of the European maritime transport space without barriers; (c) to establish and maintain co-operation with expert group(s) for specific tasks related to the operation, use and functioning of the Union maritime information and exchange system, the national single window, the national SafeSeaNet or other electronic systems and their interoperability, under terms of reference established by the HLSG; (d) to establish co-operation between the Member States bodies and the Commission regarding Article 23 of Directive 2002/59, questions related to conditions for use of the system and the integrated maritime services; (e) to monitor the interconnection and interoperability of the national single window and the Union maritime information and exchange system as well as other relevant European systems used for managing the information; and (f) to bring about an exchange of experience and good practice for the purposes of Article 20(3) of Directive 2002/59.

39.079 Article 3 provides for consultation. It states that the Commission may consult the HLSG on any matter relating to the tasks set out in Article 2 and the technical operation of current and future developments of the single window, the Union maritime information and exchange system, both at centralised and de-centralised level, including its contribution to maritime monitoring and surveillance from a holistic perspective for the aims and purposes laid down in Directive 2002/59 and Directive 2010/65.

39.080 Article 4 is entitled "Membership-Appointment". The HLSG shall be composed of representatives of the Member States and of the Commission. The members of the HLSG to be appointed by the Commission shall be senior officials. Each Member State shall designate no more than two members and a corresponding number of alternates. Alternates shall be appointed in accordance with the same conditions as members; alternates automatically replace any members who are absent or indisposed. Members and alternates shall be senior officials. Current members of the high-level steering group on SafeSeaNet shall remain appointed until the end of their term under Article 3(2) of Decision 2009/584. Members designated in accordance with paragraph 3 are appointed for three years. They shall remain in office until such time as they are replaced or their term of office ends. Their term of office may be renewed. Members who are no longer capable of contributing effectively to the group's deliberations, who resign or who do not comply with the conditions set out in paragraph 3 of Article 4, or Article 339 of the Treaty, may be replaced for the remainder of their term of office. A representative of the European Maritime Safety Agency ("EMSA") shall attend the HLSG meetings as permanent observer. The EMSA shall be represented at a high level. Representatives of the European Free Trade Association states that are parties to the Agreement on the European

Economic Area may attend HLSG meetings as observers. Personal data shall be collected, processed and published in accordance with Regulation 45/2001.

39.081 Article 5 deals with the operation of the HLSG. The HLSG shall be chaired by a representative of the Commission.[61] The Commission's representative chairing the HLSG may ask experts with specific competence on a subject on the agenda to participate in the HLSG or sub-group's discussion if this is useful or necessary. In addition, the Commission's representative may give observer status to individuals, organisations as defined in Rule 8(3) of the horizontal rules on expert groups and candidate countries. Members and their representatives, as well as invited experts and observers, shall comply with the obligations of professional secrecy laid down by the Treaties and their implementing rules, as well as with the Commission's rules on security regarding the protection of EU classified information, laid down in the annex to Commission Decisions (EU, Euratom) 2015/443[62] and 2015/444.[63] Should they fail to respect these obligations, the Commission may take all appropriate measures. The HLSG shall normally meet on Commission premises. The Commission shall provide the secretariat of the HLSG. Other Commission officials with an interest in the proceedings may attend meetings of the group. The HLSG shall adopt its rules of procedure on the basis of the standard rules of procedure for expert groups adopted by the Commission. All relevant documents (such as agendas, minutes and participants' submissions) shall be made available either in the Register of expert groups or via a link from the Register to a dedicated website, where information can be found. Exceptions to publication shall be made in accordance with Regulation (EC) No 1049/2001 of the European Parliament and of the Council.[64]

---

61 Dec. 2016/566, Art. 5(1),

62 Commission Decision (EU, Euratom) 2015/443 of 13 March 2015 on Security in the Commission (OJ L72, 17 March 2015, p. 41).

63 Commission Decision (EU, Euratom) 2015/444 of 13 March 2015 on the security rules for protecting EU classified information (OJ L72, 17 March 2015, p. 53).

64 Regulation (EC) No 1049/2001 of the European Parliament and of the Council of 30 May 2001 regarding public access to European Parliament, Council and Commission documents (OJ L145, 31 May 2001, p. 43).

CHAPTER 40

Pilotage

A. INTRODUCTION

40.001 This short chapter discusses the European Union ("EU") law relating to pilotage. Most of the EU rules discussed elsewhere in this book may well apply to pilotage: for example, the prohibition on discrimination by Member States between EU citizens on the basis of nationality;[1] rules on employment (in so far as pilots are employees);[2] the rules on competition in so far as pilots are undertakings;[3] State authorities and how they organise markets;[4] and State aid[5] are applicable to pilotage. This chapter concentrates on some specific issues which are not dealt with elsewhere in the book.

B. THE 1978 NORTH SEA PILOTAGE DIRECTIVE

Introduction

40.002 On 21 December 1978, the Council adopted a directive concerning pilotage of vessels by deep-sea pilots in the North Sea and English Channel. This was Directive 79/115.[6]

Legal bases

40.003 The legal bases of this directive are what is now the Treaty on the Functioning of the European Union ("TFEU") generally and, what is now, Article 100(2) of the Treaty in particular.

Purpose

40.004 The purpose of the directive is set out in its Preamble which reads:

"[w]hereas for the sake of safety at sea and of preventing marine pollution, it is necessary to ensure that vessels wishing to use the services of pilots in the North Sea and English Channel can call on adequately qualified deep-sea pilots, and to promote the employment of such pilots in vessels flying the flags of Member States".

---

1 See, for example, TFEU, Art. 18. This would mean, for example, that Member State X may not prefer its own citizens over those of other Member States in regard to pilotage issues (e.g. employment, pay, rights and so on); there might be a very limited exception (which should be construed narrowly in any event) relating to public service functions but that would be very exceptional.
2 See chap. 8.
3 See chap. 9.
4 Ibid.
5 See chap. 15 in the case of subsidised pilotage.
6 OJ L33/32, 8 February 1979.

Obligation on certain States to provide qualified pilots

40.005 Article 1(1) of the directive provides that the Member States which have coasts bordering on the North Sea or English Channel are obliged to take all necessary and appropriate measures to ensure that vessels availing themselves of the services of a deep-sea pilot for pilotage in the North Sea or the English Channel be provided with adequately qualified deep-sea pilots in possession of a certificate delivered by a competent authority of one of these Member States certifying that such pilots are qualified to pilot vessels in the North Sea and the English Channel.

Member States are obliged to encourage ships which fly their flags to use qualified pilots

40.006 Article 1(2) of the directive is apparently addressed to all Member States of the European Community ("EC") in that it provides that "[e]ach Member State" is obliged to take all necessary and appropriate measures to encourage vessels flying its national flag to avail themselves, in the North Sea and the English Channel, of the services of only those deep-sea pilots who are in possession of a certificate as referred to in Article 1(1) or of an equivalent certificate delivered by another North Sea coastal State, when seeking the assistance of deep-sea pilots.

Implementation

40.007 Article 2 provides that after consulting the Commission, Member States were obliged to bring into force the laws, regulations and administrative provisions necessary to comply with the directive not later than 1 January 1980 and were obliged to inform the Commission thereof.

Implementation opinions

40.008 There were then a series of opinions expressed by the Commission on the implementation (or otherwise) of the Council Directive.

40.009 On 16 June 1980 adopted Opinion 80/638 addressed to the Belgian government in respect of the implementation of Council Directive 79/115 for Belgium. The Commission was concerned about nationality requirements for pilots:

"1. In a letter dated 9 January 1980, the office of the Permanent Representation of Belgium to the European Communities submitted the following documents to the Commission for consultation pursuant to Article 2 of the above Directive: – a preliminary draft law on the introduction of a deep-sea pilot's certificate for North Sea and English Channel waters;

  – a draft Royal Decree implementing the above law;
  – a draft Ministerial Decree implementing the above Royal Decree;
  – a draft Royal Decree setting up a Maritime Control Commission.

2. From an examination of the draft Royal Decree implementing the draft law on the introduction of a deep-sea pilot's certificate for North Sea and English Channel waters it emerges that one of the conditions for granting the certificate in question is the possession of Belgian or Luxembourg nationality.

The Commission considers that the deep-sea pilots in question will simply give technical assistance to ships' masters, the latter retaining sole responsibility for sailing and manoeuvring the ship (cf. Article 3 of the draft law). Moreover, Article 7 of the preliminary draft law provides that the Belgian State shall not be held in any way responsible for any damage which the holder of a deep-sea pilot's certificate might cause in the exercise of his profession.

In these circumstances the Commission is of the opinion that the deep-sea pilots will not be involved in the exercise of official authority within the meaning of Article 55 of the EEC Treaty and that the prescribed condition of Belgian or Luxembourg nationality is therefore incompatible with Articles 48 and 52 of the Treaty.

It therefore has the honour to request the Belgian Government to re-examine, in the light of the above Articles of the Treaty, the provisions of the draft Royal Decree relating to the condition of nationality for the grant of the certificate in question."

40.010 On 24 September 1980, the Commission adopted an opinion addressed to Italy regarding the implementation of Council Directive 79/115.[7] This was Opinion 80/946. The operative provisions were:

"1. On 8 May 1980, pursuant to Article 2 of Directive 79/115/EEC, the Permanent Representation of Italy to the European Communities forwarded to the Commission a memorandum from the Ministry for Merchant Shipping requesting the National Shipping Federation and the National Shipowners Federation to encourage vessels flying the Italian flag seeking pilotage to avail themselves, in the North Sea and the English Channel, only of the services of adequately qualified deep-sea pilots in possession of either a certificate issued by the competent authority of a Member State on the North Sea or English Channel as laid down in Article 1 (1) of the Directive, or a certificate considered to be equivalent.

2. Examination of this memorandum showed the Commission that the Italian Government has complied fully with its obligations regarding implementation of the Directive concerned."

40.011 On 25 September 1980, the Commission adopted an opinion addressed to the government of the Netherlands regarding the implementation of Directive 79/115. This was Opinion 80/947. The operative provisions were:

"1. In a letter dated 22 April 1980, the Permanent Representation of the Netherlands to the European Communities submitted the following documents for the opinion of the Commission under Article 2 of Directive 79/115/EEC: – an order issued by the Minister of Defence introducing certificates for deep-sea pilots,

   - a regulation dealing with tests for deep-sea pilots,
   - the text of implementing provisions concerning pilotage,
   - a letter from the Director-General for Navigation.

2. Examination of the order issued by the Minister of Defence has revealed that one of the requirements for obtaining a deep-sea pilot's certificate is possession of Dutch nationality.

   The Commission holds the view that a deep-sea pilot's function is confined to providing technical assistance to the captain of a sea-going vessel, who remains solely responsible for the navigation and manoeuvring of his ship (cf. Article 2 of the implementing regulations concerning pilotage).

   The Commission is accordingly of the opinion that deep-sea pilots are not involved in exercising official authority within the meaning of Article 55 of the EEC Treaty and that the requirement of Dutch nationality is consequently incompatible with Articles 48 and 52 of the Treaty.

---

7 OJ 1980 L267/32.

The Commission has the honour, therefore, to invite the Government of the Netherlands to review that part of the above order dealing with nationality as a criterion for obtaining the certificate in question in the light of the Articles of the Treaty cited here."

40.012 On 25 September 1980, the Commission adopted an opinion (Opinion 80/948) addressed to the French government regarding the implementation of Council Directive 79/115. The operative provisions were:

"1 The Permanent Representation of France to the European Communities, in letters dated 16 January and 30 May 1980, submitted the following documents to the Commission under Article 2 of Directive 79/115/EEC: – a decree dated 2 May 1979 introducing certificates for deep-sea pilots,

- an order dated 27 December 1979 dealing with the conditions for obtaining a deep-sea pilot's certificate and with the scope of expertise required,
- a copy of a letter dated 28 April 1980 to the Chairman of the Central Committee of French Shipowners.

2. An examination of these documents has shown the Commission that the French Government has complied fully with its obligations regarding implementation of the Directive concerned."

40.013 On 10 February 1981, the Commission adopted an opinion (Opinion 81/110) addressed to the German government regarding the implementation of Directive 79/115.[8] The operative provisions were not clear-cut:

"1. In a letter dated 27 November 1979, the Permanent Representation of the Federal Republic of Germany to the European Communities sent to the Commission under Article 2 of Directive 79/115/EEC ... a statutory order dealing with deep-sea pilots dated 25 August 1978 (Verordnung über das Seelotsenwesen außerhalb der Reviere).
2. Examination of this document and the letter sent on 5 November 1979 by the Ministry of Transport to the German Shipowners' Association (Verband Deutscher Reeder) has led the Commission to find that the Federal Government has met, in full, its obligations regarding implementation of the Directive.
3. However, examination was also made at the same time of the Law of 13 October 1954, which deals with pilotage in general, including therefore deep-sea pilotage, and this revealed, with reference to Sections 10 and 12 of the Law, that exercise of the profession is subject to possession of German nationality.
4. In the course of earlier contacts with representatives of the Federal Government, the Commission noted that that Government expects to amend the legislation in question by 1983 and that, in the intervening period, the said restriction would not debar nationals from other Member States. The Commission however, invites the Federal Government to bring this engagement to the notice of the competent authorities, as well as of all interested parties, through an appropriate official publication, and to communicate this publication to the Commission.
5. Subject to this assurance, the Commission considers the Directive to be fully implemented in the Federal Republic of Germany."

40.014 On 15 May 1981, the Commission adopted an opinion addressed to the Irish government on the implementation of Council Directive 79/115.[9] This was Opinion 81/399. The operative provisions were:

---

8 Opinion 81/110, OJ 1981 L64/14.
9 OJ 1981 L152/36.

"1. In its letter of 28 July 1980 the Irish Permanent Representation to the European Communities sent to the Commission, under Article 2 of Directive 79/115/EEC,[10] the draft of a Ministerial measure whereby shipowners and captains of Irish ships are instructed to ensure that vessels flying the Irish flag which wish to be piloted, use in the North Sea and the English Channel only adequately qualified deep-sea pilots holding a certificate issued by the competent authority within a State bordering on the North Sea or English Channel in accordance with Article 1(1) of the Directive, or holding a certificate considered to be equivalent.

2. Examination of this document has satisfied the Commission that the publication of the aforesaid measure will fully implement the provisions of the Directive which concern Ireland. The Commission suggests that the Irish Government should, while waiting for detailed information from the other governments concerned which would allow them to complete the text of the measure in question, already consider issuing a communication to its shipowners and sea captains covering points 1 and 2 of the draft submitted to the Commission."

40.015 On 17 July 1981, the Commission adopted an opinion addressed to the UK government regarding the implementation of Directive 79/115.[11] This was Opinion 81/635. The operative provisions were succinct:

"In its letter of 17 February 1981, the Permanent Representation of the United Kingdom to the European Communities sent the Commission, pursuant to Article 2 of the Directive referred to above, the draft 'Merchant Shipping ("M") Notice' by means of which the Government intends to implement the provisions of that Directive.
    Examination of this document has enabled the Commission to confirm that the Government of the United Kingdom has fully implemented the provisions of the aforementioned Directive."

40.016 On 28 April 1982, the Commission adopted Opinion 82/303 addressed to the Greek government regarding the implementation of the Council Directive 79/115.[12] The operative provisions were:

"1. In a letter dated 13 August 1981, the Office of the Permanent Representative of Greece to the European Communities sent the Commission, under Article 2 of the Directive in question ..., Presidential Decree No 582/81 of 1 June 1981 on the pilotage of vessels flying the Greek flag by deep-sea pilots in the North Sea or English Channel.

2. Examination of that Decree has satisfied the Commission that the Greek Government has fully implemented those provisions of the Directive which apply to it."

40.017 On 30 November 1982, the Commission adopted an opinion addressed to the Danish government regarding the implementation of Directive 79/115.[13] This was Opinion 82/841. The operative provisions were:

"1. In a letter dated 6 April 1981, the office of the Permanent Representative of Denmark to the European Communities sent the Commission, as required by Article 2 of Directive 79/115/EEC,[14] the circular published by the Ministry of Industry on 7 July 1980 concerning deep-sea pilots in the North Sea, the English Channel and the Skagerrak.

2. The Commission regrets that, contrary to the said Article 2, the Danish Government did not comply with the obligation to consult the Commission before adopting the circular in question nor the obligation to adopt the measure before 1 January 1980.

3. Examination of the circular has, however, satisfied the Commission that the Danish Government has fully implemented the provisions of Article 1 (2) of the Directive. As regards

---

10 OJ 1979 L33/32.
11 OJ 1981 L231/33.
12 OJ 1982 L137/15.
13 Opinion 82/841, OJ 1982 L356/44.
14 Ed., OJ 1979 L33/32.

implementation of Article 1 (1), the Commission considers that if, under the present policy, there are not sufficient pilots available to meet the demand, the Danish authorities themselves will have to issue certificates for deep-sea pilots, in which case the Commission asks to be shown all the documents in question.

4. Subject to this reservation, the Commission considers that the Danish Government has fully implemented Directive 79/115/EEC."

40.018 On 26 November 1986, the Commission adopted an opinion addressed to the Portuguese government regarding the implementation of Directive 79/115.[15] This was Opinion 82/597. The operative provisions were:

"1. In a letter dated 24 July 1986, the Office of the Permanent Representative of Portugal to the European Communities informed the Commission, as required by Article 2 of the above-mentioned Directive, of an administrative measure published by the Portuguese Directorate-General for Merchant Shipping on 7 March 1986 on pilotage of vessels flying the Portuguese flag by deep-sea pilots operating in the North Sea and in the English Channel.

2. Examination of this administrative measure has assured the Commission that the Portuguese Government has fully implemented the provisions of the Directive applicable to it."

C. 1985 COMMISSION MEMORANDUM ON SHIPPING

40.019 The former European Commissioner for Transport, Lord Stanley Clinton Davis, was reported, at the time of the Commission's 1985 Memorandum[16] being published, as emphasising the need for concerted action in the field of pilotage. While that has not been achieved as such, there have been some measures over time and pilotage also forms part of the wider body of law relating to pilotage.

D. DISCRIMINATION ON THE BASIS OF NATIONALITY

40.020 It would be unlawful, as a matter of EU law, for a Member State to reserve to its own nationals or to discriminate between nationals of EU Member States any position or privilege relating to pilotage. For example, if a national of a particular coastal State may be a pilot or apply for a pilotage exemption certificate then all EU Member State nationals should be entitled to be pilots or apply for such a certificate. For a Member State to prevent a national of another Member State to operate as a pilot because the person was not a national of the Member State where he or she wanted to operate would be contrary to Article 18 of the TFEU.[17]

E. PILOTAGE EXEMPTION CERTIFICATES

40.021 As mentioned above, pilotage exemption certificates are an important example of EU shipping law being applied to pilotage. The European Commission has commented as follows:

---

15 OJ 1982 L356/44.

16 On the 1985 Memorandum, see Bulletin of the European Communities, progress towards a Common Transport Policy: Maritime Transport, Supplement S185.

17 See chap. 44 on Directive on Reporting Formalities for Ships Arriving and Departing from Ports of the Member States OJ L283/1, 29 October 2010.

"Use of a pilot is compulsory in many territorial waters. A pilot is familiar with the local waters and special conditions and can therefore guide ships through congested or dangerous areas. The pilot acts as an advisor, as the master remains in legal, overriding command of the vessel.

In most Member States legislation provides the possibility of some form of exemption from pilotage, either in the form of exemptions in the regulations for compulsory pilotage or in the form of issue of Pilotage Exemption Certificates (PEC). A Pilotage Exemption Certificate may be granted to the vessel's master, or mate, when they fulfill certain criteria showing a capacity to safely manage his vessel in the waters in question. Normally the pilotage exemption is valid only for the specified vessel and route.

The Commission Communication and action plan with a view to establishing a European maritime transport space without barriers invited Member States to create a regulatory framework which would permit easier pilotage exemptions. This communication specified that the conditions required for obtaining a PEC should be reasonable and should not contain elements of protectionism. This could induce lower costs for Short Sea Shipping operators and faster turnaround times of vessels in ports. The action required to put this recommendation into effect will need to be taken at national level and coordinated among national authorities.

Furthermore, during the adoption of the Directive on reporting formalities for ships arriving and departing from ports of the Member states (2010/65/EU), the European Parliament, the Council and the Commission agreed on a joint statement to examine a clear framework on granting Pilota[g]e Exemption Certificates. It was agreed that the Commission will examine this issue in co-operation with the interested parties and in consideration of the importance of safety at sea and the protection of the marine environment.

On 4 March 2011, the Commission held a consultation meeting to discuss which elements should be included in the external study on the Pilotage Exemption Certificates. The consultations for the study took place during the first half of 2012 and the study was published in October 2012."

The 2012 study on pilotage exemption certificates is a detailed analysis of the approach of the Member States. It is useful to consult chapter 44 on Directive 2010/65.[18]

---

18 OJ L283/1, 29 October 2010.

CHAPTER 41

Short sea shipping

A. INTRODUCTION

41.001 Short sea shipping is, as its name suggests, the transport of goods or passengers by sea but over very short distances. It often has the attraction of diverting traffic which would otherwise be on land (e.g. by road or rail) to the sea. The European Union ("EU") has been keen for various reasons (e.g. the protection of the environment) to divert cargo to short sea shipping. The EU has the aim of reducing 60% of the current level of greenhouse gas emissions generated by transport and by 2030 bringing about a shift of 30% of road freight carried over 300 kilometres to other modes. Shortsea Promotion Centres have been established in nearly all the coastal Member States. Moreover the European Commission has helped establish the European Shortsea Network.

41.002 Short sea shipping is extremely important in the EU. The total gross weight of goods transported as part of EU short sea shipping is estimated at almost 1.9 billion tonnes of goods in 2016, an increase of 2.6% from the previous year.[1] The UK remained the major short sea shipping country in the EU in 2016, with a share of more than 14% of the total tonnages of EU short sea shipping in 2016.[2]

B. 1996: COUNCIL RESOLUTION ON SHORT SEA SHIPPING

41.003 On 11 March 1996, the Council adopted a resolution on short sea shipping.[3] The resolution stated:

"A. Having regard to the Treaty establishing the European Community,
    Considering the White Paper on the future development of the common transport policy, of 2 December 1992,[4] which was welcomed by the Council at its meetings held on 7 and 8 June and 19 June 1993;
    Considering the Commission communication on short sea shipping, of 5 July 1995;[5]
    Considering the importance of transport for the economy of the European Union;
    Considering the increasing degree of congestion in general and the high costs which characterize land transport infrastructure;
    Considering the potential contribution that short sea shipping could make to the achievement of sustainable mobility;
    Considering that, in view of the foregoing, efforts are called for both at Community level and at the level of Member States to promote or improve short sea shipping, while respecting the free choice of users;

---

1 http://ec.europa.eu/eurostat/statistics-explained/index.php/Maritime_transport_statistics_-_short_sea_shipping_of_goods (2018).
2 http://ec.europa.eu/eurostat/statistics-explained/index.php/Maritime_transport_statistics_-_short_sea_shipping_of_goods (2018).
3 OJ C99/1, 2 April 1996.
4 COM(92) 494 final.
5 COM(95) 317 final.

Considering that, where obstacles prevent the development of short sea shipping, remedial action should be taken by regional, local or port authorities and by the maritime industries themselves;

B. NOTES:
1. the considerable advantages presented by short sea shipping for the European Union in comparison with land transport, in particular:

    (a) the general availability of space capacity in short sea shipping;
    (b) lower energy consumption and lower levels of emission of pollutants into the atmosphere;
    (c) potential contribution to the development of peripheral regions of the European Union;
    (d) possibility to extend short sea shipping further with few infrastructure costs;

2. the reports and the agreed multiannual work programmes adopted by various Conferences on shipping in different areas, such as the Baltic Sea, the Black Sea and the Mediterranean Sea;
3. the reports and proposals by the Maritime Industries Forum on the advisability of promoting short sea shipping as a viable alternative, in economic, energy, safety and environmental terms, to land transport;

C. STATES that the main objectives of short sea shipping policy are:
1. to achieve a balanced growth of this mode of transport; and
2. positive and active integration of short sea shipping, including feeder services, into the intermodal transport chain,

D. INTENDS to pursue these objectives by encouraging the following actions:
1. developing further the environmental benefits of short sea shipping;
2. promoting, in the interest of the users, free and fair competition between modes of transport in which all modes bear their full costs, including external costs;
3. fostering of free and fair competition between Community ports and between shipping lines;
4. improving port efficiency in order to reduce the costs of, and time spent in, port operations;
5. making use of combined transport for the development of short sea shipping;
6. promoting the confidence of shippers and transport undertakings in the possibilities of short sea shipping;
7. streamlining and, where appropriate, coordinating, harmonizing and simplifying customs procedures and other related administrative formalities which arise in harbours;
8. encouraging initiatives by shipping undertakings involved in short sea shipping;
9. drawing up and implementing pilot projects concerning short sea shipping, where these do not distort competition between transport modes or between shipping companies or ports of all Member States, and disseminating the results;
10. supporting training, research and development in the area of short sea shipping and port activities;
11. supporting and expanding electronic data interchange (EDI),

E. IN THE LIGHT OF THE ABOVE:
1. welcomes in general the action programme contained in the Communication by the Commission;
2. notes that the Commission will submit as soon as possible its Green Paper on the internalization of external costs in transport;
3. notes that the Commission will develop as soon as possible guidelines on State aid to shipping and to ports and will consult the Member States and the maritime industries on these guidelines;
4. agrees that the promotion of short sea shipping should continue to be an important element in ongoing Community and Member States' activity such as the trans-European transport network plan and the Fourth Framework Programme on Research and Development;

F. INVITES THE COMMISSION to propose to the Council or to develop, as soon as possible, the measures necessary to attain the objectives stated in part C taking into account its action programme and the subsidiarity principle, and in particular measures which:

1. prevent distortion of competition between ports;
2. promote the increased use of short sea shipping among its potential users;
3. simplify and streamline existing customs procedures and other related administrative formalities which arise in ports, with regard to short sea shipping;
4. encourage initiatives by shipping undertakings involved in short sea shipping;
5. support programmes of training, research and development in this transport sector;
6. encourage the use of information technology for the best development of this mode of transport,

G. INVITES THE MEMBER STATES:
1. to support the objectives and the means stated in parts C and D;
2. to cooperate with the Commission in setting a Community framework to promote the short sea shipping sector;
3. to carry out actions to stimulate short sea shipping, taking into account the proposed action programme of the Commission's communication and to encourage their regional, local and port authorities and maritime industries to do likewise;
4. to promote practical consultations, for example through round tables such as those of the Maritime Industries Forum in which the maritime industries and regional, local and port authorities are represented."

C. 2000: RESOLUTION ON THE PROMOTION OF SHORT SEA SHIPPING

41.004 On 14 February 2000, the Council adopted a resolution on the promotion of short sea shipping.[6] The EU, particularly the Commission, has been a strong supporter of short sea shipping. The resolution began by welcoming the second Commission communication on the development of short sea shipping in Europe and noted that it incorporated the second two-yearly report on progress in the development of short sea shipping requested by the Council in its Conclusions of 18 June 1997. It noted with satisfaction that the Commission's communication presented a thorough review of the development of short sea shipping, identified the main problem areas where further action was needed to promote short sea shipping, outlined a comprehensive long term approach for the development of short sea shipping and made recommendations for a number of actions to be undertaken by all parties. It reconfirmed the objectives and recommendations for action contained in the Council Resolution of 11 March 1996 on short sea shipping and in the Council Conclusions of 18 June 1997 and noted that actions had already been undertaken and initiated on the basis of these recommendations. The resolution confirmed that short sea shipping is an environmentally friendly transport mode which contributes to the sustainability of transport, strengthens the cohesion of the Community and contributes to an increased efficiency of the EU's transport system. The resolution also emphasised as a priority objective of the Council the development of short sea shipping into a dynamic part and a viable option in the intermodal door-to-door transport chain between all EU regions. It also considered that the promotion of short sea shipping in all its aspects, such as container and bulk transport, is an ongoing process, which needs to be accelerated with

---

6 OJ C56/3, 29 February 2000. See http://eur-lex.europa.eu/legal-content/EN/TXT/?uri=CELEX%3A52001PC0046,

short, medium and long term actions, while respecting the EU rules, among others those governing maritime cabotage. It also reconfirmed its view that it is primarily up to the industries themselves to develop short sea shipping and that the Council, the Member States and the Commission have an essential role to play, in particular concerning the framework conditions. The resolution recalls that, in its report to the European Council of Helsinki on a strategy on the integration of environment and sustainable development into the transport policy, the Council addresses the need of "promoting short sea shipping, focusing in particular on the removal of obstacles for its development as an environmentally friendly transport mode" and invited the Member States and the Commission to take measures in several areas, which equally lead to promoting short sea shipping. The resolution considered that the comprehensive approach presented in the Commission communication forms a good and constructive basis for the future work on reaching the abovementioned priority objective and welcomed, in general, the recommendations for the development of short sea shipping included in that communication.

41.005 The resolution continues:

"(10) IS OF THE VIEW that it is essential to find practical solutions to existing bottlenecks which hamper the development of short sea shipping and, at this stage of the development process, to focus on certain fields of action and, in particular, on:

(a) improving the efficiency of the maritime loading and unloading points in the logistics chain (i.e. intermodal connection points such as ports, terminals etc.) by streamlining the administrative procedures and by developing services and technical infrastructures (i.e. land-based facilities, hinterland connections, loading units etc.);

(b) promoting door-to-door package solutions with integrated facilities, such as one-stop shops, through the cooperation between the different transport modes and the different players in the logistic management of the supply chain, through the establishment of best practices, through the examination, with a view to their introduction, of measures such as benchmarking and key performance indicators, through the collection and dissemination of data and information on short sea shipping, amongst others using Eurostat, and through the active use of the cooperation framework provided by the round-tables and the focal points of the Member States and other national initiatives to promote short sea shipping such as national short sea shipping information offices;

(c) creating and testing new technical and market opportunities for short sea shipping, also over distances shorter than its current average distance, by promoting research and development, in particular in respect of land-based facilities, information technologies and ships specially adapted for short sea shipping; in addition, it is recommended to study possibilities for short term financial support for new projects and for the further development of existing projects in this field;

(d) creating a level playing field for short sea shipping by achieving further progress in fair and efficient pricing for infrastructure, taking into account the work of the Commission's High Level Group on transport infrastructure charging.

(11) INVITES the parties concerned, including the industries, the transport users, the Member States and the Commission to work actively towards fulfilling the priority objectives and the tasks identified under point 10, and to cooperate towards finding concrete solutions to obstacles standing in the way of the development of short sea shipping."

41.006 The Council invited the Commission to continue and intensify its work for the promotion of short sea shipping, in particular by:

"(a) initiating urgently an exercise of compiling, with input from the focal points and other interested parties, a detailed list of bottlenecks and other specific problems and their potential solutions, such as best practices;

(b) examining and consulting the parties concerned as soon as possible with a view to presenting proposals and/or encouraging the introduction of codes of conduct to simplify and streamline transport-related administrative formalities and documentation in short sea shipping, in particular as regards the uniform application of IMO FAL forms in the Community;[7]

(c) presenting its inventory of the public financial support to ports and proposals on the access to the market for port services, while taking into account the diversity of circumstances prevailing in the Community ports, such as their peripheral location, as well as public service obligations and the need to maintain a high level of safety;

(d) examining the possibility of earmarking more existing Community financial resources to the promotion of short sea shipping, of finding further possibilities for such funding, and of creating, in accordance with the rules of the Treaty on State aid and competition, a framework enabling the participation of national resources in initiating new short sea projects;

(e) developing tools to measure emissions from door-to-door transport chains containing a short sea leg in comparison with transport in one single mode, in order to facilitate a reasoned choice of transport modes;

(f) following short sea shipping market developments and collecting and disseminating factual information on short sea shipping and its potential;

(g) studying, in coordination with Short Sea Shipping Focal Points, the competitiveness of door-to-door transport chains containing a short sea leg as compared with other transport modes in relation to transport price in a segmented market;

(h) taking the needs of short sea shipping constantly into consideration in the application and planning of Community actions and in regional cooperation with the third countries concerned."

41.007 The Council invited the Commission to transmit to the Council its next progress report in 2001 and to extend this report to passenger transport in addition to cargo transport.

D. 2000: RESOLUTION ON THE PROMOTION OF INTERMODALITY AND INTERMODAL FREIGHT TRANSPORT IN THE EUROPEAN UNION

41.008 On 14 February 2000, the Council adopted a second resolution in the maritime field – this resolution was on the promotion of intermodality and intermodal freight transport in the EU.[8] It welcomed the Commission Communication on Intermodality and Intermodal Freight Transport in the European Union of October 1999 and the Communication on the Progress of the Implementation of the Action Programme of June 1997 contained in it. It noted, with satisfaction, that most projects in the action programme have been launched and encouraged the Commission to continue its implementation. The Council is of the opinion that functional and logistically efficient freight transport systems contribute to the development of economic activity within the Community for the benefit of its citizens and enterprises. It endorsed the objective set by the Commission to develop Intermodal Freight Transport, i.e. an optimal integration of different transport modes enabling

---

7 Ed., the IMO's Convention on Facilitation of International Maritime Traffic (the "FAL Convention") includes in its "Standard 2.1" a number of documents which public authorities may demand of a ship and recommends the maximum information and number of copies which should be required.

8 OJ C56/1, 29 February 2000.

an efficient and cost-effective use of the transport system through seamless, customer-oriented door-to-door services, whilst favouring competition between transport operators. The resolution recalled that the Council strategy of 6 October 1999 on the integration of environment and sustainable development into the transport policy

"underlines that further progress is required, notably in the ... promotion of ... intermodal and combined transport ... the standardisation and harmonisation of intermodal transport units ... the competitiveness and the quality of services of ports and other intermodal terminals and railways, e.g. by the increased use of telematics ... (and the study of) the different liability regimes."

The resolution emphasised the need determined by the same strategy "to continue to analyse the relationship between transport (demand) and ... the organisation of industrial production and services (globalisation, market deregulation, just-in-time logistics, electronic commerce)" with a view to developing actions consistent with the general goal of sustainable mobility. The Council reaffirmed its determination to promote transport modes contributing to sustainable transport, in particular rail transport, short sea shipping and inland navigations and recalled, in this context, its conclusions of 6 October 1999 on the revitalisation of the European railways referring, in particular, to the establishment of a Trans-European Rail Freight Network ("TERFN") and its resolution of 11 March 1996 on short sea shipping,[9] conclusions of 18 June 1997 and resolution of 14 February 2000 on the promotion of short sea shipping.[10] The Council also recalled the importance of the revision of the relevant legal framework of the Community as well as the importance of research, development and demonstration on intermodal transport and notes with satisfaction the role of studies in this field in key actions of the Fifth RTD[11] Framework Programme established by Decision 182/1999.[12] The resolution invited all parties concerned to work actively towards a sound operational market environment for intermodal transport, so as to make intermodality, where feasible, a viable and environmentally friendly alternative to single mode road transport. It noted that further work must be concentrated on identifying obstacles to intermodal transport in competing successfully in the market. It invited the Commission, in co-operation with the Member States, to continue and intensify its work for the promotion of intermodal transport including combined transport, in particular, by:

"(a) including intermodality in its revision of the TEN-T through reference to concrete actions with a view to achieving sustainable mobility, such as:

– setting up new tools for assessing the ability of planned infrastructures and actions to transfer some road transport demand towards more environmentally friendly modes,
– alleviating the bottlenecks for intermodalism, including those in the context of TERFN,
– developing and optimising terminals for intermodal transport;

(b) taking account of intermodalism with a view to creating a level playing field in the transport market when submitting, during the year 2000, a proposal for a revision of Regulation

---

9 OJ C99/1, 2 April 1996.
10 OJ C56/1, 29 February 2000.
11 RTD stands for Research and Technological Development.
12 OJ L26/1, 1 February 1999.

(EEC) No 1107/70 of the Council of 4 June 1970 on the granting of aids for transport by rail, road and inland waterway[13] with regard to aid to combined transport;

(c) integrating the information society into the European transport system, e.g. by submitting proposals for establishing an open architecture for data transfer and transport telematics;

(d) contributing to the realisation of an open and efficient real-time information and transaction systems, as a tool for shippers and intermodal transport operators;

(e) continuing, together with the Member States, the industry and relevant international organisations, its efforts to promote an appropriate liability regime in that area, inter alia, by exploring the aspects of a liability regime for intermodal transport and by presenting a report on the economic analysis of the consequences of the absence of a generally accepted intermodal liability regime and on the work being undertaken with the industry on the legal and economic advantages of the different solutions for a liability regime for intermodal transport;

(f) presenting a communication on 'Benchmarking in Transport' and developing key performance indicators for freight intermodalism; in this context, demonstrating the potential cost-effectiveness of intermodal transport projects and publishing examples and information on best practices, particularly taking into account the experience gained from the Pilot Actions for Combined Transport (PACT)-programme and the different projects under the Fifth RTD Framework Programme,

(g) directing, when proposing measures in the field of transport, the measures to the logistic and transport system as a whole and not solely to the individual modes of transport, focusing, inter alia, on harmonising the standards related to transport units and on technologies for cheaper, more efficient and environmentally friendly freight handling; to this end, presenting a communication on Supply Chain Management, logistics and intermodal transport by the end of year 2001;

(h) planning for an appropriate follow-up to the PACT programme, focussing on innovative projects;

(i) extending the action programme on intermodality to more integrated Intelligent Transport System applications, electronic commerce applications and demonstration projects and

(j) bolstering the role of research and development projects on intermodal transport in the RTD framework programmes."

41.009 The resolution went on to invite the applicant countries to follow the above objectives and actions when formulating national and local strategies. It intended to follow regularly the development in intermodality and intermodal freight transport in the EU. It invited the Commission to transmit to the Council, in 2001, its next progress report on intermodality and intermodal freight transport in the EU, with possible proposals.

E. 2004: COMMUNICATION FROM THE COMMISSION TO THE COUNCIL, THE EUROPEAN PARLIAMENT, THE EUROPEAN ECONOMIC AND SOCIAL COMMITTEE AND THE COMMITTEE OF THE REGIONS ON SHORT SEA SHIPPING

41.010 In 2004, the Commission prepared a key document on short sea shipping entitled "Communication from the Commission to the Council, the European Parliament, the European Economic and Social committee and the Committee of the Regions on Short Sea Shipping".[14] It was succinct and worth quoting much of it (but not the annexes):

---

13 OJ L130/1, 15.6.1970. Regulation as last amended by Regulation (EC) No 543/97 (OJ L84/6, 26.3.1997).
14 SEC(2004) 875, COM/2004/0453 final and available at: http://eur-lex.europa.eu/legal-content/EN/ALL/?uri=CELEX:52004DC0453.

"1. Background!

The Commission presented a Communication on Short Sea Shipping in 1995[15] and a progress report in 1997.[16] A further Communication in 1999[17] incorporated a second report on progress. It also analysed a number of obstacles that hinder the development of Short Sea Shipping and advocated a comprehensive door-to-door approach with one-stop shops to promote the mode.

Furthermore in 2001 the Commission White Paper on European Transport Policy for 2010[18] set a number of ambitious targets to ensure competitive and sustainable mobility in Europe.

In June 2002, the European Union Transport Ministers held an informal meeting in Gijón (Spain) dedicated entirely to Short Sea Shipping. Following this meeting, the Commission prepared a Programme for the Promotion of Short Sea Shipping.[19] The programme sets out 14 actions that have the objective to improve Short Sea Shipping and remove obstacles to its development.

The Commission now presents a further Communication on Short Sea Shipping in Europe highlighting the progress achieved since 1999 and linking it to the Programme for the Promotion of Short Sea Shipping...

2. Short Sea Shipping is Growing

In the last progress report, we examined the potential of Short Sea Shipping. However, in the meantime we have realised that it is much more than just a potential. For instance, in the 1990's it was the only mode of transport that proved able to keep up with the fast growth of road transport. Between 1995 and 2002, the tonne-kilometre performance of both Short Sea Shipping and road grew by 25%. In 2001, Short Sea Shipping performed 40% of all tonne-kilometres in Europe while the share of road transport was 45%...[20]

There is no doubt that passenger transport is an important part of Short Sea Shipping and helps increase cohesion. However, since the main objective of promoting Short Sea Shipping is to achieve a modal shift for goods transport, and since the potential of alleviating traffic congestion by shifting passengers from road to sea seems marginal in comparison with freight, this Communication concentrates on goods transport.

3. Environmental Benefits and Deficiencies

Maritime transport has a higher energy-efficiency than other modes of transport and is, in general, less harmful to the environment. Increased use of Short Sea Shipping would generally be in line with the Community transport and environmental policies...

4. Overcoming Obstacles to the Development of Short Sea Shipping

As was stated in the 1999 Communication and the subsequent 2003 Programme for the Promotion of Short Sea Shipping, a number of obstacles still hinder the mode from developing faster:

* It has not yet reached full integration in the intermodal door-to-door supply chain;
* It has not yet fully shed its past image of an old-fashioned industry;
* It involves complex administrative procedures;
* It requires high port efficiency.

---

15 Communication from the Commission on the Development of Short Sea Shipping in Europe – Prospects and Challenges, COM(95) 317 final, 5.7.1995.

16 Commission Staff Working Paper: Progress Report from the Commission Services following the Council Resolution on Short Sea Shipping of 11 March 1996, SEC(97) 877, 6.5.1997.

17 The Development of Short Sea Shipping in Europe: A Dynamic Alternative in a Sustainable Transport Chain – Second Two-yearly Progress Report, COM(1999) 317 final, 29.6.1999.

18 White Paper on European Transport Policy for 2010; Time to Decide, COM(2001) 370, 12.9.2001.

19 Communication from the Commission: Programme for the Promotion of Short Sea Shipping, COM(2003) 155 final, 7.4.2003.

20 EU Energy and Transport in Figures: Statistical Pocketbook 2003.

Developing Short Sea Shipping is primarily a task for the industries. Nevertheless, the authorities have a clear role to play in creating an appropriate framework and keeping the mode continuously high on the political agenda, as has been the case in the past years.

Logistics chains involving Short Sea Shipping should be managed and commercialised by one-stop shops, such as freight integrators.[21] These shops should offer customers a single contact point that takes responsibility for the whole intermodal supply chain door to door. This requires efforts from all parties but is a win-win situation.

4.1. 'Bottleneck Exercise'

The Commission, in co-operation with the Short Sea Shipping Focal Points[22] and industry, has been collecting a list of obstacles that hinder the development of Short Sea Shipping.[23] In 2003, two meetings of the Focal Points were dedicated to addressing those alleged bottlenecks one by one in the following categories:

* Image of Short Sea Shipping;
* Door-to-door Short Sea Shipping;
* Administration and documentation;
* Ports and port services;
* Country-specific issues.

A number of bottlenecks on the original list have been solved. ... Work on addressing the remaining 67 bottlenecks in a systematic manner will continue.

4.2. Customs Procedures for Short Sea Shipping

The Commission presented in 2002 a Guide to Customs Procedures for Short Sea Shipping.[24] The Guide has a two-fold purpose. First, it outlines the EU Customs rules that apply to Short Sea Shipping, including the opportunities that are available to use simplified Customs procedures. And, second, it gives a concise basis for identifying whether there could be concrete needs for modifications or further simplifications.

European-wide consultations on the Guide ended in April 2003 and the first analyses of the contributions indicated that concrete problems associated with the general EU Customs rules might be less numerous than was earlier thought. The main comments focused on the so-called 'Authorised Regular Shipping Service'[25] which is a service authorised by the Customs to carry Community goods between two Member States with minimum formalities. Indeed, for Community goods, this service can be compared to a road bridge between two or more points in the Customs territory of the Community where there are no Customs checks on either end of the bridge. The status of Community goods carried on this service does not need to be proven any more than is the case in road transport. For non-Community goods, this service can apply for simplified transit procedures, such as using the service provider's own manifests for Customs purposes.

To address questions surrounding this Authorised Regular Shipping Service, its practical application, and the relaxation of paperwork that it offers, the Commission presented in March 2004 a Working Document[26] explaining the modalities of the service and the procedures on how to become an Authorised Regular Shipping Service. The Document gives a direct response to the shipping industry by making the service more known and accessible to companies that could benefit from it.

---

21 Cf. http://europa.eu.int/comm/transport/logistics/index_en.htm.

22 For more details on the Short Sea Shipping Focal Points, see chapter 7.1 [of this communication].

23 See: http://europa.eu.int/comm/transport/maritime/sss/policy_bottlenecks_en.htm.

24 Commission Staff Working Document: Guide to Customs Procedures for Short Sea Shipping, SEC(2002) 632, 29.5.2002.

25 Cf. Commission Regulation (EC) No 75/98 of 12 January 1998, OJ L7. 13.1.1998, p. 3, as subsequently amended.

26 Commission Staff Working Document: Simplified Customs Procedures in Short Sea Shipping: 'Authorised Regular Shipping Service', SEC(2004) 333, 17.3.2004.

Some perceived problems in the contributions were of a purely practical nature and could often be simplified or solved by the introduction of electronic transfer of Customs and other administrative data (e-Customs).

As one of the first steps in e-Customs, some 3000 Customs offices in 22 countries have now implemented the New Computerised Transit System (NCTS) since mid-2003. Under the current system, the procedure relating to transport under the single administrative document (SAD) is replaced by electronic messages. Additional functionalities are planned to be introduced into the NCTS in the future.

The Commission presented in July 2003 a Communication on a simple and paperless environment for Customs and Trade.[27] The Communication suggests co-ordination between different authorities boarding the ship. This could ultimately lead to one-stop administrative shops (or 'single windows') for traders, who would then have to deal with just one administrative body instead of three or four at present. Accordingly, information relating to any given import consignment would have to be sent only once.

The Communication also suggests adjusting the Customs Code so that electronic declarations and messages become the rule and paper-based declarations the exception. To achieve this will, however, take some time because the necessary data flows will have to be organised and compatible IT systems set up.

A number of perceived problems that were indicated in the consultations related to national, regional or local applications of Community Customs rules. Some of these issues could be addressed under the initiatives to approximate national applications of Community Customs rules and improve co-operation between national Customs services, in particular through the action programme for Customs in the Community (Customs 2007).[28] Furthermore, two contact groups[29] of Customs offices work towards increasing practical co-operation and co-ordination between the Customs offices of major EU ports. These Groups examine practical operational issues, set standards, and aim to achieve an equivalent application of controls.

Based on the consultations and further developments in the Customs field, the Commission periodically updates the original Guide to Customs Procedures for Short Sea Shipping. The latest working version of the Guide is version No. 3, updated on 14 January 2004.

4.3. Port Services and Security

Short Sea Shipping needs efficient and short-sea friendly ports whether these are seaports, island ports or sea-river ports. It needs reasonable turnaround times, and transparent procedures and charges. Only with ports operating seamlessly in the intermodal chain, can Short Sea Shipping enhance its true role in Europe. And these pre-conditions are not always being met.

Consequently, the Commission made in 2001 a proposal on access to the port services market[30] in the European Union. This proposal aimed to increase the efficiency and lower the costs of certain port services: pilotage, towing, mooring, services to passengers and cargo handling.

However, the European Parliament voted against the proposed text after conciliation with the Council. Consequently, competition in the port services market continues to be less intense than it would have become with a specific Directive.

---

27 Communication from the Commission to the Council, the European Parliament and the European Economic and Social Committee: A simple and paperless environment for Customs and Trade, COM(2003) 452 final, 24.7.2003.

28 Decision No 253/2003/EC of the European Parliament and of the Council of 11 February 2003 adopting an action programme for customs in the Community (Customs 2007), OJ L36, 12.2.2003, p. 1.

29 RALFH dealing with major northern EU ports and ODYSSUD dealing with major southern EU ports.

30 Proposal for a Directive of the European Parliament and of the Council on market access to port services, COM(2001) 35 final, 13.2.2001, as amended by COM(2002) 101 final, 19.2.2002.

In the port security domain, Short Sea Shipping could benefit from the opportunity in the SOLAS (Safety of Life at Sea) Convention to conclude bilateral or multilateral agreements between the Member States on alternative security arrangements...

4.4. Loading Units

Harmonisation and standardisation of loading units can have a positive influence on Short Sea Shipping, for example, by enabling it to penetrate the all-land swap-body market...

5. Motorways of the Sea

The White Paper on European Transport Policy for 2010 strongly emphasised the concept of 'Motorways of the Sea'. These Motorways of the Sea should become part of the trans-European network (TEN-T) – just like land motorways and railways – and reduce road congestion and/or improve access to peripheral and island regions and States. In addition to reducing the number of lorries on the main roads, they could also in certain cases contribute to fostering the transport of passengers by sea since vessels can carry freight and passengers at the same time.

Motorways of the Sea should become an integral part of door-to-door logistics chains and offer efficient, regular, reliable and frequent services that can compete with road, for instance, in terms of transit time and price. The ports connected to the Motorways should have efficient hinterland connections, rapid administrative procedures and a high level of service that is targeted to making short-sea operations successful.

Although Short Sea Shipping would be the mode to operate on the Motorways of the Sea, its underlying concept is broader than that of Motorways of the Sea, because, apart from trans-national links between European Union Member States, Short Sea Shipping also includes connections with close third countries, domestic connections, and connections from mainland to islands.

In October 2003 the Commission proposed a revision of the Community Guidelines on the development of the TEN-T[31] including 29 priority projects to be implemented by 2020 at the latest. These priority projects would be declared to be of 'European interest' and receive priority funding from the relevant Community resources. Project No. 21 is the priority project on the development of Motorways of the Sea. Four Motorways of the Sea areas are proposed as part of that priority project...:

* Motorway of the Baltic Sea (linking the Baltic Sea Member States with Member States in Central and Western Europe, including the route through the North Sea/Baltic Sea canal);
* Motorway of the Sea of western Europe (leading from Portugal and Spain via the Atlantic Arc to the North Sea and the Irish Sea);
* Motorway of the Sea of south-east Europe (connecting the Adriatic Sea to the Ionian Sea and the Eastern Mediterranean, including Cyprus);
* Motorway of the Sea of south-west Europe (western Mediterranean, connecting Spain, France, Italy and including Malta and linking with the Motorway of the Sea of south-east Europe, including links to the Black Sea).

The European Parliament approved the Council's Common Position on the Commission's proposal in April 2004. The new article 12a on Motorways of the Sea would now allow Community aid for a series of measures in the framework of the trans-European network. The mechanism would enable Member States, with Community assistance, to support, inter alia, infrastructure, facilities and logistics management systems based on an appropriate tendering procedure.

---

31 Amended proposal for a Decision of the European Parliament and of the Council amending the amended proposal for a Decision of the European Parliament and of the Council amending Decision No 1692/96/EC on Community guidelines for the development of the trans-European transport network, COM(2003) 564 final, 1.10.2003.

Support for the development of the Motorways of the Sea should be based on the same criteria as under Marco Polo,[32] such as avoidance of distortions of competition and viability of the project on its own after the period of Community funding.[33]

To help this process, the Commission is developing guidelines that would set out the criteria and procedures for the funding of Motorways of the Sea projects under the rules of the trans-European transport network thereby facilitating the practical application of those rules. The guidelines are expected to be ready shortly after the new TEN-T Guidelines enter into force.

Shipping links with major characteristics of Motorways of the Sea already exist, ... the links across the English Channel and the strait of Kattegat (Denmark/Sweden) being most obvious examples. Nevertheless, highest quality standards and a considerable expansion of such links will be required to fulfil the ambitious target of the Commission White Paper on European Transport Policy for 2010, namely to have a significant part of transport growth absorbed by Short Sea Shipping and, in particular, by links on Motorways of the Sea.

6. Marco Polo

The programme 'Pilot Actions for Combined Transport' (PACT)[34] expired at the end of 2001. It was succeeded by a new programme, 'Marco Polo', in August 2003 ... This new programme is wider than its predecessor because it can subsidise actions in all sections of Short Sea Shipping, rail and inland waterways. Marco Polo has an ambitious goal to shift 12 billion tonne-kilometres a year from road to non-road modes. The budget of the new programme is EUR 100 million for the period 2003–2006.

The first call for proposals under Marco Polo was published in October 2003 with a budget of EUR 15 million. Under this call the Commission received 87 eligible proposals requesting subsidies totalling EUR 182.4 million.

Thirty-six per cent (36%) of the proposals related directly to Short Sea Shipping, while 34% were rail projects, 5% were inland waterway projects and 25% involved more than one non-road mode (e.g. Short Sea Shipping in combination with rail or inland waterways).

The short-sea proposals made in the selection round were generally of high quality and a substantial share of accepted projects will involve Short Sea Shipping.

7. Promotion Networks at Administrative and Practical Levels

Not everyone is, so far, aware of the modern benefits of door-to-door Short Sea Shipping. This is being tackled by general promotion at EU level[35] and two separate European networks of promotion each with their specific tasks: Short Sea Shipping Focal Points and Short Sea Promotion Centres.

7.1. Short Sea Shipping Focal Points

Short Sea Shipping Focal Points are highly-qualified civil servants in national administrations and responsible for the mode nationally within their public administrations. They work in co-ordination with the Commission and EU policy. On the initiative of the Commission, the Focal Points have networked at EU level to exchange experience, discuss ways to promote Short Sea Shipping, address bottlenecks that hinder the development of the mode,

---

32 Regulation (EC) No 1382/2003 of the European Parliament and of the Council of 22 July 2003 on the granting of Community financial assistance to improve the environmental performance of the freight transport system (Marco Polo Programme), OJ L196, 2. 8.2003, p. 1.

33 Other main conditions under Marco Polo are that the action would lead to an actual, substantial and measurable modal shift from road; have a realistic business plan (and, according to it, be viable after Community financing); the procedure for selecting third-party services would have to be transparent, objective and non-discriminatory; the action would involve the territory of at least two Member States or at least one Member State and one close third country; projects would have to be submitted by consortia of two or more undertakings established in at least two different Member States or at least one Member State and one close third country; and there would be an aggregated ceiling for Community and State aid which is compatible with the State aid arrangements laid down in the Treaty.

34 For more information, see http://europa.eu.int/comm/transport/marcopolo/pact/projects_en.htm.

35 See http://europa.eu.int/comm/transport/maritime/sss/index_en.htm.

and come up with new strategies to improve the attractiveness of the mode among transport users. On average they meet twice a year under the chairmanship of the Commission. The Maritime Industries Forum is represented as an observer in those meetings.

Almost all coastal Member States have nominated Focal Points, and so have the European Economic Area countries Norway and Iceland, and candidate countries Bulgaria, Romania and Turkey. Furthermore, Croatia has a Focal Point.

The Focal Points are the key actors in Member States' administrations to co-ordinate Short Sea Shipping policies within their administrations and with other administrations. They also ensure that Short Sea Shipping is kept high on the political agenda.

The Focal Points have been very active and have made a clear difference to the perception of Short Sea Shipping in national administrations. They also work to achieve co-operation between different administrations, between administrations and relevant industries, and between administrations and Short Sea Promotion Centres. They have been instrumental in solving a number of administrative bottlenecks to the benefit of Short Sea Shipping.

7.2.   Short Sea Promotion Centres and European Short Sea Network

Furthermore, 16 national Short Sea Shipping Promotion Centres[36] operate in Europe. These Promotion Centres work in line with the Commission policy but they demonstrate a wide variety of working methods to approach their national audiences. They are led by business interests that understand the benefits in having a neutral body that promotes the use of Short Sea Shipping.

These Centres help prospective Short Sea Shipping users with advice and information. Promotion work is done, inter alia, through the media of presentations for target audiences, bilateral meetings with targeted groups, responses to individual inquiries, mail-shots (fact sheets), press releases and exhibitions. Shippers and road-hauliers are being specifically targeted by this work to influence their mindset and work with Short Sea Shipping. Some Promotion Centres are also running specific initiatives, such as introducing young people to careers in the Short Sea/maritime logistics sector.

The establishment of further national Short Sea Promotion Centres is under consideration in a number of other European countries.

And since shipping is an international business with customers at both ends of a short-sea route, the national Promotion Centres are networked at European level. Their European Short Sea Network allows potential Short Sea Shipping users to benefit, not only from full geographic coverage but also from the collective expertise of individual Centres.

The European Short Sea Network has a mission to raise the profile of Short Sea Shipping in Europe. It aims at becoming the leading source of information on the mode. It gives added value to the work of individual Promotion Centres by providing a medium for them to exchange information and ideas, by giving guidance and support to new Centres and by ensuring on-going development of the Network's common web portal.

The European Short Sea Network offers a unique product which is available on the Internet (www.shortsea.info). This is a database of Short Sea Liner Services in Europe. The first phase of the database is already operational and is regularly extended and updated. In the second phase, enhanced possibilities will be added for extraction and exchange of data.

The financing sources of different Short Sea Promotion Centres demonstrate a wide range between public and private. For the Centres to reach their objectives, it is important for them to have, at least, medium-term financial security. Public support is a good way of ensuring the neutrality of the Centres and improving their credibility. Apart from this, wide industry participation is a prerequisite for the Centres.

The European Commission strongly supports these Promotion Centres and their Network and works to ensure their good functioning and give necessary policy guidance for their concrete activities.

---

36 Belgium, Denmark, Finland, France, Germany, Greece, Ireland, Italy, Lithuania, the Netherlands, Norway, Poland, Portugal, Spain, Sweden and the UK. For hyperlinks, see www.shortsea.info.

8. National Developments
   While preparing this Communication, the Commission requested input from the Short Sea Shipping Focal Points...

9. In Conclusion
   Whereas Short Sea Shipping was considered for many years to be a less performing mode, it has now proven its ability to reach levels of competitiveness normally attributed to road alone. Nevertheless, expected growth in European goods transport makes it necessary for Short Sea Shipping to expand even further so as to make its full contribution towards alleviating current and future transport problems in Europe.

   In spite of the clear positive message of this Communication, it should be remembered that the promotion of Short Sea Shipping is a long-term exercise and the impact of the ongoing work can be properly evaluated on a Europe-wide scale only over a longer time perspective. The Commission will continue to promote Short Sea Shipping and review its developments; to this end, it intends to present further Communications or progress reports when appropriate."

This is a very useful description of the EU's attitude towards short sea shipping but also the issues involved.

F. CURRENT EU PERSPECTIVE ON SHORT SEA SHIPPING

41.011 The Commission's current thinking on short sea shipping is as follows:

"The EU has a strategic interest in ensuring the continuous performance of Short sea shipping. As by 2050 short sea shipping has a strong role in reaching the EU transport goal of reducing 60% of greenhouse gas emission generated by transport and by 2030 the shift of 30% of road freight over 300 km to other modes.

A key challenge of the EU is to maintain the sector's dynamism and competitiveness whilst at the same time improving its environmental performance and energy efficiency.

Today, still a significant number of obstacles hampering the further harmonious development of the European shipping industry need to be addressed.

The main priority areas where the European Commission is taking action for enhancing the further development of Short Sea Shipping are threefold:

- Administrative simplification.
- Support industry in picking up new technologies for complying with new and stricter environmental legislation.
- Integration of short sea shipping in full logistics chains.

With a view to promoting Short Sea Shipping, Shortsea Promotion Centres (SPC) have been established in nearly all coastal EU Member States. The Commission encourages the coordination of the SPCs at European level, within a European Shortsea Network (ESN)."

CHAPTER 42

Security: ships and ports

A. INTRODUCTION

42.001 Security in the maritime sector is critical. There have been several security incidents involving ships and ports but there is a risk that there could be a catastrophic incident involving an enormous number of fatalities (e.g. an incident on a ferry or cruise liner or at a port) and/or severe damage (e.g. environmental damage due to an incident at a port facility). The issue relates equally to both ships and ports.

42.002 Ship security is an issue of considerable practical significance. An incident on board a ferry, cruise liner or even cargo vessel could have the most appalling consequences. Already, incidents involving some cruise liners and cargo vessels have been significant but the need for greater security continues unabated.

42.003 Port security is also a topic of enormous importance to any society because a lapse in security in ports can have very serious consequences (e.g. because of terrorist activities or the smuggling of armaments or narcotics). It is not surprising therefore that the European Union ("EU") has been concerned about security in ports.

42.004 The EU has defined the term "maritime security" as meaning the combination of preventive measures intended to protect shipping and port facilities against threats of intentional unlawful acts.[1]

42.005 Security is now a global issue. Among others, the International Maritime Organization (the "IMO") has become involved in the issue. For example, on 12 December 2002, the Diplomatic Conference of the IMO adopted amendments to the 1974 International Convention for the Safety of Life at Sea ("SOLAS" Convention) and an International Ship and Port Facility Security Code (the "ISPS" Code) to enhance the security of ships used in international trade and associated port facilities. The presence of several navies off the coast of Somalia demonstrates the international desire to combat security issues – and such efforts have been largely successful.

42.006 The European Parliament and the Council of Ministers believe that "[s]ecurity incidents resulting from terrorism are among the greatest threats to the ideals of democracy, freedom and peace, which are the very essence of the European Union"[2] and therefore "[p]eople, infrastructure and equipment in ports should be protected against security incidents and their devastating effects. Such protection would benefit transport users, the economy and society as a whole".[3] The Parliament and Council believe that the "security of [EU] shipping and of citizens using it and of the environment in the face of threats of

---

1 Reg. 725/2004, Art. 2(5). See also Commission, Report Assessing the Implementation of the Directive on Enhancing Port Security (COM (2009) 2) and Commission, Second Report Assessing the Implementation of the Directive on Enhancing Port Security (COM (2013) 792).

2 Dir. 2005/65, recital 1.

3 Dir. 2005/65, recital 2.

intentional unlawful acts such as acts of terrorism, acts of piracy or similar, should be ensured at all times".[4] The risk comes from persons and goods (especially hazardous goods).[5] While the focus is on international traffic, there is equally a threat from domestic or cabotage traffic[6] so *all* ports (and all traffic within ports) need to be secure.

42.007 If the EU shipping sector is to be secure then the EU's ports must be secure.[7] This need for increased security became clearer after the events of 11 September 2001 in the USA but also events since in various European States. It is not surprising therefore that the Commission presented various measures in May 2003[8] which were largely adopted as Regulation 725/2004[9] and there have been other measures adopted since.

42.008 While security remains very much within the sovereignty of Member States, the EU has been anxious to ensure a uniform minimum level of security and the EU believes there are some measures which require EU-wide action.[10] It is logical that the EU should have a role to play in regard to port security given the EU's role in regard to trade and the free movement of goods and persons.

B. REGULATION 725/2004 ON ENHANCING SHIP AND PORT FACILITY SECURITY

Introduction

42.009 On 31 March 2004, the Parliament and the Council adopted Regulation 725/2004 on enhancing ship and port facility security.[11] Regulation 725/2004 has been amended by: (a) Commission Decision 2009/83 of 23 January 2009 amending Regulation 725/2004 of the European Parliament and of the Council as far as the IMO Unique Company and Registered Owner Identification Number Scheme is concerned;[12] and (b) Regulation 219/2009 of the European Parliament and of the Council of 11 March 2009 adapting a number of instruments subject to the procedure referred to in Article 251 of the Treaty to Council Decision 1999/468 with regard to the regulatory procedure with

---

4 Reg. 725/2004, OJ L129/6, 29 April 2004 recital 2. Consolidated version is available at: http://eur-lex. europa.eu/legal-content/EN/TXT/?qid=1452274882126&uri=CELEX:02004R0725-20090420#E0001.

5 Reg. 725/2004, recital 3 states: "[i]n connection with the transport of goods containing especially dangerous substances, such as chemical and radioactive substances, the potential consequences of the threats posed by intentional unlawful acts for Union citizens and the environment are very serious".

6 Reg. 725/2004, recital 7 states: "[s]ecurity should be enhanced not only for ships used in international shipping and the port facilities which serve them, but also for ships operating domestic services within the Community and their port facilities, in particular passenger ships, on account of the number of human lives which such trade puts at risk".

7 Indeed, ports outside the EU must also be secure otherwise security threats could be transferred to the EU from non-secure non-EU ports (e.g. by way of dangerous goods entering EU ports).

8 COM(2003) 229 final.

9 OJ L129/6, 29 April 2004.

10 The seventeenth recital to Reg. 725/2004 provides: "[s]ince the objectives of this Regulation, namely the introduction and implementation of appropriate measures in the field of maritime transport policy, cannot be sufficiently achieved by the Member States and can therefore, by reason of the European scale of this Regulation, be better achieved at [EU] level, the [EU] may adopt measures in accordance with the principle of subsidiarity. ... In accordance with the principle of proportionality, ... this Regulation does not go beyond what is necessary in order to achieve those objectives."

11 OJ L129/6, 29 April 2004.

12 OJ L53/29, 31 January 2009, http://eur-lex.europa.eu/legal-content/EN/TXT/HTML/?uri=CELEX:32009 D0083&from=EN.

scrutiny– Adaptation to the regulatory procedure with scrutiny – Part Two.[13] Article 15 provides that the regulation entered into force on the twentieth day following its publication in the *Official Journal of the European Union*. It shall apply from 1 July 2004, apart from the provisions of Articles 3(2) and (3), and 9(4), which shall enter into force on and apply from the dates specified therein. The first annex contains amendments to the annex to the SOLAS Convention, 1974 (as amended). The second annex contains the International Code for the Security of Ships and of Port Facilities.

42.010 The legal basis for Regulation 725/2004 was the Treaty establishing the European Community ("TEC") generally and, in particular, Article 80(2) (now, Article 100(2) of the Treaty on the Functioning of the European Union ("TFEU")). The legislative history includes a proposal from the Commission, an opinion of the European Economic and Social Committee[14] and a consultation with the Committee of the Regions.

42.011 The fifth recital to Regulation 725/2004 recalls that without prejudice to the rules of the Member States in the field of national security and measures which might be taken on the basis of Title VI of the Treaty on European Union, the security objective contemplated by Regulation 725/2004 should be achieved by adopting appropriate measures in the field of maritime transport policy establishing joint standards for the interpretation, implementation and monitoring within the EU of the provisions adopted by the Diplomatic Conference of the IMO on 12 December 2002 and implementing powers should be conferred on the Commission to adopt detailed implementing provisions.

42.012 The tenth recital took an interesting but potentially dangerous approach by saying that permanently applying all the security rules provided for in this regulation to port facilities situated in ports which only occasionally serve international shipping might be disproportionate. The Member States should determine, on the basis of the security assessments which they are to conduct, which ports are concerned and which alternative measures provide an adequate level of protection.

42.013 The eleventh recital provides:

"Member States should vigorously monitor compliance with the security rules by ships intending to enter a Community port, whatever their origin. The Member State concerned should appoint a 'competent authority for maritime security' responsible for coordinating, implementing and monitoring the application of the security measures laid down in this Regulation as they apply to ships and port facilities. This authority should require each ship intending to enter the port to provide in advance information concerning its international ship security certificate and the levels of safety at which it operates and has previously operated, and any other practical information concerning security."

42.014 The thirteenth and fourteenth recitals give further background to the regulation:

"13. Security checks in the port may be carried out by the competent authorities for maritime security of the Member States, but also, as regards the international ship security certificate, by inspectors acting in the framework of port State control, as provided for in Council Directive 95/21/EC of 19 June 1995 concerning the enforcement, in respect of shipping using Community ports and sailing in the waters under the jurisdiction of the Member States, of international standards for ship safety, pollution prevention and shipboard living

---

13 OJ L109/87, 31 March 2009, http://eur-lex.europa.eu/legal-content/EN/TXT/HTML/?uri=CELEX:32009R0219&from=EN.
14 OJ C32, 5 February 2004, p. 21.

and working conditions (port State control).[15] Where different authorities are concerned, provision must therefore be made for them to complement each other.

14. In view of the number of parties involved in the implementation of security measures, each Member State should appoint a single competent authority responsible for coordinating and monitoring the application of shipping security measures at national level. Member States should put in place the necessary resources and draw up a national plan for the implementation of this Regulation in order to achieve the security objective described in recital 2, in particular by establishing a timetable for the early implementation of certain measures in accordance with the terms of Resolution 6 adopted by the Diplomatic Conference of the IMO on 12 December 2002. The effectiveness of the checks on the implementation of each national system should be the subject of inspections supervised by the Commission."

Objectives of Regulation 725/2004

42.015 Article 1(1) provides that the main objective of the regulation is to introduce and implement EU measures aimed at enhancing the security of ships used in international trade and domestic shipping and associated port facilities in the face of threats of intentional unlawful acts. Article 1(2) provides that the regulation is also intended to provide a basis for the harmonised interpretation and implementation and EU monitoring of the special measures to enhance maritime security adopted by the Diplomatic Conference of the IMO on 12 December 2002, which amended the SOLAS Convention and established the ISPS Code.

Concepts in Regulation 725/2004

42.016 Article 2 contains some definitions for the purposes of the regulation.

42.017 Article 2 defines "special measures to enhance maritime security of the SOLAS Convention" as meaning the amendments, as attached as Annex I to the regulation, inserting the new Chapter XI-2 into the annex to the SOLAS Convention of the IMO, in its up-to-date version. Article 2 defines the term "ISPS Code" as meaning the International Ship and Port Facility Security Code of the IMO, in its up-to-date version. "Part A of the ISPS Code" is defined as meaning the Preamble and the mandatory requirements forming Part A of the ISPS Code, as attached as Annex II to the regulation, concerning the provisions of Chapter XI-2 of the annex to the SOLAS Convention in its up-to-date version. "Part B of the ISPS Code' is defined as meaning the guidelines forming Part B of the ISPS Code, as attached as Annex III to the regulation, regarding the provisions of chapter XI-2 of the annex to the SOLAS Convention, as amended, and of Part A of the ISPS Code, in its up-to-date version.

42.018 The term "maritime security" means the combination of preventive measures intended to protect shipping and port facilities against threats of intentional unlawful acts.

42.019 The phrase "focal point for maritime security" means the body designated by each Member State to serve as a contact point for the Commission and other Member States and to facilitate, follow up and inform on the application of the maritime security measures laid down in the regulation.

---

15 Ed., OJ L157/1, 7 July 1995.

42.020 The term "competent authority for maritime security" means an authority designated by a Member State to co-ordinate, implement and monitor the application of the security measures laid down in the regulation in respect of ships and/or one or more port facilities. The competences of this authority may differ depending on the tasks assigned to it.

42.021 The phrase "International Shipping" means any maritime transport by ship from a port facility of a Member State to a port facility outside that Member State, while conversely "domestic shipping" means any transport service by ship in sea areas from a port facility of a Member State to the same port facility or another port facility within that Member State.

42.022 The term "scheduled service" means a series of sailings organised in such a way as to provide a service linking two or more port facilities: (a) either on the basis of a published timetable; (b) or with a regularity or frequency such as to constitute a recognisable systematic service.

42.023 The term "port facility" means a location where the ship/port interface takes place; this includes areas such as anchorages, waiting berths and approaches from seaward, as appropriate.

42.024 The phrase "ship/port interface" means the interactions that occur when a ship is directly and immediately affected by actions involving the movement of persons or goods or the provision of port services to or from the ship.

42.025 The term "intentional unlawful act" means a deliberate act, which, by its nature or context, could harm the vessels used for international or national maritime traffic, their passengers or their cargoes, or the port facilities connected therewith.

Joint measures and scope

42.026 Article 3(1) provides that in respect of international shipping, Member States must apply in full, by 1 July 2004, the special measures to enhance maritime security of the SOLAS Convention and Part A of the ISPS Code, in accordance with the conditions and with respect to the ships, companies and port facilities referred to therein.

42.027 Article 3(2) states that in respect of domestic shipping, Member States must apply, by 1 July 2005, the special measures to enhance maritime security of the SOLAS Convention and Part A of the ISPS Code to Class A passenger ships within the meaning of Article 4 of Council Directive 98/18 of 17 March 1998 on safety rules and standards for passenger ships[16] operating domestic services and to their companies, as defined in regulation IX-1 of the SOLAS Convention, and to the port facilities serving them.

42.028 Article 3(3) provides that Member States shall, after a mandatory security risk assessment, decide the extent to which they will apply, by 1 July 2007, the provisions of the regulation to different categories of ships operating domestic services other than those referred to in paragraph 2, their companies and the port facilities serving them. The overall level of security should not be compromised by such a decision. Member States must notify the Commission of such decisions when they are adopted, as well as of the periodic review, which must take place at intervals of no more than five years.

---

16 OJ L144/1, 15 May 1998.

42.029 Article 3(4) provides that when implementing the provisions required pursuant to paragraphs 1, 2 and 3, Member States must take fully into account the guidelines contained in Part B of the ISPS Code.

42.030 Member States must, under Article 3(5), conform to various paragraphs of Part B of the ISPS Code as if they were mandatory. Article 3(6) provides that notwithstanding the provisions of paragraph 15.4 of Part A of the ISPS Code, the periodic review of the port facility security assessments provided for in paragraph 1.16 of Part B of the ISPS Code must be carried out at the latest five years after the assessments were carried out or last reviewed.

42.031 Unsurprisingly, Article 3(7) provides that the regulation shall not apply to ships of war and troopships, cargo ships of less than 500 gt (gross tonnage), ships not propelled by mechanical means, wooden ships of primitive build, fishing vessels or vessels not engaged in commercial activities.

42.032 Under Article 3(8), notwithstanding the provisions of Articles 3(2) and (3), Member States must ensure, when ship security plans and port facility security plans are approved, that such plans contain appropriate provisions to ensure that the security of ships to which the regulation applies is not compromised by any ship or port interface or ship-to-ship activity with any ships not subject to this regulation.

Communication of information

42.033 Article 4(1) provides that each Member State must communicate to the IMO, the Commission and the other Member States the information required pursuant to Regulation 13 (Communication of information) of the special measures to enhance maritime security of the SOLAS Convention.

42.034 Each Member State must communicate to the Commission and the other Member States the contact details of the contact officials referred to in paragraph 4.16 of Part B of the ISPS Code and the information provided for in paragraph 4.41 of Part B of the ISPS Code when a ship is expelled from or refused entry to a Community port.[17]

42.035 Each Member State must draw up the list of port facilities concerned on the basis of the port facility security assessments carried out, and establish the scope of the measures taken to apply the provisions of paragraph 2 of regulation 2 (extent of application to port facilities which occasionally serve international voyages) of the special measures to enhance maritime security of the SOLAS Convention.[18]

42.036 Each Member State shall communicate the said list to the other Member States and to the Commission by 1 July 2004 at the latest. The Commission and any Member State concerned shall also be given sufficient details of the measures taken.

Alternative security agreements or equivalent security arrangements

42.037 Article 5(1) provides that for the purposes of the regulation, Regulation 11 (alternative security agreements) of the special measures to enhance maritime security of

---

17 Art. 4(2).
18 Art. 4(3).

the SOLAS Convention may also apply to scheduled intra-Community shipping operating on fixed routes and using associated port facilities.

42.038 Article 5(2) provides that to that end, Member States may conclude among themselves, each acting on its own behalf, the bilateral or multilateral agreements provided for in the said SOLAS regulation. Member States may, in particular, consider such agreements in order to promote intra-Community short sea shipping. The Member States concerned shall notify the agreements to the Commission and provide sufficient details of the measures to allow the Commission to consider whether the agreements compromise the level of security of other ships or port facilities not covered by the agreements. The details of the measures directly linked to national security, if any, may be omitted from the notification to the Commission. The Commission shall examine whether the agreements guarantee an adequate level of protection, in particular as regards the requirements of paragraph 2 of the abovementioned SOLAS regulation 11, and whether they conform with EU law and are in accordance with the proper functioning of the internal market. If the agreements do not meet these criteria, the Commission shall within four months adopt a decision in accordance with the procedure referred to in Article 11(3); in such cases, the Member States concerned shall revoke or adapt the agreements accordingly.

42.039 The periodic review of such agreements provided for in paragraph 4 of regulation 11 of the special measures to enhance maritime security must take place at intervals of no more than five years.[19]

42.040 Member States may adopt, for domestic shipping and the port facilities as referred to in Articles 3(2) and 3(3) of the regulation, equivalent security arrangements as provided for in regulation 12 (equivalent security arrangements) of the special measures to enhance maritime security of the SOLAS Convention, provided such security arrangements are at least as effective as those prescribed in Chapter XI-2 of the SOLAS Convention and the relevant mandatory provisions of the ISPS Code.[20]

42.041 The Member State concerned must communicate to the Commission sufficient details of such arrangements when they are adopted, and the outcome of periodic reviews thereof, at the latest five years after they were adopted or last reviewed.

42.042 The conditions of application of such arrangements must be subject to the Commission inspections provided for in Article 9(4), (5) and (6) of Regulation 725/2004 under the procedures defined therein.

Provision of security information prior to entry into a port of a Member State

42.043 Article 6(1) lays down rules on the provision of security information prior to entry into a port of a Member State. When a ship which is subject to the requirements of the special measures to enhance maritime security of the SOLAS Convention and of the ISPS Code or of Article 3 of the regulation announces its intention to enter a port of a Member State, the competent authority for maritime security of that Member State shall require that the information referred to in paragraph 2.1 of regulation 9 (Ships intending to enter a port of another Contracting Government) of the special measures to enhance

---

19 Reg. 725/2004, Art. 5(3).
20 Reg. 725/2004, Art. 5(4).

maritime security of the SOLAS Convention be provided.[21] The said authority must analyse, as far as necessary, the information provided and, where necessary, apply the procedure provided for in paragraph 2 of that SOLAS regulation.[22]

42.044 The information referred to in Article 6(1) must be provided: (a) at least 24 hours in advance; or (b) at the latest, at the time the ship leaves the previous port, if the voyage time is less than 24 hours; or (c) if the port of call is not known or if it is changed during the voyage, as soon as the port of call becomes known.

42.045 Under Article 6(3), a report must be kept of the procedure followed in respect of each ship subject to a security incident, as defined in paragraph 1.13 of regulation 1 (definitions) of the special measures to enhance maritime security of the SOLAS Convention.

Exemptions from the provision of security information prior to entry into a port

42.046 Member States may exempt scheduled services performed between port facilities located on their territory from the requirement laid down in Article 6 where the following conditions are met: (a) the company operating the scheduled services referred to above keeps and updates a list of the ships concerned and sends it to the competent authority for maritime security for the port concerned; (b) for each voyage performed, the information referred to in paragraph 2.1 of regulation 9 of the special measures to enhance maritime security of the SOLAS Convention is kept available for the competent authority for maritime security upon request.[23] The company must establish an internal system to ensure that, upon request 24 hours a day and without delay, the said information can be sent to the competent authority for maritime security.[24] When an international scheduled service is operated between two or more Member States, any of the Member States involved may request of the other Member States that an exemption be granted to that service, in accordance with the conditions laid down in Article 7(1).[25] Member States must check periodically that the conditions laid down in Article 7(1) and 7(2) are being met.[26] Where at least one of these conditions is no longer being met, Member States shall immediately withdraw the privilege of the exemption from the company concerned.[27] Member States must draw up a list of companies and ships granted exemption under Article 7, and must update that list. They must communicate the list and updates thereof to the Commission and any Member State concerned.[28] Notwithstanding the provisions of Article 7(1) and 7(2), a Member State may, on security grounds and on a case-by-case basis, request the provision of the information referred to in paragraph 2.1 of regulation 9 of the special measures to enhance maritime security of the SOLAS Convention prior to entry into a port.[29]

---

21 Reg. 725/2004, Art. 6(1).
22 Ibid.
23 Reg. 725/2004, Art. 7(1).
24 Ibid.
25 Reg. 725/2004, Art. 7(2).
26 Ibid.
27 Ibid.
28 Reg. 725/2004, Art. 7(4).
29 Reg. 725/2004, Art. 7(5).

Security checks in Member State ports

42.047 Certificate verification, as defined in paragraph 1.1 of regulation 9 (Control of ships in port) of the special measures to enhance maritime security of the SOLAS Convention, must be carried out in the port either by the competent authority for maritime security defined in Article 2(7) of the regulation or by the inspectors defined in Article 2(5) of Directive 95/21.[30] Where the officer conducting the certificate verification referred to in Article 8(1) has clear grounds for believing that the ship is not in compliance with the requirements of the special measures to enhance maritime security of the SOLAS Convention and of the ISPS Code, but does not belong to an authority which in that Member State is responsible for carrying out the measures provided for in paragraphs 1.2 and 1.3 of regulation 9 of the special measures to enhance maritime security of the SOLAS Convention, s/he shall immediately refer the matter to the said authority.[31]

Implementation and conformity checking

42.048 Member States must carry out the administrative and control tasks required pursuant to the provisions of the special measures to enhance maritime security of the SOLAS Convention and of the ISPS Code.[32] They must ensure that all necessary means are allocated and effectively provided for the implementation of the provisions of the regulation.[33] Member States must designate a focal point for maritime security by 1 July 2004.[34] Each Member State must adopt a national programme for the implementation of Regulation 725/2004.[35] Six months after the date of application of the relevant measures referred to in Article 3 of Regulation 725/2004, the Commission, in co-operation with the focal point referred to in Article 9(2), must start a series of inspections, including inspections of a suitable sample of port facilities and relevant companies, to monitor the application by Member States of Regulation 725/2004.[36] These inspections shall take account of the data supplied by the focal point referred to in Article 9(2), including monitoring reports.[37] The procedures for conducting such inspections must be adopted in accordance with the procedure referred to in Article 11(2).[38] The officials mandated by the Commission to conduct such inspections in accordance with Article 9(4) must exercise their powers upon production of an authorisation in writing issued by the Commission and specifying the subject-matter, the purpose of the inspection and the date on which it is to begin.[39] The Commission must in good time before inspections inform the Member States concerned by the inspections.[40] The Member State concerned must submit to such inspections and shall ensure that bodies or persons concerned also submit to those inspections.[41]

---

30 Reg. 725/2004, Art. 8(1).
31 Reg. 725/2004, Art. 8(2).
32 Reg. 725/2004, Art. 9(1).
33 Ibid.
34 Reg. 725/2004, Art. 9(2).
35 Reg. 725/2004, Art. 9(3).
36 Reg. 725/2004, Art. 9(4).
37 Reg. 725/2004, Art. 9(4).
38 Ibid.
39 Reg. 725/2004, Art. 9(5).
40 Ibid.
41 Ibid.

The Commission must communicate the inspection reports to the Member State concerned, which shall indicate sufficient details of the measures taken to remedy any shortcomings within three months of receipt of the report.[42] The report and the list of measures taken shall be communicated to the Committee referred to in Article 11(1).[43]

Integration of amendments to international instruments

42.049 The applicable international instruments referred to in Article 2, which are applied in accordance with Article 3(1), must be those which have entered into force, including the most recent amendments thereto, with the exception of the amendments excluded from the scope of the regulation resulting from the conformity checking procedure established by paragraph 5.[44] The Commission must decide on the integration of amendments to the international instruments referred to in Article 2 in respect of ships operating domestic services and the port facilities serving them to which the regulation applies, in so far as they constitute a technical update of the provisions of the SOLAS Convention and the ISPS Code.[45] Those measures, designed to amend non-essential elements of the regulation, must be adopted in accordance with the regulatory procedure with scrutiny referred to in Article 11(4); on imperative grounds of urgency, the Commission may have recourse to the urgency procedure referred to in Article 11(5).[46] The procedure for checking conformity established in paragraph 5 of Article 10 shall not apply in these cases.[47] The Commission may adopt provisions in order to define harmonised procedures for the application of the mandatory provisions of the ISPS Code, without broadening the scope of the regulation.[48] Those measures, designed to amend non-essential elements of this regulation by supplementing it, shall be adopted in accordance with the regulatory procedure with scrutiny referred to in Article 11(4).[49] On imperative grounds of urgency, the Commission may have recourse to the urgency procedure referred to in Article 11(5).[50] For the purposes of the regulation and with a view to reducing the risks of conflict between Community maritime legislation and international instruments, Member States and the Commission must co-operate, through co-ordination meetings and/or any other appropriate means, in order to define, as appropriate, a common position or approach in the competent international fora.[51] A procedure for checking conformity is hereby established in order to exclude from the scope of this regulation any amendment to an international instrument only if, on the basis of an evaluation by the Commission, there is a manifest risk that such an amendment will lower the standard of maritime security or be incompatible with EU legislation.[52] The procedure for checking conformity may be used solely to make amendments to the regulation in the fields expressly covered

---

42 Reg. 725/2004, Art. 9(6).
43 Ibid.
44 Reg. 725/2004, Art. 10(1).
45 Reg. 725/2004, Art. 10(2).
46 Ibid.
47 Ibid.
48 Reg. 725/2004, Art. 10(3).
49 Ibid.
50 Ibid.
51 Reg. 725/2004, Art. 10(4).
52 Reg. 725/2004, Art. 10(5).

by the procedure referred to in Article 11(2) and strictly within the framework of exercise of implementing powers conferred on the Commission.[53] In the circumstances referred to in Article 10(5), the procedure for checking conformity must be initiated by the Commission, which, where appropriate, may act at the request of a Member State.[54] The Commission must submit to the Committee set up in Article 11(1), without delay, after the adoption of an amendment to an international instrument, a proposal for measures with the aim of excluding the amendment in question from the regulation. The procedure for checking conformity, including, if applicable, the procedures set up in Article 5(6) of Decision 1999/468, must be completed at least one month before the expiration of the period established internationally for the tacit acceptance of the amendment concerned or the envisaged date for the entry into force of said amendment. If there is a risk (as referred to in the first subparagraph of Article 10(5)), Member States must refrain, during the course of the procedure for checking conformity, from taking any initiative intended to integrate the amendment in national legislation or to apply the amendment to the international instrument concerned.[55] All relevant amendments to international instruments that are integrated in EU maritime legislation, in accordance with Article 10(5) and Article 10(6), must be published, for information purposes, in the *Official Journal*.[56]

Committee procedure

42.050 The Commission is to be assisted by a Committee.[57] Where reference is made in the regulation to Article 11(2) then Articles 5 and 7 of Decision 1999/468 shall apply, having regard to the provisions of Article 8 of the latter.[58] The period laid down in Article 5(6) of Decision 1999/468 is set at one month.[59] Where reference is made to Article 11(3) then Articles 6 and 7 of Decision 1999/468 shall apply, having regard to the provisions of Article 8 of the latter.[60] The periods laid down in Article 6(b) and (c) respectively of Decision 1999/468 must be set at one month. Where reference is made to Article 11(4) then Article 5a(1) to (4) and Article 7 of Decision 1999/468 must apply, having regard to the provisions of Article 8 of the latter.[61] Where reference is made to Article 11(5) then Article 5a(1), (2), (4) and (6) and Article 7 of Decision 1999/468 must apply, having regard to the provisions of Article 8 of the latter.[62]

Confidentiality

42.051 Article 12 of Regulation 725/2004 addresses the issue of confidentiality. In applying Regulation 725/2004, the Commission must take, in accordance with the provisions of Commission Decision 2001/844 of 29 November 2001 amending its internal

---

53 Ibid.
54 Reg. 725/2004, Art. 10(6).
55 Reg. 725/2004, Art. 10(7).
56 Reg. 725/2004, Art. 10(8).
57 Reg. 725/2004, Art. 11(1).
58 Reg. 725/2004, Art. 11(2).
59 Ibid.
60 Ibid.
61 Reg. 725/2004, Art. 11(4).
62 Reg. 725/2004, Art. 11(5).

Rules of Procedure,[63] appropriate measures to protect information subject to the requirement of confidentiality to which it has access or which is communicated to it by Member States.

42.052 The Member States shall take equivalent measures in accordance with relevant national legislation.

42.053 Any personnel carrying out security inspections, or handling confidential information related to this regulation, must have an appropriate level of security vetting by the Member State of the nationality of the personnel concerned.

Dissemination of information

42.054 Article 13(1) provides that without prejudice to the public right of access to documents as laid down in Regulation 1049/2001 of the European Parliament and of the Council of 30 May 2001 regarding public access to European Parliament, Council and Commission documents,[64] the inspection reports and the answers of the Member States referred to in Articles 4(3), 5(2), 5(4) and 9(6) shall be secret and shall not be published.[65] They must only be available to the relevant authorities, which shall communicate them only to interested parties on a need-to-know basis, in accordance with applicable national rules for dissemination of sensitive information.[66] Member States must, as far as possible and in accordance with applicable national law, treat as confidential information arising from inspection reports and answers of Member States when it relates to other Member States.[67] Unless it is clear that the inspection reports and answers shall or shall not be disclosed, Member States or the Commission shall consult with the Member State concerned.[68]

Sanctions

42.055 Article 14 provides that Member States shall ensure that effective, proportionate and dissuasive sanctions for breaching the provisions of this regulation are introduced.

C. DIRECTIVE 2005/65 OF THE EUROPEAN PARLIAMENT AND OF THE COUNCIL ON ENHANCING PORT SECURITY

Introduction

42.056 Directive 2005/65 of the European Parliament and of the Council on enhancing port security was adopted on 26 October 2005.[69] It supplemented Regulation 725/2004 to

---

63 OJ L317/1, 3 December 2001.
64 OJ L145/43, 31 May 2001.
65 Reg. 725/2004, Art. 13(1).
66 Ibid.
67 Reg. 725/2004, Art. 13(2).
68 Reg. 725/2004, Art. 13(3).
69 OJ L310/28, 25 November 2005. See Bek, "Commentary on Directive 2005/65/EC on Enhancing Port Security" in Jessen and Werner (eds), EU Maritime Transport Law (2016), p. 1191.

enhance the security of ships and port infrastructure[70] and has been amended by Regulation 219/2009 of the European Parliament and of the Council of 11 March 2009.[71]

42.057 Directive 2005/65 was adopted to augment the earlier Regulation 725/2004 – as Recital 3 to the directive recorded:

"[t]he maritime security measures imposed by that Regulation constitute only part of the measures necessary to achieve an adequate level of security throughout maritime-linked transport chains. That Regulation is limited in scope to security measures on board vessels and the immediate ship/port interface."

And Recital 4 goes on to say that

"[i]n order to achieve the fullest protection possible for maritime and port industries, port security measures should be introduced, covering each port within the boundaries defined by the Member State concerned, and thereby ensuring that security measures taken pursuant to Regulation ... 725/2004 benefit from enhanced security in the areas of port activity. These measures should apply to all those ports in which one or more port facilities covered by Regulation ... 725/2004 are situated."

42.058 Some observations can be made in terms of some of the legal aspects of Directive 2005/65. The legal basis for Directive 2005/65 was the then Article 80(2) of the TEC which is now Article 100(2) of the TFEU. Recital 18 of the directive provides that it is a directive which applies only to certain Member States: "[s]ince this Directive concerns seaports, the obligations herein contained should not be applicable to Austria, the Czech Republic, Hungary, Luxembourg or Slovakia"; Article 21 states that the "Directive is addressed to the Member States which have ports as referred to in Article 2(2)" of the directive; and Article 2(2) provides that the

"measures laid down in this Directive shall apply to every port located in the territory of a Member State in which one or more port facilities covered by an approved port facility security plan pursuant to Regulation ... 725/2004 is or are situated. This Directive shall not apply to military installations in ports."

42.059 The fifth recital provides that the

"security objective of this Directive should be achieved by adopting appropriate measures without prejudice to the rules of the Member States in the field of national security and measures which might be taken on the basis of Title VI of the Treaty on European Union".

42.060 Member States should, according to the seventh recital,

"approve port security plans which incorporate the findings of the port security assessment. The effectiveness of security measures also requires the clear division of tasks between all parties involved as well as regular exercises. This clear division of tasks and the recording of exercise procedures in the format of the port security plan is considered to contribute strongly to the effectiveness of both preventive and remedial port security measures."

42.061 The eighth recital deals with roll-on roll-off vessels which are

"particularly vulnerable to security incidents, in particular if they carry passengers as well as cargo. Adequate measures should be taken on the basis of risk assessments which ensure that cars and goods vehicles destined for transport on roll-on roll-off vessels on domestic and international routes

---

70 OJ L129/6, 29 April 2004.
71 OJ L87/109, 31 March 2009.

do not cause a risk to the vessel, its passengers and crew or to the cargo. The measures should be taken in a way which impedes as little as possible the fluidity of the operations."

42.062 Member States should be able to establish port security committees entrusted with providing practical advice in the ports covered by the directive.[72]

42.063 Member States should ensure that responsibilities in port security are clearly recognised by all parties involved. Member States should monitor compliance with security rules and clearly establish a responsible authority for all their ports, approve all security assessments and plans for their ports, set and communicate as appropriate security levels and ensure that measures are well communicated, implemented and co-ordinated.[73]

42.064 Member States should approve assessments and plans and monitor their implementation in their ports. In order to keep disruption to ports and the administrative burden on inspection bodies to a minimum, the Commission's monitoring of the implementation of the directive should be conducted jointly with the inspections provided for in Article 9(4) of Regulation 725/2004.[74]

42.065 The twelfth recital provides that Member States should ensure that a focal point for port security takes up the role of contact point between the Commission and Member States. They should inform the Commission which ports are covered by the directive on the basis of the security assessments carried out.

42.066 The effective and standard implementation of measures under the EU's security policy raises important questions in relation to its funding. The funding of extra security measures should not generate distortions of competition. By 30 June 2006, the Commission should submit to the Parliament and the Council the findings of a study on the costs involved in measures taken under this directive, addressing in particular the way financing is shared between the public authorities, port authorities and operators.[75]

42.067 The fifteenth recital provide that the measures necessary for the implementation of Directive 2005/65 should be adopted in accordance with Council Decision 1999/468 of 28 June 1999 laying down the procedures for the exercise of implementing powers conferred on the Commission.[76]

42.068 The sixteenth recital provides that a procedure should be defined for the adaptation of the directive to take account of developments in international instruments and, in the light of experience, to adapt or complement the detailed provisions of the annexes to the directive, without broadening the scope of this directive.

42.069 The seventeenth recital recalls that the objectives of Directive 2065/65, namely the balanced introduction of appropriate measures in the field of maritime transport and port policy, cannot be sufficiently achieved by the Member States and can, therefore, by reason of the European scale of the directive, be better achieved at Community level: the Community may adopt measures in accordance with the principle of subsidiarity as set out in Article 5 of the Treaty. In accordance with the principle of proportionality, as set out in that article, this directive does not go beyond what is necessary in order to achieve those objectives.

---

72 Ninth recital.
73 Tenth recital.
74 Eleventh recital.
75 Dir. 2005/65, recital 13.
76 OJ L184/23, 17 July 1999.

Subject matter of Directive 2005/65

42.070 Article 1(1) provides that the main objective of Directive 2005/65 is to introduce EU measures to enhance port security in the face of threats of security incidents. The directive also ensures that security measures taken pursuant to Regulation 725/2004 benefit from enhanced port security. Article 1(2) provides that the measures referred to in Article 1(1) shall consist of: (a) common basic rules on port security measures; (b) an implementation mechanism for these rules; and (c) appropriate compliance monitoring mechanisms.

Scope of Directive 2005/65

42.071 Article 2(1) provides that the directive lays down security measures which must be observed in ports. Member States may apply the provisions of the directive to port-related areas. The measures laid down in the directive must apply to every port located in the territory of a Member State in which one or more port facilities covered by an approved port facility security plan pursuant to Regulation 725/2004 is or are situated.[77] This directive shall not apply to military installations in ports.[78] Member States must define for each port the boundaries of the port for the purposes of the directive, appropriately taking into account information resulting from the port security assessment.[79] Where the boundaries of a port facility within the meaning of Regulation 725/2004 have been defined by a Member State as effectively covering the port, the relevant provisions of Regulation 725/2004 shall take precedence over those of Directive 2005/65.[80]

Definitions

42.072 Article 3 sets out various definitions for the purpose of Directive 2005/65.

42.073 Article 3(1) of Directive 2005/65 provides that the term "port" means any specified area of land and water, with boundaries defined by the Member State in which the port is situated, containing works and equipment designed to facilitate commercial maritime transport operations.

42.074 Article 3(2) of Directive 2005/65 provides that the term "ship/port interface" means the interactions that occur when a ship is directly and immediately affected by actions involving the movement of persons or goods or the provision of port services to or from the ship.

42.075 Article 3(3) of Directive 2005/65 provides that the term "port facility" means a location where the ship/port interface takes place; this includes areas such as anchorages, waiting berths and approaches from seaward, as appropriate.

42.076 Article 3(4) of Directive 2005/65 provides that the "focal point for port security" means the body designated by each Member State to serve as contact point for the Commission and other Member States and to facilitate, follow up and provide information on the application of the port security measures laid down in the directive.

---

77 Dir. 2005/65, Art. 2(2).
78 Ibid.
79 Dir. 2005/65, Art. 2(3).
80 Dir. 2005/65, Art. 2(4).

42.077 The phrase "port security authority" means, according to Article 3(5) of Directive 2005/65, the authority responsible for security matters in a given port.

Co-ordination with measures taken in application of Regulation 725/2004

42.078 Article 4 provides that Member States must ensure that port security measures introduced by Directive 2005/65 are closely co-ordinated with measures taken pursuant to Regulation 725/2004.

Port security authority

42.079 Article 5(1) provides that Member States must designate a port security authority for each port covered by the directive and also a port security authority may be designated for more than one port.

42.080 Article 5(2) provides that the port security authority shall be responsible for the preparation and implementation of port security plans based on the findings of port security assessments.

42.081 Member States, by virtue of Article 5(3), may designate a "competent authority for maritime security" provided for under Regulation 725/2004 as port security authority.

Port security assessment

42.082 Article 6(1) provides that Member States must ensure that port security assessments are carried out for the ports covered by the directive. These assessments shall take due account of the specificities of different sections of a port and, where deemed applicable by the relevant authority of the Member State, of its adjacent areas if these have an impact on security in the port and shall take into account the assessments for port facilities within their boundaries as carried out pursuant to Regulation 725/2004.

42.083 Each port security assessment shall be carried out taking into account as a minimum the detailed requirements laid down in Annex I.[81] Port security assessments may be carried out by a recognised security organisation as referred to in Article 11.[82] Port security assessments must be approved by the Member State concerned.[83]

Port security plan

42.084 Article 7(1) provides that subject to the findings of port security assessments, Member States must ensure that port security plans are developed, maintained and updated. Port security plans must adequately address the specificities of different sections of a port and shall integrate the security plans for port facilities within their boundaries established pursuant to Regulation 725/2004.

---

81 Dir. 2005/65, Art. 6(2).
82 Dir. 2005/65, Art. 6(3).
83 Dir. 2005/65, Art. 6(4).

42.085 Article 7(2) provides that port security plans shall identify, for each of the different security levels referred to in Article 8: (a) the procedures to be followed; (b) the measures to be put in place; and (c) the actions to be undertaken.

42.086 Article 7(3) provides that each port security plan must take into account as a minimum the detailed requirements specified in Annex II. Where, and to the extent appropriate, the port security plan must, in particular, include security measures to be applied to passengers and vehicles set for embarkation on seagoing vessels which carry passengers and vehicles. In the case of international maritime transport services, the Member States concerned must co-operate in the security assessment.

42.087 Port security plans may be developed by a recognised security organisation as referred to in Article 11.[84] Port security plans shall be approved by the Member State concerned before implementation.[85] Member States must ensure that the implementation of port security plans is monitored.[86] The monitoring must be co-ordinated with other control activities carried out in the port.

42.088 Member States must ensure that adequate exercises are performed, taking into account the basic security training exercise requirements listed in Annex III.[87]

Security levels

42.089 Article 8(1) provides that Member States must introduce a system of security levels for ports or parts of ports. Article 8(2) provides that there shall be three security levels, as defined in Regulation 725/2004:

"– 'Security level 1' means the level for which minimum appropriate protective security measures shall be maintained at all times;
– 'Security level 2' means the level for which appropriate additional protective security measures shall be maintained for a period of time as a result of a heightened risk of a security incident;
– 'Security level 3' means the level for which further specific protective security measures shall be maintained for a limited period of time."

42.090 Member States must determine the security levels in use for each port or part of a port.[88] At each security level, a Member State may determine that different security measures are to be implemented in different parts of the port depending on the findings of the port security assessment.

42.091 Member States must communicate to the appropriate person or persons the security level in force for each port or part of a port as well as any changes thereto.[89]

Port security officer

42.092 Article 9(1) provides that a port security officer must be approved by the Member State concerned for each port. Each port must, where practicable, have a

---

84 Dir. 2005/65, Art. 7(4).
85 Dir. 2005/65, Art. 7(5).
86 Dir. 2005/65, Art. 7(6).
87 Dir. 2005/65, Art. 7(7).
88 Dir. 2005/65, Art. 8(3).
89 Dir. 2005/65, Art. 8(4).

different port security officer, but may, if appropriate, share a security officer. Port security officers must fulfil the role of point of contact for port security related issues.[90] Where the port security officer is not the same as the port facility(ies) security officer(s) under Regulation 725/2004, close co-operation between them must be ensured.[91]

Reviews

42.093 Article 10(1) provides that Member States must ensure that port security assessments and port security plans are reviewed as appropriate and they must be reviewed at least once every five years. Under Article 10(2), the scope of the review shall be that of Articles 6 or 7, as appropriate.

Recognised security organisations

42.094 Article 11 deals with recognised security organisations. It provides that Member States may appoint recognised security organisations for the purposes specified in this directive. Recognised security organisations shall fulfil the conditions set out in Annex IV.

Focal point for port security

42.095 Article 12 provides for a focal point for port security. Member States shall appoint for port security aspects a focal point. Member States may designate for port security aspects the focal point appointed under Regulation 725/2004. The focal point for port security shall communicate to the Commission the list of ports concerned by this directive and shall inform it of any changes to that list.

Implementation and conformity checking

42.096 Article 13 deals with implementation and conformity checking. Article 13(1) provides that Member States shall set up a system ensuring adequate and regular supervision of the port security plans and their implementation. Article 13(2) provides that the Commission shall, in co-operation with the focal points referred to in Article 12, monitor the implementation of the directive by Member States. Article 13(3) provides that the monitoring shall be conducted jointly with the inspections provided for in Article 9(4) of Regulation 725/2004.

Adaptations

42.097 Article 14 provides that the Commission may adapt Annexes I to IV without broadening the scope of this directive. Those measures, designed to amend non-essential elements of this directive, shall be adopted in accordance with the regulatory procedure with scrutiny referred to in Article 15(2). On imperative grounds of urgency, the Commission may have recourse to the urgency procedure referred to in Article 15(3).

---

90 Dir. 2005/65, Art. 9(2).
91 Dir. 2005/65, Art. 9(3).

Committee procedure

42.098 Article 15(1) provides that the Commission shall be assisted by the committee set up by Regulation 725/2004. Article 15(2) states that where reference is made to this paragraph, Article 5a(1) to (4) and Article 7 of Decision 1999/468 shall apply, having regard to the provisions of Article 8 thereof. Article 15(3) provides that where reference is made to this paragraph, Article 5a(1), (2), (4) and (6) and Article 7 of Decision 1999/468 shall apply, having regard to the provisions of Article 8.

Confidentiality and dissemination of information

42.099 Article 16(1) provides that in applying the directive, the Commission shall take, in accordance with Decision 2001/844,[92] appropriate measures to protect information subject to the requirement of confidentiality to which it has access or which is communicated to it by Member States. Member States must take equivalent measures in accordance with relevant national legislation. Article 16(2) provides that any personnel carrying out security inspections, or handling confidential information related to the directive, must have an appropriate level of security vetting by the Member State of which the person concerned is a national.

Penalties

42.100 Member States must ensure, by virtue of Article 17 of Directive 2005/65, that effective, proportionate and dissuasive penalties are introduced for infringements of the national provisions adopted pursuant to the directive.

Implementation

42.101 Article 18 dealt with the implementation of Directive 2005/65. Member States had to bring into force the laws, regulations and administrative provisions necessary to comply with the directive by 15 June 2007.[93]

Evaluation report

42.102 By 15 December 2008 and every five years since, the Commission has to submit an evaluation report to the Parliament and the Council based, among other things, on the information obtained pursuant to Article 13.[94] In the report, the Commission must analyse compliance with the directive by Member States and the effectiveness of the measures taken and, if necessary, it shall present proposals for additional measures.[95]

---

92 OJ L317, 3 December 2001, p. 1. Decision as last amended by Dec. 2005/94, Euratom (OJ L31, 4 February 2005, p. 66).
93 Dir. 2005/65, Art. 18(1).
94 Dir. 2005/65, Art. 19.
95 Dir. 2005/65, Art. 19.

Annexes

42.103 Annex I deals with port security assessment. Annex II deals with the all-important port security plan. Annex III sets out the basic security training exercise requirements. Annex IV enumerates the conditions to be fulfilled by a recognised security organisation.

D. COMMISSION REGULATION (EC) NO 324/2008 OF 9 APRIL 2008 LAYING DOWN REVISED PROCEDURES FOR CONDUCTING COMMISSION INSPECTIONS IN THE FIELD OF MARITIME SECURITY

Introduction

42.104 On 9 April 2008, the Commission adopted Regulation 324/2008 laying down Revised Procedures for Conducting Commission Inspections in the Field of Maritime Security.[96] The regulation was amended by Commission Implementing Regulation 2016/462 of 30 March 2016.[97] Article 19 provides that the regulation entered into force on the twentieth day following its publication in the *Official Journal* and it was published on 10 April 2008. The legal basis was the then TEC. Article 18 repealed Regulation 884/2005.[98]

42.105 Regulation 324/2008 references Regulation 725/2004 of the European Parliament and of the Council of 31 March 2004 on enhancing ship and port facility security[99] and in particular Article 9(4). It also references Directive 2005/65 of the European Parliament and of the Council of 26 October 2005 on enhancing port security[100] and in particular Article 13(2) and (3).

42.106 The background is evident from the recitals which provide:

"(1) In order to monitor the application by Member States of Regulation ... 725/2004 the Commission should conduct inspections starting six months after the entry into force of that Regulation. The organisation of inspections under the supervision of the Commission is necessary to verify the effectiveness of national quality control systems and maritime security measures, procedures and structures.

(2) In accordance with Article 13(3) of Directive 2005/65, ... the Commission should monitor the implementation by Member States of the said Directive jointly with the inspections provided for in Regulation ... 725/2004.

(3) The European Maritime Safety Agency ... should provide the Commission with technical assistance in the performance of the latter's inspection tasks in respect of ships, relevant companies and Recognised Security Organisations.

(4) The Commission should co-ordinate the schedule and preparation of its inspections with the Member States. The Commission's inspection teams should be able to call upon qualified national inspectors, where available.

(5) Commission inspections should be carried out according to a set procedure, including a standard methodology.

(6) Sensitive information relating to inspections should be treated as classified information.

---

96 OJ L98/5, 10 April 2008.

97 OJ L80/28, 31 March 2016.

98 Comm. Reg. 884/2005 of 10 June 2005 laying down procedures for conducting Commission inspections in the field of maritime security is now no longer in force and was repealed with effect from 29 April 2008. It was published at OJ L148/25, 11 June 2005.

99 OJ L129/6, 29 April 2004.

100 OJ L310/28, 25 November 2005.

(7) Commission Regulation ... 884/2005 of 10 June 2005 laying down procedures for conducting Commission inspections in the field of maritime security[101] should therefore be repealed.

(8) The measures provided for in this Regulation are in accordance with the opinion of the Committee instituted by Article 11(1) of Regulation ... 725/2004."

42.107 Chapter I sets out "Subject Matter and Definitions".

Subject matter of the regulation

42.108 Article 1 ("Subject matter") states that the regulation lays down procedures for conducting Commission inspections to monitor the application of Regulation 725/2004 at the level of each Member State and of individual port facilities and relevant companies. The regulation also lays down procedures for the monitoring by the Commission of the implementation of Directive 2005/65 jointly with the inspections at the level of Member States and port facilities in respect of ports as defined in Article 2(11) of the regulation. Importantly, but somewhat opaquely, Article 1 also provides that the inspections must be conducted in a transparent, effective, harmonised and consistent manner.

Definitions used in the regulation

42.109 Article 2 sets out various definitions for the purposes of the regulation.

42.110 The phrase "Commission inspection" means an examination by Commission inspectors of Member States' national maritime security quality control systems, measures, procedures and structures, to determine compliance with Regulation 725/2004 and implementation of Directive 2005/65. It may include inspections of ports, port facilities, ships, competent authorities for maritime security or companies, as defined in Annex I to Regulation 725/2004. It may also include inspections of recognised security organisations, as defined in Annex I to Regulation 725/2004 and in Annex IV to Directive 2005/65 relative to recognised security organisations.

42.111 The term "Commission inspector" means a person fulfilling the criteria set out in Article 7 employed by the Commission, or employed by the European Maritime Safety Agency ("EMSA"), or a national inspector, mandated by the Commission to participate in Commission inspections, listed by the Member States or by the European Free Trade Association States.

42.112 The phrase "national inspector" means a person employed by a Member State as a maritime security inspector, and qualified according to the requirements of that Member State.

42.113 The term "objective evidence" means quantitative or qualitative information, records or findings pertaining to security or to the existence and implementation of a requirement laid down in Regulation 725/2004 or Directive 2005/65, which are based on observation, measurement or test and which can be verified.

42.114 The word "observation" means a finding made during a Commission inspection and substantiated by objective evidence.

---

101 Ed., OJ L148/25, 11 June 2005.

42.115 The phrase "non-conformity" means an observed situation where objective evidence indicates the non-fulfilment of a requirement laid down in Regulation 725/2004 or Directive 2005/65 that requires corrective action.

42.116 The phrase "major non-conformity" means an identifiable deviation that poses a serious threat to maritime security that requires immediate corrective action and includes the lack of effective and systematic implementation of a requirement laid down in Regulation 725/2004 or Directive 2005/65.

42.117 The expression "focal point" means the body designated by each Member State to serve as a contact point for the Commission and other Member States and to facilitate, follow up and inform on the application of the maritime security measures laid down in Regulation 725/2004 and the port security measures laid down in Directive 2005/65.

42.118 The term "relevant company" means an entity that has to appoint a Company Security Officer, Ship Security Officer or Port Facility Security Officer, or is responsible for the implementation of a Ship Security Plan or Port Facility Security Plan, or has been appointed by a Member State as a Recognised Security Organisation.

42.119 The word "test" means a trial of maritime security measures, where intent to commit unlawful action is simulated for the purpose of testing efficiency in the implementation of existing security measures.

42.120 The term "port" means the area within the boundaries defined by Member States under Article 2(3) of Directive 2005/65 and notified to the Commission under Article 12 thereof.

42.121 The expression "provisional corrective measure" means a temporary measure or range of measures aimed at limiting to the maximum extent practicable the impact of a major non-conformity or a non-conformity identified during the conduct of an inspection before full correction can take place.

42.122 The phrase "classified information" means identified or identifiable information obtained during the conduct of inspection activities, disclosure of which may lead to a breach of security, classified in accordance with the provisions of Commission Decision (EU, Euratom) 2015/444[102] or in accordance with relevant national legislation of the Member States.

42.123 The expression "sensitive but non-classified information" means inspection related material or information obtained during the conduct of inspection activities, disclosure of which may lead to a breach of security and which can only be shared on a need-to-know basis.

42.124 The term "not confirmed" means a finding made during a Commission inspection which indicates non-fulfilment of Regulation 725/2004 or Directive 2005/65 but is not substantiated by objective evidence.

42.125 The word "Committee" means the Committee established by Article 11(1) of Regulation 725/2004.

42.126 The phrase "representative of a flag State" means a member of the competent authorities of the Member State whose flag the ship is flying or, if nominated by that Member State, a representative of a recognised security organisation.

---

102 I.e. Comm. Dec. 2015/444 of 13 March 2015 on the security rules for protecting EU classified information (OJ L72/53, 17 March 2015).

Structure of the regulation

42.127 Chapter II sets out the general requirements for inspections. Chapter III is entitled "Procedures for the Conduct of Commission Inspections". Chapter IV is entitled "General and Final Provisions".

Member States' duty to co-operate

42.128 Article 3 requires the co-operation of Member States in regard to inspections. Article 3(1) provides that without prejudice to Commission responsibilities, Member States must co-operate with the Commission in the accomplishment of its inspection tasks and this co-operation must be effective during the preparatory, monitoring and reporting phases. Article 3(2) goes on to provide that Member States must take all necessary steps to ensure that notification of an inspection: (a) is kept under strict measures of security to guarantee its non-disclosure in order not to compromise the inspection process; and (b) is communicated to relevant parties on a need-to-know basis.[103]

Exercise of Commission powers

42.129 Article 4 then deals with the exercise of Commission powers. Under Article 4(1), each Member State must ensure that Commission inspectors are able to exercise their authority to inspect the maritime security activities of any competent authority under Regulation 725/2004 or Directive 2005/65 and of any relevant company. Article 4(2) is then somewhat prescriptive and states that each Member State must ensure that, upon request, Commission inspectors have timely access to relevant security documentation necessary for the performance of the inspection duties, and in particular to: (a) the national programme for the implementation of Regulation 725/2004 referred to in Article 9(3) of that regulation; (b) the most recent updates of data supplied by the focal point and monitoring reports referred to in Article 9(4) of Regulation 725/2004; (c) the outcome of the Member State's monitoring of the implementation of port security plans; (d) relevant ship, port and port facility security assessments, and relevant ship, port and port facility security plans, records of training drills and exercises for ship, port and port facility while the Commission is conducting inspections; (e) notifications by the Member States of the decisions referred to in Article 3(3) of Regulation 725/2004 taken after the mandatory security risk assessment; and (f) any guideline, instruction or procedure, issued by the Member State for the implementation of Regulation 725/2004 and Directive 2005/65. By virtue of Article 4(3), wherever Commission inspectors encounter difficulties in the execution of their duties, the Member States concerned must "by any means within their legal powers"[104] assist the Commission to accomplish in full its task.

Participation of national inspectors in Commission inspections

42.130 Participation of national inspectors in Commission inspections is addressed by Article 5. Article 5(1) states that in agreement with the Commission, as far as practicable,

---

103 This is less than confidentiality. It is submitted that the test on "the need to know" should be an objective one.

104 This is a broad and onerous obligation on Member States.

Member States must make available national inspectors able to participate in Commission inspections, including the related preparatory and reporting phases. A national inspector may not, by virtue of Article 5(2), participate in Commission inspections in the Member State where he or she is employed.[105] Each Member State shall provide the Commission with a list of national inspectors on whom the Commission may call to participate in a Commission inspection. That list shall be updated, at least by the end of June each year.[106] Under Article 5(5), requests for national inspectors to participate in Commission inspections must be communicated in good time, normally at least two months[107] before the inspection is due to take place. The expenses arising from the participation of national inspectors in Commission inspections must, in compliance with EU rules, be met by the Commission.

Technical assistance from EMSA in Commission inspections

42.131 Article 6 states that in providing the Commission with technical assistance pursuant to Article 2(2)(b) of Regulation 1406/2002, the EMSA must make technical experts available to participate in Commission inspections, including the related preparatory and reporting phases.

Qualification criteria and training for Commission inspectors

42.132 Article 7(1) provides that the Commission inspectors must have appropriate qualifications, including sufficient theoretical and practical experience in maritime security. This shall normally include: (a) a good understanding of maritime security and how it is applied to the operations being examined; (b) a good working knowledge of security technologies and techniques; (c) a knowledge of inspection principles, procedures and techniques; (d) a working knowledge of the operations being examined; (e) an awareness of health, safety and security requirements for working in a maritime environment; and (f) a knowledge of the main legal requirements applicable in the field of maritime security. These requirements under Article 7(1) are quite onerous but presumably the inspector could have some of the knowledge available to him or her by experts but the inspector should have a minimum level of knowledge on each of the six subjects identified. Article 7(2) then goes on to provide that in order to qualify for Commission inspections, Commission inspectors must have successfully completed training to carry out such inspections. Commission inspectors shall periodically undergo training at least every five years in order to update their knowledge. In the case of national inspectors the training necessary for them to act as Commission inspectors must: (a) be accredited by the Commission; (b) be initial and recurrent; and (c) ensure a standard of performance adequate for the purposes of controlling whether security measures are implemented in accordance

---

105 Curiously, a person could be an inspector in a Member State of which he or she is a national but not employed (e.g. a Belgian employed by the Dutch agency may not inspect in the Netherlands but may do so in Belgium). It is submitted that this loophole ought to be closed.

106 Reg. 324/2008, Art. 5(3). Under Art. 5(4), the Commission shall communicate to the Committee instituted by Article 11(1) of Regulation (EC) No 725/2004 (hereinafter the Committee) the lists referred to in the first subparagraph of paragraph 3 of this article.

107 This seems to be a very long notice period.

with Regulation 725/2004[108] and Directive 2005/65.[109] Under Article 7(3), the Commission must ensure that Commission inspectors fulfil the criteria set out in Article 7(1) and (2). Finally, Article 7(4) provides that if during a previous inspection, the behaviour or performance of an inspector fails to meet the requirements of the regulation, that inspector shall not be nominated anymore for Commission inspection tasks.

Notice of inspections

42.133 Article 8 deals with notice of inspections. It is not as swift a process as one might imagine. Article 8(1) provides that the Commission must give at least six weeks' notice of an inspection to the focal point of the Member State in whose territory it is to be conducted. The Commission may communicate to the focal point, in parallel to the notice of the inspection, a pre-inspection questionnaire for completion by the competent authority, along with a request for any relevant documentation. The completed questionnaire and any requested documentation shall be submitted to the Commission at least two weeks before the inspection is scheduled to begin. The notice period may be reduced to not less than two weeks provided that the Commission acts in response to an exceptional event which may have significant impact on the overall level of maritime security in the EU and that the Commission consulted the focal point concerned prior to giving the notice. In that case the second subparagraph shall not apply. The focal point shall be notified in advance of the intended scope of a Commission inspection.[110] Where a port facility is to be inspected, the focal point shall be informed in the notice whether: (a) the inspection is to include ships at that port facility, or elsewhere in the port, during the inspection; and (b) the inspection will include monitoring of the port under Article 13(2) of Directive 2005/65 – for the purposes of point (b) "monitoring" means verifying whether or not the provisions of Directive 2005/65 have been implemented by Member States and by the ports in their territory that have been notified to the Commission under Article 12 of Directive 2005/65. In particular, monitoring means verifying that all provisions of Directive 2005/65 have been taken into account in the conduct of the port security assessments and the establishment of the port security plans and that the measures established thereunder are consistent with the provisions adopted under Regulation 725/2004 for the port facilities located in the ports concerned. Under Article 8(3), the focal point shall: (a) inform the relevant competent authorities in the Member State of the inspection; and (b) notify the Commission of those relevant competent authorities. The focal point must, by virtue of Article 8(4), advise the Commission at least 24 hours in advance of the inspection, of the name of the flag State and the IMO number of ships expected to be at a port facility or port notified under the second subparagraph of paragraph 2 during the inspection. Where the flag State is a Member State, the Commission shall give notice as soon as possible to the focal point of that Member State that the ship may be inspected when at the port facility.[111] If an inspection is to cover a ship flying the flag of a Member State other than that of the authority being inspected, the Commission shall inform the

---

108 OJ L191/59, 22 July 2005.
109 OJ L310/28, 25 November 2005.
110 Art. 8(2).
111 Art. 8(5).

focal point of the flag State so that the necessary practical arrangements can be made for conducting the inspection on board that ship.[112]

Preparation of inspections

42.134 Article 9 deals with the preparation of inspections. It is quite a short provision. Article 9(1) provides that Commission inspectors must undertake preparatory activities in order to ensure efficiency, accuracy and consistency of inspections. Under Article 9(2), the Commission must provide the focal point with the names of the Commission inspectors mandated to conduct the inspection, and other details as appropriate. Those names must include the name of the team leader for the inspection, who shall be a Commission inspector employed by the Commission. Article 9(3) provides that for each inspection, the focal point must ensure that a co-ordinator is designated to make the practical arrangements associated with the inspection activity to be undertaken. During the inspection, the team leader must be the primary contact for the co-ordinator.

The actual conduct of inspections

42.135 Article 10 then considers the actual conduct of inspections. Given the critical importance of the rules on the conduct of inspections, it is useful to set out the rules in full:

"1. A standard methodology shall be used to monitor the application by Member States of the maritime security requirements laid down in Regulation (EC) No 725/2004 and in Directive 2005/65/EC.

2. Commission inspectors, when carrying out inspection activities, shall be accompanied at all times by a representative of the relevant competent authority. That representative shall not prejudice the efficiency or effectiveness of the inspection activities.

The inspections shall be carried out in a way which impedes as little as possible the fluidity of the commercial operations. In order to achieve this, whenever appropriate and with the prior agreement of the flag State and of the master of the ship, an inspection of a ship that has commenced in port may continue after the ship has left port.

If a ship subject to an inspection is serving international scheduled services between two or more Member States, the inspection may also relate to the operations of embarkation and disembarkation applied to passengers and vehicles at each end of the voyage. In such a case, the Commission shall notify the Member State's focal point of the port of arrival in accordance with Article 8(1).

---

112 Ibid. Some of the other details of the regulation are set out in Art. 8(6)–(9): "6. Where the inspection of a port facility in a Member State is to include a ship of that Member State as flag State, the focal point shall liaise with the Commission to confirm whether or not the ship will be at the port facility during the inspection. 7. Where a ship previously identified to be inspected will not be berthed in the port during the inspection of the port facility, the Commission and the coordinator appointed under Article 9(3) shall agree an alternative ship to be inspected. This ship may be located at another port facility within the port. Paragraphs 5 and 8 of Article 8 shall still apply in these cases. 8. Commission inspections shall be carried out under the auspices of the Member State of the port facility exercising control and compliance measures under Regulation 9 of the special measures to enhance maritime security of the 1974 International Convention for the Safety of Life at Sea as amended (SOLAS Convention) when either: (a) the flag State of the ship is not a Member State; or (b) the ship was not included in the information provided pursuant to paragraph 4 of this Article. 9. When the Commission attends a national inspection or verification of a ship at a location outside the European Union, the Commission shall make the necessary arrangements with the focal point in order to follow inspections or verifications with the representative of the flag."

3. Where a ship at a port facility is to be inspected and the flag State of the ship is not the Member State of the port facility, the Member State of the port facility shall ensure that the Commission inspectors are accompanied by an officer of an authority referred to in Article 8(2) of Regulation (EC) No 725/2004 during the inspection of the ship.

4. Commission inspectors shall carry an identity card authorising them to carry out inspections on behalf of the Commission. The Member States shall ensure that Commission inspectors are able to obtain access to all areas required for inspection purposes.

5. A test shall only be performed after notification to and agreement with the focal point on its scope and purpose. The focal point shall undertake any necessary coordination with the competent authorities concerned.

6. Without prejudice to Article 11, the Commission inspectors shall, wherever appropriate and practicable, deliver an informal oral summary of their observations on the spot.

   The relevant focal point shall be informed promptly of any major non-conformity with Regulation (EC) No 725/2004 or Directive 2005/65/EC identified by a Commission inspection, prior to completion of an inspection report in accordance with Article 11 of this Regulation.

   However, in cases where a Commission inspector carrying out the inspection of a ship finds a major non-conformity requiring action under Article 16, the Team Leader shall inform immediately in writing the relevant focal points.

7. Commission inspectors shall conduct inspections in an efficient and effective manner, with due regard to safety and security."

Inspection report

42.136 Article 11 sets out the detail on inspection reports:

"1. Within six weeks of completion of an inspection,[113] an inspection report shall be communicated by the Commission to the Member State. This inspection report may contain as appropriate the outcomes of the monitoring of the port undertaken in respect of Article 8(2)(b).

2. Where a ship has been inspected during the inspection of a port facility, the relevant parts of the inspection report shall also be sent to the Member State that is the flag State, if different from the Member State in which the inspection took place.

3. The Member State shall inform the inspected entities of the relevant observations of the inspection. However, the inspection report itself shall not be sent to the inspected entities.

4. When assessing the implementation of Regulation ... 725/2004 and Directive 2005/65 ... in accordance with this Regulation, the findings shall be classified in one of the following categories: (a) in conformity; (b) in conformity, but improvement desirable; (c) non-conformity; (d) major non-conformity; and (e) not confirmed.

5. The report shall detail the findings of the inspection identified as 'major non-conformity', 'non-conformity', 'in conformity, but improvement desirable' and 'not confirmed' in the implementation of Regulation ... 725/2004 or Directive 2005/65 ... in accordance with the present Regulation.

The report may contain recommendations for corrective action."

Response from the Member State

42.137 Article 12(1) provides that within three months of the date of dispatch of an inspection report, the Member State must submit to the Commission in writing a response to the report which: (a) addresses the observations and recommendations; and (b) provides an action plan, specifying actions and deadlines, to remedy any identified deficiencies.

---

113 Ed., this is not as rapid as one might have imagined.

Article 12(2) provides that where the inspection report does not identify any non-conformity or major non-conformity with Regulation 725/2004 or Directive 2005/65, no response shall be required. Under Article 12(3), when a Member State proposes immediate corrective measures to address a major non-conformity found, it shall promptly notify the Commission about them before the Commission issues its inspection report. In such case, the report shall quote the corrective actions taken by the Member State. If only provisional measures are taken, the Member State shall promptly notify the Commission and shall also inform about the deadline for implementation of the complete and final corrective actions.

Action by the Commission

42.138 Article 13 enumerates the actions which the Commission may take. Under Article 13(1), the Commission may take any of the following steps in the event of non-conformity or major non-conformity with Regulation 725/2004 or Directive 2005/65 and following receipt of the response of the Member State: (a) submit comments to the Member State or request further explanation to clarify all or part of the response; (b) conduct a follow-up inspection or monitoring to check the implementation of corrective actions, the minimum notice for such follow-up being two weeks; (c) initiate an infringement procedure in respect of the Member State concerned. Where a follow-up inspection of a ship is to be conducted, the Member State that is the flag State shall, where possible, inform the Commission of the ship's future ports of call, so the Commission can decide where and when to carry out the follow-up inspection.[114]

Confidentiality of information

42.139 Article 14 deals with the confidentiality of information. Confidentiality of information is critical in security matters. So Article 14 provides that in accordance with "existing rules applicable",[115] when conducting inspections in the field of maritime security, the Commission shall take the appropriate measures to protect classified information to which it has access or which is communicated to it by Member States. Member States shall take equivalent measures in accordance with their relevant national legislations. Sensitive but non-classified information may be exchanged between Member States and the Commission, provided that they protect that information in accordance with the requirements applicable to guarantee its confidentiality.

Commission's inspection programme

42.140 Article 15 deals with the Commission's inspection programme. Article 15(1) provides that the Commission shall seek advice from the Committee on the priorities for the implementation of its inspection programme. Under Article 15(2), the Commission must regularly inform the Committee about the implementation of the inspection programme and the results of the inspections. The Commission must share good practices

---

114 Art. 13(2).
115 This is a somewhat ambiguous term.

observed during the inspections with the Member States. Inspection reports must normally be made available to the Committee: (a) as soon as the Member State's response under Article 12(1) has been received; and (b) when the file is closed.

Informing Member States of major non-conformity

42.141 Article 16 deals with informing Member States of major non-conformity. If an inspection discloses a major non-conformity with Regulation 725/2004 or Directive 2005/65 which is deemed to have a significant impact on the overall level of maritime security in the EU and that cannot be immediately addressed at least by corrective measures of a provisional nature, the Commission shall inform the other Member States after having notified that major non-conformity to the Member State concerned. Once a major non-conformity notified to the other Member States under Article 16 has been corrected to the satisfaction of the Commission, the Commission shall immediately inform the other Member States.

Review

42.142 Under Article 17, the Commission is obliged to review regularly its system of inspections and in particular the effectiveness of that system. One could envisage that such a review would be undertaken on an urgent basis after any incident.

CHAPTER 43

Ports: generally and the Port Services Regulation 2017/352

A. INTRODUCTION

43.001 For many years, European Union ("EU") law concentrated on ships and shipping services rather than ports. It has redressed the balance in recent years with developments in such areas as the law relating to State aid, electricity, the environment and so on as they relate to ports. The chapter provides a backup for other chapters which explore issues more specifically.

43.002 The EU's Transport Ministers in their 7 May 2014 Athens Declaration entitled *Mid-Term Review of the EC's Maritime Transport Policy until 2018 and Outlook to 2020*[1] stated:

> "BEARING in mind the importance of promoting the competitiveness of European seaports, the interconnection with hinterlands and multimodal transport involving shipping;
>
> RECOGNISING that the development of the TEN-T [Trans-European Network – Transport] network under the new guidelines regime using the Connecting Europe Facility funding will create opportunities for increasing the competitiveness and innovation of European seaports and the further development of sea-links such as the Motorways of the Sea;
>
> STRESSING that maritime transport is crucial for connecting peripheral and insular geographical areas to the rest of Europe."

43.003 There are various aspects to EU shipping law as it relates to ports. Some of those aspects are addressed in other chapters. It is not possible to address in this book every aspect of EU ports law which deserves its own book.

43.004 Ports are an extremely important part of the EU infrastructural regime. The European Commission has articulated the following as an expression of its views on the topic:

> "Europe's ports are vital gateways, linking its transport corridors to the rest of the world. 74% of goods entering or leaving Europe go by sea, and Europe boasts some of the finest port facilities in the world. Ports play an equally important role to support the exchange of goods within the internal market and in linking peripheral and island areas with the mainland of Europe. Ports are not only great for moving goods around, they also constitute energy hubs for conventional and renewable energies. 400 million passengers embark and disembark in European ports every year. Ports generate employment; 1.5 million workers are employed in European ports, with the same amount again employed indirectly across the 22 EU maritime Member States.

---

1 https://ec.europa.eu/transport/sites/transport/files/modes/maritime/consultations/doc/2015-mts-review/council-conclusions-on-mid-term-review-of-eu-maritime-policy.pdf.

The EU needs good performing ports across all its maritime regions. Bottlenecks in ports and their hinterland due to inadequate infrastructure or services can result in extra congestion, extra emission and extra costs for shippers, transport operators, consumers and society as a whole.

The new guidelines for the development of the trans-European transport network (TEN-T) have identified along Europe's coastline that will become part of a unified network boosting growth and competitiveness in Europe's Single Market.

The Commission adopted on 23 May 2013 an initiative aimed at improving port operations and onward transport connections at the 329 key seaports which belongs to the trans-European transport network. This initiative is progressively implemented through a set of legislative measures and non-legislative measures as follow:

Regulation (EU) 2017/352 of the European Parliament and the Council of Ministers establishing a framework for the provision of port services and common rules on the financial transparency of ports. The aim is to level the playing field in the sector, protect port operators against uncertainties and create a climate more conducive to efficient public and private investments. The Regulation defines the conditions under which the freedom to provide port services applies, for instance the type of minimum requirements that can be imposed for safety or environmental purposes, the circumstances in which the number of operators can be limited and the procedure to select the operators in such cases. It introduces common rules on the transparency of public funding and of charging for the use of port infrastructure and port services, notably by making sure that the port users are consulted. It introduces in each Member State a new mechanism to handle complaints and disputes between ports stakeholders. Finally it requires all port services providers to ensure adequate training to employees.

Application and modernization of the State aid rules, in the context of the competition policy. The decisions relevant to ports and forming the decision case practice are available here. In May 2016 the Commission published the Notice on the notion of State Aid, which gives guidance on when public investments do not involve State aid. An Analytical grid for ports infrastructure was published on 2 December 2016 to provide further guidance on the rules and case practice applicable in the port sector. The Commission has also adopted on 17 May 2017 an updated version of the General Block Exemption Regulation. The new regulation gives more flexibility to Member States to decide public funding of certain port investments without having to seek a prior Commission's approval.

Promotion and support of the European social dialogue between port workers and their employees and of training. The Commission helps the EU Social Dialogue Committee in the Port Sector to work on health & safety, training and qualifications, gender issues and promotion of female employment and attractiveness to young workers. Representatives of port employees and port employers work together for instance to produce common guidelines for training as well as national health and safety requirements. Another project of the Committee, financed by the Commission, is identifying the key challenges that EU ports are facing and how the industry is adapting to change and preparing for the future.

Support to better planning, financing and funding of port infrastructure and their connexions in the trans-European network. The Commission has integrated ports in the corridor work plans foreseen by Article 46 of the guidelines for the development of the trans-European transport network (Regulation 1315/2013) and provides targeted grants and other forms of financial supports to port infrastructure projects by using the Connecting Europe Facility. More than € 1 billion have already been awarded since 2014 to support rail or inland waterways connecting ports with the hinterland, basic port infrastructure, innovation and green port projects.

Initiatives to simplify procedures in ports. Improving the digital information flows and reducing administrative burden is vital to ensure efficient ship port calls and throughput of cargo. To contribute to this goal the Commission intends to establish a European Maritime Single Window environment with technical and legal frameworks for the submission and re-use of regulatory reporting information, including the eManifest information for customs. This initiative is currently under assessment and the proposal for the way forward is expected to follow in summer 2018.

Initiatives to raise the environmental of ports by promoting the exchange of good practices. As part of its research and innovation agenda the Commission launched in 2016 the 'Port of the

Future' call as part of the Horizon 2020 programme to encourage innovation in ports and the links with port cities."[2]

43.005 This chapter concentrates on Regulation 2017/352 of the European Parliament and of the Council of 15 February 2017 establishing a framework for the provision of port services and common rules on the financial transparency of ports.[3] Other aspects of ports activities are examined throughout this book.

B. THE EU'S PORT SERVICES REGULATION 2017/352

Introduction

43.006 Ports have long been controversial in EU law including, in particular, EU competition law. There have been published cases relating to ports as diverse as Genoa, Holyhead, Rødby, Roscoff and Rotterdam.[4] There have also been other cases relating to other ports on which there have been private disputes which have not yet entered the public domain. While ports can be controversial, they are also indispensable to the EU's economy – particularly, the EU's internal market. They therefore need to be integrated, efficient and attracting investment[5] because they provide jobs and contribute to competitiveness.[6]

43.007 The EU has had great difficulty is agreeing legislation to deal with ports. Proposals to liberalise ports were challenged by various interests (including some ports and many dock workers). The Commission published a communication on 23 May 2013 entitled "Ports: An Engine for Growth". The Commission believed that there was a need to liberalise or, at least, regulate aspects of the ways in which ports operate in the EU. This is because the EU views ports not only in the context of the maritime sector but also as serving a greater function in the wider economy[7] so it is not surprising that the Commission and the other EU institutions wanted to regulate ports in some ways. Eventually, the EU's attempts to regulate ports found expression in Regulation 2017/352 of the European Parliament and of the Council of 15 February 2017 establishing a framework for the provision of port services and common rules on the financial transparency of ports.[8]

---

2 https://ec.europa.eu/transport/modes/maritime/ports/ports_en.

3 OJ L57/1, 3 March 2017, http://eur-lex.europa.eu/legal-content/EN/TXT/HTML/?uri=CELEX:32017R035
2&from=EN.

4 See chap. 13.

5 The first recital to the regulation provides that "[t]he full integration of ports in seamless transport and logistics chains is needed to contribute to growth and a more efficient use and functioning of the trans-European transport network and the internal market. This requires modern port services that contribute to the efficient use of ports and a climate favourable to investments to develop ports in line with current and future transport and logistics requirements."

6 The second recital to the regulation provides that "[p]orts contribute to the long-term competitiveness of European industries in world markets while adding value and jobs in all Union coastal regions".

7 The third recital to the regulation provides that "[in] its Communication of 3 October of 2012 entitled 'Single Market Act II – Together for new growth', the Commission recalled that the attractiveness of maritime transport is dependent on the availability, efficiency and reliability of port services and the necessity of addressing questions regarding the transparency of public funding and port charges, as well as administrative simplification efforts in ports, and of reviewing restrictions on the provision of services at ports".

8 OJ L57/1, 3 March 2017.

Adoption of Regulation 2017/352

43.008 On 15 February 2017, after many years of dispute and debate, the final act was signed to bring to life the controversial "Regulation of the European Parliament and of the Council establishing a framework on market access to port services and financial transparency of ports". It has been a controversial measure and was part of a series of controversial proposals stretching over a number of years (including a directive which was eventually abandoned due to opposition). It came into force on 24 March 2017 and comes into effect on 24 March 2019.

Essence of Regulation 2017/352

43.009 Regulation 2017/352 is aimed at establishing: (a) a framework for the provision of port services; as well as (b) common rules on financial transparency and on port service and port infrastructure charges applied by managing bodies and providers of port services.[9] This regulation is the third part of the so-called EU Ports Package so it is sometimes called the "Ports Package III".

43.010 Chapter I deals with the subject matter and scope of the regulation as well as definitions in it. Chapter II deals with the provision of port services. Chapter III is focused on financial transparency and autonomy. Chapter IV deals with general and final provisions.

43.011 Some of the basic principles of the regulation are reflected in some of the recitals. For example, the eleventh recital states that in

> "accordance with the general principles set out in the Treaties, providers of port services should be free to provide their services in maritime ports covered by this Regulation. However, it should be possible to impose certain conditions on the exercise of that freedom."

It is useful to recall the views of the EU when Regulation 2017/352 was adopted:

> "A new set of rules to increase the financial transparency of ports and create clear and fair conditions for access to the port services market throughout Europe was formally adopted by the Council on 23 January 2017.
>
> The regulation will make it easier for new providers of certain port services to enter the market. It will create a more level playing field and reduce legal uncertainties for ports, port service providers and investors. This should encourage investment in ports, improve the quality of services provided to port users, and even help reduce prices.
>
> The new rules will ensure transparency of port charges and public funding of ports. This will lead to better use of public funds and the effective and fair application of EU competition rules in ports. At the same time the new rules are designed to take into account the diversity of the sector across Europe.
>
> Hon. Joe Mizzi, Minister for Transport and Infrastructure [of Malta who was chairing the Council], said: 'I welcome these reforms. The port sector is vital to the success of Europe's economy, and it stands to benefit from the increased transparency and clarity which these new rules bring.'
>
> This final vote by the Council concludes the procedure at first reading. The European Parliament voted on 14 December 2016. The legal act will be signed by both institutions in

---

9 Reg. 2017/352, Art. 1(1). Art. 1 ("subject matter and scope") states in Art. 1(1) that the "Regulation establishes: (a) framework for the provision of port services; [and] (b) common rules on financial transparency and on port service and port infrastructure charges". The word "framework" gives the EU institutions some flexibility but it means that there is a certain generality and vagueness associated with almost all such measures.

mid-February and published in the EU Official Journal a few weeks later. It will enter into force 20 days after its publication."[10]

43.012 By contrast, the UK Major Ports took the opposite view:

"EU Port Services Regulation
In December 2016, the UK lost a fifteen year battle to stop the EU regulating our ports. After years of negotiations and three legislative proposals (two of which were previously rejected by the European Parliament), a text has been agreed. Although it is significantly watered down it still imposes a one size fits all approach to the diverse ports of Europe, which will generate significant uncertainty, bureaucracy and additional cost in the UK, while doing little or nothing to tackle the problems of the continental ports.

At the heart of the debate is a battle between two ports models. The state owned ports of Europe, who are often reliant on state aids, and the UK model of a mix of privately or publicly owned but all privately-financed ports, which operate with no subsidy. The UK's answer of encouraging competition between ports has lost out to the EU's answer of regulating ports to ensure competition within ports.

In practical terms this means that even private companies that own their own ports will be forced to put bunkering, waste collection, mooring and towage services out to tender and choose a minimum of two service providers, even if the current arrangements work well. There are exemptions, but the whole process is time consuming and complex. The creation of a new system of penalties for infringements, combined with a new independent national complaints body whose rulings are binding, will generate uncertainty and undermine the commercial freedom of UK ports.

And we fear this is the thin end of the wedge. Inevitably the Commission will be back to include more port services as the years go by.

That's why the UK Major Ports Group has consistently opposed the PSR. Implementation of the Regulation will damage investment and threaten jobs. Our priority now is to ensure in the Brexit negotiations the UK is freed entirely from this Regulation."[11]

43.013 The UK Major Port Group also said:

"Port Services Regulation comes into force – 24 March 2017
As the EU Port Services Regulation finally comes into force, it is timely to remind Government of the importance of achieving the best possible deal for UK ports in the forthcoming Brexit negotiations.

For the UK, the ports industry is a vital part of our modern economy – supporting British jobs, driving innovation and enabling trade. Now more than ever, the UK must expand international trade to help grow our economy and deliver prosperity across the country. UK ports have pledged to ensure that Brexit is a success not only for the ports industry, but for the nation as a whole. We want to collaborate with Government to develop ambitious policies which will support UK trade and exports.

Because UK ports also sit at the heart of a pan-European supply network, we will continue to play an important role in facilitating European trade long after the UK leaves the European Union. So we need to ensure that those supply and logistics chains continue to function efficiently, whatever the final outcome of the Brexit negotiations.

Given the substantial flows of goods and people between Europe and the UK, we must ensure the best possible access to each other's markets. In particular, we want to see a Brexit deal that includes appropriate arrangements for trade between the UK and Europe, so that cross border trade with the EU is as frictionless and as seamless as possible.

We also seek a regulatory environment that supports ports in our ambition to fulfil our part in Britain's post-Brexit trading success. We therefore hope that any unnecessary legislation, that introduce uncertainty and risk damaging investment in the UK at this crucial time, do not form

---

10 www.consilium.europa.eu/en/press/press-releases/2017/01/23/agri-port-services/.
11 Cited on the website of Stuart Agnew MEP: www.stuartagnewmep.co.uk.

part of the final Brexit deal. In particular we hope the final deal excludes the Port Services Regulation, which comes into force on the 24 March 2017 and comes into effect on 24 March 2019. UK ports will continue to work with Government, as the Brexit negotiations progress, to ensure that ports can fulfil their crucial role in helping to grow and strengthen the UK economy in the years ahead."[12]

Purpose of Regulation 2017/352

43.014 The fourth recital to the regulation sets out the purposes of the measure:

"[f]acilitating access to the port services market and introducing financial transparency and autonomy of maritime ports[13] will improve the quality and efficiency of the service provided to port users and contribute to a climate that is more favourable to investment in ports, thereby helping to reduce costs for transport users and contributing to the promotion of short sea shipping[14] and a better integration of maritime transport with rail, inland waterway and road transport."

43.015 These are laudable aims but it is difficult to see how the regulation will achieve those aims. It will certainly not do so on its own but it may be part of a wider range of initiatives which include not only legislative instruments (such as the regulation) but also the application of existing law (such as the application of competition law).

43.016 Regulation 2017/352 does not advocate or prefer public or private ownership; indeed, the regulation could not do so given the fact that Article 345 of the Treaty on the Functioning of the European Union ("TFEU") provides that EU law is neutral on the public/private ownership debate. So, the regulation is not, as some suggest, a charter for privatisation of ports. Equally, the regulation allows for, and does not seek to interfere with the different port structures which are used in Member States.[15] The tenth recital to the regulation provides:

"[t]his Regulation does not impose a specific model for the management of maritime ports and does not affect in any way the competence of Member States to provide, in conformity with Union law, non-economic services of general interest. Different port management models are possible, provided that the framework for the provision of port services and the common rules on financial transparency set out in this Regulation are respected."

43.017 The regulation is without prejudice to the right of Member States to impose public service obligations ("PSOs") related to port services.[16] A PSO is defined by Article 2(14), for the purposes of the regulation, as meaning:

---

12 http://ukmajorports.org.uk/port-services-regulation-comes-into-force-24-march-2017/.

13 Ed., on the definition of "maritime port", see below but, for present purposes, Art. 2(16) defines a "maritime port" as meaning: "an area of land and water made up of such infrastructure and equipment so as to permit, principally, the reception of waterborne vessels, their loading and unloading, the storage of goods, the receipt and delivery of those goods and the embarkation and disembarkation of passengers, crew and other persons and any other infrastructure necessary for transport operators within the port area".

14 Ed., the phrase " short sea shipping" is defined as meaning "the movement of cargo and passengers by sea between ports situated in geographical Europe or between those ports and ports situated in non-European countries having a coastline on the enclosed seas bordering Europe".

15 The ninth recital to the regulation provides that the "Regulation should in no way prejudice the rules in Member States governing the system of property ownership applicable to maritime ports, and should allow for different port structures in Member States".

16 Reg. 2017/352, twenty-third recital which states categorically that the "Regulation should be without prejudice to the right of Member States to impose public service obligations related to port services."

"a requirement defined or determined in order to ensure the provision of those port services or activities of general interest that an operator, if it were considering its own commercial interests, would not assume or would not assume to the same extent or under the same conditions".

The nature of the regulation

43.018 It is worth noting that it is a regulation[17] rather than a directive. The regulation does not need to be implemented in Member State law so there is no requirement to have "implementing legislation" at the Member State level. This means that there is a greater likelihood of uniformity throughout the EU but total uniformity is neither likely nor possible given the diversity of ports and legal regimes across the EU's coastal Member States. There is nothing wrong with Member States adopting legislation to give effect to the regulation but the national legislation must not undermine the regulation.

43.019 It is worth observing that the regulation has 57 recitals – which is long in hortatory headlines and relatively short in hard detail. It also means that this measure is somewhat of a compromise document with various interests seeking to have recitals so as to copper fasten their position.

Entry into force of the regulation

43.020 As a regulation, the regulation is binding in its entirety and is directly applicable in all Member States.[18] There could well be some national measures[19] which facilitate the operation of the regulation but none is needed.

43.021 The regulation entered into force on the twentieth day after its publication in the *Official Journal of the European Union*.[20] However, the regulation will not apply until two years from the entry into force of the regulation.[21] Article 22 states that the regulation shall apply from 24 March 2019.

43.022 The legal basis of the regulation is the TFEU generally and, in particular, Article 100(2) of the TFEU. It is therefore primarily a transport rather than a competition measure. The legal history commenced with a proposal from the European Commission, the transmission of the draft legislative act to the Member State parliaments, an opinion of the Economic and Social Committee[22] as well as an opinion of the Committee of the Regions.[23] It was adopted under the ordinary legislative procedure.[24]

---

17 As a regulation, it is binding in its entirety and directly applicable in all Member States.
18 Reg. 2017/352, Art. 22.
19 E.g. amendments to existing laws or new national rules.
20 Reg. 2017/352, Art. 22.
21 Reg. 2017/352, Art. 22.
22 OJ C327/111, 12 November 2013.
23 OJ C114/57, 15 March 2014.
24 The European Parliament decided on 14 December 2016 and the Council decided on 23 January 2017 that the measure could be adopted in accordance with the ordinary legislative procedure.

43.023 Article 21 of the regulation (entitled "Transitional Measures").[25] The first paragraph provides that the regulation does not apply to port service contracts[26] which were concluded before the date of adoption of the regulation and are limited in time. The second paragraph provides that port service contracts concluded before the date of adoption of the regulation which are not limited in time, or have similar effects, shall be amended in order to comply with this regulation by 1 July 2025.

Brexit and the regulation

43.024 If Brexit occurs then whether the regulation has any relevance to UK ports post-Brexit will depend on the terms of the Withdrawal Agreement and Relationship Agreement which might be concluded by the EU and the UK. It is notable that the UK has been largely opposed to the measure so it is unlikely that the UK would be keen to be bound by the regulation post-Brexit.

Purpose of the regulation

43.025 The Port Package III has the general aim of creating a more efficient, interconnected and sustainable ports regime in the EU's transport network. The regulation is designed to play its part in that regard. The regulation is not aimed at privatising ports. The EU is neutral on public and private ownership.

Subject matter and scope of application of the regulation

43.026 The regulation applies to ports. Article 2(16) defines a "maritime port" as meaning:

> "an area of land and water made up of such infrastructure and equipment so as to permit, principally, the reception of waterborne vessels, their loading and unloading, the storage of goods, the receipt and delivery of those goods and the embarkation and disembarkation of passengers, crew and other persons and any other infrastructure necessary for transport operators within the port area."

---

25 Art. 21 ("Transitional Measures") provides: "1. This Regulation shall not apply to port service contracts which were concluded before 15 February 2017 and are limited in time. 2. Port service contracts concluded before 15 February 2017 which are not limited in time, or have similar effects, shall be amended in order to comply with this Regulation by 1 July 2025."

26 A port service contract is defined, by Art. 2(12), as meaning "a formal and legally binding agreement or an act of equivalent legal effect between a provider of port services and a managing body of the port, or a competent authority, having as its subject-matter the provision of one or more port services, without prejudice to the form of designating providers of port services".

43.027 The regulation applies to certain categories of port services. The services are primarily: (a) bunkering;[27] (b) cargo handling;[28] (c) mooring;[29] (d) passenger services;[30] (e) collection of ship-generated waste and cargo residues;[31] (f) pilotage;[32] and (g) towage.[33] These are the so-called "port services" for the purposes of the regulation. It is notable that each of these terms is defined precisely and in a closed manner (i.e. "X means ..." rather than "X includes ...") which limits the possible scope of the regulation.

43.028 Article 11(2) of the regulation also applies to dredging.[34] The term "dredging" is defined as meaning

"the removal of sand, sediment or other substances from the bottom of the waterway access to the port, or within the port area that falls within the competence of the managing body of the port, including the disposal of the removed materials, in order to allow waterborne vessels to have access to the port; it comprises both the initial removal (capital dredging) and the maintenance dredging carried out in order to keep the waterway accessible, whilst not being a port service offered to the user".[35]

---

27 Art. 2(1) of the regulation defines, for the purposes of the regulation, "bunkering" as meaning "the provision of solid, liquid or gaseous fuel or of any other energy source used for the propulsion of the waterborne vessel as well as for general and specific energy provision on board of the waterborne vessel whilst at berth". This would therefore include not just the traditional supply of oil but also shore electricity power.

28 Art. 2(2) of the regulation defines, for the purposes of the regulation, "cargo handling" as meaning "the organisation and handling of cargo between the carrying waterborne vessel and the shore, whether it be for import, export or transit of the cargo, including the processing, lashing, unlashing, stowing, transporting and temporary storage of the cargo on the relevant cargo handling terminal and directly related to the transporting of the cargo, but excluding, unless the Member State determines otherwise, warehousing, stripping, repackaging or any other value added services related to the cargo".

29 Art. 2(6) of the regulation defines, for the purposes of the regulation, "mooring" as meaning "the berthing and unberthing services, including shifting along the quayside, that are required for the safe operation of a waterborne vessel in the port or in the waterway access to the port". In turn, Art. 2(18) defines "waterway access" as meaning "water access to the port from the open sea, such as port approaches, fairways, rivers, sea canals and fjords, provided that such waterway falls within the competence of the managing body of the port".

30 Art. 2(7) of the regulation defines, for the purposes of the regulation, "passenger services" as meaning "the organisation and handling of passengers, their luggage and their vehicles between the carrying waterborne vessel and the shore, and also includes the processing of personal data and the transport of passengers inside the relevant passenger terminal".

31 Art. 2(10) of the regulation defines, for the purposes of the regulation, "collection of ship-generated waste and cargo residues" as meaning "the reception of ship-generated waste and cargo residues by any facility, which is fixed, floating or mobile and capable of receiving ship-generated waste or cargo residues as defined in Directive 2000/59/EC of the European Parliament and of the Council [Ed., Dir. 2000/59 of the European Parliament and of the Council of 27 November 2000 on port reception facilities for ship-generated waste and cargo residues (OJ L332, 28 December 2000, p. 81)]".

32 Art. 2(8) of the regulation defines, for the purposes of the regulation, "pilotage" as meaning "the guidance service of a waterborne vessel by a pilot or a pilotage station in order to allow for safe entry or exit of the waterborne vessel in the waterway access to the port or safe navigation within the port". The eighth recital to the regulation provides that deep sea pilotage services do not have a direct impact on the efficiency of ports as they are not used for the direct entry and exit of ports and therefore do not need to be included in the regulation.

33 Reg. 2017/352, Art. 1(2). Art. 2(17) of the regulation defines towage, for the purposes of the regulation, as meaning "the assistance given to a waterborne vessel by means of a tug in order to allow for a safe entry or exit of the port or safe navigation within the port by providing assistance to the manoeuvring of the waterborne vessel".

34 Reg. 2017/352, Art. 1(3).

35 Reg. 2017/352, Art. 2(4).

43.029 The regulation applies to the port services whether inside the port area or on the waterway access[36] to the port.

43.030 The regulation does not apply to all ports. The regulation applies to all maritime ports of the TEN-T, as listed in Annex II to Regulation 1315/2013[37] but Member States may extend the regulation to other ports as well if they wish to do so.[38] The seventh recital to the regulation provides:

> "The overwhelming majority of Union maritime traffic transits through the maritime ports of the trans-European transport network established by Regulation (EU) No 1315/2013 of the European Parliament and of the Council.[39] In order to achieve the aim of this Regulation in a proportionate way without imposing any unnecessary burden on other ports, this Regulation should apply to the maritime ports of the trans-European transport network, each of which plays a significant role for the European transport system either because it handles more than 0,1% of the total EU freight or the total number of passengers or because it improves the regional accessibility of island or peripheral areas. However, this Regulation should give Member States the possibility to decide whether or not to apply this Regulation to maritime ports of the comprehensive network located in the outermost regions. Member States should also have the possibility of introducing derogations in order to avoid disproportionate administrative burdens for those maritime ports of the comprehensive network the annual freight traffic of which does not justify the full application of this Regulation."

43.031 The regulation applies to the EU ports in scope but it also applies to those ports in scope in the European Economic Area.

43.032 The regulation is subject to the EU's rules generally including the rules on competition, public procurement[40] and human rights.[41]

43.033 The regulation would be administered by various parties including the so-called "managing body of the port" and the "competent authority" of the port. The term "managing body of the port" is defined by Article 2(5) as meaning:

> "any public or private body which, under national law or instruments, has the objective of carrying out, or is empowered to carry out, at a local level, whether in conjunction with other

---

36 The term "waterway access" is defined by Art. 2(18) as meaning: "[the] water access to the port from the open sea, such as port approaches, fairways, rivers, sea canals and fjords, provided that such waterway falls within the competence of the managing body of the port".

37 Reg. 2017/352, Art. 1(4). Member States with the outermost regions may decide not to apply the regulation to ports in those regions: Art. 1(5) of the regulation provides: "Member States may decide not to apply this Regulation to maritime ports of the comprehensive network located in the outermost regions referred to in Article 349 of the Treaty on the Functioning of the European Union. Where Member States decide not to apply this Regulation to such maritime ports, they shall notify such decision to the Commission."

38 Reg. 2017/352, Art. 1(6).

39 Regulation (EU) No 1315/2013 of the European Parliament and of the Council of 11 December 2013 on Union guidelines for the development of the trans-European transport network and repealing Decision No 661/2010/EU (OJ L348, 20.12.2013, p. 1).

40 Reg. 2017/352, Art. 1(7) provides that the "Regulation is without prejudice to Directive 2014/23/EU of the European Parliament and of the Council [Ed., Dir. 2014/23 of the European Parliament and of the Council of 26 February 2014 on the award of concession contracts (OJ L94, 28 March 2014, p. 1)] [and] Directive 2014/24/EU of the European Parliament and of the Council [Ed., Dir. 2014/24 of the European Parliament and of the Council of 26 February 2014 on public procurement and repealing Directive 2004/18 (OJ L94, 28 March 2014, p. 65)] and Directive 2014/25/EU [Ed., i.e. Dir. 2014/25 of the European Parliament and of the Council of 26 February 2014 on procurement by entities operating in the water, energy, transport and postal services sectors and repealing Directive 2004/17 (OJ L94/243, 28 March 2014)]" (footnotes omitted).

41 The fifty-seventh (i.e. last) recital to the regulation provides that the "Regulation respects the fundamental rights and observes the principles recognised in particular by the Charter of Fundamental Rights of the European Union".

activities or not, the administration and management of the port infrastructure and one or more of the following tasks in the port concerned: the coordination of port traffic, the management of port traffic, the coordination of the activities of the operators present in the port concerned, and the control of the activities of the operators present in the port concerned."

43.034 The "competent authority" is defined by Article 2(3) as meaning:

"any public or private body which, on behalf of a local, regional or national level, is entitled to carry out, under national law or instruments, activities related to the organisation and administration of port activities, in conjunction with or instead of the managing body of the port."

This could be a pre-existing institution and does not have to be specially created for the purposes of the regulation.

Framework on market access

43.035 Chapter II of the regulation is entitled "Provision of Port Services". It does not provide for a "free for all" or "open the doors for everyone". Chapter II does not apply to cargo handling, passenger services or pilotage[42] but Member States may decide to apply the chapter (and Article 21) to pilotage if they choose to do so (it is entirely at their discretion) but Member States must inform the Commission of any such decision.[43]

43.036 The regime relates to particular categories of port services rather than to all services.

43.037 The regime applies to such services either (a) inside the port area of a relevant seaport in the trans-European transport network or (b) on the waterway access to, and from, such a port.

43.038 Article 10 ("Exemptions") provides, in paragraph 1, that Chapter II (and Article 21) do not apply to cargo handling, passenger services or pilotage but they must inform the Commission of such a decision. Equally, Article 10(2) provides that Member States may decide to apply Chapter II (and Article 21) to pilotage but they must inform the Commission of such a decision.

Organisation of port services

43.039 It is important to emphasise that the regulation does not provide a free for all. So what then are the potential or actual restrictions?

43.040 Article 3(1) provides that access to the market for the provision of port services in maritime ports *may*, in accordance with the regulation, be subject to: (a) minimum requirements for the provision of port services; (b) limitations on the number of providers; (c) PSOs; and (d) restrictions related to internal operators. It is noteworthy that these restrictions "may" be invoked but do not have to be invoked by a particular Member State – this is emphasised by Article 3(2) which states explicitly "Member States may decide by national law not to impose any of the conditions referred to in [Article 3, paragraph 1] on one or more categories of port services." The way in which Article 3(2) is drafted is

---

42 Reg. 2017/352, Art. 10(1). Indeed, Art. 10(1) also provides that chap. II does not apply to cargo handling, passenger services or pilotage.

43 Reg. 2017/352, Art. 10(2). It is notable that Member States do not have the power to apply chap. II to cargo handling or passenger services.

interesting because it means that there could be differentiated regulation within the same port with some service providers subject to a particular rule but not others so Member States/ports need to be careful not to breach any rules such as procedural or fairness rules in selecting those who are subject, and those who are not subject, to such rules. Article 3(2) does not seem to permit individual ports to make such choices but rather for Member States to decide by "national law" which could, in turn, permit ports to make such choices.

43.041 Article 3(3) provides that the "terms of access to the facilities, installations and equipment of the port shall be fair, reasonable and non-discriminatory". This is the so-called "FRAND" concept which is so commonplace in so many areas of EU competition law. Unlike Article 3(1), this requirement is mandatory rather than discretionary.

Minimum requirements for the provision of port services

43.042 It would be poor policy if there would be no minimum requirements for the provision of port services. Thus Article 4 permits some minimum requirements but this is, pursuant to Article 4(7), subject to Article 7 which deals with PSOs. Article 4(1) provides that the managing body of the port, or the competent authority, may require providers of port services, including subcontractors, to comply with minimum requirements for the performance of the corresponding port service.[44] Article 4 is more liberal than Article 3 because the former permits decisions to be made at the port or competent authority level rather than by way of a choice enshrined in national law.

43.043 Article 4(2) provides an exhaustive list of the minimum requirements which may be imposed. It provides that the minimum requirements provided for in Article 4(1) may only relate to:

"(a) the professional qualifications of the provider of port services,[45] its personnel or the natural persons who actually and continuously manage the activities of the provider of port services;

(b) the financial capacity of the provider of port services;

(c) the equipment needed to provide the relevant port service in normal and safe conditions and the capacity to maintain this equipment at the required level;

(d) the availability of the relevant port service to all users, at all berths and without interruptions, day and night, throughout the year;

---

44 Art. 4(6) of the regulation provides that in the cases provided for in Art. 4(1), "the managing body of the port, or the competent authority, shall publish the minimum requirements referred to in paragraph 2 and the procedure for the granting of the right to provide port services under those requirements by [24 months after the entry into force of the regulation] or, in the case of minimum requirements that are to apply after that date, at least three months before the date from which those requirements are to apply. The managing body of the port, or the competent authority, shall, in advance, inform providers of port services of any change in the criteria and of the procedure."

45 Ed., the term "provider of port services" is defined by Art. 2(13) of the regulation as meaning "any natural or legal person providing, or wishing to provide, for remuneration one or more categories of port services".

(e) compliance with requirements on maritime safety or the safety and security of the port or access to it, its installations, equipment and workers and other persons;[46]

(f) compliance with local, national, Union and international environmental requirements;

(g) compliance with obligations in the field of social and labour law that apply in the Member State of the port concerned, including the terms of applicable collective agreements, manning requirements and requirements relating to hours of work and hours of rest for seafarers, and with applicable rules on labour inspections;[47]

(h) the good repute of the port service provider, as determined in accordance with any applicable national law on good repute, taking into consideration any compelling grounds to doubt the reliability of the provider of port services."

43.044 As a general rule, these minimum requirements must: (a) be transparent, objective, non-discriminatory, proportionate and relevant to the category and nature of the port service concerned; and (b) be complied with until the right to provide a port service expires.[48]

43.045 Article 4(5) provides that where the minimum requirements include specific knowledge of local conditions, the managing body of the port, or the competent authority, shall ensure that there is adequate access to information, under transparent and non-discriminatory conditions.

43.046 By virtue of Article 4(6), in the cases provided for in Article 4(1), the managing body of the port, or the competent authority, shall publish the minimum requirements referred to in Article 4(2) and the procedure for the granting of the right to provide port services under those requirements by 24 March 2019 or, in the case of minimum requirements that are to apply after that date, at least three months before the date from which those requirements are to apply. The managing body of the port, or the competent authority, shall, in advance, inform providers of port services of any change in the criteria and of the procedure.

43.047 The whole of Article 4 applies without prejudice to Article 7 according to Article 4(7).

43.048 The provision of port services often requires local knowledge (e.g. pilotage conditions in a port). Article 5(5) therefore provides that where "the minimum requirements include specific knowledge of local conditions, the managing body of the port, or

---

46 Ed., the thirteenth recital to the regulation states that in "the interest of efficient, safe and environmentally sound port management, the managing body of the port, or the competent authority, should be able to require that providers of port services are able to demonstrate that they meet minimum requirements for the performance of the service in an appropriate way. Those minimum requirements should be limited to a clearly defined set of conditions in so far as those requirements are transparent, objective, non-discriminatory, proportionate and relevant for the provision of the port service. In accordance with the general objectives of this Regulation, the minimum requirements should contribute to a high quality of port services and should not introduce market barriers".

47 Ed., Art. 4(3) of the regulation provides that without prejudice to Art. 4(4), where a Member State deems that it is necessary to impose a flag requirement in order to ensure full compliance with point (g) of paragraph 2 for waterborne vessels predominantly used for towage or mooring operations in ports located on its territory, it shall inform the Commission of its decision prior to the publication of the contract notice or, in the absence of a contract notice, prior to imposing a flag requirement. This is line with the seventeenth recital which provides that "Member States should inform the Commission prior to any decision to impose a flag requirement for vessels predominantly used for towage and mooring operations. Such a decision should be non-discriminatory, should be based on transparent and objective grounds and should not introduce disproportionate market barriers." This idea of market barriers is reflected in the twentieth recital which states that any "limitation on the number of providers of port services should be justified by clear and objective reasons and should not introduce disproportionate market barriers".

48 Reg. 2017/352, Art. 4(4).

the competent authority, shall ensure that there is adequate access to information, under transparent and non-discriminatory conditions". This means that local knowledge cannot be easily used as a deterrent or barrier to entry.

Procedural aspects

43.049 It is all very well the regulation setting out these minimum requirements but what procedure would be used to ensure compliance with these minimum requirements? In somewhat vague, but directly applicable language, Article 5 establishes something of a procedural regime. First, the managing body of the port, or the competent authority, must treat providers of port services in a transparent, objective, non-discriminatory and proportionate manner.[49] Second, there are timelines established with Article 5(2) providing that the managing body of the port (or the competent authority) must grant or refuse the right to provide port services on the basis of the minimum requirements established in accordance with Article 4 "within a reasonable period, which in any event shall not exceed four months, from receiving a request for the granting of such a right and the necessary documents". Third, the grounds for refusal are limited because Article 5(3) provides that any such refusal must be "duly justified" on the basis of the minimum requirements set out in Article 4(2). Finally, any limitation or termination by the managing body of the port (or the competent authority) of the right to provide a port service must be duly justified and must be in accordance with Article 5(1).[50]

Limiting the number of service providers

43.050 Limiting the number of service providers is a matter of some delicacy. Monopolistic, duopolistic or even oligopolistic markets are usually not as efficient or consumer welfare enhancing as more competitive ones. So, at a simple level, the easiest course of action is to permit anyone to provide a service in a port. However, that is not practical or even desirable. There can be limitations on space in a port. If there is unlikely to be a certain minimum return on investment then investment (both initial and subsequent) is less likely. There could also be safety or environmental concerns. In practice, however, it is somewhat challenging to create a regime which addresses the issue: nonetheless, Article 6 of the regulation seeks to do so.

43.051 As a general rule, and pursuant to Article 6(1), the managing body of the port (or the competent authority) may limit the number of providers of port services for a given port service for one or more of the following five reasons:

"(a) the scarcity or reserved use of land or waterside space, provided that the limitation is in accordance with the decisions or plans agreed by the managing body of the port and, where appropriate, any other public authorities competent in accordance with the national law;

(b) the absence of such a limitation is obstructing the performance of public service obligations as provided for in Article 7, including when such absence leads to excessively high costs related to the performance of such obligations for the managing body of the port, the competent authority, or the port users;

---

49 Reg. 2017/352, Art. 5(1).
50 Reg. 2017/352, Art. 5(4).

(c) the absence of such a limitation runs counter to the need to ensure safe, secure or environmentally sustainable port operations;

(d) the characteristics of the port infrastructure or the nature of the port traffic are such that the operations of multiple providers of port services in the port would not be possible;

(e) where it has been established pursuant to Article 35 of Directive 2014/25/EU that a port sector or sub-sector, together with its port services, within a Member State carries out an activity that is directly exposed to competition in accordance with Article 34 of that Directive. In such cases, paragraphs 2 and 3 of this Article shall not apply."

43.052 A port or competent authority may quietly and clandestinely limit the number of service providers. Instead, there have been some safeguards incorporated into Article 6. Article 6(2) provides that there must be advance publicity about the *proposal* to limit numbers and then to allow comments.[51] Article 6(3) states that the "managing body of the port, or the competent authority, shall publish the adopted decision to limit the number of providers of port services". Indeed, as a general rule,[52] there must be a selection procedure deployed:

"Where the managing body of the port, or the competent authority, decides to limit the number of providers of a port service, it shall follow a selection procedure which shall be open to all interested parties, non-discriminatory and transparent. The managing body of the port, or the competent authority, shall publish information on the port service to be provided and on the selection procedure, and shall ensure that all essential information that is necessary for the preparation of their applications is effectively accessible to all interested parties. Interested parties shall be given long enough to allow them to make a meaningful assessment and prepare their applications. In normal circumstances, the minimum such period shall be 30 days."[53]

43.053 There is a further control, in Article 6(6) where the port (or the competent authority) seeks to provide the services itself or through connected persons:

"Where the managing body of a port, or the competent authority, provides port services either itself or through a legally distinct entity which it directly or indirectly controls, the Member State concerned shall take such measures as are necessary to avoid conflicts of interests. In the absence of such measures, the number of providers shall not be fewer than two, unless one or more of the reasons listed in paragraph 1 justifies a limitation on the number of providers of port services to a single provider."

43.054 If there is an internal operator then Article 8 of the regulation comes into focus. Article 8(1) provides:

"Without prejudice to Article 6(6), the managing body of the port, or the competent authority, may decide either to provide a port service itself or to do so through a legally distinct entity over which it exercises a degree of control similar to that which it has over its own departments, provided that Article 4 applies equally to all operators providing the port service concerned. In such a case, the provider of port services shall be considered to be an internal operator for the purpose of this Regulation."

---

51 Art. 6(2) of the regulation provides that in "order to give interested parties the opportunity to submit comments within a reasonable period, the managing body of the port, or the competent authority, shall publish any proposal to limit the number of providers of port services in accordance with paragraph 1 together with the grounds justifying it at least three months in advance of the adoption of the decision to limit the number of providers of port services."

52 Art. 6(5) of the regulation provides that Art. 6(4) does not apply in cases referred to in point (e) of Art. 4(1) and in Art. 4(7) and in Art. 8.

53 Reg. 2017/352, Art. 6(4).

43.055 It is imperative that ports take great care to ensure that procedures are followed to minimise (it would be impossible to eliminate) the risk of court challenges.

PSOs

43.056 Article 7 of the regulation provides:

"1. Member States may decide to impose public service obligations related to port services on providers of port services and may entrust the right to impose such obligations to the managing body of the port, or to the competent authority, in order to ensure at least one of the following:

    (a) the availability of the port service to all port users, at all berths, without interruption, day and night, throughout the year;

    (b) the availability of the service to all users on equal terms;

    (c) the affordability of the service for certain categories of users;

    (d) the safety, security or environmental sustainability of port operations;

    (e) the provision of adequate transport services to the public; and

    (f) territorial cohesion.

2. The public service obligations referred to in paragraph 1 shall be clearly defined, transparent, non-discriminatory and verifiable, and shall guarantee equality of access to all providers of port services established in the Union.

3. Where a Member State decides to impose public service obligations for the same service in all its maritime ports covered by this Regulation, it shall notify those obligations to the Commission.

4. In the event of a disruption of port services for which public service obligations are imposed or when an immediate risk of such a situation occurs, the managing body of the port, or the competent authority, may take an emergency measure. The emergency measure may take the form of a direct award so as to attribute the service to a different provider for a period of up to two years. During that period, the managing body of the port, or the competent authority, shall either launch a new procedure to select a provider of port services or shall apply Article 8. Collective industrial action that takes place in accordance with national law shall not be considered a disruption of port services for which an emergency measure may be taken."

Internal operator

43.057 Article 8 addresses the issue of the internal operator. There is a risk of bias or favouritism so Article 8 seeks to address the issue:

"1. Without prejudice to Article 6(6), the managing body of the port, or the competent authority, may decide either to provide a port service itself or to do so through a legally distinct entity over which it exercises a degree of control similar to that which it has over its own departments, provided that Article 4 applies equally to all operators providing the port service concerned. In such a case, the provider of port services shall be considered to be an internal operator for the purpose of this Regulation.

2. The managing body of the port, or the competent authority, shall be considered to be exercising a degree of control over a legally distinct entity similar to that which it has over its own departments only if it has a decisive influence over both the strategic objectives and the significant decisions of the legal entity concerned.

3. In the cases provided for in points (a) to (d) of Article 6(1), the internal operator shall be limited to performing the assigned port service only in the port or ports attributed to it in the assignment to provide the port service."

Safeguarding of employees' rights

43.058 Article 9 aims at safeguarding employees' rights. This was important so as to avoid the type of industrial relations problems which dogged earlier Commission attempts adopt measures relating to ports.

43.059 Article 9(1) states categorically that the regulation shall not affect the application of the social and labour rules of the Member States.[54]

43.060 Article 9(2) provides that, without prejudice to EU and Member State law, including applicable collective agreements between social partners, the managing body of the port, or the competent authority, must require the designated provider of port services to grant staff working conditions in accordance with applicable obligations in the field of social and labour law and to comply with social standards as set out in EU law, Member State law or collective agreements – the latter element (i.e. collective agreements) is very important in practice and could, in certain cases, provide even greater protection to employees.

43.061 In the case of a change of provider of port services that is due to the award of a concession or public contract, the managing body of the port, or the competent authority, may require that the rights and obligations of the outgoing provider of port services arising from a contract of employment, or from an employment relationship as defined in national law, and existing on the date of that change, be transferred to the newly appointed provider of port services.[55] In such a case, the staff previously taken on by the outgoing provider of port services shall be granted the same rights as those to which they would have been entitled if there had been a transfer of undertaking within the meaning of Directive 2001/23.[56]

43.062 Where, in the context of the provision of port services, a transfer of staff occurs, tender documents and port service contracts shall list the staff concerned and give transparent details of their contractual rights and the conditions under which employees are deemed to be linked to the port services.[57]

Financial transparency and autonomy

43.063 Chapter III of the regulation contains three articles relating to: (a) transparency of financial relations;[58] (b) port service charges;[59] and (c) port infrastructure charges.[60] The sixth recital to the regulation recalls:

> "The establishment of a clear framework of transparent, fair and non-discriminatory provisions relating to the funding of and charges for port infrastructure and port services plays a fundamental role in ensuring that the ports' own commercial strategy and investment plans and, where relevant, the general national ports policy framework comply fully with competition rules. In particular, the transparency of financial relations allows a fair and effective control of State aid,

---

54 Reg. 2017/352, recital 16 states that "Member States should be able to require compliance with obligations in the field of social and labour law for the operation of port services in the port concerned."
55 Reg. 2017/352, Art. 9(3).
56 Ibid.
57 Reg. 2017/352, Art. 9(4).
58 Reg. 2017/352, Art. 11.
59 Reg. 2017/352, Art. 12.
60 Reg. 2017/352, Art. 13.

hence preventing market distortion. To that end, the Council conclusions of 5 June 2014 called upon the Commission to explore State aid guidelines for maritime ports, with the aim of ensuring fair competition and a stable legal framework for port investment."

Transparency of financial relations

43.064 The transparency of financial relations is extremely important in ports. There have been various informal allegations of a lack of transparency and financial relations in some ports (e.g. funds hidden in subsidiary companies, unfair or unrealistic pricing and a sense of opaqueness about arrangements). Article 11 therefore seeks to tackle the issue. Given its importance, it is worth citing it in full:

"1. The financial relations between public authorities and a managing body of a port, or other entity that provides port services on its behalf, in receipt of public funds shall be reflected in a transparent way in the accounting system in order to clearly show the following:

   (a) public funds made available directly by public authorities to the managing bodies of the port concerned;
   (b) public funds made available by public authorities through the intermediary of public undertakings or public financial institutions; and
   (c) the use for which those public funds have been attributed.

2. Where the managing body of a port in receipt of public funds provides port services or dredging itself, or another entity provides such services on its behalf, it shall keep the accounts for that publicly funded port service or dredging separate from those for its other activities in such a way that:

   (a) all costs and revenues are correctly assigned or allocated on the basis of consistently applied and objectively justifiable cost accounting principles; and
   (b) the cost accounting principles according to which separate accounts are maintained are clearly established.

3. The public funds referred to in paragraph 1 shall include share capital and quasi-capital funds, non-refundable grants, grants only refundable in certain circumstances, loans including overdrafts and advances on capital injections, guarantees given to the managing body of the port by public authorities and any other form of public financial support.

4. The managing body of the port, or other entity that provides port services on its behalf, shall keep the information concerning the financial relations as referred to in paragraphs 1 and 2 for five years from the end of the fiscal year to which the information refers.

5. The managing body of the port, or other entity that provides port services on its behalf, shall, in the event of a formal complaint and upon request, make available to the relevant authority in the Member State concerned the information referred to in paragraphs 1 and 2 and any additional information that it deems necessary in order to complete a thorough appraisal of the data submitted and to assess compliance with this Regulation in accordance with competition rules. Such information shall be made available to the Commission by the relevant authority upon request. The information shall be transmitted within three months from the date of the request.

6. Where the managing body of the port, or other entity that provides port services on its behalf, has not received public funds in previous accounting years but starts benefitting from public funds, it shall apply paragraphs 1 and 2 from the accounting year following the transfer of the public funds.

7. Where public funds are paid as compensation for a public service obligation, they shall be shown separately in the relevant accounts and may not be transferred to any other service or business activity.

8. Member States may decide that paragraph 2 of this Article shall not apply to those of their ports of the comprehensive network which do not meet the criteria set out in point (b) of Article 20(2) of Regulation … 1315/2013 where this results in disproportionate administrative burdens, provided that any public funds received, and their use for providing port services, remain fully transparent in the accounting system. Member States shall inform the Commission in advance of such a decision."

43.065 Article 11 is admirable in its ambition but it will be interesting to see whether it achieves its purpose. Article 11(1) is drafted in a very broad manner and would encompass many arrangements and practices. Article 11(2) requires books of accounts to be kept in certain circumstances and this is a prudent requirement. The other detailed provisions in Article 11 all help but it will be interesting to see whether Article 11 works and whether it will need adaptation in practice.

Port service charges

43.066 A port service charge is defined by Article 2(11) as meaning: "a charge levied for the benefit of the provider of port services and paid by the users of the relevant service".

43.067 Article 12 ("Port service charges") deals with the issue. Under Article 12(1), the charges for the services provided by an internal operator under a PSO, the charges for pilotage services that are not exposed to effective competition and the charges levied by providers of port services, referred to in point (b) of Article 6(1), shall be set in a transparent, objective and non-discriminatory way, and shall be proportionate to the cost of the service provided. This is quite an onerous obligation on ports because not only must the charges be transparent, objective and non-discriminatory when they are set but they must also be so when they are imposed therefore ports should bear in mind circumstances as they change.

43.068 Under Article 12(2), the payment of the port service charges may be integrated into other payments, such as the payment of the port infrastructure charges. In such a case, the provider of port services and, where appropriate, the managing body of the port must make sure that the amount of the port service charge remains easily identifiable by the user of the port service. This is a welcome change because it allows the various charges to be identifiable and visible to the port user but it could require the port authority to have to alter its accounting packages and presentation.

43.069 The provider of port services must under Article 12(3), in the event of a formal complaint[61] and upon request, make available to the relevant authority in the Member State concerned any relevant information on the elements that serve as the basis for determining the structure and the level of the port service charges that fall under Article 12(1).

Port infrastructure charges

43.070 A port infrastructure charge is defined by Article 2(9) as meaning:

---

61 There is no real guidance on what is meant by the term "formal complaint" so the term should be assessed in its specific context.

"a charge levied, for the direct or indirect benefit of the managing body of the port or of the competent authority, for the use of infrastructure, facilities and services, including the waterway access to the port concerned, as well as access to the processing of passengers and cargo, but excluding land lease rates and charges having equivalent effect."

43.071 Article 13 deals with port infrastructure charges. Under Article 13(1), Member States must ensure that a port infrastructure charge is levied but this shall not prevent providers of port services which are using the port infrastructure from levying port service charges. Article 13(2) provides that the payment of the port infrastructure charges may be integrated into other payments, such as the payment of the port service charges and, in such a case, the managing body of the port must ensure that the amount of the port infrastructure charge remains easily identifiable by the user of the port infrastructure, so it is submitted that the amount should be identifiable specifically on invoices much like value added tax is identifiable. By virtue of Article 13(3), in order to contribute to an efficient infrastructure charging system, the structure and the level of port infrastructure charges shall be determined according to the port's own commercial strategy and investment plans, and shall comply with competition rules. Where relevant, such charges shall also respect the general requirements set within the framework of the general ports policy of the Member State concerned. However, Article 13(4) provides that without prejudice to Article 13(3), port infrastructure charges may vary, in accordance with the port's own economic strategy and its spatial planning policy, in relation to, *inter alia*, certain categories of users, or in order to promote a more efficient use of the port infrastructure, short sea shipping or a high environmental performance, energy efficiency or carbon efficiency of transport operations. The criteria for such a variation shall be transparent, objective and non-discriminatory, and shall be consistent with competition law, including rules on State aid. Port infrastructure charges may take into account external costs and may vary depending on commercial practices.

43.072 The managing body of the port, or the competent authority, must (by virtue of Article 13(5)) ensure that port users and the representatives or associations of port users are informed about the nature and level of the port infrastructure charges. The managing body of the port, or the competent authority, shall ensure that users of the port infrastructure are informed of any changes in the nature or level of the port infrastructure charges at least two months in advance of the date on which those changes come into effect. The managing body of the port, or the competent authority, shall not be required to disclose differentiations in the charges that are the result of individual negotiations. It is submitted that such notification need not be individualised to users but may be available on the port's website or other means of general communication.

43.073 Under Article 13(6), the managing body of the port must, in the event of a formal complaint and upon request, make available to the relevant authority of the Member State concerned the information referred to in Article 13(4) and (5), and any relevant information on the elements that serve as a basis for determining the structure and the level of the port infrastructure charges. That authority shall make the information available to the Commission upon request.

General provisions

Introduction

43.074 Chapter IV of the regulation is entitled "General and Final Provisions". It contains an amalgam of provisions on such matters as training of staff, consultation of port users and other stakeholders, the handling of complaints, the relevant authorities, appeals, penalties, reports, transitional measures as well as the entry into force of the regulation.

Training of staff

43.075 There is a curious and somewhat vague provision, Article 14 of the regulation, entitled "training of staff". The article states that providers

"of port services shall ensure that employees receive the necessary training to acquire the knowledge which is essential for their work, with particular emphasis on health and safety aspects, and that training requirements are regularly updated to meet the challenges of technological innovation."

The provision is vague because it does not specify the content of the training. It is clearly not confined to training about the contents of the regulation. However, the thirty-seventh recital to the regulation provides that

"[in] a complex and competitive sector such as port services, initial and periodic training of staff is essential to ensure the quality of services and to protect the health and safety of port workers. Member States should therefore ensure that providers of port services provide adequate training to their employees."

Consultation of port users and other stakeholders

43.076 One of the features of the regulation is that there would be increased consultation – almost in a democratisation of ports manner. So Article 15 deals with consultation of port users and other stakeholders. It is relatively straightforward but port users should know that it is somewhat limited:

"1. The managing body of the port shall, in accordance with applicable national law, consult port users on its charging policy, including in cases covered by Article 8. Such consultation shall include any substantial changes to the port infrastructure charges and port service charges in cases where internal operators provide port services under public service obligations.

2. The managing body of the port shall, in accordance with applicable national law, consult port users and other relevant stakeholders on essential matters within its competence regarding:

(a) the coordination of port services within the port area;
(b) measures to improve connections with the hinterland, including measures to develop and improve the efficiency of rail and inland waterways transport;
(c) the efficiency of administrative procedures in the port and measures to simplify them;
(d) environmental matters;
(e) spatial planning; and
(f) measures to ensure safety in the port area, including, where appropriate, health and safety of port workers.

3. The providers of port services shall make available to port users adequate information about the nature and level of the port service charges.

4. The managing body of the port and providers of port services shall respect the confidentiality of commercially sensitive information when carrying out their obligations under this Article."

Complaints

43.077 Article 16 addresses how to handle the inevitable complaints. The fifty-third recital provides that in order to ensure the proper and effective application of this regulation, Member States should ensure that an effective procedure is in place to handle complaints.

43.078 Under Article 16(1), each Member State must ensure that an effective procedure is in place to handle complaints arising from the application of the regulation for its maritime ports covered by the regulation.

43.079 Article 16(2) goes on to provide that the handling of complaints shall be carried out in a manner which avoids conflicts of interest[62] and which is functionally independent of any managing body of the port or providers of port services. Member States shall ensure that there is effective functional separation between the handling of complaints, on the one hand, and the ownership and management of ports, provision of port services and port use, on the other hand. The handling of complaints shall be impartial and transparent, and shall duly respect the right to freely conduct business.

43.080 Complaints shall be filed in the Member State of the port where the dispute is presumed to have its origin.[63] In practice, this rarely raises an issue because the dispute relates to a port in a particular Member State. Member States must ensure that port users and other relevant stakeholders are informed of where and how to lodge a complaint and which authorities are responsible for handling complaints.[64] This requires Member States (and not just the ports) to set out publicly the relevant procedures (e.g. on the port website). Under Article 16(4), the authorities responsible for handling complaints must, where appropriate, co-operate for the purposes of mutual assistance in disputes involving parties established in different Member States. The authorities responsible for the handling of complaints must, in accordance with national law, have the power to require managing bodies of the ports, providers of port services and port users to provide them with information relevant to a complaint.[65] The authorities responsible for the handling of complaints must, in accordance with national law, have the power to take decisions that have binding effect, subject to judicial review, where applicable;[66] this provision would trump any contrary rule of national or constitutional law but it would not confer on administrative agency the power to adopt criminal sanctions unless it is required under EU law. Under Article 16(7), Member States shall inform the Commission of the procedure for the handling of complaints and of the authorities referred to in paragraph 3 by a date which is 24 months after the date of entry into force of the regulation and,

---

62 This could be somewhat difficult to do in practice and may require outside professionals to review matters objectively in a way which avoids a conflict of interests.

63 Reg. 2017/352, Art. 16(3).

64 Ibid.

65 Reg. 2017/352, Art. 16(5).

66 Reg. 2017/352, Art. 16(6).

subsequently, of any changes to that information.[67] The Commission shall publish and regularly update such information on its website.[68] Member States must, where appropriate, exchange general information about the application of Article 16.[69] The Commission must support such co-operation.[70]

Penalties

43.081 Article 19[71] of the regulation addresses the issue of penalties. It provides that Member States must lay down the rules on penalties applicable to infringements of the regulation and must take all measures necessary to ensure that they are implemented. These penalties must be effective, proportionate and dissuasive. Member States must notify those measures to the Commission by two years after the date of entry into force of the regulation and must, without delay, notify it of any subsequent amendment affecting them. It might be wondered why Article 19 (or the regulation generally) did not specify the penalties. EU law does not usually permit the EU institutions to set out penalties and also because the regulation permits Member States to choose the penalties then there is considerable flexibility.

Relevant authorities

43.082 Article 17 provides that Member States must ensure that "port users and other relevant stakeholders are informed of the relevant authorities referred to in Articles 11(5), 12(3) and 13(6)". It also provides that Member States must also inform the Commission of the identity of those authorities within two years of the date of entry into force of the regulation and, subsequently, of any changes to that information. The Commission shall publish and regularly update such information on its website.

Review of the regulation

43.083 As is commonplace with most measures, the regulation has an internal review mechanism. Article 20 provides that a report would be needed. It provides that the Commission must no later than 24 March 2023, submit a report to the European Parliament and the Council on the functioning and effect of the regulation. The report must take into

---

67 Reg. 2017/352, Art. 16(7).
68 Ibid.
69 Reg. 2017/352, Art. 16(8).
70 Ibid.
71 Art. 19 provides: "Member States shall lay down the rules on penalties applicable to infringements of this Regulation and shall take all measures necessary to ensure that they are implemented. The penalties provided for must be effective, proportionate and dissuasive. Member States shall notify those measures to the Commission by 24 March 2019 and shall without delay notify it of any subsequent amendment affecting them."

account any progress made in the framework of the EU Sectoral Social Dialogue Committee in the Port Sector.[72]

Practical issues

43.084 The measure is a regulation rather than a directive. This should reduce the amount of inconsistency in terms of implementation in Member States because it is a universal measure throughout the EU (i.e. a regulation) rather than a directive.

43.085 One of the difficulties about the regulation is that it is long on setting down general principles but relatively short on specifying the detail on how those principles will be applied in practice. It will be interesting to see how the Commission, the Court of Justice of the European Union ("CJEU") and Member State courts apply it in practice. It may well be that it is given a somewhat restrictive construction in jurisdictions which are less liberal and the opposite construction in other jurisdictions so it would be well to engage the CJEU through the preliminary reference mechanism to ensure a consistency of approach.

---

72 The fifty-sixth recital provides that the "EU Sectoral Social Dialogue Committee in the Port Sector provides the social partners with a framework to develop a joint approach to the social challenges related to port labour relations, including working conditions, health and safety questions, training requirements and professional qualifications. That framework should be developed in particular, in the light of market-based and technological developments, and should enhance the attractiveness of the sector for young workers and female workers, while taking into consideration the importance of safeguarding the competitiveness of European maritime ports and promoting good working conditions. With full respect for the autonomy of the social partners and taking into account technological progress and advances in transport logistics, the EU Sectoral Social Dialogue Committee in the Port Sector is invited to develop guidelines on the development of training requirements in order to prevent accidents in the workplace and to ensure the highest level of health and safety for port workers. Social partners should also explore different models for the organisation of maritime port labour that secure quality jobs and safe working conditions and that address fluctuations in the demand for port work. It is important that the Commission support and facilitate the work of the EU Sectoral Social Dialogue Committee in the Port Sector."

CHAPTER 44

Ports: reporting formalities for ships in European Union ports: Directive 2010/65

A. INTRODUCTION

44.001 It would help if the formalities for ships using European Union ("EU") ports were streamlined, simplified and harmonised.[1] Such a scenario would facilitate trade, harmonise procedures, increase predictability, reduce costs and hence improve compliance with law. It would also mean that a common minimum amount of information would be obtained by Member States and, in turn, the EU. The EU has therefore adopted a directive[2] aimed at simplifying and harmonising the administrative procedures applicable to maritime transport. The directive establishes a regime for the standard electronic transmission of information and the rationalisation of reporting formalities for ships arriving in, and departing from, EU ports.[3]

44.002 On 20 October 2010, the Parliament and Council adopted Directive 2010/65 on reporting formalities for ships arriving in and/or departing from ports of the Member States and repealing Directive 2002/6.[4] It is sometimes known as the "RFD" – the acronym for Reporting Formalities Directive.

44.003 Directive 2010/65 had not been the first measure on the topic and in fact it repealed Directive 2002/6[5] with effect from 19 May 2012. Indeed, there are (or have been) several measures in EU law dealing with various issues including notification

---

1 The ninth recital to Dir. 2010/65 (OJ L283/1, 29 October 2010) provides: "parties involved in trade and transport should be able to lodge standardised information and documents via an electronic single window to fulfil reporting formalities. Individual data elements should only be submitted once." If the UK proceeds to leave the EU (i.e. completes "Brexit") then one could see this measure as being a useful one for the UK to seek to abide by and retain as part of any post-Brexit regime because of the advantages which it gives shipping companies.

2 A directive, rather than a regulation, allows some flexibility to Member States in terms of how the regime is implemented. A regulation may have been ideal from the perspective of uniformity but it may have been too much to expect.

3 Indeed, the eleventh recital to Dir. 2010/65 emphasises that it is an electronic, rather than paper-based, system: "[w]hen adopting new Union measures, it should be ensured that Member States can maintain the electronic transmission of data and are not required to use paper formats".

4 OJ L283/1, 29 October 2010, http://eur-lex.europa.eu/legal-content/EN/TXT/HTML/?uri=CELEX:32010L 0065&from=EN. See Commission's PowerPoint on the regime: http://www.up.gov.si/fileadmin/up.gov.si/page-uploads/Predstavitve/RFD_roadmap.pdf. See also study to the Commission entitled "Study on Reporting Obligation Study on Reporting Obligation Resulting from Directive 2001/65 (Request for Services MOVE/D1/2012-376)". See PowerPoint entitled "Ship Formalities and e-Maritime" at the ECASBA Seminar, Brussels, 8 June 2011 by Patrick Norroy of DG MOVE, http://fonasba.com/wp-content/uploads/2012/06/NORROY.pdf. See also www.worldshipping.org/industry-issues/security/cargo-and-the-supply-chain/the-eu-reporting-formalities-directive for useful background.

5 Dir. 2010/65, Art. 16. It was repealed as of 19 May 2012. Recital 28 provides that in the interest of clarity, Dir. 2002/6 should be replaced by Dir. 2010/65.

requirements for ships arriving in/departing from ports of Member States (i.e. Article 4 of Directive 2002/59),[6] border checks on persons (i.e. Article 7 of Regulation 562/2006),[7] notification of dangerous or polluting goods carried on board (i.e. Article 13 of Directive 2002/59),[8] notification of ship waste and cargo residues (i.e. Article 6 of Directive 2000/59),[9] notification of security information (i.e. Article 6 of Regulation 725/2004) and entry summary declaration (i.e. Article 36a of Community Customs Code).[10]

44.004 Having a unified system on port formalities is very desirable. One has to be sure that reporting requirements, particularly linguistic requirements, should not be an obstacle to the free movement of goods or services (particularly, cabotage services); as recital 19 to Directive 2010/65 provides:

> "[n]ational language requirements are often an obstacle to the development of the coastal shipping network. The Member States should make all possible efforts to facilitate written and oral communication in maritime traffic between Member States, in accordance with international practice, with a view to finding common means of communication."

B. DIRECTIVE 2002/6 ON REPORTING FORMALITIES FOR SHIPS ARRIVING IN AND/OR DEPARTING FROM PORTS OF THE MEMBER STATES OF THE COMMUNITY

44.005 Directive 2002/6 of the European Parliament and of the Council of 18 February 2002 on "reporting formalities for ships arriving in and/or departing from ports of the Member States of the Community" had been adopted on 18 February 2002. It required Member States to accept certain standardised forms (known as "FAL Forms")[11] in order to facilitate traffic, as defined by the International Maritime Organization ("IMO") Convention on Facilitation of International Maritime Traffic ("FAL Convention"), adopted on 9 April 1965, as amended. Directive 2002/6 was repealed with effect from 19 May 2012. Directive 2002/6 was seen as costly and cumbersome[12] so Directive 2010/65 was aimed at making the regime more efficient.

---

6 OJ L208, 5 August 2002, p. 10. For text, see: http://eur-lex.europa.eu/legal-content/GA/TXT/?uri=celex: 32002L0059.

7 OJ L105, 13 April 2006, p. 1. For text, see: http://eur-lex.europa.eu/legal-content/EN/ALL/?uri=celex% 3A32006R0562.

8 OJ L208, 5 August 2002, p. 10. For text, see: http://eur-lex.europa.eu/legal-content/GA/TXT/?uri=celex: 32002L0059.

9 OJ L332, 28 December 2000, p. 81. For text, see http://eur-lex.europa.eu/LexUriServ/LexUriServ.do?uri= CELEX:32000L0059:EN:HTML.

10 See Kraft on www.harbourmaster.org.

11 The thirteenth recital to Dir. 2010/65 provides: "FAL forms are regularly updated. This Directive should therefore refer to the version of these forms that is currently in force. Any information required by Member States' legislation which goes beyond the requirements of the FAL Convention should be communicated in a format to be developed on the basis of FAL Convention standards."

12 See Malta-EU Steering & Action Group, www.shortsea.org.mt/news/userFiles/Directive%202010-65-EU%20-%20background%20note.pdf.

C. DIRECTIVE 2010/65 ON REPORTING FORMALITIES FOR SHIPS ARRIVING IN AND/OR DEPARTING FROM PORTS OF THE MEMBER STATES AND REPEALING DIRECTIVE 2002/6

Introduction

44.006 Directive 2010/65 is the mechanism by which the EU establishes a minimum reporting regime. As there are variations in the way in which the regime needs to be implemented, a directive (rather than a regulation) was more suitable as the relevant legal instrument.

Legal basis

44.007 The legal basis for Directive 2010/65 is the Treaty on the Functioning of the European Union ("TFEU") generally and, in particular, Article 100(2) of the TFEU. It was adopted in accordance with the ordinary legislative procedure. There had been a proposal from the European Commission, an opinion of the European Economic and Social Committee[13] and an opinion of the Committee of the Region.[14]

Entry into force

44.008 Article 14 of Directive 2010/65 deals with the transposition of the directive. It provides:

"1. Member States shall adopt and publish, by 19 May 2012 the laws, regulations and administrative provisions necessary to comply with this Directive. They shall forthwith communicate to the Commission the text of those provisions.

They shall apply those provisions from 19 May 2012.

When Member States adopt those provisions, they shall contain a reference to this Directive or be accompanied by such a reference on the occasion of their official publication. Member States shall determine how such reference is to be made.

2. Member States shall communicate to the Commission the text of the main provisions of national law which they adopt in the field covered by this Directive."

Factual background

44.009 The factual background is clear from the second recital to Directive 2010/65:

"For the facilitation of maritime transport and in order to reduce the administrative burdens for shipping companies, the reporting formalities required by legal acts of the Union and by Member States need to be simplified and harmonised to the greatest extent possible. However, this Directive should be without prejudice to the nature and content of the information required, and should not introduce any additional reporting requirements for ships not already under such obligation according to legislation applicable in Member States. It should deal solely with how the information procedures can be simplified and harmonised, and how the information could be gathered more effectively."

---

13 OJ C128, 18 May 2010, p. 131.
14 OJ C211, 4 September 2009, p. 65.

This recital emphasises that the administrative burdens should be simplified and harmonised as much as possible. It also emphasises that there should be no new additional requirements for ships

44.010 The third recital helps to put Directive 2010/65 into context given other measures:

"The transmission of data required upon arrival in and/or departure from ports under Directive 2000/59/EC of the European Parliament and of the Council of 27 November 2000 on port reception facilities for ship-generated waste and cargo residues,[15] Directive 2002/59/EC of the European Parliament and of the Council of 27 June 2002 establishing a Community vessel traffic monitoring and information system,[16] Regulation (EC) No 725/2004 of the European Parliament and of the Council of 31 March 2004 on enhancing ship and port facility security,[17] Directive 2009/16/EC of the European Parliament and of the Council of 23 April 2009 on port State control,[18] and, where appropriate, the International Maritime Dangerous Goods Code adopted in 1965, with the amendments thereto adopted and having entered into force, covers the information required by FAL forms. Therefore, where that information corresponds to the requirements in the above-mentioned legal acts, FAL forms should be accepted for providing it."[19]

44.011 The fourth recital is an apparently innocuous one but it is important in the context of describing how EU shipping law fits into the global (and, in particular, the IMO context): "In view of the global dimension of maritime transport, legal acts of the Union must take account of IMO requirements if simplification is to take place."

44.012 The system contemplated by Directive 2010/65 would be impossible without co-operation between Member States so the fifth recital states:

"Member States should deepen the cooperation between the competent authorities, such as their customs, border control, public health and transport authorities in order to continue to simplify and harmonise reporting formalities within the Union and make the most efficient use of electronic data transmission and information exchange systems, with a view to the, as far as possible, simultaneous elimination of barriers to maritime transport and the achievement of a European maritime transport space without barriers."

44.013 The desirability of having detailed statistics is described in the sixth recital:

"Detailed statistics on maritime transport should be available to assess the efficiency of and the need for policy measures aiming at facilitating maritime traffic within the Union, taking into account the need not to create unnecessary additional requirements with regard to the collection of statistics by the Member States and to make full use of Eurostat. For the purposes of this

---

15 Ed., OJ L332/8, 28 December 2000.
16 Ed., OJ L208/10, 5 August 2002.
17 Ed., OJ L129/6, 29 April 2004.
18 Ed., OJ L131/57, 28 May 2009.
19 The eighth recital provides: "Widespread use should be made of electronic means of data transmission for all reporting formalities as soon as possible and by 1 June 2015 at the latest, building on the international standards developed by the FAL Convention, whenever practicable. In order to streamline and accelerate the transmission of potentially very large amounts of information, electronic formats for reporting formalities should be used, whenever practicable. Within the Union, the provision of information in FAL forms in paper format should be the exception and should be accepted only for a limited period of time. Member States are encouraged to use administrative means, including economic incentives, to promote the use of electronic formats. For the above-mentioned reasons exchange of information between the competent authorities of the Member States should take place electronically. In order to facilitate such a development, electronic systems need to be technically interoperable to a greater extent and as far as possible by the same deadline to ensure the smooth functioning of the European maritime transport space without barriers."

Directive, it would be important to collect relevant data concerning ship traffic within the Union and/or ships calling at third country ports or in free zones."

Subject matter and scope of the directive

44.014 Article 1 of 2010/65 describes the subject matter and scope of the directive. Article 1(1) provides that the purpose of the directive is to simplify and harmonise the administrative procedures applied to maritime transport by making the electronic transmission of information standard and by rationalising reporting formalities. Article 1(2) provides that the directive shall apply to the reporting formalities applicable to maritime transport for ships arriving in and ships departing from ports situated in Member States. Under Article 1(3), the directive shall not apply to ships exempted from reporting formalities.

44.015 In terms of the application of Directive 2010/65, recital 24 recalls that according to the case law of the Court of Justice of the European Union, where transposition of a directive is pointless for reasons of geography, transposition is not mandatory and, therefore, requirements in the directive are not relevant for Member States which do not have any ports at which ships falling under the scope of the directive normally can call. Hence, for example, Luxembourg has not transposed the directive.

44.016 Article 2 sets out six definitions for the purposes of the directive. The first term "reporting formalities" means

"the information set out in the Annex which, in accordance with the legislation applicable in a Member State, must be provided for administrative and procedural purposes when a ship arrives in or departs from a port in that Member State."

This is the minimum amount of information which must be provided. The second definition is simply a cross-reference to the "FAL Convention" and is defined as meaning the IMO Convention on Facilitation of International Maritime Traffic, as amended, which was adopted on 9 April 1965. Third, the term "FAL forms" means the standardised forms, as provided for in the FAL Convention. Fourth, the term "ships" is defined as meaning "any seagoing vessel or craft" so there is no minimum requirement for persons to be on board. Penultimately, the term "SafeSeaNet" is defined as meaning the EU's maritime information exchange system as defined in Directive 2002/59.[20] Finally, the term "electronic transmission of data" is defined as meaning the process of transmitting information that has been encoded digitally, using a revisable structured format which can be used directly for storage and processing by computers.

44.017 The seventh recital of the directive provides that the directive

"should be easier for shipping companies to benefit from the status of 'authorised regular shipping service' in line with the objective of the Commission communication of 21 January 2009

---

20 The tenth recital to Dir. 2010/65 provides: "SafeSeaNet systems established at national and Union level should facilitate the reception, exchange and distribution of information between the information systems of Member States on maritime activity. To facilitate maritime transport and to reduce the administrative burdens for maritime transport, the SafeSeaNet system should be interoperable with other systems of the Union for reporting formalities. The SafeSeaNet system should be used for additional exchange of information for the facilitation of maritime transport. Reporting formalities regarding information for solely national purposes should not need to be introduced in the SafeSeaNet system."

entitled 'Communication and action plan with a view to establishing a European maritime transport space without barriers'."

Harmonisation and co-ordination of reporting formalities

44.018 Article 3 is entitled "harmonisation and coordination of reporting formalities". Under Article 3(1), each Member State shall take measures to ensure that the reporting facilities are requested in a harmonised and co-ordinated manner within that Member State. Under Article 3(2), the Commission must, in co-operation with the Member States, develop mechanisms for the harmonisation and co-ordination of reporting formalities within the EU.

Notification of ships prior to their arrival into ports

44.019 The notification of ships prior to their arrival into ports is addressed by Article 4:

"Subject to specific provisions on notification provided for in the applicable legal acts of the Union or under international legal instruments applicable to maritime transport and binding on the Member States, including provisions on control of persons and goods, Member States shall ensure that the master or any other person duly authorised by the operator of the ship provides notification, prior to arriving in a port situated in a Member State, of the information required under the reporting formalities to the competent authority designated by that Member State:

(a) at least 24 hours in advance; or
(b) at the latest, at the time the ship leaves the previous port, if the voyage time is less than 24 hours; or
(c) if the port of call is not known or it is changed during the voyage, as soon as this information is available."

44.020 Article 5 deals with the electronic transmission of data:

"1. Member States shall accept the fulfilment of reporting formalities in electronic format and their transmission via a single window as soon as possible and in any case no later than 1 June 2015.
   This single window, linking SafeSeaNet, e-Customs and other electronic systems, shall be the place where, in accordance with this Directive, all information is reported once and made available to various competent authorities and the Member States.
2. Without prejudice to the relevant format set out in the FAL Convention, the format referred to in paragraph 1 shall comply with Article 6.
3. Where reporting formalities are required by legal acts of the Union and to the extent necessary for the good functioning of the single window established pursuant to paragraph 1, the electronic systems referred to in paragraph 1 must be interoperable, accessible and compatible with the SafeSeaNet system established in accordance with Directive 2002/59/EC and, where applicable, with the computer systems stipulated in Decision No 70/2008/EC of the European Parliament and of the Council of 15 January 2008 on a paperless environment for customs and trade.[21]
4. Without prejudice to specific provisions on customs and border control set out in Regulation (EEC) No 2913/92 and Regulation (EC) No 562/2006, Member States shall consult economic operators and inform the Commission of progress made using the methods stipulated in Decision No 70/2008/EC."

---

21 Ed., OJ L23/21, 26 January 2008.

44.021 This reflects the twelfth recital of Directive 2010/65 which provides that the

"full benefits of electronic data transmission can only be achieved where there is smooth and effective communication between SafeSeaNet, e-Customs and the electronic systems for entering or calling up data. To that end, in order to limit the administrative burdens, recourse should be had in the first instance to the applicable standards."

44.022 The exchange of data is addressed by Article 6:

"1. Member States shall ensure that information received in accordance with the reporting formalities provided in a legal act of the Union is made available in their national SafeSeaNet systems and shall make relevant parts of such information available to other Member States via the SafeSeaNet system. Unless otherwise provided by a Member State, this shall not apply to information received pursuant to Regulation (EEC) No 2913/92, Regulation (EEC) No 2454/93, Regulation (EC) No 562/2006 and Regulation (EC) No 450/2008.

2. Member States shall ensure that the information received in accordance with paragraph 1 is accessible, upon request, to the relevant national authorities.

3. The underlying digital format of the messages to be used within national SafeSeaNet systems in accordance with paragraph 1 shall be established in accordance with Article 22a of Directive 2002/59/EC.

4. Member States may provide relevant access to the information referred to in paragraph 1 either through a national single window via an electronic data exchange system or through the national SafeSeaNet systems."

44.023 Article 7 deals with the information to be contained in FAL forms: "Member States shall accept FAL forms for the fulfilment of reporting formalities. Member States may accept that information required in accordance with a legal act of the Union is provided in a paper format until 1 June 2015 only." So, the transition period for paper forms has ended and the regime is now entirely electronic.

44.024 It is important that returns are kept confidential to an appropriate extent. In this context, there is a need to respect personal data legislation, commercial secrecy and security. Article 8(1) provides that Member States must, in accordance with the applicable legal acts of the EU or national legislation, take the necessary measures to ensure the confidentiality of commercial and other confidential information exchanged in accordance with the directive. Article 8(2) provides that Member States must take particular care to protect commercial data collected under the directive. In respect of personal data, Member States shall ensure that they comply with Directive 95/46. The EU institutions and bodies must ensure that they comply with Regulation 45/2001.

44.025 There are some exemptions provided for in Article 9:

"Member States shall ensure that ships falling within the scope of Directive 2002/59/EC and operating between ports situated in the customs territory of the Union, but which do not come from, call at or are headed towards a port situated outside that territory or a free zone subject to type I controls under customs legislation, are exempt from the obligation to send the information referred to in the FAL forms, without prejudice to the applicable legal acts of the Union and the possibility that Member States may request information in the FAL forms referred to in points 1 to 6 of Part B of the Annex to this Directive which is necessary to protect internal order and security and to enforce customs, fiscal, immigration, environmental or sanitary laws."

Amendment procedure

44.026 Articles 10–12 of the directive address the amendment procedure to the directive.[22]

Reporting on the functioning of the directive

44.027 Article 15 of the directive deals with a report to be produced by the Commission to the Parliament and the Council on the functioning of the directive. Article 15 provides that the Commission had to report to the European Parliament and the Council, by 19 November 2013, on the functioning of the directive, including on the: (a) possibility of extending the simplification introduced by this directive to cover inland waterway transport; (b) compatibility of the River Information Services with the electronic data transmission process referred to in the directive; (c) progress towards harmonisation and co-ordination of reporting formalities that has been achieved under Article 3; (d) feasibility of avoiding or simplifying formalities for ships that have called at a port in a third country or free zone; (e) available data concerning ship traffic/movement within the Union, and/or calling at third country ports or in free zones. The report shall, if appropriate, be accompanied by a legislative proposal.[23]

44.028 On 25 June 2014, the Commission sent a report to the Parliament and the Council on the functioning of Directive 2010/65 on reporting formalities for ships

---

22 "Article 10: Amendment procedure[:] 1. The Commission may adopt delegated acts, in accordance with Article 290 of the Treaty on the Functioning of the European Union, as regards the Annex to this Directive, so as to ensure that account is taken of any relevant changes to the FAL forms introduced by the IMO. These amendments shall not have the effect of widening the scope of this Directive. 2. For the delegated acts referred to in this Article, the procedures set out in Articles 11, 12 and 13 shall apply. Article 11: Exercise of the delegation[:] 1. The power to adopt the delegated acts referred to in Article 10 shall be conferred on the Commission for a period of 5 years from 18 November 2010. The Commission shall make a report in respect of the delegated powers at the latest 6 months before the end of the 5-year period. The delegation of power shall be automatically extended for periods of an identical duration, unless the European Parliament or the Council revokes it in accordance with Article 12. 2. As soon as it adopts a delegated act, the Commission shall notify it simultaneously to the European Parliament and to the Council. 3. The power to adopt delegated acts is conferred on the Commission subject to the conditions laid down in Articles 12 and 13. Article 12: Revocation of the delegation[:] 1. The delegation of powers referred to in Article 10 may be revoked by the European Parliament or by the Council at any time. 2. The institution which has commenced an internal procedure for deciding whether to revoke the delegation of powers shall endeavour to inform the other institution and the Commission within a reasonable time before the final decision is taken, indicating the delegated powers which could be subject to revocation and possible reasons for a revocation. 3. The decision of revocation shall put an end to the delegation of the powers specified in that decision. It shall take effect immediately or at a later date specified therein. It shall not affect the validity of the delegated acts already in force. It shall be published in the Official Journal of the European Union. Article 13: Objections to delegated acts[:] 1. The European Parliament or the Council may object to a delegated act within a period of 2 months from the date of notification. At the initiative of the European Parliament or the Council that period shall be extended by 2 months. 2. Where, on expiry of the initial 2-month period or, if applicable, the extended period, neither the European Parliament nor the Council has objected to the delegated act, it shall be published in the Official Journal of the European Union and enter into force on the date stated therein. The delegated act may be published in the Official Journal of the European Union and enter into force before the expiry of the initial 2-month period or, if applicable, the extended period where the European Parliament and the Council have both informed the Commission of their intention not to raise objections. 3. Where the European Parliament or the Council objects to a delegated act, it shall not enter into force. The institution which objects shall state the reasons for objecting to the delegated act."

23 See also draft report entitled "Directive 2010/65/EU On reporting formalities for ships arriving in and/or departing from ports – 8th eMS expert group meeting", 20 March 2013, http://ec.europa.eu/transparency/regexpert/index.cfm?do=groupDetail.groupDetailDoc&id=8971&no=2.

arriving in and/or departing from ports of the Member States.[24] It concluded that the implementation process of the directive was still ongoing and the final establishment of the single window. Co-operation among them, both on EU and national levels, was key and should be enhanced. The Commission believed that Member States should carefully assess their current systems, actively participate in the work of the eMS group and implement the functional and technical specifications in a correct manner and as discussed within the eMS group.[25] In addition, benefit could be taken from the work done in the IMP[26] demonstrator project and the AnNa[27] project. Both projects offered hands-on solutions for implementing national single windows. Ultimately, with regards to the other reporting requirements the following conclusions could be drawn: (a) there was no sufficient and detailed information available on the extent of the traffic/movement of ships from one EU port to another, or of ships calling intermediately at third country ports or entering free zones. There are however possibilities identified to gather more information in the future. The Commission will look into these possibilities and see if and how they could help to improve the quality and availability of statistics; and (b) the optimal use of shipping should be stimulated by avoiding or further simplifying formalities for ships that have called at a port in a third country or free zone. The recent Blue Belt initiative and the development of the eManifest, once implemented, should be a major step in this direction. As a next step, the Commission should look into further simplification measures by for example adding other (customs) functionalities to the eManifest.

Reporting requirements

44.029 It is useful to review the actual reporting requirements. The annex to the directive sets them out in detail. It deals with issues such as the reporting formalities resulting from legal acts of the EU, the FAL forms and formalities resulting from international legal instruments and any national legal requirements. There is also an appendix entitled "Ship Pre-Arrival Security Information Form for all Ships Prior to Entry into the Port of an EU Member State".

Assessment and conclusions

44.030 On 25 June 2014, the Commission adopted a report on the implementation of Directive 2010/65. The report urged Member States to step up compliance.

44.031 This report reviewed Directive 2010/65 which has helped to facilitate the transmission of data and information in a more efficient and effective manner. The World Shipping Council has summarised the directive but also commented critically about its implementation:

"The EU Reporting Formalities Directive (2010/65/EU) or RFD aims to simplify, harmonize, and rationalize administrative procedures and reporting requirements for maritime carriers

---

24 COM(2014) 320 final, http://ec.europa.eu/transport/modes/maritime/ports/doc/com(2014)320.pdf.

25 The term "eMS group" refers to the expert group on maritime simplification and electronic information service.

26 The IMP refers to the Integrated Maritime Policy.

27 This was the Advanced National Network for Administrations (www.annamsw.eu/) but it no longer operates.

calling at EU ports. It requires that by June 1, 2015 Member States implement measures to allow the electronic submission and reception of reporting formalities concerning vessels, their crew and cargo via a 'national single window'. Paper submissions will no longer be required or allowed. It also seeks to maximize the re-use among authorities of the information submitted electronically to the national single windows (NSW) both within and between Member States. It thus aims at a 'once only submission' of information. It seeks to improve EU trade facilitation and – quoting the European Commission – to create a 'maritime space without barriers' within the EU's internal market. With these objectives in focus the RFD was strongly welcomed by WSC and the maritime sector when the legislation was adopted in 2010.

Regrettably, the implementation of the Directive by Member States has very substantially undermined these positive objectives. A combination of an inadequate legal base in the Directive, which is not legally binding, and the resistance of many EU Member States, has prevented the EU from delivering the harmonized EU wide solutions necessary for the Directive to offer genuine benefits instead of net costs to shipping.

...

There are three critical problems in the implementation of the Directive:

1. No effort to harmonize the national requirements
2. Concept of a national single window has been seriously compromised
3. Each Member State is developing an independent system

First, despite a clear commitment in the legislation, there has been no effort to harmonize the national requirements that derive from Member State legislation, as opposed to those that stem from international agreements (such as the IMO FAL Convention) or EU legislative acts.

Second, the concept of a national single window – the center piece of the Directive – has been seriously compromised as many Member States will implement the Directive on the basis of port level, not national, entry points. There is significant uncertainty as to whether information submitted to port single windows will be shared automatically at a national level, let alone between Member States. These developments have steadily eroded the principles underpinning the Directive's expected benefits, in particular the principle of only having to submit required information once.

Third, in the absence of binding functional and technical specifications for the way that national single windows interface with industry, each Member State and/or port is developing its system independently of each other and without regard for consistency across the EU. Consequently, carriers face the prospect of having to connect to a multitude of differently functioning and constructed single windows across the EU.

Adding to the industry's concern, despite repeated requests to the Member States and to the Commission, the industry has at the end of 2014 still no overview concerning the state of readiness in Member States, their chosen implementation models, or IT requirements for the submission of information. This leaves no time whatsoever for the industry to introduce the documentary processes and IT adaptations and tests that will be necessary to ensure compliance with the new reporting requirements as of June 1, 2015.

This represents an unacceptable situation and eliminates all of the original, intended benefits of the legislation. The European Commission has stated that it does not intend to postpone implementation of the Directive.

Since December 2012, WSC, in cooperation with the European Community Shipowners Associations (ECSA), has been alerting the Commission and Member States to the very serious consequences that their implementation plans will have for the EU maritime sector.

In January 2013, WSC and ECSA wrote to Mr. Fotis Karamitsos, Deputy Director General of DG MOVE, European Commission, setting out serious concerns already noted at that stage and the need to refocus implementation on genuinely beneficial and harmonised solutions.

Throughout 2013 and 2014, the WSC participated at the meetings of the EC-chaired Member States Expert Group (EMS), which is the body tasked with coordinating RFD implementation. Multiple written submissions and statements were made to this group expressing the need for a fully harmonised data set of information for submission to Member States, a network of genuine national single windows that share information, and a binding set of uniform functional and technical specifications for the single window interfaces with trade. WSC/ECSA made joint statements to the EMS group in December 2013 and again in May 2014. The latter states that, in view of progress towards implementation, it is now inconceivable that the Directive could be implemented in June 2015 without imposing an unacceptable cost on the shipping industry and that to do so would be entirely without the support of the shipping industry as represented by WSC and ECSA.

Further high level meetings and discussions have taken place with the Deputy Director General of DG MOVE in October 2013 and October 2014 to try to find practical solutions. The latter took place in the presence of WSC and ECSA members on the occasion of a joint seminar in Brussels devoted to EU Customs and Reporting Formalities. On this occasion the EC repeated that the Directive could not be delayed, but that an enhanced effort would be made by the EC to ensure that the National Single Window interfaces would share common functional and technical specifications as well as harmonized message implementing guidelines. However, the EC subsequently had to acknowledge that this commitment could not be delivered.

In the meantime, a letter has been received from the Commission confirming that, in recognition of the evident flaws of the Directive, the legislation will be revised in 2016. We hope this would be used to establish a legal basis that is capable of delivering harmonized solutions. Pending this, and to avoid disruption to trade and prevent industry from investing in new processes and IT systems by June 2015 perhaps only to be replaced soon thereafter with other processes and IT solutions; WSC and ECSA call on the EC and Member States to keep their existing channels for reporting formalities in operation after June 1, 2015 and at least until the Directive is revised and suitable harmonized arrangements are delivered."[28]

44.032 In November 2017, the European Community Shipowners' Association ("ECSA") and the European Transport Workers' Federation ("ETF") both condemned the existing regime as too bureaucratic and burdensome.[29]

44.033 It is therefore clear that the directive was well-intentioned but has proved somewhat difficult in its implementation according to some in the sector.

44.034 For completeness, it is worth noting that it was proposed in 2016 to amend the directive. On 6 June 2016, the Commission proposed[30] a directive to amend Directive 98/41 on the registration of persons sailing on board passenger ships operating to or from ports of the Member States of the Community and to amend this directive. Article 2 of the proposed directive would amend Part A of the annex to Directive 2010/65 by adding a new point 7 which would read:

"7. Information on persons on board
Articles 4(2) and 5(2) of Council Directive 98/41/EC of 18 June 1998 on the registration of persons sailing on board passenger ships operating to or from ports of the Member States of the Community (OJ L188, 2.7.1998, p. 35)."

---

28 www.worldshipping.org/industry-issues/security/cargo-and-the-supply-chain/the-eu-reporting-formalities-directive.

29 www.marinelink.com/news/administrative-shipping431136.

30 See Commission, "Proposal for a Directive of the European Parliament and of the Council amending Council Directive 98/41/EC on the registration of persons sailing on board passenger ships operating to or from ports of the Member States of the Community and amending Directive 2010/65/EU of the European Parliament and of the Council on reporting formalities for ships arriving in and/or departing from ports of the Member States", COM(2016) 370 final.

CHAPTER 45

Ports: electricity for ships in ports

A. INTRODUCTION

45.001 This chapter considers the European Union ("EU") legal regime which requires ships to use shore-based electricity, where possible, rather than using their own engines. The requirement to use shore-power (rather than ship-power) is motivated by the fact that ship-power usually leads to more emissions than shore-power and so shore-power is more environmentally friendly. This chapter should be read in conjunction with the other chapters in the book, including, in particular, those dealing with the marine environment.

B. 2002: COMMISSION COMMUNICATION ON A STRATEGY TO REDUCE ATMOSPHERIC EMISSIONS FROM SEAGOING SHIPS

45.002 On 20 November 2002, the Commission adopted a communication to the European Parliament and the Council on a European Union Strategy to Reduce Atmospheric Emissions from Seagoing Ships.[1] The communication urged port authorities to require, incentivise or facilitate ships' use of land-based electricity while in port rather than relying on ship-power. The communication recognised that atmospheric emissions from seagoing ships include air pollutants, greenhouse gases and ozone-depleting substances, these emissions do not disperse harmlessly to the sea and they do not stop at national boundaries. The primary air pollutants addressed in the strategy were sulphur dioxide (SO_2 or SO_x), nitrogen oxides (NO_x), volatile organic compounds ("VOCs") and primary particulate matter ("PM"). Secondary pollutants considered in the strategy were sulphuric and nitric acids, formed by oxidation of SO_2 and NO_x; ground-level ozone, formed by photo-chemical reactions of NO_x and VOCs in sunlight; and secondary PM, including sulphate and nitrate particles created by the oxidisation of NO_x and SO_2. The principal greenhouse gas considered was carbon dioxide (CO_2). The principal ozone depleting substance at issue is halon.

45.003 The communication recognised that there are many operational measures which can be taken to reduce atmospheric emissions of air pollutants and greenhouse gases. It recognised that reducing fuel consumption was the most obvious one and applicable to all vessel categories but there were other measures too. It recognised that while in general, ships are already reasonably fuel-efficient in the interests of economy, speed reduction during steaming and, importantly for present purposes, running from shore-side electricity while in port are further means of reducing fuel consumption, and consequently emissions. Ultimately, among the communication's recommendations, the Commission urged port authorities to consider introducing voluntary speed reductions, and to require, incentivise or

---

1 COM(2002) 595 final, not published in the Official Journal.

facilitate ships' use of land-based electricity or clean on-board power while hotelling in port. In essence, the Commission urged port authorities to require, incentivise or facilitate ships' use of land-based electricity while in port so as to reduce the use of marine fuels.

C. 2003: EUROPEAN PARLIAMENT RESOLUTION ON THE STRATEGY TO REDUCE ATMOSPHERIC EMISSIONS FROM SEAGOING SHIPS

45.004 On 4 December 2003, the European Parliament adopted a resolution on the strategy to reduce atmospheric emissions from seagoing ships.[2] The Parliament pointed out that the use of land-based electricity in port can be facilitated by the production of a report describing positive examples of these measures, as well as their costs and benefits.

45.005 The resolution stated:

"*European Parliament resolution on a European Union strategy to reduce atmospheric emissions from seagoing ships*[3]
The European Parliament, – having regard to the Communication from the Commission to the European Parliament and the Council on a European Union strategy to reduce atmospheric emissions from seagoing ships (COM(2002) 595), – having regard to Decision No 1600/2002/EC[4] of the European Parliament and of the Council of 22 July 2002 laying down the Sixth Community Environment Action Programme, – having regard to Directive 2001/81/EC[5] of the European Parliament and of the Council of 23 October 2001 on national emission ceilings for certain atmospheric pollutants,

- having regard to the proposal for a Directive of the European Parliament and of the Council amending Directive 1999/32/EC[6] as regards the sulphur content of marine fuels and its position of 4 June 2003 thereon,[7]
- having regard to Rules 47(2) and 163 of its Rules of Procedure,
- having regard to the report of the Committee on the Environment, Public Health and Consumer Policy (A5–0400/2003),

A. whereas the Community's environmental policy, as set out in the action programmes on the environment and in particular in the Sixth Environmental Action Programme on the basis of principles enshrined in Article 174 of the Treaty, aims to achieve levels of air quality that do not give rise to unacceptable impacts on, and risks to, human health and the environment,
B. whereas emissions from shipping due to the combustion of marine fuels with a high sulphur content contribute to air pollution in the form of sulphur dioxide and particulate matter harming human health and contributing to acidification,

1. Welcomes the aim of the Commission, as spelled out in section 1.1 of the aforementioned Communication, to 'set out a broad series of objectives, actions and recommendations' for reducing the emissions of air pollutants from seagoing ships over the next ten years;
2. Welcomes the initiatives of the European Commission's White Paper on the 'European Transport Policy for 2010: time to decide' (COM(2001) 370), linking up the modes of transport and including short sea shipping as well as sea transport highways, emphasising the environmental benefits of waterborne transport; underlines, however, that it is crucial to oblige seagoing ships, by means of concerted action in

---

2 COM(2002) 595 – 2003/2064(INI).
3 Ibid.
4 OJ L242, 10.9.2002, pp. 1–15.
5 OJ L309, 27.11.2001, p. 22.
6 OJ L121, 11.5.1999, p. 13.
7 P5_TA(2003)0248.

the IMO and other international fora, to become cleaner and assistance should be provided to allow them [to] retain the environmental bonus of waterborne transport (similar to rail transport);

3. Agrees with the Commission that the main atmospheric emissions to be addressed in such a strategy are sulphur dioxide, nitrogen oxides, volatile organic compounds, particulates, carbon dioxide and halon; however, suggests that the Commission also consider including polycyclic aromatics (such as PAH) and heavy metals (e.g. Nickel and Vanadium) (section 1.1);

4. As one of the aims of the present strategy is to contribute to the 'Clean Air For Europe' (CAFE) programme, stresses that, whilst taking account of the conclusions following from the programme's development in the various legislative acts, an additional objective to this strategy should be the contribution to the EU's long-term goal of not exceeding critical loads and levels, as provided in Article 7, paragraph 2(f) of the Sixth Community Environment Programme (section 1.1);

5. Stresses that one of the objectives of the Sixth Environmental Action Programme is to achieve 'levels of air quality that do not give rise to significant negative impacts on, and risks to, human health and the environment'; emphasises that this wording cannot necessarily be equated to that used in section 1.2 of the Commission's strategy, namely to avoid 'unacceptable impacts';

6. Supports the Commission's overall objective (section 6.1) to reduce the contribution of ships' atmospheric emissions to environmental and human health problems in the EU; underlines, however, that this overall objective should be extended so as to explicitly aim to reduce ships' emissions of greenhouse gases (such as carbon dioxide) and their contribution to global warming;

7. Notes that emissions from international maritime traffic are currently excluded from Directive 2001/81/EC (National Emissions Ceilings), and asks the Commission to study the ways in which they could be included in the context of the review process;

8. Fully agrees with the Commission's conclusions that EU regulation on emission standards is 'the best way to reduce emissions from ships in EU ports, territorial waters and exclusive economic zones' (section 6.3), that 'economic instruments are one of the best means of promoting good environmental performance' (section 6.4), and that in order 'to achieve effective global reductions in atmospheric emissions the EU and its Member States need to work closely with key shipping nations at the International Maritime Organisation (IMO)'; consequently, calls on the Commission to adapt its policy proposals to these conclusions (section 2.2);

9. Notes with concern that the aforementioned proposal for a Directive amending Directive 1999/32/EC relating to the sulphur content of marine fuels, would only reduce sulphur emissions from seagoing ships in European sea areas by about 10%, as compared to emission levels for 2000, but that in order to achieve the objectives of the Sixth Community Environment Programme, emissions need to be reduced by at least 80% (section 6.3);

10. Considers that the Commission, in the context of the revision of Directive 1999/32/EC relating to the sulphur content of marine fuels, has set only limited targets as regards the limit values proposed and the sea areas to be covered by such limit values; calls, therefore, on the Commission to amend this proposal in accordance with the position of the European Parliament of 4 June 2003, which aims to reduce sulphur emissions by 80%;

11. Calls on the Commission to urgently analyse the costs and benefits of alternative, more far-reaching abatement measures and, in particular, the costs and benefits of the measures adopted by the European Parliament in its position of 4 June 2003;

12. Notes the Commission's intention to bring forward a proposal to reduce NOx emissions from seagoing vessels within, and in cooperation with, the IMO, and in line with the Tier 2 standards proposed by the US Environment Protection Agency; is concerned, however, that the Commission may link this action to future developments in the IMO, i.e. that the Commission will only take this action if, by the end 2006,

the IMO has not proposed higher international NOx standards for marine engines (section 6.3);

13. Calls on the Commission to present, before the end of 2004, a proposal for NOx emission standards for ships, based on the use of best available techniques (BAT), and which aims to reduce NOx emissions from ship engines, and to pursue BAT-based NOx emission standards which can be accepted also by the IMO;

14. Notes that the Commission expresses its intention to look again 'in future' at the possibility of regulating VOC emissions from ship-loading, and calls on the Commission to update its study on the cost-effectiveness of such measures in the light of recent technological developments and, if appropriate, to come forward with proposals for such a regulation before June 2005; (section 6.3)

15. Notes with concern that the Commission has not yet come forward with proposals for an EU-system of differentiated charges for all transport modes which takes into account marginal social costs including the external costs of air pollution and climate change, despite it being announced in the strategy that such a proposal was due 'early 2003' (section 6.4);

16. Calls on the Commission to present, before the end of 2004, proposals for EU-wide economic instruments aimed at reducing atmospheric emissions from ships;

17. Welcomes the Commission's initiative to launch a new 'Clean Marine Award Scheme' (section 6.5);

18. Notes that the Commission urges the international bunker industry to make available significant quantities of 1.5% sulphur marine heavy fuel oils in states bordering SOx emission control areas; underlines, however, that this request should be extended so as to also meet the demand for marine fuels with a maximum sulphur content of 0.5%, in all Community sea areas (section 6.5);

19. Notes that the Commission urges port authorities to consider introducing voluntary speed reductions and to require, provide incentives or facilitate ships' use of land-based electricity or of clean power produced on-board while in port; emphasises, however, that such measures could be facilitated by producing a report describing successful examples of these measures, as well as their costs and benefits (section 6.5); points out at the same time, that particular attention must be paid to, and derogations provided for, remote island regions;

20. Notes with concern that, despite the promising statements made by the Member States to the Commission last year, still only five Member States (Sweden, Denmark, Greece, Germany and Spain) have ratified Annex VI of the MARPOL Convention, and it consequently has not yet received the sufficient number of country ratifications needed to enter into force; calls, therefore, on all Member States and Accession countries that have not yet ratified it, to do so as a matter of urgency (sections 2.3 and 4.1);

21. Notes that the NOx emission standards contained in Annex VI of the MARPOL Convention were defined in 1997, and have already been applied to new marine engines built since 2000; calls on Member States to make submissions to the IMO as soon as Annex VI of the Convention enters into force, proposing higher global NOx standards for new marine engines which are more in line with the best available technology, and considering the introduction of NOx standards for existing vessels;

22. Notes the Commission's intention to identify and undertake specific actions to reduce greenhouse gas emissions from marine shipping if the IMO has not adopted a concrete, ambitious strategy on ship greenhouse gas emissions by 2003; calls on Member States to support the adoption of the draft resolution on its greenhouse gas strategy at the IMO Assembly of 2003, and subsequently to submit proposals to the IMO aimed at developing and implementing the strategy in a concrete and ambitious manner (sections 4.1 and 6.2);

23. Instructs its President to forward this resolution to the Council, the Commission, the governments of the Member States and the Accession countries and the International Maritime Organisation."

D. 2006: COMMISSION RECOMMENDATION ON THE PROMOTION OF SHORE-SIDE ELECTRICITY FOR USE BY SHIPS AT BERTH IN COMMUNITY PORTS

45.006 On 8 May 2006, the Commission adopted Recommendation 2006/339 on the promotion of shore-side electricity (i.e. national grid electricity) for use by ships at berth in Community ports.[8] Shore-side electricity would be used instead of ships producing electricity using their own engines. The aim, as mentioned above, is to reduce air and noise emissions from ships' engines while at berths in port. The recommendation was based on the Treaty establishing the European Community ("TEC") generally and, in particular, Article 211 of the then TEC.

45.007 The background to the recommendation is clear from the recitals:

"(1) In November 2002 the Commission adopted a Communication to the European Parliament and the Council on a European Union strategy to reduce atmospheric emissions from seagoing ships, … which urged port authorities to require, incentivise or facilitate ships' use of land-based electricity while in port.

(2) The European Parliament, in its resolution on the strategy of 4 December 2003,[9] pointed out that the use of land-based electricity in port could be facilitated by the production of a report describing positive examples of these measures, as well as their costs and benefits.

(3) The Council, in its Conclusions on the strategy of 22 December 2003,[10] recognised that not all environmental problems are properly addressed at international level and that, in particular, the contribution of seagoing ships to the concentration of particulate matter and of ozone and its precursors in ambient air needed further consideration.

(4) The Commission, in the context of its Communication 'The Clean Air for Europe (CAFE) programme: Towards a thematic strategy for air quality',[11] re-examined the contribution of shipping to the concentration of air pollutants in ambient air and found it to be significant, particularly in port areas. In some port areas, the attainment of air quality standards may be jeopardised by ship emissions.

(5) CAFE found that reducing ship emissions is increasingly cost-effective compared to further measures in other sectors. Most ship pollutant emissions at berth can only be reduced through engine and after-treatment measures or through the use of shore-side electricity.

(6) Ship engine emissions are regulated at international level through the International Maritime Organisation (IMO). The evolution of these standards is insufficient to respond to port air quality problems in the Community.

(7) Article 4b of Council Directive 1999/32/EC of 26 April 1999 relating to a reduction in the sulphur content of certain liquid fuels and amending Directive 93/12…[12] as regards the sulphur content of marine fuels, exempts ships which switch off all engines and use shore-side electricity while at berth in ports from the requirement to use 0,1% sulphur marine fuel.

(8) Council Directive 2003/96/EC of 27 October 2003 restructuring the Community framework for the taxation of energy products and electricity[13] permits Member States to apply total or partial exemptions or reductions in the level of taxation to electricity under certain conditions."

45.008 The recommendation itself provides:

"1. Member States should consider the installation of shore-side electricity for use by ships at berth in ports; particularly in ports where air quality limit values are exceeded or where

---

8 OJ L125/38, 12 May 2006.
9 Ed., OJ C89/107, 14 April 2004.
10 OJ C8/3, 13.1.2004.
11 COM(2001) 245 final.
12 Ed., OJ L121/13, 11 May 1999.
13 Ed., OJ L283/51, 31 October 2003.

public concern is expressed about high levels of noise nuisance, and especially in berths situated near residential areas.

2. Member States should take note of the advice, set out in the Annex, on the cost-effectiveness and practicality of using shore-side electricity to reduce emissions for different types of ships, routes and ports. Nevertheless, the environmental benefits and cost-effectiveness should be evaluated on a case by case basis.

3. Member States should work within the International Maritime Organization (IMO), in the context of the ongoing review of the International Convention for the Prevention of Pollution from Ships (MARPOL Convention), to promote the development of harmonised international standards for shore-side electrical connections, taking into account ongoing work.

4. Member States should consider offering economic incentives to operators to use shore-side electricity provided to ships, taking advantage of the possibilities set out in Community legislation.

5. Member States should promote awareness of shore-side electricity among local authorities whose responsibility includes port areas, maritime authorities, port authorities, classification societies and industry associations.

6. Member States should encourage port authorities and industry to exchange best practice concerning shore-side electricity supply and harmonising procedures for this service.

7. Member States should report to the Commission on the action they intend to take to reduce ship emissions in ports, particularly where air quality limit values are exceeded."

The annex provides pertinent information on the costs and benefits of shore-side electricity. More detailed information is contained in the recent report for the Commission, "Service Contract on Ship Emissions Assignment, Abatement and Market-based Instruments: Shore-side Electricity". It also contains details of the technical requirements benefits and costs.

E. CONCLUSION

45.009 The Commission concluded that shore-power was beneficial. In the annex to its 2006 Recommendation on the Promotion of Shore-side Electricity for Use by Ships at Berth in Community Ports[14] the Commission stated:

"The benefits and costs of shore-side electricity vary significantly depending on the existing configuration and location of the port, berth and ship. This means that its cost-effectiveness needs to be studied on a case-by-case basis, and that direct reduction of marine engine emissions should continue to be pursued.

In environmental terms, shore-side electricity achieves emission reductions well beyond those achieved from switching to 0,1% sulphur fuel at berth (as Directive 2005/33/EC requires from 2010), particularly for NOx and PM. It therefore merits particular consideration in ports where ship NOx and PM emissions are contributing to local air quality problems, such as exceedances of ambient air quality limit values for ozone and particles.

In general the figures suggest that for ships with larger engines regularly visiting the same port, switching to shore-side electricity should be both environmentally and economically preferable to using 0,1% sulphur fuel. In economic terms, shore-side electricity should generate savings compared to low sulphur fuel for new-build ships regularly visiting the same ports, especially, but not only, if electricity tax reductions are offered as allowed under Directive 2003/96/EC. Member States and local authorities might wish to consider other means to encourage ports to invest in shore-side electricity infrastructure and to ensure its use."

These rules help implement that laudable aim.

---

14 OJ L125/38, 12 May 2006.

CHAPTER 46

Carriage of goods and passengers

A. INTRODUCTION

46.001 European Union ("EU") law contains rules on the carriage of goods and passengers. In part, the EU's motivation is to promote maritime safety and an efficient trading environment but also to be seen as protecting the safety of its citizens and those in the EU. There is little doubt that the EU is more likely to win favour from its citizens when it is seen to be protecting them and their goods.

46.002 The chapter takes a largely chronological approach to the topic.[1] It begins by looking at the EU position relating to containers as they were among the first topics in this area to be addressed by the EU. The chapter then considers the registration of persons sailing on board passenger ships. It then considers the issue of liability of carriers of passengers by sea in the event of incidents. The regime relating to the statistical returns in respect of the carriage of goods and passengers by sea is then examined. It is proposed to examine each of the measures in turn rather than seeking to unify them under various themes because there are no discernible themes which could easily unify the measures which are disparate. This chapter should be read in conjunction with many other chapters throughout the book because, at one level, the whole of EU shipping law is about the carriage of passengers and/or goods.

B. CONTAINERS

1979: Council Recommendation 79/487 on the ratification of the International Convention for Safe Containers (CSC)

46.003 On 15 May 1979, the Council of Ministers adopted Recommendation 79/487 on the ratification of the International Convention for Safe Containers (the "CSC") before 1 July 1980.[2] It was a short and relatively simple measure. As a recommendation, it is not legally binding. The legal basis of the recommendation was the then European Economic Community ("EEC") Treaty and in particular Articles 75 and 84(2) of that Treaty.[3] The

---

1 One very early measure, in the context of the now defunct European Coal and Steel Community ("ECSC") is not considered as it irrelevant for present purposes but it is noted for completeness: Comm. Dec. 73/152 of 23 May 1973 obliging undertakings of the steel industry to publish schedules of transport charges for routes involving intra-Community sea links (OJ L172/20, 28 June 1973).

2 OJ 1979 L125/18.

3 The modern equivalent, after some amendments, of those articles are Arts 91 and 100(2) of the Treaty on the Functioning of the European Union ("TFEU"). Article 75 of the EEC Treaty provided:

"1. With a view to implementing Article 74 and taking due account of the special aspects of transport, the Council, acting on a proposal of the Commission and after the Economic and Social Committee and the Assembly have been consulted, shall, until the end of the second stage by means of a unanimous vote and subsequently by means of a qualified majority vote, lay down:

recommendation was preceded by an opinion by the Parliament[4] as well as the Economic and Social Committee ("EESC").

46.004 The factual background was that the CSC, which had been prepared within the framework of the United Nations Inter-Governmental Maritime Consultative Organization ("IMCO"), entered into force on 6 September 1977. It was open for ratification or accession by EU Member States. The (then) EEC Council of Ministers believed (as expressed in the recommendation) that it was in the interest of the EU that all the Member States should ratify the convention. The Council therefore recommended that Member States ratify the CSC, or accede to it before 1 July 1980, where they had not already done so and inform the Secretary-General of IMCO in writing that their ratification or accession had regard to the recommendation.

C. REGISTRATION OF PERSONS SAILING ON BOARD PASSENGER SHIPS

Introduction

46.005 One of the practical problems posed by a number of ferry disasters up to the mid-1990s was that ships (particularly, ferries) would be involved in casualties (including sinkings) and there would be no accurate record (at least, ashore) of not only the names of who was on board but even how many were on board . This caused safety issues and challenges for the search and rescue services as well as trauma and uncertainty for families and friends of those who might, or might not, have been on board. These issues were highlighted by a number of very serious incidents involving the *Herald of Free Enterprise* and the *Estonia* ferries. The EU became "seriously concerned by shipping accidents involving passenger ships which have resulted in massive loss of life" while equally

---

    (a) common rules applicable to international transport effected from or to the territory of a Member State or crossing the territory of one or more Member States;

    (b) conditions for the admission of non-resident carriers to national transport services within a Member State; and

    (c) any other appropriate provisions.

2. The provisions referred to under (a) and (b) of the preceding paragraph shall be laid down in the course of the transitional period.

3. Notwithstanding the procedure provided for in paragraph 1, provisions which relate to the principles governing transport and the application of which might seriously affect the standard of living and the level of employment in certain regions and also the utilisation of transport equipment, shall, due account being taken of the need for adaptation to economic developments resulting from the establishment of the Common Market, be laid down by the Council acting by means of a unanimous vote."

Article 91 of the TFEU today provides:

"1. For the purpose of implementing Article 90, and taking into account the distinctive features of transport, the European Parliament and the Council shall, acting in accordance with the ordinary legislative procedure and after consulting the Economic and Social Committee and the Committee of the Regions, lay down:

    (a) common rules applicable to international transport to or from the territory of a Member State or passing across the territory of one or more Member States;

    (b) the conditions under which non-resident carriers may operate transport services within a Member State;

    (c) measures to improve transport safety;

    (d) any other appropriate provisions.

2. When the measures referred to in paragraph 1 are adopted, account shall be taken of cases where their application might seriously affect the standard of living and level of employment in certain regions, and the operation of transport facilities."

4 OJ C93/82, 9 April 1979.

"persons using passenger ships and high-speed passenger craft throughout the Community have the right to expect and to be able to rely on an appropriate level of safety and upon an adequate information system which will facilitate search and rescue and the efficient handling of the aftermath of any accident that might occur."[5]

It is not surprising therefore that the EU adopted legislation to address the issue.

Council Directive 98/41 of 18 June 1998 on the registration of persons sailing on board passenger ships operating to or from ports of the Member States of the Community

Introduction

46.006 On 18 June 1998, the Council of Ministers adopted Directive 98/41 of 18 June 1998 on the registration of persons[6] sailing on board passenger ships[7] operating to or from ports of the Member States of the Community.[8] It has been amended by Directive 2002/84 of the European Parliament and of the Council of 5 November 2002[9] and Regulation 1137/2008 of the European Parliament and of the Council of 22 October 2008.[10] An unofficial consolidation is available.[11]

46.007 The directive was seen as a safety measure – the first recital to Directive 98/41 provided that within the framework of the Common Transport Policy further measures must be taken to enhance safety in maritime transport while the eighth recital states that "in view, in particular, of the internal-market dimension of maritime passenger transport, action at Community level is the most effective way of establishing a common minimum level of safety for ships throughout the Community".

Entry into force of the directive

46.008 In accordance with Article 16 of the directive, it entered into force on the twentieth day after its publication in the *Official Journal* and it was published on 2 July 1998. Article 15(1) provides that Member States had to bring into force the laws, regulations and administrative provisions necessary to comply with the directive by 1 January 1999 and they had to forthwith inform the Commission of the implementation. Article 5 had to be applied no later than 1 January 2000.

---

5 Council Dir. 98/41 of 18 June 1998 on the registration of persons sailing on board passenger ships operating to or from ports of the Member States of the Community (OJ L188/35, 2 July 1998, recital 2).

6 Art. 2 of Dir. 98/41 provides that for the purposes of the directive, the term "persons" shall mean all people on board irrespective of age.

7 Art. 2 of Dir. 98/41 provides that for the purposes of the directive, the term "passenger ship" shall mean a seagoing ship or a seagoing high-speed craft which carries more than 12 passengers. Art. 2 also provides that the term "high-speed craft" shall mean a high-speed craft as defined in Reg. 1 of Chapter X of the 1974 SOLAS Convention, in its up-to-date version.

8 OJ L188/35, 2 July 1998.

9 OJ L324/53, 29 November 2002.

10 OJ L311/1, 21 November 2008.

11 Unofficial consolidated version: http://eur-lex.europa.eu/legal-content/EN/TXT/HTML/?uri=CELEX:01998L0041-20081211&qid=1438981349584&from=EN.

Legal basis of Directive 98/41

46.009 The legal basis for Directive 98/41 was the then Treaty establishing the European Community ("TEC") generally and, in particular, Article 84(2).[12] The directive was preceded by a proposal from the Commission[13] as well as an opinion of the EESC.[14]

Purpose of Directive 98/41

46.010 Article 1 of Directive 98/41 provides that the purpose of the directive is

"to enhance the safety and possibilities of rescue of passengers and crew on board passenger ships operating to or from ports in Member States ... and to ensure that search and rescue and the aftermath of any accident which may occur can be dealt with more effectively."

The fourth recital to Directive 98/41 provides that

"information must be compiled on passengers and crew in order to facilitate search and rescue and the efficient handling of the aftermath of an accident, i.e. identifying the persons involved, providing clearer information on related legal issues and contributing to more appropriate medical care for rescued persons; whereas such information would prevent unnecessary anxiety on the part of relatives and other persons concerned regarding persons on board passenger ships involved in marine accidents in waters for which Member States bear responsibility under the 1979 International Convention on Maritime Search and Rescue (SAR)."

Scope and application of Directive 98/41

46.011 The directive applies, according to Article 3, to passenger ships[15] with the exception of: (a) ships of war and troop ships; and (b) pleasure yachts unless they are or will be crewed and carry more than 12 passengers for commercial purposes. In practical terms, the directive applies to almost all commercial vessels and certainly all passenger ferries and liners. It might well be asked why it should not be applied to all commercial vessels.

Counting of passengers

46.012 Article 4(1) of Directive 98/41 provides that all persons on board any passenger ship which departs from a port located in a Member State must be counted before that passenger ship departs.[16] Article 2 of the directive provides that for the purposes of the directive, the term "persons" shall mean all people on board irrespective of age so children must be counted just as adults must be counted.

---

12 This is the historical equivalent of Art. 100(2) of the TFEU.
13 OJ C31/5, 31 January 1997 and OJ C275/7, 11 September 1997.
14 OJ C206/111, 7 July 1997.
15 Art. 2 of Dir. 98/41 provides that the term "passenger ship" shall mean "a sea-going ship or a sea-going high-speed craft which carries more than twelve passengers which is the usual definition".
16 This reflects the fifth recital to the directive: "passengers should therefore be counted and registered before any ship departs".

Communication of passenger numbers before the vessel leaves port

46.013 Article 4(2) of Directive 98/41 provides that before "the passenger ship departs[,] the number of persons[17] on board shall be communicated to the master of the passenger ship and to the company's passenger registrar or to a shore-based company system that performs the same function". The use of the conjunctive "and" means that there is a record ashore and at sea of the number of persons on board; a record in both locations is needed. Article 2 provides that for the purposes of the directive, the term "company" shall mean the owner of a passenger ship or any other organisation or person such as the manager or the bareboat charterer, who has assumed responsibility for operating the passenger ship from the owner, so it has quite a wide ambit. Article 2 also provides that for the purposes of the directive the term "passenger registrar" shall mean the responsible shore-based person designated by a company to fulfil the ISM Code obligations or a shore-based person designated by a company as responsible for the keeping of information on persons who have embarked on a company passenger ship while Article 2 also provides that for the purposes of the directive, the term "ISM Code" shall mean the International Management Code for the Safe Operation of Ships and for Pollution Prevention adopted by the International Maritime Organization ("IMO") through Assembly Resolution A.741(18) of 4 November 1993.

Information which must be recorded for the purposes of the directive

46.014 Article 5 of Directive 98/41 details the type of information which must be recorded:

"1. The following information shall be recorded regarding every passenger ship that departs from a port located in a Member State to undertake a voyage of more than twenty miles[18] from the point of departure:
   - the family names of the persons on board,
   - their forenames or initials,
   - their sex,
   - an indication of the category of age (adult, child or infant) to which each person belongs, or the age, or the year of birth,
   - when volunteered by a passenger, information concerning the need for special care or assistance in emergency situations.

2. That information shall be collected before departure and communicated not later than thirty minutes after the passenger ship's departure to the company's passenger registrar or to a shore-based company system that performs the same function."

46.015 There is some leeway provided for in Article 9 (as amended). To understand Article 9, it is useful to have regard to the fourteenth recital to the directive before examining the article itself:

"for specific operational reasons, the counting of persons on board passenger ships crossing the Strait of Messina might, for a limited period of time, be done in a simpler way than individual counting; whereas Member States should enjoy the possibility of granting some relaxation from

---

17 Art. 2 of Dir. 98/41 provides that for the purposes of the directive, the term "persons" shall mean all people on board irrespective of age.

18 Ed., the term "mile" is defined by Art. 2 of Dir. 98/41 as meaning 1,852 metres (i.e. this is the nautical mile).

the obligation to communicate to the shore the number of persons in the case of passenger ships operating on regular services of short duration carried out exclusively in protected sea areas, as defined in this Directive; whereas passenger ships operating exclusively in protected sea areas constitute a more limited risk and should, therefore, enjoy the possibility of exemption; whereas in certain specific circumstances it may be impracticable for shipping companies to register persons on board and therefore a derogation from the obligation to register could be permitted under specific circumstances and well defined conditions."

46.016 Article 9 provides:

"1. A Member State from a port in which a passenger ship departs may lower the twenty-mile threshold laid down in Article 5.

   Any decision lowering that threshold for journeys between two ports in different Member States shall be taken jointly by those two Member States.

2. (a) When implementing Article 4(1) the Italian Republic may, for regular services[19] cross-ing the Strait of Messina, adopt provisions for counting the maximum number of persons permitted to be carried on board a passenger ship carrying passenger-train carriages and road vehicles on the basis of the maximum number of passengers authorised to be carried by train carriages and all other vehicles on board, if the persons cannot be counted individually for operational reasons. The application of this provision shall be limited to a period of four years. Any extension shall be decided, in accordance with paragraph 3, in the light of the experience gained.

   (b) A Member State from a port in which a ship departs may exempt passenger ships oper-ating, exclusively in protected sea areas,[20] regular services of less than one hour between port calls from the obligation laid down in Article 4(2) to communicate the number of persons on board to the passenger registrar or to a shore-based company system that performs the same function.

   (c) A Member State may exempt passenger ships sailing, exclusively in protected sea areas, between two ports or from and to the same port without intermediate calls from the obligations laid down in Article 5.

3. In the circumstances set out in paragraph 2, the following procedure shall apply:

   (a) the Member State shall without delay inform the Commission of its decision to grant an exemption or a derogation from the relevant provisions of Articles 4 and 5 giving sub-stantive reasons therefor;

   (b) if within six months of such notification the Commission considers that that decision is not justified or could have adverse effects on competition, it may, acting in accordance with the procedure laid down in Article 13(2), require the Member State to amend or withdraw its decision.

4. For regular services in an area where the annual probability of the significant wave height's exceeding two metres is less than 10%, and

   – if the voyage does not exceed about thirty miles from the point of departure or
   – where the primary purpose of the service is to provide regular links to outlying com-munities for customary purposes,

   a Member State from a port in which passenger ships sail on domestic voyages or two Member States between ports in which passenger ships sail may request the Commission, if

---

19 Ed., Art. 2 provides that for the purposes of the directive the term "regular service" shall mean a series of ship crossings operated so as to serve traffic between the same two or more ports, either: (a) according to a pub-lished timetable, or (b) with crossings so regular or frequent that they constitute a recognisable systematic series.

20 Ed., Art. 2 provides that for the purposes of the directive the term "protected sea area" shall mean a sea area sheltered from open sea effects where a ship is at no time more than six miles from a place of refuge where shipwrecked persons can land and in which the proximity of search and rescue facilities is ensured.

they consider it impracticable for companies to record the information specified in Article 5(1) to derogate, wholly or partly, from this requirement.

To this end, evidence of such impracticability shall be provided. In addition, it shall be demonstrated that in the area where such ships operate, shore-based navigational guidance and reliable weather forecasts are provided and that adequate and sufficient search and rescue facilities are available. Derogations granted under this paragraph may not have any adverse effect on competition.

A decision shall be taken in accordance with the procedure laid down in Article 13(2).

5. A Member State shall not, under the provisions of this Directive, exempt or grant derogations to any passenger ship sailing from its ports and flying the flag of a third country[21] that is a contracting party to the SOLAS Convention [International Convention for the Safety of Life at Sea] which under the relevant SOLAS provisions does not agree to the application of such exemptions."

Functional criteria for registration systems

46.017 Article 11 of Directive 98/41 provides:

"1. For the purposes of this Directive registration systems shall meet the following functional criteria:

    (i)   readability: the required data must be in a format that is easy to read,

    (ii) availability: the required data must be easily available to the designated authorities[22] for which the information contained in the system is relevant,

    (iii) facilitation: the system must be designed in such a way that no undue delay is caused for passengers embarking and/or disembarking the vessel,

    (iv) security: the data must be appropriately protected against accidental or unlawful destruction or loss and unauthorised alteration, disclosure or access.

2. A multiplicity of systems on the same or similar routes is to be avoided."

These are useful criteria for the systems and ensure that the system is useful.

Limitation on the number of passengers exceeding the permitted number

46.018 Article 7 provides that before a passenger ship departs from a port located in a Member State, its master must ensure that the number of persons on board does not exceed the number the passenger ship is permitted (i.e. licensed) to carry. This is reflective of the third recital to the directive which states that

"it is necessary to ensure that the number of passengers on board a passenger ship does not exceed the number for which the ship and its safety equipment have been certified; whereas companies should be able to inform the search and rescue services of the number of persons involved in an accident."[23]

---

21 Ed., Art. 2 provides that for the purposes of the directive the term "third country" shall mean any country which is not a Member State.

22 Ed., Art. 2 provides that for the purposes of the directive the term "designated authority" shall mean the competent authority of the Member State responsible for search and rescue or concerned with the aftermath of an accident.

23 While the term "accident" is used, the term "incident" would be more appropriate as to cover accidental and non-accidental incidents.

Obligations on companies operating passenger ships

46.019 Article 8 provides that each company assuming responsibility for operating a passenger ship must, where required under Articles 4 and 5: (a) set up a system for the registration of passenger information (the system shall meet the criteria laid down in Article 11) and (b) appoint a passenger registrar responsible for the keeping and the transmission of that information should an emergency occur or in the aftermath of an accident. The company must ensure that the information required by this directive is at all times readily available for transmission to the designated authority for search and rescue purposes in the event of an emergency or in the aftermath of an accident. Personal data collected in accordance with Article 5 shall not be kept longer than necessary for the purposes of the directive. The company must ensure that information concerning persons who have declared a need for special care or assistance in emergency situations is properly recorded and communicated to the master before the passenger ship departs.

46.020 Article 10 of Directive 94/41 provides that the registration systems set up in accordance with Article 8 must be approved by the relevant Member States. Member States must, at the very least, carry out random checks on the proper functioning of the registration systems set up pursuant to the directive within their territories. Each Member State must designate the authority to which the companies covered by Article 8 shall communicate the information required by the directive.

Ships outside the EU

46.021 Article 6 of Directive 98/41 provides for what might be generously referred to as an extraterritorial dimension to the directive:

"1. Each Member State shall, as regards every passenger ship that flies its flag and departs from a port located outwith[24] the Community and is bound for a port located within the Community, require the company to ensure that the information specified in Articles 4(1) and 5(1) is provided as laid down in Articles 4(2) and 5(2).
2. Each Member State shall, as regards every passenger ship that flies the flag of a third country and departs from a port located outwith the Community and is bound for a port located within the Community, require the company to ensure that the information specified in Articles 4(1) and 5(1) is collected and maintained so that it is available to the designated authority when needed for purposes of search and rescue and in the aftermath of an accident.
3. Where under the relevant SOLAS provisions a Member State grants an exemption or derogation relating to the information concerning passengers to a ship flying its flag arriving at a port located within the Community from a port located outwith the Community, it may do so only under the conditions laid down for exemptions or derogations in this Directive."

Relationship between Directive 98/41 and SOLAS

46.022 The sixth recital to Directive 98/41 provides that while

"Chapter III of the International Convention on the Safety of Life at Sea (the SOLAS Convention) provides for the counting and registration of all persons on board all passenger ships sailing on international voyages, from 1 July 1997 and 1 January 1999 respectively, while permitting

---

24 Ed., i.e. outside the EU.

Administrations[25] to exempt passenger ships sailing in sheltered waters from those requirements and from the requirement to register if the scheduled voyages of such ships render it impracticable for them to prepare such records; whereas that Chapter of the SOLAS Convention does not apply to domestic voyages and leaves important points of interpretation to the discretion of individual Member States."

The seventh recital to Directive 98/41 provides that the directive is in accordance with the right of Member States to impose on passenger ships sailing to or from their ports certain requirements *more* stringent than those laid down in the SOLAS Convention – this is in line with the general principle that Member States may impose more onerous obligations than the EU ones where the Member State obligations did not conflict with the EU ones. The seventeenth recital to Directive 98/41 provides that whereas certain provisions of the directive may be adapted by the Committee to take into account future amendments to the SOLAS Convention that would have entered into force. Article 12 of Directive 98/41 provides:

"Without prejudice to the procedures for amending the SOLAS Convention, this Directive may be amended in order to ensure the application, for the purposes of this Directive and without broadening its scope, of amendments to the SOLAS Convention relating to the registration systems which have entered into force after the adoption of this Directive. Those measures, designed to amend non-essential elements of this Directive, shall be adopted in accordance with the regulatory procedure with scrutiny referred to in Article 13(3).

The amendments to the international instruments referred to in Article 2 may be excluded from the scope of this Directive, pursuant to Article 5 of Regulation (EC) No 2099/2002 of the European Parliament and of the Council of 5 November 2002 establishing a Committee on Safe Seas and the Prevention of Pollution from Ships (COSS)."

Aspects of the administration of Directive 98/41

46.023 Article 13 provides:

"1. The Commission shall be assisted by the Committee on Safe Seas and the Prevention of Pollution from Ships (COSS) set up by Article 3 of Regulation (EC) No 2099/2002.
2. Where reference is made to this paragraph, Articles 5 and 7 of Council Decision 1999/468/EC of 28 June 1999 laying down the procedures for the exercise of implementing powers conferred on the Commission[26] shall apply, having regard to the provisions of Article 8 thereof.

The period provided for in Article 5(6) of Decision 1999/468/EC shall be set at two months.
3. Where reference is made to this paragraph, Article 5a(1) to (4) and Article 7 of Decision 1999/468/EC shall apply, having regard to the provisions of Article 8 thereof."

Penalties for breaching the regime

46.024 The consequence for a breach of the regime could be very serious. For example, if a ferry is lost, it might mean that there could be uncertainty forever as to whether a particular person was, or was not, on the ferry when she sunk. The ninth recital to Directive 98/41 provides that,

---

25 Ed., i.e. individual maritime authorities in States.
26 OJ L184/23, 17.7.1999.

"in view of the principle of proportionality a Council Directive is the appropriate legal instrument as it provides a framework for the Member States' uniform and compulsory application of safety standards while leaving each Member State the right to decide which implementation tools best fit its internal system."

Article 14 therefore provides that Member States shall lay down systems of penalties for breaching the national provisions adopted pursuant to the directive and shall take all the measures necessary to ensure that those penalties are applied and the penalties thus provided for shall be effective, proportionate and dissuasive. This is in line with the principles that it is for Member States rather than the EU to impose criminal corporate penalties.

D. LIABILITY OF CARRIERS OF PASSENGERS BY SEA IN THE EVENT OF ACCIDENTS

Regulation 392/2009 of the European Parliament and of the Council on the liability of carriers of passengers by sea in the event of accidents

Introduction

46.025 On 23 April 2009, the European Parliament and the Council adopted Regulation 392/2009 on the liability of carriers of passengers by sea in the event of accidents.[27] The first recital to the regulation provides that within the framework of the Common Transport Policy,[28] further measures need to be adopted in order to enhance safety in maritime transport. Those measures should include liability rules for damage caused to passengers, since it is important to ensure a proper level of compensation for passengers involved in maritime accidents.

46.026 Annex I to the regulation contains the then consolidated text of the Athens Convention relating to the Carriage of Passengers and their Luggage by Sea, 1974 and the Protocol of 2002 to the convention.

46.027 The entry into force of Regulation 392/2009 is addressed by Article 12 which provides that the regulation would enter into force on the day following that of its publication in the *Official Journal of the European Union* (i.e. it entered into force on 29 May 2009 having been published in the *Official Journal* on 28 May 2009). Article 12 also stated that the regulation applied from the date of the entry into force of the Athens Convention for the Community and in any case from no later than 31 December 2012. Transitional provisions are addressed in Article 11. In respect of carriage by sea within a single Member State on board ships of Class A under Article 4 of Directive 98/18, Member States had the right to choose to defer application of the regulation until four years after the date of its application. In respect of carriage by sea within a single Member State on board ships of Class B under Article 4 of Directive 98/18, Member States may choose to defer application of the regulation until 31 December 2018.

46.028 The legal basis of Regulation 392/2009 was the TEC generally and, in particular, Article 80(2) of the TEC.[29]

---

27 OJ L131/24, 28 May 2009, http://eur-lex.europa.eu/legal-content/EN/TXT/HTML/?uri=CELEX:32009R0392&from=EN.

28 On the common Transport Policy, see chap. 4.

29 The modern equivalent of Art. 80(2) of the TEC would be Art. 100(2) of the TFEU.

46.029 The 2002 Protocol to the 1974 Athens Convention relating to the Carriage of Passengers and their Luggage by Sea was adopted under the auspices of the IMO. At the time of the adoption of the regulation, the then ("EC") and its Member States were in the process of deciding whether to accede to or ratify that protocol. The provisions of the protocol incorporated by the regulation applied in the EU from no later than 31 December 2012 in any event.

46.030 The third recital to the regulation recalled that the Athens Convention applied to international transport only but the distinction between national and international transport had been eliminated within the internal market in maritime transport services and it was therefore appropriate to have the same level and nature of liability in both international and national transport within the EU hence the choices made in the regulation.

46.031 The insurance arrangements required under the Athens Convention, must, according to the fourth recital of Regulation 392/2009, take into consideration the financial means of shipowners and insurance companies. Shipowners must be in a position to manage their insurance arrangements in an economically acceptable way and, particularly in the case of small shipping companies operating national transport services, account must be taken of the seasonal nature of their operations. When setting insurance arrangements under the regulation, account must be taken of the different classes of ship and appropriate information on rights being conferred on passengers ought to be provided to those passengers prior to their journey or, where that is not possible, at the latest on departure. The approach is somewhat benign and protectionist to shipowners but it was fundamentally a realistic approach.

46.032 The seventh recital to Regulation 362/2009 recalled that the Legal Committee of the IMO adopted on 19 October 2006 the IMO Reservation and Guidelines for the Implementation of the Athens Convention (i.e. the IMO Guidelines) to address certain issues under the Athens Convention, such as, in particular, compensation for terrorism-related damage. As such, the IMO Guidelines may be considered a *lex specialis*. The eighth recital therefore stated that the regulation incorporates and makes binding parts of the IMO Guidelines and to that end, where it occurs in the provisions of the IMO Guidelines, the verb "should" should, in particular, be understood as "shall". Indeed, according to the ninth recital, the provisions of the Athens Convention (Annex I) and of the IMO Guidelines (Annex II) should be understood, *mutatis mutandis*, in the context of EU legislation.

46.033 The tenth recital to Regulation 392/2009 provides that the system of liability provided for by Regulation 392/2009 should be extended step-by-step to the different classes of ship as set out in Article 4 of Council Directive 98/18 of 17 March 1998 on safety rules and standards for passenger ships.[30] The same recital provides that account ought to be taken of the consequences for fares and the ability of the market to obtain affordable insurance coverage at the level required against the policy background of strengthening passengers' rights and the seasonal nature of some of the traffic.

46.034 The matters covered by Articles 17 and 17bis of the Athens Convention[31] fall within the exclusive competence of the EU in so far as those articles affect the rules established by Council Regulation 44/2001 of 22 December 2000 on jurisdiction and the

---

30 OJ L144/1, 15 May 1998.
31 Art. 17 deals with competent jurisdiction while Art. 17bis deals with recognition and enforcement.

recognition and enforcement of judgments in civil and commercial matters,[32] which is now the recent Brussels Regulation.[33] To that extent, these two provisions will form part of the EU legal order when the EU accedes to the Athens Convention.

46.035 For the purposes of the regulation, the twelfth recital recalls that the expression "or is registered in a Member State" should be considered to mean that the flag State for the purposes of bareboat charter-out registration is either a Member State or a contracting party to the Athens Convention. Necessary steps should be taken by the Member States and the Commission to invite the IMO to develop guidelines on the concept of bareboat charter-out registration.

46.036 The seventeenth recital provides that Member States have taken the firm commitment in their Statement on Maritime Safety of 9 October 2008 to express, no later than 1 January 2012, their consent to be bound by the International Convention on Limitation of Liability for Maritime Claims, 1976, as amended by the Protocol of 1996. Member States may make use of the option provided for in Article 15(3bis) of that convention to regulate, by means of specific provisions of this regulation, the system of limitation of liability to be applied to passengers.

46.037 The nineteenth recital recalls why the EU is acting. It provides that since the objective of the regulation, namely to create a single set of rules governing the rights of carriers by sea and their passengers in the event of an accident, cannot be sufficiently achieved by the Member States and can therefore, by reason of its scale and effects, be better achieved at EU level, the EU may adopt measures, in accordance with the principle of subsidiarity. In accordance with the principle of proportionality, as set out in that article, the regulation does not go beyond what is necessary in order to achieve that objective.

Adoption of the resolution

46.038 The regulation was preceded, as is normal, by a proposal from the Commission, an opinion of the European EESC[34] as well as an opinion of the Committee of the Regions.[35] The regulation was adopted after utilising the procedure laid down in Article 251 of the TEC[36] (involving the Conciliation Committee).

Purpose and subject matter of Regulation 392/2009

46.039 Article 1 describes the subject matter of the regulation in the following broad terms:

"1. This Regulation lays down the Community regime relating to liability and insurance for the carriage of passengers by sea as set out in the relevant provisions of:

---

32 OJ L12, 16 January 2001.

33 See chap. 47.

34 OJ C318/195, 23 December 2006.

35 OJ C229/38, 22 September 2006.

36 Opinion of the European Parliament of 25 April 2007 (OJ C74 E, 20 March 2008, p. 562), Council Common Position of 6 June 2008 (OJ C190 E, 29 July 2008, p. 17), Position of the European Parliament of 24 September 2008, Council Decision of 26 February 2009 and Legislative Resolution of the European Parliament of 11 March 2009.

(a) the Athens Convention relating to the Carriage of Passengers and their Luggage by Sea, 1974, as amended by the Protocol of 2002 (the Athens Convention) as set out in Annex I; and

(b) the IMO Reservation and Guidelines for Implementation of the Athens Convention adopted by the Legal Committee of the IMO on 19 October 2006 (the IMO Guidelines) as set out in Annex II.

2. Furthermore, this Regulation extends the application of those provisions to carriage of passengers by sea within a single Member State on board ships of Classes A and B under Article 4 of Directive 98/18/EC, and lays down certain supplementary requirements.

3. No later than 30 June 2013, the Commission shall, if appropriate, present a legislative proposal in order, inter alia, to extend the scope of this Regulation to ships of Classes C and D under Article 4 of Directive 98/18/EC."

Scope of Regulation 392/2009

46.040 Article 2 describes the scope of the regulation. It applies to any international carriage within the meaning of point 9 of Article 1 of the Athens Convention[37] and to carriage by sea within a single Member State on board ships of Classes A and B under Article 4 of Directive 98/18, where: (a) the ship is flying the flag of or is registered in a Member State; (b) the contract of carriage has been made in a Member State; or (c) the place of departure or destination, according to the contract of carriage, is in a Member State. Interestingly, under Article 2, Member States may choose to apply the regulation to all domestic sea-going voyages (i.e. cabotage services).

Liability and insurance under Regulation 392/2009

46.041 Article 3(1) provides that the liability regime in respect of passengers, their luggage and their vehicles and the rules on insurance or other financial security must be governed by the regulation, by Articles 1[38] and 1bis,[39] Article 2(2),[40] Articles 3 to 16[41] and Articles 18,[42] 20[43] and 21[44] of the Athens Convention set out in Annex I and by the provisions of the IMO Guidelines set out in Annex II. Article 3(2) goes on to provide that the IMO Guidelines as set out in Annex II to the regulation are binding.

---

37 Art. 1, point 9 provides that "international carriage" means any carriage in which, according to the contract of carriage, the place of departure and the place of destination are situated in two different States, or in a single State if, according to the contract of carriage or the scheduled itinerary, there is an intermediate port of call in another State.

38 Art. 1 contains definitions.

39 Art. 1bis provides that the annex to the Athens Convention forms an integral part of the convention.

40 Art. 2(2) of the Athens Convention provides that the convention shall not apply when the carriage is subject, under any other international convention concerning the carriage of passengers or luggage by another mode of transport, to a civil liability regime under the provisions of such convention, in so far as those provisions have mandatory application to carriage by sea.

41 These are the main operative provisions of the Athens Convention and cover issues such as liability of the carrier.

42 This relates to invalidity of contractual provisions.

43 This relates to nuclear damage.

44 This relates to commercial carriage by public authorities.

Compensation in respect of mobility equipment or other specific equipment

46.042 Article 4 provides for compensation in respect of mobility equipment or other specific equipment. It states that if there is a

> "loss of, or damage to, mobility equipment or other specific equipment used by a passenger with reduced mobility, the liability of the carrier shall be governed by Article 3(3) of the Athens Convention. The compensation shall correspond to the replacement value of the equipment concerned or, where applicable, to the costs relating to repairs."

This reflects the thirteenth recital to the regulation which provides that for the purposes of the regulation, the expression "mobility equipment" should be considered to mean neither luggage nor vehicles within the meaning of Article 8 of the Athens Convention.[45]

Global limitation of liability

46.043 Article 5 provides:

> "1. This Regulation shall not modify the rights or duties of the carrier or performing carrier under national legislation implementing the International Convention on Limitation of Liability for Maritime Claims, 1976, as amended by the Protocol of 1996, including any future amendment thereto.
>
> In the absence of any such applicable national legislation, the liability of the carrier or performing carrier shall be governed only by Article 3 of this Regulation.
> 2. In respect of claims for loss of life or personal injury to a passenger caused by any of the risks referred to in paragraph 2.2 of the IMO Guidelines the carrier and the performing carrier may limit their liability pursuant to the provisions referred to in paragraph 1 of this Article."

Advance payment

46.044 Advance payments to survivors to cover immediate needs where there has been a loss is addressed by Article 6 of the directive:[46]

> "1. Where the death of, or personal injury to, a passenger is caused by a shipping incident, the carrier who actually performed the whole or a part of the carriage when the shipping incident occurred shall make an advance payment sufficient to cover immediate economic needs on a basis proportionate to the damage suffered within 15 days of the identification of the person entitled to damages. In the event of the death, the payment shall not be less than EUR 21 000.
>
> This provision shall also apply where the carrier is established within the Community.

---

45 Art. 8 of the Athens Convention (the article is entitled "limit of liability for loss of or damage to luggage and vehicles" provides: "1. The liability of the carrier for the loss of or damage to cabin luggage shall in no case exceed 2 250 units of account per passenger, per carriage. 2. The liability of the carrier for the loss of or damage to vehicles including all luggage carried in or on the vehicle shall in no case exceed 12 700 units of account per vehicle, per carriage. 3. The liability of the carrier for the loss of or damage to luggage other than that mentioned in paragraphs 1 and 2 shall in no case exceed 3 375 units of account per passenger, per carriage. 4. The carrier and the passenger may agree that the liability of the carrier shall be subject to a deductible not exceeding 330 units of account in the case of damage to a vehicle and not exceeding 149 units of account per passenger in the case of loss of or damage to other luggage, such sum to be deducted from the loss or damage."

46 Art. 6 reflects the fifth recital to the regulation which provides that it "is appropriate to oblige the carrier to make an advance payment in the event of the death of or personal injury to a passenger, whereby advance payment does not constitute recognition of liability."

2. An advance payment shall not constitute recognition of liability and may be offset against any subsequent sums paid on the basis of this Regulation. It shall not be refundable, except in the cases set out in Article 3(1) or Article 6 of the Athens Convention or Appendix A to the IMO Guidelines, or where the person who received it is not the person entitled to damages."

It is worth emphasising that such an advance payment is not an admission of liability on the part of the carrier.

Information to passengers

46.045 Passengers need to be informed of their rights. Article 7 of the regulation provides that without prejudice to the obligations of tour operators set out in Council Directive 90/314 of 13 June 1990 on package travel, package holidays and package tours,[47] the carrier and/or performing carrier must ensure that passengers are provided with appropriate and comprehensible information regarding their rights under the regulation. Article 7 also states that where the contract of carriage is made in a Member State, that information must be provided at all points of sale, including sale by telephone and via the internet and where the place of departure is in a Member State, that information shall be provided prior to departure. In all other cases, it shall be provided at the latest on departure. To the extent that the information required under Article 7 has been provided by either the carrier or the performing carrier, the other shall not be obliged to provide it. The information must be provided in the most appropriate format. Article 7 concludes by saying that in order to comply with the information requirement under Article 7, the carrier and performing carrier shall provide passengers with at least the information contained in a summary of the provisions of this regulation prepared by the Commission and made public.

Reporting

46.046 Article 8 of the regulation provides that no later than three years after the date of application of the regulation (i.e. by 23 April 2012), the Commission has to draw up a report on the application of the regulation, which must, *inter alia*, take into account economic developments and developments in international fora.[48] That report may be accompanied by a proposal for amendment of the regulation, or by a proposal for a submission to be made by the Community before the relevant international fora.

Amendments

46.047 Article 9 of the regulation provides for the possibility of amendments:

"1. Measures designed to amend non-essential elements of this Regulation and relating to the incorporation of amendments to the limits set out in Article 3(1),[49] Article 4bis(1),[50] Article

---

47 OJ L158/59, 23 June 1990.

48 The sixteenth recital to the regulation provides that the European Maritime Safety Agency, should assist the Commission in preparing and drafting a progress report on the functioning of the rules laid down by the regulation.

49 Ed., this relates to liability of the carrier.

50 Ed., this relates to compulsory insurance.

7(1)[51] and Article 8[52] of the Athens Convention to take account of decisions taken pursuant to Article 23 of that Convention, as well as corresponding updates to Annex I to this Regulation, shall be adopted in accordance with the regulatory procedure with scrutiny referred to in Article 10(2) of this Regulation.

Taking into consideration the consequences for fares and the ability of the market to obtain affordable insurance coverage at the level required against the policy background of strengthening passengers' rights, as well as the seasonal nature of some of the traffic, by 31 December 2016, the Commission shall, on the basis of a suitable impact assessment, adopt a measure relating to the limits set out in Annex I for ships of Class B under Article 4 of Directive 98/18/EC. That measure, designed to amend non-essential elements of this Regulation, shall be adopted in accordance with the regulatory procedure with scrutiny referred to in Article 10(2) of this Regulation.

2. Measures designed to amend non-essential elements of this Regulation and relating to the incorporation of amendments to the provisions of the IMO Guidelines set out in Annex II shall be adopted in accordance with the regulatory procedure with scrutiny referred to in Article 10(2)."

Role of COSS

46.048 Article 10 provides that the Committee on Safe Seas and the Prevention of Pollution from Ships ("COSS") must assist the Commission in regard to the regulation.

E. STATISTICAL RETURNS IN RESPECT OF THE CARRIAGE OF GOODS AND PASSENGERS BY SEA

Introduction

46.049 It is important for a variety of reasons (e.g. safety, security, planning and smooth operations) that there are accurate statistical returns in respect of the carriage of goods and passengers by sea.

Directive 2009/42 on statistical returns in respect of carriage of goods and passengers by sea

Introduction

46.050 On 6 May 2009, the Parliament and the Council of Ministers adopted Directive 2009/42 on statistical returns in respect of carriage of goods and passengers by sea.[53] It was amended by a Commission decision of 14 April 2010[54] (i.e. Commission Decision

---

51 Ed., this relates to limit of the liability for death and personal injury.

52 Ed., Art. 8 of the Athens Convention (the article is entitled "limit of liability for loss of or damage to luggage and vehicles" provides: "1. The liability of the carrier for the loss of or damage to cabin luggage shall in no case exceed 2 250 units of account per passenger, per carriage. 2. The liability of the carrier for the loss of or damage to vehicles including all luggage carried in or on the vehicle shall in no case exceed 12 700 units of account per vehicle, per carriage. 3. The liability of the carrier for the loss of or damage to luggage other than that mentioned in paragraphs 1 and 2 shall in no case exceed 3 375 units of account per passenger, per carriage. 4. The carrier and the passenger may agree that the liability of the carrier shall be subject to a deductible not exceeding 330 units of account in the case of damage to a vehicle and not exceeding 149 units of account per passenger in the case of loss of or damage to other luggage, such sum to be deducted from the loss or damage."

53 OJ L141/29, 6 June 2009.

54 OJ L94/33, 15 April 2010.

2010/216) and Regulation 1090/2010 of the Parliament and Council 24 November 2010[55] as well as Commission Delegated Decision 2012/186 of 3 February 2012 amending Directive 2009/42 of the European Parliament and of the Council on statistical returns in respect of carriage of goods and passengers by sea.[56]

46.051 The legal basis of Directive 2009/42 was the TEC and in particular Article 285(1) of the TEC. Article 11 ("communication of national provisions") provides that Member States must communicate to the Commission the text of the main provisions of national law which they adopted in the field governed by the directive. Under Article 13, Directive 2009/42 entered into force on the twentieth day following its publication in the *Official Journal* and it was published on 6 June 2009.

Factual background

46.052 The recitals to the directive recall, among other things, that: (a) data on the transport of goods and passengers by sea have to be made comparable between Member States and between the different modes of transport; (b) in accordance with the principle of subsidiarity, the creation of common statistical standards enabling harmonised information to be produced can only be tackled efficiently at Community level and that data will be collected in each Member State under the authority of the bodies and institutions in charge of compiling official statistics; and (c) the Commission should be empowered to adopt certain detailed rules for implementing the directive.

Concepts in Directive 2009/42

46.053 Article 2 ("definitions") contains a number of definitions for the purposes of the directive. First, the term "carriage of goods and passengers by sea" means the movement of goods and passengers using seagoing vessels, on voyages which are undertaken wholly or partly at sea.[57] In this context, the scope of the directive shall also include goods: (i) shipped to offshore installations; and (ii) reclaimed from the seabed and unloaded in ports but bunkers and stores supplied to vessels are excluded from the scope of the directive. Second, the term "seagoing vessels" means vessels other than those which navigate exclusively in inland waters or in waters within, or closely adjacent to, sheltered waters or areas where port regulations apply but the directive does not apply to fish-catching vessels, fish-processing vessels, vessels for drilling and exploration, tugs, pusher craft, research and survey vessels, dredgers, naval vessels or vessels used solely for non-commercial purposes. Third, the term "port" means a place having facilities for merchant ships to moor and to load or unload cargo or to disembark or embark passengers to or from vessels.[58] Fourth, the term "nationality of the maritime transport operator" means that corresponding to the country in which the effective centre of the transport operator's commercial activity is located, thus the nationality of the company in question.

---

55 OJ L325/1, 9 December 2010.
56 OJ L101/5, 11 April 2012.
57 This should be read as carriage of goods and/or passengers as any other construction would be inappropriate.
58 This would include a pontoon and a harbour where, for example, large liners would anchor with passengers being transported to and from the land by tender.

Finally, the term "maritime transport operator" means any person by whom or on behalf of whom a contract for the transport of goods or persons by sea is concluded with a shipper or a passenger.

Collection of data

46.054 Article 1 ("collection of statistical data") provides that Member States must collect EU statistics on the carriage of goods and passengers by seagoing vessels calling at ports in their territories.

Data collection characteristics

46.055 Article 3 ("Data collection characteristics") provides in Article 3(1) that Member States must collect data relating to: (a) cargo and passenger information; and (b) information on the vessel. Member States have some discretion because vessels with a gross tonnage of less than 100 may be excluded from the data collection. Under Article 3(2), the characteristics of the data collection, namely, the statistical variables in each domain and the nomenclatures for their classification, as well as their periodicity of observation, are set out in Annexes I to VIII of the regulation. Article 3(3) provides that the data collection shall be based, in so far as possible, on available sources, limiting the burden on respondents which is very much in line with the principle of proportionality which permeates so much of EU law. Article 3(4) provides that the Commission shall adapt the data collection characteristics and the content of Annexes I to VIII to economic and technical developments in so far as such adaptation does not involve a substantial increase in cost for the Member States and/or in the burden on respondents.

Ports

46.056 Article 4 ("ports") provides in Article 4(1) that for the purposes of the directive, the Commission had to draw up a list of ports, coded and classified according to countries and maritime coastal areas. The Commission may then adopt those measures by means of delegated acts in accordance with Article 10a and subject to the conditions of Articles 10b and 10c. Article 4(2) provides that each Member State must select from the list referred to in Article 4(1) any port handling more than one million tonnes of goods or recording more than 200,000 passenger movements annually. For each such port selected, detailed data are to be provided, in conformity with Annex VIII, for the domains (i.e. goods and passengers) in which that port meets the selection criterion, and with summary data, if appropriate, for the other domain. Under Article 4(3), for the ports which are not selected from the list, summary data are to be provided in conformity with Annex VIII, data set A3.

Accuracy and processing

46.057 Article 5 ("accuracy of statistics") provides that the methods of collecting data shall be such that EU sea transport statistics display the precision required for the statistical data sets described in Annex VIII. The Commission must therefore draw up the standards of accuracy. The Commission may adopt those measures by means of delegated acts in accordance with Article 10a and subject to the conditions of Articles 10b and 10c.

46.058 Article 6 ("processing of the results of the data collection") provides that Member States must process the statistical information collected pursuant to Article 3, in order to obtain comparable statistics, with the standard of accuracy referred to in Article 5.

Transmission, reports and dissemination of data

46.059 Article 7 ("transmission of the results of the data collection") provides in Article 7(1) that Member States must transmit the results of the data collection referred to in Article 3 to the Commission (i.e. Eurostat), including the data declared confidential by the Member States pursuant to domestic legislation or practice concerning statistical confidentiality, in accordance with Regulation 223/2009 of the European Parliament and of the Council of 11 March 2009 on European statistics. The results shall be transmitted in accordance with the structure of the statistical data sets defined in Annex VIII. The technical details for transmission of the results shall be specified in accordance with the management procedure referred to in Article 10(2). Article 7(3) provides that the transmission of the results shall take place within five months of the end of the period of observation for data of quarterly periodicity and within eight months for data of annual periodicity.

46.060 Article 8 ("reports") provides that Member States must provide the Commission (i.e. Eurostat) with all relevant information on the methods used in compiling the data. They shall also forward details of substantial changes in the methods used to collect the data.

46.061 Article 9 ("Dissemination of statistical data") provides that the Commission (i.e. Eurostat) must disseminate appropriate statistical data with a periodicity comparable to that of the results transmitted. The arrangements for publication or dissemination of the statistical data by the Commission (i.e. Eurostat) must be adopted in accordance with the management procedure referred to in Article 10(2).

Committee procedure

46.062 Article 10 ("Committee procedure") provides that the Commission shall be assisted by the European Statistical System Committee set up by Regulation 223/2009.

46.063 Article 10a addresses the "exercise of the delegation". It provides that the power to adopt delegated acts referred to in Article 3(4), Article 4(1) and the third paragraph of Article 5 are conferred on the Commission for a period of five years from 29 December 2010. The Commission must draw up a report in respect of the delegated power at the latest six months before the end of the five-year period. The delegation of power must be automatically extended for periods of an identical duration, unless the Parliament or the Council revokes it in accordance with Article 10b. As soon as it adopts a delegated act, the Commission must notify it simultaneously to the Parliament and to the Council. The power to adopt delegated acts is conferred on the Commission subject to the conditions laid down in Articles 10b and 10c.

46.064 Article 10b deals with the revocation of the delegation. Article 10b(1) provides that the delegation of power referred to in Article 3(4), Article 4(1) and the third paragraph of Article 5 may be revoked at any time by the Parliament or by the Council. Article 10b(2) stipulates that the institution which has commenced an internal procedure for deciding whether to revoke a delegation of power must endeavour to inform the other institution and the Commission within a reasonable time before the final decision is taken, indicating the delegated power which could be subject to revocation and possible reasons for a revocation. Under Article 10b(3), the decision of revocation shall put an end to the delegation of the power specified in that decision. It must take effect immediately or at a later date specified therein. It shall not affect the validity of the delegated acts already in force. It must be published in the *Official Journal*.

46.065 Article 10c ("objections to delegated acts") provides in Article 10c(1) that the Parliament or the Council may object to a delegated act within a period of two months from the date of notification. At the initiative of the Parliament or the Council that period must be extended by two months. Under Article 10c(2), if, on expiry of the period referred to in paragraph 1, neither the Parliament nor the Council has objected to the delegated act, it must be published in the *Official Journal* and shall enter into force on the date stated therein. Equally, the delegated act may be published in the *Official Journal* and enter into force before the expiry of that period if the Parliament and the Council have both informed the Commission of their intention not to raise objections. Article 10c(3) provides that if either the Parliament or the Council objects to the delegated act within the period referred to in Article 10c(1), it shall not enter into force and the institution which objects must state the reasons for objecting to the delegated act.

Background to the amendments

46.066 Regulation 1090/2010 of the European Parliament and of the Council of 24 November 2010 amending Directive 2009/42 on statistical returns in respect of carriage of goods and passengers by sea.[59] Regulation 1090/2010 emphasises the importance of the Commission carrying out appropriate consultations (including at expert level) when preparing delegated acts.

46.067 Writing in 2015, the Commission commented that Regulation 1090/2010

"was adopted with two main purposes – to bring data collection on goods transported by maritime transport into line with that for goods transported by other forms of transport, and to align the powers conferred on the Commission by Directive 2009/42/EC of the European Parliament and of the Council[60] with the [TFEU]."[61]

Therefore the regulation:

"1. introduced the requirement for Member States to provide data on seaborne transport in the main European ports by type of goods, in accordance with the NST 2007 classification,[62] thus bringing data collection on goods transported by maritime transport into line with the approaches and standards used for statistics on road transport, rail transport and inland waterway transport;

---

59 OJ L325/1, 9 December 2010.

60 Dir. 2009/42 of the European Parliament and of the Council of 6 May 2009 on statistical returns in respect of carriage of goods and passengers by sea (OJ L141, 6 June 2009, p. 29).

61 COM(2015) 362 final. See http://eur-lex.europa.eu/legal-content/EN/TXT/PDF/?uri=COM:2015:362:FIN &from=EN.

62 Standard goods classification for transport statistics, 2007.

and 2. aligned the powers conferred on the Commission by Directive 2009/42/EC with Article 290 of the Treaty on the Functioning of the European Union."[63]

46.068 The Commission summarised Directive 2009/42 as empowering the Commission to adopt delegated acts serving the following purposes:

"• adapting the data collection requirements set out in Annexes I to VIII to reflect economic and technical developments, in so far as such changes do not entail a substantial increase in costs for Member States and/or in the burden placed on respondents (as described in Article 3(4) of Directive 2009/42/EC);

• drawing up a list of ports, coded and classified by country and by maritime coastal area (as described in Article 4(1) of Directive 2009/42/EC); and amending non-essential elements of Directive 2009/42/EC, in order to ensure that the methods of collecting data used for producing the statistical datasets on sea transport described in Annex VIII are such that these datasets meet the standards of accuracy set by the Commission (in Article 5 of Directive 2009/42/EC)."[64]

46.069 Article 10a(1) of Directive 2009/42 confers on the Commission the power to adopt delegated acts for a period of five years from 29 December 2010 but it requires the Commission to prepare a report in respect of the delegation of power at the latest six months before the end of the five-year period.

46.070 It transpired that the Commission deemed it necessary to exercise the power conferred on it by Directive 2009/42 in order to implement a set of recommendations for adapting and simplifying data collection proposed by the Task Force on Maritime Transport Statistics[65] and later approved by the Working Group on Maritime Transport Statistics.[66] Article 3(4) of Directive 2009/42 provides that the Commission may adopt these measures by means of delegated acts.[67] In 2015, the Commission summarised the changes introduced by Commission Delegated Decision 2012/186 as involving the following adaptations and simplifications of the data collection requirements set out in Annexes I to VIII of Directive 2009/42:

"1) Technical change to the classification of type of cargo in Annex II: the former cargo category 63 was divided into the three new cargo categories: 64 Rail wagons engaged in goods transport, 65 Shipborne port-to-port trailers engaged in goods transport and 66 Shipborne barges engaged in goods transport.

---

63 Report from the Commission to the European Parliament and the Council on the exercise of the power to adopt delegated acts conferred on the Commission pursuant to Regulation (EU) No 1090/2010 of the European Parliament and of the Council amending Dir. 2009/42 on statistical returns in respect of carriage of goods and passengers by sea (COM(2015) 362 final, p. 2). See http://eur-lex.europa.eu/legal-content/EN/TXT/PDF/?uri=COM:2015:362:FIN&from=EN.

64 Ibid., pp. 2–3. See http://eur-lex.europa.eu/legal-content/EN/TXT/PDF/?uri=COM:2015:362:FIN&from=EN.

65 The Task Force on Maritime Transport Statistics, in operation from 2006 to 2009, included experts from five Member States' statistical authorities and representatives from maritime industry organisations and the Commission.

66 The Working Group on Maritime Transport Statistics consists of experts from the national authorities with competency for maritime transport statistics in all EU Member States and European Free Trade Agreement countries and representatives from candidate countries, maritime industry organisations and the Commission. It approved these recommendations in April 2008 and March 2010.

67 In accordance with Art. 10a and subject to the conditions set out in Arts 10b and 10c of Dir. 2009/42 (as amended by Regulation (EU) No 1090/2010).

2) Technical change to the nomenclature for maritime coastal areas in Annex IV: the former maritime coastal area code for Mexico was split into the two separate codes: MX01 Mexico: Atlantic and MX02 Mexico: Pacific.

3) Simplification of the data collection for vessel traffic in the main European ports in datasets F1 and F2 in Annex VIII: the variable Direction was deleted (as only data on inwards movement into ports is to be collected).

4) Formalisation of the legal status of datasets F1 and F2 in Annex VIII: collection of data for dataset F1 is now voluntary and for dataset F2 it is now mandatory.

5) Introduction of a new dataset, C2, in Annex VIII: specifications have been added for the voluntary collection of data on Ro-Ro container units in the main European ports.

6) Technical change to the classification of type of cargo in Annex II: a set of codes has been introduced for collecting data on Ro-Ro container units for the dataset C2 (RX Large Ro-Ro containers, R1 20 ft freight units, R2 40 ft freight units, R3 Freight units > 20 ft and < 40 ft, and R4 Freight units > 40ft).

7) In addition, the descriptions of statistical variables and definitions given in Annex I were updated to reflect the technical changes listed above."

46.071 On 28 July 2015, the Commission reported to the European Parliament and the Council on the exercise of the power to adopt delegated acts conferred on the Commission pursuant to Regulation (EU) No 1090/2010 of the European Parliament and of the Council amending Directive 2009/42 on statistical returns in respect of carriage of goods and passengers by sea.[68] The Commission confirmed in the report that it had exercised its delegated powers correctly and complied with the necessary procedures:

"When preparing the Delegated Decision, the Commission consulted national experts at the annual meetings of the Coordinating Group for Statistics on Transport that took place in December 2010 and December 2011. The European Parliament and the Council were duly informed of all expert group meetings and received all relevant documents promptly and in an appropriate form. The draft Commission Delegated Decision was discussed and favourably received by Directors General of National Statistical Institutes of the European Union in November 2011.

The Commission adopted the Delegated Decision on 3 February 2012 and notified the European Parliament and the Council. Neither the European Parliament nor the Council issued any objection to the Delegated Decision within the standard two-month period allowed. On the expiry of the two-month period, the Delegated Decision was published in the Official Journal of the European Union on 11 April 2012. It entered into force on 12 April 2012 …

The Commission has exercised its delegated powers correctly."[69]

F. PASSENGER RIGHTS: REGULATION 1177/2010 CONCERNING THE RIGHTS OF PASSENGERS WHEN TRAVELLING BY SEA AND INLAND WATERWAY AND AMENDING REGULATION 2006/2004

Protection of maritime passengers

46.072 A controversial area of EU transport law generally has been the conferral by EU law on passengers of various rights. This has been particularly controversial in the case of air transport but less so in the case of sea transport where the relevant measure is

---

68 Report from the Commission to the European Parliament and the Council on the exercise of the power to adopt delegated acts conferred on the Commission pursuant to Regulation (EU) No 1090/2010 of the European Parliament and of the Council amending Directive 2009/42/EC on statistical returns in respect of carriage of goods and passengers by sea (COM(2015) 362 final). See http://eur-lex.europa.eu/legal-content/EN/TXT/PDF/?uri=COM:2015:362:FIN&from=EN.

69 Ibid., p. 5. See http://eur-lex.europa.eu/legal-content/EN/TXT/PDF/?uri=COM:2015:362:FIN&from=EN.

Regulation 1177/2010 concerning the rights of passengers when travelling by sea and inland waterway and amending Regulation 2006/2004.[70],[71] It is worth stressing that this measure is more about the stranded passenger than the passenger whose contract is breached by the carrier. It is an exception to the general rule and should be treated with some caution. It is submitted that the regulation would benefit from a careful review and amendment.

Adoption of Regulation 1177/2010

46.073 On 24 November 2010, the Parliament and Council adopted Regulation 1177/2010 concerning the rights of passengers when travelling by sea and inland waterway and amending Regulation 2006/2004.[72] Regulation 1177/2010 entered into force on the twentieth day following its publication in the *Official Journal* but it applied from 18 December 2012.

46.074 The legal basis of the regulation is the TFEU and, in particular, Articles 91(1) and 100(2) of the TFEU. The legal history included a proposal from the Commission,[73] an opinion of the European EESC[74] and a consultation with the Committee of the Regions. It was adopted in accordance with the ordinary legislative procedure.

46.075 In part, Regulation 1177/2010 is aimed at ensuring that EU action in the field of maritime transport would provide a high level of protection for passengers that is comparable with other modes of transport (particularly, air transport).[75] Moreover, the EU was seeking to take full account of the requirements of consumer protection in general.

46.076 The regulation was about rebalancing the interests of the parties. The second recital recalls that since

"maritime and inland waterway passenger is the weaker party to the transport contract, all passengers should be granted a minimum level of protection. Nothing should prevent carriers from offering contract conditions more favourable for the passenger than the conditions laid down in this Regulation. At the same time, the aim of this Regulation is not to interfere in commercial business-to-business relationships concerning the transport of goods. In particular, agreements between a road haulier and a carrier should not be construed as transport contracts for the purposes of this Regulation and should therefore not give the road haulier or its employees the right to compensation under this Regulation in the case of delays."

46.077 The background is clear from some of the regulation recitals:

---

70 Reg. 2006/2004 was published at OJ L364/1, 9 December 2004. It was Reg. (EC) No 2006/2004 of the European Parliament and of the Council of 27 October 2004 on cooperation between national authorities responsible for the enforcement of consumer protection laws (the regulation on consumer protection cooperation), ELI: http://data.europa.eu/eli/reg/2004/2006/2016-01-09. A consolidated version is available at: https://eur-lex.europa.eu/legal-content/EN/TXT/?qid=1524420623582&uri=CELEX:02004R2006-20160109.

71 OJ L334/1, 17 December 2010. The English language version has not been amended as at the time of writing.

72 OJ L334/1, 17 December 2010.

73 Proposal for a Regulation of the European Parliament and of the Council concerning the rights of passengers when travelling by sea and inland waterway and amending Regulation (EC) No 2006/2004 on cooperation between national authorities responsible for the enforcement of consumer protection laws {SEC(2008) 2950} {SEC(2008) 2951} (COM/2008/0816 final), COD 2008/0246. It is available at: http://eur-lex.europa.eu/legal-content/EN/TXT/PDF/?uri=CELEX:52008PC0816&from=EN.

74 OJ C317/89, 23 December 2009.

75 However, the levels of protection are not identical.

"(3) The protection of passengers should cover not only passenger services between ports situated in the territory of the Member States, but also passenger services between such ports and ports situated outside the territory of the Member States, taking into account the risk of distortion of competition on the passenger transport market. Therefore the term 'Union carrier' should, for the purposes of this Regulation, be interpreted as broadly as possible, but without affecting other legal acts of the Union, such as Council Regulation … 4056/86 of 22 December 1986 laying down detailed rules for the application of Articles 85 and 86 of the Treaty to maritime transport[76] and Council Regulation … 3577/92 of 7 December 1992 applying the principle of freedom to provide services to maritime transport within Member States (maritime cabotage).[77]

(4) The internal market for maritime and inland waterway passenger services should benefit citizens in general. Consequently, disabled persons and persons with reduced mobility, whether caused by disability, age or any other factor, should have opportunities for using passenger services and cruises that are comparable to those of other citizens. Disabled persons and persons with reduced mobility have the same rights as all other citizens with regard to free movement, freedom of choice and non-discrimination.

(5) Member States should promote the use of public transport and the use of integrated tickets in order to optimise the use and interoperability of the various transport modes and operators."

Persons with disabilities in the context of Regulation 1177/2010

46.078 The position of people with disabilities is recognised specifically:

"(4) The internal market for maritime and inland waterway passenger services should benefit citizens in general. Consequently, disabled persons and persons with reduced mobility, whether caused by disability, age or any other factor, should have opportunities for using passenger services and cruises that are comparable to those of other citizens. Disabled persons and persons with reduced mobility have the same rights as all other citizens with regard to free movement, freedom of choice and non-discrimination

…

(6) in the light of Article 9 of the United Nations Convention on the Rights of Persons with Disabilities and in order to give disabled persons and persons with reduced mobility opportunities for maritime and inland waterway travel comparable to those of other citizens, rules for non-discrimination and assistance during their journey should be established. Those persons should therefore be accepted for carriage and not refused transport, except for reasons which are justified on the grounds of safety and established by the competent authorities. They should enjoy the right to assistance in ports and on board passenger ships. In the interests of social inclusion, the persons concerned should receive this assistance free of charge. Carriers should establish access conditions, preferably using the European standardisation system.

(7) In deciding on the design of new ports and terminals, and as part of major refurbishments, the bodies responsible for those facilities should take into account the needs of disabled persons and persons with reduced mobility, in particular with regard to accessibility, paying particular consideration to 'design for all' requirements. Carriers should take such needs into account when deciding on the design of new and newly refurbished passenger ships in accordance with Directive 2006/87/EC of the European Parliament and of the Council of 12 December 2006 laying down technical requirements for inland waterway vessels[78] and Directive 2009/45 of the European Parliament and of the Council of 6 May 2009 on safety rules and standards for passenger ships.[79]

---

76 Ed., OJ L378/4.
77 Ed., OJ L364/7, 12 December 1992.
78 OJ L389/1, 30.12.2006.
79 OJ L163/1, 25.6.2009.

(8) Assistance given at ports situated in the territory of a Member State should, among other things, enable disabled persons and persons with reduced mobility to proceed from a designated point of arrival at a port to a passenger ship and from a passenger ship to a designated point of departure at a port, including embarking and disembarking.

(9) In organising assistance to disabled persons and persons with reduced mobility, and the training of their personnel, carriers should cooperate with organisations representative of disabled persons or persons with reduced mobility. In that work they should also take into account the relevant provisions of the International Convention and Code on Standards of Training, Certification and Watchkeeping for Seafarers as well as the Recommendation of the International Maritime Organisation (IMO) on the design and operation of passenger ships to respond to elderly and disabled persons' needs.

(10) The provisions governing the embarkation of disabled persons or persons with reduced mobility should be without prejudice to the general provisions applicable to the embarkation of passengers laid down by the international, Union or national rules in force.

(11) Legal acts of the Union on passenger rights should take into account the needs of passengers, in particular those of disabled persons and persons with reduced mobility, to use different transport modes and to transfer smoothly between different modes, subject to the applicable safety regulations for the operation of ships."

Informing passengers promptly of delays/cancellations and compensation

46.079 There is also a regulation that all passengers should be informed promptly of delays and cancellations: moreover, passengers should be compensated in accordance with the terms of Regulation 1177/2010:

"(12) Passengers should be adequately informed in the event of cancellation or delay of any passenger service or cruise. That information should help passengers to make the necessary arrangements and, if needed, to obtain information about alternative connections.

(13) Inconvenience experienced by passengers due to the cancellation or long delay of their journey should be reduced. To this end, passengers should be adequately looked after and should be able to cancel their journey and have their tickets reimbursed or to obtain re-routing under satisfactory conditions. Adequate accommodation for passengers may not necessarily consist of hotel rooms but also of any other suitable accommodation that is available, depending in particular on the circumstances relating to each specific situation, the passengers' vehicles and the characteristics of the ship. In this respect and in duly justified cases of extraordinary and urgent circumstances, carriers should be able to take full advantage of the available relevant facilities, in cooperation with civil authorities.

(14) Carriers should provide for the payment of compensation for passengers in the event of the cancellation or delay of a passenger service based on a percentage of the ticket price, except when the cancellation or delay occurs due to weather conditions endangering the safe operation of the ship or to extraordinary circumstances which could not have been avoided even if all reasonable measures had been taken.

(15) Carriers should, in accordance with generally accepted principles, bear the burden of proving that the cancellation or delay was caused by such weather conditions or extraordinary circumstances.

(16) Weather conditions endangering the safe operation of the ship should include, but not be limited to, strong winds, heavy seas, strong currents, difficult ice conditions and extremely high or low water levels, hurricanes, tornados and floods.

(17) Extraordinary circumstances should include, but not be limited to, natural disasters such as fires and earthquakes, terrorist attacks, wars and military or civil armed conflicts, uprisings, military or illegal confiscations, labour conflicts, landing any sick, injured or dead person, search and rescue operations at sea or on inland waterways, measures necessary to protect the environment, decisions taken by traffic management bodies or port authorities,

or decisions by the competent authorities with regard to public order and safety as well as to cover urgent transport needs.

(18) With the involvement of stakeholders, professional associations and associations of customers, passengers, disabled persons and persons with reduced mobility, carriers should cooperate in order to adopt arrangements at national or European level for improving care and assistance offered to passengers whenever their travel is interrupted, notably in the event of long delays or cancellation of travel. National enforcement bodies should be informed of those arrangements.

(19) The Court of Justice of the European Union has already ruled that problems leading to cancellations or delays can be covered by the concept of extraordinary circumstances only to the extent that they stem from events which are not inherent in the normal exercise of the activity of the carrier concerned and are beyond its actual control. It should be noted that weather conditions endangering the safe operation of the ship are indeed beyond the actual control of the carrier."

46.080 The protections of passenger safety is also recognised:

"(20) This Regulation should not affect the rights of passengers established by Council Directive 90/314/EEC of 13 June 1990 on package travel, package holidays and package tours.[80] This Regulation should not apply in cases where a package tour is cancelled for reasons other than cancellation of the passenger service or the cruise."

46.081 The position of different types of passenger safety is also recognised:

"(21) Passengers should be fully informed of their rights under this Regulation in formats which are accessible to everybody, so that they can effectively exercise those rights. Rights of passengers should include the receipt of information regarding the passenger service or cruise before and during the journey. All essential information provided to passengers should also be provided in formats accessible to disabled persons and persons with reduced mobility, with such accessible formats allowing passengers to access the same information using, for example, text, Braille, audio, video and/or electronic formats."

46.082 Passengers should have appropriate and accessible complaint procedures:

"(22) Passengers should be able to exercise their rights by means of appropriate and accessible complaint procedures implemented by carriers and terminal operators within their respective areas of competence or, as the case may be, by the submission of complaints to the body or bodies designated to that end by the Member State concerned. Carriers and terminal operators should respond to complaints by passengers within a set period of time, bearing in mind that the non-reaction to a complaint could be held against them.

(23) Taking into account the procedures established by a Member State for the submission of complaints, a complaint concerning assistance in a port or on board a ship should preferably be addressed to the body or bodies designated for the enforcement of this Regulation in the Member State where the port of embarkation is situated and, for passenger services from a third country, where the port of disembarkation is situated."

46.083 Member States must designate appropriate national authorities to deal with issues:

"(24) Member States should ensure compliance with this Regulation and designate a competent body or bodies to carry out supervision and enforcement tasks. This does not affect the rights of passengers to seek legal redress from courts under national law.

(25) The body or bodies designated for the enforcement of this Regulation should be independent of commercial interests. Each Member State should appoint at least one body

---

80 Ed., OJ L158/59, 23 June 1990.

which, when applicable, should have the power and capability to investigate individual complaints and to facilitate dispute settlement. Passengers should be entitled to receive a substantiated reply from the designated body, within a reasonable period of time. Given the importance of reliable statistics for the enforcement of this Regulation, in particular to ensure coherent application throughout the Union, the reports prepared by those bodies should if possible include statistics on complaints and their outcome."

46.084 Member States should also provide for penalties to deal with issues:

"(26) Member States should lay down penalties applicable to infringements of this Regulation and ensure that those penalties are applied. Those penalties should be effective, proportionate and dissuasive."

46.085 Regulation 1177/2010 also recognises the position relating to subsidiarity and the broader issues of enforcement:

"(27) Since the objectives of this Regulation, namely to ensure a high level of protection of and assistance to passengers throughout the Member States and to ensure that economic agents operate under harmonised conditions in the internal market, cannot be sufficiently achieved by the Member States and can therefore, by reason of the scale and effects of the action, be better achieved at Union level, the Union may adopt measures, in accordance with the principle of subsidiarity as set out in Article 5 of the Treaty on European Union. In accordance with the principle of proportionality as set out in that Article, this Regulation does not go beyond what is necessary in order to achieve those objectives.

(28) The enforcement of this Regulation should be based on Regulation ... 2006/2004 of the European Parliament and of the Council of 27 October 2004 on cooperation between national authorities responsible for the enforcement of consumer protection laws (the Regulation on consumer protection cooperation).[81] That Regulation should therefore be amended accordingly.

(29) Directive 95/46/EC of the European Parliament and of the Council of 24 October 1995 on the protection of individuals with regard to the processing of personal data and on the free movement of such data[82] should be strictly respected and enforced in order to guarantee respect for the privacy of natural and legal persons, and to ensure that the information and reports requested serve solely to fulfil the obligations laid down in this Regulation and are not used to the detriment of such persons.

(30) This Regulation respects the fundamental rights and observes the principles recognised in particular by the Charter of Fundamental Rights of the European Union, as referred to in Article 6 of the Treaty on European Union."

Chapter l: General provision

46.086 Chapter I of the directive ("General Provisions") contains a number of basic provisions.

46.087 Article 1 ("subject matter") provides that the regulation establishes rules for sea and inland waterway transport as regards the following: (a) non-discrimination between passengers with regard to transport conditions offered by carriers; (b) non-discrimination and assistance for disabled persons and persons with reduced mobility; (c) the rights of passengers in cases of cancellation or delay; (d) minimum information to be provided to passengers; (e) the handling of complaints; and (f) general rules on enforcement.

---

81 OJ L364/1, 9.12.2004.
82 Ed., OJ L281/31, 23 November 1995.

46.088 Article 2 ("scope") provides that the regulation must apply in respect of passengers travelling: (a) on passenger services where the port of embarkation is situated in the territory of a Member State; (b) on passenger services where the port of embarkation is situated outside the territory of a Member State and the port of disembarkation is situated in the territory of a Member State, provided that the service is operated by a Union carrier as defined in Article 3(e); and (c) on a cruise where the port of embarkation is situated in the territory of a Member State. However, Articles 16(2), 18, 19 and 20(1) and (4) shall not apply to those passengers.

46.089 Article 2(2) provides that the regulation does not apply in respect of passengers travelling: (a) on ships certified to carry up to 12 passengers; (b) on ships which have a crew responsible for the operation of the ship composed of not more than three persons or where the distance of the overall passenger service is less than 500 metres, one way; (c) on excursion and sightseeing tours other than cruises; or (d) on ships not propelled by mechanical means as well as original, and individual replicas of, historical passenger ships designed before 1965, built predominantly with the original materials, certified to carry up to 36 passengers. Article 2(3) of the regulation provides that Member States may, for a period of two years from 18 December 2012, exempt from the application of the regulation seagoing ships of less than 300 gt (gross tons) operated in domestic transport, provided that the rights of passengers under the regulation are adequately ensured under national law. Member States may, under Article 2(4), exempt from the application of the regulation passenger services covered by public service obligations, public service contracts or integrated services provided that the rights of passengers under the regulation are comparably guaranteed under national law. A caveat is added by Article 2(5) that without prejudice to Directive 2006/87[83] and to Directive 2009/45,[84] nothing in the regulation shall be understood as constituting technical requirements imposing obligations on carriers, terminal operators or other entities to modify or replace ships, infrastructure, ports or port terminals.

46.090 Article 3 contains the relevant definitions for the purposes of the regulation. First, the term "disabled person" or "person with reduced mobility" means any person whose mobility when using transport is reduced as a result of any physical disability (sensory or locomotor, permanent or temporary), intellectual disability or impairment, or any other cause of disability, or as a result of age, and whose situation needs appropriate attention and adaptation to his particular needs of the service made available to all passengers. Second, the "territory of a Member State" means a territory to which the TFEU applies as referred to in Article 355 of that Treaty. Third, "access conditions" means relevant standards, guidelines and information on the accessibility of port terminals and ships including their facilities for disabled persons or persons with reduced mobility. Fourth, the term "carrier" means a natural or legal person, other than a tour operator, travel agent or ticket vendor, offering transport by passenger services or cruises to the general public. Fifth, the term "Union carrier" means a carrier established within the territory of a Member State or offering transport by passenger services operated to or from

---

83 Dir. 2006/87 of the European Parliament and of the Council of 12 December 2006 laying down technical requirements for inland waterway vessels and repealing Council Directive 82/714 (OJ L389/1, 30 December 2006).

84 Dir. 2009/45 of the European Parliament and of the Council of 6 May 2009 on safety rules and standards for passenger ships (Recast) (OJ L163/1, 25 June 2009).

the territory of a Member State. Sixth, the term "passenger service" means a commercial passenger transport service by sea or inland waterways operated according to a published timetable. Seventh, the term "integrated services" means interconnected transport services within a determined geographical area with a single information service, ticketing scheme and timetable. The term "performing carrier" means a person, other than the carrier, who actually performs the carriage wholly or partially. The term "inland waterway" means a natural or artificial navigable inland body of water, or system of interconnected bodies of water, used for transport, such as lakes, rivers or canals or any combination of these. The term "port" means a place or a geographical area made up of such improvement works and facilities as to permit the reception of ships from which passengers regularly embark or disembark. The term "port terminal" means a terminal, staffed by a carrier or a terminal operator, in a port with facilities, such as check-in, ticket counters or lounges, and staff for the embarkation or disembarkation of passengers travelling on passenger services or on a cruise. The term "ship" means a vessel used for navigation at sea or on inland waterways. The term "transport contract" means a contract of carriage between a carrier and a passenger for the provision of one or more passenger services or cruises. The term "ticket" means a valid document or other evidence of a transport contract. The phrase "ticket vendor" means any retailer concluding transport contracts on behalf of a carrier. The term "travel agent" means any retailer acting on behalf of a passenger or a tour operator for the conclusion of transport contracts. The phrase "tour operator" means an organiser or retailer, other than a carrier, within the meaning of Article 2(2) and (3) of Directive 90/314.[85] The word "reservation" means a booking of a specific departure of a passenger service or a cruise. The term "terminal operator" means a private or public body in the territory of a Member State responsible for the administration and management of a port terminal. The word "cruise" means a transport service by sea or inland waterway, operated exclusively for the purpose of pleasure or recreation, supplemented by accommodation and other facilities, exceeding two overnight stays on board. The phrase "shipping incident" means shipwreck, capsizing, collision or stranding of the ship, explosion or fire in the ship, or defect in the ship.

Tickets and non-discriminatory contract conditions

46.091 Article 4(1) provides that carriers must issue a ticket to the passenger, unless under national law other documents give entitlement to transport. A ticket may be issued in an electronic format. Under Article 4(2), without prejudice to social tariffs, the contract conditions and tariffs applied by carriers or ticket vendors must be offered to the general public without any direct or indirect discrimination based on the nationality of the final customer or on the place of establishment of carriers or ticket vendors within the EU.

Other performing parties

46.092 Article 5 deals with "other performing parties". Article 5(1) provides that where the performance of the obligations under the regulation has been entrusted to a

---

85 This is the so-called Package Travel Directive (i.e. Council Dir. 90/314 of 13 June 1990 on package travel, package holidays and package tours (OJ L158/59, 23 June 1990)).

performing carrier, ticket vendor or any other person, the carrier, travel agent, tour operator or terminal operator who has entrusted such obligations must nevertheless be liable for the acts and omissions of that performing party, acting within that party's scope of employment. In addition to Article 5(1), the party to whom the performance of an obligation has been entrusted by the carrier, travel agent, tour operator or terminal operator must be subject to the provisions of the regulation, including provisions on liabilities and defences, with regard to the obligation entrusted.

Exclusion of waiver

46.093 Article 6 provides that rights and obligations pursuant to the regulation must not be waived or limited, in particular by a derogation or restrictive clause in the transport contract. This adds greater protection to passengers because it is impossible for their rights to be waived or limited by contract or otherwise.

Chapter II: "Rights of disabled persons and persons with reduced mobility"

46.094 Article 7 ("right to transport") provides in Article 7(1) that carriers, travel agents and tour operators must not refuse to accept a reservation, to issue or otherwise provide a ticket or to embark persons on the grounds of disability or of reduced mobility as such. Article 7(2) provides that reservations and tickets must be offered to disabled persons and persons with reduced mobility at no additional cost under the same conditions that apply to all other passengers. Article 7 is a general rule only because Article 8 provides some exceptions.

46.095 Article 8 ("exceptions and special conditions") provides in Article 8(1) that by way of derogation from Article 7(1), carriers, travel agents and tour operators may refuse to accept a reservation from, to issue or otherwise provide a ticket to or to embark a disabled person or person with reduced mobility: (a) in order to meet applicable safety requirements established by international, EU or national law or in order to meet safety requirements established by the competent authorities; and (b) where the design of the passenger ship or port infrastructure and equipment, including port terminals, makes it impossible to carry out the embarkation, disembarkation or carriage of the said person in a safe or operationally feasible manner. Article 8(2) provides that if there is a refusal to accept a reservation or to issue or otherwise provide a ticket on the grounds referred to in Article 8(1), carriers, travel agents and tour operators must make all reasonable efforts to propose to the person concerned an acceptable alternative transport on a passenger service or a cruise operated by the carrier. Article 8(3) provides that where a disabled person or a person with reduced mobility, who holds a reservation or has a ticket and has complied with the requirements referred to in Article 11(2), is nonetheless denied embarkation on the basis of the regulation, that person, and any accompanying person referred to in paragraph 4 of Article 8, must be offered the choice between the right to reimbursement and re-routing as provided for in Annex I. Annex I to the regulation is entitled the right to reimbursement or re-routing for disabled persons and persons with reduced mobility as referred to in Article 8. The right to the option of a return journey or re-routing shall be conditional upon all safety requirements being met. Article 8(4) provides that where strictly necessary and under the same conditions set out in Article 8(1), carriers, travel agents and tour operators may require that a disabled person or person with reduced mobility be accompanied by another person who is capable of providing the assistance required by the disabled person or person with reduced mobility. As regards passenger services, such an accompanying person must be carried free of charge. Under Article 8(5), when carriers, travel agents and tour operators have recourse to paragraphs 1 or 4, they must immediately inform the disabled person or person with reduced mobility of the specific reasons for the decision. On request, those reasons shall be notified to the disabled person or person with reduced mobility in writing, no later than five working days after the request. In the event of refusal according to paragraph 1(a), reference shall be made to the applicable safety requirements.

46.096 Article 9 deals with accessibility and information. Article 9(1) provides that in co-operation with organisations representative of disabled persons or persons with reduced mobility, carriers and terminal operators shall, where appropriate through their organisations, establish, or have in place, non-discriminatory access conditions for the transport of disabled persons and persons with reduced mobility and accompanying persons. The access conditions shall upon request be communicated to national enforcement bodies. Article 9(2) provides that the access conditions provided for in paragraph 1 shall be made publicly available by carriers and terminal operators physically or on the internet, in accessible formats on request, and in the same languages as those in which information is generally made available to all passengers. Particular attention shall be paid to the needs of disabled persons and persons with reduced mobility. Article 9(3) provides that tour operators shall make available the access conditions provided for in paragraph 1 which apply to journeys included in package travel, package holidays and package tours which they organise, sell or offer for sale. Article 9(4) provides that carriers, travel agents and tour operators shall ensure that all relevant information, including online reservation and information, concerning the conditions of carriage, journey information and access conditions is available in appropriate and accessible formats for disabled persons and persons with reduced mobility. Persons needing assistance shall receive confirmation of such assistance by any means available, including electronic means or Short Message Service ("SMS").

46.097 Article 10 ("right to assistance in ports and on board ships") provides that, subject to the access conditions provided for in Article 9(1), carriers and terminal operators must, within their respective areas of competence, provide assistance free of charge to disabled persons and persons with reduced mobility, as specified in Annexes II and III,[86] in ports, including embarkation and disembarkation, and on board ships. The assistance shall, if possible, be adapted to the individual needs of the disabled person or person with reduced mobility.

46.098 Article 11 ("conditions under which assistance is provided") provides in Article 11(1) that carriers and terminal operators must, within their respective areas of competence, provide assistance to disabled persons and persons with reduced mobility as set out in Article 10 provided that: (a) the carrier or the terminal operator is notified, by any means available, including electronic means or SMS, of the person's need for such assistance at the latest 48 hours before the assistance is needed, unless a shorter period is agreed between the passenger and the carrier or terminal operator; and (b) the disabled

---

86 Annex III deals with assistance on board ships as referred to in Arts 10 and 13.

person or person with reduced mobility presents himself at the port or at the designated point as referred to in Article 12(3): (i) at a time stipulated in writing by the carrier which must not be more than 60 minutes before the published embarkation time; or (ii) if no embarkation time is stipulated, no later than 60 minutes before the published departure time, unless a shorter period is agreed between the passenger and the carrier or terminal operator. Article 11(2) provides that in addition to Article 11(1), disabled persons or persons with reduced mobility must notify the carrier, at the time of reservation or advance purchase of the ticket, of their specific needs with regard to accommodation, seating or services required or their need to bring medical equipment, provided the need is known at that time. Article 11(3) provides that a notification made in accordance with paragraphs 1(a) and 2 may always be submitted to the travel agent or the tour operator from which the ticket was purchased. Where the ticket permits multiple journeys, one notification must be sufficient provided that adequate information on the timing of subsequent journeys is provided. The passenger must receive a confirmation stating that the assistance needs have been notified as required in accordance with paragraphs 1(a) and 2. Ultimately, Article 11(4) provides that where no notification is made in accordance with paragraphs 1(a) and 2, carriers and terminal operators shall nonetheless make all reasonable efforts to ensure that the assistance is provided in such a way that the disabled person or person with reduced mobility is able to embark, disembark and travel on the ship. Where a disabled person or person with reduced mobility is accompanied by a recognised assistance dog, that dog shall be accommodated together with that person, provided that the carrier, travel agent or tour operator is notified in accordance with applicable national rules on the carriage of recognised assistance dogs on board passenger ships, where such rules exist.[87]

46.099 The reception of notifications and designation of meeting points are addressed in Article 12. Article 12(1) provides that carriers, terminal operators, travel agents and tour operators shall take all measures necessary for the request for notifications, and for the reception of notifications made in accordance with Article 11(1)(a) and 11(2). That obligation shall apply at all their points of sale, including sale by telephone and over the internet. Article 12(2) provides that if travel agents or tour operators receive the notification referred to in paragraph 1 they must, within their normal office hours, transfer the information to the carrier or terminal operator without delay. Article 12(3) provides that carriers and terminal operators shall designate a point inside or outside port terminals at which disabled persons or persons with reduced mobility can announce their arrival and request assistance. That point shall be clearly signposted and shall offer basic information about the port terminal and assistance provided, in accessible formats.

46.100 Article 13 deals with quality standards for assistance. Article 13(1) provides that terminal operators and carriers operating port terminals or passenger services with a total of more than 100,000 commercial passenger movements during the previous calendar year shall, within their respective areas of competence, set quality standards for the assistance specified in Annexes II and III and shall, where appropriate through their organisations, determine resource requirements for meeting those standards, in co-operation with organisations representative of disabled persons or persons with reduced mobility. Article 13(2) provides that in setting quality standards, full account shall be

---

87 Reg. 1177/2010, Art. 11(5).

taken of internationally recognised policies and codes of conduct concerning facilitation of the transport of disabled persons or persons with reduced mobility, notably the IMO's recommendation on the design and operation of passenger ships to respond to elderly and disabled persons' needs. Article 13(3) stipulates that the quality standards provided for in Article 13(1) shall be made publicly available by terminal operators and carriers physically or on the internet in accessible formats and in the same languages as those in which information is generally made available to all passengers.

46.101 Article 14 deals with training and instructions. It provides that without prejudice to the International Convention and Code on Standards of Training, Certification and Watchkeeping for Seafarers (i.e. the "STCW") and to the regulations adopted under the Revised Convention for Rhine Navigation and the Convention regarding the Regime of Navigation on the Danube, carriers and, where appropriate, terminal operators shall establish disability-related training procedures, including instructions, and ensure that: (a) their personnel, including those employed by any other performing party, providing direct assistance to disabled persons and persons with reduced mobility are trained or instructed as described in Annex IV,[88] Parts A and B; (b) their personnel who are otherwise responsible for the reservation and selling of tickets or embarkation and disembarkation, including those employed by any other performing party, are trained or instructed as described in Annex IV, Part A; and (c) the categories of personnel referred to in points (a) and (b) maintain their competences, for example through instructions or refresher training courses when appropriate

46.102 Compensation in respect of mobility equipment or other specific equipment is provided for in Article 15. Article 15(1) provides that carriers and terminal operators are liable for loss suffered as a result of the loss of or damage to mobility equipment or other specific equipment, used by a disabled person or person with reduced mobility, if the incident which caused the loss was due to the fault or neglect of the carrier or the terminal operator. The fault or neglect of the carrier is presumed for loss caused by a shipping incident. Article 15(2) provides that the compensation referred to in Article 15(1) shall correspond to the replacement value of the equipment concerned or, where applicable, to the costs relating to repairs. Paragraphs 1 and 2 of Article 15 shall not apply if Article 4 of Regulation 392/2009 of the European Parliament and of the Council of 23 April 2009 on the liability of carriers of passengers by sea in the event of accidents applies. Article 15(4) provides that, moreover, every effort must be undertaken to provide rapidly temporary replacement equipment which is a suitable alternative.

Chapter III: "Obligations of carriers and terminal operators in the events of interrupted travel"

46.103 Chapter III is addressed to carriers and terminal operators but provides rights for passengers. This is a chapter which would undoubtedly benefit from a careful redrafting because it lacks precision and detail in various places. In particular, it should emphasise explicitly (what is already implicit) that the aim of the measure is to compensate the stranded passenger rather than one whose travel plans have been altered with ample notice of weeks or months and alternative arrangements have been put in place.

---

88 Annex IV is entitled "Disability-related training, including instructions, as referred to in Article 14."

Information in the event of cancelled or delayed departures

46.104 Article 16 deals with the issue of information in the event of cancelled or delayed departures. Curiously, the final regulation does not define either a cancellation[89] or a delayed departure.[90] Article 16 treats cancellation and delay as comparable in many ways.

46.105 Article 16(1) provides that in the case of a cancellation or a delay in departure of a passenger service or a cruise, passengers departing from port terminals or, if possible, passengers departing from ports shall be informed by the carrier or, where appropriate, by the terminal operator, of the situation as soon as possible and in any event no later than 30 minutes after the scheduled time of departure,[91] and of the estimated departure time and estimated arrival time as soon as that information is available. Article 16(1) refers to the passenger being informed "of the situation", it does not explicitly require the passenger to be informed of the cause or the solution to the situation but it would be better for the carrier to do so but there is, strictly speaking, no obligation to explain the cause or solution to the situation.[92]

46.106 Article 16(2) provides that if passengers miss a connecting transport service due to a cancellation or delay, the carrier and, where appropriate, the terminal operator must make "reasonable efforts"[93] to inform the passengers concerned of alternative connections. Article 2(1)(c) provides that Article 16(2) does not apply to cruises. In practice, it could well be the local terminal operator who will be better placed to provide the information to the passenger as the terminal operator is more likely to have the local transport connection information.

46.107 Article 16(3) states that the carrier or, where appropriate, the terminal operator, shall ensure that disabled persons or persons with reduced mobility receive the information required under paragraphs 1 and 2 in accessible formats. It is open to question whether all ferry and terminal operators have invested sufficiently to comply with this obligation.

Assistance in the event of cancelled or delayed departures

46.108 Article 17 deals with the assistance in the event of cancelled or delayed departures.[94] Article 20(1) provides that Article 17 does not apply to passengers with open tickets as long as the time of departure is not specified, except for passengers holding a

---

89 The proposal for the regulation had defined it as meaning the non-operation of a service which was previously scheduled and for which at least one reservation was made. This would have made it comparable to the definition in the air transport measure.

90 The proposal for the regulation had defined it as meaning a difference between the time the passenger was scheduled to depart or to arrive in accordance with the published timetable and the time of his actual or expected departure or arrival.

91 Nothing is preventing a carrier from informing passengers earlier.

92 A contrary view is expressed by Wersel in Jessen and Werner (eds), Brussels Commentary on EU Maritime Transport Law (2016), chap. 3, VI, para. 229 but she offers no explanation as to why a carrier is obliged to provide such explicit information. It is submitted that the carrier is obliged to inform passengers "of the situation" could include the cause and solution but there is no explicit provision requiring it and given the exceptional nature of the obligation to inform passengers as a matter of law, carriers may do so but probably not must do anything more than give the information about the situation.

93 The use of the term "reasonable" is a constraint and limitation on the level of effort required.

94 The proposal only dealt with delayed sailings so cancellation was added to the final version.

travel pass or a season ticket. Article 20(2) provides that Article 17 does not apply if the passenger is informed of the cancellation or delay before the purchase of the ticket or if the cancellation or delay is caused by the fault of the passenger.

46.109 Article 17(1) provides that where a carrier reasonably expects the departure of a passenger service or a cruise to be cancelled or delayed for more than 90[95] minutes beyond its scheduled time of departure, passengers departing from port terminals shall be offered free of charge snacks, meals or refreshments in reasonable relation to the waiting time, provided they are available or can reasonably be supplied.

46.110 It is worth considering some aspects of Article 17(1). First, there is a single time threshold (i.e. 90 minutes) in this maritime context (unlike the air transport measure in Directive 261/2004) and it is not dependent on the length of the journey. This could lead to disproportionate results (e.g. a 90 minute delay on a 90 minute voyage is of a different magnitude from a 90 minute delay on a two-day voyage). Nonetheless, the single time threshold is more convenient. Second, the phrase is "snacks, meals or refreshments" and not, as the proposal contemplated "snacks, meals and refreshments".[96] It has been commented, correctly, that it is for the carrier to decide what to provide from the list of snacks, meals or refreshments[97] but one could see the argument raised that the availability of food should be judged objectively by what is required rather than subjectively by the carrier. Third, Article 17(1) applies whenever the departure is from a "port terminal" as defined in the regulation (i.e. "a terminal, staffed by a carrier or a terminal operator, in a port with facilities, such as check-in, ticket counters or lounges, and staff for the embarkation or disembarkation of passengers travelling on passenger services or on a cruise")[98] rather than from a simple port. Fourth, the requirement to provide the catering is not absolute or unconditional – they shall be offered "in reasonable relation to the waiting time, provided they are available or can reasonably be supplied". So, if they are not reasonably available then they do not need to be made available. It is also submitted that a reasonable construction is needed for the provision, namely, they ought to be provided if the passengers have arrived at, and are waiting at, the port terminal. If, by contrast, passengers had several days of notice that the vessel was not sailing on that day or had been advised against coming to the port terminal in advance then it would seem perverse that a passenger who persisted in turning up at the time of the cancelled sailing would still be entitled to such catering.

46.111 Article 17(2) provides that in the case of a cancellation or a delay in departure where a stay of one or more nights or a stay additional to that intended by the passenger becomes necessary, where and when physically possible, the carrier shall offer passengers departing from port terminals, free of charge, adequate accommodation on board, or ashore, and transport to and from the port terminal and place of accommodation in addition to the snacks, meals or refreshments provided for in paragraph 1. For each passenger, the carrier may limit the total cost of accommodation ashore, not including transport to and from the port terminal and place of accommodation, to €80 per night, for a maximum of three nights.

---

95 This was a compromise between the Commission's 60 minutes and the Council's 120 minutes.
96 Wersel, op. cit. at fn. 92, chap. 3, VI, para. 240 comments: "it was clear to the Commission that the minimum to be provided is always access to the toilets and adequate heating/cooling or air condition[ing]".
97 Wersel, op. cit. at fn. 92, chap. 3, VI, para. 237.
98 Reg. 1177/2010, Art. 3(k).

46.112 It is worth considering some aspects of Article 17(2). First, Article 17(2) is only triggered when a cancellation or a delay[99] in departure where a stay of one or more nights or a stay additional to that intended by the passenger becomes "necessary" (i.e. it is not just desirable). This would appear to arise where there is a last minute-type delay or cancellation and there are no other alternatives available to the passenger. To take an example, if a passenger has driven to a port terminal for an evening sailing and it is cancelled and accommodation is necessary then one can see Article 17(2) being triggered however if the passenger had, say, a week's notice that the sailing had been cancelled then it is far from obvious that there should be the obligation on the carrier to provide the accommodation and this is all the more so where the passenger did not make reasonable efforts to limit his or her losses. Second, the accommodation need only be provided "where and when physically possible". Third, the accommodation is only relevant for departing passengers and not arriving passengers – the words used are: "the carrier shall offer passengers *departing* from port terminals" (emphasis added) which could appear somewhat unfair to arriving passengers but the regulation does not provide for accommodation to be provided even though their needs could be as great (or greater) than departing passengers. Moreover, the departure must be from a port terminal and not just a port. Fourth, the accommodation needs to be "adequate accommodation". Fifth, the accommodation could be on board the vessel or ashore.[100] In this context, it is worth noting that recital 13 provides that

> "adequate accommodation for passengers may not necessarily consist of hotel rooms but also of any other suitable accommodation that is available, depending in particular on the circumstances relating to each specific situation, the passengers' vehicles and the characteristics of the ship. In this respect and in duly justified cases of extraordinary and urgent circumstances, carriers should be able to take full advantage of the available relevant facilities, in cooperation with civil authorities."

This means that it does not necessarily have to be accommodation of the highest level but rather suitable and adequate accommodation taking into account the relevant circumstances. Sixth, subject to the other conditions in Article 17(2), there would also be transport provided between the port terminal and the place of accommodation. Sixth, the accommodation is in addition to, rather than in substitute for, the snacks, meals or refreshments provided for in Article 17(1). Seventh, Article 17(2) provides that for each passenger, the carrier may limit the total cost of accommodation ashore, not including transport to and from the port terminal and place of accommodation, to €80[101] per night, for a maximum of three nights. There is no indication that the limitation has to be imposed in advance of the purchase of the ticket or the incident and therefore the limitation could be imposed on the spot. What is not clear from the regulation is what happens if the only accommodation available costs more than €80 per night but it is likely that the only logical conclusion is that the accommodation is simply not available. Eighth, there is no need to provide the accommodation and refreshments where the weather conditions prevented the safe operation of the vessel. Finally, the regulation does not specify in

---

99 Both a cancellation and a delay are treated equally.

100 It would be the carrier's choice as to whether the accommodation is ashore or on board a vessel. It could be another vessel which the ferry company had in port and does not have to be the vessel on which the voyage is booked (e.g. because that vessel is not in the port or accessible).

101 This monetary limit relates to the cost of the accommodation ashore but not on the vessel.

Article 17 whether there is an obligation to provide such accommodation if the cancellation or delay is in "extraordinary circumstances". It is submitted that great care should be taken in imposing an obligation in extraordinary circumstances. This is for several reasons including the fact that it would be illogical for a carrier to be expected to pay €80 per night for accommodation under Article 17 but did not have to pay compensation in respect of a ticket that might have cost €5.

46.113 Under Article 17(3), in applying paragraphs 1 and 2, the carrier shall pay particular attention to the needs of disabled persons and persons with reduced mobility and any accompanying persons.

46.114 Article 18 ("re-routing and reimbursement in the event of cancelled or delayed departures") provides in Article 18(1) that where a carrier reasonably expects a passenger service to be cancelled or delayed in departure from a port terminal for more than 90 minutes, the passenger shall immediately be offered the choice between: (a) re-routing to the final destination, under comparable conditions, as set out in the transport contract, at the earliest opportunity and at no additional cost; (b) reimbursement of the ticket price and, where relevant, a return service free of charge to the first point of departure, as set out in the transport contract, at the earliest opportunity. Under Article 18(2), where a passenger service is cancelled or delayed in departure from a port for more than 90 minutes, passengers shall have the right to such re-routing or reimbursement of the ticket price from the carrier. Article 18(3) provides that the payment of the reimbursement provided for in Article 18 1(b) and 2 shall be made within seven days, in cash, by electronic bank transfer, bank order or bank cheque, of the full cost of the ticket at the price at which it was purchased, for the part or parts of the journey not made, and for the part or parts already made where the journey no longer serves any purpose in relation to the passenger's original travel plan. Where the passenger agrees, the full reimbursement may also be paid in the form of vouchers and/or other services in an amount equivalent to the price for which the ticket was purchased, provided that the conditions are flexible, particularly regarding the period of validity and the destination.

46.115 Article 19 ("compensation of the ticket price in the event of delay in arrival") provides that in Article 19(1) without losing the right to transport, passengers may request compensation from the carrier if they are facing a delay in arrival at the final destination as set out in the transport contract. The minimum level of compensation shall be 25% of the ticket price for a delay of at least: (a) one hour in the case of a scheduled journey of up to four hours; (b) two hours in the case of a scheduled journey of more than four hours, but not exceeding eight hours; (c) three hours in the case of a scheduled journey of more than eight hours, but not exceeding 24 hours; or (d) six hours in the case of a scheduled journey of more than 24 hours. If the delay exceeds double the time set out in points (a) to (d), the compensation shall be 50% of the ticket price. Article 19(2) provides that passengers who hold a travel pass or a season ticket and who encounter recurrent delays in arrival during its period of validity may request adequate compensation in accordance with the carrier's compensation arrangements. These arrangements shall state the criteria for determining delay in arrival and for calculation of compensation. Article 19(3) provides that compensation shall be calculated in relation to the price which the passenger actually paid for the delayed passenger service. Under Article 19(4), where the transport is for a return journey, compensation for delay in arrival on either the outward or the return leg shall be calculated in relation to half of the price paid for the transport by that passenger service. Article 19(5) provides that the compensation shall be paid within one month after the submission of the request for compensation. The compensation may be paid in vouchers and/or other services, provided that the conditions are flexible, particularly regarding the period of validity and the destination. The compensation shall be paid in money at the request of the passenger. The compensation of the ticket price shall not be reduced by financial transaction costs such as fees, telephone costs or stamps. Carriers may introduce a minimum threshold under which payments for compensation will not be paid. This threshold shall not exceed €6.

46.116 Article 20 contains a number of exemptions. Article 20(1) provides that Articles 17, 18 and 19 shall not apply to passengers with open tickets as long as the time of departure is not specified, except for passengers holding a travel pass or a season ticket. Article 20(2) provides that Articles 17 and 19 shall not apply if the passenger is informed of the cancellation or delay before the purchase of the ticket or if the cancellation or delay is caused by the fault of the passenger. Article 20(3) stipulates that Article 17(2) shall not apply where the carrier proves that the cancellation or delay is caused by weather conditions endangering the safe operation of the ship. Under Article 20(4), Article 19 shall not apply where the carrier proves that the cancellation or delay is caused by weather conditions endangering the safe operation of the ship or by extraordinary circumstances hindering the performance of the passenger service which could not have been avoided even if all reasonable measures had been taken.

46.117 Article 21 ("further claims") provides that nothing in the regulation shall preclude passengers from seeking damages in accordance with national law in respect of loss resulting from cancellation or delay of transport services before national courts, including under Directive 90/314.[102]

Chapter IV: "General rules on information and complaints"

46.118 Article 22 deals with the right to travel information. It provides that carriers and terminal operators shall, within their respective areas of competence, provide passengers with adequate information throughout their travel in formats which are accessible to everybody and in the same languages as those in which information is generally made available to all passengers. Particular attention shall be paid to the needs of disabled persons and persons with reduced mobility.

46.119 Article 23 deals with information on passenger rights. Article 23(1) provides that carriers, terminal operators and, when applicable, port authorities, shall, within their respective areas of competence, ensure that information on the rights of passengers under the regulation is publicly available on board ships, in ports, if possible, and in port terminals. The information shall be provided as far as possible in accessible formats and in the same languages as those in which information is generally made available to all passengers. When that information is provided particular attention shall be paid to the needs of disabled persons and persons with reduced mobility. Article 23(2) provides that in order to comply with the information requirement referred to in paragraph 1, carriers, terminal operators and, when applicable, port authorities, may use a summary of the

---

102 This is the so-called Package Travel Directive (i.e. Council Dir. 90/314 of 13 June 1990 on package travel, package holidays and package tours (OJ L158/59, 23 June 1990)).

provisions of this regulation prepared by the Commission in all the official languages of the EU institutions and made available to them. Under Article 23(3), carriers, terminal operators and, when applicable, port authorities shall inform passengers in an appropriate manner on board ships, in ports, if possible, and in port terminals, of the contact details of the enforcement body designated by the Member State concerned pursuant to Article 25(1).

46.120 Complaints are dealt with by Article 24. Article 24(1) provides that carriers and terminal operators shall set up or have in place an accessible complaint-handling mechanism for rights and obligations covered by the regulation. Article 24(2) provides that where a passenger covered by this regulation wants to make a complaint to the carrier or terminal operator, he shall submit it within two months from the date on which the service was performed or when a service should have been performed. Within one month of receiving the complaint, the carrier or terminal operator shall give notice to the passenger that his complaint has been substantiated, rejected or is still being considered. The time taken to provide the final reply shall not be longer than two months from the receipt of a complaint.

Chapter V: "Enforcement and national enforcement bodies"

46.121 Article 25 provides for national enforcement bodies. Article 25(1) states that each Member State shall designate a new or existing body or bodies responsible for the enforcement of the regulation as regards passenger services and cruises from ports situated on its territory and passenger services from a third country to such ports. Each body shall take the measures necessary to ensure compliance with this regulation. Each body shall, in its organisation, funding decisions, legal structure and decision-making, be independent of commercial interests. Member States must, under Article 25(2), inform the Commission of the body or bodies designated in accordance with Article 25. Under Article 25(3), any passenger may submit a complaint, in accordance with national law, to the competent body designated under paragraph 1, or to any other competent body designated by a Member State, about an alleged infringement of this regulation. The competent body shall provide passengers with a substantiated reply to their complaint within a reasonable period of time. A Member State may decide: (a) that the passenger as a first step shall submit the complaint covered by this regulation to the carrier or terminal operator; and/or (b) that the national enforcement body or any other competent body designated by the Member State shall act as an appeal body for complaints not resolved under Article 24. Article 25(4) provides that Member States that have chosen to exempt certain services pursuant to Article 2(4) shall ensure that a comparable mechanism of enforcement of passenger rights is in place.

46.122 Article 26 provides for a report on enforcement. By 1 June 2015 and every two years thereafter, the enforcement bodies designated pursuant to Article 25 must publish a report on their activity in the previous two calendar years, containing in particular a description of actions taken in order to implement the provisions of the regulation, details of sanctions applied and statistics on complaints and sanctions applied.

46.123 Co-operation between enforcement bodies is addressed by Article 27. It provides that national enforcement bodies referred to in Article 25(1) shall exchange information on their work and decision-making principles and practice to the extent necessary for the coherent application of the regulation. The Commission shall support them in that task.

46.124 Article 28 provides for penalties. The Member States must lay down rules on penalties applicable to infringements of the provisions of the regulation and shall take all the measures necessary to ensure that they are implemented. The penalties provided for shall be effective, proportionate and dissuasive. Member States shall notify those rules and measures to the Commission by 18 December 2012 and shall notify it without delay of any subsequent amendment affecting them.

Chapter VI: "Final provisions"

46.125 Article 29 contemplates a "report". The Commission must report to the Parliament and to the Council by 19 December 2015 on the operation and the effects of the regulation. The report shall be accompanied where necessary by legislative proposals implementing in further detail the provisions of this regulation, or amending it. Article 30 made various amendments to Regulation 2006/2004.[103] The report has been submitted and the Commission considered "that overall implementation of the regulation is satisfactory. The regulation is recent and appears to be sufficiently flexible to accommodate improvement without the need for amendments at this stage. This is also the stakeholders' view."[104]

G. DECISION 87/359 CONCERNING REDUCTIONS IN AIR AND SEA TRANSPORT FARES AVAILABLE ONLY TO SPANISH NATIONALS RESIDENT IN THE CANARY ISLANDS AND THE BALEARIC ISLANDS

46.126 On 22 June 1987, the Commission adopted Decision 87/359 concerning reductions in air and sea transport fares available only to Spanish nationals resident in the Canary Islands and the Balearic Islands.[105] The Commission acted on the basis of Article 90(1) and (3) of the then EEC Treaty. Spain had introduced, by way of Decree-Law 22/62 of 14 June 1962[106] and Law 46/81 of 29 December 1981[107] special arrangements relating to transport under which certain persons travelling between continental Spain and the Canary Islands as well as Balearic Islands were granted reductions in fares for air and sea transport. In specific terms, Article 2 of the Decree-Law 22/62 concerning air links with the Canary Islands provided from a State subsidy amounting to 33 per cent of the price for tickets on scheduled passenger services on that route and Article 3 required transport undertakings receiving the subsidy to reduce the price of their tickets by the same amount. Article 1 of the Decree-Law expressly provided that the State subsidies for air transport

---

103 I.e. Reg. 2006/2004 of the European Parliament and of the Council of 27 October 2004 on cooperation between national authorities responsible for the enforcement of consumer protection laws (the regulation on consumer protection cooperation) (OJ L364/1, 9 December 2004, p. 1).

104 Report from the Commission to the European Parliament and the Council, Report on the application of Regulation (EU) No 1177/2010 concerning the rights of passengers when travelling by sea and inland waterway and amending Regulation (EC) No 2006/2004 (COM(2016) 274 final, 24 May 2016), http://eur-lex.europa.eu/legal-content/EN/TXT/HTML/?uri=CELEX:52016DC0274&qid=1525628558025&from=EN.

105 OJ1987 L194/28.

106 See Decree-Law 22/62 of 14 June 1962, Boletin Oficial del Estado No 143, 15 June 1962.

107 Boletin Oficial del Estado, No 312, 30 December 1981.

services to and from the Canary Islands were applicable only to tickets used by Spanish nationals resident on the Islands. Law 46/81 concerned air and sea links with the Balearic Islands and provided in a similar way for a State subsidy allowing reduced fares to be charged on scheduled transport services between the archipelago and the rest of Spain. Article 2 of the Law provided for a reduction in fares amounting to 25% of the fare for sailings between the archipelago and the rest of Spain and to 10% of the fare for sailings between islands within the archipelago. Articles 3 and 4 of the Law provided that the relevant undertakings, which are required to grant the reductions in fares, would be reimbursed by the State for the resulting loss of revenue. Article 1 of the Law provided that only Spanish nationals resident in the Balearic Islands are eligible for the reduction in fares. The special arrangements provided for by Decree-Law 22/62 and Law 46/81 were reinforced by Article 1 of Royal Decree 3269/82 of 12 November 1982.[108] This provided that the reductions in fares for scheduled passenger transport services provided for in Decree-Law 22/62 and Law 46/81 and granted through the intermediary of the publicly owned transport companies are to be available only to Spanish nationals who, at the time of purchasing their tickets, can provide evidence that they are resident in the provinces of the Balearic Islands, Las Palmas and Santa Cruz de Tenerife. A number of private individuals as well as Members of the European Parliament objected to these arrangements and objected to the Commission. A formal complaint was ultimately lodged with the Commission.[109] The Commission later said, in the course of its decision, that:

> "By restricting eligibility for the reduced-fare air and sea transport arrangements to Spanish nationals resident in the Canary and Balearic Islands, Spain is clearly placing them at an advantage over nationals of other Member States similarly resident in the islands.
>
> The transport arrangements applied by Spain are of obvious economic importance in view of the number of nationals of other Member States in the islands, the cost of transport between the islands and continental Spain, and the scale of the reduction granted only to Spanish residents."

46.127 The Commission made representations to the Spanish government on 23 December 1986 expressing its view that the arrangements were incompatible with the Treaty. It reiterated its position on 5 February 1987. The Commission then reaffirmed its position on 4 March 1987 after the Commission had received the Spanish authorities' comments and statement that the arrangements would continue. The Commission, in its decision of 22 June 1987 reasoned thus:

> "10. Article 90(1) of the EEC Treaty provides that, in the case of public undertakings, Member States shall neither enact nor maintain in force any measure contrary to the rules contained in the Treaty, in particular to the rules provided for in Article 7 and Articles 85 to 94. The same requirement applies to undertakings to which Member States grant special or exclusive rights.
> 11. By continuing to apply after 1 January 1986[110] the preferential transport fare arrangements introduced by Decree-Law No. 22/62 of 14 June 1962 and Law No. 46/81 of 29 December 1981, Spain had maintained in force in the case of public undertakings, namely the national transport companies Iberia and Transmediterranea,[111] measures within the meaning of Article 90(1) of the EEC Treaty.

---

108 Boletin Oficial del Estado, No 287, 30 November 1982.
109 See Recital 6 of Dec. 87/359. OJ 1987 L194/28.
110 Ed., the date of accession of Spain to the EC.
111 The Spanish State held 99% and 95%, respectively, of their share capital (source: Dec. 87/359/EEC, Recital 9).

12. Article [106(3) of the TFEU] provides that the Commission shall secure the application of the provisions of Article 90 and shall, where necessary, address appropriate Directives or Decisions to Member States.

13. Pursuant to Article [106], the provisions of Article 7 of the EEC Treaty must in particular be observed. These prohibit any discrimination on grounds of nationality [the Treaty prohibition on discrimination on the basis of nationality within the field of the application of EU law].

14. Since, even though no exception clause is provided for in the transitional measures laid down in the Act of Accession…"[112]

46.128 The Commission thus decided, in Article 1 of its decision that:

"The following provisions are hereby declared incompatible with the provisions of Article [106] (1), in conjunction with those of Article 7, of the EEC Treaty:

- Article 1 of Spanish Decree-Law No. 22/62 on the subsidisation of air transport links with the Canary Islands,
- Article 1 of Spanish Law No. 46/81 on the subsidisation of fares for Spanish nationals resident in the Balearic Islands,
- Article 1 of Spanish Royal Decree No. 3269/82 on the certification of residence for the purposes of the subsidisation of fares and the payment of the subsidy towards scheduled transport services between the peninsula, the Canary Islands and the Balearic Islands, to the extent that they restrict the application of the reductions in transport fares for which they provide to Spanish nationals resident in the provinces of the Balearic Islands, Las Palmas and Santa Cruz de Tenerife to the exclusion of nationals of other Member States resident in the islands."

46.129 The Commission gave Spain two months from the date of notification of the decision of the measures to inform the Commission of the measures which Spain proposed taking to comply with the decision.[113]

H. COUNCIL DECISION 2012/22 OF 12 DECEMBER 2011 CONCERNING THE ACCESSION OF THE EUROPEAN UNION TO THE PROTOCOL OF 2002 TO THE ATHENS CONVENTION RELATING TO THE CARRIAGE OF PASSENGERS AND THEIR LUGGAGE BY SEA, 1974, WITH THE EXCEPTION OF ARTICLES 10 AND 11 THEREOF

46.130 On 12 December 2011, the Council adopted Decision 2012/22 concerning the accession of the European Union to the Protocol of 2002 to the Athens Convention relating to the Carriage of Passengers and their Luggage by Sea, 1974, with the exception of Articles 10 and 11 thereof.[114] The decision was amended by Regulation 517/2013 of 13 May 2013.[115]

46.131 The legal basis for Decision 2012/22 was the TFEU generally, and in particular Article 100(2), in conjunction with point (a) of Article 218(6) and the first subparagraph of Article 218(8) of the TFEU.

---

112 Spain has continued to apply its preferential transport arrangements. The discrimination on grounds of nationality must be brought to an end.

113 Dec. 87/359, Art. 2.

114 OJ L8/1, 12 January 2012, http://eur-lex.europa.eu/legal-content/EN/TXT/HTML/?uri=CELEX:32012D 0022&qid=1438980853467&from=EN.

115 OJ L158/1, 10 June 2013.

46.132 The recitals to the decision recall:

"(1) The Protocol of 2002 to the Athens Convention relating to the Carriage of Passengers and their Luggage by Sea, 1974 ('Athens Protocol') represents a major improvement to the regime relating to the liability of carriers and the compensation of passengers carried by sea. In particular, it provides for a strict liability of the carrier, including compulsory insurance, with a right of direct action against insurers up to specified limits, and for rules on jurisdiction and the recognition and enforcement of judgments. The Athens Protocol is therefore in accordance with the Union's objective of improving the legal regime relating to carriers' liability.

(2) The Athens Protocol modifies the Athens Convention relating to the Carriage of Passengers and their Luggage by Sea, 1974 ('Athens Convention') and establishes in Article 15 that the two instruments shall, as between the Parties to the Athens Protocol, be read and interpreted together as one single instrument.

(3) The majority of the rules of the Athens Protocol have been incorporated into Union law by means of Regulation (EC) No 392/2009 of the European Parliament and of the Council of 23 April 2009 on the liability of carriers of passengers by sea in the event of accidents .... Thus, the Union exerted competence as regards the matters governed by that Regulation. Member States, however, retain their competence regarding a number of provisions of the Athens Protocol, such as the opt out clause whereby they are allowed to fix limits of liability higher than those prescribed under the Athens Protocol. The matters of Member State competence under the Athens Protocol and those falling under the exclusive competence of the Union are interdependent. Therefore, in matters of their competence under the Athens Protocol, Member States should act in a coordinated manner, taking into account their duty of sincere cooperation.

(4) The Athens Protocol is open for ratification, acceptance, approval or accession by States and by Regional Economic Integration Organisations which are constituted by sovereign States that have transferred competence over certain matters governed by the Athens Protocol to those Organisations.

(5) According to Article 17(2)(b) and Article 19 of the Athens Protocol, Regional Economic Integration Organisations may conclude the Athens Protocol.

(6) The Legal Committee of the International Maritime Organization adopted in October 2006 the IMO Reservation and Guidelines for Implementation of the Athens Convention ('IMO Guidelines') to address certain issues within the Athens Convention, such as, in particular, compensation for terrorism-related damages.

(7) Regulation (EC) No 392/2009 reproduces in its annexes the relevant provisions of the consolidated version of the Athens Convention as amended by the Athens Protocol and the IMO Guidelines.

(8) Under the terms of Article 19 of the Athens Protocol, a Regional Economic Integration Organisation must declare at the time of signature, ratification, acceptance, approval or accession the extent of its competence in respect of the matters governed by the Athens Protocol.

(9) The Union should consequently accede to the Athens Protocol and make the reservation contained in the IMO Guidelines. The making of such a reservation should not be interpreted as altering the current division of competence between the Union and the Member States in relation to certification and the controls by State authorities.

(10) Certain provisions under the Athens Protocol concern judicial cooperation in civil matters and therefore fall within the scope of Title V of Part Three of the TFEU. A separate Decision relating to those provisions is to be adopted in parallel to this Decision.

(11) Member States which are to ratify or accede to the Athens Protocol should, if possible, do so simultaneously. Member States should therefore exchange information on the state of their ratification or accession procedures in order to prepare as far as possible the simultaneous deposit of their instruments of ratification or accession. When ratifying or acceding to the Athens Protocol, Member States should make the reservation contained in the IMO Guidelines."

46.133 In terms of accession, Article 1 provides that the EU's accession to the Protocol of 2002 to the Athens Convention relating to the Carriage of Passengers and their Luggage by Sea, 1974 ("Athens Protocol") as regards matters falling within the EUs exclusive competence, with the exception of Articles 10 and 11 of the protocol.

46.134 Article 2(1) provides that the President of the Council is authorised to designate the person or persons empowered to deposit the instrument of accession of the Union to the Athens Protocol in accordance with Articles 17(2)(c), 17(3) and 19 of that protocol.

46.135 Article 2(2) goes on to provide:

"At the time of the deposit of the instrument of accession, the Union shall make the following declaration of competence:

'1. Article 19 of the Athens Protocol of 2002 to the Athens Convention relating to the Carriage of Passengers and their Luggage by Sea, 1974 provides that Regional Economic Integration Organisations which are constituted by sovereign States that have transferred competence over certain matters governed by that Protocol to them may sign it, on condition that they make the declaration referred to in that Article. The Union has decided to accede to the Athens Protocol and is accordingly making that declaration.

2. The current Members of the European Union are the Kingdom of Belgium, the Republic of Bulgaria, the Czech Republic, the Kingdom of Denmark, the Federal Republic of Germany, the Republic of Estonia, Ireland, the Hellenic Republic, the Kingdom of Spain, the French Republic, the Republic of Croatia, the Italian Republic, the Republic of Cyprus, the Republic of Latvia, the Republic of Lithuania, the Grand Duchy of Luxembourg, Hungary, Malta, the Kingdom of the Netherlands, the Republic of Austria, the Republic of Poland, the Portuguese Republic, Romania, the Republic of Slovenia, the Slovak Republic, the Republic of Finland, the Kingdom of Sweden and the United Kingdom of Great Britain and Northern Ireland.

3. This declaration is not applicable to the territories of the Member States of the European Union in which the Treaty on the Functioning of the European Union (TFEU) does not apply and is without prejudice to such acts or positions as may be adopted under the Protocol by the Member States concerned on behalf of, and in the interests of, those territories.

4. The Member States of the European Union have conferred exclusive competence to the Union as regards measures adopted on the basis of Article 100 of the TFEU. Such measures have been adopted as regards Articles 1 and 1 bis, Article 2(2), Articles 3 to 16 and Articles 18, 20 and 21 of the Athens Convention as amended by the Athens Protocol and the provisions of the IMO Guidelines, by means of Regulation (EC) No 392/2009 of the European Parliament and of the Council of 23 April 2009 on the liability of carriers of passengers by sea in the event of accidents.

5. The exercise of competence which the Member States have transferred to the European Union pursuant to the TFEU is, by its nature, liable to continuous development. In the framework of the TFEU, the competent institutions may take decisions which determine the extent of the competence of the European Union. The European Union therefore reserves the right to amend this declaration accordingly, without this constituting a prerequisite for the exercise of its competence with regard to matters governed by the Athens Protocol. The European Union will notify the amended declaration to the Secretary-General of the International Maritime Organization.'.

3. The person or persons designated under paragraph 1 of this Article shall make the reservation contained in the IMO Guidelines when depositing the instrument of accession of the Union to the Athens Protocol."

46.136 Article 3 then provides that the EU had to deposit its instrument of accession to the Athens Protocol by 31 December 2011.

46.137 Article 4(1) provides that Member States shall take the necessary steps to deposit the instruments of ratification of, or accession to, the Athens Protocol within a reasonable time and, if possible, by 31 December 2011. Article 4(2) provides that Member States shall make the reservation contained in the IMO Guidelines when depositing their instruments of ratification of, or accession to, the Athens Protocol.

I. COUNCIL DECISION 2012/23 CONCERNING THE ACCESSION OF THE EUROPEAN UNION TO THE PROTOCOL OF 2002 TO THE ATHENS CONVENTION RELATING TO THE CARRIAGE OF PASSENGERS AND THEIR LUGGAGE BY SEA, 1974, AS REGARDS ARTICLES 10 AND 11 THEREOF

46.138 On 12 December 2011, the Council adopted Decision 2012/23 concerning the accession of the EU to the Protocol of 2002 to the Athens Convention relating to the Carriage of Passengers and their Luggage by Sea, 1974, as regards Articles 10 and 11 thereof.[116] It was amended by Council Regulation 517/2013.[117]

46.139 The legal basis for the decision was the TFEU generally, and in particular Article 81(1) and points (a) and (c) of Article 81(2), in conjunction with point (a) of Article 218(6) and the first subparagraph of Article 218(8) of the TFEU.

46.140 The first recital to Decision 2012/23 recalled that the Protocol of 2002 to the Athens Convention relating to the Carriage of Passengers and their Luggage by Sea, 1974 ("Athens Protocol") represented a major improvement to the regime relating to the liability of carriers and the compensation of passengers carried by sea. The recitals continue by recalling that the Athens Protocol modifies the Athens Convention relating to the Carriage of Passengers and their Luggage by Sea, 1974 and establishes in Article 15 that the two instruments shall, as between the Parties to the Athens Protocol, be read and interpreted together as one single instrument.[118] The third recital recalls that Articles 10 and 11 of the Athens Protocol affect Council Regulation (EC) No 44/2001 of 22 December 2000 on jurisdiction and the recognition and enforcement of judgments in civil and commercial matters.[119] The EU thus has exclusive competence as regards Articles 10 and 11 of the Athens Protocol. The fourth to the eleventh recitals state:

> "(4) Upon accession of the Union to the Athens Protocol, the rules on jurisdiction set out in Article 10 thereof should take precedence over the relevant Union rules.
> (5) However, the rules on recognition and enforcement of judgments laid down in Article 11 of the Athens Protocol should not take precedence either over the relevant rules of the Union, as extended to Denmark by the Agreement between the European Community and the Kingdom of Denmark on jurisdiction and the recognition and enforcement of judgments in civil and commercial matters,[120] or the rules of the Lugano Convention on jurisdiction and the enforcement of judgments in civil and commercial matters of 16 September 1988[121] or the Lugano Convention on jurisdiction and the recognition and enforcement of judgments

---

116 OJ L8/13, 12 January 2012, http://eur-lex.europa.eu/legal-content/EN/TXT/HTML/?uri=CELEX:32012D0023&qid=1438980594966&from=EN.
117 OJ L158/1, 10 June 2013.
118 Dec. 2012/23, recital 2.
119 OJ L12/1, 16 January 2001.
120 OJ L299, 16.11.2005, p. 62.
121 OJ L319, 25.11.1988, p. 9.

in civil and commercial matters of 30 October 2007,[122] since the effect of the application of these rules is to ensure that judgments are recognised and enforced at least to the same extent as under the rules of the Athens Protocol.

(6)   The Athens Protocol is open for ratification, acceptance, approval or accession by States and by Regional Economic Integration Organisations which are constituted by sovereign States that have transferred competence over certain matters governed by the Athens Protocol to those Organisations.

(7)   According to Article 17(2)(b) and Article 19 of the Athens Protocol, Regional Economic Integration Organisations may conclude the Athens Protocol.

(8)   The United Kingdom and Ireland, to which the Protocol (No 21) on the position of the United Kingdom and Ireland in respect of the Area of Freedom, Security and Justice, annexed to the Treaty on European Union and to the Treaty on the Functioning of the European Union, applies, will be bound as part of the European Union by Articles 10 and 11 of the Athens Protocol.

(9)   In accordance with Articles 1 and 2 of the Protocol (No 22) on the position of Denmark, annexed to the Treaty on European Union and to the Treaty on the Functioning of the European Union, Denmark is not taking part in the adoption of this Decision and is not bound by it or subject to its application in respect of Articles 10 and 11 of the Athens Protocol. It will be bound by these Articles only as a separate Contracting Party.

(10)   The majority of the rules of the Athens Protocol have been incorporated into Union law by Regulation (EC) No 392/2009 of the European Parliament and of the Council of 23 April 2009 on the liability of carriers of passengers by sea in the event of accidents.[123] Thus, the Union exerted competence as regards the matters governed by that Regulation. A separate Decision relating to those provisions is to be adopted in parallel to this Decision.

(11)   Member States which are to ratify or accede to the Athens Protocol should, if possible, do so simultaneously. Member States should therefore exchange information on the state of their ratification or accession procedures in order to prepare as far as possible the simultaneous deposit of their instruments of ratification or accession. When ratifying or acceding to the Athens Protocol, Member States should make the reservation contained in the IMO Guidelines."

46.141   Article 1 provides that the accession of the EU to the Protocol of 2002 to the Athens Convention relating to the Carriage of Passengers and their Luggage by Sea, 1974 ("Athens Protocol") is approved, by virtue of Article 1, on behalf of the EU as regards Articles 10 and 11 thereof. The text of the articles is reproduced in the annex.[124]

---

122   OJ L339, 21.12.2007, p. 3.

123   OJ L131, 28.5.2009, p. 24.

124   "ARTICLES 10 AND 11 OF THE PROTOCOL OF 2002 TO THE ATHENS CONVENTION RELATING TO THE CARRIAGE OF PASSENGERS AND THEIR LUGGAGE BY SEA, 1974

Article 10

Article 17 of the Convention is replaced by the following text:

'Article 17

Competent jurisdiction

1.   An action arising under Articles 3 and 4 of this Convention shall, at the option of the claimant, be brought before one of the courts listed below, provided that the court is located in a State Party to this Convention, and subject to the domestic law of each State Party governing proper venue within those States with multiple possible forums:

(a)   the court of the State of permanent residence or principal place of business of the defendant, or

(b)   the court of the State of departure or that of the destination according to the contract of carriage, or

(c)   the court of the State of the domicile or permanent residence of the claimant, if the defendant has a place of business and is subject to jurisdiction in that State, or

(d)   the court of the State where the contract of carriage was made, if the defendant has a place of business and is subject to jurisdiction in that State.

46.142 Article 2(1) provides that the President of the Council was thereby authorised to designate the person or persons empowered to deposit the instrument of accession of the Union to the Athens Protocol as regards Articles 10 and 11 thereof in accordance with Articles 17(2)(c), 17(3) and 19 of that protocol. Article 2(2) provides that at the time of the deposit of the instrument of accession, the EU shall make the following declaration of competence:

"As regards matters covered by Articles 10 and 11 of the Athens Protocol of 2002 to the Athens Convention relating to the Carriage of Passengers and their Luggage by Sea, 1974, which come under Article 81 of the Treaty on the Functioning of the European Union, the Member States of the European Union, with the exception of the Kingdom of Denmark, in accordance with Articles 1 and 2 of Protocol (No 22) on the position of Denmark, annexed to the Treaty on European Union and to the Treaty on the Functioning of the European Union, have conferred competences to the Union. The Union exercised this competence by adopting Council Regulation (EC) No 44/2001 of 22 December 2000 on jurisdiction and the recognition and enforcement of judgments in civil and commercial matters."

46.143 Article 2(3) provides that at the time of the deposit of the instrument of accession, the EU shall make the following declaration on Article 17bis(3) of the Athens Convention relating to the Carriage of Passengers and their Luggage by Sea, 1974, as amended by Article 11 of the Athens Protocol:

"1. Judgments on matters covered by the Athens Protocol of 2002 to the Athens Convention relating to the Carriage of Passengers and their Luggage by Sea, 1974, when given by a court of the Kingdom of Belgium, the Republic of Bulgaria, the Czech Republic, the Federal Republic of Germany, the Republic of Estonia, Ireland, the Hellenic Republic, the Kingdom of Spain, the French Republic, the Republic of Croatia, the Italian Republic, the Republic of Cyprus, the Republic of Latvia, the Republic of Lithuania, the Grand Duchy of Luxembourg, Hungary, Malta, the Kingdom of the Netherlands, the Republic of Austria, the Republic of Poland, the Portuguese Republic, Romania, the Republic of Slovenia, the Slovak Republic, the Republic of Finland, the Kingdom of Sweden or the United Kingdom of Great Britain and Northern Ireland, shall be recognised and enforced in a Member State of the European Union in accordance with the relevant rules of the European Union on the subject.

---

2. Actions under Article 4bis of this Convention shall, at the option of the claimant, be brought before one of the courts where action could be brought against the carrier or performing carrier according to paragraph 1.
3. After the occurrence of the incident which has caused the damage, the parties may agree that the claim for damages shall be submitted to any jurisdiction or to arbitration.'.

Article 11
The following text is added as Article 17bis of the Convention:

'Article 17bis

Recognition and enforcement
1. Any judgment given by a court with jurisdiction in accordance with Article 17 which is enforceable in the State of origin where it is no longer subject to ordinary forms of review, shall be recognised in any State Party, except

   (a) where the judgment was obtained by fraud; or
   (b) where the defendant was not given reasonable notice and a fair opportunity to present the case.

2. A judgment recognised under paragraph 1 shall be enforceable in each State Party as soon as the formalities required in that State have been complied with. The formalities shall not permit the merits of the case to be re-opened.
3. A State Party to this Protocol may apply other rules for the recognition and enforcement of judgments, provided that their effect is to ensure that judgments are recognised and enforced at least to the same extent as under paragraphs 1 and 2.'."

2. Judgments on matters covered by the Athens Protocol, when given by a court of the Kingdom of Denmark, shall be recognised and enforced in a Member State of the European Union in accordance with the Agreement between the European Community and the Kingdom of Denmark on jurisdiction and the recognition and enforcement of judgments in civil and commercial matters.

3. Judgments on matters covered by the Athens Protocol, when given by a court of a third State

    (a) bound by the Lugano Convention on jurisdiction and the recognition and enforcement of judgments in civil and commercial matters of 30 October 2007 shall be recognised and enforced in the Member States of the European Union in accordance with that Convention;

    (b) bound by the Lugano Convention on jurisdiction and the enforcement of judgments in civil and commercial matters of 16 September 1988 shall be recognised and enforced in the Member States of the European Union in accordance with that Convention."

46.144 Article 2(4) provides that the person or persons designated under Article 2(1) shall make the reservation contained in the IMO Guidelines when depositing the instrument of accession of the EU to the Athens Protocol as regards Articles 10 and 11 thereof.

46.145 Article 3 provides that the EU must deposit its instrument of accession to the Athens Protocol as regards Articles 10 and 11 thereof by 31 December 2011.

46.146 Article 4 provides that Member States had to take the necessary steps to deposit the instruments of ratification of, or accession to, the Athens Protocol within a reasonable time and, if possible, by 31 December 2011.

J. DIRECTIVE 2001/96 ESTABLISHING HARMONISED REQUIREMENTS AND PROCEDURES FOR THE SAFE LOADING AND UNLOADING OF BULK CARRIERS

Introduction

46.147 On 4 December 2001, the Parliament and Council adopted Directive 2001/96 establishing harmonised requirements and procedures for the safe loading and unloading of bulk carriers.[125] It was amended by Directive 2002/84 of the European Parliament and of the Council of 5 November 2002[126] and Regulation 1137/2008 of the European Parliament and of the Council of 22 October 2008.[127] The legal basis for Directive 2001/96 was the TEC and, in particular, Article 80(2) which is now Article 100(2) of the TFEU.

46.148 The factual background was described in the recitals to Directive 2001/96. The first recital recalled that in view of the high number of shipping accidents involving bulk carriers with an associated loss of human lives, further measures should be taken to enhance safety in maritime transport within the framework of the common transport policy. The second recital recalled that assessments of the causes of bulk carrier casualties indicate that loading and unloading of solid bulk cargoes, if not properly conducted, can contribute to the loss of bulk carriers, either by over-stressing the ship's structure or by mechanically damaging its structural members in the cargo holds. The protection of the safety of bulk carriers can be enhanced through the adoption of measures aimed at

---

125 OJ L13/9, 16 January 2002.
126 OJ L324/53, 29 November 2002.
127 OJ L311/1, 21 November 2008.

reducing the risk of structural damage and losses due to improper loading and unloading operations. The third recital stated that at the international level, the IMO, through a number of Assembly Resolutions, had adopted recommendations on the safety of bulk carriers addressing ship/port interface issues in general and loading and unloading operations in particular. Some other recitals are worth studying:

"(4) By Assembly Resolution A.862(20), the IMO adopted a Code of Practice for the Safe Loading and Unloading of Bulk Barriers ('the BLU Code'), and urged contracting governments to implement this Code at the earliest possible opportunity and to inform IMO of any non-compliance. In the Resolution, the IMO further urged contracting governments in whose territories solid bulk cargo loading and unloading terminals are situated to introduce laws so that a number of key principles necessary for the implementation of this Code could be enforced.

(5) The impact of loading and unloading operations on bulk carrier safety, in view of the global character of trade in dry cargo in bulk, has transboundary implications. The development of action to prevent the foundering of bulk carriers due to improper loading and unloading practices is therefore best done at Community level by establishing harmonised requirements and procedures to implement the IMO recommendations laid down in the Assembly Resolution A.862(20) and the BLU Code.

(6) In view of the subsidiarity principle set out in Article 5 of the Treaty, a Directive is the appropriate legal instrument as it provides a framework for the Member States' uniform and compulsory application of the requirements and procedures for the safe loading and unloading of bulk carriers, while leaving each Member State the right to decide which implementation tools best fit its internal system. In accordance with the principle of proportionality, this Directive does not go beyond what is necessary for the objectives pursued.

(7) The safety of bulk carriers and their crews can be enhanced by reducing the risks of improper loading and unloading at dry bulk cargo terminals. This can be implemented by establishing harmonised procedures for cooperation and communication between ship and terminal and by laying down suitability requirements for ships and terminals.

(8) In the interests of enhancing bulk carrier safety and avoiding distortion of competition, the harmonised procedures and suitability criteria should apply to all bulk carriers, irrespective of the flag they fly, and to all terminals in the Community at which, under normal circumstances, such carriers call for the purpose of loading or unloading solid bulk cargoes.

(9) Bulk carriers calling at terminals for the loading or unloading of solid bulk cargoes should be suitable for that purpose. Equally, terminals should also be suitable for receiving and loading or unloading visiting bulk carriers. For these purposes suitability criteria have been established in the BLU Code.

(10) Terminals should, in the interests of enhancing cooperation and communication with the ship's master on matters relating to the loading and unloading of solid bulk cargoes, appoint a terminal representative responsible for such operations in the terminal and make information books with the terminal's and port's requirements available to the masters. There are, for this purpose, provisions in the BLU Code.

(11) The development, implementation and maintenance of a quality management system by the terminals would ensure that the cooperation and communication procedures and the actual loading and unloading by the terminal are planned and executed in accordance with a harmonised framework that is internationally recognised and auditable. In view of its international recognition, the quality management system should be compatible with the ISO 9000 series of standards adopted by the International Standardisation Organisation. To allow new terminals sufficient time to achieve the relevant certification, it is important to ensure that a temporary authorisation to operate is available to them for a limited period of time.

(12) For the purpose of ensuring that loading and unloading operations are carefully prepared, agreed and conducted in order to avoid endangering the safety of the ship or crew, the responsibilities of the master and the terminal representative should be laid down. To this

end, relevant provisions can be found in the 1974 International Convention for the Safety of Life at Sea (1974 SOLAS Convention), IMO Assembly Resolution A.862(20) and the BLU Code. For the same purpose, procedures for the preparation, agreement and conduct of loading or unloading operations can be based on the provisions of those international instruments.

(13) In the general interests of the Community, in deflecting sub-standard shipping from its ports, the terminal representative should notify apparent deficiencies on board a bulk carrier which could prejudice the safety of loading or unloading operations.

(14) It is necessary that the competent authorities of the Member States prevent or halt loading or unloading operations whenever they have clear indications that ship or crew safety is endangered by these operations. The authorities should also intervene in the interests of safety in the event of disagreement between the master and the terminal representative as to the application of these procedures. The safety-related action of the competent authorities should not be dependent on commercial interests related to terminals.

(15) It is necessary to lay down procedures for the purpose of reporting damage to ships incurred during loading or unloading operations to the appropriate bodies, such as the relevant classification societies, and of repairing such damage if necessary. Where such damage could impair the safety or seaworthiness of the ship, the decision as to the necessity and urgency of repairs should be taken by the port State control authorities in consultation with the administration of the flag State. In view of the technical expertise necessary to take such a decision, the authorities should have the right to call upon a recognised organisation to inspect the damage and to advise them on any need for repairs.

(16) Enforcement of this Directive should be enhanced by efficient monitoring and verification procedures in the Member States. Reporting the results of this monitoring effort will provide valuable information on the effectiveness of the harmonised requirements and procedures laid down in this Directive.

(17) In IMO Assembly Resolution A.797(19) of 23 November 1995 on the safety of ships carrying solid bulk cargoes it is requested that port State authorities submit confirmation that loading and unloading terminals for solid bulk cargoes comply with the IMO Codes and recommendations on ship/shore cooperation. Notification of the adoption of this Directive to the IMO will provide an appropriate response to this request and a clear signal to the international maritime community that the Community is committed to supporting the efforts undertaken at international level to enhance the safe loading and unloading of bulk carriers.

(18) The measures necessary for the implementation of this Directive should be adopted in accordance with Council Decision 1999/468/EC of 28 June 1999 laying down the procedures for the exercise of implementing powers conferred on the Commission.[128]

(19) It should be possible to amend certain provisions of this Directive in accordance with that procedure, so as to bring them into line with international and Community instruments adopted, amended or entering into force after the entry into force of this Directive and for the implementation of the procedures laid down in this Directive, without broadening its scope.

(20) Council Directive 89/391/EEC of 12 June 1989 on the introduction of measures to encourage improvements in the safety and health of workers at work[129] and its relevant individual Directives are applicable to the work relating to the loading and unloading of bulk carriers."

Purpose of the directive

46.149 Article 1 ("purpose") provides that the purpose of the directive is to enhance the safety of bulk carriers calling at terminals in the Member States in order to load or

---

128 Ed., OJ L184/23, 17 July 1999.
129 Ed., OJ L183/1, 29 June 1989.

unload solid bulk cargoes, by reducing the risks of excessive stresses and physical damage to the ship's structure during loading or unloading, through the establishment of: (1) harmonised suitability requirements for those ships and terminals; and (2) harmonised procedures for co-operation and communication between those ships and terminals.

Scope of the directive

46.150 Article 2 sets out the scope of the directive. The directive applies to, according to Article 2: (1) all bulk carriers, irrespective of their flag, calling at a terminal for the loading or unloading of solid bulk cargoes; and (2) all terminals in the Member States visited by bulk carriers falling under the scope of the directive. Without prejudice to the provisions of Regulation VI/7 of the 1974 SOLAS Convention, this directive shall not apply to facilities that only in exceptional circumstances are used for loading and unloading dry cargo in bulk into or from bulk carriers, and shall not apply in cases where the loading or unloading is carried out solely with the equipment of the bulk carrier concerned.

Definitions used in the directive

46.151 Article 3 contains various definitions for the purposes of the directive. First, the term "international conventions" mean the conventions in force on 4 December 2001, as defined in Article 2(1) of Council Directive 95/21. The term "1974 SOLAS Convention" means the International Convention for the Safety of Life at Sea, together with the protocols and amendments thereto, in its up-to-date version. The phrase "BLU Code" means the Code of Practice for the Safe Loading and Unloading of Bulk Carriers, as contained in the annex to IMO Assembly Resolution A.862(20) of 27 November 1997, as it stands on 4 December 2001. The term "bulk carrier" shall bear the meaning given to it in Regulation IX/1.6 of the 1974 SOLAS Convention and interpreted by Resolution 6 of the 1997 SOLAS Conference, namely: a ship constructed with single deck, top-side tanks and hopper-side tanks in cargo spaces and intended primarily to carry dry cargo in bulk, or an ore carrier, meaning a seagoing single deck ship having two longitudinal bulkheads and a double bottom throughout the cargo region and intended for the carriage of ore cargoes in the centre holds only, or a combination carrier as defined in Regulation II-2/3.27 of the 1974 SOLAS Convention. The phrase "dry cargo in bulk" or "solid bulk cargo" shall mean solid bulk cargo as defined in Regulation XII/1.4 of the 1974 SOLAS Convention, excluding grain. The word "grain" shall bear the meaning given to it in Regulation VI/8.2 of the 1974 SOLAS Convention. The word "terminal" shall mean any fixed, floating or mobile facility equipped and used for the loading or unloading of dry cargo in bulk into or from bulk carriers. The phrase "terminal operator" means the owner of a terminal, or any organisation or person to whom the owner has transferred the responsibility for loading or unloading operations conducted at the terminal for a particular bulk carrier. The term "terminal representative" means any person appointed by the terminal operator, who has the overall responsibility for, and authority to, control the preparation, the conduct and the completion of loading or unloading operations conducted by the terminal for a particular bulk carrier. The word "master" means the person who has command over a bulk carrier or a ship's officer designated by the master for the loading or unloading operations. The phrase "recognised organisation" shall mean an organisation recognised in accordance with Article 4 of Council Directive 94/57. The phrase "administration of the flag State" means the competent authorities of the State whose flag the bulk carrier is entitled to fly. The label "port State control authority" means the competent authority of a Member State empowered to apply the control provisions of Directive 95/21. The phrase "competent authority" means a national, regional or local public authority in the Member State empowered by national legislation to implement and enforce the requirements of the directive. The phrase "cargo information" shall mean the cargo information required by Regulation VI/2 of the 1974 SOLAS Convention. The expression "loading or unloading plan" means a plan as referred to in Regulation VI/7.3 of the 1974 SOLAS Convention and having the format as contained in Appendix 2 of the BLU Code. The expression "ship/shore safety checklist" means the checklist as referred to in section 4 of the BLU Code and having the format as contained in Appendix 3 of the BLU Code. Finally, the phrase "solid bulk cargo density declaration" shall mean the information on the density of the cargo to be provided in compliance with Regulation XII/10 of the 1974 SOLAS Convention.

Requirements in relation to the operational suitability of bulk carriers

46.152 Article 4 ("requirements in relation to the operational suitability of bulk carriers") provides that Member States must make the necessary arrangements to ensure that terminal operators are satisfied with the operational suitability of bulk carriers for loading or unloading of solid bulk cargoes, by checking compliance with the provisions of Annex I.

46.153 Article 5 ("Requirements in relation to the suitability of terminals") provides that Member States must satisfy themselves that terminal operators ensure that, as concerns terminals for which they assume responsibilities under this directive:

"1. the terminals comply with the provisions of Annex II;
2. terminal representative(s) is (are) appointed;
3. information books are prepared containing the requirements of the terminal and competent authorities and information on the port and terminal as listed in Appendix 1, paragraph 1.2, of the BLU Code, and that these books are made available to the masters of bulk carriers calling at the terminal for loading or unloading solid bulk cargoes; and
4. a quality management system is developed, implemented and maintained. Such quality management system shall be certified in accordance with the ISO 9001:2000 standards or an equivalent standard fulfilling at least all aspects of ISO 9001:2000, and it shall be audited in accordance with the guidelines of the ISO 10011:1991 or equivalent standard fulfilling all aspects of ISO 10011:1991. Directive 98/34/EC (8) shall be complied with in relation to the said equivalent standards."

A transitional period of three years from the entry into force of the directive shall be granted to set up the quality management system and one additional year to obtain the certification of the system.

Temporary authorisation

46.154 Article 6 ("temporary authorisation") provides that by way of derogation from the requirements of Article 5(4), a temporary authorisation to operate, valid for no more than 12 months, may be issued by the competent authority for newly established terminals. The terminal must however demonstrate its plan to implement a quality management system in accordance with the ISO 9001:2000 standard or equivalent standard, as set out in Article 5(4).

Responsibilities of masters and terminal representatives

46.155 Article 7 ("responsibilities of masters and terminal representatives") provides that Member States shall make the necessary arrangements to ensure that the following principles concerning the responsibilities of masters and terminal representatives are respected and applied:

"1. Responsibilities of the master:

(a) the master shall be responsible at all times for the safe loading and unloading of the bulk carrier under his command;

(b) the master shall, well in advance of the ship's estimated time of arrival at the terminal, provide the terminal with the information set out in Annex III;

(c) before any solid bulk cargo is loaded, the master shall ensure that he has received the cargo information required by Regulation VI/2.2 of the 1974 SOLAS Convention, and, where required, a solid bulk cargo density declaration. This information shall be contained in a cargo declaration form as set out in Appendix 5 of the BLU Code;

(d) prior to the start of and during loading or unloading the master shall discharge the duties listed in Annex IV.

2. Responsibilities of the terminal representative:

(a) upon receipt of the ship's initial notification of its estimated time of arrival, the terminal representative shall provide the master with the information mentioned in Annex V;

(b) the terminal representative shall be satisfied that the master has been advised as early as possible of the information contained in the cargo declaration form;

(c) the terminal representative shall without delay notify the master and the port State control authority of apparent deficiencies he has noted on board a bulk carrier which could endanger the safe loading or unloading of solid bulk cargoes;

(d) prior to the start of and during loading or unloading, the terminal representative shall discharge the duties listed in Annex VI."

Procedures between bulk carriers and terminals

46.156 Article 8 ("procedures between bulk carriers and terminals") provides that Member States shall ensure that the following procedures are applied in respect of the loading or unloading of bulk carriers with solid bulk cargoes. It goes on to provide:

"1. Before solid bulk cargoes are loaded or unloaded, the master shall agree with the terminal representative on the loading or unloading plan in accordance with the provisions of Regulation VI/7.3 of the 1974 SOLAS Convention. The loading or unloading plan shall be prepared in the form laid down in Appendix 2 of the BLU Code, it shall contain the IMO number of the bulk carrier concerned, and the master and the terminal representative shall confirm their agreement to the plan by signing it.

Any change to the plan, which according to either party may affect the safety of the vessel or crew, shall be prepared, accepted and agreed by both parties in the form of a revised plan.

The agreed loading or unloading plan and any subsequent agreed revisions shall be kept by the ship and the terminal for a period of six months for the purpose of any necessary verification by the competent authorities.

2. Before loading or unloading is commenced, the ship/shore safety checklist shall be completed and signed jointly by the master and the terminal representative in accordance with the guidelines of Appendix 4 of the BLU Code.

3. An effective communication between the ship and the terminal shall be established and maintained at all times, capable of responding to requests for information on the loading or unloading process and to ensure prompt compliance should the master or the terminal representative order the loading or unloading operations to be suspended.

4. The master and the terminal representative shall conduct the loading or unloading operations in accordance with the agreed plan. The terminal representative shall be responsible for the loading or unloading of the solid bulk cargo as regards the hold order, quantity and rate of loading or unloading stated on that plan. He shall not deviate from the agreed loading or unloading plan, otherwise than by prior consultation and written agreement with the master.

5. On completion of the loading or unloading, the master and the terminal representative shall agree in writing that the loading or unloading has been done in accordance with the loading or unloading plan, including any agreed changes. In the case of unloading, such agreement shall include a record that the cargo holds have been emptied and cleaned to the master's requirements and shall record any damage suffered by the ship and any repairs carried out."

Role of the competent authorities

46.157 Article 9 ("role of the competent authorities") provides in Article 9(1) that without prejudice to the rights and obligations of the master provided under Regulation VI/7.7 of the 1974 SOLAS Convention, Member States shall ensure that their competent authorities prevent or halt the loading or unloading of solid bulk cargoes whenever they have clear indications that the safety of the ship or crew would be endangered thereby. Article 9(2) provides that in cases where the competent authority is informed of disagreement between the master and the terminal representative as to the application of the procedures provided for in Article 8, the competent authority shall intervene where this is required in the interests of safety and/or the marine environment.

Repair of damage incurred during loading or unloading

46.158 Article 10 ("repair of damage incurred during loading or unloading") states in Article 10(1) that if damage to the ship's structure or equipment occurs during loading or unloading, it shall be reported by the terminal representative to the master and, if necessary, repaired. Article 10(2) provides that if the damage could impair the structural capability or watertight integrity of the hull, or the ship's essential engineering systems, the administration of the flag State, or an organisation recognised by it and acting on its behalf, and the port State control ("PSC") authority shall be informed by the terminal representative and/or the master. The decision as to whether immediate repair is necessary or whether it can be deferred shall be taken by the PSC authority, due account being taken of the opinion, if any, of the administration of the flag State, or the organisation recognised by it and acting on its behalf, and of the opinion of the master. Where immediate repair is considered necessary, it shall be carried out to the satisfaction of the master and the competent authority before the ship leaves the port. Article 10(3) states that for the purpose of taking the decision referred to in paragraph 2, a PSC authority may rely upon a recognised organisation to undertake the inspection of the damage and to advise on the necessity of carrying-out repairs or their deferral. Article 10(4) provides that Article 10 applies without prejudice to Directive 95/21.[130]

Verification and reporting

46.159 Article 11 ("verification and reporting") provides in paragraph 1 that Member States shall regularly verify that terminals comply with the requirements of Article 5(1), Article 7(2) and Article 8. The procedure of verification shall include the carrying-out of unannounced inspections during loading or unloading operations. Additionally, Member States must verify that terminals comply with the requirements of Article 5(4), at the end of the period provided for therein, and for newly established terminals at the end of the period provided in Article 6. Article 11(2) provides that Member States must provide the Commission every three years with a report on the results of such verification. The report shall also provide an assessment of the effectiveness of the harmonised procedures for co-operation and communication between bulk carriers and terminals as provided for in the directive. The report shall be transmitted at the latest by 30 April of the year following the period of three calendar years upon which it reports.

46.160 Article 12 provides for an element of evaluation. The Commission must submit an evaluation report on the operation of the system as provided for in the directive to the Parliament and the Council, on the basis of the reports of the Member States provided for in Article 11(2). This report shall also include an assessment of whether it is necessary to continue the reporting by the Member States referred to in Article 11(2).

46.161 Notification to the IMO is the subject matter of Article 13: the Presidency of the Council, acting on behalf of the Member States, and the Commission shall jointly inform the IMO of the adoption of this directive, whereby reference shall be made to paragraph 1.7 of the annex to IMO Resolution A.797(19).

46.162 Article 14 deals with the committee procedure. In particular, the Commission shall be assisted by the COSS set up by Article 3 of Regulation 2099/2002 (9). Where reference is made to this paragraph, Article 5a(1) to (4) and Article 7 of Decision 1999/468 shall apply, having regard to the provisions of Article 8 thereof.

46.163 Article 15 provides for an amendment procedure. Article 15(1) provides that the definitions set out in points 1 to 6 and 15 to 18 of Article 3, the references to international conventions and codes and to IMO Resolutions and Circulars, the references to ISO standards and the references to Community instruments and the annexes thereto may be amended in order to bring them into line with international and Community instruments which have been adopted, amended or brought into force after the adoption of this

---

130 I.e. Council Dir. 95/21 of 19 June 1995 concerning the enforcement, in respect of shipping using Community ports and sailing in the waters under the jurisdiction of the Member States, of international standards for ship safety, pollution prevention and shipboard living and working conditions (port State control) (OJ L157/1, 7 July 1995).

directive, provided that the scope of the directive is not thereby broadened. Those measures, designed to amend non-essential elements of the directive, shall be adopted in accordance with the regulatory procedure with scrutiny referred to in Article 14(2). The Commission may amend Article 8 and the annexes for the implementation of the procedures laid down in the directive, and may amend or repeal the reporting obligations referred to in Articles 11(2) and 12, provided that such provisions do not broaden the scope of the directive. Those measures, designed to amend non-essential elements of the directive, shall be adopted in accordance with the regulatory procedure with scrutiny referred to in Article 14(2). The amendments to the international instruments referred to in Article 3 may be excluded from the scope of the directive, pursuant to Article 5 of Regulation 2099/2002.

46.164 Article 16 ("penalties") provides that the Member States must lay down the rules on penalties applicable to infringements of the national provisions adopted pursuant to the directive and shall take all measures necessary to ensure that they are implemented. The penalties provided for must be effective, proportionate and dissuasive.

46.165 Article 17(1) provides that Member States had to adopt and publish, before 5 August 2003, the provisions necessary to comply with the directive and they had to inform the Commission of those provisions. They had to apply those provisions from 1 March 2004. When Member States adopt those provisions, they shall contain a reference to the directive or be accompanied by such a reference on the occasion of their official publication. Member States shall determine how such reference is to be made. Member States had to notify to the Commission the provisions of their national law which they adopt in the field governed by the directive.

46.166 Article 18 provides that the directive entered into force on the twentieth day following that of its publication in the *Official Journal*.

46.167 Annex I deals with the requirements in relation to the operational suitability of bulk carriers for loading and unloading solid bulk carriers. Annex II deals with requirements in relation to the suitability of terminals for loading and unloading solid bulk cargoes. Annex III deals with information to be provided by the master to the terminal (as referred to in Article 7(1)(b)). Annex IV deals with duties of the master prior to and during loading or unloading operations (as referred to in Article 7(1)(d)). Annex V sets out the information to be provided by the terminal to the master. Annex VI enumerates the duties of the terminal representative prior to and during loading or unloading operations.

K. COMMISSION DECISION 96/513 OF 29 JULY 1996 IN APPLICATION, AT THE REQUEST OF FRANCE, OF ARTICLE 5(4) OF COUNCIL DIRECTIVE 93/75 CONCERNING MINIMUM REQUIREMENTS FOR VESSELS BOUND FOR OR LEAVING COMMUNITY PORTS AND CARRYING DANGEROUS OR POLLUTING GOODS

46.168 On 29 July 1996, the Commission adopted Decision 96/513 in application, at the request of France, of Article 5(4) of Council Directive 93/75 concerning minimum requirements for vessels bound for or leaving Community ports and carrying dangerous or polluting goods.[131] The legal basis was the TEC generally. The background included the Council Directive 93/75 of 13 September 1993 concerning minimum requirements for vessels bound for or leaving Community ports and carrying dangerous or polluting goods, and in particular Article 5(4) thereof.[132]

46.169 The Commission recalled that in order to limit the risks of serious accidents at sea and to reduce the resulting damage, Article 5 of Directive 93/75 provides that the operators of the vessels covered by the directive shall notify the information listed in Annex I to that directive to the competent authorities of the Member State concerned; whereas Article 5(4) authorises the Member States to exempt regular scheduled services of less than one hour's crossing time from that notification requirement and allows the Commission to agree to a reasonable extension of this period at the request of a Member State. In a request submitted on 12 July 1995 and amended by letter dated 29 March 1996, France asked the Commission to agree to an extension of this period for the scheduled services between Brest and Le Conquet (crossing time: two hours) and between Le Coquet and Ouessant (crossing time: two hours 30 minutes). The Commission then recalled:

"Whereas the ecological importance and hazards to shipping of the area concerned have led the French authorities to take appropriate measures to ensure a high level of safety for shipping in that area;

Whereas the measures consist of the buoyage of the area and information to sailors by means of appropriate nautical documentation; whereas in addition the Corsen-Ouessant maritime traffic service provides continuous surveillance of shipping in the area by radar and regular radio broadcasts of nautical information for sailors;

Whereas the risk of accident is limited owing to the scarce maritime traffic in the area and measures have been taken to keep vessels carrying dangerous or polluting cargoes away from the coastal navigation area;

Whereas the service in question provides local services between the islands and the mainland; whereas the quantities of pollutant goods on board are small;

Whereas the information required by Annex I to the Directive is available at any time from the operators or captains;

Whereas, in the circumstances, it is justified to accept France's request for exemption of the scheduled services referred to above from the application of Article 5 (2) and (3) of Directive 93/75/EEC…"

46.170 Article 1 provides that France was authorised to exempt the scheduled services between Brest and Le Conquet and between Le Conquet and Ouessant from the application of Article 5(2) and (3) of Directive 93/75, subject to the following conditions: the waters in which the services covered by this decision operate are duly buoyed and are drawn to the attention of sailors in appropriate nautical documents; compliance with the local navigation rules is assured; constant contact is maintained, in particular by radio links, with the competent maritime traffic service; only small quantities of dangerous or polluting goods, within the meaning of Directive 93/75, are carried on board; the information referred to in Annex I to Directive 93/75 is available from the operators and captains throughout the crossing and can at any time be provided to the authorities of the Member State on request.

---

131 OJ L215/5, 24 August 1996. See http://eur-lex.europa.eu/legal-content/EN/TXT/HTML/?uri=CELEX:3 1996D0513&qid=1439326929247&from=EN.
132 OJ No L247/19, 5 October 1993.

L. COMMISSION DECISION 96/710 OF 27 NOVEMBER 1996 IN APPLICATION, AT THE REQUEST OF GERMANY, OF ARTICLE 5(4) OF COUNCIL DIRECTIVE 93/75 OF 13 SEPTEMBER 1993 CONCERNING MINIMUM REQUIREMENTS FOR VESSELS BOUND FOR OR LEAVING COMMUNITY PORTS AND CARRYING DANGEROUS OR POLLUTING GOODS

46.171 On 27 November 1996, the Commission adopted Decision 96/710 in application, at the request of Germany, of Article 5(4) of Council Directive 93/75[133] concerning minimum requirements for vessels bound for, or leaving EU ports and carrying dangerous or polluting goods.[134]

46.172 Article 5 of Directive 93/75 provides that the operators of the vessels covered by the directive must notify the information listed in Annex I of the directive to the competent authorities of the Member State concerned. Article 5(4) authorises the Member States to exempt regular scheduled services of less than one hour's crossing time from such notification requirement and allows the Commission to agree to a reasonable extension of this period on request from a Member State. Germany had an issue about the application of the directive:

"Whereas, the information given by Germany in its request of 12 April 1994, on the basis of which scheduled services between the mainland and East Frisia Islands were exempted by Decision of the Commission[135] from the application of Article 5(4) of Directive 93/75, ... has been completed by a communication dated 23 February 1996 concerning regular services between the mainland and North Frisia Islands; whereas in this communication, Germany asked the Commission to agree to an exemption for the services operated between the ports of Dagebüll to Wittdün (Amrum Island) and Schlüttsiel to Hallig Langeness, which have crossing times of two hours;

Whereas the appropriate measures have been taken by the German competent authorities to ensure a high level of safety of navigation and protection of the marine environment in the area; whereas these measures include traffic surveillance and the provision of safety information to vessels, as well as the obligation to comply with local navigation rules;

Whereas the vessels in question provide local services between the islands and the mainland; whereas the risks of accident and marine pollution are limited owing to the scarce maritime traffic in the area and the small quantities of polluting goods on board the vessels;

Whereas the information required by Annex I to the Directive is available at any time from the operators or captains;

Whereas, in the circumstances, it is justifiable to accept the request from Germany to exempt the regular scheduled services referred to above from the application of Article 5(2) and (3) of Directive 93/75/EEC ..."

46.173 Article 1 provides that Germany was authorised to exempt the regular scheduled services between Dagebüll and Wittdün and between Schlüttsiel and Hallig Langeness from the application of Article 5(2) and (3) of Directive 93/75, subject to the following conditions: the waters in which the services covered by this decision operate are duly buoyed and are drawn to the attention of navigators in the relevant nautical documents; compliance with the local navigation rules is assured; constant contact is maintained, in particular by radio links, with the competent maritime traffic service; only small quantities of dangerous or polluting goods, within the meaning of Directive 93/75, are

---

133 OJ L247/15, 5 October 1993.
134 OJ L326/64, 17 December 1996.
135 OJ L29/8, 7.2.1996.

carried on board; the information referred to in Annex I to Directive 93/75 is made available by the operators throughout the crossing and can at any time be provided to the authorities of the Member State on request.

M. COMMISSION DECISION 1999/461 OF 24 JUNE 1999 ON THE PUBLICATION OF THE LIST OF EXISTING CLASS A AND B PASSENGER SHIPS NOTIFIED BY GREECE IN ACCORDANCE WITH COUNCIL DIRECTIVE 98/18 FOR WHICH THE DEROGATION OF ARTICLE 6(3)(G) MAY BE APPLIED

46.174 The Commission adopted Decision 1999/461 on 24 June 1999 on the publication of the list of existing class A and B passenger ships notified by Greece in accordance with Council Directive 98/18 for which the derogation of Article 6(3)(g) may be applied.[136]

The background was, first, Council Directive 98/18 of 17 March 1998 on safety rules and standards for passenger ships,[137] (and in particular Article 6(3)(g)), and, second, Greece had notified to the Commission the list of existing class A and B ships complying with the conditions for applying the derogation pursuant to Article 6(3)(g) of Directive 98/18,

46.175 Under Article 1 of the Decision 1999/461, the existing Class A and B passenger ships operating exclusively on domestic voyages between ports situated in Greece for which the derogation of Article 6(3)(g) may be applied are those listed in the annex to this decision.

N. COMMISSION DECISION 96/127 ON THE APPLICATION, AT THE REQUEST OF GERMANY, OF ARTICLE 5(4) OF COUNCIL DIRECTIVE 95/75 CONCERNING MINIMUM REQUIREMENTS FOR VESSELS BOUND FOR OR LEAVING COMMUNITY PORTS AND CARRYING DANGEROUS OR POLLUTING GOODS

46.176 On 22 January 1996, the Commission adopted Decision 96/127 on the application, at the request of Germany, of Article 5(4) of Council Directive 93/75 concerning minimum requirements for vessels bound for or leaving Community ports and carrying dangerous or polluting goods.[138] The background is clear from the recitals to the decision:

"Having regard to the Treaty establishing the European Community,
   Having regard to Council Directive 93/75 ... of 13 September 1993 concerning minimum requirements for vessels bound for or leaving Community ports and carrying dangerous or polluting goods,[139] and in particular Article 5(4) thereof,
   Whereas, in order to limit the risks of serious accidents at sea and to reduce the resulting damage, Article 5 of Directive 93/75 ... provides that the operators of the vessels covered by the Directive shall notify the information listed in Annex I thereto to the competent authorities of the Member State concerned; whereas Article 5 (4) authorizes the Member State to exempt regular

---

136 OJ L180/47, 15 July 1999.
137 OJ L1444/1, 15 May 1998.
138 OJ L29/8, 7 February 1996,
139 Ed., OJ L247/19, 5 October 1993.

scheduled services of less than one hour's crossing time from such notification requirement and allows the Commission to agree to a reasonable extension of this period on request from a Member State;

Whereas, by communication of 12 April 1994, the Federal Republic of Germany asked the Commission to agree to an extension of this period for the services operated between the ports of Norddeich and Juist, Norddeich and Baltrum, and Emden and Borkum (East Frisia), which have crossing times respectively of 1 hour 30 minutes, 2 hours, and 2 hours and 15 minutes;

Whereas those services are operated as regular scheduled services between the ports concerned, on a fixed timetable;

Whereas the services are operated in sheltered sea areas close to the coastline and with favourable mean maritime weather conditions; whereas the waters in which the vessels operate are duly buoyed and are marked for the attention of navigators in the relevant nautical documents; whereas the vessels concerned are required to comply with the local navigation rules and are in constant contact, in particular by radio, with the sea traffic management centre ashore;

Whereas only small quantities of dangerous or polluting goods are carried on board; whereas the risk to the environment is therefore minimal;

Whereas the information referred to in Annex I to Directive 93/75 ... concerning the kind of cargo carried is available to the captain and the operator of the vessels concerned throughout the crossing and can at any time be transmitted to the competent authorities on request;

Whereas, in the circumstances, it is justifiable to accept the request from Germany to exempt the regular scheduled services referred to above from the application of Article 5(2) and (3) of Directive 93/75 ..."

46.177 Article 1 provides that Germany is authorised to exempt the following regular scheduled services: (a) between Norddeich and Juist; (b) between Norddeich and Baltrum; and (c) between Emden and Borkum from the application of Article 5(2) and (3) of Directive 93/75, provided that the following requirements are met:

"– the waters in which the services covered by this Decision operate shall be duly buoyed and marked for the attention of navigators in the relevant nautical documents,
– the vessels concerned shall be required to comply with the local navigation rules,
– the vessels concerned shall be required to keep in constant contact, in particular by radio links, with the competent sea traffic service,
– only small quantities of dangerous or polluting goods, within the meaning of Directive 93/75/EEC, shall be carried on board,
– the information referred to in Annex I to Directive 93/75/EEC shall be available to the operators and captains of the vessel concerned throughout the crossing and shall at any time be transmissible to the authorities of the Member State."

O. COMMISSION DECISION 96/710 OF 27 NOVEMBER 1996 IN APPLICATION, AT THE REQUEST OF GERMANY, OF ARTICLE 5(4) OF COUNCIL DIRECTIVE 93/75 OF 13 SEPTEMBER 1993 CONCERNING MINIMUM REQUIREMENTS FOR VESSELS BOUND FOR OR LEAVING COMMUNITY PORTS AND CARRYING DANGEROUS OR POLLUTING GOODS

46.178 On 27 November 1996, the Commission adopted Decision 96/710 in application, at the request of Germany, of Article 5(4) of Council Directive 93/75 of 13 September 1993 concerning minimum requirements for vessels bound for or leaving Community ports and carrying dangerous or polluting goods.[140]

---

140 OJ L326/64, 12 December 1996.

46.179 Council Directive 93/75 of 13 September 1993 sets out the minimum require-ments for vessels bound for or leaving EU ports and carrying dangerous or polluting goods,[141] as amended by Commission Directive 96/39,[142] and in particular Article 5(4) of the directive. The recitals set out the background:

> "Whereas, in order to limit the risks of serious accidents at sea and to reduce the resulting damage, Article 5 of Directive 93/75 provides that the operators of the vessels covered by the Directive shall notify the information listed in Annex I thereto to the competent authorities of the Member State concerned; whereas Article 5(4) authorizes the Member States to exempt regular scheduled services of less than one hour's crossing time from such notification requirement and allows the Commission to agree to a reasonable extension of this period on request from a Member State;
>
> Whereas, the information given by Germany in its request of 12 April 1994, on the basis of which scheduled services between the mainland and East Frisia Islands were exempted by Deci-sion of the Commission[143] from the application of Article 5(4) of Directive 93/75, ... has been completed by a communication dated 23 February 1996 concerning regular services between the mainland and North Frisia Islands; whereas in this communication, Germany asked the Commis-sion to agree to an exemption for the services operated between the ports of Dagebüll to Wittdün (Amrum Island) and Schlüttsiel to Hallig Langeness, which have crossing times of two hours;
>
> Whereas the appropriate measures have been taken by the German competent authorities to ensure a high level of safety of navigation and protection of the marine environment in the area; whereas these measures include traffic surveillance and the provision of safety information to vessels, as well as the obligation to comply with local navigation rules;
>
> Whereas the vessels in question provide local services between the islands and the mainland; whereas the risks of accident and marine pollution are limited owing to the scarce maritime traffic in the area and the small quantities of polluting goods on board the vessels;
>
> Whereas the information required by Annex I to the Directive is available at any time from the operators or captains;
>
> Whereas, in the circumstances, it is justifiable to accept the request from Germany to exempt the regular scheduled services referred to above from the application of Article 5(2) and (3) of Directive 93/75 ..."

46.180 Article 1 – the operative provision – states that Germany was authorised to exempt the regular scheduled services between Dagebüll and Wittdün and between Schlüttsiel and Hallig Langeness from the application of Article (2) and (3) of Directive 93/75, subject to the following conditions: (a) the waters in which the services covered by the decision operate are duly buoyed and are drawn to the attention of navigators in the relevant nautical documents; (b) compliance with the local navigation rules is assured; (c) constant contact is maintained, in particular by radio links, with the competent mari-time traffic service; (d) only small quantities of dangerous or polluting goods, within the meaning of Directive 93/75, are carried on board; (e) the information referred to in Annex I to Directive 93/75 is made available by the operators throughout the crossing and can at any time be provided to the authorities of the Member State on request.

---

141 OJ L247/19, 5 October 1993.
142 OJ L196/7, 7 August 1996.
143 OJ L29/8, 7.2.1996.

P. DIRECTIVE 2009/20 OF THE EUROPEAN PARLIAMENT AND OF THE COUNCIL OF 23 APRIL 2009 ON THE INSURANCE OF SHIPOWNERS FOR MARITIME CLAIMS

46.181 On 23 April 2009, the Parliament and the Council adopted Directive 2009/20 on the insurance of shipowners for maritime claims.[144] The legal basis of the directive is now the TFEU generally and Article 100(2) of the TFEU. The basis of the directive is:

"(1) One element of Community maritime transport policy is to improve the quality of merchant shipping by making all economic operators act more responsibly.

(2) Dissuasive measures have already been adopted under Directive 2005/35 … of the European Parliament and of the Council of 7 September 2005 on ship source pollution and on the introduction of penalties for infringements.[145]

(3) On 9 October 2008, the Member States adopted a statement in which they unanimously recognised the importance of the application of the 1996 Protocol to the 1976 Convention on Limitation of Liability for Maritime Claims by all Member States.

(4) The obligation to have insurance should make it possible to ensure better protection for victims. It should also help to eliminate substandard ships and make it possible to reestablish competition between operators. Furthermore, in Resolution A.898(21), the International Maritime Organisation invited States to urge shipowners to be properly insured.

(5) Non compliance with the provisions of this Directive should be rectified. Directive 2009/16 … of the European Parliament and of the Council of 23 April 2009 on port State control (recast) … already provides for the detention of ships in the case of absence of certificates which have to be carried on board. However, it is appropriate to provide for the possibility of expelling a ship which does not carry a certificate of insurance. The modalities of the expulsion should allow the situation to be rectified within a reasonable time period.

(6) Since the objectives of this Directive, namely the introduction and implementation of appropriate measures in the field of maritime transport policy, cannot be sufficiently achieved by the Member States and can therefore, by reason of its scale and effects, be better achieved at Community level, the Community may adopt measures, in accordance with the principle of subsidiarity as set out in Article 5 of the Treaty. In accordance with the principle of proportionality, as set out in that Article, this Directive does not go beyond what is necessary in order to achieve those objectives."

46.182 Article 1 describes the subject matter of the directive as laying "down rules applicable to certain aspects of the obligations on shipowners as regards their insurance for maritime claims".

46.183 Article 2 describes the scope of the directive. Article 2(1) provides that Directive 2009/20 applies to ships of 300 gt or more. The directive does not apply to warships, auxiliary warships or other State owned or operated ships used for a non-commercial public service.[146] Article 2(3) provides that the directive "shall be without prejudice to the regimes established by the instruments in force in the Member State concerned and listed in the Annex hereto". There is a short annex listing the instruments for the purposes of Article 2: (a) the International Convention on Civil Liability for Oil Pollution Damage, 1992; (b) the International Convention on Liability and Compensation for Damage in Connection with the Carriage of Hazardous and Noxious Substances by Sea, 1996 (HNS Convention); (c) the International Convention on Civil Liability for Bunker Oil Pollution Damage, 2001 ("Bunker Oil" Convention); (d) the Nairobi International Convention on

---

144 OJ L131/128, 28 May 2009.
145 Ed., OJ L255/11, 30 September 2005.
146 Dir. 2009/20, Art. 2(2).

the Removal of Wrecks, 2007 ("Wrecks Removal" Convention); (e) Regulation (EC) No 392/2009 of the European Parliament and of the Council of 23 April 2009 on the liability of carriers of passengers by sea in the event of accidents.

46.184 Various works are defined by Article 3 for the purpose of the directive. The following definitions apply.

> "(a) 'shipowner' means the registered owner of a seagoing ship, or any other person such as the bareboat charterer who is responsible for the operation of the ship;
>
> (b) 'insurance' means insurance with or without deductibles, and comprises, for example, indemnity insurance of the type currently provided by members of the International Group of P & I Clubs, and other effective forms of insurance (including proved self insurance) and financial security offering similar conditions of cover;
>
> (c) '1996 Convention' means the consolidated text of the 1976 Convention on Limitation of Liability for Maritime Claims, adopted by the International Maritime Organisation (IMO), as amended by the 1996 Protocol."

46.185 Insurance for maritime claims is defined by Article 4. The article provides:

> "1. Each Member State shall require that shipowners of ships flying its flag have insurance covering such ships.
>
> 2. Each Member State shall require shipowners of ships flying a flag other than its own to have insurance in place when such ships enter a port under the Member State's jurisdiction. This shall not prevent Member States, if in conformity with international law, from requiring compliance with that obligation when such ships are operating in their territorial waters.
>
> 3. The insurance referred to in paragraphs 1 and 2 shall cover maritime claims subject to limitation under the 1996 Convention. The amount of the insurance for each and every ship per incident shall be equal to the relevant maximum amount for the limitation of liability as laid down in the 1996 Convention."

46.186 Article 5 deals with inspections, compliance, expulsion from ports and denial of access to ports:

> "1. Each Member State shall ensure that any inspection of a ship in a port under its jurisdiction in accordance with Directive 2009/16, ... includes verification that a certificate referred to in Article 6 is carried on board.
>
> 2. If the certificate referred to in Article 6 is not carried on board, and without prejudice to Directive 2009/16/EC providing for detention of ships when safety issues are at stake, the competent authority may issue an expulsion order to the ship which shall be notified to the Commission, the other Member States and the flag State concerned. As a result of the issuing of such an expulsion order, every Member State shall refuse entry of this ship into any of its ports until the shipowner notifies the certificate referred to in Article 6."

46.187 Insurance certificates are addressed by Article 6:

> "1. The existence of the insurance referred to in Article 4 shall be proved by one or more certificates issued by its provider and carried on board the ship.
>
> 2. The certificates issued by the insurance provider shall include the following information:
>
>> (a) name of ship, its IMO number, and port of registry;
>> (b) shipowner's name and principal place of business;
>> (c) type and duration of the insurance;
>> (d) name and principal place of business of the provider of the insurance and, where appropriate, the place of business where the insurance is established.
>
> 3. If the language used in the certificates is neither English nor French nor Spanish, the text shall include a translation into one of these languages."

46.188 Penalties are addressed by Article 7:

"For the purposes of Article 4(1), Member States shall lay down a system of penalties for the breach of national provisions adopted pursuant to this Directive and shall take all the measures necessary to ensure that those penalties are applied. The penalties provided for shall be effective, proportionate and dissuasive."

46.189 Under Article 8, every three years, and for the first time before 1 January 2015, the Commission must present a report to the European Parliament and to the Council on the application of the directive.

46.190 Article 9 provides for transposition of the directive:

"1. Member States shall bring into force the laws, regulations and administrative provisions necessary to comply with this Directive before 1 January 2012. They shall forthwith inform the Commission thereof.

When Member States adopt these measures, they shall contain a reference to this Directive or shall be accompanied by such a reference on the occasion of their official publication. The methods of making such reference shall be laid down by Member States.

2. Member States shall communicate to the Commission the text of the main provisions of national law which they adopt in the field covered by this Directive."

CHAPTER 47

European Union law and shipping litigation: the "Brussels I" Regulation

A. INTRODUCTION

47.001 Inevitably, there is cross-border litigation in the shipping sector. The litigation can relate to issues as diverse as cargo claims, charter parties, collisions, contracts, injuries and even fatalities. This often means that there is a choice in a case between different jurisdictions. The choice between jurisdictions is primarily the choice of: (a) which jurisdiction will hear the case (i.e. the forum which will hear the dispute); and (b) which body of law will apply to the case (i.e. the governing law which will decide the dispute).[1] This choice of legal system and law can be critical: making one particular choice could favour the plaintiff while a different choice could favour the defendant. Put another way, choosing the substantive and procedural legal regimes could determine the entire outcome of the case. This often leads to so-called "forum shopping" whereby potential litigants "shop" between different jurisdictions to find the one most favourable to their case. Often, there are skirmishes between the parties about resisting choices. The conflict of laws[2] rules help to resolve some of the difficulties involved.[3] The conflict of laws rules also help to ensure that claims are not only upheld but enforced as well. This book, and hence this chapter, concentrates only on selected European Union ("EU") law aspects of the issue. Moreover, this chapter is necessarily brief as there is a great deal of information available in other more detailed publications on the topic.[4]

---

1 Mandaraka-Sheppard comments in vol. 2 of her excellent Modern Maritime Law (3rd ed., 2013), p. 259: "[u]nder English procedural law, ... there are two broad types of jurisdiction bases by which the jurisdiction of the court can be invoked, or seised, on the merits. The one depending merely on service of the proceedings on the defendant, without requiring substantive connecting factors between the claim and the jurisdiction, subject to certain exceptions. ... The other is conferred by various International Conventions, known as the 'convention jurisdiction' basis, and depends on jurisdiction rules provided by the particular Convention that applies in a particular case. ... [W]hen the English court may be restrained from determining the merits of a case and, in the event of conflict between jurisdictions, how such conflict is resolved by Convention rules that are applicable to maritime disputes."

2 On conflict of laws, see Briggs, The Conflict of Laws (2013); Clarkson and Hill, The Conflict of Laws (2011); Collier, Conflict of Laws (3rd ed., 2008); Dicey, Morris and Collins, Dicey, Morris & Collins on the Conflict of Laws (2014); McClean and Ruiz Abou-Nigm, Morris: The Conflict of Laws (2012); and Rogerson, Collier's Conflict of Laws (2013). See Baatz (ed.), Maritime Law (3rd ed., 2014), chap. 1; Baughen, Shipping Law (6th ed., 2015), chap. 18; and Mandaraka-Sheppard, op. cit. at fn. 1, chap. 7.

3 E.g. even if the parties choose a particular governing law and a jurisdiction then a court might refuse to recognise the choices made by the parties.

4 See, for example, the publications cited in fn. 2.

47.002 Within the EU, there are special rules adopted (typically now[5] in the form of regulations[6]) to minimise further the difficulties faced by litigants – this is done by the adoption of common rules which pre-determine choices. The principal instrument is now the so-called Recast Brussels I Regulation. This is Regulation 1215/2012 of the European Parliament and of the Council of 12 December 2012 on jurisdiction and the recognition and enforcement of judgments in civil and commercial matters.[7] There had been other earlier measures including the 1968 Brussels Convention on Jurisdiction and the Enforcement of Judgments in Civil and Commercial Matters (as amended[8])[9] and the 1988 Lugano Convention (which extended the regime to the then six European Free Trade Association Member States). The current regime is based, in many ways, on Council Regulation 44/2001 of 22 December 2000 on jurisdiction and the recognition and enforcement of judgments in civil and commercial matters[10] (which replaced the 1968 Convention) but Regulation 44/2001 had been amended a number of times so the regime is now embodied in the so-called Recast Brussels I Regulation which involved an updated measure to take into account some of the lessons learned from the operation of those measures over time.[11]

47.003 This chapter examines the Recast Regulation from the perspective of shipping[12] only and therefore omits aspects of it which are irrelevant in a maritime context (e.g. provisions about wills, trusts and so on).

47.004 The background to the Recast Brussels Regulation (which entered into force on 10 January 2015) is set out, in part, in recitals 3–5 to the Recast Regulation:

"(3) The [European] Union has set itself the objective of maintaining and developing an area of freedom, security and justice, *inter alia*, by facilitating access to justice, in particular through the principle of mutual recognition of judicial and extra-judicial decisions in civil matters. For the gradual establishment of such an area, the Union is to adopt measures

---

5 The original measure was a 1968 treaty.

6 On regulations, see chap. 3.

7 OJ L351/1, 20 December 2012. Reg. 1215/2012 (the recast Regulation) replaced EU Reg. 44/2001 (the Brussels I Regulation) for proceedings commenced on or after 10 January 2015.

8 E.g. the Accession Conventions which applied the 1968 Convention to those States which acceded to the then EU (e.g. the San Sebastian Convention relating to Portugal and Spain). The 1968 Convention (as amended) was incorporated into UK law by the Civil Jurisdiction and Judgments Act 1982 (often known as the "CJJA") which took effect on 1 January 1987. Denmark was initially not part of the 1968 Convention regime but it agreed in 2007 to be bound by Reg. 44/2001. However, Denmark has always had a somewhat strained and incomplete interaction with the EU regime in this context. Changes are inevitable to the UK regime if Brexit proceeds.

9 Recital 9 of the Recast Brussels I Regulation provides that the 1968 Brussels Convention continues to apply to the territories of the Member States which fall within the territorial scope of that convention and which are excluded from the regulation pursuant to Article 355 of the Treaty on the Functioning of the European Union ("TFEU") but this is of limited relevance for present purposes.

10 OJ L12/1, 16 January 2001.

11 The Recast Regulation will be amended in due course: Art. 79 of the Recast Regulation provides that by 11 January 2022, the Commission shall present a report to the European Parliament, to the Council and to the European Economic and Social Committee on the application of the regulation. That report shall include an evaluation of the possible need for a further extension of the rules on jurisdiction to defendants not domiciled in a Member State, taking into account the operation of this regulation and possible developments at international level. Where appropriate, the report shall be accompanied by a proposal for amendment of this regulation.

12 On the Recast Regulation generally, see the publications cited in fn. 2 and Dickinson and Lein, The Brussels I Regulation Recast (2015); Magnus and Mankowski, Brussels I Regulation (2nd rev. ed., 2012). On the Recast Regulation in a shipping context, see, in particular, Mandaraka-Sheppard, op. cit. at fn. 1, vol. 2, chap. 7.

relating to judicial cooperation in civil matters having cross-border implications, particularly when necessary for the proper functioning of the internal market."

Recital 3 demonstrates the interconnectivity between issues such as the internal market and access to justice.

"(4) Certain differences between national rules governing jurisdiction and recognition of judgments hamper the sound operation of the internal market. Provisions to unify the rules of conflict of jurisdiction in civil and commercial matters, and to ensure rapid and simple recognition and enforcement of judgments given in a Member State, are essential."

Recital 4 highlights that such unifying or harmonising measures are able to minimise the disruptive effect of differences.

"(5) Such provisions fall within the area of judicial cooperation in civil matters within the meaning of Article 81 of the Treaty on the Functioning of the European Union.[13] In order to attain the objective of free circulation of judgments in civil and commercial matters, it is necessary and appropriate that the rules governing jurisdiction and the recognition and enforcement of judgments be governed by a legal instrument of the Union which is binding and directly applicable."[14]

---

13 Ed., Art. 81 of the TFEU provides:

"1. The Union shall develop judicial cooperation in civil matters having cross-border implications, based on the principle of mutual recognition of judgments and of decisions in extrajudicial cases. Such cooperation may include the adoption of measures for the approximation of the laws and regulations of the Member States.

2. For the purposes of paragraph 1, the European Parliament and the Council, acting in accordance with the ordinary legislative procedure, shall adopt measures, particularly when necessary for the proper functioning of the internal market, aimed at ensuring:

    (a) the mutual recognition and enforcement between Member States of judgments and of decisions in extrajudicial cases;
    (b) the cross-border service of judicial and extrajudicial documents;
    (c) the compatibility of the rules applicable in the Member States concerning conflict of laws and of jurisdiction;
    (d) cooperation in the taking of evidence;
    (e) effective access to justice;
    (f) the elimination of obstacles to the proper functioning of civil proceedings, if necessary by promoting the compatibility of the rules on civil procedure applicable in the Member States;
    (g) the development of alternative methods of dispute settlement;
    (h) support for the training of the judiciary and judicial staff.

3. Notwithstanding paragraph 2, measures concerning family law with cross-border implications shall be established by the Council, acting in accordance with a special legislative procedure. The Council shall act unanimously after consulting the European Parliament.

The Council, on a proposal from the Commission, may adopt a decision determining those aspects of family law with cross-border implications which may be the subject of acts adopted by the ordinary legislative procedure. The Council shall act unanimously after consulting the European Parliament.

The proposal referred to in the second subparagraph shall be notified to the national Parliaments. If a national Parliament makes known its opposition within six months of the date of such notification, the decision shall not be adopted. In the absence of opposition, the Council may adopt the decision."

14 Mandaraka-Sheppard, op. cit. at fn. 1, commented at p. 260: "[t]he EU has set itself the objective of facilitating access to justice and promoting judicial cooperation between Member States in civil and commercial matters, which is considered necessary for the proper functioning of the internal market. The reason behind this objective has been that differences between national rules governing jurisdiction and recognition of judgments hamper the sound operation of the internal markets. Therefore, it was thought that provisions aiming to unify the rules of conflict of jurisdiction are essential."

While the regime has the admirable aim of simplicity and predictability, in reality, the regime is quite complex and complicated because there are so many exceptions to the general rules which is understandable given the need to take into account the myriad situations which can arise in practice.

47.005 Recital 26 of the Recast Regulation provides that

> "[m]utual trust in the administration of justice in the Union justifies the principle that judgments given in a Member State should be recognised in all Member States without the need for any special procedure. In addition, the aim of making cross-border litigation less time-consuming and costly justifies the abolition of the declaration of enforceability prior to enforcement in the Member State addressed. As a result, a judgment given by the courts of a Member State should be treated as if it had been given in the Member State addressed."

Unfortunately, this mutual trust can lead to a certain level of inflexibility in terms of the application of the rules.[15] However, to minimise inconsistency between the approaches taken by Member States, various concepts in the regime are given an EU, rather than national, construction/interpretation[16] which leads to a uniform meaning and minimises the likelihood of divergence.

47.006 The Recast Brussels Regulation I repeats a great deal of what went before in terms of previous regimes. However, it also made a number of changes to the regime. It aimed at making the regime more predictable. It clarified the rules on the domicile of a legal person. It upheld the notion that the parties to a contract could ordinarily choose their regime except for consumer, insurance and employment contracts where some limitations were imposed in the interests of protecting the party who is ordinarily the weaker one. It provides that arbitration does not fall within the scope of the regime.[17] It seeks to minimise the possibility of concurrent proceedings. In many ways, it was a clarification measure.

---

15 E.g. Case C-116/02 Erich Gasser GmbH v MISAT Srl [2003] ECR I-14693, ECLI:EU:C:2003:657 in relation to the rigidity of the convention regime and Case C-281/02 Owusu v Jackson, trading as "Villa Holidays Bal-Inn Villas" and Others [2005] ECR I-1383, ECLI:EU:C:2005:120.

16 E.g. concepts such as "civil and commercial matters", "lis pendens", "cause of action" and so on are given an EU meaning (see case law such as Case C-406/92 Owners of the cargo lately laden on board the ship "Tatry" v Owners of the ship "Maciej Rataj" [1994] ECR I-05439, ECLI:EU:C:1994:400 [1995] 1 Lloyd's Rep 302.)

17 Baatz, op. cit. at fn. 2, has commented (p. 7, footnotes omitted): "[t]he effectiveness of arbitration agreements in Europe has been weakened. If a party commences proceedings in an EU Member State court in breach of a London arbitration agreement, the English court cannot grant an anti-suit injunction to restrain the respondent in the English arbitration from pursuing the court proceedings in the EU Member State as a result of the decision of the European Court of Justice in Allianz SpA (formerly Riunione Adriatica di Sicurta SpA) v West Tankers Inc (The Front Comor) [Case C-185/07 [2009] 1 AC 1138, [2009] 1 Lloyd's Rep 413]. There must be mutual trust between the EU Member States and the court of the EU Member State must be trusted to come to its own correct determination as to whether there is a valid arbitration clause. If there is, all the EU Member States are parties to the New York Convention and therefore each EU Member State would be obliged to stay its court proceedings in favour of arbitration. In The Front Comor the European Court of Justice rejected the argument that as arbitration proceedings fall outside the enforcement of judgments in civil and commercial matter (the Jurisdiction Regulation), as they are excluded, … the judgment of another EU Member State in relation to the validity of the arbitration agreement was also not within the Jurisdiction Regulation and therefore for the English court to grant an anti-suit injunction was not inconsistent with the Jurisdiction Regulation. The court held that as the Italian court in that case was seised of a substantive dispute for damages in a tort claim as a result of the Front Comor hitting the Italian claimants' jetty in Syracuse, and the Italian court had jurisdiction to decide the substantive claim under … the Jurisdiction Regulation unless there was a valid preliminary issue to the substantive claims fell within the Jurisdiction Regulation. Therefore it was inconsistent with the Regulation for the English court to grant an anti-suit injunction restraining the Italian claimant from pursuing proceedings within the Jurisdiction Regulation in Italy."

B. SCOPE AND APPLICATION OF THE RECAST BRUSSELS I REGULATION

47.007 Article 81 of the Recast Regulation provides that the regulation came into force on 10 January 2012 (i.e. 20 days after its publication in the *Official Journal*)[18] but applied from 10 January 2015 (with the exception of Articles 75 and 76 of the regulation which applied from 10 January 2014).[19] As a regulation, it is binding in its entirety and is directly applicable in the Member States in accordance with the Treaties (as would be the case with any regulation). It is worth recalling that despite the changes over time, there is a great deal of overlap between the conventions, the regulation and the Recast Regulation so much of the jurisprudence and thinking on earlier provisions flow through, in whole or in part, to the current regime as well.

47.008 Chapter I of the Recast Regulation I is entitled "Scope and Definitions".

47.009 Article 1(1) states that the regulation shall apply in "civil and commercial matters"[20] whatever the nature of the court or tribunal. It may not extend to anything which is not "civil and commercial" such as, in particular, to revenue, customs or administrative matters or to the liability of the State for acts and omissions in the exercise of State authority (i.e. *acta iure imperii*).[21] As the Recast Regulation relates to civil and commercial matters, it would therefore be quite relevant in the context of the vast

---

18 OJ L351/1, 20 December 2012.

19 Art. 66 of the Recast Regulation provides: "1. This Regulation shall apply only to legal proceedings instituted, to authentic instruments formally drawn up or registered and to court settlements approved or concluded on or after 10 January 2015. 2. Notwithstanding Article 80, Regulation (EC) No 44/2001 shall continue to apply to judgments given in legal proceedings instituted, to authentic instruments formally drawn up or registered and to court settlements approved or concluded before 10 January 2015 which fall within the scope of that Regulation." Art. 72 provides that the Recast "Regulation shall not affect agreements by which Member States, prior to the entry into force of Regulation (EC) No 44/2001, undertook pursuant to Article 59 of the 1968 Brussels Convention not to recognise judgments given, in particular in other Contracting States to that Convention, against defendants domiciled or habitually resident in a third State where, in cases provided for in Article 4 of that Convention, the judgment could only be founded on a ground of jurisdiction specified in the second paragraph of Article 3 of that Convention." Art. 73(1) provides that the regulation shall not affect the application of the 2007 Lugano Convention. Art. 73(2) provides that the Recast Regulation shall not affect the application of the 1958 New York Convention (i.e. Convention on the Recognition and Enforcement of Foreign Arbitral Awards, done at New York on 10 June 1958). Art. 73(3) of the Recast Regulation provides that the regulation shall not affect the application of bilateral conventions and agreements between a third State and a Member State concluded before the date of entry into force of Reg. (EC) No 44/2001 which concern matters governed by the regulation.

20 The term "civil and commercial matters" is to be given an EU, rather than a Member State or national, construction: Case 29/76 LTU Lufttransportunternehmen GmbH & Co. KG v Eurocontrol [1976] ECR 1541, ECLI:EU:C:1976:137. It is clearly not a measure which deals with criminal matters.

21 Recital 10 of the Recast Regulation provides that the "scope of this Regulation should cover all the main civil and commercial matters apart from certain well-defined matters, in particular maintenance obligations, which should be excluded from the scope of this Regulation following the adoption of Council Regulation (EC) No 4/2009 of 18 December 2008 on jurisdiction, applicable law, recognition and enforcement of decisions and cooperation in matters relating to maintenance obligations". An interesting example would be Case 814/79 Rüffer [1980] ECR 3807, ECLI:EU:C:1980:291 which concerned a dispute about a claim for redress brought by the Netherlands against the owner of a German vessel which collided with a Dutch vessel; the Netherlands had the sunken wreck of the German vessel removed by a Dutch firm; the Dutch government sought to recover the net costs of removing the wreck (after the cargo was sold); the Court of Justice of the European Union ("CJEU") said that this was the exercise of a public function and not therefore within the scope of the 1968 Convention (or, now, the Recast Regulation). This means that the concept of acta iure imperii is wider than traditional sovereign immune acts and would cover regulatory or governmental-type functions in certain circumstances.

majority of issues in shipping but not every issue.[22] Article 1(2) of the regulation provides that the regulation does not apply to: (a) the status or legal capacity of natural persons, rights in property arising out of a matrimonial relationship or out of a relationship deemed by the law applicable to such relationship to have comparable effects to marriage; (b) bankruptcy, proceedings relating to the winding-up of insolvent companies or other legal persons, judicial arrangements, compositions and analogous proceedings; (c) social security; (d) arbitration;[23] (e) maintenance obligations arising from a family relationship, parentage, marriage or affinity; as well as (f) wills and succession, including maintenance obligations arising by reason of death. It therefore does not apply to criminal, revenue, customs, constitutional, public law or administrative matters. Nor does it apply to acts and omissions in the exercise of State authority. The exclusion of arbitration is significant in a shipping context[24] and extends to surrounding applications.[25]

47.010 Article 2 of the regulation provides that for the purposes of the regulation: (a) "judgment" means any judgment given by a court[26] or tribunal of a Member State, whatever the judgment may be called, including a decree, order, decision or writ of execution, as well as a decision on the determination of costs or expenses by an officer of the court;[27] (b) "court settlement" means a settlement which has been approved by a court of a Member State or concluded before a court of a Member State in the course of proceedings; (c) "authentic instrument" means a document which has been formally drawn

---

22 The determination of what constitutes a civil and commercial matter must be decided autonomously (see Case 29/76 LTU Lufttransportunternehmen GmbH & Co. KG v Eurocontrol [1976] ECR-1541, ECLI:EU:C:1976:137) bearing in mind the objectives of the regulation and the general principles which flow from the Member State legal systems (see Case C-292/05 Eirini Lechouritou and Others v Dimosio tis Omospondiakis Dimokratias tis Germanias [2007] ECR I-1519, ECLI:EU:C:2007:102).

23 Recital 12 of the Recast Regulation states that the regulation "should not apply to arbitration. Nothing in this Regulation should prevent the courts of a Member State, when seised of an action in a matter in respect of which the parties have entered into an arbitration agreement, from referring the parties to arbitration, from staying or dismissing the proceedings, or from examining whether the arbitration agreement is null and void, inoperative or incapable of being performed, in accordance with their national law." The Recast Regulation goes on to provide that a ruling given by a court of a Member State as to whether or not an arbitration agreement is null and void, inoperative or incapable of being performed should not be subject to the rules of recognition and enforcement laid down in the regulation, regardless of whether the court decided on this as a principal issue or as an incidental question. On the other hand, where a court of a Member State, exercising jurisdiction under the regulation or under national law, has determined that an arbitration agreement is null and void, inoperative or incapable of being performed, this should not preclude that court's judgment on the substance of the matter from being recognised or, as the case may be, enforced in accordance with this regulation. This should be without prejudice to the competence of the courts of the Member States to decide on the recognition and enforcement of arbitral awards in accordance with the Convention on the Recognition and Enforcement of Foreign Arbitral Awards, done at New York on 10 June 1958, which takes precedence over this regulation. The Recast Regulation also provides that it should not apply to any action or ancillary proceedings relating to, in particular, the establishment of an arbitral tribunal, the powers of arbitrators, the conduct of an arbitration procedure or any other aspects of such a procedure, nor to any action or judgment concerning the annulment, review, appeal, recognition or enforcement of an arbitral award.

24 Case C-190/89 Marc Rich & Co. AG v Società Italiana Impianti PA [1991] ECR I-3855, ECLI:EU:C:1991:319.

25 Case C-391/95 Van Uden Maritime BV, trading as Van Uden Africa Line v Kommanditgesellschaft in Firma Deco-Line [1998] ECR I-7091, ECLI:EU:C:1998:543.

26 Art. 3 expands the definition of "court" to include certain entities in Hungary and Sweden.

27 Art. 1(2) of the Recast Regulation provides that for the purposes of Chapter III, "judgment" includes provisional, including protective, measures ordered by a court or tribunal which by virtue of this regulation has jurisdiction as to the substance of the matter. It does not include a provisional, including protective, measure which is ordered by such a court or tribunal without the defendant being summoned to appear, unless the judgment containing the measure is served on the defendant prior to enforcement.

up or registered as an authentic instrument in the Member State of origin and the authenticity of which: (i) relates to the signature and the content of the instrument; and (ii) has been established by a public authority or other authority empowered for that purpose; (d) "Member State of origin" means the Member State in which, as the case may be, the judgment has been given, the court settlement has been approved or concluded, or the authentic instrument has been formally drawn up or registered; (e) "Member State addressed" means the Member State in which the recognition of the judgment is invoked or in which the enforcement of the judgment, the court settlement or the authentic instrument is sought; and (f) "court of origin" means the court which has given the judgment the recognition of which is invoked or the enforcement of which is sought.

C. JURISDICTION

Introduction

47.011 Chapter II of the Recast Regulation deals with jurisdiction. This is a critical chapter of the regulation because it outlines the threshold jurisdictional issue. Section 1 of Chapter II is entitled "General Provisions". Section 2 deals with the so-called "Special Jurisdiction" rules. Section 3 deals with jurisdiction in matters relating to insurance. Section 4 deals with jurisdiction over consumer contracts. Section 5 is entitled "Jurisdiction over individual contracts of employment". Section 6 is entitled "Exclusive Jurisdiction". Section 7 is entitled "Prorogation of jurisdiction".

Basic rule on jurisdiction

47.012 Article 4 of the Recast Regulation sets out the basic rules on jurisdiction:

"1. Subject to this Regulation, persons domiciled in a Member State shall, whatever their nationality, be sued in the courts of that Member State.
2. Persons who are not nationals of the Member State in which they are domiciled shall be governed by the rules of jurisdiction applicable to nationals of that Member State."

47.013 Put another way, defendants are entitled to be sued in the courts of their domicile irrespective of their nationality. This provision helps to ensure that there is some real connection or nexus between the defendant and the place where the case is being instituted.[28] It prefers domicile over nationality. This rule protects defendants who are

---

28 It is useful to review some of the recitals to the Recast Regulation. Recital 13 provides that there must be a connection between proceedings to which the regulation applies and the territory of the Member State. Accordingly, common rules of jurisdiction should, in principle, apply when the defendant is domiciled in a Member State. Recital 14 provides that a defendant not domiciled in a Member State should in general (note: "in general") be subject to the national rules of jurisdiction applicable in the territory of the Member State of the court seised. However, in order to ensure the protection of consumers and employees, to safeguard the jurisdiction of the courts of the Member States in situations where they have exclusive jurisdiction and to respect the autonomy of the parties, certain rules of jurisdiction in the regulation should apply regardless of the defendant's domicile (this aim of the recital is very admirable). Recital 15 states that the rules of jurisdiction should be highly predictable and founded on the principle that jurisdiction is generally based on the defendant's domicile. Jurisdiction should always be available on this ground save in a few well-defined situations in which the subject-matter of the dispute or the autonomy of the parties warrants a different connecting factor. The domicile of a legal person must be defined autonomously so as to make the common rules more transparent and avoid conflicts of jurisdiction. Finally, Recital 16 provides that in addition to the defendant's domicile, there should be

domiciled in a Member State from being sued in the courts of other Member States except in specific circumstances. The principal exception is where there is a weaker party (e.g. insured parties, consumers and employees) then the weaker party would be protected. The domicile of the claimant or plaintiff is irrelevant.[29] A person's domicile may change so one determines domicile at the time when the proceedings are instituted and one does so by reference to the law of the Member State whose court is seised of the matter.[30] Article 63 of the Recast Regulation provides (and this could be relevant in a maritime law context):

"1. For the purposes of this Regulation, a company or other legal person or association of natural or legal persons is domiciled at the place where it has its:

    (a) statutory seat;
    (b) central administration;[31] or
    (c) principal place of business.

2. For the purposes of Ireland, Cyprus and the United Kingdom, 'statutory seat' means the registered office or, where there is no such office anywhere, the place of incorporation or, where there is no such place anywhere, the place under the law of which the formation took place.

3. In order to determine whether a trust is domiciled in the Member State whose courts are seised of the matter, the court shall apply its rules of private international law."[32]

It has been observed that

"it is not immediately obvious who constitutes 'the defendant' in an action *in rem*. The claim form will name a ship and, until the action is defended, when it will proceed as a parallel action *in personam* against the shipowner, it could be argued that the only defendant is that ship. This fiction formed the basis of the judgment of Hobhouse J in *The Nordlimt*,[33] in the context of an application of [Article 29 of the regulation]. However, the Court of Appeal was to take a radically different approach in *The Deichland*.[34] For the purposes of [Article 4], it held that 'the defendant' in an *in rem* action, even at a stage when the action was proceeding solely *in rem*, was the person who would be interested in defending the action – that is, the person potentially liable *in personam*. On the facts, that person was the demise charterer of the vessel at the time that the cargo claim arose. As they were domiciled in Germany, they were entitled to be sued in

---

alternative grounds of jurisdiction based on a close connection between the court and the action or in order to facilitate the sound administration of justice. The existence of a close connection should ensure legal certainty and avoid the possibility of the defendant being sued in a court of a Member State which it could not reasonably have foreseen. This is important, particularly in disputes concerning non-contractual obligations arising out of violations of privacy and rights relating to personality, including defamation.

29 Case C-351/89 Overseas Union Insurance Ltd and Deutsche Ruck UK Reinsurance Ltd and Pine Top Insurance Company Ltd v New Hampshire Insurance Company [1991] ECR I-3317, ECLI:EU:C:1991:279 and Case C-412/98 Group Josi Reinsurance Company SA v Universal General Insurance Company [2000] ECR I-5925, ECLI:EU:C:2000:399.

30 See Art. 62 of the Recast Regulation: "1. In order to determine whether a party is domiciled in the Member State whose courts are seised of a matter, the court shall apply its internal law. 2. If a party is not domiciled in the Member State whose courts are seised of the matter, then, in order to determine whether the party is domiciled in another Member State, the court shall apply the law of that Member State." See also Canada Trust Company v Stozenberg (No.2) [2002] 1 AC 1.

31 Ed., the central administration is located where decisions are made and entrepreneurial management occurs (i.e. not just where annual general meetings and board meetings are held): Vava & Ors v Anglo American South Africa Ltd [2013] EWHC 2131.

32 The CJEU held in Case C-412/98 Group Josi Reinsurance Company SA v Universal General Insurance Company (UGIC) [2000] ECR I-5925, ECLI:EU:C:2000:399 that a claimant is entitled to rely on Art. 63 even if it is not domiciled in a Member State.

33 [1988] 1 QB 183.

34 [1990] 1 QB 361.

Germany under [Article 4] and the Admiralty Court had no jurisdiction over the claim against them."[35]

47.014 Article 5 of the Recast Regulation provides:

"1. Persons domiciled in a Member State may be sued in the courts of another Member State only by virtue of the rules set out in Sections 2 to 7 of this Chapter.
2. In particular, the rules of national jurisdiction of which the Member States are to notify the Commission pursuant to point (a) of Article 76(1) shall not be applicable as against the persons referred to in paragraph 1."

In this context, the phrase "this Chapter" in Article 5(1) refers to Chapter II ("Jurisdiction") of Regulation 1215/2012 so it sets the tone in a fundamental way.

47.015 Article 6 of the Recast Regulation provides:

"1. If the defendant is not domiciled in a Member State, the jurisdiction of the courts of each Member State shall, subject to Article 18(1),[36] Article 21(2)[37] and Articles 24[38] and 25,[39] be determined by the law of that Member State.
2. As against such a defendant, any person domiciled in a Member State may, whatever his nationality, avail himself in that Member State of the rules of jurisdiction there in force, and in particular those of which the Member States are to notify the Commission pursuant to point (a) of Article 76(1), in the same way as nationals of that Member State."

47.016 The words "and in particular those ... State" in Article 6 are new. If the defendant is domiciled outside the regulation Member States then the courts of the Member State may exercise jurisdiction in accordance with their own national law.

Special jurisdiction

47.017 Section 2 deals with the so-called "special jurisdiction" rules. This means that a claimant may, in certain limited circumstances, sue in a court of a Member State which is not the defendant's domicile. Article 7 provides:

"A person domiciled in a Member State may be sued in another Member State:

(1) (a) in matters relating to a contract, in the courts for the place of performance of the obligation in question;
    (b) for the purpose of this provision and unless otherwise agreed, the place of performance of the obligation in question shall be:

    – in the case of the sale of goods, the place in a Member State where, under the contract, the goods were delivered or should have been delivered,
    – in the case of the provision of services, the place in a Member State where, under the contract, the services were provided or should have been provided;

    (c) if point (b) does not apply then point (a) applies;
(2) in matters relating to tort, delict or quasi-delict, in the courts for the place where the harmful event occurred or may occur;

---

35 Baughen, op. cit. at fn. 2, p. 349, footnote omitted.
36 Ed., see para. 47.027.
37 Ed., see para. 47.030.
38 Ed., see para. 47.033.
39 Ed., see para. 47.035.

(3) as regards a civil claim for damages or restitution which is based on an act giving rise to criminal proceedings, in the court seised of those proceedings, to the extent that that court has jurisdiction under its own law to entertain civil proceedings;

(4) as regards a civil claim for the recovery, based on ownership, of a cultural object as defined in point 1 of Article 1 of Directive 93/7/EEC initiated by the person claiming the right to recover such an object, in the courts for the place where the cultural object is situated at the time when the court is seised;[40]

(5) as regards a dispute arising out of the operations of a branch, agency or other establishment, in the courts for the place where the branch, agency or other establishment is situated;

...

(7) as regards a dispute concerning the payment of remuneration claimed in respect of the salvage of a cargo or freight, in the court under the authority of which the cargo or freight in question:

(a) has been arrested to secure such payment; or
(b) could have been so arrested, but bail or other security has been given;
   provided that this provision shall apply only if it is claimed that the defendant has an interest in the cargo or freight or had such an interest at the time of salvage."

There are a number of comments which should be made about Article 7. A court must determine the place of performance by reference to its own choice of law rules.[41] Where the court has jurisdiction under Article 7 then it has no power to stay its own proceedings and must hear the case.[42] Article 7(1)(a) does not apply where the contract gives a choice to pay one of two parties where one is in the jurisdiction and the other is outside.[43] A claim for unseaworthiness under a bill of lading in respect of a cargo claim would typically be linked to the place where the cargo was loaded.[44] In respect of Article 7(3), a tort claim may be instituted before the courts of the State where the event occurred or may occur and includes the place where the damage occurred and the place of event giving rise to the damage.[45] Article 7(7) is directly relevant to shipping: the "provision is needed to maintain the existing admiralty jurisdiction over salvage claims against cargo and freight. The [1952 Arrest Convention] confers jurisdiction in relation to salvage claims, but only in relation to claims against ship."[46]

47.018 Article 8 of the Recast Regulation provides that a person domiciled in a Member State may also be sued:

"(1) Where he is one of a number of defendants, in the courts for the place where any one of them is domiciled, provided the claims are so closely connected that it is expedient to hear

---

40 Ed., recital 17 of the Recast Regulation provides that the owner of a cultural object as defined in Art. 1(1) of Council Dir. 93/7 of 15 March 1993 on the return of cultural objects unlawfully removed from the territory of a Member State (OJ L74, 27 March 1993, p. 74) should be able under this regulation to initiate proceedings as regards a civil claim for the recovery, based on ownership, of such a cultural object in the courts for the place where the cultural object is situated at the time the court is seised. Such proceedings should be without prejudice to proceedings initiated under Dir. 93/7.

41 Case 12/76 Industrie Tessili Italiana Como v Dunlop AG [1976] ECR-1473, ECLI:EU:C:1976:133.

42 Oceanfix International Ltd v AGIP Kazahkstan North Caspian Operating Co NV [2009] ScotSC 9.

43 Mom Shipping Inc v AXA Corporate Solutions Assurance SA [2005] EWCA Civ 1069, [2005] 2 Lloyd's Rep 769.

44 The Sea Maas [1999] 2 Lloyd's Rep 281.

45 Case 21/76 Handelskwekerij G. J. Bier BV v Mines de potasse d'Alsace SA [1976] ECR 1735, ECLI:EU:C:1976:166.

46 Baughen, op. cit. at fn. 2, p. 350.

and determine them together to avoid the risk of irreconcilable judgments resulting from separate proceedings;[47]

(2) as a third party in an action on a warranty or guarantee or in any other third-party proceedings, in the court seised of the original proceedings, unless these were instituted solely with the object of removing him from the jurisdiction of the court which would be competent in his case;

(3) on a counter-claim arising from the same contract or facts on which the original claim was based, in the court in which the original claim is pending;

(4) in matters relating to a contract, if the action may be combined with an action against the same defendant in matters relating to rights in rem in immovable property, in the court of the Member State in which the property is situated."

It is useful to make a number of observations about Article 8. If a claimant sues several defendants then there must be a connection between the actions so that it is expedient to determine them together to avoid the risk of irreconcilable judgments.[48] Article 8(1) no longer applies where proceedings are discontinued against the co-defendant that is domiciled in the Member State of the court before which those proceedings have been instituted.[49] Articles 7 and 8 are clear indicators of how the simplicity of the rules expressed early in the regulation are not borne out in reality.

Limitations actions

47.019 Article 9 is critically important for the shipping sector. The article provides that where by virtue of the regulation, a court of a Member State has jurisdiction in actions relating to liability from the use or operation of a ship, that court, or any other court substituted for this purpose by the internal law of that Member State, shall also have jurisdiction over claims for limitation of such liability. Hence the integrity of the limitation of liability regime is preserved. It has been commented that

> "Article 11 of the [1976 Limitation Convention] entitles the defendant to constitute a limitation fund 'in any State Party in which legal proceedings are instituted in respect of claims subject to limitation', but gives the shipowner no right to launch a 'pre-emptive' strike. However, it does not prevent the shipowner doing so, provided that it can establish jurisdiction in its chosen court under either domestic grounds or, where appropriate, on Judgments Regulation grounds. Accordingly, shipowners can rely on [Article 4] to proceed, against the cargo owner in the courts of a Member State in which it is domiciled.[50] However, such a shipowner would not be able to initiate limitation proceedings in the Member State in which it was itself domiciled."[51]

Insurance

47.020 Section 3 ("Jurisdiction in matters relating to insurance") of Chapter II ("Jurisdiction") deals with jurisdiction in matters relating to insurance. Article 10 provides that in matters relating to insurance, jurisdiction shall be determined by that section, without

---

47 Ed., see Case 189/87 Kalfelis v Bankhaus Schröder, Münchmeyer, Hengst and Co [1988] ECR 5565, ECLI:EU:C:1988:459 and Andrew Weir Shipping Ltd v Wartsila UK Ltd [2004] EWHC 1284.

48 Case 189/87 Athanasios Kalfelis v Bankhaus Schröder, Münchmeyer, Hengst and Co and others [1988] ECR-5565, ECLI:EU:C:1988:459.

49 The Xing Su Hai [1995] 2 Lloyd's Rep.15.

50 It can also rely on Arts 7 and 8.

51 Baughen, op. cit. at fn. 2, p. 351.

prejudice to Article 6[52] and point 5 of Article 7.[53] Recital 18 describes the rationale: in relation to insurance, consumer and employment contracts, the weaker party should be protected by rules of jurisdiction more favourable to his or her interests than the general rules. Article 11 provides:

> "1. An insurer domiciled in a Member State may be sued:
>
>> (a) in the courts of the Member State in which he is domiciled;
>> (b) in another Member State, in the case of actions brought by the policyholder, the insured or a beneficiary, in the courts for the place where the claimant is domiciled; or
>> (c) if he is a co-insurer, in the courts of a Member State in which proceedings are brought against the leading insurer.
>
> 2. An insurer who is not domiciled in a Member State but has a branch, agency or other establishment in one of the Member States shall, in disputes arising out of the operations of the branch, agency or establishment, be deemed to be domiciled in that Member State."

47.021 Article 12 provides that in respect of liability insurance or insurance of immovable property, the insurer may also be sued in the courts of the place where the harmful event occurred. The same applies if movable and immovable property are covered by the same insurance policy and both are adversely affected by the same contingency. This is not of much relevance in the context of shipping but may be relevant in the context of port law.

47.022 Article 13 deals with liability insurance. It provides:

> "1. In respect of liability insurance, the insurer may also, if the law of the court permits it, be joined in proceedings which the injured party has brought against the insured.
> 2. Articles 10, 11 and 12 shall apply to actions brought by the injured party directly against the insurer, where such direct actions are permitted.
> 3. If the law governing such direct actions provides that the policyholder or the insured may be joined as a party to the action, the same court shall have jurisdiction over them."

47.023 Article 14 provides an exception to Article 13(3). Article 14 states:

> "1. Without prejudice to Article 13(3), an insurer may bring proceedings only in the courts of the Member State in which the defendant is domiciled, irrespective of whether he is the policyholder, the insured or a beneficiary.
> 2. The provisions of this Section shall not affect the right to bring a counter-claim in the court in which, in accordance with this Section, the original claim is pending."

47.024 Article 15 provides:

> "The provisions of this Section may be departed from only by an agreement:
>
>> (1) which is entered into after the dispute has arisen;
>> (2) which allows the policyholder, the insured or a beneficiary to bring proceedings in courts other than those indicated in this Section;
>> (3) which is concluded between a policyholder and an insurer, both of whom are at the time of conclusion of the contract domiciled or habitually resident in the same Member State, and which has the effect of conferring jurisdiction on the courts of that Member State

---

52 On Art. 6, see para. 47.015.
53 On point 5 of Art. 7, see para. 47.017.

even if the harmful event were to occur abroad, provided that such an agreement is not contrary to the law of that Member State;

(4) which is concluded with a policyholder who is not domiciled in a Member State, except in so far as the insurance is compulsory or relates to immovable property in a Member State; or

(5) which relates to a contract of insurance in so far as it covers one or more of the risks set out in Article 16."

Article 15(5) must be read in conjunction with Article 16 which is directly relevant to shipping matters.

47.025 Article 15(5) – which is also important in a shipping context – is elaborated upon in Article 16 which provides:

"The following are the risks referred to in point 5 of Article 15:

(1) any loss of or damage to:

   (a) seagoing ships, installations situated offshore or on the high seas, or aircraft, arising from perils which relate to their use for commercial purposes;

   (b) goods in transit other than passengers' baggage where the transit consists of or includes carriage by such ships or aircraft;

(2) any liability, other than for bodily injury to passengers or loss of or damage to their baggage:

   (a) arising out of the use or operation of ships, installations or aircraft as referred to in point 1(a) in so far as, in respect of the latter, the law of the Member State in which such aircraft are registered does not prohibit agreements on jurisdiction regarding insurance of such risks;

   (b) for loss or damage caused by goods in transit as described in point 1(b);

(3) any financial loss connected with the use or operation of ships, installations or aircraft as referred to in point 1(a), in particular loss of freight or charter-hire;

(4) any risk or interest connected with any of those referred to in points 1 to 3;

(5) notwithstanding points 1 to 4, all 'large risks' as defined in Directive 2009/138/EC of the European Parliament and of the Council of 25 November 2009 on the taking-up and pursuit of the business of Insurance and Reinsurance (Solvency II)."[54]

Consumer contracts

47.026 Section 4 ("Consumer Contracts") deals with jurisdiction over consumer contracts but it has limited relevance for shipping other than Article 17(3) which is of some limited significance (e.g. cruise trips). Article 17 provides:

"1. In matters relating to a contract concluded by a person, the consumer, for a purpose which can be regarded as being outside his trade or profession, jurisdiction shall be determined by this Section, without prejudice to Article 6 and point 5 of Article 7, if:

   (a) it is a contract for the sale of goods on instalment credit terms;

   (b) it is a contract for a loan repayable by instalments, or for any other form of credit, made to finance the sale of goods; or

   (c) in all other cases, the contract has been concluded with a person who pursues commercial or professional activities in the Member State of the consumer's domicile or,

---

54 OJ L335/1, 17 December 2009.

by any means, directs such activities to that Member State or to several States including that Member State, and the contract falls within the scope of such activities.

2. Where a consumer enters into a contract with a party who is not domiciled in a Member State but has a branch, agency or other establishment in one of the Member States, that party shall, in disputes arising out of the operations of the branch, agency or establishment, be deemed to be domiciled in that Member State.

3. This Section shall not apply to a contract of transport other than a contract which, for an inclusive price, provides for a combination of travel and accommodation."

47.027 Article 18 aims at easing the ability of consumers to bring proceedings to vindicate their positions. It provides:

"1. A consumer may bring proceedings against the other party to a contract either in the courts of the Member State in which that party is domiciled or, regardless of the domicile of the other party, in the courts for the place where the consumer is domiciled.

2. Proceedings may be brought against a consumer by the other party to the contract only in the courts of the Member State in which the consumer is domiciled.

3. This Article shall not affect the right to bring a counter-claim in the court in which, in accordance with this Section, the original claim is pending."

47.028 Article 19 provides that the provisions of the section on jurisdiction over consumer contracts may be departed from only by an agreement: (1) which is entered into after the dispute has arisen; (2) which allows the consumer to bring proceedings in courts other than those indicated in the Section; or (3) which is entered into by the consumer and the other party to the contract, both of whom are at the time of conclusion of the contract domiciled or habitually resident in the same Member State, and which confers jurisdiction on the courts of that Member State, provided that such an agreement is not contrary to the law of that Member State.

Employment contracts

47.029 Section 5 is entitled "Jurisdiction over individual contracts of employment". Article 20 provides:

"1. In matters relating to individual contracts of employment, jurisdiction shall be determined by this Section, without prejudice to Article 6, point 5 of Article 7 and, in the case of proceedings brought against an employer, point 1 of Article 8.

2. Where an employee enters into an individual contract of employment with an employer who is not domiciled in a Member State but has a branch, agency or other establishment in one of the Member States, the employer shall, in disputes arising out of the operations of the branch, agency or establishment, be deemed to be domiciled in that Member State."

47.030 Article 21 then provides in the context of employment:

"1. An employer domiciled in a Member State may be sued:

    (a) in the courts of the Member State in which he is domiciled; or
    (b) in another Member State:

        (i) in the courts for the place where or from where the employee habitually carries out his work or in the courts for the last place where he did so; or
        (ii) if the employee does not or did not habitually carry out his work in any one country, in the courts for the place where the business which engaged the employee is or was situated.

2. An employer not domiciled in a Member State may be sued in a court of a Member State in accordance with point (b) of paragraph 1."

47.031 Article 22 deals with proceedings instituted by employees:

"1. An employer may bring proceedings only in the courts of the Member State in which the employee is domiciled.
2. The provisions of this Section shall not affect the right to bring a counter-claim in the court in which, in accordance with this Section, the original claim is pending."

Article 22 helps to protect the position of the (usually weaker) employee who is usually the weaker party in the employer–employee relationship.

47.032 Article 23 states that the provisions of Section 5 may be departed from only by an agreement: (1) which is entered into *after* the dispute has arisen; or (2) which allows the employee to bring proceedings in courts other than those indicated in this Section.

Exclusive jurisdiction

47.033 Section 6 is entitled "Exclusive Jurisdiction". Article 24 confers jurisdiction on Member State courts, regardless of domicile, in respect of certain types of proceedings. This article is yet another exception. The article provides:

"The following courts of a Member State shall have exclusive jurisdiction, regardless of the domicile of the parties:

(1) in proceedings which have as their object rights *in rem* in immovable property or tenancies of immovable property, the courts of the Member State in which the property is situated.
    However, in proceedings which have as their object tenancies of immovable property concluded for temporary private use for a maximum period of six consecutive months, the courts of the Member State in which the defendant is domiciled shall also have jurisdiction, provided that the tenant is a natural person and that the landlord and the tenant are domiciled in the same Member State;
(2) in proceedings which have as their object the validity of the constitution, the nullity or the dissolution of companies or other legal persons or associations of natural or legal persons, or the validity of the decisions of their organs, the courts of the Member State in which the company, legal person or association has its seat. In order to determine that seat, the court shall apply its rules of private international law;[55]
(3) in proceedings which have as their object the validity of entries in public registers, the courts of the Member State in which the register is kept;
(4) in proceedings concerned with the registration or validity of patents, trade marks, designs, or other similar rights required to be deposited or registered, irrespective of whether the issue is raised by way of an action or as a defence, the courts of the Member State in which the deposit or registration has been applied for, has taken place or is under the terms of an instrument of the Union or an international convention deemed to have taken place.
    Without prejudice to the jurisdiction of the European Patent Office under the Convention on the Grant of European Patents, signed at Munich on 5 October 1973, the courts of each Member State shall have exclusive jurisdiction in proceedings concerned with the registration or validity of any European patent granted for that Member State;
(5) in proceedings concerned with the enforcement of judgments, the courts of the Member State In which the judgment has been or is to be enforced."

---

55 Ed., see Ferrexpo AG v Gilson Investments Ltd & Ors [2012] EWHC 721.

In practice, Article 24(5) is the most relevant provision in Article 24 in a shipping context.

Prorogation of jurisdiction

47.034 Section 7 of Chapter II ("Jurisdiction") is entitled "Prorogation of Jurisdiction".

47.035 Article 25 confers exclusive jurisdiction on any Member State that the parties have agreed should have jurisdiction to settle any dispute that has arisen or which may arise in connection with a particular legal relationship. The article states:

> "1. If the parties, regardless of their domicile, have agreed that a court or the courts of a Member State are to have jurisdiction to settle any disputes which have arisen or which may arise in connection with a particular legal relationship, that court or those courts shall have jurisdiction, unless the agreement is null and void as to its substantive validity under the law of that Member State. Such jurisdiction shall be exclusive unless the parties have agreed otherwise. The agreement conferring jurisdiction shall be either:
>
> > (a) in writing or evidenced in writing;
> > (b) in a form which accords with practices which the parties have established between themselves; or
> > (c) in international trade or commerce, in a form which accords with a usage of which the parties are or ought to have been aware and which in such trade or commerce is widely known to, and regularly observed by, parties to contracts of the type involved in the particular trade or commerce concerned.
>
> 2. Any communication by electronic means which provides a durable record of the agreement shall be equivalent to 'writing'.
> 3. The court or courts of a Member State on which a trust instrument has conferred jurisdiction shall have exclusive jurisdiction in any proceedings brought against a settlor, trustee or beneficiary, if relations between those persons or their rights or obligations under the trust are involved.
> 4. Agreements or provisions of a trust instrument conferring jurisdiction shall have no legal force if they are contrary to Articles 15, 19 or 23, or if the courts whose jurisdiction they purport to exclude have exclusive jurisdiction by virtue of Article 24.
> 5. An agreement conferring jurisdiction which forms part of a contract shall be treated as an agreement independent of the other terms of the contract.
>
> The validity of the agreement conferring jurisdiction cannot be contested solely on the ground that the contract is not valid."

47.036 Article 25 is very relevant in commercial life and hence in shipping because commercial parties invariably choose the courts or the Member State which would have jurisdiction to deal with issues. A jurisdiction clause in a charterparty would fall within the category of an agreement in writing.[56] If there is a jurisdiction clause in a written bill of lading where the contract is oral then the issue is more complicated: the CJEU opined in *Tilly Russ*:[57]

> "1. A jurisdiction clause contained in the printed conditions on a bill of lading satisfies the conditions ...:

---

56 Okretowe v Rallo Vito & C. Snc & Anr [2009] EWHC 2249 (Comm), [2010] 1 Lloyd's Rep 384.
57 Case 71/83 Partenreederei ms. Tilly Russ and Ernest Russ v NV Haven- & Vervoerbedrijf Nova and NV Goeminne Hout [1984] ECR-2417, ECLI:EU:C:1984:217.

If the agreement of both parties to the conditions containing that clause has been expressed in writing, or

If the jurisdiction clause has been the subject-matter of a prior oral agreement between the parties expressly relating to that clause, in which case the bill of lading, signed by the carrier, must be regarded as confirmation in writing of the oral agreement, or

If the bill of lading comes within the framework of a continuing business relationship between the parties, in so far as it is thereby established that that relationship is governed by general conditions containing the jurisdiction clause;

2. As regards the relationship between the carrier and a third party holding the bill of lading, the conditions ... are satisfied if the jurisdiction clause has been adjudged valid as between the carrier and the shipper and if, by virtue of the relevant national law, the third party, upon acquiring the bill of lading, succeeded to the shipper's rights and obligations."

47.037 Under the previous Brussels Regulation, an agreement would be recognised for its purposes only where at least one party was EU domiciled. However, Article 25 of the Recast Regulation is more embracive. So, for example, a dispute between an Austrian party and a Russian domiciled party could be made subject to being decided by a German court if that is what the parties want and the German court accepts jurisdiction.

47.038 Article 26 of the regulation provides:

"1. Apart from jurisdiction derived from other provisions of this Regulation, a court of a Member State before which a defendant enters an appearance shall have jurisdiction. This rule shall not apply where appearance was entered to contest the jurisdiction, or where another court has exclusive jurisdiction by virtue of Article 24.

2. In matters referred to in Sections 3, 4 or 5 where the policyholder, the insured, a beneficiary of the insurance contract, the injured party, the consumer or the employee is the defendant, the court shall, before assuming jurisdiction under paragraph 1, ensure that the defendant is informed of his right to contest the jurisdiction of the court and of the consequences of entering or not entering an appearance."

Article 26(2) is designed to give some protection to weaker parties in certain circumstances. The CJEU held in *Elefanten Schuh GmbH v Pierre Jacqmain*[58] that Article 26 takes priority over that of Article 25.

Examination as to jurisdiction and admissibility

47.039 Section 8 (entitled "Examination as to Jurisdiction and Admissibility") deals with a variety of issues and is very relevant for present purposes. Article 27 provides that where a Member State court is seised of a claim which is principally concerned with a matter over which the courts of another Member State have exclusive jurisdiction by virtue of Article 24, it *shall* declare of its own motion that it has no jurisdiction (i.e. it has no discretion).

47.040 Article 28 of the regulation provides:

"1. Where a defendant domiciled in one Member State is sued in a court of another Member State and does not enter an appearance, the court shall declare of its own motion that it has no jurisdiction unless its jurisdiction is derived from the provisions of this Regulation.

2. The court shall stay the proceedings so long as it is not shown that the defendant has been able to receive the document instituting the proceedings or an equivalent document in

---

58 Case 150/80 [1981] ECR-1671, ECLI:EU:C:1981:148.

sufficient time to enable him to arrange for his defence, or that all necessary steps have been taken to this end.

3. Article 19 of Regulation (EC) No 1393/2007 of the European Parliament and of the Council of 13 November 2007 on the service in the Member States of judicial and extrajudicial documents in civil or commercial matters (service of documents) ... shall apply instead of paragraph 2 of this Article if the document instituting the proceedings or an equivalent document had to be transmitted from one Member State to another pursuant to that Regulation.

4. Where Regulation ... 1393/2007 is not applicable, Article 15 of the Hague Convention of 15 November 1965 on the Service Abroad of Judicial and Extrajudicial Documents in Civil or Commercial Matters shall apply if the document instituting the proceedings or an equivalent document had to be transmitted abroad pursuant to that Convention."

Lis pendens (or related articles)

47.041 Section 9 of Chapter II ("Jurisdiction") deals with the very difficult issue of *lis pendens* or related actions. Put another way, the issue relates to a situation where there are proceedings involving the same cause of action pending in more than one jurisdiction. There is an obvious conflict of jurisdiction in such circumstances with the possibility of contradictory outcomes. Recitals 21–23 of the Recast Regulation give some useful background:

"(21) In the interests of the harmonious administration of justice it is necessary to minimise the possibility of concurrent proceedings and to ensure that irreconcilable judgments will not be given in different Member States. There should be a clear and effective mechanism for resolving cases of *lis pendens* and related actions, and for obviating problems flowing from national differences as to the determination of the time when a case is regarded as pending. For the purposes of this Regulation, that time should be defined autonomously.

(22) However, in order to enhance the effectiveness of exclusive choice-of-court agreements and to avoid abusive litigation tactics, it is necessary to provide for an exception to the general *lis pendens* rule in order to deal satisfactorily with a particular situation in which concurrent proceedings may arise. This is the situation where a court not designated in an exclusive choice-of-court agreement has been seised of proceedings and the designated court is seised subsequently of proceedings involving the same cause of action and between the same parties. In such a case, the court first seised should be required to stay its proceedings as soon as the designated court has been seised and until such time as the latter court declares that it has no jurisdiction under the exclusive choice-of-court agreement. This is to ensure that, in such a situation, the designated court has priority to decide on the validity of the agreement and on the extent to which the agreement applies to the dispute pending before it. The designated court should be able to proceed irrespective of whether the non-designated court has already decided on the stay of proceedings.

This exception should not cover situations where the parties have entered into conflicting exclusive choice-of-court agreements or where a court designated in an exclusive choice-of-court agreement has been seised first. In such cases, the general *lis pendens* rule of this Regulation should apply.

(23) This Regulation should provide for a flexible mechanism allowing the courts of the Member States to take into account proceedings pending before the courts of third States, considering in particular whether a judgment of a third State will be capable of recognition and enforcement in the Member State concerned under the law of that Member State and the proper administration of justice."

47.042 The Recast Regulation sought to deal with the so-called "torpedo" action. Such an action was possible under the previous Brussels Regulation. It involved the following scenario: although the parties agreed an exclusive jurisdiction clause, one of the parties could ignore that clause and institute proceedings in a different slower or more awkward (from the defendant's perspective) jurisdiction to frustrate the plaintiff's actions. Such an action was possible because the Brussels Regulation provided that where there were proceedings involving the same parties and the same cause of action then any court other than the court first seised had to stay its proceedings until the court first seised decided whether it had jurisdiction to hear the action so by the slower/more awkward court being seised first, the proceedings were frustrated. The Recast Regulation seeks to close that loophole by virtue of Article 31(2).

47.043 Articles 29–32 of the Recast Regulation address the issue (including analysing the situation where there is *lis pendens* between a Member State and a third State). It is useful to parse each article separately.

47.044 Article 29 provides:

> "1. Without prejudice to Article 31(2),[59] where proceedings involving the same cause of action and between the same parties are brought in the courts of different Member States, any court other than the court first seised shall of its own motion stay its proceedings until such time as the jurisdiction of the court first seised is established.
> 2. In cases referred to in paragraph 1, upon request by a court seised of the dispute, any other court seised shall without delay inform the former court of the date when it was seised in accordance with Article 32.
> 3. Where the jurisdiction of the court first seised is established, any court other than the court first seised shall decline jurisdiction in favour of that court."

As a general rule, under Article 29(1), there must be the "same cause of action" and the "same parties". In terms of the same cause of action, it does not have to be absolutely identical[60] – that may be impossible anyway because of the different legal regimes – so the test is whether the two actions have the same legal and factual matrix as well as the same object or purpose.[61]

47.045 Article 30 goes on to deal with the issue of related actions as between Member States (i.e. there is not the same cause of action but they are related):

> "1. Where related actions are pending in the courts of different Member States, any court other than the court first seised may stay its proceedings.
> 2. Where the action in the court first seised is pending at first instance, any other court may also, on the application of one of the parties, decline jurisdiction if the court first seised has jurisdiction over the actions in question and its law permits the consolidation thereof.
> 3. For the purposes of this Article, actions are deemed to be related where they are so closely connected that it is expedient to hear and determine them together to avoid the risk of irreconcilable judgments resulting from separate proceedings."

47.046 Article 31 of the Recast Regulation provides:

> "1. Where actions come within the exclusive jurisdiction of several courts, any court other than the court first seised shall decline jurisdiction in favour of that court.

---

59 Ed., Art. 31(2) provides that without prejudice to Art. 26 where a court of a Member State on which an agreement as referred to in Art. 25 confers exclusive jurisdiction is seised, any court of another Member State shall stay the proceedings until such time as the court seised on the basis of the agreement declares that it has no jurisdiction under the agreement."

60 Case 144/86 Gubisch v Guilio Palumbo [1987] ECR 4861, ECLI:EU:C:1987:528.

61 Case C-406/92 Owners of the cargo lately laden on board the ship "Tatry" v Owners of the ship "Maciej Rataj" [1994] ECR I-05439, ECLI:EU:C:1994:400, [1995] 1 Lloyd's Rep 302, para. 41. See also Case C-39/02 Maersk Oil & Gas AS [2004] ECR I-9657, ECLI:EU:C:2004:615, [2005] 1 Lloyd's Rep 210.

2. Without prejudice to Article 26, where a court of a Member State on which an agreement as referred to in Article 25 confers exclusive jurisdiction is seised, any court of another Member State shall stay the proceedings until such time as the court seised on the basis of the agreement declares that it has no jurisdiction under the agreement.

3. Where the court designated in the agreement has established jurisdiction in accordance with the agreement, any court of another Member State shall decline jurisdiction in favour of that court.

4. Paragraphs 2 and 3 shall not apply to matters referred to in Sections 3, 4 or 5 where the policyholder, the insured, a beneficiary of the insurance contract, the injured party, the consumer or the employee is the claimant and the agreement is not valid under a provision contained within those Sections."

47.047 Article 31 is aimed at solving the torpedo problem. It is probably not a perfect solution. Proceedings must be instituted in the agreed chosen court. The new rule applies only where there is an exclusive jurisdiction clause. There is no doubt about the rule applying in the case of a unilateral jurisdiction clause.[62]

47.048 Article 32 of the Recast Regulation provides:

"1. For the purposes of this Section, a court shall be deemed to be seised:

   (a) at the time when the document instituting the proceedings or an equivalent document is lodged with the court, provided that the claimant has not subsequently failed to take the steps he was required to take to have service effected on the defendant; or

   (b) if the document has to be served before being lodged with the court, at the time when it is received by the authority responsible for service, provided that the claimant has not subsequently failed to take the steps he was required to take to have the document lodged with the court.

The authority responsible for service referred to in point (b) shall be the first authority receiving the documents to be served.

2. The court, or the authority responsible for service, referred to in paragraph 1, shall note, respectively, the date of the lodging of the document instituting the proceedings or the equivalent document, or the date of receipt of the documents to be served."

Pending proceedings in a third State

47.049 So-called "third State proceedings" are often difficult in practice – Article 33–34 of the Recast Regulation attempt to deal with the issue.

47.050 Article 33 of the Recast Regulation deals with *pending proceedings* in a court of a third State:

"1. Where jurisdiction is based on Article 4 or on Articles 7, 8 or 9 and proceedings are pending before a court of a third State at the time when a court in a Member State is seised of an action involving the same cause of action and between the same parties as the proceedings in the court of the third State, the court of the Member State may stay the proceedings if:

   (a) it is expected that the court of the third State will give a judgment capable of recognition and, where applicable, of enforcement in that Member State; and

   (b) the court of the Member State is satisfied that a stay is necessary for the proper administration of justice.

---

62 A unilateral jurisdiction clause arises where one party has an obligation to bring proceedings in a particular jurisdiction but the other party has the option to sue in several jurisdictions.

2. The court of the Member State may continue the proceedings at any time if:

    (a) the proceedings in the court of the third State are themselves stayed or discontinued;

    (b) it appears to the court of the Member State that the proceedings in the court of the third State are unlikely to be concluded within a reasonable time; or

    (c) the continuation of the proceedings is required for the proper administration of justice.

3. The court of the Member State shall dismiss the proceedings if the proceedings in the court of the third State are concluded and have resulted in a judgment capable of recognition and, where applicable, of enforcement in that Member State.

4. The court of the Member State shall apply this Article on the application of one of the parties or, where possible under national law, of its own motion."

47.051 Article 34 of the Recast Regulation deals with pending proceedings in a court of a third State. It provides:

"1. Where jurisdiction is based on Article 4 or on Articles 7, 8 or 9 and an action is pending before a court of a third State at the time when a court in a Member State is seised of an action which is related to the action in the court of the third State, the court of the Member State may stay the proceedings if:

    (a) it is expedient to hear and determine the related actions together to avoid the risk of irreconcilable judgments resulting from separate proceedings;

    (b) it is expected that the court of the third State will give a judgment capable of recognition and, where applicable, of enforcement in that Member State; and

    (c) the court of the Member State is satisfied that a stay is necessary for the proper administration of justice.

2. The court of the Member State may continue the proceedings at any time if:

    (a) it appears to the court of the Member State that there is no longer a risk of irreconcilable judgments;

    (b) the proceedings in the court of the third State are themselves stayed or discontinued;

    (c) it appears to the court of the Member State that the proceedings in the court of the third State are unlikely to be concluded within a reasonable time; or

    (d) the continuation of the proceedings is required for the proper administration of justice.

3. The court of the Member State may dismiss the proceedings if the proceedings in the court of the third State are concluded and have resulted in a judgment capable of recognition and, where applicable, of enforcement in that Member State.

4. The court of the Member State shall apply this Article on the application of one of the parties or, where possible under national law, of its own motion."

Provisional and protective measures

47.052 Section 10 of Chapter II of the regulation is entitled "Provisional, including protective, measures". It contains a single article. Article 35 provides quite simply that application may be made to the courts of a Member State for such provisional, including protective, measures as may be available under the law of that Member State, even if the courts of another Member State have jurisdiction as to the substance of the matter – an example would be a freezing order.

D. RECOGNITION AND ENFORCEMENT OF JUDGMENTS

47.053 Chapter III of the convention is entitled "Recognition and Enforcement". Section 1 of Chapter III is entitled "Recognition" of judgments.

47.054 Article 36 provides:

"1. A judgment given in a Member State shall be recognised in the other Member States without any special procedure being required.
2. Any interested party may, in accordance with the procedure provided for in Subsection 2 of Section 3, apply for a decision that there are no grounds for refusal of recognition as referred to in Article 45.
3. If the outcome of proceedings in a court of a Member State depends on the determination of an incidental question of refusal of recognition, that court shall have jurisdiction over that question."

47.055 Article 37 states:

"1. A party who wishes to invoke in a Member State a judgment given in another Member State shall produce:

    (a) a copy of the judgment which satisfies the conditions necessary to establish its authenticity; and
    (b) the certificate issued pursuant to Article 53.[63]

2. The court or authority before which a judgment given in another Member State is invoked may, where necessary, require the party invoking it to provide, in accordance with Article 57, a translation or a transliteration of the contents of the certificate referred to in point (b) of paragraph 1. The court or authority may require the party to provide a translation of the judgment instead of a translation of the contents of the certificate if it is unable to proceed without such a translation."

47.056 Article 38 of the Recast Regulation provides:

"The court or authority before which a judgment given in another Member State is invoked may suspend the proceedings, in whole or in part, if:

    (a) the judgment is challenged in the Member State of origin; or
    (b) an application has been submitted for a decision that there are no grounds for refusal of recognition as referred to in Article 45 or for a decision that the recognition is to be refused on the basis of one of those grounds."

47.057 Section 2 of Chapter III ("Recognition and Enforcement") deals with enforcement.

47.058 Article 39 provides that a judgment given in a Member State which is enforceable in that Member State must be enforceable in the other Member States without any declaration of enforceability being required.

47.059 Article 40 goes on to provide that an enforceable judgment must carry with it, by operation of law, the power to proceed to any protective measures which exist under the law of the Member State addressed.

47.060 Article 41 provides:

---

[63] Ed., Art. 53 provides that the court of origin, must at the request of any interested party, issue the certificate with the form set out in Annex I of the Recast Regulation.

"1. Subject to the provisions of this Section, the procedure for the enforcement of judgments given in another Member State shall be governed by the law of the Member State addressed. A judgment given in a Member State which is enforceable in the Member State addressed shall be enforced there under the same conditions as a judgment given in the Member State addressed.

2. Notwithstanding paragraph 1, the grounds for refusal or of suspension of enforcement under the law of the Member State addressed shall apply in so far as they are not incompatible with the grounds referred to in Article 45.

3. The party seeking the enforcement of a judgment given in another Member State shall not be required to have a postal address in the Member State addressed. Nor shall that party be required to have an authorised representative in the Member State addressed unless such a representative is mandatory irrespective of the nationality or the domicile of the parties."

47.061 Article 42 of the Recast Regulation provides:

"1. For the purposes of enforcement in a Member State of a judgment given in another Member State, the applicant shall provide the competent enforcement authority with:

(a) a copy of the judgment which satisfies the conditions necessary to establish its authenticity; and

(b) the certificate issued pursuant to Article 53, certifying that the judgment is enforceable and containing an extract of the judgment as well as, where appropriate, relevant information on the recoverable costs of the proceedings and the calculation of interest.

2. For the purposes of enforcement in a Member State of a judgment given in another Member State ordering a provisional, including a protective, measure, the applicant shall provide the competent enforcement authority with:

(a) a copy of the judgment which satisfies the conditions necessary to establish its authenticity;

(b) the certificate issued pursuant to Article 53, containing a description of the measure and certifying that:

(i) the court has jurisdiction as to the substance of the matter;
(ii) the judgment is enforceable in the Member State of origin; and

(c) where the measure was ordered without the defendant being summoned to appear, proof of service of the judgment.

3. The competent enforcement authority may, where necessary, require the applicant to provide, in accordance with Article 57, a translation or a transliteration of the contents of the certificate.

4. The competent enforcement authority may require the applicant to provide a translation of the judgment only if it is unable to proceed without such a translation."

47.062 Article 43 of the Recast Regulation provides:

"1. Where enforcement is sought of a judgment given in another Member State, the certificate issued pursuant to Article 53 shall be served on the person against whom the enforcement is sought prior to the first enforcement measure. The certificate shall be accompanied by the judgment, if not already served on that person.

2. Where the person against whom enforcement is sought is domiciled in a Member State other than the Member State of origin, he may request a translation of the judgment in order to contest the enforcement if the judgment is not written in or accompanied by a translation into either of the following languages:

(a) a language which he understands; or

(b) the official language of the Member State in which he is domiciled or, where there are several official languages in that Member State, the official language or one of the official languages of the place where he is domiciled.

Where a translation of the judgment is requested under the first subparagraph, no measures of enforcement may be taken other than protective measures until that translation has been provided to the person against whom enforcement is sought.

This paragraph shall not apply if the judgment has already been served on the person against whom enforcement is sought in one of the languages referred to in the first subparagraph or is accompanied by a translation into one of those languages.

3.   This Article shall not apply to the enforcement of a protective measure in a judgment or where the person seeking enforcement proceeds to protective measures in accordance with Article 40."

47.063 Article 44 of the Recast Regulation provides:

"1. In the event of an application for refusal of enforcement of a judgment pursuant to Subsection 2 of Section 3, the court in the Member State addressed may, on the application of the person against whom enforcement is sought:

(a) limit the enforcement proceedings to protective measures;

(b) make enforcement conditional on the provision of such security as it shall determine; or

(c) suspend, either wholly or in part, the enforcement proceedings.

2.   The competent authority in the Member State addressed shall, on the application of the person against whom enforcement is sought, suspend the enforcement proceedings where the enforceability of the judgment is suspended in the Member State of origin."

47.064 Section 3 of Chapter III ("Recognition and Enforcement") deals with the refusal of recognition and enforcement of judgments. Subsection 1 of Section 3 is entitled "refusal of recognition".

47.065 Article 45 provides:

"1. On the application of any interested party, the recognition of a judgment shall be refused:

(a) if such recognition is manifestly contrary to public policy (*ordre public*) in the Member State addressed;

(b) where the judgment was given in default of appearance, if the defendant was not served with the document which instituted the proceedings or with an equivalent document in sufficient time and in such a way as to enable him to arrange for his defence, unless the defendant failed to commence proceedings to challenge the judgment when it was possible for him to do so;

(c) if the judgment is irreconcilable with a judgment given between the same parties in the Member State addressed;

(d) if the judgment is irreconcilable with an earlier judgment given in another Member State or in a third State involving the same cause of action and between the same parties, provided that the earlier judgment fulfils the conditions necessary for its recognition in the Member State addressed; or

(e) if the judgment conflicts with:

(i)   Sections 3, 4 or 5 of Chapter II where the policyholder, the insured, a beneficiary of the insurance contract, the injured party, the consumer or the employee was the defendant; or

(ii) Section 6 of Chapter II.

2. In its examination of the grounds of jurisdiction referred to in point (e) of paragraph 1, the court to which the application was submitted shall be bound by the findings of fact on which the court of origin based its jurisdiction.

3. Without prejudice to point (e) of paragraph 1, the jurisdiction of the court of origin may not be reviewed. The test of public policy referred to in point (a) of paragraph 1 may not be applied to the rules relating to jurisdiction.

4. The application for refusal of recognition shall be made in accordance with the procedures provided for in Subsection 2 and, where appropriate, Section 4."

47.066 Subsection 2 is entitled "refusal of enforcement".

47.067 Article 46 provides that on the application of the person against whom enforcement is sought, the enforcement of a judgment shall be refused where one of the grounds referred to in Article 45 is found to exist.

47.068 Article 47 provides:

"1. The application for refusal of enforcement shall be submitted to the court which the Member State concerned has communicated to the Commission pursuant to point (a) of Article 75 as the court to which the application is to be submitted.

2. The procedure for refusal of enforcement shall, in so far as it is not covered by this Regulation, be governed by the law of the Member State addressed.

3. The applicant shall provide the court with a copy of the judgment and, where necessary, a translation or transliteration of it.

   The court may dispense with the production of the documents referred to in the first subparagraph if it already possesses them or if it considers it unreasonable to require the applicant to provide them. In the latter case, the court may require the other party to provide those documents.

4. The party seeking the refusal of enforcement of a judgment given in another Member State shall not be required to have a postal address in the Member State addressed. Nor shall that party be required to have an authorised representative in the Member State addressed unless such a representative is mandatory irrespective of the nationality or the domicile of the parties."

47.069 Article 48 of the Recast Regulation provides that the court must decide on the application for refusal of enforcement without delay.

47.070 Article 49(1) provides that the decision on the application for refusal of enforcement may be appealed against by either party. Article 49(2) provides that the appeal is to be lodged with the court which the Member State concerned has communicated to the Commission pursuant to point (b) of Article 75 as the court with which such an appeal is to be lodged.

47.071 Article 50 states that the decision given on the appeal may only be contested by an appeal where the courts with which any further appeal is to be lodged have been communicated by the Member State concerned to the Commission pursuant to point (c) of Article 75.

47.072 Article 51 states:

"1. The court to which an application for refusal of enforcement is submitted or the court which hears an appeal lodged under Article 49 or Article 50 may stay the proceedings if an ordinary appeal has been lodged against the judgment in the Member State of origin or if the time for such an appeal has not yet expired. In the latter case, the court may specify the time within which such an appeal is to be lodged.

2. Where the judgment was given in Ireland, Cyprus or the United Kingdom, any form of appeal available in the Member State of origin shall be treated as an ordinary appeal for the purposes of paragraph 1."

47.073 Section 4 of Chapter III ("Recognition and Enforcement") deals with common provisions.

47.074 Article 52 provides that under no circumstances may a judgment given in a Member State be reviewed as to its substance in the Member State addressed.

47.075 Article 53 provides that the court of origin shall, at the request of any interested party, issue the certificate using the form set out in Annex I to the Recast Regulation.

47.076 Article 54 provides:

"1. If a judgment contains a measure or an order which is not known in the law of the Member State addressed, that measure or order shall, to the extent possible, be adapted to a measure or an order known in the law of that Member State which has equivalent effects attached to it and which pursues similar aims and interests.

Such adaptation shall not result in effects going beyond those provided for in the law of the Member State of origin.

2. Any party may challenge the adaptation of the measure or order before a court.

3. If necessary, the party invoking the judgment or seeking its enforcement may be required to provide a translation or a transliteration of the judgment."

47.077 Article 55 provides that a judgment given in a Member State which orders a payment by way of a penalty shall be enforceable in the Member State addressed only if the amount of the payment has been finally determined by the court of origin.

47.078 Article 56 states that no security, bond or deposit, however described, shall be required of a party who in one Member State applies for the enforcement of a judgment given in another Member State on the ground that he is a foreign national or that he is not domiciled or resident in the Member State addressed. This is designed to make enforcement easier.

47.079 Article 57 of the Recast Regulation provides:

"1. When a translation or a transliteration is required under this Regulation, such translation or transliteration shall be into the official language of the Member State concerned or, where there are several official languages in that Member State, into the official language or one of the official languages of court proceedings of the place where a judgment given in another Member State is invoked or an application is made, in accordance with the law of that Member State.

2. For the purposes of the forms referred to in Articles 53 and 60, translations or transliterations may also be into any other official language or languages of the institutions of the Union that the Member State concerned has indicated it can accept.

3. Any translation made under this Regulation shall be done by a person qualified to do translations in one of the Member States."

47.080 Chapter IV of the Recast Regulation is entitled "Authentic Instruments and Court Settlements".

47.081 Article 58 provides:

"1. An authentic instrument which is enforceable in the Member State of origin shall be enforceable in the other Member States without any declaration of enforceability being required. Enforcement of the authentic instrument may be refused only if such enforcement is manifestly contrary to public policy (*ordre public*) in the Member State addressed.

The provisions of Section 2, Subsection 2 of Section 3, and Section 4 of Chapter III shall apply as appropriate to authentic instruments.

2. The authentic instrument produced must satisfy the conditions necessary to establish its authenticity in the Member State of origin."

47.082 Article 59 provides that a court settlement which is enforceable in the Member State of origin shall be enforced in the other Member States under the same conditions as authentic instruments.

47.083 Article 60 provides that the competent authority or court of the Member State of origin shall, at the request of any interested party, issue the certificate using the form set out in Annex II containing a summary of the enforceable obligation recorded in the authentic instrument or of the agreement between the parties recorded in the court settlement.

47.084 Chapter V of the Recast Regulation is entitled "General Provisions".

47.085 Article 61 provides that no legalisation or other similar formality shall be required for documents issued in a Member State in the context of this regulation.

47.086 Article 64 provides:

"Without prejudice to any more favourable provisions of national laws, persons domiciled in a Member State who are being prosecuted in the criminal courts of another Member State of which they are not nationals for an offence which was not intentionally committed may be defended by persons qualified to do so, even if they do not appear in person. However, the court seised of the matter may order appearance in person; in the case of failure to appear, a judgment given in the civil action without the person concerned having had the opportunity to arrange for his defence need not be recognised or enforced in the other Member States."

47.087 Article 65 provides:

"1. The jurisdiction specified in point 2 of Article 8 and Article 13 in actions on a warranty or guarantee or in any other third-party proceedings may be resorted to in the Member States included in the list established by the Commission pursuant to point (b) of Article 76(1) and Article 76(2) only in so far as permitted under national law. A person domiciled in another Member State may be invited to join the proceedings before the courts of those Member States pursuant to the rules on third-party notice referred to in that list.

2. Judgments given in a Member State by virtue of point 2 of Article 8 or Article 13 shall be recognised and enforced in accordance with Chapter III in any other Member State. Any effects which judgments given in the Member States included in the list referred to in paragraph 1 may have, in accordance with the law of those Member States, on third parties by application of paragraph 1 shall be recognised in all Member States.

3. The Member States included in the list referred to in paragraph 1 shall, within the framework of the European Judicial Network in civil and commercial matters established by Council Decision 2001/470/EC ... ('the European Judicial Network') provide information on how to determine, in accordance with their national law, the effects of the judgments referred to in the second sentence of paragraph 2."

47.088 Chapter VII deals with the relationship with other instruments. Article 67 provides that the Recast Regulation shall not prejudice the application of provisions governing jurisdiction and the recognition and enforcement of judgments in specific matters which are contained in instruments of the Union or in national legislation harmonised pursuant to such instruments. Article 68(1) provides that the Recast Regulation shall, as between the Member States, supersede the 1968 Brussels Convention, except as regards the territories of the Member States which fall within the territorial scope of that convention and which are excluded from this regulation pursuant to Article 355 of the TFEU. Article 68(2) provides that in so far as this regulation replaces the provisions of the 1968

Brussels Convention between the Member States, any reference to that convention shall be understood as a reference to the regulation.

E. RELATIONSHIP BETWEEN THE RECAST REGULATION AND SPECIALISED CONVENTIONS

47.089 Article 71 of the Recast Regulation deals with the relationship between the Recast Regulation regime and specialised conventions.[64] It is useful, before examining Article 71, to consider the two preceding articles.

47.090 Article 69 of the Recast Regulation provides:

> "Subject to Articles 70 and 71, this Regulation shall, as between the Member States, supersede the conventions that cover the same matters as those to which this Regulation applies. In particular, the conventions included in the list established by the Commission pursuant to point (c) of Article 76(1) and Article 76(2) shall be superseded."

47.091 Article 70 of the Recast Regulation states:

> "1. The conventions referred to in Article 69 shall continue to have effect in relation to matters to which this Regulation does not apply.
> 2. They shall continue to have effect in respect of judgments given, authentic instruments formally drawn up or registered and court settlements approved or concluded before the date of entry into force of Regulation (EC) No 44/2001."

47.092 Article 71 of the Recast Regulation deals with the relationship between this regime and specialised conventions:

> "1. This Regulation shall not affect any conventions to which the Member States are parties and which, in relation to particular matters, govern jurisdiction or the recognition or enforcement of judgments.
> 2. With a view to its uniform interpretation, paragraph 1 shall be applied in the following manner:
>
>   (a) this Regulation shall not prevent a court of a Member State which is party to a convention on a particular matter from assuming jurisdiction in accordance with that convention, even where the defendant is domiciled in another Member State which is not party to that convention. The court hearing the action shall, in any event, apply Article 28 of this Regulation;
>   (b) judgments given in a Member State by a court in the exercise of jurisdiction provided for in a convention on a particular matter shall be recognised and enforced in the other Member States in accordance with this Regulation.
>
> Where a convention on a particular matter to which both the Member State of origin and the Member State addressed are parties lays down conditions for the recognition or enforcement of judgments, those conditions shall apply. In any event, the provisions of this Regulation on recognition and enforcement of judgments may be applied."

---

64 See Case C-148/03 Nürnberger Allgemeine Versicherungs AG v Portbridge Transport International BV [2004] ECR I-10327, ECLI:EU:C:2004:677 and Case C-533/08 TNT Express Nederland BV v AXA Versicherung AG [2010] ECR I-04107, ECLI:EU:C:2010:243.

F. CONCLUSIONS

47.093 This chapter has not been, for reasons of space and relevance, a complete description of the law relating to the Recast Regulation. Instead, it has been an attempt to set out in broad terms the Recast Regulation and it is obvious that the measure has considerable significance for shipping litigation in the EU context.

CHAPTER 48

Brexit

A. INTRODUCTION

48.001 This chapter considers selected[1] implications of Brexit[2] for European Union ("EU") shipping and ports law.[3]

48.002 "Brexit" is the term used to describe the withdrawal or secession of the United Kingdom of Great Britain and Northern Ireland ("UK") as well as Gibraltar from the EU and the European Atomic Energy Community ("EAEC").

48.003 It is widely anticipated that the UK will leave the EU on 29 March 2019 (i.e. Brexit) but it is not inevitable.[4] However, for the purposes of this chapter, it is assumed that the UK will leave the EU on that date and at 23:00 hours (UK time). It is worth noting that all the arrangements relating to Brexit have not been agreed at the time of writing. It is even possible that all arrangements for the UK's withdrawal and the post-Brexit arrangement will not be concluded before the UK actually leaves the EU.[5] This chapter relies on the position as it is understood at the time of writing.

48.004 Brexit would affect the maritime sector more immediately and more obviously than many other economic sectors. If there is more or less trade because of Brexit then the maritime sector will be an obvious indicator by virtue of the levels of trade which would be carried by ships and transported through ports. If there is a diversion in trade

---

1 No chapter could identify all of the implications given the facts that, for example, the final arrangements have not yet been agreed and the scope of EU law is so broad that there is almost no end to the possible implications.

2 On Brexit generally see, among others, Armour and Eidenmüller, Negotiating Brexit (2017); Armstrong, Brexit Time: Leaving the EU – Why, How and When? (2017); Dougan, The UK After Brexit: Legal and Policy Challenges (2017); Fabbrini (ed.), The Law & Politics of Brexit (2017); Hillman and Horlick (eds), Legal Aspects of Brexit: Implications of the United Kingdom's Decision to Withdraw from the European Union (2017); Peers, The Brexit: The Legal Framework for Withdrawal from the EU or Renegotiation of EU Membership (2016); and Tse, Doing Business After Brexit: A Practical Guide to the Legal Changes (2017). See also Clare, Goodwin and Whiteley, Brexit: Why Britain Voted to Leave the European Union (2017); and Evans and Menon, Brexit and British Politics (2017).

3 See Power, "Brexit and Shipping" (2016) 22 JIML 77. See also the presentation by Randolph, "Impact of Brexit on Competition Law in the UK", KNect365 "Competition Law Challenges in the Shipping Sector" Conference, Brussels, 7 March 2018. There are many internet articles on the topic providing contemporary commentary on this evolving subject.

4 The notion that the UK would remain in the EU ("Britstay") or return to the EU ("Britreturn") are not entirely theoretical but the odds are, at the time of writing, against either occurring. It would require various events to occur such as the EU reforming itself, EU being keener on the UK remaining, a change of mind on the part of the UK's population and perhaps a downturn in the fortunes of the UK due to Brexit which could be undone by the UK not leaving or returning to the EU. See MacShane, Brexit, No Exit: Why (in the End) Britain Won't Leave Europe (2017).

5 In many ways, that is not too surprising as EU law has always been a living dynamic body of law. Indeed, on 25 March 1957 when the Treaty of Rome (to establish the European Economic Community ("EEC")) was signed, all of its terms had not been agreed.

patterns (e.g. more or less trade is moving through the UK[6] or, alternatively, by-passing the UK and instead going between EU ports only[7]) then shipping and ports will be barometers of the changes due to Brexit. Equally, if there are more or fewer passengers moving because of Brexit then that could also be evident in the shipping and ports sector. Therefore the shipping and ports sector is a bellwether or early warning system for the impact (whether positive or negative) of Brexit on the economy generally or parts of the economy.

48.005 The essence of the change is that UK shipping and port interests would no longer have the rights and privileges of EU membership because the UK would become, after leaving the EU, a "third country" or "third State" under EU law (i.e. it would no longer be an EU Member State). Those in favour of Brexit would argue that UK shipping and port interests would be rid of the bureaucracy and burden of EU law. However, many of the rules (e.g. those EU environmental and safety rules relating to vessels (of whatever flag) entering EU ports would still apply as would EU competition law where trade in the EU was affected) and the UK would not be part of the EU's decision-making process in regard to any of the rules which the EU would adopt or amend after the UK leaves the EU but which would still impact on the UK and its interests (e.g. shipping companies). It is unclear whether, in this context and indeed generally, the UK would be a simple "third State" or will have a special and deeper relationship with the EU than most other third States – whether it has a more enhanced relationship is dependent on the terms of the arrangements which the EU and the UK agree.

48.006 It is very difficult to contemplate how all that has been done over the last five decades[8] to integrate the UK into the EU could be undone – and replaced – in two years (i.e. the time between issuing the so-called "Article 50" notice under the Treaty on European Union ("TEU") on 29 March 2017 and the UK leaving the EU on 29 March 2019). It took the UK 12 and two attempts to join a much simpler European Communities in 1973 so a total reversal now, after all the EU law that has been grafted on to the UK system, seems very difficult to imagine in a very short timescale. And yet those who supported "Brexit" claiming that the EU was inefficient and incapable of making decisions efficiently now believe that the EU and the UK could agree a "Withdrawal Agreement" and a "Relationship Agreement" in 23 months.

48.007 There will certainly be – and already are – commercial implications because of Brexit. As a backdrop, it is quite likely that there will be some reduction in trade volumes due to the uncertainty leading businesses and consumers to invest and consume less during the uncertainty. The vote in favour of Brexit has had a negative effect on business and consumer sentiment generally (but not universally) leading to a reduction in trade so it is quite likely that there will be commercial consequences. While UK exporters have benefited in the short term from being able to sell exports from the UK more competitively because of the fall in the value of sterling, this is not likely to be sustained in the

---

6 E.g. because of an increase or a decrease in trade involving the UK because the country is no longer in the EU.

7 E.g. goods avoiding the UK (i.e. the so-called "Landbridge" route between Ireland and Continental Europe) and instead those goods are going directly from Ireland to France (or vice versa) (thereby avoiding the UK) so as to remain in the EU.

8 While the UK joined the European Communities in 1973, there had been preparation undertaken in the run-up to the UK's accession.

long run because the cost of imports (particularly imported raw materials) is rising (because of the fall in the value of sterling) and hedging arrangements will come to an end. It is also unclear how the UK economy would fare if tariffs (even at the World Trade Organization ("WTO") levels) were imposed on exports from the UK.[9] While supporters of Brexit would say that there has not been the dramatic impact on the UK economy that some Remainers foresaw, it is probably more accurate to recall that it is still too early to see the full impact on the UK economy – the UK is still a Member State of the EU, the country is still part of the internal market/customs union, no post-Brexit arrangements between the EU and the UK have yet been finalised and the consequences of these decisions take time to manifest.

48.008 As well as commercial implications, there could also be operational implications to Brexit with, for example, new shipping routes being opened to bypass the UK and any customs posts which it might have – for example, all other things being equal, it would make sense to open more shipping routes between Ireland and the Continent of Europe than to have goods delayed at UK, Irish and Continental European ports due to customs operations which would otherwise slow down the movement of goods.

48.009 As mentioned at the outset, the purpose of this short chapter is to consider the legal implications of Brexit on shipping and ports. Obviously, a great deal of this analysis is purely speculative and preliminary in nature given the fact that the post-Brexit political and legal landscapes have not yet been negotiated let alone agreed. The chapter is also naturally selective given that it is impossible to identify each and every implication of Brexit for the shipping and port sector. There are dire warnings on both sides of the "Remain" and "Brexit" debate. Ultimately, it would be as wrong to see the UK as being a wilderness outside the EU[10] as to see the EU as an entity on the brink of collapse simply because the UK could be leaving because, in reality, the situation is more nuanced and sophisticated than either of those extreme views. The EU will be weaker because of a departure by the UK but the UK's departure would not cause the EU's demise; indeed, some would argue that the EU would prosper without the "slowest wheel on the wagon".[11] It is also clear that the UK would be weaker by virtue of leaving the EU (e.g. leaving the world's largest internal market) but it is unlikely to become an economic wilderness simply because of Brexit.

B. CHRONOLOGY OF BREXIT

48.010 In the immediate aftermath of the ending of the Second World War, there was an intensification of the movement towards European integration. There had always been a desire to integrate Europe but the horrors and loss of life in the Second World War (which had been the third time that France and Germany had fought each other since 1870) meant that there was a further intensification of the move towards integration. This found expression in the establishment of the Council of Europe in 1950 (which still

---

9 Moreover, the WTO regime does not cover all goods and services.
10 See Hannan, What Next: How to Get the Best from Brexit? (2016).
11 This is a reference to the fact that the UK has often been the Member State which is the slowest to agree to changes in the EU and the most sceptical of the Member States.

survives today but which is mainly concerned with human rights),[12] the European Coal and Steel Community ("ECSC") in 1952, the EEC in 1957, and the EAEC (or "Euratom") in 1957. While the Council of Europe included the UK (indeed, the UK was central to its establishment), the UK was not important in the formation of the ECSC, the EEC or the EAEC – indeed, the UK was very much an outsider. Equally, the shipping sector was not particularly important to these organisations. It is very likely that shipping was not important for the ECSC, EEC and EAEC in the initial years because there were few shipping services between the initial six Member States (i.e. Belgium, France, Germany, Italy, Luxembourg and the Netherlands) although there were shipping services between five of those six countries as well as between the EU and the rest of the world. Ports were also heavily regulated and largely State-owned. The ECSC, EEC and EAEC were largely (but not entirely) successful so it was not surprising that the UK eventually wanted to join the three European Communities.[13] The UK applied in 1961 to join the European Communities but that application was vetoed by General De Gaulle's France. The UK applied again in 1967 and this time it was successful. The UK signed the Treaty of Accession in Brussels on 22 January 1972 which had the effect, following ratification, of bringing the UK into the European Communities the following year.

48.011 On 1 January 1973, the UK acceded to the three European Communities: (a) the EEC; (b) the EAEC; and (c) the ECSC. There had already been six other Member States of those communities (namely, Belgium, France, Germany, Italy, Luxembourg and the Netherlands) – these six were the founding Member States. The UK joined those six founding Member States on the same day as Denmark and Ireland. Since then, the EEC has become the European Union and the ECSC has ceased to exist with its activities and functions being absorbed by the EU.[14] The arrival of the UK and Denmark (two significant shipping nations) in 1973 meant that shipping was more of an issue for the then European Communities than it had been before then.[15]

48.012 Ironically, while other countries which accede to the EU generally have referendums of the people *before* joining to determine whether the people wish to join the EU, the UK only had a parliamentary vote in 1972 and proceeded to acceded on that basis. It was not until 5 June 1975, two years after acceding, that the UK had a referendum of its people on whether it should remain in the then European Communities; on that occasion a majority (67.2%) voted in favour of remaining in the European Communities. Politicians were deeply divided on the issue and politicians from the same party voted in different ways on the issue. The fact that a referendum was needed at all and that there was such division among politicians was reflective of the relative unease in many parts of the UK about membership of what was to become the EU. This is indicative of the fact that the outcome of the Brexit Referendum on 23 June 2016 was not such an unusual phenomenon as many people now suspect.

---

12 The European Convention on Human Rights has some relevant for shipping (e.g. in terms of property rights (see Art. 1 of Protocol No 1 to the convention) and piracy (see e.g. Piedimonte Bodini, "Fighting Maritime Piracy under the European Convention on Human Rights" (2011) 22(3) Eur J Int Law 829).

13 It is sometimes now forgotten as to the perilous state of the UK economy before, and just after, it joined the European Communities (e.g. the International Monetary Fund had to bail out the UK economy).

14 The treaty establishing the ECSC had set a 50-year mandate for the organisation.

15 See chap. 5 generally.

48.013 While the UK was a very important Member State of the EU, it was always a somewhat semi-detached one. It sought carve-outs or exemptions from various EU rules. It did not join the EU's Economic and Monetary Union and therefore did not adopt the euro as its currency (unlike all the other major EU Member States). It had fought for a rebate of some of its financial contributions to the EU. It did not take as active a part in the EU as the likes of France and Germany. Over time, there was growing Euro-scepticism and, indeed, Euro-phobia in the UK. This found some expression in parts of the UK's Labour Party (particularly in the 1970s and 1980s)[16] but was most pronounced in parts of the UK's Conservative (or Tory) Party and ultimately led to the establishment of the separate United Kingdom Independence Party ("UKIP") which has the avowed aim of taking the UK out of the EU and took votes from both the Labour and Tory parties (but particularly, the latter). UKIP attracted significant but minority support; for example, it attracted 12.5% of the total vote in the 2015 General Election.[17] UKIP was not an isolated phenomenon because in 1994 Sir James Goldsmith had formed the Referendum Party which advocated that there ought to be a referendum on the UK's membership of the EU. The Referendum Party won 810,860 votes or 2.6% of the total votes cast in the 1997 General Election. While the Referendum Party was disbanded after Goldsmith's death in 1997, the thread of Euroscepticism/Europhobia was still present, and growing, in UK political discourse.

48.014 The Tory Party was divided deeply because of its pro- and its anti-EU factions over several decades; indeed, the internal debate within the party and the external threat from the UKIP were serious threats to the survival and well-being of the Tory Party and its various leaders over four decades.

48.015 Ultimately, the then Tory Party leader and UK Prime Minister, David Cameron, announced on 23 January 2013 that a Conservative government would hold an "in"/"out" referendum on EU membership before the end of 2017, on the basis of a rene-gotiated package between the EU and the UK, if (and this was important) the Conservative Party was re-elected in the 2015 General Election. His aim was probably three-fold: put the issue of the UK's continued membership to rest and thereby quell dissension in his own party, secure re-election but also discourage people from voting for UKIP in the 2015 General Election.[18] It was an attempt to "lance the boil" once and for all. Following the Conservative Party's victory in the 2015 General Election and the return to 10 Downing Street of David Cameron as Prime Minister, he commenced negoti-ations with the EU on revised terms of membership. In hindsight, the package agreed in February 2016[19] was too little, too late and too limited. It did not do enough to sway voters in the UK who had concerns about the EU and, ultimately, was hardly mentioned

---

16 E.g. the Labour Party pledged in the 1983 General Election (under the leadership of Michael Foot) that it would withdraw the UK from the then European Communities if it were elected to office (and without a referen-dum). Following a heavy loss of seats and not being re-elected, the Labour Party changed its policy.

17 This was a significant vote given that the Conservatives were offering an "in"/"out" referendum should they be returned to power hence, in the UK's first past-the-post electoral system, many would-be UKIP voters could have switched to Tory so as to increase the chances of the referendum occurring rather than using the vote for a UKIP candidate who would not be elected and letting a Labour Party or other party candidate win.

18 The theory was that those voters who were keen to have a referendum would have been better to vote for the Tories who had a realistic chance of being in office and delivering on the promised referendum than voting for UKIP which had no realistic prospect of being in government and could not cause a referendum to occur.

19 See http://data.consilium.europa.eu/doc/document/ST-1-2016-INIT/en/pdf.

in the subsequent referendum. Following the agreement on the package, Cameron announced in a speech to the House of Commons on 22 February 2016 that there would be a referendum on 23 June 2016.[20] It was a divisive campaign. Those who advocated that the UK should remain in the EU were more inclined to adopt a "negative" approach about the dangers of what would happen if the UK did leave rather than a more positive or upbeat approach about the positive value of remaining. By contrast, those who campaigned for the UK to leave the EU spoke positively and optimistically about "taking back control" and "winning back sovereignty" but glossed over a great many of the details and consequences. Many commentators and politicians from all sides believed that the result would be a majority for the "Remain" side of the argument but it was not to be.

48.016 On 23 June 2016, 33,577,342 people voted in only the third ever UK-wide referendum. The question the people were asked was a deceptively simple one: "Should the United Kingdom remain a member of the European Union or leave the European Union?" A total of 17,410,742 (or 51.89% of the valid vote) voted in favour of leaving the EU while 16,141,241 (or 48.11%) voted in favour of remaining in the EU. In the immediate aftermath of the result, the pound sterling fell sharply in value against other currencies, the value of shares fell worldwide but they fell particularly sharply in the UK and, ultimately, David Cameron announced, the morning after the referendum, his intention to step down from the job of UK Prime Minister given that he had campaigned to remain but a majority of those who voted had opted to leave. While he had intended to stay for a few months more until September 2016, he was replaced on 13 July 2016 by Theresa May who had been Home Secretary in Cameron's government and had campaigned, relatively mutely, for the UK to remain but now saw it as her mission to deliver the Brexit which a majority of the UK's voters had chosen.

48.017 While referendums are rare in the UK, it is true that never have so many voters in the UK ever opted for a single proposition as they did on 23 June 2016 in regard to Brexit. Equally, the margin of 51.89% to 48.11% is seen as being tight but it is comparable to the Swiss margin to reject membership of the European Economic Area ("EEA") (50.3% to 49.7%) (a decision which has never been reversed) and comparable to the margin in Greenland (53% to 47%) (a decision which has also never been reversed).

48.018 The UK government then began its preparations for Brexit.[21] In July 2016, the UK government established a new government department, the Department for Exiting the European Union ("DExEU"). The Department was headed by David Davis MP who became central to the UK's negotiations with the EU. Theresa May announced that the UK would not seek membership of the Internal/Single Market or the EU's Customs Union after it left the EU even though this was not articulated to any great extent during the referendum campaign. The UK was intent on repealing the UK's European Communities Act 1972 but then incorporating the EU law existing on the day it left the EU into UK domestic law; however, this does not really align EU and UK law because there will be an almost immediate growing divergence between the two regimes.[22]

---

20 See e.g., www.gov.uk/government/speeches/pm-commons-statement-on-eu-reform-and-referendum-22-february-2016.

21 While it was said that some preparations had been made by the UK for Brexit, in reality, the UK government had not prepared adequately for Brexit.

22 An example of this phenomenon would be Ireland which gained independence from the UK in 1922, adopted (with some minor modifications) the UK rules, and then divergences started to emerge over time.

48.019 The EU also began its preparations for the Brexit negotiations and to date, at least, the EU preparations have been more effective. The EU has had a clear, consistent and reasoned approach to the negotiations while the UK has altered course at different times and not achieved a great deal of what it set out to achieve. The European Commission was given the critical role with a task force headed up by Michel Barnier.[23] The European Parliament is also critical but more in terms of voting because the European Commission is really driving the negotiations. The EU has published a series of detailed documents on the process as well as its negotiated mandates.[24]

48.020 On 29 March 2017, the UK submitted to the EU the UK's notification of its intention to withdraw from the EU pursuant to Article 50 of the TEU. A popular misconception – in parts of the media and among some politicians – was that the triggering of Article 50 meant that the UK will leave precisely two years after it was triggered. This is not necessarily so. Article 50 of the TEU provides:

"1. Any Member State may decide to withdraw from the Union in accordance with its own constitutional requirements.

2. A Member State which decides to withdraw shall notify the European Council of its intention. In the light of the guidelines provided by the European Council, the Union shall negotiate and conclude an agreement with that State, setting out the arrangements for its withdrawal, taking account of the framework for its future relationship with the Union. That agreement shall be negotiated in accordance with Article 218(3) of the Treaty on the Functioning of the European Union. It shall be concluded on behalf of the Union by the Council, acting by a qualified majority, after obtaining the consent of the European Parliament.

3. The Treaties shall cease to apply to the State in question from the date of entry into force of the withdrawal agreement or, failing that, two years after the notification referred to in paragraph 2, unless the European Council, in agreement with the Member State concerned, unanimously decides to extend this period.

4. For the purposes of paragraphs 2 and 3, the member of the European Council or of the Council representing the withdrawing Member State shall not participate in the discussions of the European Council or Council or in decisions concerning it.

A qualified majority shall be defined in accordance with Article 238(3)(b) of the Treaty on the Functioning of the European Union.

5. If a State which has withdrawn from the Union asks to rejoin, its request shall be subject to the procedure referred to in Article 49."[25]

48.021 While the UK remains a Member State of the EU then it remains subject to EU law. The serving of the Article 50 notice has not diminished its rights or duties under EU law while it is still a Member State of the EU.

---

23 https://ec.europa.eu/info/departments/taskforce-article-50-negotiations-united-kingdom_en.

24 https://ec.europa.eu/commission/brexit-negotiations/negotiating-documents-article-50-negotiations-united-kingdom_en?field_core_tags_tid_i18n=351.

25 Art. 49 TEU, in turn, provides:

"Any European State which respects the values referred to in Article 2 and is committed to promoting them may apply to become a member of the Union. The European Parliament and national Parliaments shall be notified of this application. The applicant State shall address its application to the Council, which shall act unanimously after consulting the Commission and after receiving the consent of the European Parliament, which shall act by a majority of its component members. The conditions of eligibility agreed upon by the European Council shall be taken into account.

The conditions of admission and the adjustments to the Treaties on which the Union is founded, which such admission entails, shall be the subject of an agreement between the Member States and the applicant State. This agreement shall be submitted for ratification by all the contracting States in accordance with their respective constitutional requirements."

48.022 During 2017, negotiations commenced between the EU and the UK with a view to a withdrawal agreement being adopted. It was decided that the rights of the people affected (e.g. UK citizens living in the EU and EU citizens living in the UK post-Brexit), Ireland/Northern Ireland (e.g. trade across the border between Ireland and Northern Ireland)[26] and the UK's financial contribution to the EU would be the first three issues to be negotiated. Eventually, after a protracted and sometimes difficult process, a joint report was sent on 8 December 2017 by the European Commission and the UK to the European Council which the latter endorsed.[27] During the negotiations, the EU remained firm and fixed in its negotiating approach while the UK approach was evolutionary. There was more unity on the EU than the UK side with the latter having quite divergent objectives both in the UK Cabinet and the UK Parliament.

48.023 On 19 March 2018, the EU and the UK published a Draft Agreement on the withdrawal of the United Kingdom of Great Britain and Northern Ireland from the European Union and the European Atomic Energy Community.[28] It is only a draft agreement but the parties reached tentative agreement on various aspects of it. There are many issues yet to resolve (including what to do about the border between Ireland and Northern Ireland as well as the trade arrangements between the EU and a post-Brexit UK). Many of the issues which are yet to be negotiated and decided are not easy ones so it is not inevitable that there will be a comprehensive deal, or indeed any meaningful deal,[29] reached between the parties. It is hoped by both sides that there would be a withdrawal agreement as well as an agreement dealing with issues such as the relationship between the EU and the post-Brexit UK.

48.024 It is anticipated that on 29 March 2019 at 23:00 hours UK time, the UK would leave the EU. It is possible that there could be another date for the UK to leave because Article 50(3) TEU provides

> "[t]he Treaties shall cease to apply to the State in question from the date of entry into force of the withdrawal agreement or, failing that, two years after the notification referred to in paragraph 2, unless the European Council, in agreement with the Member State concerned, unanimously decides to extend this period."

However, the current expectation is that the UK will leave at that time which would be two years after the UK served notice under Article 50. To vary the date, there would have to be an agreement between the UK and the remaining Member States.

48.025 After 23:00 hours UK time on 29 March 2019, there will be several consequences. All primary and secondary EU law would cease to apply to the UK unless agreed otherwise – and there are indications that the UK and the EU would agree that EU law would apply until 31 December 2020 even though the UK would have left the EU. On leaving in 2019, the UK will become a "third country" or "third State" (i.e. a State

---

26 On this issue, see, e.g. Dougan, "The 'Brexit' Threat to the Northern Irish Border: Clarifying the Constitutional Framework" in Dougan, op. cit. at fn. 2, chap. 3 as well as Doyle and Connolly, "Brexit and the Northern Ireland Question" in Fabbrini (ed.), op. cit. at fn. 2, chap. 7.

27 https://ec.europa.eu/commission/publications/joint-report-negotiators-european-union-and-united-kingdom-government-progress-during-phase-1-negotiations-under-article-50-teu-united-kingdoms-orderly-withdrawal-european-union_en.

28 https://ec.europa.eu/commission/publications/draft-agreement-withdrawal-united-kingdom-great-britain-and-northern-ireland-european-union-and-european-atomic-energy-community-0_en.

29 There ought to be a minimal agreement to deal with the ending of the application of the EU treaties to the UK otherwise they would continue to apply but it is unclear as to how much more will be agreed.

which is not a Member State) as far as the EU and EU law are concerned. The UK will continue have to pay money to the EU for some years[30] (the current expectation is that the obligation will continue until 2064). It is currently expected that there would be, using the EU's phrase, a "transition phase" or the UK's phrase, an "implementation phase" until 31 December 2020 but during this time, the UK would be bound by much of EU law but would not have any role to play in the EU's institutions or law-making processes.

48.026 There is a need to ensure that not only the UK, the EU Member States and indeed all States prepare for Brexit but also private parties must also prepare for Brexit. To assist with this process, the EU has published various notices; for example, on 27 February 2018, the European Commission's Directorate-General for Mobility and Transport ("DG MOVE") issued a four-page "Notice to Stakeholders" entitled "Withdrawal of the United Kingdom and EU Rules in the Field of Maritime Transport".[31] Preparing for Brexit is however very difficult because it is unclear as to what will be the exact scope of the relationship between the EU and the UK outside the EU. Unlike the 1992 Internal Market Programme (where one knew what the rules were because there were 279 proposed measures) or the introduction of the euro (where one knew the conversion rate between the national currency and the euro), the rules of Brexit have not yet been written let alone agreed or known. The popular media and many politicians have referred to the notion that there could be a "Hard Brexit" or a "Soft Brexit" – the former meaning that the post-Brexit relationship between the EU and the UK would be very distant and the UK would face the type of obstacles to trading with the EU as would any third State without a special deal with the EU, while the latter term indicates that the EU and the UK would be quite close and there would be some (but lower) barriers and considerable cooperation between the two. In reality, the notion that there is a simple binary choice between a Hard Brexit and a Soft Brexit is too simplistic. It is too simplistic because different issues, sectors and regions will be affected in different ways over time meaning that a more accurate term is "Spectrum Brexit" (rather than a Hard Brexit or a Soft Brexit) because there will be different impacts across the whole spectrum.

48.027 As mentioned above, it is currently anticipated that the UK will continue having to make a financial contribution to the EU until 2064 so as to meet the UK's liabilities to the EU (e.g. to fund the pension of UK citizens working for the EU). The size of this financial contribution to the EU could be in the region of €38 billion or more. It is quite likely that the length of this commitment until 2064 is commensurate, in broad terms, with how long it could take to understand all of the implications of Brexit!

C. BACKGROUND OBSERVATIONS ON THE IMPACT OF BREXIT ON EU SHIPPING LAW AND POLICY

48.028 While there is an intensive and often divisive debate on the implications generally of the UK leaving the EU, the purpose of this chapter is to consider the implications from the narrow perspective of shipping and ports so the wider consequences and dimensions of Brexit will not be examined in this chapter other than to say that the majority of

---

30 This is very much connected with the UK's obligation (like any Member State) to pay for the pensions of UK citizens who retire from their employment in the EU.
31 https://ec.europa.eu/transport/sites/transport/files/legislation/brexit-notice-to-stakeholders-maritime-transport.pdf.

views expressed would indicate that Brexit would have a negative and damaging impact on the UK, its economy and place in the world but some supporters of Brexit are convinced that it will bring rich benefits and dividends to the UK; while time will tell, it is more likely to be negative than positive. The outlook is made all the more difficult because the UK's ambition to conclude free trade agreements with the likes of the USA and Russia could be thwarted by political events and policies in those countries, while some other regions of the world (e.g. Japan) have said that they are keen to first conclude arrangements with the EU before addressing potential agreements with the UK. Indeed, it is interesting to note at a maritime level how so many of the assets and services in the UK maritime sphere are no longer owned by UK interests (e.g. the ferry services between Ireland and the UK and the largest ferry ports in the UK serving those routes are owned by non-UK interests).

48.029 The UK has been central to the espousal and advocacy of the liberal and open market philosophy in EU shipping law. The UK has long opened its coast to cabotage services (which means that ships of any flag could carry cargo or persons between ports in the UK) but it took many years and some difficult battles for the EU to follow suit.[32] The UK has been critical to the liberalisation of EU shipping law and policy. The famous December 1986 package which provided for *international* maritime services (by virtue of Regulation 4055/86) was adopted under the UK's Presidency of the Council of Ministers in the second half of 1986.[33] The UK opposed what it saw as the introduction of excessive bureaucracy and administration in regard to the operation of ports.[34] The country generally espoused liberalism, privatisation, a rejection of State interference and more private enterprise in the maritime sector. It is quite likely that the EU shipping law and policy would not be as open and liberal as they would be if the UK were to remain a Member State and one could see a certain level of protectionism being espoused on occasion so the Commission will have to be vigilant.

48.030 While acceding to the EU carries with it considerable uncertainty, the UK's departure is shrouded in even deeper uncertainty as it is an unprecedented step. No Member State has ever left the EU so unlike the UK's accession where it was following in the footsteps of six countries which had been in the European Communities for two decades and had a detailed accession treaty which had been negotiated and agreed over more than a decade, this is an untrodden path with no clear plan. There is no template for the rules involved in a Member State leaving. The contents of any withdrawal agreement or relationship agreement have not yet been settled so the terms are unclear. While the UK would become, post-Brexit, a "third country", it is unclear whether it would become a third country with or without special rights and privileges vis-à-vis the EU. No EU or EEA State has ever left the EU or the EEA,[35] so it is unclear as to how the UK and the EU will interact post-Brexit. Unless there are specific and special provisions adopted (e.g. in any transitional arrangements in a withdrawal agreement) then as of the withdrawal date (i.e. scheduled to be 29 March 2019), then the rights currently afforded to UK shipping

---

32 Maritime cabotage was not mandated in the EU until the entry into force of Council Reg. 3577/92 of 7 December 1992 applying the principle of freedom to provide services to maritime transport within Member States (maritime cabotage) OJ L364/7, 12 December 1992; see chap. 7.

33 See chap. 5 generally.

34 See chap. 5 generally.

35 The three EEA States are Norway, Iceland and Liechtenstein.

and port interests by virtue of EU shipping law rules would no longer apply to such UK interests. Ironically, UK interests could still be subject to complying with certain obligations (e.g. (a) UK-flagged vessels would still have to comply with EU safety and environmental rules while using EU ports or (b) transactions involving UK companies would be subject to EU competition laws) but it would have little or no real role in the adoption or enforcement of those rules unless something special is agreed between the parties.

D. FREEDOM OF ESTABLISHMENT AND REGISTRATION OF VESSELS

48.031 The EU is built around the "fundamental freedoms" meaning that people, goods, capital/payments and services may move freely around the EU. One of these freedoms, the freedom of establishment, means that a company or individual who is a national of one Member State may, subject to very few exceptions, establish a business in another Member State on the same basis as a national of another Member State.[36] Before Brexit, therefore, a UK national may establish a business elsewhere in the EU pretty much on the same basis as a national of the host Member State but that right is likely to disappear post-Brexit. So, for example, a UK company may or may not be able to establish a business in the likes of Germany, Greece, Italy or the Netherlands on the same basis as a host company – while nothing has been finalised yet, it is widely anticipated that there would be no automatic right for UK nationals to be treated the same as the host's own entities and could therefore, all things being equal, be discriminated against. This also means that the current regime allowing for the easier transfer of vessels between registers of EU Member States would no longer be available to UK nationals.[37] It may well be that host States are still willing to allow UK nationals to establish businesses in their States but the right to do so is no longer enshrined in EU law.

E. FREE MOVEMENT OF SERVICES IN THE MARITIME SECTOR

48.032 A fundamental feature of the EU is the internal market which includes the notion of free movement of services.[38] The EU adopted measures in 1986 and 1992 to ensure that there would be free movement of services in the maritime sector; the first measure, Regulation 4055/86,[39] was designed to ensure that *international* maritime services (where the EU was involved) would be possible while the second measure, Regulation 3577/92,[40] was designed to ensure that *domestic* maritime services within Member States would be possible. Only nationals of EU Member States may avail of the rights afforded under the two regulations. Presumably, unless there is agreement to the contrary, UK nationals will no longer be able to avail of such rights. Indeed, the EU has already anticipated this outcome by warning stakeholders that, unless something is agreed to the contrary, the freedom to provide services will no longer be available to UK nationals. On 27 February 2018, the European Commission's DG MOVE issued a "Notice to

---

36 See chap. 6.
37 See chap. 6.
38 See chap. 7.
39 OJ L378/1, 31 December 1986.
40 OJ L364/7, 12 December 1992.

Stakeholders" on the "Withdrawal of The United Kingdom and EU Rules in the Field of Maritime Transport".[41]

48.033 There are features to the Notice which are irrelevant but key provisions include:

"Subject to any transitional arrangement that may be contained in a possible withdrawal agreement, as of the withdrawal date, the EU rules in the field of maritime transport no longer apply to the United Kingdom. This has in particular the following consequences in the different areas of Union law in the field of maritime transport:[42]

... MARKET ACCESS
- Intra-Union shipping services and third-country traffic: Regulation (EEC) No 4055/86[43] stipulates the freedom to provide maritime transport services between Member States, as well as between Member States and third countries, in respect of:
  - 'nationals of Member States who are established in a Member State other than that of the person for whom the services are intended';[44] and
  - 'nationals of the Member States established outside the EU', or 'shipping companies established outside the EU and controlled by nationals of a Member State, if their vessels are registered in that Member State in accordance with its legislation.'
  Persons or companies who, as of the withdrawal date, do not meet those criteria will no longer benefit from this Regulation, notably in terms of non-discriminatory treatment as regards international maritime transport connections.
- Cabotage: According to Article 1(1) of Regulation (EEC) No 3577/92,[45] the provision of maritime transport services within EU Member States (maritime cabotage) is restricted to Community[46] shipowners (as defined in Article 2(2) of that Regulation). As of the withdrawal date it will no longer be possible to provide maritime transport services in accordance with this Regulation if the conditions for constituting a Community shipowner are no longer fulfilled, unless national legislation[47] allows access to cabotage to vessels flying the flag of a third country."[48]

48.034 Brexit would appear to have little or no impact on the ability of UK interests to pursue international shipping activities and services outside the EU. However, there are some features of the EU's international agreements (e.g. the agreement between the EU and Canada known as the Comprehensive Economic and Trade Agreement ("CETA")[49]) which the UK would no longer be able to enjoy with the result that the UK would have to

---

41 https://ec.europa.eu/transport/sites/transport/files/legislation/brexit-notice-to-stakeholders-maritime-transport.pdf.

42 This notice does not address marine equipment (which is addressed in the Notice to stakeholders – Withdrawal of the United Kingdom and EU rules in the field of industrial products, https://ec.europa.eu/growth/single-market/goods_en) nor seafarer qualifications (which is addressed in the Notice to stakeholders – Withdrawal of the United Kingdom and EU rules on the minimum level of training of seafarers and the mutual recognition of seafarers' certificates, https://ec.europa.eu/transport/transport-modes/news/2017-12-11-brexit-notice-stakeholders_en).

43 Council Regulation (EEC) No 4055/86 of 22 December 1986 applying the principle of freedom to provide services to maritime transport between Member States and between Member States and third countries, OJ L378, 31.12.1986, p.1.

44 Article 1(1) of Regulation (EEC) No 4055/86.

45 Council Regulation (EEC) No 3577/92 of 7 December 1992 applying the principle of freedom to provide services to maritime transport within Member States (maritime cabotage), OJ L364, 12.12.1992, p.7.

46 Ed., i.e. EU shipowners.

47 E.g. the legislation of Denmark, Ireland, Belgium, and the Netherlands.

48 https://ec.europa.eu/transport/sites/transport/files/legislation/brexit-notice-to-stakeholders-maritime-transport.pdf.

49 See e.g. http://trade.ec.europa.eu/doclib/docs/2017/september/tradoc_156062.pdf, http://www.ecsa.eu/news/ceta-will-greatly-benefit-maritime-transport.

negotiate its own arrangements with regions, associations or countries with which the EU has already reached agreement. (More generally, the EU believes that the UK might have to agree up to 750 agreements with parties around the world if it wishes to replicate the treaty network which the UK already enjoys by virtue of its EU membership.)

F. DISCRIMINATION ON THE BASIS OF NATIONALITY

48.035 At present, Member States may not discriminate against UK nationals (e.g. individuals or companies) in matters falling within the scope of EU law.[50] For example, Article 18 of the Treaty on the Functioning of the European Union ("TFEU") provides:

> "Within the scope of application of the Treaties, and without prejudice to any special provisions contained therein, any discrimination on grounds of nationality shall be prohibited.
> The European Parliament and the Council, acting in accordance with the ordinary legislative procedure, may adopt rules designed to prohibit such discrimination."

This can have quite practical implications. For example, an Italian port may not, as a general rule, impose different dues or charges on a British vessel as opposed to an Italian vessel but post-Brexit and unless there is an agreement to the contrary, there could be discrimination in EU ports against UK vessels and even UK seafarers (e.g. pilotage exemption certificates) in certain circumstances. This means, for example, that a UK national may not be discriminated against by, say, a Belgian, French, German or Italian authority. However, post-Brexit, unless something is agreed to the contrary, it will be possible as a general rule, as a matter of EU law, to discriminate against UK nationals.

G. MARITIME SAFETY LAW

48.036 The EU has become deeply involved in, and concerned with, maritime safety matters.[51] These safety issues have covered issues such as the safety of passengers and crew members as well as the protection of the environment. Many of these measures have emerged from particular maritime incidents. It is open to question as to whether a post-Brexit UK will be inclined to, or moreover, able to adopt its own position on such issues. In practice, it is thought that the leeway for the UK to adopt its own rules would be very limited to the point of being negligible. Many of the EU rules are not dependent on the flag flown by the vessel – they are often flag-blind rules – so if UK vessels want to continue to visit EU ports or even sail EU waters then those vessels will probably opt for the EU rules in preference to any contradictory UK rules (unless, for example, the UK rules were providing greater protection but adoption of the UK rules was not incompatible with adherence to the EU ones).

48.037 On 27 February 2018, the European Commission's DG MOVE issued a "Notice to Stakeholders" on the "Withdrawal of The United Kingdom and EU Rules in the Field of Maritime Transport".[52] There are features to the Notice which are irrelevant to the issue of safety but key provisions include:

---

50 See the discussion of the Factortame litigation in chaps 5 and 6.

51 See various chapters throughout this book.

52 https://ec.europa.eu/transport/sites/transport/files/legislation/brexit-notice-to-stakeholders-maritime-transport.pdf.

"Subject to any transitional arrangement that may be contained in a possible withdrawal agreement, as of the withdrawal date, the EU rules in the field of maritime transport no longer apply to the United Kingdom. This has in particular the following consequences in the different areas of Union law in the field of maritime transport:[53]

...

MARITIME SAFETY

- Recognition of organisations: The withdrawal of the United Kingdom does not as such affect the recognitions by the Commission in accordance with Article 4 of Regulation (EC) No 391/2009[54] of organisations referred to in Article 2(c) of that Regulation. However, according to Article 8 of Regulation (EC) No 391/2009 Recognised Organisations are to be assessed on a regular basis (at least every two years) by the Commission, together with the Member State that initially submitted the request for recognition for the organisation in question. This also applies to the organisations which had initially been recognised by the relevant Member State and which now enjoy recognition pursuant to Article 15 of Regulation (EC) No 391/2009. As of the withdrawal date, the United Kingdom will no longer be in a position to participate in the assessments carried out in accordance with Article 8 of Regulation (EC) No 391/2009 of organisations initially recognised by it. With respect to this procedural requirement, the Commission is considering the necessary and appropriate steps to allow for the assessment in accordance with the terms of the Regulation.
- Port State Control: Directive 2009/16/EC[55] sets out the EU Port State Control system. The Directive requires Member States to inspect foreign ships in ports by Port State Control officers for the purpose of verifying that the condition of a ship and its equipment comply with the requirements of international conventions, and that the vessel is manned and operated in compliance with applicable international law. Directive 2009/16/EC also requires verification of compliance with a number of other EU-law based requirements,[56] including insurance certificates under Directive 2009/20/EC.[57] While EU-27 Member States will continue to verify United Kingdom ships calling to EU ports, as of the withdrawal date, the Port State Control inspection system set out in Directive 2009/16/EC no longer applies in the United Kingdom.[58] Relations between the United Kingdom and the EU in respect of Port State Control will be governed by the Paris Memorandum of Understanding on Port State Control.[59]

---

53 This notice does not address marine equipment (which is addressed in the Notice to stakeholders – Withdrawal of the United Kingdom and EU rules in the field of industrial products, https://ec.europa.eu/growth/single-market/goods_en) nor seafarer qualifications (which is addressed in the Notice to stakeholders – Withdrawal of the United Kingdom and EU rules on the minimum level of training of seafarers and the mutual recognition of seafarers' certificates, https://ec.europa.eu/transport/transport-modes/news/2017-12-11-brexit-notice-stakeholders_en).

54 Regulation (EC) No 391/2009 of the European Parliament and of the Council of 23 April 2009 on common rules and standards for ship inspection and survey organisations, OJ L131, 28.5.2009, p.11.

55 Directive 2009/16/EC of the European Parliament and of the Council of 23 April 2009 on port State control, OJ L131, 28.5.2009, p. 57.

56 Article 13 and Annex IV of Directive 2009/16/EC.

57 Point 41 of Annex IV to Directive 2009/16/EC and Article 4(1) of Directive 2009/20/EC of the European Parliament and of the Council of 23 April 2009 on the insurance of shipowners for maritime claims, OJ L131/128, 28.05.2009.

58 Note that, as of the withdrawal date, United Kingdom flagged ships will no longer be required to carry the inventory of hazardous materials that complies with Article 5(2) of Regulation 1257/2013 on ship recycling. However, this obligation becomes applicable again to ships flying the flag of a third country as of 31 December 2020 (Articles 12 and 32(2)(b) of Regulation (EU) No 1257/2013 of the European Parliament and of the Council of 20 November 2013 on ship recycling, OJ L330, 10.12.2013, p. 1). The certificate will be verified in accordance with Point 49 of Annex IV to Directive 2009/16/EC.

59 All EU Member States with sea ports, including the United Kingdom, are members of the Paris Memorandum of Understanding.

- Operations of passenger ships: According to Articles 4, 5 and 6 of Council Directive 1999/35/EC,[60] host States, as defined in that Directive, are to carry out mandatory inspections to provide for assurance of safe operation of regular ro-ro ferry and high-speed passenger craft services to or from ports of the EU. While these ships will continue to be subject to such inspections in the EU-27 Member States to or from which they operate, as of the withdrawal date, the United Kingdom will no longer have to carry out such inspections in accordance with Directive 1999/35/EC.

  …

The Commission services stand ready to provide further clarifications to interested stakeholders. The website of the Commission on maritime transport (https://ec.europa.eu/transport/modes/maritime_en) provide for general information.

These pages will be updated with further information, where necessary. Further information on other maritime safety related questions is available on European Maritime Safety Agency's website at the following link: www.emsa.europa.eu/."[61]

H. EMPLOYMENT AND SEAFARER QUALIFICATIONS

48.038 The EU has adopted several measures in the area of employment.[62] A great deal of UK employment law is thus based on EU employment law. It is assumed by many commentators that there will be some arrangements concluded between the EU and the UK on continuity of rights for those non-UK EU nationals based in the UK as well as the UK nationals based in the EU. However, it is not clear how these rules will apply to new arrivals in both locations. Brexit will impact on employment law in the UK.[63] The main rules governing employment on board vessels is the International Labour Organization's Maritime Labour Convention 2006 ("ILO Convention"). The UK government ratified the ILO Convention on 7 August 2013. The UK would probably abide by the ILO Convention. The UK may nonetheless dilute some of the rights which have been conferred on employees by virtue of EU law. The UK may have a great degree of flexibility in regard to employment law as it would not be bound by the EU employment law regime but employees (principally, seafarers) could suffer by virtue of having fewer rights and lower levels of protection.

48.039 In regard to seafarer qualifications, the European Commission's DG MOVE issued a notice to stakeholders on 19 January 2018.[64] It is entitled "Notice to stakeholders – Withdrawal of the United Kingdom and EU rules on the minimum level of training of seafarers and the mutual recognition of seafarers' certificates".[65] After reciting that the UK had served notice under Article 50 of the TEU and would therefore become a "third country" if it leaves the EU, the Notice continues:

---

60 Council Directive 1999/35 of 29 April 1999 on a system of mandatory surveys for the safe operation of regular ro-ro ferry and high-speed passenger craft services, OJ L138, 1.6.1999, p. 1. Note that this Directive is being repealed and replaced by Directive (EU) 2017/2110 that entered into force on 20 December 2017 and will have as deadline for transposition 21 December 2019 (after the withdrawal date).

61 https://ec.europa.eu/transport/sites/transport/files/legislation/brexit-notice-to-stakeholders-maritime-transport.pdf.

62 See chap. 8.

63 On this issue, see, e.g., Barnard, "Brexit and Employment Law" in Dougan, op. cit. at fn. 2 (2017), chap. 5.

64 https://ec.europa.eu/transport/transport-modes/news/2017-12-11-brexit-notice-stakeholders_en.

65 Ibid.

"In view of the considerable uncertainties, in particular concerning the content of a possible withdrawal agreement, all seafarers subject to Directive 2008/106/EC on the minimum level of training of seafarers[66] and Directive 2005/45/EC on the mutual recognition of seafarers' certificates issued by the Member States[67] are reminded of legal repercussions, which need to be considered when the United Kingdom becomes a third country.

Subject to any transitional arrangement that may be contained in a possible withdrawal agreement, as of the withdrawal date, the EU rules in the field of minimum level and mutual recognition of seafarers' certificates no longer apply to the United Kingdom. This has in particular the following consequences for the validity of certificates:

- According to Article 3 of Directive 2008/106/EC, seafarers serving on board a vessel flying the flag of an EU Member State have to hold the requisite certificate of competency or certificate of proficiency (hereafter 'certificates') issued by that Member State, by another EU Member State or by one of the third countries recognised under Article 19 of Directive 2008/106/EC. The Member State of the vessel recognises the certificates issued to seafarers by the other Member States or the recognised third countries, for such certificates to be valid in that Member State. There are two distinct recognition procedures:
  - Article 3 of Directive 2005/45/EC provides that every Member State shall recognise the certificates issued to seafarers by the other Member States: the recognition of these certificates (by the Member State of the vessel) must be accompanied by an 'endorsement attesting such recognition'.
  - Article 19(4) of Directive 2008/106/EC provides that a Member State may decide to endorse the certificates issued by the recognised third countries.
- As of the withdrawal date, the certificates issued to seafarers by the United Kingdom can no longer be presented for an 'endorsement attesting recognition' by an EU-27 Member State under Directive 2005/45/EC.

  The 'endorsement[s] attesting recognition' issued prior to the withdrawal date by EU-27 Member States under Directive 2005/45/EC of certificates issued to seafarers by the United Kingdom will continue to be valid until their expiry. A master or an officer holding an 'endorsement attesting recognition' issued by a Member State will be able to continue working on board vessels flying the flag of that Member State. However, they will not be able to change and work on board a vessel flying the flag of another Member State on the basis of their existing UK-issued certificates, given that the basis for the recognition of their certificates by that Member State (Directive 2005/45/EC) would no longer be applicable.
- As of the withdrawal date, recognition by an EU-27 Member State of certificates issued to seafarers by the United Kingdom will be subject to the conditions set out in Article 19 of Directive 2008/106/EC,[68] in line with the new status of the United Kingdom as a third country.

Preparing for the withdrawal is not just a matter for Union and national authorities, but also for private parties.

The website of the Commission on maritime transport (https://ec.europa.eu/transport/modes/maritime/seafarers_en) provides general information. These pages will be updated with further information, where necessary."[69]

---

66 Directive 2008/106/EC of the European Parliament and of the Council of 19 November 2008 on the minimum level of training of seafarers, OJ L323, 3.12.2008, p. 33.

67 Directive 2005/45/EC of the European Parliament and of the Council of 7 September 2005 on the mutual recognition of seafarers' certificates issued by the Member States and amending Directive 2001/25/EC, J L255, 30.9.2005, p. 160.

68 The list of third countries recognised at EU level was published in OJ C261, 8.8.2015, p. 25. Following the publication of this list, Montenegro was recognised by the Commission Implementing Decision published in OJ L107, 25.4.2017, p. 31, Ethiopia was recognised by the Commission Implementing Decision published in OJ L177, 8.7.2017, p. 43 and Fiji was recognised by the Commission Implementing Decision published in OJ L202, 3.8.2017, p. 6.

69 https://ec.europa.eu/transport/transport-modes/news/2017-12-11-brexit-notice-stakeholders_en.

I. MARINE EQUIPMENT

48.040 The EU has sophisticated rules in regard to marine equipment.[70] Brexit would have an impact in this context as well. On 22 January 2018, the European Commission issued a "Notice to stakeholders – Withdrawal of the United Kingdom and EU rules in the field of industrial products"[71] which touches on marine equipment as well. The Notice states:

> "Currently, Union product legislation does not generally oblige the manufacturer to designate an authorised representative.[72] However, if the manufacturer chooses to do so, the applicable legislation requires the authorised representative to be established in the Union. In addition, specific Union legislation does provide for the obligation to have an authorised representative (e.g.... marine equipment[73]) or a responsible person (cosmetic products...) established in the Union.
> Authorised representatives or responsible persons established in the United Kingdom will not, as from the withdrawal date, be recognised as authorised representatives or responsible persons for the purposes of the applicable Union product legislation. Therefore, manufacturers are advised to take the necessary steps to ensure that, as from the withdrawal date, their designated authorised representatives or responsible persons are established in the EU-27."[74]

J. SHIP RECYCLING

48.041 On 28 March 2018, the European Commission's Directorate General for Environment issued a Notice to Stakeholders entitled "Withdrawal of The United Kingdom and the EU Ship Recycling Regulation".[75] The Notice recalled that the UK submitted on 29 March 2017 the notification of its intention to withdraw from the Union pursuant to Article 50 of the TEU and the Notice continued, this

> "means that, unless a ratified withdrawal agreement[76] establishes another date, all Union primary and secondary law will cease to apply to the United Kingdom from 30 March 2019, 00:00h (CET) ('the withdrawal date').[77] The United Kingdom will then become a 'third country'."[78,79]

Turning to the specific of recycling, the Notice states:

> "Subject to any transitional arrangement that may be contained in a possible withdrawal agreement, as of the withdrawal date, the EU rules on ship recycling, and in particular Regulation (EU) No 1257/2013 of the European Parliament and of the Council of 20 November 2013 on ship recycling[80] no longer apply to the United Kingdom.

---

70 See various chapters throughout this book.

71 https://ec.europa.eu/growth/single-market/goods_en.

72 The Commission proposal for a Regulation of the European Parliament and of the Council laying down rules and procedures for compliance with and enforcement of Union harmonisation legislation on products (COM (2017) 795 final of 19.12.2017: https://ec.europa.eu/docsroom/documents/26976) provides for the obligation to have a person responsible for compliance information established in the Union in respect of all products that are subject to the Union harmonisation legislation set out in the Annex to the proposed Regulation.

73 Article 13 of Directive 2014/90/EU of the European Parliament and of the Council on marine equipment, OJ L257, 28.8.2014, p. 146.

74 https://ec.europa.eu/docsroom/documents/27401/attachments/1/translations/en/renditions/native.

75 https://ec.europa.eu/info/sites/info/files/notice_to_stakeholders_brexit_ship_recycling_final.pdf.

76 Negotiations are ongoing with the United Kingdom with a view to reaching a withdrawal agreement.

77 Furthermore, in accordance with Article 50(3) of the Treaty on European Union, the European Council, in agreement with the United Kingdom, may unanimously decide that the Treaties cease to apply at a later date.

78 A third country is a country not member of the EU.

79 https://ec.europa.eu/info/sites/info/files/notice_to_stakeholders_brexit_ship_recycling_final.pdf.

80 Ed., OJ L330/1, 10 December 2013.

This has in particular the following consequences:[81]

According to Article 6(2)(a) of Regulation (EU) No 1257/2013, owners of ships flying the flag of a Member State[82] shall ensure that ships destined to be recycled are only recycled at ship recycling facilities that are included in the European List of ship recycling facilities ('the European List'). As of the withdrawal date, the entries in the European List[83] of ship recycling facilities for facilities located in the United Kingdom will become void. As a consequence, ships flying the flag of a Member State of the Union may no longer be recycled at these ship recycling facilities.

The above is without prejudice to the possibility for the Commission to list facilities located in third countries in the European List in accordance with Article 16 of Regulation (EU) No 1257/2013.

The website of the Commission on the European Union's ship recycling policy (http://ec.europa.eu/environment/waste/ships/index.htm) provides general information concerning shipments of waste and the recycling of specific waste streams. These pages will be updated with further information, where necessary."

K. COMPETITION LAW GENERALLY

48.042 EU competition law could still apply to anti-competitive arrangements and practices in the UK notwithstanding that the UK would have left the EU.[84] This is because EU competition law applies whenever there is an effect on trade in the EU and it is irrelevant that the parties involved are not EU nationals or that any arrangements or practices were decided on outside the EU. This means that, by virtue of Article 101 of the TFEU, an anti-competitive arrangement (i.e. an agreement between undertakings, a decision by an association of undertakings or a concerted practice involving undertakings) which has the object or effect of preventing, restricting or distorting competition in the EU's internal market (or any part of it) would be prohibited and void (unless it could be exempted according to the criteria set out in Article 101(3) of the TFEU) notwithstanding that the parties to the arrangement are all from the UK and/or the arrangement was concluded in the UK. Equally, by virtue of Article 102 of the TFEU, an abuse of dominance by any undertaking having a dominant position in the internal market (or a substantial part of it) would be prohibited absolutely notwithstanding that the undertaking abusing the dominance was from the UK and/or the decision to abuse the dominance was taken in the UK. This means that notwithstanding that the UK would leave the EU, the rules of EU competition law could still be applicable to UK undertakings and arrangements/practices which were, for example, decided upon in the UK or by UK nationals.

---

81 This notice does not address EU rules on maritime transport. On these aspects, including controls in the framework of the EU port state control inspection system, see the "Notice to Stakeholders – Withdrawal of the United Kingdom and EU rules in the field of maritime transport" (https://ec.europa.eu/info/brexit/brexit-preparedness_en?page=1).

82 Article 2(1) of Regulation (EU) No 1257/2013.

83 Commission Implementing Decision (EU) 2016/2323 of 19 December 2016 establishing the European List of ship recycling facilities pursuant to Regulation (EU) No 1257/2013 of the European Parliament and of the Council on ship recycling (OJ L345, 20.12.2016, p. 119).

84 See various chapters throughout this book on EU competition and merger control law.

L. MERGER CONTROL IN THE MARITIME SECTOR

48.043 EU competition law could still apply to mergers, acquisitions and concentrative joint ventures (i.e. "concentrations") in the UK notwithstanding that the UK would have left the EU. This would occur where the undertakings involved in a proposed concentration had the requisite turnover in the EU (as well as worldwide) and the proposed transaction fell within the scope of the EU's Merger Control Regulation (i.e. Regulation 139/2004)[85] notwithstanding that the parties involved were non-EU nationals (e.g. UK nationals). So, it is quite possible that, post-Brexit, the European Commission could block a proposed transaction involving one or more UK interests and/or involving one or more UK assets notwithstanding the fact that the UK would have left the EU at that time. This type of phenomenon has occurred in the past when the EU prohibited a proposed concentration involving US corporations notwithstanding that the US authorities had approved it.[86] Such a decision could be controversial but would be entirely foreseeable so the notion that Brexit would "take back control" is not entirely accurate.

M. STATE AID

48.044 The EU's State aid regime is a very significant constraint on the ability of EU Member States in terms of their ability to aid or assist, in a discriminatory manner, certain businesses or industries. The potency of the State aid rules is clear in that Member States could not assist their banks during the Financial Crisis commencing in 2007 without the EU (specifically, the European Commission) first approving the aid. It would therefore be unfortunate for the EU if the UK were able to provide harmful State aid to its chosen undertakings or sectors to the prejudice of EU undertakings and sectors. While the EU and its interests could resort to, for example, EU anti-dumping law, it would be better to be able to invoke EU State aid law. If the EU and the UK do not agree on a special State aid regime post-Brexit then the UK would appear to be immune from the EU State aid law post-Brexit. A practical example from the maritime sector would be the tonnage tax regime. The UK's tonnage tax regime currently has to comply with EU State aid law. It is possible that the UK could liberalise its tonnage tax regime because it would no longer have to comply with the EU State Aid Guidelines – for example, the requirement to be flagged under EU flags could disappear, a wider range of vessels could be covered and the regime generally loosened. Equally, if the UK was not constrained by State aid rules then it would be possible that the UK could give assistance to certain shipping companies and ports to cover costs (e.g. by way of direct grants, subsidised loans and tax breaks). Shipping companies and port companies in the UK could get State aid from the UK which their EU counterparts could not get from their Member State governments unless there is an agreement reached between the EU and the UK in the longer term. It would be important, from the perspective of the EU and maritime interests in the EU, that the EU insists that, as part of the Brexit negotiations, post-Brexit UK is subject to some controls on its ability to grant uncontrolled State aid.

---

85 OJ L24/1, 29 January 2004.

86 Case No COMP/M.2220 General Electric/Honeywell, http://ec.europa.eu/competition/mergers/cases/decisions/m2220_en.pdf.

N. LITIGATION

48.045 The EU has had a significant impact on litigation generally including in the area of maritime matters.[87] For example, the Rome Convention sets out many key rules on contracts[88] and the Brussels Recast Regulation deals with many issues of jurisdiction as well as the recognition and enforcement of judgments.[89] Equally, while the UK is a Member State, questions of EU law may be referred by UK courts and certain other tribunals to the Court of Justice of the European Union ("CJEU") by way of the preliminary reference procedure under Article 267 of the TFEU which means that the UK courts are deciding cases in a manner which is influenced by, and more likely to be consistent with, the jurisprudence of the EU and the CJEU. It is not clear how such matters will be addressed post-Brexit given the absence of an agreement but it is likely that there will be a divergence of approach and therefore a divergence in outcome.

48.046 There is no doubt that London will continue to be a major centre for maritime litigation and arbitration. This is all the more so in matters which are unconnected with the EU and EU law. The history, concentration of talent and experience as well as its infrastructure and the nexus to London incorporated into shipping contracts by lawyers based in London will all help ensure that London will remain a world capital in the area. Nonetheless, it would be wrong for those involved to deny the fact that other locations which are remaining in the EU will strive to improve their claim to a role in the arena and the simple fact that the UK will have left the EU and that for the UK law, EU law is like a "stopped watch".

48.047 On 21 November 2017, the European Commission's Directorate-General Justice and Consumers issued a "Notice to Stakeholders: Withdrawal of the United Kingdom and EU Rules in the Field of Civil Justice and Private International Law".[90] The operative parts are:

> "In view of the considerable uncertainties, in particular concerning the content of a possible withdrawal agreement, members of the legal professions as well as other stakeholders are reminded of legal repercussions, which need to be considered when the United Kingdom becomes a third country.[91]
>
> Subject to any transitional arrangement that may be contained in a possible withdrawal agreement, as of the withdrawal date, the EU rules in the field of civil justice and private international law no longer apply to the United Kingdom. This has in particular the following consequences in the different areas of civil justice:
>
> • International jurisdiction: the rules on international jurisdiction in EU instruments in the area of civil and commercial law as well as family law no longer apply to judicial proceedings in the United Kingdom and under certain circumstances (in civil and commercial cases where the defendant is domiciled in the United Kingdom) to judicial proceedings in the EU.

---

87 On this issue, see e.g. Horsley, "Brexit and UK Courts: Awaiting Fresh Instructions" in Dougan, op. cit. at fn. 2, chap. 4.

88 https://eur-lex.europa.eu/legal-content/EN/TXT/?uri=LEGISSUM%3Al33109.

89 Regulation (EU) No 1215/2012 of the European Parliament and of the Council of 12 December 2012 on jurisdiction and the recognition and enforcement of judgments in civil and commercial matters (recast) (OJ L351/1, 20 December 2012).

90 http://ec.europa.eu/newsroom/just/document.cfm?action=display&doc_id=48468.

91 For procedures and proceedings pending on the withdrawal date, the EU is trying to agree solutions for some of the situations that might arise. The relevant essential principles of the EU position in the field of judicial cooperation in civil and commercial matters have been published on the webpage: https://ec.europa.eu/commission/publications/position-paper-judicial-cooperation-civil-and-commercial-matters_en.

International jurisdiction will be governed by the national rules of the State in which a court has been seized.

- Recognition and enforcement: judgments issued in the United Kingdom are no longer recognised and enforced in EU Member States under the rules of the EU instruments in the area of civil and commercial law as well as family law, and vice versa. Recognition and enforcement of judgments between the United Kingdom and an EU Member State will be governed by the national law of the State in which recognition and enforcement is sought or by international Conventions where both the EU (or EU Member States) and the United Kingdom are contracting parties.
- Judicial cooperation procedures: EU instruments facilitating judicial cooperation (e.g. in relation to the service of documents, taking of evidence or within the context of the European Judicial Network in Civil and Commercial Matters) no longer apply between EU Member States and the United Kingdom.
- Specific EU procedures: EU instruments making available specific procedures, in particular the European Payment Order Procedure or the European Procedure for Small Claims, will no longer be available in courts of the United Kingdom and will not be available in the courts of EU Member States where one or more parties are domiciled in the United Kingdom.

The website of the Commission on civil justice https://ec.europa.eu/info/strategy/justice-and-fundamental-rights/civil-justice_en as well as the dedicated webpage of the European Judicial Network in civil and commercial matters https://ejustice.europa.eu/content_ejn_in_civil_and_commercial_matters-21-en.do provides general information concerning the field of civil justice. These pages will be updated with further information, where necessary."[92]

O. DIVERGENCE BETWEEN EU AND UK LAW

48.048 The UK has made much of the notion that because the UK will adopt various elements of EU law as UK law on the day in which the country leaves the EU, then the risk of divergence is minimised. This notion that there would be convergence or even identical laws is grossly inaccurate. First, the laws of the EU and the UK will not be the same at the moment when the UK leaves because the way in which these laws will be interpreted by the UK courts would differ from the ways in which the CJEU would interpret them and, in any event, some of the general principles of EU law are not easily incorporated into UK law. Second, the way in which the EU law and the "EU laws dressed as UK laws" would be applied and implemented would differ (not least because of the divergent objectives of the EU (e.g. internal market and EU interests) and the UK (e.g. a more national-centred approach). Third, the EU adopts laws on an ongoing basis – several hundred measures are adopted each year by the EU. Fourth, if Brexit is to be in anyway meaningful then it makes sense that the UK will choose different rules. Ultimately, it is to be assumed that there will be greater divergence between the EU and the UK legal regimes both substantively and procedurally.

P. SANCTIONS REGIME

48.049 The EU has a developing international sanctions regime to impose sanctions on countries, companies or persons connected with regimes of which the EU does not approve (e.g. because of a violation of international law). To date, the EU and the UK have been aligned but differences between the EU and the UK (which are more likely

---

92 http://ec.europa.eu/newsroom/just/document.cfm?action=display&doc_id=48468.

post-Brexit) could complicate matters considerably. An example of the complications would be when the EU and the US sanctions regimes in regard to Cuba diverged. It is possible that there could be a divergence between the sanctions regimes espoused by the EU and the UK post-Brexit. This means further complication and complexity for those in the shipping sector because of, for example, the EU, UK, USA and United Nations sanction regimes.

Q. SHIP FINANCE

48.050 The ship finance market is generally very resilient. This market is likely to continue to adapt to changes including Brexit. However if a ship finance bank is based in the UK (typically, London) with a view to servicing the EU through the EU passport regime then it is quite likely, based on current expectations, that the current "passporting" regime whereby a UK-based bank (even if owned by non-EU interests) may serve the whole of the EU and the EEA from its UK base would disappear. As a result, such financiers may move some or all operations from the UK to the EU. While many of the incumbents could well decide to stay, Brexit is more likely to have an impact on future establishment and expansion decisions in terms of whether to enter into, or expand in, the UK or in the EU.

R. ENVIRONMENTAL LAW

48.051 The implications of Brexit on environmental law are still unclear but are likely to be significant.[93] There have been some on the Brexit side of the referendum who have argued that EU environmental laws have been excessive and intrusive. If the UK leaves the EU then it will certainly have more freedom of action subject to international legal obligations but also the willingness of UK citizens to accept that its country might decide to adopt lower standards of protection for its citizens than their neighbours enjoy. In reality, many of the EU's measures on environmental law will apply irrespective of whether Brexit occurs or not; for example, a British vessel entering an EU port must comply with the EU regime in so far as it applies to port users irrespective of the flag of the vessel. Brexiteers would argue that they can choose their own environmental laws in the future and not be concerned with the agenda of the European Commission or the decision-making by the CJEU.

S. IMPLICATIONS OF BREXIT ON CONTRACTS

48.052 Brexit may well impact on contracts in several ways. There is the issue of the geographical scope of contracts. Contracts which have a geographical application clause (e.g. "this contract shall apply to the European Union") should be reviewed to ensure whether the parties are content with such an expression of intent on application. In the past, the geographical reach of such a contract which had such a clause was extended to include other States as the EU's membership expanded. Now, however, it would be logical that the geographical reach should be narrowed because the EU would contract. If

---

93 On this issue, see e.g. Heyvaert and Cavoski, "UK Environmental Law Post-Brexit" in Dougan, op. cit. at fn. 2, chap. 6.

the parties want the contract to apply to the EU and the UK then that should be specified explicitly. Indeed, given the possibility of changes in the UK's composition, the contract could well specify territories such as England, Wales, Scotland and Northern Ireland specifically. Contracts should also identify Gibraltar explicitly if that is what the parties want after Gibraltar leaves the EU. Contracts which are in existence now may well be affected by Brexit so it is prudent to monitor the implications of Brexit for such contracts including, in particular, the negotiations.

T. PASSENGER RIGHTS

48.053 Passengers enjoy various legal rights under EU law both as consumers and as passengers. They could lose some of those rights depending on what is agreed under Brexit. On 27 February 2018, the European Commission's Directorate-General Justice and Consumers as well as DG MOVE published a "Notice to Stakeholders" entitled "Withdrawal of the United Kingdom and EU Rules on Consumer Protection and Passenger Rights".[94] Given its importance, it is useful to set out the pertinent provisions:

"Subject to any transitional arrangement that may be contained in a possible withdrawal agreement, as of the withdrawal date, the general EU rules in the field of consumer law (such as the Unfair Commercial Practices Directive,[95] the Consumer Rights Directive,[96] the Unfair Contract Terms Directive,[97] the Consumer Sales and Guarantees Directive,[98] the Package Travel Directive[99] – see sections 1 and 2 below) and the EU passenger rights legislation (see section 3 below) no longer apply to the United Kingdom.[100]
   This has in particular the following consequences:

1. PURCHASE BY CONSUMERS IN THE EU OF PRODUCTS OR SERVICES FROM TRADERS ESTABLISHED IN THE UNITED KINGDOM[101]
   On or after the withdrawal date, consumers in the EU might purchase products or services from traders established in the United Kingdom.
      According to EU law, where a consumer concludes a contract with a professional in another country who, by any means, directs his commercial activities to the consumer's country of

---

94 https://ec.europa.eu/transport/sites/transport/files/legislation/brexit-notice-to-stakeholders-consumer-protection-passenger-rights.pdf.

95 Directive 2005/29/EC of the European Parliament and of the Council of 11 May 2005 concerning unfair business-to-consumer commercial practices in the internal market and amending Council Directive 84/450/EEC, Directives 97/7/EC, 98/27/EC and 2002/65/EC of the European Parliament and of the Council and Regulation (EC) No 2006/2004 of the European Parliament and of the Council ("Unfair Commercial Practices Directive"), OJ L149, 11.6.2005, p. 22.

96 Directive 2011/83/EU of the European Parliament and of the Council of 25 October 2011 on consumer rights, amending Council Directive 93/13/EEC and Directive 1999/44/EC of the European Parliament and of the Council and repealing Council Directive 85/577/EEC and Directive 97/7/EC of the European Parliament and of the Council, OJ L304, 22.11.2011, p. 64.

97 Council Directive of 5 April 1993 on unfair terms in consumer contracts, OJ L95, 21.4.1993, p. 29.

98 Directive 1999/44/EC of the European Parliament and of the Council of 25 May 1999 on certain aspects of the sale of consumer goods and associated guarantees, OJ L171, 7.7.1999, p. 12.

99 Directive (EU) 2015/2302 of the European Parliament and of the Council of 25 November 2015 on package travel and linked travel arrangements, OJ L326, 11.12.2015, p. 1.

100 This notice does not address the specific EU rules on e-commerce, and in particular, the Directive 2000/31/EC of the European Parliament and of the Council of 8 June 2000 on certain legal aspects of information society services, in particular electronic commerce, in the Internal Market ('Directive on electronic commerce') OJ L178, 17.7.2000, p. 1.

101 This notice does not address other practical aspects of cross-border purchase in third countries, such as EU rules related to value added tax, customs, and limitation and restrictions of importation.

residence, the contract is generally governed by the law of the country where the consumer has his or her habitual residence. It is possible to choose another law but that choice cannot deprive the consumer of the protection afforded by the law of the habitual residence which cannot be derogated from by agreement under that law.[102] On that basis EU courts will continue to apply the EU rules on consumer protection even though the trader is in the United Kingdom. This includes in particular the rules set out in:
- the Unfair Commercial Practices Directive;[103]
- the Consumer Rights Directive;[104]
- the Unfair Contract Terms Directive;[105]
- the Consumer Sales and Guarantees Directive;[106]
- the Price Indication Directive;[107] and
- the Package Travel Directive.[108]

If a EU-27 consumer were to bring an individual legal action[109] before a court of the EU-27 against a trader domiciled in the United Kingdom, the withdrawal has no implications for establishing international jurisdiction where the trader has directed his activities to the Member State of the consumer's domicile;[110] in these cases the EU jurisdictional rules which allow the consumer to sue the trader in the EU-27 Member State where the consumer is domiciled apply, irrespective of whether the trader is domiciled in the EU or in a third country.[111] However, the recognition and enforcement of an EU judgement in the United Kingdom and vice versa will be governed, as of the withdrawal date by national rules in the EU-27 and in the United Kingdom.[112]

As of the withdrawal date, EU law ensuring the availability of out-of-court dispute resolution[113] and facilitating access to alternative dispute resolution[114] no longer applies to the

---

102 Article 6(1) of Regulation (EC) No 593/2008 of the European Parliament and of the Council of 17 June 2008 on the law applicable to contractual obligations (Rome I), OJ L177, 4.7.2008, p. 6. For exceptions to this general rule, see Article 6(2)–(4) of Regulation (EC) No 593/2008.

103 Directive 2005/29/EC of the European Parliament and of the Council of 11 May 2005 concerning unfair business-to-consumer commercial practices in the internal market and amending Council Directive 84/450/EEC, Directives 97/7/EC, 98/27/EC and 2002/65/EC of the European Parliament and of the Council and Regulation (EC) No 2006/2004 of the European Parliament and of the Council (Unfair Commercial Practices Directive), OJ L149, 11.6.2005, p. 22.

104 Directive 2011/83/EU of the European Parliament and of the Council of 25 October 2011 on consumer rights, OJ L304, 22.11.2011, p. 64.

105 Council Directive of 5 April 1993 on unfair terms in consumer contracts, OJ L95, 21.4.1993, p. 29.

106 Directive 1999/44/EC of the European Parliament and of the Council of 25 May 1999 on certain aspects of the sale of consumer goods and associated guarantees, OJ L171, 7.7.1999, p. 12.

107 Directive 98/6/EC of the European Parliament and of the Council of 16 February 1998 on consumer protection in the indication of prices of products offered to consumers, OJ L80, 18.3.1998, p. 27.

108 Directive (EU) 2015/2302 of the European Parliament and of the Council of 25 November 2015 on package travel and linked travel arrangements, OJ L326, 11.12.2015, p. 1.

109 While cross-border litigation by consumers is relatively rare, this aspect is addressed here to provide a complete overview.

110 Consumer contracts covered in Article 17(1)(a)–(c) of Regulation (EU) No 1215/2012 of the European Parliament and of the Council of 12 December 2012 on jurisdiction and the recognition and enforcement of judgments in civil and commercial matters, OJ L351, 20.12.2012, p. 1.

111 Article 18(1) of Regulation (EU) No 1215/2012 of the European Parliament and of the Council of 12 December 2012 on jurisdiction and the recognition and enforcement of judgments in civil and commercial matters, OJ L351, 20.12.2012, p. 1.

112 For procedures and proceedings pending on the withdrawal date, the EU is trying to agree solutions for some of the situations that might arise. The relevant essential principles of the EU position in the field of judicial cooperation in civil and commercial matters have been published here: https://ec.europa.eu/commission/publications/position-paper-judicial-cooperation-civil-andcommercial-matters_en.

113 Directive 2013/11/EU of the European Parliament and of the Council of 21 May 2013 on alternative dispute resolution for consumer disputes (Directive on consumer ADR), OJ L165, 18.6.2013, p. 63.

114 Regulation (EU) No 524/2013 of the European Parliament and of the Council of 21 May 2013 on online dispute resolution for consumer disputes (Regulation on consumer ODR), OJ L165, 18.6.2013, p. 1.

United Kingdom and the EU online dispute resolution platform is no longer available in relation to traders established in the United Kingdom.

Concerning public enforcement (e.g. to achieve the cessation of a commercial practice) the Regulation (EC) No 2006/2004 of the European Parliament and of the Council of 27 October 2004 on cooperation between national authorities responsible for the enforcement of consumer protection laws (the Regulation on consumer protection cooperation)[115] no longer applies to the United Kingdom. This means that, as from the withdrawal date, United Kingdom authorities will not be obliged under EU law to cooperate in the case of cross-border claims.

In addition, as of the withdrawal date, EU law giving to certain 'qualified entities', designated by EU Member States, legal standing for bringing injunction actions in another Member State no longer applies to the United Kingdom.[116]

2. INSOLVENCY PROTECTION OF TRAVELLERS (PACKAGE TRAVEL)

• According to EU law, package travel organisers established in the EU are obliged to provide securities for the refund and for the traveller's repatriation in case of the organiser's insolvency.[117] Organisers not established in the EU which sell or offer travel packages to consumers in the EU, or which by any means direct such activities to the EU, also must provide such insolvency protection in each of the Member States they are selling to.[118] However, where an organiser established in a third country does not offer travel packages to consumers in the EU and does not direct its selling activities to the EU (passive sales), EU law providing mandatory insolvency protection does not apply. This means that in such cases insolvency protection granted by EU law will not apply to insolvencies of organisers established in the United Kingdom occurring as of the withdrawal date.

• As of the withdrawal date, EU law providing for the mutual recognition of insolvency protection taken out in accordance with the requirements of the home country of an organiser no longer applies with regard to insolvency protection taken out in accordance with requirements applicable in the United Kingdom.[119] This means that, as of the withdrawal date, insolvency protection taken out in the United Kingdom no longer serves to comply with the requirements for insolvency protection of package travel organisers in accordance with Article 17 of Directive (EU) 2015/2302.

3. EU PASSENGER RIGHTS

…

• Ship passengers: EU law on ship passenger rights[120] continues to apply on and after the withdrawal date to passengers where the port of embarkation is in the EU-27[121] or in the United Kingdom, provided that the port of disembarkation is in the EU-27 and the service is operated by a carrier established within the territory of a Member State or offering passenger transport services to or from a Member State ('Union carrier').[122]

…

The websites of the Commission on consumer protection (https://europa.eu/youreurope/citizens/consumers/) and passenger rights (https://europa.eu/youreurope/citizens/travel/passenger-rights/index_en.htm) provide general information. These pages will be updated with further information, where necessary."

---

115 OJ L364, 9.12.2004, p. 1.

116 Article 4 of Directive 2009/22/EC of the European Parliament and of the Council of 23 April 2009 on injunctions for the protection of consumers' interests, OJ L110, 1.5.2009, p. 30.

117 See first sub-paragraph of Article 17(1) of Directive (EU) 2015/2302.

118 See second sub-paragraph of Article 17(1) of Directive (EU) 2015/2302.

119 Article 18(1) of Directive (EU) 2015/2302.

120 Regulation (EU) No 1177/2010 of the European Parliament and of the Council of 24 November 2010 concerning the rights of passengers when travelling by sea and inland waterway, OJ L334, 17.12.2010, p. 1.

121 Article 2(1)(a) of Regulation (EU) No 1177/2010.

122 Article 2(1)(b) and 3(e) of Regulation (EU) No 1177/2010. Specific rules apply to cruise passengers, see Article 2(1)(c) of Regulation (EU) No 1177/2010.

48.054 It is also possible that there could be increased bureaucracy associated with the movement of people between the UK and the EU with the need for passports and work visas delaying the movement of people causing delays and difficulties at ports.

U. CARRIAGE OF LIVE ANIMALS

48.055 On 27 February 2018, the European Commission's Directorate-General for Health and Food Safety issued a "Notice to Stakeholders" entitled "Withdrawal of the United Kingdom and EU Rules on Animal Health and Welfare and Public Health related to the Movement of Live Animals".[123] The purpose of the general[124] notice is to remind economic operators involved in trade in live animals[125] of some of the legal repercussions which need to be considered if and when the UK becomes a third country.[126] Given the detail involved, it is useful to set out the key elements of the notice in full:

"Subject to any transitional arrangement that may be contained in a possible withdrawal agreement, as of the withdrawal date, the EU public and animal health rules in the field of intra-Union trade in live animals,[127],[128],[129],[130],[131] the placing on the market of aquaculture animals,[132] the controls carried out on such movements[133] and EU law on animal transport[134] no longer apply to the United Kingdom.

---

123 https://ec.europa.eu/food/sites/food/files/animals/docs/notice_brexit_animal_health_welfare_movement_live_animals.pdf.

124 Since the EU veterinary acquis is very detailed, the notice can only set out the essential rules. The website of the Commission on imports of live animals (https://ec.europa.eu/food/animals/live_animals_en) provides for general information concerning EU animal health legislation for imported live animals.

125 The notice does not address non-commercial movements of pet animals (Reg. 576/2013 of the European Parliament and of the Council of 12 June 2013 on the non-commercial movement of pet animals, OJ L178/1, 28 June 2013).

126 For live animals the movement of which is ongoing on the withdrawal date, the EU is trying to agree solutions with the UK in the withdrawal agreement. The essential principles of the EU's position on goods placed on the market, including live animals the movement of which has started before the withdrawal date are available here: https://ec.europa.eu/commission/publications/position-paper-goods-placed-market-under-union-law-withdrawal-date_en.

127 Council Directive 64/432/EEC of 26 June 1964 on animal health problems affecting intra-Community trade in bovine animals and swine (OJ 121, 29.7.1964, p. 1977/64).

128 Council Directive 91/68/EEC of 28 January 1991 on animal health conditions governing intra-Community trade in ovine and caprine animals (OJ L46, 19.2.1991, p. 19).

129 Council Directive 2009/156/EC of 30 November 2009 on animal health conditions governing the movement and importation from third countries of equidae (OJ L192, 23.7.2010, p. 1).

130 Council Directive 2009/158/EC of 30 November 2009 on animal health conditions governing intra-Community trade in, and imports from third countries of, poultry and hatching eggs (OJ L343, 22.12.2009, p. 74).

131 Council Directive 92/65/EEC of 13 July 1992 laying down animal health requirements governing trade in and imports into the Community of animals, semen, ova and embryos not subject to animal health requirements laid down in specific Community rules referred to in Annex A (I) to Directive 90/425/EEC (OJ L268, 14.9.1992, p. 54).

132 Council Directive 2006/88/EC of 24 October 2006 on animal health requirements for aquaculture animals and products thereof, and on the prevention and control of certain diseases in aquatic animals OJ L328, 24.11.2006, p. 14).

133 Council Directive 90/425/EEC of 26 June 1990 concerning veterinary and zootechnical checks applicable in intra- Community trade in certain live animals and products with a view to the completion of the internal market (OJ L224, 18.8.1990, p. 29).

134 Council Regulation (EC) No 1/2005 of 22 December 2004 on the protection of animals during transport and related operations (OJ L3, 5.1.2005, p. 1).

This notice is also relevant for the movement of live animals and hatching eggs from and to the Channel Islands and the Isle of Man.[135]

1. ENTRY OF LIVE ANIMALS INTO THE EU

Public and animal health:

As of the withdrawal date, the entry of live animals[136],[137] from the United Kingdom into the EU-27[138] is prohibited for public and animal health reasons, unless:

- The United Kingdom is 'listed' as a third country by the Commission for animal health[139] purposes. For the 'listing', Directive 2004/68/EC as well as specific legislation applies;
- The specific animal health requirements and veterinary certification conditions set out with the 'listing' for the species or categories of animals from the United Kingdom are fulfilled;
- The United Kingdom is 'listed' by the Commission as a third country having a residue control plan approved in accordance with Directive 96/23/EC[140] for the animals and animal products specified therein. For the 'listing' Chapter VI of Directive 96/23/EC applies.

The 'Tripartite Agreement' concluded in accordance with Article 6 of Directive 2009/156/EC between France, Ireland and the United Kingdom no longer applies to the United Kingdom as of the withdrawal date.

As of the withdrawal date, these substantial requirements are controlled upon entry into the EU-27 by applying mandatory border checks, including veterinary checks, at the first point of entry into the Union territory:

- Live animals can only enter the EU-27 through 'border inspection posts'[141] approved for the species and categories of animals concerned;
- Each consignment has to be accompanied by a duly completed health certificate in compliance with EU animal health import legislation;[142]
- Each consignment undergoes documentary, identity and physical checks;[143]
- Live animals are only allowed to enter the EU-27 with the official document (Common Veterinary Entry Document) attesting that the border checks were satisfactorily carried out in compliance with the applicable animal and, public health rules.

These conditions also apply to the entry into the EU-27, as of the withdrawal date, of live animals from the United Kingdom for the purpose of transit from the United Kingdom to another third country or to another part of the United Kingdom.[144] In addition, the consignment has to

---

135 Regulation (EEC) No 706/73 of the Council of 12 March 1973 concerning the Community arrangements applicable to the Channel Islands and the Isle of Man for trade in agricultural products (OJ L68, 15.3.1973. p. 1).

136 Cattle, pigs, sheep and goats, equidae, poultry and hatching eggs, aquaculture animals, bees and bumble bees, other "ungulates" listed in Directive 2004/68/EC. Dogs, cats and ferrets in commercial movements.

137 For other animals than those in [the previous] footnote, including certain animals consigned to and from bodies, institutes or centres approved in accordance with Annex C to Directive 92/65/EEC, national animal health conditions may apply to the entry from third countries of animals (Article 18(2) of Directive 92/65/EEC). However, the EU rules on border checks apply.

138 Ed., i.e. the remaining EU Member States.

139 Council Directive 2004/68/EC of 26 April 2004 laying down animal health rules for the importation into and transit through the Community of certain live ungulate animals (OJ L139, 30.4.2004, p. 321). For equidae, poultry, aquaculture animals, and other animals see footnotes above.

140 Council Directive 96/23/EC of 29 April 1996 on measures to monitor certain substances and residues thereof in live animals and animal products (OJ L125, 23.5.1996, p. 10).

141 Commission Decision 2009/821/EC of 28 September 2009 drawing up a list of approved border inspection posts, laying down certain rules on the inspections carried out by Commission veterinary experts and laying down the veterinary units in Traces (OJ L296, 12.11.2009, p. 1).

142 Article 4 of Council Directive 91/496/EEC.

143 Article 4 of Council Directive 91/496/EEC.

144 For equidae, specific transit rules are laid down in Commission Decision 2010/57/EU of 3 February 2010 laying down health guarantees for the transit of equidae being transported through the territories listed in Annex I to Council Directive 97/78/EC (OJ L32, 4.2.2010, p. 9).

pass through border inspection posts both at entry into and exit from the Union, including the respective notifications in the EU Trade Control and Expert System (TRACES).[145,146]

In case of transit from the EU-27 through the United Kingdom to the EU-27, live animals have to be accompanied by an intra-Union trade certificate and pass through a border inspection post at entry into the EU-27, including the respective notifications in TRACES.[147,148]

Animal welfare:

Live animals admitted to enter the EU-27 will have to be transported according to all the animal welfare rules laid down in Council Regulation (EC) No 1/2005,[149] and will be submitted to checks at border inspection posts by the competent authorities as laid down in Article 21 of that Regulation.[150]

2. EXIT OF LIVE ANIMALS FROM THE EU

Public and animal health:

As of the withdrawal date, the exit of live animals[151] from a Member State to the United Kingdom through the territory of another Member State is subject to the following conditions:

- The transport operation must ensure that in accordance with Decision 93/444/EEC[152] the consignment remains under customs supervision up to the point of exit[153] from Union territory;
- Each consignment of animals is accompanied by veterinary documents or veterinary certificates meeting relevant veterinary requirements of the United Kingdom and health certificates for intra-Union trade, which contain, where necessary and applicable, the additional guarantees provided for by Union legislation for animals intended for slaughter;
- A message must be addressed in TRACES to the place of destination, which is the border inspection post of exit or the local authority of the place in which the point of exit is situated, and to the central authorities of the place of destination and of the Member State(s) of transit.

Animal welfare:

The transport of live animals exiting the EU to the United Kingdom will have to comply with Council Regulation (EC) No 1/2005 up to the final place of destination and will be submitted to checks at the exit point by the competent authorities as laid down in Article 21 of that Regulation.

Private parties are advised that the specific conditions regarding the movement and importation of live animals are regularly updated. The website of the Commission on imports of live animals (https://ec.europa.eu/food/animals/live_animals_en) provides for general information

---

145 Commission Decision 2003/623/EC of 19 August 2003 concerning the development of an integrated computerised veterinary system known as Traces (OJ L216, 28.8.2003, p. 58).

146 Article 9 of Council Directive 91/496/EEC of 15 July 1991 laying down the principles governing the organization of veterinary checks on animals entering the Community from third countries (OJ L268, 24.9.1991, p. 56).

147 In addition, for the transit of certain ungulates, Article 12 of Commission Regulation (EC) No 206/2010 applies.

148 In addition, the rules on exit of live animals apply, see section 2 of this Notice.

149 Council Regulation (EC) No 1/2005 of 22 December 2004 on the protection of animals during transport and related operations (OJ L3, 5.1.2005, p. 1).

150 See also the Commission Notice to stakeholders withdrawal of the United Kingdom and EU rules for authorisations and certificates for transporters of live animals, drivers and attendants (https://ec.europa.eu/food/animals/welfare/practice/transport_en).

151 Cattle, pigs, sheep, goats, equidae, poultry and hatching eggs, dogs, cats and ferrets, bees and bumble bees and aquaculture animals.

152 Commission Decision 93/444/EEC of 2 July 1993 on detailed rules governing intra-Community trade in certain live animals and products intended for exportation to third countries (OJ L208, 19.8.1993, p. 34). For the exit of live animals to a third country without passing through another Member State, no specific EU rules apply.

153 In accordance with Article 1(2)(a) of Decision 93/444/EEC "exit point" means any place situated in close proximity to the external frontier of one of the territories listed in Annex I to Council Directive 90/675/EEC (5) offering customs supervision facilities.

concerning EU animal health legislation for imported live animals. These pages will be updated with further information, where necessary."

V. CUSTOMS

48.056 On 30 January 2018, the European Commission's Directorate-General Taxation and Customs Union and Directorate-General for Trade issued a "Notice to Stakeholders" entitled "Withdrawal of the United Kingdom and EU Rules in the Field of Customs and Indirect Taxation".[154] The key elements of the text of the Notice include:

"In view of the considerable uncertainties, in particular concerning the content of a possible withdrawal agreement, economic operators are reminded of legal repercussions, which need to be considered when the United Kingdom becomes a third country.[155]

Subject to any transitional arrangement that may be contained in a possible withdrawal agreement, as of the withdrawal date, the EU rules in the field of customs (see below, 1) and indirect taxation (VAT and excise duties – see below, 2) no longer apply to the United Kingdom.[156]

This has in particular the following consequences as of the withdrawal date[157]:

1. CUSTOMS
• Goods which are brought into the customs territory of the EU from the United Kingdom or are to be taken out of that territory for transport to the United Kingdom, are subject to customs supervision and may be subject to customs controls in accordance with Regulation (EU) No 952/2013 of 9 October 2013 laying down the Union Customs Code.[158] This implies inter alia that customs formalities apply, declarations have to be lodged and customs authorities may require guarantees for potential or existing customs debts.
• Goods which are brought into the customs territory of the EU from the United Kingdom are subject to Council Regulation (EEC) No 2658/87 of 23 July 1987 on the tariff and statistical nomenclature and on the Common Customs Tariff.[159] This implies the application of the relevant customs duties.
• Certain goods which enter the EU from the United Kingdom or are leaving the EU to the United Kingdom are subject to prohibitions or restrictions on grounds of public policy or public security, the protection of health and life of humans, animals or plants, or the protection of national treasures.[160]
• Authorisations granting the status of Authorised Economic Operator (AEO) and other authorisations for customs simplifications, issued by the customs authorities of the United Kingdom will no longer be valid in the customs territory of the Union.

---

154 http://trade.ec.europa.eu/doclib/docs/2018/january/tradoc_156573.pdf.

155 For a movement of goods that has started before and ends on or after the withdrawal date, the EU undertakes to agree solutions with the United Kingdom in the withdrawal agreement on the basis of the EU's position on Customs related matters needed for an orderly withdrawal of the United Kingdom from the Union (https://ec.europa.eu/commission/publications/position-paper-customs-related-matters-needed-orderly-withdrawal-uk-union_en). The position paper also addresses administrative cooperation procedures on or after the withdrawal date between the EU-27 and the United Kingdom related to facts that have occurred prior to the withdrawal date (for example, mutual assistance related to the verification of proofs of origin).

156 This note does not address the general customs and tax free allowances applicable to goods in the personal luggage of travellers entering the EU.

157 The listing illustrates some important consequences in the field of customs and indirect taxation of the withdrawal of the United Kingdom from the Union but is not meant to be exhaustive.

158 OJ L269, 10.10.2013, p. 1.

159 OJ L256, 7.9.1987, p. 1.

160 A list with such prohibitions and restrictions is published on the website of DG TAXUD and can be accessed here: https://ec.europa.eu/taxation_customs/sites/taxation/files/prohibition_restriction_list_customs_en.pdf.

- Goods originating in the United Kingdom that are incorporated in goods exported from the EU to third countries will no longer qualify as 'EU content' for the purpose of the EU's Common Commercial Policy. This affects the ability of EU exporters to cumulate with goods originating in the United Kingdom and may affect the applicability of preferential tariffs agreed by the Union with third countries.

2. INDIRECT TAXATION (VAT AND EXCISE DUTIES)

- Goods which enter the VAT territory of the EU from the United Kingdom or are dispatched or transported from the VAT territory of the EU to the United Kingdom will respectively be treated as importation or exportation of goods in accordance with Council Directive 2006/112/EC of 28 November 2006 on the common system of value added tax (the 'VAT Directive').[161] This implies charging VAT at importation, while exports are exempt from VAT.
- Taxable persons wishing to use one of the special schemes of Chapter 6 of Title XII of the VAT Directive (the so-called Mini One-Stop Shop or MOSS), who supply telecommunications services, broadcasting services or electronic services to non-taxable persons in the EU, will have to be registered for the MOSS in a Member State of the EU.
- Taxable persons established in the United Kingdom purchasing goods and services or importing goods subject to VAT in a Member State of the EU who wish to claim a refund of that VAT may no longer file electronically in accordance with Council Directive 2008/9/EC[162] but have to claim in accordance with Council Directive 86/560/EEC.[163] Member States may make refunds under the latter Directive subject to reciprocity.
- A company established in the United Kingdom carrying out taxable transactions in a Member State of the EU may be required by that Member State to designate a tax representative as the person liable for payment of the VAT in accordance with the VAT Directive.
- The movement of goods which enter the excise territory of the EU from the United Kingdom or are dispatched or transported from the excise territory of the EU to the United Kingdom will respectively be treated as importation or exportation of excise goods in accordance with Council Directive 2008/118/EC of 16 December 2008 concerning the general arrangements for excise duty.[164] This implies, inter alia, that the Excise Movement and Control System (EMCS) on its own will no longer be applicable to excise duty suspended movements of excise goods from the EU into the United Kingdom, but those movements will be treated as exports, where excise supervision ends at the place of exit from the EU. Movements of excise goods to the United Kingdom will therefore require an export declaration as well as an electronic administrative document (e-AD). Movements of excise goods from the United Kingdom to the EU will have to be released from customs formalities before a movement under EMCS can begin.

The websites of the Commission on taxation and customs union (https://ec.europa.eu/taxation_customs/index_en) and external trade (http://ec.europa.eu/trade/import-and-export-rules/) provides for general information on the rules as they apply currently to the importation and exportation of goods. The relevant pages will be updated with further information, whenever available."

---

161 OJ L347, 11.12.2006, p. 1.

162 Council Directive 2008/9/EC of 12 February 2008 laying down detailed rules for the refund of value added tax, provided for in Directive 2006/112/EC, to taxable persons not established in the Member State of refund but established in another Member State (OJ L44, 20.2.2008, p. 23).

163 Thirteenth Council Directive 86/560/EEC of 17 November 1986 on the harmonisation of the laws of the Member States relating to turnover taxes – Arrangements for the refund of value added tax to taxable persons not established in Community territory (OJ L326, 21.11.1986, p. 40).

164 OJ L9, 14.1.2009, p. 12.

W. OTHER ISSUES

48.057 Brexiteers and Remainers would agree that the EU has either, depending on their perspective, interfered with or involved itself with so many areas of law and life. Identifying and addressing all of those issues are a mammoth task. This chapter must, by definition, only touch on some of the various issues involved. Before concluding and having considered many of the main issues, it is useful to identify some of the remaining issues.

48.058 If borders, burdens and bureaucracy are re-introduced in terms of trade between the UK and the remaining EU Member States then trade will become slower and more cumbersome. There is no doubt that trade has speeded up enormously since the creation of the EU's completion of the internal market by virtue of the so-called "1992 Programme". If there is extra bureaucracy and checks then trade will become slower with costs for operators of vessels and ports with implications for business generally (e.g. in the context of so-called "Just In Time" ("JIT") contracts and delivery. Shippers, carriers, ports and customers would all be well-advised to check their contracts and terms because there could well be disputes and debates as to who is liable and for what in a post-Brexit environment with delays and so on.

48.059 Some ferry operators on the English Channel could well be concerned that there would be special rules or special deals for the Eurotunnel/Channel Tunnel services which would not apply to the ferry operators.

48.060 A recurring theme in the Brexit negotiations has been the relationship between the UK and Ireland as well as, in particular, the impact of Brexit on the border between the two countries. While no agreement has been reached on these "Irish"-related aspects of Brexit, it seems that it could be difficult to reach agreement on this issue without some, or all, parties compromising. It is quite possible that this will be a point of division for some time to come unless the matter can be agreed upon. It could impact on issues such as migration controls at ferry ports and delays in the handling of cargo.

X. CONCLUSIONS

48.061 The imprecision of Brexit has meant that commentators and politicians have resorted to clichés and stock phrases. In the context of shipping and ports, phrases such as "unchartered waters", "choppy waters" and so on prevail. However, when one removes these clichés, the position is only a little clearer. It is impossible to say what will be the long term consequences because the terms of the post-Brexit arrangements between the UK and the EU have not yet been agreed. There is still no rule book. There are however some key messages. There is uncertainty about the regime and the rules. Trade will be impacted negatively for so long as there is uncertainty. Issues relating to people (and, in particular, their free movement) will be of concern to the UK and so there is little guarantee that the free movement of people post-Brexit will be as free as it is easy today.[165] There has been a great deal of "talking up" the economy generally and the sector in particular by various parties but this may not be enough to overcome the challenges which lie ahead.

---

165 Perhaps there could be relatively easy free movement of people between Ireland and the UK because of the so-called Common Travel Area but this is not certain.

48.062 If the UK and Gibraltar leave the EU, which is very likely but not inevitable, then the implications for the UK and Gibraltar will be profound but as yet unclear. In an increasingly globalised and integrated world, it is difficult to conceive that a country with such a proud history of operating on a grand world-scale would seek to "go it alone". While it may well have the fifth largest economy in the world, one is struck by the fact that it is *leaving* the world's largest trading bloc (i.e. the EU) with members which include the fourth, sixth and eighth biggest economies in the world (i.e. Germany, France and Italy respectively). Moreover, the UK represents only about 3% of the world's trade. It is also seeking to establish "free trade" agreements with various States in the world at a very time which some of those States are either ambiguous or even hostile towards free trade.

48.063 The presence of the UK in the EU has generally been seen as a force for liberal economics and open market philosophy. This has been particularly so in regard to shipping and ports. The UK has, for example, opposed cabotage restrictions and what it perceives as bureaucracy in ports. It has influenced EU law in a very constructive and intelligent manner. The UK's well-established interest groups and institutions have considered, in a thoughtful manner, various proposals which have been made by the Commission. Entities as diverse as the House of Lords, the UK Chamber of Shipping as well as London-centred groups such as the European Maritime Law Organisation have all taken time to reflect on, and comment on, EU proposals. There is little doubt that the UK has thus shaped and influenced EU shipping law. Indeed, there are some commentators who trace the early evolution of EU shipping law in the early 1970s to the very accession of the UK (and, to a much lesser extent, Denmark and Ireland) because of the arrival in the (then) European Communities family of an island as well as maritime nation.

48.064 If the UK leaves the EU then it is unlikely that the UK will have no interest in EU shipping matters – on the contrary, it will need to remain interested and should have a greater incentive to comment because it will not be part of the EU's deliberations – but it is quite likely that there would be some reduction in terms of the intensity of the scrutiny and the level of analysis by UK maritime interest in the affairs of a club which it has left. If that were so then it would be a great pity because the rules which the EU adopts will continue to apply, and even affect, UK shipping interests without meaningful formal input from the UK.

CHAPTER 49

Conclusions

A. INTRODUCTION

49.001 A number of conclusions emerge after reviewing the law of the European Union ("EU") as it relates to shipping. These conclusions are interesting in their own right but are also important in trying to understand the historical evolution, current nature and possible future development of EU shipping law.

49.002 Before examining these conclusions, it is worth reflecting on some observations which have been made by others because they provide a useful background.

49.003 It is useful to see shipping in the broader maritime context. It has been written:

"Europe is much more than just the territorial area of the Member States. Europe also includes the oceans and seas which surround it and the activities that take place therein – therefore: the vast coastal areas, the islands, the fisheries, the maritime transport and the ports, the shipbuilding and the marine equipment industries, the exploitation of energy and the tourism industry. It is by dealing with all of these, within a future maritime policy for the Union, that we are somehow redefining Europe's traditional borders and amplifying the scope of action for the Union to factor in the extensive maritime dimension of our continent."[1]

49.004 The European Commission has written:

"The seas are Europe's lifeblood. Europe's maritime spaces and its coasts are central to its well-being and prosperity – they are Europe's trade routes, climate regulator, sources of food, energy and resources, and a favoured site for its citizens' residence and recreation.

Our interactions with the sea are more intense, more varied, and create more value for Europe than ever before. Yet the strain is showing. We are at a crossroads in our relationship with the oceans.

On the one hand technology and know-how allow us to extract ever more value from the sea, and more and more people flow to Europe's coasts to benefit from that value. On the other hand, the cumulated effect of all this activity is leading to conflicts of use and to the deterioration of the marine environment that everything else depends on.

Europe must respond to this challenge; in a context of rapid globalisation and climate change the urgency is great."[2]

49.005 Shipping is an extremely valuable industry for the EU in terms of employment (both direct and indirect) as well as earnings (both direct and indirect) from the shipping sector. Moreover, however, and even if shipping earned not a cent of profit for those involved, shipping provides the indispensable means by which many of the fundamental free movements of the EU work; without a shipping sector, the free movement of goods

---

1 Borg, "Redefining Europe's Borders: Bringing the Sea to the Forefront", 11 May 2007, Speech/07/304.

2 Communication from the European Commission, An Integrated Maritime Policy for the European Union (COM(2007) 575, 10 October 2007), p. 1. On the economic contribution and value of shipping, see Oxford Economics, The Economic Value of the EU Shipping Industry (2014) available at: www.ecsa.eu/images/2014-04-01%20Oxford%20Economics%20ECSA%20Report%20FINAL.pdf.

and people (and, to a lesser extent, services, establishment and capital) would have been impossible.

49.006 The European Commission has also observed:

"Europe plays a major role in today's shipping world, with European companies owning 41% of the world's total fleet (in dwt). The adaptation of European shipping to the requirements of the global economy has brought about significant structural changes in the sector. Competitive pressure from shipping nations around the world has also increased significantly as a result of globalisation."[3]

49.007 The European Commission has written in 2018:

"For Europe, maritime transport has been a catalyst for economic development and prosperity throughout its history. Maritime Transport enables trade and contacts between all European nations. It ensures the security of supply of energy, food and commodities and provides the main vehicle for European imports and exports to the rest of the world. Almost 90% of the EU's external freight trade is seaborne. Short sea shipping represents one third of intra-EU exchanges in terms of ton-kilometres. Ensuring a good quality of life on Europe's islands and in peripheral maritime regions depends on good maritime transport services. Each year, more than 400 million passengers embark and disembark at European ports. Overall, maritime industries are an important source of employment and income for the European economy.

The European Commission's objective is to protect Europe with very strict safety rules preventing sub-standard shipping, reducing the risk of serious maritime accidents and minimising the environmental impact of maritime transport. It also safeguards access to the maritime transport market and promotes reduction of administrative burden through digitalisation. The Commission also works actively against piracy and terrorism threats. Another important activity concerns the social dimension: looking after working conditions, health and safety issues and regulating the professional qualifications of seafarers. Finally, the Commission works for the protection of citizens as users of maritime transport services, ensuring safe and secure conditions, looking after their rights as passengers and examining the quality of public service connections proposed by Member States.

The Commission's strategic goals and recommendations for the EU had been set out in 2009 in the Maritime Transport Policy until 2018. An implementation report was published in September 2016, presenting main developments and achievement as identifying areas for further work. Action in the area of maritime transport aims at ensuring the long-term performance of the European maritime transport system as a whole to the benefit of all other economic sectors and to the final consumer. The Commission actively supports the efforts of EU Member States and of the European shipping sector offering quality shipping services in Europe and all over the world."[4]

49.008 There is hardly an aspect of shipping which is not permeated by EU law. The provisions relating to shipping in the Treaties are scant. However, the secondary law on the area has developed in an intensive and detailed manner. The law has developed in different ways. The Court of Justice of the European Union ("CJEU") has developed the law through its interpretation of EU law particularly in the early days but the European Commission also provided the Court with the opportunity to adjudicate on these matters.[5] The European Commission has proposed a great number of measures over time but has not been as active in recent years as it sometimes was. The Parliament has also been active in nudging developments over time. Sometimes the developments in EU maritime

---

3 Commission, Communication from the Commission to the European Parliament, the Council, the European Economic and Social Committee and the Committee of the Regions – Strategic Goals and Recommendations for the EU's Maritime Transport Policy until 2018 (COM(2009) 0008 final, 21 January 2009), part 2.

4 https://ec.europa.eu/transport/modes/maritime_en.

5 E.g. Case 167/73 Commission v French Republic [1974] ECR 359, ECLI:EU:C:1974:35.

law have been stimulated by individual maritime casualties and incidents. The EU is increasingly developing EU shipping law in a proactive, rather than reactive, manner and it is hoped that this will continue despite Brexit and the absence of the UK. In many ways, the EU is now a significant source of law in regard to shipping in the EU.

B. THE EU AS A FORCE IN THE WORLD GENERALLY

Introduction

49.009 EU shipping law cannot be seen in isolation from the EU generally. As an international organisation, the EU is on a trajectory of growth. The 27 Member States (some of the richest and most economically advanced in the world) are moving closer together (economically, monetarily, politically as well as in many other ways). They are a force to be reckoned with by the rest of the world. The EU will expand further and may establish further arrangements with other non-European States. The EU operates to the extent that it has competence conferred on it by the Member States. It presents itself as a single block to the world and co-ordinates its position in many international organisations.

The place of the EU in world shipping

49.010 The boundaries of the EU are not the boundaries of shipping – shipping is global industry. There is no way that the EU will ever control all aspects of shipping as if the industry were contained in an EU-controlled incubator. Nonetheless, the EU is concerned with shipping and the legal regulation of this international industry within the EU. While the EU may only legislate for within the EU, EU shipping law has a wider impact because ships which cannot use EU ports have less attraction for charterers and may be prematurely scrapped.

C. EU SHIPPING LAW WAS NOT AN EARLY FEATURE OF EU LAW

49.011 While EU law has always applied to shipping (albeit in a modified form), the body of EU shipping law is of recent origin. The 1974 case of *Commission v France*[6] was the first major judicial development in EU shipping law: yet the opportunities afforded by the CJEU in that case were not grasped by the other institutions for many years. The 1979 Brussels Package was the first significant legislative package. The Foundation Treaties left considerable initiative in the hands of the Commission and discretion at the feet of the Council: the hesitancy of the latter and the paralysis of the former hampered the development of the law in this area for many years, but now the EU is very active and vibrant. While EU law is, in reality, little more than a quarter of a century old, it is very potent and dynamic. Even in its short life, there have been dramatic changes; for example, the Commission could not regulate liner conferences on competition grounds but then a block exemption was granted by the Council which has since been taken away. Today, it is clear that shipping is as subject to EU law as almost every other sector of the economy.

---

6 Case 167/73 Commission v France [1974] ECR 359, ECLI:EU:C:1974:35.

D. THERE IS HARDLY ANY LIMIT TO THE POSSIBLE APPLICATION OF EU LAW TO SHIPPING YET THERE IS A LIMIT TO THE POSSIBLE DEVELOPMENT OF EU SHIPPING LAW

49.012 EU law applies to virtually every economic activity including shipping. Thus, the application of EU law to shipping must not be underestimated. The decisions of the CJEU in cases such as *R. v Secretary of State for Transport, ex parte Factortame (No. 2)*[7] demonstrate the application of this body of law to shipping matters.

49.013 In 1977, the European Parliament's Committee on Regional Policy, Regional Planning and Transport published an Interim Report on the Sea Transport Problems in the Community and stated:

> "[A] frequently heard argument is that since sea transport is subject to world-wide ramifications and world-wide rules, it should not be forced into the 'narrow confines' of [EU] regulations, which would only represent a step backwards compared with world-wide arrangements.
> There is no logic to this argument, popular though it may be. What European industry is not subject to world-wide ramifications? Is it not simply true to say of the European economy, with its dependence on imports of raw materials and its vital need to export, that everything we do has world-wide ramifications? Even the cereals which grow in our fields are subject to world-wide rules, which in some respects go further than world arrangements for sea transport."[8]

The argument that shipping should not be regulated by the EU because the sector is subject to global forces and rules has been so roundly defeated that it is no longer viable. EU law applies to very many activities in the shipping sector including areas not covered in this book such as the tax implications of the sale of ships and businesses.[9]

E. EU TRANSPORT POLICY WAS SLOW TO DEVELOP

49.014 The EU's transport policy has been slow to develop and, in so far as it has developed, has done so in a piecemeal fashion. Critics would say that some Member States have been unwilling to confer on the EU any real purpose or power in the sphere but that has changed. Critics would also argue that the Commission has perhaps spent too much time analysing the various options and has produced too many discussion papers but such papers and analysis are necessary as a way of facilitating the development of the area and, in particular, the adoption of rules.

49.015 Pallis has written an interesting and stimulating book entitled *The Common EU Maritime Transport Policy.*[10] A reviewer of the book, Nesterowicz, has incisively catalogued Pallis' main conclusions and it is worth considering Nesterowicz's summary:

> "[Pallis] comes to five conclusions. In the first, he states that the changes in the economic environment of maritime transport, especially its internationalization, [were] not followed quickly enough by [a] sufficient regulatory framework [which] resulted in 'policy gaps'. As the previously existing policy-making levels – international (especially in the case of maritime security), national (especially in the case of shortsea shipping) and self-regulation – did not prove to be effective enough, the EU had to intervene by creating a Common Maritime Transport

---

7 Case C-213/89 [1990] ECR I-02433, ECLI:EU:C:1990:257, [1991] AC 603, [1990] 3 WLR 818, [1991] 1 All ER 70.
8 Working Documents; Doc. 5/77; 23 March 1977; Rapporteur: Mr H Seefeld, para. 9.
9 Case C-178/05 Commission v Hellenic Republic [2007] ECR I-04185, ECLI:EU:C:2007:317.
10 2002.

Policy ["CMTP"]. ... The second conclusion is that the EU decision-making institutions, primarily the Commission, played a decisive role in [CMTP] developments because of their ability to deploy their formal powers and the inter-institutional partnership and support that they granted to each other (especially in the case of Commission, Parliament and the [CJEU]). The second element allowed them especially to act with more autonomy as regards national administrations. At the same time the role of the consultative bodies was not significant. ... Third, the author maintains that, while Member States retained a prominent role in CMTP developments, none of them was able to act independently. The policy is a result of a compromise – the extreme positions of some Member States were shaped by the EU membership per se, ie, the dynamism of the formal powers that they had ceded to the EU decision-making institutions and the feedback that 'non-active Member States' (not having a special interest in maritime transport) provided to the institutions. ... Fourthly, the author underlines the role of interest groups representing maritime industries. They provided – some to a greater, some to a lesser extent – a distinctive input into the policy-making process. The influence of each industry depended on its own economic position and on the knowledge of how to play 'the Brussels game' (ie, the resources devoted to the representation of the industry and lobbying). ... Fifthly, the author sums up the previous four conclusions by holding that all the actors are autonomous but interdependent, and that the present shape of the CMTP is a result of bargaining and coalitions where the position of one actor influenced another and at the end the dynamic of the process affects all of them."[11]

F. EU SHIPPING POLICY HAS NOT BEEN ENTIRELY SUCCESSFUL

49.016 The Select Committee of the House of Lords wrote in its report entitled *Community Shipping Measures*:[12]

"[m]ost – though not all – of the measures ... proposed [in 1985] were adopted by the Council in December 1986. ... So far as they went, they seem to have worked well. But they have not stopped the decline in the Community merchant fleet. The haemorrhage of economic and potential military resources continues."[13]

49.017 The Commission did not however stand idly while the EU's fleet declined. In August 1990, it proposed the Positive Measures package. Over the last two decades and more, it has produced papers and proposals as well as adopted concrete measures in the area. The Commission has also sought to integrate the EU's whole approach to the area.[14] Despite the EU not succeeding in all respects, it has been largely successful and it is important that it keeps trying.

G. IS SHIPPING A PUBLIC SERVICE OR MERELY ANOTHER SERVICE IN THE MARKETPLACE?

49.018 Is shipping an entirely commercial activity or is there some element of public policy involved? The answer is that it is primarily an economic activity but some

---

11 [2007] LMCLQ 267 at 268.

12 European Communities Committee 28th Report 1989–90 (HL Paper 90).

13 Ibid., para. 1.

14 E.g. communication from the European Commission, An Integrated Maritime Policy for the European Union (COM(2007) 575, 10 October 2007) generally but, at p. 1, the Commission states: "the Commission proposes an Integrated Maritime Policy for the European Union, based on the clear recognition that all matters relating to Europe's oceans and seas are interlinked, and that sea-related policies must develop in a joined-up way if we are to reap the desired results".

elements involve public service obligations ("PSOs"). PSOs are relatively rare in practice and would relate to such routes as loss-making services to islands and remote regions.[15]

H. EU SHIPPING LAW IS ONLY A COMPONENT OF INTERNATIONAL SHIPPING LAW

49.019 The advent of such organisations as the United Nations, the United Nations Conference on Trade and Development ("UNCTAD"), the International Labour Organization, the Comité Maritime International, the International Maritime Organization ("IMO") and specific treaty relationships between States (falling short of international organisations) means that EU law is only one of the constituent elements of international shipping law. The EU must maintain a unified front at these organisations if it is to prove powerful and influential. The international dimension of shipping[16] means that the law of the EU relating to it will always be only a component part. Despite EU shipping law being only a component part, the EU must keeping trying and working to develop this area because there is a very good chance that the tighter and more unified EU will be able to achieve more than the near-global international community involved in organisations such as the IMO. The EU can achieve more for its citizens if it works on these issues than the more global organisations. This is not to say that there is no role for the global or near-global organisations – there is most certainly a role – but the smaller, more nimble and agile organisations can achieve more.

I. THE FORMULATION OF EU SHIPPING LAW REQUIRES THE INVOLVEMENT OF ALL PARTNERS

49.020 The former Commissioner for Transport, Stanley Clinton Davis, said there had to be a strengthening of the dialogue between the social partners: "Each has to comprehend the problems of the other; each has to be mutually supportive."[17] Three decades later, the point is still valid. It is imperative that all Member States "buy in" to EU shipping law but also that the various constituents do so too and it is, for that reason, vital that the EU continues to listen to, and engage with, constituencies such as shipowners, seafarers, passengers, shippers, port owners, financiers, lawyers, environmentalists and so on. The mechanisms for lobbying and engagement are well-established and it is important that they continue to be active.

---

15 See Mikroulea, "Competition and Public Service in Greek Cabotage" in Antapassis, Athanassiou and Røsæg (eds), Competition and Regulation in Shipping and Shipping Related Industries (2009).

16 Clough and Randolph, Shipping and EC Competition Law (1991) comment (at para. 2.1): "EEC Sea Transport Policy must … take into account the existence of bilateral agreements, the different systems of regulation in different parts of the world including national cargo reservation systems, total cargo allocation measures such as those in West and Central Africa, the open conference system in the United States and the closed conference system which has prevailed in Europe for over a century."

17 "Maritime Transport", IP(85) 60, 7 March 1985.

J. EU SHIPPING LAW AND POLICY MUST SEEK TO PROTECT EU SHIPOWNERS, SEAFARERS AND ALL THOSE INVOLVED IN THE EU SHIPPING INDUSTRY

49.021 The EU must be vigilant in ensuring that non-Member States and other organisations do not damage EU shipping interests.[18] Mrs Bredima-Savopoulou was Rapporteur for the Economic and Social Committee ("EESC") in its Opinion on the Proposal for a Council Directive concerning minimum requirements for vessels entering or leaving Community ports carrying packages of dangerous or polluting goods. She wrote in her opinion:

> "The [EU] has two alternatives: it could either introduce different standards and requirements of its own, or it could work towards effective implementation of international standards. ... The Committee recommends that the [EU] follow the second course of action by complying with the international standards laid down by specialized international maritime agencies, by incorporating these into [EU] legislation and by ensuring that these standards are strictly observed."[19]

49.022 EU shipping policy might well include a co-ordinated grant, taxation, research, qualifications and services policy so as to improve the lot of EU's shipowners, seafarers and all those involved in the EU shipping industry. EU shipping law should seek to protect weaker interests (in particular, seafarers).

K. EU SHIPPING LAW IN AN ENVIRONMENT OF SELF-REGULATION?

49.023 Shipping has long been characterised by self-regulation.[20] In some ways, the presumption is self-regulation except in so far as the law interferes with the sector. Over the last two decades, the EU has become much more interventionist – particularly in areas such as safety and the environment – but such intervention has proven to be necessary as a reaction to events when self-regulation did not work.

L. IS EU SHIPPING LAW CHARACTERISED BY KNEE-JERK REACTIONS?

49.024 Some of the measures which have been adopted by the EU could be seen as knee-jerk reactions to particular events (such as environmental and safety incidents) rather than as the culmination of careful planning. Sometimes it would appear as if the EU adopted measures in a knee-jerk manner (indeed the naming of certain measures after certain maritime disasters (e.g. the *Erika* package)) only strengthens the argument that EU measures have been a reaction to events. However, in reality, while some of these measures were adopted in response to particular events (which is admirable in itself), it is also the case that the EU had draft measures in preparation before the events occurred (e.g. safety or environmental measures in gestation before an accident or incident) which were then adopted quickly after events because the EU wanted to adopt (or be seen to adopt) measures responding to such events. If there were knee-jerk measures then it is comforting to see that newer measures are generally more the result of strategic planning.

---

18 See "EEC sends Lawyers into UKWAL Offices", Lloyd's List, 24 July 1989, p. 1.
19 OJ No. C329, 30 December 1989.
20 Pons, "After Taca? Towards a More Competitive and Innovative Liner Shipping Market", http:llempaeu. int/comm/competition (19 August 1999).

M. LIMITATIONS TO THE DEVELOPMENT OF EU SHIPPING LAW

49.025 There are *limits* to the EU's work in this area because, for example, the EU has relatively limited tonnage in a global context and is not pivotal (despite being very important) in the world of shipping. The EU-flagged fleet represents a fraction of the world's fleet. If the EU seeks to over-regulate the industry then there is a serious risk that there would be further flagging-out by EU shipowners. The Member States must be careful not to breach any general international rules on dumping or unlawful State aid. Ultimately, the EU will only be able to have power in these areas where the Member States gives it competence.

N. ROLE OF THE EU IN SHIPPING MATTERS BY COMPARISON WITH OTHER INTERNATIONAL ORGANISATIONS

49.026 In regard to shipping, the EU has a different *role* from other international organisations. Unlike global organisations such as the United Nations and its specialised agencies, the EU benefits from the cohesion which follows from having a relatively small and closely aligned membership. The EU also has the power to adopt laws and rules which are binding on Member States. The EU does not have the narrow sectoral approach of the likes of the IMO. Nor does the EU have any of the representative functions of many of the non-governmental organisations. Instead, the EU has a broader role in terms of stimulating and regulating the shipping sector in the broader economic context. The extent of this role is an important policy issue for the EU as a whole.

O. UNEVEN DISTRIBUTION OF MARINE RESOURCES IN THE EU

49.027 There is an uneven distribution of marine resources in the EU. Apart from the fact that there are some landlocked Member States, some Member States are more important than others in terms of the ownership of ships or ports. The Atlantic Arc, an organisation of certain ports on the Atlantic coast, claimed that 30 or so North Sea ports handle more than a billion tonnes of sea cargo annually while the 180 Atlantic ports handle 350 million tonnes.[21]

P. MODAL ISOLATION

49.028 Some of the rules being developed in regard to air transport and other modes (particularly in regard to competition) are apparently developed in isolation from other modes. These developments in other modes could also apply in the area of shipping so careful regard must be had to the work done in the other modes. There is an over-emphasis by the EU on the development of individual modal regimes. There is clearly a need to see transport as a seamless series of steps in the movement of goods and persons.

---

21 Lloyd's List, 8 April 1995.

Q. INFORMED APPROACH

49.029 There is a need for an "informed" approach to shipping, that is to say, the valuable work of the EU institutions should be supplemented by information (but not propaganda) from the industry and various interests. The Maritime Industries Forum is helping to provide this input. There should be greater formal and informal consultation and discussion. This discussion should not be the dialogue of the deaf but rather the exchange of opinions and views. The need for "joined-up policy-making" has been recognised by the Commission itself.[22] And now concrete steps are being taken to achieve this co-ordination.

R. OPEN MARKETS

49.030 The thrust of EU shipping policy is towards an open and non-protectionist shipping market. EU measures on competition, dumping, freedom to provide international shipping services, cabotage and so on has all attempted to open (however slowly)[23] the market. This openness is admirable. However, one wonders whether Member States are as open with each other while there may also be the fear that the EU is sacrificing some of its own operators for the sake of the greater good. It is quite possible that if the UK leaves the EU then the open market philosophy espoused by the UK will be missed, meaning that the EU shipping law regime could become more protectionist and less liberal.

S. RECURRING THEMES

49.031 Despite the notion that so much has changed, sometimes it is clear that the arguments or issues remain the same: for example, it has been written that a Commission Proposal

> "suggesting the abolition of duty-free sales at airports and on planes and ships might be included in the 'common shipping policy'. Its adoption would certainly present problems, since it would mean an important loss of revenue for the shipowner (especially on ferry services)."

That argument is not new: the passage was written in 1973 in *European Report*[24] and the proposal was made by the Commission in 1972! The demise of intra-Member States duty free in the post-1992 internal market environment has not caused undue difficulties for EU operators but its demise was perceived to be traumatic.

T. SHORT SEA TRANSPORT

49.032 The Commission has taken a special interest in the short sea sector. This is particularly important in the context of the Trans-European Network and the internal market programmes. There is no doubt that a significant part of the future of the EU is short sea

---

22 Commissioner Borg, "Redefining Europe's Borders: Bringing the Sea to the Forefront", 11 May 2007, Speech/07/304.
23 The liberalisation of cabotage has been a long drawn-out process (see chap. 7).
24 19 September 1973, No 75, p. 3.

transport. Short sea shipping is also important in transferring cargo from congested roads to the less congested sea. In this regard, the EU institutions must see transport as an integral whole and not simply as a series of separate modal steps.

U. SWOT ANALYSIS OF EU SHIPPING

Introduction

49.033 It is worth conducting a SWOT (strengths, weaknesses, opportunities and threats) analysis in EU shipping describing the commercial background generally.[25]

Strengths

49.034 The size of the fleet owned by EU interests means that the EU is inevitably a major force in the world shipping market. The size of the EU fleet is not only the ships registered in the Member States but also the ships registered elsewhere but owned by EU entities.

49.035 The maritime tradition found in some parts of the Member States is an important feature of shipping in Europe. Such tradition is at the backbone of a strong EU shipping industry. It is difficult to convince most young people to go to sea because it is quite different from many other careers – it involves long absences from home, working in a precarious and often unsafe environment, the acquisition of dedicated and perhaps not very interchangeable skills as well as the need to work in confined spaces often with a multicultural crew. There are still some parts of the EU in which the tradition of going to sea is still very much alive.

49.036 Shipping is a hugely capital intensive industry. Some of the world's biggest capital markets are found in the EU. This fact has always been significant but should be used even more in terms of developing the industry. It is still fascinating to see that some of the complex financing techniques used in the aviation industry have still not been utilised by the shipping industry generally.

49.037 Ships are increasingly more technical and sophisticated. Europe has a lead in this sector and it should build on this strength.

49.038 The EU has a strength in certain shipping sectors and sub-sectors. For example, the EU's container fleet represents about 27% of the world's container fleet in terms of tonnage.

49.039 The EU fleet has increased in recent times, going from 72.3 million grt (gross registered tonnage) in 1990 to 83.1 million grt in 1995, with most of this increase taking place in 1994.[26] This expansion needs to be sustained and built upon.

49.040 Despite its many critics, one gets the impression that the European Commission is genuinely behind the development of shipping in the EU generally (although its decisions in certain areas have not won universal support) and this is a great strength which should be capitalised on by the shipping industry in the EU. There is a conflict between some of the aims of competition law and the aims of developing a healthy EU fleet and this conflict must be overcome.

---

25 On the commercial background to shipping in each of the Member States, see chap. 2.
26 "European Shipping Fleet up to 83m GRT", Lloyd's List, 30 May 1995.

Weaknesses

49.041 The EU's shipping fortunes have been declining over time. From 1957 (when the then European Economic Community ("EEC") Treaty was signed in Rome), the number of ships worldwide has doubled and the tonnage of ships quadrupled. However, growth within the EU was not as dramatic as it was elsewhere in the world: the Far Eastern countries, the former USSR, China and the open registry States grew more significantly than the Member States. Moreover, during the shipping crisis of the 1980s, the EU suffered more deeply and earlier than the rest of the world: for example, in 1989, the Member States had only 50% of the gross tonnage and 73% of the number of ships they had in 1980. The decline is even more dramatic when viewed over a longer time-scale: the EU-flagged tonnage represented 32.7% of the world tonnage in 1967 but this had fallen to 14.7% by 1989. In more recent years, the fortunes of world shipping have improved somewhat but the EU still needs to strengthen its position in the world market. Today, the wider EU/EEA (European Economic Area) fleet represents about 18% of the world fleet in terms of tonnage.[27]

49.042 The maritime tradition which was found in many Member States is in decline. Shipyards are closing. Seafarers are turning to shore-based employment. Cheaper foreign crews are being used. Skills of seamanship, ship repair and shipbuilding are being lost.

49.043 There is a regional imbalance in the allocation of cargoes between ports: the 30 or so North Sea ports handle more than one billion tonnes of seagoing cargo each year while the 180 Atlantic ports handle more than 350 million tonnes and the Mediterranean ports handle about 500 million tonnes.[28]

49.044 It is trite but true to say that shipbuilding in the EU is in serious difficulties. These difficulties have been accentuated with the ending of the Cold War. South Korea alone now has more shipbuilding capacity than the whole of Western Europe.[29] It is hoped that the Organisation for Economic Co-operation and Development ("OECD") agreement on aids for shipbuilding and ship repair may foster a healthy industry but it will be a healthier *smaller* industry.

Opportunities

49.045 The creation of the EU internal market has been a tremendous opportunity for shipping – particularly short sea shipping.[30] The EU now arguably represents the largest single market in the world. The opportunities for shipping in the internal market are much greater than the comparable opportunities in the North American Free Trade Agreement ("NAFTA") Single Market which will benefit land-based transport much more than maritime transport. Already about 70% of the trade between Member States is carried by ships registered in the EU but this could easily fall given the cheaper shipping services available from some non-EU operators. Crises such as the Falklands War, the Gulf War and so

---

27 The share has artificially grown with the accession of Finland and Sweden on 1 January 1995.
28 "Atlantic Arc Ports Conference Plan", Lloyd's List, 8 April 1995.
29 See "Fincantieri Urges Equal Conditions on Subsidies", Lloyd's List, 7 April 1995.
30 On the short sea industry, see Wijnolst, Peeters and Liebman (eds), European Shortsea Shipping (1993). See Dibner's "Shortsea Shipping in Europe and the Americas: Status and Prospects" at p. 289 of Wijnolst et al.'s book.

on clearly show the importance of having a ready stock not only of merchant ships but also seafarers. The European Commission has written:

"a strong [EU] fleet is essential to the [EU] both for economic and strategic reasons. As the leading world trading entity, the [EU] should not be excessively dependent on third country fleets for its imports and exports, so losing control and influence on the price and quality of transport to and from its territory."[31]

49.046 This theme has been echoed by the EESC,[32] the European Parliament[33] as well as the European Commission[34] on other occasions.

49.047 The increasing mobility of passengers around the EU means that there are great opportunities in ferry traffic. Passengers are however better informed and more safety conscious then ever and this will mean that ferry operators have to comply with the highest standards.

49.048 There has been a suggestion that there be a European quality label for ships. This would be in line with the IMO's white list classification scheme. Such ships would have to match the latest safety standards and social conditions. The advantage of such a label is that such ships would benefit from a more favourable regime in terms of port State control.

Threats

49.049 The availability of cheaper[35] and less regulated crews as well as tonnage from outside the EU pose serious threats to the EU shipping fleet. There are now too few officers who are EU citizens to run an EU fleet. There are growing concerns about the safety of certain types of ships (e.g. ro-ro ferries and tankers) a large number of which are based in the EU. This will be problematical for many EU shipowners and operators. Despite the growing mobility of passengers there may be an increased tendency to travel by air rather than by sea were there to be further safety incidents. Many shipyards outside the EU can be and are cheaper than their EU counterparts. This means that the strengths of the EU in the shipping world will be lost over time. Varying regulatory and training standards in the EU can cause serious distortions and can threaten the reputation of shipping in the EU generally.

49.050 The EU's Transport Ministers recalled in their 7 May 2014 Athens Declaration: "that the European maritime sector faces significant challenges and that further

31 Guidelines for the Examination of State Aids to Community Shipping Companies, 1990 (COM(85) 90 final), p. 3.

32 E.g. in EEC Shipping Policy: Flags of Convenience (OJ 1979 C171/35) the ECOSOC wrote that "there is no disputing the fact that if Member States do not want to lose their economic independence, and if they desire to keep control over their own means of transport and maintaining jobs, they must under all circumstances have a merchant fleet at their disposal" and in the Opinion of the Economic and Social Committee on the Communication and Proposals (II.3, II.4) by the Commission to the Council on Progress towards a Common Transport Policy: Maritime Transport, the ECOSOC wrote that a "cheap and efficient sea transport system is a basic prerequisite for expansion of [EC] trade, especially with non-member countries".

33 E.g. the address of Georgios Anastassopoulos, the then Chairman of the Transport Committee of the European Parliament to the Antwerp Shipping Symposium, "A Future for the Community Fleet", 6 May 1987: reprinted in (1987) XXII ETL 197–198.

34 See Communication from the Commission to the Council on the Community's Relations with Non-Member Countries in Shipping Matters (COM(76) 341 final), para. 2.

35 In terms of wages and social security costs.

action is needed to maintain and further develop attractive, safe and sustainable quality shipping and to ensure open maritime markets and access to cargoes without restraints".[36]

V. CONSIDERATION OF OTHER ISSUES

Introduction

49.051 It is useful to consider a variety of other issues in EU shipping law as a general level.

Do Member States act in their own self-interest?

49.052 It is a truism that States almost invariably act in their own self-interest and, in the context of EU shipping law, this is no different. It is true that the UK was the principal proponent of liberalisation of cabotage services but it is equally true that the UK had by far the largest cabotage fleet and therefore it was in the interests of its own fleet to have cabotage restrictions removed.

Contrast with the USA

49.053 Too often some people assume that the EU is like the USA and vice versa. There are similarities but there are also radical differences to the point where it is dangerous to assume or presume that what happens in one location would also occur in the other location. Unlike the USA, the EU is composed of sovereign States without any system of federal law prevailing or controlling those States. In the USA, federal maritime law is pre-eminent in many areas of shipping and maritime life[37] but this is not the case in the EU. The role and realm of the EU Member States has to be respected by the EU.

Contrast with the IMO

49.054 It is useful to contrast the EU and the IMO. The EU is a general organisation in that it covers all economic sectors (apart from nuclear energy) while the IMO is specifically aimed at the maritime sector. The EU has the ability to adopt legislation, through the means of its own institutions, which would be binding on the Member States. By contrast the IMO has, by virtue of Article 1 of the IMO Convention,[38] "machinery for cooperation among Governments in the field of governmental regulation" – the IMO is therefore a co-operation forum whereas the EU may adopt legislation which is binding on Member States. The IMO is more concerned with technical matters relating to shipping while the EU is concerned with technical matters to some extent, it is even more concerned with issues such as competition and regulatory issues. It is clear that the EU needs to enhance its standing and visibility internationally in maritime matters and this includes its role in the IMO.

---

36 http://register.consilium.europa.eu/doc/srv?l=EN&f=ST%2010041%202014%20INIT.
37 E.g. the Coastal Zone Management Act and the Marine Protection, Research and Sanctuaries Act.
38 289 UNTS 48.

An integrated approach is essential

49.055 The Commission has recognised rightly that an integrated and co-ordinated approach to maritime matters is needed. Shipping is one part of that jigsaw. Hopefully, the Commission is correct when it states that an

"Integrated Maritime Policy will enhance Europe's capacity to face the challenges of globalisation and competitiveness, climate change, degradation of the marine environment, maritime safety and security, and energy security and sustainability. It must be based on excellence in marine research, technology and innovation, and will be anchored in the Lisbon agenda for jobs and growth, and the Gothenburg agenda for sustainability."[39]

The EU's maritime transport strategy until 2018 recognises the need for a comprehensive and harmonised set of policies for Europe.

New areas will continue to emerge

49.056 EU shipping law is likely to evolve and emerge into new areas over time such as research and development. While there may not be too many new areas, there is little doubt that existing areas will become even more important and will grow. Future editions of this book will no doubt touch on new areas such as taxation because already there are questions as to whether, for example, partial chartering is subject to value added taxation.[40] This evolution and dynamism ensure that the subject will remain both relevant and interesting.

Technology

49.057 In many ways, the secret of European success in shipping in the past was due to its technological superiority. This technology gap has now been narrowed to the point where non-EU ships are now as technologically advanced (or more so, in some cases) than their EU counterparts. It is submitted that the EU could do a great deal for shipping in the EU by promoting technological development in shipping so as to ensure that the non-human "cost base" improves as much as possible. A programme of technical grants and loans would be conducive to the improvement of the fortunes of EU shipping. Thankfully, the EU has begun to take an interest in the technological aspects of shipping.

Taxation

49.058 The taxation of shipping activities is a critical concern. A company established in an open registry does not pay much or any income tax in certain circumstances. The availability of low or no taxes in other jurisdictions has resulted in some EU shipping companies re-registering their fleets in other registries around the world. The EU has seen the need for a positive policy on taxation within the shipping industry and has responded (with various approvals under State aid law) for employment regimes involving reduced social security and tax contributions.

---

39 Communication from the European Commission, An Integrated Maritime Policy for the European Union (COM(2007) 575, 10 October 2007), p. 1.

40 Case C-97/06 Navicon SA v Administració del Estado [2007] ECR I-8755, ECLI:EU:C:2007:609. See also Chuah, "Exemption from VAT to apply to Partial Chartering" (2007) 13 JIML 366.

Role of competition law

49.059 While there have been fines imposed on undertakings in the shipping sector, there is no doubt further and larger fines may well be imposed in the future. Competition law has proved to be a very prominent part of EU shipping law generally. It has also proved to be controversial and somewhat complicated. However, there is little doubt that EU competition law has helped to reduce costs and enhance competition in the sector.

State aid

49.060 So many shipping activities are State aided or funded: it would not be surprising if the battle shifted more and more to State aid and shipping. The long-running battles over State aid to airlines as well as airports demonstrate clearly the possibility that State aid will become a very lively issue in regard to shipping.

Non-discrimination on the basis of nationality

49.061 It is useful to stay with the future trends. EU law prohibits discrimination on the basis of nationality between nationals of Member States. There has been clear and flagrant discrimination on the basis of nationality in shipping in certain contexts but there are situations when discrimination on the basis of nationality is permitted.

Brussels as benefactor or bully?

49.062 Is it "Brussels: The Bully" or is it "Brussels: The Benefactor"? There is widespread criticism of the EU in shipping matters and in all matters. Is this criticism justified in the realm of shipping? Some port authorities criticise the interventionist nature of the EU.[41] It is submitted that the EU has, through its actions, benefited the shipping industry. The EU has not always favoured the shipping industry in an uncritical way but has evaluated the situation and assisted the sector where appropriate.

Inefficiency in the industry

49.063 There is no doubt that there are aspects of the EU shipping sector which are inefficient and could benefit from efficiency enhancing measures. The development of the jurisprudence on inefficient public undertakings may be very significant in the context of shipping and port operations generally. Such cases as *Höfner and Elser v Macnotron GmbH*[42] are extremely important and can be used to eradicate anti-competitive practices and activities in ports.

---

41 E.g. "EU: Port Slams Brussels Bureaucrats", Lloyd's List, 25 March 1995 which was reflected two decades later when the UK's Major Ports Group criticised the Port Services Regulation: see chap. 44.
42 Case C-41/90 [1991] ECR I-1979, [1993] 4 CMLR 306, ECLI:EU:C:1991:161.

Role of the EU in international maritime affairs

49.064 On 10 October 2007, the Commission adopted a communication setting out its vision for an Integrated Maritime Policy for the EU, together with a detailed action plan setting out an ambitious work programme for the years ahead. It has become known as either a "blue paper" or a "blue book". In it, the Commission stated:

"Promoting Europe's Leadership in International Maritime Affairs
The EU will work towards more efficient international governance of maritime affairs and effective enforcement of international maritime law, urging Member states to ratify the relevant instruments. It will promote coordination of European interests in key international fora.

Access to international markets for Europe's maritime industries and services, sustainable scientific and commercial exploitation of the deep seas, protection of global marine biodiversity, improvement of maritime safety and security, working conditions, reduced ship pollution and the fight against illegal activities in international waters will be the external priorities for the Union's Integrated Maritime Policy.

Attention will also be given to the geopolitical implications of climate change. In this context, the Commission will present in 2008 a report on strategic issues relating to the Arctic Ocean.

Maritime affairs will be a regular topic in discussions with the EU's partners that have already taken steps towards an integrated maritime approach, such as Australia, Canada, Japan, Norway and the US, as well as with other partners such as Brazil, China, India and Russia.

The EU will also develop shared responsibility over the seas it shares with its closest neighbours. In particular, it will make proposals for increased co-operation in managing the Mediterranean and the Black Seas. It will promote cooperation on maritime affairs under the Northern Dimension of its external relations' policy and will bring maritime affairs into the EU's agenda of cooperation with developing states, including small island developing states.

In this context it will support maritime policy and law of the sea capacity building in developing countries.

The Commission will propose an Implementing Agreement of UNCLOS[43] on marine biodiversity in areas beyond national jurisdiction and work towards successful conclusion of international negotiations on Marine Protected Areas on the high seas."[44]

Climate change

49.065 Climate change is a serious challenge for the shipping sector. EU law has adopted legislation to address the issue and the Treaty on the Functioning of the European Union ("TFEU") contains specific provisions on the topic. There is a belief that the emissions from ships of substances such as carbon dioxide, sulphur dioxide and nitrogen oxide will have to be reduced because such emissions can be greater than from aircrafts. Emissions trading may also have to become a more prominent feature of the shipping sector. There may also be the possibility of developing solar and wind power for shipping. There is a need to co-ordinate these issues within the shipping sector and co-ordinate this policy across other policies (e.g. agricultural policy where discharges from agricultural activity cause maritime pollution).

---

43 United Nations Convention on the Law of the Sea.
44 Pp. 13–14.

More legislation?

49.066 Many members of the shipping community resent and resist the enactment of too much EU legislation. There is a danger in not having enough legislation! The CJEU and the General Court have to reach decisions on the cases brought before them and therefore if there are no hard and fast legal rules embodied in either the Foundation Treaties or the secondary legislation then the court will invoke some of the soft legal principles which means that results can be even more unpredictable.

EU shipping law can be used pro-actively

49.067 EU shipping law can be used pro-actively to take on Member States, competitors, ports, trade associations and others who are not acting legally. Competition law, in particular, provides a very real route for challenging the behaviour of others. Undertakings which have dominant positions have a specific responsibility not to act unfairly or in a way which distorts competition so, for example, dominant ports may not refuse unjustifiably access to their ports on fair and non-discriminatory terms. Let the message go out: EU shipping law is not just a straitjacket but also a lifejacket!

Role of the Member States, institutions and industry

49.068 Member States, the EU institutions and the various interest groups have been described as being in a triangular relationship:

> "[e]ach one strengthens its bargaining position against the other by referring to its relationship to the third. The hunt for a balance that advances policy responses to the changing economic environment, intensify these exchanges and the search for 'winning' coalitions. Both this intensification and this search work at the expense of each actor's 'autonomy'."[45]

It is interesting to recall the large and diverse number of interest groups which are involved in maritime policy matters in the EU; Pallis has recorded at least 37 different associations, confederations, councils groups and similar bodies.[46] These different entities sometimes co-operate and collaborate on various issues.

Role of shipping in the EU

49.069 Shipping is an important stimulant and participant in the EU's economic and social life generally. People and goods move by sea throughout much of the EU. The sea is the main artery of trade in the EU. Around 400 million people move annually by sea within the EU. Around 90% of the EU's external freight trade is by sea. Short sea shipping represents some 40% of intra-EU trade. The EU Maritime Transport Policy until 2018 recognises the importance of these features and attempts to build a policy into the future.

---

45 Pallis, "Maritime Interests in the EU Policy-Making" (2007) World Maritime University Journal of Maritime Affairs 3 at 6. See also Pallis, The Common EU Maritime Transport Policy (2002), generally as well as Selkou and Roe, Globalisation, Policy and Shipping Fordism, Post-Fordism and the European Union Maritime Sector (2004).

46 Pallis, "Maritime Interests in the EU Policy-Making" (2007) World Maritime University Journal of Maritime Affairs 3 at 7.

W. PROTECTIONISM

49.070 Many non-EU States have protected their shipping fleets by protectionist measures. This has materially affected EU fleets. Unfair pricing practices have been particularly harmful. The EU has responded in part. Unfortunately, some EU States have also been unfairly protective of their own fleets and have forced national companies (especially the State-owned ones) to build and repair their ships in the shipyards of those States and these requirements have forced up these companies' costs.

X. ATTITUDES AND POLICIES OF MEMBER STATES

49.071 As a general rule, the stance taken by each Member State in regard to shipping matters at the EU level is nearly always a direct correlation of the level of importance attached to shipping in that particular Member State and the relationship of shipping to other sectors such as shipbuilding, steel manufacture, ports, ship finance operations and industry generally.

49.072 The relative weight attached to shipping depends on the economic magnitude of the sector in the context of the national economy, the strategic importance attached to it for defence purposes and the political pressure that interested parties (e.g. maritime trade unions) can exercise.

49.073 It should also be pointed out that in some countries maritime policy is extricably linked to policies pursued for shipbuilding whilst in others the shipping industry is treated in isolation from other sectors of the national economy.

49.074 It is clear that despite shipping being an important industry for the EU as a whole, it is not a major industry in each of the Member States of the EU, with the obvious exceptions of Cyprus, Denmark, Greece, Malta, the Netherlands, Poland and the UK. It is of lesser significance (but still of significance) in France, Germany, Italy and Spain. It is interesting to observe that shipbuilding is in some ways more important than shipping in Belgium, France and Germany. All EU maritime Member States are protectionist of their shipping industries to some extent but much less so than many non-EU Member States. Such protectionism takes such forms as building aids, purchase aids, employment restrictions, rules on cabotage, taxation, international registries as well as cargo reservation policies. On balance, however, the EU Member States are in favour of an open shipping policy and have committed themselves to safeguarding and promoting open trade within the confines of free competition on a fair and commercial basis in international shipping. The Member States have adopted such openness in their own right and within the EU as well as in international organisations such as the OECD and UNCTAD. Even when the Member States are protectionist, there is no clear-cut connection between the degree of protectionism afforded to national shipping and flag shares in the external trade of EU countries. It is also true that the approach of Member States to shipping matters can be a factor of how well organised the shipping industry is in the particular Member State.

Y. THE INSTITUTIONAL DIMENSION TO THE EVOLUTION OF EU SHIPPING LAW

49.075 It would be tempting to ascribe to one institution, as opposed to another, the label of the institution that contributed most to the evolution and development of EU shipping law. Such an exercise would have to be an imprecise art rather than a science. It is very likely that credit for most of the initiatives in EU shipping law should go to the Commission (particularly the Directorates-General with responsibility for transport (and, in particular, the safety aspects of maritime transport), competition, maritime affairs and the environment). In some ways, this is natural because it is the Commission's task to initiate and propose legislation but it did require the Commission to do so but it only did so in earnest after some prodding by the Parliament and Member States. The Commission was also responding to events (stimulated, in part, because the Council would have wanted to be able to adopt measures (whose job it was for the Commission to initiate)) so the Commission was centre-stage. The Council also deserves recognition for its role: it could have ignored or rejected all that was proposed by the Commission but it did not do so. However, special recognition must go to the CJEU because it has upheld measures and gave impetus at the outset with its *Commission v France (French Seafarers)*[47] judgment. The Parliament has a growing role in the evolution of EU shipping law and that is likely to continue. Ultimately, the Member States adopted the most far-reaching measures[48] so this is an important dimension. Some Member States have been more ambitious for EU shipping law (e.g. the UK in regard to competition and removing cabotage restrictions) so it will be interesting to see how the loss of the UK as a member would impact on EU shipping law – a liberal voice would be lost.

Z. THE FUTURE

49.076 EU shipping law is now well-established and well-founded. The scope of the subject has widened over time.[49] The rules have become more specific, more robust and more pervasive. The EU has established itself as a player in the world maritime law arena and any hope (on the part of some of the detractors of the EU having a role in this space) that the EU would yield to the IMO has been dashed and is unlikely now to be ever fulfilled. It is likely, but not inevitable, that the EU will be able to continue to operate in this area. The EU and IMO operate in tandem. Indeed, the EU with its own rules has become very powerful. It began in the 1970s and 1980s but is now a recognisable body of law. The themes which are likely to remain constant include safety, the environment and competition but also security (particularly, cyber security), employment, relations with the rest of the world (including, perhaps, the UK). The citizen (as passenger, consumer, business person and stakeholder in the EU's environment) will become even more important

---

47 Case 167/73, [1974] ECR 359, ECLI:EU:C:1974:35.
48 The balance would have been adopted by the Commission under delegated powers.
49 E.g. while EU shipping law was always seen as a public law matter, it has now become involved in private law issues as well.

as a point of reference for the evolution of EU shipping law.[50] However, there is no doubt that safety, the environment and competition will be centre-stage in the future evolution of EU shipping law. It is remarkable how the issues in EU shipping law have not changed too radically over the last three decades but the importance of those issues has become clearer.

---

50 It is fair to assume that the reaction of citizens to environmental and safety incidents stimulated activity and measures on the part of the EU.

INDEX